Decedents' Estates

Decedents' Estates

Cases and Materials

Raymond C. O'Brien
Professor of Law
The Catholic University of America
Georgetown University Law Center

Michael T. Flannery
Associate Professor of Law
University of Arkansas, Little Rock

Carolina Academic Press
Durham, North Carolina

ISBN 1-59460-214-X
LCCN 2005936583

Carolina Academic Press
700 Kent St.
Durham, NC 27701
Telephone (919) 489-7486
Fax (919) 493-5668
www.cap-press.com

Printed in the United States of America

This book is dedicated to
Walter Wadlington,
teacher, mentor, friend.
ROB

This book is also dedicated to
Kerry and Sadie,
my love and my family.
MTF

Summary of Contents

Contents

Table of Cases

Principal cases are in bold type. Non-principal cases are in roman type. References are to pages.

Table of Authors

Table of Web-Based Resources

529 Plans
Rodney Koenig, *Creating College Scholarships with Qualified State Tuition Programs*,
http://www.abanet.org/rppt/publications/magazine/2000/mj00koenig.html (accessed
Oct. 12, 2005), p. 388.

California Probate Laws and Resources
California Probate, Trusts, Wills & Estates: Related Laws and Law Links,
http://www.megalaw.com/ca/top/caprobate.php (accessed Oct. 12, 2005), pp. 21-22.

Sacramento County Public Law Library - Probate Resources,
http://www.saclaw.lib.ca.us/LegalGuides/LegalGuidesFS.html; select Probate Law
(accessed Oct. 12, 2005), p. 22.

Census Bureau Information
U.S. Census Bureau, Subject Index,
http://www.census.gov/main/www/subjects.html (accessed Oct. 12, 2005), p. 67.

Civil Unions
Vermont Secretary of State, *The Vermont Guide to Civil Unions*,
http://www.sec.state.vt.us/otherprg//civilunions/civilunions.html (accessed Oct. 12,
2005), p. 78.

http://www.gaydemographics.org/USA/USA.htmhttp://www.gaydemographics.org/USA
/states/vermont/2000Census_state_vt_civilunions, p. 78.

Disclaimer Trusts
Daniel B. Evans, *The "Disclaimer" Trust: An Ideal Plan for the Medium Size Estate*,
http://evans-legal.com/dan/disclaimtr.html (accessed Oct. 12, 2005), p. 132.

Sebastian V. Grassi, Jr., *Drafting the Marital Deduction Disclaimer Trust After the 2001
Tax Act*,
http://d2d.ali-aba.org/_files/thumbs/rtf/ACFA3C_thumb.pdf (accessed Oct. 12, 2005),
p. 132.

DNA Evidence
Charles H. Brenner, *The Larry Hillblom Inheritance*,
http://dna-view.com/hillblom.htm (accessed Oct. 12, 2005), p. 387.

Employee Retirement Income Security Act of 1974 (ERISA)
United States Department of Labor, PWBA Office of Regulations and Interpretations,
Advisory Opinion by Robert J. Doyle, Director of Regulations and Interpretations, to
Mr. Thomas R. Giltner, Dec. 7, 1994,
http://www.dol.gov/ebsa/programs/ori/advisory94/94-41a.htm#tof (accessed Oct. 12,
2005), p. 66.

Equitable Adoption
William G. Reeves, *Inheritance by Equitable Adoption: An Overview of Theory and Proof,*
http://www.mobar.org/journal/2001/mayjun/reeves.htm (accessed Oct. 12, 2005), p. 92.

Escheat
Richard L. Field, *Forgotten But Not Gone: Escheatment of Stored Value Cards,*
http://www.abanet.org/scitech/ec/ecp/escheat.html (accessed Oct. 12, 2005), p. 65.

Office of the Attorney General, State of Texas, Advisory Opinion of Dan Morales,
http://www.oag.state.tx.us/opinions/op48morales/dm-258.htm (accessed Oct. 12, 2005), p. 66.

State of Delaware, Department of Finance, Division of Revenue, *Escheat - Unclaimed Property,*
http://www.state.de.us/revenue/information/Escheat.shtml (accessed Oct. 12, 2005), p. 66.

Families and Living Arrangements
U.S. Census Bureau, *Families and Living Arrangements,*
http://www.census.gov/population/www/socdemo/hh-fam.html (accessed Oct. 12, 2005), p. 76.

Federal Estate Tax
Federation of Tax Administrators,
http://www.taxadmin.org; select State Comparisons (accessed Oct. 12, 2005), p. 26.

Federal Tax
Center on Budget and Policy Priorities, Federal Tax Policies,
http://www.cbpp.org; path Areas of Research/Federal Tax (accessed Oct. 10, 2005), p. 26.

Form Wills
http://www.calbar.ca.gov/calbar/pdfs/publications/Will-Form.pdf (accessed Oct. 12, 2005), p. 147.

Legalzoom, Wills,
http://www.legalzoom.com/legalzip/wills/will_procedure.html (accessed Oct. 12, 2005), p. 147.

Will Forms for Your State,
http://www.uslegalforms.com/last_will_and_testament.htm; select Will Forms - All States - Free Law (accessed Oct. 12, 2005), p. 147.

Legacy Writer, Online Estate Planning Tools for Life,
http://www.legacywriter.com/CreateYourWill_Process.html (accessed Oct. 12, 2005), p. 147.

Generation-Skipping Transfer Tax
Internal Revenue Service, Generation-Skipping Transfer Tax Return,
http://www.irs.gov/pub/irs-pdf/f706gsd.pdf (accessed Oct. 12, 2005), p. 153.

California Bureau of Tax Administration, California Generation-Skipping Transfer Tax Return,
http://www.sco.ca.gov/col/taxinfo/estate/distributions/gstd.pdf (accessed Oct. 12, 2005), pp. 153-154.

New York State, Department of Taxation and Finance, Estate/Generation Skipping Transfer Tax Forms,
http://www.tax.state.ny.us/pdf/2005/et/et500_105.pdf (accessed Oct. 12, 2005), p. 154.

Office of the Auditor, State of Hawaii, *Study of the Fiscal Impact of Providing Certain Benefits to Reciprocal Beneficiaries*, http://www.state.hi.us/auditor/Overviews/1999/99-17.htm (accessed Oct. 12, 2005), p. 78.

Renunciation of Succession
State of Hawaii, Department of the Attorney General, Formal Opinion Letter from Katherine C. Desmarais, Deputy Attorney General, to Ms. Pilialoha E. Lee Loy, Apr. 11, 1997, http://www.state.hi.us/ag/opinions_formal_letters/9703.htm (accessed Oct. 12, 2005), p. 133.

Social Security
Social Security Administration Online, Press Office, Facts and Figures, http://www.ssa.gov/SSA_Home.html; *path* The Press/Facts and Figures (accessed Oct. 21, 2005), p. 775.

Social Security Administration Online, Press Office, http://www.socialsecurity.gov/policy/docs/quickfacts/stat_snapshot/index.html (accessed Oct. 12, 2005), p. 775

Social Security Administration Online, Press Office, http://www.ssa.gov/policy/docs/progdesc/ssptw/2004-2005/europe/index.html (accessed Oct. 12, 2005), p. 775.

Social Security Administration Online, Geographic Statistics Fact Sheets (2005), http://www.socialsecurity.gov/pressoffice/statefctshts.htm (accessed Oct. 21, 2005), p. 775.

Supreme Court of Tasmania
Supreme Court of Tasmania, http://www.supremecourt.tas.gov.au/; select Wills and Probate (accessed Oct. 12, 2005), p. 188.

Preface

Decedents' estates may harken the reader to a time when courses on wills, trusts, and estates focused on the execution of Wills, the intestate status of heirs, and the vagaries of disappointed legatees. There was such a time, but as the Twenty-First Century begins, any course on decedents' estates is more aptly characterized by the creation of inter vivos trusts, the proliferation of non-probate transfers, the easing of the "harsh formalism" of ancient formulae, the disclaimer of inheritance and contest through prenuptial agreements, and the casting of lifelines as an ever-increasing generation of older persons plans for incapacity. Any student-or professor-never would have predicted that states would limit the Rule Against Perpetuities, or abolish it altogether. No one would have predicted that academics would tinker with the share of a pretermitted heir, discount the word "survivor," or rationalize the introduction of extrinsic evidence to change the plain meaning of words. All of these things have come to pass, but a few things have remained the same. For example, no matter what the federal outcome, taxation of estates has always been the tail that wags the dog, and even amidst the lessening grip of federal levies, the states remain vigilant in collection of gift, estate, and inheritance taxes. And the human desire to make a difference in life remains the same, evidencing itself in gifts to charity, educational trusts for children, spousal trusts, and a myriad of trusts to provide "care, comfort and support" for everyone and everything, including pets. Remaining the same is the public policy of any government that seeks to provide an orderly, efficient, and fair administration of wealth transfer.

A final factor that has remained the same, and is consistently present in each generation but is often averted, is the reality that, at some point in time, each person seeking to transfer wealth will become a decedent. No matter what legal changes have taken place, no matter what strategies have been adopted, and no matter what taxes have been imposed and paid, each person is amassing a decedent's estate. Even though we are conscious observers of the scene and realize that inter vivos transfers and planning options are the focus of the modern course material, this is the reason why we chose the title for this book. In assembling the material for the book, choosing cases, writing the Notes, and incorporating code provisions, we have made a purposeful effort to concentrate on the modern adaptations of inter vivos planning, but we are ignoring neither our indebtedness to what has gone before, nor the things that have remained the same. We hope that the reader will recognize and appreciate this balance in the following themes.

First, our primary concern is to make this book a good teaching vehicle. To facilitate this, we have placed a Tool Bar at the start of each chapter, hoping that this will allow for a brief introductory summary before entering the thicket of material. Often students miss the forest for the trees, and we hope that the Tool Bar will assist in providing a comprehensive overview from which the reader will be able to start, refer to throughout, and summarize at the conclusion. We have painstakingly chosen cases with fact patterns that invite interest, creativity, and debate. Good cases make good classes! We wrote the Manual for Teachers to assist with these cases, integrate the code provisions, and explain interconnectedness.

A second theme of the book is informational. While we do ask a few questions in the Notes, far more often we explain, elaborate on the case, and highlight. And while we believe in the practice of providing students with problems, we prefer to allow the cases or the professor to present the problems. The Manual for Teachers contains many former exam questions with feedback provided. Furthermore, students and professors have embraced the Web—it is even available during class. Therefore, the casebook has many Web addresses. There is a Table of Web Sites, and the Web addresses throughout the material provide the students and the professors with a chance to update statistics, view forms, and obtain further sources and information. Plus, we hope you will utilize the many international statutes provided, which furnish a glimpse into such arenas as spousal rights and fiduciary administration in foreign countries. Finally, we offer a device that we have used to teach some of the material—what we refer to as the "Analytical Principle." This is a tool that consists of time frames and points of reference, and is used to explain complicated issues such as lapse, powers of appointment, and vesting. We explain it in Chapter Six: Utilizing Future Interests, but its applicability will be shown in Chapter Seven: Creation, Classification, and Utilization of Trusts.

A third theme of the casebook is confrontational—to incorporate into the text the thorny issue of estate and gift taxation. We have omitted a separate chapter on taxation, preferring instead to place Tax Considerations throughout the casebook. Some of these Tax Considerations consist of material presented in Notes, and some are cases, but each offers a glimpse into the interrelationship between the material being studied and taxation. We think this must be confronted in any course on decedents' estate. Professors wishing to avoid taxation issues may utilize a syllabus that consistently omits these considerations. We hope that others will find the inclusion of taxation to be a dose of reality for students, acknowledging that many of our trusts are premised on avoiding incidents of ownership that will subject the estate to taxation, or structured so as to achieve income or gift tax benefits. Admittedly, some of the tax cases are complicated and unfamiliar, but we think that modern planning for decedents must accommodate their presence and utility.

The final theme inculcated throughout the chapters is statutory construction analysis. Too often students become imbued with a lopsided appreciation for the common law to the detriment of statutory interpretations. To address this, included within the text are various code provisions, such as the international codes previously mention and a number of state and uniform statutes, many from community property states. For example, there are numerous references to both the older and the newer version of the Uniform Probate Code. Also, we find that the Uniform Trust Code has increasing application, as well as the Uniform Prudent Investor Act and the Uniform Health Care Decisions Act. Repeated reference will be made to these, and more individualized attention will be given to the Uniform Parentage Act, the Uniform Premarital Agreement Act, the Uniform Simultaneous Death Act, and the Uniform Statutory Rule Against Perpetuities Act. Of course, individual cases will discuss other state statutes in the context of decisions rendered, and admittedly, sometimes these cases were included because of the extensive discussion by the court of the state's statute. Although the statutes may lack the factual context, including the drama, of decisional law, they are the indisputable first step in any analysis.

The casebook is divided into eight chapters. Chapter One: An Introduction, introduces the student to the issues to arise in the succeeding chapters. We have provided you with "A Family Affair," which concerns a family confronting death, incapacity, wealth transfer, and how the government, attorneys, and the family's own decisions will interconnect. The clients that are factually portrayed confront a reoccurring dilemma in modern society—how to plan for incapacity and transmit wealth to others. Addressing this will invite what is to come in all the other chapters. But this is the chapter where the student is likely to first be introduced to the significance of non-probate transfers in the transmission of wealth, the struggle between state and federal tax entities, the overwhelming effort to avoid either gift or estate taxes, and the possibility that they may be held liable for negligence.

Chapter Two: Intestate Succession, is traditional, statutory and yet is very modern. Every state has an intestate statute defining heirs—this is both traditional and statutory—but extensive consideration is given to the changing definition of family in American society. After establishing the pattern of distribution of wealth when there is neither a Last Will and Testament nor a non-probate substitute, the chapter explores how spouses, issue, and the biological revolution has affected status and the distribution of wealth under intestate statutes. Same-sex partners are achieving increasing status as spouses, and science has increased opportunities for parenthood and heirs. Who is an issue of whom? This is very exciting! And although they will have applicability to other forms of wealth transfer, this chapter provides the opportunity for students to discuss simultaneous death, assignment of expectancy, and disclaimers. These, too, are traditional, but private ordering and non-probate opportunities provide modern applicability.

Chapter Three: The Last Will and Testament, details the historical rules meant to safeguard the Testator's last wishes. We will examine the different types of Wills and then explore the formalities and intentionalities needed to execute any of them. When faced with many historical precedents establishing the validity of Wills, it is interesting to introduce the students to the modern doctrines of substantial compliance and primary intent. This is the chapter in which we seek to balance the old against the new, the evolution of presence at execution, and how much influence is undue. These cases mirror the human condition. And once the students have mastered professional execution with all of its competing interests, we discuss revocation and revival of Wills. As with execution, we have sought to balance the old with the new.

Chapter Four: The Meaning of Words, invites the students to become attorneys and to make a "fortress out of the dictionary." The law has accepted facts of independent significance and incorporation, but legal lists and exoneration are evolving. Likewise, the law regarding contracts to make Wills is fairly settled, but commentators have suggested, and offered legislation, proposing changes to the rules addressing mistake and the distribution of property when there has been a lapse. Comparing the age-old rules with the new exigencies is like pouring new wine into old bottles and precipitates good class participation. But our objective is to provide the grist by offering a chance to explore textualism and evolution.

Chapter Five: Restraints on Transfer of Wealth, confronts the student with a premise they learned in Chapter One—that they have a right under the Constitution to pass their property to others at death. But in this chapter, we learn that there are restraints upon that right. For example, you cannot create a trust that promotes lawlessness, you cannot simply forget your issue, and since your spouse equivalent is your economic partner, she or he has a right to part of the wealth amassed prior to death. These restraints are the ones that students expect, fresh from classes on constitutional law. But we also address a final restraint—the bureaucratic process that will offer considerable restraint upon transfer at death. The costs, forms, delays, taxes, administration, and contests can be a bureaucratic nightmare. Finally, extensive treatment is provided for spouse equivalents. The listing of statutory entitlements available to a spouse equivalent who is able to benefit is a valuable reminder of public policy's attentiveness to committed unions. And the statutory and judicial models to provide for augmenting the estate for election by a surviving spouse equivalent are meant to promote dialogue about public policy's deficiencies and changes.

Chapter Six: Utilizing Future Interests, provides an explanation of the words, phrases, and constructions that have divided "interests" from "possession" for hundreds of years. Anticipating the next chapter, which is devoted exclusively to trusts, this chapter provides definitions, cases, the Analytical Principle that may be used to chart the interests that will pass under anti-lapse statutes, class gifts, powers of appointment, the Rule Against Perpetuities, and vesting. Rather than study the material in a vacuum, the cases and statutes seek to provide what is necessary to use future interests in estate planning instruments. Students will have had an introduction to this material in their first-year property classes, for better or for worse, so what we provide here is the practical application of those words and phrases to trusts and what goes into them.

Chapter Seven: Creation, Classification, and Utilization of Trusts, is the longest chapter in the casebook, but we thought it was justified to assemble all of the trust material in one place to provide a comprehensive approach to the topic. We think it essential that the students understand the five elements of a trust. The cases complement the statutes, and we have sought to distinguish gifts and highlight fiduciary responsibility. We are particularly pleased with the extensive Notes concerning trusts for pets, as these are far more common than anyone may think.

If the five elements of a trust are traditional, the ten classifications of trusts that are provided present the modern evolution. Please note the grantor, dynasty, and pour-over trusts, all of which are part of the modern estate planning scheme. These ten trusts and the five non-probate contractual arrangements are meant to provide the student with modern applicability, placing the material firmly in the context of what occurs each day in law offices. We anticipate that these classifications will prompt interesting class discussion. Likewise, modification and termination of trusts have historical roots and, therefore, rules, but more modern statutes have made substantial inroads, which offers a discussion as to preference and, most importantly, professional responsibility.

Too often, trust administration is given little attention. Yet, in speaking with trustees, there is extensive consideration given to what is prudent, the duty of loyalty, and how to maintain income for beneficiaries and still maintain principal for remainder beneficiaries. Additionally, how should a trustee invest, repair, sell, or administer the trust property? These issues are discussed under powers of the trustee, and appropriate statutory guidelines are provided.

Finally, in Chapter Seven, we discuss three legal constructions that rest upon the validity of trusts, they are: class gifts, powers of appointment, and the Rule Against Perpetuities. With class gifts and powers of appointment, it is possible to present the rules pertaining to definition, scope, and validity, but the Rule Against Perpetuities offers a considerable challenge because of its changing status. It is possible to speculate that the Rule began to lose its binding force when states sought to ameliorate its harshness with doctrines such as wait and see, second look, and cy pres. These are all explained. But when states, and eventually the Uniform Probate Code, adopted the Uniform Statutory Rule Against Perpetuities, extending wait and see to ninety years, it was possible to imagine eliminating the Rule completely. Some states have done so. We provide a state statute abolishing the Rule. Goodness! This provides an opportunity to discuss the public policy behind the Rule. Hopefully, having learned about trusts in the same chapter, it will all come together.

Chapter Eight: Planning for Incapacity, offers an opportunity to return to the family affair presented in the first chapter, and then to discuss options in light of what has been learned between then and now. For example, students will have thought about and discussed the utility of a Will, the consequences of intestate succession, the necessity of clear language, the avoidance of restraints, and the use of trusts to provide for care and support. That done, practicality demands assessment of resources and, specifically, payments from entitlement programs such as Social Security, Medicare, and Medicaid. So as to provide for personal dignity, privacy, and easing the burden on family members, there are state forms and cases concerning durable powers, health care decision delegation, and the powers of conservators and guardians. The facts of these cases command headlines. These are pertinent issues to persons of every age, and the cases provide a good context.

As you use this book we welcome your comments and suggestions. We wish to express our deep appreciation to so many who contributed to this enterprise. Although any errors are our own, we wish to acknowledge our former decedents' estates professors, John L. Garvey and Neill Alford. Also, the grace, friendship, and exactitude of the late Jesse Dukeminier provide inspiration. And finally, we thank all of our present and former students who contributed more than they know and more than we can acknowledge.

January 2006

Raymond C. O'Brien
obrien@law.edu

Michael T. Flannery
mxflannery@ualr.edu

Acknowledgments

We especially thank the National Conference of Commissioners on Uniform State Laws for its permission to reprint excerpts from its copyrighted text of the Uniform Probate Code, the Uniform Trust Code, the Uniform Parentage Act, the Uniform Simultaneous Death Act, the Uniform Prudent Investor Act, the Uniform Statutory Rule Against Perpetuities, the Uniform Anatomical Gift Act, the Uniform Health Care Decisions Act, and the Uniform Custodial Trust Act.

We also thank Haworth Press, Inc., for its permission to reprint excerpts from its copyrighted text of LONG-TERM CARE: FEDERAL STATE AND PRIVATE OPTIONS FOR THE FUTURE.

Note on Editing

Some text, footnotes, and citations have been edited to make the cases we have included more manageable and relevant to the teaching tools applicable to a three- or four-credit course. The footnotes that are included contain the original footnote numbers from the original source. All omissions are indicated with an appropriate ellipses symbol to indicate that material has been omitted.

Decedents' Estates

Chapter One

An Introduction

Tool Bar

I. A Family Affair

Once upon a time, in an average American city, in a modest three bedroom rambler, along a quiet suburban street, lived a man, woman, and three children. Howard and Lisa were married ten years ago; this was the second marriage for Howard and the first for Lisa. Howard and his first wife had two children before their divorce, and Howard was awarded physical and legal custody of them. His former wife lives nearby and sees the children only once or twice a year under the visitation agreement. One child is seventeen and the other is twelve. Howard and Lisa have one daughter who is seven years of age.

The family kitchen is the gathering space for the family, and Howard looks older than his forty-two years indicate as he sits at the kitchen table. He is a high-school principal and met his wife Lisa at the high school, where she still works as a teacher. She is thirty-nine years of age. The three children, Terry (17), Michael (12), and Sarah (7), are either watching television or playing with the computer.

The family has just returned from the funeral of Lisa's father. He died after a lengthy battle with cancer. He is survived by his wife of fifty years and their two daughters, Lisa and Nicole. Nicole is a stock broker. She is unmarried and lives about a thousand miles away. Nicole has taken her mother to the house after the funeral so her mother could rest from the ordeal of the last few days. Howard and Lisa are discussing the mother right now. Lisa is concerned that her mother may no longer be able to live by herself, and she is wondering if Howard would object to her mother coming to live with them. They could fix-up the basement, put in a bathroom, and perhaps get one of those devices that would allow the mother to go up the stairs while sitting down. They could pay for the changes with the money that the father left in his estate. Surely Nicole would contribute, and the mother receives Social Security.

"Well, why can't she continue to live in her own house?" Howard asks.

"You don't know my mother like I do," Lisa responded. "Have you seen how mother has lost so much weight? And at the funeral, she couldn't remember the names of people she has known all her life. And Howard, I certainly wouldn't say this to anyone else, but she just smelled. I don't think she is bathing or taking care of herself. Dad's long illness and death have taken a toll on her. She's becoming very frail."

"How about if we get someone to look in on her from time to time?" Howard responded.

"That's just so expensive. And frankly, I'm afraid to have a stranger in the house with her. You just don't know what will happen. And you hear so many things today. Mother has always been a private person. She will certainly put up a fuss if we say we are going to have a nurse or a caretaker spending a lot of time in her house."

"But she would have to put up with us here, and she will be alone here while we are working," Howard replied.

"Yes," Lisa admitted, "but I'm home early in the afternoon, and I'm always off during the summers. We would be having someone into our house rather than forcing it on her in her own house."

"Maybe we ought to first see how much money your father left before we start making plans. Do you have any idea?"

"Nicole and I looked through the papers Dad left and we found the deed for the house. It is listed as tenancy by the entirety between Mom and Dad. My guess is that the house is worth around $200,000. I know there is a life insurance policy payable to Mom for around $10,000, and there must be joint savings and checking accounts; my guess is that they are worth around $5,000 combined. The car is only two years old and that is listed in Dad's name, alone. Mom never worked, and Dad's Social Security check comes to $1,200 a month. They have been contributing to an IRA, but I don't know how much it is worth. I do know that it is in the form of mutual funds; I have the phone number of the broker. The form says the IRA is payable 'to the estate' and that there is no alternate. I also have to ask about a Fidelity Destiny mutual fund account, into which Dad has been paying $25.00 a month for the last twenty years. I know the number of shares he owns and, when I looked it up on the computer late last night, it indicated that it is worth about $300,000, at least. But what is very weird is that the beneficiary on that Fidelity account is listed as 'The Society for the Prevention of Cruelty to Animals.'"

"I'm surprised he cared so much for animals," Howard quirked.

"So am I," Lisa answered. "But he has had it for so long and probably never thought it would amount to much. I know that Mom and Dad liked to feed the birds and enjoyed going for long walks."

"Is that everything you could find then?" Howard asked.

"Just about." Lisa replied. "There are his clothes, some cuff links and a watch, books, fishing equipment, and a Washington Senators baseball, signed by all of the team and managers and dated around 1954. I doubt Mom even knew he had it, but Nicole and I found it when we were searching for clothes for the burial. Oh! And I almost forgot. We found a Last Will and Testament, dated nearly sixty years ago—long before he and Mom were married and before Nicole and I were born. It has his signature and the signature of three witnesses, too, although the ink has faded and we cannot read the names. But the amazing thing is that it names 'The Society for the Prevention of Cruelty to Animals' as the only beneficiary. That just amazes me!"

"Me too. Does that mean they get everything? Do we have to call them? In fact, what do we do? Have you asked your sister about this? I guess we should talk about this. Where do we start?"

Sitting around the kitchen table, the man and the woman confront a frequent reality in American life: the death of a parent, long-term care of a surviving parent and meeting the human, financial, and practical necessities involved. Howard and Lisa's issues are the subject of any course on decedents' estates. In prior days, the course simply referred to the manner in which wealth was transferred from one generation to another—usually through gift or a valid Last Will and Testament. Today, this is not always so. Today, vast amounts of wealth pass according to three different patterns: (1) non-probate transfers, (2) last wills and testaments, and (3) intestate statutes. Non-probate transfers, such as will substitutes, may pass property outside of the rules governing a Last Will and Testament. Last Wills and Testaments still serve to pass wealth and establish funeral plans, but the rules surrounding their validity have changed. Finally, states still seek to guess what the decedent may have wanted through an intestate statute—a statutory scheme meant to distribute property when neither a will substitute nor a Last Will and Testament is available to do so. Thus, wealth passes through three patterns, and each generates different questions when applied to the family affair of Lisa and Howard.

A. Will Substitution: Non-Probate Transfers

(a) Social Security benefits, life insurance, retirement accounts, and the IRA—for most people, these funds comprise the majority of assets passing from one generation to another. How would you provide for the legal and efficient transfer of the funds described in the fact pattern? What would you need to provide for a transfer? Where should you start the process?

(b) Real Property. How does title to the home in which the father and mother lived control the manner in which the title may be transferred to a survivor? If the daughter asks her husband if they should place title in the elderly mother or pass it to herself and her husband, what would you tell her? How would Nicole, the sister, react? How would you value the house for tax purposes?

(c) What are the federal and state tax consequences of will substitutes (non-probate transfers)? For example, joint accounts, tenancies by the entirety, Individual Retirement Accounts (IRA), payable on death contracts. All of these pass outside of the government controlled probate structure—testate and intestate succession—raising the question as to whether there should be taxes levied on these particular forms of wealth transfer. The obvious answer is "yes," as the government is not about to omit these familiar and often-used wealth transfers to escape taxation. But the decedent's property interest must be a beneficial interest to be taxable, and this determination is often made by state law, with the state's highest court making the determination of beneficial interest. Thus, important questions are raised: How should the state and federal legislatures and courts interact in imposing taxes upon citizens? With the federal taxes on estates receding to possible extinction, how will taxation at the state level respond? Consider the following decision in the context of these questions.

Commissioner v. Estate of Bosch

Supreme Court of the United States, 1967
387 U.S. 456, 87 S. Ct. 1776

Mr. Justice CLARK delivered the opinion of the Court.

These two federal estate tax cases present a common issue for our determination: Whether a federal court or agency in a federal estate tax controversy is conclusively bound by a state trial court adjudication of property rights or characterization of property interests when the United States is not made a party to such proceeding.

In No. 673, Commissioner of Internal Revenue v. Estate of Bosch, 363 F.2d 1009, the Court of Appeals for the Second Circuit held that since the state trial court had 'authoritatively determined' the rights of the parties, it was not required to delve into the correctness of that state court decree. In No. 240, Second National Bank of New Haven, Executor v. United States, 351 F.2d 489, another panel of the same Circuit held that the 'decrees of the Connecticut Probate Court * * * under no circumstances can be construed as binding' on a federal court in subsequent litigation involving federal revenue laws. Whether these cases conflict in principle or not, which is disputed here, there does exist a widespread conflict among the circuits * * * over the question and we granted certiorari to resolve it. 385 U.S. 966, 968, 87 S.Ct. 499, 512, 17 L.Ed.2d 432. We hold that where the federal estate tax liability turns upon the character of a property interest held and transferred by the decedent under state law, federal authorities are not bound by the determination made of such property interest by a state trial court.

* * *

(a) No. 673, Commissioner v. Estate of Bosch.

In 1930, decedent, a resident of New York, created a revocable trust which, as amended in 1931, provided that the income from the corpus was to be paid to his wife during her lifetime. The instrument also gave her a general power of appointment, in default of which it provided that half of the corpus was to go to his heirs and the remaining half was to go to those of his wife.

In 1951 the wife executed an instrument purporting to release the general power of appointment and convert it into a special power. Upon decedent's death in 1957, respondent, in paying federal estate taxes, claimed a marital deduction for the value of the widow's trust. The Commissioner determined, however, that the trust corpus did not qualify for the deduction under §2056(b)(5)[2] of the 1954 Internal Revenue Code and

---

2. Section 2056(b)(5) of the Internal Revenue Code of 1954, 26 U.S.C. §2056(b)(5), provides:
   '(5) Life estate with power of appointment in surviving spouse.—In the case of an interest in property passing from the decedent, if his surviving spouse is entitled for life to all the income from the entire interest, * * * with power in the surviving spouse to appoint the entire interest, * * * (exercisable in favor of such surviving spouse, or of the estate of such surviving spouse, or in favor of either, whether or not in each case the power is exercisable in favor of others), and with no power in any other person to appoint any part of the interest, or such specific portion, to any person other than the surviving spouse—
   '(A) the interest * * * thereof so passing shall, for purposes of subsection (a), be considered as passing to the surviving spouse, and

levied a deficiency. Respondent then filed a petition for redetermination in the Tax Court. The ultimate outcome of the controversy hinged on whether the release executed by Mrs. Bosch in 1951 was invalid—as she claimed it to be—in which case she would have enjoyed a general power of appointment at her husband's death and the trust would therefore qualify for the marital deduction. While the Tax Court proceeding was pending, the respondent filed a petition in the Supreme Court of New York for settlement of the trustee's account; it also sought a determination as to the validity of the release under state law. The Tax Court, with the Commissioner's consent, abstained from making its decision pending the outcome of the state court action. The state court found the release to be a nullity; the Tax Court then accepted the state court judgment as being an 'authoritative exposition of New York law and adjudication of the property rights involved,' 43 T.C. 120, 124, and permitted the deduction. On appeal, a divided Court of Appeals affirmed. It held that '[t]he issue is * * * not whether the federal court is 'bound by' the decision of the state tribunal, but whether or not a state tribunal has authoritatively determined the rights under state law of a party to the federal action.' 363 F.2d, at 1013. The court concluded that the 'New York judgment, rendered by a court which had jurisdiction over parties and subject matter, authoritatively settled the rights of the parties, not only for New York, but also for purposes of the application to those rights of the relevant provisions of federal tax law.' Id., at 1014. It declared that since the state court had held the wife to have a general power of appointment under its law, the corpus of the trust qualified for the marital deduction. We do not agree and reverse.

(b) No. 240, Second National Bank of New Haven, Executor v. United States.

Petitioner in this case is the executor of the will of one Brewster, a resident of Connecticut who died in September of 1958. The decedent's will, together with a codicil thereto, was admitted to probate by the Probate Court for the District of Hamden, Connecticut. The will was executed in 1958 and directed the payment 'out of my estate my just debts and funeral expenses and any death taxes which may be legally assessed * * *.' It further directed that the 'provisions of any statute requiring the apportionment or proration of such taxes among the beneficiaries of this will or the transferees of such property, or the ultimate payment of such taxes by them, shall be without effect in the settlement of my estate.' The will also provided for certain bequests and left the residue in trust; one-third of the income from such trust was to be given to decedent's wife for life, and the other two-thirds for the benefit of his grandchildren that were living at the time of his death. In July of 1958, the decedent executed a codicil to his will, the pertinent part of which gave his wife a general testamentary power of appointment over the corpus of the trust provided for her. This qualified it for the marital deduction as provided by the Internal Revenue Code of 1954, §2056(b)(5). In the federal estate tax return filed in 1959, the widow's trust was claimed as part of the marital deduction and that was computed as one-third of the residue of the estate before the payment of federal estate taxes. It was then deducted, along with other deductions not involved here, from the total value of the estate and the estate tax was then computed on the basis of the balance. The Commissioner disallowed the claimed deduction and levied a defi-

---

'(B) no part of the interest so passing shall, for purposes of paragraph (1) (A), be considered as passing to any person other than the surviving spouse.
'This paragraph shall apply only if such power in the surviving spouse to appoint the entire interest, or such specific portion thereof, whether exercisable by will or during life, is exercisable by such spouse alone and in all events.'

ciency which was based on the denial of the widow's allowance as part of the marital deduction and the reduction of the marital deduction for the widow's trust, by requiring that the estate tax be charged to the full estate prior to the deduction of the widow's trust. After receipt of the deficiency notice, the petitioner filed an application in the state probate court to determine, under state law, the proration of the federal estate taxes paid. Notice of such proceeding was given all interested parties and the District Director of Internal Revenue. The guardian ad litem for the minor grandchildren filed a verified report stating that there was no legal objection to the proration of the federal estate tax as set out in the application of the executor. Neither the adult grandchildren nor the District Director of Internal Revenue filed or appeared in the Probate Court. The court then approved the application, found that the decedent's will did not negate the application of the state proration statute and ordered that the entire federal tax be prorated and charged against the grandchildren's trusts. This interpretation allowed the widow a marital deduction of some $3,600,000 clear of all federal estate tax. The Commissioner, however, subsequently concluded that the ruling of the Probate Court was erroneous and not binding on him, and he assessed a deficiency. After payment of the deficiency, petitioner brought this suit in the United States District Court for a refund. On petitioner's motion for summary judgment, the Government claimed that there was a genuine issue of material fact, i.e., whether the probate proceedings had been adversary in nature. The District Court held that the 'decrees of the Connecticut Probate Court * * * under no circumstances can be construed as binding and conclusive upon a federal court in construing and applying the federal revenue laws.' 222 F.Supp. 446, 457. The court went on to hold that under the standard applied by the state courts, there was no 'clear and unambiguous direction against proration,' and that therefore the state proration statute applied. Id., at 454. The Court of Appeals reversed, holding that the decedent's will 'would seem to be clear and unambiguous to the effect that taxes were to come out of his residual estate and that despite any contrary statute the testator specifically wished to avoid any proration.' 351 F.2d, at 491. It agreed with the District Court that, in any event, the judgment of the State Probate Court was not binding on the federal court.

* * *

Petitioner in No. 240 raises the additional point that the Court of Appeals was incorrect in holding that decedent's will clearly negated the application of the state proration statute. While we did not limit the grant of certiorari, we affirm without discussion the holding of the Court of Appeals on the point. The issue presents solely a question of state law and '[w]e ordinarily accept the determination of local law by the Court of Appeals * * * and we will not disturb it here.' * * * The Court of Appeals did not pass on the correctness of the resolution of the state law problem involved in Bosch, No. 673, and it is remanded for that purpose.

* * *

The problem of what effect must be given a state trial court decree where the matter decided there is determinative of federal estate tax consequences has long burdened the Bar and the courts. This Court has not addressed itself to the problem for nearly a third of a century. In Freuler v. Helvering, 291 U.S. 35, 54 S.Ct. 308, 78 L.Ed. 634 (1934), this Court, declining to find collusion between the parties on the record as presented there, held that a prior in personam judgment in the state court to which the United States was not made a party, '[o]bviously * * * had not the effect of res judicata, and could not furnish the basis for invocation of the full faith and credit clause * * *.' At 43, 54 S.Ct. at

311. In Freuler's wake, at least three positions have emerged among the circuits. The first of these holds that

> '* * * if the question at issue is fairly presented to the state court for its independent decision and is so decided by the court the resulting judgment if binding upon the parties under the state law is conclusive as to their property rights in the federal tax case * * *.' Gallagher v. Smith, 223 F.2d 218, at 225.

The opposite view is expressed in Faulkerson's Estate v. United States, 301 F.2d 231. This view seems to approach that of Erie R. Co. v. Tompkins, 304 U.S. 64, 58 S.Ct. 817, 82 L.Ed. 1188 (1938), in that the federal court will consider itself bound by the state court decree only after independent examination of the state law as determined by the highest court of the State. The Government urges that an intermediate position be adopted; it suggests that a state trial court adjudication is binding in such cases only when the judgment is the result of an adversary proceeding in the state court. Pierpont v. C.I.R., 336 F.2d 277. Also see the dissent of Friendly, J., in Bosch, No. 673.

We look at the problem differently. First, the Commissioner was not made a party to either of the state proceedings here and neither had the effect of *res judicata*, Freuler v. Helvering, supra; nor did the principle of collateral estoppel apply. It can hardly be denied that both state proceedings were brought for the purpose of directly affecting federal estate tax liability. Next, it must be remembered that it was a federal taxing statute that the Congress enacted and upon which we are here passing. Therefore, in construing it, we must look to the legislative history surrounding it. We find that the report of the Senate Finance Committee recommending enactment of the marital deduction used very guarded language in referring to the very question involved here. It said that 'proper regard,' not finality, 'should be given to interpretations of the will' by state courts and then only when entered by a court 'in a bona fide adversary proceeding.' S.Rep. No. 1013, Pt. 2, 80th Cong., 2d Sess., 4. We cannot say that the authors of this directive intended that the decrees of state trial courts were to be conclusive and binding on the computation of the federal estate tax as levied by the Congress. If the Congress had intended state trial court determinations to have that effect on the federal actions, it certainly would have said so—which it did not do. On the contrary, we believe it intended the marital deduction to be strictly construed and applied. Not only did it indicate that only 'proper regard' was to be accorded state decrees but it placed specific limitations on the allowance of the deduction as set out in §2056(b), (c), and (d). These restrictive limitations clearly indicate the great care that Congress exercised in the drawing of the Act and indicate also a definite concern with the elimination of loopholes and escape hatches that might jeopardize the federal revenue. This also is in keeping with the long-established policy of the Congress, as expressed in the Rules of Decision Act, 28 U.S.C. §1652. There it is provided that in the absence of federal requirements such as the Constitution or Acts of Congress, the 'laws of the several states * * * shall be regarded as rules of decision in civil actions in the courts of the United States, in cases where they apply.' This Court has held that judicial decisions are 'laws of the * * * state' within the section. Erie R. Co. v. Tompkins, supra; Cohen v. Beneficial Loan Corp., 337 U.S. 541, 69 S.Ct. 1221, 93 L.Ed. 1528 (1949); King v. Order of United Commercial Travelers, 333 U.S. 153, 68 S.Ct. 488, 92 L.Ed. 608 (1948). Moreover, even in diversity cases this Court has further held that while the decrees of 'lower state courts' should be 'attributed some weight * * * the decision [is] not controlling * * *' where the highest court of the State has not spoken on the point. King v. Order of United Commercial Travelers, supra, at 160—161, 68 S.Ct. at 492. And in West v. American Tel. & Tel. Co.,

311 U.S. 223, 61 S.Ct. 179, 85 L.Ed. 139 (1940), this Court further held that 'an inter-mediate appellate state court * * * is a datum for ascertaining state law which is not to be disregarded by a federal court *unless it is convinced by other persuasive data that the highest court of the state would decide otherwise.*' At 237, 61 S.Ct. at 183 (Emphasis sup-plied.) Thus, under some conditions, federal authority may not be bound even by an intermediate state appellate court ruling. It follows here then, that when the application of a federal statute is involved, the decision of a state trial court as to an underlying issue of state law should *a fortiori* not be controlling. This is but an application of the rule of Erie R. Co. v. Tompkins, supra, where state law as announced by the highest court of the State is to be followed. This is not a diversity case but the same principle may be applied for the same reasons, viz., the underlying substantive rule involved is based on state law and the State's highest court is the best authority on its own law. If there be no decision by that court then federal authorities must apply what they find to be the state law after giving 'proper regard' to relevant rulings of other courts of the State. In this respect, it may be said to be, in effect, sitting as a state court. Bernhardt v. Polygraphic Co., 350 U.S. 198, 76 S.Ct. 273, 100 L.Ed. 199 (1956).

We believe that this would avoid much of the uncertainty that would result from the 'non-adversary' approach and at the same time would be fair to the taxpayer and pro-tect the federal revenue as well.

The judgment in No. 240 is therefore affirmed while that in No. 673 is reversed and remanded for further proceedings not inconsistent with this opinion. It is so ordered.

Judgment in No. 240 affirmed and judgment in No. 673 reversed and case remanded.

Mr. Justice DOUGLAS, dissenting.

As the Court says, the issue in these cases is not whether the Commissioner is 'bound' by the state court decrees. He was not a party to the state court proceedings and therefore cannot be bound in the sense of res judicata. The question simply is whether, absent fraud or collusion, a federal court can ignore a state court judgment when fed-eral taxation depends upon property rights and when property rights rest on state law, as they do here.

Since our 1938 decision in Erie R. Co. v. Tompkins, 304 U.S. 64, 58 S.Ct. 817, 82 L.Ed. 1188, an unbroken line of cases has held that the federal courts must look to state legislation, state decisions, state administrative practice, for the state law that is to be applied. See, e.g., Cities Service Oil Co. v. Dunlap, 308 U.S. 208, 60 S.Ct. 201, 84 L.Ed. 196; Bernhardt v. Polygraphic Co. of America, 350 U.S. 198, 76 S.Ct. 273, 100 L.Ed. 199. Those were diversity cases; and in them we have never suggested that the federal court may ignore a relevant state court decision because it was not entered by the high-est state court. Indeed, we have held that the federal court is obligated to follow the de-cision of a lower state court in the absence of decisions of the State Supreme Court showing that the state law is other than announced by the lower court. * * *

Even before it was held that federal courts must apply state law in diversity cases, it was incumbent upon federal courts to take state law from state court decisions when federal tax consequences turned on state law. In Freuler v. Helvering, 291 U.S. 35, 54 S.Ct. 308, 78 L.Ed. 634, the trustee under a decedent's will had included in in-come distributed to the life beneficiaries amounts representing depreciation of the corpus. The life beneficiaries did not include the amounts constituting depreciation and the Commissioner asserted a deficiency. While the case was on appeal to the Board of Tax Appeals, the trustee filed an accounting in the state probate court, requesting its approval. The state court held that the life beneficiaries were not entitled to the distribution of depreciation of the corpus, and ordered that the life beneficiaries repay the trustee for the amount improperly distributed to them. In the tax litigation, the Court of Appeals ignored the state court determination on the ground that 'no orders of the probate court, the effect of which would relate to what are deductions to be allowed under the national income taxing law, are conclusive and binding on the federal courts * * *.' Commissioner of Internal Revenue v. Freuler, 9 Cir., 62 F.2d 733, 735. The Court reversed, holding that the probate court order was an order governing distribution within §219 of the Revenue Act of 1921. It went on to say:

> 'Moreover, the decision of [the probate] court, until reversed or overruled, establishes the law of California respecting distribution of the trust estate. It is none the less a declaration of the law of the state because not based on a statute, or earlier decisions. The rights of the beneficiaries are property rights and the court has adjudicated them. What the law as announced by that court adjudges distributable is, we think, to be so considered in applying section 219 of the Revenue Act of 1921.' 291 U.S. at 45, 54 S.Ct. at 312.

The issue of the effect of a state court determination came up again in Blair v. Commissioner, 300 U.S. 5, 57 S.Ct. 330, 81 L.Ed. 465. The issue in that case was whether a beneficiary had effectively assigned income from a trust. In prior tax litigation, a federal court held that the trust was a spendthrift trust and that, therefore, the assignments were invalid and the income taxable to the beneficiary. The trustees then brought an action in the state court; the state courts determined that the trust was not a spendthrift trust and that the assignments were valid. The Board of Tax Appeals accepted the decision of the state court and rejected the Commissioner's claim that petitioner was liable for tax on the income. The Court rejected the Commissioner's argument that the trust was a spendthrift trust, noting that:

> 'The question of the validity of the assignments is a question of local law. * * * By that law the character of the trust, the nature and extent of the interest of the beneficiary, and the power of the beneficiary to assign that interest in whole or in part, are to be determined. The decision of the state court upon these questions is final. * * * It matters not that the decision was by an intermediate appellate court. * * * In this instance, it is not necessary to go beyond the obvious point that the decision was in a suit between the trustees and the beneficiary and his assignees, and the decree which was entered in pursuance of the decision determined as between these parties the validity of the particular assignments. Nor is there any basis for a charge that the suit was collusive and the decree inoperative. * * * The trustees were entitled to seek the instructions of the court having supervision of the trust. That court entertained the suit and the appellate court, with the first decision of the Circuit Court of Appeals before it, reviewed the decisions of the Supreme Court of the State and reached a deliberate conclusion. To derogate from the authority of that conclusion and of the decree it commanded, so far as the question is one of state law, would be wholly unwarranted in the exercise of federal jurisdiction.
>
> 'In the face of this ruling of the state court it is not open to the Government to argue that the trust 'was, under the [state] law, a spendthrift trust.' The point of the argument is that, the trust being of that character, the state law barred

the voluntary alienation by the beneficiary of his interest. The state court held precisely the contrary.' Id., 9—10, 57 S.Ct. 332.

I would adhere to Freuler v. Helvering, supra, and Blair v, Commissioner, supra. There was no indication in those cases that the state court decision would not be followed if it was not from the highest state court.

The idea that these state proceedings are not to be respected reflects the premise that such proceedings are brought solely to avoid federal taxes. But there are some instances in which an adversary proceeding is impossible (see, e.g., Estate of Darlington v. Commissioner, 3 Cir., 302 F.2d 693; Braverman & Gerson, The Conclusiveness of State Court Decrees in Federal Tax Litigation, 17 Tax L.Rev. 545, 570—572 (1962)), and many instances in which the parties desire a determination of their rights for other than tax reasons.

Not giving effect to a state court determination may be unfair to the taxpayer and is contrary to the congressional purpose of making federal tax consequences depend upon rights under state law. The result will be to tax the taxpayer or his estate for benefits which he does not have under state law. This aspect is emphasized in Blair v. Commissioner, supra, where the Government attempted to tax the taxpayer for income to which he had no right under state law. In Second National Bank v. United States, the grandchildren's trust will be assessed for the estate taxes, since the state court held that the proration statute applied; but the estate tax will be computed as if the proration statute did not apply—the marital deduction will be decreased and the tax increased. Or take the case where a state court determines that X does not own a house. After X dies, a federal court determines that the state court was wrong and that X owned the house, and it must be included in his gross estate even though it does not pass to his heirs. I cannot believe that Congress intended such unjust results.

This is not to say that a federal court is bound by all state court decrees. A federal court might not be bound by a consent decree, for it does not purport to be a declaration of state law; it may be merely a judicial stamp placed upon the parties' contractual settlement. Nor need the federal court defer to a state court decree which has been obtained by fraud or collusion. But where, absent those considerations, a state court has reached a deliberate conclusion, where it has construed state law, the federal court should consider the decision to be an exposition of the controlling state law and give it effect as such.

* * *

B. Probate Transfers: The Last Will and Testament

(a) What claims does The Society for the Prevention of Cruelty to Animals have against the estate of the decedent? Do you favor allowing property to pass outside of the family? Does time make a difference? Who would have standing to contest the claims of the Society? Since the Society is a charity, are there any other considerations that may affect the true intent of the decedent?

(b) Since the IRA proceeds are payable to the estate of the decedent, does the Last Will and Testament give the IRA to the Society as well? What is the relationship between the will-substitute IRA and the testamentary Last Will and Testament?

(c) Should the surviving spouse or the two children of the decedent, Lisa and Nicole, have any priority claim against the estate of the decedent? What role does public policy play in affecting the ability of a person to pass wealth through a valid Last Will and Testament? Should there be greater restrictions on your ability to pass wealth at death than during life?

(d) What formalities and intentionalities should a state require before allowing transfer of property at death? Since the decedent is not present to provide assurance of his or her wishes, should the formalities and intentionalities be strict? What public policy is served? Do the future extended needs of the elderly spouse of the decedent justify changes in the estate plan of the decedent so that the spouse may be provided for through additional assets? What if one of the daughters of the decedent needed expensive medical care? What if one of the daughters has fled the home and has not spoken to the decedent for decades? Should any of these possibilities have an effect upon the Last Will and Testament? What if "everyone knows" the decedent intended this to be a valid Will, but it lacks proper formalities? Would you still allow it to pass the property?

(e) Does one state have the right to require stricter standards for a Last Will and Testament than another state? What happens if a person meets all of the requirements for a valid Will in one state—the state of execution of the Will—but then dies domiciled in another state that enforces stricter formalities and that does not wish to probate the Will? Should there be a uniform system of probate in the United States to meet this dilemma?

C. Probate Transfers: Intestate Succession

(a) If there is no valid Last Will and Testament, how should the property of the decedent be distributed? Does it make a difference that the decedent died with a spouse and children? Should the spouse get everything? Does it matter how long the couple was married? If you were a part of the state legislature, how would you provide for property distribution upon death when there is no Will? Would oral arrangements suffice? What if there were a list of instructions left by the decedent? If there were no instructions, how would you take charge of the property distribution to best provide for public policy? Which is preeminent in your mind: the possible wishes of the decedent or the benefit of the potential beneficiaries? Should beneficiaries be prioritized by blood family members or by persons with whom the decedent shared a purposeful commitment?

(b) Suppose the decedent had two daughters. If he had provided for one with lavish gifts, such as an expensive education, gifts, or a wedding, would this mean that this daughter should receive less from her father's intestate estate? Should the parent's verbal or written opinion make a difference?

(c) What is the relationship among the following: the intestate estate, the will substitutes, and the Last Will and Testament? As an attorney, what responsibilities do you have to your client, to possible beneficiaries chosen by your client, and to the administration of a process through which each living person will pass? Do you favor a "privity" requirement between the decedent and the attorney, thereby eliminating any claims made by disappointed beneficiaries?

(d) Since the intestate system is governed by state statute, should there be a federal standard by which each state will have similar requirements, and by which public confusion will lessen? Do you favor a system, as in the United Kingdom, where judges are given great flexibility in making decisions?

(e) Finally, examine the family structure of Howard and Lisa. They have one child of their own, and Howard has two children from a prior marriage. The children are related by the half-blood, and Lisa is a step-mother to Terry and Michael. How would you plan an estate plan for them in a manner that would be equitable and lessen future discord?

II. Government's Role

Hodel v. Irving

Supreme Court of the United States, 1987
481 U.S. 704, 107 S. Ct. 2076

O'CONNOR, Justice.

The question presented is whether the original version of the "escheat" provision of the Indian Land Consolidation Act of 1983 * * * effected a "taking" of appellees' decedents' property without just compensation.

* * *

Towards the end of the 19th century, Congress enacted a series of land Acts which divided the communal reservations of Indian tribes into individual allotments for Indians and unallotted lands for non-Indian settlement. This legislation seems to have been in part animated by a desire to force Indians to abandon their nomadic ways in order to "speed the Indians' assimilation into American society," Solem v. Bartlett, 465 U.S. 463, 466, 104 S.Ct. 1161, 1164, 79 L.Ed.2d 443 (1984), and in part a result of pressure to free new lands for further white settlement. Ibid. Two years after the enactment of the General Allotment Act of 1887, ch. 119, 24 Stat. 388, Congress adopted a specific statute authorizing the division of the Great Reservation of the Sioux Nation into separate reservations and the allotment of specific tracts of reservation land to individual Indians, conditioned on the consent of three-fourths of the adult male Sioux. Act of Mar. 2, 1889, ch. 405, 25 Stat. 888. Under the Act, each male Sioux head of household took 320 acres of land and most other individuals 160 acres. 25 Stat. 890. In order to protect the allottees from the improvident disposition of their lands to white settlers, the Sioux allotment statute provided that the allotted lands were to be held in trust by the United States. Id., at 891. Until 1910, the lands of deceased allottees passed to their heirs "according to the laws of the State or Territory" where the land was located, ibid., and after 1910, allottees were permitted to dispose of their interests by will in accordance with regulations promulgated by the Secretary of the Interior. 36 Stat. 856, 25 U.S.C. § 373. Those regulations generally served to protect Indian ownership of the allotted lands.

The policy of allotment of Indian lands quickly proved disastrous for the Indians. Cash generated by land sales to whites was quickly dissipated, and the Indians, rather than farming the land themselves, evolved into petty landlords, leasing their allotted lands to white ranchers and farmers and living off the meager rentals. Lawson, Heirship: The Indian Amoeba, reprinted in Hearing on S. 2480 and S. 2663 before the Senate Select Committee on Indian Affairs, 98th Cong., 2d Sess., 82–83 (1984). The failure of the allotment program became even clearer as successive generations came to hold the allotted lands. Thus 40-, 80-, and 160-acre parcels became splintered into multiple undivided interests in land, with some parcels having hundreds, and many parcels having dozens, of owners. Because the land was held in trust and often could not be alienated or partitioned, the fractionation problem grew and grew over time.

A 1928 report commissioned by the Congress found the situation administratively unworkable and economically wasteful. L. Meriam, Institute for Government Research, The Problem of Indian Administration 40–41. Good, potentially productive, land was allowed to lie fallow, amidst great poverty, because of the difficulties of managing property held in this manner. Hearings on H.R. 11113 before the Subcommittee on Indian Affairs of the House Committee on Interior and Insular Affairs, 89th Cong., 2d Sess., 10 (1966) (remarks of Rep. Aspinall). In discussing the Indian Reorganization Act of 1934, Representative Howard said:

> "It is in the case of the inherited allotments, however, that the administrative costs become incredible.... On allotted reservations, numerous cases exist where the shares of each individual heir from lease money may be 1 cent a month. Or one heir may own minute fractional shares in 30 or 40 different allotments. The cost of leasing, bookkeeping, and distributing the proceeds in many cases far exceeds the total income. The Indians and the Indian Service personnel are thus trapped in a meaningless system of minute partition in which all thought of the possible use of land to satisfy human needs is lost in a mathematical haze of bookkeeping." 78 Cong. Rec. 11728 (1934).

In 1934, in response to arguments such as these, the Congress acknowledged the failure of its policy and ended further allotment of Indian lands. Indian Reorganization Act of 1934, ch. 576, 48 Stat. 984, 25 U.S.C. §461 et seq.

But the end of future allotment by itself could not prevent the further compounding of the existing problem caused by the passage of time. Ownership continued to fragment as succeeding generations came to hold the property, since, in the order of things, each property owner was apt to have more than one heir. In 1960, both the House and the Senate undertook comprehensive studies of the problem. See House Committee on Interior and Insular Affairs, Indian Heirship Land Study, 86th Cong., 2d Sess. (Comm.Print 1961); Senate Committee on Interior and Insular Affairs, Indian Heirship Land Survey, 86th Cong., 2d Sess. (Comm.Print 1960–1961). These studies indicated that one-half of the approximately 12 million acres of allotted trust lands were held in fractionated ownership, with over 3 million acres held by more than six heirs to a parcel. Id., at pt. 2, p. X. Further hearings were held in 1966, Hearings on H.R. 11113, supra, but not until the Indian Land Consolidation Act of 1983 did the Congress take action to ameliorate the problem of fractionated ownership of Indian lands.

Section 207 of the Indian Land Consolidation Act—the escheat provision at issue in this case—provided:

> "No undivided fractional interest in any tract of trust or restricted land within a tribe's reservation or otherwise subjected to a tribe's jurisdiction shall descedent [sic] by intestacy or devise but shall escheat to that tribe if such interest represents 2 per centum or less of the total acreage in such tract and has earned to its owner less than $100 in the preceding year before it is due to escheat." 96 Stat. 2519.

Congress made no provision for the payment of compensation to the owners of the interests covered by §207. The statute was signed into law on January 12, 1983, and became effective immediately.

The three appellees—Mary Irving, Patrick Pumpkin Seed, and Eileen Bissonette— are enrolled members of the Oglala Sioux Tribe. They are, or represent, heirs or devisees of members of the Tribe who died in March, April, and June 1983. Eileen Bissonette's decedent, Mary Poor Bear-Little Hoop Cross, purported to will all her property, including property subject to §207, to her five minor children in whose name Bissonette claims the property. Chester Irving, Charles Leroy Pumpkin Seed, and Edgar Pumpkin Seed all died intestate. At the time of their deaths, the four decedents owned 41 fractional interests subject to the provisions of §207. App. 20, 22–28, 32–33, 37–39. The Irving estate lost two interests whose value together was approximately $100; the Bureau of Indian Affairs placed total values of approximately $2,700 on the 26 escheatable interests in the Cross estate and $1,816 on the 13 escheatable interests in the Pumpkin Seed estates. But for §207, this property would have passed, in the ordinary course, to appellees or those they represent.

Appellees filed suit in the United States District Court for the District of South Dakota, claiming that §207 resulted in a taking of property without just compensation in violation of the Fifth Amendment. The District Court concluded that the statute was constitutional. It held that appellees had no vested interest in the property of the decedents prior to their deaths and that Congress had plenary authority to abolish the power of testamentary disposition of Indian property and to alter the rules of intestate succession. App. to Juris.Statement 21a–26a.

The Court of Appeals for the Eighth Circuit reversed. Irving v. Clark, 758 F.2d 1260 (1985). Although it agreed that appellees had no vested rights in the decedents' property, it concluded that their decedents had a right, derived from the original Sioux allotment statute, to control disposition of their property at death. The Court of Appeals held that appellees had standing to invoke that right and that the taking of that right without compensation to decedents' estates violated the Fifth Amendment. * * *

The Congress, acting pursuant to its broad authority to regulate the descent and devise of Indian trust lands, Jefferson v. Fink, 247 U.S. 288, 294, 38 S.Ct. 516, 518, 62 L.Ed. 1117 (1918), enacted §207 as a means of ameliorating, over time, the problem of extreme fractionation of certain Indian lands. By forbidding the passing on at death of small, undivided interests in Indian lands, Congress hoped that future generations of Indians would be able to make more productive use of the Indians' ancestral lands. We agree with the Government that encouraging the consolidation of Indian lands is a public purpose of high order. The fractionation problem on Indian reservations is extraordinary and may call for dramatic action to encourage consolidation. The Sisseton-Wahpeton Sioux Tribe, appearing as amicus curiae in support of the Secretary of the Interior, is a quintessential victim of fractionation. Forty-acre tracts on the Sisseton-Wahpeton Lake Traverse Reservation, leasing for about $1,000 annually, are commonly subdivided into hundreds of undivided interests, many of which generate only pennies a year in rent. The average tract has 196 owners and the average owner undivided interests in 14 tracts. The administrative headache this represents can be fathomed by examining Tract 1305, dubbed "one of the most fractionated parcels of land in the world." Lawson, Heirship: The Indian Amoeba, reprinted in Hearing on S. 2480 and S. 2663 before the Senate Select Committee on Indian Affairs, 98th Cong., 2d Sess., 85 (1984). Tract 1305 is 40 acres and produces $1,080 in income annually. It is valued at $8,000. It has 439 owners, one-third of whom receive less than $.05 in annual rent and two-thirds of whom receive less than $1. The largest interest holder receives $82.85 annually. The common denominator used to compute fractional interests in the property is 3,394,923,840,000. The smallest heir receives $.01 every 177 years. If the tract were sold (assuming the 439 owners could agree) for its estimated $8,000 value, he would be entitled to $.000418. The administrative costs of handling this tract are estimated by the

Bureau of Indian Affairs at $17,560 annually. Id., at 86, 87. See also Comment, Too Little Land, Too Many Heirs—The Indian Heirship Land Problem, 46 Wash.L.Rev. 709, 711–713 (1971).

This Court has held that the Government has considerable latitude in regulating property rights in ways that may adversely affect the owners. See Keystone Bituminous Coal Assn. v. DeBenedictis, 480 U.S. 470, 491–492, 107 S.Ct. 1232, 1245–1246, 94 L.Ed.2d 472 (1987); Penn Central Transportation Co. v. New York City, 438 U.S. 104, 125–127, 98 S.Ct. 2646, 2659–2661, 57 L.Ed.2d 631 (1978); Goldblatt v. Hempstead, 369 U.S. 590, 592–593, 82 S.Ct. 987, 988–989, 8 L.Ed.2d 130 (1962). The framework for examining the question whether a regulation of property amounts to a taking requiring just compensation is firmly established and has been regularly and recently reaffirmed. See, e.g., Keystone Bituminous Coal Assn. v. DeBenedictis, supra, 480 U.S., at 485, 107 S.Ct., at 1241–1242; Ruckelshaus v. Monsanto Co., 467 U.S. 986, 1004–1005, 104 S.Ct. 2862, 2873–2874, 81 L.Ed.2d 815 (1984); Hodel v. Virginia Surface Mining and Reclamation Assn., Inc., 452 U.S. 264, 295, 101 S.Ct. 2352, 2370, 69 L.Ed.2d 1 (1981); Agins v. Tiburon, 447 U.S. 255, 260–261, 100 S.Ct. 2138, 2141, 65 L.Ed.2d 106 (1980); Kaiser Aetna v. United States, 444 U.S. 164, 174–175, 100 S.Ct. 383, 389–390, 62 L.Ed.2d 332 (1979); Penn Central Transportation Co. v. New York City, supra, 438 U.S., at 124, 98 S.Ct., at 2659. As THE CHIEF JUSTICE has written:

> "[T]his Court has generally 'been unable to develop any "set formula" for determining when "justice and fairness" require that economic injuries caused by public action be compensated by the government, rather than remain disproportionately concentrated on a few persons.' [Penn Central Transportation Co. v. New York City, 438 U.S.], at 124 [98 S.Ct., at 2659]. Rather, it has examined the 'taking' question by engaging in essentially ad hoc, factual inquiries that have identified several factors—such as the economic impact of the regulation, its interference with reasonable investment backed expectations, and the character of the governmental action—that have particular significance...." Kaiser Aetna v. United States, supra, 444 U.S., at 175, 100 S.Ct., at 390.

There is no question that the relative economic impact of § 207 upon the owners of these property rights can be substantial. Section 207 provides for the escheat of small undivided property interests that are unproductive during the year preceding the owner's death. Even if we accept the Government's assertion that the income generated by such parcels may be properly thought of as de minimis, their value may not be. While the Irving estate lost two interests whose value together was only approximately $100, the Bureau of Indian Affairs placed total values of approximately $2,700 and $1,816 on the escheatable interests in the Cross and Pumpkin Seed estates. See App. 20, 21–28, 29–39. These are not trivial sums. There are suggestions in the legislative history regarding the 1984 amendments to § 207 that the failure to "look back" more than one year at the income generated by the property had caused the escheat of potentially valuable timber and mineral interests. S.Rep. No. 98-632, p. 12 (1984); Hearing on H.J. Res. 158 before the Senate Select Committee on Indian Affairs, 98th Cong., 2d Sess., 20, 26, 32, 75 (1984); Amendments to the Indian Land Consolidation Act: Hearing on H.J.Res. 158 before the Senate Select Committee on Indian Affairs, 98th Cong., 1st Sess., 8, 29 (1983). Of course, the whole of appellees' decedents' property interests were not taken by § 207. Appellees' decedents retained full beneficial use of the property during their lifetimes as well as the right to convey it inter vivos. There is no question, however, that the right to pass on valuable property to one's heirs is itself a valuable right. Depending on the age of the owner, much or most of the value of the parcel may inhere in this "remainder" interest. See 26 CFR § 20.2031-7(f) (Table A) (1986) (value of remainder interest when life tenant is age 65 is approximately 32% of the whole).

The extent to which any of appellees' decedents had "investment-backed expectations" in passing on the property is dubious. Though it is conceivable that some of these interests were purchased with the expectation that the owners might pass on the remainder to their heirs at death, the property has been held in trust for the Indians for 100 years and is overwhelmingly acquired by gift, descent, or devise. Because of the highly fractionated ownership, the property is generally held for lease rather than improved and used by the owners. None of the appellees here can point to any specific investment-backed expectations beyond the fact that their ancestors agreed to accept allotment only after ceding to the United States large parts of the original Great Sioux Reservation.

Also weighing weakly in favor of the statute is the fact that there is something of an "average reciprocity of advantage," Pennsylvania Coal Co. v. Mahon, 260 U.S. 393, 415, 43 S.Ct. 158, 160, 67 L.Ed. 322 (1922), to the extent that owners of escheatable interests maintain a nexus to the Tribe. Consolidation of Indian lands in the Tribe benefits the members of the Tribe. All members do not own escheatable interests, nor do all owners belong to the Tribe. Nevertheless, there is substantial overlap between the two groups. The owners of escheatable interests often benefit from the escheat of others' fractional interests. Moreover, the whole benefit gained is greater than the sum of the burdens imposed since consolidated lands are more productive than fractionated lands.

If we were to stop our analysis at this point, we might well find § 207 constitutional. But the character of the Government regulation here is extraordinary. In Kaiser Aetna v. United States, 444 U.S., at 176, 100 S.Ct., at 391, we emphasized that the regulation destroyed "one of the most essential sticks in the bundle of rights that are commonly characterized as property—the right to exclude others." Similarly, the regulation here amounts to virtually the abrogation of the right to pass on a certain type of property— the small undivided interest—to one's heirs. In one form or another, the right to pass on property—to one's family in particular—has been part of the Anglo-American legal system since feudal times. See United States v. Perkins, 163 U.S. 625, 627–628, 16 S.Ct. 1073, 1074, 41 L.Ed. 287 (1896). The fact that it may be possible for the owners of these interests to effectively control disposition upon death through complex inter vivos transactions such as revocable trusts is simply not an adequate substitute for the rights taken, given the nature of the property. Even the United States concedes that total abrogation of the right to pass property is unprecedented and likely unconstitutional. Tr. of Oral Arg. 12–14. Moreover, this statute effectively abolishes both descent and devise of these property interests even when the passing of the property to the heir might result in consolidation of property—as for instance when the heir already owns another undivided interest in the property. * * * Cf. 25 U.S.C. § 2206(b) (1982 ed., Supp. III). Since the escheatable interests are not, as the United States argues, necessarily de minimis, nor, as it also argues, does the availability of inter vivos transfer obviate the need for descent and devise, a total abrogation of these rights cannot be upheld. But cf. Andrus v. Allard, 444 U.S. 51, 100 S.Ct. 318, 62 L.Ed.2d 210 (1979) (upholding abrogation of the right to sell endangered eagles' parts as necessary to environmental protection regulatory scheme).

In holding that complete abolition of both the descent and devise of a particular class of property may be a taking, we reaffirm the continuing vitality of the long line of cases recognizing the States', and where appropriate, the United States', broad authority to adjust the rules governing the descent and devise of property without implicating the guarantees of the Just Compensation Clause. See, e.g., Irving Trust Co. v. Day, 314 U.S. 556, 562, 62 S.Ct. 398, 401, 86 L.Ed. 452 (1942); Jefferson v. Fink, 247 U.S., at 294, 38 S.Ct., at 518. The difference in this case is the fact that both descent and devise are completely abolished; indeed they are abolished even in circumstances when the governmental purpose sought to be advanced, consolidation of ownership of Indian lands, does not conflict with the further descent of the property.

There is little doubt that the extreme fractionation of Indian lands is a serious public problem. It may well be appropriate for the United States to ameliorate fractionation by means of regulating the descent and devise of Indian lands. Surely it is permissible for the United States to prevent the owners of such interests from further subdividing them among future heirs on pain of escheat. See Texaco, Inc. v. Short, 454 U.S. 516, 542, 102 S.Ct. 781, 799, 70 L.Ed.2d 738 (1982) (BRENNAN, J., dissenting). It may be appropriate to minimize further compounding of the problem by abolishing the descent of such interests by rules of intestacy, thereby forcing the owners to formally designate an heir to prevent escheat to the Tribe. What is certainly not appropriate is to take the extraordinary step of abolishing both descent and devise of these property interests even when the passing of the property to the heir might result in consolidation of property. Accordingly, we find that this regulation, in the words of Justice Holmes, "goes too far." Pennsylvania Coal Co. v. Mahon, 260 U.S., at 415, 43 S.Ct., at 160. The judgment of the Court of Appeals is

Affirmed.

* * * [Concurring opinions are omitted.]

In re Freihofer

Surrogate's Court, Albany County, 1997
172 Misc. 2d 260, 658 N.Y.S.2d 811

RAYMOND E. MARINELLI, Surrogate.

Charles Freihofer died a testate resident of Albany County on January 11, 1981, survived by his spouse, Phoebe Freihofer, and two sons, Andrew and Stephen Freihofer. By the terms of the decedent's Last Will and Testament, duly admitted to probate on January 21, 1981, the entire estate passed to his wife, Phoebe.

However, under renunciation filed in this Court on March 4, 1981 by Phoebe Freihofer, a portion of the decedent's estate made up of properties affiliated with the Charles Freihofer Baking Company, Inc. passed into testamentary trusts for the benefit of the decedent's two sons, Andrew and Stephen Freihofer.

Pursuant to the terms of the Last Will and Testament, Alan E. Steiner, Charles C. Freihofer III and Phoebe B. Freihofer, the widow, were appointed executors on January 21, 1981; letters of trusteeship for the benefit of Andrew and Stephen were issued to Alan Steiner, the sole trustee, on April 3, 1981.

An examination of the Court records in this estate reveals that a New York estate tax proceeding was filed and an Order Fixing Taxes entered on November 14, 1983. The record further indicates that the gross New York estate was valued at $1,405,201.65. There are no receipts or releases in the file, no accounting has been made to the Court, and a report filed on March 25, 1983, pursuant to 22 NYCRR former 1940.15, executed solely by co-executor/attorney Alan E. Steiner, shows that at the time the fiduciaries were still holding at least $417,446.00 in estate assets.

On August 30, 1996, Andrew G. Freihofer filed a petition with this Court seeking an Order to Compel Alan E. Steiner, as Trustee of the testamentary trust of Charles F. Freihofer, to account. Citation was issued returnable on September 10, 1996, at which time the respondent Executor filed an answer seeking dismissal of the within petition to compel accounting. Thereafter, respondent brought on a motion to dismiss the within petition and in the alternative for summary judgment based upon the following arguments:

1. release of claim

2. documentary evidence

3. there is another action pending between the same parties for the same cause of action and relief in the Supreme Court in the State of New York.

In support of the motion, an affidavit of Alan E. Steiner has been submitted, together with a memorandum of law.

In response to the motion, petitioner has submitted an affidavit and memorandum of law. It is this motion to dismiss and the underlying petition to compel an accounting which the Court now addresses.

Movant has asserted as a basis for dismissal and/or summary judgment the existence of a release of claim and a receipt, release and waiver signed by the trust beneficiary and petitioner herein, Andrew Freihofer. It is significant that the original release, receipt and waiver was never filed with the Court, and has yet to be submitted for filing, even though its existence is being relied on in the within motion. Further, it is noted that the photocopy of the release submitted is not in a form acceptable for filing in the Surrogate's Court, and fails to recite the actual consideration received. The petitioner has stated in his affidavit in response to the motion that at the time the purported release was signed discharging attorney-trustee Steiner, Mr. Steiner was representing the petitioner, and had, in fact, drafted an inter vivos trust agreement into which the testamentary trust assets would pour over, Andrew Freihofer being the grantor, and Alan Steiner, attorney-draftsman, being the sole trustee. It is further alleged, and uncontroverted by the movant, that the testamentary trust chiefly contained assets of the Freihofer Baking Company, and that the trustee, who was acting simultaneously as the petitioner's personal attorney, corporate attorney for Freihofer Baking, trustee and executor under several trusts and wills of Freihofer family members, particularly the Charles Freihofer testamentary trust FBO Andrew Freihofer, and, unbeknown at the time to the petitioner, a member of the Board of Directors of Freihofer Baking, had a personal interest in the assets held by the testamentary trust that may have been in conflict with the trust beneficiary's best interest.

The failure of the trustee-attorney Alan Steiner to fully disclose the many and potentially conflicting roles he played in the sale of Freihofer Baking, the stock of which constituted the testamentary trust assets now in question, voids any receipt release and waiver he may have obtained from his beneficiary, particularly since he sought his own discharge from liability to that beneficiary while at the same time representing that beneficiary individually.

This Court again looks at the dicta of Matter of Stalbe, 130 Misc.2d 725, 497 N.Y.S.2d 237 (Queens Surrogate's Court, 1985), holding an attorney-fiduciary to a higher standard than a lay fiduciary. Further, Mr. Steiner's legal representation of Andrew Freihofer individually as sole residuary beneficiary of a trust of which Mr. Steiner was sole trustee is an apparent violation of DR 5-101(A) of the Code of Professional Responsibility (22 NYCRR 1200.20[a]), which prohibits a lawyer, except with the client's consent *after full disclosure* [emphasis added], to accept employment if the exercise of his professional judgment on behalf of the client will or may reasonably be affected by the lawyer's own financial or personal interests. See Chang v. Chang, 190 A.D.2d 311, 317, 597 N.Y.S.2d 692.

There can be no more an egregious example of an attorney's judgment being affected than by his seeking discharge of financial liability as a fiduciary from his own client.

The attorney-fiduciary has a duty to provide full disclosure of his stewardship to the beneficiary. Here, the attorney-trustee, who also represented the sole beneficiary individually, has chosen to use none of the mechanisms under Article 22 of the SCPA to disclose, render or settle his accounts. This, despite the fact that he had knowledge of a disgruntled beneficiary, acted simultaneously as that beneficiary's legal counsel, knew the large monetary value of the trust assets and the controversial nature in which they were liquidated, and was aware of his professional duty to discharge himself as against the beneficiary. Under the circumstances, the Court finds as a matter of law that no valid release and discharge has taken place, and the movant cannot now rely upon either documentary evidence or release to avoid judicial settlement of his accounts as trustee.

Lastly, movant's request to dismiss the within proceeding based upon the existence of a similar pending proceeding in Supreme Court is dismissed. Movant has provided no proof of identity of issues, and there is a strong statutory and case law tradition of resolving questions regarding decedent's estates and testamentary trusts within the confines of the Surrogate's Court. In re Hall's Estate, 183 Misc. 672, 53 N.Y.S.2d 674 (1944); In re Meyrowitz' Estate, 137 N.Y.S.2d 677 (1954); Stortecky v. Mazzone, 85 N.Y.2d 518, 626 N.Y.S.2d 733, 650 N.E.2d 391 (1995).

SCPA § 2205, subd. 1 provides that the Court may grant an order compelling a formal accounting when it appears to be in the best interest of the estate. It appears from the records submitted that the attorney-trustee may have been paid commissions and/or attorney fees prior to judicial settlement of accounts and without consent of the beneficiary. See Matter of Crippen, 32 Misc.2d 1019, 224 N.Y.S.2d 116 (Surr.Ct. New York Co., 1961); Matter of Ross, 33 Misc. 163, 68 N.Y.S. 373 (Surr.Ct., New York Co., 1900). Under authority of these statutes and cases, together with Matter of Stortecky v. Mazzone, 84 N.Y.2d 802, 617 N.Y.S.2d 136, 641 N.E.2d 157 (1994) it appears to be in best interest of the trust for the Trustee to render and judicially settle his accounts as such. The motion is denied in its entirety, and petition granted.

Notes

Probate. The estate representative has a duty to file notice with the domicile of the decedent of the death of the decedent and then to begin the process of accounting for the assets, paying the debts, and, eventually, distributing the remaining assets to the heirs. All of this must be accomplished within an established state probate office and requires obtaining a bond, posting an official notice, and submitting forms and documented evidence. The California Probate Code contains more than five-hundred pages of statutes, not including additional statutes related to taxation and rules of court. *See* CAL. PROB. CODE §§ 1-26112 (West 2003). For links related to California Probate laws, see California Probate, Trusts, Wills & Estates: Related Laws and Law

Links, http://www.megalaw.com/ca/top/caprobate.php (accessed Oct. 12, 2005). For a list of probate resources for California, see Sacramento County Public Law Library, Probate Resources, http://www.saclaw.lib.ca.us/LegalGuides/LegalGuidesFS.html; *select* Probate Law (accessed Oct. 12, 2005). This complexity and the costs involved prompt many to seek arrangements by which their estates may pass at death through non-probate procedures—a simple plan.

Tax Considerations: The Gift Tax: The government's most intrusive role into the probate process will be through the imposition of federal and state taxes, either due during life but payable at death, or due and payable at death. For example, upon death, income taxes will have to be paid on all income made by the decedent during the taxable year prior to death. These taxes will likely be imposed by the federal and state governments, and perhaps by some localities.

In addition to the tax on income made during life, the federal government and many states impose a tax on the transfer of property, by gift, made during an individual's life. This is the gift tax. The United States Congress enacted the gift tax to supplement the estate tax. The main purpose of the gift tax was to compensate for the avoidance of estate taxes by taxing gifts of property made during the life of an individual that would otherwise be included in the donor's estate at death. For Internal Revenue Service information and links related to estate and gift taxes, see Internal Revenue Service, Tax Information for Businesses, http://www.irs.gov/businesses/index.html; *select* Estate and Gift taxes (accessed Oct. 12, 2005).

Under § 2511 of the Internal Revenue Code, the gift tax applies whether a transfer is in trust or otherwise, and whether a gift is tangible or intangible, direct or indirect, or personal or real property. Under I.R.C. § 2512, the amount subject to the gift tax is the value of the property transferred minus any consideration provided by a donee. Treasury Regulation § 25.2511-2(b) provides that any transfer of property beyond the dominion and control of the donor is a gift. Thus, the definition of gifted property is very broad and most certainly includes present and future interests, forgiveness of a debt, and even contingent interests. The following case provides an example.

Smith v. Shaughnessy

Supreme Court of the United States, 1943
318 U.S. 176, 63 S. Ct. 545

Mr. Justice BLACK delivered the opinion of the Court.

The question here is the extent of the petitioner's liability for a tax under §§501, 506 of the Revenue Act of 1932, 47 Stat. 169, 26 U.S.C.A. Int.Rev.Acts, pages 580, 588, which imposes a tax upon every transfer of property by gift, 'whether the transfer is in trust or otherwise, whether the gift is direct or indirect, and whether the property is real or personal, tangible or intangible * * *.'

The petitioner, age 72, made an irrevocable transfer in trust of 3,000 shares of stock worth $571,000. The trust income was payable to his wife, age 44, for life; upon her death, the stock was to be returned to the petitioner, if he was living; if he was not living, it was to go to such persons as his wife might designate by will, or in default of a will by her, to her intestate successors under applicable New York law. The petitioner, under protest paid a gift tax of $71,674.22, assessed on the total value of the trust principal, and brought suit for refund in the district court. Holding that the petitioner had, within the meaning of the Act, executed a completed gift of a life estate to his wife, the court sustained the Commissioner's assessment on $322,423, the determined value of her life interest; but the remainder was held not to be completely transferred and hence not subject to the gift tax. 40 F.Supp. 19. The government appealed and the Circuit Court of Appeals reversed, ordering dismissal of the petitioner's complaint on the authority of its previous decision in Herzog v. Commissioner, 116 F.2d 591. We granted certiorari because of alleged conflict with our decisions in Helvering v. Hallock, 309 U.S. 106, 60 S.Ct. 444, 84 L.Ed. 604, 125 A.L.R. 1368, and Estate of Sanford v. Commissioner, 308 U.S. 39, 60 S.Ct. 51, 84 L.Ed. 20. In these decisions, and in Burnet v. Guggenheim, 288 U.S. 280, 53 S.Ct. 369, 77 L.Ed. 748, we have considered the problems raised here in some detail, and it will therefore be unnecessary to make any elaborate re-survey of the law.

Three interests are involved here: the life estate, the remainder, and the reversion. The taxpayer concedes that the life estate is subject to the gift tax. The government concedes that the right of reversion to the donor in case he outlives his wife is an interest having value which can be calculated by an actuarial device, and that it is immune from the gift tax. The controversy, then, reduces itself to the question of the taxability of the remainder.

The taxpayer's principal argument here is that under our decision in the Hallock case, the value of the remainder will be included in the grantor's gross estate for estate tax purposes; and that in the Sanford case we intimated a general policy against allowing the same property to be taxed both as an estate and as a gift.

This view, we think, misunderstands our position in the Sanford case. As we said there, the gift and estate tax laws are closely related and the gift tax serves to supplement the estate tax.[1] We said that the taxes are not 'always mutually exclusive', and called attention to §322 of the 1924 Act, 26 U.S.C.A. Int.Rev.Acts, page 82, there involved (re-enacted with amendments in §801 of the 1932 Act, 26 U.S.C.A. Int.Rev.Acts, page 640) which charts the course for granting credits on estate taxes by reason of previous payment of gift taxes on the same property. The scope of that provision we need not now determine. It is sufficient to note here that Congress plainly pointed out that 'some' of the 'total gifts subject to gift taxes * * * may be included for estate tax purposes and some not.' House Report No. 708, 72d Cong., 1st Sess., p. 45. Under the statute the gift tax amounts in some instances to a security, a form of down-payment on the estate tax which secures the eventual payment of the latter; it is in no sense double taxation as the taxpayer suggests.

We conclude that under the present statute, Congress has provided as its plan for integrating the estate and gift taxes this system of secured payment on gifts which will later be subject to the estate tax.* * *

Unencumbered by any notion of policy against subjecting this transaction to both estate and gift taxes, we turn to the basic question of whether there was a gift of the remainder. The government argues that for gift tax purposes the taxpayer has abandoned control of the remainder and that it is therefore taxable, while the taxpayer contends

---

1. The gift tax was passed not only to prevent estate tax avoidance, but also to prevent income tax avoidance through reducing yearly income and thereby escaping the effect of progressive surtax rates. House Report No. 708, 72d Cong., 1st Sess., p. 28; Brandeis, J., dissenting in Untermyer v. Anderson, 276 U.S. 440, 450, 48 S.Ct. 353, 356, 72 L.Ed. 645; Stone, J., dissenting in Heiner v. Donnan, 285 U.S. 312, 333, 52 S.Ct. 358, 363, 76 L.Ed. 772.

that no realistic value can be placed on the contingent remainder and that it therefore should not be classed as a gift.

We cannot accept any suggestion that the complexity of a property interest created by a trust can serve to defeat a tax. For many years Congress has sought vigorously to close tax loopholes against ingenious trust instruments. * * * Even though these concepts of property and value may be slippery and elusive they can not escape taxation so long as they are used in the world of business. The language of the gift tax statute, 'property * * * real or personal, tangible or intangible', is broad enough to include property, however conceptual or contingent. And lest there be any doubt as to the amplitude of their purpose, the Senate and House Committees, reporting the bill, spelled out their meaning as follows:

> 'The terms 'property,' 'transfer,' 'gift', and 'indirectly' (in §501) are used in the broadest sense; the term 'property' reaching every species of right or interest protected by the laws and having an exchangeable value.' * * *

The essence of a gift by trust is the abandonment of control over the property put in trust. The separable interests transferred are not gifts to the extent that power remains to revoke the trust or recapture the property represented by any of them, Burnet v. Guggenheim, supra, or to modify the terms of the arrangement so as to make other disposition of the property, Sanford v. Commissioner, supra. In the Sanford case the grantor could, by modification of the trust, extinguish the donee's interest at any instant he chose. In cases such as this, where the grantor has neither the form nor substance of control and never will have unless he outlives his wife, we must conclude that he has lost all 'economic control' and that the gift is complete except for the value of his reversionary interest. * * *

The judgment of the Circuit Court of Appeals is affirmed with leave to the petitioner to apply for modification of its mandate in order that the value of the petitioner's reversionary interest may be determined and excluded.

It is so ordered.

Affirmed.

Mr. Justice ROBERTS.

I dissent. I am of opinion that, except for the life estate in the wife, the gift qua the donor was incomplete and not within the sweep of §§501 and 506, 26 U.S.C.A. Int.Rev. Acts, pages 580, 588. A contrary conclusion might well be reached were it not for Helvering v. Hallock, 309 U.S. 106, 60 S.Ct. 444, 84 L.Ed. 604, 125 A.L.R. 1368. But the decisions in Burnet v. Guggenheim, 288 U.S. 280, 53 S.Ct. 369, 77 L.Ed. 748, and Sanford v. Commissioner, 308 U.S. 39, 60 S.Ct. 51, 84 L.Ed. 20, to which the court adheres, require a reversal in view of the ruling in the Hallock case.

The first of the two cases ruled that a transfer in trust, whereby the grantor reserved a power of revocation, was not subject to a gift tax, but became so upon the renunciation of the power. The second held that where the grantor reserved a power to change the beneficiaries, but none to revoke or to make himself a beneficiary, the transfer was incomplete and not subject to gift tax. At the same term, in Porter v. Commissioner, 288 U.S. 436, 53 S.Ct. 451, 77 L.Ed. 880, the court held that where a decedent had given property inter vivos in trust, reserving a power to change the beneficiaries but no power to revoke or revest the property in himself, the transfer was incomplete until the termination of the reserved power by the donor's death and hence the corpus was subject to the estate tax.

When these cases were decided, the law, as announced by this court, was that where, in a complete and final transfer inter vivos, a grantor provided that, in a specified contingency, the corpus should pass to him, if living, but, if he should be dead, then to others, the gift was complete when made, he retained nothing which passed from him at his death, prior to the happening of the contingency, and that no part of the property given was includable in his gross estate for estate tax. * * * So long as this was the law the transfer might properly be the subject of a gift tax for the gift was, as respects the donor, complete when made.

In 1940 these decisions were overruled and it was held that such a transfer was so incomplete when made, and the grantor retained such an interest, that the cessation of that interest at death furnished the occasion for imposing an estate tax. Thus the situation here presented was placed in the same category as those where the grantor had reserved a power to revoke or a power to change beneficiaries. By analogy to the Guggenheim and Sanford cases, I suppose the gift would have become complete if the donor had, in his life, relinquished or conveyed the contingent estate reserved to him.

In the light of this history, the Sanford case requires a holding that the gifts in remainder, after the life estate, create no gift tax liability. The reasoning of that decision, the authorities, and the legislative history relied upon, are all at war with the result in this case. There is no need to quote what was there said. A reading of the decision will demonstrate that, if the principles there announced are here observed, the gifts in question are incomplete and cannot be the subject of the gift tax.

It will not square with logic to say that where the donor reserves the right to change beneficiaries, and so delays completion of the gift until his death or prior relinquishment of the right, the gift is incomplete, but where he reserves a contingent interest to himself the reverse is true,— particularly so, if the criterion of estate tax liability is important to the decision of the question, as the Sanford case affirms.

The question is not whether a gift which includes vested and contingent future interests in others than the donor is taxable as an entirety when made, but whether a reservation of such an interest in the donor negatives a completion of the gift until such time as that interest is relinquished.

All that is said in the Sanford case about the difficulties of administration and probable inequities of a contrary decision there, applies here with greater force. Indeed a system of taxation which requires valuation of the donor's retained interest, in the light of the contingencies involved, and calculation of the value of the subsequent remainders by resort to higher mathematics beyond the ken of the taxpayer, exhibits the artificiality of the Government's application of the Act. This is well illustrated in the companion cases of Robinette and Paumgarten, 318 U.S. 184, 63 S.Ct. 540, 87 L.Ed. 700. Such results argue strongly against the construction which the court adopts.

Notes

Personal services performed by a donor for a donee are not considered gifted property. *See generally* Walter D. Schwidetzky, *Estate Planning: Hyperlexis and the Annual Exclusion Rule*, 32 Suffolk L. Rev. 211 (1998). It is important to note that even though the federal estate tax is scheduled to be repealed after 2009, the federal gift tax is not. Instead, gifts made after December 31, 2009, will remain subject to a gift tax based on a progressive rate schedule, with the maximum amount being 35% on taxable gifts in excess of $500,000. What is the rationale for keeping the gift tax and eliminating the estate tax? For an overview of federal tax policies, see Center on Budget and Policy Priorities, Federal Tax Policies, http://www.cbpp.org/; *path* Areas of Research/Federal Tax (accessed Oct. 12, 2005).

Tax Considerations: The Estate Tax: The estate tax, imposed by the federal and many state governments, is a tax on property over which the decedent had an incident of ownership at death. The decedent's gross estate includes property owned outright at death as well as certain property transferred within three years of death, and many current forms of will substitutes (non-probate transfers), such as life insurance, revocable trusts and payable on death accounts. After the gross estate is determined, there are various deductions available to arrive at the taxable estate. These deductions include, among others, the debts of the decedent, expenses associated with the administration of the estate, transfers to charities, and the unlimited marital deduction for property passing to a decedent's lawful spouse. The deductions are subtracted to arrive at the taxable estate and then, once the taxable estate is computed, gifts made after 1976 are added to the taxable estate to arrive at what is called the tax base. A tentative estate tax is computed by applying the tax rates set forth in the Internal Revenue Code to the tax base and subtracting from the amount the gift tax payable on the decedent's gifts made after 1976. Then, this amount is reduced by various credits, including the unified credit, to arrive at the estate tax payable.

At present, the tax rate is gradually decreasing, with a rate of 47% in 2005 and 45% in 2007, and if the tax rate is repealed altogether, it will be 0% for persons dying after December 31, 2009. Gift and estate taxes are computed on the progressive unified rate schedule set forth in section 2001 of the Internal Revenue Code. Under the Economic Growth and Tax Relief Reconciliation Act of 2001, the personal exemption for the federal estate tax increases until reaching $2,000,000 for 2006–2008, and $3,500,000 in 2009, the year before the slated repeal of the tax altogether. Until such time as this may occur, Section 2001 of the Code makes it the responsibility of the Personal Representative to pay these taxes.

The unanswered question is the reaction of the states to the elimination of the federal estate tax. For a discussion of the effect of the repeal of the federal estate tax on states, see Federation of Tax Administrators, http://www.taxadmin.org/; *select* State Comparisons (accessed Oct. 12, 2005). Even if the federal estate tax ceases to exist, individual states may still "decouple" themselves and continue to levy a tax, necessitating continued estate planning, but on a state-by-state basis. For those states imposing a tax, there is a corresponding exemption as there is in the federal system. Any tax is imposed only on those amounts exceeding the exemption.

Finally, states impose an inheritance tax on the receipt of property by heirs. For access to a state-by-state survey of taxes, see Retirement Living Information Center, Taxes by State, http://www.retirementliving.com/; *select* Taxes by State (accessed Oct. 12, 2005). Typically, the tax is based on the heir's relationship to the decedent and deducted from the amount eventually passing to the heir. But if the decedent plans ahead and writes an appropriate provision into the Last Will and Testament, any inheritance tax may be paid from the estate residuary funds, thus leaving more value for the heirs. Many states have eliminated the inheritance tax for those closely related to the decedent, such as a spouse or issue, but each state is different and generalities are impossible. It is safe to say that government intrusion into estate administration through taxation is in a period of fluctuation, *see, e.g.,* Sarah E. Waldeck, *An Appeal to Charity: Using Philan-*

thropy to Revitalize the Estate Tax, 24 VA. TAX REV. 667 (2005); Jack Stark, *A History of the Wisconsin Inheritance Tax*, 88 MARQ. L. REV. 947 (2005), and yet, the tax considerations to follow will seek to identify the issues to monitor.

Public Policy. Increasingly, the government codifies common law restraints that restrict the ability of persons to inherit from decedents, upon whom egregious acts may have been committed during the lifetime of the decedent. *See, e.g.,* VA. CODE §64.1-16.3 (barring inheritance by a spouse who abandoned or refused to support the decedent spouse); CAL. PROB. CODE §250 (prohibiting inheritance by a person who feloniously and intentionally kills a decedent). CAL. PROB. CODE §259 provides that an heir of a decedent will be treated as having predeceased the decedent if ALL of the following apply:

(1) It has been proven by clear and convincing evidence that the person is liable for physical abuse, neglect, or fiduciary abuse of the decedent, who was an elder or dependent adult.

(2) The person is found to have acted in bad faith.

(3) The person has been found to have been reckless, oppressive, fraudulent, or malicious in the commission of any of these acts upon the decedent.

(4) The decedent, at the time those acts occurred and thereafter until the time of his or her death, has been found to have been substantially unable to manage his or her financial resources or to resist fraud or undue influence.

III. Attorney's Role

Barcelo v. Elliott

Supreme Court of Texas, 1996
923 S.W.2d 575, 39 Tex. Sup. Ct. J. 607

PHILLIPS, Chief Justice, delivered the opinion of the Court, in which GONZALEZ, HECHT, ENOCH, and BAKER, Justices, joined.

The issue presented is whether an attorney who negligently drafts a will or trust agreement owes a duty of care to persons intended to benefit under the will or trust, even though the attorney never represented the intended beneficiaries. The court of appeals held that the attorney owed no duty to the beneficiaries, affirming the trial court's summary judgment for the defendant-attorney. 927 S.W.2d 28, 1995 WL 51054. Because the attorney did not represent the beneficiaries, we likewise conclude that he owed no professional duty to them. We accordingly affirm the judgment of the court of appeals.

* * *

After Frances Barcelo retained attorney David Elliott to assist her with estate planning, Elliott drafted a will and inter vivos trust agreement for her. The will provided for specific bequests to Barcelo's children, devising the residuary of her estate to the inter vivos trust. Under the trust agreement, trust income was to be distributed to Barcelo during her lifetime. Upon her death, the trust was to terminate, assets were to be distributed in specific amounts to Barcelo's children and siblings, and the remainder was to pass to Barcelo's six grandchildren. The trust agreement contemplated that the trust would be funded by cash and shares of stock during Barcelo's lifetime, although the grandchildren contend that this never occurred. Barcelo signed the will and trust agreement in September 1990.

Barcelo died on January 22, 1991. After two of her children contested the validity of the trust, the probate court, for reasons not disclosed on the record before us, declared the trust to be invalid and unenforceable. Barcelo's grandchildren—the intended remainder beneficiaries under the trust— subsequently agreed to settle for what they contend was a substantially smaller share of the estate than what they would have received pursuant to a valid trust.

Barcelo's grandchildren then filed the present malpractice action against Elliott and his law firm (collectively "Elliott"). Plaintiffs allege that Elliott's negligence caused the trust to be invalid, resulting in foreseeable injury to the plaintiffs.[1] Elliott moved for summary judgment on the sole ground that he owed no professional duty to the grandchildren because he had never represented them. The trial court granted Elliott's motion for summary judgment.

The court of appeals affirmed, concluding that under Texas law an attorney preparing estate planning documents owes a duty only to his or her client—the testator or trust settlor—not to third parties intended to benefit under the estate plan. ——— S.W.2d at ———.

* * *

The sole issue presented is whether Elliott owes a duty to the grandchildren that could give rise to malpractice liability even though he represented only Frances Barcelo, not the grandchildren, in preparing and implementing the estate plan.

* * *

At common law, an attorney owes a duty of care only to his or her client, not to third parties who may have been damaged by the attorney's negligent representation of the client. See Savings Bank v. Ward, 100 U.S. 195, 200, 25 L.Ed. 621 (1879); Annotation, Attorney's Liability, to One Other Than Immediate Client, for Negligence in Connection with Legal Duties, 61 A.L.R. 4th 615, 624 (1988). Without this "privity barrier," the rationale goes, clients would lose control over the attorney-client relationship, and attorneys would be subject to almost unlimited liability. See Helen Jenkins, Privity—A Texas-Size Barrier to Third Parties for Negligent Will Drafting—An Assessment and Proposal, 42 Baylor L.Rev. 687, 689–90 (1990). Texas courts of appeals have uniformly applied the privity barrier in the estate planning context. See Thomas v. Pryor, 847 S.W.2d 303, 304–05 (Tex.App.—Dallas 1992), judgm't vacated by agr., 863 S.W.2d 462 (Tex.1993); Dickey v. Jansen, 731 S.W.2d 581, 582–83 (Tex.App.—Houston [1st Dist.] 1987, writ ref'd n.r.e.); Berry v. Dodson, Nunley & Taylor, 717 S.W.2d 716, 718–19 (Tex.App.—San Antonio 1986), judgm't vacated by agr., 729 S.W.2d 690 (Tex.1987).

---

1. The plaintiffs alleged that Elliott acted negligently when he:
A. provided in the trust agreement that it would not be effective until signed by the trustee, designated to be First City Bank of Houston, and then failed to obtain the execution of the trust document by the trustee;
B. drafted Mrs. Barcelo's will so as to provide that the residuary of her estate would pass into the trust he sought to create for Mrs. Barcelo, and then provided in the trust agreement that the trust would terminate upon Mrs. Barcelo's death, leaving her residuary to pass by intestacy to her children instead of her six grandchildren, including Plaintiffs, as provided in the trust agreement; and
C. failed to take the necessary steps on behalf of Mrs. Barcelo to fund the trust with the shares of stock....

Plaintiffs argue, however, that recognizing a limited exception to the privity barrier as to lawyers who negligently draft a will or trust would not thwart the rule's underlying rationales. They contend that the attorney should owe a duty of care to persons who were specific, intended beneficiaries of the estate plan. We disagree.

* * *

The majority of other states addressing this issue have relaxed the privity barrier in the estate planning context. See Lucas v. Hamm, 56 Cal.2d 583, 15 Cal.Rptr. 821, 825, 364 P.2d 685, 689 (1961), cert. denied, 368 U.S. 987, 82 S.Ct. 603, 7 L.Ed.2d 525 (1962); Stowe v. Smith, 184 Conn. 194, 441 A.2d 81, 83 (1981); Needham v. Hamilton, 459 A.2d 1060, 1062 (D.C.1983); DeMaris v. Asti, 426 So.2d 1153, 1154 (Fla.Dist.Ct.App.1983); Ogle v. Fuiten, 102 Ill.2d 356, 80 Ill.Dec. 772, 774–75, 466 N.E.2d 224, 226–27 (1984); Walker v. Lawson, 526 N.E.2d 968, 968 (Ind.1988); Schreiner v. Scoville, 410 N.W.2d 679, 682 (Iowa 1987); Pizel v. Zuspann, 247 Kan. 54, 795 P.2d 42, 51 (1990); In re Killingsworth, 292 So.2d 536, 542 (La.1973); Hale v. Groce, 304 Or. 281, 744 P.2d 1289, 1292–93 (1987); Guy v. Liederbach, 501 Pa. 47, 459 A.2d 744, 751–53 (1983); Auric v. Continental Cas. Co., 111 Wis.2d 507, 331 N.W.2d 325, 327 (1983). But see Lilyhorn v. Dier, 214 Neb. 728, 335 N.W.2d 554, 555 (1983); Viscardi v. Lerner, 125 A.D.2d 662, 510 N.Y.S.2d 183, 185 (1986); Simon v. Zipperstein, 32 Ohio St.3d 74, 512 N.E.2d 636, 638 (1987).

While some of these states have allowed a broad cause of action by those claiming to be intended beneficiaries, see Stowe, 441 A.2d at 84; Ogle, 80 Ill.Dec. at 775, 466 N.E.2d at 227; Hale, 744 P.2d at 1293, others have limited the class of plaintiffs to beneficiaries specifically identified in an invalid will or trust. See Ventura County Humane Society v. Holloway, 40 Cal.App.3d 897, 115 Cal.Rptr. 464, 468 (1974); DeMaris, 426 So.2d at 1154; Schreiner, 410 N.W.2d at 683; Kirgan v. Parks, 60 Md.App. 1, 478 A.2d 713, 718–19 (1984) (holding that, if cause of action exists, it does not extend to situation where testator's intent as expressed in the will has been carried out); Ginther v. Zimmerman, 195 Mich.App. 647, 491 N.W.2d 282, 286 (1992) (same); Guy, 459 A.2d at 751–52. The Supreme Court of Iowa, for example, held that

> a cause of action ordinarily will arise only when as a direct result of the lawyer's professional negligence the testator's intent as expressed in the testamentary instruments is frustrated in whole or in part and the beneficiary's interest in the estate is either lost, diminished, or unrealized.

Schreiner v. Scoville, 410 N.W.2d 679, 683 (Iowa 1987).

* * *

We agree with those courts that have rejected a broad cause of action in favor of beneficiaries. These courts have recognized the inevitable problems with disappointed heirs attempting to prove that the defendant-attorney failed to implement the deceased testator's intentions. Certainly allowing extrinsic evidence would create a host of difficulties. In DeMaris v. Asti, 426 So.2d 1153, 1154 (Fla.Dist.Ct.App.1983), for example, the court concluded that "[t]here is no authority—the reasons being obvious—for the proposition that a disappointed beneficiary may prove, by evidence totally extrinsic to the will, the testator's testamentary intent was other than as expressed in his solemn and properly executed will." Such a cause of action would subject attorneys to suits by heirs who simply did not receive what they believed to be their due share under the will or trust. This potential tort liability to third parties would create a conflict during the estate planning process, dividing the attorney's loyalty between his or her client and the third-party beneficiaries.

Moreover, we believe that the more limited cause of action recognized by several jurisdictions also undermines the policy rationales supporting the privity rule. These courts have limited the cause of action to beneficiaries specifically identified in an invalid will or trust. Under these circumstances, courts have reasoned, the interests of the client and the beneficiaries are necessarily aligned, negating any conflict, as the attorney owes a duty only to those parties which the testator clearly intended to benefit. See, e.g., Needham, 459 A.2d at 1062.

In most cases where a defect renders a will or trust invalid, however, there are concomitant questions as to the true intentions of the testator. Suppose, for example, that a properly drafted will is simply not executed at the time of the testator's death. The document may express the testator's true intentions, lacking signatures solely because of the attorney's negligent delay. On the other hand, the testator may have postponed execution because of second thoughts regarding the distribution scheme. In the latter situation, the attorney's representation of the testator will likely be affected if he or she knows that the existence of an unexecuted will may create malpractice liability if the testator unexpectedly dies.

The present case is indicative of the conflicts that could arise. Plaintiffs contend in part that Elliott was negligent in failing to fund the trust during Barcelo's lifetime, and in failing to obtain a signature from the trustee. These alleged deficiencies, however, could have existed pursuant to Barcelo's instructions, which may have been based on advice from her attorneys attempting to represent her best interests. An attorney's ability to render such advice would be severely compromised if the advice could be second-guessed by persons named as beneficiaries under the unconsummated trust.

In sum, we are unable to craft a bright-line rule that allows a lawsuit to proceed where alleged malpractice causes a will or trust to fail in a manner that casts no real doubt on the testator's intentions, while prohibiting actions in other situations. We believe the greater good is served by preserving a bright-line privity rule which denies a cause of action to all beneficiaries whom the attorney did not represent. This will ensure that attorneys may in all cases zealously represent their clients without the threat of suit from third parties compromising that representation.

We therefore hold that an attorney retained by a testator or settlor to draft a will or trust owes no professional duty of care to persons named as beneficiaries under the will or trust.[2]

* * *

Plaintiffs also contend that, even if there is no tort duty extending to beneficiaries of an estate plan, they may recover under a third-party-beneficiary contract theory. While the majority of jurisdictions that have recognized a cause of action in favor of will or trust beneficiaries have done so under negligence principles, * * * some have allowed recovery in contract. * * *

In Texas, however, a legal malpractice action sounds in tort and is governed by negligence principles. See Cosgrove v. Grimes, 774 S.W.2d 662, 664 (Tex.1989); Willis v. Maverick, 760 S.W.2d 642, 644 (Tex.1988). Cf. Heyer v. Flaig, 70 Cal.2d 223, 74

---

2. We express no opinion as to whether the beneficiary of a trust has standing to sue an attorney representing the trustee for malpractice. Cf. Thompson v. Vinson & Elkins, 859 S.W.2d 617, 621–23 (Tex.App. — Houston [1st Dist.] 1993, writ denied) (holding that beneficiary lacked standing to sue trustee's attorney).

Cal.Rptr. 225, 228, 449 P.2d 161, 164 (1969) (recognizing that third-party-beneficiary contract theory "is conceptually superfluous since the crux of the action must lie in tort in any case; there can be no recovery without negligence"). Even assuming that a client who retains a lawyer to draft an estate plan intends for the lawyer's work to benefit the will or trust beneficiaries, the ultimate question is whether, considering the competing policy implications, the lawyer's professional duty should extend to persons whom the lawyer never represented. For the reasons previously discussed, we conclude that the answer is no.

For the foregoing reasons, we affirm the judgment of the court of appeals.

OWEN, J., did not participate in the decision.

CORNYN, Justice, joined by ABBOTT, Justice, dissenting.

With an obscure reference to "the greater good," 923 S.W.2d at 578, the Court unjustifiably insulates an entire class of negligent lawyers from the consequences of their wrongdoing, and unjustly denies legal recourse to the grandchildren for whose benefit Ms. Barcelo hired a lawyer in the first place. I dissent.

By refusing to recognize a lawyer's duty to beneficiaries of a will, the Court embraces a rule recognized in only four states, * * * while simultaneously rejecting the rule in an overwhelming majority of jurisdictions. * * * Notwithstanding the fact that in recent years the Court has sought to align itself with the mainstream of American jurisprudence, * * * the Court inexplicably balks in this case.

The threshold question in a negligence action, including a legal malpractice suit, is duty. El Chico Corp. v. Poole, 732 S.W.2d 306, 311 (Tex.1987); see Cosgrove v. Grimes, 774 S.W.2d 662, 664 (Tex.1989) (holding that a legal malpractice action in Texas is grounded in negligence). Whether a defendant owes a duty to the plaintiff depends on several factors, including risk, foreseeability, and likelihood of injury weighed against the social utility of the actor's conduct, the magnitude of the burden of guarding against injury, and the consequences of placing the burden on the defendant. Greater Houston Transp. Co. v. Phillips, 801 S.W.2d 523, 525 (Tex.1990).

The foreseeability of harm in this case is not open to serious question. Because Ms. Barcelo hired Mr. Elliott to accomplish the transfer of her estate to her grandchildren upon her death, the potential harm to the beneficiaries if the testamentary documents were incorrectly drafted was plainly foreseeable. See Lucas, 15 Cal.Rptr. at 824, 364 P.2d at 688; see also Heyer v. Flaig, 70 Cal.2d 223, 74 Cal.Rptr. 225, 228, 449 P.2d 161, 164–65 (1969) ("The attorney's actions and omissions will affect the success of the client's testamentary scheme; and thus the possibility of thwarting the testator's wishes immediately becomes foreseeable. Equally foreseeable is the possibility of injury to an intended beneficiary."). Foreseeability of harm weighs heavily in favor of recognizing a duty to intended beneficiaries.

Additionally, the Court's decision means that, as a practical matter, no one has the right to sue for the lawyer's negligent frustration of the testator's intent. A flaw in a will or other testamentary document is not likely [to] be discovered until the client's death. And, generally, the estate suffers no harm from a negligently drafted testamentary document. Heyer, 74 Cal.Rptr. at 228, 449 P.2d at 165. Allowing beneficiaries to sue would provide accountability and thus an incentive for lawyers to use greater care in estate planning. Robert L. Rabin, Tort Recovery for Negligently Inflicted Economic Loss, 37 STAN.L.REV. 1513, 1521 (1985). Instead, the Court decides that an innocent party must bear the burden of the lawyer's error. The Court also gives no consideration to the fair adjustment of the loss between the parties, one of the traditional objectives of tort law. See W. Page Keeton et al., Prosser and Keeton on the Law of Torts §4, at 24–25 (5th ed. 1984); Robert E. Litan et al., The U.S. Liability System: Background and Trends, in Liability: Perspectives and Policy 1, 3 (Robert E. Litan and Clifford Winston eds., 1988). These grounds for the imposition of a legal duty in tort law generally, which apply to lawyers in every other context, are no less important in estate planning.

Nor do the reasons the Court gives for refusing to impose a duty under these circumstances withstand scrutiny. Contrary to the Court's view, recognizing an action by the intended beneficiaries would not extend a lawyer's duty to the general public, but only to a limited, foreseeable class. Because estate planning attorneys generally do not face any liability in this context, potential liability to the intended beneficiaries would not place them in a worse position than attorneys in any other setting.

The Court also hypothesizes that liability to estate beneficiaries may conflict with the attorney's duty to the client. Before the beneficiaries could prevail in a suit against the attorney, however, they would necessarily have to show that the attorney breached a duty to the decedent. This is because the lawyer's duty to the client is to see that the client's intentions are realized by the very documents the client has hired the lawyer to draft. No conflicting duty to the beneficiaries is imposed.

Searching for other hypothetical problems that might arise if a cause of action for the beneficiaries is recognized, the Court observes that a will not executed at the testator's death could in fact express the testator's true intentions. 923 S.W.2d at 578. Granted, such a scenario may be the result of either the testator's indecision or the attorney's negligence. Similarly, a family member might be intentionally omitted from a will at the testator's direction, or negligently omitted because of the drafting lawyer's mistake. In other words, what appears to be attorney negligence may actually reflect the testator's wishes.

But surely these are matters subject to proof, as in all other cases. Nothing distinguishes this class of cases from many others in this respect. The Court fails to consider that the beneficiaries will in each case bear the burden of establishing that the attorney breached a duty to the testator, which resulted in damages to the beneficiaries. Lawyers, wishing to protect themselves from liability, may document the testator's intentions.

In addition, Elliott suggests that allowing beneficiaries to sue the testator's attorney would interfere with the attorney-client privilege, by either encouraging attorneys to violate clients' confidences or by hindering attorneys' ability to defend their actions. This concern, too, is unfounded. Under Texas law, the attorney-client privilege does not survive the testator. Krumb v. Porter, 152 S.W.2d 495, 497 (Tex.Civ.App.—San Antonio 1941, writ ref'd); see Thomas v. Pryor, 847 S.W.2d 303, 305 (Tex.App.—Dallas 1992), writ granted and case remanded pursuant to settlement, 863 S.W.2d 462 (Tex.1993); see also Stappas v. Stappas, 271 Ala. 138, 122 So.2d 393, 396 (1960); Denver Nat'l Bank v. McLagan, 133 Colo. 487, 298 P.2d 386, 388 (1956); Manley v. Combs, 197 Ga. 768, 30 S.E.2d 485, 493 (1944); 1 McCormick on Evidence §94 (4th ed. 1992); 8 John Henry Wigmore, Wigmore on Evidence §2314 (3d ed. 1940). This is because the lawyer-client privilege applies only to confidential communications, which are "not intended to be disclosed to third persons." Tex.R.Civ.Evid. 503(a)(5). And, as

Professor Wigmore has explained, "[a]s to the *tenor and execution* of the will, it seems hardly open to dispute that they are the very facts which the testator expected and intended to be disclosed after his death." Wigmore § 2314, at 613 (emphasis in original).

In sum, I would hold that the intended beneficiary of a will or testamentary trust may bring a cause of action against an attorney whose negligence caused the beneficiary to lose a legacy in whole or in part. Accordingly, I would reverse the judgment of the court of appeals and remand this case to the trial court.

SPECTOR, Justice, dissenting.

The issue in this case is whether the attorney, David Elliott, owed a duty to Frances Barcelo's intended beneficiaries. The majority holds that he did not. The other dissenting justices would recognize a broad cause of action in favor of any person claiming to be an intended beneficiary, regardless of whether the plaintiff is identified in the will or trust instrument. Because I would recognize only a limited cause of action for the intended beneficiaries of wills and trusts, I write separately to dissent.

At common law, an attorney owes no duty to third parties who may have been damaged by the attorney's negligent representation of the attorney's client. See Savings Bank v. Ward, 100 U.S. 195, 25 L.Ed. 621 (1879). As the majority notes, although Texas courts of appeals have consistently accepted this restriction in the estate planning context, most other states addressing this issue have lowered the privity barrier in this area. * * *

I believe that recognizing such a cause of action would further public policy by requiring attorneys to exercise due care in implementing a testator's estate plan. Under current law, only the attorney's client has standing to sue for negligent preparation of the will or trust. Although the testator's personal representative would succeed to this cause of action upon the testator's death, the estate itself may suffer no damage from an invalid will or trust that frustrates the testator's intentions. See Heyer v. Flaig, 70 Cal.2d 223, 74 Cal.Rptr. 225, 228, 449 P.2d 161, 165 (1969); Guy, 459 A.2d at 749. Consequently, an attorney who negligently drafts a will or trust that is discovered to be invalid after the testator's death is accountable to no one.

I would not go so far as to hold that attorneys who draft wills and trusts have a duty to persons who are not beneficiaries named in the will or trust. Recognizing such a broad cause of action is as likely to frustrate the testator's intent as it is to carry it out. I would, however, allow beneficiaries who are specifically identified on the face of an invalid will or trust to assert a claim.

Recognizing a limited cause of action would subject attorneys who prepare wills and trusts documents to the same standard of care governing attorneys generally. Because I believe that this is sound public policy, I dissent.

Notes

In Simpson v. Calivas, 139 N.H. 1, 650 A.2d 318 (1994), the Supreme Court of New Hampshire held that, even when there is no privity between a drafting attorney and an intended beneficiary, the obvious foreseeability of injury to the beneficiary demands an exception to the privity rule. Because privity is not a bar, an intended beneficiary may file suit under tort law or as a third party beneficiary under contract law against the attorney who drafted the instrument. The *Restatement (Second) of Torts* § 74B (1979), also allows a cause of action for the intentional tortious interference with an expectancy. For an example of how this may be utilized, see Nemeth v. Banhalmi, 125 Ill. App. 3d 938, 466 N.E.2d 977 (1984). For an example of when it may not be used, see Labonte v. Giordana, 426 Mass. 319, 687 N.E.2d 1253 (1997). Hawaii allows an intended beneficiary to recover under either contract or tort theories. *See* Blair v. Ing, 95 Haw. 247 (2001). Some states will hold an attorney liable to a third party through balancing various factors. *See, e.g.,* Capitol Indem. Corp. v. Fleming, 58 P.3d 965 (Ariz. 2002)(extent to which transaction intended to affect plaintiff, foreseeability of harm, degree of certainty that plaintiff suffered injury, connection between defendant's conduct and injuries suffered, moral blame attached to defendant's conduct, and policy of preventing future harm); Leyba v. Whitley, 907 P.2d 172 (N.M. 1995)(extent to which transaction was intended to benefit plaintiff; foreseeability of harm to plaintiff; degree of certainty that plaintiff suffered injury; connection between defendant's conduct and injury; policy of preventing future harm; and extent to which profession would be unduly burdened by finding of liability). *See generally* James M. Delaney, *Where Ethics Merge With Substantive Law—An Analysis of Tax Motivated Transactions,* 38 Ind. L. Rev. 295 (2005); Carolyn L. Dessin, *Should Attorneys Have A Duty to Report Financial Abuse of the Elderly?,* 38 Akron L. Rev. 707 (2005).

IV. Client's Role

By the twenty-first century, the client's role in the transmission of wealth has expanded exorbitantly. No longer are living persons restricted to giving away money during their life time, relying upon the probate apparatus of Last Wills and Testaments, or defaulting to intestate succession laws. Today, through the evolution of trusts, persons are able to utilize a vast array of will substitutes—or non-probate transfers—to transfer wealth (during life or at death) with minimal administrative cost and, at the same time, may keep control of the income for the duration of the client's life. For example, joint bank accounts, payable-on-death accounts, such as life insurance or individual retirement accounts, deeds on land that retain a right of survivorship clause, or more complicated devices, such as living trusts with named remainder beneficiaries, allow for client control and accessible wealth during life and at death. The promised reduction or abolition of federal estate taxes and the states' elimination or erosion of the rule against perpetuities would allow for greater control by clients during life and long after death.

But two issues arise today: One is the effectiveness of a non-probate system of transfer of wealth, often marketed by persons not licensed to practice law. If the proposed non-probate transfer is to succeed, it will do so because it meets the specified legal parameter of trusts. Because these are legal devices, the intricacies must be mastered. If the trust fails, the non-probate transfer will devolve into the probate system and pass according to the laws of testate or intestate succession. Clients must have a firm grasp on the technicalities of non-probate transfers. Second, the average life expectancy of a person living in the United States continues to lengthen, thus promising greater longevity, but with concomitant issues of health care and security. This is the dilemma of long-term care—how to manage your wealth and your life into an ever-lengthening span of years, often ending in expensive assisted living or nursing home care. Medicare, a program designed to provide some medical assistance to those over the age of 65, will not meet all of these needs. Medicaid, a program for the poor, but often used to provide nursing home care for those who "spend down" into poverty, will not be able to fund all who need care. Thus, while the modern age has brought increasingly more efficient means of transferring wealth, advances in technology have introduced issues of planning for incapacity, health care directives, long-term care insurance, and surrogate decision-makers. Rather than facilitating the transfer of wealth, these factors often place wealth at the center of a contest involving surrogates, heirs, health care providers, the government, and the client who earned the wealth and who is living a very long life. See, e.g., Alyssa A. DiRusso and Kathleen M. Sablone, *Statutory Techniques for Balancing the Financial Interests of Trust Beneficiaries*, 39 U.S.F. L. Rev. 261 (2005).

Therefore, clients today must plan not only for the transfer of wealth according to the ways that we will now study, but they must plan for incapacity, the management of wealth, health, and efficient transfer when the moment is right. The roles of the government, the attorney, and the client must be integrated into this plan. These competing and complementary interests form the backdrop as we progress through the following chapters.

Chapter Two

Intestate Succession

Tool Bar

I. Public Policy of Succession

When specific intent is lacking, the law may provide for what an individual wishes. Intestate succession is one way this is accomplished. It is a statutory method by which the property of a decedent that does not pass by Last Will and Testament or by non-probate transfer may be transmitted to others. With very few exception, the "others" are always family members identified by blood, marriage, or adoption. But with the advent of expansive definitions of family to include domestic partners, civil unions, and large numbers of people living in less formal, non-marital relationships, intestate statutes may not provide for what an individual may have wanted to happen to his or her property at death. A Will or non-probate transfer is always available, yet is not always utilized by the decedent; the intestate statute is simply a last resort. This last resort will be applicable in the following situations:

(1) When there is no Last Will and Testament and no non-probate transfers to pass the property to named others.

(2) There is a Last Will and Testament, but the terms of the declaration do not make provision for all of the property owned by the decedent at death.

(3) The Last Will and Testament is revoked or found to be invalid as a result of contest, and no other Last Will and Testament is probated.

(4) The decedent directs in a Last Will and Testament that property pass according to the intestate statutes in effect in the state in which he or she is domiciled at the date of his or her death.

(5) A non-probate instrument, such as an insurance policy or a retirement account, is payable to "heirs," as compared to "estate." Language such as this would mean the property would not pass according to the terms of a valid Last Will and Testament, but according to the intestate statutes in effect at the date of the decedent's death.

The state traditionally presumes that a relative should inherit under an intestate statute if no provision is made otherwise in a Will or non-probate transfer. The closer the relative is to the decedent in terms of kinship or "blood," the more likely that relative will inherit from the decedent. Likewise, if the relative is a distant third cousin, thrice removed, the relative has less claim to the decedent's wealth. Lengthy emotional ties seldom merit the status of blood relationships. Interesting questions arise:

(1) Should the state place a blood line limit on the extent to which the property of a decedent may descend? Thus, should the state be able to limit inheritance to relatives closer to the decedent in blood relationship and eliminate completely those of more distant degree? Existing limits occur because the state wishes to provide for speedy administration of the estate and more distant relatives may be difficult to find. Plus, more distant relatives are often "laughing heirs," affected more by the joy of inheritance than grief over the death of the deceased relative. But where does the property go if the state eliminates heirs? Answer: To the state. Is there a conflict of interest? Does Internet and computer prowess provide for greater speed in locating heirs, thereby mitigating the state's rational basis for restriction of heirs?

(2) Intestate succession allows no provision for heirs that may have special needs. Handicap and youth are two examples. Does the statute thereby detract from the dece-

dent's poorly expressed intent, which may have been to benefit these individuals more than others? How may public policy remedy this oversight?

(3) What role should public policy play in preventing heirs from taking property of the decedent? For example, what of the spouse who has abused the other spouse, but the marriage remained intact? If the death did not occur because of the abuse, but the abuse can still be proven, should this, alone, be sufficient reason to bar intestate inheritance? Is the same true of adultery? Desertion? Or, if a child has not spoken to a parent for a long term of years, should the child still be able to inherit from that parent through intestate succession? Even if a step-child were closer to the decedent by caring for and loving the decedent until the moment of death? Should the step-child receive nothing and the birth child receive everything, simply by taking into account blood and not affection? *See generally* Kenneth R. Davis, *Age Discrimination and Disparate Impact: A New Look at An Age-Old Problem*, 70 BROOK. L. REV. 361 (2004–05).

(4) What role should a spouse play in intestate inheritance? Is it safe to assume that a decedent intended for his or her spouse to inherit everything? Should the parent of a decedent be able to say that he or she "deserves a return on the investment of raising the child" and benefit from intestate succession? Is it safe to assume that the surviving spouse will care for the children of the decedent, himself or herself, and that, thus, the children should receive nothing from intestate succession? Should other collateral relatives of the decedent—persons such as siblings or grandparents—have any claim to the intestate estate? Should there be a public policy claim?

(5) Should there be some connection in testate succession to what the spouse could have received had there been a divorce? Should the spouse's intestate share be equivalent to what the spouse would have received under a theory of "economic partnership" existing during the time of the couple's marriage? What should be the relationship between what the spouse would receive under the intestate provisions and what the spouse could receive if there were a valid Last Will and Testament but the spouse "elected" against it, taking a forced statutory share?

(6) Tax Considerations: The Economic Growth and Tax Relief Reconciliation Act of 2001 is scheduled to repeal the federal estate tax for those dying after December 31, 2009, and the repeal may well be permanent. The present transfer tax structure provides a number of deductions, credits, and exemptions that can be used to lessen the impact of the tax. For example, Section 2056 provides an unlimited marital deduction for property passing to a spouse, and Section 2010 provides a credit against the tax that, by 2009, will shelter $3, 500, 000 of the decedent's property from the tax. Estate planning, at a minimum, must take into consideration these tax incentives to transfer wealth to those best suited to isolate assets from the tax. When a decedent dies intestate, allowing his or her property to pass by state statute, most of the tax advantages are no longer available. As a result, the estate may pay excessive amounts of taxes that in turn will result in a lesser amount passing to the heirs, who may also be burdened if the liability should be transferred to them. In comparison, a valid Last Will and Testament allows a Testator to utilize the tax advantages provided by the Internal Revenue Code, to include the repeal of the Generation Skipping Transfer Tax (GST), gifts to a non-United States citizen spouse under a Qualified Domestic Trust (QDOT), the often-used Qualified Terminable Interest Property (QTIP) trust for domestic spouses, and a formula clause that will allow utilization of shifting exemption amounts in federal or state taxation schedules. The public policy of intestate succession does not provide any excuse for persons of more than modest means to die intestate.

II. Establishing a Pattern

Each state has its own intestate statutory scheme. Nonetheless, each will have a pattern in common with other states. The pattern will start with a surviving spouse; it will proceed, then, to issue; then to parents; and, eventually, it will proceed to more distant relatives. As an example of intestate distribution, the Uniform Probate Code has four divisions: (1) the definition of the intestate estate, (2) the share of the surviving spouse, (3) the share of heirs other than the surviving spouse, and (4) when there are no takers. The amount that each person will receive will likely differ from state-to-state, but the pattern is a consistent one among the states. If the pattern were reduced to a diagram, it would appear as such:

$$P \mp P$$
$$(X) \mp S$$
$$I$$

Terms: (X) decedent
             S spouse
             I issue
             P parents

If (X) is dead, signified by the closed parentheses, how would the intestate estate be distributed? Assuming that S is truly a spouse of the decedent or able to take as a spouse through an alternative state statute, S is likely to receive a fixed monetary amount and then a percentage of the remainder. It is very important to ascertain if S and X were validly married because only marriage or a status such as a civil union may qualify a person to occupy this pivotal position in the intestate pattern. After the surviving spouse has taken this fixed amount and percentage, what is left goes to the issue or, if none, to the parents, equally. The word "issue" is an inclusive term and is meant to include children and their issue (*e.g.*, grandchildren and great-grandchildren), should any of the children predecease the decedent. Sometimes the statute will replace the word "issue" with "descendent" but the two are synonymous. Thus, the word "issue" is far more inclusive than children and it is meant to incorporate issue of the body, marital and non-marital, and, to a degree, adopted issue. Should the surviving spouse be pregnant at the death of her deceased husband, the child-in-gestation would qualify as an issue as well; a child in gestation would qualify to inherit.

Issue of the decedent will always take to the exclusion of more remote heirs. These more remote heirs may include the parents of the decedent. Parents are termed "ancestors" and occupy a privileged status in the testate scheme, but not when issue survive. Thus, if (X) dies without a spouse but with parents and issue, the issue take the entire intestate estate. But if (X) dies with a spouse and issue, the spouse will take the bulk of the estate, sometimes the entire intestate estate, and the issue take only a portion. The parents would take nothing because issue will always trump ancestors and collaterals, which includes parents.

If there are no issue surviving the decedent, but there are parents and a spouse, then the spouse will take a significant portion of the estate, and the parents will take a minor percentage. As a practical matter, when a spouse receives the "first $200,000," for example, this is usually the entire intestate estate because the vast amount of property has usually passed by non-probate transfer. But it is possible for a parent to inherit from a child through the intestate statute, and the question arises: "Is this what the decedent intended?" It is arguable that the spouse should always inherit, and a parent should inherit only in rare circumstances. Finally, if only the spouse

Table of Consanguinity

Degrees of relatedness
are shown in parentheses.

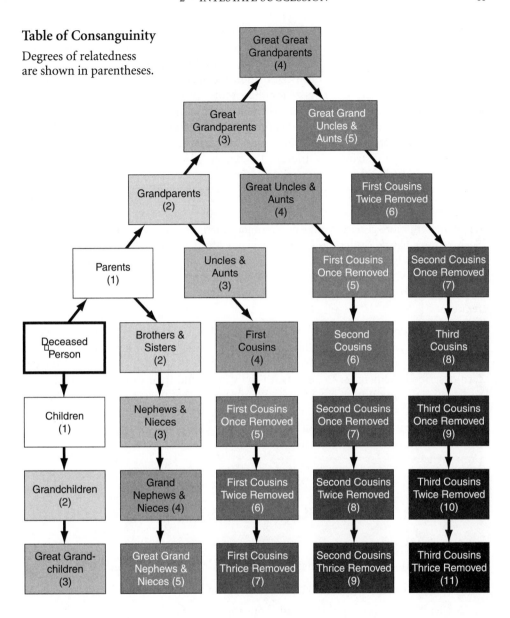

survives the decedent, and there are no issue, no ancestors, and no collaterals, the spouse takes the entire estate. Thus, the spouse occupies a pivotal role in the distribution of an intestate estate. Interestingly, the marriage could be of short or long duration.

What if there is no spouse, no issue, and no ancestors? What if the decedent is survived by only collaterals—siblings, nephews, nieces, and other, more distant relatives? How should the property be distributed then? State statues will vary, but, again, there is a pattern among them. First, only relatives by blood or adoption take; seldom do relatives by marriage take. The spouse is the only one to inherit because of marriage, and, in this situation, there is no living spouse. Thus, the statute will look to blood relatives.

Second, the statutes are likely to limit inheritance to those persons inheriting through the parents of the decedent, not those related through the grandparents. Siblings and their issue (should they be deceased as well) take to the exclusion of aunts, uncles, and first cousins. Because these latter persons descend from the grandparents and not the parents, often, they are too remote for the statute to include them. To establish with precision the relationship between a decedent and a distant collateral heir, some states utilize a Table of Consanguinity to determine degrees of kinship. The degree of kinship is important for establishing limits upon who can inherit, but the degrees do not establish the pattern of distribution. Indeed, the degree of kinship concept is more important in connection with "laughing heir" provisions.

Laughing heir provisions limit more distant relatives from taking from a decedent under the state presumption that more distant relatives will respond to the death of the decedent with more glee over sudden inheritance than remorse over the death of a relative. Such statutes have a firmer basis when they seek to make intestate administration more manageable by limiting heirs and confining inheritance to those more likely to have supported the decedent. The constitutionality of these statutes is debatable, however, when examined in the context of computer tracking of persons and state presumptions concerning remorse.

Once a pattern of intestate distribution has been established, beginning with a spouse, issue, ancestors, and collaterals, and even possible escheat to the state if none of the preceding is found, it is beneficial to look at two statutes that represent the pattern described. Remember to begin with the spouse and then work your way through to establish the amount each person would take. Note that the state statute is more representative of statutes in existence today. The Uniform Probate Code was recommended during the last decade of the Twentieth Century and is a more forward-looking statute, representative of developments in the modern American family and marital property law.

Maryland Intestate Statute (2005)

§ 3-102. Spousal share

(a) The share of a surviving spouse shall be as provided in this section.

(b) If there is a surviving minor child, the share shall be one-half.

(c) If there is no surviving minor child, but there is surviving issue, the share shall be the first $15,000 plus one-half of the residue.

(d) If there is no surviving issue but a surviving parent, the share shall be the first $15,000 plus one-half of the residue.

(e) If there is no surviving issue or parent, the share shall be the whole estate.

* * *

§ 3-103. Shares of surviving issue

The net estate, exclusive of the share of the surviving spouse, or the entire net estate if there is no surviving spouse, shall be divided equally among the surviving issue, by representation as defined in § 1-210.

§ 3-104. Absence of any surviving issue

(a) If there is no surviving issue the net estate exclusive of the share of the surviving spouse, or the entire net estate if there is no surviving spouse, shall be distributed by the personal representative pursuant to the provisions of this section.

(b) Subject to §§ 3-111 and 3-112 of this subtitle, it shall be distributed to the surviving parents equally, or if only one parent survives, to the survivor; or if neither parent survives, to the issue of the parents, by representation.

(c) If there is no surviving parent or issue of a parent, it shall be distributed one half to the surviving paternal grandparents equally, or if only one paternal grandparent survives, to the survivor, or if neither paternal grandparent survives, to the issue of the paternal grandparents, by representation, and one half to the surviving maternal grandparents equally, or if only one maternal grandparent survives, to the survivor, or if neither maternal grandparent survives, to the issue of the maternal grandparents, by representation. In the event that neither of one pair of grandparents and none of the issue of either of that pair survives, the one half share applicable shall be distributed to the other pair of grandparents, the survivor of them or the issue of either of them, in the same manner as prescribed for their half share.

(d) If there is no surviving parent or issue of a parent, or surviving grandparent or issue of a grandparent, it shall be distributed one quarter to each pair of great-grandparents equally or all to the survivor, or if neither survives, all to the issue of either or of both of that pair of great-grandparents, by representation. In the event that neither member of a pair of great-grandparents nor any issue of either of that pair survives, the quarter share applicable shall be distributed equally among the remaining pairs of great-grandparents or the survivor of a pair or issue of either of a pair of great-grandparents, in the same manner as prescribed for a quarter share.

(e) If there is no surviving blood relative entitled to inherit under this section, it shall be divided into as many equal shares as there are stepchildren of the decedent who survive the decedent and stepchildren of the decedent who did not survive the decedent but of whom issue did survive the decedent. Each stepchild of the decedent who did survive the decedent shall receive one share and the issue of each stepchild of the decedent who did not survive the decedent but of whom issue did survive the decedent shall receive one share apportioned by applying the pattern of representation set forth in § 1-210. As used in this subsection, "stepchild" shall mean the child of any spouse of the decedent if such spouse was not divorced from the decedent.

§ 3-105. Absence of heirs

(a)(1)(i) The provisions of this subsection are applicable if there is no person entitled to take under §§ 3-102 through 3-104 of this subtitle.

(ii) The provisions of this subsection do not apply to any portion of a decedent's estate that is comprised of land that is the subject of an application for a certificate of reservation for public use under Title 13, Subtitle 3 of the Real Property Article.

(2)(i) If an individual was a recipient of long-term care benefits under the Maryland Medical Assistance Program at the time of the individual's death, the net estate shall be converted to cash and paid to the Department of Health and Mental Hygiene, and shall be applied for the administration of the program.

(ii) If the provisions of subparagraph (i) of this paragraph are not applicable, the net estate shall be converted to cash and paid to the board of education in the county in which the letters were granted, and shall be applied for the use of the public schools in the county.

(b)(1) After payment has been made to the Department of Health and Mental Hygiene or to the board of education, if a claim for refund is filed by a relative within the fifth degree living at the death of the decedent or by the personal representative of the relative, and the claim is allowed, the claimant shall be entitled to a refund, without interest, of the sum paid.

(2) A claim for refund under this subsection may not be filed after the later of:

(i) 3 years after the death of the decedent; or

(ii) 1 year after the time of distribution of the property.

Uniform Probate Code (2003)

§ 2-101. Intestate Estate.

(a) Any part of a decedent's estate not effectively disposed of by will passes by intestate succession to the decedent's heirs as prescribed in this Code, except as modified by the decedent's will.

(b) A decedent by will may expressly exclude or limit the right of an individual or class to succeed to property of the decedent passing by intestate succession. If that individual or a member of that class survives the decedent, the share of the decedent's intestate estate to which that individual or class would have succeeded passes as if that individual or each member of that class had disclaimed his [or her] intestate share.

§ 2-102. Share of Spouse.

The intestate share of a decedent's surviving spouse is:

(1) the entire intestate estate if:

(i) no descendant or parent of the decedent survives the decedent; or

(ii) all of the decedent's surviving descendants are also descendants of the surviving spouse and there is no other descendant of the surviving spouse who survives the decedent;

(2) the first [$200,000], plus three-fourths of any balance of the intestate estate, if no descendant of the decedent survives the decedent, but a parent of the decedent survives the decedent;

(3) the first [$150,000], plus one-half of any balance of the intestate estate, if all of the decedent's surviving descendants are also descendants of the surviving spouse and the surviving spouse has one or more surviving descendants who are not descendants of the decedent;

(4) the first [$100,000], plus one-half of any balance of the intestate estate, if one or more of the decedent's surviving descendants are not descendants of the surviving spouse.

§ 2-102A. Share of Spouse.

[ALTERNATIVE PROVISION FOR COMMUNITY PROPERTY STATES]

(a) The intestate share of a surviving spouse in separate property is:

(1) the entire intestate estate if:

(i) no descendant or parent of the decedent survives the decedent; or

(ii) all of the decedent's surviving descendants are also descendants of the surviving spouse and there is no other descendant of the surviving spouse who survives the decedent;

(2) the first [$200,000], plus three-fourths of any balance of the intestate estate, if no descendant of the decedent survives the decedent, but a parent of the decedent survives the decedent;

(3) the first [$150,000], plus one-half of any balance of the intestate estate, if all of the decedent's surviving descendants are also descendants of the surviving spouse and the surviving spouse has one or more surviving descendants who are not descendants of the decedent;

(4) the first [$100,000], plus one-half of any balance of the intestate estate, if one or more of the decedent's surviving descendants are not descendants of the surviving spouse.

(b) The one-half of community property belonging to the decedent passes to the [surviving spouse] as the intestate share.

§ 2-103. Share of Heirs other than Surviving Spouse.

Any part of the intestate estate not passing to the decedent's surviving spouse under Section 2-102, or the entire intestate estate if there is no surviving spouse, passes in the following order to the individuals designated below who survive the decedent:

(1) to the decedent's descendants by representation;

(2) if there is no surviving descendant, to the decedent's parents equally if both survive, or to the surviving parent;

(3) if there is no surviving descendant or parent, to the descendants of the decedent's parents or either of them by representation;

(4) if there is no surviving descendant, parent, or descendant of a parent, but the decedent is survived by one or more grandparents or descendants of grandparents, half of the estate passes to the decedent's paternal grandparents equally if both survive, or to the surviving paternal grandparent, or to the descendants of the decedent's paternal grandparents or either of them if both are deceased, the descendants taking by representation; and the other half passes to the decedent's maternal relatives in the same manner; but if there is no surviving grandparent or descendant of a grandparent on either the paternal or the maternal side, the entire estate passes to the decedent's relatives on the other side in the same manner as the half.

2-105. No Taker.

If there is no taker under the provisions of this Article, the intestate estate passes to the [state].

United Kingdom Inheritance (Provision for Family and Dependents) Act (2004)

§1. Application for Financial Provision From Deceased's Estate (1) (a) through (e).

(1) Where after the commencement of this Act a person dies domiciled in England and Wales and is survived by any of the following persons:—

(a) the wife or husband of the deceased;

(b) a former wife or former husband of the deceased who has not remarried;

(ba) any person (not being a person included in paragraph (a) or (b) above) to whom subsection (1A) below applies;

(c) a child of the deceased;

(d) any person (not being a child of the deceased) who, in the case of any marriage to which the deceased was at any time a party, was treated by the deceased as a child of the family in relation to that marriage;

(e) any person (not being a person included in the foregoing paragraphs of this subsection) who immediately before the death of the deceased was being maintained, either wholly or partly, by the deceased;

that person may apply to the court for an order under section 2 of this Act on the ground that the disposition of the deceased's estate effected by his will or the law relating to intestacy, or the combination of his will and that law, is not such as to make reasonable financial provision for the applicant.

[(1A) This subsection applies to a person if the deceased died on or after 1st January 1996 and, during the whole of the period of two years ending immediately before the date when the deceased died, the person was living—

(a) in the same household as the deceased, and

(b) as the husband or wife of the deceased.] * * *

(2) In this Act "reasonable financial provision" —

(a) in the case of an application made by virtue of subsection (1)(a) above by the husband or wife of the deceased (except where the marriage with the deceased was the subject of a decree of judicial separation and at the date of death the decree was in force and the separation was continuing), means such financial provision as it would be reasonable in all the circumstances of the case for a husband or wife to receive, whether or not that provision is required for his or her maintenance;

(b) in the case of any other application made by virtue of subsection (1) above, means such financial provision as it would be reasonable in all the circumstances of the case for the applicant to receive for his maintenance.

(3) For the purposes of subsection (1)(e) above, a person shall be treated as being maintained by the deceased, either wholly or partly, as the case may be, if the deceased, otherwise than for full valuable consideration, was making a substantial contribution in money or money's worth towards the reasonable needs of that person.

§2. Powers of the Court to Make Orders (1) through (4).

(1) Subject to the provisions of this Act, where an application is made for an order under this section, the court may, if it is satisfied that the disposition of the deceased's

estate effected by his will or the law relating to intestacy, or the combination of his will and that law, is not such as to make reasonable financial provision for the applicant, make any one or more of the following orders:—

(a) an order for the making to the applicant out of the net estate of the deceased of such periodical payments and for such term as may be specified in the order;

(b) an order for the payment to the applicant out of that estate of a lump sum of such amount as may be so specified;

(c) an order for the transfer to the applicant of such property comprised in that estate as may be so specified;

(d) an order for the settlement for the benefit of the applicant of such property comprised in that estate as may be so specified;

(e) an order for the acquisition out of property comprised in that estate of such property as may be so specified and for the transfer of the property so acquired to the applicant or for the settlement thereof for his benefit;

(f) an order varying any ante-nuptial or post-nuptial settlement (including such a settlement made by will) made on the parties to a marriage to which the deceased was one of the parties, the variation being for the benefit of the surviving party to that marriage, or any child of that marriage, or any person who was treated by the deceased as a child of the family in relation to that marriage.

(2) An order under subsection (1)(a) above providing for the making out of the net estate of the deceased of periodical payments may provide for—

(a) payments of such amount as may be specified in the order,

(b) payments equal to the whole of the income of the net estate or of such portion thereof as may be so specified,

(c) payments equal to the whole of the income of such part of the net estate as the court may direct to be set aside or appropriated for the making out of the income thereof of payments under this section, or may provide for the amount of the payments or any of them to be determined in any other way the court thinks fit.

(3) Where an order under subsection (1)(a) above provides for the making of payments of an amount specified in the order, the order may direct that such part of the net estate as may be so specified shall be set aside or appropriated for the making out of the income thereof of those payments; but no larger part of the net estate shall be so set aside or appropriated than is sufficient, at the date of the order, to produce by the income thereof the amount required for the making of those payments.

(4) An order under this section may contain such consequential and supplemental provisions as the court thinks necessary or expedient for the purpose of giving effect to the order or for the purpose of securing that the order operates fairly as between one beneficiary of the estate of the deceased and another and may, in particular, but without prejudice to the generality of this subsection—

(a) order any person who holds any property which forms part of the net estate of the deceased to make such payment or transfer such property as may be specified in the order;

(b) vary the disposition of the deceased's estate effected by the will or the law relating to intestacy, or by both the will and the law relating to intestacy, in such manner as the court thinks fair and reasonable having regard to the provisions of the order and all the circumstances of the case;

(c) confer on the trustees of any property which is the subject of an order under this section such powers as appear to the court to be necessary or expedient.

III. The Surviving Spouse

Always make certain that the claimant is actually a surviving spouse. Nearly every person in America has seen the television episode of *Cheers* when Carla mourns the death of her husband at his wake but soon learns she is not the only "spouse" in attendance. In an age when people have multiple marriages, domestic partnerships, and non-marital cohabitation, the intestate process invites multiple claimants to whatever the decedent passes to others without a Last Will and Testament or non-probate transfers. A person may become a spouse through one of five ways:

(1) *Statutory Marriage*: This marriage requires a license, an officiant, and a couple meeting certain age, gender, and consanguinity/affinity requirements; a couple satisfying these requirements may acquire the status of marriage in every state.

(2) *Common Law Marriage*: Far fewer states allow for the status of marriage when a couple, meeting all of the statutory requirements except for a license and officiant, hold themselves out as married for a period of time. If the couples does, in fact, meet the requirements, the marriage is official and will be recognized in other states, unless it is contrary to strong state public policy.

(3) *Putative Spouse*: This is a curative marriage, when one or both of the parties entered into the marriage ceremony in a good faith belief that the marriage was valid, but, because of some defect in the process, the ceremony lacked validity. Good faith belief is the key ingredient. For a case where the court defines what "good faith" means, see Rebouche v. Anderson, 505 So. 2d 808 (La. App. 2d Cir. 1987).

(4) *Reciprocal Beneficiaries*: In response to litigation seeking to allow marriage between persons of the same sex, Hawaii passed legislation in 1997 allowing for persons otherwise unable to marry to enjoy certain benefits otherwise reserved to married couples. Among those benefits is intestate succession. A couple must register as Reciprocal Beneficiaries for the status to be achieved. *See* Haw. Rev. Stat. Ch. 572C et seq. (2003).

(5) *Civil Unions/Domestic Partnerships:* Through state legislation, persons of the same sex may enter into a status allowing for all of the rights and responsibilities of marriage. *See, e.g.,* Cal. Fam. Code § 297.5 (effective Jan. 1, 2005); Vt. Stat. Ann. tit. 15, §§ 1201–07 (2003). For reciprocal beneficiaries, see Vt. Stat. Ann. tit 15, §§ 1301–06 (2003).

Once the marital union has been formed, the spouse is entitled to a share unless there is a valid divorce completely separating the parties from the bonds of matrimony. But this is not always easy to define. One of the parties simply may have abandoned the other, and neither may have procured a divorce since the abandonment. The couple remains married, but perhaps public policy may bar inheritance by the abandoning party. Oftentimes, the couple simply separates and may be trying to work through a reconciliation when one of the parties dies. Marital status remains intact in spite of the separation. Many states provide for a period of separation between the parties prior to a final decree of divorce, either in preparation for a final decree of divorce or as a separate, no-fault ground which, if continued, would result in a final decree of divorce. New York state provides a statutory example, and the case that follows offers a factual context.

New York Domestic Relations Law (2004)

§ 170 An action for divorce may be maintained by a husband of a wife to procure a judgement divorcing the parties and dissolving the marriage on ... the following ground:

(6) The husband and wife have lived separate and apart pursuant to a written agreement of separation, subscribed by the parties thereto and acknowledged or proved in the form required to entitle a deed to be recorded, for a period of one or more years after the execution of such agreement and satisfactory proof has been submitted by the plaintiff that he or she has substantially performed all the terms and conditions of such agreement. Such agreement shall be filed in the office of the clerk of the county wherein either party resides. In lieu of filing such agreement, either party to such agreement may file a memorandum of such agreement, which memorandum shall be similarly subscribed and acknowledged or proved as was the agreement of separation and shall contain the following information: (a) the names and addresses of each of the parties, (b) the date of marriage of the parties, (c) the date of the agreement of separation and (d) the date of this subscription and acknowledgment or proof of such agreement of separation.

Estate of Goick
Supreme Court of Montana, 1996
275 Mont. 13, 909 P.2d 1165

ERDMANN, Justice.

This is an appeal of an order of the Seventeenth Judicial District Court, Blaine County, granting summary judgment in favor of Barbara Goick, appointing Barbara as a supervised personal representative of decedent Michael Goick's estate, approving the distribution agreement between Barbara and the decedent's children, and denying appellants' motion to compel settlement of the case. We affirm.

* * *

Michael and Barbara Goick were married in 1981 and the marriage produced three children. In December 1990, Michael filed a petition for dissolution. A hearing in the dissolution proceeding was scheduled for April 25, 1991. At that hearing, Michael and Barbara agreed to all issues except the division of household goods, which the parties were to settle within two weeks. The District Court Judge then had the parties present sufficient evidence to support a decree of divorce.

Following the hearing, the judge was apparently asked whether Barbara and Michael were divorced and he responded that they were. The parties were unable to agree on the division of the household goods and, on December 25, 1991, Barbara filed a motion to divide personal property of the marriage. In the motion, she stated her understanding was that the marriage had been dissolved on April 25, 1991, by the District Court. On December 19, 1991, the District Court Judge wrote a memorandum to the attorneys informing them that it was his understanding the parties had refused to sign the settlement agreement negotiated at the April 25 hearing and that he intended to hold the parties to that agreement. On January 7, 1992, Michael's attorney filed an application for withdrawal of attorney to which Michael consented. No further proceedings occurred in the divorce action and no final decree or order was issued. Michael died on November 30, 1992. Two days after his death, Barbara moved to dismiss the divorce proceeding for the reason that Michael had died. On December 3, 1992, an order was issued dismissing the divorce action.

On December 7, 1992, Barbara filed a petition for adjudication of intestacy, determination of heirs, and appointment of personal representative (PR). In the petition, she claimed she was the surviving spouse and was entitled to an appointment as PR. Michael's mother, brother, and sister (the appellants) filed an objection to the petition, claiming Barbara was not the surviving spouse, but rather the ex-wife of Michael. The court appointed a guardian ad litem for the children. Barbara filed a motion for summary judgment asking the court to determine that she was the surviving spouse of Michael. The appellants filed a motion for summary judgment asking the court to find that Barbara was not Michael's surviving spouse.

Subsequent to the summary judgment motion being decided, the attorneys for Barbara and the appellants, and the guardian ad litem, reached an oral settlement agreement on the telephone. That agreement was never written or signed by the parties. On August 2, 1994, the appellants filed a motion to compel a settlement, claiming that a binding agreement had been reached in the telephone conference. Barbara and the guardian ad litem objected to the motion because the oral agreement had never been approved by the parties. On October 24, 1994, the District Court issued an order denying the appellants' motion to compel settlement. The appellants filed a motion for reconsideration, which was denied.

On January 27, 1995, a distribution agreement was entered into between Barbara and the children through their guardian ad litem as the only potential heirs of Michael. A notice of distribution agreement was filed, and the appellants filed an objection to the agreement. The District Court approved the agreement on March 21, 1995. The appellants filed a motion asking the court to reconsider the distribution agreement, and the court ordered oral argument. On April 4, 1995, following the hearing, the District Court issued an order granting Barbara's motion for summary judgment on the issue of her status as a surviving spouse, approving the distribution agreement, and appointing Barbara as a supervised personal representative. From that order and the denial of their motion to compel settlement, appellants appeal.

* * *

Barbara claims the appellants have no standing to appeal. The record does not support Barbara's contention that she objected to the appellants' standing in District Court. However, as we noted in Grossman v. Dept. of Natural Resources and Conservation (1984), 209 Mont. 427, 437, 682 P.2d 1319, 1324, objections to standing cannot be waived. Therefore, Barbara is not precluded from raising this defense for the first time on appeal. *See* Stewart v. Board of County Comm'rs (1977), 175 Mont. 197, 204, 573 P.2d 184, 188.

The appellants have appealed three separate issues to this Court and it is necessary to examine their standing as to each issue. A party aggrieved may appeal an order. Rule 1,

M.R.App.P. To be aggrieved, a party must have an interest in the subject matter of the litigation which is injuriously affected by the order. Holmstrom Land Co. v. Newlan Creek Water Dist. (1979), 185 Mont. 409, 425, 605 P.2d 1060, 1069 (citing Estate of Stoian (1960), 138 Mont. 384, 357 P.2d 41).

* * *

Barbara contends that appellants were not heirs to the estate, and so, they could not be injured by Barbara's appointment as PR. The appellants claim they have standing because they are creditors of the estate. In fact, Michael's mother, Wanda Goick, is the only appellant who filed a creditor's claim against the estate. As a creditor, Wanda has priority for appointment as PR if Barbara is determined to be ineligible. See § 72-3-502, MCA. Section 72-3-503, MCA, provides that creditors can object to the appointment of a PR. Wanda objected to Barbara's appointment as PR, and for that reason she has standing to appeal the appointment. Michael's brother and sister are neither creditors nor heirs of the estate, and therefore, they have no standing to appeal her appointment as PR. See Olson v. Dept. of Revenue (1986), 223 Mont. 464, 469–70, 726 P.2d 1162, 1166.

* * *

The appellants raise the issue of whether enforcement of the distribution agreement was in error and Barbara argues that they lack standing to challenge the agreement. Under this agreement, Barbara agreed to receive a distribution of one-third of the estate, and the children agreed, through their guardian ad litem, to receive two-thirds of the estate which will be administered by a corporate trustee.

The distribution agreement provided that Barbara and the children's guardian ad litem agreed

> to enter into a private agreement among successors as to distribution of an estate, pursuant to Section 72-3-915, MCA, in order to settle the litigation in the probate matter pending in Blaine County District Court and to provide for a different distribution than provided under the laws of intestacy.

Section 72-3-915(1), MCA, provides as follows:

> Subject to the rights of creditors and taxing authorities, competent successors may agree among themselves to alter the interests, shares, or amounts to which they are entitled under the will of the decedent or under the laws of intestacy in any way that they provide in a written contract executed by all who are affected by its provisions. The personal representative shall abide by the terms of the agreement subject to his obligation to administer the estate for the benefit of creditors, to pay all taxes and costs of administration, and to carry out the responsibilities of his office for the benefit of any successors of the decedent who are not parties.

The appellants are not successors to the estate and so they are not proper parties to an agreement distributing the estate. They have no legal interest in the distribution of Michael's estate. Furthermore, Wanda's interests as a creditor of Michael's estate are completely provided for by statute.

A party has no standing where there is no personal stake in the outcome of the controversy. Northern Border Pipeline Co. v. State (1989), 237 Mont. 117, 129, 772 P.2d 829, 836 (citing Olson, 726 P.2d at 1166). The appellants have no personal stake in the validity of the agreement. We therefore conclude that the appellants have no standing to claim the distribution agreement was improper. Accordingly, the issue of whether the District Court erred in approving the distribution agreement is not properly before us.

* * *

Barbara contends the contested oral settlement agreement was a distribution of the estate to which appellants have no interest. Accordingly, she argues they have no standing to appeal the court's denial of a motion to enforce this agreement. The appellants, however, were parties to the contested settlement agreement and the agreement named Wanda as co-PR and awarded her a percentage of the estate in excess of what she would receive as a creditor. The appellants are directly affected by the validity of the agreement and thus have standing to appeal this issue. See Holmstrom, 605 P.2d at 1069.

* * *

Wanda, as the sole appellant with standing to litigate this issue, claims that both Barbara and Michael considered themselves divorced and in the April 25, 1991, hearing the District Court Judge informed the parties that they were divorced, even though no final order was ever issued. The District Court held a hearing on this issue in the probate proceeding and concluded that a divorce decree cannot be based on an oral agreement. The court further concluded that Barbara was the surviving spouse for purposes of intestate succession and granted summary judgment in her favor.

The standard we use to review a district court's grant of summary judgment is the same as that used by the district court in applying Rule 56, M.R.Civ.P. Bruner v. Yellowstone County (1995), 272 Mont. 261, 263, 900 P.2d 901, 903. Summary judgment is appropriate where there are no issues of material fact and the moving party is entitled to judgment as a matter of law. Bruner, 900 P.2d at 903.

Section 72-2-103(2)(c), MCA (1991), provides that "a person who was a party to a valid proceeding concluded by an order purporting to terminate all marital property rights" is not a surviving spouse of decedent. Wanda claims the April 25, 1991, proceeding conveyed and implied that Barbara and Michael were divorced, thereby "purporting" to terminate all marital property rights. Wanda contends that according to §72-2-103(2)(c), MCA (1991), Barbara is not a surviving spouse for the purposes of intestacy.

There was no divorce decree or order issued from the April 25, 1991, proceeding, nor was a final settlement even reached as to all marital property rights. Recently, in In re Marriage of Simms (1994), 264 Mont. 317, 871 P.2d 899, we concluded that an oral settlement agreement is not binding on a judge. Whatever settlement was reached in the April 25, 1991, proceeding was merely an oral agreement between the parties and cannot be considered the equivalent of an order where no final order was issued. Accordingly, Barbara's status as a surviving spouse was not terminated pursuant to §72-2-103(2)(c), MCA (1991).

Wanda further contends principals of equitable estoppel prevent Barbara from claiming that she is the surviving spouse in regard to Michael's estate when she has held herself out as being divorced from Michael for over one and one-half years prior to his death. Equitable estoppel requires that:

> '1. There must be conduct—acts, language, or silence—amounting to a representation or a concealment of material facts. 2. These facts must be known to the party estopped at the time of his said conduct, or at least the circumstances must be such that knowledge of them is necessarily imputed to him. 3. The truth concerning these facts must be unknown to the other party claiming the benefit of the estoppel, at the time when it was acted upon by him. 4. The conduct must be done with the intention, or at least with the expectation, that it

will be acted upon by the other party, or under such circumstances that it is both natural and probable that it will be so acted upon.... 5. The conduct must be relied upon by the other party, and, thus relying, he must be led to act upon it. 6. He must in fact act upon it in such a manner as to change his position for the worse, in other words, he must so act that he would suffer a loss if he were compelled to surrender or forego or alter what he has done by reason of the first party being permitted to repudiate his conduct and to assert rights inconsistent with it....'

Davis v. Jones (1983), 203 Mont. 464, 467, 661 P.2d 859, 861 (quoting Lindblom v. Employers' Liab. Assur. Corp. (1930), 88 Mont. 488, 494, 295 P. 1007, 1009).

In this instance, equitable estoppel would have required that Barbara's representation that they were divorced was made with the intention or expectation that Michael would act upon the representation. It would also require that Michael relied to his detriment upon the representation and that he not be aware that the divorce was not final. Both parties refused to sign the settlement negotiated at the April 25, 1991, hearing. Michael's attorney for the divorce action testified that Michael did not believe the divorce was final and that Michael insisted upon going to trial. This testimony was uncontradicted. It follows that Michael was aware that the divorce was not final and did not act to his detriment even if Barbara was found to have intentionally misrepresented the facts concerning the status of the divorce.

We conclude that Barbara is not estopped from claiming she and Michael were not divorced. The record is clear that no divorce decree or order was ever issued. We therefore conclude that the District Court did not err in holding that Barbara was the surviving spouse for purposes of intestate succession and granting summary judgment in her favor.

* * *

Wanda's position is that Barbara should not have been appointed PR because she has obvious conflicts of interest over the estate in regard to the children's interests. She argues that Barbara's claim to the estate is directly adverse to that of the children's because the children would receive the entire estate if not for Barbara's self-interest. For that reason, Wanda contends that Barbara cannot act as a fiduciary of the estate for the benefit of the children. The District Court ordered that Barbara be named PR under the court's supervision and that she not take any substantive action without the court's approval.

We review the appointment of a personal representative according to §72-3-502, MCA, to determine whether a district court has correctly interpreted the law. Estate of Peterson (1994), 265 Mont. 104, 110, 874 P.2d 1230, 1233. If a PR has not been named under will and there are no devisees, the decedent's surviving spouse has priority for appointment. Section 72-3-502, MCA.

As stated in Issue 2, Barbara is Michael's surviving spouse for purposes of intestate succession. Accordingly, she has priority for appointment over Michael's other heirs, the public administrator, and any creditor. See §72-3-502, MCA. Her appointment was agreed to by the children through their guardian ad litem. Therefore, the District Court was correct when it determined Barbara had priority for appointment. Furthermore, the children's interests are protected in this situation through the court ordered supervision of the estate's administration. We conclude that the District Court did not err in appointing Barbara as PR of Michael's estate.

* * *

Notes

Once spousal status is achieved, the spouse may receive a significant portion of the intestate estate. It should be noted that, in common law jurisdictions, the length of the marriage is not important to achieving the maximum amount allowed under the intestate statute. A couple could be newlyweds, and even if one died suddenly, the survivor would qualify to take a full share under the intestate statute as if the two had been married for fifty years or longer. Even in a community property jurisdiction, where the spouses have accumulated a community of assets while married, the surviving spouse will receive all of the community under intestate succession, even if the couple had been married for only a few days. Nonetheless, the community would be small, and the separate property of the decedent spouse presumptively would be large and not fully accessible to the surviving spouse if other heirs survive.

On the other hand, when a spouse seeks to "elect" against a valid Last Will and Testament, the amount available to the surviving spouse is based on the length of the marriage. Intestacy and election are two different means by which the spouse may take from an estate. For now, the Uniform Probate Code, for example, calibrates the elective share amount according to the length of the marriage; the longer the marriage, the more the surviving spouse will receive should she or he elect against the valid Last Will and Testament. This concept will be discussed *infra*, but the different treatment of a spouse under intestate and testate statutes should invite questions: Why does a newlywed receive a full amount from an intestate estate, but only a small portion when a Last Will and Testament leaves the decedent's estate to someone other than the surviving spouse?

Tax Considerations: Often when a spouse dies, almost all of the property is owned with the other spouse in the form of will substitutes (non-probate transfers), such as tenancy by the entirety or joint tenants with right of survivorship. Internal Revenue Code §2040(b) provides that one-half of the value of the property is included within the decedent's gross estate, recognizing thereby that the decedent owned one-half of the asset, not the entire asset. When the surviving spouse dies, I.R.C. §2033 will include the entire value of the asset within his or her estate. Obviously the arrangement for married couples allows for only one half of the property to be included within the decedent's estate for estate tax purposes, even though the decedent had a beneficial interest in the whole asset. Because of the nature of tenants in common, whereby each tenant holds his or her interest without survivorship in another at death, the arrangement does not apply, and that portion owned passes entirely as part of the gross estate of the decedent.

Also, in the case of a married couple making gifts during lifetime, spouses may elect to split a gift made by one spouse to a third person donee, each spouse being considered as a donor of one-half of the gift. Each of the spouses is able to claim the present deduction of $11,000 per donee annual exclusion, and each is able to utilize all of his or her unified credit against any gift tax that may be due. *See* I. R. C. §§2513, 2503(b), 2505.

IV. Share of Heirs Other Than a Surviving Spouse

If the spouse and issue survive the decedent, the spouse will take all or a significant portion of the intestate estate. The remaining portion will descend to issue of the decedent. Likewise, if there is no spouse surviving, all of the intestate estate will descend to the issue, or if no issue, then to the parents. If there is no surviving spouse, no surviving issue and no surviving parents, then the remaining portion will descend to the collateral heirs. Issue and collateral heirs—we will later refer to them as "classes"—are open-ended, which means that persons who qualify could predecease the decedent or additional ones could be born after the death of the decedent. For now, we are not concerned over those who may be born in the future. They will receive nothing; only those alive and ascertainable at the death of the decedent will be able to take a portion of the intestate estate.

The class of persons involved—both issue and collaterals—may consist of a mixed group. Some may be closer to the decedent in degree of kinship than others. How, then, should the estate be divided when the decedent leaves one child and three grandchildren from a predeceasing child? How should the estate be distributed when the decedent leaves no spouse, no issue and no parents, but two sisters and three nephews from a predeceasing brother? In other words, how should the estate be divided when the degrees of kinship vary and, yet, every claimant is within the statutory limit? Before these questions may be answered, certain terminology must be understood: *per capita* and *per stirpes* distribution. *Per capita* distribution means that a person receives in and of himself or herself from a decedent—he or she takes by his or her own head and not through another. When the term *per stirpes* is used, it refers to when a person takes "by representation" or through another. The following chart will provide an example for distribution among issue:

A. Issue

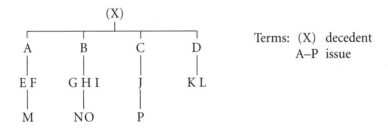

Terms: (X) decedent
       A–P issue

If (X) dies without a surviving spouse, but with issue, the issue would take before any parent would take. Thus, in the presence of issue, we are not concerned with distribution to parents or more distant collaterals. The four issue identified in the above chart are: A-B-C-D. Each is a child and each would take equally because each survived the decedent. Also, each would take per capita from the decedent because each is taking himself or herself. But now add additional facts: If B-C-D all predecease (X), A would be the only surviving child. Should A take all of (X)'s estate? No. Grandchildren of B-C-D survive: G-H-I-J-K-L. Even though they are grandchildren, they are still issue and are entitled to take under the intestate statute. But each would take through a predeceasing parent (B-C-D) and, because they take by representation or through another, the grandchildren would take per stirpes. Finally, if H and J were to predecease (X), each of them is survived by an issue as well, and that issue (N-O-P) would be able to share in (X)'s intestate estate, per stirpes, through H and J. Because the statute provides for representation among issue, it is conceivable that per stirpes distribution could continue through multiple generations.

B. Collaterals

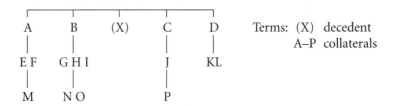

Terms: (X) decedent
A–P collaterals

As with the example concerning issue, (X) is predeceasing without a spouse. Remember that collaterals are not issue. Rather, collaterals are more distant relatives, such as brothers and sisters, and, as shown in the diagram, nephews and nieces; therefore, the presence of parents matters. Here, there are no ancestors—parents—so we are not concerned with them taking and, thereby, excluding the collaterals. Thus, how should the estate be divided? The answer is simple: the same as with issue. Thus, if A-B-C-D survive, each would take equally and per capita because each would take himself or herself. But if B-C-D predeceased (X), then A would be the only surviving sibling, and the nephews and nieces of (X) would take per stirpes through their predeceasing parent.

Once we understand how the system works in relationship to per capita and per stirpes, we must ask how much each of the parties would take if we were to make a percentage distribution. There are four methods by which we may arrive at the percentage of each of the intestate takers. The state in which you practice will apply one of these four methods. Furthermore, a person may utilize one of these methods in a valid Last Will and Testament to distribute property to heirs. States may also borrow from the four methods when implementing statutory distribution under statutes such as anti-lapse—a concept we will discover later in the course. For now, it is important to master the four methods of distribution.

C. Methods of Distribution

1. Old Uniform Probate Code (1969)

Most often referred to as the "modern" form of distribution, this method would go to the first horizontal line where there is a survivor and make a per capita distribution there, then make a per stirpes distribution at each succeeding line. The important element in the old UPC scheme is the combination of per capita and per stirpes distribution. For example, if we look at the previous chart, where (X) has died and is survived by collateral heirs, if B-C-D predecease (X), we would still start at this first horizontal line because A is still alive. A would receive one-quarter share because B-C-D, even though predeceasing, are survived by issue. There are four vertical lines of succession, and each would be entitled to receive a portion. Under this example, A would receive one-quarter share per capita and the remaining three-fourths would be divided among the other three vertical lines.

However, because B has predeceased and is survived by G-H-I, each of them would receive one-third of B's one-fourth, or one-twelfth each. Also, if H had predeceased and was survived by N and O, then N and O would have to divide per stirpes the one-twelfth share of H. Therefore, N and O would each receive a one-twenty-fourth share in the estate. The same manner of distribution would occur with C and D, but please note that J would do best among all of the nephews and nieces of (X) because J is the lone survivor of C, and B was survived by G-H-I. Thus, even though J and G-H-I are in the same degree of kinship to (X), J will receive one-fourth of the estate and G-H-I will receive one-twelfth. Because of the per stirpes method of distribution, whereby an heir is taking through another heir, there is a disparity among persons similarly related and of equal degree of kinship to the decedent. To rectify this disparity, the New Uniform Probate Code was adopted.

2. New Uniform Probate Code (1990)

The new Uniform Probate Code §2-106 is similar to the old provision in many respects, but it has one major difference: there is a per capita distribution at each level of distribution; there is no per stirpes distribution. Go the first horizontal level where there is a survivor and make a per capita distribution, then make a per capita distribution at each succeeding level. The utilization of per capita distribution at each level is the distinctive element. We can look to the previous chart for an example. Upon (X)'s death, if A is the lone survivor of the four collaterals (A-B-C-D), we begin at that level. A would receive a one-fourth share since A is a survivor and each of the predeceasing collaterals (B-C-D) is survived by issue. Thus, A would take his one-fourth share and be content. But three-fourths remains. In the old UPC, we would distribute that per stirpes among the descending heirs from B-C-D. This is not the case under the new UPC. Instead, we will take the remaining three-fourths and divide it per capita among the heirs at this second level: G-H-I-J-K-L. Each of them would receive one-sixth of three-fourths, or one-eighth each. Obviously, this method of computation would be far better for G-H-I than it would be for J. You may recall that J was receiving one-fourth under the old UPC. Yet the system does have the advantage of treating equally each of the nephews and nieces who are related to (X) by the same degree of kinship.

It is worthwhile to continue with the new UPC distribution to illustrate the per capita distribution at each level. We have seen that G-H-I-J-K-L each will receive one-eighth of the estate. The mathematics is relatively easy to this point. But what would happen if H and J had predeceased (X)? H is survived by N and O, and J is survived by P. All three (N-O-P) are related to (X) equally and, thus, under the new UPC, all three should share in the estate of (X) equally and per capita. To make this happen, we simply combine the share that H and J would have taken if each had survived. Because each would have taken one-eighth, we combine the two and arrive at one-quarter. This one quarter is then divided equally among the three heirs: N-O-P. Thus, each receives one-third of one-quarter for a share of one-twelfth each. Of course, N-O-P would take this one-twelfth share per capita.

The goal of the new UPC is to provide uniformity among heirs, and the per capita scheme is the method by which this is brought about. Uniformity is meant to bring about fairness, and this is a consistent goal among other UPC provisions as well. When some states limit inheritance to a degree of kinship, or when the UPC limits inheritance to descendants of grandparents, the goal is to limit inheritance to those who may have contributed to the decedent during life or who may partake of a direct blood kinship with the decedent after death. Because the intestate statute is simply an approximation of what the decedent may have wanted to do, certainty is elusive. The next method of intestate succession—the strict method—is seen today as less fair than others, yet, at one time, it was seen as the only method that truly and fairly represented the blood line of the decedent.

3. *Strict*

This method of distribution is similar to the old UPC, except the necessity of starting with a survivor is eliminated. Thus, under the strict method, you go to the first horizontal line, regardless of whether there is a survivor there. Once there, you make a per capita or per stirpes distribution throughout. For example, if we go back to our previous chart, we can say that A has survived (X), but not so with B-C-D. Each of them has predeceased and is survived by descendants. Just as in the old UPC, we would give A one-fourth of the estate per capita and distribute one quarter per stirpes to each of the descendants of B (G-H-I), C (J), and D (K-L). Each would receive an amount identical to what would occur if we were distributing the property under the old UPC method.

However, if the entire first horizontal line has predeceased (X), i.e., all of A-B-C-D are dead at (X)'s death, should we begin to make distribution at this point? The old and new UPC would say no; instead, go to the first line where there is a survivor and start there. But this is not how distribution would begin under the strict method of distribution. Here, you would go to the first horizontal line and distribute the property per stirpes, regardless of survivorship. Looking at our previous chart, if A-B-C-D are all predeceased, then the one-fourth distribution that each would have received if each were living will be divided among each of their respective heirs. Assuming that everyone is alive at the second horizontal line, the intestate estate would be divided among the following: E and F would each receive one-eighth, or one-half of A's one-fourth distribution; G-H-I would each receive one-twelfth, or one-third of B's one-fourth distribution; J would do the best with one-fourth, which is C's one-fourth distribution; and K and L would take one-eighth, or one-half of D's one-fourth distribution.

If fairness is a consideration, then it centers on the fact that the dead have the ability to determine the amounts the living will receive. It can be argued that this is always a factor whenever per stirpes is used. But in the strict method, it is possible to foist per stirpes upon the living through a line of persons who are all dead, not just some of them, as with the old UPC. In times past, the blood line measured through strict descent may have proven a justification for the strict method, but modern sensibilities are reluctant to apply it.

4. *Next of Kin*

The final method of distribution could be described as a completely per capita system. It is applied by going to the first level where there is a survivor of the closet degree of kinship and giving all of the intestate estate to that person or group of persons equally. No heir takes through another. Thus, if we go to the previous chart, suppose that A and B survive (X), and that J-K-L survive as well. How should the estate be divided if every other heir has predeceased? The answer under the method of next of kin distribution is that A and B would divide the entire estate. Sadly, J-K-L would receive nothing. The value of this method is that it provides for a fast and easily identifiable distribution of the estate among heirs, it lessens the chance of laughing heirs, and it provides for equality among persons of the same degree of kinship. The following decision offers an example of the old UPC and the next of kin methods.

In re Estate of Martineau

Supreme Court of New Hampshire, 1985
126 N.H. 250, 490 A.2d 779

SOUTER, Justice.

This is an appeal from a decree of distribution entered by the Probate Court for Strafford County (*Cassavechia,* J.), providing, *inter alia,* that first cousins of the intestate decedent may share in her estate by right of representation. We affirm.

Yvonne Martineau died intestate on December 8, 1981, leaving no spouse, issue, parents, siblings, issue of siblings, or grandparents. On her father's side, her survivors were an uncle and first cousins who were the issue of seven predeceased aunts and uncles. On her mother's side she was survived by first cousins and first cousins once removed who were the issue of predeceased first cousins.

The administrator petitioned the probate court for a decree of distribution that would identify the interests of those entitled to share in the estate. Since the decedent's nearest survivors are collaterals who are issue of the decedent's grandparents, the court applied RSA 561:1, II(d) to determine the interests of beneficiaries. That statute provides in part that if there is no surviving issue, parent, issue of a parent, or grandparent "but the decedent is survived by ... issue of grandparents, half of the estate passes ... to the issue of the paternal grandparents..., the issue taking equally if they are all of the same degree of kinship to the decedent, but if of unequal degree those of more remote degree take by representation; and the other half passes to the maternal relatives in the same manner...." Since in this case there are survivors in both the maternal and paternal lines, the court properly ordered that the estate be divided into halves, with one half going to the survivors in each line.

In deciding how the survivors on each side should share in their half of the estate, the court applied two statutory provisions. First, it applied the language quoted from RSA 561:1, II(d), providing that when the grandparents' issue are of unequal degree, those of more remote degree take by representation. On each side of the family in this case there are surviving issue of unequal degree. On the paternal side there is an uncle, in the third degree of kinship, and first cousins who have survived uncles or aunts, in the fourth degree. On the maternal side there are first cousins, in the fourth degree, and first cousins once removed who have survived first cousins, in the fifth degree. The court accordingly determined that some of the survivors should take by representation. To determine which survivors could so take, the court then applied a second statutory provision, RSA 561:3, that "[n]o representation shall be allowed among collaterals beyond the degree of brothers' and sisters' grandchildren."

There are, of course, no brothers' or sisters' grandchildren in the present case, since the decedent's nearest collaterals are related only through the decedent's grandparents. The court nonetheless found RSA 561:3 applicable to determine the extent of possible representation in this case. To reach this conclusion, the court did not read the statute as applying only to the specific instances of representation among siblings' children and grandchildren. The court assumed that if the statute applied only to siblings' children and grand-children it would simply have precluded representation "beyond brothers' and sisters' grandchildren."

The statute however, forbade representation "beyond the degree of brothers' and sisters' grandchildren." The court therefore read the statute as using siblings' grand-children as an example to illustrate a limitation on the right of any collateral relation to take by right of representation. Since siblings' grandchildren are in the fourth degree of kinship from a decedent, the court thus derived a general rule that in any collateral line the right to take by representation is limited to those of the fourth or nearer degrees of kinship. In applying the rule to this estate, the court denied any share by right of representation to the decedent's first cousins once removed, since they are of the fifth degree.

The result was a decree that on the maternal side the first cousins who survived the decedent would share equally. No one on the maternal side excepted to the decree.

On the paternal side the court divided the estate into eight shares, for the one surviving uncle and the surviving first cousins who would take by representation in the stead of seven aunts and uncles who had predeceased the decedent. On the paternal side only the surviving uncle excepted to the decree, by bringing this appeal.

The appellant takes the position that the court below misconstrued both of the statutes that it applied. He claims that RSA 561:1, II(d) does not provide any right to anyone to take by representation. He claims that such a right flows only from RSA 561:3, which provides that right only to those who are children or grandchildren of pre-deceased brothers and sisters. On this theory, of course, the paternal first cousins would have no right to take by representation in the place of their predeceased parents, and the uncle would take the entire paternal half, or moiety, of the estate.

In assessing the merits of the uncle's position, the words of the statutes must be our first concern. To start with the language of RSA 561:1, II(d), we have already seen that it provides that if the surviving issue of the decedent's predeceased grandparents are "of unequal degree, those of more remote degree take by representation." It is difficult to think of any language that could provide more clearly that issue of a grandparent may take by right of representation. It is likewise difficult to think of any language that could be more clearly inconsistent with the appellant's position that the statute provides no such right of representation.

The force of this language is even stronger when we contrast it with the provisions of the earlier statute that it replaced. Under the prior law, the cousins would have had no right of representation, and on the facts of this case the entire estate would have passed "to the next of kin in equal shares," 1971 Laws 179:26, enacting RSA 561:1, V (repealed by 1973 Laws 293:1), *i.e.*, to the sole surviving uncle. By the enactment of the present statute, then, the legislature expressly extended a right of representation to those in a collateral line who had not enjoyed that right before.

The appellant nonetheless argues that the express provisions of the statute do not mean what they say, and he tries to rest his argument on two facts of statutory history. The first such fact is the legislature's adoption of one section of the Uniform Probate Code but not another. The present RSA 561:1, II is a verbatim enactment of § 2-103 of the Uniform Probate Code (1969). See 1973 Laws 293:1; 1974 Laws 18:2. That is, the language providing on its face that collaterals related through a grandparent may take by representation came from the Code.

The legislature did not enact all of the Code, however. It failed to enact § 2-106, which expressly provides a formula for computing the share of one who takes by representation: the total share in question is divided by the number of "surviving heirs in the nearest degree of kinship and deceased persons in the same degree who left issue who survive the decedent, each surviving heir in the nearest degree receiving one share and the share of each deceased person in the same degree being divided among his issue in the same manner." Uniform Probate Code § 2-106 (1969). The appellant argues that the failure to enact the Code's formula for computing shares by representation suggests that the legislature did not intend to provide for representation when it enacted Code § 2-103 as RSA 561:1, II.

The argument is unpersuasive. The formula contained in § 2-106 of the Code merely states what "representation" has traditionally been taken to mean. See e.g., Preston v. Cole, 64 N.H. 459, 13 A. 788 (1887); L. Hoyt, The Law of Administration in New Hampshire 57, 59 (1916). The enactment of § 2-106 was therefore unnecessary, for its provisions were already the law. The legislature's failure to enact it suggests no more than economy.

The appellant also cites a second fact of statutory history in arguing that RSA 561:1, II(d) does not provide the right of representation that it appears to provide. He notes that the Code has no provision corresponding to RSA 561:3, which limits representation to those within the degree of siblings' grandchildren. The language of this section derives from the English statute known as 22 & 23 Car. II, ch. 10 (1672). Green v. Bancroft, 75 N.H. 204, 205, 72 A. 373, 373 (1909). See 2 W. Treat, Probate Law, New Hampshire Practice 213 (1968); 2 Laws of New Hampshire 295, 297 (adopted 1718); 5 Laws of New Hampshire 384, 385 (adopted 1789); R.S. 166:3; Laws 1883, 72:1.

The appellant asks why the legislature left this old statute on the books when it enacted the Code's scheme of distribution in RSA 561:1. He purports to find the answer by asserting that the common law allowed for no representation and that RSA 561:3 was actually a limited source of rights to take by representation, despite the fact that it appears to be a restriction on that right. Having found it to be a source, the appellant argues that the section would have been rendered wholly superfluous if RSA 561:1, II(d) had also been intended to provide for representation. Hence, he concludes that the latter statute does not provide for representation. He completes the argument by asserting that RSA 561:3 provides representation only to those in the lines of predeceased siblings, thus excluding decedent's first cousins.

This argument rests on a false premise. RSA 561:3 was not the source of representation among collaterals prior to the enactment in 1973 of the relevant portion of the present RSA 561:1. For example, under the earlier version of the statute, RSA 561:1, IV provided that in the absence of parents or issue an intestate's estate passed to "brothers and sisters or their representatives." 1971 Laws 179:26 (repealed by 1973 Laws 293:1). Since the right to take by representation did not flow from RSA 561:3 before 1973, that section did not become redundant when the legislature enacted the present RSA 561:1, and the remainder of the argument falls with its premise.

We conclude that all of the appellant's arguments are unavailing, and we hold that the probate judge was correct in his decree that the first cousins were entitled to share in the paternal moiety by right of representation. This holding is dispositive of the case before us, since the appellant could demonstrate error prejudicial to him only if we were to rule that collaterals traced through predeceased grandparents could not take by representation.

We wish nonetheless to add a word about another issue that the parties have touched upon, for we think it appropriate to bring it to the attention of the legislature. As we have already noted, the appellant has argued that RSA 561:3 does not provide a general rule limiting all representation to those in the fourth or closer degrees of kinship. Rather, he has taken the position that the statute operates only to grant and to limit representation to children or grandchildren from among all possible issue of a decedent's siblings. One early case went against the appellant's position, having treated the statute as a general limitation. Parker v. Nims, 2 N.H. 460, 461 (1822). But later cases have confined the statute's application narrowly to the class of siblings' children and grandchildren. See, e.g., Green v. Bancroft, 75 N.H. at 207, 72 A. at 374–75.

If the narrow view were to prevail today, there would be anomalous results, for representation would be limited by RSA 561:3 in the closer collateral line, but not by RSA 561:1, II(d) in the more distant. For example, a decedent's brother's great grandchild could not take by representation, but the decedent's first cousin once removed could, even though each is of the fifth degree. Such anomaly prompted counsel for appellees to argue that RSA 561:3 had been repealed by implication, upon the enactment of § 2-103 of the Code as RSA 561:1, II. Alternatively, counsel argued that the legislature had left RSA 561:3 on the books only by oversight.

We respectfully commend the legislature's attention to this issue. It may be settled best either by repeal of RSA 561:3 or by an amendment to clarify the scope of that section.

Affirmed.

* * *

Notes

After the *Martineau* decision, the New Hampshire legislature amended N.H. Rev Stat. §561:3 to provide: "No representation shall be allowed among collaterals beyond the fourth degree of relationship to the decedent."

D. The Last Resort: Escheat to the State

Board of Education of Montgomery County v. Browning
Court of Maryland, 1994
333 Md. 281, 635 A.2d 373

MURPHY, Chief Judge.

This case involves the concept of equitable adoption, and in particular, whether a person, if equitably adopted, may inherit by intestate succession from the sister of an equitably adoptive parent.

* * *

Eleanor G. Hamilton, a resident of Montgomery County, died intestate in August, 1990, leaving an estate valued at $394,405.57. At the time of her death, Hamilton had no known living blood relatives. Appellee Paula M. Browning was appointed Personal Representative of the Estate of Eleanor G. Hamilton on May 21, 1991.

Paula was born out of wedlock on October 4, 1919. Her natural father, Lawrence E. Hutchison, legally adopted Paula on October 10, 1921. In March of 1922, Hutchison married Marian Estelle Gibson. Paula grew up in the Hutchison's household in the District of Columbia; Marian, however, never formally adopted Paula. Marian, who died in 1986, was the sister of the decedent Eleanor Hamilton.

Because Eleanor apparently died without any heirs, the Board of Education of Montgomery County claimed that it was entitled to Eleanor's estate pursuant to the Maryland escheat laws. * * * Believing that she was a legal heir of Eleanor, Paula filed a complaint for declaratory judgment and a motion for summary judgment in the Circuit Court for Montgomery County. In her complaint, Paula named the Board of Education as defendant because the Board had a potential claim to the proceeds of Eleanor's estate through the escheat laws. Paula sought a declaration that she was the equitably adopted child of Marian; and as such was entitled to inherit the Estate of Eleanor G. Hamilton, Marian's sister.

In support of her motion for summary judgment, Paula submitted an affidavit in which she stated that she maintained a normal child-parent relationship with Lawrence and Marian Hutchison throughout her life. She also stated that Lawrence and Marian told her when she was a child, and later when she was an adult, that she had been adopted by them; moreover, Paula stated that Marian specifically told her in 1984 that Marian had adopted her. In 1992, when she was asked to produce proof of adoption for the instant litigation, Paula discovered that she had not been legally adopted by Marian. In her affidavit, Paula also stated that no other heirs had presented or filed claims regarding Eleanor's estate.

The Board of Education of Montgomery County, pursuant to Maryland Rule 2-322(b), filed a motion to dismiss for failure to state a claim upon which relief can be granted. The Board maintained that Paula's complaint failed to allege facts which would enable a court to declare that she was the equitably adopted child of Marian. The Board further averred that, even if Paula were adjudged to be the equitably adopted daughter of Marian, she could not, as a matter of law, inherit from the estate of her equitably adoptive mother's sister. The Board therefore argued that because Eleanor Hamilton died without a will and without any legal heirs, it was entitled to her estate under the Maryland law of escheat, as set forth in Maryland Code (1991 Repl.Vol., 1993 Cum.Supp.) §3-105(a) of the Estates and Trusts Article. Specifically, the Board asked the circuit court to grant its motion to dismiss and declare that: (1) Paula is not entitled to inherit from Eleanor's estate; and (2) the estate escheats to the Board of Education of Montgomery County.

After a December, 1992 hearing, the court concluded that the Board of Education had conceded that Paula was the equitably adopted child of Marian. * * * The court therefore framed the sole remaining issue as follows: "whether Paula Browning, as the equitably adopted daughter of Marian Hutchison, may inherit as a collateral heir to the estate of Marian Hutchison's sister, Eleanor G. Hamilton."

Relying on First Nat. Bank in Fairmont v. Phillips, 176 W.Va. 395, 344 S.E.2d 201 (1985), upon the fact that the Board of Education was the only other party interested in the Hamilton estate, and on the close relationship between Paula and her equitably adoptive mother, the court determined that Paula could inherit from the estate of her equitably adoptive mother's sister. Thus, the court denied the Board's motion to dismiss and granted Paula's motion for summary judgment. The Board appealed to the Court of Special Appeals. We granted certiorari prior to consideration of the appeal by the intermediate appellate court to decide the significant issue presented in this case 331 Md. 178, 626 A.2d 967.

* * *

Before us, the Board reasserts its view that an equitably adopted child may not inherit from her equitably adoptive parent's sibling. On the other hand, Paula argues that the lower court correctly ruled, as a matter of law, that a child may inherit by intestate succession from the sister of an equitably adoptive parent thereby defeating an escheat to the State.

The Board also contends that the lower court improperly granted Paula's motion for summary judgment because the court failed to consider the elements of equitable adoption and the evidence fell far short of the clear and convincing proof necessary to establish an equitable adoption. We need not address this argument, however, because even assuming *arguendo* that Paula was equitably adopted by Marian, we conclude that Paula may not inherit from her equitably adoptive parent's sister. Therefore, the trial court should have granted the Board's motion to dismiss and declared that the Estate of Eleanor G. Hamilton escheats to the Board of Education of Montgomery County.

When analyzing a motion to dismiss pursuant to Maryland Rule 2-322(b), we must accept as true all well-pleaded facts and allegations in the complaint. Faya v. Almaraz, 329 Md. 435, 443, 620 A.2d 327 (1993). Dismissal is only proper if the facts and allegations viewed in the light most favorable to the plaintiff fail to afford the plaintiff relief if proven. Id.; Berman v. Karvounis, 308 Md. 259, 264–65, 518 A.2d 726 (1987); Sharrow v. State Farm Mutual, 306 Md. 754, 768, 511 A.2d 492 (1986). Moreover, "any ambiguity or uncertainty in the allegations bearing on whether the complaint states a cause of action must be construed against the pleader." Figueiredo-Torres v. Nickel, 321 Md. 642, 647, 584 A.2d 69 (1991) (quoting Sharrow, supra, 306 Md. at 768, 511 A.2d 492).

For purposes of our analysis, we accept as true the factual allegations of Paula's complaint for declaratory judgment and motion for summary judgment. Thus, we will assume that Paula is the equitably adopted daughter of Marian Hutchison, Eleanor Hamilton's sister.

* * *

In the instant case, Paula seeks to inherit not from her putative mother, Marian Hutchison, but rather from Marian's sister. We agree with those cases that stand for the proposition that an equitably adopted child may not inherit *through* an equitably adoptive parent. Under both contractual and estoppel notions, the equities that clearly exist in favor of permitting an equitably adopted child to inherit from an equitably adoptive parent do not exist when that child seeks to inherit from a sibling of the child's adoptive parents. The governing law has been well summarized as follows:

> "The determinative factor, of course, is the relation of the child to the deceased in whose estate he seeks to participate. While he may recover against the estate of a defaulting promisor, the equities in his favor do not extend so far as to allow recovery against the estate of a foster parent's relative, one who has made no promise and—having done no wrong—has equities in his favor as well."

Note, supra, 58 Va.L.Rev. at 740.

Paula suggests that those cases which hold that an equitable adoptee may not inherit *through* an equitably adoptive parent are inapposite to the case at bar because in each of those cases, a legal heir of the decedent, as well as the equitably adopted child, claimed an interest in the estate, whereas in the instant case, only the Board of Education has filed a claim against the Estate of Eleanor Hamilton. Paula maintains that a party, who is not an heir, such as the Board of Education, can not defeat her claim to the Hamilton estate.

Paula's counsel conceded during oral argument before us that if an heir existed, Paula would have no interest in Eleanor's estate. Consequently, the crux of Paula's argument is that the doctrine of equitable adoption permits an equitably adopted child to inherit from the adoptive parent's sibling when the only other party seeking to inherit is the local Board of Education through the escheat laws.

This rationale was rejected by a federal district court in In re Estate of McConnell, 268 F.Supp. 346 (D.D.C.1967), aff'd, 393 F.2d 665 (D.C.Cir.1968). There, the federal district court, applying Florida law, was faced with the question of whether the natural children of the equitably adoptive parents could inherit from the equitable adoptee as "half-sisters" thereby defeating an escheat to the District of Columbia. The court held that no Florida or District of Columbia case "touching on equitable adoption is a precedent for a decree by this Court approving distribution of the estate of a deceased adoptee to the heirs of an adoptive parent who did not legally consummate the adoption." Id. at 349. Accordingly, the court found that the "half-sisters" had no interest in the estate and the estate escheated to the District of Columbia.

Although Paula correctly points out that escheats are not favored by law, see e.g., United States v. 198.73 Acres of Land, More or Less, 800 F.2d 434, 435 (4th Cir.1986); In re Estate of Wallin, 16 Ariz.App. 34, 490 P.2d 863, 864 (1971); Estate of Supeck, 225 Cal.App.3d 360, 366, 274 Cal.Rptr. 706, 710 (1990); State v. Public Service Electric & Gas Co., 119 N.J.Super. 264, 291 A.2d 32, 35 (1972); Rippeth v. Connelly, 60 Tenn.App. 430, 447 S.W.2d 380, 382 (1969), Maryland law is crystal clear that if no legal heir exists, the decedent's property escheats to the local Board of Education. See Maryland Code (1991 Repl.Vol., 1993 Cum.Supp.) §3-105 of the Estates and Trust Article. * * * In the instant case, therefore, because Paula may not inherit from her equitably adoptive mother's sister, and Eleanor Hamilton died without heirs, her estate escheats to the Board of Education.

We therefore conclude that an equitably adopted child may not inherit from her adoptive parent's sibling. Consequently, the entry of summary judgment in favor of Paula was inappropriate in this case. Furthermore, the circuit court erred in denying the Board's motion to dismiss. Because Paula may not inherit from Eleanor's estate, it escheats to the Board of Education of Montgomery County.

JUDGMENT OF THE CIRCUIT COURT FOR MONTGOMERY COUNTY REVERSED. CASE REMANDED TO THAT COURT WITH DIRECTIONS TO ENTER A DECLARATORY JUDGMENT NOT INCONSISTENT WITH THIS OPINION. COSTS TO BE PAID BY APPELLEE.

ELDRIDGE, J., * * * [dissenting opinion is omitted.]

Notes

People are living longer and are less likely than their ancestors to have children. The incidents of elder persons dying without a valid Last Will and Testament or operative non-probate transfers are greater; thus, state statutes providing for escheat are more likely. For a discussion of the history of the rule of escheat, see Richard L. Field, *Forgotten But Not Gone: Escheatment of Stored Value Cards*, http://www.abanet.org/scitech/ec/ecp/escheat.html (accessed Oct. 12, 2005). The following state statute is illustrative of what happens to estates when there are no heirs to claim inheritance:

Massachusetts General Laws (2004)

Ch. 190. Descent and Distribution of Real and Personal Property
§3.(7) Descent of land, tenements or hereditaments

If an intestate leaves no kindred and no widow or husband, his estate shall escheat to the commonwealth; provided, however, if such intestate is a veteran who died while a member of the Soldiers' Home in Massachusetts or the Soldiers' Home in Holyoke, his estate shall inure to the benefit of the legacy fund or legacy account of the soldiers' home of which he was a member.

For an Advisory Opinion from the United States Department of Labor regarding whether the Employee Retirement Income Security Act of 1974 (ERISA) preempts the Texas Unclaimed Property Statutes, see U.S. Department of Labor, PWBA Office of Regulations and Interpretations, Advisory Opinion by Robert J. Doyle, Director of Regulations and Interpretations, to Mr. Thomas R. Giltner, Dec. 7, 1994, http://www.dol.gov/ebsa/programs/ori/advisory94/94-41a.htm#tof (accessed Oct. 12, 2005). For an Advisory Opinion from the Office of the Attorney General for the State of Texas regarding whether overpayments on property taxes escheat to the state, see http://www.oag.state.tx.us/opinions/op48morales/dm-258.htm (accessed Oct. 12, 2005). For an example of a state's procedures for escheat property, see State of Delaware, Department of Finance: Division of Revenue, *Escheat - Unclaimed Property,* http://www.state.de.us/revenue/information/Escheat.shtml (accessed Oct. 12, 2005).

V. Heirs: Changing Definition of Family

Since inheritance is based on family, it stands to reason that the laws concerning inheritance should be affected by changes in the definition of the family. Historically, the definition of family was a matter of "form," and this consisted of a married couple, without the inclusion of divorce, stepchildren, protracted paternity disputes, and few adoptions. Today's families are more aptly characterized as "functional," with modern deference given to individual liberty, and, thus, far more combinations of what may be the intention of an intestate decedent. For example, the probate court may find that, at the time of his death, the decedent had two children by his second wife and three other non-marital children, each under the age of eighteen. His second wife could have a child from a previous marriage—a step-child to the decedent—and the decedent could have been supporting the child since his marriage to the child's mother. Adoption, the marvels of the new biology, and the ability to provide heirs long after the death of the decedent, contribute to the dilemmas facing legislatures and courts when seeking to discern the definition of family. The following are examples of current issues.

A. Non-Marital Relationships

Adults are entering into relationships which, while not marriage, often resemble marriage, with concomitant issues of support during life and, increasingly, upon death. In the past, claims by non-marital partners were barred because of either lack of proof or because public policy would not allow a claim where sex was a part of the relationship. Nonetheless, when California allowed for non-marital couples to enter into enforceable contracts even though sex was an incidental element, the possibility of support and claims against the estate of the decedent expanded expeditiously. *See* Marvin v. Marvin, 134 Cal. Rptr. 815, 557 P.2d 106 (1976). Today, contractual arrangements outside of marriage, where sexual relations are a part, are frequent, particularly among people with economic assets. The Internet provides up-to-date data on changing demographics. *See* U.S. Census Bureau, Subject Index, http://www.census.gov/main/www/subjects.html (accessed Oct. 12, 2005). Forms have become available for couples as well. *See, e.g.*, West's McKinney's Forms, Matrimonial and Family Law, Ch. 2, Non-Marital Rights and Liabilities (2004).

Byrne v. Laura

California Court of Appeal, 1997
52 Cal.App.4th 1054, 60 Cal.Rprt.2d 908

HANLON, J.

Appellant Gladys A. Byrne (Flo) sued respondents Charon A. Laura, et al., the administrator and heirs of the estate of Donald F. Lavezzo (respondents are hereafter referred to collectively as the Estate) to enforce her *Marvin* agreement (Marvin v. Marvin (1976) 18 Cal.3d 660 [134 Cal.Rptr. 815, 557 P.2d 106]) with the decedent (hereafter referred to as Skip). * * * The Estate cross-complained against Flo for damages for removing personal property from the home she had shared with Skip before his death, and for unpaid rent based on her occupancy of the home after his death.

The Estate's motion for summary adjudication was granted as to all of Flo's causes of action other than her quantum meruit claim, the Estate dismissed its claim for conversion without prejudice, and the case proceeded to trial before the court on Flo's quantum meruit claim and the Estate's claim for unpaid rent. The trial court found that there had been no agreement between Skip and Flo to compensate Flo for her services, and that, even if there had been such an agreement, Flo had been adequately compensated for any services she provided. Judgment was entered against Flo for $2,400 for unpaid rent, and in favor of the Estate on all of Flo's causes of action.

On appeal from the judgment, Flo contends that the court erred in granting the summary adjudication motion, and that she was entitled to a trial on her causes of action other than the one for quantum meruit. We reverse the judgment on the claims that were summarily adjudicated and on the Estate's claim for unpaid rent.

* * *

Evidence presented on the motion for summary adjudication included declarations and deposition testimony from Flo, Flo's daughter Denise, Flo's niece, a neighbor of Skip's who had known Skip and Flo since the 1930's and '40's, and two couples, the Maffeis and Simpsons, who had known Flo and Skip since their days together in high school.

Skip and Flo were childhood sweethearts who were engaged to be married when Flo was 18, but Flo broke off the engagement and they married other people. Skip was divorced from his wife in 1974, and Flo's husband died in January of 1987. Skip and Flo began dating in August of 1987, and he proposed marriage to her that December. She declined his proposal because her handicapped children, Lori and Michele, would lose insurance coverage from her deceased husband's employer if she remarried.

Skip and Flo began living together in January of 1988. She moved from San Mateo into his house in San Francisco, and they resided there together until Skip's death in 1993. When Flo was asked why she moved in with Skip, she said, "[b]ecause I loved him and we wanted to be together." The Maffeis and Simpsons said that Skip adored Flo, and called her "the queen."

When Flo moved into Skip's home in San Francisco, she brought furniture and linens from her rented house in San Mateo and commingled her belongings with Skip's. The couple eliminated some of the items Skip had in the home, purchased new furniture together, and opened a joint savings account. Flo cleaned up the house, and saw to the installation of new drapes, carpets, and appliances.

Flo said that, when she moved in, Skip told her that it "was our home, and that anything that he had was mine, and I told him ... whatever I had was his." Skip also told their friends that his possessions in the house belonged to Flo. The Simpsons recalled going over to the house for dinner, Mrs. Simpson "commenting on different pretty hand-painted Italian dishes that maybe were [Skip's] mom's," and Skip saying "well, they belong to the queen, and everything in this house is hers." Skip also said that his car was Flo's, and he apparently put their names on the license plate. When Mr. Simpson "commented about the license plate on the car," Skip said, "well, its our car, you know. It's Flo and Skip."

Skip promised Flo when she moved in, and many times thereafter, that he would take care of her for the rest of her life in exchange for her services as a homemaker. Skip repeatedly reassured Flo that she did not have to worry because he would take care of her and she would "have a roof over [her] head." Skip also assured Flo's niece and her daughter Denise, and told the Maffeis and Simpsons, that he intended to take care of Flo.

During the first four years they lived together, Skip continued working as a plumber in San Francisco, and Flo continued working part time at a school cafeteria in San Mateo. Flo did all of the couple's cooking, cleaning, laundry, and shopping. She handled their entertaining, and took care of Skip if he got sick. Their neighbor, Blanche Maffei, recalled that when she jokingly asked Skip, "'How's married life?' he answered, 'Wonderful! Flo takes very good care of me.'" They "cohabited," in Flo's words, "as husband and wife."

Flo contributed all of her earnings toward the household, and Skip paid for Flo's living expenses, including paying her monthly credit card balances and giving her grocery and spending money on a regular basis. Skip paid to set up a conservatorship for Flo's handicapped daughters, and made Flo the beneficiary of his retirement benefits. Flo was not relying solely on Skip's pension benefits to provide for her future. She said that Skip was a very private person, and that she did not "think it was my place to ask him how much money he had." But she trusted Skip, and believed him when he indicated that he had sufficient funds in the form of savings, stocks, and bonds to afford them both a comfortable retirement.

Skip retired in March of 1992. Flo continued working, but then began suffering from angina, and underwent double bypass surgery in September of 1992. Flo returned to work after a period of disability, and then retired in May of 1993. In the months when Flo did not work, Skip wrote her a check for $500, in addition to giving her money for anything she needed. Flo said she retired because "Skip wanted [her] to stay home and to retire and spend more time with him." "[H]e relied on [her] staying home so that [they] could have a good life together...."

Skip renewed his marriage proposals to Flo on many occasions while they lived together, but she continued to decline them out of concern over the insurance for her handicapped daughters. On June 15, 1993, Skip and Flo were out to dinner with the Maffeis and Simpsons, and while Flo was away from the table, Skip said that he wanted them all to take a cruise to Hawaii, where he was going to surprise Flo and arrange a marriage ceremony. Skip gave the Simpsons a wedding ring for Flo, and asked them to keep it for him. They planned to spend the July 4th holiday at the Simpsons' place in the country finalizing the dates and details of the cruise and wedding.

However, Skip died unexpectedly on June 29, 1993.

Flo said that she and Skip promised each other and agreed that all of the property they owned when they began living together and later acquired "would be jointly held and mutually owned by us and remain the property of the survivor of us." Skip repeatedly told Flo that everything he had was hers, and Flo's daughter and niece and the Maffeis and Simpsons all recalled statements by Skip to the effect that everything he had was Flo's and would someday belong to her. Skip repeatedly assured Flo that he was going to put everything, including the house, stocks and bonds, in her name. Just a week before he died, he reiterated to her that he was going to put all of his property into a living trust for her benefit.

However, according to Flo, Skip "was a procrastinator, and he'd always say ' Well, I'm going to change everything into your name, the house,' et cetera, through all the years that we lived together. But he was the type of person that didn't move too quickly on things. He procrastinated all his life. * * * So finally, like I said, the week before he died, we sat down and talked and got to the issue that we were going to do the living trust or a will because he said as of then, he didn't have anything legal. So this was something that he had to do."

Skip left an estate worth over $1.2 million. The property consisted of: $844,023.99 in stocks and bonds; $134,689.66 in various bank accounts; the house, appraised at $246,000; furnishings in the house valued at $3,000; and a 1988 Camaro valued at $5,500. Skip also left a will dated December 10, 1975, leaving all of his property to his parents or, if they did not survive him, to Claire Suy.

All of the named beneficiaries under the will had predeceased Skip. The Simpsons said that Skip never talked about family other than his parents, and as far as they knew he had no other relatives. Yolanda Maffei said that Skip "had nobody else in his life but Flo." She said that before he got together with Flo, "Skip was very much alone and very much lonesome. We one time had him for Christmas when nobody else did."

Flo said she was in a state of shock after Skip died. She considered everything of Skip's to be hers, but she did not have an attorney at the time, and did not know what her legal rights might be. She purchased the Camaro Skip had driven, and moved out of the home after she was asked to leave, taking some property in the home with her.

Flo filed a creditor's claim against Skip's estate alleging that she was the "sole and exclusive owner" of all of his property. After the claim was rejected, she filed a complaint against the Estate, which, in addition to the cause of action for quantum meruit, included causes of action for: "damages for failure to pay debt on rejected claim"; "specific performance of express oral agreement"; "imposition of constructive trust"; "temporary restraining order, preliminary injunction and permanent injunction"; "breach of oral contract"; and "declaratory relief."

The Estate moved for summary adjudication of these claims on the ground that Skip's promises were too uncertain to enforce, or, alternatively, that enforcement of the promises was barred by statutes of frauds, and there was insufficient evidence to support an estoppel to rely on a statute of frauds defense. In response, Flo argued that the evidence was sufficient to support her claims for breach of contract, and that the evidence established an inter vivos gift to her of all of Skip's property. In reply, the Estate argued inter alia that Flo's testimony and her actions in the wake of Skip's death negated any claim of a valid inter vivos transfer of any of Skip's assets.

The court determined that all of Skip's promises boiled down to an agreement to create a joint tenancy. When the court indicated that it was inclined to grant the motion for summary adjudication on the basis of this finding, and acknowledged that the Estate had not advanced an argument about joint tenancy until its reply brief on the motion, Flo requested an opportunity to submit further evidence and authorities on the point. The request was denied and the court proceeded to file its order on the motion.

* * *

The summary adjudication of Flo's claims cannot be sustained on the narrow grounds cited by the law and motion court. The ruling against Flo rested entirely on the finding of fact that she and Skip had an oral joint tenancy agreement, and the conclusion of law that equity does not allow for the enforcement of such an agreement. However, all of the promises and conduct in evidence cannot be characterized solely as an agreement for a joint tenancy, and to the extent that the agreements at issue are subject to a statute of frauds, there is a triable issue of fact as to whether the Estate is equitably estopped to assert the statute as a defense. The summary adjudication of Flo's claims must therefore be reversed.

* * *

In support of her creditor's claim in the probate proceeding, Flo declared that "at all times" she had "relied upon Skip's promises and his assurances that he would take care of me for the rest of my life." She submitted declarations from the Maffeis, and her niece and daughter, who likewise reported that Skip had said that he would take care of Flo for the rest of her life. Similar testimony was given in depositions after the rejection of the creditor's claim, and presented in opposition to the motion for summary adjudication. Skip's repeated promises to care for Flo for the rest of her life created a triable issue of fact as to the existence of a contract for her support.

Support agreements between cohabitants are enforceable under the *Marvin* case. (Marvin v. Marvin, supra, 18 Cal.3d at pp. 665, 674–675, 685, fn. 26; Friedman v. Friedman (1993) 20 Cal.App.4th 876, 889 [24 Cal.Rptr.2d 892]; Marvin v. Marvin (1981) 122 Cal.App.3d 871, 876 [176 Cal.Rptr. 555].) Skip's promise of support is indistinguishable from that of the defendant in *Marvin*, who allegedly "agreed to 'provide for all of plaintiff's financial support and needs for the rest of her life.'" (Marvin v. Marvin, supra, 18 Cal.3d at p. 666.) *Marvin* held that this agreement supported a cause of action for breach of an express contract (id. at pp. 667, 675), and there is no basis for a different conclusion in Flo's case. No issue is raised of any breach of contract on Flo's part. The record indicates that she fully performed the role of a loving spouse during all of the time they lived together.

A *Marvin* agreement is enforceable against an estate when one of the parties to the agreement dies. (See Estate of Fincher (1981) 119 Cal.App.3d 343, 348–350 [174 Cal.Rptr. 18]; Hogoboom & King, Cal. Practice Guide: Family Law 3 (The Rutter

Group 1996) ¶ 20:55, p. 20-11, rev. #1, 1995.) There is no evidence that Skip breached his promise of support during his lifetime. To the contrary, it appears that Skip gave Flo money to buy anything she needed and sought to provide her with a comfortable life while they lived together. Thus, Skip's caring for Flo during his lifetime is further evidence of the existence of a contract for support. However, the *estate* breached that contract by rejecting Flo's claim and thereby failing to provide her with means of support after Skip died. Accordingly, we conclude that it was error to grant the motion for summary adjudication of Flo's cause of action for "Damages for Failure to Pay Debt on Rejected Claim."

The Estate's various arguments with respect to Flo's case generally and her claim of support in particular do not alter this conclusion. The Estate's threshold contention is that, because Flo does not contest the outcome of the trial of her quantum meruit claim, she has waived any challenge to the grant of summary adjudication of her contract causes of action. This argument is premised on the assertion, advanced without authority, that Skip's various promises were not "severable." The Estate reasons that, because there was only one contract between Skip and Flo, and the finding after trial was that "the" contract did not exist, that finding precludes any recovery for breach of contract.

However, the claim that Skip agreed out of love and concern to care for Flo for the rest of her life is manifestly different from a claim that he had agreed to compensate her for the value of her services as if she had been his maid. As the Estate itself emphasized at the end of its closing argument at trial, "[t]he concept of quantum meruit is *not* some future I'll always be taken care [of]; it is payment for services rendered." A trier of fact could conclude that Skip had agreed to support Flo apart from any understanding about payment for her household services.

Skip's promises to care for Flo were likewise distinct from his statements about giving her his property, and those promises could be construed by a trier of fact as an agreement for support apart from any entitlement Flo might have to specific assets. Support and property division are separate issues in marital dissolutions (Fam. Code, §§ 2500 et seq., 4300 et seq.), and they are also separate issues for cohabitants. (See Marvin v. Marvin, supra, 18 Cal.3d at pp. 674–675 [distinguishing between agreement for support and agreement for sharing of property].) In granting summary adjudication, the court focused entirely on the evidence of Skip and Flo's property arrangement, and improperly ignored the evidence of a contract for Flo's support.

The Estate contends that the support claim must be rejected because it has been "newly-minted" to circumvent the summary adjudication ruling. However, while it is generally improper to assert a new theory for the first time on appeal, it is the Estate, not Flo, that has changed its position by arguing, contrary to its theory at trial, that all of Flo's contract claims were subsumed in her quantum meruit cause of action. Flo has asserted from the time she filed her creditor's claim that there was an agreement for her support, and although she has not specifically related the support agreement to the cause of action for rejection of her creditor's claim as we have done here, she has consistently and correctly maintained that the motion for summary adjudication could not be granted in light of that agreement. There are no grounds for concluding that Flo has waived her claim for support.

The Estate argues that the oral promise of support is not enforceable under Probate Code section 150, subdivision (a), which provides that a "contract to make a will or devise" must be in writing. However, this statute is inapplicable. An agreement for support, even for a lifetime, is by its terms neither a "contract to make a will," nor a contract to make a "devise," as that word is defined in the Probate Code to mean "a disposition of real or personal property by will." (Prob. Code, § 32.) No disposition by will was expressly agreed upon or necessarily implicit in the promise of support because Flo could have predeceased Skip, and in that event the contract could have been fully performed during Skip's lifetime. The fact that Skip died, and thus that the amounts owed were payable from his estate, did not transform the agreement into a promise to make a will or devise. If that were the result, then every contractual claim against an estate would involve a will or devise. * * *

The Estate contends that Skip's promises to Flo are too uncertain to enforce. However, "the modern trend of the law favors carrying out the parties' intention through the enforcement of contracts and disfavors holding them unenforceable because of uncertainty." (Hennefer v. Butcher (1986) 182 Cal.App.3d 492, 500 [227 Cal.Rptr. 318].) * * * *Marvin* endorsed "a policy based upon the fulfillment of the reasonable expectations of the parties to a nonmarital relationship." (Marvin v. Marvin, supra, 18 Cal.3d at p. 684.) If Flo's evidence is credited, as it must be for purposes of summary adjudication (Waisbren v. Peppercorn Productions, Inc. (1995) 41 Cal.App.4th 246, 252 [48 Cal.Rptr.2d 437]), then it is certain that Skip expected to provide for Flo's support. Denial of that expectation as a matter of law would be contrary to the policy enunciated in *Marvin*. Moreover, as Flo observes, her understandings with Skip were no more uncertain than the "general and nonspecific" *Marvin* agreement which was enforced in Alderson v. Alderson (1986) 180 Cal.App.3d 450, 463 [225 Cal.Rptr. 610], where "[t]he parties never bothered to actually spell out the terms of their agreement or the consideration therefor."

It is unclear how *much* support Skip intended by his promises to take care of Flo, but uncertainty about "'the precise act ... to be done'" may be resolved in light of extrinsic evidence. (Crescenta Valley Moose Lodge v. Bunt (1970) 8 Cal.App.3d 682, 689 [87 Cal.Rptr. 428].) Flo received about $96,500 from Skip's retirement benefits, and she has testified that Skip told her "'I'm putting you down as beneficiary on my retirement because I want to take care of you.'" Based on this evidence, the Estate can argue that Flo has already been "taken care of" in the manner Skip intended. On the other hand, Skip provided Flo with a certain standard of living before he died, which included a rent-free residence and money to cover all of her other needs. Flo could argue on the basis of that conduct for a level of support consistent with the lifestyle she and Skip had enjoyed. Flo could also argue for all or half of Skip's assets by way of support, based on his statements to her "that he was able to retire early because he was very careful in what he did [with his money], and that I didn't have to worry about retiring because *what he had* would take care of us for the rest of both of our lives, that we would not be limited, that we would be able to not go overboard, but do things that we would enjoy doing together."

These conflicting interpretations and any others supported by reasonable inferences from the evidence must be resolved by a trier of fact. "The fundamental goal of contractual interpretation is to give effect to the mutual intention of the parties" (Bank of the West v. Superior Court (1992) 2 Cal.4th 1254, 1264 [10 Cal.Rptr.2d 538, 833 P.2d 545]), and "questions of 'intent' and 'purpose' are ordinarily questions of fact" (Redke v. Silvertrust (1971) 6 Cal.3d 94, 103 [98 Cal.Rptr. 293, 490 P.2d 805]). Where, as here, the agreement is reasonably susceptible of different interpretations, summary adjudication is an inappropriate means of resolving the ambiguity. (See Walsh v. Walsh (1941) 18 Cal.2d 439, 444 [116 P.2d 62]; Faus v. Pacific Elec. Ry. Co. (1960) 187 Cal.App.2d 563, 570 [9 Cal.Rptr. 697]; see also Castaneda v. Dura-Vent Corp. (9th Cir. 1981) 648 F.2d

612, 619.) * * * The judgment on the cause of action based on the rejection of Flo's creditor's claim must therefore be reversed.

* * *

Equitable estoppel to rely on a statute of frauds is certainly a question of fact in Flo's case. Flo has stated that she relied on Skip's assurances that she would receive his property and that he would document this understanding. The reliance supporting an equitable estoppel need not necessarily be reliance on representations that a writing will be executed (Monarco v. Lo Greco, supra, 35 Cal.2d at pp. 625–626), but Flo's evidence that she relied on such representations constitutes a classic case for application of the doctrine. (See Wilk v. Vencill (1947) 30 Cal.2d 104, 107 [180 P.2d 351]; 5 Witkin, Cal. Procedure (4th ed. 1997) Pleading, §743, p. 200.) A trier of fact could find that Flo had "seriously" changed her position in reliance on Skip's promises by moving in with him, performing the duties of a spouse, and retiring from her job at his insistence. (See Porporato v. Devincenzi (1968) 261 Cal.App.2d 670, 673, 678–679 [68 Cal.Rptr. 210] [in reliance on decedent's oral promise to devise home to plaintiff, plaintiff remained in San Francisco and did not seek employment].) A trier of fact could also conclude that Flo would be "unconscionably" injured, under the circumstances, if the lack of a writing precluded any recovery. (Id. at p. 679.) Since equitable estoppel is a triable issue of fact in Flo's case, it was error to summarily adjudicate her claim for damages for breach of the property agreement.

The law and motion court could reach a contrary result only by first construing the property agreement to be for the creation of a joint tenancy, and then applying Estate of Seibert (1990) 226 Cal.App.3d 338 [276 Cal.Rptr. 508], which holds that joint tenancy agreements are not subject to the doctrine of equitable estoppel. The *Seibert* court found no case which had applied the doctrine to a joint tenancy, and concluded on that basis alone that the writing requirement for joint tenancies constituted "a more formidable 'statute of frauds' than the ordinary requirement pertaining to contracts having to do with real property." (Id. at p. 343.)

Seibert's reasoning is unpersuasive for a number of reasons. First, we fail to see why an agreement for a joint tenancy in real property should be treated differently for equitable purposes than any other conveyance of land, and the court does not explain the distinction. Second, it is not true that there is no precedent for equitable enforcement of an unwritten joint tenancy. While we have not undertaken an exhaustive survey of the subject, we have found at least one case in which an implied contract for a joint tenancy in real property was enforced on the basis of an equitable estoppel. (See Grant v. Long (1939) 33 Cal.App.2d 725, 739–742 [92 P.2d 940].) Third, even if there were no precedent for application of equitable estoppel in connection with a joint tenancy, that alone would not be a sufficient reason to conclude that the doctrine could not be so applied. Equitable estoppel is a "firmly rooted legal principle in this state" (Juran v. Epstein (1994) 23 Cal.App.4th 882, 894 [28 Cal.Rptr.2d 588]), which generally applies to *all* statutes of frauds. (Phillippe v. Shapell Industries, supra, 43 Cal.3d at pp. 1272–1273 (dis. opn. of Kaufman, J.); Hall v. Hall (1990) 222 Cal.App.3d 578, 585 [271 Cal.Rptr. 773].) Exceptions to this general rule may be drawn on the basis of a substantial public policy (Phillippe v. Shapell Industries, supra, at pp. 1265–1269 [consumer protection statute]) or a clear directive from the Legislature (see Juran v. Epstein, supra, at p. 896). However, neither of these grounds for an exception is identified in *Seibert*, and it is not apparent that either applies to joint tenancies.

The absence of an enforceable joint tenancy would not be fatal to Flo's claim for damages for breach of the property agreement in any event. As we have noted, joint tenancy is only one of several means by which Skip could have effected his promise to give Flo his property. It is not clear that Skip had resolved to employ a joint tenancy. Skip and Flo did not use the words "joint tenancy" to describe their property agreement, Skip did not have any particular form of agreement drawn up, and it appears from his statements shortly before his death that he may have been more inclined to use a trust than a joint tenancy. The evidence was at least susceptible of different interpretations, and did not support the court's finding as a matter of law that the agreement was for a joint tenancy. Indeed, a different finding was compelled under the court's reasoning.

"A contract must receive such an interpretation as will make it lawful, operative, definite, reasonable, and capable of being carried into effect, if it can be done without violating the intention of the parties." (Civ. Code, § 1643.) Thus, "[i]t is a fundamental rule of contractual construction that where two interpretations are reasonably permissible, courts will adopt that which renders a contract valid and effectual." (Service Employees Internat. Union, Local 18 v. American Building Maintenance Co. (1972) 29 Cal.App.3d 356, 359 [105 Cal.Rptr. 564].) While there may be little precedent for the use of equitable estoppel to enforce an oral joint tenancy, it is settled that the doctrine may be employed to enforce an oral trust in land where the beneficiary has "irrevocably change[d] his position in reliance upon the trust." (Rest.2d Trusts, § 50; see Jose v. Pacific Tile & Porcelain Co. (1967) 251 Cal.App.2d 141, 144–145 [58 Cal.Rptr. 880]; Mulli v. Mulli (1951) 105 Cal.App.2d 68, 73 [232 P.2d 556]; Haskell v. First Nat. Bank (1939) 33 Cal.App.2d 399, 402 [91 P.2d 934].) Thus, there is no question that if Skip intended to put his property in trust, Flo would have a triable claim to an estoppel against a statute of frauds defense.

Insofar as it appears from the evidence, Skip could just as well have intended to use a trust as a joint tenancy. Both interpretations are "reasonably permissible." If an oral joint tenancy were in fact absolutely unenforceable, then the rule of construction in favor of enforcement would dictate that the contract be interpreted to be for the creation of a trust, rather than a joint tenancy. * * * Such an interpretation would not "violate" Skip's intentions. According to Flo's evidence, he would have wanted her to have a chance to enforce their property agreement.

The evidence, in sum, cannot properly be construed so as to negate a claim to damages for breach of the property agreement on a theory of equitable estoppel. There are two triable issues of fact: (1) whether there was such an agreement; and (2) whether Flo should be allowed to enforce it through equitable estoppel. The form of the arrangement Skip may have intended—joint tenancy, will, or trust—is irrelevant.

The Estate contends finally that Flo cannot establish an estoppel because she fulfilled her part of the bargain with Skip out of love for him and not just out of a desire for his property. This argument is premised on a statement in the *Seibert* case that, in order to enforce "a joint tenancy commitment through estoppel ... [the plaintiff] would be required to demonstrate not only that she relied upon the alleged promise from the decedent, but that she entered into acts or performance which was 'not only referable, but unequivocally [*sic*] referable, to the particular oral agreement sought to be enforced.'" (Estate of Seibert, supra, 226 Cal.App.3d at p. 343.) *Seibert* reasoned that estoppel could not be invoked in that case because the actions taken by the plaintiff in alleged reliance on her oral joint tenancy agreement with the decedent could "just as easily [have been] explained by her renewed interest in him generally, resulting from their resumption of a conjugal relationship." (Ibid.) Since it is undisputed that

Flo performed her part of the agreement with Skip because she loved him and not solely because she wanted his property, the Estate submits that *Seibert*'s reasoning precludes any finding of estoppel in Flo's case.

However, *Seibert* is insupportable insofar as it suggests that equitable estoppel must be predicated on "performance 'unequivocally referable' to the contract." This portion of *Seibert* conflates the doctrines of equitable estoppel and part performance. When a plaintiff seeks to avoid a statute of frauds on the ground of part performance, it has sometimes been said that the performance must be "unequivocally referable" to the agreement to be enforced. (See Note, Part Performance, Estoppel, and the California Statute of Frauds (1951) 3 Stan.L.Rev. 281, 286.) "It is doubtful that acts are ever unequivocally referable to a contract," and this requirement has not been consistently applied even in part performance cases. (Ibid.) The doctrines of part performance and equitable estoppel are, in any event, separate grounds for avoiding a statute of frauds. (Id. at pp. 281–283; see, e.g., Paul v. Layne & Bowler Corp., supra, 9 Cal.2d at pp. 564–565 [considering, in turn, part performance and equitable estoppel].) *Seibert* itself, prior to the passage at issue, referred to "cases establishing part performance *and* detrimental reliance as grounds for enforcing an oral agreement." (Estate of Seibert, supra, 226 Cal.App.3d at p. 342, italics added.) The sole authority cited by *Seibert* in support of its analysis, 35 California Jurisprudence Third, Frauds, Statute of, §85, pages 121–122, concerns part performance, not equitable estoppel (as to the latter, see 35 Cal.Jur.3d, supra, §95 et seq., p. 134 et seq.). Equitable estoppel is a broader doctrine than part performance. (Note, supra, 3 Stan.L.Rev. at p. 297.) All that is required for an equitable estoppel is a "serious" change of position and "unconscionable" injury. (Monarco v. Lo Greco, supra, 35 Cal.2d at p. 623.) Performance unequivocally referable to the agreement is not an indispensable part of the equation. (See Carlson v. Richardson, *supra*, 267 Cal.App.2d at pp. 208–209.)

If such a requirement were engrafted onto the equitable estoppel doctrine, then the doctrine would be abrogated in the context of *Marvin* agreements, because the sentiments which led the parties to cohabit would prevent a finding that their actions toward each other were motivated solely by their property agreements. *Marvin* noted that most cohabitation agreements are oral, and that cases had "expressly rejected defenses [to such agreements] grounded upon the statute of frauds." (Marvin v. Marvin, *supra*, 18 Cal.3d at p. 674, fn. 9, citing Cline v. Festersen (1954) 128 Cal.App.2d 380, 386–387 [275 P.2d 149] [equitable estoppel prevented reliance on statute of frauds].) In light of *Marvin*'s endorsement of "equitable remedies to protect the expectations of the parties to a nonmarital relationship" (Marvin v. Marvin, *supra*, at p. 684, fn. 25), the court's observations on the enforcement of oral cohabitation agreements can only be interpreted as an approval of the use of equitable estoppel by cohabitants in appropriate cases. Love does not vitiate Flo's equitable estoppel claim.

* * *

Flo's causes of action for declaratory relief, specific performance, constructive trust, and injunctive relief are also viable. * * *

Marvin held that rights under a cohabitation agreement may be established by way of an action for declaratory relief. (Marvin v. Marvin, *supra*, 18 Cal.3d at p. 675.)

Flo may properly elect to pursue specific performance of the property agreement with respect to assets such as the residence and family heirlooms for which damages may be an inadequate remedy. (Civ. Code, §3387 [real property]; Rest.2d Contracts,

§ 360, com. b, at pp. 171–172 [personal property with sentimental value].) Since performance by Skip cannot be compelled, the action is one for "quasi-specific" performance. (See Porporato v. Devincenzi, *supra*, 261 Cal.App.2d at p. 674.) Such an action requires: (1) a contract that is sufficiently definite to be enforced; (2) a contract that is just and reasonable; (3) performance by the plaintiff; (4) failure to perform by the defendant; (5) adequate consideration; (6) an inadequate legal remedy; and (7) if the contract is oral and subject to a statute of frauds, a means such as estoppel of avoiding the statute. (Id. at pp. 674–675.) A trier of fact could find that all of these elements are present in Flo's case. Proof of a *Marvin* agreement for an interest in property contrary to record title must be made by "clear and convincing" evidence. (Tannehill v. Finch (1986) 188 Cal.App.3d 224, 228 [232 Cal.Rptr. 749].) A trial is needed to determine whether evidence of the property agreement in Flo's case is "sufficiently strong to command the unhesitating assent of every reasonable mind." (Ibid. [internal quotation marks omitted].)

A constructive trust can be imposed on the estate's assets to provide for quasi-specific performance of the property agreement. (Estate of Brenzikofer (1996) 49 Cal.App.4th 1461, 1466–1467 [57 Cal.Rptr.2d 401]; Porporato v. Devincenzi, *supra*, 261 Cal.App.2d at p. 674.)

Distribution under the will can be enjoined pending the trial of Flo's claims. (Estate of Anderson (1977) 68 Cal.App.3d 1010, 1016 [137 Cal.Rptr. 727]; Estate of Murphy (1964) 225 Cal.App.2d 224, 229 [37 Cal.Rptr. 205].)

The judgment against Flo for rent based on her occupancy of the home after Skip's death must be reversed pending the trial of her entitlement to that property.

* * *

The judgment against appellant on the quantum meruit cause of action is affirmed. The balance of the judgment is reversed. Appellant shall recover her costs on appeal.

Anderson, P. J., and Poché, J., concurred.

[Respondents' petition for review by the Supreme Court was denied May 28, 1997.]

Notes

Non-marital cohabitation has increased over the last decades of the Twentieth Century. According to the Census Bureau, there were more than 4 million unmarried-couple households in the United States in 1997—eight times as many as in 1970. *See* Terry A. Lugaila, U.S. Dept. of Commerce, Bureau of the Census, Current Population Reports, Population Characteristics Series P20-506, *Marital Status and Living Arrangements: March 1997 (Update)* (issued June 1998). By 2000, this number reached 5.5 million—a 72% increase from 1990. *See* U.S. Census Bureau, *Married-Couple and Unmarried Partner Households: 2000*, http://www.census.gov/prod/2003pubs/censr-5.pdf (accessed Oct. 12, 2005). For the Census Bureau's demographics on families and living arrangements, see U.S. Census Bureau, *Families and Living Arrangements*, http://www. census.gov/population/www/socdemo/hh-fam.html (accessed Oct. 12, 2005). Many of these persons have oral and written agreements, which may affect the distribution of property upon the death of one of them. The agreements may have an impact on any property passing under a Last Will and Testament or under intestate distribution.

The number of unmarried couples identified by the Census Bureau reflects opposite sex couples. Nonetheless, it is estimated that there are additional same-sex couples who are adults and who have entered into oral and written agreements. *See* Craig W. Christiansen, *Legal Ordering of Family Values: The Case of Gay and Lesbian Families*, 18 CARDOZO L. REV. 1299 (1997). The use of domestic partnerships by businesses and by state and local governments has accelerated the recognition of same-sex relationships and has identified them among the millions of couples who order their economic affairs outside of traditional marriage. *See* Raymond C. O'Brien, *Domestic Partnership: Recognition and Responsibility*, 32 S.D. L. REV. 163, 177–85 (1995). Both same-sex and opposite-sex partners may enter into a domestic partnership, which, unlike a private contract, is a public form of commitment that involves business or government benefits. But a domestic partnership does not confer on either of the two parties a status similar to marriage. Neither domestic partner has a right to intestate succession from the other or for a right of election against a Last Will and Testament, and the partner will not automatically share in a pension or Social Security benefits. To date, with the exception of CAL. FAM. CODE § 297.5 (effective Jan. 1, 2005), traditional domestic partnership benefits provide limited health care, bereavement, and employment-related benefits.

State courts are in a conundrum in deciphering the complex relationships involving non-marital, opposite, and same-sex couples. Should the courts award to the couples all of the prerogatives of marriage, with access to resources? Or as two unmarried adults with the right to contractual ordering of their property? The tendency of the courts is to protect the status of marriage and the claims of traditional marital and family claimants. Non-marital partners are especially vulnerable to rejection of their contractual claims when they conflict with the rights of a spouse. *See* Thomas v. Larosa, 184 W. Va. 374, 400 S.E.2d 809 (1990). Furthermore, enforcement of any contractual agreement between non-marital partners is more likely if the "parties structure their agreement like a business arrangement … [and not] … mirror traditional marriage." *See* Martha M. Ertman, *Sexuality: Contractual Purgatory for Sexual Marginorities: Not Heaven, but Not Hell Either*, 73 DEN. U. L. REV. 1107, 1137 (1996); Wilcox v. Trautz, 427 Mass. 326, 693 N.E.2d 141 (1998). *See also* Camille M. Quinn and Shawna S. Baker, *Essential Estate Planning for the Constitutionally Unrecognized Families in Oklahoma: Same-Sex Couples*, 40 TULSA L. REV. 479 (2005); Ralph C. Brashier, *Consanguinity, Sibling Relationships, and the Default Rules of Inheritance Law: Reshaping Half-Blood Statutes to Reflect the Evolving Family*, 58 SMU L. REV. 137 (2005); Richard L. Brown, *Disinheriting the "Legal Orphan": Inheritance Rights of Children After Termination of Parental Rights*, 70 Mo. L. REV. 125 (2005).

B. Reciprocal Beneficiaries

In an extension of domestic partnership benefits, Hawaii became the first state to extend to same-sex or opposite-sex partners, who are legally prohibited from entering into marriage, the right to obtain certain benefits previously reserved to opposite-sex married couples. The Hawaii legislation was enacted as a result of the litigation to provide same-sex couples with the right to marry. To qualify as a reciprocal beneficiary, the couple must be legally prohibited from entering into marriage; thus, for example, a mother and son would qualify if neither was already married. The reciprocal beneficiaries do not need to live together and they do not need to be domiciled in Hawaii. If the parties qualify and register as reciprocal beneficiaries, then either would have intestate succession rights and may elect against the Last Will and Testament of the other. This is a significant addition to rights gained from domestic partnership. Although not marriage, the impact of the Hawaii legislation has dramatic implications for a person seeking to chose a partner and to extend to that party benefits that more closely mirror traditional spousal benefits. To date, there have been few couples to register as reciprocal beneficiaries. *See Hawaii Domestic Partners Law A Bust*, Wash. Post, Dec. 25, 1997, at A14. For the Hawaii State Department of Health website on reciprocal beneficiary relationships, see Hawaii State Department of Health, *About Reciprocal Beneficiary Relationships*, http://www.hawaii.gov/health/vital-records/vital-records/reciprocal/index.html (accessed Oct. 12, 2005). For an Advisory Opinion by the Hawaii Attorney General regarding the Reciprocal Beneficiaries Act, see State of Hawaii, Department of the Attorney General, Formal Opinion Letter from Francis E.H. Lum and Girard D. Lau, Deputy Attorneys General, to the Honorable Kathryn S. Matayoshi, Aug. 14, 1997, http://www.state.hi.us/ag/opinions_formal_letters/9705.htm (accessed Oct. 12, 2005); State of Hawaii, Department of the Attorney General, Formal Opinion Letter from David A. Webber, Deputy Attorney General, to the Honorable Kathryn S. Matayoshi, Dec. 2, 2005, http://www.hawaii.gov/ag/opinions_formal_letters/9710.htm (accessed Oct. 12, 2005). For a study by the Office of the Auditor for the State of Hawaii regarding the fiscal impact of providing reciprocal benefits, see Office of the Auditor, State of Hawaii, *Study of the Fiscal Impact of Providing Certain Benefits to Reciprocal Beneficiaries*, http://www.state.hi.us/auditor/Overviews/1999/99-17.htm (accessed Oct. 12, 2005).

C. Civil Unions/Domestic Partnerships

In order to allow persons of the same sex to obtain "common benefits" under the Vermont Constitution, the legislature of Vermont enacted legislation providing that: "'Civil union' means that two persons have established a relationship pursuant to this chapter, and may receive the benefits and protections and be subject to the responsibilities of spouses." Vt. Stat. Ann. tit. 23, §1201(2) (2003). Subsequent issues concern the ability of two same sex persons in a civil union in Vermont to have the status recognized in other states. A United States District Court in Nebraska allowed for same sex couples to state a claim of bill of attainder to challenge state statutes seeking to deny recognition of civil unions. *See* Citizens for Equal Protection, Inc. v. Bruning, 290 F. Supp. 2d 1004 (D. Neb. 2003). An Iowa trial judge granted a dissolution of a civil union entered into by a same sex couple in Vermont. Brown v. Perez, 30 Fam. L. Rep. 1094 (Iowa Dist. Ct. No. 03971 CDCD119660 (Nov. 14, 2003)). *See also Divorce Decree for 2 Women Faces Iowa Legal Challenge*, Wash. Post, Dec. 13, 2003, at A24. For the Vermont Secretary of State's web page addressing civil unions, see Vermont Secretary of State, *The Vermont Guide to Civil Unions*, http://www.sec.state.vt.us.otherprg/civilunions/civilunions.html (accessed Oct. 12, 2005). For statistics on Vermont civil unions, see http://www.gaydemographics.org/USA/states/vermont/2000Census_state_vt_civilunions.htm (accessed Oct. 12, 2005). Connecticut has adopted civil union for same sex couples. *See* Conn. Gen. Assembly S.B. 963 (effective Oct. 1, 2005).

D. Relatives by the Half-Blood

In the age of increasing numbers of divorce and remarriage, the possibility of relatives by the half-blood increases as well. For example, suppose Joe and Lisa marry and have three children. Then Lisa dies or divorces Joe. Joe is left to raise the children by himself until he meets Patty. Joe and Patty marry and they have two children, Michael and Rachel. Joe and Patty have no additional children. The five children—three from Joe's first marriage and two from his second marriage—grow up to treat each other as members of the same family; each has the same name, each is on the same insurance policy, and each is treated as a sibling at school, although Patty never adopted the three children from Joe's marriage to Lisa. If both Joe and Patty are killed in an automobile accident and they are survived by all five children, the inheritance statutes would treat Joe as being survived by five children because all five of the children were his. But Patty would be survived by only two children because the other three are legally the children of Lisa. What if Michael or Rachel should die a year later without any spouse, issue, or parent surviving? The intestate estate would have to be divided among the siblings. Would it make a difference that Michael and Rachel had *two* parents in common and either of them had only *one* parent in common with the other three siblings? Michael and Rachel would be half-bloods to the other three children but whole bloods to each other.

The Uniform Probate Code makes no distinction between half and whole bloods. Thus, if Michael died and was survived by his sister, Rachel, and the other three children of Joe and Lisa, with whom he had only one common parent, each of the survivors would take a fourth of his estate. Just because Rachel and Michael were related by the whole blood, Rachel would take no greater amount from the estate than would the half-bloods. *See* UNIF. PROB. CODE § 2-107 (2002) (providing that relatives of the half-blood inherit the same share they would inherit if they were of the whole blood).

Inheritance among persons related by the half blood extends to persons who are not siblings. For example, a decedent could die intestate with collateral heirs related by the half-blood. The Uniform Probate Code would make no distinction between the half and whole bloods, but some state statutes adhere to the ancient principles surrounding the integrity of the blood line and would limit the inheritance. For an example, see FLA. STAT. § 732.105 (2004) (half blood kindreds inherit only half as much as those of the whole blood).

E. Relatives by Adoption

1. Statutory Adoption

Adoptions in America are in compliance with state statutes; there is no common law adoption, although equitable adoption, which shall be described *infra,* is gaining in popularity. Varying from state-to-state, the statutes will provide for a valid adoption through a two step process. The first step is the termination of the birth parent's rights in the child through that parent's surrender of the child, the involuntarily termination of the parent's rights because of abuse, neglect, or abandonment, or because termination of the parent's rights is necessary to avoid detriment to the child. Once termination has been accomplished, then the state must create a new parent-child relationship with the adoptive parent or parents. This process was more pronounced in the past; the state would issue a new birth certificate and seal the record of the adoption so the child would not have any link with the birth parents. All of this was done to promote the child's best interest in growing up in an adoptive household that was free from the interference of the birth parents. Once the adoption is final, it is as if the child never had a birth parent and is completely the child of the adopting parent. This process is best described as an unrelated adoption and is distinctive through the absence of a step-parent. Step-parent adoption is another type of adoption, with its own set of consequences; it will be discussed *infra*.

Today, the traditional process of severing ties between birth parents and adoptive parents is more blurred. The federal government seeks to promote adoptions and, to achieve this goal, passed the Adoption and Safe Families Act of 1997. The act is significant because it is a federal encouragement of state efforts to facilitate adoptions, providing, among other features, financial incentives for states to increase their adoption rates. The federal initiative is in response to an alarming increase in the number of children in foster care, child welfare dependency, and "aggravating circumstances." Thus, states are more willing to allow birth parents to surrender children for adoption. Neither the federal government nor states have control over international adoption procedures. International adoption now accounts for a substantial number of all unrelated adoptions. *See* Elizabeth Bartholet, *International Adoptions: Overview*, in ADOPTION LAW AND PRACTICE 10–11 (Joan Heifetz Hollinger, ed., Matthew Bender 1998).

The process today is further blurred because of the increase in "open adoptions." The term refers to an information exchange between the birth and the adoptive parents following the adoption itself. During the 1970s and 1980s, persons adopted argued that they were a stigmatized class because they, alone, were forbidden to view records surrounding their birth. Advances in health care techniques strengthened their petitions to view the sealed records surrounding their adoptions. Yet, while court challenges failed, states allowed for access through legislative reform. Thus, at least half of the states have some form of registry that allows persons directly involved in an adoption to solicit information concerning birth information. *See* Joan H. Hollinger, *Aftermath of Adoption: Legal and Social Consequences, in* 2 ADOPTION LAW AND PRACTICE 13–35 (Joan Heifetz Hollinger, ed., Matthew Bender, 1998). Some states provide that, if an adopted person requests birth records, the state will search for the birth parents and request their consent to the release of the records. If the birth parent does not consent, then the adopted person may still petition the court to open the adoption records. *See, e.g.,* Groves v. Clark, 277 Mont. 179, 920 P.2d 981 (1996) (enforcing specific performance of visitation agreement relevant to open adoption). But there are still restraints on an adoptee's right to information in a sealed adoption record. *See, e.g.,* In re Adoption of S.J.D., 641 N.W.2d 794 (Iowa 2002) (holding that an adult adoptee's right to free speech does not include the right to receive private information absent statutory good cause).

Nearly half of all of the adoptions in America, today, involve step-parents; these adoptions may be referred to as "related adoptions." For example, suppose two persons have a child and then divorce, or perhaps they were never married when the child was born. One of the parents receives physical custody of the child and then marries a third party; the child becomes part of a growing family as the custodial birth parent and his or her spouse has children of their own. This creates a step-parent situation, and the custodial birth parent goes to the other birth parent and asks if his or her new spouse may adopt the child to provide a single nuclear family. If the answer is yes, a version of "open adoption" may occur because the statute may actually allow both the birth parents and the new spouse to be parents to the child. By allowing the step-parent to adopt and by not severing the child's relationship with the absent birth parent, the child has three parents and maintains a multiple family network. But note the necessity of marriage as an essential agreement to the creation of step-parent adoption. Consider the following case.

In re Adoption of Luke

Supreme Court of Nebraska, 2002
263 Neb. 365, 640 N.W.2d 374

HENDRY, C.J., CONNOLLY, GERRARD, STEPHAN, McCORMACK, and MILLER-LERMAN, JJ., and INBODY, Judge.

PER CURIAM.

* * *

B.P. and A.E. (collectively appellants) appeal from the order of the Lancaster County Court which denied the adoption petition jointly filed by appellants, two nonmarried persons, in which A.E. sought to adopt Luke, the minor biological son of B.P. The outcome of this appeal is controlled by the provisions of the Nebraska adoption statutes, Neb.Rev.Stat. §43-101 et seq. (Reissue 1998 & Cum.Supp.2000). The county court correctly concluded that on the record made in this case, Luke was not eligible for adoption due to the absence of a valid relinquishment by B.P. Accordingly, we affirm.

* * *

B.P. is the biological mother of Luke, a minor child born on December 20, 1997. Luke was conceived by artificial insemination using semen from an anonymous donor from the University of Nebraska Medical Center's genetic semen bank. Accordingly, Luke's biological father is unknown and is not a party to this action. For purposes of the Nebraska adoption statutes, Luke was born "out of wedlock."

On October 2, 2000, appellants jointly filed a verified petition in which A.E. sought to adopt Luke. B.P. indicated her "consent" in the petition and in other supporting documents. B.P. did not file a relinquishment of her parental rights to Luke. To the contrary, she indicated on an affidavit attached to the petition that she did not intend to relinquish Luke. The only relief sought in this proceeding was the adoption of Luke by A.E.

A home study of appellants' household was conducted by an adoption specialist. The specialist recommended A.E.'s adoption of Luke be approved by the court.

On November 14, 2000, trial was held on the adoption petition. Appellants testified in support of the petition. A file, consisting of several documents including the home study, was admitted into evidence. No one entered an appearance, and no evidence was offered in opposition to the petition.

In an order filed December 1, 2000, the county court denied the petition for adoption. The county court concluded that Nebraska's adoption statutes do not provide for "two non-married persons to adopt a minor child, no matter how qualified they are." The county court also concluded that "the statu[t]es permit a single adult person to adopt a child after all necessary consents and relinquishments have been filed." Appellants timely appeal the county court's order denying the adoption petition.

* * *

Contending that the county court erred, appellants argue that the plain language of the adoption statute at §43-101(1), which provides that "any minor child may be adopted by any adult person or persons," permits adoption of the minor child, Luke, by A.E.; the biological parent B.P. need not relinquish her parental rights in order for A.E. to adopt Luke; and the proposed adoption is in Luke's best interests. * * *

Contending that the county court was correct, the State argues that the adoption statutes read as a whole do not provide that two nonmarried persons may jointly adopt a minor child and that the adoption statutes only provide for adoption of a child without the relinquishment of a biological parent's rights in the case of a stepparent where a spouse is the adopting party. * * *

We have long recognized that "statutes providing for adoption are of civil and not common law origin.... Adoption proceedings were unknown to the common law." (Citations omitted.) In re Petition of Ritchie, 155 Neb. 824, 827–28, 53 N.W.2d 753, 755 (1952). The adoption laws were first codified in 1897 and have been amended in 1943, 1984, 1985, and 1999. See, §43-101 et seq.; Neil v. Masterson, 187 Neb. 364, 191 N.W.2d 448 (1971). We have stated that "the matter of adoption is statutory, and the manner of procedure and terms are all specifically prescribed and must be followed." In re Adoption of Kassandra B. & Nicholas B., 248 Neb. 912, 918, 540 N.W.2d 554, 558 (1995). We have recently noted that it is inappropriate for this court to "'extend the rights of adoption beyond the plain terms of the statutes.'" In re Adoption of Hemmer, 260 Neb. 827, 830, 619 N.W.2d 848, 851 (2000) (quoting In re Petition of Ritchie, supra). Although the numerous amendments to the adoption statutes could have been crafted with greater precision, the adoption statutes as a whole are cogent and workable. Accordingly, in the instant case, the plain terms and manner of procedure of the Nebraska adoption statutes must be followed.

* * *

For an adoption to be valid under Nebraska's adoption statutes, the record must show the following factors: (1) the existence of an adult person or persons entitled to adopt, (2) the existence of a child eligible for adoption, (3) compliance with statutory procedures providing for adoption, and (4) evidence that the proposed adoption is in the child's best interests. Neb.Rev.Stat. §43-101 et seq. See In re Adoption of Kassandra B. & Nicholas B., supra. The absence of any one of the necessary factors will preclude the adoption. In this case, Luke was not eligible for adoption, the county court determined that his adoption by A.E. was precluded on this basis, and we affirm on this basis.

The county court stated that "the statu[t]es permit a single adult person to adopt a child after all necessary consents and relinquishments have been filed." On this record, B.P. did not relinquish her parental rights to Luke, and therefore, he was not eligible for adoption by A.E. The county court's denial of the petition due to an absence of a relinquishment was correct. The county court also stated that Nebraska's adoption statutes do not provide for "two non-married persons to adopt a minor child, no matter how qualified they are." Because A.E. alone sought to adopt Luke, the issue of whether two nonmarried persons are entitled to adopt was not presented to the county court in this case. Thus, that issue is not before this court on appeal, and we do not consider it.

Appellants argue that the county court erred in concluding that it could not grant the adoption of Luke by A.E. as an additional parent without a relinquishment of the parental rights of B.P. Appellants contend that "consent is an alternative to a relinquishment," brief for appellant at 12, and that where B.P. intended to preserve her parental rights upon the adoption of Luke by A.E., only B.P.'s consent, which was given, was required. Appellants refer the court to various cases in other states which concluded under the language of their adoption statutes that the biological parent need not relinquish parental rights in order to facilitate the adoption by a second adult to whom the biological parent was not married. See, e.g., In re M.M.D., 662 A.2d 837 (D.C.1995); In re Petition of K.M., 274 Ill.App.3d 189, 653 N.E.2d 888, 210 Ill.Dec. 693 (1995); Adoption of Tammy, 416 Mass. 205, 619 N.E.2d 315 (1993); Matter of Adoption of Child by J.M.G., 267 N.J.Super. 622, 632 A.2d 550 (1993); Matter of Adoption of Evan, 153 Misc.2d 844, 583 N.Y.S.2d 997 (1992); Adoption of B.L.V.B., 160 Vt. 368, 628 A.2d 1271 (1993).

The State responds that the Nebraska adoption statutory scheme does not provide for adoption without relinquishment except in the case of a stepparent where "an adult husband or wife" seeks to "adopt a child of the other spouse." §43-101(1). See, also, §43-104(3). The State contends that stepparent adoption is the only explicit adoption scenario outlined in the Nebraska adoption statutes and that it is implicit in this statutorily permitted scenario that the existing parent intends to continue parenting and, therefore, need not relinquish his or her parental rights to the child in question. The State refers the court to various cases in other states which concluded under the language of their adoption statutes that the biological parent's parental rights would terminate upon adoption of the child by the nonmarried partner of the biological parent or that an adoption was precluded because the biological parent had not relinquished parental rights. See, e.g., Sharon S. v. Superior Court of San Diego County, 93 Cal.App.4th 218, 113 Cal.Rptr.2d 107 (2001) (modified on denial of rehearing), review granted 116 Cal.Rptr.2d 496, 39 P.3d 512 (2002); Adoption of T.K.J., 931 P.2d 488 (Colo.App.1996); In re Baby Z., 247 Conn. 474, 724 A.2d 1035 (1999); In re Adoption of Doe, 130 Ohio App.3d 288, 719 N.E.2d 1071 (1998); In re Adoption of R.B.F., 762 A.2d 739 (Pa.Super.2000); In Interest of Angel Lace M., 184 Wis.2d 492, 516 N.W.2d 678 (1994).

Section 43-101 is entitled "Children eligible for adoption." Section 43-101(1) provides as follows:

> Except as otherwise provided in the Nebraska Indian Child Welfare Act, any minor child may be adopted by any adult person or persons and any adult child may be adopted by the spouse of such child's parent in the cases and subject to sections 43-101 to 43-115, except that no person having a husband or wife may adopt a minor child unless the husband or wife joins in the petition therefor. If the husband or wife so joins in the petition therefor, the adoption shall be by them jointly, except that an adult husband or wife may adopt a child of the other spouse whether born in or out of wedlock.

With respect to the non-Indian minor child, Luke, who is the subject of this case, §43-101 provides that "any minor child may be adopted." Elsewhere in chapter 43, however, numerous statutory substantive and procedural provisions are set forth which must be read together with §43-101 and met before "any minor child," §43-101, is in fact eligible for adoption and a decree of adoption may be properly entered. The statutes which provide for the consequences of adoption also bear on the issue of Luke's eligibility. Reading the various provisions of chapter 43 in pari materia, Foote v. O'Neill Packing, 262 Neb. 467, 632 N.W.2d 313 (2001), we conclude that with the exception of the stepparent adoption, the parent or parents possessing existing parental rights must relinquish the child before "any minor child may be adopted by any adult person or persons." Under Nebraska's statutory adoption scheme, the minor child, Luke, was not eligible for adoption by A.E. because B.P. had not relinquished him and the county court's reading of the statute was correct.

In In re Adoption of Kassandra B. & Nicholas B., 248 Neb. 912, 918, 540 N.W.2d 554, 558 (1995), we observed that as to the biological parent, "termination of his or her parental rights is the foundation of our adoption statutes." This pronouncement is reflected in the adoption statutes, which require relinquishment or termination prior to adoption, except when a stepparent adopts, and is further reflected in case law interpreting the adoption statutes.

Appellants argue that B.P.'s consent was the equivalent of relinquishment for purposes of the present case. We do not agree. Section §43-104 provides that "no adoption shall be decreed unless written consents thereto are filed in the court of the county in which the person or persons desiring to adopt reside." Under §43-104, such consent must be executed by

> (1) the minor child, if over fourteen years of age, or the adult child, (2) any district court, county court, or separate juvenile court in the State of Nebraska having jurisdiction of the custody of a minor child by virtue of divorce proceedings had in any district court, county court, or separate juvenile court in the State of Nebraska or by virtue of section 43-1203, and (3) both parents of a child born in lawful wedlock if living, the surviving parent of a child born in lawful wedlock, the mother of a child born out of wedlock, or both the mother and father of a child born out of wedlock as determined pursuant to sections 43-104.08 to 43-104.24, except that consent shall not be required of any parent who (a) has relinquished the child for adoption by a written instrument, (b) has abandoned the child for at least six months next preceding the filing of the adoption petition, (c) has been deprived of his or her parental rights to such child by the order of any court of competent jurisdiction, or (d) is incapable of consenting.

A consent to the proceedings by a parent or parents under §43-104 is not required when a relinquishment has been executed. §43-104(3)(a). A relinquishment would preclude the necessity of a consent. B.P. did not sign a relinquishment in this case, and her "consent" is not the equivalent of relinquishment.

We have stated that the consent granted by a court under §43-104 does nothing more than permit the trial court to entertain the adoption proceedings. Klein v. Klein, 230 Neb. 385, 431 N.W.2d 646 (1988). We read "consent" in §43-104 to mean that the person, persons, or entity authorized to consent to the proceedings has agreed that the proposed adoption should be entertained by the trial court. See, also, In re Adoption of Kassandra B. & Nicholas B., supra. In the instant case, B.P. "consented" to the proceedings and Luke is not ineligible for adoption due to a lack of such consent; however, B.P.'s consent to the proceedings was not tantamount to a relinquishment of parental rights.

The importance of "relinquishment" in the adoption statutes is apparent in §43-109, which provides in relevant part:

> If, upon the hearing, the court finds that such adoption is for the best interests of such minor child or such adult child, a decree of adoption shall be entered. No decree of adoption shall be entered unless (a) it appears that the child has resided with the person or persons petitioning for such adoption for at least six months next preceding the entering of the decree of adoption, except that such residency requirement shall not apply in an adoption of an adult child, (b) the medical histories required by subsection (2) of section 43-107 have been made a part of the court record, and (c) the court record

includes an affidavit or affidavits signed by the *relinquishing biological parent,* or parents if both are available, in which it is affirmed that, pursuant to section 43-106.02, prior to the relinquishment of the child for adoption, the *relinquishing parent* was, or parents if both are available were, (i) presented a copy or copies of the nonconsent form provided for in section 43-146.06 and (ii) given an explanation of the effects of filing or not filing the nonconsent form.

(Emphasis supplied.) The affidavit noted in §43-109(c) refers to the form completed by the relinquishing parent or parents which indicates whether the parent or parents agree to the release of information about the relinquishing parent or parents to the adopted child.

Under §43-109, "[n]o decree of adoption shall be entered unless ... (c) the court record includes an affidavit [pertaining to whether or not information regarding the *relinquishing biological parent* should be released to the adopted person] signed by the *relinquishing biological parent.*" (Emphasis supplied.) Thus, under §43-109, an adoption is not authorized unless the biological parent relinquishes the child and files the particular affidavit identified in the statute. Although the effect of a relinquishment in terms of finality is not the same in private adoptions as in agency adoptions, see Gray v. Maxwell, 206 Neb. 385, 293 N.W.2d 90 (1980), and, notwithstanding that a relinquishment of parental rights in a private adoption is not totally extinguished until the child is adopted, Yopp v. Batt, 237 Neb. 779, 467 N.W.2d 868 (1991), a relinquishment is nevertheless required.

We have held that in a private adoption case where the prospective adoptive parent was not a spouse of the biological parent, there must be a relinquishment by the biological parent and the relinquishment must be valid in order for the child to become eligible for adoption. See Gray v. Maxwell, supra (stating that where biological mother was paid sum of money in excess of legitimate expenses of confinement and birth in consideration for executing relinquishment, such relinquishment was against public policy and was invalid). In the instant case, B.P. swore in the affidavit required under §43-109 that "I do not intend to relinquish [Luke] for the ultimate purpose of adoption." Having refused to relinquish Luke, B.P. is not a "relinquishing biological parent." The affidavit B.P. signed did not meet the requirements of §43-109. Therefore, Luke was not eligible for adoption and "[n]o decree of adoption shall be entered."

The provisions contained in the adoption statutes found at §§43-110 and 43-111, pertaining to the consequences of adoption, further buttress our conclusion that "termination" of existing parental rights is the foundation of our adoption statutes. See In re Adoption of Kassandra B. & Nicholas B., 248 Neb. 912, 540 N.W.2d 554 (1995). Section 43-110, entitled "Decree; effect as between parties," provides as follows:

> After a decree of adoption is entered, the usual relation of parent and child and all the rights, duties and other legal consequences of the natural relation of child and parent shall thereafter exist between such adopted child and the person or persons adopting such child and his, her or their kindred.

We have stated that the "purpose of §43-110 is to terminate any relationship which existed between the natural parent and the child and to create a new relationship between the adoptive parent and the child." In re Estate of Luckey; Bailey v. Luckey, 206 Neb. 53, 56, 291 N.W.2d 235, 237–38 (1980).

Section 43-111, entitled "Decree; effect as to natural parents," provides:

Except as provided in section 43-106.01 and the Nebraska Indian Child Welfare Act, after a decree of adoption has been entered, the natural parents of the adopted child shall be relieved of all parental duties toward and all responsibilities for such child and have no rights over such adopted child or to his or her property by descent and distribution.

We have read this section as requiring a relinquishment prior to a private placement adoption. Gray v. Maxwell, supra.

Thus, under Nebraska's adoption statutes, the legal consequence of an adoption is that "the natural relation of child and parent shall thereafter exist between such adopted child and the person or persons adopting such child," § 43-110, and the adoption serves to relieve the natural parents of "all parental duties toward and all responsibilities for such child and have no rights over such adopted child," § 43-111. The pleadings in this case indicate that only A.E. sought to adopt Luke. Had the county court permitted the adoption of Luke by A.E., a new relationship between A.E. and Luke would have been created pursuant to § 43-110, and, as an unintended consequence, B.P. would have been relieved of her natural rights to Luke pursuant to § 43-111. In the instant case, B.P. manifestly did not want the consequences ordained by § 43-111 to attach had the county court granted the petition for adoption of Luke by A.E.

In order for A.E. to adopt Luke, he must be eligible for adoption. With the exception of stepparent adoptions, which are statutorily permitted, the Nebraska adoption statutes provide that an eligible child is one over whom parental rights have been relinquished or terminated and with respect to whom, upon entry of the adoption decree, a new relationship between the child and adoptive parent is created and the natural parents are relieved of all parental duties. In the instant case, Luke was not eligible for adoption by A.E. because B.P. had not relinquished her parental rights, and the county court's determination that the absence of such relinquishment precluded adoption of Luke by A.E. is not error.

Appellants urge this court to ignore the language of § 43-111 and to interpret the adoption statutes as permitting the adoption of Luke by A.E. as a parent in addition to the existing parent, B.P., without consequence to the parental rights of B.P. Appellants acknowledge that the exception providing for a stepparent adoption under § 43-101 permits the addition of a stepparent without relieving the natural parent of rights which would otherwise result under § 43-111. Appellants urge this court to read into the adoption statutes an additional exception for second-parent adoptions and to disregard the fact that the adoption statutes explicitly provide for stepparent adoptions and do not explicitly provide for second-parent adoptions.

The adoption statutes permit only the paradigms which are explicit. With the exception of the statutory stepparent adoption scenario outlined in § 43-101, the adoption statutes neither provide for nor expressly designate who may adopt. When construing a statute, appellate courts are guided by the presumption that the Legislature intended a sensible, rather than an absurd, result in enacting a statute. Fay v. Dowding, Dowding, 261 Neb. 216, 623 N.W.2d 287 (2001). Because the Nebraska adoption statutes explicitly provide for a stepparent adoption following which the existing parent will inherently continue raising the child, we conclude it would be an absurd result under the statutes as written to require relinquishment by the existing parent in the explicit statutorily permitted case of a stepparent adoption. As compared to a stepparent adoption, however, it is not inherent in § 43-101 that the "person or persons" seeking to adopt will necessarily be in addition to the existing parent who will continue to raise the child. Reading the adoption statutes in their entirety, it is clear that aside from the stepparent adoption scenario, the parents' parental rights must be terminated or the child must be relinquished in order for the child to be eligible for adoption by "any adult person or persons" under §43-101.

For the reasons given above, we conclude that the county court did not err when it concluded on this record that A.E. could not adopt Luke for the reason that Luke was not eligible for adoption because B.P. had not relinquished her parental rights to him.

* * *

Adoption is statutory in Nebraska, and the outcome of this case is controlled by the Nebraska adoption statutes, §43-101 et seq. The constitutional issues which may be implicated in this case were neither presented to nor ruled upon at trial and are not considered for the first time on appeal.

For an adoption to be properly decreed, the following factors must be met: There must be a person or persons entitled to adopt, a child must be eligible for adoption, the procedures and terms of the Nebraska adoption statutes must be followed, and the adoption must be in the child's best interests. In this case, because Luke was not eligible for adoption, a decree could not be properly entered, the denial of the petition on this basis was correct, and we need not consider the existence of the other factors.

According to the record, appellants, two nonmarried adults, jointly petitioned the county court of Lancaster County. The only relief sought in the proceeding was the adoption of Luke, B.P.'s biological minor son, by A.E. B.P. did not sign a relinquishment of Luke.

The county court ruled that Nebraska's adoption statutes do not provide for "two non-married persons to adopt a minor child, no matter how qualified they are." The issue of whether two nonmarried persons are entitled to adopt was not before the county court nor before this court on appeal.

The county court also concluded that a single adult person could adopt only when the child had been relinquished and that therefore, since B.P. had not relinquished Luke, A.E. could not adopt Luke because he was not eligible for adoption. With the exception of a stepparent adoption which is explicitly provided for in the Nebraska adoption statutes and for which no relinquishment is required, when the parent or parents' rights have not been terminated, a child must be relinquished by the existing parent or parents to be eligible for adoption "by any adult person or persons." §43-101(1). Because B.P. had not relinquished her parental rights to Luke, he was not eligible for adoption by A.E. Because Luke was not eligible for adoption due to the absence of a relinquishment, on the record in this case, the county court did not err in denying the petition for adoption.

AFFIRMED.

* * *

GERRARD, J., dissenting.

* * *

Even if the county court had reached the issue whether B.P.'s relinquishment of Luke was valid, I do not agree with the majority's affirmance of the county court's judgment on that basis. In my opinion, the Nebraska adoption statutes do not support the majority's conclusion that B.P. was required to relinquish Luke before Luke was eligible for adoption by A.E.

Neb.Rev.Stat. §43-102 (Cum.Supp.2000) provides, in relevant part, that "any person or persons desiring to adopt a minor child or an adult child shall file a petition for adoption signed and sworn to by the person or persons desiring to adopt. The consent or consents required by sections 43-104 and 43-105 ... shall be filed prior to the hearing." Neb.Rev.Stat. §43-104 (Cum.Supp.2000) in turn provides, in relevant part, that

> no adoption shall be decreed unless written consents thereto are filed in the court of the county in which the person or persons desiring to adopt reside and the written consents are executed by ... the mother of a child born out of wedlock ... except that consent shall not be required of any parent who (a) has relinquished the child for adoption by a written instrument....

This section establishes a distinction between a consent and a relinquishment. Moreover, the statute clearly contemplates that there will be circumstances under which there is a consent to an adoption, but not a relinquishment. The statute states that a consent is required *except* when the biological parent has executed a relinquishment. If a relinquishment by a biological parent is necessary in all cases, then the statutory language requiring consent in all other cases would be a redundancy.

The effect of a parental relinquishment is set forth in Neb.Rev.Stat. §43-106.01 (Reissue 1998), which provides in relevant part:

> When a child shall have been relinquished by written instrument ... to the Department of Health and Human Services or to a licensed child placement agency ... the person so relinquishing shall be relieved of all parental duties toward and all responsibilities for such child and have no rights over such child.

In addition, this court has held that in the case of private adoptions, a biological parent who relinquishes his or her rights to a child by a valid written instrument gives up all rights to the child at the time of the relinquishment. Yopp v. Batt, 237 Neb. 779, 467 N.W.2d 868 (1991). See, also, Gomez v. Savage, 254 Neb. 836, 580 N.W.2d 523 (1998).

While §43-106.01 and *Yopp,* supra, establish the legal effect of a voluntary relinquishment, they do not, however, provide that a relinquishment is required from a biological parent for a petition for a decree of adoption to be considered when that biological parent is one of the parties to the adoption petition. In the search for such a requirement, the majority relies on Neb.Rev.Stat. §43-109 (Cum.Supp.2000), which provides in relevant part:

> If, upon the hearing, the court finds that such adoption is for the best interests of such minor child or such adult child, a decree of adoption shall be entered. No decree of adoption shall be entered unless (a) it appears that the child has resided with the person or persons petitioning for such adoption for at least six months next preceding the entering of the decree of adoption ... (c) the court record includes an affidavit or affidavits signed by the relinquishing biological parent, or parents if both are available, in which it is affirmed that, pursuant to section 43-106.02, prior to the relinquishment of the child for adoption, the relinquishing parent was, or parents if both are available were, (i) presented a copy or copies of the nonconsent form provided for in section 43-146.06 and (ii) given an explanation of the effects of filing or not filing the nonconsent form.

The majority reads this section to imply that a relinquishment from a biological parent must be present in all cases. However, there are clearly circumstances in which there will not be such a relinquishment. The majority acknowledges that there need be—indeed, can be—no relinquishment when the biological parent's parental rights have been terminated and concludes that relinquishment is unnecessary in the case of a spousal second-parent adoption. There can also obviously be no relinquishment when the child's biological parents are deceased or the child has been abandoned. Because the Legislature could not have been unaware of these situations, it is evident that the Legislature could not have intended § 43-109 to require an affidavit from a relinquishing parent where there is no relinquishing parent. While § 43-109 requires that the record include affidavits from the relinquishing parents if there are relinquishing parents, the statute does not address when relinquishment is and is not necessary. Simply put, if there is a statutory source for the majority's conclusion that a relinquishment from a biological parent is required before a child is eligible for adoption, that source is not § 43-109.

* * *

The majority further bases its holding on the conclusion that B.P. must "relinquish" her parental rights because A.E. cannot adopt Luke without extinguishing B.P.'s parental rights. I also disagree with this conclusion, as an appropriate interpretation of Nebraska's adoption statutes reveals no basis for mandating this result.

Neb.Rev.Stat. § 43-101(1) (Cum.Supp.2000) provides:

> Except as otherwise provided in the Nebraska Indian Child Welfare Act, any minor child may be adopted by any adult person or persons and any adult child may be adopted by the spouse of such child's parent in the cases and subject to sections 43-101 to 43-115, except that no person having a husband or wife may adopt a minor child unless the husband or wife joins in the petition therefor. If the husband or wife so joins in the petition therefor, the adoption shall be by them jointly, except that an adult husband or wife may adopt a child of the other spouse whether born in or out of wedlock.

Section 43-111 provides:

> Except as provided in section 43-106.01 ... after a decree of adoption has been entered, the natural parents of the adopted child shall be relieved of all parental duties toward and all responsibilities for such child and have no rights over such adopted child or to his or her property by descent and distribution.

In construing these statutes, the majority ignores the long-established rule that the adoption statutes should be given a liberal rather than a strict construction due to the humanitarian aspects and purposes of such statutes. See Neil v. Masterson, 187 Neb. 364, 191 N.W.2d 448 (1971). The tendency of all our decisions has been toward a liberal construction of the law in all cases of adoption. In re Estate of Taylor, 136 Neb. 227, 285 N.W. 538 (1939).

> The adoption statute is a humane provision, which looks to the interest of children primarily. This is its controlling idea and policy. Therefore, every reasonable intendment should be indulged, in case of doubt, in the line of promoting that object. Other courts have taken the same view, but, if it were otherwise, our duty to carry out an obvious legislative intent would be the same.... It has made, and is making, a multitude of happy homes, happy parents, happy children, and valuable members of society, and no narrow construction should be indulged in that will tend to defeat a result so obviously intended and in every way so beneficial.

Ferguson v. Herr, 64 Neb. 649, 665, 94 N.W. 542, 545 (1903). The best interests of the child should be kept at the forefront of such an inquiry. See Yopp v. Batt, 237 Neb. 779, 467 N.W.2d 868 (1991).

With that understanding in mind, the statutory scheme as a whole serves to advance two fundamental purposes: (1) ensuring that biological parents are informed of their rights and consent to the adoption proceedings and (2) providing for the best interests of the child. See, e.g., § 43-109. The majority analyzes the wrong issue: the question is not whether the statutes specifically permit a second-parent adoption where the adoptive parent and biological parent are not married, but instead whether the statutes explicitly prohibit such an adoption.

The statutes provide, in extremely broad language, that "any minor child may be adopted by any adult person or persons," § 43-101(1), if the county court "finds that such adoption is for the best interests of such minor child," § 43-109(1). Our Legislature, like many others, has declined to make categorical assumptions about what adoptive parents or familial relationships are preferable and has instead left it to the county court to conduct a fact-specific inquiry into whether a particular adoption is in the best interests of the child. As stated by one commentator:

> [W]hat is unmistakably clear from looking at adoption statutes is the legislative delegation of decision-making power in individual cases to judges. Compelling functional justifications support this institutional design. Adoption law is built on a premise of delegation: the legislature grants broad powers to courts to make case by case decisions and to decide what arrangement is in a child's best interests. This sort of delegation, of course, goes beyond the adoption context and describes much of family law affecting children, such as custody and visitation decisions.
>
> … The highly individualized and proceduralized fact-finding procedures used by judges enable them to engage closely with the specific circumstances in which children find themselves.

Jane S. Schacter, Constructing Families in a Democracy: Courts, Legislatures and Second-Parent Adoption, 75 Chi.-Kent L.Rev. 933, 942–43 (2000).

It is plainly inconsistent with such a scheme to interpret § 43-111 as requiring the extinguishment of a biological parent's parental rights under circumstances such as those presented in this case. * * *

Despite my disagreement with the majority's analysis, I agree with the majority insofar as it concludes that the constitutional claims raised in the parties' briefs are not pertinent to the dispositive issues on appeal. In spite of the efforts of the parties and various amici to turn this appeal into a forum for or against gay and lesbian rights, the question before this court is one of statutory interpretation, and that analysis is not affected by the gender or sexual orientation of the biological or prospective adoptive parent. While some of the cases cited above involved circumstances, like those of the instant case, in which the biological and prospective adoptive parent were of the same gender, I emphasize that Nebraska's statutes make no distinction on that point; my analysis—and that of the majority—is not premised on any distinction involving the gender and sexual orientation of the couple seeking a second-parent adoption. That distinction or other distinctions (if any are to be made within the bounds of the constitution) are the province of the Legislature, and that body has not spoken on the issue.

I would reverse the judgment of the county court dismissing the adoption petition, because I believe the county court erroneously determined that it did not have the statutory authority to enter the requested adoption decree. Because the county court did not decide whether the adoption sought was in the best interests of Luke, I would remand the cause to the county court for further proceedings relating to that issue. I respectfully dissent.

Notes

Not all states require that a birth parent forfeits all rights to his or her child upon adoption by an unrelated third party. *See, e.g.,* Sharon S. v. Sup. Ct. of San Diego, 31 Cal. 4th 417, 73 P.3d 554, 2 Cal. Rptr. 3d 699 (2003) (California Supreme Court allowed for a party to waive compliance with statutory conditions intended for his or her benefit as long as the legislature has not made the conditions mandatory). *See also In re* Adoption of K.S.P., 804 N.E.2d 1253 (Ind. App. 2004). Likewise, in *In re* Adoption of R.B.F., 569 Pa. 269, 803 A.2d 1195 (2002), the Pennsylvania Supreme Court held that a same-sex partner may adopt a child of the birth parent and the birth parent does not relinquish his or her parental rights. The court utilized a change in the adoption statute affording a trial court discretion, upon cause shown, to waive a particular statutory requirement.

Most adoptions by a third party will be in the context of a step-parent involved in a marriage and seeking to adopt the child of his or her spouse. The Uniform Probate Code provides an illustration.

Uniform Probate Code (2003)

§2-114. Parent and Child Relationship.

(a) Except as provided in subsections (b) and (c), for purposes of intestate succession by, through, or from a person, an individual is the child of his [or her] natural parents, regardless of their marital status. The parent and child relationship may be established under [the Uniform Parentage Act] [applicable state law] [insert appropriate statutory reference].

(b) An adopted individual is the child of his [or her] adopting parent or parents and not of his [or her] natural parents, but adoption of a child by the spouse of either natural parent has no effect on (i) the relationship between the child and that natural parent or (ii) the right of the child or a descendant of the child to inherit from or through the other natural parent.

(c) Inheritance from or through a child by either natural parent or his [or her] kindred is precluded unless that natural parent has openly treated the child as his [or hers], and has not refused to support the child.

The Uniform Adoption Act allows for post-adoption visitation by the non-custodial former parent, siblings, and grandparents, thereby allowing for greater contact by the child with former relatives and friends. *See* Uniform Adoption Act §4-113 (2003). Such visitation will have to pass scrutiny under Troxel v. Granville, 530 U.S. 57, 120 S. Ct. 2054 (2000) (holding that a parent has a fundamental right to object to third-party visitation with a child).

2. *Equitable Adoption*

Although adoption is a statutory creation, a number of states have recognized equitable adoption to meet the needs of particular circumstances. The equitable circumstances are most often confined to intestacy when the decedent has made no choice in the matter. Also, unlike a statute that seeks uniformity, equitable adoption derives from the facts of each situation. The doctrine seeks "to do the right thing" for a child, who is treated as if he or she were the child of the decedent. Yet, in those states that recognize it, the doctrine has an adverse effect upon the other heirs of the intestate decedent and contradicts the state's intestate statutes. For a discussion of equitable adoption and its effect on inheritance rights, see William G. Reeves, *Inheritance by Equitable Adoption: An Overview of Theory and Proof,* http://www.mobar.org/journal/2001/mayjun/reeves.htm (accessed Oct. 12, 2005). The following case offers an illustration of the conflicting interests.

Lankford v. Wright

Supreme Court of North Carolina, 1997
374 N.C. 115, 489 S.E.2d 604

FRYE, Justice.

The sole issue in this case is whether North Carolina recognizes the doctrine of equitable adoption. We hold that the doctrine should be recognized in this state, and therefore, we reverse the decision of the Court of Appeals.

Plaintiff, Barbara Ann Newton Lankford, was born to Mary M. Winebarger on 15 January 1944. When plaintiff was a child, her natural mother entered into an agreement with her neighbors, Clarence and Lula Newton, whereby the Newtons agreed to adopt and raise plaintiff as their child. Shortly thereafter, plaintiff moved into the Newton residence and became known as Barbara Ann Newton, the only child of Clarence and Lula Newton.

The Newtons held plaintiff out to the public as their own child, and plaintiff was at all times known as Barbara Ann Newton. Plaintiff's school records referred to plaintiff as Barbara Ann Newton and indicated that Clarence and Lula Newton were her parents. Plaintiff's high-school diploma also referred to plaintiff as Barbara Ann Newton. After Clarence Newton died in 1960, the newspaper obituary listed Barbara Ann Newton as his surviving daughter. Later, with Lula Newton's assistance, plaintiff obtained a Social Security card issued to her under the name of Barbara Ann Newton.

After plaintiff joined the Navy, plaintiff and Lula Newton frequently wrote letters to each other. In most of the letters, plaintiff referred to Lula Newton as her mother and Lula Newton referred to plaintiff as her daughter. Lula Newton also established several bank accounts with plaintiff, where Lula Newton deposited money plaintiff sent to her while plaintiff was in the Navy. On several occasions, plaintiff took leaves of absence from work to care for Lula Newton during her illness.

In 1975, Lula Newton prepared a will. When she died in 1994, the will was not accepted for probate because some unknown person had defaced a portion of the will. The will named plaintiff as co-executrix of the estate and made specific bequests to plaintiff. Since the will could not be probated, Lula Newton died intestate.

After Lula Newton's death, plaintiff filed for declaratory judgment seeking a declaration of her rights and status as an heir of the estate of Lula Newton. Defendants, the administrators and named heirs of Lula Newton, filed a motion for summary judgment. The trial court granted defendants' motion. The North Carolina Court of Appeals affirmed the order granting summary judgment, reasoning that plaintiff was not adopted according to N.C.G.S. §§ 48-1 to -38 and that North Carolina does not recognize the doctrine of equitable adoption. This Court granted plaintiff's petition for discretionary review, and we now conclude that the doctrine of equitable adoption should be recognized in North Carolina.

"It is a fundamental premise of equitable relief that equity regards as done that which in fairness and good conscience ought to be done." Thompson v. Soles, 299 N.C. 484, 489, 263 S.E.2d 599, 603 (1980). "Equity regards substance, not form," In re Will of Pendergrass, 251 N.C. 737, 743, 112 S.E.2d 562, 566 (1960), and "will not allow technicalities of procedure to defeat that which is eminently right and just," id. at 746, 112 S.E.2d at 568. These principles form the essence of the doctrine of equitable adoption, and it is the duty of this Court to protect and promote them.

Equitable adoption is a remedy to "protect the interest of a person who was supposed to have been adopted as a child but whose adoptive parents failed to undertake the legal steps necessary to formally accomplish the adoption." Gardner v. Hancock, 924 S.W.2d 857, 858 (Mo.Ct.App.1996). The doctrine is applied in an intestate estate to "give effect to the intent of the decedent to adopt and provide for the child." Id. It is predicated upon

> principles of contract law and equitable enforcement of the agreement to adopt for the purpose of securing the benefits of adoption that would otherwise flow from the adoptive parent under the laws of intestacy had the agreement to adopt been carried out; as such it is essentially a matter of equitable relief. Being only an equitable remedy to enforce a contract right, it is not intended or applied to create the legal relationship of parent and child, with all the legal consequences of such a relationship, nor is it meant to create a legal adoption.

2 Am.Jur.2d *Adoption* § 53 (1994) (footnotes omitted).

Adoption did not exist at common law and is of purely statutory origin. Wilson v. Anderson, 232 N.C. 212, 215, 59 S.E.2d 836, 839 (1950). Equitable adoption, however, does not confer the incidents of formal statutory adoption; rather, it merely confers rights of inheritance upon the foster child in the event of intestacy of the foster parents. * * * In essence, the doctrine invokes the principle that equity regards that as done which ought to be done. The doctrine is not intended to replace statutory requirements or to create the parent-child relationship; it simply recognizes the foster child's right to inherit from the person or persons who contracted to adopt the child and who honored that contract in all respects except through formal statutory procedures. As an equitable matter, where the child in question has faithfully performed the duties of a natural child to the foster parents, that child is entitled to be placed in the position in which he would have been had he been adopted. Likewise, based on principles of estoppel, those claiming under and through the deceased are estopped to assert that the child was not legally adopted or did not occupy the status of an adopted child.

Further, the scope of the doctrine is limited to facts comparable to those presented here. Thirty-eight jurisdictions have considered equitable adoption; at least twenty-seven have recognized and applied the doctrine. See, e.g., First Nat'l Bank in Fairmont v. Phillips, 176

W.Va. 395, 344 S.E.2d 201 (1985). A majority of the jurisdictions recognizing the doctrine have successfully limited its application to claims made by an equitably adopted child against the estate of the foster parent. Geramifar v. Geramifar, 113 Md.App. 495, 688 A.2d 475 (1997). By its own terms, equitable adoption applies only in limited circumstances. The elements necessary to establish the existence of an equitable adoption are:

(1) an express or implied agreement to adopt the child,

(2) reliance on that agreement,

(3) performance by the natural parents of the child in giving up custody,

(4) performance by the child in living in the home of the foster parents and acting as their child,

(5) partial performance by the foster parents in taking the child into their home and treating the child as their own, and

(6) the intestacy of the foster parents.

See 2 Am.Jur.2d *Adoption* §54 (1994). These elements, particularly the requirement of intestacy, limit the circumstances under which the doctrine may be applied. Specifically, the doctrine acts only to recognize the inheritance rights of a child whose foster parents died intestate and failed to perform the formalities of a legal adoption, yet treated the child as their own for all intents and purposes. The doctrine is invoked for the sole benefit of the foster child in determining heirship upon the intestate death of the person or persons contracting to adopt. Whether the doctrine applies is a factual question, and each element must be proven by clear, cogent, and convincing evidence. See, e.g., First Nat'l Bank in Fairmont v. Phillips, 176 W.Va. 395, 344 S.E.2d 201.

In this case, the evidence in the record tends to show that the above elements can be satisfied by clear, cogent, and convincing evidence. The record demonstrates that the Newtons agreed to adopt plaintiff; that the Newtons and plaintiff relied on that agreement; that plaintiff's natural mother gave up custody of plaintiff to the Newtons; that plaintiff lived in the Newtons' home, cared for them in their old age, and otherwise acted as their child; that the Newtons treated plaintiff as their child by taking her into their home, giving her their last name, and raising her as their child; and that Mrs. Newton died intestate several years after Mr. Newton died. These facts fit squarely within the parameters of the doctrine of equitable adoption and are indicative of the dilemma the doctrine is intended to remedy.

We note that our decision to recognize the doctrine of equitable adoption is not precluded by prior decisions of this Court as asserted by defendants and decided by the Court of Appeals. In Ladd v. Estate of Kellenberger, 314 N.C. 477, 334 S.E.2d 751 (1985), we specifically stated that "[w]e find no occasion to address the question of whether North Carolina recognizes the doctrine of equitable adoption." Id. at 479, 334 S.E.2d at 753. Likewise, in Chambers v. Byers, 214 N.C. 373, 199 S.E. 398 (1938), our holding was limited to whether the agreement at issue was an enforceable contract to make a will. Thus, neither *Ladd* nor *Chambers* foreclosed the possibility of future recognition of equitable adoption by this Court.

The dissent points out that a minority of jurisdictions have declined to recognize the doctrine of equitable adoption. However, we again note that an overwhelming majority of states that have addressed the question have recognized and applied the doctrine. More importantly, it is the unique role of the courts to fashion equitable remedies to protect and promote the principles of equity such as those at issue in this case. We are convinced that acting in an equitable manner in this case does not interfere with the legislative scheme for adoption, contrary to the assertions of the dissent. Recognition of the doctrine of equitable adoption does not create a legal adoption, and therefore does not impair the statutory procedures for adoption.

In conclusion, a decree of equitable adoption should be granted where justice, equity, and good faith require it. The fairness of applying the doctrine once the prerequisite facts have been established is apparent. Accordingly, we reverse the Court of Appeals' decision which affirmed the trial court's entry of summary judgment for defendants and remand to the trial court for further proceedings not inconsistent with this opinion.

REVERSED AND REMANDED.

MITCHELL, Chief Justice, dissenting.

In its opinion, the majority for the first time accepts the doctrine of equitable adoption for North Carolina. As applied by the majority in this case, the doctrine results in neither an adoption nor equity. Therefore, although I am convinced the majority is engaged in an honest but unfortunate attempt to do good in the present case, I must dissent.

"Equity" is that established set of principles under which substantial justice may be attained in particular cases where the prescribed or customary forms of ordinary law seem to be inadequate. 27A Am.Jur.2d *Equity* § 1 (1994). Equity "is a complex system of established law and is not merely a reflection of the judge's sense of what is appropriate." Id. § 2. It arose in response to the restrictive and inflexible rules of the common law, and not as a means of avoiding legislation that courts deemed unwise or inadequate.

For purposes of governing and regulating judicial action, equity courts over the centuries "have formulated certain rules or principles which are described by the term 'maxims.'" Id. § 108. It is these maxims which must control the equity jurisdiction of the courts if their judgments are to reflect anything other than the peculiar preferences of the individual judges involved.

> A court of equity has no more right than has a court of law to act on its own notion of what is right in a particular case; it must be guided by the established rules and precedents. Where rights are defined and established by existing legal principles, they may not be changed or unsettled in equity. A court of equity is thus bound by any explicit statute or directly applicable rule of law, regardless of its views of the equities.

Id. § 109 (footnotes omitted).

One maxim of equity, as the majority explains, is that equity regards as done that which in fairness and good conscience ought to be done. A court's notion of what is good or desirable does not determine what "ought to be done" in applying equity. The maxim of equity upon which the majority relies must yield to other controlling and established rules or maxims. One such maxim is that a court of equity, however benevolent its motives, is "bound by any explicit statute or directly applicable rule of law, regardless of its view of the equities." Id. Thus, no equitable remedy may properly be applied to disturb statutorily defined and established rights, such as those rights created by North Carolina statutes controlling intestate succession or those controlling legal adoption.

The North Carolina Intestate Succession Act provides a comprehensive and extensive legislative scheme controlling intestate succession by, through, and from adopted children. N.C.G.S. § 29-17(a) provides:

> A child, *adopted in accordance with Chapter 48 of the General Statutes* or in accordance with the applicable law of any other jurisdiction, and the heirs of such child, are entitled by succession to any property by, through and from his adoptive parents and their heirs the same as if he were the natural legitimate child of the adoptive parents.

N.C.G.S. § 29-17(a) (1995) (emphasis added). The extensive scheme created by the legislature is clear and unambiguous. It provides, in pertinent part, that only those children who are adopted *in compliance with chapter 48* or adopted according to the requirements of another jurisdiction are eligible to take by intestate succession. Therefore, the maxim relied upon by the majority may not properly be applied here.

> Equity will not interfere where a statute applies and dictates requirements for relief. Use of equitable principles to trump an apposite statute thus is legally indefensible. The disregard of an unambiguous law based on sympathy is unjustifiable under the rubric of equity.

27A Am.Jur.2d *Equity* § 246 (footnotes omitted).

It is well established that "[w]here an extensive legislative scheme governs, it is incumbent upon chancellors to restrain their equity powers." Id. The application of the doctrine of equitable adoption by the majority in this case violates this principle of equity requiring greater restraint when dealing with statutory law than when addressing the common law. The majority's application of the doctrine of equitable adoption here negates the rights of other heirs such as defendants which are expressly provided for in the extensive legislative scheme established by the North Carolina Intestate Succession Act. In the instant case, the application of the doctrine of equitable adoption denies other rightful heirs their statutory intestate shares, in effect voiding the intestate succession hierarchy enacted by our legislature. This result is contrary to established maxims of equity.

Further, contrary to established maxims of equity, the decision of the majority also "trumps" another applicable extensive legislative scheme. Adoption did not exist at common law in North Carolina. Therefore, we have expressly and correctly held that adoption "can be accomplished only in accordance with provisions of statutes enacted by the legislative branch of the State government." Wilson v. Anderson, 232 N.C. 212, 215, 59 S.E.2d 836, 839 (1950). The North Carolina General Assembly has enacted a comprehensive and extensive legislative scheme governing adoptions contained in chapter 48 of the General Statutes. Plaintiff does not fall within the requirements of these statutes. Therefore, I believe that the majority errs in failing to apply restraint in the exercise of its equity powers and in applying its own notion of what "ought to be done" in order to improperly "trump" an apposite statute. 27A Am.Jur.2d *Equity* § 246.

Presently, all states recognize a parent-child relationship through adoption if the certain and unambiguous statutory procedures of each specific state are followed. A strong minority of courts that have reviewed the issue have declined to recognize the doctrine of equitable adoption. See Wilks v. Langley, 248 Ark. 227, 235, 451 S.W.2d 209, 213 (1970) (holding inheritance under theory of "virtual adoption" unknown in Arkansas); Maui Land & Pineapple Co. v. Naiapaakai Heirs of Makeelani, 69 Haw. 565, 568, 751 P.2d 1020, 1022 (1988) ("to depart from the statutes by creating a doctrine of equitable adoption would import mischief and uncertainty into the law"); In re Estate of Edwards, 106 Ill.App.3d 635, 637, 62 Ill.Dec. 407, 435 N.E.2d 1379, 1381 (1982) ("Illinois has not expressly recognized the theory of equitable adoption"); Lindsey v. Wilcox, 479 N.E.2d 1330, 1333 (Ind.Ct.App.1985) ("the doctrine of equitable adoption has never been approved in Indiana and it continues to be denied judicial approval"); In re Estate of Robbins, 241 Kan. 620, 621, 738 P.2d 458, 460 (1987) ("Kansas courts do not recognize the doctrine of equitable adoption"); Pierce v. Pierce, 198 Mont. 255, 259, 645 P.2d 1353, 1356 (1982) (the adoptive parent or parents must follow the required procedures set forth in the Uniform Adoption Act in order for an adoption to occur); Alley v. Bennett, 298 S.C. 218, 221, 379 S.E.2d 294, 295 (1989) (the method of adoption provided by statute is exclusive); Couch v. Couch, 35 Tenn.App. 464, 476, 248 S.W.2d 327, 333 (1951) ("The right of adoption was unknown to the common law. It is of statutory origin, and to create the contemplated relation the procedure fixed by the statute must be substantially followed.").

Asserting their belief that adoption is singularly defined by statute, these courts have properly deferred to the judgment of their legislators and the procedures established in their state adoption statutes. These courts have also deferred to their legislative bodies to enact laws governing the many complex issues that will arise if the doctrine of equitable adoption is recognized. Such issues would include whether the equitably "adopted" child would inherit from his or her natural parents or from a natural sibling who had not been equitably adopted. Moreover, a court deciding to recognize "equitable adoption" would have to determine for inheritance purposes the relationship between the equitably adopted child's issue and the equitably adoptive parents, versus the child's biological parents. The complexities abound.

The North Carolina General Assembly clearly enacted chapter 48 of the General Statutes of North Carolina with the intent to establish the exclusive procedure by which a minor child may be adopted. The preface to chapter 48 states the legislative intent in adopting this chapter.

> The General Assembly finds that it is in the public interest to establish a *clear judicial process* for adoptions, to promote the integrity and finality of adoptions, to encourage prompt, conclusive disposition of adoption proceedings, and to structure services to adopted children, biological parents, and adoptive parents that will provide for the needs and protect the interests of all parties to an adoption, particularly adopted minors.

N.C.G.S. § 48-1-100(a) (1995) (emphasis added). The legislature intended that adoption in North Carolina be accomplished only through the formal judicial proceedings provided for in the extensive legislative scheme created in chapter 48. Therefore, equity may not properly interfere by creating a new form of partial or total adoption.

In effect, this Court preempts statutes enacted by our legislature in order to recognize the doctrine of equitable adoption. However, because our legislature has extensively, comprehensively, and unambiguously acted, both with regard to adoption and with regard to intestate succession, I am persuaded that the majority improperly "trumps" clear legislative intent in the name of equity.

Despite plaintiff's foster parents' verbal acknowledgments and holding plaintiff out as their natural child, they never legally adopted her by complying with the statutory process. "A mere contract to adopt a child, however, is not a contract to devise or bequeath property to that child." Ladd v. Estate of Kellenberger, 314 N.C. 477, 486, 334

S.E.2d 751, 758 (1985). Thus, it is my opinion that this Court should not declare plaintiff to have been "equitably adopted," thereby subrogating the rights of the statutorily determined heirs for purposes of intestate succession.

Finally, another principle of equity prevents the proper application here of the maxim that equity regards as done that which ought to be done. Defendants in this case include the heirs of Lula Newton under the North Carolina Intestate Succession Act. There is no allegation, contention, or evidence that they are anything other than innocent third parties to the transactions between plaintiff and her natural parents on the one hand and the Newtons on the other concerning any promise to adopt. This Court, like most courts, has expressly recognized and held that the maxim that equity regards as done that which ought to be done *ought not* to be and "will not be enforced to the injury of innocent third parties." Hood ex rel. N.C. Bank & Trust Co. v. N.C. Bank & Trust Co., 209 N.C. 367, 381, 184 S.E. 51, 63 (1936); see Ladd v. Estate of Kellenberger, 314 N.C. at 487, 334 S.E.2d at 758; see also Casey v. Cavaroc, 96 U.S. 467, 24 L.Ed. 779 (1877); Riganti v. McElhinney, 248 Cal.App.2d 116, 56 Cal.Rptr. 195 (1967); Kennedy v. Bank of America, 237 Cal.App.2d 637, 47 Cal.Rptr. 154 (1965); Rigby v. Liles, 505 So.2d 598 (Fla.Dist.Ct.App.1987); Bedal v. Johnson, 37 Idaho 359, 218 P. 641 (1923); Kelsey v. Kelsey, 190 N.Y.S. 52 (Sup.Ct.1921), rev'd on other grounds, 204 A.D. 116, 197 N.Y.S. 371 (1922); Crahane v. Swan, 212 Or. 143, 318 P.2d 942 (1957); Smith v. Schwartz, 398 Pa. 555, 159 A.2d 220 (1960); Crabb v. Uvalde Paving Co., 23 S.W.2d 300 (Tex.Com.App.1930). Here, the majority injures such innocent third parties.

The record in the present case does not indicate that either plaintiff or defendants are anything other than innocents. Therefore, general principles of equity do not arise concerning what "ought to be done" as between them; "where equities are equal, 'the law must prevail.'" 27A Am.Jur.2d *Equity* § 139 (footnotes omitted).

In the present case, the controlling maxims of equity clearly require that this Court restrain its equity powers so as not to overrule comprehensive statutory schemes and, thereby, do harm to innocents. For these reasons, I respectfully dissent from the decision of the majority and would affirm the holding of the Court of Appeals which affirmed the order of the trial court.

PARKER, J., joins in this dissenting opinion.

Notes

Most states have adopted equitable adoption as a judicial process. California has statutorily provided for equitable adoption under defined circumstances, specifically holding that a person claiming to be an intestate decedent's equitably adopted child for inheritance purposes must show that the decedent's conduct clearly and convincingly demonstrated an intent to adopt. *See, e.g.,* In re Estate of Ford, 2004 WL 219790 (Cal. App. 1 Dist. 2004).

California Probate Code (2004)

§ 6454. Foster parent or stepparent

For the purpose of determining intestate succession by a person or the person's issue from or through a foster parent or stepparent, the relationship of parent and child exists between that person and the person's foster parent or stepparent if both of the following requirements are satisfied:

(a) The relationship began during the person's minority and continued throughout the joint lifetimes of the person and the person's foster parent or stepparent.

(b) It is established by clear and convincing evidence that the foster parent or stepparent would have adopted the person but for a legal barrier.

A series of judicial opinions place the doctrine of equitable adoption in context. For example, a woman who had been equitably adopted by her stepfather is not entitled, following his death, to inherit from his mother, who left a valid Last Will and Testament providing for her son's "surviving issue." Thus the doctrine was limited to the equitable parent, not third parties. Estate of Furia, 103 Cal. App. 4th 1, 126 Cal. Rptr. 2d 384 (2002). Likewise, courts would not extend equitable adoption to statutory anti lapse. For example, in a case where an equitable parent died and left a valid Last Will and Testament, bequeathing property to his sons and a daughter, whom he equitably adopted, when the adopted daughter predeceased the parent, the court would not apply the state's anti-lapse statute to distribute the bequest to the adopted daughter's children. *In re* Estate of Seader, 76 P.3d 1236 (Wyo. 2003). *See* Anti Lapse, *infra*.

F. Non-Marital Children

There has been a progressive order to the rights of non-marital children. Their legal status has expanded with the number of non-marital births in the United States; close to 30% of American children are born to parents who are not married. *See* Amara Bachu, U.S. Dept. Of Commerce, Bureau of the Census, Current Population Reports, Population Characteristics, Series P20-482, *Fertility of American Women; June 1994*, at v (1995). Thus, inheritance claims by children not born to a marital union may occur in the context of intestate succession, or, if there is a valid Last Will and Testament, the child may have a claim as a pretermitted heir or a member of class designated as "children," or the child may have standing to contest the validity of the Will. The presence—or possibility—of non-marital children raises significant issues in many areas. For example, in the area of estate planning, the New Jersey Supreme Court ruled that a law firm may disclose to a wife, in the preparation of a couple's estate plan, the fact that the husband has fathered another woman's child. *See* A. v. B., 158 N.J. 51, 726 A.2d 924 (1999). Where the issue involves the right of a putative father to inherit from or through the child, inheritance from or through the child is precluded unless the putative parent has held the child out as his own and has not refused to support the child. *See* In re Estate of Turpening, 258 Mich. App. 464, 671 N.W.2d 567 (2003). Similarly, in order to inherit from or through the child, the putative parent must provide care or maintenance of the child at least one year before the child reaches the age of majority. *See* McKinney v. Richitelli, 357 N.C. 483, 586 S.E.2d 258 (2003).

California Probate Code (2004)

§ 6452. Out-of-wedlock birth

If a child is born out of wedlock, neither a natural parent nor a relative of that parent inherits from or through the child on the basis of the parent and child relationship between that parent and the child unless both of the following requirements are satisfied:

(a) The parent or a relative of the parent acknowledged the child.

(b) The parent or a relative of the parent contributed to the support or the care of the child.

Claims by non-marital children confront the state with issues of fairness in distributing decedent's property, efficient administration of the decedent's estate, and acceptable means of establishing proof of paternity. Litigation and the state statutes that prompt it center on the following issues:

1. Before or After Decedent's Death; Gender; Support Versus Probate

There are important distinctions that must be made between claims for support during the life of a putative parent and claims against the estate of the deceased parent after the parent's death. *See, e.g.*, Clark v. Jeter, 486 U.S. 456, 108 S. Ct. 1910 (1988) (unanimous Court held that a non-marital child had an Equal Protection right to the same statute of limitations for obtaining support from a living putative father as a marital child). A Louisiana court upheld a statute that provided that a non-marital child must prove paternity by clear and convincing evidence if the parent is deceased, but only needs a preponderance of the evidence if the parent is alive. *See* Sudwischer v. Estate of Hoffpauir, 705 So. 2d 724 (La. 1997), *cert denied*, 524 U.S. 940, 118 S. Ct. 2347 (1998). The state may also demand a higher level of proof for establishing paternity from a male than from a female. *See, e.g.*, Miller v. Allbright, 523 U.S. 420, 118 S. Ct. 1428 (1998). Distinctions involved in the process of proving paternity are exemplified in the following case.

Wingate v. Estate of Ryan

Supreme Court of New Jersey, 1997
149 N.J. 227, 693 A.2d 457

COLEMAN, J.

The issue raised in this appeal is whether the twenty-three-year limitations period found in N.J.S.A. 9:17-45(b) of the New Jersey Parentage Act ("Parentage Act"), codified at N.J.S.A. 9:17-38 to -59, applies to an intestacy action filed by a thirty-one-year-old claimant to prove parentage and heirship under N.J.S.A. 3B:5-10 of the Administration of Estates—Decedents and Others Act. That statute, commonly referred to as the Probate Code, is codified at N.J.S.A. 3B:1-1 to 3B:29-1. In 1991, the Legislature amended section 5-10 of the Probate Code to provide that a parent and child relationship "may be established as provided by the 'New Jersey Parentage Act,'" by persons born out of wedlock for purposes of proving heirship. L. 1991, c. 22, § 1.

Plaintiff Joanne Wingate filed a complaint under the Probate Code to establish that she and her son are heirs of John L. Ryan. The trial court denied defendants' motion for summary judgment to dismiss plaintiff's complaint for failure to file the claim by her twenty-third birthday. On defendants' appeal, the Appellate Division reversed in a published opinion, holding that the twenty-three-year limitations period in the Parentage

Act, N.J.S.A. 9:17-45(b), applied to plaintiff's claim. 290 N.J.Super. 463, 676 A.2d 144 (1996). We granted plaintiff's petition for certification, 146 N.J. 496, 683 A.2d 199 (1996), and now reverse. We hold that the limitations period under the Parentage Act does not apply to claims filed under the Probate Code.

* * *

Plaintiff Joanne Wingate was born on December 15, 1963. Plaintiff's mother, Rachel M. Parsio, was married to Willard Wingate at the time of plaintiff's birth. Parsio and Willard Wingate were divorced in 1970. Willard Wingate died in 1988. On February 6, 1995, decedent John J. Ryan died intestate. Until just before Ryan's death, plaintiff had believed that she was Willard Wingate's natural child. However, ten days before Ryan's death, plaintiff's mother informed her that Ryan was her natural father.

Decedent had a close relationship with Parsio and plaintiff. Parsio asserts that decedent purchased gifts for plaintiff on holidays and birthdays, and paid for substantial expenses, such as her braces and her wedding gown. According to Parsio, decedent acknowledged to her that he was plaintiff's biological father on several occasions, but decedent repeatedly refused to publicly acknowledge that fact because he and Parsio were not married, and such a revelation would cause embarrassment, particularly in light of his Catholic faith. Parsio claims that she did not reveal decedent's paternity because Ryan threatened to "cut off ties," including financial support, to her and plaintiff.

After filing her complaint on February 7, 1995, in the Chancery Division, Family Part, plaintiff obtained an order permitting blood and hair samples to be taken from decedent prior to embalming. Cellmark Diagnostics performed genetic testing on samples from decedent, Parsio, and plaintiff.

Cellmark's DNA fingerprint analysis revealed a match between decedent and plaintiff, the probability of which was one in twenty-three million for unrelated persons. DNA blood profiles revealed a 99.99% probability of decedent's paternity, as compared to that of a random Caucasian male. Cellmark's report concluded that decedent was plaintiff's natural father, and decedent's estate has not contested that conclusion.

Plaintiff filed an amended complaint on February 17, 1995, adding Helen Thomas, both individually as decedent's sister and as administratrix of decedent's estate, as a defendant. Defendants then filed a motion for summary judgment. The Family Part granted summary judgment to defendants dismissing the complaint, reasoning that plaintiff had failed to comply with the twenty-three-year limitations period under the Parentage Act, N.J.S.A. 9:17-45(b).

On plaintiff's motion for reconsideration, the Family Part vacated its summary judgment and transferred the matter to the Probate Part. The Appellate Division granted defendants' motion for leave to appeal and stayed further proceedings in the Probate Part pending disposition of the appeal. The Appellate Division reversed the trial court's denial of defendants' motion for summary judgment.

* * *

Our analysis must begin with the legislative enactments that will inform our ultimate decision. The Wills, Descent and Simultaneous Death Act was enacted in 1977 and amended in 1979. The predecessor to the provision that is pertinent to this case provided:

If, for purposes of intestate succession, a relationship of parent and child must be established to determine succession by, through, or from a person.

a. The relationships and rights of an adopted minor child shall be those as provided by section 14 of P.L.1977, c. 367 (C. 9:3-50), and the relationships and rights of an adopted adult shall be as provided in N.J.S. 2A:22-3.

b. In cases not covered by a., a person born out of wedlock is a child of the mother. That person is also a child of the father, if:

(1) The natural parents, before or after the birth of the child, participated in a ceremonial marriage or shall have consummated a common-law marriage where such marriage is recognized as valid in the manner authorized by the law of the place where such marriage took place, even though the attempted marriage is void; or

(2) The paternity is established by an adjudication before the death of the father or is established thereafter by clear and convincing proof, except that the paternity established under this subparagraph is ineffective to qualify the father or his kindred to inherit from or through the child unless the father has openly treated the child as his, and has not refused to support the child.

* * *

In 1982, the Legislature revised the Wills, Descent and Simultaneous Death Act and renamed it an Act for the Administration of Estates—Decedents and Others, now commonly known as the Probate Code. L. 1981, c. 405. Pertinent to this case is N.J.S.A. 3B:5-10, which repealed N.J.S.A. 3A:2A-41 and became effective in 1982. The 1982 version of N.J.S.A. 3B:5-10 provided:

If, for the purposes of intestate succession, a relationship of parent and child must be established to determine succession by, through or from a person, a child born out of wedlock is a child of the mother. That child is also a child of the father, if:

a. The natural parents, before or after the birth of the child, participated in a ceremonial marriage or shall have consummated a common-law marriage where the marriage is recognized as valid in the manner authorized by the law of the place where the marriage took place, even though the attempted marriage is void; or

b. The paternity is established by an adjudication before the death of the father or is established thereafter by clear and convincing proof, except that the paternity established under this subsection is ineffective to qualify the father or his kindred to inherit from or through the child unless the father has openly treated the child as his, and has not refused to support the child.

N.J.S.A. 3B:23-19 of the Probate Code provides a general limitations period for claims brought under that statute. Claims by persons whose names or addresses are unknown must be brought "within a reasonable time and after reasonable notice ... as may be prescribed by the court." N.J.S.A. 3B:23-19. N.J.S.A. 3B:23-20 provides that a person who fails to file a claim within the time required by the court pursuant to N.J.S.A. 3B:23-19 "shall be forever thereafter debarred from all right, title or claim to the decedent's estate."

The 1982 version of N.J.S.A. 3B:5-10(b) is identical to a provision in the Uniform Probate Code of 1969. Unif. Probate Code § 2-109(2)(ii), 8 U.L.A. 67 (1983). That section has alternative provisions, one for jurisdictions that have adopted the Uniform Parentage Act, and the other, followed by New Jersey, for those jurisdictions that have not adopted the Uniform Parentage Act. Id. at 67–68 cmt. Thus, when the Probate Code was modified in 1982, New Jersey had not yet adopted a Parentage Act. That, however, was changed the next year, creating inconsistent methods and standards of proof for establishing parentage under New Jersey's Probate Code and Parentage Act.

* * *

In 1983, the Legislature passed the Parentage Act, which is modeled after the Uniform Parentage Act of 1973. Assembly Judiciary, Law, Public Safety and Defense Committee Statement to Senate Bill No. 888—L. 1983, c. 17. The Legislature enacted the Parentage Act "to establish the principle that regardless of the marital status of the parents, all children and parents have equal rights with respect to each other and to provide a procedure to establish parentage in disputed cases." Ibid.

Procedurally, the Parentage Act establishes several presumptions of paternity in N.J.S.A. 9:17-43(a), and sets forth in section 43(d) the burden of proving paternity absent the existence of such a presumption. Claims to establish paternity must be filed timely: "[n]o action shall be brought under this act more than 5 years after the child attains the age of majority." N.J.S.A. 9:17-45(b). That section effectively imposes a twenty-three-year statute of repose for actions under the Parentage Act, running from the child's date of birth.

N.J.S.A. 9:17-45(b) is analogous to a provision of the Uniform Parentage Act that requires an action to be brought within three years of a child's majority. Unif. Parentage Act §7, 9B U.L.A. 306 (1987). The comment to that Uniform Parentage Act section states that, "[i]n effect, ... this Section provides for a twenty-one-year statute of limitations, except that a late paternity action does not affect laws relating to distribution and closing of decedents' estates or to the determination of heirship." Ibid. cmt. Because the Probate Code and the Parentage Act prior to 1991 provided different methods and standards for establishing parentage, steps were taken to resolve the conflicts.

* * *

The responsibility for attempting to reconcile the conflicting methods and standards of proof in the two acts fell on the New Jersey Law Revision Commission ("Commission"). N.J.S.A. 1:12A-8. In its 1987 annual report to the Legislature pursuant to N.J.S.A. 1:12A-9, the Commission reported that the methods and standards for proving parentage under the Probate Code and the Parentage Act were inconsistent. First Annual Report of the New Jersey Law Revision Commission 3 (1987) ("Law Revision Commission Report"). The focus of the report was limited to the inconsistent burdens of proof required by those two statutes. Ibid. The Commission noted that the Parentage Act specified several presumptions of paternity that could be rebutted by clear and convincing evidence. Ibid. If no presumption of parentage existed, then that issue would be determined by a preponderance of the evidence. N.J.S.A. 9:17-43(d). The Probate Code, on the other hand, required claimants to prove paternity by clear and convincing evidence for post-mortem claims under the 1982 version of N.J.S.A. 3B:5-10(b).

The Commission explained that "the version of the [Uniform] Probate Code chosen for N.J.S. 3B:5-10 was never intended to be enacted in jurisdictions which accepted the [Uniform] Parentage Act," and that the Legislature had enacted the version of the Uniform Probate Code provision that reflected the absence of a Parentage Act in New Jersey at that time. Law Revision Commission Report, supra, at 3–4. The Commission recommended that the Legislature amend the Probate Code to reflect New Jersey's adoption of the Uniform Parentage Act in 1983, and to allow children born out of wedlock to prove paternity for heirship purposes by using the more permissive standards of the Parentage Act. Id. at 4. The Commission stated that such an amendment would promote "the modern principle that the parent-child relationship extends equally, irrespective of the marital state of the parents." Ibid.

Consistent with the Commission's recommendation, in 1991 the Legislature revised N.J.S.A. 3B:5-10 to provide:

> If, for the purposes of intestate succession, a relationship of parent and child must be established to determine succession by, through, or from a person, in cases not covered by N.J.S. 3B:5-9, [for adoption,] a person is the child of the person's parents regardless of the marital state of the person's parents, and the parent and child relationship may be established as provided by the "New Jersey Parentage Act," P.L.1983, c. 17 (C. 9:17-38 et seq.).

* * *

The parties agree that in view of the 1991 amendment, plaintiff must follow the methods and standards of proof outlined in the Parentage Act. They also agree that the DNA test results establish that John Ryan is plaintiff's father. The parties disagree, however, on whether plaintiff's claim against the estate is time barred.

* * *

Plaintiff argues that the Probate Code's statute of limitations, N.J.S.A. 3B:23-19, applies to her claim. That section provides that "the court may require all those persons whose names or addresses are unknown, to appear or file their [intestacy] claims … within a reasonable time and after reasonable notice by publication or otherwise, as may be prescribed by the court." Ibid. Plaintiff contends that the 1991 amendment to the Probate Code was intended to incorporate only the favorable methods and standards of proof found in the Parentage Act without altering the limitations period for filing her claim under N.J.S.A. 3B:23-19.

Defendants argue that the Appellate Division was correct in applying the limitations provision of the Parentage Act, N.J.S.A. 9:17-45(b), because it is more specific and was enacted more recently than N.J.S.A. 3B:23-19. 290 N.J.Super. at 471, 676 A.2d 144 (citing 3A Norman J. Singer, Sutherland on Statutory Construction, § 70.03 (5th ed. 1992) ("When two or more statutes of limitation deal with the same subject matter, the statute which is more recent and specific will prevail over the older and more general one.")).

The critical question is whether the Legislature intended in 1991 to change the Probate Code's statute of limitations, N.J.S.A. 3B:23-19. To answer that question, we must interpret the amendment. We have consistently held that when interpreting a statute, "courts must seek to fulfill the statutory objective 'so far as the terms of the legislation and proper consideration of the interests of those subject to it will fairly permit.'" State v. Haliski, 140 N.J. 1, 9, 656 A.2d 1246 (1995) (quoting State v. Gill, 47 N.J. 441, 444, 221 A.2d 521 (1966)); Merin v. Maglaki, 126 N.J. 430, 435, 599 A.2d 1256 (1992). A court should interpret a statute in a way that advances "the sense and meaning fairly deducible from the context." Lesniak v. Budzash, 133 N.J. 1, 14, 626 A.2d 1073 (1993).

The first consideration when interpreting a statute is the statute's plain meaning. State v. Szemple, 135 N.J. 406, 421, 640 A.2d 817 (1994); Merin, supra, 126 N.J. at

434, 599 A.2d 1256; Town of Morristown v. Woman's Club, 124 N.J. 605, 610, 592 A.2d 216 (1991). If different interpretations exist, then the statute's meaning is not obvious or self-evident on its face. Szemple, supra, 135 N.J. at 422, 640 A.2d 817; GE Solid State, Inc. v. Director, Div. of Taxation, 132 N.J. 298, 307, 625 A.2d 468 (1993). When a statute is ambiguous, a court's function is to ascertain and to effectuate the Legislature's intent. Szemple, supra, 135 N.J. at 422, 640 A.2d 817 (citing Cedar Cove, Inc. v. Stanzione, 122 N.J. 202, 213, 584 A.2d 784 (1991)). Extrinsic aids, such as legislative history, committee reports, and contemporaneous construction, may be used to help resolve any ambiguity and to ascertain the true intent of the Legislature. Ibid.

The legislative history regarding the 1991 amendment includes the Senate Judiciary Committee's Statement that accompanied the proposed amendment. It provides:

'This bill is intended to resolve a potential conflict between N.J.S.A. 3B:5-10 part of New Jersey's Probate Code and the 'New Jersey Parentage Act,' P.L.1983, c. 17 (C. 9:17-38 et seq.) with regard to the standard for the determination of the parentage of children born out of wedlock.

* * *

The Parentage Act which was enacted in 1983 sets procedures and standards for determining parentage of children born out of wedlock. *These procedures were intended to be applicable in all actions. In order to insure that a determination of parentage under the Parentage Act would also be applicable in probate matters, this bill would amend 3B:5-10 to provide that for purposes of intestate succession the parent-child relationship may be established as provided in the Parentage Act.*'

* * *

As noted earlier, the 1991 amendment to N.J.S.A. 3B:5-10 was in response to the 1987 report submitted by the Law Revision Commission that emphasized the different burdens of proof for establishing parentage under the Parentage Act and under the Probate Code. The Parentage Act creates rebuttable presumptions of parentage under some circumstances. N.J.S.A. 9:17-43(a). In those circumstances, a putative father may overcome that presumption only by clear and convincing evidence. N.J.S.A. 9:17-43(b). Absent a designated presumption of parentage, the burden of proof is by a preponderance of the evidence. N.J.S.A. 9:17-43(d). In contrast, under the Probate Code prior to the 1991 amendment, a parentage action to prove heirship after the decedent's death required a claimant to establish heirship by clear and convincing proof. N.J.S.A. 3B:5-10(b).

What emerges from a review of the legislative history is an intent to change the Probate Code's provision, N.J.S.A. 3B:5-10, to create the same burden of proof existing under the Parentage Act. Consistent with that intent, the Senate Committee's Statement reveals that the only articulated purpose of the amendment was to resolve a potential conflict between the Probate Code and the Parentage Act regarding "the standard for the determination of the parentage of children born out of wedlock." Senate Judiciary Committee Statement to Senate Bill No. 1346—L. 1991, c. 22. The word "standard" most commonly refers to the burden of proof in a cause of action. See Del Tufo v. Township of Old Bridge, 147 N.J. 90, 98, 685 A.2d 1267 (1996) (using term "standard" to refer to burden of proof); see also SSI Med. Servs., Inc. v. State, 146 N.J. 614, 617, 685 A.2d 1 (1996) (same).

That conclusion is supported by the fact that the Commission discussed only the inconsistent burden of proof issue. The Commission recommended changing the burden of proof under the Probate Code because of the increased reliance on scientific tests under the Parentage Act to establish paternity. Hence, the Commission recommended that the Legislature

> accept the more clear and specific rules for the determination of parent-child relationships of the Parentage Act and its reflection of the modern principle that scientific tests can be used to make an accurate determination of parentage in the majority of cases.

* * *

We conclude that the Legislature intended the 1991 amendment to N.J.S.A. 3B:5-10 to amend only the standard of proof. The Legislature was convinced that, given the reliable scientific tests used under the Parentage Act to establish parentage, it no longer made sense to require a higher burden of proof under the Probate Code to establish the identical fact. Consequently, the Legislature's use of the terms "standard for the determination of parentage of children," intended for the word "standard" to have its common meaning, namely, the burden of proof.

* * *

Apart from the legislative history revealing that the 1991 amendment intended to change only the burden of proof for establishing parentage under the Probate Code, the Parentage Act and the Probate Code are independent statutes designed to address different primary rights. The purpose of the Parentage Act is to establish "the legal relationship ... between a child and the child's natural or adoptive parents, incident to which the law confers or imposes rights, privileges, duties, and obligations." N.J.S.A. 9:17-39. Child support is the major concern under the Parentage Act. The purpose of the Probate Code, on the other hand, is to determine the devolution of a decedent's real and personal property. N.J.S.A. 3B:1-3. The different purposes the two statutes serve, help to explain why the Legislature contemplated different periods of limitations for filing claims under those statutes.

It is well established in New Jersey that parents have a duty to support their children from the date of birth until the children are emancipated, which is presumed to occur upon the age of majority. Newburgh v. Arrigo, 88 N.J. 529, 543, 443 A.2d 1031 (1982). Because the right to support accrues on the date of birth and ends on emancipation, it is fair to apply N.J.S.A. 9:17-45(b) to claims for support.

Although plaintiff received financial and emotional support from decedent for many years before his death, decedent's parentage was not established before plaintiff reached her twenty-third birthday as required by N.J.S.A. 9:17-45(b). She was not told that decedent was her father until she was thirty-one-years old, at which time she was not in need of his support. Indeed, the law imposed no obligation for him to support her at that time. Consequently, application of the Parentage Act's statute of limitations to any support claim that she might have filed at the age of thirty-one would have been fair because (1) that period balances a claimant's right to support with the State's interest in requiring prompt filing of parentage actions, see Unif. Parentage Act §7, 9B U.L.A. 306-07 cmt. (1987); and (2) a parent is relieved of the duty to provide support upon the child's emancipation. Newburgh, supra, 88 N.J. at 543, 443 A.2d 1031.

In contrast to children who file support claims, which accrue on the date of birth, potential heirs have no right to share in an estate until the death of the decedent. By definition under the Probate Code, heirs are "those persons ... who are entitled under the statutes of intestate succession to the property of a decedent." N.J.S.A. 3B:1-1. Applying N.J.S.A. 9:17-45(b) to actions under the Probate Code would create a statute of repose that commences on the birth of a potential heir, rather than a statute of limitations running from the decedent's death. Indeed, the Parentage Act provides that it does not affect the time within which an heirship claim must be filed. N.J.S.A. 9:17-45(f). That section provides further evidence that claims under the Probate Code and Parentage Act are subject to independent limitations periods. To hold otherwise would grant heirship immunity to parents of children who are born out of wedlock and do not establish parentage before reaching age twenty-three. That would terminate many claims before they accrue. E.A. Williams, Inc. v. Russo Dev. Corp., 82 N.J. 160, 167, 411 A.2d 697 (1980). To allow that to occur would be contrary to the Legislature's recognition in 1991 that "a person is the child of the person's parents regardless of the marital state of the person's parents." N.J.S.A. 3B:5-10.

Furthermore, the purpose of the 1991 amendment was to make it easier, not harder or impossible, for persons born out of wedlock to establish heirship. Before the 1991 amendment, a child's heirship could be established after the death of a parent, regardless of the age of the child. N.J.S.A. 3A:2A-41(b)(2) (repealed 1982). Absent some express contrary indication, it is highly unlikely that the Legislature would reduce the limitations period for filing heirship claims. A reduction in the limitations period would indeed be anomalous, given that our society has been moving gradually away from imposing legal disadvantages on children born out of wedlock who bear no responsibility for their parents'"irresponsible liaisons beyond the bonds of marriage." Weber v. Aetna Cas. & Sur. Co., 406 U.S. 164, 175, 92 S.Ct. 1400, 1406, 31 L.Ed.2d 768, 779 (1972). "[P]enalizing the illegitimate child is an ineffectual—as well as an unjust—way of deterring the parent." Id. at 175, 92 S.Ct. at 1407, 31 L.Ed.2d at 779. Finally, the comment to the limitations provision of the Uniform Parentage Act §7, 9B U.L.A. 306 (1987), is persuasive. That comment states that, "[i]n effect, ... this Section provides for a twenty-one-year statute of limitations, except that *a late paternity action does not affect laws relating to distribution and closing of decedents' estates or to the determination of heirship.*" Ibid. cmt. (emphasis added). Thus, the Uniform Parentage Act was not intended to affect the limitations period for actions to prove heirship. Because our Parentage Act is modeled after the Uniform Parentage Act, and for the other reasons stated, we hold that the Legislature did not intend its 1991 amendment to change the Probate Code's limitation on when claims can be filed thereunder for determination of heirship.

Our holding that the 1991 amendment changes only the standard for proving parentage for heirship purposes should have no effect on estate planning. It is inconceivable that since the amendment, fathers of children born out of wedlock have made their estate planning decisions based on whether post-mortem parentage claims for heirship purposes had to be established by a preponderance of the evidence or by clear and convincing evidence, as was required before the amendment. In the present case, the social opprobrium associated with having a liaison with a married woman is more likely to have influenced decedent not to include plaintiff in his estate planning by publicly acknowledging her as his daughter or by providing for her in a will.

* * *

We also reject the Appellate Division's reasoning that the twenty-three-year period of repose should be imposed in order to guard against spurious claims. 290 N.J.Super. at 476–77, 676 A.2d 144. The need to prevent fraudulent claims has been "substantially alleviated by recent scientific developments in blood testing dramatically reducing the possibility that a defendant will be falsely accused of being the illegitimate child's father." Mills v. Habluetzel, 456 U.S. 91, 104 n. 2, 102 S.Ct. 1549, 1557 n. 2, 71 L.Ed.2d 770, 781 n. 2 (1982) (O'Connor, J., concurring); see also Pickett v. Brown, 462 U.S. 1, 17, 103 S.Ct. 2199, 2208, 76 L.Ed.2d 372, 385 (1983) (stating that "the relationship between a statute of limitations and the State's interest in preventing the litigation of stale or fraudulent paternity claims has become more attenuated as scientific advances in blood testing have alleviated the problems of proof surrounding paternity actions"); State v. Marcus, 294 N.J.Super. 267, 279, 683 A.2d 221 (App.Div.1996) (noting general acceptance of DNA analysis by scientific community and courts); State v. Williams, 252 N.J.Super. 369, 380, 599 A.2d 960 (Law Div.1991) (stating that "[i]t is generally accepted that [DNA testing] can limit the spectrum of potential donors of a blood specimen to one out of every 10 million persons").

Another source has noted that

> [j]udicial recognition of the scientific acceptance of the foundations of DNA analysis is consistent with our conclusion that the methods of DNA analysis surveyed in this report are firmly grounded in molecular biology. When [DNA] profiling is done with due care, the results are highly reproducible.... [T]here seems little doubt in the courtroom, as in the laboratory, that properly conducted [DNA] profiling is a scientifically acceptable procedure....
>
> [Committee on DNA Forensic Science, National Research Council, The Evaluation of Forensic DNA Evidence 176 (1996) (footnote omitted).] * * *

In another decision, the United States Supreme Court noted that "increasingly sophisticated tests for genetic markers permit the exclusion of over 99% of those who might be accused of paternity, regardless of the age of the child." Clark v. Jeter, 486 U.S. 456, 465, 108 S.Ct. 1910, 1916, 100 L.Ed.2d 465, 474 (1988) (emphasis added). Indeed, in the present case, the Cellmark report has revealed a 99.99% probability of decedent's paternity and a DNA fingerprint match with decedent, the probability of which is one in twenty-three million for unrelated people. In the face of such compelling evidence, few spurious claims will go undetected.

* * *

We hold that N.J.S.A. 3B:23-19 controls and that the 1991 amendment to N.J.S.A. 3B:5-10 did not change the Probate Code's statute of limitations. That statute allows an out-of-wedlock child of a deceased parent to file an heirship claim with the personal representative of the decedent's estate within the time the court has deemed reasonable for the filing of claims. Here, there can be no dispute over whether plaintiff filed her claim within a reasonable time. Ryan died on February 6, 1995, and plaintiff filed her claim on February 7, 1995.

* * *

The judgment of the Appellate Division is reversed. The matter is remanded to the Chancery Division, Probate Part to dispose of the complaint on the merits.

For reversal and remandment—Chief Justice PORITZ, and Justices HANDLER, POLLOCK, O'HERN, GARIBALDI, STEIN and COLEMAN * * * .

2. *Constitutionality of Claims*

Since 1968, the United States Supreme Court has decided more than 20 cases involving statutory tests by which states have sought to establish claims by non-marital children. Most of the state statutes were invalidated as violating the Equal Protection Clause of the Fourteenth Amendment. *See, e.g.,* Trimble v. Gordon, 430 U.S. 762, 97 S. Ct. 1459 (1977) (difficulties of proving paternity do not justify the total statutory disinheritance of illegitimate children, whose fathers die intestate). Some of the state statutes were upheld as rationally related to the state's interest in maintaining an accurate and efficient system for the disposition of property at death. *See, e.g.,* Parham v. Hughes, 441 U.S. 347, 99 S. Ct. 1742 (1979). Unmarried, biological fathers who develop a substantial relationship with their children must be afforded the same rights in regard to the child as the child's mother. *See, e.g.,* Lehr v. Robertson, 463 U.S. 248, 103 S. Ct. 2895 (1983). The Supreme Court will allow the states to make rational demands in providing for a fair and speedy administration of decedents' estates if the demands are applied equally and without gender bias.

3. *Proof of Paternity*

Increasingly, family paternity is being identified through advanced technology— DNA testing being the most recent method—allowing for suits by non-marital children against the estates of putative fathers. *See* Angela R. Arkin, *Evidentiary and Related Issues in Paternity Proceedings, in* VITECK, DISPUTED PATERNITY PROCEEDINGS, 5th ed., § 3.07 (Matthew Bender, 1998). Because DNA testing is relatively new, the admissibility of test results and procedures differ from state to state. Increasingly, courts admit the evidence, holding that the tests are simply extensions of existing state statutes that admit blood tests and genetic evidence to prove paternity. State acceptance is spurred, in part, by federal legislation, anxious to prove paternity and collect child support from putative fathers. *See, e.g.,* 42 U.S.C. §666(a)(5)(F)(I) (2003) (providing that genetic test results must be admitted as evidence so long as they are of a type generally acknowledged as reliable and are performed by an accredited laboratory).

It appears that DNA testing will allow for accurate paternity testing long after the death of the decedent. For example, DHL Corporation founder Larry Lee Hillbloom left his $500 million estate to charity but, allegedly, left behind a number of non-marital children from different Pacific-Island women, with whom he allegedly had sex. After his death, the women petitioned on behalf of their children to establish the children as pretermitted heirs to Mr. Hillbloom's estate. Proof of paternity was based on DNA samples taken from a mole from his body, years before, during a routine surgical procedure and stored in medical laboratories. *See* Peter Waldman, *Heir Freight: How the Strange Life of a DHL Founder Left His Estate a Mess,* WALL ST. J., May 15, 1996, at A1. *See also* Charles Nelson Le Ray, *Implications of DNA Technology on Posthumous Paternity Determination: Deciding the Facts When Daddy Can't Give His Opinion,* 35 B.C. L. REV. 747 (1994). Courts have even allowed exhumation of an alleged father's remains where the petitioner has established reasonable cause. *See* Wawrykow v. Simonich, 438 Pa. Super. 340, 652 A.2d 843 (1994).

Additional issues arise because of advances in technology. For example, DNA testing allows for the testing of third parties to establish paternity; this procedure invites further issues of privacy protection. *See, e.g.,* Lach v. Welch, 1997 WL 536330 (Conn.

Super. 1997) (court ordered DNA testing of putative grandparents). A minority of states have passed statutes limiting the accessibility of genetic information because of the potential of abuse. *See, e.g.,* Or. REV. STAT. ANN. §§ 192.531–549 (2003). It is certain that additional privacy issues will arise as the need to establish paternity clashes with the right of individuals to be secure in the privacy of their bodily composition. *See, e.g.,* Christopher L. Blakesley, *Scientific Testing and Proof of Paternity: Some Controversy and Key Issues for Family Law Counsel,* 57 LA. L. REV. 379 (1997); Michael M.J. Lin, *Conferring a Federal Property Right in Genetic Material: Stepping into the Future with the Genetic Privacy Act,* 22 AM. J. L. & MED. 109 (1996).

4. Presumptive Paternity

DNA testing is expensive and involves issues of privacy. Thus, many states use presumptions to establish paternity. Genetic testing is a means by which to rebut the presumption. States use these presumptions differently. For example, some states may provide that, if a putative father seeks to rebut the presumption of paternity that arises because of marriage, the putative father must make a preliminary showing that rebutting paternity would serve the best interests of the child. Thus, if a child is born to a married couple and another man, not married to the mother, wishes to rebut the presumption that the child is the natural child of the man to whom the mother is married, the putative father must make a preliminary showing that it would be in the child's bet interest for the presumption of paternity to be rebutted. Other courts presume paternity by the married husband if the child is conceived when the mother is married. *Cf.* Aichele v. Hodge, 259 Mich. App. 146, 673 N.W.2d 452 (2003) *and* In re Paternity of Adam, 273 Mont. 351, 903 P.2d 207 (1995), *cert. denied,* 517 U.S. 1156, 116 S. Ct. 1544 (1996).

The presumption of paternity arising because of marriage is based on the best interests of the child and the aversion to declaring a child illegitimate. *See* Michael H. v. Gerald D., 491 U.S. 110, 109 S. Ct. 2333 (1989). If a child grows up in a household thinking that his or her parents are just that—parents—what is the impact on the child if paternity is established in another person? California has gone through a long history of presumptions of paternity, each seeking to protect the best interest of a child. Today, California statutorily provides that a child of a marriage in which the husband is not sterile or impotent is conclusively presumed to be a child of the marriage unless a blood test, filed within two years of the child's birth, proves otherwise. The motion for a blood test may be brought by the husband, the wife, the presumed father, or the child, through the guardian ad litem. Exceptions are made for artificial insemination. For these provisions, see CAL. FAM. CODE §§ 7540, 7541, 7613 (2004).

Uniform Parentage Act of 2000

§ 204. Presumption of Paternity.

(a) A man is presumed to be the father of a child if:

(1) he and the mother of the child are married to each other and the child is born during the marriage;

(2) he and the mother of the child were married to each other and the child is born within 300 days after the marriage is terminated by death, annulment, declaration of invalidity, or divorce [, or after a decree of separation];

(3) before the birth of the child, he and the mother of the child married each other in apparent compliance with law, even if the attempted marriage is or could be declared invalid, and the child is born during the invalid marriage or within 300 days after its termination by death, annulment, declaration of invalidity, or divorce [, or after a decree of separation];

(4) after the birth of the child, he and the mother of the child married each other in apparent compliance with law, whether or not the marriage is or could be declared invalid, and he voluntarily asserted his paternity of the child, and:

> (A) the assertion is in a record filed with [state agency maintaining birth records];

> (B) he agreed to be and is named as the child's father on the child's birth certificate; or

> (C) he promised in a record to support the child as his own; or

(5) for the first two years of the child's life, he resided in the same household with the child and openly held out the child as his own.

(b) A presumption of paternity established under this section may be rebutted only by an adjudication under [Article] 6 [proceeding to adjudicate parentage].

G. Reproduction and the Biological Revolution

With the birth of "Baby Louise" in 1978, human fertilization through artificial means became a part of the process by which children are born. Baby Louise was the first child conceived through in vitro fertilization. First developed in Great Britain, the procedure involved taking eggs from a woman's ovary and fertilizing them with sperm from the prospective father. The fertilized egg was then artificially inserted into the mother, who carried the embryo to term. *See* Roy Reed, N.Y. TIMES, July 27, 1978, at A1, col. 2. The procedure and the legal ramifications of paternity have invited discussion and confusion in the courts. The following decision is an example.

In re Marriage of Buzzanca
Court of Appeal, Fourth District, 1998
61 Cal.App.4th 1410, 72 Cal.Rptr.2d 280.

SILLS, P. J.

* * *

Jaycee was born because Luanne and John Buzzanca agreed to have an embryo genetically unrelated to either of them implanted in a woman—a surrogate—who would carry and give birth to the child for them. After the fertilization, implantation and pregnancy, Luanne and John split up, and the question of who are Jaycee's lawful parents came before the trial court.

Luanne claimed that she and her erstwhile husband were the lawful parents, but John disclaimed any responsibility, financial or otherwise. The woman who gave birth also appeared in the case to make it clear that she made no claim to the child.

The trial court then reached an extraordinary conclusion: Jaycee had *no* lawful parents. First, the woman who gave birth to Jaycee was not the mother; the court had—astonishingly—already accepted a stipulation that neither she nor her husband were the "biological" parents. Second, Luanne was not the mother. According to the trial court, she could not be the mother because she had neither contributed the egg nor given birth. And John could not be the father, because, not having contributed the sperm, he had no biological relationship with the child.

We disagree. Let us get right to the point: Jaycee never would have been born had not Luanne and John both agreed to have a fertilized egg implanted in a surrogate.

The trial judge erred because he assumed that legal motherhood, under the relevant California statutes, could *only* be established in one of two ways, either by giving birth or by contributing an egg. He failed to consider the substantial and well-settled body of law holding that there are times when *fatherhood* can be established by conduct apart from giving birth or being genetically related to a child. The typical example is when an infertile husband consents to allowing his wife to be artificially inseminated. As our Supreme Court noted in such a situation over 30 years ago, the husband is the "lawful father" because he *consented* to the procreation of the child. (See People v. Sorensen (1968) 68 Cal.2d 280, 284–286 [66 Cal.Rptr. 7, 437 P.2d 495, 25 A.L.R.3d 1093].)

The same rule which makes a husband the lawful father of a child born because of his consent to artificial insemination should be applied here—by the same parity of reasoning that guided our Supreme Court in the first surrogacy case, Johnson v. Calvert (1993) 5 Cal.4th 84 [19 Cal.Rptr.2d 494, 851 P.2d 776]—to both husband and wife. Just as a husband is deemed to be the lawful father of a child unrelated to him when his wife gives birth after artificial insemination, so should a husband *and* wife be deemed the lawful parents of a child after a surrogate bears a biologically unrelated child on their behalf. In each instance, a child is procreated because a medical procedure was initiated and consented to by intended parents. The only difference is that in this case—unlike artificial insemination—there is no reason to distinguish between husband and wife. We therefore must reverse the trial court's judgment and direct that a new judgment be entered, declaring that both Luanne and John are the lawful parents of Jaycee. * * *

John filed his petition for dissolution of marriage on March 30, 1995, alleging there were no children of the marriage. Luanne filed her response on April 20, alleging that the parties were expecting a child by way of surrogate contract. Jaycee was born six days later. In September 1996 Luanne filed a separate petition to establish herself as Jaycee's mother. Her action was consolidated into the dissolution case. In February 1997, the court accepted a stipulation that the woman who agreed to carry the child, and her husband, were not the "biological parents" of the child. * * * At a hearing held in March, based entirely on oral argument and offers of proof, the trial court determined that Luanne was not the lawful mother of the child and therefore John could not be the lawful father or owe any support.

* * *

In addition to blood tests there are several other ways the [Uniform Parentage] Act allows paternity to be established. Those ways are not necessarily related at all to any biological tie. Thus, under the Act, paternity may be established by:

-marrying, remaining married to, or attempting to marry the child's mother when she gives birth (see Fam. Code, § 7611, subds. (a) & (b));

-marrying the child's mother after the child's birth and either consenting to being named as the father on the birth certificate (Fam. Code, § 7611, subd. (c)(1)) or making a written promise to support the child (see Fam. Code, § 7611, subd. (c)(2)).

A man may also be deemed a father under the Act in the case of artificial insemination of his wife, as provided by section 7613 of the Family Code. * * * To track the words of the statute: "If, under the supervision of a licensed physician and surgeon and with the consent of her husband, a wife is inseminated artificially with semen donated by a man not her husband, the husband is treated in law as if he were the natural father of a child thereby conceived." * * *

As noted in *Johnson*, "courts must construe statutes in factual settings not contemplated by the enacting legislature." (Johnson v. Calvert, supra, 5 Cal.4th at p. 89.) So it is, of course, true that application of the artificial insemination statute to a gestational surrogacy case where the genetic donors are unknown to the court may not have been contemplated by the Legislature. Even so, the two kinds of artificial reproduction are *exactly* analogous in this crucial respect: Both contemplate the procreation of a child by the consent to a medical procedure of someone who intends to raise the child but who otherwise does not have any biological tie.

If a husband who consents to artificial insemination under Family Code section 7613 is "treated in law" as the father of the child by virtue of his consent, there is no reason the result should be any different in the case of a married couple who consent to in vitro fertilization by unknown donors and subsequent implantation into a woman who is, as a surrogate, willing to carry the embryo to term for them. The statute is, after all, the clearest expression of past legislative intent when the Legislature did contemplate a situation where a person who caused a child to come into being had no biological relationship to the child.

Indeed, the establishment of fatherhood and the consequent duty to support when a husband consents to the artificial insemination of his wife is one of the well-established rules in family law. * * * The leading case in the country (so described by a New York family court in In re Adoption of Anonymous (1973) 74 Misc.2d 99 [345 N.Y.S.2d 430, 433]) is People v. Sorensen, supra, 68 Cal.2d 280, in which our Supreme Court held that a man could even be *criminally* liable for failing to pay for the support of a child born to his wife during the marriage as a result of artificial insemination using sperm from an anonymous donor.

In *Sorensen*, the high court emphasized the role of the husband in *causing* the birth, even though he had no biological connection to the child: "[A] reasonable man who … actively participates and consents to his wife's artificial insemination in the hope that a child will be produced whom they will treat as their own, *knows that such behavior carries with it the legal responsibilities of fatherhood and criminal responsibility for nonsupport.*" (68 Cal.2d at p. 285, italics added.) The court went on to say that the husband was "directly responsible" for the "existence" of the child and repeated the point that "without defendant's active participation and consent the child would not have been procreated." (Ibid.)

Sorensen expresses a rule universally in tune with other jurisdictions. "Almost exclusively, courts which have addressed this issue have assigned parental responsibility to the husband based on conduct evidencing his consent to the artificial insemination." (In re Baby Doe (1987) 291 S.C. 389 [353 S.E.2d 877, 878]; accord, Gursky v. Gursky (1963) 39 Misc.2d 1083 [242 N.Y.S.2d 406, 411–412] [even though child was not technically "legitimate" under New York law at the time, husband's conduct in consenting to the artificial insemination properly invoked application of the doctrine of equitable estoppel requiring him to support the child]; Anonymous v. Anonymous (1964) 41 Misc.2d 886 [246 N.Y.S.2d 835, 836–837] [following *Gursky*]; K.S. v. G.S. (1981) 182 N.J. Super. 102 [440 A.2d 64, 68] [because husband did not offer clear and convincing evidence that he had *withdrawn* his consent to artificial insemination procedure, he was bound by initial consent given earlier and accordingly held to be lawful father of the child]; In re Marriage of Adams (1988) 174 Ill.App.3d 595 [124 Ill.Dec. 184, 528 N.E.2d 1075, 1087] [affirming child support award where trial court had determined there was "actual consent" to artificial insemination]; * * * K.B. v. N.B. (Tex.Ct.App. 1991) 811 S.W.2d 634, 639] [even though husband did not consent in writing to insemination procedure, his full knowledge of the facts and willing participation in the artificial insemination, involvement in child birth classes, speaking of the child as "our baby" and passage of time before repudiation established that he ratified procedure and was therefore liable for child support]; Levin v. Levin (Ind. 1994) 645 N.E.2d 601, 605 [consent of husband to wife's artificial insemination meant obligation to support because child was a "child of the marriage," the same as if the child had been adopted during the marriage].)

One New York family court even went so far as to hold the lesbian partner of a woman who was artificially inseminated responsible for the support of two children where the partner had dressed as a man and the couple had obtained a marriage license and a wedding ceremony had been performed prior to the inseminations. (Karin T. v. Michael T. (1985) 127 Misc.2d 14 [484 N.Y.S.2d 780].) * * * Echoing the themes of causation and estoppel which underlie the cases, the court noted that the lesbian partner had "by her course of conduct in this case ... brought into the world two innocent children" and should not "be allowed to benefit" from her acts to the detriment of the children and public generally. (484 N.Y.S.2d at p. 784.) * * *

Indeed, in the one case we are aware of where the court did not hold that the husband had a support obligation, the reason was *not* the absence of a biological relationship as such, but because of actual lack of consent to the insemination procedure. (See In re Marriage of Witbeck-Wildhagen (1996) 281 Ill.App.3d 502 [217 Ill.Dec. 329, 667 N.E.2d 122, 125-126] [it would be "unjust" to impose support obligation on husband who never consented to the artificial insemination].)

It must also be noted that in applying the artificial insemination statute to a case where a party has caused a child to be brought into the world, the statutory policy is really echoing a more fundamental idea—a sort of *grundnorm* to borrow Hans Kelsen's famous jurisprudential word—already established in the case law. That idea is often summed up in the legal term "estoppel." Estoppel is an ungainly word from the Middle French (from the word meaning "bung" or "stopper") expressing the law's distaste for inconsistent actions and positions—like consenting to an act which brings a child into existence and then turning around and disclaiming any responsibility.

While the Johnson v. Calvert court was able to predicate its decision on the Act rather than making up the result out of whole cloth, it is also true that California courts, prior to the enactment of the Act, had based certain decisions establishing paternity merely on the common law doctrine of estoppel. We have already discussed one of those decisions, People v. Sorensen, in detail. There an ex-husband was held, in light of his role in causing the birth of the child, to be estopped from disclaiming responsibility. Common law estoppel was also the basis for establishing paternity and its concomitant responsibility as far back as the 1961 decision of Clevenger v. Clevenger (1961) 189 Cal.App.2d 658, 662 [11 Cal.Rptr. 707, 90 A.L.R.2d 569] (husband who took illegitimate child into his home and held child out as his own "estopped" to assert illegitimacy and "avoid liability for its support").

There is no need in the present case to predicate our decision on common law estoppel alone, though the doctrine certainly applies. The estoppel concept, after all, is *already* inherent in the artificial insemination statute. In essence, Family Code section 7613 is nothing more than the codification of the common law rule articulated in *Sorensen*: By consenting to a medical procedure which results in the birth of a child—which the *Sorensen* court has held establishes parenthood by common law estoppel—a husband incurs the legal status and responsibility of fatherhood. (See People v. Sorensen, supra, 68 Cal.2d at p. 285.)

John argues that the artificial insemination statute should not be applied because, after all, his wife did not give birth. But for purposes of the statute with its core idea of estoppel, the fact that Luanne did not give birth is irrelevant. The statute contemplates the establishment of lawful fatherhood in a situation where an intended father has no biological relationship to a child who is procreated as a result of the father's (as well as the mother's) *consent* to a medical procedure.

* * *

In the present case Luanne is situated like a husband in an artificial insemination case whose consent triggers a medical procedure which results in a pregnancy and eventual birth of a child. Her motherhood may therefore be established "under this part," by virtue of that consent. In light of our conclusion, John's argument that the surrogate should be declared the lawful mother disintegrates. The case is now postured like the Johnson v. Calvert case, where motherhood could have been "established" in either of two women under the Act, and the tie broken by noting the intent to parent as expressed in the surrogacy contract. (See Johnson v. Calvert, supra, 5 Cal.4th at p. 93.) The only difference is that this case is not even close as between Luanne and the surrogate. Not only was Luanne the clearly intended mother, no bona fide attempt has been made to establish the surrogate as the lawful mother. * * *

We should also add that neither could the woman whose egg was used in the fertilization or implantation make any claim to motherhood, even if she were to come forward at this late date. Again, as between two women who would both be able to establish motherhood under the Act, the *Johnson* decision would mandate that the tie be broken in favor of the intended parent, in this case, Luanne.

* * *

In the case before us, we are not concerned, as John would have us believe, with a question of the enforceability of the oral and written surrogacy contracts into which he entered with Luanne. This case is not about "transferring" parenthood pursuant to those agreements. We are, rather, concerned with the consequences of those agreements as *acts* which *caused the birth* of a child.

The legal paradigm adopted by the trial court, and now urged upon us by John, is one where all forms of artificial reproduction in which intended parents have no biological relationship with the child result in legal parentlessness. It means that, absent adoption, such children will be dependents of the state. One might describe this paradigm as the "adoption default" model: The idea is that by not specifically addressing some permutation of artificial reproduction, the Legislature has, in effect, set the default switch on adoption. The underlying theory seems to be that when intended parents resort to artificial reproduction without biological tie the Legislature wanted them to be *screened* first through the adoption system. (Thus John, in his brief, argues that a surrogacy contract must be "subject to state oversight.")

The "adoption default" model is, however, inconsistent with both statutory law and the Supreme Court's *Johnson* decision. As to the statutory law, the Legislature has already made it perfectly clear that public policy (and, we might add, common sense) favors, whenever possible, the establishment of legal parenthood with the concomitant responsibility. Family Code section 7570, subdivision (a) states that "There is a compelling state interest in establishing paternity for all children." The statute then goes on to elaborate why establishing paternity is a good thing: It means someone besides the taxpayers will be responsible for the child: "Establishing paternity is the first step toward a child support award, which, in turn, provides children with equal rights and access to benefits...." (Ibid.) In light of this strong public policy, the statutes which follow section 7570, subdivision (a) seek to provide a "simple system allowing for the establishment of voluntary paternity." (Fam. Code, § 7570, subd. (b).)

Section 7570 necessarily expresses a legislative policy applicable to maternity as well. It would be lunatic for the Legislature to declare that establishing paternity is a compelling state interest yet conclude that establishing maternity is not. The obvious reason the Legislature did not include an explicit parallel statement on "maternity" is that the issue almost never arises except for extraordinary cases involving artificial reproduction.

Very plainly, the Legislature has declared its preference for assigning *individual* responsibility for the care and maintenance of children; not leaving the task to the taxpayers. That is why it has gone to considerable lengths to ensure that parents will live up to their support obligations. (Cf. Moss v. Superior Court (1998) 17 Cal.4th 396, 424 [71 Cal.Rptr.2d 215, 950 P.2d 59] [noting legislative priority put on child support obligations].) The adoption default theory flies in the face of that legislative value judgment.

* * *

In the case before us, there is absolutely no dispute that Luanne caused Jaycee's conception and birth by initiating the surrogacy arrangement whereby an embryo was implanted into a woman who agreed to carry the baby to term on Luanne's behalf. In applying the artificial insemination statute to a gestational surrogacy case where the genetic donors are unknown, there is, as we have indicated above, no reason to distinguish *between* husbands and wives. Both are equally situated from the point of view of consenting to an act which brings a child into being. * * * Accordingly, Luanne should have been declared the lawful mother of Jaycee.

* * *

Even though neither Luanne nor John are biologically related to Jaycee, they are still her lawful parents given their initiating role as the intended parents in her conception and birth. And, while the absence of a biological connection is what makes this case extraordinary, this court is hardly without statutory basis and legal precedent in so deciding. * * * Fortunately, as the *Johnson* court also noted, intent to parent "'correlate[s] significantly'" with a child's best interests. (Johnson v. Calvert, supra, 5 Cal.4th at p. 94, quoting Schultz, op. cit. supra, Wis. L.Rev., at p. 397.) That is far more than can be said for a model of the law that renders a child a legal orphan. * * *

Again we must call on the Legislature to sort out the parental rights and responsibilities of those involved in artificial reproduction. No matter what one thinks of artificial insemination, traditional and gestational surrogacy (in all its permutations), and—as now appears in the not-too-distant future, cloning and even gene splicing—courts are still going to be faced with the problem of determining lawful parentage. A child cannot be ignored. Even if all means of artificial reproduction were outlawed with draconian criminal penalties visited on the doctors and parties involved, courts will still be called upon to decide who the lawful parents really are and who—other than the tax-payers—is obligated to provide maintenance and support for the child. These cases will not go away.

Courts can continue to make decisions on an ad hoc basis without necessarily imposing some grand scheme, looking to the imperfectly designed Uniform Parentage Act and a growing body of case law for guidance in the light of applicable family law principles. Or the Legislature can act to impose a broader order which, even though it might not be perfect on a case-by-case basis, would bring some predictability to those who seek to make use of artificial reproductive techniques. As jurists, we recognize the traditional role of the common (i.e., judge-formulated) law in applying old legal principles to new technology. (See, e.g., Hurtado v. State of California (1884) 110 U.S. 516, 530 [4 S.Ct. 111, 118, 28 L.Ed. 232] ["This flexibility and capacity for growth and adaptation is the peculiar boast and excellence of the common law."]; Rodriguez v. Bethlehem Steel Corp. (1974) 12 Cal.3d 382, 394 [115 Cal.Rptr. 765, 525 P.2d 669] ["in the common law system the primary instruments of this evolution are the courts, adjudicating on a regular basis the rich variety of individual cases brought before them"].) However, we still believe it is the Legislature, with its ability to formulate general rules based on input from all its constituencies, which is the more desirable forum for lawmaking.

That said, we must now conclude the business at hand.

(1) The portion of the judgment which declares that Luanne Buzzanca is not the lawful mother of Jaycee is reversed. The matter is remanded with directions to enter a new judgment declaring her the lawful mother. The trial court shall make all appropriate orders to ensure that Luanne Buzzanca shall have legal custody of Jaycee, including entering an order that Jaycee's birth certificate shall be amended to reflect Luanne Buzzanca as the mother.

(2) The judgment is reversed to the extent that it provides that John Buzzanca is not the lawful father of Jaycee. The matter is remanded with directions to enter a new judgment declaring him the lawful father. Consonant with this determination, today's ruling is without prejudice to John in future proceedings as regards child custody and visitation as his relationship with Jaycee may develop. * * * The judgment shall also reflect that the birth certificate shall be amended to reflect John Buzzanca as the lawful father.

(3) To the degree that the judgment makes no provision for child support it is reversed. The matter is remanded to make an appropriate permanent child support order. Until that time, the temporary child support order shall remain in effect. (See Jaycee B. v. Superior Court, supra, 42 Cal.App.4th at p. 730.)

Luanne and Jaycee will recover their costs on appeal.

Wallin, J., and Crosby, J., concurred.

[Respondent's petition for review by the Supreme Court was denied June 10, 1998.]

Notes

Paternity, as the word implies, was thought to only concern males. But advances in technology involve women in a determination of maternity. There is also the issue of whether sperm, ova, or embryos may be bequeathed through the probate process. Should such a process with its inherent ability to bring about conception, birth, and additional heirs, long into the future, violate public policy? California recently decided to allow a man to bequeath sperm to his former female partner over the objections of his children. *See* Kane v. Superior Ct., 37 Cal. App. 4th 1577, 44 Cal. Rptr. 2d 578 (1995). *See also* Bonnie Steinbock, *Sperm as Property*, 6 STAN. L. & POL. REV. 57 (1995). Do current statutes provide sufficient guidance for courts? Or should each of the cases be decided separately on the facts?

Uniform Parentage Act of 2000

§ 702. Parental Status of Donor.

A donor is not a parent of a child conceived by means of assisted reproduction.

§ 703. Paternity of Child of Assisted Reproduction.

A man who provides sperm for, or consents to, assisted reproduction by a woman as provided in Section 704 with the intent to be the parent of her child, is a parent of the resulting child.

§ 704. Consent to Assisted Reproduction.

(a) Consent by a woman, and a man who intends to be a parent of a child born to the woman by assisted reproduction must be in a record signed by the woman and the man. This requirement does not apply to a donor.

(b) Failure [by] a man to sign a consent required by subsection (a), before or after birth of the child, does not preclude a finding of paternity if the woman and the man, during the first two years of the child's life resided together in the same household with the child and openly held out the child as their own.

§ 705. Limitation on Husband's Dispute of Paternity.

(a) Except as otherwise provided in subsection (b), the husband of a wife who gives birth to a child by means of assisted reproduction may not challenge his paternity of the child unless:

(1) within two years after learning of the birth of the child he commences a proceeding to adjudicate his paternity; and

(2) the court finds that he did not consent to the assisted reproduction, before or after birth of the child.

(b) A proceeding to adjudicate paternity may be maintained at any time if the court determines that:

(1) the husband did not provide sperm for, or before or after the birth of the child consent to, assisted reproduction by his wife;

(2) the husband and the mother of the child have not cohabited since the probable time of assisted reproduction; and

(3) the husband never openly held out the child as his own.

(c) The limitation * * * applies to a marriage declared invalid after assisted reproduction.

§ 707. Parental Status of Deceased Individual.

If an individual who consented in a record to be a parent by assisted reproduction dies before placement of eggs, sperm, or embryos, the deceased individual is not a parent of the resulting child unless the deceased spouse consented in a record that if assisted reproduction were to occur after death, the deceased individual would be a parent of the child.

VI. Simultaneous Death

If a person wishes to transfer property to another at death, this may be done through a Last Will and Testament, a state statute of intestate succession, or a will substitute, which, for example, pays the benefits of a life insurance policy to another. In each of these three situations, the person wishing to transfer wealth must have intended that the recipient survive. But for how long? If the survivor lives for a very short period of time, he or she will have other plans for the wealth received, and, thus, the wealth could quickly go to persons the original decedent neither knew nor intended to benefit from his or her transfer. Thus, the law implies that any beneficiary should survive for at least a while in order to enjoy the inheritance. Otherwise, the purpose of the transfer is negated and, in addition, probate costs come too rapidly.

For example, if a married woman dies with a valid Last Will and Testament and leaves all of her property to her husband, this is both logical and appropriate. But if she and her husband are both victims of the same traffic accident, and the husband dies a day after his wife, he still survives. His estate would receive the property of the wife, and this property will pass according to his Last Will and Testament. His estate plan was to provide for his wife if she survived him, otherwise, for his property to pass to his own sisters and brothers. Because his wife did not survive, the property goes to his own sisters and brothers. Of course, this includes the property of the wife since he inherited it from her the day before. Her family will not share in her assets, it all will go to her husband's brothers and sisters.

Various approaches have been adopted to address what the law regards as the unfairness of passing property to a beneficiary who dies too quickly. In the most obvious case, if a decedent has a valid Last Will and Testament, the will may provide for a time in which the survivor must survive to take under the Last Will and Testament. For example: "Any beneficiary under this, my Last Will and Testament, must survive me by at least nine months. In the event that he or she does not survive me by this time, then I direct that his or her bequest or devise pass to the alternate taker or to the residuary clause." But if the decedent does not provide in a valid Will for a time in which a beneficiary must survive, there are statutes that will provide some guidance. For example, the Uniform Simultaneous Death Act has been adopted in nearly every state and provides that an heir must survive by at least 120 hours. However, it only applies if there is no proof of survivorship. To determine whether this is a good approach, the following case is illustrative.

Janus v. Tarasewicz
Illinois Appellate Court, 1985
135 Ill. App. 3d 936, 482 N.E.2d 418

O'CONNOR, Justice:

This non-jury declaratory judgment action arose out of the death of a husband and wife, Stanley and Theresa Janus, who died after ingesting Tylenol capsules which had been laced with cyanide by an unknown perpetrator prior to its sale in stores. Stanley Janus was pronounced dead shortly after he was admitted to the hospital. However, Theresa Janus was placed on life support systems for almost two days before being pronounced dead. Claiming that there was no sufficient evidence that Theresa Janus survived her husband, plaintiff Alojza Janus, Stanley's mother, brought this action for the proceeds of Stanley's $100,000 life insurance policy which named Theresa as the primary beneficiary and plaintiff as the contingent beneficiary. Defendant Metropolitan Life Insurance Company paid the proceeds to defendant Jan Tarasewicz, Theresa's father and the administrator of her estate. The trial court found sufficient evidence that Theresa survived Stanley Janus. We affirm.

The facts of this case are particularly poignant and complex. Stanley and Theresa Janus had recently returned from their honeymoon when, on the evening of September 29, 1982, they gathered with other family members to mourn the death of Stanley's brother, Adam Janus, who had died earlier that day from what was later determined to be cyanide-laced Tylenol capsules. While the family was at Adam's home, Stanley and Theresa Janus unknowingly took some of the contaminated Tylenol. Soon afterwards, Stanley collapsed on the kitchen floor.

Theresa was still standing when Diane O'Sullivan, a registered nurse and a neighbor of Adam Janus, was called to the scene. Stanley's pulse was weak so she began cardiopulmonary resuscitation (CPR) on him. Within minutes, Theresa Janus began having seizures. After paramedic teams began arriving, Ms. O'Sullivan went into the living room to assist with Theresa. While she was working on Theresa, Ms. O'Sullivan could hear Stanley's "heavy and labored breathing." She believed that both Stanley and Theresa died before they were taken to the ambulance, but she could not tell who died first.

Ronald Mahon, a paramedic for the Arlington Heights Fire Department, arrived at approximately 5:45 p.m. He saw Theresa faint and go into a seizure. Her pupils did not respond to light but she was breathing on her own during the time that he worked on her. Mahon also assisted with Stanley, giving him drugs to stimulate heart contractions. Mahon later prepared the paramedic's report on Stanley. One entry in the report shows that at 18:00 hours Stanley had "zero blood pressure, zero pulse, and zero respiration." However, Mahon stated that the times in the report were merely approximations. He was able to say that Stanley was in the ambulance en route to the hospital when his vital signs disappeared.

When paramedic Robert Lockhart arrived at 5:55 p.m., both victims were unconscious with non-reactive pupils. Theresa's seizures had ceased but she was in a decerebrate posture in which her arms and legs were rigidly extended and her arms were rotated inward toward her body, thus, indicating severe neurological dysfunction. At that time, she was breathing only four or five times a minute and, shortly thereafter, she stopped breathing on her own altogether. Lockhart intubated them both by placing tubes down their tracheae to keep their air passages open. Prior to being taken to the ambulance, they were put on "ambu-bags" which is a form of artificial respiration whereby the paramedic respirates the patient by squeezing a bag. Neither Stanley nor Theresa showed any signs of being able to breathe on their own while they were being transported to Northwest Community Hospital in Arlington Heights, Illinois. However, Lockhart stated that when Theresa was turned over to the hospital personnel, she had a palpable pulse and blood pressure.

The medical director of the intensive care unit at the hospital, Dr. Thomas Kim, examined them when they arrived in the emergency room at approximately 6:30 p.m.

Stanley had no blood pressure or pulse. An electrocardiogram detected electrical activity in Stanley Janus' heart but there was no synchronization between his heart's electrical activity and its pumping activity. A temporary pacemaker was inserted in an unsuccessful attempt to resuscitate him. Because he never developed spontaneous blood pressure, pulse or signs of respiration, Stanley Janus was pronounced dead at 8:15 p.m. on September 29, 1982.

Like Stanley, Theresa Janus showed no visible vital signs when she was admitted to the emergency room. However, hospital personnel were able to get her heart beating on its own again, so they did not insert a pacemaker. They were also able to establish a measurable, though unsatisfactory, blood pressure. Theresa was taken off the "ambu-bag" and put on a mechanical respirator. In Dr. Kim's opinion, Theresa was in a deep coma with "very unstable vital signs" when she was moved to the intensive care unit at 9:30 p.m. on September 29, 1982.

While Theresa was in the intensive care unit, numerous entries in her hospital records indicated that she had fixed and dilated pupils. However, one entry made at 2:32 a.m. on September 30, 1982, indicated that a nurse apparently detected a minimal reaction to light in Theresa's right pupil but not in her left pupil.

On September 30, 1982, various tests were performed in order to assess Theresa's brain function. These tests included an electroencephalogram (EEG) to measure electrical activity in her brain and a cerebral blood flow test to determine whether there was any blood circulating in her brain. In addition, Theresa exhibited no gag or cord reflexes, no response to pain or other external stimuli. As a result of these tests, Theresa Janus was diagnosed as having sustained total brain death, her life support systems then were terminated, and she was pronounced dead at 1:15 p.m. on October 1, 1982.

Death certificates were issued for Stanley and Theresa Janus more than three weeks later by a medical examiner's physician who never examined them. The certificates listed Stanley Janus' date of death as September 29, 1982, and Theresa Janus' date of death as October 1, 1982. Concluding that Theresa survived Stanley, the Metropolitan Life Insurance Company paid the proceeds of Stanley's life insurance policy to the administrator of Theresa's estate.

On January 6, 1983, plaintiff brought the instant declaratory judgment action against the insurance company and the administrators of Stanley and Theresa's estates, claiming the proceeds of the insurance policy as the contingent beneficiary of the policy. Also, the administrator of Stanley's estate filed a counterclaim against Theresa's estate seeking a declaration as to the disposition of the assets of Stanley's estate.

During the trial, the court heard the testimony of Ms. O'Sullivan, the paramedics, and Dr. Kim. There was also testimony that, while Theresa was in the intensive care unit, members of Theresa's family requested that termination of her life support system be delayed until the arrival of her brother who was serving in the military. However, Theresa's family denied making such a request.

In addition, Dr. Kenneth Vatz, a neurologist on the hospital staff, was called as an expert witness by plaintiff. Although he never actually examined Theresa, he had originally read her EEG as part of hospital routine. Without having seen her other hospital records, his initial evaluation of her EEG was that it showed some minimal electrical activity of living brain cells in the frontal portion of Theresa's brain. After reading her records and reviewing the EEG, however, he stated that the electrical activity measured by the EEG was "very likely" the result of interference from surrounding equipment in the intensive care unit. He concluded that Theresa was brain dead at the time of her admission to the hospital but he could not give an opinion as to who died first.

The trial court also heard an evidence deposition of Dr. Joseph George Hanley, a neurosurgeon who testified as an expert witness on behalf of the defendants. Based on his examination of their records, Dr. Hanley concluded that Stanley Janus died on September 29, 1982. He further concluded that Theresa Janus did not die until her vital signs disappeared on October 1, 1982. His conclusion that she did not die prior to that time was based on: (1) the observations by hospital personnel that Theresa Janus had spontaneous pulse and blood pressure which did not have to be artificially maintained; (2) the instance when Theresa Janus' right pupil allegedly reacted to light; and (3) Theresa's EEG which showed some brain function and which, in his opinion, could not have resulted from outside interference.

At the conclusion of the trial, the court held that the evidence was sufficient to show that Theresa survived Stanley, but the court was not prepared to say by how long she survived him. Plaintiff and the administrator of Stanley's estate appeal. In essence, their main contention is that there is not sufficient evidence to prove that both victims did not suffer brain death prior to their arrival at the hospital on September 29, 1982.

Dual standards for determining when legal death occurs in Illinois were set forth in the case of In Re Haymer (1983), 115 Ill.App.3d 349, 71 Ill.Dec. 252, 450 N.E.2d 940. There, the court determined that a comatose child attached to a mechanical life support system was legally dead on the date he was medically determined to have sustained total brain death, rather than on the date that his heart stopped functioning. The court stated that in most instances death could be determined in accordance with the common law standard which is based upon the irreversible cessation of circulatory and respiratory functions. (115 Ill.App.3d 349, 355, 71 Ill.Dec. 252, 450 N.E.2d 940.) If these functions are artificially maintained, a brain death standard of death could be used if a person has sustained irreversible cessation of total brain function. (115 Ill.App.3d 349, 355, 71 Ill.Dec. 252, 450 N.E.2d 940.) In a footnote, the court stated that widely accepted characteristics of brain death include: (1) unreceptivity and unresponsivity to intensely painful stimuli; (2) no spontaneous movement or breathing for at least one hour; (3) no blinking, no swallowing, and fixed and dilated pupils; (4) flat EEG's taken twice with at least a 24-hour intervening period; and (5) absence of drug intoxication or hyperthermia. (115 Ill.App.3d 349, 354 n. 9, 71 Ill.Dec. 252, 450 N.E.2d 940; see Report of the Ad. Hoc Committee of the Harvard Medical School to Examine the Definition of Brain Death: A Definition of Irreversible Coma, 205 J.A.M.A. 337 (1968); Lovato v. District Court (1979), 198 Colo. 419, 601 P2d 1072, 1076–77; see also Report of the Medical Consultants on the Diagnosis of Death to the President's Commission for the Study of Ethical Problems in Medicine and Biomedical and Behavioral Research, 246 J.A.M.A. 2184 (proposing other criteria.) However, the court refused to establish criteria for determining brain death because it noted that the advent of new research and technologies would continue to change the tests used for determining cessation of brain function. (115 Ill.App.3d 349, 354 n. 9, 71 Ill.Dec. 252, 450 N.E.2d 940.) Instead, the court merely required that the diagnosis of death under either standard must be made in accordance with "the usual and customary standards of medical practice." 115 Ill.App.3d 349, 355, 71 Ill.Dec. 252, 450 N.E.2d 940.

Even though *Haymer* was decided after the deaths of Stanley and Theresa, we find that the trial court properly applied the *Haymer* standards under the general rule that a civil case is governed by the law as it exists when judgment is rendered, not when the facts underlying the case occur. (See GTE Automatic Electric, Inc. v. Allphin (1976), 38 Ill.App.3d 910, 913–14, 349 N.E.2d 654, affirmed 68 Ill.2d 326, 12 Ill.Dec. 134, 369 N.E.2d 841; In Re Estate of Mertes (1975), 34 Ill.App.3d 557, 559, 340 N.E.2d 25.) The application of *Haymer* is not unfair since the treating physicians made brain death diagnoses at the time of the deaths, and the parties presented evidence at trial regarding brain death.

Regardless of which standard of death is applied, survivorship is a fact which must be proven by a preponderance of the evidence by the party whose claim depends on survivorship. (In Re Estate of Moran (1979), 77 Ill.2d 147, 150, 32 Ill.Dec. 349, 395 N.E.2d 579.) The operative provisions of the Illinois version of the Uniform Simultaneous Death Act provides in pertinent part:

> If the title to property or its devolution depends upon the priority of death and there is no sufficient evidence that the persons have died otherwise than simultaneously and there is no other provision in the will, trust agreement, deed, contract of insurance or other governing instrument for distribution of the property different from the provisions of this Section:
>
> (a) The property of each person shall be disposed of as if he had survived.
>
> * * *
>
> (d) If the insured and the beneficiary of a policy of life or accident insurance have so died, the proceeds of the policy shall be distributed as if the insured had survived the beneficiary.

Ill.Rev.Stat.1981, ch. 110 1/2, par. 3-1.

In cases where the question of survivorship is determined by the testimony of lay witnesses, the burden of sufficient evidence may be met by evidence of a positive sign of life in one body and the absence of any such sign in the other. (In Re Estate of Lowrance (1978), 66 Ill.App.3d 159, 162, 22 Ill.Dec. 895, 383 N.E.2d 703; Prudential Insurance Co. v. Spain (1950), 339 Ill.App. 476, 90 N.E.2d 256.) In cases such as the instant case where the death process is monitored by medical professionals, their testimony as to "the usual and customary standards of medical practice" will be highly relevant when considering what constitutes a positive sign of life and what constitutes a criteria for determining death. (See In Re Haymer (1983), 115 Ill.App.3d 349, 71 Ill.Dec. 252, 450 N.E.2d 940.) Although the use of sophisticated medical technology can also make it difficult to determine when death occurs, the context of this case does not require a determination as to the exact moment at which the decedents died. Rather, the trial court's task was to determine whether or not there was sufficient evidence that Theresa Janus survived her husband. Our task on review of this factually disputed case is to determine whether the trial court's finding was against the manifest weight of the evidence. (See Fransen Construction Co. v. Industrial Commission (1943), 384 Ill. 616, 628–29, 52 N.E.2d 241; In Re Estate of Adams (1952), 348 Ill.App. 115, 121, 108 N.E.2d 32.) We hold that it was not.

In the case at bar, both victims arrived at the hospital with artificial respirators and no obvious vital signs. There is no dispute among the treating physicians and expert witnesses that Stanley Janus died in both a cardiopulmonary sense and a brain death sense when his vital signs disappeared en route to the hospital and were never reestablished. He was pronounced dead at 8:15 p.m. on September 29, 1982, only after intensive procedures such as electro-shock, medication, and the insertion of a pacemaker failed to resuscitate him.

In contrast, these intensive procedures were not necessary with Theresa Janus because hospital personnel were able to reestablish a spontaneous blood pressure and pulse which did not have to be artificially maintained by a pacemaker or medication. Once spontaneous circulation was restored in the emergency room, Theresa was put on a mechanical respirator and transferred to the intensive care unit. Clearly, efforts to preserve Theresa Janus' life continued after more intensive efforts on Stanley's behalf had failed.

It is argued that the significance of Theresa Janus' cardiopulmonary functions, as a sign of life, was rendered ambiguous by the use of artificial respiration. In particular, reliance is placed upon expert testimony that a person can be brain dead and still have a spontaneous pulse and blood pressure which is indirectly maintained by artificial respiration. The fact remains, however, that Dr. Kim, an intensive care specialist who treated Theresa, testified that her condition in the emergency room did not warrant a diagnosis of brain death. In his opinion, Theresa Janus did not suffer irreversible brain death until much later, when extensive treatment failed to preserve her brain function and vital signs. This diagnosis was confirmed by a consulting neurologist after a battery of tests were performed to assess her brain function. Dr. Kim denied that these examinations were made merely to see if brain death had already occurred. At trial, only Dr. Vatz disagreed with their finding, but even he admitted that the diagnosis and tests performed on Theresa Janus were in keeping with the usual and customary standards of medical practice.

There was also other evidence presented at trial which indicated that Theresa Janus was not brain dead on September 29, 1982. Theresa's EEG, taken on September 30, 1982, was not flat but rather it showed some delta waves of extremely low amplitude. Dr. Hanley concluded that Theresa's EEG taken on September 30 exhibited brain activity. Dr. Vatz disagreed. Since the trier of fact determines the credibility of expert witnesses and the weight to be given to their testimony (Anderson v. General Grinding Wheel Corp. (1979), 74 Ill.App.3d 270, 281, 30 Ill.Dec. 354, 393 N.E.2d 9), the trial court in this case could have reasonably given greater weight to Dr. Hanley's opinion than to Dr. Vatz'. In addition, there is evidence that Theresa's pupil reacted to light on one occasion. It is argued that this evidence merely represents the subjective impression of a hospital staff member which is not corroborated by any other instance where Theresa's pupils reacted to light. However, this argument goes to the weight of this evidence and not to its admissibility. While these additional pieces of neurological data were by no means conclusive, they were competent evidence which tended to support the trial court's finding, and which also tended to disprove the contention that these tests merely verified that brain death had already taken place.

In support of the contention that Theresa Janus did not survive Stanley Janus, evidence was presented which showed that only Theresa Janus suffered seizures and exhibited a decerebrate posture shortly after ingesting the poisoned Tylenol. However, evidence that persons with these symptoms tend to die very quickly does not prove that Theresa Janus did not in fact survive Stanley Janus. Moreover, the evidence introduced is similar in nature to medical presumptions of survivorship based on decedents' health or physical condition which are considered too speculative to prove or disprove survivorship. (See In Re Estate of Moran (1979), 77 Ill.2d 147, 153, 32 Ill.Dec. 349, 395

N.E.2d 579.) Similarly, we find no support for the allegation that the hospital kept Theresa Janus on a mechanical respirator because her family requested that termination of her life support systems be delayed until the arrival of her brother, particularly since members of Theresa's family denied making such a request.

In conclusion, we believe that the record clearly established that the treating physicians' diagnoses of death with respect to Stanley and Theresa Janus were made in accordance with "the usual and customary standards of medical practice." Stanley Janus was diagnosed as having sustained irreversible cessation of circulatory and respiratory functions on September 29, 1982. These same physicians concluded that Theresa Janus' condition on that date did not warrant a diagnosis of death and, therefore, they continued their efforts to preserve her life. Their conclusion that Theresa Janus did not die until October 1, 1982, was based on various factors including the restoration of certain of her vital signs as well as other neurological evidence. The trial court found that these facts and circumstances constituted sufficient evidence that Theresa Janus survived her husband. It was not necessary to determine the exact moment at which Theresa died or by how long she survived him, and the trial court properly declined to do so. Viewing the record in its entirety, we cannot say that the trial court's finding of sufficient evidence of Theresa's survivorship was against the manifest weight of the evidence.

Because of our disposition of this case, we need not and do not consider whether the date of death listed on the victims' death certificates should be considered "facts" which constitute *prima facie* evidence of the date of their deaths. See Ill.Rev.Stat. 1981, ch. 111 1/2, par. 73-25; People v. Fiddler (1970), 45 Ill.2d 181, 184–86, 258 N.E.2d 359.

Accordingly, there being sufficient evidence that Theresa Janus survived Stanley Janus, the judgment of the circuit court of Cook County is affirmed.

Affirmed.

BUCKLEY, P.J., and CAMPBELL and O'CONNOR, JJ., concur.

Notes

The Uniform Probate Code has a different approach, which has been adopted by the most recent Uniform Simultaneous Death Act, although not every state has adopted the modification. How is the Uniform Probate Code different? May it be utilized with nonprobate transfers? Compare it with the Uniform Simultaneous Death Act immediately following.

Uniform Probate Code (2003)

§ 2-702. Requirement of Survival by 120 Hours.

(a) [**Requirement of Survival by 120 Hours Under Probate Code.**] For the purposes of this Code, except as provided in subsection (d), an individual who is not established by clear and convincing evidence to have survived an event, including the death of another individual, by 120 hours is deemed to have predeceased the event.

(b) [**Requirement of Survival by 120 Hours under Governing Instrument.**] Except as provided in subsection (d), for purposes of a provision of a governing instrument that relates to an individual surviving an event, including the death of another individual, an individual who is not established by clear and convincing evidence to have survived the event by 120 hours is deemed to have predeceased the event.

(c) [Co-owners With Right of Survivorship; Requirement of Survival by 120 Hours.] Except as provided in subsection (d), if (i) it is not established by clear and convincing evidence that one of two co-owners with right of survivorship survived the other co-owner by 120 hours, one-half of the property passes as if one had survived by 120 hours and one-half as if the other had survived by 120 hours and (ii) there are more than two co-owners and it is not established by clear and convincing evidence that at least one of them survived the others by 120 hours, the property passes in the proportion that one bears to the whole number of co-owners. For the purposes of this subsection, "co-owners with right of survivorship" includes joint tenants, tenants by the entireties, and other co-owners of property or accounts held under circumstances that entitles one or more to the whole of the property or account on the death of the other or others.

(d) [Exceptions.] Survival by 120 hours is not required if:

(1) the governing instrument contains language dealing explicitly with simultaneous deaths or deaths in a common disaster and that language is operable under the facts of the case;

(2) the governing instrument expressly indicates that an individual is not required to survive an event, including the death of another individual, by any specified period or expressly requires the individual to survive the event by a specified period; but survival of the event or the specified period must be established by clear and convincing evidence;

(3) the imposition of a 120-hour requirement of survival would cause a nonvested property interest or a power of appointment to fail to qualify for validity under Section 2-901(a)(1), (b)(1), or (c)(1) or to become invalid under Section 2-901(a)(2), (b)(2), or (c)(2); but survival must be established by clear and convincing evidence; or

(4) the application of a 120-hour requirement of survival to multiple governing instruments would result in an unintended failure or duplication of a disposition; but survival must be established by clear and convincing evidence.

(e) [Protection of Payors and Other Third Parties.]

(1) A payor or other third party is not liable for having made a payment or transferred an item of property or any other benefit to a beneficiary designated in a governing instrument who, under this section, is not entitled to the payment or item of property, or for having taken any other action in good faith reliance on the beneficiary's apparent entitlement under the terms of the governing instrument, before the payor or other third party received written notice of a claimed lack of entitlement under this section. A payor or other third party is liable for a payment made or other action taken after the payor or other third party received written notice of a claimed lack of entitlement under this section.

(2) Written notice of a claimed lack of entitlement under paragraph (1) must be mailed to the payor's or other third party's main office or home by registered or certified mail, return receipt requested, or served upon the payor or other third party in the same manner as a summons in a civil action. Upon receipt of written notice of a claimed lack of entitlement under this section, a payor or other third party may pay any amount

owed or transfer or deposit any item of property held by it to or with the court having jurisdiction of the probate proceedings relating to the decedent's estate, or if no proceedings have been commenced, to or with the court having jurisdiction of probate proceedings relating to decedents' estates located in the county of the decedent's residence. The court shall hold the funds or item of property and, upon its determination under this section, shall order disbursement in accordance with the determination. Payments, transfers, or deposits made to or with the court discharge the payor or other third party from all claims for the value of amounts paid to or items of property transferred to or deposited with the court.

(f) [**Protection of Bona Fide Purchasers; Personal Liability of Recipient.**]

(1) A person who purchases property for value and without notice, or who receives a payment or other item of property in partial or full satisfaction of a legally enforceable obligation, is neither obligated under this section to return the payment, item of property, or benefit nor is liable under this section for the amount of the payment or the value of the item of property or benefit. But a person who, not for value, receives a payment, item of property, or any other benefit to which the person is not entitled under this section is obligated to return the payment, item of property, or benefit, or is personally liable for the amount of the payment or the value of the item of property or benefit, to the person who is entitled to it under this section.

(2) If this section or any part of this section is preempted by federal law with respect to a payment, an item of property, or any other benefit covered by this section, a person who, not for value, receives the payment, item of property, or any other benefit to which the person is not entitled under this section is obligated to return the payment, item of property, or benefit, or is personally liable for the amount of the payment or the value of the item of property or benefit, to the person who would have been entitled to it were this section or part of this section not preempted.

Uniform Simultaneous Death Act (1993)

§4. Co-owners with Right of Survivorship; Requirement of Survival by 120 Hours.

Except as provided in Section 6, if (i) it is not established by clear and convincing evidence that one of two co-owners with right of survivorship survived the other co-owner by 120 hours, one-half of the property passes as if one had survived by 120 hours and one-half as if the other had survived by 120 hours and (ii) there are more than two co-owners and it is not established by clear and convincing evidence that at least one of them survived the others by 120 hours, the property passes in the proportion that one bears to the whole number of co-owners.

§6. Exceptions.

Survival by 120 hours is not required if:

(1) the governing instrument contains language dealing explicitly with simultaneous deaths or deaths in a common disaster and that language is operable under the facts of the case;

(2) the governing instrument expressly indicates that an individual is not required to survive an event, including the death of another individual, by any specified period or

expressly requires the individual to survive the event for a specified period; but survival of the event or the specified period must be established by clear and convincing evidence;

(3) the imposition of a 120-hour requirement of survival would cause a nonvested property interest or a power of appointment to [be invalid under the Rule Against Perpetuities] [fail to qualify for validity under Section 1(a)(1), (b)(1), or (c)(1) or to become invalid under Section 1(a)(2), (b)(2), or (c)(2), of the Uniform Statutory Rule Against Perpetuities]; but survival must be established by clear and convincing evidence; or

(4) the application of a 120-hour requirement of survival to multiple governing instruments would result in an unintended failure or duplication of a disposition; but survival must be established by clear and convincing evidence.

VII. Assignment of Expectancy

Scott v. First National Bank of Baltimore

Maryland Court of Appeals, 1961
224 Md. 462, 168 A.2d 349

HENDERSON, Judge.

This appeal is from a decree of an equity court declaring valid the assignment of a one-half expectancy from the estate of the assignor's father, then living, in favor of the assignor's daughter Virginia. The assignment was alluded to in Kelly v. Scott, 215 Md. 530, 532, 137 A.2d 704, although that case is not in point here, and the effect of that decision was modified by subsequent legislation. See Code (1960 Supp.), art. 16, sec. 135A (ch. 93, Acts of 1958).

The facts are not in dispute. Wilmer Scott became enamoured of another woman in 1947 and told his wife Grace he intended to leave her. The marital home was in Connecticut. On January 31, 1948, Wilmer and Grace entered into a separation agreement whereby she was to have custody of the child and he agreed to pay $250 per month for the support of Grace and Virginia, then just two years of age. In the event of Grace's remarriage he agreed to pay $150 a month for Virginia's support until she reached the age of twenty-one. Wilmer transferred to Grace his interest in their house at Rowayton, Conn., subject to a $10,000 mortgage which she assumed, his 1935 car, his modest bank account, his interest in a bank partnership trust, and a $10,000 service life insurance policy, provided Grace continue the payments. In a separate instrument he assigned under seal to Virginia one-half of his expectancy in his father's estate 'for the consideration of one dollar and other valuable considerations received to my full satisfaction from my wife * * * on behalf of my daughter'. Grace sued for divorce in August, 1948, and obtained a decree *a vinculo* on March 11, 1949, from the Fairfield County Court. The decree did not mention the assignment, although the decree for alimony and support incorporated the provisions set out in the separation agreement, but the agreement was not made a part of the decree. Evidently the separation agreement was exhibited to the court, but it was not shown that the assignment was so exhibited.

Wilmer married the other woman in 1949, but this marriage ended in a divorce and another alimony decree against him. In 1952 he married his present wife, by whom he has two children. Grace remarried in 1950. Wilmer did not comply with the support decree, indeed, he has made no payments at all since 1952. In March, 1959, Grace recovered a judgment for over $12,000 in back payments. On September 11, 1958, Wilmer's father died intestate. At the time of his death and since 1936 the father, Thomas A. Scott, had been mentally incompetent and committed to the Sheppard & Enoch Pratt Hospital in Baltimore, Maryland. He left surviving him two children, of whom Wilmer was one. His administrator, the First National Bank of Baltimore, filed an inventory showing a personal estate of about $490,000. It brought this proceeding by way of interpleader.

Wilmer was in financial straits at the time of the separation in 1948. He was earning about $300 a month and receiving $150 a month from the committee of his father, but he had numerous unpaid bills and unpaid small loans. Although he was an educated man he had difficulty in holding jobs, he claims, because of the fact that he suffered from epilepsy, although there was other testimony that it was due to his excessive drinking. Whatever cash he turned over to Grace was used to pay bills then unpaid. His history is one of improvidence and living beyond his means.

The parties agree and concede that the validity and effect of the assignment is to be determined under the law of Connecticut, where it was executed and delivered. That, of course, is the general rule applicable to foreign contracts dealing with personalty. See Restatement, Conflict of Laws § 332, and Baltimore & O. R. Co. v. Glenn, 28 Md. 287, 321. It is also agreed that at common law the transfer of a mere possibility or expectancy, not coupled with an interest, is void. Dart v. Dart, 1928, 7 Conn. 250; cf. Keys v. Keys, 148 Md. 397, 400, 129 A. 504. The parties further agree that under some circumstances, at least, equity will enforce the assignment of an expectancy after the death of the ancestor despite its invalidity at law. It is generally recognized that since the relief sought is in the nature of specific performance of a contract, equity will enforce the contract only where it is fair and equitable and supported by an adequate consideration. Keys v. Keys, supra; 6 Williston, Contracts (Rev. ed.) § 1681A; Pomeroy, Equity Jurisprudence (5th ed.) §§ 953a and 1287; 1 Bogert, Trusts § 112; 1 Scott, Trusts (2d ed.) § 86.1; Restatement, Property § 316. See also Notes, 17 A.L.R. 597, 44 A.L.R. 1465, and 121 A.L.R. 450, and Notes, 25 Colum.L.Rev. 215, and 35 No.Car.L.Rev. 127, 131. The appellant contends that the necessary consideration is lacking in the instant case.

Both parties cite and rely upon the case of Hooker v. Hooker, 130 Conn. 41, 32 A.2d 68, but they place a different interpretation upon it. The facts are strikingly similar to those in the instant case, but the posture of the case was somewhat different. In that case the Hookers executed a separation agreement in Connecticut in which, among other things, Mr. Hooker agreed to pay a certain sum to his wife in lieu of support and to establish two *inter vivos* trusts in favor of the minor children. He further agreed to assign in trust for each child any amounts he might thereafter receive from his mother's estate. It did not appear that any particular consideration passed to the husband in exchange for this agreement. Mrs. Hooker subsequently obtained a divorce in Nevada, and the decree incorporated the terms of the separation agreement by reference; the decree declaring it to be 'fair, just and equitable.' After the death of the mother the ex-wife sued to enforce the assignment of the husband's interest in his mother's estate.

The Connecticut court first held that the husband's contention that the agreement merged in the Nevada decree and that no action could be brought upon the agreement, as such, was not raised in the trial court and could not be raised for the first time on appeal. The authorities seem to hold generally that a property settlement does not merge in a decree. See Note, 32 A.L.R.2d 1145. But see Whitney v. Heublein, 145 Conn. 154, 139 A.2d 605. The court in the Hooker case, supra, also held that the trial court was correct in excluding testimony attacking the Nevada decree because, although the question of domicile would ordinarily be open to show a lack of jurisdiction, the husband, who had remarried, was not in a position to contest the divorce under the doctrine of clean hands, if not by way of estoppel. The court also stated that the husband did not contend that there was any public policy against property settlements made in view of divorce proceedings, instituted or determined upon, if submitted to and approved by a court with full opportunity for scrutiny, as would justify the Connecticut court in disregarding a decision of the Nevada court that the agreement was valid. It may be noted that this was stated as a contention and not as a holding. The appellant in the instant case contends that the Connecticut court relied upon the Nevada decree to establish the validity of the agreement, as a matter of collateral estoppel by judgment, if not as *res judicata*. For a statement of the principle, see Restatement, Judgments §§ 68 and 70.

We think that contention is untenable. The suit was on the agreement, and although the court stated that the wife claimed that the Nevada decree conclusively established the validity of the agreement, whereas the husband claimed its approval by the Nevada court was irrelevant, the court made no express reference to estoppel by judgment. Instead, the court discussed, in connection with the agreement to place additional sums in trust for the children, the husband's claim that the agreement was void as one for the transfer of an expectancy. Citing the case of Brown v. Brown, 66 Conn. 493, 498, 34 A. 490, 491, the court stated that an agreement to assign an expectancy is enforceable in equity and that the rule is supported by the great weight of authority 'where the agreement is fairly made upon adequate consideration and without oppression or unjust advantage being taken of the heir.' The court discussed authorities, pro and con, as to the necessity that the ancestor have knowledge of the purported assignment but said: 'The danger that such an agreement will defeat his intent is not so great as to require that his knowledge of its existence be proved in order to render it valid.' The court further said: 'We have no statute in this state changing the common law in such a situation as the one before us, and our courts have jurisdiction in equity to enforce the agreement by compelling compliance with it.' [130 Conn. 41, 32 A.2d 73].

It is true that the adequacy of the consideration was not discussed. But the court did discuss the validity of the agreement and its enforceability in Connecticut. It would hardly have been necessary to discuss the point at all if the Nevada decision were given conclusive effect. If the Connecticut court did not discuss the adequacy of the consideration because the point was not raised, as the appellant suggests, and the question was left open, we must still determine, as best we can, what the Connecticut court would hold, were the question presented.

All of the authorities seem to agree that a gratuitous assignment is unenforceable, because there is no contract to enforce. 1 Scott, Trusts, supra at p. 655. Some courts, notably in Kentucky, refuse to enforce any agreements to assign an expectancy because of a public policy against sales to moneylenders and the danger of overreaching in the case of impoverished prospective heirs. Others enforce agreements to sell, provided the consideration amounts to a fair equivalent. Some of the commentators suggest that the adequacy of consideration is only one element in determining whether equity will enforce and that contracts to assign an expectancy should not be placed in any special category. See the Note, 25 Colum.L.Rev., supra. In this connection we may quote the language of Judge Hammond in Ledingham v. Bayless, 218 Md. 108, 115, 145 A.2d 434, 439, a case involving a contract to make a will, where it was said: 'As in other contracts, the parties may agree on the surrender or acquisition of any legal rights as consideration, and the adequacy of such consideration is material only as an element of fraud or undue influence or as one of the factors which a court will take into consideration in determining whether or not to grant specific performance.' Cf. Sidor v. Kravec, 135 Conn. 571, 66 A.2d 812. In 1 Scott, Trusts, supra at p. 654, the learned author states that the courts uniformly find adequate consideration present in the case of marriage settlements and separation agreements. We find nothing in the Connecticut cases cited to indicate that a property settlement in contemplation of divorce would be unenforceable because lacking in consideration amounting to equivalence. We think the cases cited point in the opposite direction.

We do not suggest that any weight should be attached to the seal or recited consideration. Nor do we suggest that love and affection alone would suffice, although there are cases that suggest a more liberal rule in the case of family settlements. See 6 Williston, Contracts, supra, and Warner v. Warner, 124 Conn. 625, 1 A.2d 911, 118 A.L.R. 1348. Of course, both parties in the instant case were concerned with the welfare of the child Virginia. Grace assumed the burden of the care and education of Virginia, over and above the rather small sum stipulated for her support. It is true that the divorce court could not be bound by the parties' agreement, insofar as it might affect the welfare of the child. But the wife may well have tempered her demands because of the assignment in order to insure that the child would receive a share of the expectancy which might otherwise be frittered away. She also assumed liability for the unpaid bills and loans and the mortgage. We find adequate consideration in these undertakings. There is no claim of fraud or overreaching and the chancellor found that the agreement was not unfair or inequitable under the circumstances. The bargain was at arm's length and the husband had an opportunity to seek independent advice.

The appellant argues that the real consideration was that the wife should obtain a divorce and thus permit him to marry the paramour. We find nothing collusive in the separation agreement. She undoubtedly had grounds for divorce before the separation, and the Connecticut cases seem to clearly hold that a property settlement in contemplation of divorce is not invalid. The appellant argues that this is true only if the settlement is submitted to and approved by the divorce court. As we read the cases the requirement is simply that it not be concealed from the divorce court, because concealment may have a material bearing upon the issues presented. In this connection see Mills v. Mills, 119 Conn. 612, 179 A. 5; Maisch v. Maisch, 87 Conn. 377, 87 A. 729; cf. Koster v. Koster, 137 Conn. 707, 81 A.2d 355. That was not the situation in the instant case.

The passage we have quoted from the Hooker case is a sufficient answer to the appellant's contention that the assignment is invalid because made without the knowledge of the assignor's father. It is true that it was not shown in that case that the mother was unaware of the agreement, although knowledge was not affirmatively shown. But we think the Connecticut court indicated that it would follow the weight of authority to the effect that knowledge is immaterial. See Restatement, Property § 316 comment j, and Keys v. Keys, supra. See also Hofmeister v. Hunter, 230 Wis. 81, 283 N.W. 330, 121 A.L.R. 444, where a conveyance was enforced although the ancestor was insane.

Decree affirmed, with costs.

Notes

A Florida court has held that the test to enforce an assignment of an expectancy is two-pronged: first, there must be sufficient consideration to support the assignment, but then, too, the assignment must be fairly entered into, without fraud, duress, or any breach of a fiduciary relationship. Diaz v. Rood, 851 So. 2d 843 (Fla. 2d. Dist. App. 2003). Assignment of expectancy often takes place in the context of nursing home care. If an individual qualifies for Medicaid assistance in payment of nursing home care, an entitlement most often achieved by spending down assets, the nursing home resident or his or her guardian will be required to assign any expectancy the resident may currently or one day receive. For example, in return for the "consideration" of government assistance in the payment of nursing home care, the resident will assign his or her Social Security check to the nursing home. In addition, if the resident should win the lottery, inherit a fortune, or receive a gift, the resident would be required to assign that lottery winning, inheritance, or gift to the nursing home. The consideration is the cost of the care received. In order to qualify for Medicaid, persons or their guardians often seek to disclaim assets; this procedure is discussed *infra*. But courts have been very reluctant to allow the disclaimer. The assets should be counted in determining if a person reaches the poverty threshold necessary for Medicaid assistance. *See, e.g.,* Molloy v. Bane, 214 A.D.2d 171, 631 N.Y.S.2d 910 (1995).

VIII. Disclaimer: Release and Renunciation

Disclaimer is an umbrella term that incorporates both release and renunciation. All refer to the prospective beneficiary's ability and conduct in rejecting proposed benefits. Today, particularly under the Uniform Probate Code, disclaimer is possible in reference to benefits under a Last Will and Testament, intestacy, and even under non-probate transfers or will substitutes. If a potential beneficiary wishes to disclaim benefits during the lifetime of a donor or testator, he or she "releases" any claim. Because the claim is still a mere expectancy, consideration is required to provide substance. A common form of release today is a prenuptial agreement between two parties not to take from one another's estate. Particularly among older persons who are marrying for the second time, with children from prior unions, the mutuality of the release provides the consideration. *See* Uniform Premarital Agreement Act, 9B U.LA. 369 (1987); Eric Rasmusen and Jeffrey E. Stake, *Lifting the Veil of Ignorance: Personalizing the Marriage Contract*, 73 IND. L. J. 453 (1998). For discussion and hypotheticals, see Daniel B. Evans, *The "Disclaimer" Trust: An Ideal Plan for the Medium Size Estate*, http://evans-legal.com/dan/disclaimtr.html (accessed Oct. 20, 2005). For discussion on drafting the disclaimer trust, with sample provisions and forms, see Sebastian V. Grassi, Jr., *Drafting the Marital Deduction Disclaimer Trust After the 2001 Tax Act*, http://d2d.ali-aba.org/_files/thumbs/ rtf/ACFA3F_thumb.pdf (accessed Oct. 20, 2005).

Incorporated within disclaimer, "renunciation" refers to actions by the beneficiary after the death of the donor or testator to reject any claim to the property. Because the donor or testator is dead, the interest is identifiable and consideration is unnecessary. Renunciation is often a tool for tax planning. By rejecting a bequest or legacy, an individual may be able to provide for an alternative provision to become effective, which would benefit a family member or loved-one. For an Advisory Opinion by the Attorney General of Hawaii on the effect of renunciation of succession, see State of Hawaii, Department of the Attorney General, Formal Opinion Letter from Katherine C. Desmarais, Deputy Attorney General, to Ms. Pilialoha E. Lee Loy, Apr. 11, 1997, http://www.state. hi.us/ag/opinions_formal_letters/9703.htm (accessed Oct. 12, 2005). Such a benefit would be accomplished without gift tax consequences. To effectuate a "qualified disclaimer" and avoid transfer tax consequences, the provisions of section 2518 of the Internal Revenue Code must be followed. Issues concerning taxation are discussed elsewhere in this book, but because taxes motivate nearly every consideration, the applicability must be raised.

The applicability of disclaimer to testate, intestate, and non-probate transfers is important in an age when contract and individual concerns predominate. Examine the Uniform Probate Code for the applicability of disclaimer to all aspects of wealth transfer.

Uniform Probate Code (2003)

§2-1105. Power to Disclaim; General Requirements; When Irrevocable.

(a) A person may disclaim, in whole or part, any interest in or power over property, including a power of appointment. A person may disclaim the interest or power even if its creator imposed a spendthrift provision or similar restriction on transfer or a restriction or limitation on the right to disclaim.

(b) Except to the extent a fiduciary's right to disclaim is expressly restricted or limited by another statute of this State or by the instrument creating the fiduciary relationship, a fiduciary may disclaim, in whole or part, any interest in or power over property, including a power of appointment, whether acting in a personal or representative capacity. A fiduciary may disclaim the interest or power even if its creator imposed a spendthrift provision or similar restriction on transfer or a restriction or limitation on the right to disclaim or an instrument other than the instrument that created the fiduciary relationship imposed a restriction or limitation on the right to disclaim.

(c) To be effective, a disclaimer must be in a writing or other record, declare the disclaimer, describe the interest or power disclaimed, be signed by the person making the disclaimer, and be delivered or filed in the manner provided in Section 2-1112. In this subsection:

  (1) "record" means information that is inscribed on a tangible medium or that is stored in an electronic or other medium and is retrievable in perceivable form; and

  (2) "signed" means, with present intent to authenticate or adopt a record, to;

    (A) execute or adopt a tangible symbol; or

    (B) attach to or logically associate with the record an electronic sound, symbol, or process.

(d) A partial disclaimer may be expressed as a fraction, percentage, monetary amount, term of years, limitation of a power, or any other interest or estate in the property.

(e) A disclaimer becomes irrevocable when it is delivered or filed pursuant to Section 2-1112 or when it becomes effective as provided in Sections 2-1106 through 2-1111, whichever occurs later.

(f) A disclaimer made under this Part is not a transfer, assignment, or release.

§ 2-1107. Disclaimer of Rights of Survivorship in Jointly Held Property.

(a) Upon the death of a holder of jointly held property, a surviving holder may disclaim, in whole or part, the greater of:

    (1) a fractional share of the property determined by dividing the number one by the number of joint holders alive immediately before the death of the holder to whose death the disclaimer relates; or

    (2) all of the property except that part of the value of the entire interest attributable to the contribution furnished by the disclaimant.

(b) A disclaimer under subsection (a) takes effect as of the death of the holder of jointly held property to whose death the disclaimer relates.

(c) An interest in jointly held property disclaimed by a surviving holder of the property passes as if the disclaimant predeceased the holder to whose death the disclaimer relates.

§ 2-1113. When Disclaimer Barred or Limited.

(a) A disclaimer is barred by a written waiver of the right to disclaim.

(b) A disclaimer of an interest in property is barred if any of the following events occur before the disclaimer becomes effective:

    (1) the disclaimant accepts the interest sought to be disclaimed;

    (2) the disclaimant voluntarily assigns, conveys, encumbers, pledges, or transfers the interest sought to be disclaimed or contracts to do so; or

    (3) a judicial sale of the interest sought to be disclaimed occurs.

(c) A disclaimer, in whole or part, of the future exercise of a power held in a fiduciary capacity is not barred by its previous exercise.

(d) A disclaimer, in whole or part, of the future exercise of a power not held in a fiduciary capacity is not barred by its previous exercise unless the power is exercisable in favor of the disclaimant.

(e) A disclaimer is barred or limited if so provided by law other than this Part.

(f) A disclaimer of a power over property which is barred by this section is ineffective. A disclaimer of an interest in property which is barred by this section takes effect as a transfer of the interest disclaimed to the persons who would have taken the interest under this Part had the disclaimer not been barred.

Tax Considerations: While it may seem strange behavior to disclaim any monetary advantage, most disclaimers are motivated by federal, or perhaps state, tax considerations. For example, a parent with sufficient assets may wish to "disclaim" assets so that an issue, a descendant, a child, or grandchild may receive the asset instead. Disclaimer avoids any gift tax consequences associated with giving the asset to the child. Or in another example, disclaimer by anyone other than a spouse, may have the effect of increasing the share that would go to the spouse and thus increase the marital deduction. These are valid considerations and motivations under the present federal tax code, and should the estate tax be repealed, they may remain as motivations under state regimes. Failure to advise clients of the tax ramifications of disclaimers has been considered as malpractice by attorneys. *See, e.g.,* Kinney v. Shinholser, 663 So.2d 643 (Fla. App. 1995). So as to make the rules standard within the federal tax code, Congress has set forth the following provision:

Internal Revenue Code

Section 2518. Disclaimers
(a) General Rule.

For purposes of this subtitle, if a person makes a qualified disclaimer with respect to any interest in property, this subtitle shall apply with respect to such interest as if the interest had never been transferred to such person.

(b) Qualified disclaimer defined.

For purposes of subsection (a), the term "qualified disclaimer" means an irrevocable and unqualified refusal by a person to accept an interest in property but only if–

(1) such refusal is in writing,

(2) such writing is received by the transferor of the interest, his legal representative, or the holder of the legal title to the property to which the interest relates not later than the date which is 9 months after the later of-

(A) the day on which the transfer creating the interest in such person is made, or

(B) the day on which such person attains the age of 21,

(3) such person has not accepted the interest or any of its benefits, and

(4) as a result of such refusal, the interest passes without any direction on the part of the person making the disclaimer and passes either–

(A) to the spouse of the decedent, or

(B) to a person other that the person making the disclaimer.

* * *

DePaoli v. C.I.R.
10th Circuit Court of Appeals, 1995
62 F.3d 1259

JENKINS, Senior District Judge.

This case arises out of the taxpayers' efforts to escape estate taxes by disclaiming a testamentary transfer of property. The Tax Court held the purported disclaimer invalid for estate tax purposes, subjecting the taxpayers to liability not only for estate taxes but also for a gift tax and an addition to tax under section 6651(a)(1) of the Internal Revenue Code. See 66 T.C.M. (CCH) 1493, 1993 WL 500190 (1993). The taxpayers appeal. We have jurisdiction under I.R.C. §7482(a)(1) and reverse.

* * *

Quinto DePaoli, Sr., a resident of New Mexico, died in 1987. He was survived by his wife, Soila DePaoli, and his only son, Quinto DePaoli, Jr. Quinto Senior's will left his entire estate to Quinto Junior. The will was formally probated on December 30, 1987. On

July 21, 1988, shortly before the estate tax return was due, Soila and Quinto Junior moved to have the probated will set aside. They claimed that the original will had been destroyed, that the will admitted to probate was actually a duplicate copy and that Quinto Senior had intended to make a new will leaving Quinto Junior the greatest amount he could receive without any tax liability (namely, $600,000) and leaving the bulk of the estate to Soila but that he had died before he could execute the new will. Quinto Junior acknowledged that he could claim a substantial part of the estate but agreed to receive only $600,000 to settle the will contest. The probate court granted the motion and ordered the estate distributed accordingly.

The federal estate tax return filed for Quinto Senior's estate indicated that the entire estate passed to Soila, less certain expenses and a $600,000 bequest to Quinto Junior. The bequest to Soila was classified as a deductible bequest to a surviving spouse. The return indicated that no property passed to the surviving spouse as a result of a qualified disclaimer under I.R.C. § 2518(b), and no written disclaimer was attached to the return. The return indicated that no tax was due, since the tax on the $600,000 taxable estate was within the unified credit available to the estate.

The Commissioner denied the entire marital deduction on the grounds that Quinto Senior's will, as probated, bequeathed all his property to his son and the agreement between Quinto Junior and Soila was invalid. The Commissioner also determined that the agreement between Quinto Junior and Soila constituted a taxable gift for gift tax purposes and assessed an addition to tax against Quinto Junior under I.R.C. § 6651(a)(1) for failing to file a gift tax return.[1]

The Tax Court upheld the Commissioner's determinations. The court held that Quinto Junior's agreement to forego all but $600,000 of his father's estate did not entitle the estate to the marital deduction because the portion of the estate passing to Soila passed to her from Quinto Junior and not from Quinto Senior. The court further held that the property passing to Soila constituted a taxable gift from Quinto Junior, making Quinto Junior liable for the federal gift tax. Finally, the court held that Quinto Junior's failure to file a gift tax return was not "due to reasonable cause" and that Quinto Junior was therefore liable for an addition to tax under I.R.C. § 6651(a)(1). The Tax Court concluded that the deficiency in estate tax due was $1,633,250, the deficiency in gift tax due was $1,297,750 and the addition to tax was $324,438. Quinto Junior, the estate, and Quinto Senior's personal representatives (Soila and Rachel Craig) appealed.

* * *

The appellants claim that the Tax Court erred by denying the estate a marital deduction. They claim that, as a result of Quinto Junior's disclaimer of his property rights under Quinto Senior's will, Quinto Senior's property passed to his surviving spouse (Soila) as a matter of law and was therefore properly deducted.[2] The parties agree that this issue is subject to de novo review.

---

1. Section 6651(a)(1) imposes an addition to tax for failure to file a gift tax return "unless it is shown that such failure is due to reasonable cause and not due to willful neglect." I.R.C. § 6651(a)(1). The penalty ranges from 5 to 25 percent of the gift tax due, depending on how delinquent the taxpayer is. Id.

2. Before the Tax Court, the petitioners also argued that they had properly claimed the marital deduction under former section 20.2056(e)-2(d) of the estate tax regulations because the decedent's property had passed to Soila in settlement of a will contest. The Tax Court rejected this argument, and the petitioners have not challenged that ruling on appeal.

Estate taxes are imposed on the value of a decedent's taxable estate. I.R.C. §2001. In determining the value of the taxable estate, the value of property that passes to a surviving spouse is deducted. Id. §2056(a). If property passes from a decedent to someone other than the surviving spouse and that person makes a "qualified" disclaimer that results in the surviving spouse being entitled to the property, the disclaimed interest is treated as passing directly from the decedent to the surviving spouse and therefore qualifies for the marital deduction. See Treas.Reg. §20.2056(d)-1(b).

To qualify, a disclaimer must meet certain requirements, chief of which, for purposes of this appeal, is that, as a result of the disclaimer, the interest passes to the surviving spouse "without any direction on the part of the person making the disclaimer." I.R.C. §2518(b)(4). The Tax Court held that Quinto Junior's agreement to forego all but $600,000 of his father's estate was not a qualified disclaimer because his interest would not have passed to Soila without his direction.[3]

The requirement that the disclaimed property pass without any direction from the person making the disclaimer means that the disclaimer must result in a valid passing of the disclaimed interest to the surviving spouse by operation of state law. Federal law does not prescribe rules for the passing of disclaimed property interests, so any disclaimed property passing other than by operation of state law must be at the direction of the disclaimant. See Estate of Goree v. Commissioner, 68 T.C.M. (CCH) 123, 125–26, 1994 WL 379246 (1994); Estate of Bennett v. Commissioner, 100 T.C. 42, 67, 72–73, 1993 WL 19583 (1993).

Under New Mexico law, unless the decedent indicates otherwise in his will, any disclaimed property passes as if the disclaimant had predeceased the decedent. See N.M.Stat.Ann. §45-2-801(C) (Michie 1989 Repl.).[4] Under New Mexico's antilapse statute, if a devisee who is related to the testator by kinship is treated as if he had predeceased the testator, the devisee's "issue" who survive the testator by 120 hours "take in place of" the devisee. Id. §45-2-605. Thus, if Quinto Junior had "issue," his disclaimer would not have caused the disclaimed property to pass to his stepmother, Soila, by operation of law and therefore would not have been a qualified disclaimer under I.R.C. §2518(b) entitling the estate to the marital deduction.

Quinto Junior has never been married but has two illegitimate children—Thomas Derrick DePaoli and Christopher Noel Contreras DePaoli. Derrick was five years old at the time of Quinto Senior's death, and Christopher was four. The Tax Court concluded that the property Quinto Junior disclaimed would not have passed to Soila absent his

3. The Commissioner does not claim and the Tax Court did not hold that the disclaimer failed to meet the requirements for a valid disclaimer under New Mexico law, contained in N.M.Stat.Ann. §45-2-801 (Michie Repl.1989). The Tax Court doubted whether Quinto Junior intended to make a qualified disclaimer under federal law when he entered into the settlement agreement with Soila, since the estate tax return did not indicate that any property passed to Soila as a result of a qualified disclaimer. The court called the argument "patently an afterthought with weak factual support." See 66 T.C.M. (CCH) at 1495, 1993 WL 500190. However, the Commissioner concedes that the Tax Court did not reject the taxpayers' claim on that ground. It held only that the disclaimer was not a qualified disclaimer under I.R.C. §2518(b)(4) because it directed that the disclaimed property pass to Soila. See Br. for Appellee at 22–23 n. 6. It is only that issue that we need address.

4. Article II of the Uniform Probate Code (dealing with intestate succession) and section 1-201 (the general definitional section) were revised in 1990. In accordance with this revision, New Mexico substantially revised its probate code in 1993. Unless otherwise indicated, citations to the New Mexico Probate Code, N.M.Stat.Ann. ch. 45, are to the code in effect at the time of the events giving rise to this action.

agreement that Soila take the property but would have passed to Derrick and Christopher. The petitioners claim that Quinto Junior's illegitimate children were not his "issue" within the meaning of the antilapse statute and therefore would not have taken in his place as a result of his disclaimer.

The New Mexico Probate Code in effect at the time of Quinto Senior's death and Quinto Junior's disclaimer defines "issue" as "all of a person's lineal descendants of all generations, with the relationship of parent and child at each generation being determined by the definitions of child and parent contained in the Probate Code." N.M.Stat.Ann. § 45-1-201(A)(21). The Probate Code defines "child" as "any individual entitled to take as a child under the Probate Code by intestate succession from the parent whose relationship is involved" and excludes stepchildren, foster children and grandchildren. Id. § 45-1-201(A)(3). For purposes of intestate succession, the Probate Code provides that a child born out of wedlock is considered a "child" of the father if, among other things, "the reputed father has recognized the child in writing by an instrument signed by him, which shows upon its face that it was so signed with the intent of recognizing the child as an heir." Id. § 45-2-109(B)(2).[5] The code makes declarations of deceased persons admissible to prove that such an instrument was lost or destroyed, as well as to prove the existence, contents and genuineness of such an instrument. The statute further provides, "Such declarations shall be corroborated by proof of general and notorious recognition of such child by the father." Id. § 45-2-109(B)(2). Finally, the code defines "heirs" as "those persons ... who are entitled under the statutes of intestate succession to the property of a decedent." Id. § 45-1-201(A)(17). Under the statutes of intestate succession, the part of the intestate estate not passing to the surviving spouse passes "to the issue of the decedent." Id. § 45-2-103(A).

In other words, under New Mexico law as it existed in 1987 and 1988, an illegitimate child was considered "issue" of his natural father and therefore entitled to take in place of the natural father under the antilapse statute if the natural father recognized the child by a signed, written instrument that "shows upon its face" that the father signed it "with the intent of recognizing the child as an heir," id. § 45-2-109(B)(2), that is, as someone entitled to succeed to the father's property under the intestate succession statutes, see id. § 45-1-201(A)(17).

The Tax Court concluded that Quinto Junior had recognized his illegitimate children as his heirs when he filed his federal income tax returns for the years 1987 through 1990 listing each of them as his "son" and claiming dependency exemptions for them. The Internal Revenue Code defines "dependent" to include a "son or daughter of the taxpayer" and any other individual who "has as his principal place of abode the home of the taxpayer and is a member of the taxpayer's household" for the tax year. See I.R.C. § 152(a). The Tax Court reasoned that, if Quinto Junior had intended to take an exemption for his children without recognizing them as his heirs, he would have listed them simply as dependents or household members, as he did for the children's mother, Gloria Contreras.[6] The court concluded: "Because petitioner chose to identify Thomas and Christopher specifically as his 'sons,' instead of as just members of his household, we are

---

5. Under the Probate Code as it existed before 1993, an illegitimate child could also be considered a child of his natural father for purposes of intestate succession if the child's natural parents participated in a marriage ceremony or if paternity was established by an adjudication. See N.M.Stat.Ann. § 45-2-109(B)(1) & (3). Neither of those conditions has been met here.

6. Quinto Junior claimed an exemption for Ms. Contreras on his 1987 and 1990 income tax returns, identifying her as "Girlfriend" and "Fam[ily] Mem [ber]," respectively.

persuaded that these returns, signed by petitioner under penalties of perjury, constitute a written instrument signed with the intent of recognizing the children as heirs." 66 T.C.M. (CCH) at 1497, 1993 WL 500190.[7]

The problem with the Tax Court's reasoning is that it equates "son" under the Internal Revenue Code with "heir" under the New Mexico Probate Code. The term "son" is ambiguous. See Lalli v. Lalli, 439 U.S. 259, 274 n. 11, 99 S.Ct. 518, 528 n. 11, 58 L.Ed.2d 503 (1978). It may refer to a natural child, an adopted child, a stepchild, a legitimate child or an illegitimate child. The Internal Revenue Code's definition of a child is broader than the Probate Code's. For example, a stepchild can be a "child" within the meaning of the Internal Revenue Code and therefore a dependent for purposes of the dependency exemption but is not a "child" and therefore an heir for purposes of intestate succession. Compare I.R.C. § 151(c)(3) (formerly § 151(e)(3)) with N.M.Stat.Ann. § 45-1-201(A)(3).

Similarly, an illegitimate child may be a child (and hence a dependent) under the Internal Revenue Code without being a child (and hence an heir) under the Probate Code. A son or daughter need not be legitimate for the father to qualify for a dependency exemption under the Internal Revenue Code. * * * By listing Derrick and Christopher as his "sons" on his tax returns, Quinto Junior may have recognized them as his children but did not necessarily recognize them as his "heirs."

The Commissioner argues that New Mexico law recognizes no distinction between a child and an heir, that all New Mexico law requires is that the natural father recognize his illegitimate child as his child, since a child is entitled to inherit under New Mexico's intestacy statutes and thus is an "heir." However, not all children are entitled to inherit by intestate succession under New Mexico law. A child must satisfy the statutory definition of "child" to be considered "issue" under the Probate Code. Cf. Coleman v. Offutt (In re Estate of Coleman), 104 N.M. 192, 194, 718 P.2d 702, 704 (Ct.App.1986) (an adopted son who satisfies the statutory definition of "child" is also "issue" of his father). For present purposes, an illegitimate child is not entitled to succeed to his or her fathers' property by intestate succession unless the father (1) "has recognized the child in writing," (2) "by an instrument signed by him," (3) "which shows upon its face that it was so signed with the intent of recognizing the child as an heir." N.M.Stat.Ann. § 45-2-109(B)(2). At best, Quinto Junior's tax returns only satisfy the first two requirements. They do not show "upon [their] face" that they were signed "with the intent of recognizing" Derrick and Christopher as Quinto Junior's heirs. The only intent evident from the returns is the intent to claim a dependency exemption, which, the Commissioner concedes, a taxpayer can claim without intending to make the dependent an heir (as Quinto Junior did when he filed his 1987 and 1990 returns claiming an exemption for his mistress).

In construing section 45-2-109(B)(2), we are required to give effect to all its provisions and not to render any part of the statute surplusage. See, e.g., Whitely v. New Mexico State Personnel Bd., 115 N.M. 308, 311, 850 P.2d 1011, 1014 (1993); Roberts v. Southwest Community Health Servs., 114 N.M. 248, 251, 837 P.2d 442, 445 (1992). The Commissioner's argument, which equates "heir" with "child," would read the phrase "which shows upon its face that it was so signed with the intent of recognizing

---

7. The Tax Court further held that Quinto Junior had not met his burden of proving that he had any contrary intention. In fact, the only direct evidence on this issue was Quinto Junior's own testimony. He testified that he had never acknowledged in writing the intent to recognize a child as an heir. Tr. at 6.

the child as an heir" out of the statute. It would be enough if the father of an illegitimate child "recognized the child in writing by an instrument signed by him." We believe that the next phrase—"which shows upon its face that it was so signed with the intent of recognizing the child as an heir"—requires something different from recognition of parentage, namely, an intent to recognize the child as an heir, that is, as someone entitled to inherit from the father by intestate succession. In other words, we believe that section 45-2-109(B)(2), properly construed, requires both recognition of paternity and evidence of an intent that the child inherit.

For that reason, this case is distinguishable from the cases the Commissioner relies on. In each of those cases state law required only proof of paternity; it did not require evidence of an intent to recognize the child as an heir. The relevant statute in each case provided that an illegitimate child is an heir of "the person who, in writing, signed in the presence of a competent witness, acknowledges himself to be the father" of the child. See In re Estate of Jerrido, 339 So.2d 237, 239 (Fla.Dist.Ct.App.1976), cert. denied, 346 So.2d 1249 (Fla.1977); Glick v. Knoll (In re Estate of Glick), 136 Mont. 176, 346 P.2d 987, 987 (1959); Schalla v. Roberts (In re Estate of Schalla), 2 Wis.2d 38, 86 N.W.2d 5, 8 (1957). Moreover, in each of those cases, the court relied on governing case law to the effect that the form and purpose of the writing acknowledging paternity was immaterial. See Jerrido, 339 So.2d at 240 (relying on Florida case law holding that "the written acknowledgment of parenthood need not assume any particular formality") (citations omitted); Glick, 346 P.2d at 989 (relying on Montana case law holding that a writing acknowledging paternity "is a sufficient compliance with the statute without regard to the purpose for which the instrument was executed") (citation omitted); Schalla, 86 N.W.2d at 9 (under the relevant statute, the written acknowledgment did not have to be made for the express purpose of establishing heirship). By contrast, the New Mexico statute requires that the writing "show[ ] upon its face that it was ... signed with the intent of recognizing the child as an heir." Where a statute prescribes the form a written acknowledgment must take, other courts have held that a tax return that identified the taxpayer's illegitimate child as his son or daughter did not constitute a sufficient written acknowledgment where the return did not strictly comply with all the requirements of the statute. See, e.g., Smith v. Smith, 40 Conn.Supp. 151, 483 A.2d 629, 630–31 (1984); Distefano v. Commonwealth, 201 Va. 23, 109 S.E.2d 497, 500–01 (1959).

The parties have not provided any legislative history for section 45-2-109(B)(2),[8] and we have not found any New Mexico cases directly on point. However, we believe our construction of the statute is consistent with New Mexico law. The New Mexico

---

8. The phrase "which shows upon its face that it was so signed with the intent of recognizing the child as an heir" is of obscure (though not illegitimate) parentage. The language dates back to at least 1915, see 1915 N.M.Laws ch. 69, § 1, and was carried over into subsequent revisions of the New Mexico Probate Code until the latest revision, in 1993. Although New Mexico borrowed its probate statutes from Kansas, which in turn adopted Iowa statutes, see State v. Chavez, 42 N.M. 569, 572–74, 82 P.2d 900, 903 (1938), the quoted language appears to be unique to New Mexico. The corresponding Iowa and Kansas statutes only required that the putative father recognize his illegitimate children as his children by "general and notorious" recognition "or else in writing." See McKellar v. Harkins, 183 Iowa 1030, 166 N.W. 1061, 1063 (1918) (quoting Iowa Code § 3385 (1897)); Estate of McKay v. Davis, 208 Kan. 282, 491 P.2d 932, 933 (1971) (quoting Kan.G.S. § 3845 (1915)). Under New Mexico law, proof of general and notorious recognition was required to corroborate a declaration of a deceased person regarding a written recognition, but alone it was not sufficient to make an illegitimate child an heir. See N.M.Stat.Ann. § 45-2-109(B)(2).

Supreme Court has recognized a distinction between paternity and heirship.[9] In Gallup v. Bailey (In re Gossett's Estate), 46 N.M. 344, 129 P.2d 56 (1942), the court held that the so-called bastardy act, which required the putative father of an illegitimate child to support and maintain the child if the father had acknowledged paternity in writing, "has no application to the descent and distribution and inheritance of estates; in which case the writing must be made for the purpose of recognizing the child as an heir, but this is not so as to the Bastardy Act." 46 N.M. at 351–52, 129 P.2d at 61.

In Haskew v. Haskew (In re Haskew's Estate), 56 N.M. 506, 245 P.2d 841 (1952), the court considered whether the putative father of an illegitimate child had sufficiently recognized the child so as to make the child his heir. The statute in effect at the time provided that, absent written recognition, the father must have recognized the child as his child and "such recognition must have been general and notorious." There was no written recognition in that case. The court held that there was sufficient evidence that the father had recognized the child as his own, but there was not sufficient evidence that the recognition was general and notorious. See 56 N.M. at 507, 245 P.2d at 841. Thus, the illegitimate child was not entitled to inherit from his father, even though paternity had been established.

Quinto Junior's tax returns do not show on their face that he intended his illegitimate children to be his heirs, that is, to inherit from him under New Mexico's intestate succession statutes. Consequently, they were not his "issue" within the meaning of the antilapse statute and would not have succeeded to any disclaimed property under section 45-2-605.[10] Therefore, when Quinto Junior disclaimed an interest in his father's estate, that interest passed to his stepmother, Soila, by operation of law, making the disclaimer a "qualified disclaimer" within the meaning of I.R.C. § 2518(b). Because the property passing to Soila, the surviving spouse, passed as a result of a qualified disclaimer, the estate properly claimed the marital deduction. Moreover, because the property is deemed to have passed directly from Quinto Senior to Soila, the disclaimer did not make Quinto Junior liable for the federal gift tax. Finally, because Quinto Junior was not required to file a gift tax return as a result of the disclaimer, he is not liable for the addition to tax under I.R.C. § 6651(a)(1) for failing to file a gift tax return.[11]

We recognize that the parties' settlement, which provided the basis for their disclaimer argument, may be nothing more than a blatant attempt to avoid paying estate

9. New Mexico is not alone in recognizing the distinction. See, e.g., Wong v. Wong Hing Young, 80 Cal.App.2d 391, 181 P.2d 741, 743 (1947) (an admission of paternity sufficient under the probate code was not sufficient to impose a support obligation on the putative father under the civil code); In re Flemm, 85 Misc.2d 855, 381 N.Y.S.2d 573, 577 (Sur.Ct.1975) (recognizing that under prior New York law an order of filiation establishing paternity entitled an illegitimate child to the support of the putative father but did not entitle the child to inherit from the putative father).

10. Our holding that Derrick and Christopher could not have inherited from their father at the time of Quinto Senior's death does not necessarily mean that the children will be denied an inheritance. The New Mexico Legislature repealed section 45-2-109 when it revised the Probate Code in 1993. The current statute provides that, for purposes of intestate succession, a person is "the child of his natural parents, regardless of their marital status," provided the natural parent "has openly treated the child as his and has not refused to support the child." N.M.Stat.Ann. § 45-2-114(A) & (C) (Michie Repl.1993). Quinto Junior's tax returns may well be evidence that he has "openly treated" the children as his and "not refused" to support them. However, that issue is not before us, and we express no opinion on it.

11. Our conclusion that the Tax Court erred in holding that the disclaimer did not meet the requirement of I.R.C. § 2518(b)(4) that the property pass "without any direction on the part of the person making the disclaimer" makes it unnecessary to reach the other issues the petitioners raise.

taxes. However, neither the probate court nor the Tax Court found anything wrong with the disclaimer other than its purported direction that the estate pass to Soila. The validity of the disclaimer is not properly before us. We have concluded that the effect of the disclaimer under the unique New Mexico probate statutes in effect at the time was to cause the estate to pass to Soila regardless of any direction on the part of Quinto Junior, thus making the estate eligible for the marital deduction under federal law. There is nothing wrong with trying to escape tax liability if the law allows a taxpayer to do so. See, e.g., Rothschild v. United States, 407 F.2d 404, 413 (Ct.Cl.1969); Prentis v. United States, 273 F.Supp. 449, 457 (S.D.N.Y.1964), aff'd in part, rev'd in part, 364 F.2d 525 (2d Cir.1966). Cf. Re Weston's Settlements, [1968] 3 All E.R. 338, 342 (C.A.1968) (per Lord Denning) ("no-one has ever suggested that [tax avoidance] is undesirable or contrary to public policy"; but although the avoidance of tax "may be lawful, ... it is not yet a virtue"). We believe in this case the law allowed the estate to claim the marital deduction. That does not mean that the petitioners can successfully escape taxation altogether. It simply means that the Commissioner may have to wait until Soila dies to collect taxes on the estate.

REVERSED.

IX. Advancements

Under the common law, it was presumed that a parent intended equality among his or her children. Thus, if a parent died intestate, and children—sometimes issue—survived the parent, the intestate statute would make an equal distribution among the surviving children. But what if one or more of the children had received his or her "portion" during lifetime in the form of tuition assistance, an expensive wedding, a car, or other significant gift? If, in relation to the deceased parent's estate, the child received something substantial during life, it was then presumed that this child had received what was his or her share of the intestate estate; therefore, this child was presumed to receive a proportionally less amount from the intestate statute. The child would rebut this by saying that the item that was received was a gift, free and simple, and was not intended to be part of the parent's intestate estate. Of course, it also may be a loan. There are three possibilities: advancement, gift, or loan. But the child would wish it to be a gift and, thus, would need to rebut the presumption that it was an advancement.

If, in fact, the parent intended an advancement, the amount of the advancement must be taken into consideration in calculating the amount the child will now receive. The advanced amount does not go through probate, but the value of the advancement at the time it was made comes into "hotchpot"—a fictitious amount, which includes the advancement and the intestate estate going to all of the children. Each child would then receive his or her share, and if the recipient of the advancement chooses to take from the intestate estate, the advanced amount is subtracted from what the child would have received. See, e.g., Miss. Code Ann. § 91-1-17 (Advancement from Intestate) (2005).

Because the burden of proof is on the child, the child would have to produce evidence of the parent's desire to make this a gift or a loan. Because the parent is dead and it is the siblings who are litigating, the process is involved and factional. There are few winners.

The Uniform Probate Code both enlarges the possibility of advancement in the context of intestate succession and, at the same time, reduces the possibility. Many states have followed the lead of the Code and now reject the presumption of advancement by requiring written proof of advancement, contemporaneously with the gift. *See, e.g.,* VA. CODE ANN. §64.1-63.1 (2003). Compare the common law rule with that of the Uniform Probate Code.

Uniform Probate Code (2003)

§2-109. Advancements.

(a) If an individual dies intestate as to all or a portion of his [or her] estate, property the decedent gave during the decedent's lifetime to an individual who, at the decedent's death, is an heir is treated as an advancement against the heir's intestate share only if (i) the decedent declared in a contemporaneous writing or the heir acknowledged in writing that the gift is an advancement or (ii) the decedent's contemporaneous writing or the heir's written acknowledgment otherwise indicates that the gift is to be taken into account in computing the division and distribution of the decedent's intestate estate.

(b) For purposes of subsection (a), property advanced is valued as of the time the heir came into possession or enjoyment of the property or as of the time of the decedent's death, whichever first occurs.

(c) If the recipient of the property fails to survive the decedent, the property is not taken into account in computing the division and distribution of the decedent's intestate estate, unless the decedent's contemporaneous writing provides otherwise.

Chapter Three

The Last Will and Testament

Tool Bar

A Little Background

The prominence of a Last Will and Testament has waned with the closing of the second millennium. Whereas previously a person of sufficient age, intent, and capacity needed to fulfill the commands of the Statute of Frauds (1677) and the Wills Act (1837) to bequeath and devise property to succeeding generations upon death, the third millennium has fully embraced a less formalistic mode of property transfer. Today, much of wealth is transferred at death through non-probate transfers or will substitutes. It is arguable that this has lowered the bar for Last Wills and Testaments. For example, today, the formalities of the Last Will and Testament may often be met with the clear and convincing proof of substantial compliance, and the rigidity of the demonstration of what was meant by a plain meaning word or phrase may be captured with clear and convincing proof of primary intent. These non-probate devices result, in part, from the explosion of non-probate transfers.

Professor John H. Langbein was among the first to conclude that the Last Will and Testament no longer exclusively served the needs of a modern society. First, the non-probate or will substitute transfer used by so many people today reflects the need of modern people to be individualistic in making decisions on how to transfer wealth. The probate system, with its strict requirements, forced people into a monopoly that stultified initiative and often resulted in failure to achieve individually desired goals. On the other hand, using living trusts, insurance policies, joint bank accounts, rights of survivorship, and payable on death beneficiaries allows a vast array of options to property owners. These modern options are fast, inexpensive, and far more accurate. Also, modern wealth does not consist so much of real estate but, rather, of contract rights or wealth in the form of stocks, pension funds, intellectual property, and bank deposits. These may more speedily be transferred at death through alternatives to a Last Will and Testament. *See* John H. Langbein, *The Nonprobate Revolution and the Future of the Law of Succession*, 97 HARV. L. REV. 1108 (1984). Finally, the business of selling non-probate devices and plans has firmly established itself in older, wealthier communities, and is able to reach millions of potential customers through advertisements, web sites, and community associations.

In reviewing the following material, ask yourself if you think the traditional requirements surrounding the execution of a probate transfer, especially in the context of a Last Will and Testament, are necessary or effective, and if they serve the public interest. Remember that there is a public policy obligation to those persons who earned the wealth and who seek to transfer it at death. And there is a concomitant obligation to those expecting a transfer. We should also admit that third parties, such as creditors, taxing agencies, and family members have a stake in the transfer of wealth as well. It is easy to get lost in the rules and fail to ask about the point of it all.

I. Categories of Wills

A. Statutory and Form Wills

California is one of a few states that offers to persons seeking a simple Last Will and Testament a form to complete that will serve as a valid instrument with which to transfer property at death. For the majority of people using the forms, the objective is to avoid the use of an attorney yet to meet the requirements of the probate code in that particular jurisdiction. California provides for a form will through statute. *See* CAL. PROB. CODE ANN. §§ 6240 et seq. (West 2004). To access the forms on the web, see http://www.calbar.ca.gov/calbar/pdfs/publications/Will-Form.pdf (accessed Oct. 12, 2005). The statute provides instructions to include filling in the blanks and proper execution and it repeatedly advises seeking assistance from an attorney concerning avoidance of taxes, estate planning, and the proper role of a form will. The forms provide printed wording with blanks for the testator to complete. Because the blanks are meant to refer to traditional family structure, they involve spouses (and domestic partners in the case of California), children, and trusts for the care and maintenance of these status individuals. Obviously, persons seeking more creative objectives would find the statutory and form wills lacking in creativity. So too, because the forms allow for completion and execution by persons without the supervision of an attorney, the process is often flawed, and, thus, the form is often ineffective. If the form will is ineffective, the property passes according to another mode of transfer—perhaps intestate succession—which often defeats the intention of the decedent. *See* Herbert T. Krimmel, *A Criticism of the California Statutory Will*, 19 W. STATE U. L. REV. 77 (1991).

The Internet has expanded creative approaches to form wills, and software companies provide usable forms that may be modified to meet individual objectives. For example, see Will Forms for Your State, http://www.uslegalforms.com/last_will_and_testament.html; *select* Will Forms - All States - Free Law (accessed Oct. 12, 2005); Legalzoom, Wills, http://www.legalzoom.com/legalzip/wills/will_procedure.html (accessed Oct. 12, 2005); Legacy Writer, Online Estate Planning Tools for Life, http://www.legacywriter.com/CreatYourWill_Process.html (accessed Oct. 12, 2005). Downloaded from web services, these forms allow persons to individualize testamentary transfers, but they most often lack professional assistance, which invites mistakes and, often, invalidity. Questions then arise as to the liability of companies that provide the forms to potential heirs, who would have benefitted if the forms had met the statutory requirements for a valid testamentary transfer.

B. Nuncupative Wills

The practice of permitting property to pass by nuncupative (oral) wills is very restricted. The oral character permits confusion and litigation, yet, in a few states, personal property of a very limited amount may be transferred at death through an oral transfer. Most often, the state will require that the oral will transpire in connection with a last illness and that it be stated in the presence of at least three people, who must reduce the statement to writing within a specified time. For an example, see Kay v. Sandler, 718 S.W.2d 872 (Tex. App. 14th Dist. 1986); OHIO REV. CODE ANN. § 2107.60 (West 2003). The Uniform Probate Code (1990) makes no provision for a nuncupative will.

C. Holographic Wills

Less than half of the states allow for holographic wills. Many of these states adopt the common law requirements that the purported holographic will be totally in the handwriting of the decedent, signed, and dated. The Uniform Probate Code makes minor adjustments to these requirements by minimizing them, however, it provides for the validity of holographic instruments as a means by which property may be transferred at death. Note the difference between the common law requirements and the following code provision.

Uniform Probate Code (2003)

§ 2-502. Execution; Witnessed Wills; Holographic Wills.

(a) Except as provided in subsection (b) and in Sections 2-503, 2-506, and 2-513, a will must be:

(1) in writing;

(2) signed by the testator or in the testator's name by some other individual in the testator's conscious presence and by the testator's direction; and

(3) signed by at least two individuals, each of whom signed within a reasonable time after he [or she] witnessed either the signing of the will as described in paragraph (2) or the testator's acknowledgment of that signature or acknowledgment of the will.

(b) A will that does not comply with subsection (a) is valid as a holographic will, whether or not witnessed, if the signature and material portions of the document are in the testator's handwriting.

(c) Intent that the document constitute the testator's will can be established by extrinsic evidence, including, for holographic wills, portions of the document that are not in the testator's handwriting.

In re Kimmel's Estate

Supreme Court of Pennsylvania, 1924
278 Pa. 435, 123 A. 405

SIMPSON, J.

One of decedent's heirs at law appeals from a decree of the orphans' court, directing the register of wills to probate the following letter:

'Johnstown, Dec. 12.

'The Kimmel Bro. and Famly We are all well as you can espec fore the time of the Year. I received you kind & welcome letter from Geo & Irvin all OK glad you poot your Pork down in Pickle it is the true way to keep meet every piece gets the same, now always poot it down that way & you will not miss it & you will have good pork fore smoking you can keep it from butchern to butchern the hole year round. Boys, I wont agree with you about the open winter I think we are gone to have one of the hardest. Plenty of snow & Verry cold verry cold! I dont want to see it this way but it will will come see to the old sow & take her away when the time comes well I cant say if I will come over yet. I will wright in my next letter it may be to ruff we will see in the next letter if I come I have some very valuable papers I want you to keep fore me so if enny thing hapens all the scock money in the 3 Bank liberty lones Post office stamps and my home on Horner St goes to George Darl & Irvin Kepp this letter lock it up it may help you out. Earl sent after his Christmas Tree & Trimmings I sent them he is in the Post office in Phila working.

'Will clost your Truly,

Father.'

This letter was mailed by decedent at Johnstown, Pa., on the morning of its date— Monday, December 12, 1921—to two of his children, George and Irvin, who were named in it as beneficiaries; the envelope being addressed to them at their residence in Glencoe, Pa. He died suddenly on the afternoon of the same day.

Two questions are raised: First. Is the paper testamentary in character? Second. Is the signature to it a sufficient compliance with our Wills Act? Before answering them directly, there are a few principles, now well settled, which, perhaps, should be preliminarily stated.

While the informal character of a paper is an element in determining whether or not it was intended to be testamentary (Kisecker's Estate, 190 Pa. 476, 42 Atl. 886), this becomes a matter of no moment when it appears thereby that the decedent's purpose was to make a posthumous gift. On this point the court below well said:

'Deeds, mortgages, letters, powers of attorney, agreements, checks, notes, etc., have all been held to be, in legal effect, wills. Hence, an assignment (Coulter v. Shelmadine, 204 Pa. 120, 53 Atl. 638), * * * a deed (Turner v. Scott, 51 Pa. 126), a letter of instructions (Scott's Estate, 147 Pa. 89, 23 Atl. 212, 30 Am. St. Rep. 713), a power of attorney (Rose v. Quick, 30 Pa. 225), and an informal letter of requests (Knox's Estate, 131 Pa. 220, 18 Atl. 1021, 6 L. R. A. 353, 17 Am. St. Rep. 798), were all held as wills.'

It is equally clear that where, as here, the words 'if enny thing hapens,' condition the gift, they strongly support the idea of a testamentary intent; indeed they exactly state what is expressed in or must be implied from every will. True, if the particular contingency stated in a paper, as the condition upon which it shall become effective, has never in fact occurred, it will not be admitted to probate. Morrow's Appeal, 116 Pa. 440, 9 Atl. 660, 2 Am. St. Rep. 616; Forquer's Estate, 216 Pa. 331, 66 Atl. 92, 8 Ann. Cas. 1146. In the present case, however, it is clear the contingency, 'if enny thing hapens,' was still existing when testator died suddenly on the same day he wrote and mailed the letter; hence, the facts not being disputed, the question of testamentary intent was one of law for the court. Davis' Estate, 275 Pa. 126, 118 Atl. 645.

As is often the case in holographic wills of an informal character, much of that which is written is not dispositive; and the difficulty, in ascertaining the writer's intent, arises largely from the fact that he had little, if any, knowledge of either law, punctuation, or grammar. In the present case this is apparent from the paper itself; and in this light the language now quoted must be construed:

'I think we are gone to have one of the hardest [winters]. Plenty of snow & Verry cold Verry cold! I dont want to see it this way but it will come * * * well I cant say if I will come over yet. I will wright in my next letter it may be to ruff we will see in the next letter if I come I have some very valuable papers I want you to keep fore me so if enny thing hapens all * * * [the real and personal property specified] goes to George Darl and Irvin Kepp this letter lock it up it may help you out.'

When resolved into plainer English, it is clear to us that all of the quotation, preceding the words 'I have some very valuable papers,' relate to the predicted bad weather, a doubt as to whether decedent will be able to go to Glencoe because of it, and a possible resolution of it in his next letter; the present one stating 'we will see in the next letter if I come.' This being so, the clause relating to the valuable papers begins a new subject of thought, and since the clearly dispositive gifts which follow are made dependent on no other contingency than 'if enny thing happens,' and death did happen suddenly on the same day, the paper, so far as respects those gifts, must be treated as testamentary.

It is difficult to understand how the decedent, probably expecting an early demise— as appears by the letter itself, and the fact of his sickness and inability to work, during the last three days of the first or second week preceding—could have possibly meant anything else than a testamentary gift, when he said 'so if enny thing hapens [the property specified] goes to George Darl and Irvin'; and why, if this was not intended to be effective in and of itself, he should have sent it to two of the distributees named in it, telling them to 'Kepp this letter lock it up it may help you out.'

The second question to be determined depends on the proper construction of section 2 of the Wills Act of June 7, 1917 (P. L. 403, 405; Pa. St. 1920, §8308), which is a re-enactment of section 6 of the Wills Act of April 8, 1833 (P. L. 249), reading as follows:

> 'Every will shall be in writing, and, unless the person making the same shall be prevented by the extremity of his last sickness, shall be signed by him at the end thereof, or by some person in his presence and by his express direction.'

The letter now being considered was all in the handwriting of decedent, including the word 'Father,' at the end of it; and hence the point to be decided would appear to resolve itself into this: Does the word 'Father,' when taken in connection with the contents of the paper, show that it was 'signed by him?' When stated thus bluntly—in the very language of the statute—the answer seems free from doubt; but since we said in Brennan's Estate, 244 Pa. 574, 581, 91 Atl. 220, 222, that 'signing in the usual acceptation of the word and in the sense in which, presumably, it is used in the act is the writing of a name or the affixing of what is meant as a signature,' we must go further and determine whether or not the word 'Father' was 'meant as a signature.'

In Vernon v. Kirk, 30 Pa. 218, 223, it is said:

> 'The purpose of the Legislature seems rather to have been to designate the place where the signature should be, to wit, at the end of the will, than to prescribe the manner in which it should be made. * * * It was not, as was supposed in the earlier cases, to furnish, in the handwriting, evidence of identity, and protection against fraud; for the name might be signed by the testator or by another at his request, in which last case no such proof is deducible from the handwriting. The authentication of the instrument was left to the witnesses. * * * While the place of the signature is rigidly defined, its made is left unfetered.'

In Knox's Estate, 131 Pa. 220, 229, 18 Atl. 1021, 1022 (6 L. R. A. 353, 17 Am. St. Rep. 798), this subject was fully considered, and we there said:

> 'The purposes of the act of 1833 were accuracy in the transmission of the testator's wishes, the authentication of the instrument transmitting them, the identification of the testator, and certainty as to his completed testamentary purpose. The first was attained by requiring writing instead of mere memory of witnesses, the second and third by the signature of testator, and the last by placing the signature at the end of the instrument. The first two requirements were derived from the English statute; the third was new (since followed by the act of 1 Vict. c. 26), and was the result of experience of the dangers of having mere memoranda or incomplete directions taken for the expression of final intention. Baker's Appeal, 107 Pa. 381; Vernon v. Kirk, 30 Pa. 223. These being the purposes of the act, and the Legislature not having concerned itself with what should be deemed a signing, we must look dehors the statute for a definition. As already said, the act is founded on the statute of frauds, 29 Car. 2. Under that act it has been held that the signing may be by a mark, or by initials only, or by a fictitious or assumed name, or by a name different from that by which the testator is designated in the body of the will. 1 Jarman on Wills, 78; 1 Redf. of Wills, c. 6, § 18, and cases there cited.'

This has been approved and followed in Plate's Estate, 148 Pa. 55, 23 Atl. 1038, 33 Am. St. Rep. 805; Swire's Estate, 225 Pa. 188, 192, 73 Atl. 1110; and Churchill's Estate, 260 Pa. 94, 100, 103 Atl. 533, and has never been doubted. If, then, the word 'Father,' was intended as a completed signature to this particular character of paper, it answers all the purposes of the Wills Act. That it was so intended we have no doubt. It was the method employed by decedent in signing all such letters, and was mailed by him as a finished document. In these respects it varies from Brennan's Estate, supra, so much relied on by appellant, where the writing of 'your misserable father,' was construed to be not a signature, but part of an unfinished paper, which decedent retained, and to which his signature was not subsequently attached.

It is of course true—and upon this point Plate's Estate, supra, and Brennan's Estate, supra, were decided—that while 'exactly what constitutes a signing has never been reduced to a judicial formula,' if that which is written at the end of the paper is not 'a full and complete signature according to the intention and understanding of the testator,' it is not a compliance with the statute. The same cases decide, however, it will be held to be so, 'if the intent to execute is apparent.' In the present case, as already pointed out, testator used the word 'Father,' as a complete signature, and mailed the paper as a finished document. True, a formal will would not be so executed; but this is not a formal will. It is a letter, signed by him in the way he executed all such letters, and, from this circumstance, his 'intent to execute is apparent' beyond all question.

Decree affirmed and appeal dismissed, the costs in this court to be paid by the estate of Harry A. Kimmel, deceased.

D. Witnessed Wills

When people think of a Last Will and Testament, they think of a process described in print, television, and the movies. That is, an attorney invites a well-dressed person into a dignified room and, in the presence of two or three disinterested persons, invites the lead character to admit that this document is his or her Will and to signify this with a signature on the last page. This signing is then followed by inviting the witnesses to sign and then departing after the attorney makes a grand show of handing the completed document to the client. The entire procedure seems quite staged and, in fact, it is. And the procedure has a lengthy history.

The formalities and the procedure for the execution of a witnessed Will derive from two English statutes: the Statute of Frauds (1677) and the Wills Act (1837). These two statutes form the basis of a procedure that dominated Will attestation for decades but now may vary from state to state. It can be argued that to be secure in due execution, a Will should be executed in conformity with the strictest requirements (the Statute of Frauds and the Wills Act) in order to meet the requirements of any state within which the testator may one day die domiciled. Even though the Uniform Probate Code may be enacted in whole or in part, the requirements contained therein vary from those of the two much earlier English statutes. Thus, examine the historical requirements of the English statutes and compare them to the Uniform Probate Code:

Statute of Frauds

29 Car. II, c. 3, § V (1677)

And be it further enacted by the authority aforesaid, that from and after the said four and twentieth day of June all devises and bequests of any lands or tenements, devisable either by force of the Statute of Wills, or by this Statute, or by force of the custom of Kent, or the custom of any borough, or any other particular custom, shall be in writing, and signed by the party so devising the same, or by some other person in his presence and by his express directions, and shall be attested and subscribed in the presence of the said devisor by three or four credible witnesses, or else they shall be utterly void and of none effect.

Wills Act

7 Wm. IV& 1 Vict., c. 26, § IX (1837)

And be it further enacted, that no will shall be valid unless it shall be in writing and executed in manner hereinafter mentioned; (that is to say), it shall be signed at the foot or end thereof by the testator, or by some other person in his presence and by his direction; and such signature shall be made or acknowledged by the testator in the presence of two or more witnesses present at the same time, and such witnesses shall attest and shall subscribe the will in the presence of the testator, but no form of attestation shall be necessary.

California Probate Code (2003)

§ 6110. Necessity of writing; other requirements

(a) Except as provided in this part, a will shall be in writing and satisfy the requirements of this section.

(b) The will shall be signed by one of the following:

(1) By the testator.

(2) In the testator's name by some other person in the testator's presence and by the testator's direction.

(3) By a conservator pursuant to a court order to make a will under Section 2580.

(c) The will shall be witnessed by being signed by at least two persons each of whom (1) being present at the same time, witnessed either the signing of the will or the testator's acknowledgment of the signature or of the will and (2) understand that the instrument they sign is the testator's will.

Notes

Like the California Code above, the Uniform Probate Code relaxes the requirements of the English statutes in reference to witnesses and the testator's acknowledgment. Note Unif. Prob. Code § 2-502(a)(3) (allowing for witnesses to sign "within a reasonable time after either the signing of the will ... or the testator's acknowledgment...."). Whether or not any of the statute's formalities have been met is a matter for contest of the will. The requirements contained in the previous statutes may be divided into two separate grounds of contest: formalities and intentionalities. The statutes explicitly define the formalities required, yet there is a corresponding requirement that, at the time the formality was executed, the testator must possess proper intentionalities. These intentionalities will be discussed later in the context of contest of Wills. For now, we examine each of the formalities recited in the previously identified statutes. While each state may or may not require each of these, each formality may decide whether or not the Will may be probated.

Tax Considerations: A valid Last Will and Testament is an essential document in any estate plan that seeks to maximize tax advantages. Although not exhaustive, consider the following examples: (1) Charities are not heirs, and, thus, are not automatically able to inherit under any state intestate statute. Yet a valid Last Will and Testament may donate an unlimited amount to any charity and qualify for a charitable deduction. See I.R.C. § 2055. (2) Since intestate statutes do not always provide that a surviving spouse takes all of the estate assets, only a Last Will and Testament can guarantee that the decedent's estate qualifies for the unlimited marital deduction. See I.R.C. § 2056. (3) If the decedent was the Donee of a general testamentary power of appointment, the general power will be included within the decedent's gross estate whether the power is exercised or not. See I.R.C. § 2041. Failure to consider the tax ramifications of possessing such a power may result in significant tax liability. A Last Will and Testament may manage this liability in a better fashion. See, e.g., John G. Steinkamp, *Estate and Gift Taxation of Powers of Appointment Limited by Ascertainable Standards,* 79 MARQ. L. REV. 1996 (1995). (4) The Last Will and Testament allows a decedent to create a trust that will benefit the decedent's children and succeeding generations, such as grandchildren and great-grandchildren. These trusts are commonly referred to as generation skipping trusts and receive advantageous treatment under changes to the Generation Skipping Transfer Tax (GST). For the I.R.S. Generation-Skipping Transfer Tax form, see Internal Revenue Service, Generation-Skipping Transfer Tax Return, http://www.irs.gov/pub/irs-pdf/f706gsd.pdf (accessed Oct. 12, 2005). For the Generation-Skipping Transfer Tax form for California, see California Bureau of Tax Administration, California Generation-Skipping Transfer Tax Return, http://www.sco.ca.gov/col/taxinfo/estate/distributions/gstd.pdf (accessed Oct. 12, 2005). For the Generation-Skipping Transfer Tax Form for the State of New York, see New York State, Department of Taxation and Finance, Estate/Generation Skipping Transfer Tax Forms, http://www.tax.state.ny.us/pdf/2005/et/et500_105.pdf (accessed Oct. 10, 2005). Like the federal estate tax, the generation skipping tax is scheduled to be repealed and the amounts subject to taxation continue to decline as the exemption rises. Chapter 13 of the Internal Revenue Code provides detailed rules in assigning intergenerational tax liability. *See* I.R.C. §§ 2601–2663. (5) The intent of the Testator controls the apportionment of debt among the estate's beneficiaries. Whether this includes those persons benefitting from will substitutes, and how the apportionment occurs within the Last Will and Testament, depends upon the intent expressed by the Testator.

An example of how a decedent's estate may be surprised by unanticipated "economic dominion" is illustrated by the following decision.

Estate of Kurz v. Commissioner
United States Court of Appeals, Seventh Circuit, 1995
68 F.3d 1027

EASTERBROOK, Circuit Judge.

Between her husband's death, in 1971, and her own, in 1986, Ethel H. Kurz was the beneficiary of two trusts. Kurz received the income from each. She was entitled to as much of the principal of one (which we call the Marital Trust) as she wanted; all she had to do was notify the trustee in writing. She could take only 5% of the other (which we call the Family Trust) in any year, and then only if the Marital Trust was exhausted. When Kurz died, the Marital Trust contained assets worth some $3.5 million, and the Family Trust was worth about $3.4 million. The estate tax return included in the gross estate the whole value of the Marital Trust and none of the value of the Family Trust. The Tax Court held that Kurz held a general power of appointment over 5% of the Family Trust, requiring the inclusion of another $170,000 under 26 U.S.C. § 2041(a)(2). 101 T.C. 44, 1993 WL 270973 (1993); see also T.C. Memo 1994-221, 1994 WL 193870 (computing a tax due of approximately $31,000).

Section 2041(b)(1) defines a general power of appointment as "a power which is exercisable in favor of the decedent, his estate, his creditors, or the creditors of his estate". Kurz had the power to consume or appoint the corpus of the Marital Trust to anyone she pleased whenever she wanted, and the Estate therefore concedes that it belongs in the gross estate. For her part, the Commissioner of Internal Revenue concedes that the 95% of the Family Trust that was beyond Kurz's reach even if the Marital Trust had been empty was not subject to a general power of appointment. What of the other 5%? None of the Family Trust could be reached while the Marital Trust contained 1¢, and the Estate submits that, until the exhaustion condition was satisfied (which it never was), the power to appoint 5% in a given year was not "exercisable", keeping the Family Trust outside the gross estate. To this the Commissioner replies that a power is "exercis*able*" if a beneficiary has the ability to remove the blocking condition. Suppose, for example, that the Family Trust could not have been touched until Ethel Kurz said "Boo!". Her power to utter the magic word would have been no different from her power, under the Marital Trust, to send written instructions to the trustee.

The Tax Court was troubled by an implication of the Commissioner's argument. Suppose the Family Trust had provided that Kurz could reach 5% of the principal if and only if she lost 20 pounds, or achieved a chess rating of 1600, or survived all of her children. She *could* have gone on a crash diet, or studied the games of Gary Kasparov, or even murdered her children. These are not financial decisions, however, and it would be absurd to have taxes measured by one's ability to lose weight, or lack of moral scruples. Imagine the trial, five years after a person's death, at which friends and relatives troop to the stand to debate whether the decedent was ruthless enough to kill her children, had enough willpower to lay off chocolates, or was smart enough to succeed at chess. The Tax Court accordingly rejected the Commissioner's principal argument, ruling that raw ability to satisfy a condition is insufficient to make a power of appointment "exercisable".

If not the Commissioner's position, then what? The Estate's position, 180° opposed, is that the condition must be actually satisfied before a power can be deemed "exercisable". The Tax Court came down in the middle, writing that a condition may be disregarded when it is "illusory" and lacks any "significant non-tax consequence independent of the decedent's ability to exercise the power." Of course, illusions are in the eye of the beholder, and we are hesitant to adopt a legal rule that incorporates a standard well suited to stage magicians (though some legal drafters can give prestidigitators a run for their money). No one doubts that the Kurz family had good, non-tax reasons for the structure of the trust funds. The only question we need resolve is whether a sequence of withdrawal rights prevents a power of appointment from being "exercisable". Despite the large number of trusts in the United States, many of them arranged as the Kurz trusts were, this appears to be an unresolved issue. Neither side could find another case dealing with stacked trusts, and we came up empty handed after independent research.

For a question of first principles, this one seems remarkably simple. Section 2041 is designed to include in the taxable estate all assets that the decedent possessed or effectively controlled. If only a lever must be pulled to dispense money, then the power is exercisable. The funds are effectively under the control of the beneficiary, which is enough to put them into the gross estate. Whether the lever is a single-clutch or double-clutch mechanism can't matter. Imagine a trust divided into 1,000 equal funds numbered 1 to 1,000, Fund 1 of which may be invaded at any time, and Fund n of which may be reached if and only if Fund n-1 has been exhausted. Suppose the beneficiary depletes Funds 1 through 9 and dies when $10 remains in Fund 10. Under the Kurz Estate's view, only $10 is included in the gross estate, because Funds 11 through 1,000 could not have been touched until that $10 had been withdrawn. But that would be a ridiculously artificial way of looking at things. Tax often is all about form, see Howell v. United States, 775 F.2d 887 (7th Cir.1985), but § 2041 is an anti-formal rule. It looks through the trust to ask how much wealth the decedent actually controlled at death. The decedent's real wealth in our hypothetical is $10 plus the balance of Funds 11 through 1,000; the decedent could have withdrawn and spent the entire amount in a trice. Whether this series of trusts has spend-thrift features (as the Kurz trusts did) or is invested in illiquid instruments (as the Kurz trusts were) would not matter. The Estate does not deny that Kurz had a general power of appointment over the entire Marital Trust, despite these features. If the costs of removing wealth from the trust do not prevent including in the gross estate the entire corpus of the first trust in a sequence (they don't), then the rest of the sequence also is includable.

Wait!, the Estate exclaims. How did first principles get into a tax case? After consulting the statute, a court turns next to the regulations. 26 C.F.R. § 20.2041-3(b) provides:

For purposes of section 2041(a)(2), a power of appointment is considered to exist on the date of a decedent's death even though the exercise of the power is subject to the precedent of giving of notice, or even though the exercise of the power takes effect only on the expiration of a stated period after its exercise, whether or not on or before the decedent's death notice has been given or the power has been exercised. However, a power which by its terms is exercisable only upon the occurrence during the decedent's lifetime of an event or a contingency which did not in fact take place or occur during such time is not a power in existence on the date of the decedent's death. For example, if a decedent was given a general power of appointment exercisable only after he reached a certain age, only if he survived another person, or only if he died without descendants, the power would not be in existence on the date of the decedent's death if the condition precedent to its exercise had not occurred.

The Kurz Estate takes heart from the provision that "a power which by its terms is exercisable only upon the occurrence during the decedent's lifetime of an event or a contingency which did not in fact take place or occur during such time is not a power in existence on the date of the decedent's death." Like the Tax Court, however, we do not find in this language the strict sequencing principle the Estate needs.

This is the Commissioner's language, and the Commissioner thinks that it refers only to conditions that could not have been satisfied. Regulation-writers have substantial leeway in their interpretation, see Shalala v. Guernsey Memorial Hospital, 514 U.S. 87, 115 S.Ct. 1232, 1236–37, 131 L.Ed.2d 106 (1995), because the delegation of the power to make substantive regulations is the delegation of a law-creation power, and interpretation is a vital part of the law-creation process. See Homemakers North Shore, Inc. v. Bowen, 832 F.2d 408 (7th Cir.1987). A reading must of course be reasonable—must be an interpretation—else the rulemaker is revising the law without the requisite notice and opportunity for comment. Pettibone Corp. v. United States, 34 F.3d 536, 541–42 (7th Cir.1994). The Commissioner's understanding of the regulation tracks its third sentence, which is designed to illustrate the second. It says: "For example, if a decedent was given a general power of appointment exercisable only after he reached a certain age, only if he survived another person, or only if he died without descendants, the power would not be in existence on the date of the decedent's death if the condition precedent to its exercise had not occurred." All three examples in the third sentence deal with conditions the decedent could not have controlled, at least not in the short run, or lawfully. The rate of chronological aging is outside anyone's control, whether one person survives another does not present an option that may be exercised lawfully, and whether a person has descendants on the date of death is something that depends on the course of an entire life, rather than a single choice made in the administration of one's wealth.

By contrast, the sequence in which a beneficiary withdraws the principal of a series of trusts barely comes within the common understanding of "event or … contingency". No one could say of a single account: "You cannot withdraw the second dollar from this account until you have withdrawn the first." The existence of this sequence is tautological, but a check for $2 removes that sum without satisfying a contingency in ordinary, or legal, parlance. Zeno's paradox does not apply to financial transactions. Breaking one account into two or more does not make the sequence of withdrawal more of a "contingency"—at least not in the sense that §20.2041-3(b) uses that term.

No matter how the second sentence of § 20.2041-3(b) should be applied to a contingency like losing 20 pounds or achieving a chess rating of 1600, the regulation does not permit the beneficiary of multiple trusts to exclude all but the first from the estate by the expedient of arranging the trusts in a sequence. No matter how long the sequence, the beneficiary exercises economic dominion over all funds that can be withdrawn at any given moment. The estate tax is a wealth tax, and dominion over property is wealth. Until her death, Ethel Kurz could have withdrawn all of the Marital Trust and 5% of the Family Trust by notifying the Trustee of her wish to do so. This case is nicely covered by the first sentence of § 20.2041-3(b), the notice provision, and the judgment of the Tax Court is therefore

AFFIRMED.

II. Statutory Formalities

A. Presence

In re Demaris' Estate
Circuit Court of Oregon, 1941
166 Or. 36, 110 P.2d 571

ROSSMAN, Justice.

This is an appeal from an order of the circuit court which, after dismissing a contest of an instrument testamentary in form which was presented to the county court for probate as the last will and testament of George Demaris, deceased, held that the said instrument was in truth the last will and testament of said deceased and was entitled to probate as such.

George Demaris, a bachelor, 39 years of age, died in Milton, Umatilla County, April 11, 1939, leaving an estate which was appraised as worth $7,347.57. The contested instrument made the deceased's sister, Ida Fuller, sole beneficiary. She is the proponent. The original contestant was Amos Demaris, father of the deceased. He died after the proceeding had begun and was succeeded as contestant by Arch Demaris, his son and executor of his estate. The petition made two charges against the script: (a) improper execution; and (b) undue influence. The latter charge has been virtually abandoned. The findings of fact of the circuit court state: "At the time of the execution of said will George Demaris was not acting under duress, fraud or undue influence." We have carefully read the transcript of evidence and are fully satisfied that there was no room for any other finding. The evidence shows that when he signed this instrument the deceased was free from all improper influences and acted purely upon his own volition. His mind was clear.

The portion of the petition which recites the charge of improper execution says: "Said instrument of writing was prepared by Harold B. Gillis, in the absence of George Demaris and it was never read by nor read to him and he did not know the contents thereof at the time he subscribed his name thereto; that after the said George Demaris subscribed his name thereto, the said instrument of writing was taken from the room occupied by the said George Demaris into another room more than twenty-five feet from the said George Demaris, entirely out of his sight and wholly out of his presence, where it was then signed by the said Harold B. Gillis and Jean I. Gillis, his wife, as pretended witnesses, and the said George Demaris did not see either of said witnesses subscribe his or her name to the said instrument of writing and he did not know and never did know who were witnesses to the said instrument of writing or whether the same was witnessed by anyone or at all."

It will be observed that the signatures of the testator and of the two attesting witnesses are conceded. The only issues, therefore, are: did the testator know (1) the contents of the instrument, and (2) the identity of the attesters; and did the attesting witnesses sign "in the presence of the testator" within the contemplation of § 18-201, O.C.L.A., which says: "Every will shall be in writing, signed by the testator, or by some other person under his direction, in his presence, and shall be attested by two or more competent witnesses, subscribing their names to the will, in the presence of the testator."

George Demaris' mother had predeceased him. His father was still living at the time of George's death, but died shortly thereafter. He left no estate, unless George's descended to him. Since George left no issue, and since his mother had predeceased him, his estate descended to his father, if the will under attack is invalid. The father's will bequeathed the sum of $1 to Ida Fuller, sole beneficiary of George's will, and of the remainder of the estate left to Ann Kelly and Arch Demaris one-fourth each. All three of those persons were children of Amos Demaris; Ann and Ida were sisters of George, and Arch was his brother. We shall refer to those three frequently hereafter. As has already been said, Ida Fuller is the proponent and Arch Demaris is the contestant. Ann Kelly was one of the latter's principal witnesses. George was the youngest of the nine children of Amos Demaris and his wife. Some time before their deaths the parents had separated. This and other circumstances caused friction to develop, not only between some of the children and the father, but also between some of the children themselves. George was one of the children who sympathized with his mother and evidenced displeasure at his father's course. He and Ida were near in age and shared the same views. Ida did not marry until a year or so before George's death.

We shall now give a resume of the evidence which bears upon the above charges. George Demaris lived upon a farm situated near Milton. April 2, 1939, he was taken ill and summoned his sister, Mrs. Ann Kelly, who lived nearby. Shortly she took him to the office of Dr. Harold B. Gillis in Milton. Dr. Gillis is the person named in the contestant's petition. At the time of George's arrival Dr. Gillis was absent, but his wife, a registered nurse, who was in charge of the office, communicated with her husband by telephone. Pursuant to instructions which she received over the telephone, Mrs. Gillis administered to George a quarter grain of morphine, the purpose being to relieve the intense pain from which he was suffering. George weighed 190 pounds. The uncontradicted evidence indicates that a man of that weight, experiencing pain as intense as that which George was suffering, could sustain no lessening of mental powers from the administration of a quarter grain of morphine.

The witnesses referred to Dr. Gillis' office as a clinic. It was a one-story building, 30 by 30 feet in ground dimensions, divided into eight rooms. We are concerned with only the three front rooms. These were a waiting room with a consultation room to its left and a treatment room to its right. * * * The two doors connecting these three rooms were 29 inches wide. [There was] ... a cot and a bed in the treatment room and a desk in the consultation room.

* * *

When George entered the clinic he was taken at once into the treatment room and was placed upon the cot. In order to make him more comfortable a bed was then brought into the room and he was placed upon it with his head toward the west. The cot was 22 inches wide and the bed 36 inches wide. The two were placed within a few inches of each other. When the door was open it touched the foot of the cot. Next to the north wall of the treatment room was some electrical equipment. Between the equipment and the bed there remained a space about a foot and a half wide. It was in this space, of narrow corridor, that Mrs. Kelly and Dr. Gillis stood when the incidents which we shall shortly describe took place. After the bed had been moved into the room George was placed upon it. * * *

After Dr. Gillis had made his examination he arrived at the conclusion that an operation was necessary and so told the members of the family that had gathered. He suggested that it might be advisable to secure a consultant. It was agreed that Dr. J. W. Ingram of Walla Walla should be called. He did not arrive, however, until after the incidents with which we are concerned had taken place, and hence we shall have no occasion to mention him again. Before Dr. Ingram arrived, which was about 10 P. M., Dr. Gillis was told that George wanted to speak to him. Dr. Gillis had been in Milton for only two years and had not known George prior to this evening. Likewise, Mrs. Fuller was a stranger to him, but he had attended other members of the Demaris family. After George had made known his wish to speak to Dr. Gillis alone, the physician asked those in the room to leave. Apparently those who were in the room were Mrs. Fuller and Mrs. Kelly. After they had stepped into the waiting room Dr. Gillis closed the door. We now quote from his testimony: "After everybody had left there he said, 'Doc, I am in an awful serious condition and I don't know whether I will live. If I don't live, I want my sister Ide to have everything I have got.'" "Ide" was George's nickname for his sister Ida Fuller. Continuing, the physician said, "I believe the first thing that I did, I asked if he had a previous will and he said 'No.' Then, I asked if he wanted to leave all of his money and real estate and personal properties, and he said 'Yes.' And so, I said, 'I will draw it up as to that effect.' And I went into my office and got out my stationery and started to typewrite that down but I didn't know the complete name of the beneficiary or her address. (Q.) That was Mrs. Fuller? (A.) Mrs. Fuller. And so I called her into my private office to ask her name and address and I don't believe at that time I told her it was for a will, and I merely asked her her name and address in Walla Walla." When he said that he repaired to his private office for the purpose of typewriting the will he meant * * * the consultation room. [There was] a desk in that room. Upon the desk stood a typewriter and it was upon that instrument that he wrote the will. Before Dr. Gillis left the room George had asked him not to mention to those in the waiting room the request which he had just made for the preparation of the will. A copy of the script which the witness prepared follows:

"Milton, Oregon
"April 2, 1939

"Being sound of mind I, George Demaris, do will and bequeath all real and personal properties as well as monies to my sister, Ida Fuller, 846 N. 9th St., Walla Walla, Washington.

"Signed_____

"Witnessed by_____."

Dr. Gillis said that this was the first will he had ever prepared, and added, "the last."

Only two or three minutes were consumed in typing the will and thereupon Dr. Gillis re-entered George's room, bringing with him not only the writing but also a pen and a magazine. He swore that when he re-entered the room Mrs. Gillis was there attending to George and that they were the only two persons in the room. He could not recall whether he closed the door after re-entering. We now quote from his testimony: "I took a pen with me and a magazine for him to write on and propped him up in bed. He was lying on his left side. I put him up so he could write and I said, 'George, here's the will,' and it 'bequeathed all your monies and real and personal properties to your sister Ida Fuller' and to sign here." He said that George, who was in severe pain, did not read the will before signing and that he (Dr. Gillis) did not read it to him. Further testifying, he swore that while George was signing his name to the instrument he had another attack of cystic vomiting and thereupon Mrs. Gillis departed for the purpose of obtaining some towels. He explained that George refused to use an emesis basin, hence, the need for the towels. As Mrs. Gillis hurried out of the room "someone came into the room," so the physician swore. After George had completed his signature Dr. Gillis left the room and took the script with him. Twenty to thirty minutes later he and his wife entered the consultation room and there, as attesting witnesses, signed the will. The witness said that George had not expressly asked him to sign. He could not recall whether the doors of the waiting room were closed at that time. When he signed he was seated in a chair on the north side of the desk, and when his wife signed she was standing on the south side of the desk. The desk was 34 by 60 inches in size. The witness swore that it was impossible for George to have seen him (the witness) when he signed the will, but that it was physically possible for George to have seen Mrs. Gillis sign. After the two had signed as attesting witnesses, Dr. Gillis placed the will in a compartment of his desk. Before doing so he did not show it to George; in fact, after George had signed the will he never saw it again.

Dr. Gillis testified that following the operation George's condition showed marked improvement until 3:30 in the morning of the day of his death, which was nine days after the operation. The cause of the death, according to the physician, was cerebral embolism. In the period in which George seemed on the way to recovery, "I kidded him," so Dr. Gillis testified, "about not needing his will." George's only response, according to the witness, was "he smiled and felt pretty good." Upon cross-examination the witness slightly elaborated upon the above narrative. Among other matters, he said, "I remember I told him that here was his will, and that he had bequeathed-willed all of his monies and properties to his sister Ida." Some time after George had signed the operation was performed.

Mrs. Gillis testified that she knew nothing about the preparation of the will. Her first information about the writing came when her husband entered the room where she was attending George and "said, 'Here, George, this is what I have written' or something to that effect, and read—he didn't read it, he just told him the contents of what he had written * * *. I believe it was something like this, 'I bequeath all of my real and personal property to Ida Fuller.' Something like that. That was the contents anyway." Upon cross-examination, her words were: "He came in and shut the door and said, 'Here it is, George.' And he told him the contents—I don't remember the words. He told him the contents and he held it in his hand and he picked up the magazine and put the will on the magazine and put the will so he could see it." She testified that she remained in the room until George had written "George D" whereupon George began to vomit and she rushed out of the room for a supply of towels. About twenty to thirty minutes later she met her husband in the consultation room and was then asked by him to sign as an attesting witness. George had not asked her to do so. She said that when her husband made this request she at first demurred, explaining that she did not care to have anything to do with wills, but yielded and signed when he said, "You are the only one here that is not a relative." She too swore that her husband was seated in his office chair and that she signed while standing on the south side of the desk. Both doors of the waiting room stood open. She said that George, while lying in the bed, could have seen her in the act of signing the will had he looked, and added that while she was signing she could plainly see George. She too said that it was impossible for George to have seen Dr. Gillis sign. The will was not signed sooner, she explained, because in the interval she was engaged in performing various duties for other persons in the clinic. At the time of the signing there were in the reception room, according to her testimony, Mr. and Mrs. Arch Demaris and Mr. and Mrs. Fuller. Mrs. Kelly at that moment was attending George. Upon cross-examination, she was asked to estimate how far George was from her when she signed. She answered that the distance was 15 or 16 feet. She was unable to say whether George saw her sign.

Like her husband, Mrs. Gillis testified that a day or two after the operation George showed great improvement. In fact, he shortly talked about returning home and made arrangements for Ida Fuller to stay with him then. In his conversations with Mrs. Gillis he said, so she swore, "If anything does happen to me, I want Mrs. Fuller to have everything." She was then asked, "Did he mention the will itself?" Her reply follows: "Yes. Yes, he asked me if the doctor had the will, but he never at any time asked to see it. He asked me if it was in safekeeping. * * * He asked me if I had witnessed the will and I said 'Yes.' And he said, 'I thought so.' and that was about all of the conversation there was about witnessing." She thought that conversation occurred the third day after the execution of the will. Upon further questioning, she added, "He asked me if I didn't sign it, and I said, 'Yes.' And he said, 'Yes, I thought you did.' And he said, 'I know Doc did.'" Mrs. Gillis swore that she had never seen either George or Ida Fuller prior to the evening when the two entered on account of George's illness.

The bed upon which George lay was more than 6 feet long and was higher than an ordinary bed. Since the treatment room was only 9 feet long, the foot of the bed was less than 3 feet from the door opening.

* * *

Arch Demaris, the contestant, who helped to place George in the bed, remained near at hand until George was taken to the operating room. We shall now review his testimony. He saw Dr. Gillis in the course of the evening enter George's room and heard him to say, "Clear the room." Following this direction, Ida Fuller and Ann Kelly stepped into the waiting room where Arch was seated. In a few minutes he saw Dr. Gillis return to the consultation room and at that moment, since "George started to throw up, she (Mrs. Kelly) run in the room." After Dr. Gillis had seated himself at his desk he asked Arch's wife whether a capital or a small M was used in the name Demaris. In three or four minutes the doctor "went into George's room and he said, 'Here, George, sign this.' * * * Well, the doctor—my sister Ann Kelly was standing right at the head of the bed and the doctor walked in, and there was a passage probably a foot wide, as near as I can remember. He was kind of stooped over and he kind of reached that book or whatever he had with him out there and said, 'George, sign this.'" According to Arch, Ann Kelly, and not Mrs. Gillis, was with George at that time. Arch at that time was seated upon the aforementioned davenport and, according to his testimony, "I seen George lift his hand up like he was going to sign it." He was then asked whether he could see any movement of George's hand, and replied, "I seen him raise his hand but I never paid any more attention about him signing." At that point, according to Arch, "the doctor came back out," and went to the consultation room. Upon cross-examination, Arch testified that after Dr. Gillis had typed the instrument he carried it into George's room, not in his pocket, but openly, where it was visible to those who cared to look. He also swore that from his position on the davenport "I couldn't say that I could see all of the bed; * * * I could see, oh, I would say half of the bed anyway." He was positive he could see George's hands, face and head.

Bessie Demaris, wife of Arch, was another of his witnesses. She had known Dr. Gillis about a year and said that she and the physician's wife were good friends. She was seated upon the davenport when the incidents which she described occurred. She saw Dr. Gillis enter George's room were Ida Fuller and Ann Kelly were endeavoring to comfort George. According to her testimony, she then heard Dr. Gillis say, "Clear the room, all of you, clear the room." The two women then left and the door was closed. In a few minutes Dr. Gillis left George's room, went into the consultation room, and seated himself by his typewriter and began to type. Next, "he motioned for me to come like that (indicating) and I went and stood at the end of the desk and he said, 'How do you spell Demaris, with a capital M or a small M?'" After the typing had been concluded she saw Dr. Gillis re-enter George's room and heard him say "Sign this George." At that moment, according to this witness, Mrs. Ann Kelly was at the head of George's bed. We now quote further from her testimony: "And George raised up but I couldn't see him sign his name on that, but I could see his arm move. * * * He said 'Sign this George' and George raised up and signed." She swore that she did not know the nature of the paper that George signed and said that its contents had not been read to George.

The only other witness whose testimony we shall mention is that of Ida Fuller. We shall mention only a minor part of hers. She testified that Dr. Gillis inquired of her, and not of Mrs. Kelly or of Mrs. Bessie Demaris, for the manner of spelling the name Demaris. She further testified that besides asking for that information, the doctor also asked for her (Mrs. Fuller's) address. By reverting to the copy of the will, set forth in a preceding paragraph, it will be observed that Mrs. Fuller's name, street and post office addresses all appear in the will. Since that is true, and since none of the other witnesses who contradicted Mrs. Fuller claim that they gave that information, this circumstance speaks strongly in favor of Mrs. Fuller as a truthful witness. However, we are free to confess that this issue is minor.

A high degree of affection was manifested between George and his sister Ida Fuller, sole beneficiary of the challenged document. The last fact that we shall mention will be stated in the words of the memorandum decision of the circuit judge who tried this case. His description is apt and well sustained by the record. It follows: "* * * the beneficiary of the will, Ida Fuller, throughout her entire life, has displayed a tireless devotion to the testator. It is true that her brothers and sisters are honest, industrious and splendid law-abiding citizens; but in sickness and distress, in good times and bad, she was the one who was always ready to sacrifice her own time and energy, whenever the testator, her brother, needed help. When he was sick, no matter where she might be, she was the one who was called upon to return, and care for him. Freely and gladly she answered the call and nursed him back to health. If he had not remembered her in his will, it would have appeared strange. While she is not old, she is no longer young, and is poor financially. He chose the honorable course, and it was only to be expected, that when he was stricken, and on his death-bed, and no doubt with a foreboding that he was approaching the end, his thoughts should turn towards this sister, who had been so unselfish and devoted to him. * * *"

None of the contestant's witnesses were questioned about the attestation of the will, nor were they asked whether Dr. and Mrs. Gillis met in the consultation room after George had signed the script. Since there is no testimony at variance with what the attesters said upon the subject of attestation, their testimony stands unchallenged.

The above will have to suffice as a narrative of the evidence. The findings of fact of the circuit court state: "* * * Dr. Gillis, after receiving the instructions to prepare the will from the testator, went to his own office and there prepared the last will and testament which is in controversy. That the doors were not again closed during the time while the document was being prepared and signed. That after completing the Will, Dr. Gillis and his wife took the Will to the testator on the cot; that at said time the contents of the Will were explained to the testator; that the testator thereupon started to subscribe his name to the will in the presence of Dr. Gillis and Mrs. Gillis; that Dr. Gillis was there all the time while the testator signed the will; that Mrs. Gillis saw the testator sign the name 'George' and saw him start to sign his surname 'Demaris'; that thereupon Mrs. Gillis left the receiving room to go to the rear of the hospital for some towels; that shortly thereafter Dr. Gillis and his wife went to the doctor's office, and the doctor signed his name as a witness and requested Mrs. Gillis to sign her name as a witness, which she did; that from the point where Mrs. Gillis stood in front of the desk Mrs. Gillis was able to look through the door and see the patient, and that she was watching him because of his condition; that Dr. Gillis subscribed his name as a witness while sitting in a chair on the left side of the desk and could not see or be seen by the testator while actually witnessing the document; that while witnessing the document Dr. Gillis was directly in front of his wife across the table who could see the testator as well as the doctor; that George Demaris could have seen the witness Mrs. Gillis sign when she signed if he had looked; that he could not have seen Dr. Gillis sign; that the testator knew that Dr. Gillis had signed the Will as a witness, and some days later determined that Mrs. Gillis had signed the Will as a witness; * * *".

* * *

We now return to the statute which the contestant says was disregarded when George and the Gillises subscribed their signatures to the questioned instrument. The part which is applicable says that the witnesses must sign the will "in the presence of the testator." By reverting to the language of the contestant's petition, it will be seen that the contestant admits that the document under consideration actually bears the testator's and attesters' signatures. The contestant, therefore, does not challenge the genuineness of any of the three signatures, nor does he claim that the instrument under review is a document which George did not intend to sign. Nevertheless, since the requirements of the statute are mandatory, it is necessary that the evidence should show that the attesters signed "in the presence of the testator." In other words, it is essential, not only that the signatures be genuine and that they be found upon an instrument which all three persons intended to sign, but also that the attesters signed in the testator's presence. We shall shortly take note of the reason for the requirement.

The admissions made by the contestant are well justified by the facts. It will be recalled that Mrs. Kelly said that she was alongside the bed within arm's reach of her brother's hand when he signed the will. Harold Biggs, Arch Demaris and the latter's wife described the execution of a paper by George which, it develops, was his will. This is, therefore, a case in which the signatures of all three people are not only admitted, but were made under the very noses of the contestant, his wife, his sister and the latter's employee. Since the will was written upon a single sheet of paper, and since Mrs. Kelly took such careful note of her brother's act in signing the will that she was in a position to comment upon the peculiar slant of the letters, the circumstances afforded no opportunity for the substitution of a spurious copy. Indeed, no one even intimates that a substitution took place. This is a case in which (1) the will was typed in the presence of the contestant and of his witnesses, one of whom says she helped the draftsman by spelling for him the name of the testator; and (2) the will after being typed was carried by the draftsman openly into the room of the testator where, in a voice loud enough to be heard not only by the testator but also by those in the waiting room, he presented it to the testator for his approval and signature.

The meaning of the phrase "in the presence of the testator" has been the subject of much controversy and of diversity of opinion. Decisions directly opposite to one another can be readily found. Some of the decisions restrict a testator to his sense of sight in ascertaining whether his attesting witnesses are in his presence when they sign. They hold that if he and the attesters are in the same room all are prima facie in each other's presence, but if the attesting signatures are written in another room, then, prima facie, the statutory requirement was violated. If a counterpane stretched between the bedposts, to shield the testator from drafts, is between him and the attesters, the attestation is invalid. Reed v. Roberts, 26 Ga. 294, 71 Am.Dec. 210. These strict interpretation courts go further. For instance, in Re Beggans' Will, 68 N.J.Eq. 572, 59 A. 874, and Graham v. Graham, 32 N.C. 219, the courts held that before a finding could be authorized that the attesting witnesses signed in the testator's presence it must appear, not only that the testator would have seen them sign had he chosen to look, but that he did actually see the will and the writing of the signatures as the attestation took place. Burney v. Allen, 125 N.C. 314, 34 S.E. 500, 502, 74 Am.St.Rep. 637, represents a slight restriction upon the interpretation just noticed. The court there merely demanded proof that the testator could have seen had he cared to look. It said: "He must have the opportunity, through the evidence of ocular observation, to see the attestation." It took pains to point out, however, that if illness rendered it impossible or dangerous for the testator to move his head in order to watch the attesting witnesses, the attestation would be deemed invalid. It will be observed that those courts insist upon the sight test as the medium to be employed in determining the validity of the attestation. Many other decisions to like effect appear in the reports. The courts which insist upon the sight test disregard all others. For instance, in Calkins v. Calkins, 216 Ill. 458, 75 N.E. 182, 183, 1 L.R.A.,N.S., 393, 108 Am.St.Rep. 233, the facts were that after the testator had signed his will in the presence of the attesters, they withdrew to a table in an adjacent room outside the range of his vision and there signed. Then the witnesses returned to the testator, read the will to him, including their signatures, and showed him the latter. He expressed his approval. The court, after reiterating that "the test of presence of the testator is contiguity, with an uninterrupted view between the testator and the subscribing witnesses," held that the execution was invalid. It repudiated all substitutes for the statutory requirement, and declared that the above was not a compliance with the statute, but an attempted substitute for it. Even where an attester, who had previously signed the will, retraced his old signature with a dry pen in the presence of the testator, the attestation was held invalid. Playne v. Scriven, 1 Rob.Eccl. 772, 163 Reprint 1209.

The strict interpretation states, confining as they do the test of presence to the element of vision, experience difficulty in determining what the testator must see when he looks. One of the decisions, Graham v. Graham, 32 N.C. 219, which is typical of many others, holds that a view of the attesters' backs is not sufficient; the testator must be able to see the hands and forearms and the paper itself.

For a further interpretation of the word "presence" as employed in the strict interpretation jurisdictions, see Witt v. Gardiner, 158 Ill. 176, 41 N.E. 781, 49 Am.St.Rep. 150.

The same courts which insist upon the sight test employ a different one—mental apprehension—when they deal with a blind man's will. They hold that if the blind person's intellect and hearing are good and if he is conscious of what is going on around him, attestation made within the range of his senses of touch and hearing is valid. See, for instance, In re Allred's Will, 170 N.C. 153, 86 S.E. 1047, L.R.A.1916C, 946, Ann.Cas. 1916D, 788.

Other courts adopt a liberal point of view. They speak of the circumstances of the individual case and of the purpose of the statute. One decision says: "This requisite of the statute is designed to prevent substitution and fraud upon an intending testator." In re Beggans' Will, supra [68 N.J.Eq. 572, 59 A. 875]. Our court has spoken to like effect in Re Estate of Shaff, 125 Or. 288, 266 P. 630, 632: "The reason of the rule, as before remarked, is to obviate any opportunity of the witnesses, committing a fraud upon the testator, by changing or altering the document."

* * *

As we said, the liberal rule states apply what might be termed the mental apprehension test. Its essence is thus stated in Healey v. Bartlett, 73 N.H. 110, 59 A. 617, 618, 6 Ann.Cas. 413: "When a testator is not prevented by physical infirmities from seeing and hearing what goes on around him, it is the general, if not the universal, rule that his will is attested in his presence if he understands and is conscious of what the witnesses are doing when they write their names, and can, if he is so disposed, readily change his position so that he can see and hear what they do and say. * * * In other words, if he has knowledge of their presence, and can, if he is so disposed, readily see them write their names, the will is attested in his presence, even if he does not see them do it, and could not without some slight physical exertion. It is not necessary that he should actually see the witnesses, for them to be in his presence. They are in his presence whenever they are so near him that he is conscious of where they are and of what they are doing, through any of his senses, and are where he can readily see them if he is so disposed. The test, therefore, to determine whether the will of a person who has the use of all his faculties is attested in his presence, is to inquire whether he understood what the witnesses were doing when they affixed their names to his will, and could, if he had been so disposed, readily have seen them do it."

* * *

We are, of course, satisfied that the attestation must occur in the presence of the testator and that no substitution for the statutory requirement is permissible. But we do not believe that sight is the only test of presence. We are convinced that any of the senses that a testator possesses, which enable him to know whether another is near at hand and what he is doing, may be employed by him in determining whether the attesters are in his presence as they sign his will. Had George been suddenly stricken blind instead of having become afflicted with an abdominal illness, the circumstances determining whether the attestation took place in his presence would have been no different. It is unnecessary, we believe, that the attestation and execution occur in the same room. And, as just stated, it is unnecessary that the attesters be within the range of vision of the testator when they sign. If they are so near at hand that they are within the range of any of his senses, so that he knows what is going on, the requirement has been met.

At least one of the objects of the statute was served in the present instance; that is, two disinterested persons were brought to the testator's bedside to be present while he executed his will. When two disinterested persons, who later tell the truth, are present, the testator has been afforded, in our opinion, the best protection against fraud that this statute is capable of yielding. As we have just said, as a result of the demands of this statute, Dr. Gillis and his wife came to George's bedside at the time when he signed. Later, one of the two signed her signature to the will within the testator's range of vision, voice and hearing. All that George had to do to see Mrs. Gillis sign was to look through the two doors which were in alignment between himself and her. A glance would enable him to see Mrs. Gillis, including her hand, while she wrote her signature. It should not be inferred that George was incapable of moving or sitting up; he could do either without assistance. Since the floor covering in all three rooms was linoleum, it seems fair to assume that footsteps in any of the rooms could be easily heard by the testator. The other attesting witness, like Mrs. Gillis, was within 20 feet of George's hand when the attesting signature was written. It is no misstatement of the fact to say that both witnesses were within the immediate nearness and vicinity of the testator. Although Dr. Gillis was not within George's range of vision, he was within his range of voice and hearing. These three small rooms, if combined, would make nothing more than one room of fair length but of narrow width. Present at the time were some of George's brothers, sisters and other relatives. Although George had not told them that the instrument under preparation was his will, he was surely justified in believing that they would not be entirely inattentive to his interests. Those are circumstances which can properly be considered, we believe, in determining whether Dr. Gillis signed in the presence of George. When the doctor signed he was within direct sight and almost within arm's reach of the relatives who were seated upon the waiting room davenport. Since much that was said about the preparation of the paper was heard by those who were in these small rooms, we feel justified in assuming that Dr. Gillis was within the range of George's voice when he signed. These circumstances, together with the fact that both of the Gillises throughout the entire evening were frequently in George's room and were available at all times at his beck and call, convince us that they were in his presence at the time when they signed their attesting signatures.

The question occurs whether George was conscious of the fact that Dr. and Mrs. Gillis were signing their attesting signatures at the moment when they wrote them. Consciousness of the fact that the attesting signatures are being written is an indispensable element of the conscious presence rule. In determining whether George was aware of the fact that the signatures were being written, we may properly take into consideration, we believe, the fact that he had asked that the will be prepared, and that both of the Gillises were present when he signed. Undoubtedly, the request for the preparation of a will, under the circumstances disclosed by the record, carried with it an implied request for an attestation. Therefore, since Dr. Gillis' wife was present with her husband at the moment when George signed, he must have known that those two persons would shortly sign as attesters. We may also take into consideration the fact that two or three days later, while referring to the attestation of the will, he said, "I know that Doc did." Just before making that remark he was assured that Mrs. Gillis had signed and that, in compliance with his request, the will had been deposited in a safe repository. As previously stated, Mrs. Gillis was within the direct range of George's vision when she signed. It seems safe to infer that in a small space of the kind with which we are concerned the attention of a testator, who had just signed a will, would be attracted when he saw his two attesting witnesses go into an office room and there, taking pen in hand, proceed to use it. George lay upon his back at least a part of the time that evening. These circumstances persuade us that George was conscious of the attestation when it took place.

* * *

In conclusion, we express the belief that if Dr. Gillis and his wife failed to comply with the strict letter of the statute when they attested the will, they, nevertheless, substantially complied with its requirements. To hold otherwise would be to observe the letter of the statute as interpreted strictly, and fail to give heed to the statute's obvious purpose. Thus, the statute would be turned against those for whose protection it had been written. The circuit court, in sustaining the will, committed no error.

The evidence reviewed above convinces us, as it did the trial judge, that the testator knew the contents of the will before he signed it, and, further, that if he did not know the identity of both attesters at the moment when he signed, he discovered the name of the unfamiliar one two or three days later and then expressed his approval.

The above disposes of all issues presented by the contestant. The circumstances, therefore, afford no occasion for an expression of our views upon other matters.

The decree of the circuit court is affirmed.

KELLY, C. J., and RAND and BELT, JJ., concur.

BAILEY, J., dissents.

BEAN and LUSK, JJ., took no part in this decision.

Notes

A review of the Statute of Frauds and the Wills Act reveals that the presence requirement for execution was originally a three-prong test: (1) the witnesses saw the testator sign, (2) the testator saw the witnesses sign, and (3) the witnesses saw each other sign. The test implied a requirement of *sight*: that any of those named could actually see the others if he or she were to look. Exceptions were often made for those who were sight impaired, and more modern jurisdictions have rejected the absoluteness of sight in favor of the conscious presence test. An example of the incorporation of conscious presence may be found in the Uniform Probate Code § 2-502(a)(2). This test does not require actual sight, but only that the persons involved comprehend the signing through a *consciousness* of the events taking place, even in different proximate locations. And even if the testator were to sign the Will in an isolated moment, but later "acknowledge that signature or acknowledge the Will" as his or her own, then the sight or consciousness of that event would allow for a valid attestation of the Will. *See* Unif. Prob. Code § 2-502 (a)(3) (2003).

A time sequence is implied, and at least one decision has held that the witnesses must sign while the testator is still alive. *See In re* Estate of Royal, 826 P.2d 1236 (Colo. 1992). Some states provide a number of days for witnesses to sign after a testator has signed: New York requires witnesses to sign within 30 days, and the Uniform Probate Code provides for signing within a reasonable time. *See* N.Y. Est. Powers & Trusts L. § 3-2.1(a)(4)(McKinney 2003); Unif. Prob. Code § 2-502(a)(3) (2003).

B. Signature

In re Estate of Wait

Tennessee Court of Appeals, 1957
43 Tenn. App. 217, 306 S.W.2d 345

CARNEY, Judge.

The appellant, Sylvia Sunderland, executrix and principal beneficiary under the will of Georgie Miriam Wait, deceased, appeals from an order of the Probate Court of Shelby County, Tennessee, which refused to admit said will for probate. The appellees are the next of kin of the deceased, Georgie Miriam Wait, and will inherit the estate of Miss Wait if said will is not admitted to probate. The estate consists of approximately $22,000 in personalty and a house and lot located in Memphis, Tennessee.

Said paper writing was on three pages partly typewritten and partly filled in in pen and ink and is as follows:

'Last Will and Testament of Georgie Miriam Wait

* * *

'I, Georgie Miriam Wait, a resident of Memphis, Shelby County, State of Tennessee, being of sound and disposing memory do hereby make, publish and declare this to be my last will and testament, hereby revoking all other and former wills or codicils to wills by me at anytime heretofore made. I request and direct and it is my will as follows:

Item I

'I direct that all of my just debts, and the expense of my last illness and for my funeral and burial shall be paid from my estate by my Executor or Executrix as the case may be, hereinafter named, as soon after my death as may be practicable.

Item II

'I do hereby give and bequeath to Anne C. Wait, widow, of my deceased brother Jonathon Wait, the sum of one ($1.00) dollar.

Item III

'I do hereby give, grant, convey, devise and bequeath all the real property which I may own or to which I am or may be in any way entitled to <u>my friend of many years—Sylvia Sunderland.</u>

Item IV

'I do hereby give and bequeath all the rest, residue and remainder of my estate consisting of personalty only which I may own at my death or to which I am or may be entitled in any way to: <u>To my cousins—Minnie Gill, Alice Wait and Mattie Bailey, I give $1.00 (one dollar) each, and the balance of my personalty including house furnishings to my dear friend Sylvia Sunderland.</u>

Item V

'I do hereby appoint <u>Sylvia Sunderland</u> Executrix of my will, and dispense with, and ask that she be not required to give any bond as such.

'Witness my hand in the presence of <u>Lessie M. Cunningham</u> and <u>Mrs. Dock White</u> who are requested to sign this, my last will, as witnesses, at Memphis, Tennessee, on this the <u>30th</u> day of <u>March</u>, 1956.

'x <u>Georgie Miriam Wait</u>

'The above Georgie Miriam Wait, did on this the <u>30th</u> day of <u>March</u>, 1956, declare to us the foregoing instrument to be her last will and testament, and called on us to witness same, and did in our presence and sight, and each of us, sign her name thereto as and for her last will and testament, and we at her request, and in her presence and sight and of each other, sign our names as witnesses, this <u>30th</u> day of <u>March</u>, 1956.

'<u>Lessie M. Cunningham</u>

'<u>Mrs. Dock White</u>'

Those parts of the will which were filled in in pen and ink have been underscored.

The beneficiary, Sylvia Sunderland, at the request of the testatrix, completed in pen and ink Items III and IV of the will and also wrote her name as executrix in the first paragraph of Item V of the will. The testatrix was old and feeble and could not write very well. The beneficiary, Miss Sunderland, was not present at the time of the attempted execution of the will on March 30, 1956.

It is to be noted that the attestation clause appears in all things regular and indicates that the will was executed and witnessed in conformity with the provisions of T.C.A. § 32-104.

However, it developed from the testimony of the attesting witnesses in the proceeding to probate the will in common form that the testatrix, Miss Wait, had not signed the will at the time the two attesting witnesses signed it but that she signed it a day or two later. It is the contention of the appellant that the testatrix showed the will to the attesting witnesses and declared the same to be her last will; that she touched the pen to the will at the place indicated for her signature and made a mark sufficient in law to constitute her signature under the statute and that thereupon the two attesting witnesses at her request and in her presence and in the presence of each other signed their names thereto as attesting and subscribing witnesses to said will.

The two attesting witnesses are in substantial agreement as to most of the circumstances surrounding the attempted signing of the will by the testatrix, Miss Wait. However, they do differ somewhat in just what the testatrix said at the time.

Both attesting witnesses were neighbors of the testatrix and testified that they were requested by Miss Wait to come to her home and to witness her will.

One of the attesting witnesses, Mrs. Dock White, testified that Miss Wait, the testatrix, was sitting at a table and that she placed a pen to the will on the table as if to sign and her hand was shaking and she said, 'Oh, I can't write; you all go ahead and sign it and I will sign it later when I can control my hand.'

Further, Mrs. White testified that she could not see whether Miss Wait had written anything or any part of her signature on the line because when Miss Wait handed the will over to the two witnesses she had placed a piece of paper over the line indicated for the signature of the testatrix. A few days later she was in the home of Miss Wait and the testatrix showed her the will which had been signed saying, 'At last I got to where I could control my hand and I signed this will.'

The other attesting witness, Mrs. Cunningham, corroborated the testimony of Mrs. White to the effect that the testatrix was sitting at the table and tried to write her name; that she was shaking and trying to write and that the pen was moving but that she did not know just exactly what, if anything, the testatrix had written at that time.

Mrs. Cunningham testified that she did not hear the testatrix say that she would sign the will later but that she did hear her say, 'I am so nervous I can't sign it' and that she asked the two witnesses to go ahead and sign the will which they did.

Both of the witnesses were positive in their testimony that while they could not testify that Miss Wait had actually written anything on the signature line because the paper was placed over this line, yet they could not say that she had not actually made a mark on the signature line.

The judge of the Probate Court held that the proof was insufficient to establish that Miss Wait had executed the will in accordance with the provisions of T.C.A. §32-104; i.e. (1) That Miss Wait herself had not signed the will in the presence of the two witnesses; nor (2) did she acknowledge her signature already made; nor (3) did she direct that some other person sign her name for her.

It is the contention of appellant that since the witnesses testified that Miss Wait was actually attempting to execute a will and that she placed a pen to the paper that she thereby made some sort of a mark on the paper which was sufficient in law to constitute her legal signature.

Appellees contend, (1) that there was no evidence that Miss Wait intended to make a signature by mark; (2) that under the provisions of T.C.A. §32-104 a signature by mark is not recognized and that therefore, the will would not be entitled to probate even if the proof were sufficient to show that the testatrix attempted to make a signature by mark on the paper writing.

Appellant relies upon the language of the Supreme Court in the case of Leathers v. Binkley, 196 Tenn. 80, 264 S.W.2d 561, 563, which was as follows:

'To protect the right of testamentary disposition of property, we must sustain a will as legally executed if it is possible to do so, Sizer's Pritchard on Wills, Secs. 384, 386 et seq.; 57 Am.Jur., Wills, Sec. 218. Compare: Ball v. Miller, 31 Tenn.App. 271, 214 S.W.2d 446.'

However, in our opinion, the facts in the Leathers case were substantially different from the case at bar. The attesting witnesses in that case testified that they did not remember whether they signed before or after the testator. In the present case both attesting witnesses affirmatively testified that the testatrix did not sign the will until after they had signed and that it was signed by her out of their presence. For that reason we think the decision in the Leathers case is not controlling of the case at bar.

In the case of Ball v. Miller, 1948, 31 Tenn.App. 271, 214 S.W.2d 446, the testatrix was in the hospital and had signed the will in the presence of two witnesses whom she had requested to witness her will. One of the witnesses, a doctor, had signed but before the other witness could sign, the testatrix suffered a coughing spell and the second attesting witness went to seek a nurse. The condition of the testatrix became considerably worse and the second attesting witness failed or neglected to sign the will before the death of the testatrix.

Prior to the execution of the Uniform Wills Act in 1941, now T.C.A. §32-104, said will would have been entitled to probate as a will of personality even though it would not have been sufficiently valid to devise real estate. The Court of Appeals, following the case of Fann v. Fann, 186 Tenn. 127, 208 S.W.2d 542, reannounced the rule that there is no difference in the requirements for the execution of a will bequeathing personalty and a will devising real estate. The Court of Appeals held in the Ball case that since only one witness had actually signed the will that it was not executed in compliance with the provisions of Code Section 8098.4, T.C.A. §32-104, and therefore not entitled to probate as a will.

In the case of Eslick v. Wodicka, 1948, 31 Tenn.App. 333, 215 S.W.2d 12, the proof showed that the testator signed the will privately and subsequently acknowledged his signature before both attesting witnesses. The attesting witnesses signed the will out of the presence of each other though they later were jointly in the presence of the testator and he thanked both of them for acting as subscribing witnesses. At this subsequent meeting the testator did not have the will with him though it had been actually signed by each subscribing witness in the presence of the testator prior to the meeting. In the Eslick case the Court of Appeals held that the failure of the attesting witnesses to sign the will both in the presence of the testator and in the presence of each other as required by Code Section 32-104 was fatal to the validity of the will and that the subsequent acknowledgement of their signatures in the presence of the testator and in the presence of each other was not authorized by the statute and ineffective to validate the will.

We do not find it necessary or proper for this court to rule whether or not a testator may legally sign a will by mark. A careful reading of the testimony of the attesting witnesses indicates clearly to us that the testatrix may have made a mark of some sort, either an initial or one or more letters of her signature, on the will but she clearly indicated that she did not consider such mark or marks to constitute her signature. In our opinion neither the testatrix nor the attesting witnesses understood the requirements of the statute that the testatrix must (1) signify to the attesting witnesses that the instrument is his will and then take one of three courses: (a) Himself sign the will or (b) acknowledge his signature already made or (c) at the direction of the testator and in the testator's presence have someone else sign the name of the testator to the document.

The statute is very clear that regardless which one of the three courses is pursued the act must be done in the presence of two or more attesting witnesses. We think the evidence clearly shows that on the day in question the testatrix had not signed the will or attempted to sign the will before the attesting witnesses were called to her home.

Further, we think the evidence shows that she complied with a portion of the statute by signifying to the attesting witnesses that the paper writing was her will and that she then set about to sign the will by writing her usual signature thereon; that due to her physical infirmity her hand shook so that she decided to defer her signature until a later date and asked the attesting witnesses to go ahead at that time and sign their names to the will which they did; that the testatrix did not consider that she had signed the will until after the attesting witnesses had signed the will and had left her presence. At some later date her hand became more steady and she did actually sign the will but not in the presence of either attesting witness though at a later date she did acknowledge her signature to one of the attesting witnesses.

There is simply no proof on which the Probate Court or this Court could find that the testatrix intended any mark she may have made on the paper as her signature. On the contrary, we think the overwhelming proof is that she did not intend any such mark to be her signature but that she intended to and did actually sign the will at some later date after the attesting witnesses had already signed it and were out of her presence. This the statute does not permit.

Therefore, we feel constrained to hold that His Honor, the Judge of the Probate Court of Shelby County, correctly held that the purported will of Miss Wait was not executed in accordance with the requirements of Code Section 32-104 and therefore, it is not entitled to probate and the assignment of error is overruled.

A decree will be entered affirming the judgment of the lower court and taxing the appellant and her surety with the costs of this appeal.

AVERY P. J. (W. D.), and BEJACH, J., concur.

Notes

While the case demonstrates that presence and the requirement of a "full intended signature" overlap, there are additional requirements surrounding the signatures. For example, what should be the order of signing? Should the testator always sign first? Logic would appear to require this, but in the absence of statutory requirement, the issue seems moot. And the signature may be by "proxy;" such is allowed by the UNIF. PROB. CODE § 2-502(a)(2). A proxy signature occurs when the testator, for any reason, does not sign personally but, instead, asks another to sign the testator's name in the testator's presence. This is different from signature by assistance. There, the testator's hand is assisted by another, but the physical signing is done by the testator. Signing by proxy has particular requirements; it must be in the presence of the testator and at the direction of the testator. The Wills Act (1837) requires that the testator sign at the Foot or End of the Will. But what will happen if dispositions of property appear physically after the signature? Under the common law, any provision appearing after the signature would be denied probate as simply an unexecuted codicil. However, at least one state has interpreted the "end" as the "logical end" of the instrument and not the physical end, thus allowing dispositions to be probated that appear after the signature in terms of physical location, but that, logically, may be accommodated within the entire instrument through language or sequence numbering. *See* Stinson's Estate, 228 Pa. 475, 77 A. 807 (1910).

C. Witnesses

The Statute of Frauds (1677) requires three or four credible witnesses, but the Wills Act (1837) requires only two. Today, almost all states require only two witnesses, but if the decedent were to die domiciled in a state requiring three witnesses, the Last Will and Testament would be in jeopardy if it were executed in a state requiring only two witnesses but submitted for probate in a state requiring three witnesses. For example, in Vermont, more than two witnesses are required for a Last Will and Testament to be entitled to probate. *See* VT. STAT. ANN. tit. 14, §5 (2003). Are there any remedies here? A state may, by statute, accept a Will for probate if it meets the requirements of the testator's domicile or place of execution. *See* UNIF. PROB. CODE § 2-506 (2003) (choice of law as to execution). With few exceptions, age of the witnesses is not specifically mentioned in statutes, but the witness must be able to testify in court as to the intentionalities of the testator, and the witness' youth will be a detriment.

Because the Statute of Frauds refers to credible witnesses, the issue of competence of the witnesses arises, most often in the context of self interest. If a witness receives something under the Last Will and Testament that he or she would not receive under intestate succession or an otherwise valid Will, does that mean he or she is incompetent to serve as a witness because he or she is an interested party? Under the common law interest rules, the answer was, "Yes." But to deny probate to the entire Will because of a lack of sufficient witnesses due to interest seems harsh to many legislatures. Thus, several states take an intermediate approach. Compare the Uniform Probate Code with the provisions of New York and California as examples.

Uniform Probate Code (2003)

§ 2-505. Who May Witness.

(a) An individual generally competent to be a witness may act as a witness to a will.

(b) The signing of a will by an interested witness does not invalidate the will or any provision of it.

N.Y. Est., Powers & Trusts L. (2003)

§ 3-3.2 Competence of attesting witness who is beneficiary; application to nuncupative will

(a) An attesting witness to a will to whom a beneficial disposition or appointment of property is made is a competent witness and compellable to testify respecting the execution of such will as if no such disposition or appointment had been made, subject to the following:

(1) Any such disposition or appointment made to an attesting witness is void unless there are, at the time of execution and attestation, at least two other attesting witnesses to the will who receive no beneficial disposition or appointment thereunder.

(2) Subject to subparagraph (1), any such disposition or appointment to an attesting witness is effective unless the will cannot be proved without the testimony of such witness, in which case the disposition or appointment is void.

(3) Any attesting witness whose disposition is void hereunder, who would be a distributee if the will were not established, is entitled to receive so much of his intestate share as does not exceed the value of the disposition made to him in the will, such share to be recovered as follows:

(A) In case the void disposition becomes part of the residuary disposition, from the residuary disposition only.

(B) In case the void disposition passes in intestacy, ratibly * * * from the distributees who succeed to such interest. For this purpose, the void disposition shall be distributed under 4-1.1 as though the attesting witness were not a distributee.

* * *

Cal. Prob. Code (West 2003)

§ 6112. Witnesses; interested witnesses

(a) Any person generally competent to be a witness may act as a witness to a will.

(b) A will or any provision thereof is not invalid because the will is signed by an interested witness.

(c) Unless there are at least two other subscribing witnesses to the will who are disinterested witnesses, the fact that the will makes a devise to a subscribing witness creates a presumption that the witness procured the devise by duress, menace, fraud, or undue influence. This presumption is a presumption affecting the burden of proof. This presumption does not apply where the witness is a person to whom the devise is made solely in a fiduciary capacity.

(d) If a devise made by the will to an interested witness fails because the presumption established by subdivision (c) applies to the devise and the witness fails to rebut the presumption, the interested witness shall take such proportion of the devise made to the witness in the will as does not exceed the share of the estate which would be distributed to the witness if the will were not established. Nothing in this subdivision affects the law that applies where it is established that the witness procured a devise by duress, menace, fraud, or undue influence.

In re Estate of Parsons

California Court of Appeal, First District, 1980
103 Cal. App. 3d 384, 163 Cal. Rptr. 70

GRODIN, J.

This case requires us to determine whether a subscribing witness to a will who is named in the will as a beneficiary becomes "disinterested" within the meaning of Probate Code section 51 by filing a disclaimer of her interest after the testatrix's death. While our own policy preferences tempt us to an affirmative answer, we feel constrained by existing law to hold that a disclaimer is ineffective for that purpose.

* * *

Geneve Parsons executed her will on May 3, 1976. Three persons signed the will as attesting witnesses: Evelyne Nielson, respondent Marie Gower, and Bob Warda, a notary public. Two of the witnesses, Nielson and Gower, were named in the will as beneficiaries. Nielson was given $100; Gower was given certain real property. Mrs. Parsons died on December 13, 1976, and her will was admitted to probate on the petition of her executors, respondents Gower and Lenice Haymond. On September 12, 1977, Nielson filed a disclaimer of her $100 bequest.[1] Appellants then claimed an interest in the estate on the ground that the devise to Gower was invalid.[2] The trial court rejected their argument, which is now the sole contention on appeal.

---

1. The disclaimer was filed pursuant to Probate Code section 190.1, which provides in part: "A beneficiary may disclaim any interest, in whole or in part, by filing a disclaimer as provided in this chapter." The disclaimer here was filed within the statutory period set forth in Probate Code section 190.3, subdivision (a), which provides in part: "[A] disclaimer shall be conclusively presumed to have been filed within a reasonable time if filed as follows: [¶] (1) In case of interests created by will, within nine months after the death of the person creating the interest...."

2. Appellants Phyllis Maschke and Roger, Donald, and Clifford Winelander are the assignees of their uncle Sydney Winelander, the decedent's first cousin once removed. Appellants Frances Areitio, Florence Rennaker, and Josephine, Henry, and Walter Marion are also the decedent's first cousins once removed.

Mrs. Parsons' will contained no residuary clause. If the devise to Gower fails, appellants and other next of kin of equal degree will inherit the property.

Appellants base their claim on Probate Code section 51, which provides that a gift to a subscribing witness is void "unless there are two other and disinterested subscribing witnesses to the will."[3] Although Nielson disclaimed her bequest after subscribing the will, appellants submit that "a subsequent disclaimer is ineffective to transform an interested witness into a disinterested one." Appellants assert that because there was only one disinterested witness at the time of attestation, the devise to Gower is void by operation of law.

Respondents contend that appellants' argument is "purely technical" and "completely disregards the obvious and ascertainable intent" of the testatrix. They urge that the property should go to the person named as devisee rather than to distant relatives who, as the testatrix stated in her will, "have not been overlooked, but have been intentionally omitted." They stress that there has been no suggestion of any fraud or undue influence in this case, and they characterize Nielson's interest as a "token gift" which she relinquished pursuant to the disclaimer statute. (Prob. Code, § 190 et seq.) Finally, respondents point to the following language of Probate Code section 190.6: "In every case, the disclaimer shall relate back for all purposes to the date of the creation of the interest." On the basis of that language, respondents conclude that Nielson "effectively became disinterested" by reason of her timely disclaimer. According to respondents, the conditions of Probate Code section 51 have therefore been satisfied, and the devise to Gower should stand.

* * *

This appears to be a case of first impression in California, * * * and our interpretation of Probate Code section 51 will determine its outcome. * * * We are required to construe the statute "so as to effectuate the purpose of the law." (Select Base Materials v. Board of Equal. (1959) 51 Cal.2d 640, 645 [335 P.2d 672].) To ascertain that purpose, we may consider its history. (Estate of Ryan (1943) 21 Cal.2d 498, 513 [133 P.2d 626].)

At common law a party to an action, or one who had a direct interest in its outcome, was not competent to testify in court because it was thought that an interested witness would be tempted to perjure himself in favor of his interest. (See Davis v. Davis (1864) 26 Cal. 23, 35.) Centuries ago, this principle concerning the competence of witnesses in litigation was injected into the substantive law of wills. (See Estate of Zeile (1910) 5 Coffey's Prob. Dec. 292, 294.) The statute of frauds of 1676 required that devises of land be attested and subscribed "by three or four credible witnesses, or else they shall be utterly void and of none effect." (29 Car. II, ch. 3, § 5.) The word "credible" was construed to mean "competent" according to the common law principles then prevailing, and "competent" meant "disinterested"—so that persons having an interest under the will could not be "credible witnesses" within the meaning of the statute. The entire will would therefore fail if any one of the requisite number of attesting witnesses was also a beneficiary. (Holdfast v. Dowsing (K.B. 1746) 2 Str. 1253 [93 Eng.Rep. 1164].) In 1752 Parliament enacted a statute which saved the will by providing that the interest of an attesting witness was void. (25 Geo. II, ch. 6, § I.) Under

---

3. Probate Code section 51 reads as follows: "All beneficial devises, bequests and legacies to a subscribing witness are void unless there are two other and disinterested subscribing witnesses to the will, except that if such interested witness would be entitled to any share of the estate of the testator in case the will were not established, he shall take such proportion of the devise or bequest made to him in the will as does not exceed the share of the estate which would be distributed to him if the will were not established."

such legislation, the competence of the witness is restored by invalidating his gift. (Estate of Zeile, supra, 5 Coffey's Prob. Dec. at p. 294.) The majority of American jurisdictions today have similar statutes; and California Probate Code section 51 falls into this category. (Rees, American Wills Statutes (1960) 46 Va.L.Rev. 613, 629–633. See generally 2 Bowe-Parker: Page on Wills (3d rev. ed. 1960) Formalities of Execution, §§ 19.73–19.110, pp. 169–216; Evans, The Competency of Testamentary Witnesses (1927) 25 Mich.L.Rev. 238.)

The common law disabilities to testify on account of interest have long been abolished. (Evid. Code, § 700; Davis v. Davis, supra, 26 Cal. at p. 35; II Wigmore, Evidence (3d ed. 1940) Testimonial Qualifications, § 488, p. 525, fn. 2.) Having become a part of the substantive law of wills, Probate Code section 51, on the other hand, survives. (See Evans, supra, 25 Mich.L.Rev. at pp. 238–239; II Wigmore, supra, § 582, pp. 722–723.) Our task is to ascertain and effectuate its present purpose. * * * When a court seeks to interpret legislation, "the various parts of a statutory enactment must be harmonized by considering the particular clause or section in the context of the statutory framework as a whole." (Moyer v. Workmen's Comp. Appeals Bd. (1973) 10 Cal.3d 222, 230 [110 Cal.Rptr. 144, 514 P.2d 1224].) We therefore turn to the Probate Code.

In order to establish a will as genuine, it is not always necessary that each and every one of the subscribing witnesses testify in court. (Prob. Code, §§ 329, 372.) Moreover, Probate Code section 51 does not by its terms preclude any witness from testifying; nor does the section void the interest of a subscribing witness when "two other and disinterested" witnesses have also subscribed the will. It is therefore entirely conceivable and perfectly consistent with the statutory scheme that a will might be proved on the sole testimony of a subscribing witness who is named in the will as a beneficiary; and if the will had been attested by "two other and disinterested subscribing witnesses," the interested witness whose sole testimony established the will would also be permitted to take his gift, as provided in the instrument. (Prob. Code, §§ 51, 329, 372.) If Probate Code section 51 serves any purpose under such circumstances, its purpose must necessarily have been accomplished before the will was offered for probate. Otherwise, in its statutory context, the provision would have no effect at all.

The quintessential function of a subscribing witness is performed when the will is executed. (Prob. Code, § 50; Estate of LaMont (1952) 39 Cal.2d 566, 569 [248 P.2d 1].) We believe that Probate Code section 51 looks in its operation solely to that time. (See 2 Bowe-Parker: Page on Wills, supra, § 19.85, p. 185, and § 19.102, pp. 204–205; Evans, supra, 25 Mich.L.Rev. at p. 238.) The section operates to ensure that at least two of the subscribing witnesses are disinterested. Although disinterest may be a token of credibility, as at common law, it also connotes an absence of selfish motives. We conclude that the purpose of the statute is to protect the testator from fraud and undue influence at the very moment when he executes his will, by ensuring that at least two persons are present "who would not be financially motivated to join in a scheme to procure the execution of a spurious will by dishonest methods, and who therefore presumably might be led by human impulses of fairness to resist the efforts of others in that direction." (Gulliver & Tilson, Classification of Gratuitous Transfers (1941) 51 Yale L.J. 1, 11. See also 2 Bowe-Parker: Page on Wills, supra, § 19.74, p. 173.) No other possible construction which has been brought to our attention squares so closely with the statutory framework.

* * *

Because we hold that Probate Code section 51 looks solely to the time of execution and attestation of the will, it follows that a subsequent disclaimer will be ineffective to transform an interested witness into a "disinterested" one within the meaning of that section. If the execution of a release or the filing of a disclaimer after the will has been attested could effect such a transformation, the purpose of the statute as we have defined it would be undermined. Respondents' reliance on Probate Code section 190.6[5] is misplaced. * * * That section serves to equalize the tax consequences of disclaimers as between heirs at law and testamentary beneficiaries. (See Estate of Meyer (1951) 107 Cal.App.2d 799, 810 [238 P.2d 587]; Estate of Nash (1967) 256 Cal.App.2d 560, 561 [64 Cal.Rptr. 298, 27 A.L.R.3d 1349].) Probate Code section 190, subdivision (a) defines "beneficiary" to mean "any person entitled, *but for his disclaimer*, to take an interest" by various means. (Italics added.) Even assuming that an "interest" arises within the meaning of the disclaimer statute from the execution of a will (cf. Prob. Code, § 190, subd. (b)), Evelyn Nielson would *not* have been entitled to take under the will by reason of Probate Code section 51; and she was, therefore, not a "beneficiary" within the meaning of the disclaimer statute. The disclaimer statute therefore has no application here. In this case, when the will was executed and attested, only one of the subscribing witnesses was disinterested. The gifts to the other witnesses were therefore void, by operation of law. (Prob. Code, § 51.) Nielson's disclaimer was a nullity, because she had no interest to disclaim.

Respondents' concern for the intentions of the testatrix is likewise misplaced. The construction of the will (Prob. Code, § 101) is not at issue here. We are faced instead with the operation of Probate Code section 51, which makes no reference to the intentions of the testatrix. Legislation voiding the interest of an attesting witness "often upsets genuine expressions of the testator's intent." (Chaffin, Execution, Revocation, and Revalidation of Wills: A Critique of Existing Statutory Formalities (1977) 11 Ga.L.Rev. 297, 317.) But that legislation controls the outcome of this case.

It has been said that statutes such as this are ill suited to guard against fraud and undue influence. "If the potential malefactor does not know of the rules, he will not be deterred. If he does know of them, which is unlikely, he will realize the impossibility of the financial gain supposed to be the motive of the legatee witness, and so will probably escape the operation of the remedy against himself." (Gulliver & Tilson, supra, 51 Yale L.J. at pp. 12–13.) Lord Mansfield observed over 200 years ago, "In all my experience at the Court of Delegates, I never knew a fraudulent will, but what was legally attested; and I have heard the same from many learned civilians." (Wyndham v. Chetwynd (K.B. 1757) 1 Black. W. 95, 100 [96 Eng.Rep. 53].) * * * Yet Probate Code section 51 remains the law in California.

We are mindful that there has been no suggestion of any fraud or other misconduct in the case before us, and it may well be that "the vast majority of testators in modern

---

5. Probate Code section 190.6 provides:

Unless otherwise provided in the will, inter vivos trust, exercise of the power of appointment, or other written instrument creating or finally determining an interest, the interest disclaimed and any future interest which is to take effect in possession or enjoyment at or after the termination of the interest disclaimed, shall descend, go, be distributed or continue to be held as if the beneficiary disclaiming had predeceased the person creating the interest. In every case, the disclaimer shall relate back for all purposes to the date of the creation of the interest.

society do not need the type of 'protection' that is afforded by our statute." (Chaffin, Improving Georgia's Probate Code (1970) 4 Ga.L.Rev. 505, 507.) "[T]he reported decisions give the impression that the remedies are employed more frequently against innocent parties who have accidentally transgressed the requirement than against deliberate wrongdoers, and this further confirms the imaginary character of the difficulty sought to be prevented." (Gulliver & Tilson, supra, 51 Yale L.J. at p. 12.) But the Legislature has spoken here, and in matters such as this, "the legislature has a wide discretion in determining the conditions to be imposed." (Estate of Mintaberry (1920) 183 Cal. 566, 568 [191 P. 909].)

Respondents note that a growing number of states have enacted statutes similar to Uniform Probate Code section 2-505, which dispenses with the rule contained in the California statute.* * * Perhaps statutes like California Probate Code section 51 represent a "mediaeval point of view" concerning the proper function of an attesting witness; and perhaps "the question whether he has abused his position should be made one of fact, like any other question having to do with the motives and conduct of parties who take part in the testamentary transaction." (Mechem, Why Not a Modern Wills Act? (1948) 33 Iowa L.Rev. 501, 506–507.) We cannot ignore what the statute commands, however, "merely because we do not agree that the statute as written is wise or beneficial legislation." (Estate of Carter (1935) 9 Cal.App.2d 714, 718 [50 P.2d 1057].) Any remedial change must come from the Legislature.

That portion of the judgment from which this appeal is taken is therefore reversed.

Racanelli, P. J., and Elkington, J., concurred.

The petition of respondent Gower for a hearing by the Supreme Court was denied June 4, 1980.

Tobriner, J., and Mosk, J., were of the opinion that the petition should be granted.

Notes

Witnesses are seldom called to give testimony concerning the execution of the Will unless there is a contest. The court may dispense with the testimony of witnesses. *See, e.g.,* N.Y. SURROG. CT. PROC. L. § 1405 (2004). Also, the presence of an attestation clause provides a rebuttable presumption that everything recited therein was performed. If the state has adopted a procedure for a self-proved will, *see infra,* then the formalities recited become irrebuttable.

D. Compliance Devices

1. Substantial Compliance

In re Alleged Will of Ranney
Supreme Court of New Jersey, 1991
124 N.J. 1, 589 A.2d 1339

POLLOCK, J. [delivered the opinion of the court.]

The sole issue is whether an instrument purporting to be a last will and testament that includes the signature of two witnesses on an attached self-proving affidavit, but not on the will itself, should be admitted to probate. At issue is the will of Russell G. Ranney. The Monmouth County Surrogate ordered probate of the will, but the Superior Court, Law Division, Probate Part, reversed, ruling that the will did not contain the signatures of two witnesses as required by N.J.S.A. 3B:3-2. The Appellate Division found that the self-proving affidavit formed part of the will and, therefore, that the witnesses had signed the will as required by the statute. 240 N.J.Super. 337, 573 A.2d 467 (1990). It reversed the judgment of the Law Division and remanded the matter for a plenary hearing on the issue of execution. We granted the contestant's petition for certification, 122 N.J. 163, 584 A.2d 230 (1990), and now affirm the judgment of the Appellate Division.

* * *

The following facts emerge from the uncontested affidavits submitted in support of probate of the will. On October 26, 1982, Russell and his wife, Betty (now known as Betty McGregor), visited the law offices of Kantor, Mandia, and Schuster to execute their wills. Russell's will consisted of four pages and a fifth page containing a self-proving affidavit, entitled "ACKNOWLEDGMENT AND AFFIDAVIT RELATING TO EXECUTION OF WILL." The pages of Russell's will were neither numbered nor attached before execution. After Russell and Betty had reviewed their wills, they and their attorney, Robert Kantor, proceeded to a conference room, where they were joined by Kantor's partner John Schuster III and by two secretaries, Laura Stout and Carmella Mattox, who was also a notary.

Consistent with his usual practice, Kantor asked Russell if the instrument represented Russell's will and if Russell wanted Schuster and Stout to act as witnesses. Russell answered both questions affirmatively, and signed the will on the fourth page:

IN WITNESS WHEREOF, I have hereunto set my hand and seal this 26th day of October, One Thousand Nine Hundred and Eighty Two.

/s/ Russell G. Ranney

Russell G. Ranney

No one else signed the fourth page of the will. Russell, followed by Schuster and Stout, then signed the self-proving affidavit on the fifth page. Both Schuster and Stout believed that they were signing and attesting the will when they signed the affidavit. Furthermore, both Kantor, who had supervised the similar execution of many wills, and Schuster believed that the witnesses' signatures on the "Acknowledgment and Affidavit" complied with the attestation requirements of N.J.S.A. 3B:3-2. Mattox, whose practice was to notarize a document only if she witnessed the signature, notarized all the signatures.

After execution of the will, Stout stapled its four pages to the self-proving affidavit. The fifth and critical page reads:

ACKNOWLEDGMENT AND AFFIDAVIT RELATING TO
EXECUTION OF WILL

STATE OF NEW JERSEY
ss.
COUNTY OF MONMOUTH

RUSSELL G. RANNEY, JOHN SCHUSTER III, and LAURA J. STOUT, the Testator and the witnesses, respectively whose names are signed to the attached instrument, being first duly sworn, do hereby declare to the undersigned authority that the Testator signed and executed the instrument as his Last Will and Testament and that he signed willingly and that he executed it as his free and voluntary act for the purposes therein expressed; and that each witness states that he or she signed the Will as witnesses in the presence and hearing of the Testator and that to the best of his or her knowledge, the Testator was at the time 18 or more years of age, of sound mind and under no constraint or undue influence.

/s/   Russell G. Ranney

RUSSELL G. RANNEY

/s/   John Schuster III

/s/   Laura J. Stout

Subscribed, sworn to, and acknowledged before me, by Russell G. Ranney, the Testator, and subscribed and sworn to before me by JOHN SCHUSTER III and LAURA J. STOUT, witnesses, this 26 day of October 1982.

/s/   Carmella Mattox

Notary

The acknowledgment and affidavit is almost identical to the language suggested by N.J.S.A. 3B:3-5 for a self-proving affidavit signed subsequent to the time of execution. The form for making a will self-proved at the time of execution, as occurred here, is set forth in the preceding section, N.J.S.A. 3B:3-4. Although the subject affidavit was executed simultaneously with the execution of the will, the affidavit refers to the execution of the will in the past tense and incorrectly states that the witnesses had already signed the will.

Immediately after the execution of Russell's will, Betty executed her will in the presence of the same witnesses. As with Russell's will, Schuster and Stout signed the page containing the self-proving affidavit, but did not sign the will. Betty's will contained somewhat different dispositive provisions, and each page bore a legend identifying it as one page of "a three page will." The acknowledgment and affidavit, which appeared on the fourth page of the document, bore the legend "attached to a three page will."

Russell's will gives Betty a life estate in their apartment in a building at 111 Avenue of Two Rivers in Rumson, the rental income from other apartments in that building, and the tuition and rental income from the Rumson Reading Institute, which was merged into the Ranney School after the execution of Russell's will. The will further directs that on Betty's death, the Avenue of Two Rivers property and the proceeds of the Institute are to be turned over to the trustees of the Ranney School. Additionally, Betty receives all of Russell's personal property except that necessary for the operation of the Institute.

The residue of Russell's estate is to be paid in trust to Betty, Kantor, and Henry Bass, Russell's son-in-law, who were also appointed as executors. Betty and Harland Ranney and Suzanne Bass, Russell's two children, are to receive thirty-two percent each of the trust income, and are to share equally the net income from the operation of Ransco Corporation. Nancy Orlow, Betty's daughter and Russell's step-daughter, is to receive the remaining four percent of the trust income. Russell's will provides further that after Betty's death the income from Ransco Corporation is to be distributed equally between Harland Ranney and Suzanne Bass, and on their deaths is to be distributed to the Ranney School.

Russell died on April 4, 1987, and the Monmouth County Surrogate admitted the will to probate on April 21, 1987. Kantor represented Betty during the probate proceedings, but on March 8, 1988, he was disbarred for reasons unrelated to this case. See In re Kantor, 109 N.J. 647 (1988). Subsequently, Betty retained new counsel and contested the probate of Russell's will. She did not, however, assert that the will was the product of fraud or undue influence. Nor did she contend that it failed to express Russell's intent. Her sole challenge was that the will failed to comply literally with the formalities of N.J.S.A. 3B:3-2. Suzanne R. Bass, Harland Ranney, Henry Bass, and the Ranney School urged that the will be admitted to probate.

Without taking any testimony, the Law Division heard the matter on the return date of Betty's order to show cause. The court was satisfied that the will was Russell's last will and testament, but felt constrained to deny probate because the attesting witnesses had not strictly complied with the requirements of N.J.S.A. 3B:3-2.

Although the Appellate Division "decline[d] to hold that the placement of the witnesses' signatures is immaterial," 240 N.J.Super. at 344, 573 A.2d 467, it ruled that the self-proving affidavit was part of the will and that the witnesses' signatures on the affidavit constituted signatures on the will, id. at 344–45, 573 A.2d 467. Treating Russell's will as if it contained a defective attestation clause, the court remanded for a hearing to determine whether Russell had executed the document as his will, whether Schuster and Stout had signed the self-proving affidavit in response to Russell's request to witness the will, and whether they had witnessed either Russell's signature or his acknowledgment of that signature. Id. at 345, 573 A.2d 467.

We disagree with the Appellate Division that signatures on the subsequently-executed self-proving affidavit literally satisfied the requirements of N.J.S.A. 3B:3-2 as signatures on a will. We further hold, however, that the will may be admitted to probate if it substantially complies with these requirements.

* * *

The first question is whether Russell's will literally complies with the requirements of N.J.S.A. 3B:3-2, which provides:

> [E]very will shall be in writing, signed by the testator or in his name by some other person in his presence and at his direction, and shall be signed by at least two persons each of whom witnessed either the signing or the testator's acknowledgment of the signature or of the will.

In holding that signatures on the self-proving affidavit satisfy N.J.S.A. 3B:3-2, the Appellate Division relied on out-of-state decisions that permitted the probate of wills when the witnesses signed a self-proving affidavit, but not the will. 240 N.J.Super. at 344, 573 A.2d 467. The rationale of those cases is that a self-proving affidavit and an attestation clause are sufficiently similar to justify the conclusion that signatures on a self-proving affidavit, like signatures on the attestation clause, satisfy the requirement that the signatures be on the will. See In re Estate of Charry, 359 So.2d 544, 545 (Fla.Dist.Ct.App.1978) (witnesses' signatures on self-proving affidavit on same page as testator's signature satisfied attestation requirements); In re Estate of Petty, 227 Kan. 697, 702–03, 608 P.2d 987, 992–93 (1980) (self-proving affidavit on same page as testator's signature substantially complies with attestation requirements); In re Cutsinger, 445 P.2d 778, 782 (Okla.1968) (self-proving affidavit executed on same page as testator's signature is an attestation clause in substantial compliance with statutory requirement); see also In re Will of Leitstein, 46 Misc.2d 656, 657, 260 N.Y.S.2d 406, 407–08 (Sur.1965) (probating will when witnesses signed affidavit purporting to be attestation clause). The Appellate Division found that the similarity between self-proving affidavits and attestation clauses warrants treating the affidavit attached to Russell's will as the equivalent of an attestation clause. 240 N.J.Super. at 345, 573 A.2d 467. Noting that the absence of an attestation clause does not void a will, but merely requires the proponents to prove due execution, the Appellate Division could find "no reason, either in logic or policy, to deny a similar opportunity to the proponents" of Russell's will. Ibid. That conclusion fails to consider, however, the fundamental differences between a subsequently-executed, self-proving affidavit and an attestation clause. We are unable to conclude that a will containing the signatures of witnesses only on such an affidavit literally complies with the attestation requirements of N.J.S.A. 3B:3-2.

Self-proving affidavits and attestation clauses, although substantially similar in content, serve different functions. Mann, Self-Proving Affidavits and Formalism in Wills Adjudication, 63 Wash.U.L.Q. 39, 41 (1985). Attestation clauses facilitate probate by providing "prima facie evidence" that the testator voluntarily signed the will in the presence of the witnesses. 5 A. Clapp, N.J. Practice: Wills and Administration § 133 at 335 (3d ed.1982). An attestation clause also permits probate of a will when a witness forgets the circumstances of the will's execution or dies before the testator. Id. at 337.

Self-proving affidavits, by comparison, are sworn statements by eyewitnesses that the will has been duly executed. Mann, supra, 63 Wash.U.L.Q. at 40. The affidavit performs virtually all the functions of an attestation clause, and has the further effect of permitting probate without requiring the appearance of either witness. Id. at 41; 8 A. Clapp, supra, § 2063 at 9, comment 1. Wills may be made self-proving simultaneously with or after execution. N.J.S.A. 3B:3-4, -5. One difference between an attestation clause and a subsequently-signed, self-proving affidavit is that in an attestation clause, the attestant expresses the present intent to act as a witness, but in the affidavit, the affiant swears that the will has already been witnessed. This difference is more apparent than real when, as here, the affiants, with the intent to act as witnesses, sign the self-proving affidavit immediately after witnessing the testator's execution of the will.

The Legislature first authorized self-proving affidavits in the 1977 amendments to the Probate Code, specifically N.J.S.A. 3A:2A-6. Nothing in the statutory language or history intimates that the Legislature contemplated a subsequently-executed affidavit as a substitute for the attestation clause. Instead, the 1977 amendments indicate that the Legislature envisioned the will, including the attestation clause, as independent from such an affidavit. Hence, the form provided in N.J.S.A. 3B:3-5 for a subsequently-signed affidavit refers to the will as a separate instrument and states that the testator and witnesses have signed the will. Thus, the Legislature indicated its intention that subsequently-executed, self-proving affidavits be used solely in conjunction with duly-executed wills. Although the execution of Russell's will and of the self-proving affidavit apparently were contemporaneous, the affidavit follows the form provided in N.J.S.A. 3B:3-5. Consequently, the signatures of the witnesses on the subject self-proving affidavit do not literally comply with the statutory requirements.

That finding does not end the analysis. As we stated in In re Estate of Peters, 107 N.J. 263, 526 A.2d 1005 (1987), in limited circumstances a will may be probated if it substantially complies with those requirements. Id. at 281 n. 4, 526 A.2d 1005.

Other states have recognized that a will failing to satisfy the attestation requirements should not be denied probate when the witnesses have substantially complied with those requirements and the testator clearly intended to make a will. See, e.g., In re LaMont's Estate, 39 Cal.2d 566, 569–70, 248 P.2d 1, 2–3 (1952) (signature of witness substantially complied with execution requirements even if witness thought he was signing as executor); In re Estate of Petty, supra, 227 Kan. at 702–03, 608 P.2d at 992–93 (witnesses' signatures on self-proving affidavit substantially comply with attestation requirements); Smith v. Neikirk, 548 S.W.2d 156, 158 (Ky.Ct.App.1977) (will substantially satisfies statutory requirements even though witness turned back on testator at moment of signing and another witness signed as notary); In re Will of Kiefer, 78 Misc.2d 262, 264, 356 N.Y.S.2d 520, 522–23 (Sur.1974) (will admitted to probate when only one of two witnesses signed); see also 2 Bowe & Parker, Page on Wills § 19.4 nn. 15–21 (1960) (collecting cases applying rule of substantial compliance).

Scholars also have supported the doctrine of substantial compliance. Langbein, Substantial Compliance with the Wills Act, 88 Harv.L.Rev. 489 (1975); Nelson & Starck, Formalities and Formalism: A Critical Look at the Execution of Wills, 6 Pepperdine L.Rev. 331, 356 (1979). At the 1990 annual conference, the Commissioners on Uniform State Laws added a section to the Uniform Probate Code explicitly advocating the adoption of the doctrine. Uniform Probate Code § 2-503 (National Conference of Commissioners on Uniform State Laws 1990). That section, 2-503, provides:

> Although a document * * * was not executed in compliance with § 2-502 [enumerating the wills formalities], the document * * * is treated as if it had been executed in compliance with that section if the proponent of the document * * * establishes by clear and convincing evidence that the decedent intended the document to constitute (i) the decedent's will * * *.

In the 1990 edition of the Restatement (Second) of Property (Donative Transfers) (Restatement), moreover, the American Law Institute encourages courts to permit probate of wills that substantially comply with will formalities. § 33.1 comment g Tentative Draft No. 13) (approved by the American Law Institute at 1990 annual meeting). The Restatement concludes that in the absence of legislative action, courts "should apply a rule of excused noncompliance, under which a will is found validly executed if the proponent establishes by clear and convincing evidence that the decedent intended the document to constitute his or her will." Ibid. Thus, courts and scholars have determined that substantial compliance better serves the goals of statutory formalities by permitting probate of formally-defective wills that nevertheless represent the intent of the testator.

* * *

Substantial compliance is a functional rule designed to cure the inequity caused by the "harsh and relentless formalism" of the law of wills. Langbein, supra, 88 Harv.L.Rev. at 489; see also L. Waggoner, R. Wellman, G. Alexander & M. Fellows, Family Property Law: Wills, Trusts and Future Interests 32–35 (Tentative Draft 1990) (discussing genesis of substantial compliance doctrine). The underlying rationale is that the

> finding of a formal defect should lead not to automatic invalidity, but to a further inquiry: does the noncomplying document express the decedent's testamentary intent, and does its form sufficiently approximate Wills Act formality to enable the court to conclude that it serves the purposes of the Wills Act? [Langbein, supra, 88 Harv.L.Rev. at 489.]

Scholars have identified various reasons for formalities in the execution of wills. The primary purpose of those formalities is to ensure that the document reflects the uncoerced intent of the testator. Id. at 492; Mann, supra, 63 Wash.U.L.Q. at 49. Requirements that the will be in writing and signed by the testator also serve an evidentiary function by providing courts with reliable evidence of the terms of the will and of the testamentary intent. Gulliver & Tilson, Classification of Gratuitous Transfers, 51 Yale

L.J. 1, 6–7 (1941). Additionally, attestation requirements prevent fraud and undue influence. Id. at 9–10; In re Estate of Peters, supra, 107 N.J. at 276, 526 A.2d 1005. Further, the formalities perform a "channeling function" by requiring a certain degree of uniformity in the organization, language, and content of wills. Langbein, supra, 88 Harv.L.Rev. at 494. Finally, the ceremony serves as a ritual that impresses the testator with the seriousness of the occasion. Gulliver & Tilson, supra, 51 Yale L.J. at 5.

Rigid insistence on literal compliance often frustrates these purposes. Restatement, supra, § 33.1 comment g (strict compliance has in many cases led courts to results that defeated the intent of the testator). To avoid such frustration, some courts, although purporting to require literal compliance, have allowed probate of technically-defective wills. See In re Estate of Bochner, 119 Misc.2d 937, 938, 464 N.Y.S.2d 958, 959 (Sur.1983); In re Will of Leitstein, supra, 46 Misc.2d at 657, 260 N.Y.S.2d at 408. Other courts have refused to probate wills because of technical defects despite evidence that the testator meant the document to be a will. See In re Estate of Sample, 175 Mont. 93, 96–97, 572 P.2d 1232, 1234 (1977) (refusing to probate will signed only on attached self-proving affidavit); Boren v. Boren, 402 S.W.2d 728, 729 (Tex.1966). Leading authorities have criticized the *Boren* rule, finding no basis in logic or policy for its blind insistence on voiding wills for "the most minute defect[s] in formal compliance * * * no matter how abundant the evidence that the defect [is] inconsequential." Langbein, supra, 88 Harv.L.Rev. at 489; accord In re Estate of Charry, supra, 359 So.2d at 545 (declining to follow *Boren* rule because it elevated form over substance); Mann, supra, 63 Wash.U.L.Q. at 39–40 (characterizing *Boren* line of cases as "odd and rather perverse"); Nelson & Starck, supra, 6 Pepperdine L.Rev. at 356–57.

We agree with those authorities. Compliance with statutory formalities is important not because of the inherent value that those formalities possess, but because of the purposes they serve. Mann, supra, 63 Wash.U.L.Q. at 60; Nelson & Starck, supra, 6 Pepperdine L.Rev. at 355. It would be ironic to insist on literal compliance with statutory formalities when that insistence would invalidate a will that is the deliberate and voluntary act of the testator. Such a result would frustrate rather than further the purpose of the formalities. Nelson & Starck, supra, 6 Pepperdine L.Rev. at 353–55.

Concerned about inequities resulting from excessive adherence to formalism, the Commissioners on Uniform State Laws proposed the Uniform Probate Code. The goals of the Code were to simplify the execution of wills, Uniform Probate Code, art. 2, pt. 5, General Comment at 46 (1974), and to recognize the intent of the testator in the distribution of his property, id. at § 1-102(b)(2). Consequently, the Commissioners minimized the formalities of execution and diminished "the ceremonial value of attestation." Langbein, supra, 88 Harv.L.Rev. at 510–11. Responding to similar concerns in 1977, the New Jersey Legislature adopted a variation of the Uniform Probate Code that differed significantly from its pre-Code predecessor. 1977 N.J. Laws, ch. 412, § 1; see In re Estate of Peters, supra, 107 N.J. at 271, 526 A.2d 1005. Thus, N.J.S.A. 3B:3-2, like its identical 1977 counterpart, N.J.S.A. 3A:2A-4, does not require that witnesses sign in the presence of the testator and of each other. In re Estate of Peters, supra, 107 N.J. at 273, 526 A.2d 1005. The 1977 amendments also removed the interested-witness provisions, N.J.S.A. 3A:2A-7, with the result that a beneficiary who acts as a witness is no longer prevented from taking under a will, N.J.S.A. 3B:3-8. As a result of those amendments, moreover, unwitnessed holographic wills could be admitted to probate. N.J.S.A. 3A:2A-5. Under the current provision, N.J.S.A. 3B:3-3, a holographic will is valid whether or not witnessed, so long as the signature and material provisions of the will are in the handwriting of the testator. N.J.S.A. 3B:3-3. The approval of unwitnessed holographic wills, like the diminution of attestation requirements, reflects a more relaxed attitude toward the execution of wills.

Legislative history confirms that N.J.S.A. 3B:3-2 was enacted to free will execution from the ritualism of pre-Code law and to prevent technical defects from invalidating otherwise valid wills. Senate Judiciary Committee Public Hearing on Uniform Probate Code Bills at 20 (comments of Harrison Durand) (reduction of statutory formalities meant to prevent failure of testamentary plans); see In re Estate of Peters, supra, 107 N.J. at 272 n. 2, 526 A.2d 1005 (noting that former statute often resulted in wills being refused probate because some formality not followed). Generally, when strict construction would frustrate the purposes of the statute, the spirit of the law should control over its letter. New Jersey Builders, Owners & Managers Ass'n v. Blair, 60 N.J. 330, 338, 288 A.2d 855 (1972). Accordingly, we believe that the Legislature did not intend that a will should be denied probate because the witnesses signed in the wrong place.

The execution of a last will and testament, however, remains a solemn event. A careful practitioner will still observe the formalities surrounding the execution of wills. When formal defects occur, proponents should prove by clear and convincing evidence that the will substantially complies with statutory requirements. See Uniform Probate Code, supra, §2-503; Restatement, supra, §33.1 comment g. Our adoption of the doctrine of substantial compliance should not be construed as an invitation either to carelessness or chicanery. The purpose of the doctrine is to remove procedural peccadillos as a bar to probate.

Furthermore, as previously described, ante at 1342–1343, a subsequently-signed self-proving affidavit serves a unique function in the probate of wills. We are reluctant to permit the signatures on such an affidavit both to validate the execution of the will and to render the will self-proving. Accordingly, if the witnesses, with the intent to attest, sign a self-proving affidavit, but do not sign the will or an attestation clause, clear and convincing evidence of their intent should be adduced to establish substantial compliance with the statute. For that reason, probate in these circumstances should proceed in solemn form. See N.J.S.A. 3B:3-23; R. 4:84-1. Probate in solemn form, which is an added precaution to assure proof of valid execution, may be initiated on an order to show cause, R. 4:84-1(b), and need not unduly delay probate of a qualified will.

* * *

The record suggests that the proffered instrument is the will of Russell Ranney, that he signed it voluntarily, that Schuster and Stout signed the self-proving affidavit at Russell's request, and that they witnessed his signature. Furthermore, Betty has certified that Russell executed the will and that she is unaware of the existence of any other will. Before us, however, her attorney questions whether Russell "actually signed" the will. If, after conducting a hearing in solemn form, the trial court is satisfied that the execution of the will substantially complies with the statutory requirements, it may reinstate the judgment of the Surrogate admitting the will to probate.

Following the judgment of the Appellate Division, this Court amended the Rules of Civil Procedure pertaining to probate practice. Those amendments resulted in the allocation of the probate jurisdiction of the Chancery Division to the Chancery Division, Probate Part. See R. 4:83.

The judgment of the Appellate Division is affirmed, and the matter is remanded to the Chancery Division, Probate Part.

For affirmance and remandment—Justices CLIFFORD, HANDLER, POLLOCK, O'HERN, GARIBALDI, and STEIN—6.

Opposed—None.

Uniform Probate Code (2003)

§ 2-503. Harmless Error.

Although a document or writing added upon a document was not executed in compliance with Section 2-502, the document or writing is treated as if it had been executed in compliance with that section if the proponent of the document or writing establishes by clear and convincing evidence that the decedent intended the document or writing to constitute (i) the decedent's will, (ii) a partial or complete revocation of the will, (iii) an addition to or an alteration of the will, or (iv) a partial or complete revival of his [or her] formerly revoked will or of a formerly revoked portion of the will.

Restatement (Third) of Property, Wills and Other Donative Transfers (1999)

§ 3.3 Excusing Harmless Errors

A harmless error in executing a will may be excused if the proponent establishes by clear and convincing evidence that the decedent adopted the document as his or her will.

Australian Capital Territory Wills Act § 11A

Validity of will etc. not executed with required formalities.

(1) A document, or a part of a document, purporting to embody testamentary intentions of a deceased person shall, notwithstanding that it has not been executed in accordance with the formal requirements of this Act, constitute a will of the deceased person, an amendment of the will of the deceased person or a revocation of the will of the deceased person if the Supreme Court is satisfied that the deceased person intended the document or part of the document to constitute his or her will, an amendment of his or her will or the revocation of his or her will respectively.

(2) In forming a view of whether a deceased person intended a document or part of a document to constitute his or her will, an amendment of his or her will or a revocation of his or her will, the Supreme Court may, in addition to having regard to the document, have regard to—

(a) any evidence relating to the manner of execution of the document; or

(b) any evidence of the testamentary intentions of the deceased person, including evidence (whether admissible before the commencement of this section or not) of statements made by the deceased person.

New South Wales Wills, Probate and Administration Act § 18A

(1) A document purporting to embody the testamentary intentions of a deceased person, even though it has not been executed in accordance with the formal requirements of this Act, constitutes a will of the deceased person, an amendment of such a will or the revocation of such a will if the Court is satisfied that the deceased person intended the document to constitute his or her will, an amendment of his or her will or the revocation of his or her will.

(2) In forming its view, the Court may have regard (in addition to the document) to any other evidence relating to the manner of execution or testamentary intentions of the deceased person, including evidence (whether admissible before the commencement of this section or otherwise) of statements made by the deceased person.

Northern Territory Wills Act (1987) § 12. *Validity of Will*

(2) A document purporting to embody the testamentary intentions of a deceased person, notwithstanding that it has not been executed with the formalities required by this Act, is deemed to be a will of the deceased person where the Supreme Court [the court of first instance in probate matters], upon application for admission of the document to probate as the last will of the deceased, is satisfied that there can be no reasonable doubt that the deceased intended the document to constitute his will.

Queensland Succession Act of 1981, § 9

(a) the court may admit to probate a testamentary instrument executed in substantial compliance with the formalities prescribed by this section if the court is satisfied that the instrument expresses the testamentary intention of the testator; and

(b) the court may admit extrinsic evidence including evidence of statements made at any time by the testator as to the manner of execution of a testamentary instrument.

South Australia, Wills Act 1946, as amended by Wills (Miscellaneous) Amendment Act 1994, § 12

(2) Subject to this Act, if the Court is satisfied that a document that has not been executed with the formalities required by this Act expresses testamentary intentions of a deceased person, the document will be admitted to probate as a will of the deceased person.

(3) If the Court is satisfied that a document that has not been executed with the formalities required by this Act expresses an intention by a deceased person to revoke a document that might otherwise have been admitted to probate as a will of the deceased person, that document is not to be admitted to probate as a will of the deceased person.

(4) This section applies to a document whether is came into existence within or outside the State.

(5) Rules of Court may authorise the Registrar to exercise the powers of the Court under this section.

Tasmania Wills Act 1992 § 26

(1) A document purporting to embody the testamentary intentions of a deceased person is taken, notwithstanding that it has not been executed in accordance with Division 3, to be a will of the deceased person, an amendment of such a will or the revocation of such a will if the Court, on application for a grant of probate of the last will of the deceased person, is satisfied that there can be no reasonable doubt that that person intended the document to constitute the will of that person, an amendment of such a will or the revocation of such a will.

(2) In considering a document for the purposes of subsection (1), the Court may have regard, in addition to the document, to any other evidence relating to the manner of execution or the testamentary intentions of the deceased person, including evidence, whether admissible before the commencement of this Act or otherwise, of statements made by the deceased person.

For the official web site on probate for the Supreme Court of Tasmania, see Supreme Court of Tasmania, http://www.courts.tas/gov.au/; *select* Wills and Probate (accessed Oct. 12, 2005).

Canada

Uniform Wills Act of Canada § 19 (1988). Notwithstanding a lack of compliance with all the formal requirements as to execution that are imposed by this Act, a [court] that is satisfied that

(a) a document intended by a deceased to constitute a will embodies the testamentary intentions of the deceased, or

(b) a document or writing on a document embodies the intention of a deceased to revoke, alter or revive a will of the deceased or a document described in clause (a),

may order that the document or writing is fully effective, as though it had been executed in compliance with all the formal requirements imposed by this Act, as the will of the deceased or as the revocation, alteration or revival of a will of the deceased or of a document described in clause (a).

Israel

Israel Succession Law, 5725-1965, in Ministry of Justice, 19 Laws of the State of Israel 62, ch. 1, § 25 (1965). Where the Court has no doubt as to the genuineness of a will, it may grant probate thereof notwithstanding any defect with regard to the signature of the testator or of the witnesses, the date of the will, the procedure set out [for attested wills] or the capacity of the witnesses.

2. Self-Proving Affidavit

The attorney who supervised the execution of the Last Will and Testament in the *Ranney* decision utilized a new statutory device known as a self-proving affidavit. The device is similar to an attestation clause in that a presumption is involved. When an attestation clause is used, a *rebuttable* presumption arises that every formality recited in the clause has been accomplished. This presumption excuses the witnesses from having to give testimony at a later date as to the accomplishment of the formalities. A self-proving affidavit goes one step further. In states that allow for self-proving affidavits by statute, the affidavit raises an *irrebuttable* presumption that all of the formalities recited in the clause were accomplished. The state statute may require a one-step method or a two-step method (the *Ranney* approach); the signature of a notary public to effectuate the irrebuttable presumption is an added requirement to the formalities. The Uniform Probate Code provides for both the one-step and the two-step self-proving affidavit. *See* UNIF. PROB. CODE § 2-504 (a)–(b) (2003). *See also*, Hickox v. Wilson, 269 Ga. 180, 496 S.E.2d 711 (1998) (court probated a will after it had not been signed by a testator; the testator and two witnesses signed only the self-proving affidavit). Note, too, that the self-proving affidavit does not make the intentionalities irrebuttable, it only makes the formalities irrebuttable. Intentionalities are treated separately from formalities.

3. Changing Jurisdictions

Uniform Probate Code (2003)

§ 2-506. Choice of Law as to Execution.

A written will is valid if executed in compliance with Section 2-502 or 2-503 or if its execution complies with the law at the time of execution of the place where the will is executed, or of the law of the place where at the time of execution or at the time of death the testator is domiciled, has a place of abode, or is a national.

III. Intentionalities

Proper intent is a necessary complement to testamentary formalities. "It takes two to tango!" The list of intentionalities that follows is often associated with grounds of contest—legal actions that challenge the validity of the Last Will and Testament. But before any one of them may become the subject of contest, each must have been present or absent when the Will was executed. Each involves the mind of the testator at the crucial moment—the moment of execution.

Note that when the statutory formalities were described in the previous section, cases and statutes provided for a presumption that the formalities were accomplished if they were recited in the attestation clause as present at the time of execution. State statutes made the presumption irrebuttable if a self-proving affidavit accompanied the properly executed attestation clause. Such irrebuttability is available in the context of intentionalities in only a few states, such as Arkansas, North Dakota and Ohio. Each state has a statute permitting pre-mortem probate. That is, a testator may probate his or her Will prior to death and, by doing so in an adversary proceeding before the probate clerk, may make irrebuttable the presumptions about testamentary capacity, freedom from undue influence, and intent to make this his or her Last Will and Testament. *See* ARK. CODE ANN. §28-40-202 (2003); N.D. CENT. CODE §30.1-08.1-01 (2003); OHIO REV. CODE ANN. §2107.081 (2003). Some commentators have welcomed the possibility of freedom from litigation over so personal an issue as intentionalities. *See, e.g.,* Aloysius A. Leopold & Gerry W. Beyer, *Ante-Mortem Probate: A Viable Alternative,* 43 ARK. L. REV. 131 (1990).

The following intentionalities involve medical testimony, judges and juries, bias and dashed expectations, sex and intrigue, and a sibling or two with more than one ax to grind. The law seems hard-pressed to provide a remedy.

A. Testamentary Intent

In re Estate of Beale
Supreme Court of Wisconsin, 1962
15 Wis.2d 546, 113 N.W.2d 380

BROWN, Justice.

* * *

Appellant begins with the assertion that the 1959 will is an unnatural one in that it disinherited Beale's ten year old son. Then he states his proposition that 'proponents of an unnatural will have burden to give a reasonable explanation for its unnatural provisions.' The learned trial court filed a written decision which demonstrated the meticulous study which the court gave to the will itself and to the evidence adduced in the several hearings, and the court concluded that the will was not 'unnatural.' Thomas' inheritance was reduced by the 1959 will to a contingent remainder but whether this rendered the will an unnatural one seems to us to be immaterial in the absence of any contention by appellant that, because of testamentary incapacity, undue influence or other factors appearing in the evidence, the will does not express the testator's true desires and intent. There are present no such factors to impugn the conclusion that the 1959 will exactly stated Professor Beale's own wish and purpose in respect to provision for his son Thomas. As the provisions or the lack of them are within the permission of the law neither Beale nor anyone else has to justify them or please any other person.

Appellant's brief further informs us that 'the right to make a will is not a constitutional or natural right, but a 'creature of statutory law", citing a Pennsylvania case. We have frequently held to the contrary, even so recently as in Estate of Ogg (1952), 262 Wis. 181, 54 N.W.2d 175, and Will of Wright (1961), 12 Wis.2d 375, 107 N.W.2d 146. See also Will of Rice (1912), 150 Wis. 401, 450, 136 N.W. 956, 137 N.W. 778. In each of those cases we have emphasized that the right to make a will is a sacred and constitutional right, which right includes a right of equal dignity to have the will carried out. And see Will of Hopkins (1956), 273 Wis. 632, 639, 79 N.W.2d 131, where we said:

> 'Appellant claims that the will was an unnatural will, because after the administration of the specific bequests, the bulk of which was to the Masons, no residue remained to distribute to the surviving relatives. When a valid last will and testament has disposed of the owner's estate, the interest of surviving relatives is controlled by its provisions and not by the statute of descent. As said by

the trial court, 'the law gives the testator the right to dispose of his property in any manner he may desire as long as it is his own act and free will, and the court is fully satisfied in this instance that the testator knew what he was doing at the time he signed his will and disposed of his property in the manner indicated therein * * * it is the responsibility of this court to respect his wishes."

In the Rice case, supra, at page 446, 136 N.W. at page 974, we cited with approval Will of Dardis (1908), 135 Wis. 457, 115 N.W. 332, 23 L.R.A., N.S., 783, to the effect that '* * * regardless of holdings elsewhere, in this state a will, once validly made and subsisting to the death of the testator, must be taken and judicially enforced according to his intent, if that can be ascertained; * * *.'

The long line of Wisconsin decisions does not permit the probate court to entertain the argument that a will can be denied probate only because it appears to be unjust to a natural object of a testator's bounty. Here appellant has made no attack on the testamentary capacity of Beale nor has he claimed he was unduly influenced. Will of Dobson (1951), 258 Wis. 587, 46 N.W.2d 758, states the following, relying upon Will of Schaefer (1932), 207 Wis. 404, 241 N.W. 382:

'* * * We might, without great difficulty, conclude that in equity the instrument provides an unjust distribution of the estate. However, we may not consider it in the light of what we may deem just or unjust. If it was made by Joseph Dobson with full testamentary capacity, expresses his desires and is not the result of undue influence, it is our duty to give it effect. That it does not divide the estate equally between the natural objects of testator's bounty is not controlling.'

Thus this court, as well as the county court, is precluded from considering whether Professor Beale's 1959 will is an 'unnatural will', with a view to denying probate to it.

* * *

While appellant concedes, or at least does not dispute, that when Professor Beale signed the purported 1959 will he had testamentary capacity and was not subject to undue influence appellant vigorously denies that the 14 pages of the 1959 instrument were legally published and declared to be his will and legally signed and witnessed as such and, in the alternative, that these pages did not constitute his will at the moment of execution.

In this record there are a few indisputable facts. From then there are a number of conflicting inferences reasonably to be drawn.

It cannot be questioned that on June 16 or 17, 1959, Professor Beale dictated a 14 page Document in the form of a last will, revoking all prior wills; that his secretary typed the original will, with three carbon copies, and delivered all of them to him in loose-leaf form the afternoon of June 20th; that Beale was in New York City at the home of a friend, a professor of Columbia University, on the evening of June 21st and on that evening he exhibited 'a pile' of sheets of paper and declared to his three friends that this was his will and desired them to witness his will; that they saw him sign the sheet which was on top of the pile and that immediately thereafter, at his request, they signed as witnesses in his presence and in the presence of each other; that the place where they put their signatures was immediately below the usual testamentary clause declaring this to be Professor Beale's will; that none of the witnesses paid any detailed attention to the number of pages in the pile nor could they identify later any of the pages except the one where they had written their names; that when all four participants had signed, Beale put all papers in his briefcase and the meeting ended.

It is uncontradicted that on the next day, or shortly thereafter, Beale and his two sons left by plane for Moscow; that a few days after June 21st Mrs. Burleigh, Beale's secretary, received a letter from him on Columbia University note paper, bearing date June 21, 1959, mailed in New York or in London on a day not given; that the letter asked Mrs. Burleigh to make several changes in pages 12 and 13 of the will which she had previously typed, to carry out marginal penciled notes in Beale's handwriting on those pages; that enclosed with the letter were the original pages 12 and 13; that Mrs. Burleigh made the alterations as directed and mailed them back to him in Moscow; that these pages were later found in a sealed envelope addressed to Beale in Beale's handwriting and mailed from London, England to him at his Madison address.

There is nothing legally invalid in the execution of a will because the separate pages of the will have not been fastened together. It is a requirement, though, that all the pages be present at the time of execution.

Thompson on Wills (3rd Ed.), sec. 124, page 197, states:

> '* * * It is not necessary that they [the witnesses] see or examine all the pages of the will to see that all the sheets of paper were in place when the will was executed. * * *' Citing In Re Sleeper's Appeal, 129 Maine 194, 151 Atl. 150, 71 A.L.R. 518.

In Sleeper's Appeal, supra, the court stated:

> '* * * nor is it essential that the witnesses should see and examine all the pages of a will at the time of execution, if the court is satisfied, from other evidence or the circumstances surrounding the execution, that all the sheets of paper offered for probate were present at the time of execution. * * *'

> 2 Page on Wills (Bowe-Parker Revision), sec. 19.147, page 277, is to the same effect, citing Sleeper's Appeal, supra, and 11 B.U.L.Rev. 148; 5 Temp.L.Q. 152; 17 La.L.Rev. 69; and 40 Yale L.J. 144.

In the case at bar the witnesses are unable to say whether or not the 14 pages were on the table before them when, on June 21st, they signed the last page. The determination then, comes down to the reasonable inferences to be drawn from the established facts. Appellant relies on the undisputed fact that two pages of the will were received in Madison within a few days following June 21st, enclosed in a letter dated June 21st. And appellant infers that those two pages had already been sent off to Madison when, late in the evening of June 21st, the testator and witnesses signed the last page.

On the other hand the trial court put weight on the fact that all 14 original pages are clearly identified and legible as they were dictated by Beale before the corrections or amendments. This intact original was handed to Beale by his secretary and was taken by him to New York. The very next day Beale presented 'a pile' of papers to his witnesses and declared that such papers were his will. It is not impossible or improbable that Beale was speaking the truth and the pile of pages were the complete 14 page will, as the trial court found. The fact that Beale sent off two pages to Mrs. Burleigh with a letter dated June 21st may raise an inference that Beale did this before he went to the party and he had there only the remaining pages, which he falsely declared to be his will. Certainly that is not the only permissible inference. When Beale and his friends had signed the will and he had gathered up the pages and departed June 21st was not over; Beale could still have written the letter, less than 100 words, on that date after the party and enclosed with it pages 12 and 13. There is no evidence at all of when the letter and the pages were mailed and there is some evidence that they were mailed in London.

The question is one of inference and when the inferences can reasonably go either way the appellate court must adopt the view taken by the trial court.

'1. It is the function of the trial court, in cases tried to the court, to draw such inferences from the established facts as deemed proper, and the supreme court cannot disturb the same unless they are against the great weight and clear preponderance of the evidence.' Hull v. Pfister & Vogel Leather Co. (1940), 235 Wis. 653, 294 N.W. 18, (Headnote).

'As the trial court's function is to determine the facts and to weigh them, In re Will of Russell, 1950, 257 Wis. 510, 44 N.W.2d 231, so, too, the inferences to be drawn from established facts are for the trier of the fact, in this case the trial court. Its findings in these respects should not be interfered with unless contrary to the great weight and clear preponderance of the evidence, * * *.' Estate of Miller (1953), 265 Wis. 420, 424–425, 61 N.W.2d 813.

'It is well established that findings of a trial court are not to be disturbed on appeal unless they are contrary to the great weight and clear preponderance of the evidence. Swazee v. Lee, 1951, 259 Wis. 136, 137, 47 N.W.2d 733.' Drott Tractor Co. v. Kehrein (1957), 275 Wis. 320, 323, 81 N.W.2d 500.

'* * * The most that can be said is that on some of the contested issues of fact, the proof might have sustained a finding contrary to that made by the court. Upon such a state of the record this court may not disturb the findings of the trial court.' Drott Tractor Co. v. Kehrein, supra, p. 328, 81 N.W.2d p. 504.

While the present facts permit the inference urged by appellant they do not compel that inference in opposition to the one drawn by the trial court, and the evidence and reasonable inferences sustain the trial court's conclusion that the entire original will, as dictated by Professor Beale to his secretary, was before the witnesses and the execution of that will complied with the requirements of law.

* * *

Appellant, however, has other shots in his locker, the first of which is that even if the entire 14 pages of the will, as originally typed, were before the testator and witnesses at the time of execution the fact that Beale so quickly chose to make changes in it must persuade the court that at the moment of execution Beale did not intend this to be his will, no matter what he may have declared. The burden is on appellant to show that although Beale had himself dictated this will in the very recent past and had declared it to his three friends to be his will, he had already changed his mind concerning it.

As before, the court might have drawn that inference but it was not compelled to do so. The trial court considered Beale's express declaration that this was his will as of that moment was entitled to the greater weight. That court said, in its written decision:

'The objectors contend that the proper *Animus Testandi* is lacking in this case. Such an objection cannot be sustained. It certainly cannot be said that a man who dictates a document consisting of fourteen pages which purports to be his last will and testament, takes the finished typewritten document from Madison, Wisconsin to New York City, secures three personal friends to witness the document, telling them it is his will, all of which takes place shortly before he is to take a long trip to a foreign land, lacks the necessary testamentary intent to make that document his last will. The necessary testamentary intent existed at the time the will was executed, and that is all that is required.'

The inference drawn by the trial court is reasonable and we must adopt its conclusion.

* * *

Next, appellant submits that Beale had revoked the 1959 will. Sec. 238.14, Stats. of 1959, states:

> 'Will, how revoked. No will nor any part thereof shall be revoked unless by burning, tearing, canceling or obliterating the same, with the intention of revoking it, by the testator or by some person in his presence and by his direction, or by some other will or codicil in writing, executed as prescribed in this chapter, or by some other writing, signed, attested and subscribed in the manner provided in this chapter for the execution of a will; excepting only that nothing contained in this section shall prevent the revocation implied by law from subsequent changes in the condition or circumstances of the testator. The power to make a will implies the power to revoke the same.'

These are the only ways by which a will can be revoked in this state. Deck v. Deck (1900), 106 Wis. 470, 82 N.W. 293. The burden is upon the objectors to establish by competent evidence that there was a valid and effective revocation. Estate of Sweeney (1946), 248 Wis. 607, 22 N.W.2d 657, 24 N.W.2d 406.

In contending that Bale intended to revoke the 1959 will, appellant first points to the several alterations requested by Beale and the fact that the date was changed from June 21st to June 22nd. Beale, himself, never said or wrote that he intended to revoke the will. He wrote a direction to modify one sentence. Such attempted alterations, according to appellant, were themselves sufficient to revoke the 1959 will. None of these alterations pertained to the distribution of Beale's property. As already mentioned, the change in executors was the only significant substitution. Such a change does not operate as a revocation of the will in its entirety. 57 Am.Jur., Wills, sec. 510, page 355, states:

> 'Clearly, a will is not revoked in its entirety by the act of the testator in striking out the name of the person designated executor and writing in the name of another person as executor, notwithstanding this occurs after the will has been executed and attested and without a reattestation or republication. * * *'

Respondents contend that the substitution of executors, as it did not comply with statutory will standards (sec. 238.06, Stats.), is invalid. Thus, the attempted changes cannot have the effect of invalidating the will. Even if the changes were valid they would have no effect on the property distribution directed by the will. Will of Home (1939), 231 Wis. 227, 233, 284 N.W. 766, 285 N.W. 754, held: 'Aside from this the alterations have no effect to invalidate the will as a whole. They would only invalidate the change.' In the same case we said, page 234, 284 N.W. page 768: '* * * The recent case of Byrne's Will, 223 Wis. 503, 271 N.W. 48, clearly implies that alterations in a will do not render it void and have no effect except as they operate as partial revocations. * * *'

2 Page on Wills, sec. 537, pages 3–4, says:

'If the will which is altered by testator after execution is one which is required, by statute, to be attested and subscribed by witnesses, interlineations which testator makes after execution, are of no effect unless the will is subsequently re-executed or republished; and such a will must be admitted to probate as though the interlineations had never been made. * * *

'If the name of an executor is added after execution, such addition is of no effect. * * *'

Will of Marvin (1920), 172 Wis. 457, 179 N.W. 508, (headnotes 1 and 2) states:

'If a testator cancels or destroys a will with the present intention of making a new disposition of his property, and the proposed new disposition fails to be carried into effect, the presumption in favor of a revocation by the canceling is repelled, and the will stands as originally made.

'Where testatrix left all her property to one of four grandchildren, and after her death the will was found to have pencil marks through the words bequeathing the property to such grandchild, and below the attestation clause there was written with a pen a clause in the handwriting of the testatrix giving all her property, after payment of all her debts, to an orphans' home, but such clause was not signed by testatrix nor witnessed, the attempted changes did not become effective and the will remained as originally drawn.'

We determine that the 1959 will was not revoked by the alterations nor were the attempted modifications effective.

We then come to a fact whose effect, if any, until now we have found no occasion to consider, viz.:

Promptly after Professor Beale's death his family searched his office in the University Library for a will. What they found there was the 1959 will, without the first page, and a complete copy of the will, including the first page. Several months later the missing original first page was discovered in a folder containing Beale's notes for a history lecture. These papers were found in Beale's second office in another university building. This page was delivered to the court and the complete will as originally transcribed and legible in spite of the alterations was then before the county court.

Page 1 contained the introductory clause revoking all prior wills. Appellant submits that the abstraction of this page from the remainder of the will manifested Beale's intent to destroy the will of which page 1 was a part. The trial court concluded that page 1 had merely been misplaced and no contrary intent has been proved. Once the execution and validity of a will has been established, valid and effective revocation is a burden which falls upon the objectors. Estate of Sweeney, supra. The county court's conclusion that appellant has not met this burden is consistent with the proof. A contrary view, that revocation by this means was intended, depends not even upon inference but on mere speculation.

* * *

At least one more mystery appears worth mentioning, although in our view it presents no fact to affect the outcome:

A few days before Christmas, 1959, Beale, who had returned to Madison, directed Mrs. Burleigh to re-type the altered pages 12 and 13 on the same typewriter she had used when she first typed the will. We may guess that Beale wanted pages which did not show they had been tampered with, as was apparent on the two original sheets now showing erasures and re-typed corrections. We may guess, further, that Beale intended to insert in the will without discovery the new pages without republication and re-execution of the will. This is no more than guesswork and is of no consequence. Before Mrs. Burleigh typed the two new sheets Beale's death intervened on December 27, 1959. Whatever his purpose, nefarious or not, he did not accomplish it. Mrs. Burleigh had not begun this final typing when she was told that Professor Beale had died. She then typed the two pages as Professor Beale directed and gave them to Beale's son, Henry. There were then no marginal initials on them. These pages are in evidence and, although Professor Beale never in his life had them or saw them, his initials are now on the margin of each of these pages and, as Mrs. Burleigh testified, are in his handwriting.

We began with a consideration of the unnatural. At the end we are confronted by the supernatural. We consider ourselves fortunate that this weird addition to the facts turns out to be immaterial.

We conclude that the trial court's findings and conclusions are not against the great weight and the clear preponderance of the evidence and the judgment admitting the will to probate as the will existed when it was executed and as Mrs. Burleigh first typed it must be affirmed.

Judgment affirmed.

CURRIE, Justice (dissenting).

On the record here presented, the paramount issue is whether, at time of execution of the 1959 will, testator intended the then existing fourteen typewritten pages to be his will. As the majority opinion intimates, if it was testator's intent to keep the instrument ambulatory in character, so that from time to time he could substitute pages for any except the last, which bore the signature of himself and witnesses, then this instrument would not qualify as his last will and testament because the requisite testamentary intent would be lacking. The crucial piece of evidence on this issue is testator's letter of June 21, 1959, to Mrs. Burleigh forwarding for retyping the two pages on which he had made alterations. If this letter was written before testator and the witnesses affixed their signatures, it would carry great weight in establishing that testator had intended an ambulatory instrument.

The June 21st letter was written on Columbia University stationery. A reasonable inference is that he procured this stationery at the apartment of his friend, Professor Forcey, a member of the Columbia University faculty, and the host of the June 21st party given in honor of testator. However, Professor Forcey, who testified as a subscribing witness to the 1959 will, was asked no questions about furnishing stationery to testator or about whether he possessed any knowledge concerning the writing of the June 21st letter.

Forcey did testify that both Howard Kennedy Beale, Jr., and Henry Barton Beale were present with their father in the Forcey apartment at the June 21st party. Neither of these two sons of testator were called as witnesses at the trial. The general rule is that failure of a party to call a material witness within his control, or whom it would be more natural for such party to call than the opposing party, raises an inference against such party. Feldstein v. Harrington (1958), 4 Wis.2d 380, 388, 90 N.W.2d 566; 2 Wigmore, Evidence (3rd ed.), p. 162, et seq., secs. 285, 286. This rule is applicable in situations of family relationship, such as parent and child. Anno., 5 A.L.R.(2d) 893, 934. Thus, the failure to call either of these two sons as a witness raised an inference against the proponents of the 1959 will. However, the trial court's memorandum opinion does not comment upon the fact that these two older sons were not called to testify as to their knowledge with respect to the writing of the June 21st letter.

It may very well be that the *guardians ad litem* for all three sons interviewed the two older sons about the June 21st letter and found they possessed no knowledge or recollection with respect to their father writing it. However, this is a situation where the trial court might very well have drawn the opposite inference from that which it did. Additional testimony with respect to the June 21st letter might have tipped the scales the other way. This is very important considering the fact that a ten year old boy, who is a ward of the court, has been virtually disinherited by his father's will.

Under these circumstances I would exercise our discretionary power under sec. 251.09, Stats. to reverse and remand for the purpose of taking the testimony of the two older boys with respect to the June 21st letter.

I am authorized to state that DIETERICH, J., joins in this dissenting opinion.

Notes

The issue in *Beale* was whether the testator intended the assemblage of pages to be his Last Will and Testament or whether he intended it to be a draft of one that would follow. The difficulty of discerning the intent of a decedent is captured in Will phrases such as: "I am going on a journey and may not return. If I do not, I leave everything to my adopted son." Eaton v. Brown, 193 U.S. 411, 24 S. Ct. 487 (1904). Did the testatrix intend this to be a term will, valid only for the length of her journey? Did the testatrix thus imply that if she does, in fact, return from the trip safely, the Last Will and Testament is no longer effective? Or was the trip merely an inducement for her to execute the Will?

Obviously, holographic Wills, written without the supervision of an attorney, are the most likely to contain phrases that precipitate confusion. Added to this is the problem of determining if a written instrument, wholly in the handwriting of the decedent, dated and signed, is a holographic Will or merely a letter to a friend or relative. The distinguishing feature is the necessity of finding "death talk" in the language used by the scrivener. The language must anticipate that death is the motivating factor behind the letter and that the future disposition of property is the intended result. *See, e.g.,* In re Kimmel's Estate, 278 Pa. 435, 123 A. 405 (1924) (court held that a letter sent by the decedent to two of his children on the same day on which he died had proper testamentary intent and could be probated as a Last Will and Testament). The facts of each case, particularly regarding beneficiaries, the availability of other testamentary instruments, and the circumstances surrounding the death of the scrivener, are all pertinent.

B. Incorporation by Reference

Clark v. Greenhalge

Supreme Judicial Court of Massachusetts, 1991
411 Mass. 410, 582 N.E.2d 949

NOLAN, Justice.

We consider in this case whether a probate judge correctly concluded that specific, written bequests of personal property contained in a notebook maintained by a testatrix were incorporated by reference into the terms of the testatrix's will.

We set forth the relevant facts as found by the probate judge. The testatrix, Helen Nesmith, duly executed a will in 1977, which named her cousin, Frederic T. Greenhalge, II, as executor of her estate. The will further identified Greenhalge as the principal beneficiary of the estate, entitling him to receive all of Helen Nesmith's tangible personal property upon her death except those items which she "designate[d] by a memorandum left by [her] and known to [Greenhalge], or in accordance with [her] known wishes," to be given to others living at the time of her death.[2] Among Helen Nesmith's possessions was a large oil painting of a farm scene signed by T.H. Muckley and dated 1833. The value of the painting, as assessed for estate tax purposes, was $1,800.00.

In 1972, Greenhalge assisted Helen Nesmith in drafting a document entitled "MEMORANDUM" and identified as "a list of items of personal property prepared with Miss Helen Nesmith upon September 5, 1972, for the guidance of myself in the distribution of personal tangible property." This list consisted of forty-nine specific bequests of Ms. Nesmith's tangible personal property. In 1976, Helen Nesmith modified the 1972 list by interlineations, additions and deletions. Neither edition of the list involved a bequest of the farm scene painting.

Ms. Nesmith kept a plastic-covered notebook in the drawer of a desk in her study. She periodically made entries in this notebook, which bore the title "List to be given Helen Nesmith 1979." One such entry read: "Ginny Clark farm picture hanging over fireplace. Ma's room." Imogene Conway and Joan Dragoumanos, Ms. Nesmith's private home care nurses, knew of the existence of the notebook and had observed Helen Nesmith write in it. On several occasions, Helen Nesmith orally expressed to these nurses her intentions regarding the disposition of particular pieces of her property upon her death, including the farm scene painting. Helen Nesmith told Conway and Dragoumanos that the farm scene painting was to be given to Virginia Clark, upon Helen Nesmith's death.

Virginia Clark and Helen Nesmith first became acquainted in or about 1940. The women lived next door to each other for approximately ten years (1945 through 1955), during which time they enjoyed a close friendship. The Nesmith-Clark friendship remained constant through the years. In more recent years, Ms. Clark frequently spent time at Ms. Nesmith's home, often visiting Helen Nesmith while she rested in the room which originally was her mother's bedroom. The farm scene painting hung in this room above the fireplace. Virginia Clark openly admired the picture.

According to Ms. Clark, sometime during either January or February of 1980, Helen Nesmith told Ms. Clark that the farm scene painting would belong to Ms. Clark after Helen Nesmith's death. Helen Nesmith then mentioned to Virginia Clark that she would record this gift in a book she kept for the purpose of memorializing her wishes with respect to the disposition of certain of her belongings. * * * After that conversation, Helen Nesmith often alluded to the fact that Ms. Clark someday would own the farm scene painting.

Ms. Nesmith executed two codicils to her 1977 will: one on May 30, 1980, and a second on October 23, 1980. The codicils amended certain bequests and deleted others, while ratifying the will in all other respects.

---

2. The value of Ms. Nesmith's estate at the time of her death exceeded $2,000,000.00, including both tangible and nontangible assets.

Greenhalge received Helen Nesmith's notebook on or shortly after January 28, 1986, the date of Ms. Nesmith's death. Thereafter, Greenhalge, as executor, distributed Ms. Nesmith's property in accordance with the will as amended, the 1972 memorandum as amended in 1976, and certain of the provisions contained in the notebook.[4] Greenhalge refused, however, to deliver the farm scene painting to Virginia Clark because the painting interested him and he wanted to keep it. Mr. Greenhalge claimed that he was not bound to give effect to the expressions of Helen Nesmith's wishes and intentions stated in the notebook, particularly as to the disposition of the farm scene painting. Notwithstanding this opinion, Greenhalge distributed to himself all of the property bequeathed to him in the notebook. Ms. Clark thereafter commenced an action against Mr. Greenhalge seeking to compel him to deliver the farm scene painting to her.

The probate judge found that Helen Nesmith wanted Ms. Clark to have the farm scene painting. The judge concluded that Helen Nesmith's notebook qualified as a "memorandum" of her known wishes with respect to the distribution of her tangible personal property, within the meaning of Article Fifth of Helen Nesmith's will.[5] The judge further found that the notebook was in existence at the time of the execution of the 1980 codicils, which ratified the language of Article Fifth in its entirety. Based on these findings, the judge ruled that the notebook was incorporated by reference into the terms of the will. Newton v. Seaman's Friend Soc'y, 130 Mass. 91, 93 (1881). The judge awarded the painting to Ms. Clark.

The Appeals Court affirmed the probate judge's decision in an unpublished memorandum and order, 30 Mass.App.Ct. 1109, 570 N.E.2d 184 (1991). * * * We allowed the appellee's petition for further appellate review and now hold that the probate judge correctly awarded the painting to Ms. Clark.

A properly executed will may incorporate by reference into its provisions any "document or paper not so executed and witnessed, whether the paper referred to be in the form of … a mere list or memorandum, … if it was in existence at the time of the execution of the will, and is identified by clear and satisfactory proof as the paper referred to therein." Newton v. Seaman's Friend Soc'y, supra at 93. The parties agree that the document entitled "memorandum," dated 1972 and amended in 1976, was in existence as of the date of the execution of Helen Nesmith's will. The parties further agree that this document is a memorandum regarding the distribution of certain items of Helen Nesmith's tangible personal property upon her death, as identified in Article Fifth of her will. There is no dispute, therefore, that the 1972 memorandum was incorporated by reference into the terms of the will. *Newton,* supra.

The parties do not agree, however, as to whether the documentation contained in the notebook, dated 1979, similarly was incorporated into the will through the language of Article Fifth. Greenhalge advances several arguments to support his contention that the purported bequest of the farm scene painting written in the notebook was not incorpo-

---

4. Helen Nesmith's will provided that Virginia Clark and her husband, Peter Hayden Clark, receive $20,000.00 upon Helen Nesmith's death. Under the terms of the 1972 memorandum, as amended in 1976, Helen Nesmith also bequeathed to Virginia Clark a portrait of Isabel Nesmith, Helen Nesmith's sister with whom Virginia Clark had been acquainted. Greenhalge honored these bequests and delivered the money and painting to Virginia Clark.

5. Article Fifth of Helen Nesmith's will reads, in pertinent part, as follows: "that [Greenhalge] distribute such of the tangible property to and among such persons *as I may designate by a memorandum left by me and known to him, or in accordance with my known wishes,* provided that said persons are living at the time of my decease" (emphasis added).

rated into the will and thus fails as a testamentary devise. The points raised by Green-halge in this regard are not persuasive. First, Greenhalge contends that the judge wrongly concluded that the notebook could be considered a "memorandum" within the meaning of Article Fifth, because it is not specifically identified as a "memorandum." Such a literal interpretation of the language and meaning of Article Fifth is not appropriate.

"The 'cardinal rule in the interpretation of wills, to which all other rules must bend, is that the intention of the testator shall prevail, provided it is consistent with the rules of law.'" Boston Safe Deposit & Trust Co. v. Park, 307 Mass. 255, 259, 29 N.E.2d 977 (1940), quoting McCurdy v. McCallum, 186 Mass. 464, 469, 72 N.E. 75 (1904). The in-tent of the testator is ascertained through consideration of "the language which [the tes-tatrix] has used to express [her] testamentary designs," Taft v. Stearns, 234 Mass. 273, 277, 125 N.E. 570 (1920), as well as the circumstances existing at the time of the execu-tion of the will. Boston Safe Deposit & Trust Co., supra 307 Mass. at 259, 29 N.E.2d 977, and cases cited. The circumstances existing at the time of the execution of a codicil to a will are equally relevant, because the codicil serves to ratify the language in the will which has not been altered or affected by the terms of the codicil. See Taft, supra 234 Mass. at 275–277, 125 N.E. 570.

Applying these principles in the present case, it appears clear that Helen Nesmith in-tended by the language used in Article Fifth of her will to retain the right to alter and amend the bequests of tangible personal property in her will, without having to amend formally the will. The text of Article Fifth provides a mechanism by which Helen Ne-smith could accomplish the result she desired; i.e., by expressing her wishes "in a mem-orandum." The statements in the notebook unquestionably reflect Helen Nesmith's ex-ercise of her retained right to restructure the distribution of her tangible personal property upon her death. That the notebook is not entitled "memorandum" is of no consequence, since its apparent purpose is consistent with that of a memorandum under Article Fifth: It is a written instrument which is intended to guide Greenhalge in "distribut[ing] such of [Helen Nesmith's] tangible personal property to and among ... persons [who] are living at the time of her decease." In this connection, the distinction between the notebook and "a memorandum" is illusory.

The appellant acknowledges that the subject documentation in the notebook estab-lishes that Helen Nesmith wanted Virginia Clark to receive the farm scene painting upon Ms. Nesmith's death. The appellant argues, however, that the notebook cannot take effect as a testamentary instrument under Article Fifth, because the language of Article Fifth limits its application to "a" memorandum, or the 1972 memorandum. We reject this strict construction of Article Fifth. The language of Article Fifth does not preclude the existence of more than one memorandum which serves the intended purpose of that article. As pre-viously suggested, the phrase "a memorandum" in Article Fifth appears as an expression of the manner in which Helen Nesmith could exercise her right to alter her will after its exe-cution, but it does not denote a requirement that she do so within a particular format. To construe narrowly Article Fifth and to exclude the possibility that Helen Nesmith drafted the notebook contents as "a memorandum" under that Article, would undermine our long-standing policy of interpreting wills in a manner which best carries out the known wishes of the testatrix. See Boston Safe Deposit & Trust Co., supra. The evidence supports the conclusion that Helen Nesmith intended that the bequests in her notebook be ac-corded the same power and effect as those contained in the 1972 memorandum under Ar-ticle Fifth. We conclude, therefore, that the judge properly accepted the notebook as a memorandum of Helen Nesmith's known wishes as referenced in Article Fifth of her will.

The appellant also contends that the judge erred in finding that Helen Nesmith intended to incorporate the notebook into her will, since the evidence established, at most, that she intended to bequeath the painting to Clark, and not that she intended to incorporate the notebook into her will. Our review of the judge's findings on this point, which is limited to a consideration of whether such findings are "clearly erroneous," proves the appellant argument to be without merit. First Pa. Mortgage Trust v. Dorchester Sav. Bank, 395 Mass. 614, 621, 481 N.E.2d 1132 (1985). The judge found that Helen Nesmith drafted the notebook contents with the expectation that Greenhalge would distribute the property accordingly. The judge further found that the notebook was in existence on the dates Helen Nesmith executed the codicils to her will, which affirmed the language of Article Fifth, and that it thereby was incorporated into the will pursuant to the language and spirit of Article Fifth. It is clear that the judge fairly construed the evidence in reaching the determination that Helen Nesmith intended the notebook to serve as a memorandum of her wishes as contemplated under Article Fifth of her will.

Lastly, the appellant complains that the notebook fails to meet the specific requirements of a memorandum under Article Fifth of the will, because it was not "known to him" until after Helen Nesmith's death. For this reason, Greenhalge states that the judge improperly ruled that the notebook was incorporated into the will. One of Helen Nesmith's nurses testified, however, that Greenhalge was aware of the notebook and its contents, and that he at no time made an effort to determine the validity of the bequest of the farm scene painting to Virginia Clark as stated therein. There is ample support in the record, therefore, to support the judge's conclusion that the notebook met the criteria set forth in Article Fifth regarding memoranda.

We note, as did the Appeals Court, that "one who seeks equity must do equity and that a court will not permit its equitable powers to be employed to accomplish an injustice." Pitts v. Halifax Country Club, Inc., 19 Mass.App.Ct. 525, 533, 476 N.E.2d 222 (1985). To this point, we remark that Greenhalge's conduct in handling this controversy fell short of the standard imposed by common social norms, not to mention the standard of conduct attending his fiduciary responsibility as executor, particularly with respect to his selective distribution of Helen Nesmith's assets. We can discern no reason in the record as to why this matter had to proceed along the protracted and costly route that it did.

Judgment affirmed.

Uniform Probate Code (2003)

§2-510. Incorporation by Reference.

A writing in existence when a will is executed may be incorporated by reference if the language of the will manifests this intent and describes the writing sufficiently to permit its identification.

§2-512. Events of Independent Significance.

A will may dispose of property by reference to acts and events that have significance apart from their effect upon the dispositions made by the will, whether they occur before or after the execution of the will or before or after the testator's death. The execution or revocation of another individual's will is such an event.

§ 2-513. Separate Writing Identifying Devise of Certain Types of Tangible Personal Property.

Whether or not the provisions relating to holographic wills apply, a will may refer to a written statement or list to dispose of items of tangible personal property not otherwise specifically disposed of by the will, other than money. To be admissible under this section as evidence of the intended disposition, the writing must be signed by the testator and must describe the items and the devisees with reasonable certainty. The writing may be referred to as one to be in existence at the time of the testator's death; it may be prepared before or after the execution of the will; it may be altered by the testator after its preparation; and it may be a writing that has no significance apart from its effect on the dispositions made by the will.

Notes

Incorporation by reference is different from events of independent significance. The latter refers to a person or event that will be ascertained at the effective date of the Last Will and Testament. For example, "I hereby give and bequeath the automobile of which I am possessed at the date of my death to my youngest child, issue of my body or adopted by me." Both the automobile and the youngest child are yet to be determined and their identities will come about independently.

Devices such as pour-over trusts are often associated with events of independent significance, and we will see this, *infra*. For example, an individual may create an inter vivos trust to provide for the education of his or her grandchildren. The trust will be funded while the individual is still alive, additional grandchildren are being born, and expenditures are being made for their education. Tax advantages could be achieved through such planning as well. But in the Last Will and Testament of this same individual is a clause that provides that assets will be bequeathed to this same trust. Thus, the Will accomplishes "pour-over" into the inter vivos trust, even though the inter vivos trust may be revoked or modified. The termination or modification occurs as an event of independent significance and yet is incorporated into the Last Will and Testament. *See, e.g.,* Clymer v. Mayo, 393 Mass. 754, 473 N.E.2d 1084 (1985) (court allowed pour-over into an unfunded, revocable, and amenable inter vivos trust). The Uniform Probate Code provides for such pour-over arrangements in UNIF. PROB. CODE § 2-511 (2003) (Testamentary Additions to Trusts).

C. Changes in Property

If an individual executes a Last Will and Testament, it may be many years before death occurs and the Will becomes effective. During that period of time, property may change or be destroyed. This change may occur because the property must be sold to pay estate debts, the property cannot be found, or the property has been given to the beneficiary or another entity during the lifetime of the decedent. The issue then arises as to how to effectuate the intent of the testator, who wanted to provide for a beneficiary, but the purpose cannot be accomplished with the property described in the Will. After reviewing tax considerations, see the following categories as examples:

Tax Considerations: Between the time of execution of the Last Will and Testament and the decedent's death, the value in items bequeathed or devised may shift radically. To accurately include within estate planning considerations formulae to meet these shifts and avoid catastrophic tax consequences is the goal of every estate planner. However, there are advantages in allowing property that has increased in value to be included in the decedent's estate. The present law provides that the tax basis of property that passes to an heir is the fair market value at the decedent's death and not the date of purchase. For example, if a decedent purchases property for $100,000, and when he or she dies the property is worth $500,000, the estate tax value is now $500,000, and this amount is included in the gross estate. The benefit to the heir is that, when the heir seeks to sell the property, the basis for any gain will be the "stepped up" basis of $500,000, rather than the original cost of $100,000. *See* I.R.C. §1014. However, if the value of the property decreased during this period, the heirs cannot use the loss. Also, all assets included in the gross estate are valued under a fair market test. However, under certain circumstances, the Personal Representative may elect an alternate valuation date. Under such a circumstance, the value of the property for estate tax purposes will be either the value on the date of the sale if it is sold within six months of the decedent's death, or the value as of six months after the decedent's death. *See* I.R.C. §§2031-1; 2032-1. Also, when considering the time frame between when the decedent executed his or her last Will and Testament and the date of death, be aware that the decedent's estate will include any gift taxes paid within three years of death. The decedent's estate will also include transfers made within three years of death that, if they had not been made, would be includable in the decedent's estate because the decedent retained an interest in the property. *See* I.R.C. §2035. These are rules of estate tax computation and important to the overall tax liability.

1. Ademption Generally

McGee v. McGee

Supreme Court of Rhode Island, 1980
122 R.I. 837, 413 A.2d 72

WEISBERGER, Justice.

This is a complaint for declaratory judgment, in which the plaintiff administrator, Richard J. McGee (Richard), sought directions from the Superior Court in respect to the construction of certain provisions of the will of his mother, Claire E. McGee, and instructions relating to payment of debts and distribution of assets from the testatrix's estate. The sole issue presented by this appeal concerns the question of the ademption of an allegedly specific legacy to the grandchildren of the decedent and the consequent effect of such ademption upon payment of a bequest in the amount of $20,000 to Fedelma Hurd (Hurd), a friend of the testatrix. The provisions of the will pertinent to this appeal read as follows:

"CLAUSE ELEVENTH:

I give and bequeath to my good and faithful friend FEDELMA HURD, the sum of Twenty Thousand ($20,000.00) Dollars, as an expression to her of my appreciation for her many kindnesses.

"CLAUSE TWELFTH:

I give and bequeath all of my shares of stock in the Texaco Company, and any and all monies standing in my name on deposit in any banking institution as follows:

(a) My Executor shall divide the shares of stock, or the proceeds thereof from a sale of same, *with all of my monies, standing on deposit in my name, in any bank*, into three (3) equal parts and shall pay 1/3 over to the living children of my beloved son, PHILIP; 1/3 to the living children of my beloved son, RICHARD and 1/3 over to the living children of my beloved son, JOSEPH. Each of my grandchildren shall share equally the 1/3 portion given to them. " (Emphasis added.)

At the time of the execution of the will and up until a short time before the death of the testatrix, a substantial sum of money was on deposit in her name at the People's Savings Bank in Providence. About five weeks prior to his mother's death, Richard, proceeding pursuant to a written power of attorney as modified by an addendum executed the following month, withdrew approximately $50,000 from these savings accounts. Of this amount, he applied nearly $30,000 towards the purchase of four United States Treasury bonds, commonly denominated as "flower bonds," from the Federal Trust Company in Waterville, Maine (Richard then resided in that state). His objective in executing this transaction was to effect an advantageous method of satisfying potential federal estate tax liability. * * * The bonds, however, did not serve the intended purpose since at the time of Mrs. McGee's death her gross estate was such that apparently no federal estate tax liability was incurred. The remainder of the monies withdrawn from the savings accounts were deposited in Claire McGee's checking account to pay current bills and in a savings account in Richard's name to be transferred to his mother's account as the need might arise for the payment of her debts and future obligations. The sole sum that is now the subject of this appeal is the approximately $30,000 held in the form of United States Treasury bonds.

The complaint for declaratory judgment sought instructions concerning whether the administrator should first satisfy the specific legacy to the grandchildren from the proceeds of the sale of the flower bonds or whether he should first pay the $20,000 bequest to Fedelma Hurd, since the estate lacked assets sufficient to satisfy both bequests.

After hearing evidence and considering legal memoranda filed by the parties, the trial justice found that the bequest to the grandchildren contained in the twelfth clause of the will constituted a specific legacy. He held further, however, that Rhode Island regarded the concept of ademption with disfavor and he sought, therefore, to effectuate the intent of the testatrix. He proceeded to determine that since there is an assumption that one intends to leave his property to those who are the natural objects of his bounty, rather than to strangers, the administrator "should trace the funds used to purchase the Flower Bonds and should satisfy the specific legacy to the grandchildren" under the twelfth clause of the will. Consequently, the trial justice held that the legacy to Fedelma Hurd under the eleventh clause of the will must fail. This appeal ensued.

The McGee grandchildren suggest that the principal design of the testatrix's estate plan, ascertainable from a contemplation of the testamentary disposition of her property, was to benefit her family rather than "outsiders." They urge us to consider her intentions which they assure us were concerned, in part, with protecting the family interests from an anticipated reduction of the estate's value by taxes in determining whether the transfer of the funds in her accounts did in fact work an ademption. In addition, Richard points out that the decedent did not herself purchase these bonds. On the contrary, Richard acquired them in order to help discharge anticipated tax obligations of the estate and informed his mother of them only subsequently to the purchase. He argues, furthermore, not only that the funds with which he purchased the flower bonds originated in his mother's accounts, but also that since these bonds "are as liquid as cash" they are indeed monies standing in the decedent's name on deposit in a banking institution. He suggests that this description conforms in every respect to the formula drafted into the twelfth clause of her will. Merely the form of the legacy has changed, according to Richard, not its essential character, quality, or substance.

In response, appellant asserts that an ademption occurred by the voluntary act of the testatrix during her lifetime, since her son withdrew the funds as an authorized agent operating under a lawful power of attorney. There is evidence, moreover, that the testatrix subsequently ratified the purchase of the bonds when Richard afterwards told her of his actions and their intended effect upon estate taxes. * * * As a consequence, Hurd asserts that there was no longer any money standing on deposit in the name of the testatrix in any bank with which to discharge the specific legacy to the grandchildren. These transactions resulted in an extinction of the subject matter of the legacy. Hurd argues, in addition, that the intention of the testatrix, even if discernible, is irrelevant to the question of the ademption of the bequest. She therefore contends that her general legacy should be payable from the proceeds of the sale of the flower bonds.

At the outset, we recognize that the instant case concerns specifically the concept of ademption by extinction, a legal consequence that may attend a variety of circumstances occasioned either by operation of law or by the actions of a testator himself or through his guardian, conservator, or agent. Gardner v. McNeal, 117 Md. 27, 82 A. 988 (1911); In re Wright, 7 N.Y.2d 365, 165 N.E.2d 561, 197 N.Y.S.2d 711 (1960). In particular, a testamentary gift of specific real or personal property may be adeemed— fail completely to pass as prescribed in the testator's will—when the particular article devised or bequeathed no longer exists as part of the testator's estate at the moment of his death because of its prior consumption, loss, destruction, substantial change, sale, or other alienation subsequent to the execution of the will. In consequence, neither the gift, its proceeds, nor similar substitute passes to the beneficiary, and this claim to the legacy is thereby barred. Atkinson, Handbook of the Law of Wills § 134 at 741, 743–44 (2d ed. 1953); 6 Bowe & Parker, Page on the Law of Wills § 54.1 at 242, § 54.9 at 256–57 (1962); Note, Wills: Ademption of Specific Legacies and Devises, 43 Cal.L.Rev. 151 (1955).

The principle of ademption by extinction has reference only to specific devises and bequests and is thus inapplicable to demonstrative or general testamentary gifts. 6 Page, supra § 54.3 at 245, § 54.5 at 248. In Haslam v. de Alvarez, 70 R.I. 212, 38 A.2d 158 (1944), we prescribed the criteria for determining the character of a legacy, relying on the earlier case of Dean v. Rounds, 18 R.I. 436, 27 A. 515 (1893), wherein we held that "(a) specific legacy, as the term imports, is a gift or bequest of some definite specific thing, something which is capable of being designated and identified." Id. When the testator intends that the legatee shall receive the exact property bequeathed rather than its corresponding quantitative or *ad valorem* equivalent, the gift is a specific one, and when "the main intention is that the legacy be paid by the delivery of the identical thing, and that thing only, and in the event that at the time of the testator's death such thing is no longer in existence, the legacy will not be paid out of his general assets." Hanley v. Fernell, 54 R.I. 84, 86, 170 A. 88, 89 (1934). In particular, the designation and identification of the specific legacy in a testator's will describe the gift in a manner that serves to distinguish it from all other articles of the same general nature and prevents its distribution from the general assets of the testator's estate. 6 Page, supra § 48.3 at 11–12.

In the case at bar, the trial justice construed the twelfth clause of Mrs. McGee's will as bequeathing a specific legacy to her grandchildren. While it is true that the party who contends the legacy is a specific one must bear the burden of proof on this issue, Di-Cristofaro v. Beaudry, 113 R.I. 313, 320 A.2d 597 (1974), and appellant, in her brief, characterized the twelfth clause as a bequest of a particular residuary gift, the trial justice apparently found that petitioner's contentions met the burden and that the testatrix clearly considered the bequest a specific one.

Without a doubt, the trial justice properly interpreted the McGee grandchildren's bequest, primarily because of the tone of the other provisions, the tenor of the entire instrument, see Hanley v. Fernell, 54 R.I. at 86, 170 A. at 89; Gardner v. Viall, 36 R.I. 436, 90 A. 760 (1914), and the specificity with which the testatrix described that portion of the twelfth clause relative to the Texaco stock. Additionally, money payable out of a fund rather than out of the estate generally described with sufficient accuracy and satisfiable only out of the payment of such fund, Haslam v. de Alvarez, or a bequest of money deposited in a specific bank, Hanley v. Fernell, is, as a rule, a specific legacy. When a will bequeaths "the money owned by one which is on deposit" in a designated bank, although the amount remains unspecified, the gift is nevertheless identifiable and definite, apart from all other funds or property in the testator's estate; and the legacy is specific. Willis v. Barrow, 218 Ala. 549, 552, 119 So. 678, 680 (1929); Prendergast v. Walsh, 58 N.J.Eq. 149, 42 A. 1049 (Ch.1899). Despite the fact that Mrs. McGee did not name any particular bank in the twelfth clause of her will, she bequeathed all the money in her name "in any bank." In view of the fact that she expected all of her money remaining at her death to go to her grandchildren and, further, the money to be payable from a particular source that is, accounts in her name in banking institutions we conclude that the legacy was sufficiently susceptible of identification to render it a specific one.

Accordingly, since the bequest to the grandchildren is specific, we must now determine whether or not it was adeemed by the purchase of the bonds. Note, Ademption and the Testator's Intent, 74 Harv.L.Rev. 741 (1961). In connection with the early theory of ademption, the courts looked to the intention of the testator as the basis of their decisions. 6 Page, supra § 54.14 at 265. But ever since the landmark case of Ashburner v. MacGuire, 2 Bro.C.C. 108, 29 Eng.Rep. 62 (Ch.1786), wherein Lord Thurlow enunciated the "modern theory," courts have utilized the identity doctrine or "in specie" test. This test focuses on two questions only: (1) whether the gift is a specific legacy and, if it is, (2) whether it is found in the estate at the time of the testator's death. Atkinson, supra § 134 at 742; Note, 74 Harv.L.Rev. at 742; Comment, Ademption in Iowa—A Closer Look at the Testator's Intent, 57 Iowa L.Rev. 1211 (1972). The extinction of the property bequeathed works an ademption regardless of the testator's intent. In re Tillinghast, 23 R.I. 121, 123–24, 49 A. 634, 635 (1901); Humphreys v. Humphreys, 2 Cox Ch. 184, 30 Eng.Rep. 85 (Ch.1789); 6 Page, supra § 54.15 at 266.

The legatees of the twelfth clause argue that the subject matter of the specific bequest, although apparently now unidentifiable in its previous form, actually does exist in the estate of their grandmother but in another form as the result of an exchange or transfer of the original property. But there is a recognized distinction between a bequest of a particular item and a gift of its proceeds, see generally Annot., 45 A.L.R.3d 10 (1972); and the testatrix, in the instant case, did recognize the distinction in the twelfth clause of her will by bequeathing the Texaco stock "or the proceeds thereof from a sale of same" but omitting to include similar provisions regarding proceeds in connection with the language immediately following which described the bank-money legacy. It appears that the testatrix's intention, manifest on the face of her will, was that her grandchildren receive only the money in her bank accounts and not the money's proceeds or the investments that represent the conversion of that money into other holdings. Atkinson, supra § 134 at 743–44; 6 Page, supra § 54.9 at 256–57, § 54.16 at 268–70; see Gardner v. McNeal, 117 Md. 27, 82 A. 988 (1911).

In accordance with the generally accepted "form and substance rule," a substantial change in the nature or character of the subject matter of a bequest will operate as an ademption; but a merely nominal or formal change will not. In re Peirce, 25 R.I. 34, 54 A. 588 (1903) (no ademption since transfer of stock after consolidation of banks without formal liquidation was exchange and not sale); Willis v. Barrow, 218 Ala. 549, 119 So. 678 (1929) (no ademption by transfer of money from named bank to another since place of deposit was merely descriptive); In re Hall, 60 N.J.Super. 597, 160 A.2d 49 (1960) (no ademption by transfer of the money from banks designated in will to another one since location was formal description only and did not affect substance of testamentary gift).

Since the money previously on deposit in Mrs. McGee's bank accounts no longer exists at the time of her death, the question arises whether the change was one of form only, rather than substance. We have determined that the change effected by Richard was not merely formal but was substantial. There is no language in the will that can be construed as reflecting an intention of the testatrix to bequeath a gift of bond investments to her grandchildren. The plain and explicit direction of the twelfth clause of the will is that they should receive whatever remained in her bank accounts at the time of her death. Since no sums of money were then on deposit, the specific legacy was adeemed. Clearly, this case is dissimilar to those in which the fund, at all times kept intact, is transferred to a different location, as in Willis and Prendergast, where the money merely "changed hands," not character. See also In re Tillinghast, 23 R.I. 121, 49 A. 634 (1901) (no ademption by mere act of transferring mortgages to own name since they were in specie at the time of testatrix's death). The fact that Mrs. McGee did not herself purchase the bonds is not significant. Disposal or distribution of the subject matter of a bequest by an agent of the testator or with the testator's authorization or ratification similarly operates to adeem the legacy. Gardner v. McNeal, 117 Md. 27, 82 A. 988 (1911); In re Wright, 7 N.Y.2d 365, 165 N.E.2d 561, 197 N.Y.S.2d 711 (1960); Glasscock v. Layle, 21 Ky.Law.Rep. 860, 53 S.W. 270 (Ky.1899).

The petitioner improperly relies upon the case of Morse v. Converse, 80 N.H. 24, 113 A. 214 (1921). In that case the testatrix voluntarily placed her property into the hands of a conservator to care for and use for her support. The conservator purchased a Liberty bond out of bank deposits bequeathed in the testatrix's will, and the legacies were not adeemed thereby. But, contrary to the case at bar, the testatrix in Morse neither knew about nor consented to the conservator's acts; therefore, the court explained, the change "furnishes no evidence of an intentional revocation by her." Id. at 26, 113 A. at 215. But see In re Wright, citing Matter of Ireland's Estate, 257 N.Y. 155, 177 N.E. 405 (1931) (specifically bequeathed stock adeemed even though sold by conservator after testator had become incompetent).

Moreover, under the principles enunciated by Lord Thurlow in Ashburner v. MacGuire, and more fully expressed in the case of Humphreys v. Humphreys, only the fact of change or extinction, not the reason for the change or extinction, is truly relevant. The vast majority of jurisdictions adhere to this rule. See Atkinson, supra § 134 at 741–42; 6 Page, supra § 54.15 at 266–68. This "in specie" theory of ademption, although it may occasionally result in a failure to effectuate the actual intent of a testator, has many advantages. Significant among these advantages is simplicity of application, as opposed to ad hoc determination of intent from extrinsic evidence in each particular case. This theory further has the advantages of stability, uniformity, and predictability. The argument in support of Lord Thurlow's rule is well expressed in 6 Page, supra § 54.15 at 266:

> If the sale or collection of the bequest works an ademption or not depending upon testator's intention as inferred from the surrounding circumstances, many cases will arise in which it is difficult or impossible to ascertain what testator's intention was; and probably, in many cases, testator did not think of the consequences which would follow from his conduct. If the sale or collection of the bequest operates as an ademption or not, depending upon his intentions, and such intention may be shown by his oral declarations, then the controlling evidence in the case will consist of the written will, executed in accordance with statute, together with testator's oral declarations. This violates both the letter and the spirit of state wills statutes, which insist on the formalities of writing and execution in order to avoid opportunities for perjury. For these reasons, it is now held that the sale, destruction, or collection, of the bequest or devise, adeems it without regard to the actual intention of the testator.

Accordingly, we hold that the trial justice erred in allowing the admission of extrinsic evidence regarding Mrs. McGee's intent. We further hold that the specific legacy in the twelfth clause of the testatrix's will is adeemed and the legatees' claim to this bequest is thereby barred. We direct the trial justice to order the petitioner to satisfy the general pecuniary legacy bequeathed in the eleventh clause of the will from the sale of the flower bonds, with the excess to pass under the residuary (fourteenth) clause of the will.

The respondent's appeal is sustained, the judgment below is reversed, and the cause is remanded to the Superior Court for proceedings consistent with this opinion.

Uniform Probate Code(2003)

§ 2-606. Nonademption of Specific Devises; Unpaid Proceeds of Sale, Condemnation, or Insurance; Sale by Conservator or Agent.

(a) A specific devisee has a right to specifically devised property in the testator's estate at the testator's death and to:

(1) any balance of the purchase price, together with any security agreement, owed by a purchaser at the testator's death by reason of sale of the property;

(2) any amount of a condemnation award for the taking of the property unpaid at death;

(3) any proceeds unpaid at death on fire or casualty insurance on or other recovery for injury to the property;

(4) any property owned by the testator at death and acquired as a result of foreclosure, or obtained in lieu of foreclosure, of the security interest for a specifically devised obligation;

(5) any real property or tangible personal property owned by the testator at death which the testator acquired as a replacement for specifically devised real property or tangible personal property; and

(6) if not covered by paragraphs (1) through (5), a pecuniary devise equal to the value as of its date of disposition of other specifically devised property disposed of during the testator's lifetime but only to the extent it is established that ademption would be inconsistent with the testator's manifested plan of distribution or that at the time the will was made, the date of disposition or otherwise, the testator did not intend ademption of the devise.

(b) If specifically devised property is sold or mortgaged by a conservator or by an agent acting within the authority of a durable power of attorney for an incapacitated principal, or a condemnation award, insurance proceeds, or recovery for injury to the property is paid to a conservator or to an agent acting within the authority of a durable power of attorney for an incapacitated principal, the specific devisee has the right to a general pecuniary devise equal to the net sale price, the amount of the unpaid loan, the condemnation award, the insurance proceeds, or the recovery.

(c) The right of a specific devisee under subsection (b) is reduced by any right the devisee has under subsection (a).

(d) For the purposes of the references in subsection (b) to a conservator, subsection (b) does not apply if, after the sale, mortgage, condemnation, casualty, or recovery, it was adjudicated that the testator's incapacity ceased and the testator survived the adjudication for at least one year.

(e) For the purposes of the references in subsection (b) to an agent acting within the authority of a durable power of attorney for an incapacitated principal, (i) "incapacitated principal" means a principal who is an incapacitated person, (ii) no adjudication of incapacity before death is necessary, and (iii) the acts of an agent within the authority of a durable power of attorney are presumed to be for an incapacitated principal.

2. *Ademption by Satisfaction*

Uniform Probate Code (2003)

§ 2-609. Ademption by Satisfaction.

(a) Property a testator gave in his [or her] lifetime to a person is treated as a satisfaction of a devise in whole or in part, only if (i) the will provides for deduction of the gift, (ii) the testator declared in a contemporaneous writing that the gift is in satisfaction of the devise or that its value is to be deducted from the value of the devise, or (iii) the devisee acknowledged in writing that the gift is in satisfaction of the devise or that its value is to be deducted from the value of the devise.

(b) For purposes of partial satisfaction, property given during lifetime is valued as of the time the devisee came into possession or enjoyment of the property or at the testator's death, whichever occurs first.

(c) If the devisee fails to survive the testator, the gift is treated as a full or partial satisfaction of the devise, as appropriate, in applying Sections 2-603 and 2-604, unless the testator's contemporaneous writing provides otherwise.

Tax Considerations: Bequests and devises made within a valid Last Will and Testament or intestate succession (the probate estate) exclude assets passing through will substitutes (non-probate transfers). Thus, excluded are items such as joint tenancies, inter vivos powers of appointment, life insurance, and other payable on death contracts. Nonetheless, because these items are property owned at death, even though not passing through a Last Will and Testament, they are includable within the decedent's gross estate for federal estate tax purposes. *See* I.R.C. §§ 2031–2046. On the other hand, the tax ramifications of making an irrevocable transfer during lifetime involve gift taxes, which are described as part of the larger transfer tax scheme at Internal Revenue Code § 2001. Presently, there is an $11,000 annual exclusion for gifts to each donee. *See* Rev. Proc. 2004-71, 2004-50 I.R.B. 970. To qualify for the annual exclusion, the gift must be a gift of a present interest in the property transferred, which generally is defined as an "unrestricted right to the immediate use, possession, or enjoyment of property or income from property." *See* Treasury Regulation § 25.2503-3(b). The $11,000 annual exclusion per donee is doubled if the gift is made by two spouses. *See* Treasury Regulation 25.2513-1.

3. *Ademption by Extinction*

Wasserman v. Cohen

Supreme Court of Massachusetts, 1993
414 Mass. 172, 606 N.E.2d 901

LYNCH, Justice.

This appeal raises the question whether the doctrine of ademption by extinction applies to a specific gift of real estate contained in a revocable inter vivos trust. The plaintiff, Elaine Wasserman, brought an action for declaratory judgment in the Middlesex Division of the Probate and Family Court against the defendant, David E. Cohen (trustee), as he is the surviving trustee of a trust established by Frieda M. Drapkin (Drapkin). In her complaint the plaintiff requested that the trustee be ordered to pay her the proceeds of the sale of an apartment building which, under the trust, would have been conveyed to the plaintiff had it not been sold by Drapkin prior to her death. Pursuant to the trustee's motion to dismiss under Mass.R.Civ.P. 12(b)(6), 365 Mass. 754 (1974), the probate judge dismissed the action. The plaintiff appealed. We granted the plaintiff's application for direct appellate review and now affirm.

1. We summarize the relevant facts. Frieda Drapkin created the Joseph and Frieda Drapkin Memorial Trust (trust) in December, 1982, naming herself both settlor and trustee. She funded the trust with "certain property" delivered on the date of execution, and retained the right to add property by inter vivos transfer and by will. Drapkin also reserved the right to receive and to direct the payment of income or principal during her lifetime, to amend or to revoke the trust, and to withdraw property from the trust. On her death, the trustee was directed to distribute the property as set out in the trust. The trustee was ordered to convey to the plaintiff "12-14 Newton Street, Waltham, Massachusetts, Apartment Building, (consisting of approximately 11,296 square feet)."

When she executed the trust, Drapkin held record title to the property at 12-14 Newton Street in Waltham, as trustee of Z.P.Q. Realty Trust. However, she sold the property on September 29, 1988, for $575,000, and had never conveyed her interest in the property to the trust. * * *

Drapkin died on March 28, 1989. Her will, dated December 26, 1982, devised all property in her residuary estate to the trust to be disposed of in accordance with the trust's provisions.

2. The plaintiff first contends that the probate judge erred in failing to consider Drapkin's intent in regard to the gift when she sold the property. We disagree.

We have long adhered to the rule that, when a testator disposes, during his lifetime, of the subject of a specific legacy or devise in his will, that legacy or devise is held to be adeemed, "whatever may have been the intent or motive of the testator in doing so." Walsh v. Gillespie, 338 Mass. 278, 280, 154 N.E.2d 906 (1959), quoting Richards v. Humphreys, 15 Pick. 133, 135 (1833). Baybank Harvard Trust Co. v. Grant, 23 Mass. App.Ct. 653, 655, 504 N.E.2d 1072 (1987). The focus is on the actual existence or nonexistence of the bequeathed property, and not on the intent of the testator with respect to it. Bostwick v. Hurstel, 364 Mass. 282, 295, 304 N.E.2d 186 (1973). To be effective, a specific legacy or devise must be in existence and owned by the testator at the time of his death. Moffatt v. Heon, 242 Mass. 201, 203–204, 136 N.E. 123 (1922). Baybank Harvard Trust Co. v. Grant, supra.

The plaintiff asks us to abandon the doctrine of ademption. She contends that, because the doctrine ignores the testator's intent, it produces harsh and inequitable results and thus fosters litigation that the rule was intended to preclude. See Note, Ademption and the Testator's Intent, 74 Harv.L.Rev. 741 (1961). This rule has been followed in this Commonwealth for nearly 160 years. See Richards v. Humphreys, supra. Whatever else may be said about it, it is easily understood and applied by draftsmen, testators, and fiduciaries. The doctrine seeks to give effect to a testator's probable intent by presuming he intended to extinguish a specific gift of property when he disposed of that property prior to his death. As with any rule, exceptions have emerged.[3] These limited exceptions do not lead us to the abandonment of the rule. Its so-called harsh results can be easily avoided by careful draftsmanship and its existence must be recognized by any competent practitioner. When we consider the myriad of instruments drafted in reliance on its application, we conclude that stability in the field of trusts and estates requires that we continue the doctrine.

3. The plaintiff also argues that deciding ademption questions based on a determination that a devise is general or specific is overly formalistic and fails to serve the testator's likely intent. She maintains that the court in Bostwick v. Hurstel, supra, moved away from making such classifications. In *Bostwick*, the court held that a gift of stock was not adeemed where the stock had been sold and repurchased prior to the death of the testatrix, and where it had been subject to two stock splits. However, the court confined the holding specifically to its facts. * * * See Bostwick v. Hurstel, supra at 294–295, 304 N.E.2d 186. In addition, the court stated: "Our holding does not indicate that we have

---

3. This court has created two exceptions to the "identity" theory. In Walsh v. Gillespie, 338 Mass. 278, 154 N.E.2d 906 (1959), a conservator appointed for the testatrix five years after her will was executed sold shares of stock that were the subject of a specific legacy. The court held that the sale did not operate as an ademption as to the unexpended balance remaining in the hands of the conservator at the death of the testatrix. Id. at 284, 154 N.E.2d 906. In Bostwick v. Hurstel, 364 Mass. 282, 304 N.E.2d 186 (1973), a conservator had sold, then repurchased, stock that was the subject of a specific legacy and that had been split twice, before the death of the testatrix. The court held that the bequest of stock was not adeemed but emphasized, "we do not violate our rule that 'identity' and not 'intent' governs ademption cases." Id. at 296, 304 N.E.2d 186. See Baybank Harvard Trust Co. v. Grant, 23 Mass.App.Ct. 653, 655, 504 N.E.2d 1072 (1987).

abandoned the classification of bequests as general or specific for all purposes. We have no occasion at this time to express any opinion on the continuing validity of such distinctions in those cases where abatement or ademption of the legacy is at issue...." Id. at 292, 304 N.E.2d 186. * * * We now have such an occasion, and we hold that, at least in regard to the conveyance of real estate at issue here, the practice of determining whether a devise is general or specific is the proper first step in deciding questions of ademption.

4. We have held that a trust, particularly when executed as part of a comprehensive estate plan, should be construed according to the same rules traditionally applied to wills. See Second Bank-State St. Trust Co. v. Pinion, 341 Mass. 366, 371, 170 N.E.2d 350 (1960) (doctrine of independent legal significance applied to pour-over trusts); Clymer v. Mayo, 393 Mass. 754, 473 N.E.2d 1084 (1985) (G.L. c. 191, §9, which revokes dispositions made in will to former spouses on divorce or annulment, applied to trust executed along with will as part of comprehensive estate plan). In Clymer v. Mayo, supra at 766, 473 N.E.2d 1084, we reasoned that "[t]reating the components of the decedent's estate plan separately, and not as parts of an interrelated whole, brings about inconsistent results." We also quoted one commentator who wrote, "The subsidiary rules [of wills] are the product of centuries of legal experience in attempting to discern transferors' wishes and suppress litigation. These rules should be treated presumptively correct for will substitutes as well as for wills." Id. at 768, 473 N.E.2d 1084, quoting Langbien, The Nonprobate Revolution and the Future of the Law of Succession, 97 Harv.L.Rev. 1108, 1136–1137 (1984). We agree with this reasoning. As discussed above, the doctrine of ademption has a "long established recognition" in Massachusetts. See Second Bank-State St. Trust Co. v. Pinion, supra, 341 Mass. at 371, 170 N.E.2d 350. Furthermore, Drapkin created the trust along with her will as part of a comprehensive estate plan. Under the residuary clause of her will, Drapkin gave the majority of her estate to the trustee, who was then to dispose of the property on her death according to the terms of the trust. We see no reason to apply a different rule because she conveyed the property under the terms of the trust, rather than her will. Thus, we conclude that the doctrine of ademption, as traditionally applied to wills, should also apply to the trust in the instant case.

5. *Conclusion.* Since the plaintiff does not contest that the devise of 12-14 Newton Street was a specific devise, * * * it follows that the devise was adeemed by the act of Drapkin.

So ordered.

4. *Accessions*

Uniform Probate Code (2003)

§2-605. Increase in Securities; Accessions.

(a) If a testator executes a will that devises securities and the testator then owned securities that meet the description in the will, the devise includes additional securities owned by the testator at death to the extent the additional securities were acquired by the testator after the will was executed as a result of the testator's ownership of the described securities and are securities of any of the following types:

(1) securities of the same organization acquired by reason of action initiated by the organization or any successor, related, or acquiring organization, excluding any acquired by exercise of purchase options;

(2) securities of another organization acquired as a result of a merger, consolidation, reorganization, or other distribution by the organization or any successor, related, or acquiring organization; or

(3) securities of the same organization acquired as a result of a plan of reinvestment.

(b) Distributions in cash before death with respect to a described security are not part of the devise.

5. *Exoneration*

Ashkenazy v. Ashkenazy's Estate

Florida Court of Appeals, 1962
140 So.2d 331

HENDRY, Judge.

The appellant, Jeanne Ashkenazy, specific devisee under the will of Saul Ashkenazy, filed a petition in the County Judge's Court in and for Dade County, Florida to require the executors-appellees to exonerate certain real property from the lien of the mortgage encumbering such property; three days after the filing of the said petition the executors filed a petition in the said court for instructions. The county judge considered the petitions to be in effect petitions for the construction of the will of the deceased, Saul Ashkenazy, pursuant to § 732.41 of the Florida Statutes, F.S.A.

The petitions raised two main questions for the county judge's consideration. First, whether the appellant as the beneficiary of real property (Paragraph 'Tenth' of the will set forth hereinbelow) is entitled to have such property exonerated from the lien of a mortgage. The second question is concerned with the shares of stock left to one of the specific legatees (Paragraph 'Twelfth' of the will set forth hereinbelow) as to whether such legatee is entitled to recover the stock free from a lien on such stock where the lien was to secure a loan made after the execution of the will and where a timely claim was filed in the estate by the holder of such lien.

The facts in the case were presented to the trial court by way of the following stipulation:

'The following facts are hereby stipulated to by the attorneys for the Executors herein, by the attorneys for the residuary legatee, DAVID B. ASHKENAZY; and, by the attorney for the specific legatee, JEANNE ASHKENAZY; however, this Stipulation is limited to an agreement of the truth of the following facts without acknowledgment as to their materiality, relevancy or admissability [sic].

'1. That the decedent herein, SAUL ASHKENAZY, and the specific legatee herein, JEANNE ASHKENAZY, were married each to the other on the 10th day of September, 1950, in the City of Stuart, County of Martin, State of Florida.

'2. While married, the aforesaid decedent and his aforesaid wife purchased improved real property located in Dade County, Florida, subject to an existing First Mortgage; the date of warranty deed conveying title to said property to them was the 6th day of May, 1952, and said deed was recorded on the 8th day of May, 1952, and provided as follows:

"Subject to mortgage for $7,200.00 made by Homecraft Corporation, a Florida corporation, to National Title Insurance Company, a Florida corporation, dated August 15, 1959, and recorded in Mortgage Book 2352, page 299, and assigned to John Hancock Mutual Life Insurance Company, a Massachusetts corporation, by Assignment of Mortgage dated December 27, 1950, and recorded in Assignment Book 326, page 96, of the Public Records of Dade County, Florida. Balance on said mortgage was $6,977.81 on April 1, 1952, with interest paid to that date which balance with the grantees herein specifically assume and agree to pay."

That said mortgage was payable at the rate of $55.00 per month. At the time decedent executed his Will, he resided on the property in question and used the same as his home; that after the execution of said Will, to-wit on or about November, 1960, decedent leased said property, and did thereafter, until the time of his death, derive rental income therefrom, and that from and after November, 1960, the same was not homestead property.

'3. The aforesaid decedent and his aforesaid wife were divorced by Final Decree of Divorce entered on the 16th day of December 1957, in Dade County Circuit Court, Chancery No. 205,751. The divorce decree ratified and incorporated a Separation Agreement executed by the parties, dated September 24, 1957, which agreement provided for conveyance of the aforesaid real property by the wife to the husband and for the husband to assume the payment of the aforesaid mortgage. Pursuant to said decree and said Separation Agreement, the former wife conveyed said property to the decedent by Warranty Deed dated January 28, 1958, recorded on February 24, 1958, which deed specifically provided for the decedent to assume and agree to pay the aforesaid mortgage. The decedent continued to make the payments on said mortgage until his death, and the present principal balance of same is approximately $5,000.00.

'4. On June 6, 1960, the decedent executed a valid Last Will and Testament which provided, inter alia, as follows:

"SECOND: I instruct my hereinafter named Executrix and Executor to pay all of my just debts as soon after my death as shall be practicable."

"TENTH: Unto my former wife, JEANNE ASHKENAZY, I give, devise and bequeath my house, located on Douglas Road in Coral Gables, Florida, to do with as she sees fit; unto my said former wife I likewise give, devise and bequeath my cemetary lots in Mount Sinai Far Band Cemetary in Miami to do with as she sees fit."

"TWELFTH: I give, devise and bequeath unto my friend, LILLIAN CONROY FINE of Miami, Florida, all of my shares in The Wellington Fund, the property legally described as:

"Lots 1 and 2 in Block 1 of LAKE LETTA ESTATES, according to the Plat thereof, recorded in Plat Book 1, Page 70-B of Highlands County, Florida and my automobile."

"FOURTEENTH: All of the rest, residue and remainder of my estate, whether real, mixed or personal, wheresoever situate, I give, devise and bequeath to my beloved nephew, DAVID B. ASHKENAZY, absolutely."

'5. The shares referred to in Paragraph TWELFTH of the decedent's Will were unencumbered at the time of the execution of said Will, but at the time of decedent's death they, together with 513 shares of National Securities Growth Series Stock, which was part of the residual estate, were encumbered to Mercantile National Bank of Miami Beach, Florida, to secure a loan in the sum of $4,000.00, dated October 19, 1960, due and payable on April 19, 1961, with quarterly interest of 5 1/2% per annum.

'6. The decedent died on February 5, 1961.

'7. The decedent's will was admitted to Probate on February 14, 1961.

'8. No claim has been filed in the estate by the mortgagee of the above described real property.

'9. Claim has been filed in the estate by the aforesaid bank.'

The county judge entered his order construing the will of the deceased which reads in part as follows:

'It is ORDERED AND ADJUDGED that the devise of the following described property located on Douglas Road in Coral Gables * * * is subject to the mortgage which encumbered said property at the death of Saul Ashkenazy, and that Jeanne Ashkenazy is obligated to make the payments on the mortgage subsequent to the date of death in order to protect her interest, and that Jeanne Ashkenazy is entitled to all income from said property subsequent to the death of the testator, less any payments made for her by the executors on account of the mortgage debt or for maintenance of the property.

'It is FURTHER ORDERED AND ADJUDGED that the bequest of 'all of my shares in the Wellington Fund' (133 shares of Wellington Fund, Inc.) to Lillian Conway Fine is free and clear of liens and encumbrances, and that the executors are authorized and directed to pay and satisfy the claim of the Mercantile National Bank of Miami Beach out of the residuary assets of this estate.'

The first question is presented by the appellant, Jeanne Ashkenazy, who asserts that she is entitled to have the real property free and clear from the lien of the mortgage encumbering such property. The second question is presented by the appellee, David Ashkenazy, the residuary legatee, who urges, by cross-assignment of error, that the court erred in holding that the shares of stock 'to Lillian Conway Fine is free and clear of liens and encumbrances'.

It is the appellant's contention as to the initial question that the law is that the testator's intent controls only where the will specifically provides either for or against exoneration; that the instruction in the will for payment of debts (under paragraph 'Second' above) is evidence that the intent of the testator was to have the real property exonerated from the mortgage lien; that, in the absence of the testator's intent to the contrary, the specific devisee of real property has a common law right of exoneration; and that the facts and surrounding circumstances herein, show that the testator intended that the appellant take the real property free and clear of the mortgage lien.

The executors, as one of their three principal grounds in support of the lower court's order construing the will, cite In re Comstock's Estate, 143 Fla. 500, 197 So. 121; Furlong v. Coral Gables Federal Savings & Loan Association, Fla.App.1960, 121 So.2d 797, and In re Simpson's Estate, Fla.App.1959, 113 So.2d 766, as controlling, notwithstanding the lower court's holding that the said cases were 'of little or no value in the deter-

mination of the questions before this Court in this case because the property involved
in each of [these] Florida cases was not a part of the assets in the Probate Court.' The
executor's second contention for affirmance is based on the county judge's finding that
the testator intended 'that Jeanne Ashkenazy take her devise subject to the mortgage encumbering the devised property, and that she is not entitled to exoneration'. The third
ground urged by the executors is that any common law right of exoneration has been
abrogated or overturned by § 734.05 of the Florida Statutes, F.S.A. * * * wherein all distinctions between real and personal property were abolished and by § 733.16 of the
Florida Statutes, F.S.A. * * * wherein no payment of debts may be made on claims
which have not been timely filed.

The lower court, inter alia, found that the Comstock, Furlong and Simpson cases,
supra, are homestead property cases which deal with the right of exoneration solely as
a question of law; that the said cases are concerned with property passing outside the
will whereas the instant case concerns a specific devise of property passing under the
will and therefore, the intent of the testator must be determined from the will itself;
that the only part of the will of the deceased, Saul Ashkenazy referring to the payments of debts or liens is paragraph 'Second', supra, which is a standard clause included in substantially all wills prepared by an attorney as well as most purchased
printed forms and that the better judicial rule is that such a standard clause is of no
value in determining the intent of the testator; that therefore the will offers no clue as
to the intention of the testator with respect to the right of exoneration of the appellant, Jeanne Ashkenazy; that it is thus incumbent on the court to examine the surrounding facts and circumstances to ascertain the intention of the testator; that the
court finds that it was the intention of the testator, Saul Ashkenazy, that Jeanne Ashkenazy take her devise subject to the mortgage encumbering the devised property without any right of exoneration because (1) the property was encumbered when the will
was made, (2) the testator intended to devise property he then owned, which was the
equity in the property and (3) the mortgage was a long term obligation which might
not be paid during the lifetime of the testator; and that the filing of a claim by the
mortgagee under § 733.16 of the Florida Statutes, F.S.A. is inapposite to the right of
exoneration.

We have carefully studied the contentions of the parties and the findings of the lower
court and it is our opinion that as to the initial question presented by the appellant,
Jeanne Ashkenazy, i. e., her right as specific devisee to have the real property exonerated
from the mortgage lien, the lower court was in error.

Our research has confirmed appellant's position that this exact question is one of
first impression in this state. We agree with the learned county judge that the homestead cases, cited supra, and the case of Lopez v. Lopez, Fla.1956, 90 So.2d 456, which
deals with the right of exoneration with respect to an estate by the entireties, are readily distinguishable from the case at bar. Those cases are concerned with exoneration
rights as to property passing outside the will and therefore present a materially different query.

We hold that since no statute has been passed changing the common-law rule of exoneration, * * * the common-law rule remains in full force and effect by reason of § 2 of
Article XVIII of the Constitution of Florida, 26 F.S.A. * * * The decisive determination
therefore is the application of the common-law rule to the situation at hand. We find
the common-law rule to be that the specific devisee of real property is entitled to have
the mortgage on the devised property paid at the expense of the residue of the estate

* * * unless the will expressly shows a contrary intent * * * or an implied intent not to exonerate can be extracted from the provisions of the will as a whole when viewed in light of the surrounding circumstances. * * *

In the case at bar, we find that the deceased, Saul Ashkenazy, did not expressly signify any intention not to exonerate the property here involved from the mortgage lien. In so finding, we fully concur with the lower court that the general direction in paragraph 'Second' of the decedent's will, i. e., 'to pay all of my just debts as soon after my death as shall be practicable' does not, of itself, indicate a positive intent to exonerate the real property. * * * Hence, unless an implied intent not to exonerate can be elicited from the entire will when scrutinized in the light of the surrounding circumstances, * * * the appellant, Jeanne Ashkenazy, is entitled to have the real property exonerated.

The lower court, in concluding that it was the intent of the deceased not to exonerate the specific devise of real property, stated that the grounds for such a conclusion were:

'1. The land was encumbered when the will was made.

2. The testator intended to devise the property he then owned, which was the equity in the property.

3. The mortgage was a long term obligation which might not be paid in the lifetime of the testator.'

While we are in accord that the above quoted grounds were indicative of an implied intent not to exonerate, we feel that the lower court failed to take into consideration other factors which, at the very least, counterbalanced those indicators that there was an implied intent not to exonerate. These factors were:

1. The fact that as part of the separation agreement between the decedent and the appellant, the decedent assumed payment of the mortgage in return for the appellant-wife's conveying such property to the decedent. It is our belief that this evinced an intention to exonerate. This is so, because the failure to exonerate the real property from the mortgage lien would put the appellant in almost the same position as before the separation agreement and would, in effect, nullify the obvious gift intended to the former wife by the devise in question.

2. The will and the entire record reveal that the deceased, Saul Ashkenazy, was a very benevolent man who was in the habit of making charitable gifts all over the world. * * * An interpretation of paragraph 'Tenth' (which is the provision in favor of appellant, Jeanne Ashkenazy) as the executors so interpret it, would leave the deceased's former wife little, if anything. This is in contravention of the will read as a whole in that the applicable provisions show that there was still some closeness of relationship between the decedent and his former wife. * * *

3. The fact that the mortgage is not of such size in relation to the residuary estate that application of the common-law rule of exoneration would operate to deprive the residuary legatee of most of his estate and thus prevent, to a large extent, the testamentary plan of disposition.

It is our belief that these further factors divulge an intention by the decedent, Saul Ashkenazy, to exonerate the real property in question. Assuming arguendo, however, that these factors do no more than counteract the aforesaid findings of the lower court, we would still reverse the order appealed as to this question because the common-law rule was that a specific devisee was entitled to exoneration absent an intent to the contrary. In other words, the burden of proof in such a situation is on the residuary legatee.

We hold that the common-law rule as to the right of exoneration is here controlling and there being no contrary testamentary intent shown, either express or implied, the appellant, Jeanne Ashkenazy was entitled to have the real property exonerated from the mortgage lien.

As to the second question, i.e., the right of the specific legatee, Lillian Conroy Fine, to have the shares of stock (under paragraph 'Twelfth') exonerated from all liens thereon, we affirm the lower court's holding that it was the intention of the testator that this legacy be exonerated from all liens. We concur with the lower court that the factors which evince an intention of exoneration as to the shares were:

'1. The shares of stock were not encumbered when the will was made.

'2. The testator intended to bequeath the property he then owned, which was free and clear.

'3. The bank loan was a short term obligation which the testator expected to pay in his lifetime.'

We have reviewed the other contentions of the parties and have found them to be without merit. * * *

It follows, therefore, that the order appealed is in all respects affirmed except that it is reversed so that the appellant, Jeanne Ashkenazy, shall have a right to have the real property in question exonerated from the mortgage lien.

Affirmed in part and reversed in part.

Uniform Probate Code (2003)

§ 2-607. Nonexoneration.

A specific devise passes subject to any mortgage interest existing at the date of death, without right of exoneration, regardless of a general directive in the will to pay debts.

Tax Considerations: In the event that exoneration applies, and, indeed, any time the estate is called upon to pay taxes or other expenses associated with probate, such as the spouse's elective share, the liability for these expenses should be apportioned among the estate's beneficiaries. Not to apportion the expenses will exhaust the residuary estate, defeat the intent of the Testator, and burden estate administration. Integration of the probate and non-probate (will substitute) transfers is the difficult dilemma. The following decision is illustrative.

In re Valma M. Hanson Revocable Trust

Indiana Court of Appeals, 2002
779 N.E.2d 1218

KIRSCH, Judge.

Barry C. Bergstrom, Trustee of the Valma M. Hanson Revocable Trust ("Trust"), brings this interlocutory appeal of the trial court's order denying his motion to dismiss the action filed by Elizabeth Hanson and Bonnie Kuczkowski ("Petitioners") wherein they allege that Bergstrom had violated the terms of the Trust in his administration thereof. The issue Bergstrom presents upon appeal is whether the trial court erred in denying his motion to dismiss for failure to state a claim upon which relief can be granted.

We affirm.

* * *

On December 2, 1983, in Illinois, Valma Hanson executed an instrument that established the Trust. Hanson named herself as the original Trustee, but later she named Bergstrom as Trustee by amendment in 1992. Article Five of the Trust instrument directed the Trustee to pay the various taxes payable upon her death. Article Eight created a separate "Trust B" and directed that after her death, Trust B of the "Trust as then constituted" was to be divided and distributed pursuant to the provisions of "Schedule 'C'" of the Trust. Appellant's Appendix at 24. Schedule C, as amended in 1992, stated that the "Trust Estate as provided in Article Eight shall be divided and distributed" upon her death "as follows: 1. SPECIFIC DEVISE OF REAL ESTATE " then held in the Trust Estate was bequeathed to Bergstrom, and "2.... the balance of the assets included in the Trust Estate as constituted" was to be divided according to specified percentages among nine individuals[1] and one church. Appellant's Appendix at 47. The Trust instrument also specified that the "Trust Agreement and the trusts created hereby shall be construed, regulated and governed by and in accordance with the laws of the State of Illinois." Appellant's Appendix at 33.

On March 31, 1992, Hanson executed a last will and testament. In Article I of her will, she bequeathed all of her personal property to Bergstrom. In Article II, she exercised her testamentary power of appointment over the principal assets that were held in Trust A from her late husband's revocable trust to appoint Bergstrom and bequeath those assets to him. In Article III, the will provided the "GIFT OF RESIDUE TO TRUST," whereby "all the residue of [her] estate" was "give[n] and devise[d]" to Trust B of her Trust. Appellant's Appendix at 85. The will named Bergstrom as executor thereof. Also, the will stated that Hanson was "a resident of Lake County, Indiana," and the will was to be "construed and interpreted under the laws of the State of which I am now a resident." Appellant's Appendix at 85, 88.

Hanson died on December 1, 1998. Indiana inheritance tax and Federal estate tax returns were filed, and the taxes and expenses were paid from the residuary assets of Trust B. Bergstrom allocated the payment of the taxes and expenses exclusively to the non-real estate assets in Schedule C and did not assess a contribution against the balance of the assets in Trust B, which included the devise of realty to Bergstrom. After Bergstrom had distributed to himself the real estate held by Hanson at the time of her death and paid the taxes and expenses, no property was available for those identified to receive the specified percentage shares of "the balance of the assets" in Trust B. Appellant's Appendix at 47.

On behalf of the residuary beneficiaries other than Bergstrom, the instant petition was filed, asserting that as Trustee, Bergstrom had violated the terms of the Trust by failing to apportion the federal estate tax and Indiana inheritance tax against all the property in Trust B.[2] Petitioners asked that the Trust be docketed concerning "all issues

---

1. One of the individuals named as a residuary beneficiary was Bergstrom with a 25% share indicated.

2. In their appellate brief, Petitioners assert that they "also raised issues which are related to the accuracy and completeness of the accounting of Bergstrom." Appellee's Brief at 9. However, they do not direct us to any such assertions in their petition, and we find only the assertion that he failed to apportion taxes.

with respect to the accounting and distribution of assets within the Trust," Appellant's Appendix at 16, while also seeking the removal of Bergstrom and payment of attorney's fees.

Bergstrom filed a motion to dismiss, arguing that the petition failed to state a claim upon which relief could be granted. Specifically, Bergstrom contended that (1) the terms of the Trust authorized the payment of death taxes to be made at his discretion as Trustee, and (2) Indiana's statute on the apportionment of federal estate taxes was "inapplicable ... because the trust agreement specifies the application of Illinois law, which has no similar rule on apportionment." Appellant's Appendix at 72. The trial court denied Bergstrom's motion to dismiss, finding that the petition "states a claim on which relief can be granted because the Trust Agreement, as amended, should not be interpreted to permit payment of all death taxes from the residuary of the Trust." Appellant's Appendix at 7–8.

* * *

Bergstrom argues that the motion to dismiss should have been granted because the Trust instrument itself authorized his discretion in the payment of estate and inheritance taxes. The provision he relies upon is Article Five of the Trust, which as amended, reads as follows:

DISCRETIONARY PROVISIONS FOR TRUSTEE TO DEAL WITH SETTLOR'S ESTATE AND MAKE PAYMENTS OF DEBTS AND TAXES

After the Settlor's death, the Trustee, if in its discretion it deems it advisable, may pay all or any part of the Settlor's funeral expenses, legally enforceable claims against the Settlor or her estate, reasonable expenses of administration of her estate, any allowances by court order to those dependent upon the Settlor, *any estate, inheritance, succession, death or similar taxes payable by reason of the Settlor's death*, together with any interest thereon or other additions thereto, without reimbursement from the Settlor's executor or administrator, from any beneficiary of insurance upon the Settlor's life, or from any other person. *All such payments*, except of interest, *shall be charged generally against the principal of the Trust Estate includable in the Settlor's estate for Federal estate tax purposes* and any interest so paid shall be charged generally against the income thereof, provided, however, *any such payments of estate, inheritance, succession, death or similar taxes shall be charged against the principal constituting Trust B* and any interest so paid shall be charged against the income thereof....

Appellant's Appendix at 39–40 (emphasis added).

Petitioners argue that because this Trust provision specifically directs that taxes are payable *generally* from the principal of Trust B, and the real estate distributed to Bergstrom was a part of the principal of the Trust, that real estate must not be excluded from being subject to the payment of a share of the estate taxes.[3] Petitioners further assert that "[t]he intent of Hanson in her Trust is clear on its face" and requires apportionment across all of the assets in Trust B. Appellees' Brief at 8. We agree.

---

3. In their brief to the trial court opposing the motion to dismiss and in their appellate brief, Petitioners asserted that the expenses of administration should also have been so apportioned. However, no such assertion was presented to the trial court in Petitioners' amended petition for docketing of the Trust. See Appellant's Appendix at 12–16.

Petitioners note that "both Indiana and Illinois law recognize the legal proposition that in construing a trust, the prime goal is to determine the settlor's intent by first looking at the plain language of the document." Appellant's Brief at 10. If the settlor's intent is clear from the plain language of instrument, and not against public policy, then we must honor the settlor's intent. Appellant's Brief at 10. Indeed, we have said that the primary objective "in interpreting a trust is to determine the intent of the settlor," which is an "age-old proposition." Matter of Fitton, 605 N.E.2d 1164, 1169 (Ind.Ct.App.1992). We must ascertain the settlor's intent and "give effect to" that intent. Ind. Dep't of State Revenue v. Nichols, 659 N.E.2d 694, 699 (Ind.Tax 1995). We examine the trust document as a whole to determine "the plain and unambiguous purpose of the settlor" as that intent appears "within the 'four corners' of the trust document." Id. (citations omitted). When interpreting a trust, we "must look to the language used in the instrument." Stowers v. Norwest Bank Indiana, 624 N.E.2d 485, 489 (Ind.Ct.App.1993), trans. denied (1995). Our determination of the settlor's intent based upon unambiguous trust document terms is a question of law. Id. Indiana's Trust Code provides that its rules of law are to "be interpreted and applied to the terms of the trust so as to implement the intent of the settlor and the purposes of the trust." IC 30-4-1-3. "If the rules of law and the terms of the trust conflict, the terms of the trust shall control unless the rules of law clearly prohibit or restrict the article which the terms of the trust purport to authorize." Id.

The trust language authorizes the Trustee, in its discretion, to pay the various taxes due upon the settlor's death by charging them *generally* against the principal of the Trust Estate that was included in the settlor's estate for Federal estate tax purposes. "Principal" is defined as "the corpus or main body of an estate ... distinguished from income." WEBSTER's THIRD INT'L DICTIONARY 1802 (1976). Hence, the "balance of the assets," which the Trust directed to be distributed by percentage to the Petitioners, was part of the principal of the Trust Estate. Here, the principal of Trust B as shown on the federal estate tax return filed by Bergstrom consists of a Trust value of $1,027,351.00 and includes real estate valued at $388,046.00, which Bergstom passed to himself without any contribution for payment of taxes and expenses. Bergstrom paid taxes, including federal estate tax and Indiana inheritance tax, in the amount of $228,412.31 without assessing a proportionate share against each beneficiary's distribution. He specifically failed to allocate payment of the taxes to the balance of the assets in Trust B, which included the real estate.

As the primary beneficiary, Bergstrom inherited over three-quarters of a million dollars after taxes, while the other named beneficiaries received nothing. We are left with the sense that Bergstrom had an irreconcilable conflict of interest and that paying the taxes from the assets set aside for the other beneficiaries thwarted Hanson's testamentary intent that they share in her estate.[4] The Trust specified a number of gifts to nine individuals and a church and if Hanson had intended Bergstrom to be the sole beneficiary (the net effect of non-apportionment), she could easily have stated this in the instrument. She made her intent clear by specifically stating that the taxes be charged *generally* against the principal of the Trust included in her estate. The principal included the real estate, and taxes paid from the trust were to be charged against it as is the case with the non-real property assets.

Bergstrom argues that we should be guided by Illinois law because Hanson specified the application of Illinois law in her Trust. Illinois has not adopted an apportionment

---

4. Most egregious is the fact that the share set aside for the United Methodist Church was utilized to pay death taxes notwithstanding the fact that it is a charitable donation exempt from such taxes and that it appears Bergstrom took a deduction on the federal estate tax return for the gift.

rule. In Estate of Maierhofer, 328 Ill.App.3d 987, 989, 263 Ill.Dec. 124, 767 N.E.2d 850, 852 (2002), the Appellate Court of Illinois most recently affirmed that Illinois does not follow "the principle of equitable apportionment"[5] *when the instrument is silent as to the source of probate tax payment.* Rather, "the burden on the residue rule"— that "taxes, debts and expenses of administration attributable to probate assets are borne by the residuary estate *in the absence of a contrary indication in the [instrument]"*—is the rule for "estate tax liability in Illinois." Id. at 990, 263 Ill.Dec. 124, 767 N.E.2d at 853. The Illinois court noted that "courts of this state have consistently applied the burden on the residue rule," a rule that "Illinois lawyers have long relied on," with countless instruments "drafted on this assumption." Id. at 990, 263 Ill.Dec. 124, 767 N.E.2d at 852 (citations omitted).

Contrary to Bergstrom's argument, because the intent of the settlor is clear from the language of the trust instrument, we conclude that apportioning the payment of taxes across all of the assets in Trust B, not just those going to the remaining beneficiaries, is consistent with Illinois law that payment should be from the residuary estate "in the absence of a contrary indication." Id. at 989, 263 Ill.Dec. 124, 767 N.E.2d at 852. Bergstrom's argument must fail because it ignores the plain language used by Hanson herself concerning payment of the taxes.

Based upon the language of the Trust instrument, we find that Petitioners have stated a set of facts and circumstances that can support the relief they requested. Consequently, the trial court did not err in denying Bergstrom's motion to dismiss.

Affirmed.

BROOK, C.J., concurs.

DARDEN, J., dissents with separate opinion.

DARDEN, Judge, dissenting.

I must respectfully disagree with the majority's conclusion that the trust instrument expressed the clear intent that the payment of taxes be apportioned "across all of the assets in Trust B." Slip Op. at 9. In my opinion, the trust instrument expressed Hanson's clear intent that it be entirely a matter of the Trustee's discretion as to what assets constituting the principal of her estate would be utilized to pay taxes. Although I am more than willing to acknowledge that the result of the Trustee's exercise of that discretion can be seen as inequitable when the Petitioners had been named as potential residuary beneficiaries, I cannot turn a blind eye to the unambiguous language of the trust instrument written by Hanson.[6]

As the majority notes, the trust instrument authorizes the Trustee, in its discretion, to pay the various taxes owing upon the settlor's death from the principal of the Trust Estate that was included in the settlor's estate for Federal estate tax purposes. However, in my opinion, that is exactly what happened. "Principal" is defined as "the corpus or

---

5. The Illinois court explained that equitable apportionment "is a term used to describe the process of distributing the burden of estate expenses among beneficiaries in the same proportion they cause such expenses to be incurred." 328 Ill.App.3d at 990, 263 Ill.Dec. 124, 767 N.E.2d at 852.

6. It is worth noting that there is no assertion that undue influence or fraud induced Hanson in her drafting of the trust instrument; nor do Petitioners claim a lack of capacity on the part of Hanson. I am also mindful of the effect of time—from when Hanson drafted the trust instrument until her death—on the total assets remaining at the time of her death, both as to her need to use resources for her own maintenance and the fluctuation of the value of equities in her estate based on market forces.

main body of an estate … distinguished from income." WEBSTER'S THIRD INT'L DICTIO-
NARY (1976) p. 1802. Hence, the "balance of the assets," which (after the specific devise
of real estate to Bergstrom) the Trust directed to be distributed by percentage to the Petitioners, was part of the principal of the Trust Estate. If Hanson had desired that the
Trustee pay the taxes by assessing a proportionate share against each beneficiary's distribution—the real estate specifically devised to Bergstrom as well as the Petitioners'
shares—she could have written the trust instrument to so state. For example, the Trust
could have provided that the tax payments by the Trustee should be "charged generally,
in shares proportionate to the respective beneficiaries' distributions, against the principal of the Trust Estate.…" However, by the clear language she used in the trust instrument, Hanson did not direct the Trustee to apportion among the beneficiaries the tax
burden owing upon her death.

Absent such a specific direction upon the part of Hanson, I would next consider the
fact that Hanson specified the application of Illinois law. As the majority notes, Indiana's Trust Code provides that its rules of law are to "be interpreted and applied to the
terms of the trust so as to implement the intent of the settlor and the purposes of the
trust." See Ind.Code § 30-4-1-3. "If the rules of law and the terms of the trust conflict,
the terms of the trust shall control unless the rules of law clearly prohibit or restrict the
article which the terms of the trust purport to authorize." Id. Petitioners direct us to no
authority that would prohibit Hanson, as settlor, from specifying the application of Illinois law in the administration of her trust. Consequently, because it was her intent that
Illinois law apply, I would turn to the law of that state and its application to the terms of
the Trust.

In Estate of Maierhofer, 328 Ill.App.3d 987, 989, 263 Ill.Dec. 124, 767 N.E.2d 850,
852 (2002), the Appellate Court of Illinois most recently affirmed that Illinois does not
follow "the principle of equitable apportionment" when the instrument is silent as to
source of probate tax payment. Rather, "the burden on the residue rule" is the rule for
"estate tax liability in Illinois." 328 Ill.App.3d at 989, 990, 767 N.E.2d at 852, 853. The
Illinois court noted that its courts "have consistently applied the burden on the residue
rule," a rule that "Illinois lawyers have long relied on," with countless instruments
"drafted on this assumption." 328 Ill.App.3d at 990, 767 N.E.2d at 852 (citations omitted). Therefore, the fact that as Trustee, Bergstrom used the discretion given to him to
pay the death taxes from the residuary estate[7] is not only consistent with the terms of
the Trust, but it is consistent with Illinois law that payment should be from the residuary estate "in the absence of a contrary indication." 328 Ill.App.3d at 989, 767 N.E.2d
at 852.

The Petitioners also argued to the trial court that Indiana law should apply because
Hanson executed her will in Indiana, her real and personal property were located in Indiana, and she was a resident of Indiana at the time of her death. However, I would also
find this argument to fail because it ignores the plain language used in the will by Hanson concerning payment of the taxes.

Indiana law provides that federal estate taxes "shall be" apportioned "among all" of
the estate's beneficiaries "unless" the decedent has "otherwise" directed in the will.
Ind.Code § 29-2-12-2. Hanson's will directed that taxes "payable by reason of [her]

---

7. BLACK'S defines "residuary estate" as "[t]he part of a decedent's estate remaining after all
debts, expenses, taxes, and specific bequests and devises have been satisfied." BLACK'S LAW DICTIO-
NARY 569 (7th ed. 1999).

death" be paid "out of the principal of [her] residuary estate." (App. 86). Under Hanson's will, the principal of her "residuary estate" can be read to be either (1) all of Trust B or (2) the "balance of the assets" to be distributed to Petitioners after the specific devise of real estate to Bergstrom. Under either interpretation, the payment of taxes by Bergstrom does comport with the specific direction of Hanson's will that taxes be paid from the residuary estate, and the statute does not dictate a contrary result.[8] Consistent with the statute, I would find that the Trust directed the Trustee to make the tax payment from the principal—and, as previously noted, that is what I find Bergstrom to have done.

Based upon the language of the Trust instrument and of Hanson's will, it appears to me that the Petitioners have stated a set of facts and circumstances that cannot support the relief they requested; therefore, I believe Bergstrom's motion to dismiss should have been granted.

D. Ambiguity

Often a testator may say one thing and mean another. Even when the language is clear on its face and it describes with clarity an object or person in existence, this may not be the object or person intended. Such legal disputes are often categorized as resulting from three possibilities: (1) plain meaning: where the words or phrases appear to describe with complete accuracy the testator's objective; (2) latent ambiguity: where the description, although accurate in its possibilities, may be open to more than one meaning or objective of the testator; and (3) patent ambiguity: where the description is clearly erroneous and cannot be what the testator had as an objective. Because of the court's reluctance to re-write the Last Will and Testament, rules have developed that insulate the court from attempts at judicial modification by plaintiffs. The following case invites consideration of how a court may respond to any dispute over ambiguity in what the testator has written.

In re Estate of Gibbs
Supreme Court of Wisconsin, 1961
14 Wis.2d 490, 111 N.W.2d 413

FAIRCHILD, Justice.

* * * The evidence leads irresistibly to the conclusion that Mr. and Mrs. Gibbs intended legacies to respondent, and that the use of the middle initial 'J.' and the address of North 46th street resulted from some sort of mistake.

Respondent testified that he met Mr. Gibbs about 1928. From 1930 to 1949 he was employed as superintendent of a steel warehouse where Mr. Gibbs was his superior. They worked in close contact. Until 1945 the business belonged to the Gibbs Steel Company. In that year the business was sold, but Mr. Gibbs stayed on for four years in a supervisory capacity. Respondent remained with the new company until 1960. After 1949 Mr. Gibbs occasionally visited the plant and saw the respondent when there. From 1935

---

8. The statute specifies that for apportionment purposes, the term "will" includes a trust. I.C. § 29-2-12-1.5.

to 1955 respondent took men occasionally to the Gibbs home to do necessary work about the place. He also visited there socially several times a year and saw both Mr. and Mrs. Gibbs. Mrs. Gibbs had made a few visits at the plant before 1949 and respondent had seen her there. Mr. Gibbs did not visit respondent's home, although on a few occasions had telephoned him at home. Mr. Gibbs always called respondent 'Bob.'

Miss Krueger, who had been the Gibbs' housekeeper for 24 years up to 1958 and was a legatee under both wills, corroborated much of respondent's testimony. She also testified that Mr. Gibbs had told her he made a will remembering various people including 'the boys at the shop,' referring to them as 'Mike, Ed and Bob.'

Miss Pacius, a legatee under both wills, who had been Mr. Gibbs' private secretary for many years while he was in business, testified to Mr. Gibbs' expressions of high regard for respondent. Another former employee also testified to a similar effect.

Of the individuals named in the wills as legatees, all except two were shown to be relatives of Mr. or Mrs. Gibbs, former employees, neighbors, friends, or children of friends. The two exceptions were named near the end of the will and proof as to them may have been inadvertently omitted. 'Mike,' named in the will, was a warehouse employee under the supervision of respondent.

The attorney who drew several wills for Mr. and Mrs. Gibbs produced copies of most of them. They were similar in outline to the wills admitted to probate except that Mr. Gibbs' wills executed before Mrs. Gibb's death bequeathed his property to her, if she survived. The first ones were drawn in 1953 and each contained a bequest to 'Robert Krause, of Milwaukee, Wisconsin, if he survives me, one per cent (1%).' There was testimony that Mrs. Gibbs' will, executed in August, 1955, contained the same language. In the 1957 wills the same bequest was made to 'Robert Krause, now of 4708 North 46th Street, Milwaukee, Wisconsin.' In several other instances street addresses of legatees were given for the first time in 1957. In the 1958 wills the same bequest was made to 'Robert J. Krause, now of 4708 North 46th Street, Milwaukee, Wisconsin.' The scrivener also produced a hand-written memorandum given to him by Mr. Gibbs for the purpose of preparing Mr. Gibbs' 1958 will, and the reference on that memorandum corresponding to the Krause bequest is 'Bob, 1%.' Four bequests (to Gruener, Krause, Preuschl and Owen) appear in the same order in each of the wills and are reflected in the memorandum referred to as 'Fred Gruener, Bob, Mike, and Ed.' Gruener, Preuschl and Owen were former employees of Gibbs Steel Company, as was respondent. Owen's residence is given as Jefferson, Wisconsin, in all the wills. In the 1953 wills, the residence of Gruener, Krause and Preuschl was given only as Milwaukee, Wisconsin. At street address was inserted for the first time in each case in the 1957 wills, and repeated in the later ones.

Prior to 1950 respondent had lived at several different locations. From 1950 until April, 1960, he lived at 2325 North Sherman boulevard. We take judicial notice that this address and 4708 North 46th street are in the same general section of the city of Milwaukee, and that both are a number of miles distant from the Gibbs' home. We also take judicial notice that the telephone directory for Milwaukee and vicinity listed 14 subscribers by the name of Robert Krause with varying initials in October, 1958, and 15 in October of 1959. The listing for appellant gives his middle initial J. as well as his street address.

The only evidence which suggests even a possibility that Mr. or Mrs. Gibbs may have known of appellant may be summarized as follows:

For a time, appellant had a second job as a part time taxi driver, and he recalled an elderly lady who was his passenger on a lengthy taxi trip in June, 1955. He did not recall where he picked her up. He had driven her across the city, waiting for her while she visited in a hospital, and then driven her back across the city. The place where he let her out, however, was not her home. He did not recall that she had given him her name, but she had inquired as to his. They had conversed about the illness of appellant's wife and his working at an extra job in order to make ends meet. She had expressed sympathy and approval of his efforts. Presumably when he was notified that his name appeared in the Gibbs' wills as legatee, he endeavored to find an explanation of his good fortune and concluded that the lady in question must have been Mrs. Gibbs. The 1955 taxi ride, however, could not explain the gift to Robert Krause in the 1953 wills, and it is clear that the same legatee was intended in the Krause bequests in all the wills. Moreover, appellant's description of his taxi passenger differed in several particulars from the description of Mrs. Gibbs given by other witnesses.

* * * As stated above, the county court could reach no other conclusion upon consideration of the extrinsic evidence than that Mr. and Mrs. Gibbs intended to designate respondent as their legatee. The difficult question is whether the court could properly consider such evidence in determining testamentary intent.

Under rules as to construction of a will, unless there is ambiguity in the text of the will read in the light of surrounding circumstances, extrinsic evidence is inadmissible for the purpose of determining intent. * * *

A latent ambiguity exists where the language of the will, though clear on its face, is susceptible of more than one meaning, when applied to the extrinsic facts to which it refers. * * *

There are two classes of latent ambiguity. One, where there are two or more persons or things exactly measuring up to the description in the will; * * * the other where no person or thing exactly answers the declarations and descriptions of the will, but two or more persons or things answer the description imperfectly. Extrinsic evidence must be resorted to under these circumstances to identify which of the parties, unspecified with particularity in the will, was intended by the testator. * * *

Had the probated wills used the language of the 1953 wills 'To Robert Krause of Milwaukee,' such terms would have described both appellant and respondent, as well as a number of other people. Upon such ambiguity of the first type above mentioned becoming apparent, extrinsic evidence would be admissible in order to determine which Robert Krause Mr. and Mrs. Gibbs had in mind as their legatee.

Had the will said 'To my former employee, Robert J. Krause of 4708 North 46th Street,' neither appellant nor respondent would have exactly fulfilled the terms. Latent ambiguity of the second type would thus have appeared, and again extrinsic evidence would be admissible to determine what individual testators had in mind.

The wills containing, as they do, similar bequests to a long list of individuals, each bearing some relationship of blood, friendship, or former employment to Mr. or Mrs. Gibbs, come close to implying that every legatee named has some such relationship. Nevertheless the wills do not refer to Krause as standing in any particular relationship.

The terms of the bequest exactly fit appellant and no one else. There is no ambiguity.

'An ambiguity is not that which may be made doubtful by extrinsic proof tending to show an intention different from that manifested in the will, but it must grow out of the difficulty of identifying the person whose name and description correspond with the terms of the will.' * * *

Under the circumstances before us, can a court properly consider evidence showing that some of the words were used by mistake and should be stricken or disregarded? It is traditional doctrine that wills must not be reformed even in the case of demonstrable mistake. * * * This doctrine doubtless rests upon policy reasons. The courts deem it wise to avoid entertaining claims of disappointed persons who may be able to make very plausible claims of mistake after the testator is no longer able to refute them.

Although the courts subscribe to an inflexible rule against reformation of a will, it seems that they have often strained a point in matters of identification of property or beneficiaries in order to reach a desired result by way of construction. In Will of Stack, [214 Wis. 98, 251 N.W. 470 (1934)], * * * where the will devised 'Block 64,' the court included part of block 175 in the provision to conform to the unexpressed intent of the testator. In Will of Boeck, * * * [160 Wis. 577, 152 N.W. 155 (1915)], * * * where the will devised the 'northeast quarter of the northwest quarter' of a section, which was not owned by the testator, the court held such provision passed the southeast quarter of the northwest quarter, to conform to the misexpressed intent of the testator. In Moseley v. Goodman, [138 Tenn. 10, 195 S.W. 590 (1917)], * * * where testator bequeathed property to 'Mrs. Moseley,' the court denied the claim of Mrs. Lenoir Moseley to the gift and held that Mrs. Trimble had been intended by the testator. Mrs. Trimble was known to the testator by the nickname 'Mrs. Moseley.'

In Miller's Estate, [26 Pa. Super. 443 (1904)], * * * testator left property to 'William Wilson's children.' Relying on evidence that testator frequently confused William Wilson with his brother Seth, the court held the gift should go to the children of Seth Wilson, who had been intended by the testator. In Groves v. Culph, [132 Ind. 186, 31 N.E. 569 (1892)], * * * testator devised a remainder interest in part of lot 15 to his daughter. The court, to conform to testator's true intent, included part of lot 16 in this devise. In Castell v. Togg [163 Eng.Rep. 102 (1836)], * * * and Geer v. Winds, [4 S.C.Eq., 4 Desaus 85 (1810)], * * * the testator omitted a child from his will by mistake. The court inserted in the will the gift which had been intended for the child by the parent. In Beaumont v. Feld, [24 Eng.Rep. 673 (1723)], * * * a bequest to 'Catharine Earnley' was proven to have been intended for Gertrude Yardley, and was given to the latter, and in Masters v. Masters, [24 Eng.Rep. 454 (1718)], * * * a gift to 'Mrs. Sawyer' was given to Mrs. Swopper, because testator knew no one by the former name. In the two cases last mentioned, no one with the name given in the will claimed the gift.

We are also aware of the rule which allows a court in probating a will to deny probate to a provision in the document which was included by mistake. British courts will deny probate to a single word, or part of a sentence, thereby completely altering the provided dispositions. * * *

We conclude that details of identification, particularly such matters as middle initials, street addresses, and the like, which are highly susceptible to mistake, particularly in metropolitan areas, should not be accorded such sanctity as to frustrate an otherwise clearly demonstrable intent. Where such details of identification are involved, courts should receive evidence tending to show that a mistake has been made and should disregard the details when the proof establishes to the highest degree of certainty that a mistake was, in fact, made.

We therefore consider that the county court properly disregarded the middle initial and street address, and determined that respondent was the Robert Krause whom testators had in mind.

Orders affirmed.

BROADFOOT and BROWN, JJ., dissenting.

Notes

The use of extrinsic evidence to affect words of plain meaning has traditionally been forbidden. *See, e.g.,* Mahoney v. Grainger, 283 Mass. 189, 186 N.E. 86 (1933); Estate of Carroll, 764 S.W.2d 736 (Mo. App. 1989) (holding that intention must be determined by the Will itself and not by guessing what a testator may have meant). Not all commentators agree with the "harsh and relentless formalism" of such a rule. *See, e.g.,* 9 John H. Wigmore, EVIDENCE § 2462 at 198 (James H. Chadbourn rev. 1981). But the rule is still the cornerstone of Will construction. Modern arguments of mistake may allow for the introduction of extrinsic evidence if that evidence is clear and convincing, however, there is a reluctance to allow courts to change the plain meaning of words based on complaints by a disappointed plaintiff. For a discussion of mistake and means to effectuate a remedy when there is dispute over plain meaning, see Joseph W. de Furia, Jr., *Mistakes in Wills Resulting from Scriveners' Errors: The Argument for Reformation*, 40 CATH. U. L. REV. 1 (1990). Some courts imply gifts to fill gaps when the use of extrinsic evidence would otherwise be impermissible. *See, e.g.,* In re Bieley, 91 N.Y.2d 520, 695 N.E.2d 1119, 673 N.Y.S.2d 38 (1998). But other courts are reluctant to sacrifice predictability for something called "paramount intent." *See, e.g.,* Matter of Gustafson,74 N.Y.2d 448, 547 N.E.2d 1152, 548 N.Y.S.2d 625 (1989).

E. Mistake

Erickson v. Erickson

Supreme Court of Connecticut, 1998
246 Conn. 359, 716 A.2d 92

BORDEN, Associate Justice.

The dispositive issue in this appeal is whether, pursuant to General Statutes (Rev. to 1995) § 45a-257 (a), the trial court should have admitted extrinsic evidence regarding the decedent's intent that his will would not be revoked automatically by his subsequent marriage.[2] The named plaintiff, Alicia Erickson, * * * who is the daughter of the decedent,

---

2. General Statutes (Rev. to 1995) § 45a-257 (a) provides: "If, after the making of a will, the testator marries or is divorced or his marriage is annulled or dissolved or a child is born to the testator or a minor child is legally adopted by him, or a child is born as a result of A.I.D. as defined in section 45a-771, to which the testator has consented in accordance with subsection (a) of section 45a-772, and no provision has been made in such will for such contingency, such marriage, divorce, annulment, dissolution, birth or adoption of a minor child shall operate as a revocation of such will * * *."

Section 45a-257 (a) was repealed by 1996 Public Acts, No. 96-95, and, to the extent that § 45a-

Ronald K. Erickson, appeals * * * from the judgment of the trial court in favor of the defendant, Dorothy Erickson, [formerly Dorothy A. Mehring] * * * the executrix of the estate of the decedent, dismissing the plaintiff's appeal from the decree of the Probate Court for the district of Madison. The Probate Court had admitted the will of the decedent to probate. The trial court ruled that the decedent's will, which had been executed shortly before his marriage to the defendant, provided for the contingency of marriage.

The plaintiff claims on her appeal that the trial court improperly concluded that the decedent's will provided for the contingency of marriage. * * * The defendant claims on her cross appeal that the trial court improperly excluded certain extrinsic evidence regarding the decedent's intent. We conclude that the trial court should have permitted the defendant to introduce extrinsic evidence of the decedent's intent. Accordingly, we reverse the judgment of the trial court and order a new trial.

Certain facts in this appeal are undisputed. On September 1, 1988, the decedent executed a will. At that time, he had three daughters and was unmarried. Two days later, on September 3, 1988, he married the defendant. He died on February 22, 1996.

The six articles of his will provide as follows.[7] The first article provides for the payment of funeral expenses and debts by the estate. The second article states that the

---

257 (a) dealt with the effect of marriage on a will, it has been replaced by General Statutes § 45a-257a, which provides: Failure of testator to provide for surviving spouse who married testator after execution of will. Determination of share of estate. (a) If a testator fails to provide by will for the testator's surviving spouse who married the testator after the execution of the will, the surviving spouse shall receive the same share of the estate the surviving spouse would have received if the decedent left no will unless: (1) It appears from the will that the omission was intentional; or (2) the testator provided for the spouse by transfer outside the will and the intent that the transfer be in lieu of a testamentary provision is shown by the testator's statements, or is reasonably inferred from the amount of the transfer or other evidence.

'(b) In satisfying a share provided in subsection (a) of this section, devises and legacies made by the will abate in accordance with section 45a-426.'

The effective date of § 45a-257a was January 1, 1997. Therefore, that statute does not apply to this case because the will in question was executed in 1988. At that time, the applicable statute was General Statutes § 45-162, which was transferred to § 45a-257 in 1991. Because that statute remained unchanged until Public Act 96-95, hereafter references to § 45a-257 are to the 1995 revision of the statute.

7. The decedent's will provides in relevant part:

"Article I: I order and direct that my funeral expenses and my just debts, if any, except such as are barred by the Statute of Limitations or otherwise outlawed, be paid as soon as may be practicable; provided, however, that if any such debts are secured by mortgages, my Executrix or Executor, as the case may be, shall pay such debts so secured only if, in her or his discretion, such payment shall appear to be for the benefit of my estate; and provided further that all legacy, succession, inheritance, transfer and estate taxes which may become payable by reason of my death, whether or not levied on property or estate passing by this, my Last Will and Testament, shall be paid by my Executrix or Executor out of my residuary estate in the same manner as an expense of administration, and shall not be pro rated or apportioned among or charged against the respective devisees, legatees, beneficiaries, transferees or other recipients, nor charged against any property passing or which may have passed to any of them, and that my Executrix or Executor shall not be entitled to reimbursement for any portion of any such tax from any person.

"Article II: All the rest, residue and remainder of my estate and property (hereinafter called my residuary estate) of every nature, character and description, whether real, personal or mixed, and wheresoever situate, of which I may die seized or possessed, or in or to which I may in any wise be interested or entitled at the time of my death, or under or with respect to which I shall have any power of disposition or appointment at the time of my death, I give, devise and bequeath to DOROTHY A. MEHRING, of Madison, Con-

residue of the estate will pass to the defendant. The third article provides that if the defendant predeceases the decedent, one half of the residuary estate will pass in equal parts to the decedent's three daughters, Laura Erickson Kusy, Ellen Erickson Cates and Alicia Erickson, and one half of the residuary estate will pass in equal parts to Thomas Mehring, Christopher Mehring, Maureen Mehring and Kathleen Mehring, the children of the defendant. The fourth article appoints the defendant as the executrix of the will, with Attorney Robert O'Brien as the contingent executor in the event that the defendant is unable to or refuses to serve as executrix. The fifth article gives the executrix or executor the power to dispose of property of the estate as necessary. The sixth article appoints the defendant as the guardian of any of the decedent's children who have not reached the age of eighteen at the time of his death.

The Probate Court admitted the decedent's will to probate. The plaintiff appealed from the Probate Court's judgment. Prior to trial, the plaintiff filed a motion in limine to exclude extrinsic evidence of the decedent's intent. The plaintiff argued that "[§] 45a-257 makes the Court's inquiry very simple: to determine whether the will was revoked, the Court need examine only [the decedent's] will, his marriage certificate to [the defendant], and his death certificate. Extrinsic evidence regarding [the decedent's] intentions is inadmissible because the language of [the decedent's] will is unambiguous, and therefore under ... [§] 45a-257 the operation of the marriage to revoke the will is automatic and mandatory." The defendant, in opposition to the plaintiff's motion, made a detailed offer of proof to show the contrary intent of the decedent.[8]

---

necticut, provided she survives me.

"Article III: If said DOROTHY A. MEHRING predeceases me, I give, devise and bequeath my said residuary estate as follows:

"A. ONE-HALF (1/2), in equal parts, to my daughters, LAURA ERICKSON, ELLEN ERICKSON and ALICIA ERICKSON, all of Madison, Connecticut, or to the survivors or survivor of them.

"B. ONE-HALF (1/2), in equal parts, to THOMAS MEHRING and CHRISTOPHER MEHRING, both of Madison, Connecticut, and MAUREEN MEHRING and KATHLEEN MEHRING, both of Guilford, Connecticut, or to the survivors or survivor of them.

"Article IV: I hereby nominate, constitute, designate and appoint said DOROTHY A. MEHRING to be the Executrix of this, my Last Will and Testament, or in the event of her inability or refusal to act, I hereby nominate, constitute, designate and appoint ATTORNEY ROBERT J. O'BRIEN, of West Hartford, Connecticut, to be the Executor of this, my Last Will and Testament, and I order and direct that in no event shall my Executrix or Executor, as the case may be, be required to give any bond, undertaking or other security for the faithful performance of her or his duties as Executrix or Executor.

    * * *

8. The defendant's offer of proof provided: "May it please the court, if [O'Brien and the defendant] were permitted to testify they would testify as follows. [O'Brien] would testify that he is an attorney before the Hartford [bar], that he was for many years prior to the marriage in 1988 the attorney for [the decedent].

In addition to being his attorney on a variety of business and personal matters, he was also a close friend of [the decedent]. He was aware that [the decedent] was courting [the defendant] who became [his wife] and he was invited to their wedding which was scheduled for September 3, 1988.

About one week prior to that time he received a call from [the decedent] saying he and [the defendant] immediately after the wedding were going to go to New York and then take a Concorde flight to Ireland and they wanted to arrange, as many of us do prior to events like that, for their wills to be drafted prior to the marriage ceremony.

He gave him instructions that the wills would be identical, that is, that all of his estate was to go to [the defendant]. If [the defendant] should predecease him it should go to, half should go to his children, half to [the defendant's] children. That [the defendant] should be the administratrix of

The admission of certain evidence was undisputed, namely, the will, the marriage certificate of the decedent and the defendant, and the decedent's death certificate. The trial court denied the plaintiff's motion in limine with respect to the evidence that Thomas Mehring, Christopher Mehring, Maureen Mehring and Kathleen Mehring, who were named beneficiaries in the will, are the children of the defendant. The court granted the motion in limine, however, with respect to any other evidence regarding the decedent's intent.

With respect to the other issue at trial, namely, whether the decedent's will provided for the contingency of his marriage to the defendant, the trial court, in a de novo proceeding, concluded that the Probate Court properly had admitted the will to probate because the will provided for the contingency of marriage. The trial court reasoned that "[the decedent's] will bequeathed all of his estate to the woman he was licensed to marry and did marry two days later. In his will, he named her executrix and designated her the guardian of his daughters, whose mother had previously died. The nature of these provisions, coupled with the extreme closeness in time of the marriage constitutes clear and convincing evidence of provision for the contingency of marriage. It would be preposterous to assume that [the decedent] was instead executing a will to make provisions that were to be revoked two days later." Accordingly, the trial court rendered judgment affirming the Probate Court's judgment admitting the will, and denied the plaintiff's appeal. This appeal followed.

The plaintiff claims that because the will did not expressly provide for the contingency of marriage, the trial court improperly concluded that the decedent's will provided for the contingency of marriage and, therefore, that his subsequent marriage did not automatically revoke his will under § 45a-257 (a). The plaintiff argues that in determining whether a will provides for contingency of a subsequent marriage, the court may consider only the language of the will, and that the will in question in this case does not include any language referring to the contingency of marriage, such as "the

---

the will, the executrix, excuse me, the executrix of the will and that she would be appointed guardian of his children, and that [her] will be exactly the same.

On Thursday, September 1, two days before the wedding, the two of them went to Hartford and executed the wills. I would offer [the defendant's] will as a piece of evidence. And I represent to the court that it is a mirror image of [the decedent's] will that you have admitted as an exhibit. She, like [the decedent], leaves everything to him. If he should predecease her half of her estate goes to his children, half to her children. He appoints her guardian of his children and appoints [her] executor of his estate.

During the course of the execution of the wills there was no conversation whatsoever about the fact that the Saturday marriage would revoke the will that had been drafted on Thursday. The wedding to take place two days later would revoke the will that had been drafted on Thursday, although there was considerable discussion about the marriage itself and the festivities and the guests and things like that.

[O'Brien] would testify that the reason that he did not place in the will any specific mention of the marriage or talk about it at all with [the defendant] or [the decedent] was because in his view when a man executes a will two days before his marriage in which he leaves everything to the woman that he's about to marry, makes her guardian of his children, makes her administrator of the, executor, executrix of the estate, and if she should predecease him, leaves half of his estate to her kids.

Clearly makes provision in the will for not just a contingency, but the imminent [inevitability] of the marriage that's going to take place two days later. So he didn't think there was any necessary that he had to put in words when it was so clear that it was making—

* * *

words 'if I marry,' 'when I marry,' 'my future wife' or even 'my fiancee.' In fact the words 'wife,' 'spouse' and 'marry' do not appear within the four corners of the will."

In contrast, the defendant claims that the trial court improperly excluded extrinsic evidence of the decedent's intent establishing that his subsequent marriage to her would not result in the revocation of his will. * * * In the alternative, the defendant argues that there is sufficient language within the will itself, without resort to extrinsic evidence, to indicate that the decedent did not intend for his will to be revoked upon his marriage to her.

We conclude that the will, in and of itself, did not provide for the contingency of the subsequent marriage of the decedent and, therefore, under existing case law, properly would have been revoked by that marriage pursuant to § 45a-257 (a). We also conclude, however, that under the circumstances of this case, the trial court improperly excluded evidence of a mistake by the scrivener that, if believed, would permit a finding that the will provided for the contingency of marriage. We therefore reverse the judgment of the trial court and order a new trial in which such evidence may be considered by the trial court.

On the basis of existing case law, the question of whether a will provides for the contingency of a subsequent marriage must be determined: (1) from the language of the will itself; and (2) without resort to extrinsic evidence of the testator's intent. * * * Fulton Trust Co. v. Trowbridge, 126 Conn. 369, 372, 11 A.2d 393 (1940) (execution of will followed by adoption of child; no language in will providing for such contingency); Strong v. Strong, 106 Conn. 76, 79–80, 137 A. 17 (1927) (execution of will followed by birth of child; no language in will providing for such contingency); cf. Czepiel v. Czepiel, 146 Conn. 439, 442, 151 A.2d 878 (1959) (language in will provided for possible subsequent marriage); Blake v. Union & New Haven Trust Co., 95 Conn. 194, 196–97, 110 A. 833 (1920) (language in will provided for subsequent birth of child). Applying this standard, we conclude that the trial court should not have admitted the will because, notwithstanding the inferences that the trial court drew from the dates of the marriage license and the will, and from the identity of certain of the named beneficiaries in the will, there was *no language in the will* providing for the contingency of the subsequent marriage of the decedent. Thus, this will fell on that side of the dividing line encompassing those wills that do not, in and of themselves, provide for such a contingency; see Fulton Trust Co. v. Trowbridge, supra, at 372, 11 A.2d 393; Strong v. Strong, supra, at 80, 137 A. 17; and beyond that side of the line encompassing those wills that do provide for such a contingency. See Czepiel v. Czepiel, supra, at 440, 151 A.2d 878; Blake v. Union & New Haven Trust Co., supra, at 196, 110 A. 833.

This conclusion does not, however, end our inquiry in this case. In Connecticut Junior Republic v. Sharon Hospital, 188 Conn. 1, 2, 448 A.2d 190 (1982), this court considered the issue of "whether extrinsic evidence of a mistake by a scrivener of a testamentary instrument is admissible in a proceeding to determine the validity of the testamentary instrument." In a three to two decision, this court held that such evidence is not admissible. Id., at 9, 448 A.2d 190. Upon further consideration, we now conclude that the reasons given by the dissent in that case are persuasive and apply to the facts of the present case. We, therefore, overrule *Connecticut Junior Republic,* and hold that if a scrivener's error has misled the testator into executing a will on the belief that it will be valid notwithstanding the testator's subsequent marriage, extrinsic evidence of that error is admissible to establish the intent of the testator that his or her will be valid notwithstanding the subsequent marriage. Furthermore, if those two facts, namely, the scrivener's error and its effect on the testator's intent, are established by clear and convincing evidence, they will be sufficient to establish that "provision has been made in such will for such contingency," within the meaning of § 45a-257 (a).

In Connecticut Junior Republic v. Sharon Hospital, supra, 188 Conn. at 9, 448 A.2d 190, this court reasserted the familiar rule that, although extrinsic evidence is not admissible to prove an intention not expressed in the will itself or to prove a devise or bequest not contained in the will, such evidence is admissible to identify a named devisee or legatee, to identify property described in the will, to clarify ambiguous language in the will, and to prove fraud, incapacity or undue influence. In rejecting the claim that extrinsic evidence should also be admissible to prove a scrivener's error, the majority relied principally on our existing case law and on the risk of subverting the policy of the statute of wills. Id., at 23, 448 A.2d 190 (Peters, J., dissenting). The majority acknowledged, however, that, as with any rule of law, time and experience could persuade to the contrary. "[P]rinciples of law which serve one generation well may, by reason of changing conditions, disserve a later one.... Experience can and often does demonstrate that a rule, once believed sound, needs modification to serve justice better." (Citations omitted; internal quotation marks omitted.) Id., at 17–18, 448 A.2d 190. We are now persuaded to the contrary.

The dissent in that case by Justice Peters and joined by Justice Shea, concluded that it "would permit extrinsic evidence of a scrivener's error to be introduced in litigation concerned with the admissibility of a disputed will to probate." Id., at 22, 448 A.2d 190. The dissent gave three principal reasons for its conclusion, each of which we consider to be persuasive and each of which applies to this case. See id., at 22–26, 448 A.2d 190.

First, given that extrinsic evidence is admissible to prove that a will was executed by the testator "in reliance on erroneous beliefs induced by fraud, duress, or undue influence"; id., at 22, 448 A.2d 190; there is no discernible policy difference between that case and a case in which "a will is executed in reliance on erroneous beliefs induced by the innocent error, by the innocent misrepresentation, of the scrivener of a will." Id., at 23, 448 A.2d 190. In each instance, "the testamentary process is distorted by the interference of a third person who misleads the testator into making a testamentary disposition that would not otherwise have occurred." Id., at 22–23, 448 A.2d 190. "In each instance, extrinsic evidence is required to demonstrate that a will, despite its formally proper execution, substantially misrepresents the true intent of the testator." Id., at 23, 448 A.2d 190.

Similarly, in the present case, there is no discernible policy difference between extrinsic evidence offered to show fraud, duress or undue influence, and extrinsic evidence offered to show that a scrivener's error induced the decedent to execute a will that he believed would survive his subsequent marriage. In both instances, the testamentary process was distorted by the interference of a third person who misled the testator into executing a will that would not otherwise have been executed—in the present case, a will that would be revoked upon his marriage because it did not contain language providing for the contingency of marriage. Thus, as in the case of fraud, duress or undue influence, extrinsic evidence is required to demonstrate that the will that the testator executed did not substantially state his true intention. * * *

Second, the dissent recognized that, based on the policy of the statute of wills, the "risk of subversion of the intent of a testator, who cannot personally defend his testamentary bequest, is without doubt a serious concern." Id., at 24, 448 A.2d 190. The dissent, however, persuasively underscored the counterbalancing "risk of blindly enforcing a testamentary disposition that substantially misstates the testator's true intent." Id.

Again drawing on the analogy to the case of fraud, duress or undue influence, the dissent stated that "[h]ad the decedent's lawyer deliberately and fraudulently altered the second codicil, the relevant extrinsic evidence would unquestionably have been admitted." Id., at 25, 448 A.2d 190. The dissent contended that "innocent misrepresentation is treated as generally equivalent to fraud in terms of its legal consequences." Id. Therefore, the dissent asserted, the "[s]tatute of [w]ills does not compel enforcement of testamentary dispositions that a testator never intended to make." Id.

Similarly, in the present case, had the decedent's attorney deliberately and fraudulently, rather than innocently but mistakenly, misrepresented to the decedent that his will would be valid despite his subsequent marriage, it is at least arguable that the beneficiaries of that fraudulent conduct, namely, the heirs-at-law of the decedent who would inherit in the event of his intestacy, would not be permitted to take advantage of that fraud, and that a court of equity could impress a constructive trust on their inheritance. We conclude that, analogously, in this case, the extrinsic evidence should be admissible to establish the decedent's true intent.

Third, the dissent examined and rejected the two main objections to the admission of extrinsic evidence of a scrivener's error. One objection was "that whatever error the scrivener may have made was validated and ratified by the testator's act in signing his will." Id., at 26, 448 A.2d 190. The dissent responded, correctly in our view, that, although "signing [a] will creates a strong presumption that the will accurately represents the intentions of the testator, that presumption is a rebuttable one." Id. Similarly, in the present case, although the fact that the decedent signed the will may create a rebuttable presumption that he did not intend it to survive his subsequent marriage, that presumption should be rebuttable by persuasive extrinsic evidence to the contrary.

The other objection was "that allowing extrinsic evidence of mistake will give rise to a proliferation of groundless will contests." Id. The dissent presented a two part response, with which we also agree. First, it noted that, "[i]n the law of contracts, where the parol evidence rule has undergone considerable erosion, this risk has not been found to have been unmanageable. In the law of wills, the risk is limited by the narrowness of the exception that this case would warrant ... [namely, to] permit the opponent of a will to introduce extrinsic evidence of the error of a scrivener, and [to] require proof of such an extrinsic error to be established by clear and convincing evidence." Id., at 26–27, 448 A.2d 190

Similarly, in the present case, the admissibility of such extrinsic evidence, in our view, will not prove to be any less manageable than in cases of parol evidence in contract disputes. Furthermore, we would impose the same elevated burden of proof on the proponent of the will in a case such as this. The proponent would have to establish the scrivener's error by clear and convincing evidence.

We recognize that the dissent's position in *Connecticut Junior Republic* would have resulted in the consideration of extrinsic evidence of a scrivener's error offered for the purpose of *preventing* admission of a testamentary document to probate, rather than for the purpose of *procuring* such admission, as in the present case. Regardless of that distinction, however, the mistake doctrine advocated by the dissent in *Connecticut Junior Republic* applies equally to the present case. The dissent in *Connecticut Junior Republic* phrased the issue in that case as follows: "Must the true intent of the testator be thwarted when, because of the mistake of a scrivener, he has formally subscribed to a written bequest that substantially misstates his testamentary intention?" Id., at 22, 448 A.2d 190. That is precisely the issue in the present case. The dissent in *Connecticut Ju-*

nior Republic answered that question in the negative, recognizing that evidence of a scrivener's mistake should be admissible where offered to establish that a written bequest *should not be admitted* to probate because its execution was the product of a mistake of the scrivener and, therefore, did not embody the disposition intended by the testator. Id., at 22–23, 448 A.2d 190. Likewise, in the present case, evidence of a scrivener's mistake should be admissible to establish that a written bequest *should be admitted* to probate because the disposition provided by the bequest would have obtained, in accordance with the decedent's intent, but for the scrivener's mistake.

Finally, we address one other consideration that was not present in *Connecticut Junior Republic,* which might be perceived to be present in this case. That is the potential for past reliance by testators on our prior case law. We do not believe that this is a persuasive consideration. It is very unlikely that, in reliance on such case law, any testators executed wills and deliberately omitted language providing for the contingency of marriage in order to be sure that their wills would be revoked by a subsequent marriage. Moreover, it is very unlikely that any testators, having married after executing such wills, deliberately did not make new testamentary dispositions in reliance on the proposition that their prior wills had been revoked by that subsequent marriage.

Applying these principles to the facts of the present case, we conclude that the extrinsic evidence offered, if believed, could prove clearly and convincingly that there was a scrivener's error that induced the decedent to execute a will that he intended to be valid despite his subsequent marriage. The offer of proof indicates that the evidence would be susceptible to an inference by the fact finder that there had been an implied assertion by the scrivener that the will would be valid despite the decedent's subsequent marriage. This inference could have been bolstered, moreover, by the evidence of the conversations between the decedent and the scrivener shortly before the decedent's death.

The judgment is reversed and the case is remanded for a new trial.

In this opinion KATZ, PALMER and PETERS, JJ., concurred.

BERDON, Associate Justice, concurring.

Although I have some reservation with identifying the error on the part of the attorney as a "scrivener's error" in this case, I concur in the result reached by the majority. More specifically, I agree that Connecticut Junior Republic v. Sharon Hospital, 188 Conn. 1, 448 A.2d 190 (1982) should be overruled. Justice Peters' dissent in *Connecticut Junior Republic,* as joined by Justice Shea, points out that the opponent of a will should be allowed "to introduce extrinsic evidence of the error of a scrivener, and [that] ... proof of such an extrinsic error [must] be established by clear and convincing evidence." Id., at 26, 448 A.2d 190. Although "antiquity does not automatically disqualify common law precedents"; id., at 23, 448 A.2d 190 (Peters, J., dissenting); our law should serve modern needs.

Restatement (Third) of Property, Wills & Donative Transfers (2003)

§ 12.1 Reforming Donative Documents To Correct Mistakes

A donative document, though unambiguous, may be reformed to conform the text to the donor's intention if it is established by clear and convincing evidence (1) that a mistake of fact or law, whether in expression or inducement, affected specific terms of the document; and (2) what the donor's intention was. In determining whether these elements have been established by clear and convincing evidence, direct evidence of intention contradicting the plain meaning of the text as well as other evidence of intention may be considered.

F. Testamentary Capacity

Barnes v. Marshall
Supreme Court of Missouri, 1971
467 S.W.2d 70

HOLMAN, Judge.

This action was filed to contest a will and two codicils executed by Dr. A. H. Marshall a short time before his death which occurred on July 29, 1968. The plaintiff is a daughter of the testator. The defendants are the beneficiaries of the alleged will. A number are relatives of testator, but many are religious, charitable, and fraternal organizations. A trial resulted in a verdict that the paper writings were not the last will and codicils of Dr. Marshall. A number of the defendants have appealed. We will hereinafter refer to the appellants as defendants. We have appellate jurisdiction because the will devises real estate and also because of the amount in dispute.

One of the 'Points Relied On' by defendants is that the verdict is against the greater weight of the credible evidence. Since this court will not weigh the evidence in a case of this nature this point, strictly speaking, would not present anything for review. However, in considering the argument under that point we have concluded that defendants actually intended to present the contention that plaintiff did not make a submissible case and that the trial court erred in not directing a verdict for defendants, and we will so consider the point. The petition charged that testator was not of sound mind and did not have the mental capacity to make a will. The transcript contains more than 1,100 pages and there are a large number of exhibits. We will state the facts as briefly as possible and we think they will clearly support our conclusion that the submission is amply supported by the evidence.

The will, executed April 30, 1968, made specific bequests of testator's home and office furniture and equipment. The remainder of the net estate was devised to trustees, with annual payments to be made from the income to various individuals, churches, charities, and fraternal organizations. Plaintiff, her husband and two children were to receive $5.00 each per year. The estate was appraised in the inventory at $525,400.

The Marshalls had three children: plaintiff who lived in St. Louis, Mary Taylor Myers who lived in Dexter, Missouri, and died in May 1965, and Anetta Ester Vogel who lived near Chicago and who died about a month after her father's death.

In stating the evidence offered by plaintiff we will deal specifically with five witnesses: three lay witnesses because of contentions concerning their testimony, hereinafter discussed, and the two medical witnesses because of the importance we attribute to their testimony. There were many other witnesses whose testimony we will endeavor to summarize in a general way.

Ward Barnes, husband of plaintiff, testified that he visited in the Marshall home frequently from the time of his marriage in 1930 until Dr. Marshall's death; that Mrs. Marshall was a very cultured, refined, patient, and accommodating woman; that he spent a great deal of time with testator and soon learned that testator would dominate the conversation in accordance with a certain pattern; that testator told him that he discontinued his medical practice at the command of the Lord so that he might use his time in saving the nation and the world; that testator had told him 'that the Lord had revealed to him the secrets of heaven; that he was the only man on earth to whom the Lord had revealed these secrets; that he had told him that heaven was a glorious place and that when he went to heaven he would have a beautiful crown and a wonderful throne sitting next to Thee Lord. He said that there were three powers in heaven, the Lord, Thee Lord, and God, and he said that this throne that he would have would be on the right hand side of Thee Lord in heaven. He said that heaven was a wonderful place, Thee Lord had revealed to him that whatever pleasures man had on earth he would have in heaven. If it was whiskey, if it was gambling, if it was women, that these would be provided him.' He stated that testator had also told him that the Lord had given him a special power of calling upon the Lord to right the wrongs which people had done to him; that many times he related instances of various people whom he had 'turned over to the Lord' and the Lord had meted out justice at his instance by taking away the person's wealth, and usually that the person lost his health, had a long period of suffering, and eventually died; that when testator related stories about the men he had turned over to the Lord he would become highly emotional, would pound on the table with his fists, would call these men dirty profane names, his face would become flushed, and the veins in his neck would stand out; that testator had told him that he (testator) had run for Congress on two occasions and had run for President of the United States (although apparently never nominated by any party) on two or three occasions; that he had told him that 'if he were made President of the United States he would cancel all public debt, that he would call in all government bonds and discontinue the interest on all of these obligations, and that he would then print money and control the currency, and that he would kill the damn bankers and the crooks and the thieves that were robbing the people in political office and that the world would then be able to settle down and live in peace.' He stated that on one occasion testator took him to his office and showed him a number of young women who were mailing out material in the interest of his candidacy; that he had said it was costing him 'thousands of dollars to mail this material out, but the Lord had told him to do it and he had no right to go counter to what the Lord had told him to do.' He further stated that in one of his campaigns for President testator had purchased a new car and had many biblical quotations and sayings of his own printed all over the automobile; that he had observed him, campaigning from this car, at the corner of Grand and Lindell Boulevard in St. Louis.

Witness Barnes further testified that testator had told him that Mrs. Marshall had inherited a piece of land and that when it was sold he took part of the money and gave her a note for $3,500; that later Mrs. Marshall had pressed him for payment and had conferred with Moore Haw, an attorney, and that because of that testator had locked her out of the house; that Mrs. Marshall then filed a suit and caused him to pay her the $3,500; that eventually the Marshalls were reconciled and resumed their life together; that at the time Mrs. Marshall died he and plaintiff went immediately to Charleston and at testator's request plaintiff made the funeral arrangements; that testator went to his wife's bedroom and searched the room looking for money and called him and plaintiff in to help him; that he found only a few dollars and then became enraged, 'his fists clenched * * * his hands were shaking, his body was trembling; his face was red and he was—you could see he was in a terrible emotional state as he stood there shaking his fists and shouting. He said, 'I know she had more money than that. * * * Your mother made me pay and that scoundrel Moore Haw, the dirty, low down * * * made me pay that thirty-five hundred dollars,' and he said, 'I want my money back. I want you to give it to me.'" Witness further testified that of the $3,500 testator had paid his wife in 1941 Mrs. Marshall had given plaintiff $1,500; that from the time of his wife's death until his own death testator had frequently demanded that plaintiff send him $3,500 and stated that if she didn't he would cut her out of his will; that it was his opinion that from the time he first became acquainted with him until his death Dr. Marshall was not of sound mind.

Frank Eaves testified that he had known testator for about eight years before his death; that he was Plant Supervisor for Crenshaw Packing Company and that testator would come to the plant about once a week; that he had heard testator talk about having the Lord come down on people, making them suffer, and having them killed; that he said his furnace didn't work and he had the Lord put a curse on it and it had worked good ever since; that he said he 'talked directly to God and God told him things'; that when he would discuss subjects of that kind 'his face would get real red, his eyes would bug out, the vessels would stand out on his neck, he would slobber and shout, and pound on anything available'; that he would sometimes come in dressed in nothing but his nightgown and his house shoes; that on one occasion he came to the plant with nothing on but a housecoat; that he was talking about a rash on his body and opened his housecoat and exposed his private parts to the female secretary and others present. Mr. Eaves was of the opinion that testator was of unsound mind over the period he had known him.

William West testified that he was a drug clerk in the Myers Drug Store in Dexter; that he had known testator from 1951 until his death; that testator came in the drug store about once a month during that period; that he had heard testator say that he talked directly to the Lord and the Lord told him the things he was to do; that one of these was that he should save the world and should be prime minister of the United States; that he also talked about turning people over to the Lord for punishment and when he did so the Lord would mete out the punishment and the men would die, or lose their wealth or something of that nature; that when he would talk about such things he used loud abusive language, his face would be flushed, and he would pound the table; that at the funeral of testator's daughter, Mrs. Myers, he (the witness) started to assist Mrs. Marshall, who was then about 80 years old, out of her chair and Dr. Marshall 'slapped me on the arm and told me to keep my hands off of her'; that he was present when Mrs. Marshall was trying to get out of the car and in so doing exposed a portion of her leg and testator 'bawled her out for it.' Witness was of the opinion that testator, during the time he had known him, was of unsound mind.

Dr. Charles Rolwing testified that he first saw testator professionally in 1940; that at that time testator complained of heart trouble but he was unable to find any evidence of such; that he was of the opinion that he was then suffering from manic-depressive psychosis for which there is no cure and that it would gradually get worse; that he also attended testator from the first part of May 1968 until his death in July; that at that time he was suffering from a serious heart ailment; that he was at that time still suffering from manic-depressive psychosis; that he was of the opinion that on April 30, May 17, and May 24, 1968, testator was of unsound mind.

Plaintiff also presented the testimony of Dr. Paul Hartman, a specialist in psychiatry and neurology, who testified in response to a hypothetical question. This question hypothesized much of the evidence related by the other witnesses for plaintiff and utilizes ten pages of the transcript. In response thereto Dr. Hartman expressed the opinion that

Dr. Marshall was of unsound mind on the dates he executed his will and codicils; that he would classify Dr. Marshall's mental disease as manic-depressive psychosis with paranoid tendencies; that it was his opinion that Dr. Marshall was incapable of generalized logical thinking.

In addition to the foregoing evidence plaintiff testified herself and offered more than a dozen other witnesses, all of whom related unusual conduct and statements of testator. Plaintiff also offered a large number of exhibits in the nature of letters from testator and various publications containing advertisements and statements written by testator. There was evidence that plaintiff had been a dutiful daughter, had been solicitous of testator and her mother, had visited them frequently and often would take prepared food which she knew they liked. A number of these witnesses testified that testator had told them of various men who had wronged him and that he had turned them over to the Lord who meted out punishment in the form of financial loss, illness, death, or all three; that when he would tell of these things he would speak loud, get excited, his face would become red, his eyes bulge out, and he would gesture violently; that testator was unreasonably jealous of his wife and often said that all women who wore short skirts, or smoked, were immoral.

There was testimony that on the Christmas before the death of his daughter, Mary Myers, the Myers and Barnes families ate Christmas dinner with the Marshalls, and after the dinner testator 'jumped on' Mary about her skirt being short and continued doing so until Mary became so upset that she and her husband had to leave.

A number of witnesses testified concerning the fact that testator would go to various public establishments dressed in his nightgown and bathrobe. An article written by testator and published in a local newspaper under date of June 4, 1942, under the heading of 'DR. MARSHALL SAYS,' contained the following: 'Providence they say always raises up a great leader in every crisis * * *. I am that great leader. I am that prophet that Moses and all the other prophets have spoken about. I am the Messiah that the people of this world have been talking and praying about and believing and hoping that he would soon show up. I am the inspired prophet.'

In contending that plaintiff did not make a submissible case defendants point to the testimony of their witnesses to the effect that testator was of sound mind and was calm, quiet, and collected on the day the will was executed. The difficulty with that argument is that in determining this question 'we must disregard the evidence offered by defendants unless it aids plaintiffs' case, accept plaintiffs' evidence as true, and give them the benefit of every inference which may legitimately be drawn from it.' Sturm v. Routh, Mo.Sup., 373 S.W.2d 922, 923.

It is also contended that most of plaintiff's evidence dealt with testator's 'sickness, peculiarities, eccentricities, miserliness, neglect of person or clothing, forgetfulness, anger, high temper, unusual or peculiar political and religious views, jealousy, mistreatment of family, unusual moral views, and repeating of stories, which are not evidence of testamentary incapacity or of unsound mind.'

As we have indicated, we do not agree with defendants' contentions. We have stated a portion of the evidence and it need not be repeated here. It is sufficient to say that we think testator's stated views on government, religion, morals, and finances go beyond the classification of peculiarities and eccentricities and are sufficient evidence from which a jury could reasonably find he was of unsound mind. When we add the strong medical testimony to that of the lay witnesses there would seem to be no doubt that a submissible case was made.

Defendants also point out that there is evidence that a person suffering from manic-depressive psychosis has periods of normalcy between the abnormal periods of elation or depression and that testator was in a normal period at the time the will was executed. The mental condition of testator at the precise time the will was executed was a question for the jury to decide. The jury was obviously persuaded that he was not of sound mind and since there was evidence to support that verdict it is conclusive.

* * *

Plaintiff's evidence relating to the mental condition of testator encompassed the period from 1940 until his death in 1968. The next point briefed by defendants is that the court erred in admitting evidence of occurrences years prior to the execution of the will because it was too remote to have any probative value. It is true, as defendants contend, that '[e]vidence, not too remote, of mental unsoundness either before or after the will's execution is admissible, provided it indicates that such unsoundness existed at the time the will was made.' Rothwell v. Love, Mo.Sup., 241 S.W.2d 893, 895. There can be no question, however, but that evidence concerning testator's mental condition long prior to the execution of the will is admissible if it tends to show his condition at the time of said execution. Holton v. Cochran, 208 Mo. 314, 106 S.W. 1035, l.c. 1069; Buford v. Gruber, 223 Mo. 231, 122 S.W. 717; Clingenpeel v. Citizens' Trust Co., Mo.Sup., 240 S.W. 177. Dr. Rolwing testified that he treated testator in 1940 and that he was of unsound mind at that time; that he was suffering from manic-depressive psychosis, an incurable mental disease which would gradually get worse. That testimony was certainly admissible as it would have a direct bearing on testator's mental condition at the time the will was executed. And in view of that testimony it was appropriate to admit other evidence concerning testator's statements and conduct tending to support the submission of mental incapacity occurring during the intervening period. This point is accordingly ruled adversely to defendants' contention.

The next point briefed by defendants is that the court erred in permitting lay witnesses Ward Barnes, Frank Eaves, and William L. West to express an opinion that testator was of unsound mind. This for the reason that the facts related by those witnesses were not inconsistent with sanity and hence the necessary foundation was not established. The rule regarding the competency of lay witnesses to express an opinion on the issue as to whether a person is or is not of sound mind is that 'a lay witness is not competent to testify that, in the opinion of such witness, a person is of unsound mind or insane, without first relating the facts upon which such opinion is based; and, when the facts have been stated by such lay witness, unless such facts are inconsistent with such person's sanity, the opinion of such lay witness that the person under consideration was insane or of unsound mind, is not admissible in evidence and may not be received. * * * In this connection it has repeatedly been determined that evidence of sickness, old age, peculiarities, eccentricities in dress or oddities of habit, forgetfulness, inability to recognize friends, feebleness resulting from illness, and other facts or circumstances not inconsistent with the ability to understand the ordinary affairs of life, comprehend the nature and extent of one's property and the natural objects of his bounty, and which are not inconsistent with sanity, cannot be used as a basis for the opinion testimony of a lay witness that a person is of unsound mind or insane. * * * 'The rule is well settled that, ordinarily, before a lay witness will be permitted to give his opinion that a person is of unsound mind, he must first detail the facts upon which he bases such opinion, but if he expresses an opinion that such person is of sound mind, he is not required to detail the facts upon which he founds his opinion. The reason for the rule is obvious. An opinion that a person is of unsound mind is based upon abnormal or unnatural acts and conduct of such person, while an opinion of soundness of mind is founded upon the absence of such acts and conduct." Lee v. Ullery, 346 Mo. 236, 140 S.W.2d 5, l.c. 9, 10.

Because of this point we have heretofore detailed the testimony of these three witnesses in the factual statement and such need not be repeated here. We think it is obvious that each witness detailed sufficient facts upon which to base the opinion stated. Those facts went far beyond a mere showing of peculiarities and eccentricities. They were clearly inconsistent with the conclusion that testator was of sound mind. The facts detailed by these witnesses are quite different from those stated by the witnesses in Lewis v. McCullough, Mo.Sup., 413 S.W.2d 499, the case upon which defendants rely.

The defendants also contend that the court erred in refusing to permit their witness, Harris D. Rodgers, to express an opinion that testator was of sound mind. This witness operated an abstract business in Benton, Missouri, which is about 20 miles from Charleston. However, he had known testator for about 35 years and had seen and visited with him on an average of from two to four times a year. We have concluded that we need not determine whether or not the court erred in excluding this testimony. This for the reason that it is 'well settled that, if in a specific instance the evidence should not have been excluded, the error is harmless if the same evidence is found in the testimony of the same or other witnesses, given before or after the objection was sustained.' Steffen v. Southwestern Bell Telephone Co., 331 Mo. 574, 56 S.W.2d 47, 48. In this instance defendants offered ten lay witnesses who were permitted to testify that in their opinion testator was of sound mind. With such an abundance of testimony on that issue it seems apparent to us that the exclusion of the opinion of one additional witness could not have been prejudicial. No reversible error appearing this point is ruled adversely to defendants.

Defendants' final contention is that the court erred in refusing to give their proffered Instruction No. P—1. They say that the instructions given were not sufficient to properly instruct the jury and that P—1 was necessary to clarify the issues. The instructions given submitted the issue as to whether testator was of sound and disposing mind and memory at the time he signed the documents. Also given was Instruction No. 8 which is MAI 15.01 and which defines the phrase 'sound and disposing mind and memory.'

Instruction P—1 reads as follows:

'The Court instructs the jury that, in determining the issue of whether Dr. A. H. Marshall was of sound and disposing mind and memory, you may take into consideration the instrument itself and all its provisions, in connection with all other facts and circumstances in evidence. But, under the law of the State of Missouri, Dr. A. H. Marshall was not obligated to leave any part of his estate to the plaintiff, Julia Amma Barnes, and he was not obliged to mention plaintiff in his will. A man who is of sound and disposing mind and memory as defined by Instruction No. _ _ has the right to dispose of his property by will as he may choose, even to the entire exclusion of those who, but for the will, would be the heirs of his estate; and if after considering all the evidence in the case, including the instrument itself and all its provisions, you believe that Dr. A. H. Marshall was of sound and disposing mind and memory, you will not further consider whether said disposition was appropriate or unappropriate. The jury should not substitute its judgment for the testator's judgment, nor should they determine the case upon the wisdom or the justice of the disposition made by the testator of his property; whether such disposition is just or right is a question for the testator, and for none other than the testator.'

It will be noted that P—1 is clearly a cautionary instruction. And the rule is well established that '[t]he giving of cautionary instructions is largely within the discretion of the trial court and unless such discretion is abused it will not be interfered with on appeal.' Bucks v. Hamill, 358 Mo. 617, 216 S.W.2d 423, 425. We also have the view that the instruction is somewhat argumentative in its nature. In that connection this court recently said that 'Missouri Approved Instructions were adopted so that questions of fact may be accurately and concisely submitted to a jury in lieu of the vast amount of surplusage that formerly was found in many instructions.' Stemme v. Siedhoff, Mo.Sup., 427 S.W.2d 461, 466. Moreover, it appears that the manner in which P—1 is prepared is out of harmony with the direction that 'instructions shall be simple, brief, impartial, free from argument * * *.' S.Ct. Rule 70.01(e), V.A.M.R. The ultimate issues were properly submitted to the jury and we do not consider it necessary or desirable that P—1 should have been given. The trial court did not abuse its discretion in refusing to give it and hence no reversible error occurred.

The judgment is affirmed.

All concur.

Notes

In addition to mental capacity, the lack of testamentary capacity could occur because the testator was of insufficient age to execute a Last Will and Testament in that jurisdiction. Most states require that the testator be at least eighteen years-of-age. Lack of age and lack of the requisite mental capacity at the moment of execution would make the entire Last Will and Testament null and void. But the legal test for testamentary capacity is a minimal one. To make a valid Will, it is sufficient that the testator "understands the nature of the business in which he is engaged and when making a will, has a recollection of the property he means to dispose of, the object or objects of his bounty, and how he wishes to dispose of his property." Milhoan v. Koenig, 196 W. Va. 163, 166, 469 S.E.2d 99, 102 (1996). This test may be met even when the testator is under guardianship or has been committed to a mental facility. See, e.g., In re Estate of Gentry, 32 Or. App. 45, 573 P.2d 322 (1978). Even if the testator lacks capacity, he or she may be within a "lucid interval" and, thus, possess capacity at the moment of execution but not otherwise. See, e.g., Lee v. Lee, 337 So. 2d 713 (Miss. 1976); Daley v. Boroughs, 310 Ark. 274, 835 S.W.2d 858 (1992). Often it is the attorney who must make the initial and pivotal decision of whether the client possesses testamentary capacity; failure to inquire could raise professional responsibility consequences. See, e.g., Gonsalves v. Superior Court, 19 Cal. App. 4th 1366, 24 Cal. Rptr. 2d 52 (1993) (court held that an attorney who fails to investigate the testamentary capacity of his or her client was not liable in tort to a former beneficiary disinherited by the Will drawn by the attorney; the attorney's primary duty is to the client for whom he or she is drafting the Will). Ethical ramifications arise from this responsibility. See Jan E. Rein, *Ethics and the Questionably Competent Client: What the Model Rules Say and Don't Say*, 9 STAN. L. & POLICY REV. 241 (1998).

Most states place the burden of proof in contesting the Will on any contestant, but the proponents of the Will have the burden of proof for due execution of the formalities. See CAL. PROB. CODE § 8252(a) (2004). A jury may play an instrumental role in determining capacity, as was illustrated in the *Barnes* decision, but some states, like California, for example, ban juries from Will contest cases. *See* CAL. PROB. CODE § 8252(b) (2004): "The court shall try and determine any contested issue of fact that affects the validity of the will." Similar proposals to abolish jury participation have been made in other states. *See, e.g.,* Comment, *The Pros and Cons of Jury Trials in Will Contests*, 1990 U. CHI. LEGAL F. 529 (1990).

Uniform Probate Code (2003)

§ 3-407. [Formal Testacy Proceedings; Burdens in Contested Cases].

In contested cases, petitioners who seek to establish intestacy have the burden of establishing prima facie proof of death, venue, and heirship. Proponents of a will have the burden of establishing prima facie proof of due execution in all cases, and, if they are also petitioners, prima facie proof of death and venue. Contestants of a will have the burden of establishing lack of testamentary intent or capacity, undue influence, fraud, duress, mistake or revocation. Parties have the ultimate burden of persuasion as to matters with respect to which they have the initial burden of proof. If a will is opposed by the petition for probate of a later will revoking the former, it shall be determined first whether the later will is entitled to probate, and if a will is opposed by a petition for a declaration of intestacy, it shall be determined first whether the will is entitled to probate.

G. Delusion

In re Hargrove's Will

Supreme Court, Appellate Division, First Department, 1941
262 A.D. 202, 28 N.Y.S.2d 571, aff'd 288 N.Y. 604, 42 N.E.2d 608 (1942)

TOWNLEY, J.

The decree appealed from denies probate to the will of Ernest Temple Hargrove. This decree was based upon the verdict of the jury which by a vote of ten to two found the deceased lacking in testamentary capacity. The jury's finding was based upon its conclusion that the testator suffered from an insane delusion that two children born to his wife during their marriage were not his and that as a consequence the testator did not know the true objects of his bounty. The will made no provision for these children but left all of his property to Mrs. Clement Griscom 'as an inadequate acknowledgment of the lifelong kindness shown to me by my business associate and intimate personal friend, her late husband.'

With the exception of this claimed delusion about the paternity of his children there is no serious claim of mental deficiency. The testator appears to have been a very successful business man, capable of managing large interests with conspicuous success and equally successful in the management of many charitable and religious activities in which he became interested. He was active as president and head of the Griscom-Russell Company, manufacturers of heavy machinery, up to within a month of his death, on April 8, 1939. The instrument offered for probate was in his own handwriting and executed by him on December 17, 1923. Ten witnesses, all men of importance in New York city, testified that decedent was at all times of sound mind and a man of unusual intelligence and four of these witnesses were called by the contestants.

The only witnesses to the contrary were an alienist who had never seen him and the testator's divorced wife who had not seen him for thirty-one years prior to his death except for an accidental meeting in a book store twenty years prior to his death. As bearing on the credibility of the latter it is significant that she denied here that the testator prior to his death had ever accused her of being indiscreet, whereas she had obtained a Colorado divorce from the testator in which she alleged that about three years prior to the date of her complaint, the decedent had accused her of being indiscreet in her association with certain persons and that in November, 1905, he had also made similar charges. In that action the jury found the decedent guilty of the matters charged in the complaint.

The law is that assuming that decedent was mistaken in his belief that he was not the father of the children of his divorced wife, that fact would not necessarily establish testator's incapacity. The rule applicable to the determination of the question was clearly stated in Matter of White (121 N. Y. 406, 413) as follows: 'Delusion is insanity, where one persistently believes supposed facts, which have no real existence, except in his perverted imagination, and against all evidence and probability, and conducts himself, however logically, upon the assumption of their existence. That was so held in Seamen's Society v. Hopper [33 N. Y. 624]. But, if there are facts, however insufficient they may in reality be, from which a prejudiced, or a narrow or a bigoted mind might derive a particular idea, or belief, it cannot be said that the mind is diseased in that respect. The belief may be illogical, or preposterous, but it is not, therefore, evidence of insanity in the person. Persons do not always reason logically, or correctly, from facts, and that may be because of their prejudices, or of the perversity, or peculiar construction of their minds. Wills, however, do not depend for their validity upon the testator's ability to reason logically, or upon his freedom from prejudice.'

The question presented, therefore, is whether there is any rational basis, however slight, for the decedent's belief that he was not the father. The story of the married life of the Hargroves may be summarized as follows: The deceased married Aimee Neresheimer in 1899. For the next six years he traveled in Europe, Africa and Australia with her. A son was born in Brussels in February, 1902, and a daughter in Dresden in 1904. In 1905 the decedent and his children returned to the United States and took up a residence in Denver, Col. In Denver, the testator became interested in the business of his then father-in-law and in that connection met and became friendly with one Smith, a friend of his father-in-law and his attorney. In the latter part of 1906 the testator's wife asked him for a divorce, claiming incompatibility. This led to many conferences in which testator's father-in-law and Smith assumed to act as friendly advisers. An action for divorce on the ground of cruelty was brought. The entire proceeding from the service of process to the entry of judgment was accomplished in a single day. Within an hour after the entry of the decree Smith, whom decedent had consulted about his divorce, procured a divorce from his own wife and announced that he would marry the wife of the testator.

The conditions surrounding these decrees created a considerable scandal in Denver. Within a month Smith and the testator's wife were married at the alleged insistence of her father. The testator apparently did not discover the remarriage for some months. He then applied to have the divorce set aside on the ground of fraud and alleged that his wife prior thereto had been guilty of improper relations with Smith. This application was denied upon technical grounds. He thereafter left Denver and came to New York where he was befriended by Clement Griscom, became associated with him in business and died the president of his company. Mr. Griscom's wife is named as beneficiary in this will. Neither the divorced wife nor the children communicated with the deceased during the thirty-one years intervening before his death.

Decedent left an affidavit with his executor stating that his divorced wife had confessed to him that the children were not his and that he had satisfied himself that that was so. He spoke of this belief only to his intimate friends and then only when necessary. His entire conduct in this connection was that of a dignified considerate gentleman and there is nothing in connection therewith which justifies the belief that his opinion was based on an insane delusion. All of his reasons for his belief, of course, cannot be known. They relate to the intimate personal affairs incident to the marriage relation. When consideration is given, however, to his unfortunate experiences in connection with his divorce, the fact of his belief in his wife's infidelity certified to by her under oath in her divorce proceeding and confirmed by the formal affidavit left by him with his executor, it cannot be said that his belief on this subject was entirely without reason, although possibly mistaken.

Upon the foregoing facts the finding that the decedent lacked testamentary capacity cannot be sustained. The conclusion we have reached, however, must not be considered as involving any finding as to the legitimacy of the children involved.

That part of the decree that held that the instrument offered for probate was not revoked by the subsequent codicil was clearly correct. This codicil concededly contained no terms of revocation of the will. The precise terms were not established. There was no inherent inconsistency with the original testamentary plan of the decedent. The revocation of the codicil, therefore, did not necessarily result in the destruction of the will, even assuming the codicil was sufficiently proved. As was said in Osburn v. Rochester Trust & S. D. Co. (209 N. Y. 54, 56): 'While it might often happen that the codicil would be so related to and dependent on the will that it would be impossible to destroy the latter without carrying down the former, the reverse would ordinarily not be true. There would seem to be no good reason why a testator should not be allowed to revoke a codicil, which might be as in this case an entirely separate and distinct instrument, without destroying his will, in itself a full and complete instrument.'

The decree so far as appealed from by the contestants should be affirmed. In so far as appealed from by the proponent, it should be reversed, with costs to said appellant payable out of the estate, and the will admitted to probate.

MARTIN, P. J., and CALLAHAN, J., concur.

GLENNON and DORE, JJ., dissent.

GLENNON, Justice (dissenting).

There is ample testimony in the record to support the verdict of the jury that Ernest Temple Hargrove, at the time of the execution of the paper offered for probate, was not of sound and disposing mind and memory. In the course of his charge to the jury, the surrogate clearly stated the issue between the parties to the will contest in the following language: 'You can well see that this question is a comparatively simple one. I do not mean by that that it may be simple for you to decide, but I think the issue is simple. It comes down to the issue as to whether or not Mrs. Neres did tell Mr. Hargrove that these children were not his, for of course, if she told him that, and she was the mother of these children, then of course he had ample basis in fact for his belief that these children were not his. However, if her testimony is truthful, that she never told him of this as he says she did, then if this was the mere creature of his imagination, you may find that he was suffering from an insane delusion on this subject.'

At the conclusion of the charge, counsel for the proponent said in part: 'With that addition, if your Honor please, the proponent is entirely satisfied with your Honor's charge.'

The evidence clearly shows that William Archibald Temple Hargrove, who was born in Brussels, Belgium, in February, 1902, is the legitimate son of Ernest Temple Hargrove, deceased, and the latter's former wife, Aimee Neres, and that Joan Leona Constance Hargrove, who was born on August 14, 1904, in Dresden, Germany, is the legitimate daughter of the same parents. At the outset it might be well to note that the son bears in part the given name of the decedent, whereas the daughter, as part of her name, was christened Constance, after the decedent's sister.

The decedent first became acquainted with Aimee Neres, nee Neresheimer, when she was about twelve years of age. At that time she lived with her parents in Bayside, Long Island.

When Mrs. Neres was fourteen years of age, in 1897, the decedent proposed marriage to her and took her to England, under the chaperonage of his sister Constance, to meet his parents. He repeated his proposal upon their return from England, but her father objected to the marriage at that time on account of her age and sent her to a convent in Canada, where she remained for a year and a half. When Mrs. Neres became sixteen years of age, the marriage took place.

They went to England on their honeymoon and thence to the Peace Conference at the Hague. In connection with his work, which we do not deem necessary to go into at this time, they traveled throughout the world. The testimony of Mrs. Neres indicates that their son was conceived in Australia and born in Brussels, while the daughter was conceived in Paris and born, as heretofore noted, in Dresden.

About 1905, they returned to the United States and went to Boulder, Col., to the home where Mrs. Neres' parents then resided and later they moved to Denver, where they took up a residence. We do not believe it necessary to refer at any length to the divorce which was obtained by Mrs. Neres in 1906, since the speed with which it was effected has been covered in the majority opinion.

In his application, sworn to by the decedent on December 12, 1907, to set aside the divorce which Mrs. Neres had obtained, the decedent said in part: 'That your petitioner then and there informed said Smith, as his said attorney, that such divorce proceedings would bring disgrace upon the children of said plaintiff and your petitioner, and that he, your petitioner, would resist such proceedings to the utmost, and asked said Smith to aid him in pacifying and conciliating said plaintiff in order to avoid said proposed action for divorce.'

It must be conceded that the children, to whom reference was made in the quoted sentence, were his son William and his daughter Joan, and still the decedent under date of February 20, 1920, made the following affidavit which appears in the record:

'ERNEST TEMPLE HARGROVE
10 Horatio Street
New York

'Ernest Temple Hargrove of the city and county of New York, being duly sworn, deposeth and saith that he was married to a girl named Amy Neresheimer of Bayside, Long Island, toward the end of the year 1899, though he is not certain of this date; that he took this woman to Europe with him as his wife and that they also visited South Africa and Australia; that said woman gave birth to two children, the first a boy, born in Brussels, and the second a girl born near Dresden; that in 1894 or 1895, deponent took this woman with the two said children to Denver, Colorado, where her parents were then living; that deponent engaged in business with said woman's father, and with a Denver lawyer named Milton Smith; that within a year of their arrival in Denver, said woman declared her determination to obtain a divorce from deponent; that deponent, knowing she had no grounds for a divorce, thereupon requested said Milton Smith to speak to said woman and to tell her she could not obtain a divorce; that said Milton Smith, to the amazement of deponent, assured him that any woman could get a divorce in Colorado who for any reason whatever was dissatisfied with her husband, showing deponent law books and recent decisions to substantiate this statement; that said Milton Smith urged deponent, so as to avoid publicity and scandal, to concede said woman a divorce, stating to deponent that in all probability a reconciliation would take place in six months; that deponent was at last persuaded and that said woman obtained a decree of divorce within a few weeks thereafter; that within two weeks after said divorce had been obtained by her, deponent learned that Milton Smith had at the same time divorced his own wife, and that Milton Smith had at once married deponent's former wife; that deponent, realizing he had been tricked, was angry, and at an interview with his former wife insisted that she must confess the whole truth to deponent about the past; that said woman thereupon confessed that she had cohabited with a number of men, whose names she gave, after her marriage with deponent, and that two of these men, one a citizen of Chicago, whose name deponent has forgotten, and another a German doctor, whose name was Weidner, were respectively the fathers of her two children; said woman reminded deponent of certain facts, which at the time he had not understood, and which tended to prove that he himself could not have been the father of said children; that deponent shortly thereafter visited Chicago and accused said man, a citizen of Chicago, of being the father of the older of two said children; that said man confessed that he had cohabited with said woman and that said woman at that time had declared her intense desire to have a child by him and that they had cohabited together a number of times at her solicitation; that deponent later verified the other statements said woman made to him during said interview, and that deponent obtained absolute evidence that neither of said children was his; that deponent also investigated said woman's life prior to her marriage to him and learned that she had been common property in and around Bayside, Flushing, and other small towns on Long Island, prior to said marriage, and that she had been notorious as an immoral character; that deponent knows said woman to be grasping and unscrupulous, and that he makes this affidavit to facilitate the task of the executors of his will in the event that said woman or her children should dare to claim any share of deponent's estate in spite of the explicit terms of said will; and that deponent swears that said woman married deponent under false pretenses and by lying and by concealing vital facts, and that deponent has no children, by her or by any other woman.

'In testimony whereof, deponent hath hereunto subscribed his name and affixed his seal on this twentieth day of February in the year 1920.

'ERNEST TEMPLE HARGROVE.'

Since the jury had this exhibit before it, they must have realized that the alleged confession of Aimee Neres as to her intimacy with the citizen of Chicago, who might be styled as the forgotten man, and the German doctor, were the expressions of a mind afflicted with a delusion as to the paternity of his children who would be, under normal conditions, the natural objects of his bounty. If the vigorous denials of Aimee Neres as to these groundless charges of misconduct be cast aside, although the jury had the right to believe her denials and did so, we may ask when was the so-called confession obtained? Manifestly, it could not have been immediately subsequent to her marriage with Milton Smith since, as we have heretofore pointed out, in his affidavit of December, 1907, the decedent indicated that these, his two children, were then uppermost in his mind. Neither could it have been at the chance meeting in a book store in New York in September, 1921, where in the first instance the decedent failed to recognize his former wife and upon being apprised of her identity, the record shows that he fled. Furthermore, that meeting took place about a year after the affidavit of February 20, 1920, was sworn to.

The jury undoubtedly noted that part of the affidavit wherein the decedent referred to his investigations of Aimee Neres' life as a child and stated that she had been 'common property' in and around Bayside, Flushing, and other small towns on Long Island. The marriage it will be remembered took place when she was only sixteen years of age, very shortly after she left the school in Canada.

It seems almost absurd to believe that an intensely religious man, which concededly the decedent was, could have subscribed his name, affixed his seal and sworn to a document containing such outlandish statements if he was not suffering from an insane delusion concerning his children who normally would be the proper objects of his bounty.

We of the minority do not doubt for a moment that in other matters the decedent was capable of sound reasoning. He was, what might be termed, an outstanding success in the business world. Still we repeat that in so far as his children were concerned, he was suffering from an insane delusion.

The question here involved is similar to that which appeared in Riggs v. American Tract Society (95 N. Y. 503) wherein Judge DANFORTH said, in part:

'The trial judge * * * confined their [the jury's] inquiry to the question whether he was affected with insane delusions in regard to the persons who were the natural objects of his bounty * * * and left them to say * * * whether that delusion * * * 'so took possession of his mind that he could not act upon that subject with sense.' * * *.

'The law was well stated. If delusion existed upon one subject, he was as to that of unsound mind, although in regard to other subjects he might reason and act like a rational man.'

The facts disclosed in the case now under consideration clearly raised an issue for the jury and may not be disposed of by the court as an issue of law. In Matter of Barney (185 App. Div. 782, 794), this court, through LAUGHLIN, J., said: 'The well-settled rule in this class of cases is that if there be more than a mere scintilla of evidence tending to show incompetency to make a will and of such a character that different inferences may fairly be drawn therefrom, the case must be decided as one of fact and if the trial be before a jury it must be left with the jury. (Hagan v. Sone, 174 N. Y. 317.)' (See, also, Matter of Eno, 196 App. Div. 131, 155.)

We are in accord with the views expressed in the majority opinion with reference to the contestants' cross-appeal which pertains to the so-called codicil. We rest our conclusion solely upon the proposition that the jury had ample evidence before it to reach a verdict to sustain the finding that at the time of the execution of the paper offered for probate Ernest Temple Hargrove was not of sound and disposing mind and memory.

DORE, J., concurs.

Decree, so far as appealed from by the contestants, unanimously affirmed. Decree, so far as appealed from by the proponent, reversed, with costs to said appellant payable out of the estate, the will admitted to probate, and proceeding remitted to the Surrogate's Court in accordance with opinion.

H. Undue Influence

It is safe to say that influence is a consistent factor in motivating a testator to devise or bequeath property to a beneficiary. The difficulty is in defining what is undue influence. As the American family becomes more "functional" and less "form" oriented in its definition, expectancy of inheritance becomes less precise, and more surprises occur in the distribution of assets upon death. Divorce, increasing numbers of stepchildren, and remarriage contribute to a rise in Will contest litigation. Many of these contests originate from disappointment over asset distribution, and litigants assert undue influence. *See* Jeffrey P. Rosenfeld, *Will Contests, Legacies of Aging and Social Change, in* INHERITANCE AND WEALTH IN AMERICA, 173 (Robert K. Miller, Jr. & Stephen J. McNamee eds., 1998). Often a person with standing—for example, a blood relative—argues that the Will is a product of the undue influence of another individual. The other person could be in a social, charitable, sexual, or supportive role with the testator, and the blood relative argues that this role provided the opportunity for undue influence and unjust enrichment.

In analyzing the next three cases, utilize these analytical steps to determine if the testator was unduly influenced by the beneficiary of the Last Will and Testament:

(1) Upon whom is the burden of proof placed—the proponent of the Will (the beneficiary interest) or the contestant asserting undue influence?

(2) Does the burden of proof shift because of the presence of a confidential relationship between the testator and the beneficiary? Confidential relationships include attorney-client, doctor-patient, priest-penitent, and guardian-ward relationships, or a relationship of trust.

(3) If the burden shifts and a presumption of confidentiality is created, what is the level of proof needed to rebut that presumption and to allow the Will's provision to be probated? If the burden does not shift, what is the level of proof needed to prove the undue influence?

(4) Are there suspicious circumstances that assist in creating a presumption of undue influence?

(5) Is the focus on the mind of the testator or on the conduct of the beneficiary?

(6) What is the remedy to be imposed if undue influence is established? Should all or a portion of the Will be voided?

1. Family

Haynes v. First National State Bank of New Jersey

Supreme Court of New Jersey, 1981
87 N.J. 163, 432 A.2d 890

HANDLER, J.

This is a will contest in which the plaintiffs, two of the decedent's six grandchildren, seek to set aside the probate of their grandmother's will and two related trust agreements. The major issue presented is whether the will is invalid on the grounds of "undue influence" attributable to the fact that the attorney, who advised the testatrix and prepared the testamentary instruments, was also the attorney for the principal beneficiary, the testatrix's daughter, in whom the testatrix had reposed trust, confidence and dependency. A second question concerns the enforceability of a "non-contestability" or *in terrorem* clause in the testamentary documents under New Jersey common law since the decedent died before the effective date of the new probate code, N.J.S.A. 3A:2A-32, which invalidates such clauses in wills.

In an unreported opinion upholding the probate of the will and related trusts, the trial court held that the circumstances created a presumption of undue influence but that this presumption had been rebutted by defendants. It ruled further that the *in terrorem* clause was unenforceable. The case was appealed to the Appellate Division, which affirmed the trial court as to the lack of undue influence, sustaining the probate of the will and its judgment upholding the related trust agreements, but disagreed with the trial court's ruling that the *in terrorem* clause was unenforceable. Plaintiffs then filed their petition for certification which was granted. 85 N.J. 99, 425 A.2d 264 (1980).

* * *

The issues raised by this appeal, particularly whether the contested will was invalid as a result of "undue influence," require a full exposition of the facts.

Mrs. Isabel Dutrow, the testatrix, was the widow of Charles E. Dutrow, an employee of Ralston Purina Co. who had acquired substantial stock in that corporation. Upon his death the stock, aggregating almost eight million dollars, was distributed to his widow and their two daughters, both outright and in trust.

Betty Haynes, one of the daughters of Charles and Isabel Dutrow, came with her two sons to live with her parents in the Dutrow family home in York, Pennsylvania in 1941 while Betty's husband was in military service during World War II. Following Charles Dutrow's death in 1945 and her own divorce, Betty and her sons continued to live with Mrs. Dutrow in York. The relationships between mother and daughter were extremely close, Mrs. Dutrow having deep affection for Betty, as well as her grandsons whom she practically raised. The two boys, however, left the York home sometime around 1968 to the considerable aggravation and disappointment of their grandmother.[1] But Betty remained with her mother until Betty's death in June 1973.

At the time of Betty's death, she had been living with her mother for more than 30 years. Mrs. Dutrow was then 84 years old and suffered from a number of ailments in-

---

1. The Haynes children apparently undertook lifestyles which caused both their mother and grandmother great anguish: one son resisted military service and took refuge in Canada during the Vietnam war and both had live-in girlfriends whom they eventually married.

cluding glaucoma, cataracts and diverticulitis, and had recently broken her hip. Mrs. Dutrow, distraught over the death of her closest daughter and somewhat alienated from the Haynes children, decided to move in with her younger daughter, Dorcas Cotsworth, and Dorcas' husband, John, who had homes in Short Hills and Bay Head, New Jersey. This decision was a reasonable one, freely made by Mrs. Dutrow, who despite her age, physical condition and feelings of despair was and remained an alert, intelligent and commanding personality until the time of her death.

During her lifetime, Mrs. Dutrow executed a great many wills and trust agreements. All of these instruments, as well as those her husband had executed prior to his death, were prepared by the longstanding family attorney, Richard Stevens, of Philadelphia. By June 1967 Stevens had prepared five wills and several codicils for Mrs. Dutrow.

As of the time she moved in with the Cotsworths, Mrs. Dutrow's estate plan reflected a basic disposition to treat the Haynes and the Cotsworth family branches equally. During the last four years of her life, however, while living with daughter Dorcas, Mrs. Dutrow's will went through a series of changes which drastically favored Dorcas and her children while diminishing and excluding the interests of the Haynes brothers. These changes, and their surrounding circumstances, bear most weightily upon the issue of undue influence.

Shortly after moving in with Dorcas, following a conference between her daughter and Stevens, the first of many will and trust changes was made by Mrs. Dutrow on July 25, 1973. Under the new provisions of the will, Mrs. Dutrow's residuary estate was to be divided into two equal trusts, one for Dorcas, the principal of which Dorcas could invade up to certain limits and the other a trust with income to each of the Haynes boys without a power of invasion. A new will and an inter vivos trust with almost identical provisions, including approximately 60,000 shares of Ralston Purina stock, were later executed on November 24, 1973 and December 4, 1973, respectively. Mrs. Dutrow also gave Dorcas 5,000 shares of stock outright to compensate her for the expense of having Mrs. Dutrow live with her.

During the time these instruments were being drawn, Dorcas and her husband, John Cotsworth, began actively to express their views about Mrs. Dutrow's estate plans to Stevens. In a meeting between Stevens, Mrs. Dutrow, and the Cotsworths on November 13, 1973 at the Cotsworth home in Short Hills, John Cotsworth gave Stevens two charts of Mrs. Dutrow's estate which Cotsworth had prepared. According to Stevens' testimony at trial, the import of the charts was to make "substantial outright gifts to the members of the Cotsworth family and smaller gifts to [plaintiffs, the Haynes children]." Stevens further testified that Mrs. Dutrow had told him at this meeting that the pressure upon her by the Cotsworths to change her will was enormous. On November 19, 1973, John Cotsworth wrote Stevens a long letter in which he summarized what he, Cotsworth, saw as Mrs. Dutrow's "objectives" with regard to her estate plans and then detailing in over five pages the calculations as to how these "objectives" could be achieved. An important aspect of his proposal was to deplete substantially the estate to simplify Mrs. Dutrow's "money worries." Cotsworth further noted at the beginning of this letter to Stevens that

> [o]ur joint obligation—you and the family—is to accomplish these objectives with minimum tax effects upon the total estate. Obviously you are in a far better position to work out the details than I am, but you appear reluctant to go as fast or as far as I have suggested for reasons that are not clear to us.

Then, on November 26, 1973, Cotsworth proceeded to consult Grant Buttermore, his own lawyer, regarding Mrs. Dutrow's estate plans. Buttermore had been the attorney for the Cotsworth family and the Cotsworth family business, the Berry Steel Corporation, for six to seven years and had provided substantial legal advice concerning the corporation. He had also prepared wills for both Mr. and Mrs. Cotsworth and some of their children. For all intents and purposes, Buttermore can be viewed as having been the family attorney for the Cotsworths.

On November 29, 1973, following the initial contact by her husband, Dorcas Cotsworth went to Buttermore concerning the trust agreement of November 24 that Stevens had prepared for her mother. As a result, Buttermore called Stevens while Dorcas was in his office and discussed the matter of Mrs. Dutrow's domicile. This subject, in addition to a proposal concerning "gifting" by Mrs. Dutrow, had earlier been broached to Buttermore by John Cotsworth. Both lawyers agreed that Mrs. Dutrow's domicile should be changed to New Jersey for tax purposes and Buttermore made the change on the instrument by hand. Later that day Buttermore wrote to Stevens to confirm the results of the call, as well as the fact that the Cotsworths were personally involved in Mrs. Dutrow's estate planning, viz:

> We are in the process of reviewing Mrs. Dutrow's estate with her and Mr. and Mrs. Cotsworth along the lines suggested by Mr. Cotsworth in his outline heretofore submitted to you.

Buttermore concluded this letter by relaying Mrs. Dutrow's request to Stevens to provide "a complete list of all [her] assets ... in order that we may make a proper analysis."

Stevens immediately responded, writing separate letters to Buttermore and Mrs. Dutrow on November 30. He gave Buttermore a skeletal list of Mrs. Dutrow's assets with no detail. At the same time he also undertook to make some technical corrections of Mrs. Dutrow's will, which was executed, as noted, on December 4. In the letter accompanying the will, he mentioned his conversation with Buttermore and his "assumption" that Mrs. Dutrow wanted him to give Buttermore the information he was requesting.

The response to this communication was a letter written to Stevens on December 3, 1973 in Dorcas Cotsworth's handwriting on her personal stationary, and signed by Dorcas and Mrs. Dutrow, which contained the following:

> These are my mother's observations as she sits here besides me and she insists she is not being pressured....

> Mother and I have discussed this so often — now she says get it over and let me forget it — as it worries her with everything undone....

> Her desire and intent is to have Dorcas rewarded while alive — to have an Irrevocable Trust set up to let Dorcas have income and right to sprinkle money to Grandchildren when necessary....

> When Dorcas dies then the per stirpes takes over....

> Mother approves of Mr. Grant Buttermore knowing all details and keeping in this estate.

A meeting of Buttermore and John Cotsworth with Stevens was scheduled for December 13, 1973. Prior to this meeting Buttermore met with Mrs. Dutrow alone, as he testified was his customary practice, "so that I could get the intent directly from ... the testatrix." During this two hour conference, according to Buttermore, he explained various legal and tax aspects of estate planning to Mrs. Dutrow. He also told her "that intent was much more important and controlled over the other two items, meaning taxation and liquidity." Buttermore also reviewed at length Mrs. Dutrow's assets and her present will and trusts. Among other things, Mrs. Dutrow, according to Buttermore's testimony, said that "her first priority was to make sure she had enough to last during her lifetime," for which purpose Mrs. Dutrow said she would need $26,000 per year. Buttermore also explained to Mrs. Dutrow that the practical effect of the per stirpes disposition of the November 24 trust agreement would be to enable the two plaintiffs, the Haynes brothers, ultimately to "receive twice as much as each of the other grandchildren," to which Mrs. Dutrow responded, according to Buttermore, "I didn't realize that."

Buttermore testified that he told Stevens at the December 13 meeting that Mrs. Dutrow "wanted to go to the per capita basis equally among the grandchildren." Stevens, according to Buttermore, was very skeptical that Mrs. Dutrow wanted to do this and asked Buttermore to doublecheck it with her. Buttermore replied that "[i]n my mind she'd already made that decision after our talk on December the eleventh."

On December 17 and 18, a concerned Stevens wrote Buttermore letters confirming the discussion of December 13, and on December 18, specifically adverted to the possibility of "undue influence." There is no indication in the record that Buttermore responded to Stevens on this matter.

Buttermore, in response to a call from Dorcas Cotsworth, again met alone with Mrs. Dutrow in Short Hills on January 11 to discuss a problem concerning some back dividends. While he was with her, Buttermore, at his own initiative, told her what had happened during his December 13 meeting with Stevens and John Cotsworth and reviewed with her Stevens' letter of December 17 concerning her estate plans. Following that exchange, Buttermore related, Mrs. Dutrow instructed *him* to "draw the papers." Although Stevens had previously asked Buttermore to write him in Vermont, where he was vacationing, if there were any further developments concerning Mrs. Dutrow's estate planning, Buttermore did not do so, apparently believing that Mrs. Dutrow, who complained of Stevens' absence, did not desire or need Stevens to be further involved. Thus, Buttermore, still the Cotsworths' attorney, also stepped in, exclusively, as Mrs. Dutrow's attorney for purposes of planning her estate.

Significantly, at this juncture, drastic changes in Mrs. Dutrow's estate planning materialized. According to Buttermore, he and Mrs. Dutrow then proceeded to discuss in detail her wishes for a new will and trust agreements. Mrs. Dutrow assertedly indicated that she wanted "to leave [her estate] equally ... between the grandchildren," and did not care about the adverse tax consequence which Buttermore claimed he had explained to her. Buttermore also seemed to minimize the effect of the proposed change allegedly requested by Mrs. Dutrow by pointing out to her that altering the particular trust in question would not accomplish her goals; although all six grandchildren would inherit equally under the particular trust in question, the consequence of other trusts already in existence would be that the two Haynes grandchildren would "still be getting greater in the end" than Mrs. Cotsworth's children. During that meeting, Buttermore also apparently showed Stevens' letter of December 18 concerning undue influence to Mrs. Dutrow.

These discussions resulted in the near total severance of the Haynes children from their grandmother's estate. Assertedly, at Mrs. Dutrow's request, Buttermore promptly prepared two new trust agreements, which provided for the payment of income with full right of invasion of principal to Dorcas Cotsworth during her lifetime and that, upon Dorcas' death, "the then remaining balance in said trust shall be divided equally among settlor's grandchildren." In addition, Mrs. Dutrow's new will provided for the bequest of all her tangible personal property to Dorcas Cotsworth, "or if she does not survive me to my grandchildren who survive me, equally." These instruments were executed by Mrs. Dutrow on January 16, 1974.

On January 19 Buttermore sent Stevens copies of the new instruments along with a letter in which he explained that after going over everything "meticulously with Mrs. Dutrow," the new instruments had been prepared "along the lines we have discussed" and that, in Stevens' absence, Mrs. Dutrow had become "quite upset with the Fidelity Bank and decided that she wanted to immediately revoke" the existing trust agreements and will. Stevens testified to astonishment at the proposed distribution. He also expressed surprise about the provision in both trust agreements, which permitted Dorcas Cotsworth to withdraw the principal each year so that, if exercised, there might be nothing left when she died.

In early May 1974 Buttermore again met with Mrs. Dutrow to make some changes in the trust agreements. The most important change allowed the corporate trustee First National State Bank of New Jersey to distribute principal, "in its sole discretion," to Dorcas Cotsworth and any of Mrs. Dutrow's grandchildren (i.e., plaintiffs as well as Dorcas' children). This was in contrast to the original terms of this trust agreement, as executed by Mrs. Dutrow in January 1974, which allowed for such discretionary distribution by the bank only to Mrs. Cotsworth and her children, not to plaintiffs. According to Buttermore's testimony, this change was clearly Mrs. Dutrow's idea.

On April 24, 1975, Mrs. Dutrow amended the revocable trust agreement and added a codicil to her will in order to add *in terrorem* clauses to each instrument. Both the amendment and the codicil were prepared by Buttermore. At trial, Buttermore said that Mrs. Dutrow had decided to add the clause after reading that J. Paul Getty had included such a clause in his will to prevent litigation.

Buttermore next met with Mrs. Dutrow to discuss her estate on December 11, 1975. At this meeting, according to Buttermore's testimony, Mrs. Dutrow told him that she had decided to give her estate, other than special bequests or amounts, to Dorcas Cotsworth, to enable Dorcas to enjoy it during Dorcas' lifetime. Buttermore testified that he was "taken by surprise" by this proposal and tried to explain to Mrs. Dutrow that this change would result in additional taxes of between $700,000 and $800,000 when Dorcas died. But, according to Buttermore, Mrs. Dutrow insisted on making the change. The necessary amendments to the revocable trust agreement were prepared by Buttermore and executed by Mrs. Dutrow on January 9, 1976, providing for distribution of the principal to Dorcas upon Mrs. Dutrow's death, or, if Dorcas was not then living, equally among Mrs. Dutrow's grandchildren. A new will executed the same day provided, as had previous wills, that Dorcas would inherit all of Mrs. Dutrow's tangible personal property. The final change made by Mrs. Dutrow in her estate plans before she died in September 1977, was to amend the revocable trust to give $10,000 to each of her grandchildren at her death, apparently realizing that otherwise the Haynes children would likely not inherit anything.

The last testamentary document executed by the testatrix was a will dated April 8, 1976. It contained no further major changes in her dispositions. Mrs. Dutrow died on September 27, 1977 and her final will was admitted to probate by the Surrogate of Ocean County on October 12, 1977, with the First National State Bank of New Jersey as executor.

* * *

In any attack upon the validity of a will, it is generally presumed that "the testator was of sound mind and competent when he executed the will." Gellert v. Livingston, 5 N.J. 65, 71, 73 A.2d 916 (1950). If a will is tainted by "undue influence," it may be overturned. "Undue influence" has been defined as "mental, moral or physical" exertion which has destroyed the "free agency of a testator" by preventing the testator "from following the dictates of his own mind and will and accepting instead the domination and influence of another." In re Neuman, 133 N.J.Eq. 532, 534, 32 A.2d 826 (E. & A. 1943). When such a contention is made

> the burden of proving undue influence lies upon the contestant unless the will benefits one who stood in a confidential relationship to the testatrix and there are additional circumstances of a suspicious character present which require explanation. In such case the law raises a presumption of undue influence and the burden of proof is shifted to the proponent. [In re Rittenhouse's Will, 19 N.J. 376, 378–379, 117 A.2d 401 (1955)]

Accord, In re Blake's Will, 21 N.J. 50, 55–56, 120 A.2d 745 (1956); In re Davis, 14 N.J. 166, 169, 101 A.2d 521 (1953); In re Hopper, 9 N.J. 280, 282, 88 A.2d 193 (1952), 5 N.J. Practice (Clapp, Wills and Administration) §62 (3rd ed. 1962).

The first element necessary to raise a presumption of undue influence, a "confidential relationship" between the testator and a beneficiary, arises

> where trust is reposed by reason of the testator's weakness or dependence or where the parties occupied relations in which reliance is naturally inspired or in fact exists.... [In re Hopper, supra, 9 N.J. at 282, 88 A.2d 193]

Here, the aged Mrs. Dutrow, afflicted by the debilitations of advanced years, was dependent upon her sole surviving child with whom she lived and upon whom she relied for companionship, care and support. This was a relationship sustained by confidence and trust. The determination of the trial court, in this case, that there was a confidential relationship between the testatrix and the chief beneficiary of her will is unassailable.

The second element necessary to create the presumption of undue influence is the presence of suspicious circumstances which, in combination with such a confidential relationship, will shift the burden of proof to the proponent. Such circumstances need be no more than "slight." In re Blake's Will, supra, 21 N.J. at 55–56, 120 A.2d 745; In re Rittenhouse's Will, supra, 19 N.J. at 379, 117 A.2d 401; Gellert v. Livingston, supra, 5 N.J. at 71, 73 A.2d 916; In re Week's Estate, 29 N.J.Super. 533, 540, 103 A.2d 43 (App.Div.1954).

In this case there were suspicious circumstances attendant upon the execution of the will. There was a confidential relationship between the testatrix and her attorney, who was also the attorney for the daughter and the daughter's immediate family. Furthermore, following the establishment of the confidential relationship of the daughter's attorney with the testatrix, there was a drastic change in the testamentary dispositions of the testatrix, which favored the daughter. These factors collectively triggered the presumption that there was undue influence in the execution of the will.

On this record, the trial court correctly posited a presumption of undue influence that shifted the burden of proof on this issue to the proponents of the will. The court concluded ultimately on this issue, however, that the proponents, the defendants, had overcome the presumption of undue influence. The trial judge determined that Mrs. Dutrow was of firm mind and resolve, that the final testamentary disposition, though markedly different from previous plans, was not unnatural or instinctively unsound and it represented her actual intent. Further, the court found the explanation for Mrs. Dutrow's final testamentary disposition to be candid and satisfactory.

The plaintiffs argue vigorously that the trial court's findings of fact and conclusions are not supported by sufficient evidence. They contend that in view of the strength of the presumption of undue influence created by the confidential relationships and the peculiarly suspicious circumstances of this case, there is an unusually heavy burden of proof required to disprove undue influence, which defendants failed to meet.

In this jurisdiction, once a presumption of undue influence has been established the burden of proof shifts to the proponent of the will, who must, under normal circumstances, overcome that presumption by a preponderance of the evidence. In re Week's Estate, supra, 29 N.J.Super. at 538–539, 103 A.2d 43. Accord, In re Estate of Churick, 165 N.J.Super. 1, 5, 397 A.2d 677 (App.Div.1978), aff'd o. b., 78 N.J. 563, 397 A.2d 655 (1979); In re Baker's Will, 68 N.J.Super. 574, 587, 173 A.2d 422 (App.Div.1971). See Gellert v. Livingston, supra, 5 N.J. at 71, 73 A.2d 916 (1950). See generally 5 N.J. Practice, supra, §62. As stated by Judge Clapp in In re Week's Estate, supra:

> In the case of a presumption of undue influence, apparently because the presumption is fortified by policy, the proponent must, according to the language of the cases, prove, to the satisfaction of the trier of fact, that there was no undue influence. In connection with this presumption, unlike other presumptions, the courts do not speak as to the burden of going forward with the evidence. However, we conclude, the moment this presumption is erected, both the burden of proof ... and the burden of going forward with proof, shift to the proponent and are identical and coincident. To meet each of these assignments, the proponent must establish by the same quantum of proof that is, by a preponderance of the proof that there is no undue influence. [29 N.J.Super. at 538–539, 103 A.2d 43 (citations omitted)]

In re Week's Estate, supra, recognized, however, that there were situations calling for a stronger presumption of undue influence and a commensurately heavier burden of proof to rebut the presumption. While in that case the presumption of undue influence was deemed to be rebuttable by a preponderance of evidence, the court acknowledged other

> cases where the presumption of undue influence is so heavily weighted with policy that the courts have demanded a sterner measure of proof than that usually obtaining upon civil issues. That is the situation, for instance, where an attorney benefits by the will of his client and especially where he draws it himself. [29 N.J.Super. at 539, 103 A.2d 43.]

It has been often recognized that a conflict on the part of an attorney in a testimonial situation is fraught with a high potential for undue influence, generating a strong presumption that there was such improper influence and warranting a greater quantum of proof to dispel the presumption. Thus, where the attorney who drew the will was the sole beneficiary, the Court required "substantial and trustworthy evidence of explanatory facts" and "candid and full disclosure" to dispel the presumption of undue influence. In re Blake's Will, 21 N.J. 50, 58–59, 120 A.2d 745 (1956). And, where an attorney-beneficiary, who had a preexisting attorney-client relationship with the testatrix, introduced the testatrix to the lawyer who actually drafted the challenged will, this Court has required evidence that was "convincing or impeccable," In re Rittenhouse's Will, supra, 19 N.J. at 382, 117 A.2d 401, "convincing," In re Hopper, supra, 9 N.J. at 285, 88 A.2d 193, and, "clear and convincing," In re Davis, supra, 14 N.J. at 170, 101 A.2d 521. Accord, In re

Baker's Will, supra; see In re Estate of Lehner, 142 N.J.Super. 56, 360 A.2d 400 (App.Div.1975), rev'd on other grounds, 70 N.J. 434, 360 A.2d 383 (1976); cf. In re Estate of Churick, supra, 165 N.J.Super. at 5, 397 A.2d 677 (applying lower burden of proof where testator advised by independent attorney); In re Week's Estate, supra (same).

In imposing the higher burden of proof in this genre of cases, our courts have continually emphasized the need for a lawyer of independence and undivided loyalty, owing professional allegiance to no one but the testator. In In re Rittenhouse's Will, supra, 19 N.J. at 380–382, 117 A.2d 401, the Court questioned the attorney's independence and loyalty in view of the attorney-beneficiary's role in bringing the draftsman and the testatrix together, noting that the beneficiary had been "unable to give a satisfactory explanation of the relationship" between himself, the draftsman and the testatrix, viz:

> [I]t would appear the testatrix did not independently choose [the draftsman]as the scrivener of her will. It is fair to assume from the record that she was influenced to do so by [the beneficiary].

Similarly, in In re Davis, supra, 14 N.J. at 171, 101 A.2d 521, the Court observed:

> We wish to reiterate what has been said repeatedly by our courts as to the proprieties of a situation where the testatrix wishes to make her attorney or a member of his immediate family a beneficiary under a will. Ordinary prudence requires that such a will be drawn by some other lawyer of the testatrix' own choosing, so that any suspicion of undue influence is thereby avoided. Such steps are in conformance with the spirit of Canons 6, 11, of the Canons of Professional Ethics promulgated by this court.* * *

See also In re Hopper, supra, 9 N.J. at 282, 88 A.2d 193.

It is not difficult to appreciate the policy reasons for creating an especially strong presumption of undue influence in cases of attorney misconduct. Such professional delinquency is encompassed by our official rules governing the professional ethics of attorneys. Our disciplinary rules cover all gradations of professional departures from ethical norms, and, the existence of an ethical conflict exemplified in this case is squarely posited under DR 5-105.* * * This ethical rule prohibits an attorney from engaging in professional relationships that may impair his independent and untrammeled judgment with respect to his client. This disciplinary stricture

> should be practically self-demonstrative to any conscientious attorney. There is nothing novel about the ethical dilemma dealt with by DR 5-105. A lawyer cannot serve two masters in the same subject matter if their interests are or may become actually or potentially in conflict. [In re Chase, 68 N.J. 392, 396, 346 A.2d 89 (1975)]

So pervasive and fundamental is the ethical reach of DR 5-105 that ethical violations of this disciplinary rule based upon conflicts of interest have been found in a myriad of situations and in almost every walk of professional life. * * * Such conflicts often arise where there is dual representation. E. g., In re Krakauer, 81 N.J. 32, 404 A.2d 1137 (1979); In re Dolan, 76 N.J. 1, 384 A.2d 1076 (1978). See "Developments of the Law—Conflicts of Interest in the Legal Profession," 94 Harv.L.Rev. 1244, 1292–1315 (1961). A conflict of interest, moreover, need not be obvious or actual to create an ethical impropriety. The mere possibility of such a conflict at the outset of the relationship is sufficient to establish an ethical breach on the part of the attorney. In re Kushinsky, 53 N.J. 1, 5, 247 A.2d 665 (1968); In re Braun, 49 N.J. 16, 18, 227 A.2d 506 (1967); In re Blatt, 42 N.J. 522, 524, 201 A.2d 715 (1964); In re Kamp, 40

N.J. 588, 595, 194 A.2d 236 (1963). Even where the representation of two clients has become a routine practice on the part of the bar generally, when the latent conflict becomes real, the attorney must fully disclose all material information and, if need be, extricate himself from the conflict by terminating his relationship with at least one party. Cf. Lieberman v. Employers Ins. of Wausau, 84 N.J. 325, 338–340, 419 A.2d 417 (1980) (conflict of interest on part of insurance defense counsel who normally represented both the insured and the insurer).

Accordingly, it is our determination that there must be imposed a significant burden of proof upon the advocates of a will where a presumption of undue influence has arisen because the testator's attorney has placed himself in a conflict of interest and professional loyalty between the testator and the beneficiary. * * * In view of the gravity of the presumption in such cases, the appropriate burden of proof must be heavier than that which normally obtains in civil litigation. The cited decisions which have dealt with the quantum of evidence needed to dispel the presumption of influence in this context have essayed various descriptions of this greater burden, viz: "convincing," "impeccable," "substantial," "trustworthy," "candid," and "full." Our present rules of evidence, however, do not employ such terminology. The need for clarity impels us to be more definitive in the designation of the appropriate burden of proof and to select one which most suitably measures the issue to be determined. See, e. g., In re Week's Estate, supra. Only three burdens of proof are provided by the evidence rules, namely, a preponderance, clear and convincing, and beyond a reasonable doubt. Evid.R. 1(4). The standard in our evidence rules that conforms most comfortably with the level of proofs required by our decisions in this context is the burden of proof by clear and convincing evidence. * * * In re Davis, supra, 14 N.J. at 170, 101 A.2d 521; cf. Sarte v. Pidoto, 129 N.J.Super. 405, 411, 324 A.2d 48 (App.Div.1974) (de facto use of a standard stricter than preponderance of the evidence entails proof by clear and convincing evidence under rules of evidence). Hence, the presumption of undue influence created by a professional conflict of interest on the part of an attorney, coupled with confidential relationships between a testator and the beneficiary as well as the attorney, must be rebutted by clear and convincing evidence.

Applying these principles to this case, it is clear that attorney Buttermore was in a position of irreconcilable conflict within the common sense and literal meaning of DR 5-105. In this case, Buttermore was required, at a minimum, to provide full disclosure and complete advice to Mrs. Dutrow, as well as the Cotsworths, as to the existence and nature of the conflict and to secure knowing and intelligent waivers from each in order to continue his professional relationship with Mrs. Dutrow. DR 5-105(C). Even these prophylactic measures, however, might not have overcome the conflict, nor have been sufficient to enable the attorney to render unimpaired "independent professional judgment" on behalf of his client, DR 5-105(B); see Lieberman v. Employers Ins. of Wausau, supra, 84 N.J. at 338–340, 419 A.2d 417. Any conflict, of course, could have been avoided by Buttermore simply refusing to represent Mrs. Dutrow. DR 5-105(A), (B); see In re Davis, supra, at 171, 101 A.2d 521. But, Buttermore was apparently insensitive or impervious to the presence or extent of the professional conflict presented by these circumstances. He undertook none of these measures to eliminate the dual representation or overcome the conflict.[7] Consequently, a strong taint of undue influence was permitted, presumptively, to be injected into the testamentary disposition of Mrs. Dutrow.

---

7. In this case, we recognize that Buttermore believed in good faith that he was taking proper precautions to overcome or avoid the consequences of the improper conflict and did not believe or

Accordingly, the attorney's conduct here, together with all of the other factors contributing to the likelihood of wrongful influence exerted upon the testatrix, has engendered a heavy presumption of undue influence which the proponents of the will must overcome by clear and convincing evidence.

This determination that clear and convincing evidence must be marshalled to overcome the presumption of undue influence appropriately requires that the matter be remanded to the trial court for new findings of fact and legal conclusions based upon application of this burden of proof. We remand, recognizing that there is considerable evidence in the record as to Mrs. Dutrow's intelligence, independence and persistence, of her alienation, to some extent, from the Haynes children, and as to her natural intent primarily to benefit her children, rather than her grandchildren. Moreover, all of this evidence is based upon the credibility of witnesses, which we cannot independently evaluate. We are also mindful that the trial court found that the explanation for Mrs. Dutrow's testamentary disposition was candid and satisfactory.

Nevertheless, the trial court does not appear to have given full weight to the additional significant factor generating the heightened presumption of undue influence in this case, namely, that occasioned by the conflict of interest on the part of the attorney drafting the will, whose testimony was crucial to the outcome of this case. Most importantly, the court's conclusion was premised upon an application of the conventional standard of proof entailing only a preponderance of the evidence. We therefore cannot with any certitude predict that the trial court's findings of fact and resultant conclusions would be the same were he to reassess the evidence, imposing upon the proponents of the will the burden of proof of lack of undue influence by clear and convincing evidence. Consequently, the fair disposition, which we now direct, is to remand the matter to the trial court for a redetermination of facts and conclusions based upon the record.

* * *

The second issue involves the enforceability of the *in terrorem* clauses challenged by the plaintiffs. The trial court noted that under the State's common law, *in terrorem* clauses are enforceable when the contest is based upon an allegation of undue influence, even if probable cause and good faith are present. The trial judge nonetheless declared the clauses unenforceable because the new probate code, N.J.S.A. 3A:2A-32, admittedly not controlling in this case because of the date of Mrs. Dutrow's death, "provides that *in terrorem* clauses are unenforceable if probable cause exists" and, following the lead of the new code on this point, the court refused to enforce the clauses, noting that its ruling was "in accord with the authoritative view and the modern trend."

On this latter issue, the Appellate Division found that there was no basis in law for the trial court's decision, and that although the new probate code, N.J.S.A. 3A:2A-32, changed the law with respect to wills, the change applied only to wills of decedents who died on or after September 1, 1978, nearly a year after Mrs. Dutrow's death. In addi-

---

perceive that his position involved an impermissible conflict of interest in light of these measures. He also expressed the view that frequently estate planning involves members of an entire family and therefore no conflict exists for an attorney who has professional relationships with members of the family, in addition to the testator. This position is, of course, inconsistent with our explicit holding that such conduct, as exemplified by the facts of this case, violates DR 5-105. Since this application of DR 5-105 to such situations has not been generally acknowledged, we do not think it fair that ethical sanctions be pursued retroactively in this case for such conduct, since there are no additional aggravating circumstances. See In re Smock, 86 N.J. 426, 432 A.2d 34 (1981).

tion, the Appellate Division found no indication that the new statute is meant to apply to trusts. Furthermore, the court said in support of reversal on this issue, "[e]nforcement of the *in terrorem* clause is particularly equitable here."

As noted earlier, on April 24, 1975, Mrs. Dutrow amended the revocable trust agreement and added a codicil to her will in order to add *in terrorem* clauses to each instrument. The clause in the amendment to the revocable trust agreement, almost identical to that in the will, provided:

> If any beneficiary under this trust shall contest the validity of, or object to this instrument, or attempt to vacate the same, or to alter or change any of the provisions hereof, such person shall be thereby deprived of all beneficial interest thereunder and of any share in this Trust and the share of such person shall become part of the residue of the trust, and such person shall be excluded from taking any part of such residue and the same shall be divided among the other persons entitled to take such residue. * * *

In 1977 the Legislature enacted N.J.S.A. 3A:2A-32 as part of the new probate code [Uniform Probate Code (U.L.A.) § 3-905 (1969)] * * *. This statute renders *in terrorem* clauses in wills unenforceable if probable cause for a will contest exists:

> A provision in a will purporting to penalize any interested person for contesting the will or instituting other proceedings relating to the estate is unenforceable if probable cause exists for instituting proceedings.

In Alper v. Alper, 2 N.J. 105, 65 A.2d 737 (1949), the Court said that the existence of probable cause to bring the challenge to the will should result in nonenforcement of an *in terrorem* clause "where the contest of the will is waged on the ground of forgery or subsequent revocation by a later will or codicil." However, where typical grounds of challenge were advanced "fraud, undue influence, improper execution or lack of testamentary capacity" the clause was deemed to be enforceable, notwithstanding probable cause, as a safeguard against deleterious, acrimonious and wasteful family litigation. Id. at 112–113, 65 A.2d 737. Accord, Provident Trust Co. v. Osborne, 133 N.J.Eq. 518, 521, 33 A.2d 103 (Ch.1943). See also In re Estate of Badenhop, 61 N.J.Super. 526, 535, 161 A.2d 318 (Cty.Ct.1960).

The new statute, N.J.S.A. 3A:2A-32, however, abolishes the distinction drawn by the Court in Alper between cases in which *in terrorem* clauses in wills shall be enforced, and those in which they shall not, stating quite simply that whenever there is probable cause to contest a will, the clause should not be enforced. While the statute applies neither to the will in this case, which was probated prior to the statute's effective date, nor to the trust agreement, since the statute applies only to wills, the statute is indicative of a legislative intent to create a policy less inhibitory to the bringing of challenges to testamentary instruments. There does not appear to be any logical reason why the purpose of the statute should not be presently recognized and be applied equally to trust instruments or should not be applied in the circumstances of this case.

There are public policy considerations both favoring and disfavoring the enforcement of *in terrorem* clauses. On the one hand, such provisions seek to reduce vexatious litigation, avoid expenses that debilitate estates and give effect to a testator's clearly expressed intentions. * * *

On the other hand, a majority of jurisdictions have declined to enforce *in terrorem* clauses where challenges to testamentary instruments are brought in good faith and with probable cause. * * *

Given this relative equipoise of considerations, it is entirely appropriate for the courts to be sensitive and responsive to the Legislature's perception of the public interest and policy in these matters. See Knight v. Margate, 86 N.J. 374, 431 A.2d 833 (1981); Kruvant v. Mayor & Council Tp. of Cedar Grove, 82 N.J. 435, 414 A.2d 9 (1980). The assessment, balancing and resolution of these concerns by the Legislature, now reflected in the statute law, is, of course, not binding upon the judiciary's decisional authority in a matter not governed by such enactments. Nevertheless, the legislative handling of the subject is, and should be, strongly influential in the judicial quest for the important societal values which are constituent elements of the common law and find appropriate voice in the decisions of the court expounding the common law. See Van Beeck v. Sabine Towing Co., 300 U.S. 342, 351, 57 S.Ct. 452, 456, 81 L.Ed. 685, 690 (1937).

We therefore decline to enforce an *in terrorem* clause in a will or trust agreement where there is probable cause to challenge the instrument. The trial court concluded that the plaintiffs in this case "proceeded in good faith and on probable cause." That finding is amply supported by evidence of record.

* * *

We have determined that *in terrorem* clauses in the will and trust instruments are not enforceable. We have also directed, for reasons set forth in this opinion, that the case be remanded for new findings of fact and legal conclusions with respect to the major issue of undue influence in the execution of the will.

Accordingly, the judgment below is reversed and the matter remanded. Jurisdiction is not retained.

CLIFFORD, J., dissenting in part [is omitted].

* * *

For reversal—Justices SULLIVAN, PASHMAN, CLIFFORD, SCHREIBER and HANDLER—5.

For affirmance—None.

2. Heterosexuality

In re Will of Moses
Supreme Court of Mississippi, 1969
227 So. 2d 829

SMITH, Justice:

Mrs. Fannie Traylor Moses died on February 6, 1967. An instrument, dated December 23, 1957 and purporting to be her last will and testament, was duly admitted to probate in common form in the Chancery Court of the First Judicial District of Hinds County. Thereafter, on February 14, 1967, appellant, Clarence H. Holland, an attorney at law, not related to Mrs. Moses, filed a petition in that court tendering for probate in solemn form, as the true last will and testament of Mrs. Moses, a document dated May 26, 1964, under the terms of which he would take virtually her entire estate. This document contained a clause revoking former wills and Holland's petition prayed that the earlier probate of the 1957 will be set aside.

The beneficiaries under the 1957 will (the principal beneficiary was an elder sister of Mrs. Moses) responded to Holland's petition, denied that the document tendered by him was Mrs. Moses' will, and asserted, among other things, that it was (1) the product of Holland's undue influence upon her, (2) that at the time of its signing, Mrs. Moses lacked testamentary capacity, and, (3) that the 1957 will was Mrs. Moses' true last will and testament and its probate should be confirmed. By cross bill, respondents prayed that Holland's apparent ownership of an interest in certain real estate had been procured by undue influence and that it should be cancelled as a cloud upon the title of Mrs. Moses, the true owner.

By agreement, the case was heard by the chancellor without a jury.

After hearing and considering a great deal of evidence, oral and documentary, together with briefs of counsel, the chancellor, in a carefully considered opinion, found that (1) the 1964 document, tendered for probate by Holland, was the product of undue influence and was not entitled to be admitted to probate, (2) the earlier probate of the 1957 will should be confirmed and, (3) Mrs. Moses had been the true owner of the interest claimed by Holland in the real estate and his claim of ownership should be cancelled as a cloud upon the title of Mrs. Moses.

Holland's appeal is from the decree entered denying probate to the 1964 document and cancelling his claim to an undivided one-half interest in the real estate.

A number of grounds are assigned for reversal. However, appellant's chief argument is addressed to the proposition that even if Holland, as Mrs. Moses' attorney, occupied a continuing fiduciary relationship with respect to her on May 26, 1964, the date of the execution of the document under which he claimed her estate, the presumption of undue influence was overcome because, in making the will, Mrs. Moses had the independent advice and counsel of one entirely devoted to her interests. It is argued that, for this reason, a decree should be entered here reversing the chancellor and admitting the 1964 will to probate. The question as to the land would then become moot as Holland would take it under the residuary clause of the 1964 will.

A brief summary of facts found by the chancellor and upon which he based his conclusion that the presumption was not overcome, follows:

Mrs. Moses died at the age of 57 years, leaving an estate valued at $125,000. She had lost three husbands in less than 20 years. Throughout the latter years of her life her health became seriously impaired. She suffered from serious heart trouble and cancer had required the surgical removal of one of her breasts. For 6 or 7 years preceding her death she was an alcoholic.

On several occasions Mrs. Moses had declared her intention of making an elder sister her testamentary beneficiary. She had once lived with this sister and was grateful for the many kindnesses shown her. Mrs. Moses' will of December 23, 1957 did, in fact, bequeath the bulk of her estate to this sister.

The exact date on which Holland entered Mrs. Moses' life is unclear. There is a suggestion that she had met him as early as 1951. Their personal relationship became what the chancellor, somewhat inaccurately, characterized, as one of 'dubious' morality. The record, however, leaves no doubt as to its nature. Soon after the death of Mrs. Moses' last husband, Holland, although 15 years her junior, began seeing Mrs. Moses with marked regularity, there having been testimony to the effect that he attended her almost daily. Holland was an attorney and in that capacity represented Mrs. Moses. She declared that he was not only her attorney but her 'boyfriend' as well. On August 22, 1961, a date during the period in which the evidence shows that Holland was Mrs.

Moses' attorney, she executed a document purporting to be her will. This instrument was drawn by an attorney with whom Holland was then associated and shared offices, and was typed by a secretary who served them both. It was witnessed by Holland's associate and their secretary. In addition to other testamentary dispositions, this document undertook to bequeath to Holland 'my wedding ring, my diamond solitare ring and my three gold bracelets containing twenty-five (25) pearls each.' In it Holland is referred to as 'my good friend.' The validity of this document is not an issue in the present case.

After Mrs. Moses died, the 1964 will was brought forward by another attorney, also an associate of Holland, who said that it had been entrusted to him by Mrs. Moses, together with other papers, for safekeeping. He distinguished his relation with Holland from that of a partner, saying that he and Holland only occupied offices together and shared facilities and expenses in the practice of law. He also stated that he saw Mrs. Moses on an 'average' of once a week, most often in the company of Holland.

Throughout this period, Mrs. Moses was a frequent visitor at Holland's office, and there is ample evidence to support the chancellor's finding that there existed a continuing fiduciary relationship between Mrs. Moses and Holland, as her attorney.

In May, 1962, Holland and the husband of Holland's first cousin, one Gibson, had contracted to buy 480 acres of land for $36,000. Mrs. Moses was not, it appears, originally a party to the contract. Gibson paid the $5,000 earnest money but testified that he did not know where it had come from and assumed that it came from Mrs. Moses. At the time, Mrs. Moses had annuity contracts with a total maturity value of some $40,000 on which she obtained $31,341.11. This sum was deposited in a bank account called 'Cedar Hills Ranch.' She gave Holland authority to check on this account, as well as upon her personal account. About this time, Gibson disappeared from the land transaction. On June 7, 1962, the deal was closed. At closing, the persons present, in addition to the grantors and their agents and attorney, were Mrs. Moses and Holland, her attorney. Mrs. Moses had no other counsel. Holland issued a check on the Cedar Hills Ranch account (in which only Mrs. Moses had any money) for the $31,000 balance. Although none of the consideration was paid by Holland, the deed from the owners purported to convey the land to Holland and Mrs. Moses in equal shares, as tenants in common. On the day following, Holland issued another check on the Cedar Hills Ranch account (in which he still had deposited no money) for $835.00 purportedly in payment for a tractor. This check was issued by Holland to his brother. Eight days later Holland drew another check on this account for $2,100.00 purportedly for an undisclosed number of cattle. This check was issued to Holland's father.

The evidence supports the chancellor's finding that the confidential or fiduciary relationship which existed between Mrs. Moses and Holland, her attorney, was a subsisting and continuing relationship, having begun before the making by Mrs. Moses of the will of August 22, 1961, under the terms of which her jewelry had been bequeathed to Holland, and having ended only with Mrs. Moses' death. Moreover, its effect was enhanced by the fact that throughout this period, Holland was in almost daily attendance upon Mrs. Moses on terms of the utmost intimacy. There was strong evidence that this aging woman, seriously ill, disfigured by surgery, and hopelessly addicted to alcoholic excesses, was completely bemused by the constant and amorous attentions of Holland, a man 15 years her junior. There was testimony too indicating that she entertained the pathetic hope that he might marry her. Although the evidence was not without conflict and was, in some of its aspects, circumstantial, it was sufficient to support the finding that the relationship existed on May 26, 1964, the date of the will tendered for probate by Holland.

The chancellor's factual finding of the existence of this relationship on that date is supported by evidence and is not manifestly wrong. Moreover, he was correct in his conclusion of law that such relationship gave rise to a presumption of undue influence which could be overcome only by evidence that, in making the 1964 will, Mrs. Moses had acted upon the independent advice and counsel of one entirely devoted to her interest.

Appellant takes the position that there was undisputed evidence that Mrs. Moses, in making the 1964 will, did, in fact, have such advice and counsel. He relies upon the testimony of the attorney in whose office that document was prepared to support his assertion.

This attorney was and is a reputable and respected member of the bar, who had no prior connection with Holland and no knowledge of Mrs. Moses' relationship with him. He had never seen nor represented Mrs. Moses previously and never represented her afterward. He was acquainted with Holland and was aware that Holland was a lawyer.

A brief summary of his testimony, with respect to the writing of the will, follows:

Mrs. Moses had telephoned him for an appointment and had come alone to his office on March 31, 1964. She was not intoxicated and in his opinion knew what she was doing. He asked her about her property and 'marital background.' He did this in order, he said, to advise her as to possible renunciation by a husband. She was also asked if she had children in order to determine whether she wished to 'pretermit them.' As she had neither husband nor children this subject was pursued no further. He asked as to the values of various items of property in order to consider possible tax problems. He told her it would be better if she had more accurate descriptions of the several items of real and personal property comprising her estate. No further 'advice or counsel' was given her.

On some later date, Mrs. Moses sent in (the attorney did not think she came personally and in any event he did not see her), some tax receipts for purposes of supplying property descriptions. He prepared the will and mailed a draft to her. Upon receiving it, she telephoned that he had made a mistake in the devise of certain realty, in that he had provided that a relatively low valued property should go to Holland rather than a substantially more valuable property which she said she wanted Holland to have. He rewrote the will, making this change, and mailed it to her, as revised, on May 21, 1964. On the one occasion when he saw Mrs. Moses, there were no questions and no discussion of any kind as to Holland being preferred to the exclusion of her blood relatives. Nor was there any inquiry or discussion as to a possible client-attorney relationship with Holland. The attorney-draftsman wrote the will according to Mrs. Moses' instructions and said that he had 'no interest in' how she disposed of her property. He testified 'I try to draw the will to suit their purposes and if she (Mrs. Moses) wanted to leave him (Holland) everything she had, that was her business as far as I was concerned. I was trying to represent her in putting on paper in her will her desires, and it didn't matter to me to whom she left it * * * I couldn't have cared less.'

When Mrs. Moses returned to the office to execute the will, the attorney was not there and it was witnessed by two secretaries. One of these secretaries, coincidentally, had written and witnessed the 1961 will when working for Holland and his associate.

The attorney's testimony supports the chancellor's finding that nowhere in the conversations with Mrs. Moses was there touched upon in any way the proposed testamentary disposition whereby preference was to be given a nonrelative to the exclusion of her blood relatives. There was no discussion of her relationship with Holland, nor as to who her legal heirs might be, nor as to their relationship to her, after it was discovered that she had neither a husband nor children.

It is clear from his own testimony that, in writing the will, the attorney-draftsman, did no more than write down, according to the forms of law, what Mrs. Moses told him. There was no meaningful independent advice or counsel touching upon the area in question and it is manifest that the role of the attorney in writing the will, as it relates to the present issue, was little more than that of scrivener. The chancellor was justified in holding that this did not meet the burden nor overcome the presumption.

In Croft v. Alder, 237 Miss. 713, 724, 115 So.2d 683, 686 (1959) there was an extensive review of the authorities relating to the question here under consideration. This Court said:

> Meek v. Perry, 1858, 36 Miss. 190, 243, 244, 252, 259, is perhaps the leading case. It involved a will by a ward leaving a substantial amount of her property to her guardian. The Court held that the presumption of invalidity applies to wills as well as deeds. It was said the law watches with the greatest jealousy transactions between persons in confidential relations and will not permit them to stand, unless the circumstances demonstrate the fullest deliberation on the part of the testator and the most abundant good faith on the part of the beneficiary. Hence the law presumes the existence of undue influence, and such dealings are *prima facie* void, and will be so held 'unless the guardian show by *clearest proof* that he took no advantage over the testator, and the *cestui's* act was a result of his own volition and upon the fullest deliberation. * * *

> Moreover, even where there is no presumption of undue influence, the burden of proof rests upon the proponents throughout and never shifts to the contestants, both on undue influence and mental incapacity. Cheatham v. Burnside, 1954, 222 Miss. 872, 77 So.2d 719. From its very nature, evidence to show undue influence must be largely circumstantial. Undue influence is an intangible thing, which only rarely is susceptible of direct or positive proof. As was stated in Jamison v. Jamison, 1909, 96 Miss. 288, 51 So. 130, 'the only positive and affirmative proof required is of facts and circumstances from which the undue influence may be reasonably inferred.' * * *

> The able and respected attorney who prepared the will upon data furnished him by Barney, who stated he was acting for Mr. Alder, testified that, in his opinion, the testator was mentally competent and the instrument reflected testator's independent purpose. However, the record indicates that the witness had not conferred with Mr. Alder about the will prior to its drafting. Moreover, *his testimony does not negative the presumption of undue influence resulting from 'antecedent agencies' and prior actions by the principal beneficiary who was in the confidential relation.* In Jamison v. Jamison, 1909, 96 Miss. 288, 298, 51 So. 130, 131, it was said: 'The difficulty is also enhanced by the fact, universally recognized, that he who seeks to use undue influence does so in privacy. He seldom uses brute force or open threats to terrorize his intended victim, and if he does he is careful that no witnesses are about to take note of and testify to the fact. He observes, too, the same precautions if he seeks by cajolery, flattery,

or other methods to obtain power and control over the will of another, and direct it improperly to the accomplishment of the purpose which he desires. Subscribing witnesses are called to attest the execution of wills, and testify as to the testamentary capacity of the testator, and the circumstances attending the immediate execution of the instrument; but *they are not called upon to testify as to the antecedent agencies by which the execution of the paper was secured, even if they had any knowledge of them, which they seldom have.'* In re Coins' Will (Fortner v. Coins), 1959, [237 Miss. 322] 114 So.2d 759.

We do not think that the testimony of the attorney who attested the will, as to his observations at that particular time, can suffice to rebut the already existing presumption. *As stated in Jamison, he naturally would have had no knowledge of any precedent activities by Barney.* (emphasis added).

In Croft, supra, this Court quoted the rule as stated in 57 Am.Jur. Wills sections 389, 390 as follows:

> * * * [A]lthough the mere existence of confidential relations between a testator and a beneficiary under his will does not raise a presumption that the beneficiary exercised undue influence over the testator, as it does with gifts *inter vivos,* such consequence follows where the beneficiary 'has been actively concerned in some way with the preparation or execution of the will, or where the relationship is coupled with *some suspicious circumstances, such as mental infirmity of the testator;' * * * (emphasis added).*

See also Young v. Martin, 239 Miss. 861, 125 So.2d 734, 126 So.2d 529 (1961).

Holland, of course, did not personally participate in the actual preparation or execution of the will. If he had, under the circumstances in evidence, unquestionably the will could not stand. It may be assumed that Holland, as a lawyer, knew this.

In Croft, supra, this Court said that the presumption of undue influence in the production of a will may arise from 'antecedent circumstances' about which its draftsman and the witnesses knew nothing. The rule, as stated in that case, is that undue influence will be presumed where the beneficiary 'has been actively concerned in some way with the preparation or execution of the will, or where the *relationship* is coupled with some *suspicious circumstances,* such as mental infirmity of the testator.' (emphasis added).

Undue influence operates upon the will as well as upon the mind. It is not dependent upon a lack of testamentary capacity.

The chancellor's finding that the will was the product of Holland's undue influence is not inconsistent with his conclusion that 'Her (Mrs. Moses) mind was capable of understanding the essential matters necessary to the execution of her will on May 26, 1964, at the time of such execution.' A weak or infirm mind may, of course, be more easily over persuaded. In the case under review, Mrs. Moses was in ill health, she was an alcoholic, and was an aging woman infatuated with a young lover, 15 years her junior, who was also her lawyer. If this combination of circumstances cannot be said to support the view that Mrs. Moses suffered from a 'weakness or infirmity' of mind, vis-a-vis Holland, it was hardly calculated to enhance her power of will where he was concerned. Circumstances in evidence, both antecedent and subsequent to the making of the will, tend to accord with that conclusion.

The sexual morality of the personal relationship is not an issue. However, the intimate nature of this relationship is relevant to the present inquiry to the extent that its existence, under the circumstances, warranted an inference of undue influence, extending and augmenting that which flowed from the attorney-client relationship. Particularly is this true when viewed in the light of evidence indicating its employment for the personal aggrandizement of Holland. For that purpose, it was properly taken into consideration by the chancellor.

In 94 C.J.S. Wills § 263 (1956) it is stated:

> The mere existence of illicit, improper, unlawful, or meretricious relations between the testator and the beneficiary or the beneficiary's mother is insufficient of itself to prove fraud or undue influence, although the existence of such relations is an important fact to be considered by the jury along with other evidence of undue influence, giving to other circumstances a significance which they might not otherwise have; and much less evidence will be required to establish undue influence on the part of one holding wrongful and meretricious relations with the testator.

In Croft and Taylor, supra, the beneficiary was present at or participated at some stage or in some way in the preparation or execution of the will. However, it is to be noted that it was the 'antecedent circumstances' which gave rise to the presumption of undue influence, and that this was not overcome by testimony of an independent lawyer-draftsman who testified that the will reflected the independent wishes of the testator who had been of sound mind and had known what he was doing.

The rule laid down in Croft, supra, would have little, if any, practical worth, if, under circumstances such as those established in this case, it could be nullified by a mere showing that the beneficiary was not physically present when the will was prepared and executed.

The rule that where a fiduciary relationship has been established, a presumption of undue influence arises, is not limited to holographs, nor confined to wills otherwise prepared by the testator himself. It encompasses with equal force wills written for the testator by a third person. There is no sound reason supporting the view that a testator, whose will has become subservient to the undue influence of another, is purged of the effects of that influence merely because the desired testamentary document is prepared by an attorney who knows nothing of the antecedent circumstances.

The chancellor was justified in finding that the physical absence of Holland during Mrs. Moses' brief visit to the office of the attorney who wrote the will did not suffice to abate or destroy the presumption of undue influence.

The chancellor was the judge of the credibility of the witnesses and the weight and worth of their testimony. Moreover, as trier of facts, it was for him to resolve conflicts and to interpret evidence where it was susceptible of more than one reasonable interpretation. It was also his prerogative to draw reasonable inferences from facts proved. As said in Croft, supra, '[T]he only positive and affirmative proof required is of facts and circumstances from which the undue influence may be reasonably inferred.' This Court, in passing upon the sufficiency of the evidence to support the factual findings of the chancellor, must accept as true all that the evidence proved or reasonably tended to prove, together with all reasonable inferences to be drawn from it, supporting such findings.

Viewed in the light of the above rules, it cannot be said that chancellor was manifestly wrong in finding that Holland occupied a dual fiduciary relationship with respect to Mrs. Moses, both conventional and actual, attended by suspicious circumstances as set forth in his opinion, which gave rise to a presumption of undue influence in the production of the 1964 will, nor that he was manifestly wrong in finding that this presumption was not overcome by 'clearest proof' that in making and executing the will Mrs. Moses acted upon her 'own volition and upon the fullest deliberation,' or upon independent advice and counsel of one wholly devoted to her interest.

* * *

As stated in Croft, supra, the rule that a presumption of undue influence arises when a fiduciary relationship is established applies with even greater stringency in cases of transactions *inter vivos*. In the land transaction, Holland attended as Mrs. Moses' attorney. She had no other advice or counsel. The chancellor correctly held that, under the circumstances, Holland, as her attorney, could take no interest adverse to Mrs. Moses in the land purchased by her. He took title to the half interest in the land as trustee for Mrs. Moses and not otherwise. His apparent claim of ownership of a half interest was properly cancelled and removed as a cloud upon the title of Mrs. Moses to the complete fee. Johnson v. Outlaw, 56 Miss. 541 (1879) and Cameron v. Lewis, 56 Miss. 601 (1879). See also Sojourner v. Sojourner, 247 Miss. 342, 153 So.2d 803, 156 So.2d 579 (1963) and Smith v. Dean, 240 S.W.2d 789 (Tex.Civ.App.) (1951).

For the foregoing reasons, the petition for rehearing is sustained, the original majority opinion is withdrawn, this opinion will be that of the Court, and the decree of the chancery court will be affirmed.

Petition for rehearing sustained, original opinion withdrawn, and decree of chancery court affirmed.

ETHRIDGE, C.J., and GILLESPIE, RODGERS and JONES, JJ., concur.

BRADY, PATTERSON, INZER and ROBERTSON, JJ., dissent.

ROBERTSON, Justice (dissenting):

I am unable to agree with the majority of the Court that Mrs. Moses should not be allowed to dispose of her property as she so clearly intended.

Since 1848 it has been the law of this state that every person twenty-one years of age, male of female, married or unmarried, being of sound and disposing mind, has the power by last will and testament or codicil in writing to dispose of all of his or her worldly possessions as he or she sees fit. § 657 Miss.Code 1942 Ann. (1956).

In 1848 the Legislature also said:

> 'Whenever any last will and testament shall empower and direct the executor as to the sale of property, the payment of debts and legacies, and the management of the estate, *the directions of the will shall be followed by the executor* * * *.' § 518 Miss.Code 1942 Ann. (1956). (Emphasis added).

The intent and purpose of the lawmakers was crystal clear: No matter what the form of the instrument, if it represented the free, voluntary and knowledgeable act of the testator or testatrix it was a good will, and the directions of the will should be followed. We said in Gillis v. Smith, 114 Miss. 665, 75 So. 451 (1917):

> "A man of sound mind may execute a will or a deed from any sort of motive satisfactory to him, *whether that motive be love, affection, gratitude, partiality, prejudice, or even a whim or caprice.*" 114 Miss. at 677, 75 So. at 453. (Emphasis added).

Mrs. Fannie T. Moses was 54 years of age when she executed her last will and testament on May 26, 1964, leaving most of her considerable estate to Clarence H. Holland, her good friend, but a man fifteen years her junior. She had been married three times, and each of these marriages was dissolved by the death of her husband. Holland's friendship with Mrs. Moses dated back to the days of her second husband, Robert L. Dickson. He was also a friend of her third husband, Walter Moses.

She was the active manager of commercial property in the heart of Jackson, four apartment buildings containing ten rental units, and a 480-acre farm until the day of her death. All of the witnesses conceded that she was a good businesswoman, maintaining and repairing her properties with promptness and dispatch, and paying her bills promptly so that she would get the cash discount. She was a strong personality and pursued her own course, even though her manner of living did at times embarrass her sisters and estranged her from them.

The chancellor found that she was of sound and disposing mind and memory on May 26, 1964, when she executed her last will and testament, and I think he was correct in this finding.

The chancellor found that there was a confidential relationship between Mrs. Moses and Holland, who had acted as her attorney in the past, and who was, in addition, a close and intimate friend, and that because of this relationship and some suspicious circumstances a presumption of undue influence arose.

In Croft v. Alder, 237 Miss. 713, 115 So.2d 683 (1959), this Court said:

> '57 Am.Jur., Wills, Secs. 389, 390, state that, although *the mere existence of confidential relations between a testator and a beneficiary under his will does not raise a presumption that the beneficiary exercised undue influence over the testator,* as it does with gifts *inter vivos,* such consequence follows *where the beneficiary 'has been actively concerned in some way with the preparation or execution of the will, or where the relationship is coupled with some suspicious circumstances, such as mental infirmity of the testator;'* or where the beneficiary in the confidential relation was active directly in preparing the will or procuring its execution, and obtained under it a substantial benefit. * * *' 237 Miss. at 723–724, 115 So.2d at 686. (Emphasis added).

There is no proof in this voluminous record that Holland ever did or said anything to Mrs. Moses about devising her property to anybody, much less him. It is conceded that in the absence of the presumption of undue influence that there is no basis to support a finding that Holland exercised undue influence over Mrs. Moses. This being true, the first question to be decided is whether the presumption of undue influence arises under the circumstances of this case.

It is my opinion that the presumption did not arise. The fact, alone, that a confidential relationship existed between Holland and Mrs. Moses is not sufficient to give rise to the presumption of undue influence in a will case. We said in Croft, supra:

> '[S]uch consequence follows where the beneficiary *'has been actively concerned in some way with the preparation or execution of the will,* or where the relationship is coupled with some suspicious circumstances, *such as mental infirmity of the testator;'* or where *the beneficiary* in the confidential relation *was active directly in preparing the will or procuring its execution,* and obtained under it a substantial benefit.' 237 Miss. at 723–724, 115 So.2d at 686. (Emphasis added).

It was not contended in this case that Holland was in any way actively concerned with the preparation or execution of the will. Appellees rely solely upon the finding of the chancellor that there were suspicious circumstances. However, the suspicious circumstances listed by the chancellor in his opinion had nothing whatsoever to do with the preparation or execution of the will. These were remote antecedent circumstances having to do with the meretricious relationship of the parties, and the fact that at times Mrs. Moses drank to excess and could be termed an alcoholic, but there is no proof in this long record that her use of alcohol affected her will power or her ability to look after her extensive real estate holdings. It is common knowledge that many persons who could be termed alcoholics, own, operate and manage large business enterprises with success. The fact that she chose to leave most of her property to the man she loved in preference to her sisters and brother is not such an unnatural disposition of her property as to render it invalid.

* * *

In this case, there were no suspicious circumstances surrounding the preparation or execution of the will, and in my opinion the chancellor was wrong in so holding. However, even if it be conceded that the presumption of undue influence did arise, this presumption was overcome by clear and convincing evidence of good faith, full knowledge and independent consent and advice.

* * *

What else could she have done? She met all the tests that this Court and other courts have carefully outlined and delineated. The majority opinion says that this still was not enough, that there were 'suspicious circumstances' and 'antecedent agencies', but even these were not connected in any shape, form or fashion with the preparation or execution of her will. They had to do with her love life and her drinking habits and propensities.

It would appear that the new procedure will be to fine-tooth comb all the events of a person's life and if, in the mind of the judge on the bench at that particular time, there are any 'suspicious circumstances' or 'antecedent agencies' in that person's life even though they are in nowise connected with the preparation or execution of that person's will, such last will and testament will be set aside and held for naught. With all time-honored tests out the window, the trial judge will be in the dangerous predicament of embarking on an unknown sea, without chart or compass.

If full knowledge, deliberate and voluntary action, and independent consent and advice have not been proved in this case, then they just cannot be proved. We should be bound by the uncontradicted testimony in the record; we should not go completely outside the record and guess, speculate and surmise as to what happened.

I think that the judgment of the lower court should be reversed and the last will and testament of Fannie T. Moses executed on May 26, 1964, admitted to probate in solemn form.

BRADY, PATTERSON and INZER, JJ., join in this dissent.

3. Homosexuality

In re Will of Kaufmann

Supreme Court of New York, Appellate Division, 1964
20 A.D.2d 464, 247 N.Y.S.2d 664, *aff'd*, 15 N.Y.2d 825, 257 N.Y.S.2d 941,
205 N.E.2d 864 (1965)

McNally, J.

This will contest is limited to the issue of undue influence. The contestants are the distributees of, and the proponent is unrelated to, the decedent. Two juries have found undue influence. On the prior appeal, by a divided court, the decree denying probate was reversed and a new trial directed because of error (14 A.D.2d 411). Appellant argues the proof in its totality fails to establish a jury question on the issue of undue influence. This court's prior determination impliedly held that the contestants had established a prima facie case on the issue of undue influence. (Politi v. Irvmar Realty Corp., 13 A.D.2d 469.) As a matter of sound policy, the law of the case should apply.

The instrument offered for probate is dated June 19, 1958. The decedent, Robert D. Kaufmann, was then 44, unmarried, a millionaire with a substantial income. Robert's sole distributees were two brothers, Joel and Aron. Joel is married and his sons are Richard and Lee, infants over 14 years of age. Aron is unmarried and an invalid.

Robert had inherited all his wealth from his parents. He had no liking or aptitude for business. His inherited wealth consisted principally of minority interests in various family enterprises in which he did not actually participate.

In and prior to 1947 Robert was intimately and warmly associated and identified with his relatives; he lived with his brother Joel in Washington and was particularly attached to and fond of his nephews, Richard and Lee. In 1947 Robert took up painting, an interest which he pursued and developed with increasing involvement with the passage of time and with a great measure of artistic success. During the latter part of 1947 or early 1948, Robert came to New York City and set up his own establishment. He was then about 34.

Until about 1951 Robert maintained his apartment at 965 Fifth Avenue. In 1951 he purchased a five-story town house at 42 East 74th Street. In addition, in 1955 Robert acquired a Summer house in Quogue, Long Island, and in 1958 a Winter home in Key West, Florida.

It would appear that Robert and the proponent, Walter A. Weiss, met in 1948. Weiss was the senior of Robert by five years. Weiss did not testify at either of the two trials. In his pretrial examination Weiss stated he was an attorney who did not practice. His pedigree, resources and means of income in 1948 do not appear.

On June 15, 1948 an agreement prepared by Weiss was entered into between Robert and Weiss whereby Weiss was retained as "financial advisor and business consultant" at an annual "retainer" of $10,000 for the period of one year with the right in Weiss to terminate the arrangement on "one weeks' notice, if he [Weiss] finds conditions make it impossible in his opinion to function effectively". The agreement recites the purpose of Weiss to advise Robert as to his then investments and towards the end of "developing new opportunities for financial profit", it also recites: "It is contemplated an office will be maintained and probably a corporation will be formed, as dictated by maximum business gain."

Robert paid Weiss annually thereafter the sum of $10,000; in addition, he made tax-free gifts to Weiss of about $3,000 during the years 1956, 1957 and 1958. Weiss also received from Robert $4,500 for his services in the sale of a hotel owned by Robert.

Soon after June, 1948 the books and records of Robert were transferred from Washington to New York. Theretofore Robert's records had been kept by employees of Robert's family in Washington at no expense to Robert. Washington was the main business headquarters of the family.

During the latter part of 1948 offices were established at 630 Fifth Avenue and announcements printed of the opening on January 6, 1949 of offices as "financial con-

sultants" by "Walter A. Weiss and Robert D. Kaufmann". Robert paid all office expenses; Weiss contributed his time. The venture earned no fees for financial consultations during the 10 years of its existence. The sole investment made was in a garage
construction enterprise adverted to as "Multi-Deck" in which Weiss' brother was the
principal. On Weiss' advice Robert invested $120,000 therein and the end result was a
total loss.

In 1949 Weiss moved into Robert's apartment at 965 Fifth Avenue. Weiss lived with
Robert until the latter's death on April 18, 1959.

The five-story town house at 42 East 74th Street, purchased in 1951, was extensively
renovated. The top floor was made an office, a full-time secretary employed; the remainder of the building was elaborately furnished and appointed as living quarters. A
full-time cook was employed. Weiss took full charge of the establishment, its furnishing, the employment of help and the maintenance of the household. All mail and in-
coming telephone calls were routed to and through Weiss.

Robert and Weiss travelled to Paris in 1950 for a few months; to Europe, West In-
dies, the Virgin Islands, Haiti, Greece and other countries during 1952 and 1953 and
around the world in 1956. Robert paid all expenses. Weiss claims to have paid his share
of living and travel expenses but we have no evidence other than his declaration on
that score.

On April 19, 1950 Robert made a will providing for bequests to his father's and
brother's wives, his father's secretary who had for many years been in charge of Robert's
records, his housekeeper and art teacher, the Institute for Psycho-Therapy, Inc., and the
Lillian Swope Foundation. To Weiss he devised the stock in Multi-Deck. In addition,
Robert cancelled Weiss' indebtedness to him. The will recited provision had been made
for an aunt of Robert by way of insurance. The residue was divided into four parts: two
for the benefit of his brothers and two for the benefit of his two nephews. Three executors were nominated—Robert's father, his brother Joel and his cousin Donald.

The 1950 will reflects a natural testamentary disposition in the light of the nature
and extent of Robert's estate, his family and his known relations to and with others.

Weiss had made efforts to insinuate himself into the good graces of Robert's family
without success. The investment counseling project was his brainchild. In his view it contemplated the exploitation of his knowledge by Robert's family. Weiss' pretrial deposition
is that "he [Robert] understood that on the facts his main contribution would be his con-
tacts and the possibility for new business that might arise through his family and his companies, or through other connections that he might have. And we sent announcements of
the opening of this business to all of his friends and business connections".

No business was forthcoming. Robert's family was unimpressed. Weiss was frustrated. He had succeeded in inducing Robert to place the utmost confidence in him but
had been totally rejected by Robert's family. On April 4, 1951 Weiss' confidential memorandum to Robert states:

> "It would be a good thing for me if I were able to achieve polite, formal
> business relations with your brother [Joel]. What he thinks of me personally
> cannot concern my business life. I have always felt that he has no faith in me
> and his surface facade was a 'double-dealing', painful, and embarrassing to us
> both. It would surprise me if we were able to work well together, in the light of
> the record. At your request I am willing to try, and a full discussion of these

present communications is a likely starting point. I repeat—Joel's personal appraisal of me is not in issue since I feel he does not know me. Your own continued confidence is naturally very gratifying, particularly in the face of so much family unpleasantness. That, too, however, I must reject from my door, as an inevitable part of your own family set-up. * * *

It cannot be doubted that prior to 1948 Robert was dependent on Joel in financial matters; that Robert was not involved in decision making; he had shown no interest in such involvement; that he was warmly attached to his family and had no serious differences with them. Weiss' pretrial statement does not suggest otherwise.

Shortly after taking up with Weiss, Robert's financial records were transferred from Washington to New York; Robert employed Weiss as financial adviser, and they launched the venture of financial consultants. There is no reality to support the marked changes. There is no evidence of any particular qualifications on the part of Weiss in financial matters; there is no suggestion of any practical reason for assuming the burden and expense of the maintenance of records in New York and the transaction of business away from the center of the family financial activities in Washington. There is no realistic expectancy of any demand for the services of either Robert or Weiss as financial consultants. On the other hand, these activities may have served to inspire Robert with a false feeling of accomplishment and independence.

Weiss' pretrial statement is: "I remember his [Robert] asking me if I would undertake to represent him and to handle his affairs and to help him be independent so that he could take his affairs unto himself." In addition, Weiss said that Robert was obsessed with the idea of independence and Weiss offered to help him towards that end. If Weiss successfully persuaded Robert that he was achieving independence when, in fact, Weiss was extending and exploiting Robert's dependence and estranging Robert from his family, then he violated his undertaking and the issue is presented whether the instrument offered for probate is a product of the breach of faith.

In 1949 Robert opened a checking account with Bankers Trust Company. Weiss was given power to draw against this account. Soon thereafter a similar arrangement was made as to an account with Chemical Bank New York Trust Co. Thereafter, until Robert's death, Weiss had the power to draw against all Robert's bank accounts. In 1951 Weiss acquired a general power of attorney from Robert. Weiss had unrestricted access to Robert's safe-deposit box.

The record establishes that since 1950 those selected by Weiss rendered medical and legal services to Robert. In 1951 Robert changed his attorneys. On June 13, 1951 he executed a new will. This enlarged Weiss' share of Robert's estate. In addition to personal effects and paintings, the will devises to Weiss the 74th Street residence and one half of the residue, and he is made the trustee of several trusts and one of three executors, the others being Robert's brother, Joel, and Robert's psychiatrist, Dr. Janet M. Rioch. Weiss' expectancy under the provisions of this will was over $500,000.

Contemporaneously with the will of June 13, 1951 Robert signed a letter of the same date purporting to explain his will. The letter affirms the will contains unusual provisions in that "a sizeable portion" of Robert's estate is devised to a man "not a member of my family". The letter to Robert's brothers proceeds to state the reasons for the provisions. It recites that Robert first met Weiss in 1946; that Robert's outlook was then "approaching the nadir"; he was a "frustrated time-wasting little boy"; he was "terribly unhappy, highly emotional and filled to the brim with a grandly variegated group of fears, guilt and assorted complexes". It states that Robert fortunately met Walter who encouraged him to submit to psychoanalysis. In addition, the letter goes on to state:

> Walter gave me the courage to start something which slowly but eventually permitted me to supply for myself everything my life had heretofore lacked: an outlet for my long-latent but strong creative ability in painting,... a balanced, healthy sex life which before had been spotty, furtive and destructive; an ability to reorientate myself to actual life and to face it calmly and realistically. All of this adds up to Peace of Mind—and what a delight, what a relief after so many wasted, dark, groping, fumbling immature years to be reborn and become adult!
>
> I am eternally grateful to my dearest friend—best pal, Walter A. Weiss. What could be more wonderful than a fruitful, contented life and who more deserving of gratitude now, in the form of an inheritance, than the person who helped most in securing that life? I cannot believe my family could be anything else but glad and happy for my own comfortable self-determination and contentment and equally grateful to the friend who made it possible.
>
> Love to you all,
>
> Bob.

The letter is accompanied by an envelope addressed to Robert's brothers and the Kaufmann family. The envelope is unsealed. The letter and envelope thereafter accompanied the three succeeding wills prepared by attorneys other than the one who drew the will of 1951. Prior to 1954, the 1951 letter was in the possession of the attorney who had drawn the 1951 and the 1953 wills. In or about May, 1954, the letter of June 13, 1951 and the letter of October 23, 1952, hereafter described, came into the possession of Weiss who caused them to be delivered with the 1953 will to the attorneys who thereafter prepared the last two wills.

The letter of 1951 fixes the year 1946 as the year of meeting between Robert and Weiss. The record evidence is that this event occurred in 1948. The anticipation of their meeting by more than one year is significant in that it was during 1947 and before Robert met Weiss that Robert took up and commenced his career in art. It is in the artistic area that Robert was productive and accomplished. Weiss was not an artist. Robert's art teacher was provided for in the wills prior to but was excluded from the will offered for probate.

* * *

To the extent that the letter implies or suggests a marked improvement of a previously disoriented and fearful personality, it is again at odds with reality as will appear.

Assuming, however, the content of the letter, it completely fails to explain the extent of the testamentary gift to Weiss tantamount to over a half million dollars.

* * *

The record shows beyond dispute that prior to 1948 Robert had no financial responsibilities and had assumed none. His affairs were in the hands of his brother Joel, whose holdings and financial interests were the same as Robert's. Robert had a large fortune, a substantial income and no responsibilities. Unquestionably Robert was dependent on Joel as to matters of investments and management of his various interests. All of this was being attended to without expense to Robert.

Robert was endowed with a good mind, sensitivity, artistic ability and generous disposition. He earnestly sought independence. However, he had no prior experience in assuming responsibility; all decisions had been made for him. He sought help and direction to satisfy his drive for independence. He turned to Weiss for that help. Weiss acknowledges he was originally retained by Robert "to represent him and to handle his affairs and to help him be independent so that he could take his affairs unto himself".

The arrangement was not one of master and servant or principal and agent; it was a confidential relationship more in the nature of teacher and pupil in the area of finance with specific application to the resources and assets of Robert. It had a very ominous inception. The agreement dated June 15, 1948 prepared by Weiss, a lawyer by training, obligated Robert for one year, provided for annual compensation of $10,000, the sum demanded by Weiss and not objected to by Robert, and was terminable at the option of Weiss on one week's notice. Weiss was retained as "financial advisor and business consultant". This one-sided agreement may, perhaps, be justified on the premise that Weiss was entitled to make the best bargain and was not then under any legal obligation to protect Robert. Weiss' attitude did not augur well for the qualities of fairness and loyalty required on his part to achieve Robert's desire for the capacity to be independent in matters of business.

* * *

Weiss and Robert lived together from 1949 to the date of Robert's death. The evidence enabled the jury to find that Robert became increasingly dependent on Weiss socially and businesswise. Moreover, it supports the view that this dependence was encouraged and that Weiss took affirmative steps to insulate Robert from his family and persons he sought to cultivate.

Robert gave Weiss his unbounded confidence and trust. Weiss exploited Robert, induced him to transfer to him the stewardship formerly exercised by Joel, increased Robert's need for dependency, prevented and curtailed associations which threatened his absolute control of Robert and alienated him from his family.

Weiss, in his memorandum of April 4, 1951, attributes to Joel the following description of his role which the jury could have found to be the fact: "I believe Joel finds it most acceptable to his pride to consider that I have instigated an independent will in you for my own purposes; that you serve my selfish desire to mix into his all-important, fascinating business machinations—all out of some kind of misguided weakness of will!"

Weiss was responsible for the displacement of the attorneys who prepared the 1950 will; he introduced Robert to Garrison who prepared the instrument offered for probate. Weiss recommended the doctors who treated Robert; he employed all help who came in contact with Robert. Mail and telephone communications were routed through Weiss. Family mail at times was destroyed and did not reach Robert. Correspondence purporting to be from Robert was dictated by Weiss.

Weiss saw to it none other than himself took advantage of Robert. Weiss warned Mapson, Robert's companion on the trip, not to take advantage of Robert during their stay in Paris in 1953. Finally, Weiss arrived in Paris unannounced and in the presence of Robert, who stood by mutely, told Mapson to remove himself. Robert attempted to maintain secretly his contact with Mapson in New York but was found out by Weiss who physically intervened. Again Robert submitted silently.

Anne McDonnell, the housekeeper and cook, testified Weiss was master of the household and brooked no interference from Robert. She also testified there were occasions when Weiss insisted that Robert sign papers without opportunity to read them and that Robert complied.

Watkins, a banker friend of Robert's father, testified he talked at length with Robert about the Fairfax matter. On one occasion Weiss was present and did all the talking while Robert was mute. On another occasion Watkins was alone with Robert and his only response was: "That's the way Walter [Weiss] wants it."

Robert perceptibly lost weight during the latter years, in part due to a low cholesterol diet. He became disinterested in his attire and appearance. After 1950 he received extensive psychiatric treatment, the nature of which does not appear.

In 1955 Robert complained of inability to sleep. His inability to sleep continued until his death. He took large quantities of pills for the condition which included doriden, miltown, seconal and nembutal—medication to reduce tension and induce sleep. He was unable to sleep without medication. On April 18, 1959, asleep at his home in Key West, Robert died in a fire which destroyed the house.

* * *

Following the death of Robert, Weiss disclaimed knowledge of the letter of June 13, 1951; disclaimed knowledge of the details of the change of beneficiaries as to the insurance policies and averred initial knowledge after Robert's death of the instrument offered for probate. In all of these respects the jury could have found Weiss lied deliberately.

Contestants' medical expert testified the record evidence delineated a personality with pathological dependency; one unable to deal with reality, insecure, unstable and who tends to submit unreasonably to the will of another. There was no expert medical testimony to the contrary.

One may make testamentary disposition of his worldly goods as he pleases. The motives and vagaries or morality of the testator are not determinative provided the will is the free and voluntary disposition of the testator and is not the product of deceit. There are two principal categories of undue influence in the law of wills, the forms of which are circumscribed only by the ingenuity and resourcefulness of man. One class is the gross, obvious and palpable type of undue influence which does not destroy the intent or will of the testator but prevents it from being exercised by force and threats of harm to the testator or those close to him. The other class is the insidious, subtle and impalpable kind which subverts the intent or will of the testator, internalizes within the mind of the testator the desire to do that which is not his intent but the intent and end of another. (Marx v. McGlynn, 88 N. Y. 357; Rollwagen v. Rollwagen, 63 N. Y. 504, 519.)

If it appeared to the satisfaction of the jury that Weiss willfully alienated Robert from his family by falsely accusing Joel of fraud and mismanagement in the conduct of the family business enterprises for the purpose of causing Robert to disinherit members of his family, then the jury properly could have found undue influence. (Matter of Anna, 248 N. Y. 421, supra.; Tyler v. Gardiner, 35 N. Y. 559, 595.)

The fact that the relation between Robert and Weiss may have afforded Robert some satisfaction did not enable Weiss deceitfully, improperly and insidiously to turn Robert against his family. (Matter of Budlong, 126 N. Y. 423, 432, supra.; Rollwagen v. Rollwagen, supra, p. 520.)

We are concerned with the testamentary mind, intent and purpose of Robert on June 19, 1958, when the instrument offered for probate was executed. To what extent Weiss affected Robert's mind and whether, if at all, he influenced his testamentary intent can only be determined upon a close examination of the interaction between the two over the course of the period between 1948 and the time of death, April 18, 1959. When the influence, if any, is ascertained, we can then address ourselves to the question whether it was within legally permissible bounds or exceeded them and was therefore undue influence.

* * *

If Weiss was in Europe at the times he became beneficiary of the life insurance policies and at the times when the four wills were executed in which he is named, and Robert was living in New York near or with his family, much of the argument made by counsel for appellant would be compelling. The assumed situation is what was present in Marx v. McGlynn (88 N. Y. 357, supra.). There, Bradley was in Europe, 3,000 miles away from the testatrix in New York when she executed the will. The testatrix lived with her sister and was among friends with whom she was brought up. However, there had been a long close relation between Bradley and the testatrix. Bradley had been spiritual advisor of the testatrix; had been her traveling companion and had shown great influence over her. The court there observed that Bradley did not influence the testatrix as to her property, or alienate her from her relatives; that at all times she had and kept control and that Bradley was given no control over her property; moreover, that Bradley was not her agent with respect to her property.

All of the elements adverted to in *Marx* and not present there are here conclusively established. In addition, there is here proximity to the point of oneness, and the presence of Weiss within the same household at the times the wills were made and the beneficiaries displaced in respect of the life insurance.

In *Marx* the court held there was a presumption of undue influence on the part of Bradley which, however, the Surrogate held had been overcome and the Court of Appeals affirmed, saying (p. 371): "But there are certain cases in which the law indulges in the presumption that undue influence has been used, and those cases are * * * a will * * * of * * * a ward in favor of his guardian, or any person in favor of his priest or religious adviser, or where other close confidential relationships exist."

Here, the circumstances spell out a confidential relation between proponent and the decedent which gave rise to an obligation on the part of the proponent-devisee to offer an explanation. The language of this court in Matter of Satterlee (281 App. Div. 251, 254) is apropos: "Surely, in the light of the unusual setting and the highly fiduciary relationship which proponent had assumed toward decedent, it was incumbent on him to come forward and explain his becoming the principal beneficiary under her will".

Matter of Walther (6 N Y 2d 49) is distinguishable on the facts. Here, we are concerned with a marked departure from a prior, natural plan of testamentary disposition which excessively and unnaturally favors a nonrelative under circumstances establishing motive, opportunity, overreaching and persistent involvement in transfers and dispositions of property in contemplation of death.

The issue of undue influence was submitted to the jury without the benefit to the contestants of any presumption. The charge placed the unrelieved burden of establishing undue influence upon the contestants. The issue was given to the jury in the aspect most favorable to the appellant; appellant made no exception to the charge. The record overwhelmingly sustains the verdict on undue influence on the basis of the charge made.

The decree denying probate of the instrument dated June 19, 1958 should be affirmed, with costs to respondents payable out of the estate.

* * *

Witmer, J. (dissenting).

* * *

The case for the contestants is grounded completely upon circumstantial evidence, and consists of evidence of a relationship between the testator and the proponent Weiss begun in the late 1940's and continuing until testator's death in April, 1959. No specific act is relied upon as constituting the alleged undue influence inducing the propounded will; but the claim is that from about 1950 testator was under the complete domination of Weiss.

* * *

Testator relied heavily upon Weiss to attend to most administrative details and relied upon his business advice. The record shows that at an early date testator's father and brother Joel, and other members of his family and friends, resented testator's close relationship with Weiss. It also shows that Weiss knew this, and he had little love for them. Contestants charge that Weiss was the cause of their business differences with testator. They assert that Weiss was the mastermind behind all of testator's demands in his business relations with them, and who in the background prepared the letters which testator sent to them, many of which are in evidence. They also contend that Weiss used the differences thus arising between testator and his brothers as a means of encouraging testator to change his will in Weiss' favor; and there is evidence that Weiss had a hand from time to time in advising testator's attorneys as to testamentary changes testator desired. In support of the charge of undue influence contestants have also presented evidence that testator was subservient to Weiss' wishes on a number of occasions from 1952 onward, with particular reference to social relations. There is also evidence that testator used sleeping pills, lost weight and submitted to psychoanalysis.

This evidence has been sufficient to cause two juries to declare that testator's will was induced by undue influence. Was it sufficient therefor under the laws of this State?

It is elementary that the statutory right of a competent person to dispose of his property as he wishes may not be thwarted by disappointed relatives nor by jurors who think that the testator used bad judgment or was misled.

> "Undue influence is a fact which must be proved by the contestant and not merely assumed to exist. (Matter of Smith, 95 N. Y. 516; Matter of Ruef, 180 App. Div. 203, affd. 223 N. Y. 582; Matter of Rundles, 216 App. Div. 658.) Like any other fact, it may be proved by circumstantial evidence but the circumstances must lead to it not only by fair inference but as a necessary conclusion. To avoid the will of a competent testator on the ground of undue influence, the contestant must show facts entirely inconsistent with the hypothesis of the execution of the will by any means other than undue influence. (Cases cited.)" (Matter of Henderson, 253 App. Div. 140, 145.)

> "So, too, the mere fact that one is the sole legatee or sole distributee is not in itself evidence of the exercise of undue influence. (Matter of Dowdle, 224 App. Div. 450, affd. 256 N. Y. 629.)

"A mere showing of opportunity and even of a motive to exercise undue influence does not justify a submission of that issue to the jury, unless there is in addition evidence that such influence was actually utilized (Cudney v. Cudney, 68 N. Y. 148, 152; Matter of Reid, 298 N. Y. 878). (Matter of Walther, 6 N Y 2d 49, 55.)

The verdict in this case rests upon surmise, suspicion, conjecture and moral indignation and resentment, not upon the legally required proof of undue influence; and it cannot stand.

The record shows that the testator was intelligent and generally healthy. The evidence that he lost weight was explained by his doctor who said that he had placed him upon a no-fat diet. True, the testator was not wholly like other people. He had little zest for business, which fact set him apart from his family. He had artistic ability, and particularly loved to paint. So did Weiss. They had common interests. Testator felt and said that he had uncommon ability as a painter and that some day he would be known for his artistic work. In this, he was not wholly wrong, for it appears that eighty museums have accepted his work for permanent display.

The record is replete with evidence of the friendly relation, indeed love and affection, that existed between testator and Weiss for a decade. There is no substantial evidence that their relationship was not one of mutual esteem and self-respect. The isolated incidents of testator bowing to Weiss' wishes on certain occasions over this period fall far short of conclusively pointing to a subserviency, when viewed in the light of all the evidence. True, testator relied upon Weiss in business and administrative matters, but that is not to say that testator was not essentially in command. There is evidence that at times testator made his own business decisions. The fact that Weiss advised testator in his business dealings with his brothers is not inconsistent with his position as testator's financial advisor. * * *

The issue in this case is not what were the morals of these men, nor whether testator led a normal life, nor whether Weiss has been proved a liar. The issue is, does the propounded instrument represent the intrinsic wishes and will of the testator, or was it the product of the command of Weiss which the testator did not really want to follow, but was unable to resist? The veracity of Weiss, it is true, may not be ignored in considering this issue.

* * *

Of course, the court does not condone the relationship, but the moral law may not be substituted for the law of wills; and it should not be overlooked that difficult cases tend to make bad law. Undoubtedly the testator was influenced, but the evidence in this case is entirely consistent with the complete lack of undue influence. Yet, because of the suspicious circumstances involved, the majority of this court as well as the court below would deny him his legal right to dispose of his property as he has chosen to do.

Contestants' psychiatrist, Dr. Herman, testified that he did not know for what reason the testator was psychoanalyzed; that the testator was an introvert; and that another psychiatrist could reach a different conclusion than did Dr. Herman concerning testator's independence. However misguided testator was, in view of his admitted competence and the equivocation by Dr. Herman "[t]he evidence is in no way inconsistent with the assumption that the will expresses the voluntary intent of the [testator] and does not satisfy the test that intervention and undue influence can only be established by evidence that is not inconsistent with a contrary hypothesis". (Matter of Walther, 6 N.Y.2d 49, 56, 188 N.Y.S.2d 168, 174, 159 N.E.2d 665.)

There was, thus, no question of fact for the jury; and proponents' motion for a directed verdict should have been granted. The decree appealed from should therefore be reversed, with costs to all parties appearing separately and filing briefs, payable out of the estate, and the matter remitted to the Surrogate's Court with directions to admit the will to probate.

Stevens, J., concurs in dissent.

Notes

Undue influence cases often appear as sensational headlines, movies, and books. *See, e.g.*, David Margolick, UNDUE INFLUENCE: THE EPIC BATTLE FOR THE JOHNSON & JOHNSON FORTUNE (1993) (describing the suit brought by the children of J. Seward Johnson against their stepmother, Barbara Piasecka, and the attorneys who played an instrumental role in the preparation of Mr. Johnson's Will). For a legal review, see John H. Langbein, *Will Contests*, 103 YALE L.J. 2039 (1994). Sexuality plays a major role in developing cases. *See, e.g.*, Joseph W. de Furia, Jr., *Testamentary Gifts Resulting from Meretricious Relationships: Undue Influence or Natural Beneficence?*, 64 NOTRE DAME L. REV. 200 (1989); Lawrence A. Frolik, *The Biological Roots of the Undue Influence Doctrine: What's Love Got To Do With It?*, 57 U. PITT L. REV. 841 (1996). There are special repercussions if a testator deviates from sexual norms. *See, e.g.*, Ray D. Madoff, *Unmasking Undue Influence*, 81 MINN. L. REV. 571 (1997).

Attorneys and those serving in confidential relationships with testators must be especially careful in anticipating contest. *See, e.g.*, Disciplinary Counsel v. Galinas, 76 Ohio St. 3d 87, 666 N.E.2d 1083 (1996) (attorney suspended for drafting a Will that gave him an interest in the estate). California has a statute that invalidates any bequest to named individuals, including any attorney who drafts the Will, unless the attorney is related by blood or marriage to the testator. See CAL. PROB. CODE ANN. § 21350 (2004). *But see* Vaupel v. Barr, 194 W. Va. 296, 460 S.E.2d 431 (1995) (attorney-friend was able to keep the bequest). Religious organizations are vulnerable to contest because of the confidentiality that resides between pastor and parishioner. *See* Estate of Maheras, 897 P.2d 268 (Okla. 1995). Nursing homes are certain to become the subject of more litigation as increasing numbers of persons trust in their care. *See* Matter of Burke, 82 A.D.2d 260, 441 N.Y.S.2d 542 (N.Y. App. Div. 2 Dept. 1981). The California Probate Code provides a certificate of independent review and should be considered when any form of confidentiality is present. *See* CAL. PROB. CODE § 21351 (2004).

I. Fraud

In re Roblin's Estate
Supreme Court of Oregon, 1957
210 Or. 371, 311 P.2d 459

ROSSMAN, Justice.

This is an appeal by Charles Dana Roblin, contestant, from a decree of the Circuit Court for Marion County which dismissed proceedings he had instituted to contest the will of his father, Charles Ernest Roblin, and which ordered that the will be admitted to probate.

Charles Ernest and Ollie M. Roblin, both now deceased, were the parents of the appellant, Charles Dana Roblin, and of a daughter, Ruth Emily Shantz, proponent and respondent. For convenience we will refer to the elder Charles Roblin as Mr. Roblin and to the younger as Charles.

The family resided for many years in Salem. When Ruth Married Carl Shantz they took their residence in Milwaukie, Oregon. Charles became a peripatetic, but during summer months returned to Salem for extended visits in the family home. In 1950 Mr. Roblin left the family home and made his abode in a Salem hotel. Ruth testified that he left in aggravation over his wife's conduct in sending money to Charles and paying his bills. In 1951 Mr. Roblin suffered a stroke and shortly repaired to a nursing home in Salem.

In the fall of 1951, Ruth, at her father's instance, arranged for him to undergo an eye operation in Portland. In that period he resided with Ruth and her husband for seven months. After he had recovered from the operation he returned to the nursing home where Ruth visited him every two weeks. Mrs. Roblin also called upon him from time to time, being driven to the nursing home in the Roblins' car by Charles. The latter, however, did not enter the home. Upon an earlier occasion when he attempted to visit his father, the latter ordered him out of the room in no unmistakable language.

Mrs. Roblin executed a will on July 3, 1953, and died five days later. Her will bequeathed all of her property equally to both children. Its terms were operative on property appraised at $1,581. But Charles received, in addition to his half of that sum, property worth $12,301.06 which was not part of the estate proper. This greater amount represented accounts and chattels the title to which was in Charles and the mother jointly, and to which he survived.

On either the evening of July 8 or the morning of July 9, 1953, Ruth visited her father in the nursing home and informed him, perhaps in response to his inquiry, that her mother had left everything to Charles except a diamond ring. Immediately Mr. Roblin ordered Ruth to obtain for him a lawyer. Ruth suggested a Mr. Steelhammer who was her husband's cousin. The suggestion was acceptable to her father, he having known Mr. Steelhammer through their mutual membership in the Salem Elks Lodge. On the morning of July 9 Mr. Steelhammer went to the nursing home and conversed in privacy with Mr. Roblin, who directed him to prepare a will, leaving Charles one dollar only and the remainder to Ruth. The father also requested Mr. Steelhammer to prepare a petition for a conservatorship of the father's property with Ruth as conservator. That afternoon, Ruth, upon Mr. Steelhammer's request, drove him to the nursing home. When they arrived, the attorney alone met with the testator, who then executed his will, with Steelhammer and the operator of the home as witnesses. The will nominated Ruth as executrix and left to her everything except one dollar which was bequeathed to Charles. The petition for conservatorship was filed on July 20. Mr. Roblin died September 6, 1953, aged 83.

* * *

Courts set aside wills whose provisions reflect the testator's belief in false data arising from fraudulent misrepresentation made to him by a beneficiary. In re Estate of Rosenberg, 196 Or. 219, 246 P.2d 858, 248 P.2d 340.

'Fraud which causes testator to execute a will consists of statements which are false, which are known to be false by the party who makes them, which are material, which are made with the intention of deceiving testator, which deceive testator, and which cause testator to act in reliance upon such statements.'

I Page on Wills, 3d Ed. 347, § 176. Absent any one of the elements of that definition of fraud, no ground for contest is established.

The statement which we are considering, and the consequences of its utterance, must be measured against the elements of fraud which vitiates a solemnly executed will.

The statement must be false and known to be such by the maker. In fact, Ruth's mother did not leave everything, except a ring, to her brother. Ruth was to receive half of $1,581; the other half of which went to Charles along with the $12,301.06 in jointly held property to which Charles survived. After the expenses of administration and taxes were paid by that estate, Ruth received $61.90. Charles received from his mother $12,367.96. The disparity is so great that Ruth may be excused for having been piqued, as is Charles now.

We must distinguish between a belief in the literal truth and falsity of a statement and that type of belief in falsity that underlies the fraudulent misrepresentation. Ruth testified at trial that 'The only thing one could say, or I did say, was that Mother had left everything to Charlie.' In this context a belief in the falsity of an utterance must be defined with regard to the nature of man and his reactions to an unexpected disappointment. The testimony just quoted demonstrates that at the time of utterance, and indeed at the time of trial, after reflection, Ruth doubted not that the hyperbole fairly described the division of her mother's estate.

The speaker must intend to deceive, and succeed. We are unwilling to decide that even a conscious exaggeration necessarily imports an intent to deceive. Even people of high character often exaggerate in order to express their belief with clarity and force. The purpose in instances of that kind is not to deceive, but better to communicate the belief. We are convinced that the statement made by Ruth is an example of that process. The speaker may in perfect good faith omit what he considers to be a non-material qualification upon his broad statement, thinking that a recital of all the details merely obfuscates the main point.

The misrepresentation must cause the testator to act upon it. In other words, the will must be the fruit of the fraud. In the Roblin family, little family unity or mutuality of attitude toward life bound father and son together. We know that the father emphatically expressed a desire that Charles stay away from the nursing home so that the two would not meet. Evidently, the wanderlust of the son was a canker to the parent. The learned trial judge would have been justified in a conclusion that the statement made by Ruth did not cause her father to rely upon it in the execution of his will, but rather that the statement merely provided an occasion for the taking of a step which the disappointed parent may have independently taken even if the statement had never been uttered.

The testimony of Ruth and of Charles conflicts in that she states, and he denies, that all her information about the division of their mother's estate came from him. If one believes her account, which the judge below may have done, her statement to her father cannot be objectionable. In that event, she merely relayed information which Charles gave her.

Both parties testified on direct and on cross-examination at some length about the amount of money each had received from Mr. and Mrs. Roblin inter vivos. We deem this evidence irrelevant. The statement of Ruth which is objected to refers only to the disposition of her mother's property upon her death. It does not relate to the inter vivos gifts to the children, of which Ruth received the greater share. Consequently the truth or falsity of the statement stands independent of the history of inter vivos donations.

Agreeing, as we do, with the disposition of this matter by the judge below, we affirm his decree.

Affirmed.

Latham v. Father Divine

Court of Appeals of New York, 1949
299 N.Y. 22, 85 N.E.2d 168

DESMOND, J.

The amended complaint herein has, in response to a motion under rule 106 of the Rules of Civil Practice, been dismissed for insufficiency. Its principal allegations are these: plaintiffs are first cousins, but not distributees, of Mary Sheldon Lyon, who died in October, 1946, leaving a will, executed in 1943, which gave almost her whole estate to defendant Father Divine, leader of a religious cult, and to two corporate defendants in some way connected with that cult, and to an individual defendant (Patience Budd) said to be one of Father Divine's active followers; that said will has been, after a contest instituted by distributees, probated under a compromise agreement with the distributees, by the terms of which agreement, to which plaintiffs were not parties, the defendants just above referred to will receive a large sum from the estate; that after the making of said will, decedent on several occasions expressed 'a desire and a determination to revoke the said will, and to execute a new will by which the plaintiffs would receive a substantial portion of the estate', 'that shortly prior to the death of the deceased she had certain attorneys draft a new will in which the plaintiffs were named as legatees for a very substantial amount, totalling approximately $350,000'; that 'by reason of the said false representations, the said undue influence and the said physical force' certain of the defendants 'prevented the deceased from executing the said new Will'; that, shortly before decedent's death, decedent again expressed her determination to execute the proposed new will which favored plaintiffs, and that defendants 'thereupon conspired to kill, and did kill, the deceased by means of a surgical operation performed by a doctor engaged by the defendants without the consent or knowledge of any of the relatives of the deceased.'

Nothing is better settled than that, on such a motion as this, all the averments of the attacked pleading are taken as true. For present purposes, then, we have a case where one possessed of a large property and having already made a will leaving it to certain persons, expressed an intent to make a new testament to contain legacies to other persons, attempted to carry out that intention by having a new will drawn which contained a large legacy to those others, but was, by means of misrepresentations, undue influence, force, and indeed, murder, prevented, by the beneficiaries named in the existing will, from signing the new one. Plaintiffs say that those facts, if proven, would entitle them to a judicial declaration, which their prayer for judgment demands, that defendants, taking under the already probated will, hold what they have so taken as constructive trustees for plaintiffs, whom decedent wished to, tried to, and was kept from, benefiting.

We find in New York no decision directly answering the question as to whether or not the allegations above summarized state a case for relief in equity. But reliable texts, and cases elsewhere (see 98 A. L. R. 474 et seq.) answer it in the affirmative. Leading writers (3 Scott on Trusts, pp. 2371–2376; 3 Bogert on Trusts and Trustees, Part 1, §§ 473–474, 498, 499; 1 Perry on Trusts and Trustees [7th ed.], pp. 265, 371) in one form or another, state the law of the subject to be about as it is expressed in comment i under section 184 of the Restatement of the Law of Restitution: '*Preventing revocation of will and making new will*. Where a devisee or legatee under a will already executed prevents the testator by fraud, duress or undue influence from revoking the will and executing a new will in favor of another or from making a codicil, so that the testator dies leaving the original will in force, the devisee or legatee holds the property thus acquired upon a constructive trust for the intended devisee or legatee.'

A frequently-cited case is Ransdel v. Moore (153 Ind. 393) where, with listing of many authorities, the rule is given thus (pp. 407–408): 'when an heir or devisee in a will prevents the testator from providing for one for whom he would have provided but for the interference of the heir or devisee, such heir or devisee will be deemed a trustee, by operation of law, of the property, real or personal, received by him from the testator's estate, to the amount or extent that the defrauded party would have received had not the intention of the deceased been interfered with. This rule applies also when an heir prevents the making of a will or deed in favor of another, and thereby inherits the property that would otherwise have been given such other person.' (To the same effect, see 4 Page on Wills [3d ed.], p. 961.)

While there is no New York case decreeing a constructive trust on the exact facts alleged here, there are several decisions in this court which, we think, suggest such a result, and none which forbids it. Matter of O'Hara (95 N. Y. 403), Trustees of Amherst College v. Ritch (151 N. Y. 282), Edson v. Bartow (154 N. Y. 199), and Ahrens v. Jones (169 N. Y. 555) which need not be closely analyzed here as to their facts, all announce, in one form or another, the rule that, where a legatee has taken property under a will, after agreeing, outside the will, to devote that property to a purpose intended and declared by the testator, equity will enforce a constructive trust to effectuate that purpose, lest there be a fraud on the testator. (In Williams v. Fitch, 18 N. Y. 546, a similar result was achieved in a suit for money had and received.) In each of those four cases first above cited in this paragraph, the particular fraud consisted of the legatee's failure or refusal to carry out the testator's designs, after tacitly or expressly promising so to do. But we do not think that a breach of such an engagement is the only kind of fraud which will impel equity to action. A constructive trust will be erected whenever necessary to satisfy the demands of justice. Since a constructive trust is merely 'the formula through which the conscience of equity finds expression' (Beatty v. Guggenheim Exploration Co., 225 N. Y. 380, 386; see 3 Bogert on Trusts and Trustees, Part 1, § 471; Lightfoot v. Davis, 198 N. Y. 261; Falk v. Hoffman, 233 N. Y. 199; Meinhard v. Salmon, 249 N. Y. 458; also, see, Warren in 41 Harv. L. Rev. 309 et seq.), its applicability is limited only by the inventiveness of men who find new ways to enrich themselves unjustly by grasping what should not belong to them. Nothing short of true and complete justice satisfies equity, and, always assuming these allegations to be true, there seems no way of achieving total justice except by the procedure used here.

The Appellate Division held that Hutchins v. Hutchins (7 Hill 104) decided by the Supreme Court, our predecessor, in 1845, was a bar to the maintenance of this suit. Hutchins v. Hutchins (supra) was a suit at law, dismissed for insufficiency in the days when law suits and equity causes had to be brought in different tribunals; the law court could give nothing but a judgment for damages (see discussion in 41 Harv. L. Rev. 313, supra). Testator Hutchins' son, named in an earlier will, charged that defendant had, by fraud, caused his father to revoke that will and execute a new one, disinheriting plaintiff. The court sustained a demurrer to the complaint, on the ground that the earlier will gave the son no title, interest or estate in his father's assets and no more than a hope or expectancy, the loss of which was too theoretical and tenuous a deprivation to serve as a basis for the award of damages (see, also, Simar v. Canaday, 53 N. Y. 298, 302, 303). Plaintiffs' disappointed hopes in the present case, held the Appellate Division, were similarly lacking in substance. But disappointed hopes and unrealized expectations were all that the secretly intended beneficiaries, not named in the wills, had in Matter of O'Hara, Trustees of Amherst College v. Ritch and Edson v. Bartow (supra) but that in itself was not enough to prevent the creation of constructive trusts in their favor. Hutchins v. Hutchins (supra), it seems, holds only this: that in a suit at law there must, as a basis for damages, be an invasion of a common-law right. To use that same standard in a suit for the declaration and enforcement of a constructive trust would be to deny and destroy the whole equitable theory of constructive trusts.

Nor do we agree that anything in the Decedent Estate Law or the Statute of Frauds stands in the way of recovery herein. This is not a proceeding to probate or establish the will which plaintiffs say testatrix was prevented from signing, nor is it an attempt to accomplish a revocation of the earlier will, as were Matter of Evans (113 App. Div. 373) and Matter of McGill (229 N. Y. 405, 411). The will Mary Sheldon Lyon did sign has been probated and plaintiffs are not contesting, but proceeding on, that probate, trying to reach property which has effectively passed thereunder (see Ahrens v. Jones, 169 N. Y. 555, 561, supra). Nor is this a suit to enforce an agreement to make a will or create a trust, or any other promise by decedent (Personal Property Law, §31; see Frankenberger v. Schneller, 258 N. Y. 270; Bayreuther v. Reinisch, 264 App. Div. 138, affd. 290 N. Y. 553; Blanco v. Velez, 295 N. Y. 224). This complaint does not say that decedent, or defendants, promised plaintiffs anything, or that defendants made any promise to decedent. The story is, simply, that defendants, by force and fraud, kept the testatrix from making a will in favor of plaintiffs. We cannot say, as matter of law, that no constructive trust can arise therefrom.

The ultimate determinations in Matter of O'Hara and Edson v. Bartow (supra) that the estates went to testators' distributees do not help defendants here, since, after the theory of constructive trust had been indorsed by this court in those cases, the distributees won out in the end, but only because the secret trusts intended by the two testators were, in each case, of kinds forbidden by statutes.

We do not agree with appellants that Riggs v. Palmer (115 N. Y. 506) completely controls our decision here. That was the famous case where a grandson, overeager to get the remainder interest set up for him in his grandfather's will, murdered his grandsire. After the will had been probated, two daughters of the testator who, under the will, would take if the grandson should predecease testator, sued and got judgment decreeing a constructive trust in their favor. It may be, as respondents assert, that the application of Riggs v. Palmer (supra) here would benefit not plaintiffs, but this testator's distributees. We need not pass on that now. But Riggs v. Palmer (supra) is generally helpful to appellants, since it forbade the grandson profiting by his own wrong in connection with a will; and, despite an already probated will and the Decedent Estate Law, Riggs v. Palmer (supra) used the device or formula of constructive trust to right the attempted wrong, and prevent unjust enrichment.

The reference to a conspiracy in the complaint herein makes it appropriate to mention Keviczky v. Lorber (290 N. Y. 297). Keviczky, a real estate broker, got judgment on findings that a conspiracy by defendants had prevented him from earning a commission which he would otherwise have gotten. All sides agreed that he had not in fact performed the engagement which would have entitled him to a commission as such; thus, when the conspiracy intervened to defeat his efforts, he had no contractual right to a commission but only an expectation thereof which was frustrated by the conspirators. Thus again we see, despite the broad language of Hutchins v. Hutchins (supra) that it is not the law that disappointed expectations and unrealized probabilities may never, under any circumstances, be a basis for recovery.

This suit cannot be defeated by any argument that to give plaintiffs judgment would be to annul those provisions of the Statute of Wills requiring due execution by the testator. Such a contention, if valid, would have required the dismissal in a number of the suits herein cited. The answer is in Ahrens v. Jones (169 N. Y. 555, 561, supra): "The trust does not act directly upon the will by modifying the gift, for the law requires wills to be wholly in writing, but it acts upon the gift itself as it reaches the possession of the legatee, or as soon as he is entitled to receive it. The theory is that the will has full effect by passing an absolute legacy to the legatee, and that then equity, in order to defeat fraud, raises a trust in favor of those intended to be benefited by the testator, and compels the legatee, as a trustee ex maleficio, to turn over the gift to them."

The judgment of the Appellate Division, insofar as it dismissed the complaint herein, should be reversed, and the order of Special Term affirmed, with costs in this court and in the Appellate Division. [See 299 N. Y. 599.]

LOUGHRAN, Ch. J., CONWAY and FULD, JJ., concur with DESMOND, J.;

LEWIS and DYE, JJ., dissent and vote for affirmance upon the grounds stated by VAUGHAN, J., writing for the Appellate Division.

Judgment reversed, etc.

IV. Revocation

Once a Last Will and Testament has been executed with proper formalities and intentionalities, it may be revoked under certain circumstances. Traditionally, the circumstances appear within statutes providing for the formalities of execution. Nonetheless, circumstances often occur that blur the fine lines delineated by the statutes, inviting court interpretation and construction. But in reviewing the material concerning revocation, we remain focused on the acts done by the Testator or the Testator's agent, and the intent evidenced by the Testator at the time of the act.

A. Physical Act

Uniform Probate Code (2003)

§ 2-507 Revocation by Writing or by Act.

(a) A will or any part thereof is revoked:

(1) by executing a subsequent will that revokes the previous will or part expressly or by inconsistency; or

(2) by performing a revocatory act on the will, if the testator performed the act with the intent and for the purpose of revoking the will or part or if another individual performed the act in the testator's conscious presence and by the testator's direction. For purposes of this paragraph, "revocatory act on the will" includes burning, tearing, canceling, obliterating, or destroying the will or any part of it. A burning, tearing, or canceling is a "revocatory act on the will," whether or not the burn, tear, or cancellation touched any of the words on the will.

(b) If a subsequent will does not expressly revoke a previous will, the execution of the subsequent will wholly revokes the previous will by inconsistency if the testator intended the subsequent will to replace rather than supplement the previous will.

(c) The testator is presumed to have intended a subsequent will to replace rather than supplement a previous will if the subsequent will makes a complete disposition of the testator's estate. If this presumption arises and is not rebutted by clear and convincing evidence, the previous will is revoked; only the subsequent will is operative on the testator's death.

(d) The testator is presumed to have intended a subsequent will to supplement rather than replace a previous will if the subsequent will does not make a complete disposition of the testator's estate. If this presumption arises and is not rebutted by clear and convincing evidence, the subsequent will revokes the previous will only to the extent the subsequent will is inconsistent with the previous will; each will is fully operative on the testator's death to the extent they are not inconsistent.

Notes

The Uniform Probate Code provides an example of the typical revocation by physical act statute, allowing for revocation if there is a specified act done to the Will. But note that the act need not touch the writing itself to be considered a valid revocation by physical act. This issue and its consequences appear in the following decision.

Thompson v. Royall
Supreme Court of Virginia, 1934
163 Va. 492, 175 S.E. 748

HUDGINS, J., delivered the opinion of the court.

The only question presented by this record, is whether the will of Mrs. M. Lou Bowen Kroll had been revoked shortly before her death.

The uncontroverted facts are as follows: On the 4th day of September, 1932, Mrs. Kroll signed a will, typewritten on five sheets of legal cap paper; the signature appeared on the last page duly attested by three subscribing witnesses. H. P. Brittain, the executor named in the will, was given possession of the instrument for safe-keeping. A codicil typed on the top third of one sheet of paper dated September 15, 1932, was signed by the testatrix in the presence of two subscribing witnesses. Possession of this instrument was given to Judge S. M. B. Coulling, the attorney who prepared both documents.

On September 19, 1932, at the request of Mrs. Kroll, Judge Coulling, and Mr. Brittain took the will and the codicil to her home where she told her attorney, in the presence of Mr. Brittain and another, to destroy both. But instead of destroying the papers, at the suggestion of Judge Coulling, she decided to retain them as memoranda, to be used as such in the event she decided to execute a new will. Upon the back of the manuscript cover, which was fastened to the five sheets by metal clasps, in the handwriting of Judge Coulling, signed by Mrs. Kroll, there is the following notation:

> This will null and void and to be only held by H. P. Brittain, instead of being destroyed, as a memorandum for another will if I desire to make same. This 19 Sept 1932.

> M. LOU BOWEN KROLL.

The same notation was made upon the back of the sheet on which the codicil was written, except that the name, S. M. B. Coulling, was substituted for H. P. Brittain; this was likewise signed by Mrs. Kroll.

Mrs. Kroll died October 2, 1932, leaving numerous nephews and nieces, some of whom were not mentioned in her will, and an estate valued at approximately $200,000. On motion of some of the beneficiaries, the will and codicil were offered for probate. All the interested parties including the heirs at law were convened, and on the issue, *devisavit vel non*, the jury found that the instruments dated September 4th and 15, 1932, were the last will and testament of Mrs. M. Lou Bowen Kroll. From an order sustaining the verdict and probating the will this writ of error was allowed.

For more than one hundred years, the means by which a duly executed will may be revoked, have been prescribed by statute. These requirements are found in section 5233 of the 1919 Code, the pertinent parts of which read thus:

> No will or codicil, or any part thereof, shall be revoked, unless * * * by a subsequent will or codicil, or by some writing declaring an intention to revoke the same, and executed in the manner in which a will is required to be executed, or by the testator, or some person in his presence and by his direction, cutting, tearing, burning, obliterating, canceling, or destroying the same, or the signature thereto, with the intent to revoke.

The notations, dated September 19, 1932, are not wholly in the handwriting of the testatrix, nor are her signatures thereto attached attested by subscribing witnesses; hence under the statute they are ineffectual as 'some writing declaring an intention to revoke.' The faces of the two instruments bear no physical evidence of any cutting, tearing, burning, obliterating, canceling, or destroying. The only contention made by appellants is, that the notation written in the presence, and with the approval, of Mrs. Kroll, on the back of the manuscript cover in the one instance, and on the back of the sheet containing the codicil in the other, constitute 'canceling' within the meaning of the statute.

Both parties concede that to effect revocation of a duly executed will, in any of the methods prescribed by statute, two things are necessary: (1) The doing of one of the acts specified, (2) accompanied by the intent to revoke—the *animo revocandi*. Proof of either, without proof of the other, is insufficient. Malone v. Hobbs, 1 Rob. (40 Va.) 346, 39 Am.Dec. 263; 2 Minor Ins. 925. The proof established the intention to revoke. The entire controversy is confined to the acts used in carrying out that purpose. The testatrix adopted the suggestion of her attorney to revoke her will by written memoranda, admittedly ineffectual as revocations by subsequent writings, but appellants contend the memoranda, in the handwriting of another, and testatrix's signatures, are sufficient to effect revocation by cancellation. To support this contention appellants cite a number of authorities which hold that the modern definition of cancellation includes, 'any act which would destroy, revoke, recall, do away with, overrule, render null and void, the instrument.'

Most of the authorities cited, that approve the above, or a similar meaning of the word, were dealing with the cancellation of simple contracts, or other instruments that require little or no formality in execution. However there is one line of cases which apply this extended meaning of 'canceling' to the revocation of wills. The leading case so holding is Warner v. Warner's Estate, 37 Vt. 356. In this case proof of the intent and the act were a notation on the same page with, and below the signature of the testator, reading: 'This will is hereby cancelled and annulled. In full this the 15th day of March in the year 1859,' and written lengthwise on the back of the fourth page of the foolscap paper, upon which no part of the written will appeared, were these words, 'Cancelled and is null and void. (Signed) I. Warner.' It was held this was sufficient to revoke the will under a statute similar to the one here under consideration.

In Evans' Appeal, 58 Pa.St. 238, the Pennsylvania court approved the reasoning of the Vermont court in Warner v. Warner's Estate, supra, but the force of the opinion is weakened when the facts are considered. It seems that there were lines drawn through two of the three signatures of the testator appearing in the Evans will, and the paper on which material parts of the will were written was torn in four places. It therefore appeared on the face of the instrument, when offered for probate, that there was a sufficient defacement to bring it within the meaning of both obliteration and cancellation.

The construction of the statute in Warner v. Warner's Estate, supra, has been criticized by eminent textwriters on wills, and the courts in the majority of the states in construing similar statutes have refused to follow the reasoning in that case. * * *

The above, and other authorities that might be cited, hold that revocation of a will by cancellation within the meaning of the statute, contemplates marks or lines across the written parts of the instrument, or a physical defacement, or some mutilation of the writing itself, with the intent to revoke. If written words are used for the purpose, they must be so placed as to physically affect the written portion of the will, not merely on blank parts of the paper on which the will is written. If the writing intended to be the act of cancelling, does not mutilate, or erase, or deface, or otherwise physically come in contact with any part of written words of the will, it cannot be given any greater weight than a similar writing on a separate sheet of paper, which identifies the will referred to, just as definitely, as does the writing on the back. If a will may be revoked by writing on the back, separable from the will, it may be done by a writing not on the will. This the statute forbids.

* * *

The attempted revocation is ineffectual, because testatrix intended to revoke her will by subsequent writings not executed as required by statute, and because it does not in any wise physically obliterate, mutilate, deface, or cancel any written parts of the will.

For the reasons stated, the judgment of the trial court is affirmed.

Affirmed.

Notes

Even though Uniform Probate Code § 2-507(a)(2) would seem to change the holding of the *Thompson* decision, the issue arises as to what must occur for the physical act to be sufficient for a revocation to occur. Must the act be on the same piece of paper as the Will itself? Is a mere line sufficient or is there a requirement of a level of proof, such as clear and convincing? Would physical acts done to a "copy" of the Will but not the Will itself be sufficient? *See, e.g., Restatement (Third) of Property* § 4.1 cmt. f. (1999). Finally, if physical revocation of the entire Will is allowed, and physical revocation of part of the Will is allowed, how may we tell when the Testator intended the act to revoke only part of the Will and not the whole Will? Sometimes the Testator may partially obliterate a word or phrase and then write something next to it, intending that this be substituted for that which was in the original. Why will the subsequent addition be ineffective, and why will the physical act done to the original be effective or not?

Harrison v. Bird

Supreme Court of Alabama, 1993
621 So.2d 972

HOUSTON, Justice.

The proponent of a will appeals from a judgment of the Circuit Court of Montgomery County holding that the estate of Daisy Virginia Speer, deceased, should be administered as an intestate estate and confirming the letters of administration granted by the probate court to Mae S. Bird.

The following pertinent facts are undisputed:

Daisy Virginia Speer executed a will in November 1989, in which she named Katherine Crapps Harrison as the main beneficiary of her estate. The original of the will was retained by Ms. Speer's attorney and a duplicate original was given to Ms. Harrison. On March 4, 1991, Ms. Speer telephoned her attorney and advised him that she wanted to revoke her will. Thereafter, Ms. Speer's attorney or his secretary, in the presence of each other, tore the will into four pieces. The attorney then wrote Ms. Speer a letter, informing her that he had "revoked" her will as she had instructed and that he was enclosing the pieces of the will so that she could verify that he had torn up the original. In the letter, the attorney specifically stated, "As it now stands, you are without a will."

Ms. Speer died on September 3, 1991. Upon her death, the postmarked letter from her attorney was found among her personal effects, but the four pieces of the will were not found. Thereafter, on September 17, 1991, the Probate Court of Montgomery County granted letters of administration on the estate of Ms. Speer, to Mae S. Bird, a cousin of Ms. Speer. On October 11, 1991, Ms. Harrison filed for probate a document purporting to be the last will and testament of Ms. Speer and naming Ms. Harrison as executrix. On Ms. Bird's petition, the case was removed to the Circuit Court of Montgomery County. Thereafter, Ms. Bird filed an "Answer to Petition to Probate Will and Answer to Petition to Have Administratrix Removed," contesting the will on the grounds that Ms. Speer had revoked her will.

Thereafter, Ms. Bird and Ms. Harrison moved for summary judgments, which the circuit court denied. Upon denying their motions, the circuit court ruled in part (1) that Ms. Speer's will was not lawfully revoked when it was destroyed by her attorney at her direction and with her consent, but not in her presence, see Ala.Code 1975, § 43-8-136(b); (2) that there could be no ratification of the destruction of Ms. Speer's will, which was not accomplished pursuant to the strict requirements of § 43-8-136(b); and

(3) that, based on the fact that the pieces of the destroyed will were delivered to Ms. Speer's home but were not found after her death, there arose a presumption that Ms. Speer thereafter revoked the will herself. * * *

[F]inding that the presumption in favor of revocation of Ms. Speer's will had not been rebutted and therefore that the duplicate original will offered for probate by Ms. Harrison was not the last will and testament of Daisy Virginia Speer, the circuit court held that the estate should be administered as an intestate estate and confirmed the letters of administration issued by the probate court to Ms. Bird.

If the evidence establishes that Ms. Speer had possession of the will before her death, but the will is not found among her personal effects after her death, a presumption arises that she destroyed the will. See Barksdale v. Pendergrass, 294 Ala. 526, 319 So.2d 267 (1975). Furthermore, if she destroys the copy of the will in her possession, a presumption arises that she has revoked her will and all duplicates, even though a duplicate exists that is not in her possession. See Stiles v. Brown, 380 So.2d 792 (Ala.1980); see, also, Snider v. Burks, 84 Ala. 53, 4 So. 225 (1887). However, this presumption of revocation is rebuttable and the burden of rebutting the presumption is on the proponent of the will. See *Barksdale,* supra.

Based on the foregoing, we conclude that under the facts of this case there existed a presumption that Ms. Speer destroyed her will and thus revoked it. Therefore, the burden shifted to Ms. Harrison to present sufficient evidence to rebut that presumption— to present sufficient evidence to convince the trier of fact that the absence of the will from Ms. Speer's personal effects after her death was not due to Ms. Speer's destroying and thus revoking the will. See Stiles v. Brown, supra.

From a careful review of the record, we conclude, as did the trial court, that the evidence presented by Ms. Harrison was not sufficient to rebut the presumption that Ms. Speer destroyed her will with the intent to revoke it. We, therefore, affirm the trial court's judgment.

We note Ms. Harrison's argument that under the particular facts of this case, because Ms. Speer's attorney destroyed the will outside of Ms. Speer's presence, "[t]he fact that Ms. Speer may have had possession of the pieces of her will and that such pieces were not found upon her death is not sufficient to invoke the presumption [of revocation] imposed by the trial court." We find that argument to be without merit.

AFFIRMED.

HORNSBY, C.J., and MADDOX, SHORES and KENNEDY, JJ., concur.

Notes

The decision raises an issue that arises in many cases—that of a lost will. While the case demonstrates the attempt at physical revocation, the Will was actually revoked because the torn pieces were returned to the possession of the Testatrix and could not be found in her possession. The issue raised is the presumption of revocation by physical act brought on by the Will, which is traceable to the possession of the Testatrix but which cannot be found. How should the presumption of a lost Will be addressed if the person who would most benefit from its non-production had access to the Will? Perhaps the best recourse is a shift in the burden of proof necessary to rebut the presumption. *See, e.g.,* Estate of Travers, 121 Ariz. 282, 589 P.2d 1314 (1978); Lonergan v. Estate of Budahazi, 669 So.2d 1062 (Fla. App. 1996). Once the presumption of revocation has been rebutted, what will you admit to probate to prove the intentions of the Testator?

B. Subsequent Instrument

In re Wolfe's Will

Supreme Court of North Carolina, 1923
185 N.C. 563, 117 S.E. 804

ADAMS, J.

* * *

A will may be revoked by a subsequent instrument executed solely for that purpose, or by a subsequent will containing a revoking clause or provisions inconsistent with those of the previous will, or by any of the other methods prescribed by law; but the mere fact that a second will was made, although it purports to be the last, does not create a presumption that it revokes or is inconsistent with one of prior date. * * *

The propounder admits that the instrument dated August 14th (herein for convenience referred to as the second will) is a part of the maker's testamentary disposition, but insists that it does not affect the validity of the instrument dated July 31st, herein designated as the first will. By reason of this admission the appeal presents the single question whether the two wills are so inconsistent that they cannot stand together and whether the first is revoked by the second.

It has often been held that in the construction of wills the primary purpose is to ascertain and give effect to the testator's intention as expressed in the words employed, and if the language is free from ambiguity and doubt, and expresses plainly, clearly, and distinctly the maker's intention, there is no occasion to resort to other means of interpretation. * * *

In the instant case, the language being clear and unequivocal, the chief controversy between the parties involves the meaning of the words "all my effects" as used in the second will. The propounder contends that they include only personal property; the respondents insist that the term embraces real as well as personal property, and that the second will revokes the first, the two being necessarily inconsistent.

The observation has been made that the individual cases construing "effects" are of value only for the purpose of illustration, each case being a law unto itself; but there seems to be a practical unanimity of judicial decision, with the exception of certain English cases, that the word "effects," used simpliciter or in a general or unlimited sense and unaffected by the context, signifies all that is embraced in the words "personal property," but is not sufficiently comprehensive to include real estate. "Effects," however, may include land when used as referring to antecedent words which describe real estate, or when used in written instruments in which the usual technical terms are not controlling * * *.

In the second will there are no words which ex vi termini import a disposition of real property; there is no residuary clause or clause of revocation; and in these circumstances, as the courts do not favor the revocation of wills by implication, there appears to be no sound reason for holding that the two instruments are so inconsistent as to be incapable of standing together and that the first is necessarily revoked by the second. It is true there is a presumption that the testator intended to dispose of all his estate, and under our construction the testator died intestate as to the land not devised to Mary Lillie Luffman, but, as said in Andrews v. Applegate, supra, such presumption, however strong, will not justify or warrant a construction incorporating in the second will any kind of property which cannot be brought within its terms.

Having admitted that the second will is a valid testamentary disposition of the property therein described, the propounder is entitled to have the jury determine whether the instrument dated July 31, 1911, is any part of the maker's will. The judgment and verdict are therefore set aside and a new trial is awarded.

New trial.

Notes

Subsequent instruments may revoke previous valid instruments explicitly or impliedly. A subsequent explicit revocation occurs when the valid subsequent instrument states that it explicitly "revokes all Wills and Codicils to Wills executed by me." There could be a million previous Wills but if this last one is valid, it revokes all of them. Revocation by subsequent instrument occurs by implication when there is no explicit clause included, but a specific item is given in the first Will, and the same specific item is given in the second Will, but to a different legatee. The second legatee trumps the first. *See* UNIF. PROB. CODE § 2-507(a)(1)(2005).

C. Revocation by Operation of Law

Uniform Probate Code (2003)

§ 2-804. Revocation of Probate and Nonprobate Transfers by Divorce; No Revocation by other Changes of Circumstances.

(a) [**Definitions.**] In this section:

(1) "Disposition or appointment of property" includes a transfer of an item of property or any other benefit to a beneficiary designated in a governing instrument.

(2) "Divorce or annulment" means any divorce or annulment, or any dissolution or declaration of invalidity of a marriage, that would exclude the spouse as a surviving spouse within the meaning of Section 2-802. A decree of separation that does not terminate the status of husband and wife is not a divorce for purposes of this section.

(3) "Divorced individual" includes an individual whose marriage has been annulled.

(4) "Governing instrument" means a governing instrument executed by the divorced individual before the divorce or annulment of his [or her] marriage to his [or her] former spouse.

(5) "Relative of the divorced individual's former spouse" means an individual who is related to the divorced individual's former spouse by blood, adoption, or affinity and who, after the divorce or annulment, is not related to the divorced individual by blood, adoption, or affinity.

(6) "Revocable," with respect to a disposition, appointment, provision, or nomination, means one under which the divorced individual, at the time of the divorce or annulment, was alone empowered, by law or under the governing instrument, to cancel the designation in favor of his [or her] former spouse or former spouse's relative,

whether or not the divorced individual was then empowered to designate himself [or herself] in place of his [or her] former spouse or in place of his [or her] former spouse's relative and whether or not the divorced individual then had the capacity to exercise the power.

(b) [**Revocation Upon Divorce.**] Except as provided by the express terms of a governing instrument, a court order, or a contract relating to the division of the marital estate made between the divorced individuals before or after the marriage, divorce, or annulment, the divorce or annulment of a marriage:

(1) revokes any revocable (i) disposition or appointment of property made by a divorced individual to his [or her] former spouse in a governing instrument and any disposition or appointment created by law or in a governing instrument to a relative of the divorced individual's former spouse, (ii) provision in a governing instrument conferring a general or nongeneral power of appointment on the divorced individual's former spouse or on a relative of the divorced individual's former spouse, and (iii) nomination in a governing instrument, nominating a divorced individual's former spouse or a relative of the divorced individual's former spouse to serve in any fiduciary or representative capacity, including a personal representative, executor, trustee, conservator, agent, or guardian; and

(2) severs the interests of the former spouses in property held by them at the time of the divorce or annulment as joint tenants with the right of survivorship [or as community property with the right of survivorship], transforming the interests of the former spouses into equal tenancies in common.

* * *

(d) [**Effect of Revocation.**] Provisions of a governing instrument are given effect as if the former spouse and relatives of the former spouse disclaimed all provisions revoked by this section or, in the case of a revoked nomination in a fiduciary or representative capacity, as if the former spouse and relatives of the former spouse died immediately before the divorce or annulment.

(e) [**Revival if Divorce Nullified.**] Provisions revoked solely by this section are revived by the divorced individual's remarriage to the former spouse or by a nullification of the divorce or annulment.

(f) [**No Revocation for Other Change of Circumstances.**] No change of circumstances other than as described in this section and in Section 2-803 effects a revocation.

* * *

Notes

When we discuss protection of spouses and children in Chapter Five, we examine pretermitted heir statutes (protection of issue, usually children) and pretermitted spouse statutes (protection of spouses). These state statutes are shown to further the public policy of the protection of children who were born after the execution of the Will, or spouses who married the Testator after the execution of the Will. The statutes provide a presumption of intention; if the Testator forgot these persons, the state will provide for them. Now we see in the Uniform Probate Code provision another attempt at assisting the Testator's intent. That is, the statute provides that, if a Testator divorces or the marriage is annulled after execution of the Last Will and Testament, any provision in the Will for the former spouse or a relative of the former spouse who is not a relative of the decedent is revoked from the Will. Note that this applies to non-probate transfers also, which is not a surprising development for the Uniform Probate Code. Of course, the provisions of the Code will not apply if the Testator's intent has been stated otherwise in the Will, a court order, or a pre- or post-nuptial agreement. The Will remains valid; only the relevant provisions are stricken. If the couple has only separated, does the Code's provisions apply? Would the provisions apply if the couple legally separated, divided all of the marital assets, but have not yet received a final decree of divorce? *See, e.g., In re* Estate of Bullotta, 575 Pa. 587, 838 A.2d 594 (2003) (holding husband's estate to terms of settlement agreement that he and wife had reached before his death, even though divorce action abated upon death and parties could no longer divorce).

V. Revival

Like revocation, revival of any Last Will and Testament occurs because of statutory or common law procedures. What follows are the five methods for revival—some resulting from common sense, such as writing a new Will or re-executing a revoked Will—but each reflects an intent on the part of the Testator to reapply the formalities and intentionalities necessary for a valid instrument.

A. Revoking the Revoking Will

Uniform Probate Code (2003)

§ 2-509. Revival of Revoked Will.

(a) If a subsequent will that wholly revoked a previous will is thereafter revoked by a revocatory act under Section 2-507(a)(2), the previous will remains revoked unless it is revived. The previous will is revived if it is evident from the circumstances of the revocation of the subsequent will or from the testator's contemporary or subsequent declarations that the testator intended the previous will to take effect as executed.

(b) If a subsequent will that partly revoked a previous will is thereafter revoked by a revocatory act under Section 2-507(a)(2), a revoked part of the previous will is revived unless it is evident from the circumstances of the revocation of the subsequent will or from the testator's contemporary or subsequent declarations that the testator did not intend the revoked part to take effect as executed.

(c) If a subsequent will that revoked a previous will in whole or in part is thereafter revoked by another, later, will, the previous will remains revoked in whole or in part, unless it or its revoked part is revived. The previous will or its revoked part is revived to the extent it appears from the terms of the later will that the testator intended the previous will to take effect.

Notes

Once a Last Will and Testament has been effectively executed in accordance with formalities and intentionalities, it may only be revoked in accordance with similar formalities and intentionalities. Thus, if a valid Last Will and Testament is revoked by a subsequently valid Last Will and Testament, is that revocation valid? The answer is, "Yes." But what if that second Last Will and Testament is then revoked—perhaps by physical act—and the first Will, although revoked by subsequent instrument, has no other methods of revocation associated with it? May it then be probated? This is the issue of revoking the revoking Will. The common law provided that the first Will should be automatically revived as long as there were no other acts of revocation. States adopting this view analyze the issue as one in which the court should look at the date of the death of the Testator and not what occurred prior to that time. Because the first Will is valid as of that date, it should be probated. Other states adopt the position of the Uniform Probate Code, which provides that, before automatically reviving the first Will, the court should look at the circumstances of revocation, the subsequent Will, and the declarations of the Testator. *See, e.g.,* Estate of Alburn, 18 Wis. 2d 340, 118 N.W.2d 919 (1963). Some states take the position that a revoked Will cannot be revived unless it is re-executed. *See, e.g., In re* Eberhardt's Estate, 1 Wis. 2d 439, 85 N.W.2d 483 (1957). Finally, should it make a difference that the second Will wholly or partially revoked the first Will? According to the Uniform Probate Code § 2-509(b), it should.

B. Dependent Relative Revocation and Mistake

Carter v. First United Methodist Church of Albany

Supreme Court of Georgia, 1980
246 Ga. 352, 271 S.E.2d 493

NICHOLS, Justice.

The caveator, Luther Reynolds Carter, appeals from judgment entered in the superior court in behalf of the propounder, First United Methodist Church, admitting to probate, as the will of Mildred C. Tipton, an instrument bearing the date of August 21, 1963.

The 1963 instrument, typed and signed in the form of and purporting to be the last will and testament of Mildred C. Tipton, was found among Mrs. Tipton's other personal papers in her dining room chest after her death on February 14, 1979. It was folded together with a handwritten instrument dated May 22, 1978, captioned as her will but unsigned and unwitnessed, purporting to establish a different scheme of distribution of her property. Pencil marks had been made diagonally through the property disposition provisions of the 1963 document and through the name of one of the co-executors.

The superior court found that from time to time prior to her death, Mrs. Tipton had made it known to her attorney that she needed his services in order to change or revise her will, or to make a new will; that at one time she had written out some proposed changes on tablet paper to be suggested to her lawyer when he prepared a new will for her; and that she did not intend to revoke her will by scratching through some of its provisions and by writing out the proposed changes.

* * * The parties stipulated that the 1963 instrument offered for probate had been found among Mrs. Tipton's records and papers in a drawer of a chest in her dining room, and that the 1963 will was executed by Mrs. Tipton and attested by the witnesses to the will. * * *

The case was submitted to the trial court on stipulated facts, and under stipulation that the depositions of Mrs. Tipton's attorney and one of her friends, relating to her intentions, be admitted in evidence. There is no transcript, and the record is sparse as to facts. Each party seems to have felt that the burden of proof properly was to be placed upon the other party and, accordingly, neither made much effort to develop the facts. The issue resolves itself, however, if certain presumptions are placed into proper perspective with each other.

"As a general rule, the burden is on a person attacking a paper offered for probate as a will to sustain the grounds of his attack. But by express provision of our statute, where a will has been canceled or obliterated in a material part, a presumption of revocation arises, and the burden is on the propounder to show that no revocation was intended ... Where the paper is found among the testator's effects, there is also a presumption that he made the cancellations or obliterations ... It having been shown that the paper offered for probate in this case had been in the custody of the deceased up to the time of his death, the propounder was met with both of the presumptions above alluded to." McIntyre v. McIntyre, 120 Ga. 67, 70, 47 S.E. 501 (1904).

The deposition of Mrs. Tipton's attorney, introduced by stipulation in behalf of the propounder, establishes, without contradiction, that Mrs. Tipton had written out some changes in her will on tablet paper and repeatedly had attempted to get her attorney to change or to revise her will, or to make a new will. The parties stipulated that the two writings, the 1963 will and the 1978 manuscript, were found after her death among her personal effects. No evidence appears in the record, and no contention is made, that Mrs. Tipton did not make the marks on the 1963 will or write the 1978 instrument. The presumption that Mrs. Tipton made the pencil marks and wrote the memorandum of her intentions stands unrebutted. Langan v. Cheshire, 208 Ga. 107, 65 S.E.2d 415 (1951); Porch v. Farmer, 158 Ga. 55, 122 S.E. 557 (1924); Howard v. Hunter, 115 Ga. 357, 41 S.E. 638 (1902). The other presumption, that of absolute revocation, is the focal point of our remaining inquiry.

The statute to which McIntyre refers is Code Ann. §113-404, which provides, in part, that an intention to revoke will be presumed from the obliteration or canceling of a material portion of the will. In Georgia, the drawing of pencil lines through provisions of a will is a sufficient "canceling". McIntyre, supra, at p. 70, 47 S.E. 501. The question of whether or not the canceled provision is "material" is one of law. Howard v. Cotten, 223 Ga. 118, 122, 153 S.E.2d 557 (1967). The caveator contends that the propounder introduced no evidence to rebut the statutory presumption of revocation, and the propounder contends that under the doctrine of dependent relative revocation, or conditional revocation, the facts proven give rise to a presumption in favor of the propounder (which the caveator failed to rebut) that Mrs. Tipton did not intend for her 1963 will to be revoked unless her new dispositions of her property became effective in law. The caveator thus contends that the propounder failed to rebut the presumption of absolute or unconditional revocation, and the propounder contends he rebutted that presumption by evidence giving rise to another presumption, that of conditional revocation, which the caveator failed to rebut.

The doctrine of dependent relative revocation (conditional revocation) has been stated by this court as follows:

"It is a doctrine of *presumed intention*, and has grown up as a result of an effort which courts always make to arrive at the real intention of the testator. Some of the cases appear to go to extreme lengths in the application of this doctrine, and seem to defeat the very intention at which they were seeking to arrive. The doctrine, as we understand it and are willing to apply it, is this: The mere fact that the testator intended to make a new will, or made one which failed of effect, will not alone, in every case, prevent a cancellation or obliteration of a will from operating as a revocation. If it is clear that the cancellation and the making of the new will were parts of one scheme, and the revocation of the old will was so related to the making of the new as to be dependent upon it, then if the new will be not made, or if made is invalid, the old will, though canceled, should be given effect, if its contents can be ascertained in any legal way. But if the old will is once revoked—if the act of revocation is completed—as if the will be totally destroyed by burning and the like, or if any other act is done which evidences an unmistakable intention to revoke, though the will be not totally destroyed, the fact that the testator intended to make a new will, or made one which can not take effect, counts for nothing. In other words, evidence that the testator intended to make or did actually make a new will, which was inoperative, may throw light on the question of intention to revoke the old one, but it can never revive a will once completely revoked." (Emphasis added.) McIntyre v. McIntyre, 120 Ga. 67, 71, 47 S.E. 501, 503 supra. The doctrine has been recognized and applied by the highest courts of many states. Annos. 62 ALR 1401, 115 ALR 721. It has been the subject of considerable discussion by the text writers. 1 Redfearn, Wills And Administration In Georgia (4th Ed.), p. 188, § 96; Chaffin, Studies In The Georgia Law of Decedent's Estates and Future Interests, pp. 184, 186.

Professor Chaffin is of the opinion that "McIntyre represents a sound approach to the doctrine of dependent relative revocation." He writes that in McIntyre, "The doctrine was correctly perceived to be a rule of presumed intention rather than a rule of substantive law. The court refused to set aside the revocation until evidence bearing on testator's intent, including his oral declarations, was examined in an effort to discern what he would have desired if he had been aware of the true facts." He also concludes, correctly, this court believes, that "Most courts have taken the position that dependent relative revocation is judged by a stricter standard in a situation involving revocation by subsequent instrument as opposed to physical act." He is strongly of the opinion that "if the purpose of the doctrine is to effect testator's intent, there is no point in distinguishing between revocation by physical act and by subsequent instrument." Chaffin, supra, pp. 186–187. This court agrees. In Georgia, the doctrine is one of presumed intention. The principle is the same whether the revocation is by physical act or by subsequent instrument. * * *

In the present case, the testatrix wrote the 1978 instrument which the parties have conceded (by the absence of their contentions) cannot be admitted to probate because it lacks some of the requisites of a will. The propounder says, in effect, if not in express words, that the testatrix would have preferred the property disposition clauses of the 1963 will over the only other alternative—intestacy. The caveator contends, in essence, that the testatrix would have preferred intestacy. How stands the record?

The fact that the old will, with pencil lines drawn by Mrs. Tipton through the property disposition provisions, was found among her personal papers folded together with the 1978 writing, that makes a somewhat different disposition of her property, is some evidence tending to establish that "the cancellation and the making of the new will were parts of one scheme, and the revocation of the old will was so related to the making of the new as to be dependent upon it." 120 Ga. at 71, 47 S.E. at 503. This evidence was sufficient to rebut the statutory presumption of revocation (Code Ann. § 113-404) and to give rise to a presumption in favor of the propounder under the doctrine of dependent relative revocation or conditional revocation. McIntyre, supra. The stipulation that these two instruments were found together thus shifted the burden of proof to the caveator to prove, in essence, that Mrs. Tipton would have preferred intestacy.

* * * The presumption against intestacy (or in favor of the continued validity of the 1963 will) stands unrebutted in the present case. * * *

Accordingly, the trial court, as finder of the facts, did not err in admitting the will to probate.

Judgment affirmed.

Notes

Dependent relative revocation is a doctrine of failed intent. The Restatement applies this doctrine by providing that a partial or complete revocation is presumptively ineffective if the Testator made the revocation in connection with an attempted disposition that fails, or because of a false belief of law or fact that is either recited in the Will or proven by clear and convincing evidence. *See Restatement (Third) of Property* §4.3 (1999). This sounds a great deal like the level of proof associated with the doctrine of mistake, *see infra*, and this seems like a more modern application of the solution applied under dependent relative revocation. *See, e.g.,* Estate of Anderson, 56 Cal. App. 4th 435, 65 Cal. Rptr. 2d 307 (1997).

C. Republication by Codicil

If there is a valid Codicil to a valid Last Will and Testament and the Codicil is revoked, the Last Will and Testament remains valid and subject to probate. But if the Will is revoked, then all Codicils to that Will are revoked as well. But what if there is a Last Will and Testament that had been valid, but then was revoked under any of the three methods available? Would a valid Codicil be able to revive that Last Will and Testament? The answer is, "Yes," as long as the Codicil referred to the Will and successfully overcame any facts that may make it appear that the revocation occurred after the execution of the Codicil. *See generally In re* Estate of Stormong, 34 Ohio App. 3d 92, 517 N.E.2d 259 (1986). But what if the Last Will and Testament had never been valid to begin with because it lacked the proper testamentary formalities or intentionalities? Would the Codicil be able to make the Last Will and Testament valid? *See Restatement (Third) of Property* §3.4 (1999) (treating a Will as executed when its most recent codicil was executed).

D. Re-execution and New Will

These last two means of revival complete the list of five but are added with the caution that re-execution of the revoked Last Will and Testament invites a level of confusion and negligence as to what may precipitate a charge of malpractice. Indeed, being properly attentive to all of the issues heretofore discussed, executing a new Will seems to be the best course of action for client and attorney. *See generally* Espinosa v. Sparber, Shevin, Shapo, Rosen & Heilbronner, 612 So. 2d 1378 (Fla. 1993).

Chapter Four

The Meaning of Words

Tool Bar

Once a Last Will and Testament becomes effective through the accomplishment of the formalities and intentionalities mandated by the particular state, or once the non-probate transfer effectively creates an interest that is transferrable at death, the issue arises as to what the words contained within the Will or the Will Substitute mean. To paraphrase the poet T.S. Eliot, when we think we have done our legal duty, we are still left "with the intolerable wrestle with words and meaning."[1] For example, if in my Will I write: "Jennifer is to receive all that I have within my safe deposit box," what is Jennifer to receive if the contents of that box changes repeatedly between the time I execute the Will and the date of my death? Or, in another example, if I write: "Jimmy is to receive the motor vehicle that I own at the date of my death," and the vehicle is replaced between the time of execution and the date of my death, what is Jimmy to receive? Should the law be conscious of the need to balance certainty in fixing intent with changing circumstances, mistake, and ambiguity?

---

1. T.S. Eliot, *East Coker in* FOUR QUARTETS, at II (1940).

As you progress through the following material, concentrate on the fact that you have a valid instrument but are now asked to define what is encompassed by that instrument. Often that which is encompassed may not make sense when viewed in the context of surrounding circumstances. Was a mistake made by the decedent or by the attorney who drafted the instrument? If there is a mistake, what may the law do about it to help the decedent obtain the benefit of having his or her estate pass according to his or her wishes? And what may the law do to protect the legitimate expectations of actual and potential beneficiaries? There will be a struggle in the pages that follow between what has been termed "harsh and relentless formalism"[2] and what less formal evidence indicates was the true intent of the decedent. The task is not so much to pick one side or the other, but to identify the issue and make a firm resolve to do what is necessary to avoid this pitfall in the future drafting of similar instruments.

I. Incorporation by Reference

Clark v. Greenhalge

Supreme Judicial Court of Massachusetts, 1991
411 Mass. 410, 582 N.E.2d 949

(For the text of the opinion, see *supra* at 197.)

Uniform Probate Code (2003)

§ 2-510. Incorporation by Reference.

A writing in existence when a will is executed may be incorporated by reference if the language of the will manifests this intent and describes the writing sufficiently to permit its identification.

Estate of Nielson

California Court of Appeal, 1980
105 Cal. App. 3d 796, 165 Cal. Rptr. 319

STANIFORTH, Acting P. J.

Arthur G. Nielson (contestant) opposed the admission to probate of the will of his deceased nephew, Lloyd M. Nielson (testator). At the close of contestant's evidence, the trial court granted the proponent's motion for judgment made pursuant to Code of Civil Procedure section 631.8, denied the contest and admitted the will to probate. The court found contestant had failed to meet his burden of proof to overcome the presumption of validity of the will. The court concluded there was no evidence to show that the testator had made the strikeover, interlineations appearing on the face of his 1969 will. * * *

---

2. John Langbein, *Substantial Compliance With the Wills Act*, 88 HARV. L. REV. 489 (1975).

Contestant appeals asserting his evidence had established the absence of any valid will and therefore testator's estate was required to pass by rules of intestate succession to the nearest heirs-at-law.

* * *

Testator executed a typewritten witnessed will dated February 25, 1969 (1969 will) disposing of the bulk of his estate to his mother. If the mother predeceased him, it would go to the Salvation Army of San Diego, the Braille Club of San Diego, the San Diego County Association for Retarded Children, and the National Anti-Vivisection Society (Chicago, Ill.) Paragraph sixth of the 1969 will indicated the testator intentionally omitted provision for any of his heirs.

This will was validly executed; however, on its face numerous lines have been drawn through the dispositive provisions to the above enumerated charities. Interlineated in their place were the handwritten words "Bulk of Estate-1.-Shrine Hospital for Crippled Children-Los Angeles. $10,000-2.-Society for Prevention of Cruelty to Animals (nearest chapter)." Appearing at the margin of these cancellations and interlineations were the testator's initials. Additionally, the date of the 1969 will was cancelled followed by the date "November 29, 1974." At both the top and bottom of this typewritten will were the handwritten words "*Revised* by Lloyd M. Nielson November 29, 1974."

Contestant asserts these deletions and interlineations (1) revoke the 1969 will and (2) were ineffective as a holographic will or codicil for failure to comply with Probate Code section 53.

Upon trial contestant testified he was the testator's closest living heir. He offered no testimonial evidence as to the authorship, the intent with which the deletions, interlineations were made on the will. The trial court found "[t]here was no evidence admitted concerning the handwriting of the interlineations which appear on the decedent's will of February 25, 1969 except for signature of the decedent and the signatures of the subscribing witnesses and their addresses." Accordingly, the trial court found "[t]hat the handwriting and interlineations ... are of no force and effect except for signature of the testator...."

* * *

Once the proponent of a will proves a prima facie case of due execution, the contestant has the burden of proving by competent evidence the issues raised by his contest. (Estate of Relph (1923) 192 Cal. 451, 459 [221 P. 361]; Estate of Darilek (1957) 151 Cal.App.2d 322, 325 [311 P.2d 615].)

Direct evidence, however, is not essential to prove the destruction, cancellation, alterations in a will were made by the testator. A presumption of cancellation can arise from circumstantial evidence alone. (Estate of Streeton (1920) 183 Cal. 284, 290 [191 P. 16]; Estate of Olmsted (1898) 122 Cal. 224, 230 [54 P. 745].)

For example, where the will is in the possession or under the control of a decedent until his last illness, the inference is the changes and alterations were made by the testator. (Estate of Stickney (1951) 101 Cal.App.2d 572, 575 [225 P.2d 649]; Estate of Hewitt (1923) 63 Cal.App. 440, 447 [218 P. 778].)

Furthermore, the handwriting on the will may speak for itself. Where the issue is the questioned authorship of a will, the trier of fact can determine the issue by comparison of the questioned writing with "genuine" or admitted handwriting of the testator without the aid of the oral testimony of any witness. (Evid. Code, § 1417; Estate of Johnson (1927) 200 Cal. 299, 304 [252 P. 1049]; Castor v. Bernstein (1906) 2 Cal.App. 703, 706

[84 P. 244].) Thus, no handwriting expert or testimony was necessary. The court—the trier of fact—had the testator's admitted handwriting before it in the proffered will. It was authorized by law to determine the authenticity of the "questioned handwriting by comparison" with the conceded handwriting of the testator.

Since the trial court erroneously concluded there was "no evidence" presented as to authorship of the deletions/interlineations on the face of the will, we must reverse and remand for further proceedings consistent with this opinion. (Cf., Heap v. General Motors Corp. (1977) 66 Cal.App.3d 824 [136 Cal.Rptr. 304].) For guidance of the trial court upon any retrial of this cause, we resolve these further contentions of error.

* * *

Upon the assumed premise the trial court will find the deletions and interlineations to be in the testator's handwriting, * * * contestant argues that a holographic will or codicil did not result from the testator's writings on the face of his formal witnessed will. Section 53 of the Probate Code provides:

> A holographic will is one that is entirely written, dated and signed by the hand of the testator himself. It is subject to no other form, and need not be witnessed. No address, date or other matter written, printed or stamped upon the document, which is not incorporated in the provisions which are in the handwriting of the decedent, shall be considered as any part of the will.

If the handwriting on the face of the formal will is "*entirely* [italics added] written, dated and signed by the hand of the testator," then the statutory requisites of section 53 are met. Contestant argues the handwriting was united with, integrated, incorporated into the type-written portions of the 1969 will, therefore no valid holograph resulted. The resolution of this contention requires an examination of several well-established rules relating to wills and particularly holographic wills or codicils.

First, there is no requirement that a holograph be written on a separate paper or denominated by the testator as a will or codicil. (Estate of Spitzer (1925) 196 Cal. 301, 307 [237 P. 739]; Estate of French (1964) 225 Cal.App.2d 9, 15 [36 Cal.Rptr. 908].)

Second, the mere presence of typewritten words on the paper upon which a holographic will or codicil is written, of which such words are no part, does not render the holograph invalid. (Prob. Code, §53.)

> [A]s declared in Estate of Bower ... 'the mere presence of printed matter on the paper is not fatal to the validity of an holographic will written thereon if such printed matter be not included or incorporated, directly or indirectly, in the will as written by the hand of the decedent.' (Estate of Baker (1963) 59 Cal.2d 680, 683 [31 Cal.Rptr. 33, 381 P.2d 913]; see also Estate of Helmar (1973) 33 Cal.App.3d 109 [109 Cal.Rptr. 6].)

The Supreme Court in Estate of Baker, supra, tells us the test is not whether the handwritten portion of the document independently evidences the decedent's intent as to the disposition of his property and to matters essential to the validity of the will *but whether the handwritten portion evidences an intent to include any printed or typed matter* which, when read with the handwritten words, *is relevant* to the decedent's will.

The *Baker* court further indicated that unless the printed or typed matter is relevant to the "substance" of the decedent's will, it can be disregarded as surplusage. (Estate of Baker, supra, 59 Cal.2d 680, 683.) In *Baker*, supra, the place of execution of the will (Modesto, California) was not relevant to the decedent's testamentary intent or to the validity of the will, therefore, the printed words were held not to be incorporated into the handwritten portions of the will. (Id., at pp. 683–684; Estate of Christian (1976) 60 Cal.App.3d 975, 981 [131 Cal.Rptr. 841].)

A second set of relevant rules pertains to the reverse process, the incorporation by reference of *extrinsic documents* into an otherwise valid witnessed or holographic will.

In Estate of Smith (1948) 31 Cal.2d 563 [191 P.2d 413], the decedent had written a holographic revocatory clause across the face of a copy of an attested will (the original of which had been left with the decedent's attorney). The Supreme Court held the decedent had incorporated the attested will in the holographic clause, and said (p. 567):

> It has long been settled in this state that either a holographic or an attested testamentary instrument may refer to and incorporate another testamentary instrument executed with different statutory formalities or an informal or unattested document, so long as the reference is unmistakable or with the aid of extrinsic proof can be made so. (See 7 Witkin, Summary of Cal. Law (8th ed. 1974) Wills and Probate, § 144, p. 5660.)

"The papers incorporated by reference are used to construe and apply the will, and do not become part of the will in the same sense as those integrated. Hence the holographic will may be regarded as entirely in the testator's handwriting, as required by the statute." (7 Witkin, supra, p. 5661; Estate of Smith, supra, 31 Cal.2d 563, 567–568; see also Estate of Atkinson (1930) 110 Cal.App. 499, 502 [294 P. 425].)

The requisites of incorporation by reference are (1) the extrinsic paper must be in existence at the time the will makes reference to it; (2) the will must identify the paper by a sufficiently certain description, and extrinsic evidence is admissible as an aid to such identification; and (3) it must appear that the testator intended to incorporate the paper for the purpose of carrying out his testamentary desires. (Estate of Foxworth (1966) 240 Cal.App.2d 784, 788, 789 [50 Cal.Rptr. 237].)

Finally, a prior will is revoked by a subsequent will which contains an "express revocation or provisions wholly inconsistent" with its terms. (Prob. Code, § 72.) The revoking instrument must be executed with the same formalities required for the execution of a will. (Prob. Code, § 74.) Thus a formal will may be revoked by a valid holographic will or codicil.

Applying these statutes and judicial declarations to the document under scrutiny we conclude the following: First, if the handwriting on the face of the formal will were written, dated and signed by the testator, then it meets the statutory requisites of a holographic will (Prob. Code, § 53) unless "other written matter" was expressly or impliedly, directly or indirectly, incorporated into and relevant to the handwritten words. The word "incorporate" as used in section 53 means "formed or combined into one body or unit; intimately united, joined, or blended" (Webster's New World Dict. of the English Language (1966) p. 738) or "to unite with or introduce into something already existent" (Webster's Third New Internat. Dict. (1961) p. 1145.)

An examination of the document, in its entirety, leads to these conclusions: the typewritten words are not relevant to the substance of the holograph or essential to its validity as a will or codicil. Nor do the written or express words or physical ordering of relationships indicate any intention that the holograph unite, form or blend with the provisions of the typewritten will. Nor does the word-content of the holograph indicate any intent to integrate the handwriting with the typewritten will. We conclude no evidence from the face of this document tells us the author intended to "incorporate" directly or indirectly the typewritten will into the provisions which are in his handwriting so as to render the handwriting ineffective as a will or codicil and thereby defeat the author's declared testamentary intent.

We further conclude that the handwriting when viewed as a whole authorizes an inference of an intent to incorporate by reference those portions of the typewritten will not modified or revoked by the holographic codicil and to give validity to, republish the typewritten will as modified by the holograph. The words used by the writer reasonably compel this conclusion.

Estate of Atkinson, supra, (110 Cal.App. 499) bears a striking factual resemblance to the case at bench and is sound authority supporting these conclusions. In *Atkinson*, the decedent had executed a formal written will. Thereafter,

> "On July 9, 1913, the decedent drew ink lines through the words of the second and third clauses of [that] will and wrote, in red ink, across the typewritten lines thereof the following:
>
> "'July 9 1913
>
> "'I cut out this part of will
>
> "'T. G. Atkinson'
>
> "At the same time and in the same manner he wrote across the lines of the sixth paragraph, but without drawing any lines through the words thereof, the following:
>
> "'July 9th 1913
>
> "'John Atkinson children are to get John share in this will
>
> "'T. G. Atkinson.'
>
> "Appellants admit that the second and third clauses were effectively canceled and the only contentions made by them relate to the writing over the sixth clause." (Id., at p. 501.)

The court stated (p. 502):

> The mere presence of typewritten words upon the paper upon which the codicil is written does not render the olographic codicil, of which such words form no part, invalid. [Citations.]
>
> Appellants contend that by the olographic codicil the testator 'sought to make a new will by making certain changes on the face of the old will and retaining the remaining provisions thereof that were not scratched out or written over. The altered document, as thus changed was intended to be his revised original will'. It is of no materiality that the codicil is written upon one of the sheets of the original will, except that the document referred to in the codicil is thereby more clearly identified. 'It has long been settled that a will or codicil executed in accordance with the requirements of statute may, by an appropriate reference, incorporate within itself a document or paper not so executed.' [Citation.] The codicil considered in the case cited was olographic. It certainly is no objection that a document so incorporated has been formally executed as a will. 'The execution of a codicil, referring to a previous will, has the effect to republish the will, as modified by the codicil.' [Citation.] In the case of *In re Soher*, ... it is said: 'The argument is, that the olographic codicil cannot be understood without reference to the attested will; that the latter is in contempla-

tion of law "a part" of the former, and that therefore it does not come within the definition of an olographic will, which is a will 'entirely written, dated and signed by the hand of the testator himself'.... The only difference between an olographic and an attested will is in the form of execution.... One form is the precise equivalent of the other.... Whatever may be done in or by the one may be done in or by the other.'

Thus, the *Atkinson* court relied upon two well-established principles of the law of wills to reach the conclusion that the interlineations, written, signed, dated by the testator, constitute a holographic codicil and the doctrine of incorporation by reference gave validity to republish the will as modified by the holographic codicil. (Estate of Atkinson, supra, 110 Cal.App. 499, 502.)

Those principles relied upon by the *Atkinson* court have been approved by the Supreme Court (Estate of Baker, supra, 59 Cal.2d 680, 683; Estate of Smith, supra, 31 Cal.2d 563, 567) and there is no reason to doubt their present viability. These rules as applied in *Atkinson* and here do not erode the legislative mandate of section 53. Rather such construction is in accord with the current policy of law with respect to construction of wills. (7)As stated in Estate of Baker, supra, 59 Cal.2d 680, 683:

> The policy of the law is toward 'a construction favoring validity, in determining whether a will has been executed in conformity with statutory requirements.' [Citations.] Further, 'the tendency of both the courts and the Legislature has been toward greater liberality in accepting of a writing as an holographic will [citation].... '

* * *

Nor are the cases of Estate of Baker, supra, Estate of Christian, supra, and Estate of Helmar, supra, in conflict with the *Atkinson* rule. Estate of Christian, supra, 60 Cal.App.3d 975, involved the use of the printed form will and the filling in of the blanks by the testator. Thus, there was a physical incorporation or tying together of the printed and handwritten portions.

Christian, supra, makes this most significant analysis of *Baker*, supra:

> 'In reversing, the Supreme Court noted the tendency of both the courts and the Legislature toward greater liberality in accepting a writing as a holographic will and reaffirmed the rule that the mere presence of printed matter on paper is not fatal if such matter is not included or incorporated directly or indirectly in the will as written by the hand of the decedent. [Citation.] It then declared that the printed words, 'Modesto, California,' had not been incorporated into the handwritten portion because the two words were '... not relevant to [the will's] substance or essential to its validity as a will ...' that decedent did not refer to or adopt [the words]as part of the "provisions which are in the handwriting of the decedent" [citation]; ...' [Citation.] * * *

> '*Baker* also held that the fact that the decedent had crossed out the printed language at the top of the page but had not crossed out 'Modesto, California,' before writing the date '[did] not provide a reference in the will to the latter two words or warrant the conclusion that he intended to or did incorporate in the handwritten provisions, such two words which were immaterial to [the] validity of the document as a holographic will.' The court held this to be true even though it could be inferred by reason of an earlier will that the decedent mis-

takenly may have believed that designation of locality was necessary in a testamentary document. [Citation.]

'Appellant would have us glean from *Baker* a rule that any printed matter on the document not relevant to the testamentary disposition of the decedent's property or to the validity of the document as a will is to be treated as surplusage even though the printed matter is impliedly incorporated into or referred to in the handwritten portion of the will.'

The court's footnote 1 provides:

Baker expressly overruled any contrary statements or implications in the Estate of Bower.... What the *Baker* court apparently had reference to in *Bower* was the statement that in determining the validity of the document the court must consider all parts thereof 'whether or not indispensable thereto' [citation] and the following language: 'True, such introductory written and printed matters are not essential to a testamentary document. But, the fact remains that decedent herein concluded that they were indispensable to and should be a part of *his* will and he manifestly made them a part of *his* will.... As stated above, we are to read the decedent's will as *he* wrote it and not as we would write it in order to cause it to comply with established legal principles.' [Citation.] (Italics in original.) (Estate of Christian, supra, 60 Cal.App.3d 975, 980.)

Without question the Supreme Court in *Baker* overruled the *Bower* (Estate of Bower (1938) 11 Cal.2d 180 [78 P.2d 1012]) language which would have required the court in measuring compliance of the writing with Probate Code section 53 to "consider all parts thereof 'whether or not indispensable thereto.'" Here the printed portions of the formal will are not physically connected or merged into the holograph nor are they indispensable to the question of its validity. Thus, *Christian*, supra, is not only distinguishable factually but in its reasoning and citation of authority (*Baker's* reversal of *Bower*) supported the *Atkinson* reasoning and result.

In *Helmar*, supra, there was a typewritten introduction to the handwritten will reciting inter alia not only the testamentary intent but the date of the writing. Thus, the typewritten portion was not only essential but was "physically incorporated," "tied to" the provisions of the handwritten portions by the decedent. (Estate of Helmar, supra, 33 Cal.App.3d 109, 113.)

Our discussion concerning the cogency, applicability of the rules of law expressed in the Estate of Atkinson, supra, does not preclude—dependent upon the nature of the findings of fact yet to be made as to authorship and intent with which the deletions, interlineations were made—an application of yet other rules of law, including the doctrine of dependent relative revocation. (See Estate of Kaufman (1945) 25 Cal.2d 854, 858–859 [155 P.2d 831]; Estate of Cuneo (1963) 60 Cal.2d 196, 202–203 [32 Cal.Rptr. 409, 384 P.2d 1, A.L.R.3d 1132].)

Finally, we find no error in the trial court's refusal to consider evidence of a settlement among the six charities—proponents—as a basis for granting the Code of Civil Procedure section 631.8 motion. This potential settlement had absolutely no relevance to the validity of the testator's will. This appeal offers no basis for imposition of sanctions.

Judgment reversed and cause remanded for proceedings conformable to this opinion.

Henderson, J., * * * concurred.

II. Facts of Independent Significance

Uniform Probate Code (2003)

§ 2-512. Events of Independent Significance.

A will may dispose of property by reference to acts and events that have significance apart from their effect upon the dispositions made by the will, whether they occur before or after the execution of the will or before or after the testator's death. The execution or revocation of another individual's will is such an event.

Notes

Modern estate planning utilizes a device known as a pour-over trust. The device allows for a living person to create a legal arrangement—a trust—which may accomplish stated objectives either during the person's life or after the person's death. If the trust has no assets when it is created, it is called an unfunded trust. If there are assets at the time of creation, it is called a funded trust. If the trust is unfunded, the person may direct that his or her Last Will and Testament fund the trust at death, thus allowing for a "pour over" from the Will to the trust. But this "pour-over" practice created a difficulty in the law because, if there were no funding at creation, then no valid trust was created since every trust must have a corpus. Thus, the Will could not "pour over" into the trust since no trust was ever created. This sounds confusing, however, of even greater importance is the fact that this interfered with estate planning objectives. To rectify this dilemma and to facilitate the modern estate planning culture, statutes were enacted to enable unfunded inter-vivos trusts to be created as events of independent significance, into which Last Wills and Testaments may "pour over" assets.

Uniform Probate Code (2003)

§ 2-511. Testamentary Additions to Trusts.

(a) A will may validly devise property to the trustee of a trust established or to be established (i) during the testator's lifetime by the testator, by the testator and some other person, or by some other person, including a funded or unfunded life insurance trust, although the settlor has reserved any or all rights of ownership of the insurance contracts, or (ii) at the testator's death by the testator's devise to the trustee, if the trust is identified in the testator's will and its terms are set forth in a written instrument, other than a will, executed before, concurrently with, or after the execution of the testator's will or in another individual's will if that other individual has predeceased the testator, regardless of the existence, size, or character of the corpus of the trust. The devise is not invalid because the trust is amendable or revocable, or because the trust was amended after the execution of the will or the testator's death.

(b) Unless the testator's will provides otherwise, property devised to a trust described in subsection (a) is not held under a testamentary trust of the testator, but it becomes a part of the trust to which it is devised, and must be administered and disposed of in accordance with the provisions of the governing instrument setting forth the terms of the trust, including any amendments thereto made before or after the testator's death.

(c) Unless the testator's will provides otherwise, a revocation or termination of the trust before the testator's death causes the devise to lapse.

Tax Considerations: Pour-over trusts are very popular as estate planning tools, gaining validity through the use of the doctrine of independent significance and the Uniform Probate Code's Section 2-511 recognition. Greater detail will be provided concerning them in our discussion on trusts, *infra*, but the tax ramifications should be introduced now. With the exception of charitable gifts and bequests, and, obviously, gifts made to a surviving spouse, there are no tax advantages as the funds "pour-over" from a valid Last Will and Testament into an inter vivos trust or from another form of will substitute into a testamentary estate plan. Hence, a taxable interest results. Any tax advantages result from charitable or spousal exceptions and not because they are pour-over devices. The taxable feature is that all are considered as "property owned at death" of the decedent. Indeed, any number of devices may be used to "pour over" but each would be considered as part of the gross estate. For example, revocable transfers (I.R.C. § 2038), annuities (I.R.C. § 2039), general testamentary powers of appointment (I.R.C. § 2041), and life insurance (I.R.C. § 2042).

III. Legal List

Uniform Probate Code (2003)

§ 2-513. Separate Writing Identifying Devise of Certain Types of Tangible Personal Property.

Whether or not the provisions relating to holographic wills apply, a will may refer to a written statement or list to dispose of items of tangible personal property not otherwise specifically disposed of by the will, other than money. To be admissible under this section as evidence of the intended disposition, the writing must be signed by the testator and must describe the items and the devisees with reasonable certainty. The writing may be referred to as one to be in existence at the time of the testator's death; it may be prepared before or after the execution of the will; it may be altered by the testator after its preparation; and it may be a writing that has no significance apart from its effect on the dispositions made by the will.

Notes

Few can refute the flexibility that a legal list provides. Before or after execution of the Last Will and Testament, a testator may create a list and frequently change items of personal property—jewelry, art, furniture—without the necessity of writing a new Will. True, the list must be signed and the Will must refer to the list as being in existence or to come into existence, but a legal list provides far greater flexibility and is a by-product of the relaxation of testamentary formalities. But some questions remain: Would stocks, money market funds, and bonds be considered money or tangible personal property?

Does a file on the computer constitute a written legal list? If the list provides for a personal item to go to X and the Will provides that it go to Y, who gets the item? If a legal list and a holographic will serve as sufficient writings, which would be better to employ?

IV. Plain Meaning Versus Ambiguity

A. Latent and Patent Ambiguity

In re Estate of Russell

Supreme Court of California, 1968
69 Cal. 2d 200, 444 P.2d 353

SULLIVAN, J.

Georgia Nan Russell Hembree appeals from a judgment (Prob. Code, § 1240 * * *) entered in proceedings for the determination of heirship (§§ 1080–1082) decreeing inter alia that under the terms of the will of Thelma L. Russell, deceased, all of the residue of her estate should be distributed to Chester H. Quinn.

Thelma L. Russell died testate on September 8, 1965, leaving a validly executed holographic will written on a small card. The front of the card reads:

'Turn
the card   March 18–1957
          I leave everything
          I own Real &
          Personal to Chester
          H. Quinn & Roxy Russell
          Thelma L. Russell'

The reverse side reads:

          My ($10.) Ten dollar gold
          Piece & diamonds I leave
          to Georgia Nan Russell.
          Alverata, Geogia [sic].'

Chester H. Quinn was a close friend and companion of testatrix, who for over 25 years prior to her death had resided in one of the living units on her property and had stood in a relation of personal trust and confidence toward her. Roxy Russell was testatrix' pet dog which was alive on the date of the execution of testatrix' will but predeceased her.[2] Plaintiff is testatrix' niece and her only heir-at-law.

In her petition for determination of heirship plaintiff alleges, inter alia, that 'Roxy Russell is an Airedale dog'; * * * that section 27 enumerates those entitled to take by

---

2. Actually the record indicates the existence of two Roxy Russells. The original Roxy was an Airedale dog which testatrix owned at the time she made her will, but which, according to Quinn, died after having had a fox tail removed from its nose, and which, according to the testimony of one Arthur Turner, owner of a pet cemetery, was buried on June 9, 1958. Roxy was replaced with another dog (breed not indicated in the record before us) which, although it answered to the name Roxy, was, according to the record, in fact registered with the American Kennel Club as 'Russel's [sic] Royal Kick Roxy.'

will; that 'Dogs are not included among those listed in ... Section 27. Not even Airedale dogs'; that the gift of one-half of the residue of testatrix' estate to Roxy Russell is invalid and void; and that plaintiff was entitled to such one-half as testatrix' sole heir-at-law.

At the hearing on the petition, plaintiff introduced without objection extrinsic evidence establishing that Roxy Russell was testatrix' Airedale dog which died on June 9, 1958. To this end plaintiff, in addition to an independent witness, called defendant pursuant to former Code of Civil Procedure section 2055 (now Evid. Code, § 776). Upon redirect examination, counsel for Quinn then sought to introduce evidence of the latter's relationship with testatrix 'in the event that your Honor feels that there is any necessity for further ascertainment of the intent above and beyond the document.' Plaintiff's objections on the ground that it was inadmissible under the statute of wills and the parole evidence rule 'because there is no ambiguity' and that it was inadmissible under section 105, were overruled. Over plaintiff's objection, counsel for Quinn also introduced certain documentary evidence consisting of testatrix' address book and a certain quitclaim deed 'for the purpose of demonstrating the intention on the part of the deceased that she not die intestate.' Of all this extrinsic evidence only the following infinitesimal portion of Quinn's testimony relates to care of the dog: 'Q. [Counsel for Quinn] Prior to the first Roxy's death did you ever discuss with Miss Russell taking care of Roxy if anything should ever happen to her? A. Yes.' Plaintiff carefully preserved an objection running to all of the above line of testimony and at the conclusion of the hearing moved to strike such evidence. Her motion was denied.

The trial court found, so far as is here material, that it was the intention of the testatrix 'that CHESTER H. QUINN was to receive her entire estate, excepting the gold coin and diamonds bequeathed to' plaintiff and that Quinn 'was to care for the dog, ROXY RUSSELL, in the event of Testatrix's death. The language contained in the Will concerning the dog, ROXY RUSSELL, was precatory in nature only, and merely indicative of the wish, desire and concern of Testatrix that CHESTER H. QUINN was to care for the dog, ROXY RUSSELL, subsequent to Testatrix's death.'[4] The court concluded that testatrix intended to and did make an absolute and outright gift to Mr. Quinn of all the residue of her estate, adding: 'There occurred no lapse as to any portion of the resid-

---

4. The memorandum decision elaborates on this point, stating in part: 'The obvious concern of the human who loves her pet is to see that it is properly cared for by someone who may be trusted to honor that concern and through resources the person may make available in the will to carry out this entreaty, desire, wish, recommendation or prayer. This, in other words, is a most logical example of a precatory provision. It is the only logical conclusion one can come to which would not do violence to the apparent intent of Mrs. Russell.'

The trial court found further: 'Testatrix intended that GEORGIA NAN RUSSELL HEMBREE was not to have any other real or personal property belonging to Testatrix, other than the gold coin and diamonds.' This finding also was elaborated on in the memorandum decision: 'In making the will it is apparent she had Georgia on her mind. While there is other evidence in the case about Thelma Russell's frame of mind concerning her real property and her niece, which was admitted by the Court, over counsel's vigorous objection, because it concerned testatrix' frame of mind, a condition relevant to the material issue of intent, nevertheless this additional evidence was not necessary to this Court in reaching its conclusion.' The additional evidence, referred to included an address book of testatrix upon which she had written: 'Chester, Don't let Augusta and Georgia have one penny of my place if it takes it all to fight it in Court. Thelma.'

uary gift to CHESTER H. QUINN by reason of the language contained in the Will concerning the dog, ROXY RUSSELL, such language not having the effect of being an attempted outright gift or gift in trust to the dog. The effect of such language is merely to indicate the intention of Testatrix that CHESTER H. QUINN was to take the entire residuary estate and to use whatever portion thereof as might be necessary to care for and maintain the dog, ROXY RUSSELL.' Judgment was entered accordingly. This appeal followed.

Plaintiff's position before us may be summarized thusly: That the gift of one-half of the residue of the estate to testatrix' dog was clear and unambiguous; that such gift was void and the property subject thereof passed to plaintiff under the laws of intestate succession; and that the court erred in admitting the extrinsic evidence offered by Quinn but that in any event the uncontradicted evidence in the record did not cure the invalidity of the gift.

We proceed to set forth the rules here applicable which govern the interpretation of wills.

First, as we have said many times: 'The paramount rule in the construction of wills, to which all other rules must yield, is that a will is to be construed according to the intention of the testator as expressed therein, and this intention must be given effect as far as possible.' (Estate of Wilson (1920) 184 Cal. 63, 66–67 [193 P. 581].) * * * The rule is imbedded in the Probate Code. (§ 101.)[6] Its objective is to ascertain what the testator meant by the language he used. * * *

When the language of a will is ambiguous or uncertain resort may be had to extrinsic evidence in order to ascertain the intention of the testator.[8] We have said that extrinsic evidence is admissible 'to explain any ambiguity arising on the face of a will, or to resolve a latent ambiguity which does not so appear.' (Estate of Torregano (1960) 54 Cal.2d 234, 246 [5 Cal.Rptr. 137, 352 P.2d 505, 88 A.L.R.2d 597], citing § 105.)[9] A latent ambiguity is one which is not apparent on the face of the will but is disclosed by some fact collateral to it. (See 4 Page on Wills (Bowe-Parker Rev.) § 32.7, p. 255; Comment:

---

6. Section 101 in pertinent part provides: 'A will is to be construed according to the intention of the testator. Where his intention cannot have effect to its full extent, it must have effect as far as possible.'

8. 'It is a fundamental and indisputable proposition that wherever doubt arises as to the meaning of a will, such doubt is resolved by construction and that construction is one of law. It is an application of legal rules governing construction either to the will alone or to properly admitted facts to explain what the testator meant by the doubtful language. In those cases where extrinsic evidence is permissible there may be a conflict in the extrinsic evidence itself, in which case the determination of that conflict results in a finding of pure fact. But when the facts are thus found, those facts do not solve the difficulty. They still are to be applied to the written directions of the will for the latter's construction, and that construction still remains a construction at law.' (Estate of Donnellan (1912) 164 Cal. 14, 19 [127 P. 166], per Henshaw, J.; accord: Estate of Platt (1942) 21 Cal.2d 343, 352 [131 P.2d 825]; see Parsons v. Bristol Dev. Co. (1965) 62 Cal.2d 861, 865 [44 Cal.Rptr. 767, 402 P.2d 839].)

9. Section 105 provides: 'When there is an imperfect description, or no person or property exactly answers the description, mistakes and omissions must be corrected, if the error appears from the context of the will or from extrinsic evidence, excluding the oral declarations of the testator as to his intentions; and when an uncertainty arises upon the face of a will, as to the application of any of its provisions, the testator's intention is to be ascertained from the words of the will, taking into view the circumstances under which it was made, excluding such oral declarations.'

Extrinsic Evidence and the Construction of Wills in California (1962) 50 Cal.L.Rev. 283, 284–291.)

As to latent ambiguities, this court in the *Donnellan* case said: 'Broadly speaking, there are two classes of wills presenting latent ambiguities, for the removal of which ambiguities resort to extrinsic evidence is permissible. The one class is where there are two or more persons or things exactly measuring up to the description and conditions of the will, … The other class is where no person or thing exactly answers the declarations and descriptions of the will, but where two or more persons or things in part though imperfectly do so answer.' (Estate of Donnellan (1912) 164 Cal. 14, 20 [127 P. 166].) * * * Extrinsic evidence always may be introduced initially in order to show that under the circumstances of a particular case the seemingly clear language of a will describing either the subject of or the object of the gift actually embodies a latent ambiguity for it is only by the introduction of extrinsic evidence that the existence of such an ambiguity can be shown. Once shown, such ambiguity may be resolved by extrinsic evidence. (Estate of Dominici (1907) 151 Cal. 181, 184 [90 P. 448]; Taylor v. McCowen (1908) 154 Cal. 798, 802 [99 P. 351]; Estate of Donnellan, supra, 164 Cal. 14, 20, 22–24; cf. Estate of Sargavak (1953) 41 Cal.2d 314, 320 [259 P.2d 897]; Estate of Carter (1956) 47 Cal.2d 200, 207–208 [302 P.2d 301].)

A patent ambiguity is an uncertainty which appears on the face of the will. (Estate of Womersley (1912) 164 Cal. 85, 87 [127 P. 645]; Estate of Willson (1915) 171 Cal. 449, 456–457 [153 P. 927]; Estate of Salmonski (1951) 38 Cal.2d 199, 214 [238 P.2d 966]; see generally 4 Page on Wills, op.cit. supra, §32.7, p. 255; Comment: supra, 50 Cal.L.Rev. 283, 284–291.) 'When an uncertainty arises upon the face of a will as to the meaning of any of its provisions, the testator's intent is to be ascertained from the words of the will, but the circumstances of the execution thereof may be taken into consideration, excluding the oral declarations of the testator as to his intentions.' (Estate of Salmonski, supra, 38 Cal.2d 199, 214.) * * * This is but a corollary derived from an older formalism. Long before *Salmonski* it was said in Estate of Willson, supra, 171 Cal. 449, 456: 'The rule is well established that where the meaning of the will, on its face, taking the words in the ordinary sense, is entirely clear, and where no latent ambiguity is made to appear by extrinsic evidence, there can be no evidence of extrinsic circumstances to show that the testatrix intended or desired to do something not expressed in the will.' * * * However, this ancient touchstone has not necessarily uncovered judicial material of unquestioned purity.

In order to determine initially whether the terms of *any written instrument* are clear, definite and free from ambiguity the court must examine the instrument in the light of the circumstances surroundings its execution so as to ascertain what the parties meant by the words used. Only then can it be determined whether the seemingly clear language of the instrument is in fact ambiguous. 'Words are used in an endless variety of contexts. Their meaning is not subsequently attached to them by the reader but is formulated by the writer and can only be found by interpretation in the light of all the circumstances that reveal the sense in which the writer used the words. The exclusion of parol evidence regarding such circumstances merely because the words do not appear ambiguous to the reader can easily lead to the attribution to a written instrument of a meaning that was never intended.' (Universal Sales Corp. v. California etc. Mfg. Co. (1942) 20 Cal.2d 751, 776 [128 P.2d 665] (Traynor, J., concurring).) 'The court must determine the true meaning of the instrument in the light of the evidence available. It can neither exclude extrinsic evidence relevant to that determination nor invoke such evidence to write a new or different instrument.' (Laux v. Freed (1960) 53 Cal.2d 512,

527 [2 Cal.Rptr. 265, 348 P.2d 873] (Traynor, J., concurring); see also Corbin, The Interpretation of Words and the Parol Evidence Rule (1965) 50 Cornell L.Q. 161, 164:
'[W]hen a judge refuses to consider relevant extrinsic evidence on the ground that the
meaning of written words is to him plain and clear, his decision is formed by and
wholly based upon the completely extrinsic evidence of his own personal education and
experience'; Corbin, op.cit. supra, pp. 189–190; Farnsworth, 'Meaning' in the Law of
Contracts (1967) 76 Yale L.J. 939, 957–965; Holmes, The Theory of Legal Interpretation
(1899) 12 Harv.L.Rev. 417, 420; Rest., Contracts, §230, coms. a, b, §235, cls. (a), (d),
coms. a, f, §238, cl. (a), com. a, §242, com. a; 3 Corbin on Contracts (1960) §535, pp.
17–21, §536, pp. 27–30 et seq.; 4 Page on Wills, op.cit. supra, §30.8, p. 59, §32.1, pp.
232–233, §32.2 pp. 236–237; 9 Wigmore on Evidence (3d ed. 1940) §2470 et seq.; 4
Williston on Contracts (3d ed. 1961) §610, pp. 499–503; §610A, pp. 517–519, §629,
pp. 923–925; Witkin, Cal. Evidence (2d ed. 1966) §730, p. 675 et seq.)

The foregoing reflects the modern development of rules governing interpretation, for in
the words of Wigmore 'The history of the law of Interpretation is the history of a progress
from a stiff and superstitious formalism to a flexible rationalism.' (9 Wigmore, op.cit.
supra, §2461, p. 187.) While 'still surviving to us, in many Courts, from the old formalism … [is] the rule that you *cannot disturb a plain meaning*' (9 Wigmore, op.cit. supra, p.
191, original emphasis) nevertheless decisions and authorities like those cited above be-
speak the current tendency to abandon the 'stiff formalism of earlier interpretation' and to
show the meaning of words even though no ambiguity appears on the face of the document.

There is nothing in these rules of interpretation which confines their application to
contracts. Indeed quite the contrary. The rules are a response to 'problems which run
through all the varieties of jural acts,' are therefore not necessarily solvable separately for
deeds, contracts and wills, are not peculiar to any one kind of jural act, but involve a
general principle applicable to all. (9 Wigmore, op.cit. supra, §2401, pp. 6–7, §2458,
pp. 179–181, §2463, §2467.) Thus Wigmore says: 'In the field of *wills,* where there is
none but the individual standard [* * *] of meaning to be considered, this principle is
seen in unrestricted operation;…'[14] (§2470, p. 228.)

Accordingly, we think it is self-evident that in the interpretation of a will, a court
cannot determine whether the terms of the will are clear and definite in the first place
until it considers the circumstances under which the will was made so that the judge

---

14. 'The truth had finally to be recognized that words *always* need interpretation; that the
process of interpretation inherently and invariably means the ascertainment of the association between words and external objects; and that this makes inevitable a free resort to extrinsic matters for
applying and enforcing the document. 'Words *must* be translated into things and facts.' Instead of
the fallacious notion that 'there should be interpretation only when it is needed,' the fact is that there
must always be interpretation. Perhaps the range of search need not be extensive, and perhaps the
application of the document will be apparent at the first view; but there must always be a traveling
out of the document, a comparison of its words with people and things. The deed must be applied
'physically to the ground.' Perhaps the standard of interpretation will limit our search; perhaps the
obligation (as some Courts maintain) to enforce the ordinary standard as against the mutual or the
individual standard…, or to enforce the mutual as against the individual standard…, will render
certain data immaterial. But these restrictions are independent of the present principle. Once freed
from the primitive formalism which views the document as a self-contained and self-operative formula, we can fully appreciate the modern principle that the words of a document are never anything but indices to extrinsic things, and that therefore *all the circumstances must be considered
which go to make clear the sense of the words,*—that is, their associations with things.' (9 Wigmore,
op.cit. supra, p. 227, original emphasis.)

may be placed in the position of the testator whose language he is interpreting. (Cf. Code Civ. Proc., § 1860.) * * * Failure to enter upon such an inquiry is failure to recognize that the 'ordinary standard or 'plain meaning,' is simply the meaning of the people who did *not* write the document.' (9 Wigmore, op.cit. supra, § 2462, p. 191.)

Thus we have declared in a slightly different context that extrinsic evidence as to the circumstances under which a written instrument was made is ' 'admissible to interpret the instrument, but not to give it a meaning to which it is not reasonably susceptible' (Coast Bank v. Minderhout, 61 Cal.2d 311, 315 [38 Cal.Rptr. 505, 392 P.2d 265]; ...), and it is the instrument itself that must be given effect. (Civ. Code, §§ 1638, 1639; Code Civ. Proc., § 1856.)' (Parsons v. Bristol Dev. Co. (1965) 62 Cal.2d 861, 865 [44 Cal.Rptr. 767, 402 P.2d 839].) * * * 'If the evidence offered would not persuade a reasonable man that the instrument meant anything other than the ordinary meaning of its words, it is useless.' (Estate of Rule (1944) 25 Cal.2d 1, 22 [152 P.2d 1003, 155 A.L.R. 1319] (Traynor, J., dissenting), disapproved on other grounds, Parsons v. Bristol Dev. Co., supra, 62 Cal.2d 861, 866, fn. 2.) * * * On the other hand an ambiguity is said to exist when, in the light of the circumstances surrounding the execution of an instrument, 'the written language is fairly susceptible of two or more constructions.' (Hulse v. Juillard Fancy Foods Co. (1964) 61 Cal.2d 571, 573 [39 Cal.Rptr. 529, 394 P.2d 65]; Nofziger v. Holman (1964) 61 Cal.2d 526, 528 [39 Cal.Rptr. 384, 393 P.2d 696]; Coast Bank v. Minderhout (1964) 61 Cal.2d 311, 315 [38 Cal.Rptr. 505, 392 P.2d 265], citing cases; see Pacific Gas & E. Co. v. G. W. Thomas Drayage etc. Co., ante, p. 40.)

As we have explained, what is here involved is a general principle of interpretation of written instruments, applicable to wills as well as to deeds and contracts. Even when the answer to the problem of interpretation is different for different kinds of written instruments, 'it appears in all cases as a variation from some general doctrine.' (9 Wigmore, op.cit. supra, § 2401, p. 7.) Under the application of this general principle in the field of wills, extrinsic evidence of the circumstances under which a will is made (except evidence expressly excluded by statute) * * * may be considered by the court in ascertaining what the testator meant by the words used in the will. If in the light of such extrinsic evidence, the provisions of the will are reasonably susceptible of two or more meanings claimed to have been intended by the testator, 'an uncertainty arises upon the face of a will' (§ 105) and extrinsic evidence relevant to prove any of such meanings is admissible (see § 106), * * * subject to the restrictions imposed by statute (§ 105). If, on the other hand, in the light of such extrinsic evidence, the provisions of the will are not reasonably susceptible of two or more meanings, there is no uncertainty arising upon the face of the will (§ 105; see Estate of Beldon (1938) 11 Cal.2d 108, 117 [77 P.2d 1052]; Estate of Pierce (1948) 32 Cal.2d 265, 272 [196 P.2d 1]; Estate of Carter, supra, 47 Cal.2d 200, 207) and any proffered evidence attempting to show an intention *different* from that expressed by the words therein, giving them the only meaning to which they are reasonably susceptible, is inadmissible. In the latter case the provisions of the will are to be interpreted according to such meaning. In short, we hold that while section 105 delineates the manner of ascertaining the testator's intention 'when an uncertainty arises upon the face of a will,' it cannot always be determined whether the will is ambiguous or not until the surrounding circumstances are first considered.

Finally, before taking up testatrix' will, we add a brief word concerning our proper function on this appeal. This function must subserve the paramount rule that the 'will is to be construed according to the intention of the testator.' (See fns. 5 and 6, ante, and accompanying text.) As we said in Parsons v. Bristol Dev. Co., supra, 62

Cal.2d 861, 865, it is 'solely a judicial function to interpret a written instrument unless the interpretation turns upon the credibility of extrinsic evidence.' (See fn. 8, ante.) Accordingly, 'an appellate court is not bound by a construction of a document based solely upon the terms of the written instrument without the aid of extrinsic evidence, where there is no conflict in the evidence, or a determination has been made upon incompetent evidence. [Citations.]' (Estate of Wunderle (1947) 30 Cal.2d 274, 280 [181 P.2d 874]; see Estate of Donnellan, supra, 164 Cal. 14, 19; Estate of Platt (1942) 21 Cal.2d 343, 352 [131 P.2d 825]; Parsons v. Bristol Dev. Co., supra, 62 Cal.2d 861, 865.)

We said in Estate of Beldon, supra, 11 Cal.2d 108, 111–112, ' 'The making of a will raises a presumption that the testator intended to dispose of all his property. Residuary clauses are generally inserted for the purpose of making that disposition complete, and these clauses are always to receive a broad and liberal interpretation, with a view of preventing intestacy as to any portion of the estate of the testator, and this general rule is in harmony with the declaration of our code that the provisions of a will must be construed, if possible, so as to effect that purpose.' (O'Connor v. Murphy, 147 Cal. 148, 153 [81 P. 406].) But there is no room for application of the rule if the testator's language, taken in the light of surrounding circumstances, will not reasonably admit of more than one construction.... If [testator] used language which results in intestacy, and there can be no doubt about the meaning of the language which was used, the court must hold that intestacy was intended.' Therefore, if having ascertained in the instant case that the provisions of the will are not reasonably susceptible of two or more meanings, we conclude that the only meaning to which the words expressed by testatrix are reasonably susceptible results in intestacy, we must give effect to her will accordingly. (Estate of Beldon, supra, 11 Cal.2d 108, 112; Estate of Akeley (1950) 35 Cal.2d 26, 32 [215 P.2d 921, 17 A.L.R.2d 647] (Traynor, J. dissenting); Estate of Barnes (1965) 63 Cal.2d 580, 583–584 [47 Cal.Rptr. 480, 407 P.2d 656].)

Examining testatrix' will in the light of the foregoing rules, we arrive at the following conclusions: Extrinsic evidence offered by plaintiff was admitted without objection and indeed would have been properly admitted over objection to raise and resolve the latent ambiguity as to Roxy Russell and ultimately to establish that Roxy Russell was a dog. Extrinsic evidence of the surrounding circumstances * * * was properly considered in order to ascertain what testatrix meant by the words of the will, including the words: 'I leave everything I own Real & Personal to Chester H. Quinn & Roxy Russell' or as those words can now be read 'to Chester H. Quinn and my dog Roxy Russell.'

However, viewing the will in the light of the surrounding circumstances as are disclosed by the record, we conclude that the will cannot reasonably be construed as urged by Quinn and determined by the trial court as providing that testatrix intended to make an absolute and outright gift of the entire residue of her estate to Quinn who was 'to use whatever portion thereof as might be necessary to care for and maintain the dog.' No words of the will gave the entire residuum to Quinn, much less indicate that the provision for the dog is merely precatory in nature. Such an interpretation is not consistent with a disposition which by its language leaves the residuum in equal shares to Quinn and the dog. A disposition in equal shares to two beneficiaries cannot be equated with a disposition of the whole to one of them who may use 'whatever portion thereof as might be necessary' on behalf of the other. (See § 104; cf. Estate of Kearns (1950) 36 Cal.2d 531, 534–536 [225 P.2d 218].) (8) Neither can the bare language of a gift of one-half of the residue to the dog be so expanded as to mean a gift to Quinn in trust for the care of the dog, there being no words indicating an enforceable duty upon Quinn to do so or indicating to whom the trust property is to go upon termination of the trust. 'While no particular form of expression is necessary for the creation of a trust, nevertheless some expression of intent to that end is requisite.' (Estate of Doane, supra, 190 Cal. 412, 415; see § 104; Estate of Marti (1901) 132 Cal. 666, 669 [61 P. 964, 64 P. 1071]; Estate of McCray (1928) 204 Cal. 399, 402 [268 P. 647]; Estate of Sargavak, supra, 41 Cal.2d 314, 319, citing cases.)

Accordingly, since in the light of the extrinsic evidence introduced below, the terms of the will are not reasonably susceptible of the meaning claimed by Quinn to have been intended by testatrix, the extrinsic evidence offered to show such an intention should have been excluded by the trial court. * * * Upon an independent examination of the will we conclude that the trial court's interpretation of the terms thereof was erroneous. Interpreting the provisions relating to testatrix' residuary estate in accordance with the only meaning to which they are reasonably susceptible, we conclude that testatrix intended to make a disposition of all of the residue of the estate to Quinn and the dog in equal shares; therefore, as tenants in common. (§ 29; Estate of Hittell (1903) 141 Cal. 432, 434–436 [75 P. 53]; Estate of Murphy (1909) 157 Cal. 63, 66–72 [106 P. 230, 137 Am.St.Rep. 110]; Estate of Kunkler (1912) 163 Cal. 797, 800 [127 P. 43]; Noble v. Beach (1942) 21 Cal.2d 91, 94 [130 P.2d 426].) As a dog cannot be the beneficiary under a will (§ 27; see 1 Page on Wills, op.cit. supra, § 17.21, p. 851) the attempted gift to Roxy Russell is void.[22] (§ 27; Estate of Burnison (1949) 33 Cal.2d 638, 646 [204 P.2d 330], affd. 339 U.S. 87 [94 L.Ed. 675, 70 S.Ct. 503]; Estate of Doane, supra, 190 Cal. 412.)

There remains only the necessity of determining the effect of the void gift to the dog upon the disposition of the residuary estate. That portion of any residuary estate that is the subject of a lapsed gift to one of the residuary beneficiaries remains undisposed of by the will and passes to the heirs-at-law. (§§ 92, 220; Estate of Hittell, supra, 141 Cal. 432, 437; Estate of Kunkler, supra, 163 Cal. 797, 800; Estate of Hall (1920) 183 Cal. 61, 63 [190 P. 364].) The rule is equally applicable with respect to a void gift to one of the residuary beneficiaries. (§ 220; see 96 C.J.S., Wills, § 1226; 53 Cal.Jur.2d, Wills, § 271, p. 531.) Therefore, notwithstanding testatrix' expressed intention to limit the extent of her gift by will to plaintiff (see Estate of Barnes, supra, 63 Cal.2d 580, 583) one-half of the residuary estate passes to plaintiff as testatrix' only heir-at-law (§ 225). We conclude that the residue of testatrix' estate should be distributed in equal shares to Chester H. Quinn and Georgia Nan Russell Hembree, testatrix' niece.

The judgment is reversed and the cause is remanded with directions to the trial court to set aside the findings of fact and conclusions of law; to make and file findings of fact and conclusions of law in conformity with the views herein expressed; and to enter judgment accordingly. Such findings of fact, conclusions of law and judgment shall be prepared, signed, filed and entered in the manner provided by law. Plaintiff shall recover costs on appeal.

Traynor, C. J., Peters, J., Tobriner, J., Mosk, J., and Burke, J., concurred.

---

22. As a consequence, the fact that Roxy Russell predeceased the testatrix is of no legal import. As appears, we have disposed of the issue raised by plaintiff's frontal attack on the eligibility of the dog to take a testamentary gift and therefore need not concern ourselves with the novel question as to whether the death of the dog during the lifetime of the testatrix resulted in a lapsed gift. (§ 92.)

McCOMB, J. (dissenting) [opinion omitted] * * *

Restatement (Third) of Property: Wills & Donative Transfers (2003)

§ 11.1 Ambiguity Defined

An ambiguity in a donative document is an uncertainty in meaning that is revealed by the text or by extrinsic evidence other than direct evidence of intention contradicting the plain meaning of the text.

Comment:

a. Scope note. This section defines an ambiguity in a donative document as an uncertainty in meaning that is revealed by the text or by extrinsic evidence other than direct evidence of intention contradicting the plain meaning of the text. An uncertainty in meaning shows that the document contains an inadequate expression of the donor's intention. Ambiguities often but not necessarily arise in situations in which two or more constructions of the document are plausible.

Certain types of ambiguity arise recurrently. These are ambiguous descriptions, mistaken inclusions or omissions, and cases in which the donor's customary usage of terms differs from the ordinary meaning of terms used in the document. Each of these types is treated in § 11.2.

When the text of a donative document is ambiguous, the donor's intention is not always ascertainable from the text alone. Although it is customary to distinguish between latent and patent ambiguities, no legal consequences attach to the distinction. The terms are used for descriptive purposes only. A patent ambiguity is an ambiguity that appears from the text alone (Comment *b*) and a latent ambiguity is one that is revealed by extrinsic evidence other than direct evidence of intention contradicting the plain meaning of the text (Comment *c*).

B. Plain Meaning Rule and Mistake

In re Pavlinko's Estate

Supreme Court of Pennsylvania, 1959
394 Pa. 564, 148 A.2d 528

BELL, Justice.

Vasil Pavlinko died February 8, 1957; his wife, Hellen, died October 15, 1951. A testamentary writing dated March 9, 1949, which purported to be the will of Hellen Pavlinko, was signed by Vasil Pavlinko, her husband. The residuary legatee named therein, a brother of Hellen, offered the writing for probate as the will of Vasil Pavlinko, but probate was refused. The Orphans' Court, after hearing and argument, affirmed the decision of the Register of Wills.

The facts are unusual and the result very unfortunate. Vasil Pavlinko and Hellen, his wife, retained a lawyer to draw their wills and wished to leave their property to each other. By mistake Hellen signed the will which was prepared for her husband, and Vasil signed the will which was prepared for his wife, each instrument being signed at the end thereof. The lawyer who drew the will and his secretary, Dorothy Zinkham, both signed as witnesses. Miss Zinkham admitted that she was unable to speak the language of Vasil and Hellen, and that no conversation took place between them. The wills were kept by Vasil and Hellen. For some undisclosed reason, Hellen's will was never offered for probate at her death; in this case it was offered merely as an exhibit.

The instrument which was offered for probate was short. It stated:

'I, *Hellen* Pavlinko, of * * *, do hereby make, publish and declare this to be *my* * * * [Italics thoughout [*sic*], ours] Last Will and Testament, * * *.'

In the first paragraph she directed her executor to pay her debts and funeral expenses. In the second paragraph she gave her entire residuary estate to 'my husband, Vasil Pavlinko * * * absolutely'. She then provided:

'Third: If my aforesaid husband, Vasil Pavlinko, should predecease me, then and in that event, I give and bequeath:

'(a) To my brother-in-law, Mike Pavlinko, of McKees Rocks, Pennsylvania, the sum of Two hundred ($200) Dollars.

'(b) To my sister-in-law, Maria Gerber, (nee Pavlinko), of Pittsburgh, Pennsylvania, the sum of Two Hundred ($200) Dollars.

'(c) The rest, residue and remainder of *my* estate, of whatsoever kind and nature and wheresoever situate, I give, devise and bequeath, absolutely, to *my brother*, Elias Martin, now residing at 520 Aidyl Avenue, Pittsburgh, Pennsylvania.

'I do hereby nominate, constitute and appoint my husband, Vasil Pavlinko, as Executor of this my Last Will and Testament.' It was then mistakenly signed: 'Vasil Pavlinko [Seal]'.

While no attempt was made to probate, as Vasil's will, the writing which purported to be his will but was signed by Hellen, it could not have been probated as Vasil's will, because it was not signed by him at the end thereof.

The Wills Act of 1947 provides in clear, plain and unmistakable language in § 2: 'Every will, * * * shall be in writing and shall be signed *by the testator* at the end thereof', 20 P.S. § 180.2, with certain exceptions not here relevant. The Court below correctly held that the paper which *recited* that it was the will of Hellen Pavlinko and intended and purported to give Hellen's estate to her husband, could not be probated as the will of Vasil and was a nullity.

In order to decide in favor of the residuary legatee, almost the entire will would have to be rewritten. The Court would have to substitute the words 'Vasil Pavlinko' for 'Hellen Pavlinko' and the words 'my wife' wherever the words 'my husband' appear in the will, and the relationship of the contingent residuary legatees would likewise have to be changed. To consider this paper— as written—as Vasil's will, it would give his entire residuary estate to 'my husband, Vasil Pavlinko, absolutely' and 'Third: If my husband, Vasil Pavlinko, should predecease me, then * * * I give and bequeath my residuary estate to my brother, Elias Martin.' The language of this writing, which is signed at the end thereof by *Vasil* Pavlinko, is unambiguous, clear and unmistakable, and it is obvious that it is a meaningless nullity.

While no authority is needed to demonstrate what is so obvious, there is a case which is directly in point and holds that such a writing cannot be probated as the will of

Vasil Pavlinko. This exact situation arose in Alter's Appeal, 67 Pa. 341. The facts are recited in the unanimous opinion of the Court, speaking through Mr. Justice Agnew (at page 344):

'This is a hard case, but it seems to be without a remedy. An aged couple, husband and wife, having no lineal descendants, and each owning property, determined to make their wills in favor of each other, so that the survivor should have all they possessed. Their wills were drawn precisely alike, mutatis mutandis, and laid down on a table for execution. Each signed a paper, which was duly witnessed by three subscribing witnesses, and the papers were enclosed in separate envelopes, endorsed and sealed up. After the death of George A. Alter, the envelopes were opened and it was found that each had by mistake signed the will of the other. To remedy this error the legislature, by an Act approved the 23rd day of February 1870, conferred authority upon the Register's Court of this county to take proof of the mistake, and proceed as a court of chancery, to reform the will of George A. Alter and decree accordingly. * * * Was the paper signed by George A. Alter his will? Was it capable of being reformed by the Register's Court? The paper drawn up for his will was not a will in law, for it was not 'signed by him at the end thereof,' as the Wills Act requires. *The paper he signed was not his will, for it was drawn up for the will of his wife and gave the property to himself. It was insensible and absurd.* It is clear, therefore, that he had executed no will, and there was nothing to be reformed. There was a mistake, it is true, but that mistake was the same as if he had signed a blank sheet of paper. He had written his name, but not to his will. He had never signed his will, and the signature where it was, was the same as if he had not written it at all. He therefore died intestate, and his property descended as at law.' The Court further decided that the Legislative Act was void because it had no power to divest estates which were already vested at law on the death of George A. Alter without a will.

How firmly and without exception the Courts have carried out the provisions of the Wills Act, when the language thereof is clear and unmistakable, is further evident from the following authorities: In re Bryen's Estate, 328 Pa. 122, 195 A. 17; In re Churchill's Estate, 260 Pa. 94, 103 A. 533; In re Gray's Will, 365 Pa. 411, 76 A.2d 169.

In re Bryen's Estate, 328 Pa. 122, 195 A. 17, a testator received from his lawyer a three page will. He wished to add an additional clause providing for a grandchild. The lawyer thereupon rewrote the last page 'backed and bound together with brass eyelets the first, second and new third page, unnumbered, and inserted the original third page loosely between the last of the fastened pages and the backer.' Bryen executed the loose sheet at the end thereof in the presence of two subscribing witnesses. He then placed the enclosure in his safe deposit box where it was found after his death. The Court held that the instrument could not be probated as Bryen's last will because it was not signed at the end thereof in conformity with the statute, nor could any part or pages thereof be probated as his last will. This Court, speaking through Mr. Justice, later Chief Justice, Stern, said (328 Pa. at page 128, 195 A. at page 20):

'The obvious truth of the matter is that the loose sheet was signed by mistake, * * *. While decedent's mistake is regrettable, it cannot be judicially corrected; the situation thus created must be accepted as it exists. Alter's Appeal, 67 Pa. 341. The question is not what a testator mistakenly thinks he is doing, but what he actually does. In re Churchill's Estate, 260 Pa. 94, 100, 103 A. 533; In re Dietterich's Estate, 127 Pa.Super. 315, 322, 323, 193 A. 158. It is of paramount importance to uphold the legal requirements as to the execution of wills, so that the possibility of fraud may be reduced to a minimum.'

In re Churchill's Estate, 260 Pa. 94, 103 A. 533, 535, the Court refused to probate Churchill's will, which was written by him. He failed to sign his name 'at what was so clearly the end of the paper as a will. What he did do was to write his name in three blank spaces in the paper, first at the top and then in the testimonium and attestation clauses * * * he said to one of the two attesting witnesses, 'This is my will, I have signed it,' and to the other, 'I wish you to witness my name to a paper,' and subsequently handed it to a physician, saying, 'This is my will, and I want you to keep it for me,' * * *

'The decedent may have thought he had made a will, but the statute says he had not. The question is not one of his intention, but of what he actually did, or rather what he failed to do. He failed to sign the paper at the end thereof, and this essential requirement of the statute is not met by the insertion of his name in his own handwriting in three blank spaces in the printed form of the paper which he may have intended to use in executing his will. 'It may happen, even frequently, that genuine wills, namely, wills truly expressing the intentions of the testators, are made without observation of the required forms; and whenever that happens, the genuine intention if frustrated by the act of the Legislature, of which the general object is to give effect to the intention. The courts must consider that the Legislature, having regard to all probable circumstances, has thought it best, and has therefore determined, to run the risk of frustrating the intention sometimes, in preference to the risk of giving effect to or facilitating the formation of spurious wills, by the absence of forms. * * * 'Our Act of 1833 as well as the statute of Victoria, are in part borrowed from the British statute of frauds, two sections of which have been so evaded by judicial construction as to be practically repealed. We do not propose that the act of 1833 shall meet with the same fate. The Legislature have laid down a rule so plain that it cannot be evaded without a clear violation of its terms. No room is left for judicial construction or interpretation. It says a will must be signed at the end thereof, and that's the end of it. We are of opinion that this paper was not a will within the meaning of the act of 1833, and that it was error to admit it to probate.'

In re Gray's Will, 365 Pa. 411, 76 A.2d 169, 170, testatrix signed her will 'Mrs. Ella X (her mark) Gray. Witness: Fannie Graff.' Mrs. Anderson was also present and saw Mrs. Gray make her mark, but did not sign her name on the paper as a subscribing witness. The Court said (365 Pa. at pages 414–415, 76 A.2d at page 170):

'The first question that arises is, was this writing of January 22, 1946, a will and if so, was it probatable as such? The learned trial judge found and we agree that this writing was testamentary in character. In re Davis' Estate, 275 Pa. 126, 118 A. 645; Kimmel's Estate, 278 Pa. 435, 123 A. 405, 31 A.L.R. 678; In re Wenz's Estate, 345 Pa. 393, 29 A.2d 13. It is however equally clear that even if it be a will, *it is not a valid or probatable will*. Section 2, subsection (2) of the Wills Act of April 24, 1947, P.L. 89 provides: 'If the testator is unable to sign his name for any reason, a will to which he makes his mark and to which his name is subscribed in his presence before or after he makes his mark, shall be as valid as though he had signed his name thereto: Provided, He makes his mark in the presence of two witnesses who sign their names to the will in his presence.'

This Court held that the instrument did not comply with §2 of the Wills Act of 1947 and could not be probated as Mrs. Gray's will.

Once a Court starts to ignore or alter or rewrite or make exceptions to clear, plain and unmistakable provisions of the Wills Act in order to accomplish equity and justice in that particular case, the Wills Act will become a meaningless, although well intentioned, scrap of paper, and the door will be opened wide to countless fraudulent claims which the Act successfully bars.

Decree affirmed. Each party shall pay their respective costs.

MUSMANNO, Justice (dissenting).

Vasil Pavlinko and his wife, Hellen Pavlinko, being unlettered in English and un-learned in the ways of the law, wisely decided to have an attorney draw up their wills, since they were both approaching the age when reflecting persons must give thought to that voyage from which there is no return. They explained to the attorney, whose services they sought, that he should draw two wills which would state that when either of the partners had sailed away, the one remaining ashore would become the owner of the prop-erty of the departing voyager. Vasil Pavlinko knew but little English. However, his lawyer, fortunately, was well versed in his clients's native language, known as Little Russian or Carpathian. The attorney thus discussed the whole matter with his two visitors in their language. He then dictated appropriate wills to his stenographer in English and then, after they had been transcribed, he translated the documents, paragraph by paragraph, to Mr. and Mrs. Pavlinko, who approved of all that he had written. The wills were laid be-fore them and each signed the document purporting to be his or her will. The attorney gave Mrs. Pavlinko the paper she had signed and handed to her husband the paper he had signed. In accordance with customs they had brought with them from the old coun-try, Mrs. Pavlinko turned her paper over to her husband. It did not matter, however, who held the papers since they were complementary of each other. Mrs. Pavlinko left her property to Mr. Pavlinko and Mr. Pavlinko left his property to Mrs. Pavlinko. They also agreed on a common residuary legatee, Elias Martin, the brother of Mrs. Pavlinko.

Mrs. Pavlinko died first, but for some reason her will was not probated. Then Mr. Pavlinko died and Elias Martin came forth to claim his inheritance. The Register of Wills of Allegheny County refused to accept the Vasil Pavlinko will for probate. It now developed for the first time that, despite every care used by her attorney, a strange thing had happened. Mr. Pavlinko had signed his wife's will and Mrs. Pavlinko had signed her husband's will.

At the hearing before the Register of Wills, the will signed by Vasil Pavlinko was in-troduced as Exhibit No. 1 and the will signed by Hellen Pavlinko was introduced as Ex-hibit No. 2. The attorney, who had drawn the wills and had witnessed the signatures of the testator and testatrix, testified to what had occurred in his office; his secretary who had typed the wills and had witnessed the signatures, also testified to the events which spelled out the little mishap of the unintentional exchange of the wills.

The Orphans' Court of Allegheny County sustained the action of the Register of Wills. Elias Martin appealed to this Court, which now affirms the lower court and, in doing so, I submit, creates another enigma for the layman to ponder over, regarding the mysterious manner in which the law operates, it wonders to perform. Everyone in this case admits that a mistake was made: an honest, innocent, unambiguous, simple mis-take, the innocent, drowsy mistake of a man who sleeps all day and, on awakening, ac-cepts the sunset for the dawn.

Nothing is more common to mankind than mistakes. Volumes, even libraries have been written on mistakes: mistakes of law and mistakes of fact. In every phase of life, mis-takes occur and there are but few people who will not attempt to lend a helping hand to the person who mistakes a step for a landing and falls, or the one who mistakes a nut for a grape and chokes, or the one who steps through a glass so clear that he does not see it. This Court, however, says that it can do nothing for the victim of the mistake in this case, a mistake which was caused through no fault of his own, nor of his intended benefactors.

Next to the love which the Pavlinkos bore to each other, they were devoted to Mrs. Pavlinko's brother, Elias Martin. They wholeheartedly agreed that after they had quitted the earth, this devoted kinsman of theirs should have all that they would leave behind them. No one disputes this brute fact, no one can dispute this granitic, unbudgeable truth. Cannot the law, therefore, dedicated as it is to the truth, and will all its wisdom and majestic power, correct this mistake which cries our for correction? May the law not untie the loose knot of error which begs to be freed? I know that the law is founded on precedent and in many ways we are bound by the dead hand of the past. But even, with obeisance to precedent, I still do not believe that the medicine of the law is incapable of curing the simple ailment here which has not, because of any passage of time, become aggravated by complications.

We have said more times than there are tombstones in the cemetery where the Pavlinkos lie buried, that the primary rule to be followed in the interpretation of a will is to ascertain the intention of the testator. Can anyone go to the graves of the Pavlinkos and say that we do not know what they meant? They said in English and in Carpathian that they wanted their property to go to Elias Martin.

We have also said time without number that the intent of the testator must be gathered from the four corners of his will. Whether it be from the four corners of the will signed by Vasil Pavlinko or whether from the eight corners of the wills signed by Vasil and Hellen Pavlinko, all set out before the court below, the net result is always the same, namely that the residue of the property of the last surviving member of the Pavlinko couple was to go to Elias Martin. In the face of all the pronouncements of the law as to the fidelity with which the intention of the testator must be followed, on what possible basis can we now ignore the intention expressed by the Pavlinkos so clearly, so conclusively, and so all-encompassingly?

The Majority says that there is nothing we can do to effectuate the expressed intention of Vasil Pavlinko. But, I respectfully submit, the Majority does not make a serious effort to effectuate that expressed intent. The Majority contents itself with saying that 'the facts are unusual and the result very unfortunate.' But the results do not need to be unfortunate. In re King's Will, 369 Pa. 523, 531, 87 A.2d 469, 474, we said that: 'What offends against an innate sense of justice, decency and fair play offends against good law.' Certainly the results being affirmed by this Court offend against an innate sense of justice. Elias Martin is being turned out of Court when there is no need for such a peremptory eviction. The Majority authorizes the eviction on the basis of a decision rendered by this Court in 1878 in the case of Alter's Appeal, 67 Pa. 341. There, wife and husband, also signed wrong papers and the Court in that post-Civil War period, held nothing could be done to correct the error. But even if we say that the Alter decision makes impossible the transferring of the signature of Vasil Pavlinko to the will written in his name, I still do not see how it prevents this Court from enforcing the provision in the will which *was* signed by Vasil Pavlinko. In the Alter case an attempt was made to reform the will 'by striking off the signature 'Catherine Alter,' and causing the name 'George A. Alter' to be signed thereto' so that the paper so signed could be 'admitted to probate as the will of George A. Alter.' But in our case here, no such substitution is being sought. What Elias Martin seeks is admission to probate of a testamentary writing *actually signed by the testator Vasil Pavlinko.*

Moreover, in the Alter case, as distinguished from the Pavlinko will, George A. Alter left everything to himself. Even if we accept the Majority's conclusion, based on the Alter case, that all provisions in the Pavlinko will, which refer to himself, must be regarded as nullities, not correctable by parol evidence because they evince no latent ambiguities, it does not follow that the residuary clause must perish. The fact that some of the provisions in the Pavlinko will cannot be executed does not strike down the residuary clause, which is meaningful and stands on its own two feet. * * * We know that one of the very purposes of a residuary clause is to provide a catch-all for undisposed-of or ineffectually disposed-of property.

> 'A residuary gift carries with it, and is presumed to have been so intended, not only all the estate which remains not specifically disposed of at the time the will is executed, *but all that, for any reason, which is illy disposed of, or fails as to the legatees originally intended.* In re Wood's Estate, 209 Pa. 16, (57 A. 1103).' (In re Jull's Estate, 370 Pa. 434, 442, 88 A.2d 753, 756.) (Emphasis supplied.)

And the Wills Act itself specifically provides:

> 'A devise or bequest not being part of the residuary estate which shall fail or be void because the beneficiary fails to survive the testator or because it is contrary to law *or otherwise incapable of taking effect* or which has been revoked by the testator or is undisposed of or is released or disclaimed by the beneficiary, if it shall not pass to the issue of the beneficiary under the provisions * * * provided for by law, shall be included in the residuary devise or bequest, if any, contained in the will.' (Emphasis supplied.) 20 P.S. § 180.14(9).

The Majority also relies on In re Bryen's Estate, 218 Pa. 122, 195 A. 17, 20, but in that case the testator failed to sign the prepared will at the end. He affixed his signature to a page which was 'in effect nothing more than a detached and independent paper not sequentially integrated with the others to form with them a testamentary instrument.' But here, I repeat, there was a complete testamentary instrument signed by Vasil Pavlinko at the end thereof and with testamentary intent.

The Majority calls upon In re Churchill's Estate, 260 Pa. 94, 103 A. 533, as further substantiation of its position, but the testator in that case failed to sign the testamentary writing at the end.

And, so far as In re Gray's Will, 365 Pa. 411, 76 A.2d 169, additionally cited by the Majority, is concerned, it clearly is not applicable to the facts in the case at bar because, there, the mark of the testator was not made in accordance with the provisions of the Wills Act.

I see no insuperable obstacle to probating the will signed by Vasil Pavlinko. Even though it was originally prepared as the will of his wife, Hellen, he did adopt its testamentary provisions as his own. Some of its provisions are not effective but their ineffectuality in no way bars the legality and validity of the residuary clause which is complete in itself. I would, therefore, probate the paper signed by Vasil Pavlinko. Here, indeed, is a situation where we could, if we wished, consistent with authority and precedent, and without endangering the integrity of the Wills Act, put in to effect the time-honored proverb that 'where there's a will, there's a way.'

In fact, we have here two wills, with signposts unerringly pointing to the just and proper destination, but the Court still cannot find the way.

* * *

Estate of Gibbs

Supreme Court of Wisconsin, 1961
14 Wis.2d 490, 111 N.W.2d 413

(For the text of the opinion, see *supra* at 224.)

Erickson v. Erickson

Supreme Court of Connecticut, 1998
246 Conn. 350, 716 A.2d 92

(For the text of the opinion, see *supra* at 228.)

Espinosa v. Sparber, Shevin, Shapo, Rosen & Heilbronner

Supreme Court of Florida, 1993
612 So.2d 1378

McDONALD, Justice.

We review Espinosa v. Sparber, Shevin, Shapo, Rosen & Heilbronner, 586 So.2d 1221 (Fla. 3d DCA 1991), which involves the following question of great public importance certified in an unpublished order dated September 17, 1991:

> UNDER THE FACTS OF THIS CASE ... MAY A LAWSUIT ALLEGING PRO-
> FESSIONAL MALPRACTICE BE BROUGHT, ON BEHALF OF PATRICIA
> AZCUNCE, AGAINST THE DRAFTSMAN OF THE SECOND CODICIL?

We have jurisdiction pursuant to article V, section 3(b)(4) of the Florida Constitution. We answer the question in the negative and approve the decision of the district court.

Howard Roskin, a member of the Sparber, Shevin law firm, drafted a will for Rene Azcunce, the testator. At the time he signed his will, Rene and his wife, Marta, had three children, Lisette, Natalie, and Gabriel. Article Seventeenth of the Will specifically provided that:

> (a) References in this, my Last Will and Testament, to my children, shall be construed to mean my daughters, LISSETE AZCUNCE and NATALIE AZ-CUNCE, and my son, GABRIEL AZCUNCE.

> (b) References in this, my Last Will and Testament, to my "issue," shall be construed to mean my children [as defined in Paragraph (a), above] and their legitimate natural born and legally adopted lineal descendants.

Article Fourth of the will established a trust for the benefit of Marta and the three named children and also granted Marta a power of appointment to distribute all or a portion of the trust to the named children and their issue. In addition, the will provided that, upon Marta's death, the trust was to be divided into equal shares for each of the three named children.

Neither the will nor the first codicil to the will, executed on August 8, 1983, made any provisions for after-born children. On March 14, 1984, Patricia Azcunce was born as the fourth child of Rene and Marta. Rene contacted Roskin and communicated his desire to include Patricia in his will. In response, Roskin drafted a new will that provided for Patricia and also restructured the trust. However, due to a disagreement between Rene and Roskin on the amount of available assets, Rene never signed the second will. Instead, on June 25, 1986, he executed a second codicil drafted by Roskin that changed the identity of the co-trustee and co-personal representative, but did not provide for the after-born child, Patricia. When Rene died on December 30, 1986, he had never executed any document that provided for Patricia.[1]

---

1. Patricia brought suit in probate court to be classified as a pretermitted child, which would have entitled her to a share of Rene's estate. Her mother and adult sibling consented to Patricia's pe-

Marta brought a malpractice action on behalf of Patricia and the estate against Roskin and his law firm. The trial court dismissed the complaint with prejudice for lack of privity and entered final summary judgment for Roskin and his firm. The Third District Court of Appeal reversed the dismissal with regard to the estate, affirmed it with regard to Patricia, and certified the question of whether Patricia has standing to bring a legal malpractice action under the facts of this case.

An attorney's liability for negligence in the performance of his or her professional duties is limited to clients with whom the attorney shares privity of contract. Angel, Cohen & Rogovin v. Oberon Investments, N.V., 512 So.2d 192 (Fla.1987). In a legal context, the term "privity" is a word of art derived from the common law of contracts and used to describe the relationship of persons who are parties to a contract. Baskerville-Donovan Engineers, Inc. v. Pensacola Executive House Condominium Ass'n, Inc., 581 So.2d 1301 (Fla.1991). To bring a legal malpractice action, the plaintiff must either be in privity with the attorney, wherein one party has a direct obligation to another, or, alternatively, the plaintiff must be an intended third-party beneficiary. In the instant case, Patricia Azcunce does not fit into either category of proper plaintiffs.

In the area of will drafting, a limited exception to the strict privity requirement has been allowed where it can be demonstrated that the apparent intent of the client in engaging the services of the lawyer was to benefit a third party. Rosenstone v. Satchell, 560 So.2d 1229 (Fla. 4th DCA 1990); Lorraine v. Grover, Ciment, Weinstein & Stauber, P.A., 467 So.2d 315 (Fla. 3d DCA 1985). Because the client is no longer alive and is unable to testify, the task of identifying those persons who are intended third-party beneficiaries causes an evidentiary problem closely akin to the problem of determining the client's general testamentary intent. To minimize such evidentiary problems, the will was designed as a legal document that affords people a clear opportunity to express the way in which they desire to have their property distributed upon death. To the greatest extent possible, courts and personal representatives are obligated to honor the testator's intent in conformity with the contents of the will. In re Blocks' Estate, 143 Fla. 163, 196 So. 410 (1940).

If extrinsic evidence is admitted to explain testamentary intent, as recommended by the petitioners, the risk of misinterpreting the testator's intent increases dramatically. Furthermore, admitting extrinsic evidence heightens the tendency to manufacture false evidence that cannot be rebutted due to the unavailability of the testator. For these reasons, we adhere to the rule that standing in legal malpractice actions is limited to those who can show that the testator's intent *as expressed in the will* is frustrated by the negligence of the testator's attorney. Although Rene did not express in his will and codicils any intention to exclude Patricia, his will and codicils do not, unfortunately, express any affirmative intent to provide for her. Because Patricia cannot be described as one in

---

tition being granted. The probate court judge appointed a guardian ad litem for Patricia's two minor siblings, and the guardian opposed the petition. Subsequently, the court ruled that the second codicil destroyed Patricia's status as a pretermitted child, and the decision was upheld on appeal. Azcunce v. Estate of Azcunce, 586 So.2d 1216 (Fla. 3d DCA 1991).

We are not privy to the factors that the guardian ad litem considered in deciding not to consent to Patricia's classification as a pretermitted child, a decision that deprived Patricia of a share in the estate and ultimately led to costly litigation. We hope, however, that a guardian evaluating the facts of this case would not focus strictly on the financial consequences for the child, but would also consider such important factors as family harmony and stability.

privity with the attorney or as an intended third-party beneficiary, a lawsuit alleging professional malpractice cannot be brought on her behalf.

Rene's estate, however, stands in the shoes of the testator and clearly satisfies the privity requirement. Therefore, we agree with the district court's decision that the estate may maintain a legal malpractice action against Roskin for any acts of professional negligence committed by him during his representation of Rene. Because the alleged damages to the estate are an element of the liability claim and are not relevant to the standing question in this particular case, we do not address that issue.

For the reasons stated above, we answer the certified question in the negative and approve the decision of the district court.

It is so ordered.

BARKETT, C.J., and OVERTON, SHAW, GRIMES, KOGAN and HARDING, JJ., concur.

* * *

Restatement (Third) of Property, Wills & Donative Transfers (2003)

§ 12.1 Reforming Donative Documents To Correct Mistakes

A donative document, though unambiguous, may be reformed to conform the text to the donor's intention if it is established by clear and convincing evidence (1) that a mistake of fact or law, whether in expression or inducement, affected specific terms of the document; and (2) what the donor's intention was. In determining whether these elements have been established by clear and convincing evidence, direct evidence of intention contradicting the plain meaning of the text as well as other evidence of intention may be considered.

Notes

The remedy for mistake is different from the remedy for failure to complete the necessary formalities. Formality deficiency is addressed through Professor Langbein's doctrine of substantial compliance, *see* John H. Langbein, *Substantial Compliance With the Wills Act*, 88 HARV. L. REV. 489 (1975), or is incorporated into the Uniform Probate Code, *see* UNIF. PROB. CODE §2-503 (1990) (Harmless Error), or in the *Restatement (Third) of Property*, §3.3 (1999) (Wills and Other Donative Transfers) ("A harmless error in executing a will may be excused if the proponent establishes by clear and convincing evidence that the decedent adopted the document as his or her will.") A mistake in the Will—particularly if the mistake is of the plain meaning variety—is more like a deficiency in an intentionality and may be addressed by courts, as was done in cases like *Estate of Gibbs*, or through the *Restatement (Third) of Property*, § 12.1 (Donative Transfers), which allows for clear and convincing evidence to correct the mistake. In addition, New Jersey uses a doctrine of probable intent to fill gaps in Wills. *See* Engle v. Seigel, 74 N.J. 287, 377 A.2d 892 (1977). But other courts retain a strict approach to the introduction of extrinsic evidence to resolve any inconsistencies. *See, e.g.*, Knupp v. District of Columbia, 578 A.2d 702 (1990). For some analysis of the approaches, see

Pamela R. Champine, *My Will Be Done: Accommodating the Erring and the Atypical Testator*, 80 Neb. L. Rev. 387 (2001).

V. Contract and Wills

Competent adults may enter into contracts that affect the terms of a Will or inheritance in general. But in examining these contracts, it is important to understand that there are two distinct claims at issue: contractual remedies and Will remedies. Thus, if an adult enters into a contract to make or revoke a Will or to appoint under a power of appointment, or agrees not to contest a Will, what is at issue is merely the validity of the contract, itself, and not the validity of the Will or the power of appointment, or the contest of the Will. The two issues are distinct, and claims may be based on either contract law or the law of Wills. *See generally* Kent Greenawalt, *A Pluralist Approach to Interpretation: Wills and Contracts*, 42 San Diego L. Rev. 533 (2005). What follows are examples of an integrated state statute addressing the interaction between contracts and Wills, and the most common forms of contracts affecting Last Wills and Testaments—prenuptial agreements.

A. Integrating Statute

California Probate Code (2004)

§ 21700. Contract to make will or devise; establishment; effect of execution of joint will or mutual wills; applicable law

(a) A contract to make a will or devise or other instrument, or not to revoke a will or devise or other instrument, or to die intestate, if made after the effective date of this statute, can be established only by one of the following:

(1) Provisions of a will or other instrument stating the material provisions of the contract.

(2) An expressed reference in a will or other instrument to a contract and extrinsic evidence proving the terms of the contract.

(3) A writing signed by the decedent evidencing the contract.

(4) Clear and convincing evidence of an agreement between the decedent and the claimant or a promise by the decedent to the claimant that is enforceable in equity.

(5) Clear and convincing evidence of an agreement between the decedent and another person for the benefit of the claimant or a promise by the decedent to another person for the benefit of the claimant that is enforceable in equity.

(b) The execution of a joint will or mutual wills does not create a presumption of a contract not to revoke the will or wills.

(c) A contract to make a will or devise or other instrument, or not to revoke a will or devise or other instrument, or to die intestate, if made prior to the effective date of this section, shall be construed under the law applicable to the contract prior to the effective date of this section.

B. Disclaimers by Spouses

Geddings v. Geddings
Supreme Court of South Carolina, 1995
319 S.C. 213, 460 S.E.2d 376

FINNEY, Chief Justice:

Respondent (Pinkie Geddings) initiated this action seeking to invoke her right to an elective share of the decedent's probate estate pursuant to S.C.Code Ann. §62-2-201 (Supp.1994). Appellants answered alleging Mrs. Geddings had waived her right to an elective share by signing a waiver agreement. After a hearing, the probate judge granted Mrs. Geddings an elective share finding that the purported waiver was void because she did not receive the required statutory fair disclosure. S.C.Code Ann. §62-2-204 (1987). Appellants appealed the matter to the circuit court which affirmed the probate court's determination. We affirm.

The Geddings were married in 1979. Both had children by their former spouses. In 1988 Mrs. Geddings signed a document presented to her by her husband titled "Waiver of Right to Elect and of Other Rights." In summary the document acknowledged that each had made a will; each desired that the bulk of his/her property go to his/her children by previous marriages; each disclaimed interest in the spouse's estate except as provided in the will admitted to probate at the death of the other spouse; and each had made a full, fair and complete disclosure to each other of all presently-owned assets.

Appellants contend the court erred in concluding the waiver agreement was invalid because Mrs. Geddings did not receive fair disclosure.

As an initial matter, appellants assert the probate court allowed Mrs. Geddings to testify in violation of the Dead Man's Statute S.C.Code Ann. §19-11-20 (1985). Based on that testimony, appellants claim the court erroneously concluded she had signed the agreement acknowledging fair disclosure when in fact she did not receive fair disclosure. Appellants did not object to Mrs. Geddings' testimony on the ground of violation of the Dead Man's Statute. Therefore appellants are precluded from raising the question now. Branton v. Martin, 243 S.C. 90, 132 S.E.2d 285 (1963).

The right of election of a surviving spouse may be waived by a written contract signed by the party waiving after fair disclosure. S.C.Code Ann. §62-2-204 (1987). While South Carolina has not defined what constitutes fair disclosure in this context, other states have in the similar context of antenuptial agreements. Considering the confidential relationship between parties to an antenuptial agreement, the affirmative duty imposed upon each party to disclose his or her financial status transcends what is normally required for a commercial transaction. In re Estate of Lebsock, 44 Colo.App. 220, 618 P.2d 683 (1980). "Fair disclosure contemplates that each spouse should be given information, of a general and approximate nature, concerning the net worth of the other. Each party has a duty to consider and evaluate the information received before signing an agreement." In re Estate of Lopata, 641 P.2d 952 (Colo.1982); In re Estate of Hill, 214 Neb. 702, 335 N.W.2d 750 (1983).

> Fair disclosure means that before signing an antenuptial agreement, each party must disclose to the other the facts that exist at the time of the agreement and which, in the absence of the antenuptial agreement, affect or determine the prospective intestate share of a surviving spouse in the disclosing party's estate

or which otherwise affect or determine distribution of property at the disclosing party's death.

In re Estate of Stephenson, 243 Neb. 890, 503 N.W.2d 540 (1993).

Both judges found the evidence presented by Mrs. Geddings established she had no real or general knowledge of the total extent of her husband's assets. While Mrs. Geddings had fully disclosed her assets to the decedent, she had no knowledge of the value of husband's estate. The attorney preparing the waiver document testified he did not discuss assets with Mrs. Geddings when it was executed. Mrs. Geddings was excluded from the annual corporate meetings held in her home at Christmas which included only the decedent and his children. There was substantial testimony that decedent was secretive about his financial affairs.

In an action at equity, tried first by the master or special referee and concurred in by the trial judge, the findings of fact will not be disturbed on appeal unless found to be without evidentiary support or against the clear preponderance of the evidence. Townes Assoc., Ltd. v. City of Greenville, 266 S.C. 81, 221 S.E.2d 773 (1976); Dean v. Kilgore, 313 S.C. 257, 437 S.E.2d 154 (Ct.App.1993) (two-judge rule would apply in appeal from circuit court of an equity case originating in probate court where both courts agreed on material issues).

There was sufficient evidence supporting the factual findings of the probate court concurred in by the circuit court. Accordingly, we

AFFIRM.

TOAL, MOORE and WALLER, JJ., and GEORGE T. GREGORY, Jr., Acting Associate Justice, concur.

* * *

Notes

Whether a premarital agreement may be enforced so as to waive election against the decedent's estate, inheritance under intestate succession, or the taking of non-probate transfers, is still unsettled. Some courts void the agreement, as did the court in *Geddings,* because of failure to disclose all assets at the time of the signing. Some courts have held that agreements may be void if they are a product of duress and, therefore, are involuntary. *See, e.g.,* In re Estate of Hollett, 150 N.H. 39, 834 A.2d 348 (2003). But other courts sustain agreements upon public policy grounds, even if a spouse waives alimony, support, and additional benefits. *See, e.g.,* Hardee v. Hardee, 355 S.C. 382, 585 S.E.2d 501 (2003) (holding that parties are adults and should be able to contract away rights and privileges). Because of the Uniform Premarital Agreement Act (1983), there is some uniformity among the states adopting it, with respect to a requirement of a written signed contract, that it be conscionable and voluntary and that there be fair and reasonable disclosure. The Uniform Probate Code adopts similar requirements.

Uniform Probate Code (2003)

§ 2-213. Waiver of Right to Elect and of Other Rights.

(a) The right of election of a surviving spouse and the rights of the surviving spouse to homestead allowance, exempt property, and family allowance, or any of them, may be waived, wholly or partially, before or after marriage, by a written contract, agreement, or waiver signed by the surviving spouse.

(b) A surviving spouse's waiver is not enforceable if the surviving spouse proves that:

(1) he [or she] did not execute the waiver voluntarily; or

(2) the waiver was unconscionable when it was executed and, before execution of the waiver, he [or she]:

(i) was not provided a fair and reasonable disclosure of the property or financial obligations of the decedent;

(ii) did not voluntarily and expressly waive, in writing, any right to disclosure of the property or financial obligations of the decedent beyond the disclosure provided; and

(iii) did not have, or reasonably could not have had, an adequate knowledge of the property or financial obligations of the decedent.

(c) An issue of unconscionability of a waiver is for decision by the court as a matter of law.

(d) Unless it provides to the contrary, a waiver of "all rights," or equivalent language, in the property or estate of a present or prospective spouse or a complete property settlement entered into after or in anticipation of separation or divorce is a waiver of all rights of elective share, homestead allowance, exempt property, and family allowance by each spouse in the property of the other and a renunciation by each of all benefits that would otherwise pass to him [or her] from the other by intestate succession or by virtue of any will executed before the waiver or property settlement.

VI. Ademption and Exoneration

Often a testator in a valid Last Will and Testament may devise or bequeath a specific piece of property to a named individual, but when the testator dies, the property has been lost, sold, or given away. Sometimes the item of property is given away during the lifetime of the testator to the intended beneficiary named in the Will and then the bequest or devise may be satisfied according to the Will, or there is a contemporaneous writing by the testator or the recipient that the gift was in satisfaction of the Will provision. *See* UNIF. PROB. CODE §2-609 (1996). If the property item is gone, for whatever reason, the law refers to it as adeemed by extinction or satisfaction. If it is gone, does the testator want the estate to provide the disappointed devisee or legatee with the value of what is not there? Or does the testator intend that, since the specific item is not there—and it was so specific—that the item is adeemed and eliminated, and the estate pays nothing? The answer will depend on whether the item was specific, as compared to demonstrative, general, or residuary. But the issue remains the same: What is the intent of the testator in a valid Will?

A. Ademption

Wasserman v. Cohen

Supreme Judicial Court of Massachusetts, 1993
414 Mass. 172, 606 N.E.2d 901

(For the text of the opinion, see *supra* at 210.)

Uniform Probate Code (2003)

§ 2-606. Nonademption of Specific Devises; Unpaid Proceeds of Sale, Condemnation, or Insurance; Sale by Conservator or Agent.

(a) A specific devisee has a right to specifically devised property in the testator's estate at the testator's death and to:

(1) any balance of the purchase price, together with any security agreement, owed by a purchaser at the testator's death by reason of sale of the property;

(2) any amount of a condemnation award for the taking of the property unpaid at death;

(3) any proceeds unpaid at death on fire or casualty insurance on or other recovery for injury to the property;

(4) any property owned by the testator at death and acquired as a result of foreclosure, or obtained in lieu of foreclosure, of the security interest for a specifically devised obligation;

(5) any real property or tangible personal property owned by the testator at death which the testator acquired as a replacement for specifically devised real property or tangible personal property; and

(6) if not covered by paragraphs (1) through (5), a pecuniary devise equal to the value as of its date of disposition of other specifically devised property disposed of during the testator's lifetime but only to the extent it is established that ademption would be inconsistent with the testator's manifested plan of distribution or that at the time the will was made, the date of disposition or otherwise, the testator did not intend ademption of the devise.

(b) If specifically devised property is sold or mortgaged by a conservator or by an agent acting within the authority of a durable power of attorney for an incapacitated principal, or a condemnation award, insurance proceeds, or recovery for injury to the property is paid to a conservator or to an agent acting within the authority of a durable power of attorney for an incapacitated principal, the specific devisee has the right to a general pecuniary devise equal to the net sale price, the amount of the unpaid loan, the condemnation award, the insurance proceeds, or the recovery.

(c) The right of a specific devisee under subsection (b) is reduced by any right the devisee has under subsection (a).

(d) For the purposes of the references in subsection (b) to a conservator, subsection (b) does not apply if, after the sale, mortgage, condemnation, casualty, or recovery, it was adjudicated that the testator's incapacity ceased and the testator survived the adjudication for at least one year.

(e) For the purposes of the references in subsection (b) to an agent acting within the authority of a durable power of attorney for an incapacitated principal, (i) "incapacitated principal" means a principal who is an incapacitated person, (ii) no adjudication of incapacity before death is necessary, and (iii) the acts of an agent within the authority of a durable power of attorney are presumed to be for an incapacitated principal.

Uniform Probate Code (2003)

§ 2-605. Increase in Securities; Accessions.

(a) If a testator executes a will that devises securities and the testator then owned securities that meet the description in the will, the devise includes additional securities owned by the testator at death to the extent the additional securities were acquired by the testator after the will was executed as a result of the testator's ownership of the described securities and are securities of any of the following types:

(1) securities of the same organization acquired by reason of action initiated by the organization or any successor, related, or acquiring organization, excluding any acquired by exercise of purchase options;

(2) securities of another organization acquired as a result of a merger, consolidation, reorganization, or other distribution by the organization or any successor, related, or acquiring organization; or

(3) securities of the same organization acquired as a result of a plan of reinvestment.

(b) Distributions in cash before death with respect to a described security are not part of the devise.

B. Exoneration

Under the common law, a specific devise of real estate to a devisee required that any mortgage existing at the death of the testator be paid off from the residuary assets of the estate. The law assumed that the testator wanted the debt, like all debts incurred by the testator during life, to be paid. Thus, the devisee would take title clear of any debt. Such a practice was beneficial to the devisee but detrimental to the residuary legatee. Compare the common law rule with the following statute.

Uniform Probate Code (2003)

§ 2-607. Nonexoneration.

A specific devise passes subject to any mortgage interest existing at the date of death, without right of exoneration, regardless of a general directive in the will to pay debts.

VII. Lapse

If ademption by extinction or satisfaction concerns an item of property missing between the execution of the Will and the death of the testator, the doctrine of lapse concerns a human person who dies between the time of execution and the date of the decedent's death taking under the Will (or even some non-probate transfers). Thus, if a valid Will is executed in the year 2000 and contains the phrase: "One million dollars to my sister, Sadie," and Sadie dies in 2002 with the Will being probated at the death of the testator in 2005, the bequest to Sadie could be said to "lapse" because you cannot give property to a dead person. If it does lapse, then the bequest may pass to an alternate legatee, the residuary estate, or the decedent's intestate estate. Is this what was intended by the testator? Or should the state make some allowance for any perceived lack of clarity on the part of the testator and provide a substitution for the testator's intent? This entire chapter has provided examples of substitutions for testators' intent. The following case illustrates how a state anti-lapse statute substitutes for testators' intent, and the sections that follow explore attendant issues.

Estate of Kehler

Supreme Court of Pennsylvania, 1980
488 Pa. 165, 411 A.2d 748

ROBERTS, Justice.

Testator, Emerson Kehler, died in April of 1975. By paragraph THIRD of his will, he disposed of the residue of his estate:

> All the rest, residue and remainder of my estate, real, personal and mixed, of whatsoever nature and wheresoever situated, I give, devise and bequeath unto my brother, RALPH KEHLER, of Reading, Pennsylvania, and my sisters, VIOLA WELKER, of Lavelle, Pennsylvania, ADA SHARTEL, of Reading, Pennsylvania, and GERTRUDE KRAPF, of Stroudsburg, Pennsylvania, and to the survivor or survivors of them, equally, share and share alike, to have and to hold unto themselves, their heirs and assigns forever.

Ralph Kehler predeceased testator, but Ralph Kehler's daughter, appellant Ethel Chupp, survived testator.

At issue on this appeal is whether appellant may take the share of the residue her father Ralph Kehler would have received had he survived testator. Appellant takes the position that testator's intent concerning the disposition of the bequest to a predeceased sibling is ambiguous. She maintains, therefore, that the relevant "anti-lapse" statute, 20 Pa.C.S. § 2514(9), applies. Section 2514(9) provides:

> *Rules of interpretation*

> In the absence of a contrary intent appearing therein, wills shall be construed as to real and personal estate in accordance with the following rules:

> * * *

> (9) Lapsed and void devises and legacies; substitution of issue. A devise or bequest to a child or other issue of the testator or to his brother or sister or to a child of his brother or sister whether designated by name or as one of a class shall not lapse if the beneficiary shall fail to survive the testator and shall leave issue surviving the testator but shall pass to such surviving issue who shall take per stirpes the share which their deceased ancestor would have taken had he survived the testator: Provided, That such a devise or bequest to a brother or sister or to the child of a brother or sister shall lapse to the extent to which it will pass to the testator's spouse or issue as a part of the residuary estate or under the intestate laws. * * *

The Orphans' Court Division of the Court of Common Pleas of Northumberland County disagreed. It concluded that the language of testator's will, particularly "and to the survivor or survivors of them," manifests testator's "contrary intent" within the meaning of section 2514 to limit takers to those named siblings who are living at testator's death, thus precluding operation of subsection (9). We agree with appellant that the orphans' court misinterpreted testator's will.

This Court has not yet held that a testator must expressly provide for a possible lapse to manifest "contrary intent" overcoming operation of the anti-lapse statute. See Corbett Estate, 430 Pa. 54, 61 n.7, 241 A.2d 524, 527 n.7 (1968). Surely, however, a "contrary intent" must appear with reasonable certainty. See id. at 62–63, 241 A.2d at 527–28. Accord, Sykes Estate, 477 Pa. 254, 257, 383 A.2d 920, 921 (1978).

Testator's will here permits no such certainty. In paragraph THIRD of his will, Testator fails to make an express statement concerning his intended disposition of residue in the event a named beneficiary predeceases him. Instead, he merely states his desire to leave the residue to his named siblings "and to the survivor or survivors of them." By contrast, in other paragraphs of his will, testator expressly provides for the possibility of lapse. In paragraph FIRST, in which testator gives his nephew Emerson Asher Shoemaker a monetary gift, testator provides:

> I give and bequeath the sum of One Thousand ($1,000.00) Dollars, unto my nephew, EMERSON ASHER SHOEMAKER, of Reading, Pennsylvania, should he survive me, but if he predeceases me, then this paragraph of my Will shall be null and void and of no effect.

In Paragraph SECOND, testator employs the identical language manifesting an intent to provide a lapse in another bequest of $1,000 to another nephew, Larry Welker. There, testator again stated "if he predeceases me, then this paragraph of my Will shall be null and void and of no effect."

Testator's careful use of express language directing a lapse of these bequests in his will raises considerable doubt that he intended a lapse in paragraph THIRD, where no such language is used. It cannot now be said with the requisite reasonable certainty that testator intended a lapse of residuary bequests under paragraph THIRD. In accordance with the Legislature's directive contained in 20 Pa.C.S. § 2514(9), it must be presumed that testator did not intend his bequest to Ralph Kehler to lapse. By way of the same statute, appellant may share in the residuary estate.

Decree vacated and case remanded for proceedings consistent with this opinion. Each party pays own costs.

NIX, J., did not participate in the consideration or decision of this case.

LARSEN, J., filed a dissenting opinion, in which EAGEN, C. J., joins.

LARSEN, Justice, dissenting.

I dissent. I believe the testator clearly expressed his intention in Paragraph Third to distribute the residue of his estate to the survivor or survivors of the four named siblings. It is not surprising that testator used different language in the first and second paragraphs as those paragraphs mentioned only one individual each each paragraph was a specific monetary legacy to a specific individual.

The majority observes the testator "merely states his desire to leave the residue to his named siblings 'and to the survivor or survivors of them.'" I agree with this observation, but contrary to the majority, I would affirm the Orphans' Court because of this "merely stated" expression of intent, and would affirm the distribution of the estate in accordance with his intent.

EAGEN, C. J., joins in this dissenting opinion.

* * *

A. Intent of the Testator

An expressed intent of the testator will prevent application of any statute seeking to prohibit lapse. "Any statute seeking to prohibit lapse shall not apply" would be an example. But seldom is intent expressed so clearly. Is there sufficient intent to prohibit applicability of any applicable lapse statute if the testator were to write: "One million dollars to Sadie if she survives me"? Survivorship language seems to express the intent of the testator that the statute not apply, but the 1990 version of the Uniform Probate Code §2-603(b)(3) provides: "words of survivorship, such as in a devise to an individual 'if he survives me,' or in a devise to 'my surviving children,' are not, in the absence of additional evidence, a sufficient indication of an intent contrary to the application of [the statute]." Admittedly, this is the minority approach, but it has been adopted in other countries, *see, e.g.,* QUEENSLAND SUCCESSION ACT OF 1981, §33(2), and some judicial opinions, *see, e.g.,* Estate of Ulrickson, 290 N.W.2d 757 (Minn. 1980), and found reputable by some commentators, *see, e.g.,* Susan F. French, *Antilapse Statutes Are Blunt Instruments: A Blueprint for Reform,* 37 HASTINGS L. J. 335, 369 (1985). An alternate gift to another in case there is no survivorship would satisfy the conditional language of survivorship and, in all cases, because the statute is a rule of construction, the overall intent of the testator should be given effect.

B. Simultaneous Death

In order to prevent inheritance by those who die simultaneously with the decedent, states have enacted simultaneous death statutes similar to that contained in Uniform Probate Code §2-702(a), which provides that "an individual who is not established to have survived an event ... by 120 hours is deemed to have predeceased the [testator's death]." This time requirement, rather than mere survivorship, also has been adopted by the Uniform Simultaneous Death Act, §4 (1991). Thus, even though, technically, a beneficiary under a Will may survive the testator, if the survivorship is not by at least 120 hours, the beneficiary will be treated as if he or she predeceased the testator, and the anti-lapse statute will apply.

C. Relatives

Legislators seek to protect families, and, thus, anti-lapse statutes almost always apply to predeceasing relatives of the testator. Thus, if a testator dies with a valid Will in existence, devising or bequeathing property to a named relative, that relative is protected under the statute. These relatives tend to be by consanguinity rather than affinity, thus a testator's grandparents and their descendants would be covered by the statute, but a spouse and the spouse's relatives would not. There are some exceptions. For example, the UNIF. PROB. CODE, §2-603(b) (1990) (Substitute Gift) includes a stepchild of the decedent as protected. Some states make the statute applicable to all. *See, e.g.,* N.H. REV. STAT. ANN. §551.12 (2003) ("The heirs in the descending line of a legatee or devisee, deceased before the testator, shall take the estate bequeathed or devised, in the same manner the legatee or devisee would have taken it if he had survived.") Establishing a relationship between the testator and the predeceasing legatee is the first step. Afterwards, there is the necessity that this relative have issue (descendants) who survive the testator to take by representation.

D. Time Applicability

At common law, if a bequest or devise were made to a legatee or devisee who was dead at the time of the execution of the Will, the gift was void; if made to a legatee or devisee who died between the time of the execution of the Will and the death of the decedent, the bequest or devise lapsed. Thus, there was a distinction and it most often arose in the context of a bequest such as "to the children of my sister, Sadie." If Sadie had children die before execution of the Will, and children who died after execution of the Will but before the death of the testator, and each predeceasing child was survived by issue, the question arose as to the applicability of any anti-lapse statute. Some statutes allow for the anti-lapse provision to apply to all predeceasing relatives, regardless of whether they die prior to execution of the Will or between execution and the date of death of the decedent. *See, e.g.,* VA. CODE ANN. §64.1-***. Some states still retain the common law distinction and prohibit applicability of the anti-lapse statute to relatives predeceasing execution of the Will. *See, e.g.,* N.Y. EST., POWERS & TRUSTS L. §3-3.3 (2004); TEX. PROB. CODE §68(a) (1997).

E. Class Gifts

If a testator provided: "One million dollars to the children of Sadie," and Sadie had three children survive the testator by more than 120 hours, but one died prior to the testator, survived by one child of her own, should the anti-lapse statute apply to the predeceasing child of Sadie? Or should the surviving members of the class we call "Sadie's children" take all of the money to the exclusion of the other? This is the dilemma of whether anti-lapse should apply to class gifts, since it is arguable that, when the testator used class (children) language, the testator intended to prevent the application of any anti-lapse statute and allow the survivor to take all. Consider the approaches in the following cases:

Dawson v. Yucus
Illinois Appellate Court, 1968
97 Ill. App. 2d 101, 239 N.E.2d 305

CHARLES E. JONES, Justice.

In this will construction case plaintiffs seek a decree finding Clause Two of the will of Nelle G. Stewart, deceased, is a devise to a class. Plaintiffs appeal a trial court decree rendered for defendants.

Nelle G. Stewart, of Girard, Illinois, died on May 29, 1965, leaving a duly executed will dated March 3, 1959, and containing ten dispositive clauses. The first clause directed payment of debts and funeral expenses. The second clause, the interpretation of which is the sole issue in this case, provided:

'Through the Will of my late husband, Dr. Frank A. Stewart, I received an undivided one-fifth (1/5) interest in two hundred sixty-one and thirty-eight hundredths (261.38) acres of farm lands located in Sections Twenty-eight (28), Twenty-nine (29), Thirty-two (32) and Thirty-three (33) in Township Fourteen (14) North, Range Four (4) West of the Third Principal Meridian in Sangamon County, Illinois, and believing as I do that those farm lands should go back to my late husband's side of the house, I therefore give; devise and bequeath my one-fifth (1/5) interest in said farm lands as follows: One-half (1/2) of my interest therein to Stewart Wilson, a nephew, now living in Birmingham, Michigan and One-half (1/2) of my interest to Gene Burtle, a nephew, now living in Mission, Kansas.'

Clauses three and four made bequests of personalty to Ina Mae Yucus, Lola Eades, Hazel Degelow and Ella Hickey. Clauses five, six and seven made bequests of cash to charities. Clause eight provided for the payment of reasonable allowance to Ina Mae Yucus or Hazel Degelow should illness make it necessary for the testatrix to live in either of their homes. Clause nine directed the executrix to convert all 'the rest, residue and remainder of my property * * * of whatever kind and character and wheresoever situate, including void or lapsed legacies * * * into cash * * * and the proceeds divided equally between Ina Mae Yucus and Hazel Degelow, or to the survivor or survivors of them, should any of said named persons predecease me.' Clause ten appoints Ina Mae Yucus executrix and waives bond.

After the will was admitted to probate, Stewart Wilson filed suit to construe the will alleging that the devise in clause two was a class gift, that Gene Burtle, one of the devisees in clause two, died after the date of execution of the will but before the testatrix and that plaintiff, as the survivor of the class, was entitled to the entire one-fifth interest in the farm. After the complaint was filed, Stewart Wilson conveyed the interest he allegedly received as survivor of the class to the two children of the deceased Gene Burtle and they were substituted as plaintiffs. The defendants, the executrix and the beneficiaries named in the residuary clause of the will, filed answer denying that clause two was a gift to a class, asserting that it was a devise to two specific individuals and that upon the death of Gene Burtle prior to that of the testatrix, the gift to him lapsed and passed into the residuary clause of the will.

At the trial the court found that the death of Gene Burtle prior to that of the testatrix created a latent ambiguity and admitted extrinsic evidence relating to testatrix' intentions. There is no serious dispute over the facts shown by the evidence presented by plaintiffs. Nelle G. Stewart was the widow of Dr. Frank A. Stewart and received as a devisee in his will a one-fifth interest in a 261 acre farm in Sangamon County. Nelle G. Stewart and Dr. Frank A. Stewart had no children. At the death of Dr. Stewart his surviving blood relatives were Gene Burtle, Stewart Wilson, William C. Stewart and Robert T. Stewart, his nephews and Patti S. Lusby, his niece. Nelle G. Stewart knew all of these relatives of Dr. Stewart. Of these relatives of Dr. Stewart, only Gene Burtle and Stewart Wilson had a close personal relationship with the testatrix. Gene Burtle died on May 15, 1963, and the testatrix knew of his death but made no changes in her previously executed will. There was evidence from four witnesses that in conversations had with testatrix she stated she wanted the one-fifth interest in the farm to go either to her husband's side of the house, or to Gene Burtle and Stewart Wilson because she felt especially close to them and none other of Dr. Stewart's relatives had any contact with her.

The trial court held, we think correctly, that clause two of testatrix' will did not create a class gift and that the gift in that clause to Gene Burtle lapsed and, pursuant to the Illinois Lapse Statute, Chapt. 3, Sec. 49, I. R.S.1965, passed into the residue of her estate.

The definition of class gifts and pertinent rules of construction as followed by Illinois courts are set forth in the case of Strohm v. McMullen, 404 Ill. 453, 89 N.E.2d 383:

'The definition of a class gift adopted by this court, as laid down by Mr. Jarman in his work on Wills, Vol. 1, p. 534, 5th Am.Ed., is: 'A gift to a class is defined * * * as a gift of an aggregate sum to a body of persons uncertain in number at the time of the gift, to be ascertained at a future time, and who are all to take in equal or in some other definite proportions, the share of each being dependent for its amount upon the ultimate number of persons.' Volunteers of America v. Peirce, 267 Ill. 406, 108 N.E. 318; Blackstone v. Althouse, 278 Ill. 481, 116 N.E. 154, L.R.A.1918B, 230; Henry v. Henry, 378 Ill. 581, 39 N.E.2d 18.

A class, in its ordinary acceptation, is a number or body of persons with common characteristics or in like circumstances, or having some common attribute, and, as applied to a devise, it is generally understood to mean a number of persons who stand in the same relation to each other or to the testator.' Blackstone v. Althouse, 278 Ill. 481, 116 N.E. 154, 157, L.R.A.1918B, 230. And it has been definitely decided in this State that in determining whether a devise is to a class or to individuals depends upon the language of the will. If from such language it appears that the amounts of their shares are uncertain until the devise or bequest takes effect, the beneficiaries will generally be held to take as a class; but where at the time of making the gifts the number of beneficiaries is certain, and the share each is to receive is also certain, and in no way dependent for its amount upon the number who shall survive, it is not a gift to a class, but to the individuals. Volunteers of America v. Peirce, 267 Ill. 406, 108 N.E. 318; Blackstone v. Althouse, 278 Ill. 481, 116 N.E. 154, L.R.A.1918B, 230; Strauss v. Strauss, 363 Ill. 442, 2 N.E.2d 699, 105 A.L.R. 1386; Henry v. Henry, 378 Ill. 581, 39 N.E.2d 18; Peadro v. Peadro, 400 Ill. 482, 81 N.E.2d 192.

'There is an exception to the rule that naming the individual prevents the gift from becoming a class gift, stated in Strauss v. Strauss, 363 Ill. 442, 2 N.E.2d 699, 105 A.L.R. 1386, holding that the mere fact that the testator mentions by name the individuals who make up the class is not conclusive, and that if the intention to give a right of *survivorship* is collected from the remaining provisions of the will, as applied to the existing facts, such an intention must prevail. This is in accord with the general rule applying to construction of wills, that the intention of the testator, if clearly manifested from the whole will, must prevail over rules of construction. This rule was recognized in the late case of Peadro v. Peadro, 400 Ill. 482, 81 N.E.2d 192, 194, where the gift after a life estate was devised as follows: 'shall be equally divided, share and share alike, between Earl D. Peadro, Berniece F. Peadro, Roy F. Peadro and Irtys A. Peadro, or the survivor of them to be their sole and absolute property.' In that case we held there was no class gift, saying: 'This court recognizes the rule that a gift to persons named is a gift to them individually and not as a class, and will treat the gift as one to individuals, unless reasons are found in the language and structure of the will for deciding that the intent of the testator, which is, of course, paramount to the rule, would be best subserved by disregarding the rule and treating the gift as one to a class.'

Also, see Restatement of Property, Future Interests, Sections 279, 280 and 281.

Admittedly the gift in clause two is not made with the usual generic class description such as 'children', 'brothers', 'nephews', 'cousins', 'issues', 'decedents', or 'family' but is in fact to two named individuals, conditions which militate against construction of the clause as a class gift. However, plaintiffs argue that because of the death of Gene Burtle prior to that of the testatrix a latent ambiguity exists and extrinsic evidence was properly received to show the true intention of the testatrix in clause two of her will, and that the phrase in clause two, 'and believing as I do that these farm lands should go back to my husband's side of the house,' together with the extrinsic evidence, clearly requires class gift construction.

Plaintiffs rely largely upon the cases of Strauss v. Strauss, supra, and Krog v. Hafka, 413 Ill. 290, 109 N.E.2d 213. The Strauss case, as quoted above, recognizes the general rule that naming of individuals prevents the gift from becoming a class gift, but holds that merely naming the individuals is not conclusive if the intention to give a right of survivorship is collected from the remaining provisions of the will and the existing facts. In the Krog case, which plaintiffs contend is on all fours with this case, one Frieda Studtmann left a will consisting of four paragraphs. The first paragraph directed payment of debts and funeral expenses; the second made a specific legacy to a church; and the third was as follows: 'Third, I hereby give, devise and bequeath to Harry E. Hafka and his wife, Ethel May Hafka, of New Lenox, Illinois, all of my estate both real and personal of every kind and nature whatsoever to have and to hold the same to them and their heirs and assigns forever.'; the last paragraph appointed Harry E. Hafka executor. Harry E. Hafka died eight months prior to the death of testatrix. Extrinsic evidence showed that testatrix, a spinster, spent the later part of her life residing on her 170 acre farm; that for approximately seven years prior to her death Harry Hafka and his wife Ethel May Hafka lived with her, operated the farm and furnished extensive care for testatrix, who was under the doctor's attention for four or five years with a goitre and heart ailment; that the testatrix did not care for her cousins (her only relatives); their paths crossed infrequently and she entertained resentment toward them. Testatrix told witnesses she was not interested in leaving her estate to her relatives inasmuch as they had more money than she did; that at her request a nonlawyer friend, eighty years of age, prepared her will and she told him and the witnesses that she was living with the Hafkas, she liked them well, that it was her desire that everything should go to them, that they had agreed to take care of her until she died and to give her a decent burial. She also mentioned her relatives and stated she did not owe them anything, 'they are not going to get any of my estate.' Other evidence was that the testatrix told her personal physician that she wanted everything she had to go to the Hafkas for they had taken good care of her. The Supreme Court made an extensive review of the law of latent ambiguity and class gifts and concluded by reciting eight controlling factors that made the conclusion inescapable that Frieda Studtmann intended that all her property was to go to the Hafkas as a class, and that Ethel May Hafka, as the survivor of the class, took the entire residue of the estate.

We think, and hold, that this case is more nearly akin to Strohm v. McMullen, supra, and O'Connell v. Gaffney, 23 Ill.2d 611, 179 N.E.2d 647. The will under consideration in Strohm contained a clause expressly excluding a sister and nephew from any benefits from the testator's estate. It then gave the residue of the estate to three named persons, share and share alike. Two of the three persons named in the residuary clause predeceased the testator, the third claimed the entire residue as the survivor of a class. The court rejected the class construction and held that:

> 'The fact that the testator did not want certain relatives to share in his estate does not indicate that he desired that the named residuary devisees be clothed with the right of survivorship. * * *

'The sixth clause of the will in this case not only named the individuals who were to take, but also who were to take 'share and share alike.' No more precise description of a donee, or of the amount to be given, could be made, leaving no room to construe the individuals into a class so that the survivor of such class would take all the residue.'

The reiduary [sic] clause of the will considered in the O'Connell case provided, '* * * I direct that one part be paid in equal shares, to my two brothers, James Gaffney and Edward Gaffney of Ireland.' Edward died before the testator. The court held:

'Considering the fact that the instant will devises to two brothers of the testator, who are named, and that they are to take in equal shares, it seems clear that Owen Gaffney was thinking simply of his two brothers then living and not of a person or persons to be ascertained at a future time. In our opinion, nothing appears from the general plan of disposition, or from any special relationship of Owen Gaffney to his two brothers, or from the failure of Owen Gaffney to change his will after the death of Edward to overcome the initial presumption that the gift was to James and Edward as individuals. The gift to the two brothers in equal shares further strengthens this conclusion that a class gift was not intended by the testator.'

In this case the testatrix named the individuals, Stewart Wilson and Gene Burtle, and gave them each a one-half portion of her interest in the farm, thus making certain the number of beneficiaries and the share each is to receive. The shares in no way depend upon the number who shall survive the death of the testatrix. There is nothing in the language of the will that indicates the testatrix intended to create a class or survivorship gift. The only other provision of the will, also contained in clause two, that has any bearing on the question is the statement, '* * * believing as I do that those farm lands should go back to my late husband's side of the house * * *.' While it is true that this language recites testatrix' desire that the one-fifth interest in the farm go back to her husband's side of the house, it does not indicate a survivorship gift was intended. Her intention to return the farm to her husband's side of the house was fulfilled when she named Stewart Wilson and Gene Burtle as the donees of the interest. And we are not persuaded that the extrinsic evidence offered by plaintiffs is sufficient to require a finding that the testatrix intended a class or survivorship gift as in the Strauss and Krog cases. There is no evidence which requires, or, in view of the Strohm and O'Connell cases, would even permit, construing this specific devise of equal one-half portions to two named individuals as a class gift.

Further emphasis for the result we have reached is supplied by other factors found in the will and extrinsic evidence. First, the testatrix created a survivorship gift of the residue of her estate in the ninth clause of her will, thus indicating she knew how to manifest an intent to create a class or survivorship gift; hence, the language of clause two, phrased differently, was intended to create a gift to individuals distributively. Restatement of Property, Future Interests, Sec. 280, Comment g., No. 1. Paragraph No. 2 of the same Restatement citation provides, 'The specification * * * of an exact proportion in the subject matter of the conveyance, which is to be received by each of the named and described persons, is strongly indicative of an intent to make a gift to individuals distributively whenever the * * * proportions so specified equals the entire subject matter given by the limitation in question.' Secondly, the common characteristic of the alleged class described by plaintiffs is that of relation to Dr. Stewart, or, in the words of clause two, the class is of 'my late husband's side of the house.' However, this characteristic is also shared by three other heirs of Dr. Stewart of the same degree of relationship to him as Stewart Wilson and Gene Burtle. It thus appears that Gene Burtle and Stewart Wilson do not constitute the alleged class but are individuals named from the class.

The factors that distinguish the Strauss case from this case were furnished by the Supreme Court in Strohm v. McMullen, supra, where they analyzed the Strauss case and found that the 'mentioning of the names of the children (in the Strauss case) was only one of four different ways in which the residuary legatees were designated, the others in themselves being sufficient to bring the donees within a class.' Nor do we feel that the Krog case is 'on all fours' with this one. In that case the language found to create a class gift was much different than that used in the instant will, and the testatrix enjoyed a much closer relationship with the Hafkas than that between Mrs. Stewart and Gene Burtle and Stewart Wilson. Extrinsic evidence shows that the 'close personal relationship' consisted of friendly visits by the Burtles and Wilsons about every summer when they came from their homes in Michigan and Kansas to visit in Springfield and Girard. In Krog, the testatrix received many years of personal services from the Hafkas and stated upon several occasions that she did not want any of her heirs to have any of her property. Further, few of the controlling factors enumerated by the court in deciding that case are present here. For instance, the always present presumption that the testatrix intended not to die intestate as to any of her property was relied upon in the Krog case, but here no partial intestacy will result from the non-class construction. Here there is a general testamentary scheme favoring the beneficiaries of the residue of Mrs. Stewart's estate; namely, Ina Mae Yucus and Hazel Degelow—persons with whom she was obviously on an intimate and friendly basis as shown by the fact that she left them the residue of her estate and, per clause eight of her will, contemplated living in either of their homes.

The devise in clause two was not to persons who come within the designation of a class but was to individuals distributively. It was not so made or limited to prevent the operation of the Illinois Lapse Statute which must be given its intended effect. The court below correctly held that upon the death of Gene Burtle prior to that of the testatrix the devise to him lapsed and passed under the residuary clause of the will. The Decree will be affirmed.

Affirmed.

CRAVEN, Acting P.J., and TRAPP, J., concur.

* * *

In re Moss

Court of Appeal, England, 1899
[1899] 2 Ch. 314, aff'd [1901] A.C. 187 (H.L.)

WALTER Moss by his will dated in 1876, after appointing his wife Elizabeth Moss and his niece Elizabeth Jane Fowler his executrixes, and making sundry devises and bequests, gave all his share or interest in the Daily Telegraph newspaper unto the said E. Moss and E. J. Fowler "upon trust to pay the income thereof to my said wife for her life, and after her decease, upon trust for the said E. J. Fowler and the child or children of my sister Emily Walter who shall attain the age of twenty-one years equally to be divided between them as tenants in common." And he gave the residue of his estate and effects to his wife. And he empowered his trustees with the consent of his wife * * * .

The testator died in 1893, and his will was proved by his widow, Elizabeth Moss, alone. At the date of his will there were living his niece Elizabeth Jane Fowler, who was then slightly under twenty-one, his sister Emily Walter, and five children of Emily Walter.

Elizabeth Jane Fowler died in 1891, in the testator's lifetime, a spinster. Emily Walter and her five children survived the testator.

The testator's widow, Elizabeth Moss, the tenant for life of his Daily Telegraph share and his residuary legatee, died in 1897, having by her will given her residuary estate, including any share or portion of a share in the Daily Telegraph newspaper which might belong to her at her death, to her trustees in trust for sale and to stand possessed of the proceeds, after payment of her funeral and testamentary expenses, debts, and legacies, in trust for William George Kingsbury absolutely; and she appointed him and another her trustees and executors.

At her death all the five children of Emily Walter were living and had attained twenty-one.

The question was whether, in consequence of the death of Elizabeth Jane Fowler in the lifetime of her uncle, the testator, the share bequeathed to her in his Daily Telegraph share had lapsed and fallen into his residuary estate, or whether the entirety passed to Emily Walter's five children: in other words, whether the gift by the testator of his Daily Telegraph share was a gift to a class, so that these five children, as the survivors of the class, took the whole.

To have this question decided, an originating summons was taken out by W. G. Kingsbury and his co-trustee and co-executor of the testator's widow, Elizabeth Moss, W. G. Kingsbury being also her residuary legatee, against Emily Walter's five children and also against Emily Walter as the present trustee of the Daily Telegraph share, to have it declared that the bequest of the testator's share in the Daily Telegraph newspaper upon trust, after the death of his wife, for Elizabeth Jane Fowler and the child or children of Emily Walter who should attain twenty-one equally, was not a gift to a class, but that the share bequeathed to Elizabeth Jane Fowler had lapsed by her death in the testator's lifetime and thus fell into the residue of the estate.

The summons was heard on December 14, 1898, by North J., who, after saying the cases upon the point were so irreconcilable that he should act independently of them, held that, as he could find nothing in the will to shew that Elizabeth Jane Fowler was included in the class, the share given to her lapsed by reason of her death in the testator's lifetime, and so passed to the plaintiffs.

The defendants, the five children of Emily Walter, appealed.

LINDLEY M.R.

It is very difficult to construe this will by the light of the authorities. I entirely agree with North J. that the authorities do not help one much, because they are in inextricable confusion. I do not think there is any case which can be cited by either side which cannot be matched by a case on the other side more or less difficult to distinguish from it. The practical question which we have to decide on this will is, Who are the persons now entitled to the share of the testator in the *Daily Telegraph* newspaper? There are several rival views. One view is, and that is the one adopted by the learned judge below, that the share which Elizabeth Jane Fowler would have taken if she were alive—that is, one-sixth, as I understand it—has lapsed and has fallen into the residuary estate, so that, according to that view, one-sixth of that share has gone to persons who were certainly never intended to take it. That is obvious. That may be the legal result of the gift, but it is obvious it was never dreamt of by the testator. What he intended was that his share should go amongst the persons he has named and to no one else.

Now the difficulty lies in this. We hear about classes, and gifts to classes, and definitions of classes. You may define a class in a thousand ways: anybody may make any number of things or persons a class by setting out an attribute more or less common to them all and making that the definition of the class. We have been referred, and not improperly at all, to Mr. Jarman's definition of a class for the purpose for which lawyers want it—that is, in construing a will—and I think Mr. Swinfen Eady is right in saying that, looking at that definition, this case does come within it. But after all, whether you call this a class or whether you call it a number of persons who are treated by the testator as if they were the class, appears to me to be merely a matter of language. One is very reluctant to frame definitions unless one can make a law to accord with the definitions, which judges cannot do. Now what is to be done with the share of this lady who has died? The testator says it is to be equally divided between her and the children of Emily Walter, to be equally divided between them all. If some of them are dead, are the shares of those who are dead to go to those who survive, or are they to go to someone else? That is the practical question; and whether you call the persons a class or "in effect" a class—as Mr. Theobald does in a passage of his work on wills, where he says (4th ed. p. 645), "it is clear that a gift to A., and the children of B., may in effect be a gift to a class, if the testator treats the legatees as a class"—or whether you call them a number of persons who are to be treated as a class, is quite immaterial. The guiding question here is, What is to be done with this *Daily Telegraph* share which is to be divided amongst these legatees? It seems to me that it is to go to such of them as shall be living. That is the obvious intention. The alternative view takes the share away where it was never intended to go, and upon that ground it appears to me that we ought to differ from the learned judge. I confess, and I say so frankly, that if this case had come before me in the first instance I should have decided it as North J. did, but my brother Romer has convinced me that is not right.

SIR F. H. JEUNE.

I agree. I do not propose to add anything that may tend to make the decisions which are already contradictory and complicated still more so.

ROMER L.J.

In the absence of any context negativing this view, I think that, when a testator gives property X. to A. and a class of persons—say the children of B.—in equal shares, he intends that the whole of X. shall pass by his gift if any one of the children of B. survive him, even although A. does not. Clearly, if A. survived and none of the children of B. survived so as to share, then A. would take the whole, for A. would either have to take the whole or nothing, unless indeed it could be said that you are to look at the number of children of B. living at the date of the will and say there is an intestacy as to the share of each child dying between the date of the will and the testator's death; but that to my mind is clearly an untenable proposition. If then the testator intended that A. should take the whole if none of the children of B. survived him to share, I think also he intended the children of B. to take the whole if A. did not survive so as to share. There is no satisfactory distinction, to my mind, between those two cases. I think that, in such a gift as I have mentioned, what the testator really means is that the property is to be shared equally by a body constituted of such of the following as should be existing at the date of the testator's death, that is to say, A. and the children of B. And generally, when the testator—there being nothing to negative the view in the rest of the will—gives property to be shared at a particular period equally between a class properly so called and an individual or individuals, I think that what the testator prima facie must be taken to mean is that you are to see which part of that aggregated body is to share in that property at the time it comes for distribution, and that such a gift is really a gift to a class: and though I am perfectly well aware of the danger there is in attempting to lay down general propositions—and few judges would more shrink from doing so than I, knowing as I do how a general proposition laid down often hampers judges in dealing with succeeding cases—yet I do think in the present case I may venture to make the following statement, especially as the cases are so complicated and there is no express decision of the Court of Appeal or of the House of Lords upon the point. In my opinion it is correct to say that a gift by will to a class properly so called and a named individual such as A. equally, so that the testator contemplates A. taking the same share that each member of the class will take, is prima facie a gift to a class.

For those reasons, applying those principles to the case before us, I have no hesitation in saying that, in my opinion, the gift here was a gift to a class, and that Elizabeth Jane Fowler was only intended to share as one of a class; and that inasmuch as she did not survive so as to share, the rest of the class takes the whole of the property.

* * *

F. Non-Probate Transfers

Traditionally, anti-lapse statutes applied only to Wills, but with the increase in the use of non-probate transfers (will substitutes) and with the attendant issues surrounding intent, anti-lapse is applicable to certain forms of non-probate transfers. Thus, the following would be applicable to anti-lapse protection under statutes such as the Uniform Probate Code: life insurance beneficiaries, bank accounts in payable-on-death form, or any contract with a payable-on-death beneficiary, such as a pension plan.

Uniform Probate Code (2003)

§ 2-706. Life Insurance; Retirement Plan; Account With POD Designation; Transfer-on-Death Registration; Deceased Beneficiary.

(b) [**Substitute Gift.**] If a beneficiary fails to survive the decedent and is a grandparent, a descendant of a grandparent, or a stepchild of the decedent, the following apply:

(1) Except as provided in paragraph (4), if the beneficiary designation is not in the form of a class gift and the deceased beneficiary leaves surviving descendants, a substitute gift is created in the beneficiary's surviving descendants. They take by representation the property to which the beneficiary would have been entitled had the beneficiary survived the decedent.

(2) Except as provided in paragraph (4), if the beneficiary designation is in the form of a class gift, other than a beneficiary designation to "issue," "descendants," "heirs of the body," "heirs," "next of kin," "relatives," or "family," or a class described by language of similar import, a substitute gift is created in the surviving descendants of any deceased beneficiary. The property to which the beneficiaries would have been entitled had all of them survived the decedent passes to the surviving beneficiaries and the surviving descendants of the deceased beneficiaries. Each surviving beneficiary takes the share to which he [or she] would have been entitled had the deceased

beneficiaries survived the decedent. Each deceased beneficiary's surviving descendants who are substituted for the deceased beneficiary take by representation the share to which the deceased beneficiary would have been entitled had the deceased beneficiary survived the decedent. For the purposes of this paragraph, "deceased beneficiary" means a class member who failed to survive the decedent and left one or more surviving descendants.

(3) For the purposes of Section 2-701, words of survivorship, such as in a beneficiary designation to an individual "if he survives me," or in a beneficiary designation to "my surviving children," are not, in the absence of additional evidence, a sufficient indication of an intent contrary to the application of this section.

(4) If a governing instrument creates an alternative beneficiary designation with respect to a beneficiary designation for which a substitute gift is created by paragraph (1) or (2), the substitute gift is superseded by the alternative beneficiary designation only if an expressly designated beneficiary of the alternative beneficiary designation is entitled to take.

G. Powers of Appointment

In a power of appointment, assets are transferred to a trustee, who will administer the trust for the benefit of a named beneficiary for life. If the beneficiary may "appoint" these assets at his or her death, the legal description is that this is a general testamentary power of appointment. For example, if a trust were declared by which someone were to transfer one million dollars in trust for the support of Sadie for her life, and then, as he appoints the remainder, to whomever Sadie designates in her Will, Sadie would have a life estate in a support trust. But Sadie would also have what we will later refer to as a general testamentary power of appointment. That means that she may appoint to (bequeath to) anyone she wishes in her valid Will. If, in that Will, she appoints to someone who predeceases her, may the anti-lapse apply even though the trust was created by someone other than Sadie? The short answer is, "Yes," if the applicable issues we have identified so far apply to allow it. The Uniform Probate Code specifically applies the anti-lapse statute to powers of appointment: "'Devise' includes an alternate devise, a devise in the form of a class gift, and an exercise of a power of appointment." *See* UNIF. PROB. CODE § 2-603(a)(3) (2003). "'Testator' includes the donee of a power of appointment if the power is exercised in the testator's will." *Id.* at (a)(7). Furthermore, the predeceasing devisee may be a relative of either the testator or the person exercising the power of appointment. *See id.* at (b) (Substitute Gift). We will examine powers of appointment in greater depth *infra*.

Chapter Five

Restraints on Transfer of Wealth

Tool Bar

Any person with standing has a right to contest the formalities and intentionalities of a Last Will and Testament. Chapter Three explores these possibilities. But states have developed procedures by which they may object to decisions made by a decedent at death which, if made during lifetime, the decision would have greater probability of success. For example, an elderly widow may be able to demolish her memory-laden home during her lifetime if she is afraid her children may vandalize it. But if she directs her personal representative to do the demolishing after her death, her wishes will most likely be thwarted by general public policy concerns. *See* Eyerman v. Mercantile Trust Co., 524 S.W.2d 210 (Mo. App. 1975). And nearly everyone would agree that a person should not inherit under probate or non-probate transfer if the inheritance only came about because of an intentional homicide by the heir, but what if the potential heir perpetrated domestic violence, elder abuse, or abandoned the decedent during life? *See, e.g.,* Diane J. Klein, *A Disappointed Yankee in Connecticut (or Nearby) Probate Court: Tortious Interference With Expectation of Inheritance—A Survey With Analysis of State Approaches in the First, Second, and Third Circuits*, 66 U. PITT. L. REV. 235 (2004). There are other issues, like to what extent should the state be responsible for protecting the economic rights of a surviving spouse or minor and adult children? What is the responsibility of the state to provide citizens an efficient and cost-effective means of transferring property at death? These are the issues raised in this chapter. As an attorney, you will be directly involved in the administration of the probate system and, thus, you should consider this chapter in the context of striving for efficiency and fairness.

I. General Public Policy

A. Common Law Restraints

Clark v. Office of Personnel Management
U.S. Court of Appeals for the Federal Circuit, 2001
256 F.3d 1360

MICHEL, Circuit Judge.

Phillip Clark ("Clark") petitions for review of the final decision of the Merit Systems Protection Board ("Board"), made final on March 13, 2000, when the full Board declined to review the initial decision of the Administrative Judge ("AJ"). The AJ had affirmed the Office of Personnel Management's ("OPM") denial of Clark's application for the Basic Employee Death Benefit ("BEDB"), to which the surviving spouse of a federal employee is entitled if the employee worked for at least 18 months under the Federal Employees Retirement System ("FERS"). Clark v. Office of Pers. Mgmt., No. AT-0843-99-683-I-1 (M.S.P.B. Oct. 14, 1999). As executor of the estate of Michael Clark ("Michael"), Clark filed a timely petition for review with this court under 5 U.S.C. §7703 (1994), and we have jurisdiction pursuant to 28 U.S.C. §1295(a)(9) (1994). Because the federal statute regarding the BEDB, 5 U.S.C. §8442(b) (1994), is silent as to whether a killer or his or her estate may receive federal death benefits earned by his or her victim, and because OPM concluded, based on the Alabama state authorities' substantial evidence, that Michael killed Melonie Clark ("Melonie"), OPM was thus correct in following the principle of Alabama law to prevent Michael's estate from collecting the BEDB earned by his victim. Accordingly, we affirm.

* * *

Melonie, a Department of Defense ("DOD") civilian employee at Fort McClellan, Alabama, was married to Michael. The couple had two children together. On August 19, 1994, allegedly in the midst of a child custody dispute, Michael traveled to the home of Melonie's parents, where Melonie and the children were temporarily staying. While the details of what occurred that day are not entirely clear, there was an exchange of gunfire that left Michael, Melonie and both of Melonie's parents dead.

The two children, ages three and seven, apparently witnessed the events. One of the children allegedly told investigators that his father had killed himself. An investigation by the Talladega County Sheriff's Office revealed that Michael intentionally caused the death of Melonie by shooting her, and that he then committed suicide. A postmortem examination found that Michael had been shot once in the abdomen and once in the hand before he committed suicide. The examination further revealed that the bullets which wounded Michael had been fired from a different gun than that which Michael used to commit suicide. Melonie's death certificate states that her death was a "homicide" caused by a "gunshot to face," and lists her time of death as 5:10 p.m., August 19, 1994. Michael's death certificate states that his death was a "suicide" caused by a "gunshot to head," and lists his time of death as 5:14 p.m., August 19, 1994.

Pursuant to 5 U.S.C §8442(b) and its implementing regulation, 5 C.F.R. §843.309(a) (1994), if a federal employee dies after completing at least 18 months of civilian service, that employee's spouse is entitled to receive the BEDB, as a result of that employee's participation in FERS.[1] Clark, Michael's brother, is the executor and conservator of Michael's estate, as well as the guardian of the two children. As executor of Michael's estate, Clark submitted an application to OPM in order to obtain the BEDB to which he claims Michael was entitled as a result of Melonie's participation in FERS.

In a letter dated August 10, 1998, which formalized an initial decision dated June 19, 1998, and subsequently in a final reconsideration decision dated June 16, 1999, OPM

---

1. Section 8442(b), chapter 5, of the U.S.C., entitled "Rights of a widow or widower," states that, "[i]f an employee or Member dies after completing at least 18 months of civilian service creditable under section 8411 and is survived by a widow or widower, the widow or widower is entitled to ... [a survivor benefit]." Section 843.309(a), chapter 5 of the C.F.R., entitled "Federal Employees Retirement System—Death Benefits and Employee Refunds—Current and Former Spouse Benefits," similarly states that "if an employee or Member dies after completing at least 18 months of civilian service creditable under Subpart C of Part 842 of this chapter and is survived by a current spouse who meets the requirements of §843.303, the current spouse is entitled to the basic employee death benefit ..."

denied Clark's application, citing the principle that one who kills his spouse cannot inherit from that spouse. OPM noted in its final decision that "because it is against public policy to permit an individual to profit from his or her own wrongdoing, Mr. Clark's estate's claim for FERS basic employee death benefit as the estate of the widower of Mrs. Melonie G. Clark was disallowed. OPM follows the common law concept that you cannot profit from a crime." Letter from OPM to Clark of 6/16/99, at 2.

Clark appealed OPM's decision to the Board. In an initial decision dated October 14, 1999, the AJ held that pursuant to the Code of Alabama § 43-8-253 (1994) ("Slayer Statute"), one who kills his or her spouse is deemed to have predeceased the decedent. The Slayer Statute provides in relevant part that "[a] final judgment of conviction of felonious and intentional killing is conclusive for purposes of this section. In the absence of a conviction of felonious and intentional killing the court may determine by a preponderance of the evidence whether the killing was felonious and intentional for purposes of this section."

The AJ reasoned that Michael, being deemed to have "died before" Melonie, was never considered a "surviving spouse" and consequently neither he nor his estate is entitled to the BEDB. In response to Clark's argument that the Slayer Statute does not apply to a determination of eligibility for *federal* benefits, the AJ held that state law is used to determine relevant familial relationships, in particular to determine who may be deemed "the surviving spouse" for purposes of distributing survivor benefits: "Although the death benefit is provided for by statute, questions involving the relationships of individuals such as Michael and Melonie are determined by state law and not Federal law." *Clark,* slip op. at 3.

On March 13, 2000, the full Board denied Clark's petition for review, making the AJ's decision the final decision of the Board. Subsequently, Clark filed a timely petition for review with this court.

* * *

The scope of judicial review of decisions of the Board is narrowly limited by statute. Specifically, this court must affirm the Board's decision unless we find it to be arbitrary, capricious, an abuse of discretion, or otherwise not in accordance with law; obtained without procedures required by law, rule or regulation having been followed; or unsupported by substantial evidence. 5 U.S .C. § 7703(c) (1994); Kewley v. Dep't of Health & Human Servs., 153 F.3d 1357, 1361 (Fed.Cir.1998).

OPM is a federal agency charged with the distribution of the BEDB, pursuant to 5 U.S.C. § 8442(b) and 5 C.F.R. § 843.309(a). The statute and its implementing regulation provide in relevant part that if an employee dies after completing at least 18 months of civilian service and is survived by a spouse, that spouse will receive a benefit. However, neither the statute nor its implementing regulation explicitly addresses whether a survivor benefit should be given to one who has become a widow or widower by intentionally killing his or her spouse. OPM and the Board thus relied on state law principles to determine whether Michael was deemed to be a "surviving spouse," and hence whether Clark, as the executor of Michael's estate, was entitled to receive the BEDB.

As noted by the Board, we have previously affirmed reliance on state law principles to determine eligibility for federal benefits. See *Clark,* slip op. at 3, citing Rogers v. Office of Pers. Mgmt., 87 F.3d 471, 473 (Fed.Cir.1996) (relying in part on the presumption of validity under Texas *state law* in favor of the latest marriage to determine which of two "wives" was married to the deceased federal employee at the time of his death and thus which "wife" was entitled to his survivor annuity) (emphasis added); Money v. Office of Pers. Mgmt., 811 F.2d 1474, 1479 (Fed.Cir.1987) (affirming the Board's determination that eligibility for federal benefits should be decided based upon which one of two marriages would be recognized as valid by California *state* courts) (emphasis added).

OPM determined that Alabama state law prohibits killers from profiting from their crimes. In Weaver v. Hollis, 247 Ala. 57, 22 So.2d 525 (1945), a case cited by OPM, Letter from OPM to Clark of 6/16/99, at 2, the Supreme Court of Alabama held that, "[t]he basic reasons behind the denial of the right of the husband to inherit from the wife whom he has feloniously killed is so compelling, we now declare that in this jurisdiction he cannot do so." *Weaver,* 22 So.2d at 529. We note that *Weaver* in fact predates by decades the Slayer Statute, which was not passed by the Alabama Legislature until 1982.

Alabama's intent to preclude killers from profiting from their crimes is further evidenced through the Slayer Statute. In enacting the Slayer Statute, the Alabama Legislature decided that one who "feloniously and intentionally" kills his or her spouse is deemed to have predeceased the decedent and is thus ineligible to receive "surviving spouse" benefits. See Ala.Code § 43-8-253(a). In the opinion affirming OPM's denial of Clark's BEDB application, the Board reasoned that, "the FERS death benefit [BEDB] is a benefit that accrues only to a surviving spouse … [a]nd since the Alabama law provides that Michael should be deemed to have predeceased Melonie, then his estate is not entitled to the benefit." *Clark,* slip op. at 2–3.

However, before applying the principle of Alabama law to deny Clark's BEDB application, OPM first examined the evidence before it to determine whether Michael had intentionally and feloniously caused the death of his wife. OPM reviewed the death certificates from the Deputy Coroner, which stated that Melonie's death had been deemed a "homicide" and Michael's death a "suicide." OPM also submitted a written request to the Talladega County Sheriff's Office to obtain further information regarding the case. In response to its request, OPM received and considered a letter from the County Sheriff's Office, dated June 14, 1999, which detailed the conclusions of the Chief Investigator: "[T]he investigation did reveal that Michael H. Clark did intentionally cause the death of his wife, Melonie Gentry Clark, by shooting her with a firearm, along with other members of her family, and then committed suicide prior to the arrival of law enforcement on the scene." Letter from the Talladega County Sheriff's Office to OPM of 6/14/99.

Based on this evidence from appropriate state authorities, OPM in its final decision concluded that it should follow the principle of Alabama law in the instant case, and that therefore Michael's intentional killing of Melonie prevented his estate from obtaining the BEDB: "We have a report from the Talladega County Sheriff's Office indicating that Mr. Clark intentionally caused the death of Mrs. Clark by shooting her with a firearm. Based on this information, we found that Mr. Clark and subsequently his estate were not entitled to a basic employee death benefit." Letter from OPM to Clark of 6/16/99, at 1. While neither OPM nor the Board was bound by the conclusions of the state authorities, both reasonably concluded, based on the content of the documents before them, that the principle of Alabama law should be followed to deny Clark's BEDB application. Their conclusions were supported by substantial evidence and were in accordance with law.

We additionally note that this principle of Alabama law is long-standing and widespread. As stated above, the policy that a killer may not profit from his or her crime precedes by decades the Slayer Statute, which was not passed by the Alabama Legislature until 1982. In fact, the Supreme Court recently noted in dictum that the principles underlying state slayer statutes are "well established in the law and ha[ve] a long historical pedigree." Egelhoff v. Egelhoff, 532 U.S. 141, —, 121 S.Ct. 1322, 1330, 149 L.Ed.2d 264 (2001) (citing Riggs v. Palmer, 115 N.Y. 506, 22 N.E. 188 (1889)). Similarly, in this court, we have upheld the propriety of this principle in order to prevent one who has intentionally killed a spouse from benefitting from the crime. In Lofton v. West, 198 F.3d 846 (Fed.Cir.1999), we stated that the Department of Veterans Affairs ("DVA"), in light of the universality of this principle, acted reasonably in promulgating a regulation which adopted the rule that a "slayer" may not obtain benefits as a result of "intentionally and wrongfully" causing the death of his or her spouse. Id. at 850. We reasoned in *Lofton* that "Congress legislates against a common law background, and [the relevant regulation] simply codifies a long-standing common law principle known as the 'slayer's rule,' which bars wrongdoers from obtaining insurance and other benefits as a direct consequence of their wrongful acts." Id.

Clark argues to this court that he is entitled to the BEDB because, in the absence of a conviction, the Slayer Statute requires a finding by an Alabama probate court that Michael intentionally killed Melonie. Clark asserts that absent such a finding, the Slayer Statute is inapplicable and consequently he is entitled to the BEDB from OPM. On the other hand, OPM argues that Clark is not entitled to the BEDB because the Code of Alabama does not limit the term "court" in the Slayer Statute to only include an Alabama probate court, and that therefore OPM and the Board can constitute "courts" for purposes of the statute.

We disagree with both contentions. The plain language of the Code of Alabama clearly contemplates that, absent a conviction, determinations of intentional killings for purposes of the Slayer Statute will be made by an Alabama "court." See Ala.Code § 43-8-253(e). However, merely because the Slayer Statute is technically inapplicable to the instant case does not preclude OPM, nor the Board, from relying on the state law principle behind the statute. As stated above, the Slayer Statute codified a long-standing Alabama state principle, which is also found in virtually all other states, see *Egelhoff*, 532 U.S. at ——, 121 S.Ct. at 1330, as well as in federal common law. See *Lofton*, 198 F.3d at 850. If there had been a conviction or an Alabama court finding, OPM would have been required to apply the Slayer Statute. However, the absence of a conviction and of a probate court finding did not necessarily preclude OPM from lawfully relying on the Slayer Statute's underlying principles.

We certainly do not hold that it is always appropriate for OPM to rely on state law to deny an individual federal benefits. In some instances, the federal statute might contain an explicit provision which contradicts a state principle, in which case OPM would not be able to rely on such principle. Nor do we hold that OPM was required to accept the state authorities' conclusions that Michael had intentionally killed his wife. Rather, we hold only that because the federal statute in question was silent on the subject of killers obtaining the BEDB earned by their victims, OPM was entitled to look to Alabama state law to determine that the estate of a "slayer" may not obtain "surviving spouse" benefits. Furthermore, because there was substantial evidence that Michael did indeed intentionally cause the death of his wife, we hold that OPM lawfully concluded that the principle of Alabama's "slayer's rule" applied to the instant case, and consequently OPM correctly denied Clark's BEDB application.

Furthermore, we note that in regard to the instant case, federal common law is in accordance with the state law principle. See *Lofton*, 198 F.3d at 850; Mutual Life Insurance Co. v. Armstrong, 117 U.S. 591, 6 S.Ct. 877, 881, 29 L.Ed. 997 (1886). Thus, Clark would still not be entitled to the BEDB even had the Board relied on federal common law. Consequently, we do not reach the hypothetical, and unlikely, question of whether, if a state court should rule in the future that slayers may obtain benefits from their victims, OPM may rely on such a state law principle that contradicts federal common law. See *Egelhoff*, 532 U.S. at ——, 121 S.Ct. at 1330 (stating in dictum that "the principles underlying the [slayer] statutes ... have been adopted by nearly every State").

* * *

Based on substantial evidence from Alabama state authorities that Michael intentionally killed Melonie, OPM reasonably relied on the principle of Alabama law in order to deny Clark's BEDB application. Thus, the Board's approval of OPM's reliance on Alabama law, and its decision affirming OPM's ruling, was based on substantial evidence and was in accordance with law. Accordingly, the Board's decision is

AFFIRMED.

Notes

The case demonstrates the effect of a state slayer statute, but also the court's willingness to utilize the "statute's underlying principles" to bar inheritance where it may reasonably be concluded that an heir intentionally killed the person from whom he or she was to inherit. The court allows title to pass to the "slayer," but because no one should be able to profit from his or her own wrongdoing, the court applies the equitable device of a constructive trust to then transfer title to persons other than the slayer. *See, e.g., In re* Estate of Mahoney, 220 A.2d 475 (Vt. 1966). Because equity is involved, courts may fashion a constructive trust remedy that not only deprives the slayer but also deprives heirs of the slayer from inheriting too. This would make certain that the slayer does not eventually inherit from them and, thus, gain by his or her own wrongdoing. *See, e.g., In re* Estate of Mueller, 275 Ill. App. 3d 128, 655 N.E.2d 1040, *rev. denied,* 660 N.E.2d 1269 (1995); UNIF. PROB. CODE § 2-803(f) (2003) ("A wrongful acquisition of property or interest by a killer not covered by this section must be treated in accordance with the principle that a killer cannot profit from his [or her] wrong doing.")

Applicability of any slayer statute may be had through a civil determination under a "preponderance of the evidence" test, or through a criminal determination under a "beyond a reasonable doubt" test. *See Restatement (Third) of Property; Wills and Other Donative Transfers,* §8.4 (2003) (Homicide-The Slayer Rule). In California, if one spouse is convicted of attempted murder, the injured spouse is entitled to 100 percent of the community interest in the retirement and pension benefits of the injured spouse. *See* CAL. FAM. CODE §782.5 (2003).

Shapira v. Union National Bank

Ohio Court of Common Pleas, Mahoning County, 1974
39 Ohio Misc. 28, 315 N.E.2d 825

HENDERSON, Judge.

This is an action for a declaratory judgment and the construction of the will of David Shapira, M.D., who died April 13, 1973, a resident of this county. By agreement of the parties, the case has been submitted upon the pleadings and the exhibit.

The portions of the will in controversy are as follows:

'Item VIII. All the rest, residue and remainder of my estate, real and personal, of every kind and description and wheresoever situated, which I may own or have the right to dispose of at the time of my decease, I give, devise and bequeath to my three (3) beloved children, to wit: Ruth Shapira Aharoni, of Tel Aviv, Israel, or wherever she may reside at the time of my death; to my son Daniel Jacob Shapira, and to my son Mark Benjamin Simon Shapira in equal shares, with the following qualifications: * * *

'(b) My son Daniel Jacob Shapira should receive his share of the bequest only, if he is married at the time of my death to a Jewish girl whose both parents were Jewish. In the event that at the time of my death he is not married to a Jewish girl whose both parents were Jewish, then his share of this bequest should be kept by my executor for a period of not longer than seven (7) years and if my said son Daniel Jacob gets married within the seven year period to a Jewish girl whose both parents were Jewish, my executor is hereby instructed to turn over his share of my bequest to him. In the event, however, that my said son Daniel Jacob is unmarried within the seven (7) years after my death to a Jewish girl whose both parents were Jewish, or if he is married to a non Jewish girl, then his share of my estate, as provided in item 8 above should go to The State of Israel, absolutely.'

The provision for the testator's other son Mark, is conditioned substantially similarly. Daniel Jacob Shapira, the plaintiff, alleges that the condition upon his inheritance is unconstitutional, contrary to public policy and unenforceable because of its unreasonableness, and that he should be given his bequest free of the restriction. Daniel is 21 years of age, unmarried and a student at Youngstown State University.

The provision in controversy is an executory devise or legacy, under which vesting of the estate of Daniel Jacob Shapira or the State of Israel is not intended to take place necessarily at the death of the testator, but rather conditionally, at a time not later than seven years after the testator's death. The executory aspect of the provision, though rather unusual, does not render it invalid. Heath v. City of Cleveland (1926), 114 Ohio St. 535, 151 N.E. 649.

* * *

Plaintiff's argument that the condition in question violates constitutional safeguards is based upon the premise that the right to marry is protected by the Fourteenth Amendment to the Constitution of the United States. Meyer v. Nebraska (1923), 262 U.S. 390, 43 S.Ct. 625, 67 L.Ed. 1042; Skinner v. Oklahoma (1942), 316 U.S. 535, 62 S.Ct. 1110, 86 L.Ed. 1655; Loving v. Virginia (1967), 388 U.S. 1, 87 S.Ct. 1817, 18 L.Ed.2d 1010. In Meyer v. Nebraska, holding unconstitutional a state statute prohibiting the teaching of languages other than English, the court stated that the Fourteenth Amendment denotes the right to marry among other basic rights. In Skinner v. Oklahoma, holding unconstitutional a state statute providing for the sterilization of certain habitual criminals, the court stated that marriage and procreation are fundamental to the very existence and survival of the race. In Loving v. Virginia, the court held unconstitutional as violative of the Equal Protection and Due Process Clauses of the Fourteenth Amendment an antimiscegenation statute under which a black person and a white person were convicted for marrying. In its opinion the United States Supreme Court made the following statements, 388 U.S. at page 12, 87 S.Ct. at page 1823:

'There can be no doubt that restricting the freedom to marry solely because of racial classifications violates the central meaning of the Equal Protection Clause.

'* * * The freedom to marry has long been recognized as one of the vital personal rights essential to the orderly pursuit of happiness by free men.

'Marriage is one of the 'basic civil rights of man,' fundamental to our very existence and survival. * * * The Fourteenth Amendment requires that the freedom of choice to marry not be restricted by invidious racial discriminations. Under our Constitution, the freedom to marry, or not marry, a person of another race resides with the individual and cannot be infringed by the State.'

From the foregoing, it appears clear, as plaintiff contends, that the right to marry is constitutionally protected from restrictive state legislative action. Plaintiff submits, then, that under the doctrine of Shelley v. Kraemer (1948), 334 U.S. 1, 68 S.Ct. 836, 92 L.Ed. 1161, the constitutional protection of the Fourteenth Amendment is extended from direct state legislative action to the enforcement by state judicial proceedings of private provisions restricting the right to marry. Plaintiff contends that a judgment of this court upholding the condition restricting marriage would, under Shelley v. Kraemer, constitute state action prohibited by the Fourteenth Amendment as much as a state statute.

In Shelley v. Kraemer the United States Supreme Court held that the action of the states to which the Fourteenth Amendment has reference includes action of state courts and state judicial officials. Prior to this decision the court had invalidated city ordinances which denied blacks the right to live in white neighborhoods. In Shelley v. Kraemer owners of neighboring properties sought to enjoin blacks from occupying properties which they had bought, but which were subjected to privately executed restrictions against use or occupation by any persons except those of the Caucasian race. Chief Justice Vinson noted, in the course of his opinion at page 13, 68 S.Ct. at page 842: 'These are cases in which the purposes of the agreements were secured only by judicial enforcement by state courts of the restrictive terms of the agreements.'

In the case at bar, this court is not being asked to enforce any restriction upon Daniel Jacob Shapira's constitutional right to marry. Rather, this court is being asked to enforce the testator's restriction upon his son's inheritance. If the facts and circumstances of this case were such that the aid of this court were sought to enjoin Daniel's marrying a non-Jewish girl, then the doctrine of Shelley v. Kraemer would be applicable, but not, it is believed, upon the facts as they are.

Counsel for plaintiff asserts, however, that his position with respect to the applicability of Shelley v. Kraemer to this case is fortified by two later decisions of the United States Supreme Court: Evans v. Newton (1966), 382 U.S. 296, 86 S.Ct. 486, 15 L.Ed.2d 373 and Pennsylvania v. Board of Directors of City Trusts of the City of Philadelphia (1957), 353 U.S. 230, 77 S.Ct. 806, 1 L.Ed.2d 792.

Evans v. Newton involved land willed in trust to the mayor and city council of Macon, Georgia, as a park for white people only, and to be controlled by a white board of managers. To avoid the city's having to enforce racial segregation in the park, the city officials resigned as trustees and private individuals were installed. The court held that such successor trustees, even though private individuals, became agencies or instrumentalities of the state and subject to the Fourteenth Amendment by reason of their exercising powers or carrying on functions governmental in nature. The following comment of Justice Douglas seems revealing: 'If a testator wanted to leave a school or center for the use of one race only and in no way implicated the State in the supervision, control, or management of that facility, we assume arguendo that no constitutional difficulty would be encountered.' 382 U.S. 300, 86 S.Ct. 489.

The case of Pennsylvania v. Board, as the full title, above, suggests, is a case in which money was left by will to the city of Philadelphia in trust for a college to admit poor white male orphans. The court held that the board which operated the college was an agency of the state of Pennsylvania, and that, therefore, its refusal to admit the plaintiffs because they were negroes was discrimination by the state forbidden by the Fourteenth Amendment.

So, in neither Evans v. Newton nor Pennsylvania v. Board was the doctrine of the earlier Shelley v. Kraemer applied or extended. Both of them involved restrictive actions by state governing agencies, in one case with respect to a park, in the other case with respect to a college. Although both the park and the college were founded upon testamentary gifts, the state action struck down by the court was not the judicial completion of the gifts, but rather the subsequent enforcement of the racial restrictions by the public management.

Basically, the right to receive property by will is a creature of the law, and is not a natural right or one guaranteed or protected by either the Ohio or the United States constitution. Patton v. Patton (1883), 39 Ohio St. 590; Hagerty v. State (1897), 55 Ohio St. 613, 45 N.E. 1046; State, ex rel. Taylor v. Guilbert (1904), 70 Ohio St. 229, 71 N.E. 636; Magoun v. Illinois Trust and Savings Bank (1898), 170 U.S. 283, 18 S.Ct. 594, 42 L.Ed. 1037; 55 Ohio Jurisprudence 2d 535, Wills, Section 64; 57 American Jurisprudence 138, Wills, Section 153. It is a fundamental rule of law in Ohio that a testator may legally entirely disinherit his children. 56 Ohio Jurisprudence 2d 252, Wills, Section 742; 55 Ohio Jurisprudence 2d 564, Wills, Section 101; Wilson v. Behr (C.A. Hamilton (1936)), 57 Ohio App. 117, 121, 12 N.E.2d 300, 5 O.O. 424. This would seem to demonstrate that, from a constitutional standpoint, a testator may restrict a child's inheritance. The court concludes, therefore, that the upholding and enforcement of the provisions of Dr. Shapira's will conditioning the bequests to his sons upon their marrying Jewish girls does not offend the Constitution of Ohio or of the United States. United States National Bank of Portland v. Snodgrass (1954), 202 Or. 530, 275 P.2d 860, 50 A.L.R.2d 725; Gordon v. Gordon (1955), 332 Mass. 197, 124 N.E.2d 228; 54 Mich.L.Rev. 297 (1955); cf. 39 Minn.L.Rev. 809 (1955).

* * *

The condition that Daniel's share should be 'turned over to him if he should marry a Jewish girl whose both parents were Jewish' constitutes a partial restraint upon marriage. If the condition were that the beneficiary not marry anyone, the restraint would be general or total, and, at least in the case of a first marriage, would be held to be contrary to public policy and void. A partial restraint of marriage which imposes only reasonable restrictions is valid, and not contrary to public policy: 5 Bowe-Parker: Page on Wills 460, Section 44.25; 56 Ohio Jurisprudence 2d 243, Wills, Section 729; 52 American Jurisprudence 2d 1023, Marriage, Section 181. The great weight of authority in the United States is that gifts conditioned upon the beneficiary's marrying within a particular religious class or faith are reasonable. 5 Bowe-Parker; Page on Wills 461, Section 44.25; 52 American Jurisprudence 2d 1025, Marriage, Section 183; 56 Ohio Jurisprudence 2d 245, Wills, Section 731; 1 Prentice-Hall, Estate Planning, Law of Wills, 373, Paragraph 375.20; 1 Restatement of the Law, Trusts 2d, 166, Section 62(h); National Bank v. Snodgrass (supra), annotation, 50 A.L.R.2d 740; Gordon v. Gordon, supra; In re Harris (1955), 143 N.Y.2d 746; Matter of Seaman (1916), 218 N.Y. 77, 112 N.E. 576;

Matter of Liberman (1939), 279 N.Y. 458, 18 N.E.2d 658; In re Silverstein's Will (1956), 155 N.Y.S.2d 598; In re Clayton's Estate (Phila.Co.Pa.1930), 13 Pa.D. & C. 413; Pacholder v. Rosenheim (1916), 129 Md. 455, 99 A. 672.

Plaintiff contends, however, that in Ohio a condition such as the one in this case is void as against the public policy of this state. In Ohio, as elsewhere, a testator may not attach a condition to a gift which is in violation of public policy. 56 Ohio Jurisprudence 2d 238, Wills, Section 722; Neidler v. Donaldson (P.C. Seneca 1966), 9 Ohio Misc. 208, 224 N.E.2d 404, 38 O.O.2d 360. There can be no question about the soundness of plaintiff's position that the public policy of Ohio favors freedom of religion and that it is guaranteed by Section 7, Article I of the Ohio Constitution, providing that 'all men have a natural and indefeasible right to worship Almighty God according to the dictates of their own conscience.' Plaintiff's position that the free choice of religious practice cannot be circumscribed or controlled by contract is substantiated by Hackett v. Hackett (C.A. Lucas 1958), 78 Ohio Law Abs. 485, 150 N.E.2d 431. This case held that a covenant in a separation agreement, incorporated in a divorce decree, that the mother would rear a daughter in the Roman Catholic faith was unenforceable. However, the controversial condition in the case at bar is a partial restraint upon marriage and not a covenant to restrain the freedom of religious practice; and, of course, this court is not being asked to hold the plaintiff in contempt for failing to marry a Jewish girl of Jewish parentage.

Counsel contends that if 'Dr. David Shapira, during his life, had tried to impose upon his son those restrictions set out in his Will he would have violated the public policy of Ohio as shown in Hackett v. Hackett. The public policy is equally violated by the restrictions Dr. Shapira has placed on his son by his Will.' This would be true, by analogy, if Dr. Shapira, in his lifetime, had tried to force his son to marry a Jewish girl as the condition of a completed gift. But it is not true that if Dr. Shapira had agreed to make his son an inter-vivos gift if he married a Jewish girl within seven years, that his son could have forced him to make the gift free of the condition.

It is noted, furthermore, in this connection, that the courts of Pennsylvania distinguish between testamentary gifts conditioned upon the religious faith of the beneficiary and those conditioned upon marriage to persons of a particular religious faith. In In re Clayton's Estate, supra (13 Pa.D. & C. 413), the court upheld a gift of a life estate conditioned upon the beneficiary's not marrying a woman of the Catholic faith. In its opinion the court distinguishes the earlier case of Drace v. Klinedinst (1922), 275 Pa. 266, 118 A. 907, in which a life estate willed to grandchildren, provided they remained faithful to a particular religion, was held to violate the public policy of Pennsylvania. In Clayton's Estate, the court said that the condition concerning marriage did not affect the faith of the beneficiary, and that the condition, operating only on the choice of a wife, was too remote to be regarded as coercive of religious faith.

But counsel relies upon an Ohio case much more nearly in point, that of Moses v. Zook (C.A. Wayne 1934), 18 Ohio Law Abs. 373. This case involves a will in which the testatrix gave the income of her residual estate in trust to her niece and nephews for two years and then the remainder to them. Item twelve provides as follows: 'If any of my nieces or nephews should marry outside of the Protestant Faith, then they shall not receive any part of my estate devised or bequeathed to them.' The will contained no gift over upon violation of the marriage condition. The holding of the trial court was that item twelve was null and void as being against public policy and the seven other items of the will should be administered as specified in detail by the court. There is nothing in the reported opinion to show to what extent, if at all, the question of public policy was in issue or contested in the trial court; only one of the several other unrelated holdings of the trial court (not including the public policy holding) was assigned as error; and although the Court of Appeals adopted the unexcepted-to holdings of the trial court, there is no citation of authorities or discussion concerning the public policy question itself. The case was apparently not appealed to the Supreme Court, and no other cases in Ohio have been cited or found. Moses v. Zook differs in its facts in not containing a gift over upon breach of the condition, and appears not to have been a sufficiently litigated or reasoned establishment of the public policy of Ohio which this court should be obliged to follow.

The only cases cited by plaintiff's counsel in accord with the holding in Moses v. Zook are some English cases and one American decision. In England the courts have held that partial restrictions upon marriage to persons not of the Jewish faith, or of Jewish parentage, were not contrary to public policy or invalid. Hodgson v. Halford (1879 Eng.) L.R. 11 Ch.Div. 959, 50 A.L.R.2d 742. Other cases in England, however, have invalidated forfeitures of similarly conditioned provisions for children upon the basis of uncertainty or indefiniteness. Re Blaiberg (1940), Ch. 385 (1940), 1 All.Eng. 632, 50 A.L.R.2d 746; Clayton v. Ramsden (1943), A.C. 320 (1943), 1 All.Eng. 16-H.L., 50 A.L.R.2d 746; Re Donn (1944), Ch. 8 (1943), 2 All.Eng. 564, 50 A.L.R.2d 746; Re Moss' Trusts (1945), 1 All.Eng. 207, 61 Times L. 147, 50 A.L.R.2d 747. Since the foregoing decisions, a later English case has upheld a condition precedent that a granddaughter-beneficiary marry a person of Jewish faith and the child of Jewish parents. The court distinguished the cases cited above as not applicable to a condition precedent under which the legatee must qualify for the gift by marrying as specified, and there was found to be no difficulty with indefiniteness where the legatee married unquestionably outside the Jewish faith. Re Wolffe (1953), 1 Week L.R. 1211 (1953), 2 All.Eng. 697, 50 A.L.R.2d 747.

The American case cited by plaintiff is that of Maddox v. Maddox (1854), 52 Va. (11 Grattain's) 804. The testator in this case willed a remainder to his niece if she remain a member of the Society of Friends. When the niece arrived at a marriageable age there were but five or six unmarried men of the society in the neighborhood in which she lived. She married a non-member and thus lost her own membership. The court held the condition to be an unreasonable restraint upon marriage and void, and that there being no gift over upon breach of the condition, the condition was in terrorem, and did not avoid the bequest. It can be seen that while the court considered the testamentary condition to be a restraint upon marriage, it was primarily one in restraint of religious faith. The court said that with the small number of eligible bachelors in the area the condition would have operated as a virtual prohibition of the niece's marrying, and that she could not be expected to 'go abroad' in search of a helpmate or to be subjected to the chance of being sought after by a stranger. The court distinguished the facts of its case from those in England upholding conditions upon marriage by observing that England was 'already overstocked with inhabitants' while this country had 'an unbounded extent of territory, a large portion of which is yet unsettled, and in which increase of population is one of the main elements of national prosperity.' The other ground upon which the Virginia court rested its decision, that the condition was in terrorem because of the absence of a gift over, is clearly not applicable to the case at bar, even if it were in accord with Ohio law, because of the gift over to the State of Israel contained in the Shapira will.

In arguing for the applicability of the Maddox v. Maddox test of reasonableness to the case at bar, counsel for the plaintiff asserts that the number of eligible Jewish females in this county would be an extremely small minority of the total population especially as compared with the comparatively much greater number in New York, whence have come many of the cases comprising the weight of authority upholding the validity of such clauses. There are no census figures in evidence. While this court could probably take judicial notice of the fact that the Jewish community is a minor, though important segment of our total local population, nevertheless the court is by no means justified in judicial knowledge that there is an insufficient number of eligible young ladies of Jewish parentage in this area from which Daniel would have a reasonable latitude of choice. And of course, Daniel is not at all confined in his choice to residents of this county, which is a very different circumstance in this day of travel by plane and freeway and communication by telephone, from the horse and buggy days of the 1854 Maddox v. Maddox decision. Consequently, the decision does not appear to be an appropriate yardstick of reasonableness under modern living conditions.

Plaintiff's counsel contends that the Shapira will falls within the principle of Fineman v. Central National Bank (1961), 87 Ohio Law Abs. 236, 175 N.E.2d 837, 18 O.O.2d 33, holding that the public policy of Ohio does not countenance a bequest or device conditioned on the beneficiary's obtaining a separation or divorce from his wife. Counsel argues that the Shapira condition would encourage the beneficiary to marry a qualified girl just to receive the bequest, and then to divorce her afterward. This possibility seems too remote to be a pertinent application of the policy against bequests conditioned upon divorce. Most other authorities agree with Fineman v. Bank that as a general proposition, a testamentary gift effective only on condition that the recipient divorce or separate from his or her spouse is against public policy and invalid. 14 A.L.R.3d 1222. But no authorities have been found extending the principle to support plaintiff's position. Indeed, in measuring the reasonableness of the condition in question, both the father and the court should be able to assume that the son's motive would be proper. And surely the son should not gain the advantage of the avoidance of the condition by the possibility of his own impropriety.

Finally, counsel urges that the Shapira condition tends to pressure Daniel, by the reward of money, to marry within seven years without opportunity for mature reflection, and jeopardizes his college education. It seems to the court, on the contrary, that the seven year time limit would be a most reasonable grace period, and one which would give the son ample opportunity for exhaustive reflection and fulfillment of the condition without constraint or oppression. Daniel is no more being 'blackmailed into a marriage by immediate financial gain,' as suggested by counsel, than would be the beneficiary of a living gift or conveyance upon consideration of a future marriage—an arrangement which has long been sanctioned by the courts of this state. Thompson v. Thompson (1867), 17 Ohio St. 649.

In the opinion of this court, the provision made by the testator for the benefit of the State of Israel upon breach or failure of the condition is most significant for two reasons. First, it distinguishes this case from the bare forfeitures in Moses v. Zook, and in Maddox v. Maddox (including the technical in terrorem objection), and, in a way, from the vagueness and indefiniteness doctrine of some of the English cases. Second, and of greater importance, it demonstrates the depth of the testator's conviction. His purpose was not merely a negative one designed to punish his son for not carrying out his wishes. His unmistakable testamentary plan was that his possessions be used to encourage the preservation of the Jewish faith and blood, hopefully through his sons, but, if not, then through the State of Israel. Whether this judgment was wise is not for this court to determine. But it is the duty of this court to honor the testator's intention within the limitations of law and of public policy. The prerogative granted to a testator by the laws of this state to dispose of his estate according to his conscience is entitled to as much judicial protection and enforcement as the prerogative of a beneficiary to receive an inheritance.

It is the conclusion of this court that public policy should not, and does not preclude the fulfillment of Dr. Shapira's purpose, and that in accordance with the weight of authority in this country, the conditions contained in his will are reasonable restrictions upon marriage, and valid.

B. Statutory Restraints

McKinney v. Richitelli

North Carolina Supreme Court, 2003
586 S.E.2d 258, 357 N.C. 483

EDMUNDS, Justice.

Plaintiff Karen McKinney, acting individually and as the personal representative of the estate of her deceased son, Michael Edward McKinney * * * (Michael), brought this declaratory action against Michael's father, James Everett Richitelli (defendant), to determine the rights of the parties with respect to any proceeds of Michael's estate and to any proceeds of a wrongful death action brought on Michael's behalf. The Court of Appeals reversed the trial court's entry of summary judgment in favor of plaintiff. For the reasons discussed herein, we reverse the decision of the Court of Appeals.

Taken in the light most favorable to defendant, the evidence shows that plaintiff and defendant were married in 1976 and that their son, Michael, was born on 30 July 1977. Plaintiff and defendant were divorced in 1981. The district court entered a custody order awarding primary custody of Michael to plaintiff, while providing defendant visitation rights. Although the custody order required defendant to pay child support of $240.00 per month beginning on 1 October 1980, he failed to make any payments from 1 January 1981 through Michael's eighteenth birthday, 30 July 1995. Defendant admits that he had no contact or communication with Michael during this period, but explains that for most of these years, he was either incarcerated for theft and robbery convictions or suffering from drug and alcohol abuse.

Defendant's first contact with Michael after 1981 came when he wrote Michael in March 1997. At this time, Michael was nineteen years old, had been diagnosed with cancer, and would later file a medical malpractice action in which he alleged that a radiologist caused his illness. By defendant's accounts, after their initial contact, he and Michael visited with each other on at least three occasions and spoke regularly by telephone before Michael's death. Between October 1997 and December 1998, defendant sent Michael six checks totaling $3,150.

Michael's medical malpractice suit was filed on 13 May 1998, and he died intestate on 21 February 1999. After plaintiff was appointed as the personal representative of Michael's estate on 19 March 1999, she amended Michael's suit to include a wrongful death claim. While the wrongful death claim was pending, plaintiff on 6 July 2000 filed a declaratory judgment complaint against defendant, seeking a judicial determination of defendant's rights to any potential award resulting from the wrongful death suit. Defendant answered and moved to dismiss the declaratory judgment action pursuant to N.C. R. Civ. P. 12(b)(6). Following discovery, plaintiff filed a motion for summary judgment claiming she was entitled to judgment as a matter of law because defendant's behavior "during the period of 1981 through July 30, 1995 constituted a willful abandonment resulting in the loss of his right to intestate succession in any part of [Michael's] estate including wrongful death proceeds."

The motions were heard in the Superior Court, Wake County, on 31 January 2001. The key issue was the interpretation of N.C.G.S. §31A-2, "Acts barring rights of parents," which provides as follows:

> Any parent who has wil[l]fully abandoned the care and maintenance of his or her child shall lose all right to intestate succession in any part of the child's estate and all right to administer the estate of the child, except—
>
> (1) Where the abandoning parent resumed its care and maintenance at least one year prior to the death of the child and continued the same until its death; or
>
> (2) Where a parent has been deprived of the custody of his or her child under an order of a court of competent jurisdiction and the parent has substantially complied with all orders of the court requiring contribution to the support of the child.

N.C.G.S. §31A-2 (2001). On 14 March 2001, the trial court denied defendant's motion to dismiss and granted plaintiff's motion for summary judgment by an order declaring "that pursuant to N.C.G.S. §31A-2 defendant ... has lost all right to intestate succession in any part of [Michael's] estate, including, but not limited to, the proceeds of any wrongful death claim because of his willful abandonment of the care and maintenance of [Michael] during his minority."

Defendant appealed, and in an unpublished opinion, the Court of Appeals reversed the trial court's judgment. McKinney v. Richitelli, 149 N.C.App. 973, 563 S.E.2d 100 (2002). The Court of Appeals noted that "our case law remains unclear whether a parent can resume a relationship with a child after the child reaches the age of majority and therefore fall within the first exception to N.C.G.S. §31A-2," but concluded that a genuine issue of material fact existed as to whether defendant had resumed a relationship with Michael sufficient to invoke the exception set out in N.C.G.S. §31A-2(1). The Court of Appeals' opinion and the briefs to this Court relied heavily on our order vacating In re Estate of Lunsford, 143 N.C.App. 646, 547 S.E.2d 483 (2001), a case similar to the one at issue, and remanding the case only for additional findings of fact by the trial court. In re Estate of Lunsford, 354 N.C. 571, 556 S.E.2d 292 (2001). However, in that order, we made no determinations as to questions of law. Because the record in the case at bar is sufficiently developed to allow us to reach the underlying issues, we do not consider arguments based on our order in Lunsford to be applicable.

Summary judgment may be granted in a declaratory judgment action "where 'the pleadings, depositions, answers to interrogatories, and admissions on file, together with the affidavits, if any, show that there is no genuine issue as to any material fact and that any party is entitled to a judgment as a matter of law.'" Williams v. Blue Cross Blue Shield of N.C., 357 N.C. 170, 178, 581 S.E.2d 415, 422 (2003) (quoting N.C.G.S. §1A-

1, Rule 56(c) (2001)). Plaintiff argues that the Court of Appeals erred in determining that a genuine issue of material fact existed as to whether defendant had resumed statutorily adequate care and maintenance of Michael.

In deciding whether summary judgment was proper in this case, we must undertake a three-fold inquiry. First, we must determine whether N.C.G.S. §31A-2 applies after a child has reached his or her majority to prevent an abandoning parent from recovering through an offspring that was abandoned while a minor.[2] If so, we must next consider whether defendant abandoned Michael such that N.C.G.S. §31A-2 precludes defendant from taking under intestate succession. Finally, if we find that defendant abandoned Michael, we must determine whether a parent who has abandoned his or her minor child may thereafter resume a parent-child relationship with the now-adult child and, by so doing, come under the exception set out in N.C.G.S. §31A-2(1). See Heyward D. Armstrong, In re Estate of Lunsford and Statutory Ambiguity: Trying to Reconcile Child Abandonment and the Intestate Succession Act, 81 N.C. L.Rev. 1149 (2003).

We observe at the outset that N.C.G.S §31A-2 is ambiguous because nowhere in chapter 31A of the General Statutes is the term "child" defined, nor is the meaning of the term clear from its context. Thus "child" here could reasonably mean either a minor offspring or an offspring of any age. Although defendant contends that the word "child" as used in the body of the statute logically refers to a "minor child," he argues that the word "child" as used in the exception set out in N.C.G.S. §31A-2(1) refers to a child regardless of age. Under defendant's interpretation, a parent may reconcile with his or her offspring after the child has reached majority and thereafter take if the adult child dies intestate. In contrast, plaintiff argues that under N.C.G.S. §31A-2 the continuous abandonment of a minor child by a parent permanently terminates that parent's right to participate in the intestate share when the child reaches his or her majority. Under plaintiff's interpretation, the exception set out in N.C.G.S. §31A-2(1) can take effect only if the reconciliation occurs while the child is still a minor.

In interpreting such a statutory ambiguity, we adhere to the following rules of construction:

> Where the language of a statute is clear and unambiguous, there is no room for judicial construction and the courts must construe the statute using its plain meaning. Utilities Comm. v. Edmisten, Atty. General, 291 N.C. 451, 232 S.E.2d 184 (1977). But where a statute is ambiguous, judicial construction must be used to ascertain the legislative will. Young v. Whitehall Co., 229 N.C. 360, 49 S.E.2d 797 (1948). The primary rule of construction of a statute is to ascertain the intent of the legislature and to carry out such intention to the fullest extent. Buck v. Guaranty Co., 265 N.C. 285, 144 S.E.2d 34 (1965). This intent "must be found from the language of the act, its legislative history and the circumstances surrounding its adoption which throw light upon the evil sought to be remedied." Milk Commission v. Food Stores, 270 N.C. 323, 332, 154 S.E.2d 548, 555 (1967).

---

2. Logically, N.C.G.S. §31A-2 must apply to an abandonment that initially occurs while the child is a minor. After all, a parent cannot abandon an emancipated or adult child when the parent has no further responsibility for the child.

Burgess v. Your House of Raleigh, Inc., 326 N.C. 205, 209, 388 S.E.2d 134, 136–37 (1990).

Our analysis begins with Avery v. Brantley, 191 N.C. 396, 131 S.E. 721 (1926). In Avery, the father abandoned his daughter, and the issue before us was the father's ability to recover in the negligence suit brought when his intestate daughter was killed in an accident. We considered two statutes then in effect. One statute, 1 N.C. Cons.Stat. § 189 (1920), terminated the rights of a natural parent to the care, custody, and services of a child once the parent gave up the child for adoption. The other statute, 1 N.C. Cons.Stat. 137(6) (Supp.1924), provided that a parent would inherit if a child died intestate. This second statute did not contain a provision limiting its operation when a parent had abandoned the child. Because the child in Avery had not been adopted, we held that the statutes could not be interpreted in pari materia and that the statute allowing the parents to inherit from their intestate daughter controlled. Id. at 400, 131 S.E. at 722. Accordingly, we concluded that the mother and father shared in the proceeds of the child's estate, even though the father had abandoned the child. Id. Thereafter, the General Assembly amended 137(6) to provide,

> [i]f, in the lifetime of its father and mother, a child dies intestate, without leaving husband, wife or child, or the issue of a child, its estate shall be equally divided between the father and mother. If one of the parents is dead at the time of the death of the child, the surviving parent shall be entitled to the whole of the estate.... Provided, that a parent, or parents, who has willfully abandoned the care, custody, nurture and maintenance of such child to its kindred, relatives or other person, shall forfeit all and every right to participate in any part of said child's estate under the provisions of this section.

Act of Mar. 9, 1927, ch. 231, 1927 N.C. Sess. Laws 591 (amending 1 N.C. Cons.Stat. § 137(6), later recodified as N.C.G.S. § 28-149(6) (1943)).

With the adoption in 1960 of a new Intestate Succession Act, N.C.G.S. ch. 29, N.C.G.S. § 28-149(6) was abolished. The General Statutes Commission, "cognizant of the inadequate statutory law relating to the inheritance of property by unworthy heirs," thereupon created a special committee to draft new legislation addressing the topic. Report of Drafting Committee to the General Statutes Commission, Special Report of the General Statutes Commission on an Act to Be Entitled "Acts Barring Property Rights," at 1 (Feb. 8, 1961). The committee responded by drafting a bill (enacted by the General Assembly and now codified as N.C.G.S. §31A-2) that, among other provisions, prohibited abandoning parents from recovering through their intestate children. The committee stated that the purpose of this section was to " revise, broaden, and reintroduce" abolished N.C.G.S. § 28-149(6). Id. at 4. The committee reasoned that "[i]t seems very inequitable to allow a parent who has abandoned his child to inherit from such child when the child dies intestate." Id. However, the committee also provided two exceptions that allowed an abandoning parent to share in the intestate's estate. Id. The first of these exceptions encouraged an abandoning parent to resume his or her duties of care and maintenance of the child in an effort to renew the parent-child relationship. See N.C.G.S. §31A-2(1).

It is apparent from this history that the legislative intent behind N.C.G.S. §31A-2 was both to discourage parents from shirking their responsibility of support to their children and to prevent an abandoning parent from reaping an undeserved bonanza. Were we to hold that section 31A-2 has no application once a child reaches majority, a parent who has abandoned his or her child would nevertheless automatically inherit if the still-abandoned child died intestate after reaching the age of eighteen. Such an interpretation would frustrate the statute's purpose and effectively forgive the abandoning parent's dereliction. Therefore, we hold that N.C.G.S. §31A-2 applies to any abandoned child dying intestate regardless of the child's age at death.

We next consider whether defendant abandoned Michael. While we have observed the difficulty of formulating a uniform definition of the term, we have explained "abandonment" of a child as "wil[l]ful or intentional conduct on the part of the parent which evinces a settled purpose to forego all parental duties and relinquish all parental claims to the child." Pratt v. Bishop, 257 N.C. 486, 501, 126 S.E.2d 597, 608 (1962); see also In re Young, 346 N.C. 244, 251, 485 S.E.2d 612, 617 (1997).

> Abandonment has also been defined as wil[l]ful neglect and refusal to perform the natural and legal obligations of parental care and support. It has been held that if a parent withholds his presence, his love, his care, the opportunity to display filial affection, and wil[l]fully neglects to lend support and maintenance, such parent relinquishes all parental claims and abandons the child.

Pratt v. Bishop, 257 N.C. at 501, 126 S.E.2d at 608; see also Lessard v. Lessard, 77 N.C.App. 97, 100–01, 334 S.E.2d 475, 477 (1985) (utilizing the Pratt definitions of abandonment in the context of N.C.G.S. §31A-2), aff'd per curiam, 316 N.C. 546, 342 S.E.2d 522 (1986). "Maintenance" or support refers to a parent's financial obligation to provide support during the child's minority. See generally Wells v. Wells, 227 N.C. 614, 44 S.E.2d 31 (1947).

Applying these precepts to this case, the evidence, even viewed in the light most favorable to defendant, demonstrates that defendant abandoned Michael. From the time Michael was four until after his eighteenth birthday, defendant violated the court's order by failing to make any child support payments. Both in her brief and at oral argument, plaintiff claimed defendant owed approximately $42,000 in arrearages accrued during Michael's minority. Although defendant states that for a significant amount of that time he was either unemployed or in prison, at no point during this period did defendant attempt to modify the child support order. Even though defendant was entitled under the support order to visit Michael on alternate weekends, holidays, and two weeks in the summer, he did not see his son even once in fifteen years. Defendant admits that he had no communication with Michael at all during this period even though he was allowed to write letters from prison during his periods of incarceration. These findings demonstrate "wil[l]ful or intentional conduct on the part of the parent which evinces a settled purpose to forego all parental duties and relinquish all parental claims to the child." Pratt v. Bishop, 257 N.C. at 501, 126 S.E.2d at 608. Thus, we hold that defendant abandoned Michael as contemplated by N.C.G.S. §31A-2.

Finally, we must determine whether defendant is entitled to the benefit of the exception provided in N.C.G.S. §31A-2(1). Defendant argues that this exception applies to any abandoned child, whether or not that child has reached majority. He reasons that although the duty of maintenance or financial support ends at majority, the duty of care applies to a child of any age. Because he provided sufficient evidence to establish that he resumed the care and maintenance of Michael at least one year before Michael's death, defendant argues that his conduct in the final two years of Michael's life restored defendant's right to inheritance. We find defendant's arguments unpersuasive.

The critical inquiry as to N.C.G.S. §31A-2(1) is not whether a parent can resume a relationship with a child, but whether a parent " resumed its care and maintenance at least one year prior to the death of the child and continued the same until its death." N.C.G.S. §31A-2(1). The exception requires that the parent resume both the "care and maintenance" of the child. Id. (emphasis added). These requirements may not be read in the disjunctive. As stated above, while "care" pertains to love and concern for the child, "maintenance" refers to the financial support of a child during minority. See generally Wells v. Wells, 227 N.C. 614, 44 S.E.2d 31. Our jurisprudence establishes that "[t]he authority of the court to require support for a normal child ceases when the legal obligation to support no longer exists. The parents' duty to support ... cease[s] upon emancipation." Shoaf v. Shoaf, 282 N.C. 287, 290, 192 S.E.2d 299, 302 (1972). "The age of emancipation is precisely fixed—eighteen." Id. at 291, 192 S.E.2d at 303. Although a parent may have a duty of support of an older child who is still in school, N.C.G.S. §50-13.4(c)(2) (2001), there is no evidence to indicate this provision applies here. In the case at bar, defendant did not reestablish contact with Michael until he was almost twenty years old. Even assuming that defendant presented sufficient evidence that he resumed the care of Michael, defendant cannot resume the maintenance of Michael because his legal obligation to do so ceased at eighteen.

We held above that N.C.G.S. §31A-2 pertains to the estate of a child of any age. Under the logic of that analysis—that a parent who abandons a child should benefit from the death of the child only if the parent has resumed a parental relationship with the child—an abandoning parent who seeks to come under the exception in N.C.G.S. §31A-2(1) must renew both the care and the maintenance of the child during the child's minority, when care and maintenance are most valuable. See Williford v. Williford, 288 N.C. 506, 510, 219 S.E.2d 220, 223 (1975) (although issue not squarely presented, we held that "the plaintiff father, having abandoned the deceased when the latter was a minor child, may not now share in the proceeds of the settlement of the claim for wrongful death now in the hands of the administratrix") (emphasis added). Under the terms of the statute, the care and maintenance must continue for a year before the child's death. Therefore, we hold that, in order to benefit from this provision, a parent must renew such care and maintenance at least one year before the child reaches the age of eighteen.

This holding not only follows from the preceding historical and textual analysis, it is also consistent with our understanding of the General Assembly's overall intent. When an adult or emancipated child discerns that a parent who had previously abandoned him or her now sincerely seeks reconciliation, the child is free to execute a will making provisions for the no-longer-wayward parent. Although we acknowledge that this argument is of limited application to the facts before us because any recovery for Michael's wrongful death would pass under the laws of intestate succession even if he had written a will, see N.C.G.S. §28A-18-2(a) (2001), the larger principle that the abandoned child has the power to prevent a reconciled parent from being excluded from the child's estate informs our analysis. We believe that the General Assembly has adequately demonstrated an unwillingness to allow an abandoning parent to take from an abandoned adult child as the result of a mechanical application of the rules of intestate succession.

We hold that summary judgment in favor of plaintiff was proper in this case. Accordingly, we reverse the decision of the Court of Appeals.

REVERSED.

California Probate Code (2004)

§ 259. Predeceasing a decedent

(a) Any person shall be deemed to have predeceased a decedent to the extent provided in subdivision (c) where all of the following apply:

(1) It has been proven by clear and convincing evidence that the person is liable for physical abuse, neglect, or fiduciary abuse of the decedent, who was an elder or dependent adult.

(2) The person is found to have acted in bad faith.

(3) The person has been found to have been reckless, oppressive, fraudulent, or malicious in the commission of any of these acts upon the decedent.

(4) The decedent, at the time those acts occurred and thereafter until the time of his or her death, has been found to have been substantially unable to manage his or her financial resources or to resist fraud or undue influence.

(b) Any person shall be deemed to have predeceased a decedent to the extent provided in subdivision (c) if that person has been convicted of a violation of Section 236 of the Penal Code or any offense described in Section 368 of the Penal Code.

(c) Any person found liable under subdivision (a) or convicted under subdivision (b) shall not (1) receive any property, damages, or costs that are awarded to the decedent's estate in an action described in subdivision (a) or (b), whether that person's entitlement is under a will, a trust, or the laws of intestacy; or (2) serve as a fiduciary as defined in Section 39, if the instrument nominating or appointing that person was executed during the period when the decedent was substantially unable to manage his or her financial resources or resist fraud or undue influence. This section shall not apply to a decedent who, at any time following the act or acts described in paragraph (1) of subdivision (a), or the act or acts described in subdivision (b), was substantially able to manage his or her financial resources and to resist fraud or undue influence within the meaning of subdivision (b) of Section 1801 of the Probate Code and subdivision (b) of Section 39 of the Civil Code.

* * *

Tax Considerations: The tax structure in America today is an example of the restraint on the transfer of wealth. For example, the Internal Revenue Code currently allows a donor to exclude from taxable gifts transfers totaling $11,000 for each donee of a non-charitable gift (*see* Rev. Proc. 2001-71, 2004-50 I.R.B. 970). Inter vivos gifts will decrease the size of an individual's gross estate that would otherwise be subject to the estate tax rate of 47% in 2005, but returning to 55% if the tax is not repealed following 2010. *See* I.R.C. § 2001(c). And, yes, there is an exemption amount rising to $3,500,000 by 2009, but states are not obligated to index their own rates to correspond with this phase-out of the federal estate tax, thus providing continuation of restraints at the state level. There is also an incentive to transfer wealth to a spouse so as to qualify for the marital deduction, *see* I.R.C. § 2056, but in the case of a spouse who is not a citizen of the United States, the transfer must be in the form of a Qualified Domestic Trust to qualify for the deduction. *See* I.R.C. § 2056A. Under the current law, the generation-skipping tax restricts the amount that a decedent may be able to transfer to successive generations by imposing a tax on all amounts greater than the applicable exemption. *See* I.R.C. § 2601. If an heir makes a qualified disclaimer, *see* I.R.C. § 2518(b), he or she may save taxes, but such a disclaimer acts as a restraint on the intent of the decedent. Of course, there are multiple rules restricting the rights of a decedent to control property passing to others without adverse tax consequences. Attention to careful drafting to satisfy the rules is illustrated in the following decision.

Jackson v. United States
Supreme Court of the United States, 1964
376 U.S. 503, 84 S. Ct. 869

Mr. Justice WHITE delivered the opinion of the Court.

Since 1948 § 812(e)(1)(A) of the Internal Revenue Code of 1939 has allowed a 'marital deduction' from a decedent's gross taxable estate for the value of interests in property passing from the decedent to his surviving spouse.[1] Subsection (B) adds the qualification, however, that interests defined therein as 'terminable' shall not qualify as an interest in property to which the marital deduction applies.[2] The question raised by this case is whether the allowance provided by California law for the support of a widow during the settlement of her husband's estate is a terminable interest.

Petitioners are the widow-executrix and testamentary trustee under the will of George Richards who died a resident of California on May 27, 1951. Acting under the Probate Code of California, the state court, on June 30, 1952, allowed Mrs. Richards the sum of $3,000 per month from the corpus of the estate for her support and maintenance, beginning as of May 27, 1951, and continuing for a period of 24 months from that date. Under the terms of the order, an allowance of $42,000 had accrued during the 14 months since her husband's death. This amount, plus an additional $3,000 per month for the remainder of the two-year period, making a total of $72,000, was in fact paid to Mrs. Richards as widow's allowance.

On the federal estate tax return filed on behalf of the estate, the full $72,000 was claimed as a marital deduction under § 812(e) of the Internal Revenue Code of 1939. The deduction was disallowed, as was a claim for refund after payment of the deficiency, and the present suit for refund was then brought in the District Court. The District Court granted summary judgment for the United States, holding, on the au-

---

1. The deduction allowed is: 'An amount equal to the value of any interest in property which passes or has passed from the decedent to his surviving spouse, but only to the extent that such interest is included in determining the value of the gross estate.' 26 U.S.C. (1952 ed.) § 812(e)(1)(A).

2. Subsection (B) provides in pertinent part: 'Where, upon the lapse of time, upon the occurrence of an event or contingency, or upon the failure of an event or contingency to occur, such interest passing to the surviving spouse will terminate or fail, no deduction shall be allowed with respect to such interest—

'(i) if an interest in such property passes or has passed (for less than an adequate and full consideration in money or money's worth) from the decedent to any person other than such surviving spouse (or the estate of such spouse); and

'(ii) if by reason of such passing such person (or his heirs or assigns) may possess or enjoy any part of such property after such termination or failure of the interest so passing to the surviving spouse.' 26 U.S.C. (1952 ed.) § 812(e) (1)(B).

The marital deduction and terminable interest provisions of the 1954 Code are similar to those of its 1939 counterpart. See 26 U.S.C. (1958 ed.) § 2056(a) and (b).

thority of Cunha's Estate v. Commissioner, 9 Cir., 279 F.2d 292, that the allowance to the widow was a terminable interest and not deductible under the marital provision of the Internal Revenue Code. The Court of Appeals affirmed, 9 Cir., 317 F.2d 821, and we brought the case here because of an asserted conflict between the decision below and that of the Court of Appeals for the Fifth Circuit in United States v. First National Bank & Trust Co. of Augusta, 5 Cir., 297 F.2d 312. 375 U.S. 894, 84 S.Ct. 172, 11 L.Ed.2d 123. For the reasons given below, we affirm the decision of the Court of Appeals.

In enacting the Revenue Act of 1948, 62 Stat. 110, with its provision for the marital deduction, Congress left undisturbed § 812(b)(5) of the 1939 Code, which allowed an estate tax deduction, as an expense of administration, for amounts 'reasonably required and actually expended for the support during the settlement of the estate of those dependent upon the decedent.' 26 U.S.C. (1946 ed.) § 812(b)(5). As the legislative history shows, support payments under § 812(b)(5) were not to be treated as part of the marital deduction allowed by § 812(e)(1). * * * The Revenue Act of 1950, 64 Stat. 906, however, repealed § 812(b)(5) because, among other reasons, Congress believed the section resulted in discriminations in favor of States having liberal family allowances.[4] Thereafter allowances paid for the support of a widow during the settlement of an estate 'heretofore deductible under section 812(b) will be allowable as a marital deduction subject to the conditions and limitations of section 812(e).' S.Rep. No. 2375, 81st Cong., 2d Sess., p. 130, U.S.Congressional Service, 1950, p. 3191.

The 'conditions and limitations' of the marital deduction under § 812(e) are several but we need concern ourselves with only one aspect of § 812(e)(1)(B), which disallows the deduction of 'terminable' interests passing to the surviving spouse. It was conceded in the Court of Appeals that the right to the widow's allowance here involved is an interest in property passing from the decedent within the meaning of § 812(e)(3), that it is an interest to which the terminable interest rule of § 812(e)(1)(B) is applicable, and that the conditions set forth in (i) and (ii) of § 812(e)(1)(B) were satisfied under the decedent's will and codicils thereto. The issue, therefore, is whether the interest in property passing to Mrs. Richards as widow's allowance would 'terminate or fail' upon the 'lapse of time, upon the occurrence of an event or contingency, or upon the failure of an event or contingency to occur.'

We accept the Court of Appeals' description of the nature and characteristics of the widow's allowance under California law. In that State, the right to a widow's allowance is not a vested right and nothing accrues before the order granting it. The right to an allowance is lost when the one for whom it is asked has lost the status upon which the right depends. If a widow dies or remarries prior to securing an order for a widow's allowance, the right does not survive such death or remarriage. The amount of the widow's allowance which has accrued and is unpaid at the date of death of the widow is payable to her estate but the right to future payments abates upon her death. The remarriage of a widow subsequent to an order for an allowance likewise abates her right to future payments. 317 F.2d 821, 825.

---

4. The legislative history states: 'In practice (the support allowance deduction) has discriminated in favor of estates located in States which authorize liberal allowances for the support of dependents, and it has probably also tended to delay the settlement of estates.' S.Rep. No. 2375, 81st Cong., 2d Sess., p. 57.

In light of these characteristics of the California widow's allowance, Mrs. Richards did not have an indefeasible interest in property at the moment of her husband's death since either her death or remarriage would defeat it. If the order for support allowance had been entered on the day of her husband's death, her death or remarriage at any time within two years thereafter would terminate that portion of the interest allocable to the remainder of the two-year period. As of the date of Mr. Richards' death, therefore, the allowance was subject to failure or termination 'upon the occurrence of an event or contingency.' That the support order was entered in this case 14 months later does not, in our opinion, change the defeasible nature of the interest.

Petitioners ask us to judge the terminability of the widow's interest in property represented by her allowance as of the date of the Probate Court's order rather than as of the date of her husband's death. The court's order, they argue, unconditionally entitled the widow to $42,000 in accrued allowance of which she could not be deprived by either her death or remarriage. It is true that some courts have followed this path, * * * but it is difficult to accept an approach which would allow a deduction of $42,000 on the facts of this case, a deduction of $72,000 if the order had been entered at the end of two years from Mr. Richards' death and none at all if the order had been entered immediately upon his death. Moreover, judging deductibility as of the date of the Probate Court's order ignores the Senate Committee's admonition that in considering terminability of an interest for purposes of a marital deduction 'the situation is viewed as at the date of the decedent's death.' S.Rep.No. 1013, Part 2, 80th Cong., 2d Sess., p. 10. We prefer the course followed by both the Court of Appeals for the Ninth Circuit in Cunha's Estate, supra, and by the Court of Appeals for the Eighth Circuit in United States v. Quivey, 292 F.2d 252. Both courts have held the date of death of the testator to be the correct point of time from which to judge the nature of a widow's allowance for the purpose of deciding terminability and deductibility under §812(e)(1). This is in accord with the rule uniformly followed with regard to interests other than the widow's allowance, that qualification for the marital deduction must be determined as of the time of death. * * *

Our conclusion is confirmed by §812(e)(1)(D),[7] which saves from the operation of the terminable interest rule interests which by their terms may (but do not in fact) terminate only upon failure of the widow to survive her husband for a period not in excess of six months. The premise of this provision is that an interest passing to a widow is normally to be judged as of the time of the testator's death rather than at a later time when the condition imposed may be satisfied; hence the necessity to provide an exception to the rule in the case of a six months' survivorship contingency in a will.[8] A gift

---

7. 'For the purposes of subparagraph (B) an interest passing to the surviving spouse shall not be considered as an interest which will terminate or fail upon the death of such spouse if—

'(i) such death will cause a termination or failure of such interest only if it occurs within a period not exceeding six months after the decedent's death, or only if it occurs as a result of a common disaster resulting in the death of the decedent and the surviving spouse, or only if it occurs in the case of either such event; and

'(ii) such termination or failure does not in fact occur.' 26 U.S.C. (1952 ed.) §812(e)(1)(D).

8. The Senate Report accompanying the House bill which eventually became law states that 'Subparagraph (D) of section 812(e)(1) provides an exception to the terminable interest rule under subparagraph (B) of such section. This exception is for the purpose of allowing the marital deduction in certain cases where there is a contingency with respect to the interest passing to the surviving spouse under a common-disaster clause or similar clause in the decedent's will.' S.Rep. No. 1013, Part 2, 80th Cong., 2d Sess., p. 15.

conditioned upon eight months' survivorship, rather than six, is a nondeductible terminable interest for reasons which also disqualify the statutory widow's allowance in California where the widow must survive and remain unmarried at least to the date of an allowance order to become indefeasibly entitled to any widow's allowance at all.

Petitioners contend, however, that the sole purpose of the terminable-interest provisions of the Code is to assure that interests deducted from the estate of the deceased spouse will not also escape taxation in the estate of the survivor. This argument leads to the conclusion that since it is now clear that unless consumed or given away during Mrs. Richards' life, the entire $72,000 will be taxed to her estate, it should not be included in her husband's. But as we have already seen, there is no provision in the Code for deducting all terminable interests which become nonterminable at a later date and therefore taxable in the estate of the surviving spouse if not consumed or transferred. The examples cited in the legislative history make it clear that the determinative factor is not taxability to the surviving spouse but terminability as defined by the statute. * * * Under the view advanced by petitioners all cash allowances actually paid would fall outside §812(e)(1) (B); on two different occasions the Senate has refused to give its approval to House-passed amendments to the 1954 Code which would have made the terminable-interest rule inapplicable to all widow's allowances actually paid within specified periods of time. * * *

We are mindful that the general goal of the marital deduction provisions was to achieve uniformity of federal estate tax impact between those States with community property laws and those without them. * * * But the device of the marital deduction which Congress chose to achieve uniformity was knowingly hedged with limitations, including the terminable-interest rule. These provisions may be imperfect devices to achieve the desired end, but they are the means which Congress chose. To the extent it was thought desirable to modify the rigors of the terminable-interest rule, exceptions to the rule were written into the Code. Courts should hesitate to provide still another exception by straying so far from the statutory language as to allow a marital deduction for the widow's allowance provided by the California statute. * * * The achievement of the purposes of the marital deduction is dependent to a great degree upon the careful drafting of wills; we have no fear that our decision today will prevent either the full utilization of the marital deduction or the proper support of widows during the pendency of an estate proceeding.

Affirmed.

Mr. Justice DOUGLAS dissents.

II. Protection of Issue

A. Standing

Issue is an elusive term, especially in an age of advanced biological procedures through which birth may occur many years after the death of the donor of sperm or egg. *See, e.g.,* Hecht v. Superior Court, 16 Cal. App. 4th 836, 20 Cal. Rptr. 2d 275 (1993) (man allowed to bequeath sperm to girlfriend for possible conception); *In re* Parentage of J.M.K., 121 Wash. App. 578, 89 P.3d 309 (2004) (man precluded as putative father for failure to satisfy statute requiring that artificial insemination agreement be in writing), *rev'd by*, 119 P.3d 840 (Wash. 2005). Statutes such as the Uniform Parentage Act (2002) and the Uniform Status of Children of Assisted Conception Act (2003) seek to provide a presumption of paternity and a set of rules that courts may follow, but there is still little uniformity among the states with respect to issue and parentage. The following case is illustrative.

Woodward v. Commissioner of Social Security

Massachusetts Supreme Judicial Court, 2002
760 N.E.2d 257, 435 Mass. 536

MARSHALL, C.J.

The United States District Court for the District of Massachusetts has certified the following question to this court. See S.J.C. Rule 1:03, as appearing in 382 Mass. 700 (1981).

> If a married man and woman arrange for sperm to be withdrawn from the husband for the purpose of artificially impregnating the wife, and the woman is impregnated with that sperm after the man, her husband, has died, will children resulting from such pregnancy enjoy the inheritance rights of natural children under Massachusetts' law of intestate succession?

We answer the certified question as follows: In certain limited circumstances, a child * * * resulting from posthumous reproduction may enjoy the inheritance rights of "issue" under the Massachusetts intestacy statute. These limited circumstances exist where, as a threshold matter, the surviving parent or the child's other legal representative demonstrates a genetic relationship between the child and the decedent. The survivor or representative must then establish both that the decedent affirmatively consented to posthumous conception and to the support of any resulting child. Even where such circumstances exist, time limitations may preclude commencing a claim for succession rights on behalf of a posthumously conceived child. Because the government has conceded that the timeliness of the wife's paternity action under our intestacy law is irrelevant to her Federal appeal, we do not address that question today.

The United States District Court judge has not asked us to determine whether the circumstances giving rise to succession rights for posthumously conceived children apply here. In addition, she has removed from our consideration the question whether the paternity judgment obtained by the wife in this case was valid. See note 6, infra. We answer only the certified question. *See* Canal Elec. Co. v. Westinghouse Elec. Corp., 406 Mass. 369, 370 n. 1, 548 N.E.2d 182 (1990); Cabot Corp. v. Baddour, 394 Mass. 720, 721, 477 N.E.2d 399 (1985).

* * *

The undisputed facts and relevant procedural history are as follows. In January, 1993, about three and one-half years after they were married, Lauren Woodward and Warren Woodward were informed that the husband had leukemia. At the time, the couple was childless. Advised that the husband's leukemia treatment might leave him sterile, the Woodwards arranged for a quantity of the husband's semen to be medically withdrawn and preserved, in a process commonly known as "sperm banking." The husband then underwent a bone marrow transplant. The treatment was not successful. The husband died in October, 1993, and the wife was appointed administratrix of his estate.

In October, 1995, the wife gave birth to twin girls. The children were conceived through artificial insemination using the husband's preserved semen. In January, 1996, the wife applied for two forms of Social Security survivor benefits: "child's" benefits under 42 U.S.C. § 402(d)(1) (1994 & Supp. V 1999), and "mother's" benefits under 42 U.S.C. § 402(g)(1) (1994).[3]

The Social Security Administration (SSA) rejected the wife's claims on the ground that she had not established that the twins were the husband's "children" within the meaning of the Act.[4] In February, 1996, as she pursued a series of appeals from the SSA decision, the wife filed a "complaint for correction of birth record" in the Probate and Family Court against the clerk of the city of Beverly, seeking to add her deceased husband as the "father" on the twins' birth certificates. In October, 1996, a judge in the Probate and Family Court entered a judgment of paternity and an order to amend both birth certificates declaring the deceased husband to be the children's father. In his judgment of paternity, the Probate Court judge did not make findings of fact, other than to state that he "accepts the [s]tipulations of [v]oluntary [a]cknowledgment of [p]arentage of [the children] ... executed by [the wife] as [m]other, and [the wife], [a]dministratrix of the [e]state of [the husband], for father." See G.L. c. 209C, § 11. * * *

The wife presented the judgment of paternity and the amended birth certificates to the SSA, but the agency remained unpersuaded. A United States administrative law judge, hearing the wife's claims de novo, concluded, among other things, that the children did not qualify for benefits because they "are not entitled to inherit from [the husband] under the Massachusetts intestacy and paternity laws."[6] The appeals council of

---

3. At the time of his death, the husband was a fully insured individual under the United States Social Security Act (Act). Section 402(d)(1) of 42 U.S.C. provides "child's" benefits to dependent children of deceased parents who die fully insured under the Act. See 42 U.S.C. § 402(d)(1); 20 C.F.R. § 404.350. Section 402(g)(1) of 42 U.S.C. provides "mother's" benefits to the widow of an individual who died fully insured under the Act, if, inter alia, she has care of a child or children entitled to child's benefits. See 42 U.S.C. § 402(g)(1); 20 C.F.R. § 404.339 (2001). Thus, the wife's eligibility for Social Security survivor benefits hinges on her children's eligibility for such benefits.

4. The Act defines children, in pertinent part, as the "child or legally adopted child of an individual." See 42 U.S.C. § 416(e). The term "child" includes "natural child." See 20 C.F.R. § 404.355. The Act also establishes presumptions of dependency for certain classes of children, as well as other mechanisms for establishing dependency. As stated in the certification order, the wife's

> appeal centers on only one possible basis for eligibility, which is that under SSA regulations the children are eligible if they would be treated as [the husband's] natural children for the disposition of his personal property under the Massachusetts law of intestate succession. See 42 U.S.C. §§ 402(d)(3) and 416(h)(2)(A); 20 C.F.R. § 404.355(a)(1); 20 C.F.R. § 404.361(a).

6. The administrative law judge reasoned that the children were not "ascertainable heirs as defined by the intestacy laws of Massachusetts," because they were neither born nor in utero at the date of the husband's death and "the statutes and cases contemplated an ascertainable child, one who had been conceived prior to the father's death." He also found that the children could not inherit as the husband's children under Massachusetts intestacy law because the evidence failed to establish that the husband, before his death, either acknowledged the children as his own or intended to contribute to their support. See G.L. c. 190, § 7. Further, the administrative law judge held that the SSA was not bound by the judgment of paternity because that judgment "is not only inconsistent with Massachusetts paternity laws but also constitutes a proceeding to which the [SSA] was not a party." See Soc. Sec. Rul. 83-37c; Gray v. Richardson, 474 F.2d 1370 (6th Cir.1973). In her certification order, the United State District Court judge affirmed that, as a matter of Federal law, the administrative law judge "was not compelled to give dispositive weight to the Probate Court judgment." She did not ask us to determine whether the paternity judgment is "inconsistent with Massachusetts paternity laws," as the administrative law judge concluded.

the SSA affirmed the administrative law judge's decision, which thus became the commissioner's final decision for purposes of judicial review. The wife appealed to the United States District Court for the District of Massachusetts, seeking a declaratory judgment to reverse the commissioner's ruling.

The United States District Court judge certified the above question to this court because "[t]he parties agree that a determination of these children's rights under the law of Massachusetts is dispositive of the case and ... no directly applicable Massachusetts precedent exists."

* * *

We have been asked to determine the inheritance rights under Massachusetts law of children conceived from the gametes[7] of a deceased individual and his or her surviving spouse.[8] We have not previously been asked to consider whether our intestacy statute accords inheritance rights to posthumously conceived genetic children. Nor has any American court of last resort considered, in a published opinion, the question of posthumously conceived genetic children's inheritance rights under other States' intestacy laws.[9]

This case presents a narrow set of circumstances, yet the issues it raises are far reaching. Because the law regarding the rights of posthumously conceived children is unsettled, the certified question is understandably broad. Moreover, the parties have articulated extreme positions. The wife's principal argument is that, by virtue of their genetic connection with the decedent, posthumously conceived children must always be permitted to enjoy the inheritance rights of the deceased parent's children under our law of intestate succession. The government's principal argument is that, because posthumously conceived children are not "in being" as of the date of the parent's death, they are always barred from enjoying such inheritance rights.

Neither party's position is tenable. In this developing and relatively uncharted area of human relations, bright-line rules are not favored unless the applicable statute requires them. The Massachusetts intestacy statute does not. Neither the statute's "posthumous

---

7. We use the term "gamete" here to denote "[a]ny germ cell, whether ovum or spermatozoon." Stedman's Medical Dictionary 701 (26th ed.1995).

8. Although the certified question asks us to consider an unsettled question of law concerning the paternity of children conceived from a deceased male's gametes, we see no principled reason that our conclusions should not apply equally to children posthumously conceived from a deceased female's gametes.

9. We are aware of only two cases that have addressed, in varying degrees, the question before us. In Hecht v. Superior Court, 16 Cal.App.4th 836, 20 Cal.Rptr.2d 275 (1993), the California Court of Appeal considered, among other things, whether a decedent's sperm was "property" that could be bequeathed to his girl friend. Id. at 847, 20 Cal.Rptr.2d 275. In answering in the affirmative, the court noted, in dicta and without elaboration, that, under the provisions of California's Probate Code, "it is unlikely that the estate would be subject to claims with respect to any such children" resulting from insemination of the girl friend with the decedent's sperm. Id. at 859, 20 Cal.Rptr.2d 275. In Matter of Estate of Kolacy, 332 N.J.Super. 593, 753 A.2d 1257 (2000), the plaintiff brought a declaratory judgment action to have her children, who were conceived after the death of her husband, declared the intestate heirs of her deceased husband in order to pursue the children's claims for survivor benefits with the Social Security Administration. A New Jersey Superior Court judge held that, in circumstances where the decedent left no estate and an adjudication of parentage did not unfairly intrude on the rights of others or cause "serious problems" with the orderly administration of estates, the children would be entitled to inherit under the State's intestacy law. Id. at 602, 753 A.2d 1257.

children" provision, see G.L. c. 190, §8, nor any other provision of our intestacy law limits the class of posthumous children to those in utero at the time of the decedent's death. Cf. La. Civ.Code Ann. art. 939 (West 2000) ("A successor must exist at the death of the decedent").[10] On the other hand, with the act of procreation now separated from coitus, posthumous reproduction can occur under a variety of conditions that may conflict with the purposes of the intestacy law and implicate other firmly established State and individual interests. We look to our intestacy law to resolve these tensions.

* * *

We begin our analysis with an overview of Massachusetts intestacy law. In our Commonwealth, the devolution of real and personal property in intestacy is neither a natural nor a constitutional right. It is a privilege conferred by statute. Merchants Nat'l Bank v. Merchants Nat'l Bank, 318 Mass. 563, 573, 62 N.E.2d 831 (1945). Our intestacy statute "excludes all rules of law which might otherwise be operative. It impliedly repealed all preexisting statutes and supersedes the common law." Cassidy v. Truscott, 287 Mass. 515, 521, 192 N.E. 164 (1934).

Section 1 of the intestacy statute directs that, if a decedent "leaves issue," such "issue" will inherit a fixed portion of his real and personal property, subject to debts and expenses, the rights of the surviving spouse, and other statutory payments not relevant here. See G.L. c. 190, §1. * * * To answer the certified question, then, we must first determine whether the twins are the "issue" of the husband.

The intestacy statute does not define "issue." However, in the context of intestacy the term "issue" means all lineal (genetic) descendants, and now includes both marital and nonmarital * * * descendants. See generally S.M. Dunphy, Probate Law and Practice §8.5, at 123 (2d ed. 1997 & Supp.2001), and cases cited. * * * See also G.L. c. 4, §7, Sixteenth ("Issue, as applied to the descent of estates, shall include all the lawful lineal descendants of the ancestor"); Powers v. Wilkinson, 399 Mass. 650, 662, 506 N.E.2d 842 (1987). The term "'[d]escendants'... has long been held to mean persons 'who by consanguinity trace their lineage to the designated ancestor.'" Lockwood v. Adamson, 409 Mass. 325, 329, 566 N.E.2d 96 (1991), quoting Evarts v. Davis, 348 Mass. 487, 489, 204 N.E.2d 454 (1965).

Turning to "issue" who are the nonmarital children of an intestate, the intestacy statute treats different classes of nonmarital children differently based on the presumed ease of establishing their consanguinity with the deceased parent. A nonmarital child is presumptively the child of his or her mother and is entitled by virtue of this presumption to enjoy inheritance rights as her issue. G.L. c. 190, §5. However, to enjoy inheritance rights as the issue of a deceased father, a nonmarital child, in the absence of the father's acknowledgment of paternity or marriage to the mother, must obtain a judicial determination that he or she is the father's child. G.L. c. 190, §7. The general purpose of such a specific adjudication requirement is to ensure that wealth passes from and to the actual family. See generally 2 T.H. Belknap, Newhall's

---

10. The cases relied on by the administrative law judge do no more than affirm the general common-law rule that heirs are fixed as of the date of death, see National Shawmut Bank v. Joy, 315 Mass. 457, 467, 53 N.E.2d 113 (1944); Gorey v. Guarente, 303 Mass. 569, 576–577, 22 N.E.2d 99 (1939), and that children born after death within the probable period of gestation may inherit as issue of the deceased parent in exception to the general rule. See Bowen v. Hoxie, 137 Mass. 527, 528–529, 1884 WL 10644 (1884). See also Waverley Trust Co., petitioner, 268 Mass. 181, 183, 167 N.E. 274 (1929). Our intestacy statute supersedes any Massachusetts common law in this area. * * *

Settlement of Estates and Fiduciary Law in Massachusetts § 24:2, at 38–42 (5th ed.1997). We held, at a time when the means for establishing the paternity of a child were less certain than they are today, that such disparate treatment between the mother and the father of a child advanced the Legislature's interests in preventing fraudulent claims against the estate and in administering estates in an orderly fashion. See Lowell v. Kowalski, 380 Mass. 663, 668, 405 N.E.2d 135 (1980) ("distinction between rights to inherit from a natural father and rights to inherit from a natural mother may properly be based on the greater difficulty of proving paternity than of proving maternity").

The "posthumous children" provision of the intestacy statute, G.L. c. 190, § 8, is yet another expression of the Legislature's intent to preserve wealth for consanguineous descendants. That section provides that "[p]osthumous children shall be considered as living at the death of their parent." The Legislature, however, has left the term "posthumous children" undefined. The Massachusetts intestacy statute originally made no provision for after-born children. See, e.g., St. 1805, c. 90 (approved Mar. 12, 1806). Then in Hall v. Hancock, 15 Pick. 255, 1834 WL 2638 (1834), in the context of a will contest, this court held that a child who was presumptively in utero as of the date of the decedent's death was a child "in being" as of the date of the decedent's death "in all cases where it will be for the benefit of such child to be so considered." Id. at 257, 258. Two years later, the Legislature enacted the "posthumous children" provision of the intestacy statute, bringing that devolution mechanism into conformity with our decision concerning wills. See Rev. St. 1836, c. 61, § 13. Despite numerous later amendments to our intestacy laws, the "posthumous children" provision has remained essentially unchanged for 165 years. * * *

The Massachusetts intestacy statute thus does not contain an express, affirmative requirement that posthumous children must "be in existence" as of the date of the decedent's death. The Legislature could surely have enacted such a provision had it desired to do so. Cf. La. Civ.Code Ann. art. 939 (effective July 1, 1999) (West 2000) ("A successor must exist at the death of the decedent"). See also N.D. Cent.Code Ann. 14-18-04 (Michie 1997) ("A person who dies before a conception using that person's sperm or egg is not a parent of any resulting child born of the conception"). We must therefore determine whether, under our intestacy law, there is any reason that children conceived after the decedent's death who are the decedent's direct genetic descendants—that is, children who "by consanguinity trace their lineage to the designated ancestor"—may not enjoy the same succession rights as children conceived before the decedent's death who are the decedent's direct genetic descendants. Lockwood v. Adamson, supra.

To answer that question we consider whether and to what extent such children may take as intestate heirs of the deceased genetic parent consistent with the purposes of the intestacy law, and not by any assumptions of the common law. See Cassidy v. Truscott, supra at 520–521, 192 N.E. 164. In the absence of express legislative directives, we construe the Legislature's purposes from statutory indicia and judicial decisions in a manner that advances the purposes of the intestacy law. Houghton v. Dickinson, 196 Mass. 389, 391, 82 N.E. 481 (1907).

The question whether posthumously conceived genetic children may enjoy inheritance rights under the intestacy statute implicates three powerful State interests: the best interests of children, the State's interest in the orderly administration of estates, and the reproductive rights of the genetic parent. Our task is to balance and harmonize these interests to effect the Legislature's over-all purposes.

* * * First and foremost we consider the overriding legislative concern to promote the best interests of children. "The protection of minor children, most especially those who may be stigmatized by their 'illegitimate' status ... has been a hallmark of legislative action and of the jurisprudence of this court." L.W.K. v. E.R.C., 432 Mass. 438, 447–448, 735 N.E.2d 359 (2000). Repeatedly, forcefully, and unequivocally, the Legislature has expressed its will that all children be "entitled to the same rights and protections of the law" regardless of the accidents of their birth. G.L. c. 209C, §1. See G.L. c. 119, §1 ("It is hereby declared to be the policy of the commonwealth to direct its efforts, first, to the strengthening and encouragement of family life for the protection and care of children ..."). Among the many rights and protections vouchsafed to all children are rights to financial support from their parents and their parents' estates. See G.L. c. 119A, §1 ("It is the public policy of this commonwealth that dependent children shall be maintained, as completely as possible, from the resources of their parents, thereby relieving or avoiding, at least in part, the burden borne by the citizens of the commonwealth"); G.L. c. 191, §20 (establishing inheritance rights for pretermitted children); G.L. c. 196, §§1–3 (permitting allowances from estate to widows and minor children); G.L. c. 209C, §14 (permitting paternity claims to be commenced prior to birth). See also G.L. c. 190, §§1–3, 5, 7–8 (intestacy rights). * * *

We also consider that some of the assistive reproductive technologies that make posthumous reproduction possible have been widely known and practiced for several decades. See generally Banks, Traditional Concepts and Nontraditional Conceptions: Social Security Survivor's Benefits for Posthumously Conceived Children, 32 Loy. L.A. L.Rev. 251, 267–273 (1999). In that time, the Legislature has not acted to narrow the broad statutory class of posthumous children to restrict posthumously conceived children from taking in intestacy. Moreover, the Legislature has in great measure affirmatively supported the assistive reproductive technologies that are the only means by which these children can come into being. See G.L. c. 46, §4B (artificial insemination of married woman). See also G.L. c. 175, §47H; G.L. c. 176A, §8K; G.L. c. 176B, §4J; G.L. c. 176G, §4 (insurance coverage for infertility treatments). We do not impute to the Legislature the inherently irrational conclusion that assistive reproductive technologies are to be encouraged while a class of children who are the fruit of that technology are to have fewer rights and protections than other children.

In short, we cannot, absent express legislative directive, accept the commissioner's position that the historical context of G.L. c. 190, §8, dictates as a matter of law that all posthumously conceived children are automatically barred from taking under their deceased donor parent's intestate estate. We have consistently construed statutes to effectuate the Legislature's overriding purpose to promote the welfare of all children, notwithstanding restrictive common-law rules to the contrary. See, e.g., L.W.K. v. E.R.C., supra at 447, 735 N.E.2d 359; Adoption of Tammy, 416 Mass. 205, 210, 619 N.E.2d 315 (1993); Powers v. Wilkinson, 399 Mass. 650, 661–662, 506 N.E.2d 842 (1987); Powers v. Steele, 394 Mass. 306, 310, 475 N.E.2d 395 (1985); Hall v. Hancock, 32 Mass. 255, 15 Pick. 255 (1834). * * * Posthumously conceived children may not come into the world the way the majority of children do. But they are children nonetheless. We may assume that the Legislature intended that such children be "entitled," in so far as possible, "to the same rights and protections of the law" as children conceived before death. See G.L. c. 209C, §1.

* * * However, in the context of our intestacy laws, the best interests of the posthumously conceived child, while of great importance, are not in themselves conclusive.

They must be balanced against other important State interests, not the least of which is the protection of children who are alive or conceived before the intestate parent's death. In an era in which serial marriages, serial families, and blended families are not uncommon, according succession rights under our intestacy laws to posthumously conceived children may, in a given case, have the potential to pit child against child and family against family. Any inheritance rights of posthumously conceived children will reduce the intestate share available to children born prior to the decedent's death. See G.L. c. 190, § 3(1). Such considerations, among others, lead us to examine a second important legislative purpose: to provide certainty to heirs and creditors by effecting the orderly, prompt, and accurate administration of intestate estates. See generally S.M. Dunphy, Probate Law and Practice § 8.1, at 115 (2d ed.1997).

The intestacy statute furthers the Legislature's administrative goals in two principal ways: (1) by requiring certainty of filiation between the decedent and his issue, and (2) by establishing limitations periods for the commencement of claims against the intestate estate. In answering the certified question, we must consider each of these requirements of the intestacy statute in turn.

First, as we have discussed, our intestacy law mandates that, absent the father's acknowledgment of paternity or marriage to the mother, a nonmarital child must obtain a judicial determination of paternity as a prerequisite to succeeding to a portion of the father's intestate estate. Both the United States Supreme Court and this court have long recognized that the State's strong interest in preventing fraudulent claims justifies certain disparate classifications among nonmarital children based on the relative difficulty of accurately determining a child's direct lineal ancestor. See Lowell v. Kowalski, 380 Mass. 663, 668–669, 405 N.E.2d 135 (1980). See also Trimble v. Gordon, 430 U.S. 762, 771, 97 S.Ct. 1459, 52 L.Ed.2d 31 (1977).

* * *

We now turn to the second way in which the Legislature has met its administrative goals: the establishment of a limitations period for bringing paternity claims against the intestate estate. Our discussion of this important goal, however, is necessarily circumscribed by the procedural posture of this case and by the terms of the certified question. The certification record discloses that, after one unsuccessful insemination attempt, the wife conceived using her deceased husband's sperm approximately sixteen months after his death. The children were born approximately two years after the husband's death, and the paternity action (in the form of a "complaint for correction of birth record") was filed approximately four months after the children's birth. Both the SSA and the administrative law judge concluded that the wife and the children were not entitled to Social Security survivor benefits because, among other things, the paternity actions were not brought within the one-year period for commencing paternity claims mandated by the intestacy statute. See G.L. c. 190, § 7.

However, in his brief to this court, the commissioner represented that he had informed the United States District Court judge that the wife "had been advised that she need not address" the timeliness issue on appeal in light of a change in Federal regulations. Specifically, the SSA has amended its regulations to read:

> We will not apply any State inheritance law requirement that an action to establish paternity must be taken within a specified period of time measured from the worker's death or the child's birth, or that an action to establish paternity must have been started or completed before the worker's death....

20 C.F.R. § 404.355(b)(2). * * * We understand the commissioner's representation to be a concession that the timeliness of the wife's Massachusetts paternity actions is not relevant to the Federal law question whether the wife's children will be considered the husband's "natural children" for Social Security benefits purposes, and that therefore whatever we say on this issue has no bearing on the wife's Federal action. We also note that the certified question does not specifically address the limitations matter and that, in their briefs to this court, the parties referred to the limitations question only peripherally. * * *

Nevertheless, the limitations question is inextricably tied to consideration of the intestacy statute's administrative goals. In the case of posthumously conceived children, the application of the one-year limitations period of G.L. c. 190, § 7 is not clear; it may pose significant burdens on the surviving parent, and consequently on the child. * * * It requires, in effect, that the survivor make a decision to bear children while in the freshness of grieving. It also requires that attempts at conception succeed quickly. Cf. Commentary, Modern Reproductive Technologies: Legal Issues Concerning Cryopreservation and Posthumous Conception, 17 J. Legal Med. 547, 549 (1996) ("It takes an average of seven insemination attempts over 4.4 menstrual cycles to establish pregnancy"). Because the resolution of the time constraints question is not required here, it must await the appropriate case, should one arise.

* * * Finally, the question certified to us implicates a third important State interest: to honor the reproductive choices of individuals. We need not address the wife's argument that her reproductive rights would be infringed by denying succession rights to her children under our intestacy law. Nothing in the record even remotely suggests that she was prevented by the State from choosing to conceive children using her deceased husband's semen. The husband's reproductive rights are a more complicated matter.

In A.Z. v. B.Z., 431 Mass. 150, 725 N.E.2d 1051 (2000), we considered certain issues surrounding the disposition of frozen preembryos. A woman sought to enforce written agreements between herself and her former husband. The wife argued that these agreements permitted her to implant frozen preembryos created with the couple's gametes during the marriage, even in the event of their divorce. We declined to enforce the agreements. Persuasive to us, among other factors, was the lack of credible evidence of the husband's "true intention" regarding the disposition of the frozen preembryos, and the changed family circumstance resulting from the couple's divorce. See id. at 158–159, 725 N.E.2d 1051. Recognizing that our laws strongly affirm the value of bodily and reproductive integrity, we held that "forced procreation is not an area amenable to judicial enforcement." Id. at 160, 725 N.E.2d 1051. In short, A.Z. v. B.Z., supra, recognized that individuals have a protected right to control the use of their gametes.

Consonant with the principles identified in A.Z. v. B.Z., supra, a decedent's silence, or his equivocal indications of a desire to parent posthumously, "ought not to be construed as consent." See Schiff, Arising from the Dead: Challenges of Posthumous Procreation, 75 N.C. L.Rev. 901, 951 (1997). * * * The prospective donor parent must clearly and unequivocally consent not only to posthumous reproduction but also to the support of any resulting child. Cf. Paternity of Cheryl, 434 Mass. 23, 37, 746 N.E.2d 488 (2001) ("The law places on men the burden to consider carefully the permanent consequences that flow from an acknowledgment of paternity"). After the donor-parent's death, the burden rests with the surviving parent, or the posthumously conceived child's other legal representative, to prove the deceased genetic parent's affirmative consent to both requirements for posthumous parentage: posthumous reproduction and the support of any resulting child.

This two-fold consent requirement arises from the nature of alternative reproduction itself. It will not always be the case that a person elects to have his or her gametes medically preserved to create "issue" posthumously. A man, for example, may preserve his semen for myriad reasons, including, among others: to reproduce after recovery from medical treatment, to reproduce after an event that leaves him sterile, or to reproduce when his spouse has a genetic disorder or otherwise cannot have or safely bear children. That a man has medically preserved his gametes for use by his spouse thus may indicate only that he wished to reproduce after some contingency while he was alive, and not that he consented to the different circumstance of creating a child after his death. Uncertainty as to consent may be compounded by the fact that medically preserved semen can remain viable for up to ten years after it was first extracted, long after the original decision to preserve the semen has passed and when such changed circumstances as divorce, remarriage, and a second family may have intervened. See Banks, Traditional Concepts and Nontraditional Conceptions: Social Security Survivor's Benefits for Posthumously Conceived Children, 32 Loy. L.A. L.Rev. 251, 270 (1999). * * *

Such circumstances demonstrate the inadequacy of a rule that would make the mere genetic tie of the decedent to any posthumously conceived child, or the decedent's mere election to preserve gametes, sufficient to bind his intestate estate for the benefit of any posthumously conceived child. Without evidence that the deceased intestate parent affirmatively consented (1) to the posthumous reproduction and (2) to support any resulting child, a court cannot be assured that the intestacy statute's goal of fraud prevention is satisfied.

As expressed in our intestacy and paternity laws, sound public policy dictates the requirements we have outlined above. Legal parentage imposes substantial obligations on adults for the welfare of children. Where two adults engage in the act of sexual intercourse, it is a matter of common sense and logic, expressed in well-established law, to charge them with parental responsibilities for the child who is the natural, even if unintended, consequence of their actions. Where conception results from a third-party medical procedure using a deceased person's gametes, it is entirely consistent with our laws on children, parentage, and reproductive freedom to place the burden on the surviving parent (or the posthumously conceived child's other legal representative) to demonstrate the genetic relationship of the child to the decedent and that the intestate consented both to reproduce posthumously and to support any resulting child.

* * *

The certified question does not require us to specify what proof would be sufficient to establish a successful claim under our intestacy law on behalf of a posthumously conceived child. Nor have we been asked to determine whether the wife has met her burden of proof. The record reveals that the administrative law judge repeatedly requested that the wife provide objective corroboration of her claim that the husband consented to father children after his death.[24] The administrative law judge's opinion indicates that he

---

24. In pertinent part, the factual record contains a brief affidavit that the wife submitted to the Probate Court judge in her action to amend the children's birth records, a physician's letter that was submitted in that action, and a transcript of the wife's testimony before the administrative law judge. The wife's affidavit attests only that the husband's sperm was extracted and preserved "because my husband and I wanted to have children from our union." The two-sentence notarized physician's letter, addressed to the wife's attorney, was from the director of Reproductive En-

was willing to consider "additional declarations or written statements from the decedent's family, [the wife's] family, financial records or records from the fertility institute that demonstrate any acknowledgment [of the children] made by [the husband]." Cf. Higgins v. Ripley, 16 Mass.App.Ct. 928, 450 N.E.2d 186 (1983); Wrenn v. Harris, 503 F.Supp. 223, 226–227 (D.Mass.1980). Perhaps because the law was unsettled at the time, the wife's counsel took the position that the paternity judgment and the birth certificates were sufficient, and that no further evidence was required. In the wife's Probate Court action, however, the judge held the husband to be the "father" of the children, but did not make any specific findings to support that determination. Nor did he determine whether the husband intended to support the wife's children. Moreover, although a birth certificate is prima facie evidence of the facts recorded therein, G.L. c. 46, § 19, under our laws, genetic and legal parentage are not always coterminous. See G.L. c. 210 (adoption statute).

It is undisputed in this case that the husband is the genetic father of the wife's children. However, for the reasons stated above, that fact, in itself, cannot be sufficient to establish that the husband is the children's legal father for purposes of the devolution and distribution of his intestate property. In the United States District Court, the wife may come forward with other evidence as to her husband's consent to posthumously conceive children. She may come forward with evidence of his consent to support such children. We do not speculate as to the sufficiency of evidence she may submit at trial.

* * *

We feel constrained to comment on the judgment of paternity and the issuance of the amended birth certificates. The Probate and Family Court judge should not have entered the paternity judgment, or ordered the husband's name added to the birth certificates, on the record the mother presented. The mother sought to establish her deceased husband's paternity of the twins by bringing a complaint to amend birth records against the clerk of the city of Beverly (who, according to the judgment of paternity, did not object to the action). Where an estate is at issue—which will always be the case where a parent is deceased—notice of the action to establish legal parentage should be given to every other interested party, including the potential heirs who would have taken but for the posthumous creation of the children. See Mass. R. Civ. P. 19(a)(2), 365 Mass. 765 (1974) (joinder of interested persons); Mass. R. Dom. Rel. P. 19 (West 2001) (same); Rodrigues v. Rodrigues, 286 Mass. 77, 83, 190 N.E. 20 (1934). See also Sondra S. v. Jay O., 126 Misc.2d 322, 327–328, 482 N.Y.S.2d 660 (Fam.Ct.1984) (proceeding to establish deceased father's paternity must be adversary proceeding, with notice given to all interested parties). In this case, no such notice was given. * * *

The record also discloses that the wife sought to bind the husband's estate for the benefit of her posthumously conceived children by filing stipulations of voluntary acknowledgment of parentage executed by herself as mother and by herself as administra-

---

docrinology and Fertility Services of Malden Hospital. He wrote that, on February 3, 1995, the wife "had a twin pregnancy" as a result of her insemination with the husband's "frozen/thawed semen" and that "[w]e were notified that she delivered twins in October, 1995." Before the administrative law judge the wife testified only that she and the husband had discussed with doctors whether she would "be able to have children, [the husband's] children" should the husband's bone marrow transplant not succeed. At the time, the couple had been told that the husband's leukemia treatments might render him sterile, if he survived. She further testified that the husband "agreed" with her that "if something should happen ... I would still be able to have his children."

trix of the husband's estate. See G.L. c. 209C, § 11. The Probate and Family Court judge should not have considered these stipulations, much less grounded his paternity judgment on them. Neither the statutory powers granted to administrators, see, e.g., G.L. c. 195, § 5A, nor the Massachusetts intestacy and paternity laws permit such procedures to establish paternity. See, e.g., G.L. c. 209C, § 11 (requiring voluntary acknowledgments of paternity to be signed by both parents).

* * *

For the second time this term, we have been confronted with novel questions involving the rights of children born from assistive reproductive technologies. See Culliton v. Beth Israel Deaconess Med. Ctr., 435 Mass. 285, 756 N.E.2d 1133 (2001). As these technologies advance, the number of children they produce will continue to multiply. So, too, will the complex moral, legal, social, and ethical questions that surround their birth. The questions present in this case cry out for lengthy, careful examination outside the adversary process, which can only address the specific circumstances of each controversy that presents itself. They demand a comprehensive response reflecting the considered will of the people.

In the absence of statutory directives, we have answered the certified question by identifying and harmonizing the important State interests implicated therein in a manner that advances the Legislature's over-all purposes. In so doing, we conclude that limited circumstances may exist, consistent with the mandates of our Legislature, in which posthumously conceived children may enjoy the inheritance rights of "issue" under our intestacy law. These limited circumstances exist where, as a threshold matter, the surviving parent or the child's other legal representative demonstrates a genetic relationship between the child and the decedent. The survivor or representative must then establish both that the decedent affirmatively consented to posthumous conception and to the support of any resulting child. Even where such circumstances exist, time limitations may preclude commencing a claim for succession rights on behalf of a posthumously conceived child. In any action brought to establish such inheritance rights, notice must be given to all interested parties.

The Reporter of Decisions is to furnish attested copies of this opinion to the clerk of this court. The clerk in turn will transmit one copy, under the seal of this court, to the clerk of the United States District Court for the District of Massachusetts, as the answer to the question certified, and will also transmit a copy to each party.

Uniform Parentage Act (2003)

§ 707. Parental Status of Deceased Individual.

If an individual who consented in a record to be a parent by assisted reproduction dies before placement of eggs, sperm, or embryos, the deceased individual is not a parent of the resulting child unless the deceased spouse consented in a record that if assisted reproduction were to occur after death, the deceased individual would be a parent of the child.

Notes

Restatement (Third) of Property, Wills and Other Donative Transfers, § 2.5, Comment l (1999) (Children produced by assisted reproductive technologies), provides that a child must be born within a reasonable time after the decedent's death in circumstances that indicate that the decedent would have approved of the child's right to inherit. The California Probate Code §6453 (Natural parents), provides that no parent and child relationship may exist unless "[i]t was impossible for the father to hold out the child as his own and paternity is established by clear and convincing evidence." If an issue is born during the lifetime of the decedent or born after the death of the decedent and the issue alleges that he or she has standing as a child, what would be the legal arguments by which the child could inherit from the estate? Certainly, the child may inherit as an intestate heir, have standing to contest any Last Will and Testament, and be able to take under any valid Will provisions relating to issue. In addition, once having standing, the issue may be a pretermitted heir.

B. Pretermitted Heirs

In re Estate of Laura
Supreme Court of New Hampshire, 1997
141 N.H. 628, 690 A.2d 1011

THAYER, Justice.

The testator, Edward R. Laura, Sr., died on August 23, 1990. The petitioners, two generations of the testator's heirs who were excluded from his will, appeal a decision of the Rockingham County Probate Court (Maher, J.), approving the order of the Master (Gerald Taube, Esq.), that barred them from inheriting any portion of the testator's estate. On appeal, the petitioners argue that the probate court erred in: (1) ruling that the testator did not revoke his will when he drafted an unexecuted codicil in 1990; (2) ruling that the testator's great-grandchildren were not pretermitted heirs under RSA 551:10 (1974); and (3) refusing to segregate certain assets from the testator's estate. We affirm in part, vacate in part, and remand.

The record reveals the following facts. The testator had three children. Two children, Edward R. Laura, Jr. and Shirley Chicoine, survived him. Shirley and Edward each have three children. The testator's third child, Jo Ann Laura, died in 1974. She was survived by two children, Richard Chicoine and Neil F. Chicoine, Jr. Neil died in 1988 and is survived by two children, Cecilia Chicoine and Neil F. Chicoine, III, the testator's great-grandchildren. Richard, acting on behalf of himself and the testator's great-grandchildren, and Edward are the petitioners here.

Sometime prior to September 17, 1984, the testator hired an attorney to draft his will. The will was executed on September 26, 1984. It provided that the testator's estate would pass to his daughter, Shirley, who was also designated as the executrix of his estate. In addition, the will named the testator's deceased daughter, Jo Ann, and explicitly named his son, Edward, and his grandchildren, Richard and Neil, in a paragraph designed to disinherit them. Paragraph seven of the will provided:

> I have intentionally omitted to provide in this Will for any heirs at law, next of kin, or relatives of mine, by blood, marriage or adoption, specifically but not limited to my son, Edward and my grandchildren, Richard and Neil, except as aforesaid, and such omissions are not occasioned by accident or mistake.

The will did not mention the testator's two great-grandchildren. Cecilia Chicoine was born one day before the will was executed; Neil F. Chicoine, III was not born until two years after the will was executed.

In 1990, the testator attempted to execute a codicil to his will. The codicil would have altered the disposition of his estate, giving three equal shares to Edward, Shirley, and Richard, and equal shares to Shirley's and Edward's respective children. The parties agree, however, that the codicil was not properly witnessed and therefore did not become effective. Although the petitioners presented testimony regarding the drafting of the codicil, the codicil was not produced for probate.

Following the testator's death, his 1984 will was presented to the probate court. The will was proved and allowed, and Shirley was appointed executrix on September 30, 1990. In 1991, Richard, on behalf of himself and the testator's great-grandchildren, and Edward petitioned the probate court to reexamine the 1984 will. They challenged the will on several grounds: (1) the testator revoked his will when he attempted to execute the ineffective codicil in 1990; (2) the testator's great-grandchildren were entitled to an intestate share of his estate because they qualified as pretermitted heirs under RSA 551:10; and (3) the testator's estate included assets belonging to his deceased daughter, Jo Ann, that should be segregated and turned over to Jo Ann's heirs.

* * *

The * * * issue on appeal is whether the probate court erred in ruling that the testator's great-grandchildren were not entitled to an intestate share of his estate under RSA 551:10.

RSA 551:10 protects a testator's heirs against unintentional omission from the testator's will. See 7 DeGrandpre, supra § 11.02, at 99. It provides:

> Every child born after the decease of the testator, and every child or issue of a child of the deceased not named or referred to in his will, and who is not a devisee or legatee, shall be entitled to the same portion of the estate, real and personal, as he would be if the deceased were intestate.

RSA 551:10. The statute creates a rule of law that the omission of a child or issue of a child from a will is accidental "unless there is evidence in the will itself that the omission was intentional." In re Estate of MacKay, 121 N.H. 682, 684, 433 A.2d 1289, 1290 (1981) (quotation and emphasis omitted). "[T]he statute ... is not a limitation on the power to make testamentary dispositions but rather is an attempt to effectuate a testator's presumed intent. It prevents forgetfulness, not disinheritance." Royce v. Estate of Denby, 117 N.H. 893, 896, 379 A.2d 1256, 1258 (1977).

Relying on the statute, the petitioners argue that the testator's great-grandchildren were not named or referred to in the testator's will and therefore are entitled to an intestate share of his estate. They contend that the testator's decision to specifically name Neil F. Chicoine, Jr., the father of the petitioning great-grandchildren, in paragraph seven of the will was irrelevant in determining whether they are pretermitted heirs under RSA 551:10. According to the petitioners, testators must name or refer to their children (or in this case, grandchildren) as well as the issue of their children (or in this case, great-grandchildren) in their wills; otherwise any issue not named or referred to is pretermitted. We disagree.

We hold that a testator who specifically names one heir in an effort to disinherit him has "referred to" the issue of that heir for purposes of the statute. Accord Towne v. Cottrell, 236 Or. 151, 387 P.2d 576, 578 (1963); see In re Barter's Estate, 86 Cal. 441, 25 P. 15, 16 (1890); Matter of Estate of Kane, 828 P.2d 997, 999 (Okla.Ct.App.1992). If a testator has a predeceased child who is neither named, referred to, nor a devisee or legatee under the testator's will, then the naming of the next degree of issue in the line of descent will successfully preclude issue more removed from the testator from invoking the statute. On the other hand, where an issue of a child is named, referred to, or a devisee or legatee, but the testator's child is neither named, referred to, nor a devisee or legatee, then the testator's child is pretermitted, provided the child has not predeceased the testator. See Gage v. Gage, 29 N.H. 533, 543 (1854). Our holding is supported by our case law, in which we have acknowledged that a testator's reference to an heir "need not be direct" to exclude the heir under RSA 551:10. See In re Estate of Osgood, 122 N.H. 961, 964, 453 A.2d 838, 840 (1982); cf. Gage, 29 N.H. at 543 (naming of an heir's issue is not sufficient reference to the heir to preclude application of RSA 551:10).

Here, the testator specifically named Neil Chicoine, Jr., the father of the great-grand-children, in paragraph seven of his will. As a result, the testator "referred to" the descendant great-grandchildren for purposes of the pretermitted heir statute.

Furthermore, the testator named his daughter, Jo Ann—the grandmother of petitioners Cecilia and Neil—in his will. When a testator's child has been named, referred to, or is a devisee or legatee under the will, the child's issue cannot invoke the statute even if the issue are neither named, referred to, nor devisees or legatees under the will. Accordingly, the testator's great-grandchildren were not pretermitted heirs under RSA 551:10 and were not entitled to collect an intestate share of his estate.

* * *

Affirmed in part; vacated in part; remanded.

All concurred.

Notes

The New Hampshire statute is unique in that it applies to children and issue, and includes children and issue born before or after execution of the Last Will and Testament. Any child or issue thereby "forgotten" would be able to take what he or she would take under the applicable intestate statute unless there was evidence in the Will, itself, that the omission was intentional. Most children or issue are provided for as members of a class within the language of the Will. For example, "Whenever I refer to child or children, I refer to all of my children, issue of my body, or adopted by me." All children, no matter when born, would take as members of a class of children when the Will speaks of children.

A parent may prohibit the application of a pretermitted heir statute by express provision in a Will, thus limiting the child to contesting only the validity of the Will. Such a provision would have isolated the estate plan of Larry Lee Hillblom, a co-founder of the delivery service DHL Corp. Mr. Hillblom had allegedly paid teenage girls for sex and at least four children resulted from sexual relationships with four different women. There is no evidence that he officially acknowledged these children and, when he died, he left a valid Will, leaving his estate to charity. After he died in an airplane crash in 1995, mothers came forward with children, claiming he was their father and that he had forgotten about them in his Will. Genetic testing, arranged through Mr. Hillblom's mother's donation of a sample of her blood in return for $1 million and a French villa, established Mr. Hillblom as the father of the children. After extensive litigation, each of the four children settled for $50 million from Mr. Hillblom's $600 million estate; legal fees were $40 million, and the remainder went to medical research at the University of

California. *See* Robert Frank, *Jetting In to Catch the Knicks,* WALL ST. J., Mar. 20, 2000, at A1. For more on the DNA evidence in the case, see Charles H. Brenner, *The Larry Hillblom Inheritance,* http://dna-view.com/hillblom.htm (accessed Oct. 20, 2005).

Uniform Probate Code (2003)

§ 2-302. Omitted Children.

(a) Except as provided in subsection (b), if a testator fails to provide in his [or her] will for any of his [or her] children born or adopted after the execution of the will, the omitted after-born or after-adopted child receives a share in the estate as follows:

(1) If the testator had no child living when he [or she] executed the will, an omitted after-born or after-adopted child receives a share in the estate equal in value to that which the child would have received had the testator died intestate, unless the will devised all or substantially all of the estate to the other parent of the omitted child and that other parent survives the testator and is entitled to take under the will.

(2) If the testator had one or more children living when he [or she] executed the will, and the will devised property or an interest in property to one or more of the then-living children, an omitted after-born or after-adopted child is entitled to share in the testator's estate as follows:

(i) The portion of the testator's estate in which the omitted after-born or after-adopted child is entitled to share is limited to devises made to the testator's then-living children under the will.

(ii) The omitted after-born or after-adopted child is entitled to receive the share of the testator's estate, as limited in subparagraph (i), that the child would have received had the testator included all omitted after-born and after-adopted children with the children to whom devises were made under the will and had given an equal share of the estate to each child.

(iii) To the extent feasible, the interest granted and omitted after-born or after-adopted child under this section must be of the same character, whether equitable or legal, present or future, as that devised to the testator's then-living children under the will.

(iv) In satisfying a share provided by this paragraph, devises to the testator's children who were living when the will was executed abate ratably. In abating the devises of the then-living children, the court shall preserve to the maximum extent possible the character of the testamentary plan adopted by the testator.

(b) Neither subsection (a)(1) nor subsection (a)(2) applies if:

(1) it appears from the will that the omission was intentional; or

(2) the testator provided for the omitted after-born or after-adopted child by transfer outside the will and the intent that the transfer be in lieu of a testamentary provision is shown by the testator's statements or is reasonably inferred from the amount of the transfer or other evidence.

(c) If at the time of execution of the will the testator fails to provide in his [or her] will for a living child solely because he [or she] believes the child to be dead, the child is entitled to share in the estate as if the child were an omitted after-born or after-adopted child.

(d) In satisfying a share provided by subsection (a)(1), devises made by the will abate under Section 3-902.

Notes

Because the omitted child receives an intestate portion, there could be great disparity if a parent were to provide in his or her Will for one child with a bequest or devise significantly less than what the intestate portion might be. For example, "I give and bequeath my copy of Bartlett's Familiar Quotations to my daughter, Denise, because it has great sentimental value to me." An afterborn child receiving an intestate portion because of a pretermitted child statute would provide great disparity, no matter how sentimental the book may be. To rectify this, the Uniform Probate Code adopted a provision that limits the omitted child "to devises made to the testator's then living children under the will." Under Unif. Prob. Code § 2-302(a)(2)(I), modeled after N.Y. Est., Powers & Trusts Law § 5-3.2, the Uniform Probate Code would give nothing to an omitted child if a parent gave nothing to a child already in existence at the time of execution of the Will. And if the parent devised property to one or more children in existence at the time of the execution of the Will, the omitted child or children must share in whatever that property is, thereby reducing the value of the devise to the child or children in existence. The point is that children are to share equally.

Tax Considerations: The Internal Revenue Code provides multiple benefits to spouses—an unlimited marital deduction against the estate tax, for example. Obviously this is done with the thought that the marital couple forms an economic partnership, both having contributed to the accumulation of assets. This is not true with issue (descendants), and the paucity of benefits extended to them by the Code demonstrates that reality. Nonetheless, the Economic Growth and Tax Relief Reconciliation Act of 2001 provided a significant benefit to parents or grandparents seeking to provide for their issue. This is the Qualified State Tuition Plan, often called "529 Plans" because of its designation under Internal Revenue Code Section 529. In essence, the tuition plans allow for a parent or grandparent, among others, to invest in mutual funds that are then tax-deferred. The investment program must be established and maintained by a state, state agency, or by an eligible educational institution. If the designated beneficiary uses the funds for tuition, fees, books, and board at a post-secondary educational institution, then there is no federal income tax liability at all. The new Code also allows donors to utilize five years of exclusions (5 times $11,000) in one year to accelerate the process and the plan. If the designated beneficiary dies before utilizing the funds, or decides against further education, another individual within the family may be substituted as the designated beneficiary. For more on "529 Plans," go to American Bar Association, Rodney C. Koenig, *Creating College Scholarships with Qualified State Tuition Programs,* http://www.abanet.org/rppt/publications/magazine/2000/mj00koenig.html (accessed Oct. 20, 2005).

III. Protection of Spousal Persons

A. Who Is a Spouse?

In 1997, Hawaii became the first state to enact legislation providing to same sex couples the reciprocal benefits enjoyed by married couples. *See* Haw. Rev. Stat. Ann. § 572C-1 (Michie 1997). Thereafter known as "Reciprocal Beneficiary" status, the couples had the same legal status as married couples in the state. This included the right of election against a Will and the ability to take under intestate succession. In 2000, Vermont enacted into law a new status termed "Civil Unions," providing the benefits, protections, and responsibilities of spouses to same sex persons who qualify and who complete requirements similar to marriage formalities in the state. *See* Vt. Stat. Ann. tit. 15 §§ 1201–1205 (2000). California then created an advanced form of "domestic partnership" status, providing a surviving partner with rights similar to those of a surviving spouse. *See* Cal. Fam. Code § 297.5 (effective Jan. 1, 2005).

No status, reciprocal beneficiary, civil union, or domestic partnership "travels" from state to state; all rights granted thereunder are only local. Indeed, federal legislation specifically restricts spousal benefits to opposite sex persons who are married. *See* 1 U.S.C. § 7 (1998); 28 U.S.C. § 1738C (2004). But the landscape continues to change. In 2003, the Supreme Judicial Court of Massachusetts ordered that marriage licenses be granted to same sex persons, holding that to deny them a license lacked rational basis and violated the state's guarantee of equal protection. *See* Goodridge v. Dept. of Public Health, 440 Mass. 309, 798 N.E.2d 941 (2003). Massachusetts is now the first state to allow same-sex marriages. The debate over same sex marriage continues, but it is reasonable to conclude that the status providing spousal benefits extends beyond what has traditionally been defined as marriage.

Even if a relationship appears on its face to warrant the status of spousal, state statutes still may deny validity because of a variety of impediments. For example, if marriages are incestuous, polygamous, or involve one or more persons of radical underage, then the marriage is often void from the start. *See, e.g.,* Cal. Fam. Code §§ 2200 (incestuous marriages) & 2201 (bigamous and polygamous marriages) (2004). Also, a state may establish grounds upon which a marriage may be declared voidable upon petition because of a condition or defect at the time of the marriage. *See, e.g.,* Cal. Fam. Code § 2210 (2004) (annulment, causes for; e.g., unsound mind, fraud, coercion, physical incapacity). Remedial devices that may justify finding the person still a spouse include having a potential spouse being declared a "putative" spouse. *See, e.g.,* Cal. Code Civ. Proc. § 377.60(b) (2004) ("[putative spouse] means the surviving spouse of a void or voidable marriage who is found by the court to have believed in good faith that the marriage to the decedent was valid."). Once established, by whatever means, spousal status confers the right to contest, elect against a Will, take under intestate succession and participate in the following entitlements.

B. Pretermitted Spouse

In re Estate of Shannon

California Court of Appeal. Fourth District, 1990
224 Cal. App. 3d 1148, 274 Cal. Rptr. 338

HUFFMAN, Acting Presiding Justice.

Gilbert A. Brown, executor of the will of Lila Demos Shannon (also known as Lila King Demos), appeals on behalf of Lila's estate from an order of the probate court denying her petition for determination of heirship as an omitted spouse under Probate Code * * * section 6560 in the estate of Russell Donovan Shannon. We reverse.

* * *

On January 25, 1974, Russell, an unmarried widower, executed his last will and testament, naming his daughter, Beatrice Marie Saleski, executrix and sole beneficiary. The will also provided his grandson, Donald Saleski, would inherit his estate in the event Beatrice did not survive him for "thirty (30) days" and contained a disinheritance clause which provided as follows:

> SEVENTH: I have intentionally omitted all other living persons and relatives. If any devises, legatee, beneficiary under this Will, or any legal heir of mine, person or persons claiming under any of them, or other person or persons shall contest this Will or attack or seek to impair or invalidate any of its provisions or conspire with or voluntarily assist anyone attempting to do any of those things mentioned, in that event, I specifically disinherit such person or persons. [¶] If any Court finds that such person or persons are lawful heirs and entitled to participate in my estate, then in that event I bequeath each of them the sum of one ($1.00) dollar and no more.

On April 27, 1986, Russell married Lila. On February 22, 1988, Russell died. He did not make any changes in his will after his marriage to Lila and before his death. His 1974 will was admitted to probate May 9, 1988, and Beatrice was named executrix of his estate.

On September 27, 1988, Lila filed a petition for family allowance (§ 6540), to set apart probate homestead (§ 6520) and for determination of entitlement to estate distribution as an omitted surviving spouse (§§ 1080, 6560). The court denied the petition for family allowance and Lila withdrew her petition to set apart probate homestead. The remaining issue of Lila's entitlement to share in Russell's estate was heard December 14, 1988, and taken under submission.

On March 24, 1989, the probate court issued its order denying Lila's petition to determine heirship. She timely appealed only from this latter order. * * *

During the pendency of this appeal, Lila died and her son Brown was named executor of her estate and substituted in her place as appellant. * * * He has objected to the distribution of Russell's estate until after this appeal is decided.

* * *

On appeal, Lila contends she was a pretermitted spouse within the meaning of section 6560 and does not fall under any of the exceptions under section 6561 which would preclude her from sharing in Russell's estate as an omitted spouse. We agree and reverse.

Section 6560, added to the Probate Code in 1983, amended in 1984 and applicable to estates of decedents who died on or after January 1, 1985 (Stats.1983, ch. 842, § 55; Stats.1984, ch. 892, § 45), states:

> Except as provided in Section 6561, if a testator fails to provide by will for his or her surviving spouse who married the testator after the execution of the will, the omitted spouse shall receive a share in the estate consisting of the following property in the estate: [¶] (a) The one-half of the community property that belongs to the testator.... [¶] (b) The one-half of the quasi-community property that belongs to the testator.... [¶] (c) A share of the separate property of the testator equal in value to that which the spouse would have received if the testator had died intestate, but in no event is the share to be more than one-half the value of the separate property in the estate.

Section 6561 states:

> The spouse does not receive a share of the estate under Section 6560 if any of the following is established: [¶] (a) The testator's failure to provide for the spouse in the will was intentional and that intention appears from the will. [¶] (b) The testator provided for the spouse by transfer outside the will and the intention that the transfer be in lieu of a testamentary provision is shown by statements of the testator or from the amount of the transfer or by other evidence. [¶] (c) The spouse made a valid agreement waiving the right to share in the testator's estate.

Section 6560 supersedes that portion of former section 70 which had the effect of revoking the will as to the omitted spouse and giving that spouse the same share as the spouse would have taken if the testator had died intestate. (See Cal.Law Revision Com. com., 54A, (West's Ann.Prob.Code (1990 supp.) §6560, p. 295.) Section 6561 supersedes the portion of former section 70 which stated, "unless provision has been made for the spouse by marriage contract, or unless the spouse is provided for in the will, or in such way mentioned therein as to show an intention not to make such provision; and no other evidence to rebut the presumption of revocation can be received." (Stats.1931, ch. 281, p. 590, §70.) These latter two provisions are continued in section 6561 in subdivision (a) and, in addition, section 6561 now recognizes an omitted spouse may waive the right to take property of the other spouse by testate or intestate succession (§6561(c)) and does not receive a share if the testator provided for the omitted spouse by a "transfer outside the will" that was intended to be in lieu of a testimentary provision (§6561(b)). See Cal.Law Revision Com. com., 54A West's Ann.Prob.Code, *supra*, §6561, p. 297.)

It is well established section 6560 reflects a strong statutory presumption of revocation of the will as to the omitted spouse based upon public policy. (Estate of Duke (1953) 41 Cal.2d 509, 261 P.2d 235.) Such presumption is rebutted only if circumstances are such as to fall within the literal terms of one of the exceptions listed in section 6561. (See Estate of Sheldon (1977) 75 Cal.App.3d 364, 142 Cal.Rptr. 119.) The burden of proving the presumption is rebutted is on the proponents of the will. (See Estate of Paul (1972) 29 Cal.App.3d 690, 697, 105 Cal.Rptr. 742.)

Here, Russell failed to provide for Lila in his will. Under the language of section 6560, she is thus an omitted spouse and the crucial inquiry becomes whether Beatrice met the burden of rebutting this presumption. Specifically, the issues are whether the will shows a specific intent to exclude Lila pursuant to section 6561(a) and whether Beatrice presented sufficient evidence to show Russell had intended to otherwise provide for Lila outside of his will in lieu of her taking under it pursuant to section 6561(b), or to show Lila waived her rights to share in his estate under section 6561(c).

The will on its face does not evidence an intent on Russell's part to disinherit Lila. As the presumption under section 6560 is only rebutted by a clear manifestation of such intent on the face of the will, "regardless of what may have been the wishes of the [decedent]" (Estate of Basore (1971) 19 Cal.App.3d 623, 627–628, 96 Cal.Rptr. 874; see also *Estate of Duke, supra,* 41 Cal.2d 509, 261 P.2d 235 and *Estate of Paul, supra,* 29 Cal.App.3d 690, 105 Cal.Rptr. 742), the section 6561(a) exception has not been established.

Contrary to Beatrice's reliance on Estate of Kurtz (1922) 190 Cal. 146, 210 P. 959 to argue the language "any legal heir of mine" in the disinheritance clause contained in Russell's will somehow shows his intent to disinherit Lila, whom he married 12 years after executing the will, that case has been effectively overruled by subsequent case law. (See Estate of Axcelrod (1944) 23 Cal.2d 761, 769–770, 147 P.2d 1 (conc. opn. of Carter, J.).) *Estate of Axcelrod, supra*, 23 Cal.2d at pp. 765–769, 147 P.2d 1 distinguished the *Kurtz* case and held a general provision in a will that the testator "intentionally omitted all of my heirs who are not specifically mentioned herein, intending thereby to disinherit them", may not be construed as mentioning a subsequently acquired spouse in such a way as to show an intention not to make provision for the spouse, where the testator at the time the will was executed had no spouse who could become "an heir." (Id. at p. 767, 147 P.2d 1.)

Case law has also held exclusionary clauses in wills which fail to indicate the testator contemplated the possibility of a future marriage are insufficient to avoid the statutory presumption. (Estate of Poisl (1955) 44 Cal.2d 147, 149–150, 280 P.2d 789; *Estate of Paul, supra*, 29 Cal.App.3d 690, 105 Cal.Rptr. 742.) Even testamentary clauses specifically disinheriting a named individual whom the testator planned to marry and a clause stating "any other person not specifically mentioned in this Will, whether related by marriage or not" have been held insufficient to disclose the explicit intention of a testator to omit provision for another woman the testator married after executing the will either as a member of the designated disinherited class or as a contemplated spouse. (Estate of Green (1981) 120 Cal.App.3d 589, 593, 174 Cal.Rptr. 654.) As there is no mention of Lila or the fact of a future marriage in the disinheritance clause of the will, it does not manifest Russell's intent to specifically disinherit Lila as his surviving spouse.

Nor have the circumstances of section 6561(b) or (c) been established. Beatrice asserts a retired California Highway Patrolmen Widow's and Orphan's Fund from which $2,000 was paid to Lila as Russell's beneficiary, coupled with a declaration of Russell's attorney "[t]hat in the twelve months immediately preceding [Russell's death, he] informed this declarant that he had remarried and that his wife was independently wealthy and that she had more than he had and that he wanted his daughter to have his estate upon his death …", evidence Russell's intent to provide for Lila outside the will in lieu of a testamentary provision and satisfy the requirements of section 6561(b). In support of this argument she cites a New Mexico case, Matter of Taggart (1980) 95 N.M. 117, 619 P.2d 562, which held the omission of an after-acquired spouse in a will can be shown to be intentional by a transfer outside the will such as life insurance or other joint arrangement based on evidence of the testator's statements, the amount of the transaction, or other evidence. She claims Russell's intent she take his entire estate is paramount and the presumption under section 6560 must yield to that intent. (See Estate of Smith (1985) 167 Cal.App.3d 208, 212, 212 Cal.Rptr. 923.)

However, as Lila notes, the evidence of the widow's and orphan's trust fund benefits and Beatrice's attorney's declaration were excluded from evidence at the court hearing on the probate heirship matter making it impossible for the court to base its determination on such claimed transfer.

Even assuming the evidence were properly before the probate court at the time of the hearing, such was insufficient to rebut the presumption of section 6560 because it does not show Russell provided the trust fund benefits for Lila in lieu of sharing in his estate.

Moreover, the facts presented at the probate hearing that Russell and Lila kept their property separate during the course of their marriage is not sufficient to show "a valid agreement waiving the right to share" in each other's estate pursuant to section 6561(c). (See Estate of Butler (1988) 205 Cal.App.3d 311, 318, 252 Cal.Rptr. 210.)

Beatrice has simply not met her burden of proving Russell's intent to disinherit Lila and rebut the presumption of revocation under section 6560. The probate court therefore erred in denying Lila's petition to determine heirship.

* * *

The order denying Lila's petition for heirship is reversed and remanded for further proceedings consistent with this opinion.

NARES and LIM * * * JJ., concur.

Notes

Of course, as with a pretermitted child, the testator may specifically include a clause in the Will that states that a surviving spouse is not to be considered a pretermitted spouse as defined in the *Shannon* decision. A lack of specificity will result in the disappointed spouse receiving an intestate portion, the revocation of the entire Will under operation of law, or litigation about what the testator actually intended, as was demonstrated in *Shannon*. The Uniform Probate Code differs from the California pretermitted spouse provision, favoring issue descended from a previous relationship taking under the Will. How would the following Uniform Probate Code provision affect the *Shannon* decision? Note the process of abatement to satisfy the pretermitted spouse in the California code.

Uniform Probate Code (2003)

§ 2-301. Entitlement of Spouse; Premarital Will.

(a) If a testator's surviving spouse married the testator after the testator executed his [or her] will, the surviving spouse is entitled to receive, as an intestate share, no less than the value of the share of the estate he [or she] would have received if the testator had died intestate as to that portion of the testator's estate, if any, that neither is devised to a child of the testator who was born before the testator married the surviving spouse and who is not a child of the surviving spouse nor is devised to a descendant of such a child or passes under Sections 2-603 or 2-604 to such a child or to a descendant of such a child, unless:

(1) it appears from the will or other evidence that the will was made in contemplation of the testator's marriage to the surviving spouse;

(2) the will expresses the intention that it is to be effective notwithstanding any subsequent marriage; or

(3) the testator provided for the spouse by transfer outside the will and the intent that the transfer be in lieu of a testamentary provision is shown by the testator's statements or is reasonably inferred from the amount of the transfer or other evidence.

(b) In satisfying the share provided by this section, devises made by the will to the testator's surviving spouse, if any, are applied first, and other devises, other than a devise to a child of the testator who was born before the testator married the surviving spouse and who is not a child of the surviving spouse or a devise or substitute gift under Sections 2-603 or 2-604 to a descendant of such a child, abate as provided in Section 3-902.

California Probate Code (2004)

§ 6562. Manner of satisfying share of omitted spouse

(a) Except as provided in subdivision (b), in satisfying a share provided by this article:

(1) The share shall first be taken from the testator's estate not disposed of by will, if any.

(2) If that is not sufficient, so much as may be necessary to satisfy the share shall be taken from all devisees in proportion to the value they may respectively receive under the testator's will. Such value shall be determined as of the date of the decedent's death.

(b) If the obvious intention of the testator in relation to some specific devise or other provision of the will would be defeated by the application of subdivision (a), the specific devise or provision may be exempted from the apportionment under subdivision (a), and a different apportionment, consistent with the intention of the testator, may be adopted.

C. Statutory Entitlements

1. Social Security

Because Social Security is a federal benefit, any state statutes that distribute social security property at death are inapplicable because they are preempted by Congress. Thus, even though Social Security benefits may be apportioned at divorce between the divorcing parties, at death, any Social Security benefits accumulated are solely the property of the surviving spouse. *See* Boggs v. Boggs, 520 U.S. 833, 117 S. Ct. 1754 (1997) (formerly providing a unique community property right, the ability of a spouse to transfer his or her share of the community by Last Will and Testament without surviving the other spouse, but now preempted by federal law).

2. ERISA Plans

The Employee Retirement Security Act of 1974 is a federal statute governing most pension plans and prohibits the assignment or alienation of pension benefits, with few exceptions. Thus, simply by being a surviving spouse under a covered pension plan, the spouse takes the benefits even though the decedent may have named another person as beneficiary. *See, e.g.,* In re Lefkowitz, 767 F. Supp. 501 (S.D.N.Y. 1991). A spouse may waive his or her rights to an annuity, *see* 29 U.S.C. § 1055(c)(2) (2004), but any waiver of a pension must be witnessed by a notary or a plan representative, *see* 29 U.S.C. § 1055(c)(2)(A) (2004).

3. Homestead

In order to protect the surviving spouse and, perhaps, minor children from hardship, all states have homestead laws crafted to secure the family domicile for at least the duration of a life estate of the surviving spouse. To apply, the decedent must have been domiciled in the state providing the homestead allowance. The Uniform Probate Code ignores the necessity of an actual home and, instead, provides a monetary amount of $15,000 for the surviving spouse or to be divided among the surviving minor children. *See* Unif. Prob. Code § 2-402 (2003). But Florida, for example, allows up to one-half of an acre in a municipality or 160 acres elsewhere. *See* Fla. Const. Art. 10, § 4(a)(1) (2004).

4. *Family Maintenance*

Similar to spousal maintenance at separation and divorce, support from the estate is provided to the surviving spouse and minor children during the administration. While the Uniform Probate Code provides for a "reasonable amount in money," *see* UNIF. PROB. CODE § 2-404(a) (2004), the court may take into account other resources available to the family and the current living standard in computing a figure. The allowance may be "suited to the condition in life of the surviving spouse and to the condition of the estate." 755 ILL. COMP. STAT. § 5/15-1(a) (2004). The allowance takes precedence in the administration of the estate and "is not chargeable against any benefit or share passing to the surviving spouse or children by the will of the decedent, unless otherwise provided, by intestate succession, or by elective share." UNIF. PROB. CODE § 2-404(b) (2004). Finally, note that the British courts are given vast discretion to distribute a decedent's estate among specified persons so as to make a reasonable financial provision. *See* (UNITED KINGDOM) INHERITANCE (PROVISION FOR FAMILY AND DEPENDENTS) ACT OF 1975, § 1(e) (as amended by the FAMILY LAW ACT 1996).

5. *Exempt Property*

Regardless of any need of the surviving spouse, states often allow for a set portion of personal property to be exempt from the claims of creditors. If there is no surviving spouse, then decedent's children are entitled to the exemption. Uniform Probate Code § 2-403 provides a $10,000 exemption and is in addition to anything taken under the Will, intestate succession, or election. California Probate Code § 141 allows a surviving spouse to waive in whole or in part the right to any exempt property being set aside.

6. *Dower or Curtesy*

Dower is a feudal entitlement for a surviving widow of one-third of the husband's land owned during marriage. Curtesy is a similar entitlement of a life estate for a surviving widower in all of the lands owned by the wife during marriage, as long as issue were born of the marriage. *See generally* Roger W. Anderson, UNDERSTANDING TRUSTS AND ESTATES 146 (1994); 2 F. Pollock & F. Maitland, HISTORY OF ENGLISH LAW (2d ed. 1898). However, because gender distinctions are unconstitutional, and because the protection afforded in dower and curtesy involved only land, dower and curtesy were not responsive to today's needs, thus, states were prompted to abolish both. The Uniform Probate Code replaces them with an elective share available to either spouse, equally. *See* UNIF. PROB. CODE § 2-112 (2004). This will be discussed *infra*.

7. *Universal Succession*

European administration of estates allows for "universal succession" of any estate to the heirs without the appointment of a personal representative and the other steps necessary to administer an estate. The heirs will be responsible for payment of debts or taxes, each heir taking as a tenant in common, and none of them taking a fee for administration. California allows for universal succession between spouses only. *See* CAL. PROB. CODE §§ 13500–13660 (2004). But the Uniform Probate Code more resembles the European system by allowing "the heirs of an intestate or the residuary devisees under a will, excluding minors and incapacitated, protected, or unascertained persons," to become universal successors. *See* UNIF. PROB. CODE § 3-312 (2004). The procedure is described in UNIF. PROB. CODE §§ 3-313 to 3-322 (2004).

8. Election Dilemma

At the death of a decedent, a surviving spouse is confronted with personal loss, but there are also attendant economic issues confronting him or her. The decedent may have left a valid Will devising property acquired during his or her marriage to someone other than the spouse. Or the decedent may have a Will devising all property to the surviving spouse, but there may be non-probate transfers naming someone other than the surviving spouse as beneficiary, and these transfers may make up the bulk of the estate. Or the decedent may die intestate with only a small portion of the wealth accumulated during marriage passing through the intestate statutes to the surviving spouse and the bulk of the wealth passing through non-probate transfers to other beneficiaries. Should the surviving spouse "elect" against the Will or seek to "augment" the probate estate with the non-probate transfers? What if the beneficiaries named in the Will or the non-probate transfers are issue of the decedent and the surviving spouse? Eventually, these issue will inherit from the surviving spouse, so why not make it sooner than later?

Election by a spouse at the death of a decedent is a recognition by the spouse that property acquired during marriage is a result of the partnership of the spouse and the decedent. If the property is partially owned by the survivor, then no matter how title is held, a portion of that property should not pass according to the decedent's Will or non-probate transfer. Unless the surviving spouse has waived his or her right to election through a valid antenuptial agreement or postnuptial settlement, the surviving spouse has a right to take that portion earned through election. The law of the decedent's domicile governs the elective share as to all of a decedent's property. *See* UNIF. PROB. CODE §2-202(a)(d) (2004).

There is a time limit on the right to elect. The Uniform Probate Code provides that:

> Except as provided in subsection (b), the election must be made by filing in the court and mailing or delivering to the personal representative, if any, a petition for the elective share within nine months after the date of the decedent's death, or within six months after probate of the decedent's will, whichever limitation later expires.

UNIF. PROB. CODE § 2-211(a) (2004). The right to elect may only be made by a surviving spouse, and if the spouse is incapacitated, it may be made on his or her behalf by a "conservator, guardian, or agent under the authority of a power of attorney." UNIF. PROB. CODE § 2-212(b) (2004). This could result in a guardian and intestate or testate heir of the incapacitated surviving spouse electing against the decedent's estate on behalf of the spouse. But suppose the spouse dies shortly thereafter, and the main beneficiary of the election is the guardian, not the incapacitated spouse. To rectify this possible injustice, the Uniform Probate Code offers a solution. Any proceeds obtained as a result of the election on behalf of the incapacitated spouse will be placed in a Custodial Trust, *see* UNIF. CUSTODIAL TRUST ACT (1987) to be spent as the "custodial trustee considers advisable," *see* UNIF. PROB. CODE § 2-212(c)(2) (2004) until the surviving spouse's death. At that time, "the custodial trustee shall transfer the unexpended custodial trust property [to the residuary clause] of the will of the beneficiary's predeceased spouse against whom the elective share was taken ... or ... to that predeceasing spouse's [intestate heirs]." UNIF. PROB. CODE § 2-212(c)(3) (2004).

The decision to elect or not may be a difficult one. If more of the decedent's property will pass to the surviving spouse, election may offer substantial estate tax savings because of the current marital deduction in the estate tax. Or tax savings may be generated by refusing to elect, taking a life estate under the spouse's Will, and allowing the property to pass under a bypass trust device. In spite of technicalities, it seems reasonable to think that the decision to elect may be determined by the size of the share given to the survivor when compared to what the spouse would take under election. Other factors within the decedent's Will may prove important, such as the identity of the trustee, the Will's beneficiaries, and the nature of particular assets. But the decision may rest upon the scope of non-probate assets, their beneficiaries, and whether the state will allow them to be included in the estate for purposes of election. For example, because a substantial portion of the estate assets pass through devices such as joint tenancies with right of survivorship, payable-on-death accounts, living trusts, and even inter vivos gifts, the question becomes whether these may be included in the estate against which the surviving spouse elects. If the surviving spouse is limited to only the probate estate, that which passes under the Will, or intestate succession, the amount may be so insignificant as to be devoid of meaning. In order to increase the amount against which the surviving spouse may elect, courts and legislatures have instituted different approaches. *See, e.g.*, Ronald Z. Domsky, *'Til Death Do Us Part ... After That, My Dear, You're On Your Own: A Practitioner's Guide to Disinheriting A Spouse in Illinois*, 29 S. ILL. U. L.J. 207 (2005). What follows is an explanation of the dilemma faced by a surviving spouse and present day approaches.

9. Tax Considerations: The Internal Revenue Code provides extensive benefits to distribution of assets to spouses. For example: first, spouses may utilize the unlimited gift tax marital deduction, *see* I.R.C. § 2523, as long as the gift is not disqualified under the nondeductible terminal interest rule, *see* I.R.C. § 2523(b). Second, only one-half of any marital joint tenancies is included in the gross estate of the first spouse to die. *See* I.R.C. § 2040(b). Third, there is an unlimited deduction allowed against the decedent's gross estate for all assets passing to the surviving spouse, *see* I.R.C. § 2056; the only exception to this broad policy benefit is if, "on the lapse of time, on the occurrence of an event or contingency, or on the failure of an event or contingency to occur, an interest passing to the surviving spouse will terminate or fail, no deduction will be allowed." I.R.C. § 2056(b)(1). No terminable interest applies if the decedent requires the spouse to survive by a period of six months or less, or if the decedent requires the spouse to survive a common disaster. *See* I.R.C. § 2056(b)(3). This is an important consideration in light of the rules on simultaneous death.

In spite of the restriction against devising a terminable interest, the law allows many restrictions to be placed upon the surviving spouse by the decedent and still allow for the unlimited marital deduction. For example, in a valid Last Will and Testament, the decedent may provide the spouse with the right to income from the property for life, payable at least annually, *see* I.R.C. § 2056(b)(7); the Personal Representative may have discretion in providing for the property for the marital deduction, *see* Reg. § 20.2056(b)(7). And many trusts provide a surviving spouse with a life estate and a general power of appointment. *See* I.R.C. § 2056(b)(5). Estates seeking to take advantage of the marital deduction are likely to do so through what is called a QTIP trust—a Qualified Terminable Interest Property trust. The requirements are as follows:

(1) The spouse is entitled to all of the income for life, payable at least annually.

(2) No person, including the spouse, has the power to appoint any of the property to someone other than the spouse during the spouse's lifetime.

(3) The Personal Representative has made an election that the property passing to the surviving spouse should qualify for the marital deduction.

The restraint upon the surviving spouse is formidable, especially when compared to what the (surviving) spouse would have taken under most states' divorce process, whereby either the marital or community property is distributed, depending on whether the state follows a common law or a community property perspective. *See generally* Walter Wadlington & Raymond C. O'Brien, Family Law In Perspective 82–109 (2001). At divorce, recognizing the economic partnership of marriage, it is very unlikely that the court would restrict the assets by imposing life estates on either divorcing party. Yet, under the QTIP arrangement, such restrictions are allowed in furtherance of tax policy and with prejudice to the surviving spouse's established economic interests. *See generally* Wendy C. Gerzog, *The Illogical and Sexist QTIP Provisions: I Just Can't Say It Ain't So*, 76 N.C. L. Rev. 1597 (1998); Joseph M. Dodge, *A Feminist Perspective on the QTIP Trust and the Unlimited Marital Deduction*, 76 N.C. L. Rev. 1729 (1998); Mary Moers Wenig, *Taxing Women: Thoughts on a Gendered Economy*, 6 S. Cal. Rev. L. & Women's Stud. 561 (1997). For more on the varied uses of QTIP Trusts, see Richard W. Sherman, *A Half-Dozen Uses for a QTIP (qualified terminable interest property)*, http://www.nysscpa.org/cpajournal/old/12097358.htm (accessed Oct. 20, 2005).

Of course statutory election against a Last Will and Testament by the surviving spouse is an option, and this will be explored in the casebook material discussing augmented estate, *infra*. Nonetheless, for many married couples, the marital deduction trust is an important estate planning tool. The following a decision illustrates both the nature of a QTIP trust, the history of the marital deduction, and the attendant need to be precise in formulation.

Shelfer v. Commissioner

United States Court of Appeals, Eleventh Circuit, 1996
86 F.3d 1045

KRAVITCH, Circuit Judge:

The Commissioner of the Internal Revenue Service ("Commissioner") appeals the Tax Court's decision in favor of the estate of Lucille Shelfer. The court held that Lucille's estate was not liable for a tax deficiency assessed on the value of a trust from which she had received income during her lifetime. The estate of Lucille Shelfer's husband, Elbert, previously had taken a marital deduction for these trust assets, claiming that the trust met the definition of a qualified terminable interest property trust ("QTIP") pursuant to 26 U.S.C. § 2056(b)(7).

This case presents an issue of first impression for this circuit: whether a QTIP trust is established when, under the terms of the trust, the surviving spouse is neither entitled to, nor given the power of appointment over, the trust income accumulating between the date of the last distribution and her death, otherwise known as the "stub income." The Commissioner interprets the QTIP statutory provisions to allow such trusts to qualify for the marital deduction in the decedent's estate; accordingly, the value of the trust assets must be included in the surviving spouse's estate. We agree with the Commissioner and REVERSE the Tax Court.

* * *

Elbert Shelfer died on September 13, 1986 and was survived by his wife, Lucille. Elbert's will provided that his estate was to be divided into two shares, that were to be held in separate trusts. The income from each trust was to be paid to Lucille in quarterly installments during her lifetime. The first trust was a standard marital deduction trust consisting of one-third of the estate. It is not at issue in this case. The second trust, comprising the remaining two-thirds of the estate, terminated upon Lucille's death. The principal and all undistributed income was payable to Elbert's niece, Betty Ann Shelfer.

Elbert's will designated Quincy State Bank as the personal representative for his estate, and on June 16, 1987, the bank filed a tax return on behalf of the estate. The bank elected to claim a deduction for approximately half of the assets of the second trust under the QTIP trust provisions of 26 U.S.C. § 2056(b)(7). The IRS examined the return, allowed the QTIP deduction, and issued Quincy Bank a closing letter on May 10, 1989. The statute of limitations for an assessment of deficiency with respect to Elbert's return expired on June 16, 1990.

On January 18, 1989, Lucille died; Quincy State Bank served as personal representative for her estate. The bank filed an estate tax return on October 18, 1989 and did not include the value of the assets in the trust, even though the assets previously had been deducted on her husband's estate tax return. The IRS audited the return and assessed a tax deficiency for the trust assets on the ground that the trust was a QTIP trust subject to taxation. Quincy State Bank commenced a proceeding in tax court on behalf of Lucille's estate, claiming that the trust did not meet the definition of a QTIP trust because Lucille did not control the stub income; therefore, the Bank argued, the estate was not liable for tax on the trust assets under 26 U.S.C. § 2044. The Tax Court agreed. The Commissioner appeals this decision.

* * *

The proper construction of a statutory provision is a purely legal issue; thus, we apply a *de novo* standard of review to the Tax Court's decision. Kirchman v. Commissioner, 862 F.2d 1486, 1490 (11th Cir.1989). As in any case involving the meaning of a statute, we begin our analysis with the language at issue.

26 U.S.C. § 2056(b)(7)(B) provides, in relevant part:

(i) In general.—The term "qualified terminable income interest property" means property—

(I) which passes from the decedent,

(II) in which the surviving spouse has a qualifying income interest for life, and

(III) to which an election under this paragraph applies.

(ii) Qualifying income interest for life.—The surviving spouse has a qualifying income interest for life if—

(I) *the surviving spouse is entitled to all the income from the property, payable annually or at more frequent intervals,* or has a usufruct interest for life in the property, and

(II) no person has a power to appoint any part of the property to any person other than the surviving spouse. Subclause (II) shall not apply to a power exercisable only at or after the death of the surviving spouse.[1]

---

1. This section of the code is complemented by § 2044, which provides for the inclusion of the QTIP assets in the estate tax return of the surviving spouse. It states that "[t]he value of the gross estate shall include the value of any property to which this section applies in which the decedent had a

Lucille's estate contends, and the Tax Court held, that the phrase "all of the income" includes income that has accrued between the last distribution and the date of the spouse's death, or the stub income. They argue that "all" refers to every type of income. Stub income is a kind of income, and thus the surviving spouse must be entitled to stub income in order for the trust to qualify as a QTIP trust. They conclude that because Elbert's will did not grant Lucille control over the stub income, the QTIP election fails.

In contrast, the Commissioner and amicus * * * argue that the statute is satisfied if the surviving spouse controls "all of the income" that has been distributed. They contend that the requirement that income be, "payable annually or at more frequent intervals," limits "all of the income" to distributed income, namely those payments that have been made to the surviving spouse during her life. See Estate of Howard v. Commissioner, 910 F.2d 633, 635 (9th Cir.1990) (concluding that "if [the surviving spouse] has been entitled to regular distributions at least annually, she has had an income interest for life").

The estate replies that the phrase "payable annually or at more frequent intervals" is separated from the preceding clause by commas, and thus is a parenthetical clause. Because parenthetical clauses are non-restrictive, it contends that the clause is merely a description of the distribution process and does not in any way limit the preceding requirement that the spouse must be entitled to "all of the income."

Both parties insist that their reading of the statute is "plain." We do not agree. Although the use of commas around the clause "payable annually or at more frequent intervals" does indicate a parenthetical clause, we refuse to place inordinate weight on punctuation and ignore the remainder of the sentence. It is equally plausible that the next clause is designed to provide a context from which to define "all of the income." * * * Cf. Smiley v. Citibank, 517 U.S. 735, —, 116 S.Ct. 1730, 1736, 135 L.Ed.2d 25 (1996) ("A word often takes on a more narrow connotation when it is expressly opposed to another word: 'car,' for example, has a broader meaning by itself than it does in a passage speaking of 'cars and taxis.'"). Nothing in this statutory provision on its face allows us to choose between these interpretations. Accordingly, we must look to other sources for guidance.

The Commissioner contends that the second part of the statute, subclause (ii)(II), mandates her reading of the statute. This clause states that no one can have the power to appoint any of the property to someone other than the surviving spouse. This prohibition is modified by the language beneath this clause, known as the "flush language," which states that subclause II expressly does not apply to a power exercisable only at or after the death of the surviving spouse. See Estate of Shelfer v. Commissioner, 103 T.C. 10, 21–22, 1994 WL 373509 (1994) (Wells, J., dissenting). The flush language allows the decedent to appoint the trust property to another beneficiary after the death of the surviving spouse. The Commissioner argues that the language also refers to disposition of the stub income after the spouse's death.

Although the flush language limiting subclause (ii)(II) is consistent with the Commissioner's argument, it does not directly apply to the independent requirement in subclause (ii)(I) that the spouse be entitled to "all of the income," which remains ambiguous. Thus, the statutory language alone does not resolve the issue before this court.

---

qualifying income interest for life." The statute does not further define "qualifying income interest for life," so we refer back to the definition given in §2056 above. (Emphasis added).

Our conclusion is further supported by the lack of consensus among jurists as to the clear meaning of this statute. In this case, the Tax Court split on the issue, with ten judges joining the majority and six judges dissenting. Moreover, in a Ninth Circuit case involving this same provision, the majority reversed the Tax Court and concluded that the statute plainly allowed the trust to qualify. Howard, 910 F.2d at 637. The dissent, however, agreed with the Tax Court's reading of the statute. Id. (Rymer, J., dissenting). See Smiley, at —, 116 S.Ct. at 1733 (In light of the disagreement among the courts and judges who have heard the issue, "it would be difficult indeed to contend that the word … is unambiguous.…").

Accordingly, we must look beyond the "plain language" of the statute for guidance. When faced with a similarly ambiguous tax code provision, the Supreme Court thoroughly examined the history and purpose of the tax provision at issue, past practices, and the practical implications of its ruling. Commissioner v. Engle, 464 U.S. 206, 104 S.Ct. 597, 78 L.Ed.2d 420 (1984). * * * We follow suit, beginning with the history and purpose of the marital deduction.

* * *

The marital deduction for estate taxes first appeared in §812(e) of the Internal Revenue Code of 1939, which was enacted by the Revenue Code of 1948. * * * The marital deduction provisions served the dual purposes of equalizing the tax treatment between persons in common-law and community property states * * * and "codify[ing] the longstanding notion that marital property belongs to the unitary estate of both spouses.…" Shelfer, 103 T.C. at 25 (Beghe, J., dissenting).

An essential goal of the marital deduction statutory scheme "from its very beginning, however, was that any property of the first spouse to die that passed untaxed to the surviving spouse should be taxed in the estate of the surviving spouse." Estate of Clayton v. Commissioner, 976 F.2d 1486, 1491 (5th Cir.1992). * * * In accordance with this intent, the statute proscribed deductions for terminable property interests. Terminable property interests are those interests that will terminate upon the occurrence of an event, the failure of an event to take place, or after a certain time period. * * * Because these interests could terminate prior to the death of the surviving spouse, they posed a risk that the assets would escape taxation in the spouse's estate tax return.

The original statute allowed three exceptions to the terminable property rule for interests that would not escape taxation in the spouse's estate. Property interests would qualify for the marital deduction under any of the following conditions: 1) the interest of the spouse was conditional on survival for a limited period and the spouse survived that period; 2) the spouse had a life estate in the property with the power of appointment over the corpus; or 3) the spouse received all life insurance or annuity payments during her lifetime with the power to appoint all payments under the contract. * * * To take advantage of these exceptions, however, the decedent had to relinquish all control over the marital property to the surviving spouse.

As divorce and remarriage rates rose, Congress became increasingly concerned with the difficult choice facing those in second marriages, who could either provide for their spouse to the possible detriment of the children of a prior marriage or risk under-endowing their spouse to provide directly for the children. * * * In the Economic Recovery Act of 1981, Congress addressed this problem by creating the QTIP exception to the terminable property interest rule. According to the House of Representatives Report, the QTIP trust was designed to prevent a decedent from being "forced to choose between surrendering control of the entire estate to avoid imposition of estate tax at his death or reducing his tax benefits at his death to insure inheritance by the children." H.R.Rep. No. 201, 97th Cong., 1st Sess. 160 (1981). Thus, the purpose of the QTIP trust provisions was to liberalize the marital deduction to cover trust instruments that provide ongoing income support for the surviving spouse while retaining the corpus for the children or other beneficiaries.

In addition to creating the QTIP trust provisions, the 1981 Act also substantially changed the marital deduction by lifting the limitations on the amount of the deduction. * * * The Senate Report for the 1981 Act states the reason for the change: "The committee believes that a husband and wife should be treated as one economic unit for purposes of estate and gift taxes, as they generally are for income tax purposes. Accordingly, no tax should be imposed on transfers between a husband and wife." S.Rep. No. 144, 97th Cong., 1st Sess. 127 (1981), reprinted in 1981 U.S.C.C.A.N. 105, 228.

Although the legislative history of the 1981 Act sets forth Congress's reasons for enacting the statute, it does not directly address the stub income issue. * * * When "neither the statutory language nor the legislative history are dispositive of the issue, we guide ourselves generally by the purposes" of the Act and Congress's intent in enacting it. Rickard v. Auto Publisher, Inc., 735 F.2d 450, 457 (11th Cir.1984). Accordingly, we must decide which interpretation of the statute best comports with the two general goals discussed above: expanding the marital deduction to provide for the spouse while granting the decedent more control over the ultimate disposition of the property, and treating a husband and wife as one economic entity for the purposes of estate taxation.

Under the Commissioner's interpretation of the statute, the decedent would gain the tax benefit, retain control of the trust corpus, and provide the spouse with all of the periodic payments for her personal support. The stub income, which accrues after her death and is thus not used for her maintenance, could be appointed to someone else. This result is consistent with the statutory goals of expanding the deduction while providing for the spouse's support. * * * In contrast, the Tax Court's reading of the statute would condition the tax benefit for the entire trust corpus on ceding control over a much smaller amount that is not needed for the spouse's support.

The statute's second goal, treating a married couple as one economic entity, was effected in a comprehensive statutory scheme. In addition to the QTIP provisions of § 2056(b)(7), Congress added § 2044, which requires the estate of the surviving spouse to include all property for which a marital deduction was previously allowed, and § 2056(b)(7)(B)(v), which states that a QTIP "election, once made, shall be irrevocable." Taken together, these sections of the code provide that assets can pass between spouses without being subject to taxation. * * * Upon the death of the surviving spouse, the spouse's estate will be required to pay tax on all of the previously deducted marital assets. The Commissioner's position comports with the statutory scheme because it compels the surviving spouse to abide by the irrevocable election of a QTIP trust and to pay taxes on property that had previously been subject to a deduction. * * *

The Tax Court opinion in this case reached the opposite conclusion. In addition to accepting the technical statutory arguments rejected above, the court relied upon the legislative history discussed extensively in its opinion in Howard v. Commissioner, 91 T.C. 329, 1988 WL 86347 (1988). Shelfer, 103 T.C. at 17. In Howard, the court began by acknowledging that the legislative history of the QTIP provisions in § 2056(b)(7) does not directly address the meaning of the clause "all of the income." Instead of turning to the general purposes of the Act, the court referred to the legislative history of § 2056(b)(5), a similar statute, and the accompanying regulations to that statute.

Section 2056(b)(5) allows a deduction for "property passing from the decedent, if his surviving spouse is entitled for life to all the income from the entire interest, or all the income from a specific portion thereof, payable annually or at more frequent intervals, with power in the surviving spouse to appoint the entire interest." Unlike the QTIP provisions at issue here, § 2056(b)(5) requires that the spouse exert control over the trust corpus by power of appointment.

The Senate Report discussing § 2056(b)(5) lists the conditions necessary for a power of appointment trust to qualify for the deduction. The Report lists in separate subheadings the requirement that the spouse must be entitled to all of the income for her life and the prerequisite that the income must be payable at annual or more frequent intervals. Howard, 91 T.C. at 333 (citing S.Rep. 1013, 80th Cong., 2d Sess., pt. 2, at 16–17 (1948)). The Tax Court determined that the two subheadings indicated that "all of the income" should be defined without reference to the requirement for periodic payments.

We do not read the report as compelling this result. The listing of two subheadings does not erase the possibility that Congress intended to define the first requirement by reference to or within the context of the second.

Additionally, even if we accept the Tax Court's construction of the Senate report for § 2056(b)(5), we do not reach the same conclusion with respect to § 2056(b)(7). Although this court presumes that the same words in different parts of the statute have the same meaning, such a presumption is rebuttable. Doctors Hosp., Inc. of Plantation v. Bowen, 811 F.2d 1448, 1452–53 (11th Cir.1987). In the instant case, the Commissioner has presented sufficient evidence to overcome the presumption.

First, the two sections were enacted in entirely different statutes, separated by a significant time period. The Senate report for the power of appointment trusts in § 2056(b)(5) was written over thirty years prior to the 1981 enactment of the QTIP provisions at issue here. Thus, we give more weight to the objectives stated in the more recent legislative history of the QTIP provisions. See Gulf Oil Corp. v. Panama Canal Co., 481 F.2d 561, 570 (5th Cir.1973) (holding that Congress's use of the same words many years ago "does not tie the law to an interpretation of those words or phrases fit for the past but now wholly out of keeping with the present"). * * *

Second, the QTIP provisions were a substantial break with the past. The whole purpose of § 2056(b)(7) was to eliminate the requirement that the surviving spouse retain control of all of the property, as was previously required under § 2056(b)(5). In furtherance of this goal, Congress added flush language to the QTIP statute providing that the power to appoint property to someone other than the surviving spouse is exercisable after the spouse's death.

Importantly, the Tax Court did not rely solely on the similar wording of the two statutes in reaching its conclusion. The court held that although the Shelfer trust did not qualify for a marital deduction, a trust could qualify for the deduction if the surviving spouse had a power of appointment over the stub income. Shelfer, 103 T.C. at 21 (citing Howard, 91 T.C. at 338). Neither of the statutes, however, specifically equates "entitled to all of the income" with "the power of appointment." * * * The Senate Report cited above also does not mention "power of appointment." Thus, the Tax Court had to go beyond the statutory language and the legislative history to find a realistic meaning for the critical statutory terms.

The Tax Court relied primarily upon the regulations accompanying § 2056(b)(5) for its determination that the spouse's power of appointment over the stub income would satisfy the statute. Estate Tax Regulations § 20.2056(b)-5(f). These regulations are particularly pertinent because they are referenced in the legislative history of the QTIP provisions of § 2056(b)(7). Howard, 91 T.C. at 335 (citing H.R.Rep. No. 201 at 161; Staff of Joint Committee on Taxation, 97th Cong., 1st Sess., General Explanation of the Economic Recovery Tax Act of 1981 at 435 (Comm.Print 1981)). * * * The Tax Court quoted from subsection 5(f)(8) of the regulations:

> [A]s respects the income for the period between the last distribution date and the date of the spouse's death, it is sufficient if that income is subject to the spouse's power to appoint. Thus, if the trust instrument provides that income accrued or undistributed on the date of the spouse's death is to be disposed of as if it had been received after her death, and if the spouse has a power of appointment over the trust corpus, the power necessarily extends to the undistributed income.

The court read this regulation as requiring that the stub income "must be disposed of as the spouse directs." Howard, 91 T.C. at 333.

We disagree. The regulations must be interpreted in light of the statutory provisions of § 2056(b)(5), for which it was written. As previously discussed, § 2056(b)(5) creates an exception to the terminable property rule for property over which the surviving spouse has a power of appointment. The property is subject to taxation upon the spouse's death because the tax code requires an estate to pay taxes on all property over which the decedent had the power of appointment. * * * To complete the statutory scheme and to ensure taxation, the regulations require that the stub income be subject to the spouse's power of appointment or treated as part of the corpus over which the spouse had power of appointment.

Following the logic of the regulations, the person with the power to appoint the property in the trust corpus should be permitted to have the power to appoint the stub income; the stub income will then be subject to taxation along with the corpus property. Under the QTIP provisions, that person is the decedent. The trust corpus and the stub income would be taxable pursuant to § 2044, which requires the spouse to include all previously deducted property in which she has a qualifying interest for life.[20] This

---

20. We acknowledge that § 2044 does not expressly apply to stub income because it provides that the surviving spouse's estate must include all property over which the spouse had a qualifying income interest for life. Although we have already shown that the trust property can be a qualifying income interest for life even if the surviving spouse is not given control of the stub income, we have not determined whether the stub income can be part of the qualifying income interest for life. The Commissioner's regulation, now finalized at 26 C.F.R. § 2044(b)(2), clarifies the issue by specifically including the stub income in the spouse's gross estate. We note that although the regulation was not finalized at the time of this action, it is the most consistent interpretation of the statute for the same reason that the regulations for the power of appointment trust are reasonable. Both regulations ensure that previously deducted property is taxed at the death of the surviving spouse. Moreover, both regulations are faithful to the statutory scheme. In the power of appointment regulations, the stub income is rendered subject to the power of appointment and becomes taxable. In the QTIP provisions, the stub income is included in the spouse's estate along with the trust corpus, both of which are not controlled by the spouse.

comprehensive scheme, like that of the power of appointment trust, allows an initial deduction and later taxation of the property.[21]

Our conclusion that the trust income and the stub income can be treated the same for taxation purposes is consistent with the flush language of § 2056(b)(7), which provides that any property can be appointed to someone other than the surviving spouse at or after the spouse's death. See Shelfer, 103 T.C. at 21–23 (Wells, J., dissenting). Thus, under the terms of the statute, the trust corpus and the stub income can both be appointed to someone other than the surviving spouse after her death without disqualifying the trust from a marital deduction.

Examining the legislative history of the 1981 Act, we conclude that Congress intended to liberalize the marital deduction, to treat a husband and wife as one economic unit, and to allow the stub income to be treated in the same manner as the trust corpus for taxation purposes. These goals favor a broad interpretation of the statute that would allow the QTIP election in this case. Having assessed the legislative history and purpose of the statute, we turn to the practical implications of this interpretation. * * *

* * *

Our construction of the statute has several practical advantages over the Tax Court's position. First, it would assure certainty in estate planning. See Jacques T. Schlenger, et al., Failure to Pay Stub Income to Estate Defeats QTIP Election, 21 Est.Plan. 368 (1994) (noting that the Tax Court's decision in Shelfer leaves the "stub income" issue unsettled). * * * The status of trust instruments that were set up in accordance with the Commissioner's advice will not be in question and the validity of the Commissioner's final regulation on this matter will be affirmed. * * *

Second, our result comports with standard trust practices. Under the Tax Court's approach, a trust fund that made daily payments to the surviving spouse would qualify for the deduction because there would be no undistributed income; in contrast, one that made quarterly payments would be ineligible. In Howard, the Ninth Circuit noted that "no trust pays its beneficiaries on a daily basis. The statute did not impose such an unrealistic requirement for a trust to become a QTIP." Howard, 910 F.2d at 635. * * * Our reading of the statute gives meaning to the statutory terms requiring annual or more frequent distribution, not daily disbursements. See Tramel v. Schrader, 505 F.2d 1310, 1314 (5th Cir.1975) (citing cardinal rule that a statute should be construed such that no clause shall be superfluous). * * *

Finally, a broad reading of the marital deduction provisions benefits the federal Treasury and furthers Congressional intent to ensure taxation of all previously deducted property. In the instant case, for example, the corpus of $2,829,610 would be subject to taxation, for a gain of over $1,000,000 in tax deficiencies. The Tax Court's opinion would grant similar estates a substantial windfall, encouraging other executors of wills to disclaim the previously taken deduction. * * *

---

21. Our reading of the regulation does not disqualify a trust instrument that provides for the surviving spouse to have the power of appointment over the stub income or to receive the stub income as part of her estate. Under those circumstances, congressional goals will be served because the stub income will clearly be taxable and the couple will be considered one economic unit. We merely hold that the estate planning document at issue here also qualifies for the deduction because Congress provided a statutory scheme which will require taxation of the stub income if it reverts to the trust remainderman.

For all of these reasons, we conclude that our interpretation of the statute will better serve the practical realities of trust administration and estate taxation.

* * *

After determining that the statutory language is ambiguous, we looked beyond the statute to additional sources of information, such as the legislative history. Careful consideration of these documents leads us to discern two purposes for the 1981 Act: treating the married couple as one economic unit, and expanding the deduction to include arrangements that divest the surviving spouse of control over property. These congressional goals are best served by allowing the deduction in the decedent's estate and requiring subsequent inclusion in the surviving spouse's estate when trust documents do not grant control over the stub income to the surviving spouse. Accordingly, we REVERSE the Tax Court.

D. Augmented Estate

The issue in providing for a surviving spouse's elective share is fairness. Centuries ago, when wealth consisted mainly of real estate, providing a widow with a one-third life interest in her husband's real estate (dower) was thought sufficient to safeguard her marital property rights. Likewise, a husband had a life interest in the wife's real estate, provided children were born (curtesy). But today, the nature of wealth has shifted from real estate to pensions, life insurance, revocable and irrevocable trusts, and joint accounts. Dower and curtesy are inapplicable to these. Furthermore, these interests pass outside of what is traditionally known as the probate estate—that is, property passing under a Will or by intestate succession. Thus, if title is held in the name of one spouse, and that spouse names a person other than the surviving spouse as beneficiary of a non-probate transfer, how can that asset, even though acquired during marriage as a result of the efforts of both spouses, be incorporated into the probate estate so that the surviving spouse may include it within his or her right of election? This is the challenge, and it occurs in common law states where title to property is determinative, whereas, in community property states, title is at best "sometimes presumptively controlling." See GRACE GANZ BLUMBERG, COMMUNITY PROPERTY IN CALIFORNIA, 176–228 (3d ed. 1999). Thus, all property acquired by a married couple in a community property state, no matter in whose name title is held, is community property and is subject to the surviving spouse's election, even if it passes to another under a non-probate transfer method. In a common law state with a traditional elective statute, see, e.g., MD. EST. & TRUSTS CODE ANN. § 3-203 (2001), all property acquired during marriage may not be subject to the spouse's election because title may be held solely in the name of the decedent and may pass as a non-probate transfer to another beneficiary. For a comprehensive analysis, see Angela M. Vallario, *Spousal Election: Suggested Equitable Reform for the Division of Property at Death*, 52 CATH. U. L. REV. 519, 535–43 (2003). The disparity between the community property and the common law systems results in unfair treatment of surviving spouses. What follows is a further explanation and suggestions for reform.

1. Distribution of Property at Divorce

Disparity between what a married couple would divide upon divorce and what the couple would divide at death further illustrates the deficiencies of the traditional elective share system in common law jurisdictions. At divorce, a married couple in a community property state may include in property to be divided "[a]ll property, real or personal wherever situated, acquired by a married person during marriage while domiciled in th[e] state." CAL. FAM. CODE § 760 (2003). Specifically, this would include property held as a revocable trust (a non-probate device). See CAL. FAM. CODE § 761 (2003). As for the couple itself, property included for division includes "property acquired by the parties during marriage in joint form, including property held in tenancy in common, joint tenancy, or tenancy by the entirety, or as community property." See CAL. FAM. CODE § 2581 (2003). Once defined as community property, "[e]xcept upon the written agreement of the parties, or on oral stipulation of the parties in open court ... the court shall ... divide the community estate of the parties equally." CAL. FAM. CODE § 2550 (2003). Equal division between the two parties in community property states is the likely mode of division. But in common law jurisdictions, equitable factors are used to divide property upon divorce.

For example, New York, a common law state, lists thirteen factors it uses in division of marital property at divorce. These include the duration of the marriage, any equitable claim of one party, probable future financial circumstances of either party, or wasteful dissipation of assets. See N.Y. DOM. REL. LAW § 236 (McKinney 1999 & Supp. 2003). New York and other states utilizing equitable factors in the distribution of marital property may not award a divorcing spouse an equal distribution of community assets as in community property states, but the common law equitable scheme will take into account factors to arrive at a substantial portion of the marital property for the divorcing spouse seeking to obtain a portion of those assets titled in the name of the other spouse. See, e.g., MD. FAM. LAW CODE ANN. § 4-204 (1999 & Supp. 2002). This equitable portion awarded at divorce is very likely to be substantially more than that awarded to a surviving spouse at death through the traditional election statute used in common law jurisdictions. This is a product of the fact that, while marital property distribution laws operative at dissolution of a marriage (divorce) have benefitted from modern thinking regarding marriage as an economic partnership, the traditional election statutes utilized at death still retain the outdated notion that title may be held in the name of one party as a product of only one party's contribution to the marriage. See MARY ANN GLENDON, THE TRANSFORMATION OF FAMILY LAW 131 (1989). This disparity in common law jurisdictions between what a spouse may obtain at divorce and what the spouse may obtain at death results in unfair treatment of surviving spouses at death.

2. Distribution of Property at Death

The deficiency in the common law traditional elective share approach is its inability to look beyond the decedent's probate estate to property that will pass under non-probate transfer. Because non-probate transfers may account for a substantial portion of the assets passing at death, this is a major shortfall. There are other insufficiencies. The surviving spouse is entitled to only a fixed percentage of the probate estate — sometimes only a life estate, see, e.g., CONN. GEN. STAT. ANN. § 45a-436 (West 1993 & Supp. 2003) — sometimes nothing at all, see, e.g., GA. CODE ANN. § 53-5-2 (Michie 1997). Furthermore, since election does not take into account length of marriage, a marriage of short duration will take equally from the decedent's estate with a surviving spouse of a long-term marriage. The traditional elective share approach does not take into account the wealth of a surviving spouse, nor the fact that substantial property may have been passed to the survivor during marriage. Finally, the traditional model forces any disappointed surviving spouse to litigate to recover assets that certainly would have been included in marital assets subject to distribution at divorce.

3. Statutory Models for Reform

a. New York. Because New York was the first state to codify a means by which a surviving spouse may include non-probate assets in the elective share, it is illustrative. By statute, the surviving spouse may include the following non-probate transfers within the amount to which he or she may elect: gifts causa mortis, gifts made within one year of death greater than $10,000, Totten Trusts, joint bank accounts, joint tenancies and tenancies by the entirety, payable-on-death accounts to persons other than the decedent, lifetime transfers over which the decedent retained possession or life income or a "power to revoke such dispositions or a power to consume, invade, or dispose of the principal thereof," any pension plans, and finally, any property over which the decedent had a general power of appointment. The elective share of these amounts, plus any probate assets, is $50,000 or one-third of the decedent's net estate, whichever is greater. N.Y. Est., Powers & Trusts L. §5-1.1-A (2004). The approach does not take into account the length of marriage, but it does take into account property passing from the decedent to the surviving spouse through testate, intestate, or non-probate transfers. N.Y. Est., Powers & Trusts L. § 5-1.1-A(a)(4)(A) (2004).

b. Uniform Probate Code. Following the example of the New York statute, drafters of the Uniform Probate Code inaugurated its own version in 1969. Like the New York statute, there was no provision made to distinguish a long term from a short term marriage, and the surviving spouse was entitled to a simple one-third of the augmented estate, whether the decedent died testate or intestate. *See* Unif. Prob. Code § 2-201 (1969). The statute was careful to include most non-probate transfers such as joint accounts, revocable trusts, and pension benefits, but many complained that it did not adequately recognize what had become a modern conception of marriage—that marriage is an economic partnership in which each spouse has an undivided one-half interest. *See* Unif. Prob. Code, art. II, pt. 2, gen. cmt. (2004); Alan Newman, *Incorporating the Partnership Theory of Marriage in Elective-Share Law: The Approximation System of the Uniform Probate Code and the Deferred Community-Property Alternative*, 49 Emory L. J. 487 (2000). To better address this objective, the Uniform Probate Code was revised in 1990 and amended in 1993. The new version included more assets within the purview of the statute to include life insurance, accident insurance, and even the surviving spouse's own property. *See* Unif. Prob. Code §§ 2-205–06 (2004). Because the couple also has a duty to support one another simply because of the status of marriage, the new statute included a $50,000 supplemental provision, payable no matter how long the couple was married. *See* Unif. Prob. Code § 2-202(b) (2004). As we will see in determining the amount to be paid to the surviving spouse, the amount the surviving spouse receives increases in proportion to the length of the marriage, *see* Unif. Prob. Code § 2-202(a) (2004), and the surviving spouse may take the property outright and not as an income interest. With this background in mind, we examine the components of the Uniform Probate Code elective model.

First: What is Included in the Augmented Estate? All property interests, real or personal, movable or immovable, tangible or intangible, wherever situated, are included. *See* Unif. Prob. Code § 2-203 (2004). These are then divided into four components:

(1) **decedent's probate estate** (testate or intestate property), reduced by funeral or administrative expenses, any homestead, family allowance, or exempt property that we have defined earlier, and any enforceable claims against the estate. *See* Unif. Prob. Code § 2-204 (2004);

(2) **decedent's non-probate transfers to persons other than the surviving spouse**, to include general inter vivos powers of appointment (presently exercisable), joint accounts, payable-on-death accounts, accident or life insurance, irrevocable transfers where the decedent retained the right to income or possession, any irrevocable transfer where the decedent created a power over income or property in another person for the decedent's benefit, and any property given by the decedent within two years of his or her death and during marriage, the value of which amounted to an aggregate transfer to any one donee in either of the two years to exceed $10,000. *See* UNIF. PROB. CODE § 2-205 (2004);

(3) **decedent's non-probate transfers to the surviving spouse**, to include any joint tenancies, any right of survivorship ownership, and anything included in Uniform Probate Code § 2-205 (recited in the previous section). Social Security benefits are specifically excluded from the list of transfers. *See* UNIF. PROB. CODE § 2-206(2004); and the

(4) **surviving spouse's own property and non-probate transfers to others**, to include property held in joint tenancy or with any arrangement of survivorship, property passing to the spouse due to the decedent's death except for exempt property, homestead, family allowance or Social Security, and property the surviving spouse gave away under the terms of any joint tenancy or survivorship arrangement. The value of the property is determined as of the time of the decedent's death, and the surviving spouse may reduce this amount by any enforceable claims that may be brought. *See* UNIF. PROB. CODE § 2-207 (2004).

Second: Calculate the Elective Share Amount. Once the value of the augmented estate is identified, the next step is to use the percentage table to correlate the length of marriage with the amount to which the surviving spouse would be entitled in a true partnership theory of marriage. Thus, Uniform Probate Code § 2-202(a) provides:

If the decedent and the spouse were married to each other:	The elective share is:
Less than 1 year	Supplemental amount only ($50,000)
1 year but less than 2 years	3% of the augmented estate.
2 years but less than 3 years	6% of the augmented estate.
3 years but less than 4 years	9% of the augmented estate.
4 years but less than 5 years	12% of the augmented estate.
5 years but less than 6 years	15% of the augmented estate.
6 years but less than 7 years	18% of the augmented estate.
7 years but less than 8 years	21% of the augmented estate.
8 years but less than 9 years	24% of the augmented estate.
9 years but less than 10 years	27% of the augmented estate.
10 years but less than 11 years	30% of the augmented estate.
11 years but less than 12 years	34% of the augmented estate.
12 years but less than 13 years	38% of the augmented estate.
13 years but less than 14 years	42% of the augmented estate.
14 years but less than 15 years	46% of the augmented estate.
15 years or more	50% of the augmented estate.

Third: Credits. Now that the augmented amount is calculated and the percentage allowed to the surviving spouse is fixed, the spouse is credited for those amounts he or she already owns or has received from the decedent, *see* UNIF. PROB. CODE § 2-209 (2004); thus, double-dipping is disallowed. Included at this stage are assets the spouse received by testate or intestate succession, non-probate transfers received by the surviving spouse, and property owned by the surviving spouse up to an "applicable percentage"—a mathematical calculation based in part on the length of the marriage. *See* Unif. Prob. Code § 2-209(a)(2) (2004). Thus, if the spouse already has his or her proportionate share of the estate, nothing further needs to be done. If the spouse is still entitled to an elective share amount, the question arises as to where the property may be obtained to pay the spouse his or her elective share. Uniform Probate Code § 2-209(b) provides that there should be equitable apportionment between the decedent's probate estate and the decedent's non-probate transfers to others. If there are insufficient assets at this level, then the Code allows for a contribution from the persons who have received irrevocable gifts from the decedent within the past two years in excess of $10,000 in either year. *See* Unif. Prob. Code § 209(c) (2004). Admittedly, this would be difficult to obtain. To the extent that the recipients of the decedent's property still have the property, each

> is liable to make a proportional contribution toward satisfaction of the surviving spouse's elective-share or supplemental elective share [$50,000] amount. A person liable to make a contribution may choose to give up the proportional part of the decedent's non-probate transfers to him [or her] or to pay the value of the amount for which he [or she] is liable.

Unif. Prob. Code § 2-210(a) (2004)

c. Equitable Model. Implied within both the New York statutory model and the far more complicated Uniform Probate Code model of elective share is the goal of equalizing what a spouse would receive at death with what the spouse would receive at divorce. If the economic partnership theory of marriage is to be implemented, then a spouse should not receive more at divorce than he or she would receive at death. The community property states better equalize death and divorce than do the common law states. Hence, the question arises as to why not draft an election statute for use in common law states that would mirror the manner in which property is divided at divorce, taking into consideration decedent's property passing through probate and non-probate transfers, disregarding the strict confines of title? Professor Angela M. Vallario developed such a model—an election model based on the equitable distribution of property system used by common law states at divorce. *See* Angela M. Vallario, *Spousal Election: Suggested Equitable Reform for the Division of Property at Death*, 52 Cath. U. L. Rev. 519 (2003). Her proposed statute includes for purposes of right of election by the surviving spouse the decedent's real and personal property, movable and immovable, tangible and intangible, wherever situated. *Id.* at 562. Specifically, this includes non-probate transfers "owned in substance" by the decedent immediately before death, *id.* at 563, any transfer made within a one-year period preceding decedent's death, *id.* at 564, and any probate or non-probate property owned by the surviving spouse, *id.* at 565. The surviving spouse is to take one-half of this amount, *id.* at 562 , and if the award is "insufficient," on application by the surviving spouse, the court may award an additional amount, after taking into consideration the following: (1) support available to the surviving spouse from other sources and the spouse's earning capacity; (2) such other relevant criteria as the court deems equitable and proper. *Id.* The burden of proof is upon the surviving spouse to show by a preponderance of the evidence that the elective share, alone, is insufficient. *Id.* The equitable factor of what the "court deems equitable and proper," is reflected in many state statutes providing for marital property distribution at divorce. *See, e.g.,* N.Y. Dom. Rel. L. § 236 (McKinney 1999 & Supp. 2003); Md. Fam. L. Code Ann. § 4-204 (1999 & Supp. 2002).

The equitable basis of the proposed statute resonates with a clause for making "reasonable financial provision" for, among others, a surviving spouse, in the (UNITED KINGDOM) INHERITANCE (PROVISION FOR FAMILY AND DEPENDENTS) ACT 1975, § 1(e) (AS AMENDED BY THE FAMILY LAW ACT (1996)). It also eliminates the need for the fixed $50,000 supplemental support award. *See* UNIF. PROB. CODE § 2-202(b) (2004). Also, by making the focus the "property acquired during marriage," the proposal adopts the sliding scale of the elective share, allowing for length of marriage to determine the amount of property coming under the purview of the election. This also will exclude separate property from being considered under election. Most of all, the statute provides for flexibility in approach to each marriage's dissolution at death, as is done at divorce.

4. Judicial Models for Reform

a. **Testamentary Disposition.** The task for any elective statute or judicial approach seeking to "augment" or enhance the property against which the surviving spouse may elect at death of the decedent is to incorporate the vast array of non-probate transfers or inter vivos irrevocable gifts passing outside of the traditional probate estate. One method by which these non-probate transfers may be incorporated is to find that they lacked the characteristics to effectively establish themselves as non-probate transfers during the lifetime of the decedent. Unless the decedent effectively makes a transfer during lifetime, any property remaining at death must pass according to the requirements of a valid Will. Such property would be classified as "Testamentary." Not being valid non-probate transfers, testamentary property would be included in the augmented estate for election. The following case provides an example.

Newman v. Dore

Court of Appeals of New York, 1937
275 N.Y. 371, 9 N.E.2d 966

LEHMAN, Judge.

The Decedent Estate Law (Consol Laws, c. 13, arts. 2, 3) regulates the testamentary disposition and the descent and distribution of the real and personal property of decedents. It does not limit or affect disposition of property inter vivos. In terms and in intent it applies only to decedents' estates. Property which did not belong to a decedent at his death and which does not become part of his estate does not come within its scope.

The share in the real and personal property of a decedent, not devised or bequeathed, which a husband or wife takes, is now fixed by section 83 of the Decedent Estate Law. Prior to the revision of the Decedent Estate Law which took effect on September 1, 1930, a decedent could by testamentary disposition effectively exclude a wife or husband from the share of the estate which would pass to her or him in case of intestacy. That was changed by section 18 of the revised Decedent Estate Law. By that section (subdivision 1) 'a personal right of election is given to the surviving spouse to take his or her share of the estate as in intestacy, subject to the limitations, conditions and exceptions contained in this section.' These limitations and exceptions include a case where 'the testator has devised or bequeathed in trust an amount equal to or greater than the intestate share, with income thereof payable to the surviving spouse for life.' Subdivision 1(b). The Legislature has declared that its intention in enacting these sections of the revised Decedent Estate Law was 'to increase the share of a surviving spouse in the estate of a deceased spouse, either in a case of intestacy or by an election against the terms of the will of the deceased spouse thus enlarging property rights of such surviving spouse.' Laws 1929, c. 229, § 20.

Ferdinand Straus died on July 1, 1934, leaving a last will and testament dated May 5, 1934, which contained a provision for a trust for his wife for her life of one-third of the decedent's property both real and personal. In such case the statute did not give the wife a right of election to take her share of the estate as in intestacy. She receives the income for life from a trust fund of the amount of the intestate share, but does not take the share. That share is one-third of the decedent's estate. It includes no property which does not form part of the estate at the decedent's death. The testator on June 28, 1934, three days before his death, executed trust agreements by which, in form at least, he transferred to trustees all his real and personal property. If the agreements effectively divested the settlor of title to his property, then the decedent left no estate and the widow takes nothing. The widow has challenged the validity of the transfer to the trustees. The beneficiary named in the trust agreement has brought this action to compel the trustees to carry out its terms. The trial court has found that the 'trust agreements were made, executed and delivered by said Ferdinand Straus for the purpose of evading and circumventing the laws of the State of New York, and particularly sections 18 and 83 of the Decedent Estate Law.' Undoubtedly the settlor's purpose was to provide that at his death his property should pass to beneficiaries named in the trust agreement to the exclusion of his wife. Under the provisions of the Decedent Estate Law the decedent could not effect the desired purpose by testamentary disposition of his property. The problem in this case is whether he has accomplished that result by creating a trust during his lifetime.

The validity of the attempted transfer depends upon whether 'the laws of the State of New York and particularly sections 18 and 83 of the Decedent Estate Law' prohibit or permit such transfer. If the statute, in express language or by clear implication, prohibits the transfer, it is illegal; if the laws of the state do not prohibit it, the transfer is legal. In strict accuracy, it cannot be said that a 'purpose of evading and circumventing' the law can carry any legal consequences. 'We do not speak of evasion, because, when the law draws a line, a case is on one side of it or the other, and if on the safe side is none the worse legally that a party has availed himself to the full of what the law permits. When an act is condemned as an evasion what is meant is that it is on the wrong side of the line indicated by the policy if not by the mere letter of the law.' Bullen v. Wisconsin, 240 U.S. 625, 630, 36 S.Ct. 473, 474, 60 L.Ed. 830. In a subsequent case it was said of a defendant: 'The fact that it desired to evade the law, as it is called, is immaterial, because the very meaning of a line in the law is that you intentionally may go as close to it as you can if you do not pass it.' Superior Oil Co. v. State of Mississippi, 280 U.S. 390, 395, 50 S.Ct. 169, 170, 74 L.Ed. 504, both opinions by Mr. Justice Holmes. Under the laws of the State of New York, and particularly sections 18 and 83 of the Decedent Estate Law, neither spouse has any immediate interest in the property of the other. The 'enlarged property right' which the Legislature intended to confer is only an expectant interest dependent upon the contingency that the property to which the interest attaches becomes part of a decedent's estate. The contingency does not occur, and the expectant property right does not ripen into a property right in possession, if the owner sells or gives away the property. Herrmann v. Jorgenson, 263 N.Y. 348, 189 N.E. 449; Matter of McCulloch's Will, 263 N.Y. 408, 189 N.E. 473, 91 A.L.R. 1440. Defeat of a contingent expectant interest by means available under the law cannot be regarded as an unlawful 'evasion' of the law. A duty imperfectly defined by law may at times be evaded or a right imperfectly protected by law may be violated with impunity, but to say that an act, lawful under common-law rules and not prohibited by any express or implied statutory provision, is in itself a 'fraud' on the law or an 'evasion' of the law, involves a contradiction in terms.

That does not mean, of course, that the law may not place its ban upon an intended result even though the means to effect that result may be lawful. The statute gives to a spouse a property right. The question is, how far the statute protects that right even while it remains only expectant and contingent. A right created by law may be protected by law against invasion through acts otherwise lawful. A wrong does not cease to be a wrong because it is cloaked in form of law. The test of legality, then, is whether the result is lawful and the means used to achieve that result are lawful. Here, we should point out that the courts below have not based their decision primarily upon the finding that the trust agreements were executed for the purpose of evading and circumventing the law of the state of New York. The courts have also found, and the evidence conclusively establishes, that the trust agreements were made for the purpose of depriving the decedent's widow of any rights in and to his property upon his death. Under the trust agreements executed a few days before the death of the settlor, he reserved the enjoyment of the entire income as long as he should live, and a right to revoke the trust at his will, and in general the powers granted to the trustees were in terms made 'subject to the settlor's control during his life,' and could be exercised 'in such manner only as the settlor shall from time to time direct in writing.' Thus, by the trust agreement which transferred to the trustees the settlor's entire property, the settlor reserved substantially the same rights to enjoy and control the disposition of the property as he previously had possessed, and the inference is inescapable that the trust agreements were executed by the settlor, as the court has found, 'with the intention and for the purpose of diminishing his estate and thereby to reduce in amount the share' of his wife in his estate upon his death and as a 'contrivance to deprive * * * his widow of any rights in and to his property upon his death.' They had no other purpose and substantially they had no other effect. Does the statute intend that such a transfer shall be available as a means of defeating the contingent expectant estate of a spouse?

In a few states where a wife has a similar contingent expectant interest or estate in the property of her husband, it has been held that her rights may not be defeated by any transfer made during life with intent to deprive the wife of property, which under the law would otherwise pass to her. Thayer v. Thayer, 14 Vt. 107, 39 Am.Dec. 211; Evans v. Evans, 78 N.H. 352, 100 A. 671; Dyer v. Smith, 62 Mo.App. 606; Payne v. Tatem, 236 Ky. 306, 33 S.W. (2d) 2. In those states it is the intent to defeat the wife's contingent rights which creates the invalidity and it seems that an absolute transfer of all his property by a married man during his life, if made with other purpose and intent than to cut off an unloved wife, is valid even though its effect is to deprive the wife of any share in the property of her husband at his death. Dunnett v. Shields & Conant, 97 Vt. 419, 123 A. 626; Patch v. Squires, 105 Vt. 405, 165 A. 919. The rule has been stated that 'while the wife cannot complain of reasonable gifts or advancements by a husband to his children by a former marriage, yet, if the gifts constitute the principal part of the husband's estate and be made without the wife's knowledge, a presumption of fraud arises, and it rests upon the beneficiaries to explain away that presumption.' Payne v. Tatem, supra, 236 Ky. 306, at page 308, 33 S.W.(2d) 2, 3.

Motive or intent is an unsatisfactory test of the validity of a transfer of property. In most jurisdiction it has been rejected, sometimes for the reason that it would cast doubt upon the validity of all transfers made by a married man, outside of the regular course of business; sometimes because it is difficult to find a satisfactory logical foundation for it. Intent may, at times, be relevant in determining whether an act is fraudulent, but there can be no fraud where no right of any person is invaded. 'The great weight of authority is that the intent to defeat a claim which otherwise a wife might have is not enough to defeat the deed.' Leonard v. Leonard, 181 Mass. 458, 462, 63 N.E. 1068, 1069, 92 Am.St.Rep. 426, and cases there cited. Since the law gives the wife only an expectant interest in the property of her husband which becomes part of his estate, and since the law does not restrict transfers of property by the husband during his life, it would seem that the only sound test of the validity of a challenged transfer is whether it is real or illusory. That is the test applied in Leonard v. Leonard, supra. The test has been formulated in different ways, but in most jurisdictions the test applied is essentially the test of whether the husband has in good faith divested himself of ownership of his property or has made an illusory transfer. 'The 'good faith' required of the donor or settlor in making a valid disposition of his property during life does not refer to the purpose to affect his wife but to the intent to divest himself of the ownership of the property. It is, therefore, apparent that the fraudulent intent which will defeat a gift inter vivos cannot be predicated of the husband's intent to deprive the wife of her distributive * * * share as widow.' Benkart v. Commonwealth Trust Co., of Pittsburgh, 269 Pa. 257, 259, 112 A. 62, 63. In Pennsylvania the courts have sustained the validity of the trusts even where a husband reserved to himself the income for life, power of revocation, and a considerable measure of control. Cf. Lines v. Lines, 142 Pa. 149, 21 A. 809, 24 Am.St.Rep. 487; Potter Title & Trust Co. v. Braum, 294 Pa. 482, 144 A. 401, 64 A.L.R. 463; Beirne v. Continental-Equitable Trust Co., 307 Pa. 570, 161 A. 721. In other jurisdictions transfers in trust have been upheld regardless of their purpose where a husband retained a right to enjoy the income during his life. Rabbitt v. Gaither, 67 Md. 94, 8 A. 744; Cameron v. Cameron, 10 Smedes & M. (Miss.) 394, 48 Am.Dec. 759; Gentry v. Bailey, 6 Gratt. (47 Va.) 594; Hall v. Hall, 109 Va. 117, 63 S.E. 420, 21 L.R.A. (N.S.) 533; Stewart v. Stewart, 5 Conn. 317; Osborn v. Osborn, 102 Kan. 890, 172 P. 23. In some of these cases the settlor retained, also, a power of revocation. In no jurisdiction has a transfer in trust been upheld where the conveyance is intended only to cover up the fact that the husband is retaining full control of the property though in form he has parted with it. Though a person may use means lawfully available to him to keep outside of the scope of a statute, a false appearance of legality, however attained, will not avail him. Reality, not appearance, should determine legal rights. Cf. Jenkins v. Moyse, 254 N.Y. 319, 172 N.E. 521, 74 A.L.R. 205.

In this case the decedent, as we have said, retained not only the income for life and power to revoke the trust, but also the right to control the trustees. We need not now determine whether such a trust is, for any purpose, a valid present trust. It has been said that, 'where the settlor transfers property in trust and reserves not only * * * a power to revoke and modify the trust but also such power to control the trustee as to the details of the administration of the trust that the trustee is the agent of the settlor, the disposition so far as it is intended to take effect after his death is testamentary. * * *' American Law Institute, Restatement of the Law of Trusts, §57, subd. 2. We do not now consider whether the rule so stated is in accord with the law of this state or whether in this case the reserved power of control is so great that the trustee is in fact 'the agent of the settlor.' We assume, without deciding, that except for the provisions of section 18 of the Decedent Estate Law the trust would be valid. Cf. Robb v. Washington & Jefferson College, 185 N.Y. 485, 78 N.E. 359; Von Hesse v. MacKaye, 136 N.Y. 114, 32 N.E. 615. Perhaps 'from the technical point of view such a conveyance does not quite take back all that it gives, but practically it does.' That is enough to render it an unlawful invasion of the expectant interest of the wife. Leonard v. Leonard, supra; Brownell v. Briggs, 173 Mass. 529, 54 N.E. 251.

Judged by the substance, not by the form, the testator's conveyance is illusory, intended only as a mask for the effective retention by the settlor of the property which in form he had conveyed. We do not attempt now to formulate any general test of how far a settlor must divest himself of his interest in the trust property to render the conveyance more than illusory. Question of whether reservation of the income or of a power of revocation, or both, might even without reservation of the power of control be sufficient to show that the transfer was not intended in good faith to divest the settlor of his property must await decision until such question arises. In this case it is clear that the settlor never intended to divest himself of his property. He was unwilling to do so even when death was near.

The judgment should be affirmed, with costs.

CRANE, C. J., and HUBBS, LOUGHRAN and RIPPEY, JJ., concur.

FINCH, J., concurs in result.

O'BRIEN, J., takes no part.

Judgment affirmed.

b. Illusory Transfer. As a method of enhancing the property against which the surviving spouse may elect, some courts have applied a test asking whether the transfer was "illusory." This approach rejects motive or intent and, instead, asks if the decedent, at the time of the transfer, "in good faith divested himself of ownership of his property or has made an illusory transfer." *See* Newman v. Dore, 275 N.Y. 371, 379. 9 N.E.2d 966, 969 (1937). Focus here is on the intent of the decedent to surrender ownership of the property, not whether the decedent sought to defraud the surviving spouse. The success of this test in enlarging the probate estate and, thus, the property against which election may be taken, is minimal. Courts have allowed property to escape election even though the decedent retained a life estate, income, and the power to revoke. *See, e.g.*, Smyth v. Cleveland Trust Co., 172 Ohio St. 489, 179 N.E.2d 60 (1961). South Carolina has adopted this test by statute. *See* S.C. CODE ANN. § 62-7-112 (1997) (2004).

c. Intent to Defraud. Fraud is difficult to prove. Courts have sought to establish it on the part of the decedent in making a transfer by focusing on either the subjective intent of the decedent or any objective evidence, such as the length of time between establishing the non-probate transfer and the date of decedent's death. *See, e.g.*, Mo. ANN. STAT. § 474.150(1) (1998) (subjective intent); Hanke v. Hanke, 123 N.H. 175, 459 A.2d 246 (1983) (objective factors). If established, the property may be brought within the purview of the elective share.

d. Objective factors. Confronted with the vagaries of intent, one test looks to objective factors in establishing whether the non-probate transfer should be included within the elective share property. This test is explained in the following decision and has been adopted in *Restatement (Second) of Property* § 34.1(3) (2004).

Sullivan v. Burkin

Supreme Judicial Court of Massachusetts, 1984
390 Mass. 864, 460 N.E.2d 571

WILKINS, Justice.

Mary A. Sullivan, the widow of Ernest G. Sullivan, has exercised her right, under G.L. c. 191, § 15, to take a share of her husband's estate. By this action, she seeks a determination that assets held in an inter vivos trust created by her husband during the marriage should be considered as part of the estate in determining that share. A judge of the Probate Court for the county of Suffolk rejected the widow's claim and entered judgment dismissing the complaint. The widow appealed, and, on July 12, 1983, a panel of the Appeals Court reported the case to this court. * * *

In September, 1973, Ernest G. Sullivan executed a deed of trust under which he transferred real estate to himself as sole trustee. The net income of the trust was payable to him during his life and the trustee was instructed to pay to him all or such part of the principal of the trust estate as he might request in writing from time to time. He retained the right to revoke the trust at any time. On his death, the successor trustee is directed to pay the principal and any undistributed income equally to the defendants, George F. Cronin, Sr., and Harold J. Cronin, if they should survive him, which they did. There were no witnesses to the execution of the deed of trust, but the husband acknowledged his signatures before a notary public, separately, as donor and as trustee.

The husband died on April 27, 1981, while still trustee of the inter vivos trust. He left a will in which he stated that he "intentionally neglected to make any provision for my wife, Mary A. Sullivan and my grandson, Mark Sullivan." He directed that, after the payment of debts, expenses, and all estate taxes levied by reason of his death, the residue of his estate should be paid over to the trustee of the inter vivos trust. The defendants George F. Cronin, Sr., and Harold J. Cronin were named coexecutors of the will. The defendant Burkin is successor trustee of the inter vivos trust. On October 21, 1981, the wife filed a claim, pursuant to G.L. c. 191, § 15, for a portion of the estate.* * * ["Election."]

Although it does not appear in the record, the parties state in their briefs that Ernest G. Sullivan and Mary A. Sullivan had been separated for many years. We do know that in 1962 the wife obtained a court order providing for her temporary support. No final action was taken in that proceeding. The record provides no information about the value of any property owned by the husband at his death or about the value of any assets held in the inter vivos trust. At oral argument, we were advised that the husband owned personal property worth approximately $15,000 at his death and that the only asset in the trust was a house in Boston which was sold after the husband's death for approximately $85,000.

As presented in the complaint, and perhaps as presented to the motion judge, the wife's claim was simply that the inter vivos trust was an invalid testamentary disposition and that the trust assets "constitute assets of the estate" of Ernest G. Sullivan. There is no suggestion that the wife argued initially that, even if the trust were not testamentary, she had a special claim as a widow asserting her rights under G.L. c. 191, § 15. If the wife is correct that the trust was an ineffective testamentary disposition, the trust assets would be part of the husband's probate estate. In that event, we would not have to consider any special consequences of the wife's election under G.L. c. 191, § 15, or, in the words of the Appeals Court, "the present vitality" of Kerwin v. Donaghy, 317 Mass. 559, 572, 59 N.E.2d 299 (1945).

We conclude, however, that the trust was not testamentary in character and that the husband effectively created a valid inter vivos trust. Thus, whether the issue was initially involved in this case, we are now presented with the question (which the executors will have to resolve ultimately, in any event) whether the assets of the inter vivos trust are to be considered in determining the "portion of the estate of the deceased" (G.L. c. 191, § 15) in which Mary A. Sullivan has rights. We conclude that, in this case, we should adhere to the principles expressed in Kerwin v. Donaghy, supra, that deny the surviving spouse any claim against the assets of a valid inter vivos trust created by the deceased spouse, even where the deceased spouse alone retained substantial rights and powers under the trust instrument. For the future, however, as to any inter vivos trust created or amended after the date of this opinion, we announce that the estate of a decedent, for the purposes of G.L. c. 191, § 15, shall include the value of assets held in an inter vivos trust created by the deceased spouse as to which the deceased spouse alone retained the power during his or her life to direct the disposition of those trust assets for his or her benefit, as, for example, by the exercise of a power of appointment or by revocation of the trust. Such a power would be a general power of appointment for Federal estate tax purposes (I.R.C. § 2041(b)(1) [1983]) and a "general power" as defined in the Restatement (Second) of Property § 11.4(1) (Tent. Draft No. 5, 1982).

We consider first whether the inter vivos trust was invalid because it was testamentary. A trust with remainder interests given to others on the settlor's death is not invalid as a testamentary disposition simply because the settlor retained a broad power to modify or revoke the trust, the right to receive income, and the right to invade principal during his life. Ascher v. Cohen, 333 Mass. 397, 400, 131 N.E.2d 198 (1956); Leahy v. Old Colony Trust Co., 326 Mass. 49, 51, 93 N.E.2d 238 (1950); Kerwin v. Donaghy, 317 Mass. 559, 567, 59 N.E.2d 299 (1945); National Shawmut Bank v. Joy, 315 Mass. 457, 473–475, 53 N.E.2d 113 (1944); Kelley v. Snow, 185 Mass. 288, 298–299, 70 N.E. 89 (1904). The fact that the settlor of such a trust is the sole trustee does not make the trust testamentary. In National Shawmut Bank v. Joy, supra 315 Mass. at 476–477, 53 N.E.2d 113, we held that a settlor's reservation of the power to control investments did not impair the validity of a trust and noted that "[i]n Greeley v. Flynn, 310 Mass. 23, 36 N.E.2d 394 [1941], the settlor was herself the trustee and had every power of control, including the right to withdraw principal for her own use. Yet the gift over at her death was held valid and not testamentary." We did, however, leave open the question whether such a trust would be testamentary "had the trustees been reduced to passive impotence, or something near it." Id. 315 Mass. at 476, 53 N.E.2d 113. We have held an inter vivos trust valid where a settlor, having broad powers to revoke the trust and to demand trust principal, was a cotrustee with a friend (Ascher v. Cohen, supra 333 Mass. at 400, 131 N.E.2d 198) or with a bank whose tenure as trustee was at the whim of the settlor (Leahy v. Old Colony Trust Co., supra 326 Mass. at 51, 93 N.E.2d 238). In Theodore v. Theodore, 356 Mass. 297, 249 N.E.2d 3 (1969), the settlor was the sole trustee of two trusts and had the power to revoke the trusts and to withdraw principal. The court assumed that the trusts were not testamentary simply because of this arrangement. The Theodore case involved trust assets transferred to the trust only by third persons. For the purposes of determining whether a trust is testamentary, however, the origin of the assets, totally at the disposal of the settlor once received, should make no difference. See Gordon v. Feldman, 359 Mass. 25, 267 N.E.2d 895 (1971), in which the court and the parties implicitly accepted as valid an inter vivos trust in which A conveyed to himself as sole trustee with the power in A to withdraw income and principal. We believe that the law of the Commonwealth is correctly represented by the statement in Restatement (Second) of Trusts § 57, comment h (1959), that a trust is "not testamentary and invalid for failure to comply with the requirements of the Statute of Wills merely because the settlor-trustee reserves a beneficial life interest and power to revoke and modify the trust. The fact that as trustee he controls the administration of the trust does not invalidate it."

We come then to the question whether, even if the trust was not testamentary on general principles, the widow has special interests which should be recognized. Courts in this country have differed considerably in their reasoning and in their conclusions in passing on this question. See 1 A. Scott, Trusts § 57.5 at 509–511 (3d ed. 1967 & 1983 Supp.); Restatement (Second) of Property—Donative Transfers, Supplement to Tent. Draft No. 5, reporter's note to § 13.7 (1982); Annot., 39 A.L.R.3d 14 (1971), Validity of Inter Vivos Trust Established by One Spouse Which Impairs the Other Spouse's Distributive Share or Other Statutory Rights in Property. In considering this issue at the May, 1982, annual meeting of the American Law Institute the members divided almost evenly on whether a settlor's surviving spouse should have rights, apart from specific statutory rights, with respect to the assets of an inter vivos trust over which the settlor retained a general power of appointment. See Proceedings of the American Law Institute, May, 1982, pp. 59–117; Restatement (Second) of Property—Donative Transfers, Supplement to Tent. Draft No. 5 at 28 (1982). * * *

The rule of Kerwin v. Donaghy, supra 317 Mass. at 571, 59 N.E.2d 299, is that "[t]he right of a wife to waive her husband's will, and take, with certain limitations, 'the same portion of the property of the deceased, real and personal, that … she would have taken if the deceased had died intestate' (G.L. [Ter.Ed.] c. 191, § 15), does not extend to personal property that has been conveyed by the husband in his lifetime and does not form part of his estate at his death. Fiske v. Fiske, 173 Mass. 413, 419, 53 N.E. 916 [1899]. Shelton v. Sears, 187 Mass. 455, 73 N.E. 666 [1905]. In this Commonwealth a husband has an absolute right to dispose of any or all of his personal property in his lifetime, without the knowledge or consent of his wife, with the result that it will not form part of his estate for her to share under the statute of distributions (G.L. [Ter.Ed.] c. 190, §§ 1, 2), under his will, or by virtue of a waiver of his will. That is true even though his sole purpose was to disinherit her." In the Kerwin case, we applied the rule to deny a surviving spouse the right to reach assets the deceased spouse had placed in an inter vivos trust of which the settlor's daughter by a previous marriage was trustee and over whose assets he had a general power of appointment. The rule of Kerwin v. Donaghy has been adhered to in this Commonwealth for almost forty years and was adumbrated even earlier. * * * The bar has been entitled reasonably to rely on that rule in advising clients. In the area of property law, the retroactive invalidation of an established principle is to be undertaken with great caution. See Boston Safe Deposit & Trust Co. v. Fleming, 361 Mass. 172, 181–182, 279 N.E.2d 342, appeal dismissed, 409 U.S. 813, 93 S.Ct. 46, 34 L.Ed.2d 69 (1972); Fiduciary Trust Co. v. Mishou, 321 Mass. 615, 636, 75 N.E.2d 3 (1947). Cf. Johnson Controls, Inc. v. Bowes, 381 Mass. 278, 282–283, 409 N.E.2d 185 (1980) (insurance contracts); Whitinsville Plaza, Inc. v. Kotseas, 378 Mass. 85, 97–98, 390 N.E.2d 243 (1979) (covenants not to compete made in deeds and leases); Rosenberg v. Lipnick, 377 Mass. 666, 667, 389 N.E.2d 385 (1979) (antenuptial agreements); Tucker v. Badoian, 376 Mass. 907, 918–919, 384 N.E.2d 1195 (1978) (Kaplan, J., concurring) (relative rights as to the flow of surface water). Contrast as to tort law, Payton v. Abbott Labs, 386 Mass. 540, 565–570, 437 N.E.2d 171 (1982). We conclude that, whether or not Ernest G. Sullivan established the inter vivos trust in order to defeat his wife's right to take her statutory share in the assets placed in the trust and even though he had a general power of appointment over the trust assets, Mary A. Sullivan obtained no right to share in the assets of that trust when she made her election under G.L. c. 191, § 15.

We announce for the future that, as to any inter vivos trust created or amended after the date of this opinion, we shall no longer follow the rule announced in Kerwin v. Donaghy. There have been significant changes since 1945 in public policy considerations bearing on the right of one spouse to treat his or her property as he or she wishes during marriage. The interests of one spouse in the property of the other have been substantially increased upon the dissolution of a marriage by divorce.[6] We believe that, when a marriage is terminated by the death of one spouse, the rights of the surviving spouse should not be so restricted as they are by the rule in Kerwin v. Donaghy. It is neither equitable nor logical to extend to a divorced spouse greater rights in the assets of an inter vivos trust created and controlled by the other spouse than are extended to a spouse who remains married until the death of his or her spouse.

The rule we now favor would treat as part of "the estate of the deceased" for the purposes of G.L. c. 191, § 15, assets of an inter vivos trust created during the marriage by the deceased spouse over which he or she alone had a general power of appointment, exercisable by deed or by will. This objective test would involve no consideration of the motive or intention of the spouse in creating the trust. We would not need to engage in a determination of "whether the [spouse] has in good faith divested himself [or herself] of ownership of his [or her] property or has made an illusory transfer" (Newman v. Dore, 275 N.Y. 371, 379, 9 N.E.2d 966 [1937]) or with the factual question whether the spouse "intended to surrender complete dominion over the property" (Staples v. King, 433 A.2d 407, 411 [Me.1981]). Nor would we have to participate in the rather unsatisfactory process of determining whether the inter vivos trust was, on some standard, "colorable," "fraudulent," or "illusory."

What we have announced as a rule for the future hardly resolves all the problems that may arise. There may be a different rule if some or all of the trust assets were conveyed to such a trust by a third person. Cf. Theodore v. Theodore, 356 Mass. 297, 249 N.E.2d 3 (1969). We have not, of course, dealt with a case in which the power of appointment is held jointly with another person. If the surviving spouse assented to the creation of the inter vivos trust, perhaps the rule we announce would not apply. We

---

6. At the time of a divorce or at any subsequent time, "the court may assign to either husband or wife all or any part of the estate of the other," on consideration of various factors, such as the length of the marriage, the conduct of the parties during the marriage, their ages, their employability, their liabilities and needs, and opportunity for future acquisition of capital assets and income. G.L. c. 208, § 34, as amended by St.1982, c. 642, § 1. The power to dispose completely of the property of the divorced litigants comes from a 1974 amendment to G.L. c. 208, § 34. See St.1974, c. 565. It made a significant change in the respective rights of the husband and wife and in the power of Probate Court judges. See Bianco v. Bianco, 371 Mass. 420, 422–423, 358 N.E.2d 243 (1976). We have held that the "estate" subject to disposition on divorce includes not only property acquired during the marriage from the efforts of the husband and wife, but also all property of a spouse "whenever and however acquired." Rice v. Rice, 372 Mass. 398, 400, 361 N.E.2d 1305 (1977). Without suggesting the outer limits of the meaning of the word "estate" under G.L. c. 208, § 34, as applied to trust assets over which a spouse has a general power of appointment at the time of a divorce, after this decision there should be no doubt that the "estate" of such a spouse would include trust assets held in a trust created by the other spouse and having provisions such as the trust in the case before us.

have not discussed which assets should be used to satisfy a surviving spouse's claim. We have not discussed the question whether a surviving spouse's interest in the intestate estate of a deceased spouse should reflect the value of assets held in an inter vivos trust created by the intestate spouse over which he or she had a general power of appointment. That situation and the one before us, however, do not seem readily distinguishable. See Schnakenberg v. Schnakenberg, 262 A.D. 234, 236–237, 28 N.Y.S.2d 841 (N.Y.1941). A general power of appointment over assets in a trust created by a third person is said to present a different situation. Restatement (Second) of Property—Donative Transfers, Supplement to Tent. Draft No. 5, reporter's note to § 13.7 at 29 (1982). Nor have we dealt with other assets not passing by will, such as a trust created before the marriage or insurance policies over which a deceased spouse had control. Id. at 30, 38.

The question of the rights of a surviving spouse in the estate of a deceased spouse, using the word "estate" in its broad sense, is one that can best be handled by legislation. See Uniform Probate Code, §§ 2-201, 2-202, 8 U.L.A. 74–75 (1983). See also Uniform Marital Property Act, § 18 (Nat'l Conference of Comm'rs on Uniform State Laws, July, 1983), which adopts the concept of community property as to "marital property." But, until it is, the answers to these problems will "be determined in the usual way through the decisional process." Tucker v. Badoian, 376 Mass. 907, 918–919, 384 N.E.2d 1195 (1978) (Kaplan, J., concurring).

We affirm the judgment of the Probate Court dismissing the plaintiff's complaint.

So ordered.

IV. Administration

A. Limitations: Probate Versus Non-Probate Transfers

Probate technically means establishing the validity of the Last Will and Testament, but the term is often used to refer to the entire process by which all assets of the decedent, passing by testate or intestate succession, are identified and then distributed to heirs or intended legatees or devisees, and expenses are paid. A more accurate term for this process would be administration of the decedent's estate. Recall that one of the benefits of non-probate transfers is that no administration is necessary; items such as payable-on-death accounts, revocable trusts, or joint tenancies pass immediately upon the death of the decedent to named beneficiaries without the necessity of administration. This is what makes them so popular and so private; they are fast and allow clients to by-pass the public process by which a Will is established by probate as a public document and conduit of wealth transfer. But estate taxes on non-probate transfers may still be due, and sometimes title to real estate must be cleared. With probate, real and personal property, passing as it does through administration,

> devolves to the persons to whom it is devised by [a decedent's] last will or to those indicated as substitutes for them in cases involving lapse, renunciation, or other circumstances affecting the devolution of testate estate, or in the absence of testamentary disposition, to [his or her] heirs, or to those indicated as substitutes for them in cases involving renunciation or other circumstances af-

fecting devolution of intestate estates, subject to homestead allowance, exempt property and family allowance, to rights of creditors, elective share of the surviving spouse, and to administration.

Unif. Prob. Code §3-101 (2004). Procedures associated with administration have evolved over generations and will vary among states, yet there is a process that, with variations, will apply whenever a decedent dies leaving a valid Will or property passing according to intestate succession. What follows is a sketch of that process.

B. Administrative Process

1. Venue

Upon the death of a decedent, the proper question to ask is where to begin the process of administration. For example, "[i]f the decedent was domiciled in this state at the time of death, the proper county for proceedings concerning administration of the decedent's estate is the county in which the decedent was domiciled, regardless of where the decedent died." Cal. Prob. Code §7051 (2004). Thus, domicile of the decedent governs the devolution of all personal property, wherever located, and any real property located in that state. If real property is located in another state, then there must be ancillary administration in that state, meaning that the Will must be probated there to clear title to the real estate, see Unif. Prob. Code §4-205 (2004), pay all debts, and collect all assets. See Unif. Prob. Code §§4-201 to 203 (2004). The same would be true if the decedent died intestate and owned personal and real property in more than one state.

2. Personal Representative

The Uniform Probate Code often refers to the executor (testate) or the administrator (intestate) by use of the ubiquitous term "personal representative;" the term eliminates any distinction between the two titles. To qualify as such, a person "must be appointed by order of the Registrar, qualify and be issued letters. Administration of an estate is commenced by the issuance of letters." See Unif. Prob. Code §3-103 (2004). Any valid Will may designate a Personal Representative, but if there is no Will or it fails to appoint a Personal Representative, there is a list of priority of possible appointees established by statute. See, e.g., Unif. Prob. Code §3-203 (2004). Once appointed by the court, the Personal Representative has specified duties to perform, the powers relating "back in time to give acts by the person appointed which are beneficial to the estate occurring prior to appointment the same effect as those occurring thereafter." Unif. Prob. Code §3-701 (2003). For example, one of the first duties is probate of the Will—establishing the validity of its formalities and intentionalities— but making no determination as to the substantive terms contained therein. Once the court accepts the administration of the estate, the Personal Representative is entitled to reasonable compensation unless other provisions are established in the Will. See Unif. Prob. Code §3-719 (2004); Cal. Prob. Code §§10800–10805 (2003).

3. Statute of Limitations

There are varying times as to the statute of limitations for submitting a Will for probate. The Uniform Probate Code provides a three year period following the death of the decedent, with some exceptions. *See* UNIF. PROB. CODE § 3-108 (2004). Differing from submitting a Will for probate, a proceeding to contest an informally probated Will may be commenced within twelve months after such informal probate or three years after the decedent's death, whichever is later. *Id.* In the case of small estates involving only personal property, there is a provision for minimal administration, but the process still must be commenced by the Personal Representative. *See, e.g.,* UNIF. PROB. CODE §§ 3-1201 to 1204 (2004); CAL. PROB. CODE §§ 7660–66 (2003).

4. *Informal and Formal Probate*

As the name implies, informal probate means that the Will lacks contest by any party and allows for a speedier distribution of the probate estate. *See* UNIF. PROB. CODE §§ 3-301 to 311 (2004). "Informal probate is conclusive as to all persons until superceded by an order in a formal intestacy proceeding." UNIF. PROB. CODE § 3-302 (2004).

> A formal testacy proceeding is litigation to determine whether a decedent left a valid will. A formal testacy proceeding may be commenced by an interested person filing a petition [Section 3-402(a)] in which [he or she] requests that the Court, after notice and hearing, enter an order probating a will, or a petition to set aside an informal probate of a will or to prevent informal probate of a will which is the subject of a pending application, or a petition in accordance with Section 3-402(b) for an order that the decedent died intestate.

UNIF. PROB. CODE § 3-401 (2004). As the more juridical procedure, the Uniform Probate Code formal procedure establishes the parameters of notice, proof, testimony, finality, and effect of the order. *See* UNIF. PROB. CODE §§ 3-402 to 414 (2004).

5. *Information*

A Personal Representative is a fiduciary who shall observe the standards of care applicable to trustees. UNIF. PROB. CODE § 3-703(a) (2004). *See also* UNIF. PROB. CODE § 3-712 (2004) (Improper Exercise of Power; Breach of Fiduciary Duty); CAL. PROB. CODE §§ 9600–9606 (2003). As such, he or she has a strict duty of care, and one of the responsibilities is that, no later than thirty days after appointment, the Personal Representative must give information to the heirs and devisees by ordinary mail telling them of the appointment and that they are entitled to information from the Personal Representative regarding the administration. The Representative must also inform the heirs and devisees that they have the right to petition the court in any matter relating to the estate, including distribution of assets and expenses of administration. UNIF. PROB. CODE § 3-705 (2004).

6. *Inventory and Appraisement*

Within three months of appointment, a Personal Representative must prepare and file or mail an inventory of property owned by the decedent at the time of his or her death, listing items with reasonable detail, fair market value, and any debts against the property. The filing must be with the court, but a copy shall be sent to any interested person who requests it. UNIF. PROB. CODE § 3-706 (2004). The Personal Representative has a duty to modify the inventory as needed, *see* UNIF. PROB. CODE § 3-708 (2004), and must pay taxes on and take all steps necessary for management, protection and preservation of the assets. UNIF. PROB. CODE § 3-709 (2004).

7. *Administration Powers of Personal Representative*

Unless restricted by a valid Will of the decedent, the Personal Representative is given an extensive array of powers to do such duties as selling assets, employing persons, voting stocks of other securities, *see* UNIF. PROB. CODE § 3-715 (2004), or even running decedent's business, *see, e.g.,* CAL. PROB. CODE § 9760 (2003). Employment of any person and the compensation paid to that person is subject to review by the court. *See* UNIF. PROB. CODE § 3-721 (2004). *See, e.g.,* CAL. PROB. CODE §§ 10810–10814 (2003) (compensation paid to an attorney). If, for any reason, the original Personal Representative is unable to complete the estate administration, a successor "has the same power and duty as the original personal representative to complete the administration and distribution of the estate, as expeditiously as possible, but [he or she] shall not exercise any power expressly made personal to the [personal representative] named in the will." UNIF. PROB. CODE § 3-716 (2004).

8. *Notice to Creditors*

The Personal Representative must publish a notice to creditors once a week for three successive weeks in a newspaper of general circulation in the decedent's domicile county announcing his or her appointment, address, and notice that they must present claims within four months of the date of the first publication of the notice or be barred forever. *See* UNIF. PROB. CODE § 3-801(a) (2004). California is more precise, providing that the first publication date of the notice shall be at least 15 days before the hearing.Three publications in a newspaper published once a week, or more often, with at least five days intervening between the first and last publication dates, not counting the publication dates, are sufficient. *See* CAL. PROB. CODE § 8121(a) (2003).

9. *Payment of Claims*

The Personal Representative is empowered to pay claims against the decedent's estate, waive defenses, and, if assets are insufficient to pay all claims in full, make payment in the following order: (a) costs and expenses of administration; (b) reasonable funeral expenses; (c) debts and taxes, with preference under federal law; (d) reasonable and necessary medical and hospital expenses of the last illness of the decedent, including compensation of persons attending him or her; (e) debts and taxes, with preference under other laws of the state; (f) all other claims. UNIF. PROB. CODE § 3-805 (2004). There are a number of special provisions relating to abatement of assets, UNIF. PROB. CODE § 3-902 (2004), distribution in kind, UNIF. PROB. CODE § 3-907 (2004), and liability of a distributee when there has been an improper distribution of an asset, UNIF. PROB. CODE § 3-909 (2004). In contracting in his fiduciary capacity, a Personal Representative is not individually liable unless he or she fails to reveal his representative capacity and identify the estate in his contracting. UNIF. PROB. CODE § 3-808 (2004).

10. *Closing the Estate*

After one year, the Personal Representative or any interested person may petition the court for an order of complete settlement of the estate. *See* UNIF. PROB. CODE §§ 3-1001 to 02 (2004). Most states require the Personal Representative to file a final accounting to the court, *see, e.g.,* CAL. PROB. CODE § 10900 (2003), but the Uniform Probate Code does not do this, providing, instead, an optional sworn statement of the Personal Representative. *See* UNIF. PROB. CODE § 3-1003 (2004). The Uniform Probate Code provides that, no earlier than six months of his or her original appointment, the Personal Representative may file with the court a verified statement that he or she has determined that the time limit for the creditors' presentation of claims has expired, that all claims have been paid, and a copy of the statement has been sent to all distributees, creditors, and any other claimants. UNIF. PROB. CODE § 3-1003 (2004). Successors and creditors have six months after the filing of the closing statement to bring suit against the Personal Representative for any negligence in the performance of his or her duties. UNIF. PROB. CODE § 3-1005 (2004). But the Personal Representative could bring an inter partes proceeding in which all the interested parties are joined for the purpose of obtaining a court order settling the account. This has the effect of discharging the Personal Representative from further liability and furthering the goal of finality. *See* UNIF. PROB. CODE §§ 3-1001 to 02 (2004).

11. Tax Considerations

The Personal Representative is responsible for the payment of taxes associated with the decedent's estate (*see* I.R.C. § 2002). With few exceptions, the estate tax is due nine months from the decedent's death. *See* I.R.C. § 6075. Generally, an estate will be allowed an automatic six month extension of time beyond the nine month due date to file the estate tax return so long as Form 4768 is filed on or before the original due date. *See* § 20.6081-1 of the Procedure and Administration Regulations. The taxable estate equals the value of the gross estate less the deductions allowed under I.R.C. §§ 2053 through 2058. With respect to the value of the gross estate, the Personal Representative may elect to utilize an alternate valuation date if the value of the gross estate and the amount of the estate tax due will decrease (*see* I.R.C. § 2032). The alternate valuation date may be six months after the date of death of the decedent, and once the election is made it is irrevocable.

C. Professional Responsibility

Hotz v. Minyard

Supreme Court of South Carolina, 1991
304 S.C. 225, 403 S.E.2d 634

GREGORY, Chief Justice.

This appeal is from an order granting respondents summary judgment on several causes of action. We reverse in part and affirm in part.

Respondent Minyard (Tommy) and appellant (Judy) are brother and sister. Their father, Mr. Minyard, owns two automobile dealerships, Judson T. Minyard, Inc. (Greenville Dealership), and Minyard-Waidner, Inc. (Anderson Dealership). Tommy has been the dealer in charge of the Greenville Dealership since 1977. Judy worked for her father at the Anderson Dealership beginning in 1983; she was also a vice-president and minority shareholder. In 1985, Mr. Minyard signed a contract with General Motors designating Judy the successor dealer of the Anderson Dealership.

Respondent Dobson is a South Carolina lawyer practicing in Greenville and a member of respondent Dobson & Dobson, P.A. (Law Firm). Dobson is also a certified public accountant, although he no longer practices as one. In 1985, Dobson sold the tax return preparation practice of Law Firm to respondent Dobson, Lewis & Saad, P.A. (Accounting Firm). Although his name is included in Accounting Firm's name, Dobson is merely a shareholder and director and does not receive remuneration as an employee.

Dobson did legal work for the Minyard family and its various businesses for many years. On October 24, 1984, Mr. Minyard came to Law Firm's office to execute a will with his wife, his secretary, and Tommy in attendance. At this meeting he signed a will which left Tommy the Greenville Dealership, gave other family members bequests totalling $250,000.00, and divided the remainder of his estate equally between Tommy and a trust for Judy after his wife's death. All present at the meeting were given copies of this will. Later that afternoon, however, Mr. Minyard returned to Dobson's office and signed a second will containing the same provisions as the first except that it gave the real estate upon which the Greenville dealership was located to Tommy outright. Mr. Minyard instructed Dobson not to disclose the existence of the second will. He specifically directed that Judy not be told about it.

In January 1985, Judy called Dobson requesting a copy of the will her father had signed at the morning meeting on October 24, 1984. At Mr. Minyard's direction, or at least with his express permission, Dobson showed Judy the first will and discussed it with her in detail.

Judy testified she had the impression from her discussion with Dobson that under her father's will she would receive the Anderson Dealership and would share equally with her brother in her father's estate. According to Dobson, however, he merely explained Mr. Minyard's intent to provide for Judy as he had for Tommy when and if she became capable of handling a dealership. Dobson made a notation to this effect on the copy of the will he discussed with Judy. Judy claimed she was led to believe the handwritten notes were part of her father's will.

In any event, Judy claims Dobson told her the will she was shown was in actuality her father's last will and testament. Although Dobson denies ever making this express statement, he admits he never told her the will he discussed with her had been revoked.

In January 1986, Mr. Minyard was admitted to the hospital for various health problems. In April 1986, he suffered a massive stroke. Although the date of the onset of his mental incompetence is disputed, it is uncontested he is now mentally incompetent.

Judy and Tommy agreed that while their father was ill, Judy would attend to his daily care and Tommy would temporarily run the Anderson Dealership until Judy returned. During this time, Tommy began making changes at the Anderson Dealership. Under his direction, the Anderson Dealership bought out another dealership owned by Mr. Minyard, Judson Lincoln-Mercury, Inc., which was operating at a loss. Tommy also formed a holding company which assumed ownership of Mr. Minyard's real estate leased to the Anderson Dealership. Consequently, rent paid by the dealership was greatly increased.

Judy questioned the wisdom of her brother's financial dealings. When she sought to return to the Anderson Dealership as successor dealer, Tommy refused to relinquish control. Eventually, in August 1986, he terminated Judy from the dealership's payroll.

Judy consulted an Anderson law firm concerning her problems with her brother's operation of the Anderson Dealership. As a result, on November 15, 1986, Mr. Minyard executed a codicil removing Judy and her children as beneficiaries under his will. Judy was immediately advised of this development by letter.

In March 1987, Judy met with Tommy, her mother, and Dobson at Law Firm's office. She was told if she discharged her attorneys and dropped her plans for a lawsuit, she would be restored under her father's will and could work at the Greenville Dealership with significant fringe benefits. Judy testified she understood restoration under the will meant she would inherit the Anderson Dealership and receive half her father's estate, including the real estate, as she understood from her 1985 meeting with Dobson. Judy discharged her attorneys and moved to Greenville. Eventually, however, Tommy terminated her position at the Greenville Dealership.

As a result of the above actions by Tommy and Dobson, Judy commenced this suit alleging various causes of action. The causes of action against Tommy for tortious interference with contract, a shareholder derivative suit for wrongful diversion of corporate profits, and fraud survived summary judgment and are not at issue here. Judy appeals the trial judge's order granting summary judgment on the remaining causes of action against Tommy, Dobson, and the professional associations. We address only the trial judge's ruling on the cause of action against Dobson for breach of fiduciary duty. Judy also appeals the dismissal of Minyard-Waidner, Inc. as a party defendant.

* * *

Judy's complaint alleges Dobson breached his fiduciary duty to her by misrepresenting her father's will in January 1985. As a result, in March 1987 she believed she would regain the Anderson Dealership if she refrained from pursuing her claim against her brother. This delay gave Tommy additional time in control of the Anderson Dealership during which he depleted its assets. Law Firm and Accounting Firm are charged with vicarious liability for Dobson's acts.

The trial judge granted Dobson, Law Firm, and Accounting Firm summary judgment on the ground Dobson owed Judy no fiduciary duty because he was acting as Mr. Minyard's attorney and not as Judy's attorney in connection with her father's will. We disagree.

We find the evidence indicates a factual issue whether Dobson breached a fiduciary duty to Judy when she went to his office seeking legal advice about the effect of her father's will. Law Firm had prepared Judy's tax returns for approximately twenty years until September 1985 and had prepared a will for her she signed only one week earlier. Judy testified she consulted Dobson personally in 1984 or 1985 about a suspected misappropriation of funds at one of the dealerships and as late as 1986 regarding her problems with her brother. She claimed she trusted Dobson because of her dealings with him over the years as her lawyer and accountant.

A fiduciary relationship exists when one has a special confidence in another so that the latter, in equity and good conscience, is bound to act in good faith. Island Car Wash, Inc. v. Norris, 292 S.C. 595, 599, 358 S.E.2d 150, 152 (Ct.App.1987). An attorney/client relationship is by nature a fiduciary one. In re: Green, 291 S.C. 523, 354 S.E.2d 557 (1987). Although Dobson represented Mr. Minyard and not Judy regarding her father's will, Dobson did have an ongoing attorney/client relationship with Judy and there is evidence she had "a special confidence" in him. While Dobson had no duty to disclose the existence of the second will against his client's (Mr. Minyard's) wishes, he owed Judy the duty to deal with her in good faith and not actively misrepresent the first will. We find there is a factual issue presented whether Dobson breached a fiduciary duty to Judy. We conclude summary judgment was improperly granted Dobson on this cause of action. See Standard Fire Ins. Co. v. Marine Contracting and Towing Co., 301 S.C. 418, 392 S.E.2d 460 (1990) (summary judgment).

Similarly, we find evidence to present a jury issue whether Law Firm should be held vicariously liable for Dobson's conduct since Dobson was acting in his capacity as a lawyer when he met with Judy to discuss the will in January 1985. There is no evidence, however, that Dobson was acting in his capacity as an accountant on that occasion since he was giving legal advice and not rendering accounting services. We find no basis for vicarious liability against Accounting Firm. Accordingly, we reverse the granting of summary judgment on this cause of action as to Dobson and Law Firm and affirm as to Accounting Firm.

Finally, the trial judge dismissed Minyard-Waidner, Inc., the Anderson Dealership, as a party defendant on the ground the complaint contains no allegation of wrongdoing by the corporate entity. Judy claims the corporation is the real party in interest in her shareholder's derivative action and should not be dismissed from the action.

Under former S.C.Code Ann. § 15-5-40 (1976), it was required that parties united in interest be joined as plaintiffs or defendants. A party whose consent could not be obtained could be named as a defendant. This Court never construed § 15-5-40 in the context of a shareholder derivative suit and it has now been superseded by the South Carolina Rules of Civil Procedure. Rule 23(b), SCRCP, governing derivative suits makes no mention of the need to name the corporation as a party defendant. Other jurisdictions have held that a shareholder derivative suit must be dismissed if the corporation is not named as a party defendant where the corporation is not defunct. See, e.g., Wagner v. Bisco, 190 Ga. 474, 9 S.E.2d 650 (1940). The reasoning for such a rule is that the court must have all interested parties before it to fix their respective rights. Further, because a stockholder has no power to bind the corporation, the corporation must be named as a defendant if it has not brought the action in its own right. Id. While we decline at this time to adopt such a requirement, we hold a corporate defendant may be named in a shareholder's derivative suit as a party defendant even where no wrongdoing by the corporate entity is alleged.

Pursuant to Supreme Court Rule 23, we affirm the trial judge's order granting summary judgment on the remaining causes of action. The judgment of the circuit court is

REVERSED IN PART; AFFIRMED IN PART.

HARWELL, CHANDLER, FINNEY and TOAL, JJ., concur.

Chapter Six

Utilizing Future Interests

Tool Bar

I. Interests Held by the Settlor

As a legal entity, trusts and estates is almost always premised on future events, thus differentiating itself from outright gifts here and now. Throughout the course of centuries, in the common law and community property worlds, terms and phrases have arisen to best describe what the drafters of testamentary and inter vivos instruments expect to happen in the future. These terms and phrases, denoting statutes, presumptions, rules, and doctrines, are classified as future interests. The dilemma for many practitioners is that future interests resemble the morbidity of Latin more than the alacrity of DSL. It is the task of the drafting attorney to reverse the biblical adage and put new wine into old bottles. An example of modern necessities placed within the historical framework of future interests may be found in the following case. It provides an example of future interests at work, but also the more modern demands of estate planning.

First National Bank of Bar Harbor v. Anthony

Supreme Judicial Court of Maine, 1989

557 A.2d 957

ROBERTS, Justice.

The children of John M. Anthony, Deborah Alley and Christopher Anthony Perasco, appeal from a summary judgment of the Superior Court, Hancock County (*Smith, J.*), that denied their claim to a remainder interest in an *inter vivos* trust created by their now deceased grandfather, J. Franklin Anthony. The court determined that the gift to John M. Anthony, a child of the settlor, of the remainder interest lapsed as a result of John M. Anthony's death prior to the death of the settlor. Because we hold that the remainder interest of John M. Anthony was a present, vested interest at the time of the creation of the *inter vivos* trust, we vacate the judgment.

* * *

On May 14, 1975, J. Franklin Anthony, of Bar Harbor, established a revocable *inter vivos* trust with the First National Bank of Bar Harbor. The income was payable to the settlor for life, then to his widow, Ethel L. Anthony, should she survive him. Upon the death of both J. Franklin and Ethel L. Anthony, the corpus would be divided "in equal shares to [the settlor's] children, John M. Anthony, Peter B. Anthony and Dencie S. Tripp [now Fenno] free and clear of any trust."

Ethel Anthony predeceased her husband on November 22, 1982. On September 9, 1983, John M. Anthony died unmarried, leaving three children: Deborah Alley, Christopher Anthony Perasco and Paul Anthony.

J. Franklin Anthony died on April 2, 1984. On April 10, 1984, his will was admitted to Probate by the Hancock County Probate Court. The will left two-thirds of his estate to Peter B. Anthony and one-third to Dencie S. Fenno; the heirs of John M. Anthony were expressly omitted from the will.

* * *

The First National Bank of Bar Harbor, in its capacity as trustee, filed a complaint in the Superior Court requesting construction of the Anthony Trust. The children of John M. Anthony, grandchildren of the settlor, filed a motion for summary judgment. The grandchildren asserted that John M. Anthony's interest in the trust was vested, not contingent, at the time of its creation. John M.'s heirs, therefore, were entitled to his one-third interest in the trust.

The motion was opposed by Dencie S. Fenno and Peter B. Anthony, at that time arguing that the terms of the trust were ambiguous and that extrinsic evidence should be permitted to determine the intent of the settlor. Their memorandum was accompanied by two affidavits stating that affiant's understanding that the deceased settlor wished the children of John M. Anthony to receive nothing from the settlor's estate. In granting summary judgment against the movants, the court (1) declined to consider extrinsic evidence on the ground that the language of the trust was unambiguous, (2) determined that the gift of the remainder to named individuals "in equal shares" was a gift to the individuals and not to a class, (3) held that the gift to John M. Anthony lapsed because his interest did not vest until the death of the survivor of the settlor and his wife, and (4) declined to apply the Anti-Lapse Statute, 18-A M.R.S.A. §2-605 (Supp. 1988), because the statute applies only to testamentary gifts. The court therefore directed the trustee to pay over the lapsed gift to John M. Anthony to the personal representative of the deceased settlor. This appeal followed.

* * *

Before us all parties now agree that the terms of the trust are unambiguous and that a summary judgment is appropriate. Moreover, all parties agree that the gift of the remainder interest "in equal shares" to the named children of the settlor was a gift to the individuals and not to a class. As a result, we need address only the court's holding that the gift to John M. Anthony lapsed upon his death prior to the death of the settlor.

The parties rely almost exclusively on our prior cases dealing with testamentary dispositions. These cases are of little assistance on the issue before us. Because a will is not operative until the death of the testator, an interest in a testamentary trust cannot vest prior to that event. On the other hand, an *inter vivos* trust is operative from the date of its creation. We must determine the settlor's intent as expressed in the trust instrument by examining the settlor's overall plan of disposition.

We note the following: (1) the settlor explicitly retained the right to change his beneficiaries if he wanted to alter the trust's disposition; (2) the settlor imposed no restrictions on what his children could do with their respective shares; (3) aside from his power to revoke or amend the trust, the settlor specifically limited his own benefit to income during his lifetime and payment of certain expenses associated with his death; (4) the settlor made survival an explicit condition of any benefit to his wife, but did not include such language in the case of his children. The unexercised right to make a change in beneficiaries, the absence of any control over how the children might dispose of their shares, and the overall assignment of economic benefits lead us to conclude that this plan of disposition effectively eliminated any further interest of the settlor in the trust principal unless he affirmatively chose to intervene. His failure to change the plan coupled with the omission of a survival requirement in the case of the children's shares, suggests a disposition to a predeceased child's estate rather than a reversion to the settlor's estate. As a result of this construction of the instrument, it may be said that the children's interests were vested, subject to defeasance or divestment if the settlor chose to amend or revoke the trust or change his beneficiaries.

We next address the question whether the settlor's reservation of the power of amendment or revocation should alter our conclusion that the children's interests vested. Substantial case law from other jurisdictions persuades us that it should not. A leading case decided by the Ohio Supreme Court holds that an *inter vivos* trust reserving to the settlor the income for life plus the power to revoke, with a remainder over at the death of the settlor, creates a vested interest in the remainderman subject to defeasance by the exercise of the power of revocation. First National Bank v. Tenney, 165 Ohio St. 513, 138 N.E.2d 15 (1956).

Similarly, an Illinois appellate court, reversing the trial court, held that a delay in enjoyment of possession does not imply a requirement of survival by the remainderman before the remainder is vested. First Galesburg National Bank & Trust Co. v. Robinson, 149 Ill.App.3d 584, 102 Ill.Dec. 894, 500 N.E.2d 995 (1986). The court concluded that the words "at the death of" do not refer to the time when the remainder vested, but rather to the time when the remainderman was entitled to possession. *Id.* 102 Ill.Dec. at 895, 500 N.E.2d at 996. The sons of the settlors, therefore, took a present right to the remainder upon execution of the trust instrument, although enjoyment was postponed until the termination of the life estates. *Id.* 102 Ill.Dec. at 895–96, 500 N.E.2d at 996–97.

Even when the settlor said "on [the settlor's] death the remainder shall vest," the *inter vivos* trust has been held to create a present interest subject to divestment by amendment or revocation. Randall v. Bank of America N.T. & S.A., 48 Cal.App.2d 249, 119 P.2d 754 (1941). An Indiana court has stated that the language of Restatement (Second) of Trusts § 112(f) that a person dying prior to the creation of a trust cannot be a beneficiary of that trust is inapplicable to persons living at the time of the creation of an *inter vivos* trust. Hinds v. McNair, 413 N.E.2d 586 (Ind.App.1980).... [additional citations omitted].

The trust instrument before us contains no requirement that the remainder beneficiaries survive the life tenants and we see no reason to imply a requirement of survival. Only the settlor's subsequent revocation or substitution would divest the remainder interest. Evidence presented by affidavit of the settlor's desire to revoke the contingent remainder and disinherit his son and son's heirs is simply not relevant. Although the settlor's intention is critical in interpreting the terms of a trust, that intention must be ascertained by analyzing the trust instrument. Mooney v. Northeast Bank & Trust Co., 377 A.2d 120, 122 (Me.1977). Only when the instrument is ambiguous can a court consider extrinsic evidence. *Id.* at 122.

Because John M. Anthony's interest vested at the time of the creation of the trust, we do not consider whether Maine's anti-lapse statute, 18-A M.R.S.A. § 2-605, could apply to an *inter vivos* trust.

The entry is:

Judgment vacated.

Remanded for determination of the appropriate instruction to the Trustee in accordance with the opinion herein.

Costs to be taxed against the trust estate.

All concurring.

Notes

(1) The first question to ask is whether the instrument created by the Settlor was valid. The court held that it was valid and that it was a revocable inter vivos trust. The Settlor's intent and the validity of that intent are always crucial as the Settlor creates all interests in the corpus and income.

(2) Second, ask if the Settlor retained any future control over the income or the corpus of the trust. The Settlor did retain control over the future income of the trust, specifying that it would be payable to him and his wife for the remainder of their lives. They had life estates. Future control over the corpus specified that it would be paid in equal shares to his children at the termination of the life estates. The children had remainders.

(3) Third, ask if the remainders possessed by the children were vested, contingent, or vested subject to defeasance. These are the only three possibilities. If the remainder is vested, the children own it immediately, but it will only become possessory at the termination of the life estates. If the interest is contingent, the children will own it only when the condition is met at some point in the future, which is designated by the Settlor and is most likely when it becomes possessory. Third, the children could have an interest described as vested subject to defeasance. What does this mean? The court notes that, because the Settlor retained the right to revoke the trust, it is arguable that the children had a vested interest subject to defeasance through the Settlor revoking the trust. In other words, the corpus belongs to the children now, but could be "defeased" by the Set-

tlor revoking the trust and taking it away. Perhaps a better example might be to pose a hypothetical: If the Settlor's trust were to read: "Income to myself for life and then corpus to my spouse should she survive me, but if not, then to my children." Note that, here, the children have no initial condition to meet—the interest is theirs immediately. However, they could be defeased by the spouse living longer than the Settlor. The spouse has a condition to meet, but not the children, and if the spouse meets that condition, something adverse could affect the children's interest. Under the terms of the trust and the given hypothetical, the children do not have to meet any condition, hence they are vested. But they could be "defeased" by another party—the spouse—performing an act that would deprive them of their interest. Hence, the children have a vested interest subject to defeasance.

(4) If the children have a completely vested interest, they need not meet any conditions; it is theirs immediately, even though not possessory. Please note the distinction between vested and possessory. Thus, the children do not need to survive the Settlor's death to have their estates take possession when the Settlor dies because the Settlor did not specify survivorship as a condition to be met; it was vested in the children when the trust was established by the Settlor. When the life estates end—i.e., when the Settlor and his spouse die—the living children take in possession, AND the estates of those children who predeceased will take on behalf of the predeceasing children. Thus, if, as was the case in this decision, a child predeceases the Settlor, either the child's Last Will and Testament or the child's statutory intestate estate will pass the child's share of the corpus. This means that the surviving children will take less of the estate, and part of the Settlor's corpus may go to strangers who take under the predeceasing child's Last Will and Testament. But the language of the Settlor should control and the case demonstrates the three possibilities available to the Settlor: vested, contingent, and vested subject to defeasance.

(5) Finally, it is important to note that the Settlor created these interests through an inter vivos trust—a non-probate device and very popular among estate planners. These trusts have become the subject of statutory and judicial reform efforts. For example, while the issue of vesting is the issue presented in this decision, there is another legal doctrine mentioned in the final paragraph of the decision—anti-lapse, *see* Chapter Four: Section VII, Lapse. Traditionally, anti-lapse applies only to Last Wills and Testaments, but some states have begun utilizing it with non-probate transfers, such as the inter vivos trust used in the decision here. Lapse and vesting may result in different beneficiaries taking the corpus, so it is important to compare the two doctrines as you progress through the material.

If a Settlor gives away an interest completely and presently, with no conditions, vesting, or vesting subject to defeasance, the Settlor may be said to have given the interest in fee simple. In medieval law, there were only three possibilities: fee simple, fee tail, and life estates. This means that the interest is both possessory and indefeasible, vested in another right now. Similarly, if the Settlor gives an interest to A for life and then to B, A has a life estate, and B has a vested remainder (note the absence of any condition that B survive A) that is a remainder in fee simple, too, since it belongs to B now, subject only to when B's interest becomes possessory at the death of A. The Settlor no longer has any rights to the property. While this may sound convoluted, the consequences are real. B's interest is subject to taxation and attachment by creditors, and B can even sell that which he has—a vested remainder. The law simply seeks to provide an apparatus through the language of future interests that provides for recognizable rights.

If the Settlor does not convey a fee simple interest, the Settlor is seeking to control the property in such a manner that will allow for it to come back to the Settlor or the Settlor's estate. Modern trust law provides extensive rules regarding the Settlor's ability to revoke trusts, particularly in reference to ability, method, withdrawal, contest, and liability of the trustee. *See, e.g.,* Unif. Trust Code §§ 601–04 (2004). Most often, because of taxation consideration, estate planners prefer irrevocability of trusts, by which the Settlor surrenders all rights over the property. But under the common law rules of future interests, the Settlor may retain future rights in property while conveying less than the owned fee simple. This may be accomplished through one of the following:

A. Reversion

The easiest example of a reversion is the following: "Settlor gives a life estate to A," but provides nothing further. Obviously, the Settlor retains the vested fee simple interest and possession will revert to the Settlor at the death of A. Note that this is different from a remainder, whereby, at the death of A, the interest would go to a person *other than the Settlor.*

B. Possibility of Reverter

A reversion is similar to a possibility of reverter in that this classification also keeps open the possibility that the property may return to the Settlor. The difference is one of wording, as is often the case with future interests. For example, if the Settlor conveys property to "A and his heirs for so long as A does well in school," the clause "for so long as A does well in school" is an added distinction that does not appear in a reversion. With the possibility of a reverter, here is added the special limitation that goes beyond a simple life estate and reversion to the Settlor. Here, doing well in school makes this a "possibility" of reverter. In the realm of future interests, there is also the concern as to whether this possibility of reverter would be a determinable one. Because of the use of the words "for so long as," this is a determinable fee since the event will occur as a result of consequences brought on by A. For our estate planning purposes, such distinctions are beyond the scope of inquiry, but there are historical distinctions to be made.

C. Right of Reentry

This power of reentry is most often classified as a right of termination by the Settlor of what was given initially by the Settlor. That is, if the Settlor gives to A the right to live on a parcel of land in return for rent, the payment of the rent is a condition subsequent, and non-payment will result in termination of the tenancy by the Settlor. Obviously, the use of words is important here so that it is possible to enforce the condition for termination of the estate originally given by the Settlor. Once the condition has been met, however, the Settlor has the right to terminate the estate and regain the property.

II. Interests in Persons Other Than the Settlor

A. Remainders

In First National Bank of Bar Harbor v. Anthony, discussed *supra*, the court was asked to distinguish among three types of remainders: vested, contingent, and vested subject to defeasance. Recall that the decision involved a trust with a life estate for the Settlor and the Settlor's spouse, and then the remainder to the named children at the death of the two life tenants. Nothing was to return to the Settlor, so reversion, reverter, and right of reentry were not possibilities. The court ruled that the Settlor had given the named children a vested remainder at the creation of the interest and future possession. What the court did not discuss was the effect that a "class" of remainder persons would have upon the interest conveyed.

Because the Settlor named the children, there was no class designation involved. Classes include phrases such as "my children," or "my nephews and nieces," and the like. For further discussion of decreasing class members, *see* Chapter Four: Section VII, A. These are class designations, and when a Settlor gives a remainder interest to a class, capable of increasing and decreasing according to future events, the law of remainders provides that the remainder is vested as to the present class members, but subject to partial divestment whenever any additional class member is born. Thus, if there are three class members at the execution of the Last Will and Testament, but five when the Testator actually dies and the Will speaks, then five class members will share in the bequest, not just three. Often the Settlor will provide for life estates and then the remainder to my children, issue of my body, or adopted by me. This is a class designation. If the Settlor provides for this class within an inter vivos trust—a common non-probate device—and has two children at the effective date of the conveyance, the two children have a vested remainder. But since additional children may be born to the Settlor and, thus, also may take as remainder persons, a part of the original children's remainder is defeased upon the increase of class. An exception to this is when a Settlor provides "a life estate for my life and then the remainder to my heirs at law." Since a living person has no heirs, the remainder class cannot be ascertained until the death of the Settlor, thereby eliminating any concern over increase or decrease of class. Those persons designated as heirs at law at the death of the Settlor take under the trust. *See* Chapter Seven: Section V.

B. Executory Interests

Unlike remainders, an executory interest is never vested until a point in the future, when a condition established by the Settlor takes place. At that point in time when the condition occurs, an executory interest divests the Settlor of the interest, thereby causing the vested interest to "spring" from the Settlor to the person or persons completing the condition. If an event in the future causes the interest to "shift" vesting from one person to the other, neither of whom is the Settlor, this is called a "shifting" executory interest. These interests have historical validity because of the Statute of Uses and the Wills Act; the former of these creates a legal interest arising from executory interests, rather than equitable interests.

III. Analytical Principle

Between the time when a Testator executes a valid Last Will and Testament and the date of death of the Testator, significant changes could occur in reference to property and persons. *See* Chapter Three: Section III (C) (changes in property); Chapter Four: Section VII (lapse—changes in persons). Likewise, in the event that the Testator creates a testamentary trust in a valid Last Will and Testament, with possession to occur at a point in the future, long after the death of the Testator, further changes could occur in reference to property and persons. And if we depart from Wills, if a Settlor creates an inter vivos trust in named persons and makes possession of the corpus dependent upon an event to occur in the future, significant changes could occur in reference to property and persons between the time the Settlor funds the trust and the occasion of the event in the future.

In both testamentary and inter vivos (non-probate) transactions, changes in property and persons are affected by different legal doctrines. For example, when a relative of the Testator dies prior to the Testator, survived by the relative's issue, every state and the Uniform Probate Code apply the doctrine of anti-lapse, which distributes the share the deceased relative would have received to the surviving issue of the relative in a manner resembling intestacy. *See* Chapter Four: Section VII. The modern Uniform Probate Code applies this doctrine of anti-lapse to non-probate, payable-on-death devices too. *See* Unif. Prob. Code § 2-706(b) (2004). However, if a Testator dies with a valid Last Will and Testament that creates a testamentary trust payable at a point in the future, such as when the beneficiary turns thirty, anti-lapse does not apply. The doctrine governing disposition of the trust property, when the beneficiary dies prior to the occurrence of the event signaling possession, is vesting, whether the interest created by the Testator is vested, contingent, or vested subject to defeasance.

The shifting patterns of interests and the different doctrines applicable to each can be daunting. There are testamentary and inter vivos transactions, plus different effective dates and issues dependent upon revocability or irrevocability. Thus, as a means of spatially diagraming the changes in persons and property, the corresponding legal issues, and the possible results, consider using the following chart, which delineates time frames and events to identify the issue presented and the applicable legal doctrine that should apply. The chart is called the Analytical Principle and it is described in more extensive detail at Raymond C. O'Brien, *Analytical Principle: A Guide for Lapse, Survivorship, Death Without Issue, and the Rule,* 10 Geo. Mason L. Rev. 383 (1988).

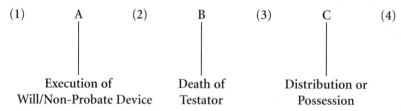

The chart moves from left to right in time progression and has three major events that may occur. The <u>A point</u> in time is most often the execution of the Last Will and Testament, but it could also be the execution of a non-probate POD (payable on death) device, such as an insurance policy or an inter vivos trust. Applicable to this point will be the concern over the formalities and intentionalities of the Will, *see* Chapter Three:

Sections II and III, or the necessary ingredients of a valid trust, *see* Chapter Eight: Section I. Assuming the Will or the non-probate device is valid, the next significant date is the date of the death of the Testator or the Settlor, in the case of a non-probate transfer. This is the B point. There are few instances when the death of the Settlor of a non-probate transfer will be of particular significance in the application of legal doctrines; taxation and the Rule Against Perpetuities are two such instances. But in reference to a valid Last Will and Testament, the death of the Testator is a significant event because, at that point, the Will speaks and the provisions set in place at the A point in time are to be performed; vesting occurs, heirs are determined, and property is distributed.

Please note that, between the A point in time and the B point in time, significant changes in property and persons may have taken place. For example, Testator may have bequeathed one-hundred shares of Starbucks at the A point in time, but between then and the B point, there have been seven stock splits. Does the legatee who is to inherit the one-hundred shares get all of the stock that resulted from the splits, or only one-hundred shares at the B point? Likewise, Testator could have bequeathed one-million dollars to "my children," and even though there were only two children at the A point, now there are five children at the B point. How many children take? And what if one of the children died between the A point and the B point, survived by issue? Would an anti-lapse statute apply to save the child's share for his or her issue?

The C point occurs when the Testator has created a testamentary trust at the B point, or created a non-probate device at the A point—an inter vivos trust, for example—and, under the terms of either process, there is a point in time in the future when distribution must be made. The C point is that specific point in time. For example, in a valid Last Will and Testament, Testator bequeaths one-million dollars to Sadie, to be paid when she turns thirty. The C point would be when Sadie turns thirty. Or another example: Settlor executes a life insurance policy on Settlor's life (A point), payable to Sadie upon Settlor's death. The C point would be the death of the Settlor, which happens to coincide with the B point.

The three points in the time chart are separated by time frames when there is likely to be changes in persons and property. Time frame (1) has few events to precipitate the application of legal doctrines, but one would be class gifts and, often, the application of the anti-lapse statute. Examples of this will be provided *infra*. But Time frame (2) includes anti-lapse in each and every state statute, as well as class gift issues to accommodate increasing and decreasing class members. Changes in property may be reflected in this Time frame (2) as well. Time frame (3) is the time between the death of the Testator and the occurrence of the event precipitating distribution of corpus. In the case of a Last Will and Testament, this is the arena of vesting, contingency, and vesting subject to defeasance. Finally, Time frame (4) provides an opportunity to analyze powers of appointment. *See* Chapter Seven: Section VI. All three points in the chart (A-B-C) and all four time frames ((1)-(2)-(3)-(4)) provide us with a spatial method through which we can identify the legal issue involved and then apply the appropriate legal doctrine. Let us look at some examples:

A. Anti-lapse

In a valid Last Will and Testament, Testator bequeaths to her sister Sadie, one-million dollars. The Will is executed in 2000 (Point A) and, at that time, Sadie is in perfect health and has two children. Nonetheless, in 2003, Sadie dies in a tragic accident. By 2005, the Testator dies with the same Last Will and Testament in effect (Point B). Sadie's legacy of one-million dollars is still a part of the Will, but the plaintiff, the residuary legatee of the Will, argues that Sadie's bequest has lapsed because of her death prior to the Testator in Time frame (2). Sadie's children, her surviving issue and the defendants in the case, argue that they should take the legacy under the state's anti-lapse statute and divide it among themselves. Who wins? First, note that the Will is valid; this is always the first and foremost question. Then note that there is the death of Sadie in Time frame (2). This signals that anti-lapse is an issue, inviting consideration of the tool bar associated with anti-lapse. *See* Chapter Four: Section VII. Could vesting—a different doctrine—apply to someone dying in Time frame (2)? Yes, but only if no Will were involved, for example, when the Settlor executes a valid non-probate trust at Point A, with possession to be at Point C. Anti-lapse, with the exception of the most modern Uniform Probate Code § 2-706, only applies when we consider Wills, not non-probate transfers.

B. Vesting

How would vesting be identified and analyzed using the chart? Of course, vesting may never be a consideration if property is to pass under a Last Will and Testament and the Testator has not died. It is a maxim in law that a Will speaks at death. Therefore, vesting may never apply to Time frame (2) if we are discussing a Last Will and Testament. However, if, in a valid Last Will and Testament, the Testator provides one-million dollars to Sadie, with income from this to be paid to her each year until she turns thirty, and Sadie dies at age 28, survived by two children, with her own Last Will and Testament bequeathing all her property to National Geographic, what happens to the one-million dollars? Using the Analytical Principle chart, we know that Sadie has died in Time frame (3), between Points B and C. She had a trust established for her by the Testator but never reached the age for distribution. Was her interest in the corpus vested at the death of the Testator? Yes, the corpus was vested in Sadie, to be paid when she turned thirty. There was no condition for her to meet to accomplish vesting. So, how should the property be distributed? If Sadie had died in Time frame (2), anti-lapse would apply, but since she died in Time frame (3), the applicable doctrine is vesting, not anti-lapse. Vesting would give the one-million dollars to her estate, passing it to the National Geographic. The only recourse Sadie's children would have would be to challenge the validity of Sadie's Will, thereby allowing the property to go to them via intestacy. This did not occur. Thus, note the difference between what happens in Time frame (2) and Time frame (3). Because of the anti-lapse statute that would pass the property only to issue of Sadie, not the National Geographic, there is a distinctive difference between the applicable legal doctrines and the results between death in Time frames (2) and (3).

To review the rules as to vesting, contingent, or vested subject to defeasance, consider the following ancient decision:

Clobberie's Case

Court of Chancery, England, 1677

2 Chan. Ca. 155, 2 Vent. 342, 86 Eng. Rep. 476

In one Clobberie's Case it was held, that where one bequeathed a sum of money to a woman, at her age of twenty-one years, or day of marriage, to be paid unto her with interest, and she died before either, that the money should go to her executor; and was so decreed by my Lord Chancellor Finch.

But he said, if money were bequeathed to one at his age of twenty-one years, if he dies before that age, the money is lost.

On the other side, if money be given to one to be paid at the age of twenty-one years; there, if the party dies before, it shall go to the executors.

C. Class Gifts

Recall that a class gift results when a Testator or a Settlor uses a term that is capable of increase and decrease; common terms are "children," "nephews," and "nieces." *See* Chapter Seven: Section V. Obviously, the Testator or the Settlor is seeking fluidity by using a term that will incorporate an expanding or contracting group of persons. For example, Testator drafts a Last Will and Testament (Point A) and writes: "One-million dollars to be divided among my children." At Point A, Testator has two children, but at Point B, Testator has four children. How many children take? Obviously, all four children will take because all four children were members of the class when the Will speaks. But recall that if one of the children had died during Time frame (2), survived by issue, then the anti-lapse statute would apply since anti-lapse is applicable during Time frame (2). Now, the Testator drafts a Will that provides: "One-million dollars to be divided among my children when the youngest of them reaches the age of thirty." At the time of Testator's death, one child is twenty-one and, thus, the condition is not met, so a testamentary trust is put into place while waiting for the youngest child to reach thirty so the money may be dispersed. Before the youngest child reaches thirty, but after the death of the Testator, a child of the Testator dies. Does the estate of the deceased child have any claim to the one-million dollars when the youngest child reaches thirty? Yes, because of vesting. Vesting applies in Time frame (3). Since there was no condition that the child live until the youngest reached thirty, each child had a vested interest at the death of the Testator. Since the deceased child had a vested interest, the estate of the child will take the child's portion when the youngest child reaches thirty and possession for all occurs. Please note that the estate of the child takes and not the issue of the child, as was the case with anti-lapse.

If we take one final example, utilizing Time frames (1), (2) and (3), we may be able to further demonstrate the utility of the chart. Testator drafts a valid Last Will and Testament and writes: "One-million dollars to be divided among my children when the youngest of them reaches thirty." When Testator writes this at Point A, one child has already died with surviving issue prior to the execution of the Will. Testator will have another child die with surviving issue after Point A and before Point B (Time frame (2)). Finally, another child will die with surviving issue after the death of Testator and before the youngest child reaches the age of thirty (Time frame (3)), between Point B and Point C. When the youngest child reaches the age or thirty (Point C), three actual children survive. How should the one-million dollar bequest be divided? The chart will allow you to spatially track the deaths of each child and suggest the legal doctrine to apply. Thus, since there was no condition of survivorship for children to live until the youngest reached thirty, the court may apply both anti-lapse and vesting doctrines.

When we look at the chart, we see that one child of the Testator died in Time frame (1), survived by issue. Does anti-lapse apply to relatives of Testator who die prior to the execution of the Last Will and Testament (Point A)? Yes, according to the Uniform Probate Code and many other state statutes. Second, should anti-lapse apply to children who die after execution of the Last Will and Testament, but prior to the death of the Testator (Time frame (2))? Yes. Since both of these children had issue surviving the Testator, the issue would take a share from the predeceasing parent under anti-lapse doctrines. Please note that anti-lapse does not provide any benefits to the estate of the deceased child; only the issue may take according to the statute, and, if there are no issue, the legacy lapses and is shared by the surviving class members. Then note that one child died with issue between the death of the Testator (Point B) and when the youngest child turned thirty (Point C). Since this is Time frame (3), vesting applies and the share of that child will go to the child's estate, not to issue, as was the case with anti-lapse. Finally, three children survived Point C when the youngest of them reached the age of thirty. Into how many shares will you divide the one-million dollars? The one-million dollars will be divided into six shares:

One share will go to the issue of the child who died in Time frame (1) survived by issue.

One share will go to the issue of the child who died in Time frame (2) survived by issue.

One share will go to the estate—because of vesting—of the child who died in Time frame (3).

Three shares, one each, will go to the three children who survived Point C.

D. Powers of Appointment

When using the chart to understand powers of appointment, it is first necessary to review the language of powers because there are terms and phrases particular to that area of the law. *See* Chapter Seven: Section VI. Once the terms are mastered, it is necessary to understand that a power of appointment is a device attached to a trust. For example, a Testator executes a valid Last Will and Testament, and then, at the death of the Testator, that Will provides: "One-million dollars to Sadie, income for life, and then, at her death, as she shall appoint in her Last Will and Testament." Sadie has an income trust with a general, testamentary power of appointment. Of course, there are many legal issues that could apply to the Testator's trust, and these may be reviewed at the materials associated with trusts in this casebook. But for now, please note that the Testator (she wrote a Will!) is also a Settlor of a testamentary trust (she established a trust!) and a Donor of a power of appointment. Sadie is a legatee under the Will, a beneficiary under the trust, and a Donee under the terms of the power of appointment. How may this be viewed spatially on the chart?

The base chart is the Last Will and Testament of the Testator, Settlor, Donor. When the Testator dies at Point B, Sadie survives and is able to begin to receive life income. Sadie's death is the condition that will bring about distribution, so Sadie's death is Point C. Up to this point, our only concerns are the validity of the Last Will and Testament of the Testator, the validity of the trust, and the validity of the power of appointment. Assuming that all of these are valid, that they do not violate the Rule Against Perpetuities, and that Sadie effectively exercises her power of appointment, we then turn our attention to Sadie, the legatee, beneficiary, donee.

Since Sadie must exercise her power of appointment in a valid Last Will and Testament, we are going to create another chart for Sadie's exercise and place it on top of the base chart we created for the Testator. But at which point? Since Point C is the point at which Sadie must exercise the power, that will be the point to which we attach Sadie's chart. Thus, since Sadie exercises with a Last Will and Testament at death, this is Sadie's Point B, and we are going to place it atop of the Testator's Point C. Our objective is to place in spatial context the reality of the fact that the power of appointment being exercised by Sadie derives from the trust created by the original Testator, Settlor, Donor.

Why is it necessary to combine the two legal devices, creation and exercise? One reason is the fact that if Sadie does not exercise the power of appointment, the corpus (appointment) will result back to the original Testator, Settlor, Donor. Plus, the Rule Against Perpetuities will be applied from creation of the power by the Donor. Another reason is to demonstrate that if Sadie does exercise the power of appointment but does so in favor of a person or group of persons who predecease her, then all of the rules of anti-lapse apply. Please recall that the anti-lapse statute will save a bequest made to a relative of the Testator who predeceases the Testator and is survived by issue; the issue take in place of the predeceasing relative. The most modern version of the Uniform Probate Code provides that anti-lapse will apply if the predeceasing appointee is a relative of the donee *or* the donor of the power of appointment, thus enlarging the scope of anti-lapse. *See* UNIF. PROB. CODE § 2-603 (2004). Another benefit of combining the base chart of the Testator with the exercise by the Donee of the power is the ability we have to estimate whether there is a violation of the Rule Against Perpetuities and possibilities to correct the violations through various savings devices.

E. Rule Against Perpetuities

The dominance of the "Rule" has diminished significantly with the ascending adoption by states of the Uniform Statutory Rule Against Perpetuities (USRAP), now adopted into the Uniform Probate Code § 2-901 (2004). Some states have abolished the Rule, *see, e.g.,* N.J. STAT. § 46:2F-9 (2004). Before using the chart to better understand the Rule, you should review the terms and variations associated with the Rule. *See* Chapter Seven: Section VII.

There are many ways in which the Rule may be stated, *see* Chapter Seven: Section VII, but perhaps this is most appropriate for our purposes:

> Standing at the creation of the interest, is there any possibility that any interest may not vest within a life in being plus twenty-one years?

A great deal of law is capsulized in that one sentence! Using it, we now revisit the example given in the preceding material on powers of appointment. That is, the Testator executed a valid Last Will and Testament and, when the Testator died, it became valid, providing for one-million dollars to Sadie, income for life, then, at her death, as she shall appoint by her Last Will and Testament. Please recall that Sadie has a life estate in trust, coupled with a general, testamentary power of appointment. Because the Testator's Last Will and Testament is linked to Sadie's trust and exercise of the power of appointment, we have linked the chart of the Testator with the chart of Sadie's exercise. Thus, the Testator's Point C and Sadie's Point B are one and the same; Sadie's valid exercise of the power is the point of distribution of the corpus (Point B) of the Testator's Last Will and Testament (Point C). The two instruments are linked for purposes of anti-lapse and powers of appointment. But they are also linked for purposes of the Rule Against Perpetuities. Why?

The Rule Against Perpetuities provides that all interests must vest within a life in being plus twenty-one years. The life must be in being at the creation of the interest, but when we look at Sadie's power of appointment, when is the interest created? You cannot say it is created when Sadie exercises the power (Point C for the Testator, Point B for Sadie), because she is simply exercising a power given to her by the Donor of the power, the Testator. Thus, creation for purposes of the Rule is when the Testator created the power in the Last Will and Testament, the Testator's Point B. We need to use the "relation back" doctrine to return to the creation by the Testator to determine if there is a Rule violation when Sadie exercises the power. And since we know that Sadie was a "life in being" at the creation of the power (Testator's Point B), and we know that Sadie exercises the power in her Last Will and Testament (Sadie's Point B, Testator's Point C), we know that all interests become vested at that point, and there is no Rule violation. Please note that we need to use the "relation back" doctrine because the Testator/Donor gave to Sadie, the beneficiary/donee, a general testamentary power of appointment. The same relation back would have occurred if the Donor had given Sadie a special power of appointment. In any power other than a general inter vivos power, most states require creation to be when the Donor creates the power, not when the Donee exercises the power. *See, e.g.*, Unif. Prob. Code § 2-902 (2004). This is one major reason why the two charts must be seen in tandem.

But let us utilize the chart in a manner that will demonstrate a violation of the Rule. We continue with the same example as before: Testator executes a valid Last Will and Testament and, when it speaks (Point B), the Testator gives Sadie one-million dollars, income for life, and then as she shall appoint in her Last Will and Testament (Point C for the Testator and Point B for Sadie). When Sadie exercises her power of appointment in her valid Last Will and Testament (Point B for Sadie), she exercises by creating a trust for her children for life and then for her grandchildren surviving. If no grandchild survives, then to National Geographic. Now return to the chart and note the following conclusions:

(1) Creation under the relation back doctrine remains the creation by the Testator in the Testator's Last Will and Testament (Testator's Point B).

(2) When we look at the exercise by Sadie, we know that all of the interests created by Sadie do not become vested until we determine if a grandchild survives at least one of Sadie's children at Sadie's Point C. Please note that the grandchildren have a contingent interest and National Geographic has a vested interest subject to defeasance.

(3) The death of the last of Sadie's children brings about indefeasible vesting in either the grandchildren or National Geographic, therefore, the children are the measuring lives.

(4) Are all of the measuring lives also lives in being? To be in being, they must all be there at the creation of the power, when the Testator dies. The answer is, "no," unless it was completely impossible for Sadie to have any more children (measuring lives) after Testator's Point B, when creation occurred. If there is any *possibility* of having an additional measuring life who would not be a life in being at the creation of the interest (Testator's Point B), then the Rule is violated, no matter what *actually* happens when the appointment of the trust becomes completely vested at Sadie's Point C.

The chart allows for a spatial examination of all of the interests involved. Furthermore, it can be of additional assistance when we examine, in more detail, reformation devises (savings clauses) to correct the violation of the Rule in the example just given.

Reformation could consist of cy pres, second look, and even the doctrine of capture. All of these are discussed in reference to the Rule in Chapter Seven: Section VII.

IV. Survival

Often courts are confronted with the issue of whether the Settlor's trust of future interests was meant to require survivorship in any beneficiary. The issue is important in considering vesting versus contingent interests, anti-lapse, the Rule Against Perpetuities, and class gifts, to name but a few circumstances. Secondly, to what point did the Settlor intend to require survivorship? Usually, the debate over point of survivorship is between the death of the Settlor or the death of a life tenant. There are significant consequences to these two issues. Consider the following decision and the Uniform Probate Code that follows.

Security Trust Co. v. Irvine
Delaware Court of Chancery, 1953
33 Del. Ch. 375, 93 A.2d 528

BRAMHALL, Vice Chancellor.

In this case this court is asked to determine two issues: (1) whether or not the residuary estate left to brothers and sisters of the testator vested as of the date of his death or at the time of the death of the last life tenant; (2) if it should be decided that the residuary estate vested as of the time of the death of the testator, do the life tenants take as members of the class of brothers and sisters receiving the residuary estate?

Plaintiff is trustee under the last will and testament of James Wilson, deceased, who died on July 29, 1918, leaving a last will and testament dated October 25, 1915. After providing for certain specific bequests, testator gave and devised all his 'real and mixed estate' to the Security Trust and Safe Deposit Company,—now the Security Trust Company,—to two sisters, Martha B. Wilson and Mary E. Wilson, during their joint lives and during the lifetime of the survivor of them. Testator further provided that in the event that his sister, Margaret W. Irvine, should be left a widow, she should share equally with the two sisters above named in the benefits of the trust so provided. As to the remainder, testator provided as follows:

> 'Upon the death of two sisters, Martha B. Wilson and Mary E. Wilson, and the survivor of them, then it is my will that all of my real and mixed estate and any proceeds that may have arisen from the sale of any part thereof, together with any unexpended income there may be, shall be equally divided among my brothers and sisters, share and share alike, their heirs and assigns forever, the issue of any deceased brother or sister to take his or her parent's share.'

Testator was survived by his five brothers and sisters: Samuel H. Wilson, Margaret W. Irvine, Martha B. Wilson, Mary E. Wilson, and Henry Wilson. At the time of the execution of the will the ages of the brothers and sisters ranged from 39 to 52 years. Martha B. Wilson and Mary E. Wilson, the two life tenants, died respectively on June 9, 1928, and August 18, 1951, unmarried and without issue, the trust therefore terminating on the latter date. The other devisees all predeceased Mary E. Wilson, the surviving life tenant. Samuel H. Wilson died on October 26, 1926, leaving to survive him three children, Frazer Wilson, Jeannette A. Wilson, and Samuel H. Wilson, Jr., and Grace Wilson Gearhart, daughter of a deceased son, Francis Paul Wilson. Samuel H. Wilson, Jr. died in 1924, unmarried and without issue.

Samuel Irvine, one of the defendants, is the sole residuary legatee under the will of Margaret W. Irvine, deceased. Martha B. Wilson died testate on June 9, 1928, leaving her residuary estate to her two nieces, Margaret Gregg Wilson, now Margaret W. Hanby, and Mary Hope Wilson, each an undivided one-half interest therein.

Mary E. Wilson died testate on August 18, 1951, leaving her entire residuary estate to Margaret W. Hanby, after providing for the payment of her debts and a legacy to Mary Hope Wilson in the sum of $100.

The estate of Martha B. Wilson has been closed, the final account having been passed on February 9, 1935; the estate of Mary E. Wilson has also been closed, the final account in that estate having been passed on September 15, 1952.

I must first determine whether or not the remainder interest of the testator became vested at the time of his death or at the time of the death of the last life tenant, Mary E. Wilson, on August 18, 1951. In order to resolve this question the intention of the testator at the time of the drafting of the will must first be ascertained. If it should be clear that testator intended this provision of the will to take effect at some future date, then the intention of the testator, so far as it may be legally carried out, will prevail. However, in reaching my conclusion, I must accept certain well recognized rules of construction.

The law favors the early vesting of devised estates and will presume that words of survivorship relate to the death of the testator, if fairly capable of that construction. In the absence of a clear and unambiguous indication of an intention to the contrary, the heirs will be determined as of the date of the death of the testator and not at some future date. When the language employed by the testator annexes futurity, clearly indicating his intention to limit his estate to take effect upon a dubious and uncertain event, the vesting is suspended until the time of the occurrence of the event. See Delaware Trust Company v. Delaware Trust Company, Del.Ch., 91 A.2d 44, and cases therein cited.

The assertion that it is indicated in the will that the testator intended the residuary estate to be vested as of the date of the death of the last life tenant is based upon the contentions: (1) the fact that testator left a life estate to two of his sisters and then gave the residuary estate to his brothers and sisters indicates that testator did not intend the two sisters to share in his residuary estate and therefore the residuary estate did not vest until the date of the death of the last life tenant; (2) the use of the words 'upon the death of two sisters' and the provision in the will of testator that his estate 'should be equally divided among my brothers and sisters' indicates an intention that testator intended a future vesting of his residuary estate

Whatever may be the law in other states it is well settled in this state that the fact that a life tenant is a member of a class, in the absence of any clear indication in the will to the contrary, does not prevent the life tenant from participating in the remainder of testator's estate as a part of the class. Wright v. Gooden, 6 Houst. 397. The opinion of this court in the case of Delaware Trust Company v. Delaware Trust Company, supra, is not in conflict. In the Delaware Trust Company case the testatrix, after creating several life estates, the last of which was to her only son, provided that the residue and remainder of her estate should go to her heirs-at-law. In her trust inter vivos executed at the same time, she provided that the remainder, consisting of the proceeds of the sale of some

Pennsylvania real estate, should go to the heirs-at-law of her husband. In that case the only son was the only heir-at-law of both the testatrix and her husband. This court decided that the intention of the testatrix as manifested by the general scheme or purpose as found in her will and in her trust agreement, was to create an estate to take effect as of the date of the death of the last life tenant. It was there stated that the use of the words 'my heirs-at-law' and 'heirs-at-law of my husband', where the son was the sole heir-at-law of both, along with other circumstances therein mentioned, demonstrated the intention of the testatrix to provide for future vesting. Here the testator in his will showed only an intention to postpone the enjoyment of the remainder until after the death of the life tenants. Where the will merely postpones the time of vesting the residuary estate would vest as of the time of the death of testator. The fact that the life tenants were also members of the class to whom the remainder of testator's estate was devised, would not prevent an early vesting of the remainder estate.

As to the use of the word 'upon', it is equally clear under the decisions in this state and elsewhere, that this word and other words of this nature refer only to the time of payment and not to the substance of the devise. Cann v. Van Sant, 24 Del.Ch. 300, 11 A.2d 388; In re Nelson's Estate, 9 Del.Ch. 1, 74 A. 851. Other Delaware cases are to the same effect. In any event, the use of this word, and the provision for dividing its remainder, under the circumstances of this case would not alone be sufficient to overcome the presumption of immediate vesting.

It is contended on behalf of certain defendants that even though it should be determined that the gift to the brothers and sisters vested as of the date of the death of testator, the life tenants should be excluded from membership in the class of brothers and sisters. They base their contention upon the fact that testator in another item of his will gave them a life interest in his residuary estate.

In endeavoring to ascertain the intention of testator, it is uniformly held that such a provision is not of itself sufficient to prevent the life tenant from participating in the remainder as part of the class. See cases cited in 13 A.L.R. 620. It is not sufficient to show the absence of an intention to include the life tenants; there must be some indication of a clear and unambiguous nature to exclude them. Dillman v. Dillman, 409 Ill. 494, 499, 100 N.E.2d 567; Carver v. Wright, 119 Me. 185, 109 A. 896. I can find no incongruity in the mere fact that testator provided a life estate for his two sisters and later gave the remainder to his brothers and sisters, of which the two sisters were part of the class. They were unmarried. They were no longer young. It seems to be clear from the several provisions in the will of the testator that it was his purpose to provide for them. Such provision does not indicate to me that testator did not intend that they should participate further in his estate. Certainly there is no legal inconsistency in life tenants participating in the remainder. The theory that the testator particularly desired to see that his sisters were provided for is at least as strong as the supposition that he intended to exclude them from participating in the remainder.

I conclude that the life tenants should participate in the remainder devised by testator to his brothers and sisters.

Having determined that the life tenants should participate in the provision for the brothers and sisters, I must next consider the effect of the provision that the 'issue of any deceased brothers or sisters to take his or her parent's share'.

As to the brothers and sisters who died leaving issue, it was specifically provided that such issue should take the interest of such brother or sister leaving issue. Their interest was thereby divested, their issue being substituted in their place. In such case, the brother or sister dying leaving issue would have no power of disposition of his or her interest in the estate. In re Nelson's Estate, supra.

The will of testator is silent as to any provision relative to any of the brothers and sisters dying without leaving issue. Martha B. Wilson, Mary E. Wilson and Margaret W. Irvine, three sisters of testator, left no issue at the time of their death. Was their interest divested by their death, even though they left no issue, or did their estates receive an absolute interest, free and clear of any conditions subsequent?

Under the will of testator, the death of the life tenants leaving issue caused their interest to be divested. I have determined that the brothers and sisters received an absolute estate, subject to the provision that the interest of any brother or sister dying prior to the death of the life tenant should go by substitution to the issue of such brother or sister. However, this provision of the will does not apply where there is no issue, since there would then be no limitation upon their estate. The decisions in this state are silent as to what would happen under such circumstances. However, the weight of authority in other states is to the effect that in the event of the death of the devisees leaving no issue, the interest of such devisees is not divested by their death. McArthur v. Scott, 113 U.S. 340, 5 S.Ct. 652, 28 L.Ed. 1015; Plitt v. Plitt, 167 Md. 252, 173 A. 35, 109 A.L.R. 1; Jacobs v. Whitney, 205 Mass. 477, 91 N.E. 1009; Rutledge v. Fishburne, 66 S.C. 155, 44 S.E. 564; Gardner v. Vanlandingham, 334 Mo. 1054, 69 S.W.2d 947. Since the estates created were absolute except for the condition subsequent, and since the subsequent condition has been removed, the estates of the sisters dying without issue would have an absolute interest unrestricted by any condition.

I believe that such a determination would be in accord with the plain intention of the testator. He apparently desired to provide for his own brothers and sisters and their issue. If he had desired to provide that the interest of any brother or sister dying without issue should go to the surviving brothers or sisters or had intended to make some other similar provision, it would have been easy for him to do so. The fact that he did not, indicates that he had no such intention. I concluded that the interests of Martha B. Wilson, Mary E. Wilson and Margaret W. Irvine, were not divested by their death without issue and that their interests in the estate of the testator under the residuary clause of the will should go to their respective estates.

The estates of Martha B. Wilson and Mary E. Wilson have been closed. In accordance with the opinion of this court in Cooling v. Security Trust Co., 29 Del.Ch. 286, 76 A.2d 1, their shares may be distributed by the trustee directly to the persons entitled to receive the same, the trustees first seeing that any taxes which may be due or any costs which may be incurred by reason thereof are paid.

An order will be signed on notice in accordance with this opinion.

Note

The holding in *Irvine* represents the traditional method of interpretation of future interests, which allows for remainders to be vested subject to divestment only if the remainderman is survived by issue. Note how the court is adamant in its adherence to recognized rules of construction that favor early vesting, and survivorship as relating to the death of the Testator. Unless clearly evidenced by the Testator, vesting occurs at the death of the Testator, not at the death of the life tenant or some other event. When the court adopted these rules into its holding, what was the result? Who received the estate under the Last Will and Testament of James Wilson?

Now compare that result to what would happen if the following Uniform Probate Code provision had been in existence and applicable at the time of the decision. Particularly, compare Unif. Prob. Code § 2-707(b): "A future interest under the terms of a trust is contingent on the beneficiary's surviving the distribution date...." then providing what happens if the beneficiary does not survive. Who would take the estate of James Wilson under this provision? As you compare, ask if there are advantages to the Uniform Probate Code provision and if they outweigh the more traditional approach. Then ask if there is a similarity between Sections 2-707 and 2-603 (anti-lapse) and how they work in practice.

Uniform Probate Code (2004)

Section 2-707. Survivorship with Respect to Future Interests Under Terms of Trust; Substitute Takers

(a) [Definitions.] In this section:

(1) "Alternative future interest" means an expressly created future interest that can take effect in possession or enjoyment instead of another future interest on the happening of one or more events, including survival of an event or failure to survive an event, whether an event is expressed in condition-precedent, condition-subsequent, or any other form. A residuary clause in a will does not create an alternative future interest with respect to a future interest created in a nonresiduary devise in the will, whether or not the will specifically provides that lapsed or failed devises are to pass under the residuary clause.

(2) "Beneficiary" means the beneficiary of a future interest and includes a class member if the future interest is in the form of a class gift.

(3) "Class member" includes an individual who fails to survive the distribution date but who would have taken under a future interest in the form of a glass gift had he [or she] survived the distribution date.

(4) "Distribution date," with respect to a future interest, means the time when the future interest is to take effect in possession or enjoyment. The distribution date need not occur at the beginning or end of a calendar day, but can occur at a time during the course of a day.

(5) "Future interest" includes an alternative future interest and a future interest in the form of a class gift.

(6) "Future interest under the terms of a trust" means a future interest that was created by a transfer creating a trust or to an existing trust or by an exercise of a power of appointment to an existing trust, directing the continuance of an existing trust, designating a beneficiary of an existing trust, or creating a trust.

(7) "Surviving beneficiary" or "surviving descendant" means a beneficiary or a descendant who neither predeceased the distribution date nor is deemed to have predeceased the distribution date under Section 2-702.

(b) [Survivorship Required; Substitute Gift.] A future interest under the terms of a trust is contingent on the beneficiary's surviving the distribution date. If a beneficiary of a future interest under the terms of a trust fails to survive the distribution date, the following apply:

(1) Except as provided in paragraph (4), if the future interest is not in the form of a class gift and the deceased beneficiary leaves surviving descendants, a substitute gift is created in the beneficiary's surviving descendants. They take by representation the property to which the beneficiary would have been entitled had the beneficiary survived the distribution date.

(2) Except as provided in paragraph (4), if the future interest is in the form of a class gift, other than a future interest to "issue," "descendants," "heirs of the body," "heirs," "next of kin," "relatives," or "family," or a class described by language of similar import, a substitute gift is created in the surviving descendants of any deceased beneficiary. The property to which the beneficiaries would have been entitled had all of them survived the distribution date passes to the surviving beneficiaries and the surviving descendants of the deceased beneficiaries. Each surviving beneficiary takes the share to which he [or she] would have been entitled had the deceased beneficiaries survived the distribution date. Each deceased beneficiary's surviving descendants who are substituted for the deceased beneficiary take by representation the share to which the deceased beneficiary would have been entitled had the deceased beneficiary survived the distribution date. For the purposes of this paragraph, "deceased beneficiary" means a class member who failed to survive the distribution date and left one or more surviving descendants.

(3) For the purposes of Section 2-701, words of survivorship attached to a future interest are not, in the absence of additional evidence, a sufficient indication of an intent contrary to the application of this section. Words of survivorship include words of survivorship that relate to the distribution date or to an earlier or an unspecified time, whether those words of survivorship are expressed in condition-precedent, condition-subsequent, or any other form.

(4) If a governing instrument creates an alternative future interest with respect to a future interest for which a substitute gift is created by paragraph (1) or (2), the substitute gift is superseded by the alternative future interest only if an expressly designated beneficiary of the alternative future interest is entitled to take in possession or enjoyment.

(c) [More Than One Substitute Gift; Which One Takes.] If, under subsection (b), substitute gifts are created and not superseded with respect to more than one future interest and the future interests are alternative future interests, one to the other, the determination of which of the substitute gifts takes effect is resolved as follows:

(1) Except as provided in paragraph (2), the property passes under the primary substitute gift.

(2) If there is a younger-generation future interest, the property passes under the younger-generation substitute gift and not under the primary substitute gift.

(3) In this subsection:

(i) "Primary future interest" means the future interest that would have taken effect had all the deceased beneficiaries of the alternative future interests who left surviving descendants survived the distribution date.

(ii) "Primary substitute gift" means the substitute gift created with respect to the primary future interest.

(iii) "Younger-generation future interest" means a future interest that (A) is to a descendant of a beneficiary of the primary future interest, (B) is an alternative future interest with respect to the primary future interest, (C) is a future interest for which a substitute gift is created, and (D) would have taken effect had all the deceased beneficiaries who left surviving descendants survived the distribution date except the deceased beneficiary or beneficiaries of the primary future interest.

(iv) "Younger-generation substitute gift" means the substitute gift created with respect to the younger-generation future interest.

(d) [If No Other Takers, Property Passes Under Residuary Clause or to Transferor's Heirs.] Except as provided in subsection (e), if, after the application of subsections (b) and (c), there is no surviving taker, the property passes in the following order:

(1) if the trust was created in a nonresiduary devise in the transferor's will or in a codicil to the transferor's will, the property passes under the residuary clause in the transferor's will; for purposes of this section, the residuary clause is treated as creating a future interest under the terms of a trust.

(2) if no taker is produced by the application of paragraph (1), the property passes to the transferor's heirs under Section 2-711.

(e) [If No Other Takers and If Future Interest Created by Exercise of Power of Appointment.] If, after the application of subsections (b) and (c), there is no surviving taker and if the future interest was created by the exercise of a power of appointment:

(1) the property passes under the donor's gift-in-default clause, if any, which clause is treated as creating a future interest under the terms of a trust; and

(2) if no taker is produced by the application of paragraph (1), the property passes as provided in subsection (d). For purposes of subsection (d), "transferor" means the donor if the power was a nongeneral power and means the donee if the power was a general power.

Uniform Probate Code (2003)

Section 2-603. Antilapse; Deceased Devisee; Class Gifts.
(B) [Substitute Gift.]

(3) For purposes of Section 2-601, words of survivorship, such as in a devise to an individual "if he survives me," or in a devise to "my surviving children," are not, in the absence of additional evidence, a sufficient indication of an intent contrary to the application of this section [antilapse].

Notes

In the debate over Unif. Prob. Code § 2-707 (2004) and its impact on practice, the common law and taxation of trusts are significant to the law of future interests. For some assistance in discussing the meaning of survivorship, the intent of the Settlor, and the role of the courts, see David M. Becker, *Uniform Probate Code § 2-707 and the Experienced Estate Planner: Unexpected Disasters and How to Avoid Them*, 47 UCLA L. REV. 339 (1999); Laura E. Cunningham, *The Hazards of Tinkering with the Common Law of Future Interests: The California Experience*, 48 HASTINGS L. J. 667 (1997); Lawrence W.

Waggoner, *The Uniform Probate Code Extends Anti-Lapse-Type Protection to Poorly Drafted Trusts*, 94 MICH. L. REV. 2309 (1996); Jesse Dukeminier, *The Uniform Probate Code Upends the Law of Remainders*, 94 MICH. L. REV. 148 (1995); Lawrence W. Waggoner, *The UPC's New Survivorship and Antilapse Provisions*, 55 ALB. L. REV. 1091 (1992); Lawrence W. Waggoner, *Future Interests Legislation: Implied Conditions of Survivorship and Substitutionary Gifts Under the New Illinois "Anti-Lapse" Provision*, 1969 U. ILL. L.F. 423; Edward C. Halbach, Jr., *Future Interests: Express and Implied Conditions of Survival*, 49 CALIF. L. REV. 297 (1961).

V. Heirs, Descendants, Issue

Estate of Woodworth

California Court of Appeal, Fifth District, 1993
18 Cal. App. 4th 936, 22 Cal. Rptr. 2d 676

DIBIASO, Acting P. J.

The Regents of the University of California (Regents) appeal from an order of the probate court which rejected their claim to the remainder of a testamentary trust. We will reverse. We will apply the common law preference for early vesting and hold that, absent evidence of the testator's intent to the contrary, the identity of "heirs" entitled to trust assets must be determined at the date of death of the named ancestor who predeceased the life tenant, not at the date of death of the life tenant.

* * *

Harold Evans Woodworth died testate in 1971. His will was there-after admitted to probate; in 1974 a decree of distribution was entered. * * * According to this decree,[1] a portion of the estate was distributed outright to the testator's surviving spouse, Mamie Barlow Woodworth. The balance of the estate was distributed to Mamie Barlow Woodworth and the Bank of America, to be held, administered and distributed in accord with the terms of a testamentary trust established by the will of Harold Evans Woodworth. The life tenant of the trust was Mamie Barlow Woodworth. Among the trust provisions was the following:

'This trust shall terminate upon the death of MAMIE BARLOW WOODWORTH. Upon the termination of this trust, my trustee shall pay, deliver and convey all of the trust estate then remaining, including all accrued and/or undistributed income thereunto appertaining, to MRS. RAY B. PLASS, also known as Elizabeth Woodworth Plass, [Elizabeth Plass] whose present address is 90 Woodland Way, Piedmont, California, if she then survives, and if not then to her heirs at law.'

Elizabeth Plass was the testator's sister; he also had two brothers who predeceased him. One died without issue. The other was survived by two children, Elizabeth Woodworth Holden, a natural daughter, and James V. Woodworth, an adopted son.

---

1. The decedent's will was not introduced in the probate court proceedings. A decree of distribution is a conclusive determination of the terms of a testamentary trust and the rights of all parties claiming any interest under it. (Estate of Easter (1944) 24 Cal.2d 191, 194 [148 P.2d 601].)

Elizabeth Plass died in 1980; she was survived by her husband, Raymond Plass. Raymond Plass died testate in 1988. In relevant part, he left the residue of his estate to the Regents for use on the university's Berkeley campus.

Mamie Woodworth, the life tenant, died in 1991. Thereafter, Wells Fargo Bank, as successor trustee of the Woodworth trust, petitioned the probate court pursuant to Probate Code section 17200 to determine those persons entitled to distribution of the trust estate. The petition alleged that "The petitioner [was] uncertain as to whether Elizabeth Plass's 'heirs at law' under [the decree] should be determined as of February 14, 1980, the date of her death, or August 13, 1991, the date of Mamie [Barlow] Woodworth's death."

It is undisputed that (1) as of February 14, 1980, Elizabeth Plass's heirs at law were her husband, Raymond Plass; her niece, Elizabeth Woodworth Holden; and her nephew, James V. Woodworth; and (2) as of August 13, 1991, Elizabeth Plass's heirs at law were Elizabeth Woodworth Holden and James V. Woodworth (the Woodworth heirs).

At the hearing in the probate court, the Woodworth heirs offered extrinsic evidence, in the form of their own declarations, concerning the purported intent of the testator. However, relying only on the language of the decree of distribution,[2] the probate court concluded that the identity of the heirs entitled to the trust assets must be determined as of the date of death of the life tenant. The probate court therefore ordered the trustee to deliver the remaining trust assets in equal shares to the Woodworth heirs.

* * *

The decree of distribution constitutes a final and conclusive adjudication of the testamentary disposition which the deceased made of his property. (Estate of Miner (1963) 214 Cal.App.2d 533, 538 [29 Cal.Rptr. 601].) Thus, the outcome of this appeal turns on the proper construction to be given to the provision in the decree which directs the distribution of the trust assets upon termination. (Estate of Easter, *supra*, 24 Cal.2d 191, 194–195.) Because the probate court's ruling was based entirely upon the language of the decree, we are not bound by the probate court's conclusion. (Estate of Dodge (1971) 6 Cal.3d 311, 318 [98 Cal.Rptr. 801, 491 P.2d 385].) Instead, we must make an independent determination of the meaning of the decree. (Parsons v. Bristol Development Co. (1965) 62 Cal.2d 861, 865–866 [44 Cal.Rptr. 767, 402 P.2d 839].) In addition, since the probate court did not rely upon any purported evidence of intent, any reference we may make to the "record" in this case will not include such evidence; we review the propriety of the probate court order as if the extrinsic evidence did not exist.

* * *

The Regents contend the probate court erroneously failed to apply the general rule of construction which requires that the identity of "heirs" entitled to take a remainder interest be determined as of the date of death of the denominated ancestor, in the absence of any contrary intent expressed by the testator. (See Estate of Stanford (1957) 49 Cal.2d 120, 124 [315 P.2d 681]; Estate of Liddle (1958) 162 Cal.App.2d 7 [328 P.2d 35]; and Estate of Newman (1924) 68 Cal.App. 420, 424 [229 P. 898].) Had the probate court construed the decree in accord with this principle, the Regents would have been entitled to

---

2. There is nothing in the record before us which suggests the trial court's ruling was founded, in whole or part, upon any extrinsic evidence.

share in the trust assets as a residuary legatee of Raymond Plass, an heir at law of Elizabeth Plass at the time of her death in 1980.

The Woodworth heirs respond by asserting the probate court's decision is consistent with an exception to the general rule which requires that the determination be made at the date of death of the life tenant. (See Wells Fargo Bank v. Title Ins. & Trust Co. (1971) 22 Cal.App.3d 295, 300 [99 Cal.Rptr. 464]; and Estate of McKenzie (1966) 246 Cal.App.2d 740 [54 Cal.Rptr. 888].) (4)(See fn. 3.), (3b) Under this principle, the Regents have no interest in the trust assets, because Raymond Plass predeceased Mamie Barlow Woodworth.[3]

* * *

Estate of Liddle, *supra*, 162 Cal.App.2d 7, reflects the common law preference for vested rather than contingent remainders.[4] Thus, unless a particular instrument disclosed a different intent on the part of the testator, a remainder to a class of persons, such as children, became vested in the class when one or more of its members came into existence and could be ascertained, even though the class was subject to open for future additional members. (Estate of Stanford, *supra*, 49 Cal.2d at p. 125.) Furthermore, the fact that takers of a postponed gift were described by a class designation did not, under the common law rule, give rise to any implied condition of survival. (Id. at p. 126.)

The circumstances involved in *Liddle* are substantially indistinguishable from those of the present case. In *Liddle*, the remainder of a testamentary trust was to be distributed to the testatrix's attorney or, in the event of his death, the attorney's heirs at law. Although the attorney survived the testatrix, he predeceased the life tenant. The attorney's only heir, his wife, died intestate several years before the death of the life tenant. (*Liddle, supra,* 162 Cal.App.2d at pp. 9–10.) The wife's heirs and the administrator of her estate clashed with certain remote cousins of the attorney over the ownership of the trust assets.

The appellate court ruled in favor of the wife's estate. (162 Cal.App.2d at pp. 20–21.) Relying upon statutes, treatises, and case law expressing common law notions, including Estate of Stanford, *supra*, 49 Cal.2d 120, the court construed the phrase "heirs at law" according to its technical meaning, that is, the person or persons who are entitled to succeed to the property of an intestate decedent. (*Liddle, supra,* 162 Cal.App.2d at pp. 14–15.) The *Liddle* court then held the members of this class must be determined as of the death of the named ancestor. The rule was summarized as follows:

> 'Normally, when a gift has been made to the "heirs" or "next of kin" of a
> named individual, the donor has said in effect that he wants the property dis-

---

3. It is undisputed that had the testator in this case died on or after January 1, 1985, the Regents would have no claim to the trust assets. Under Probate Code sections 6150 and 6151, which have been in effect since 1985 (see Prob. Code, § 6103), a devise of a future interest to a class, such as heirs, includes only those who fit the class description at the time the legacy is to take effect in enjoyment.

4. The bias for early vesting was also evident in several now repealed provisions of the Probate Code. For example, former section 28 provided: "Testamentary dispositions, including devises and bequests to a person on attaining majority, are presumed to vest at the testators's death."

Former section 123 read in part: "A testamentary disposition to a class includes every person answering the description at the testator's death; but when the possession is postponed to a future period, it includes also all persons coming within the description before the time to which possession is postponed."

tributed as the law would distribute it if the named person died intestate. Accordingly, the normal time for applying the statute of descent or distribution is at the death of the named individual. This is, however, merely a rule of construction, and if the testator or grantor manifests an intention that the statute be applied either at an earlier or a later time, such intention will be given effect.' (*Liddle, supra,* 162 Cal.App.2d at p. 19, 328 P.2d 35.)

The designated ancestor in *Liddle* was the attorney. Because his wife was his intestate heir at the time he died, the court found she was the proper recipient of the trust estate.

* * *

On the other hand, *Wells Fargo Bank, supra,* 22 Cal.App.3d 295, 300, reflects the application of an exception to the early vesting principle. In *Wells Fargo Bank,* a woman had conveyed, by a grant deed, a life estate in certain real property to her daughter, with remainders to the grantor's two other children. If the life tenant died without issue and the two other children died without issue before the grantor's death, the instrument provided that the remainder interest in the property would belong to the grantor's "heirs." (*Wells Fargo Bank, supra,* 22 Cal.App.3d 295, 297–298.) The trial court determined the heirs should be ascertained as of the date of the grantor's death.

The Court of Appeal reversed. Because the remainder to the other children or their issue was contingent upon their surviving the life tenant, the court held the substitutional gift to the heirs was also contingent, thereby requiring the identification of the class members as of the death of the life tenant:

'In this type of case ... the class of heirs is determined upon termination of the trust because the question whether the testator's heirs would take at all having been postponed until the resolution of contingency, the question of the identity of the heirs has likewise been deemed to have been postponed by the testator. [Citations.]' (*Wells Fargo Bank, supra,* 22 Cal.App.3d 295, 300, 99 Cal.Rptr. 464.)

This concept was also recognized in *Estate of McKenzie, supra,* 246 Cal.App.2d 740, a case cited in *Wells Fargo Bank:*

'There is another class of cases in which the word 'heirs' has been held to refer to persons other than those who were heirs at the time of the testator's death.... In this type of case, the class of heirs is determined upon termination of the trust, because the gift to heirs was a substituted one, the primary gift being contingent. (Simes & Smith, The Law of Future Interests (2d ed.) §735, p. 210.) The question whether the testator's heirs would take at all having been postponed until the resolution of the contingency, the question of the identity of the heirs in such cases has likewise been deemed to have been postponed by the testator. (See In Re Sayre's Will [1956] 1 App.Div.2d 475 [151 N.Y.S.2d 506, 509–512].)' (Estate of McKenzie, at p. 745.) The *McKenzie* court did not apply this exception, however, because the trust language before it did not create a contingent, substitutional gift. (*Estate of McKenzie, supra,* 246 Cal.App.2d at p. 745, 54 Cal.Rptr. 888.)

The *Liddle* court also considered but rejected the exception:

'The fact that the gift to the described group is substitutional does not cause the postponement of the application of the statute to a period subsequent to the death of the designated ancestor.' (*Liddle, supra,* 162 Cal.App.2d at p. 19, 328 P.2d 35.)

The court reasoned:

> '[i]f it were held at bar that [the attorney's wife] took a contingent estate at the death of [the testatrix], that fact did not alter the further one that the contingency was fulfilled when she survived her husband, and what was previously a contingent remainder (if it was one) became vested in her as his sole heir at law.' (*Liddle, supra*, 162 Cal.App.2d at p. 17, 328 P.2d 35.)

* * *

The will of Harold Evans Woodworth created a contingent remainder in Elizabeth Plass, with a substitutional gift to her heirs at law. Although it appears we are therefore free to choose between *Liddle* and *Wells Fargo Bank*, in reality this is not so; the contingent, substitutional gift exception to the rule of early vesting applies only to grants of remainder interests which differ materially from the one now before us.

An authority relied upon in *McKenzie*, and by implication in *Wells Fargo Bank*, for the exception is Simes & Smith, The Law of Future Interests (2d ed.) §735, page 210. (*Estate of McKenzie, supra*, 246 Cal.App.2d at p. 745.) However, under consideration at the cited portion of this treatise is the situation where "a testator devises a life estate or defeasible fee to *a person who is one of his heirs*, followed by a remainder or executory interest to the testator's heirs." (Simes & Smith, *supra*, §735, p. 206, italics added.) As Simes and Smith point out, in such circumstances, some courts have rejected the general rule that the members of the class are to be determined at the death of the ancestor (i.e., the testator), and instead have applied an exception which identifies the heirs who will take the remainder as those in being upon the death of the holder of the life estate or defeasible fee. (Id., at pp. 206–210.) The rationale for these decisions is an assumption the testator did not intend to give both a present and a future interest to the same person. (See Simes & Smith, *supra*, §735, at pp. 206–210.)

Wells Fargo Bank involved a bequest of the same type as that which is the subject of section 735 of the Simes and Smith treatise. In *Wells Fargo Bank*, the estate of the life tenant would have been entitled to receive a portion of the remainder if the identity of the grantor's heirs was determined at the time of the grantor's death rather than at the date of the life tenant's death. (*Wells Fargo Bank, supra*, 22 Cal.App.3d at p. 298.) The *Wells Fargo Bank* court essentially adopted the analysis in section 735 of Simes and Smith that:

> '[I]f the general rule is applied, an incongruous result would be reached by taking the property away from [the holder of the possessory interest] because he died without issue and giving it back to him because of the same reason.' (*Wells Fargo Bank, supra*, 22 Cal.App.3d at p. 300, 99 Cal.Rptr. 464.)

The *Wells Fargo Bank* court relied on three New York appellate decisions: In re Pelham's Will (1970) 63 Misc.2d 377 [312 N.Y.S.2d 285]; In re Patterson's Estate (1965) 45 Misc.2d 797 [257 N.Y.S.2d 742]; and In re Sayre's Will (1956) 1 A.D.2d 475 [151 N.Y.S.2d 506].[5] In each of these cases, there existed at least the possibility that the estate of an interim beneficiary who did not survive the termination of a preceding interest, and therefore did not or would not receive an outright interest in the testator's property, would nonetheless be entitled to share in the remainder. In In re Pelham's Will, supra,

---

5. This opinion was also cited in *Estate of McKenzie, supra*, 246 Cal.App.2d at page 745, as additional authority for the existence of the exception.

312 N.Y.S.2d at page 288, the two heirs determined at the testator's death were "the same persons who would take as intestate distributees had the testator made no alternative gift of the remainder." In In re Patterson's Estate, *supra*, 257 N.Y.S.2d at page 745, identifying the testator's heirs at his death could have "result[ed] in a distribution of trust remainders through the estates of the same persons who were the income beneficiaries and contingent remaindermen of the trusts." In *In re Sayre's Will*, *supra*, 151 N.Y.S.2d at page 511, "... although the specific remainder to [an interim beneficiary] failed when she predeceased the life tenant, still she could qualify for a share as an heir."

By contrast, in the instant case we do not have a contingent, substituted gift to a class of recipients which includes the deceased interim beneficiary. As in *Liddle*, the class of contingent, substituted heirs does not encompass any prior contingent interim beneficiary. The named remainderman, Elizabeth Plass, did not lose her interest because she died without issue. She lost her interest because she died before the death of the life tenant. According to the record, neither Mamie Barlow Woodworth nor—of course—Elizabeth Plass is an heir at law of Elizabeth Plass.

Thus, we believe the exception to the general rule of early vesting, as implemented in *Wells Fargo Bank*, should not be applied to the remainder interest contained in the decree of distribution here.

* * *

For the reasons which follow, we find no other justification for departing from *Liddle*. First, there is nothing in the language of the other provisions of the decree of distribution before us which reveals the testator's intent or desire. Since the record does not include Harold Evans Woodworth's will, we cannot resort to it to attempt to divine his wishes. (See *Estate of Stanford*, *supra*, 49 Cal.2d at pp. 130–134.)

Second, the fact that the university, an entity, is not a relative of Elizabeth Plass or one of her heirs at law is not material. (See *Wells Fargo Bank*, *supra*, 22 Cal.App.3d at p. 301.) Unlike the *Wells Fargo Bank* court, we are unwilling to say that application of the general rule "would result in thwarting the expressed intention of the Grantor by distributing the corpus of the trust to persons or entities other than [Elizabeth Plass's] heirs." (*Wells Fargo Bank*, *supra*, 22 Cal.App.3d at p. 301.) Had the instrument in *Wells Fargo Bank* satisfactorily disclosed the grantor's intentions regarding the distribution of the remainder interest in the property, there would have been no need for the court to have even considered the competing rules of construction in order to decide the case. (See *Estate of Stanford*, *supra*, 49 Cal.2d at p. 127.)

It would be pure speculation for us to conclude that Harold Evans Woodworth would not have wanted Raymond Plass to inherit a portion of the trust assets. It appears from the record that Raymond Plass and Elizabeth Plass were married at the time the testator executed his will. It has long been the law in California that a husband is an heir of his deceased wife. (*Estate of Liddle*, *supra*, 162 Cal.App.2d at p. 16.) Nothing in the decree forecloses the possibility the testator took into account the fact that Elizabeth Plass might predecease, and Raymond Plass might outlive, Mamie Barlow Woodworth, resulting in Raymond Plass's succession to a portion of the trust remainder.

Third, the rule of construction which favors descent according to blood in cases of ambiguity in testamentary dispositions (see *Wells Fargo Bank*, *supra*, 22 Cal.App.3d at p. 302; Estate of Boyd (1938) 24 Cal.App.2d 287, 289 [74 P.2d 1049]) should likewise not determine the result in this case. The general rule favoring early vesting was well established long before the testator died. We do not think it should be abandoned in order to carry out some purportedly perceived, but entirely speculative, notion about the intent of the testator based upon events which occurred well after the testator's death. (See *Estate of McKenzie, supra*, 246 Cal.App.2d at p. 748.) As we noted earlier, it is perfectly conceivable that Harold Evans Woodworth took into account in making his will the possibility that his property would pass to Raymond Plass and thereafter be transferred to strangers to the Woodworth line.

In this connection, the *Wells Fargo Bank* court in part rationalized its decision with the observation that:

> 'by allowing such beneficiary to take as an heir regardless of his failure to survive might well end in an unacceptable result, namely that the remainder would not vest in the heirs of the grantor, but in the beneficiary's heirs or his residuary legatees who, in turn, need not be the heirs or relatives of the grantor at all (*In re Sayre's Will, supra*, [151 N.Y.S.2d at] pp. 510–511).' (*Wells Fargo Bank, supra*, 22 Cal.App.3d at p. 300, 99 Cal.Rptr. 464.)

Such an outcome is unacceptable, however, only if it is contrary to the testator's clear intent. (6), (5b) In the absence of any firm indication of testamentary intent, the rules of construction must be implemented in order to ensure uniformity and predictability in the law, rather than disregarded in order to carry out a court's ad hoc sense of what is, with perfect hindsight, acceptable in a particular set of circumstances. (See *Estate of McKenzie, supra*, 246 Cal.App.2d at pp. 748–749.)

Former Probate Code section 122 (repealed 1985), relied upon by the Woodworth heirs as an additional reason to uphold the probate court order, is not relevant. The section read:

> 'Words in a will referring to death or survivorship, simply, relate to the time of the testator's death, unless possession is actually postponed, when they must be referred to the time of possession.'

The crucial question in this case is whether the decree's language imposes a survivorship condition to membership in the class of Elizabeth Plass's heirs. Since we have determined it does not, former section 122 has no effect. In substance, the Woodworth heirs argue that because possession of the remainder of the trust assets in this case was postponed, the statute requires that a condition of survivorship be imposed upon the recipients of the remainder. This is an unwarranted reading of the section, and one which turns its language upside down.

Last, none of the other exceptions identified in *Wells Fargo Bank* to the early vesting rule applies under the circumstances of this case. This is not a situation where the " ... life tenant is the sole heir, but the will devises the remainder to the testator's 'heirs.'" (*Wells Fargo Bank, supra*, 22 Cal.App.3d at p. 300; *Estate of Wilson* (1920) 184 Cal. 63 [193 P. 581].)

In addition, the language of the decree does not contain any "expression of futurity in the description of the ancestor's heirs" (*Wells Fargo Bank, supra*, 22 Cal.App.3d at p. 300), such as "my then living heirs-at-law" (Estate of Layton (1933) 217 Cal. 451, 454 [19 P.2d 793, 91 A.L.R. 480]; see also *Estate of McKenzie, supra*, 246 Cal.App.2d at p. 744). When, as here, "'the gift is in terms "then to the heirs" of a designated person, the word "then" merely indicates the time of enjoyment and has no significance in relation to the rule [of early vesting].'" (*Estate of Miner, supra*, 214 Cal.App.2d at p. 542.) The use of the word "then" in the instant decree did nothing more than create a contingent remainder in Elizabeth Plass. Whatever reliance the trial court placed upon the term was therefore erroneous.[6]

Further, the rule in *Estate of Easter, supra,* 24 Cal.2d 191, does not apply because the decree in the present case does not use the word "vest." In *Easter,* the California Supreme Court considered a decree of distribution which provided: "'Upon the death of the [life tenant/widow of the testator] the trust ... shall terminate and all of the property ... *shall go to and vest in* the heirs at law of the [testator].'" (Id., at p. 195, italics in original.) Certain claimants argued the remainder was determinable at the time of the testator's death, in the absence of a clearly expressed contrary intent. The Supreme Court disagreed, finding no uncertainty in the decree. By providing that two things should occur upon the death of the life tenant, i.e., (1) the trust shall terminate and (2) the property shall go to and vest in the testator's heirs at law, the decree clearly indicated an intent that the interests of the heirs should vest at the time of the termination of the trust. "Any other construction would ignore the normal and usual meaning of the words 'shall go to and vest in the heirs at law.'" (*Estate of Easter, supra,* 24 Cal.2d at p. 195.) Later, in *Estate of Stanford, supra,* 49 Cal.2d at page 130, the Supreme Court made it clear that the rule of early vesting was not applied in *Easter* because of the presence in the decree of the technical word "vest." (See also *McKenzie, supra,* 246 Cal.App.2d at p. 745; and *Wells Fargo Bank, supra,* 22 Cal.App.3d at p. 300.)

Finally, and contrary to the contention of the Woodworth heirs, we do not find the words "pay to" contained in the instant decree to be equivalent to the word "vest" or otherwise constitute an "expression of futurity" for purposes of determining the identity of the relevant heirs. (*Wells Fargo Bank, supra,* at p. 300.) Rather, the instruction pertains to the time when the recipients of the assets are entitled to have them. (*Estate of Miner, supra,* 214 Cal.App.2d at p. 542.)

* * *

Accordingly, we must reverse the probate court's ruling that the Regents have no claim to the assets of the testamentary trust. Because the trial court did not consider the extrinsic evidence presented by the parties, we take no position with respect to it or its effect. It may be evaluated by the probate court on remand.

The judgment (order) appealed from is reversed.

Thaxter, J., and Brown, J., ... concur.

Notes

The Doctrine of Worthier Title applies in some states and, as such, provides that when a Settlor transfers property in trust, retaining a life estate in the Settlor or in another, and then provides that the remainder should go to the Settlor's heirs, it is presumed that the Settlor intended to retain a reversion in the Settlor's estate and did not intend to create a remainder in the Settlor's heirs. While the rule may be rebutted with evidence of a different intent, many states have abolished the rule completely. *See, e.g.,* UNIF. PROB. CODE §2-710 (2004) (Worthier-Title Doctrine Abolished). Likewise, the

---

6. The trial court's written decision included the following statement:

"It was the intent of the decedent in using the word 'then' in relation to the disposition to Elizabeth Woodworth Plass that the determination of the identity of the heirs be made as of the time of the death of the life tenant and the termination of the trust."

Rule in Shelley's Case provides that, when land is conveyed to a donee for life, then to the donee's heirs, there is no contingent remainder in the donee's heirs; the donee retains the remainder. Likewise, state statutes have abolished the rule's application. *See, e.g., Restatement (Second) of Property, Don. Trans.* § 30.1 (2003).

Uniform Probate Code (2004)

Section 2-711. Future Interests in "Heirs" and Like.

If an applicable statute or a governing instrument calls for a present or future distribution to or creates a present or future interest in a designated individual's "heirs," "heirs at law," "next of kin," "relatives," or "family," or language of similar import, the property passes to those persons, including the state, and in such shares as would succeed to the designated individual's intestate estate under the intestate succession law of the designated individual's domicile if the designated individual died when the disposition is to take effect in possession or enjoyment. If the designated individual's surviving spouse is living but is remarried at the time the disposition is to take effect in possession or enjoyment, the surviving spouse is not an heir of the designated individual.

Section 2-708. Class Gifts to "Descendants," "Issue," or "Heirs of the Body"; Form of Distribution if None Specified.

If a class gift in favor of "descendants," "issue," or "heirs of the body" does not specify the manner in which the property is to be distributed among the class members, the property is distributed among the class members who are living when the interest is to take effect in possession or enjoyment, in such shares as they would receive, under the applicable law of intestate succession, if the designated ancestor had then died intestate owning the subject matter of the class gift.

Chapter Seven

Creation, Classification, and Utilization of Trusts

Tool Bar

I. Elements of a Valid Trust

The evolution of the equitable device that would eventually be known as a trust originated during medieval times but has since evolved into an estate planning tool used today to avoid probate, shelter the assets of many dependent persons, and reduce or eliminate tax liability. With the gradual erosion of the Rule Against Perpetuities, trusts may now span multiple generations, providing a legacy to the persons creating them, income to multiple trustees, and benefit to countless beneficiaries. Statutes have replaced the shadowy interplay of law and equity from which the earliest forms of trusts originated, so that today, American trust law is dominated by the enactment of the Uniform Trust Code (2000), the Uniform Custodial Trust Act (1987), the Uniform Prudent Investor Act (1994), and the Uniform Principal and Income Act (1997). *See, e.g.,* Lynn Foster, *The Arkansas Trust Code: Good Law for Arkansas,* 27 U. Ark. Little Rock L. Rev. 191 (2005). Federal law governs trillions of dollars held for pensions under trust management, all managed by the Employee Retirement Income Security Act of 1974 (ERISA).

While many trusts benefit charitable enterprises, such as the Pew Foundation, and some benefit cemeteries and pets (often called honorary trusts), the majority of trusts benefit private individuals. Typically, a private trust will be created by a person seeking to provide for her or his spouse and then to their children for their lives, then the remainder to their grandchildren. The trust may be created during life time (inter vivos) or at death, through a valid Last Will and Testament (testamentary). The person creating the trust (Settlor) must transfer legal title over the trust property (Res/Corpus) to a person or group of persons (Trustee(s)), with specific instructions as to what do (Trust Purpose) for the persons who benefit from the income or corpus of the trust (Beneficiaries). With modern estate planning, which allows for creative ways to manage assets and achieve personal objectives, the possibilities are endless.

But the law of trusts contains pitfalls for the unwary as there are significant differences between Wills and trusts. Termination or revocation of a trust is different from the law applicable to a Last Will and Testament, compensation for beneficiaries has changed as wealth is defined differently, *see, e.g.,* UNIF. PRINCIPAL AND INCOME ACT (1997), and transfers to minors may be made through the UNIF. TRANSFERS TO MINORS ACT (1986). Taxation of trusts is perhaps the most significant issue facing the estate planner, but there are many examples of successful avoidance of state and federal tax liability with proper planning. And, of course, the burden upon a trustee is significant: the Trustee must be prudent and administer the trust with impartiality and loyalty, and the Trustee must be properly compensated, *see, e.g.,* UNIF. TRUST CODE (2003). All of these elements will be explored as this chapter describes the creation, classification, and utilization of trusts. We begin with the elements of a successful trust.

A. Settlor

Uniform Trust Code (2003)

Section 103. Definitions.

(14) "Settlor" means a person, including a testator, who creates, or contributes property to, a trust. If more than one person creates or contributes property to a trust, each person is a settlor of the portion of the trust property attributable to that person's contribution except to the extent another person has the power to revoke or withdraw that portion.

Section 402. Requirements for Creation.

(a) A trust is only created if:

(1) the settlor has the capacity to create a trust;

(2) the settlor indicates an intention to create the trust.

Section 602. Revocation or Amendment of Revocable Trust.

(a) Unless the terms of a trust expressly provide that the trust is irrevocable, the settlor may revoke or amend the trust.

Section 603. Settlor's Powers; Powers of Withdrawal.

(a) While a trust is revocable and the settlor has capacity to revoke the trust, rights of the beneficiaries are subject to the control of, and the duties of the trustee are owed exclusively to, the settlor.

(b) During the period the power may be exercised, the holder of a power of withdrawal has the rights of a settlor of a revocable trust under this section to the extent of the property subject to the power.

Notes

While the Settlor of the trust has a significant advantage in that the Settlor creates the trust, its purpose, and its beneficiaries, once created, the prerogatives of the Settlor decrease in proportion to the duties granted to the Trustee on behalf of the beneficiaries. Once the trust is created, the beneficiaries possess an equitable right against the Trustee for any breach, and unless the Settlor is also a beneficiary or has expressly retained the power of enforcement, the Settlor has no remedy against the Trustee. Nonetheless, a number of states retain strong support for the rights of a Settlor in protecting the corpus or income derived from a trust. *See, e.g.*, Nev. Rev. Stat. § 166.080 (2004) (denying former spouse or child to take trust benefits, in spite of a spendthrift clause imposed by the Settlor, unless specifically named as beneficiary). And some states concerned about the Settlor's intent will not allow beneficiaries to terminate a trust when a Settlor's material purpose has not been accomplished and the Settlor has not cooperated with all of the beneficiaries to agree to termination. *See, e.g., In re* Estate of Brown, 148 Vt. 94, 528 A.2d 752 (1987).

While California, Texas, and the Uniform Trust Code § 602 adopt the minority rule that a trust is revocable if the trust is silent on this subject, the majority of jurisdictions follow the rule that if the trust is silent on revocation, it is irrevocable. *See Restatement (Second) of Trusts* § 330(2)(2004).

B. Trustee: Private and Corporate

Uniform Trust Code (2003)

Section 801. Duty to Administer Trust.

Upon acceptance of a trusteeship, the trustee shall administer the trust in good faith, in accordance with its terms and purposes and the interests of the beneficiaries, and in accordance with this [Code].

Section 806. Trustee's Skills.

A trustee who has special skills or expertise, or is named trustee in reliance upon the trustee's representation that the trustee has special skills or expertise, shall use those special skills or expertise.

Section 815. General Powers of Trustee.

(a) A trustee, without authorization by the court, may exercise:

(1) powers conferred by the terms of the trust; and

(2) except as limited by the terms of the trust:

(A) all powers over the trust property which an unmarried competent owner has over individually owned property;

(B) any other powers appropriate to achieve the proper investment, management, and distribution of the trust property; and

(C) any other powers conferred by this [Code].

(b) The exercise of a power is subject to the fiduciary duties prescribed by this [article].

Section 1006. Reliance on Trust Instrument.

A trustee who acts in reasonable reliance on the terms of the trust as expressed in the trust instrument is not liable to a beneficiary for a breach of trust to the extent the breach resulted from the reliance.

Section 1013. Certification of Trust.

(a) Instead of furnishing a copy of the trust instrument to a person other than a beneficiary, the trustee may furnish to the person a certification of trust containing the following information:

(1) that the trust exists and the date the trust instrument was executed;

(2) the identity of the settlor;

(3) the identity and address of the currently acting trustee;

(4) the powers of the trustee;

(5) the revocability or irrevocability of the trust and the identity of any person holding a power to revoke the trust;

(6) the authority of cotrustees to sign or otherwise authenticate and whether all or less than all are required in order to exercise powers of the trustee;

(7) the trust's taxpayer identification number;

(8) the manner of taking title to trust property.

Section 708. Compensation of Trustee.

(a) If the terms of the trust do not specify the trustee's compensation, a trustee is entitled to compensation that is reasonable under the circumstances.

(b) If the terms of a trust specify the trustee's compensation, the trustee is entitled to be compensated as specified, but the court may allow more or less compensation if:

(1) the duties of the trustee are substantially different from those contemplated when the trust was created; or

(2) the compensation specified by the terms of the trust would be unreasonably low or high.

Section 705. Resignation of Trustee.

(a) A trustee may resign:

(1) upon at least 30 days' notice to the qualified beneficiaries, the settlor, of living, and all cotrustees; or

(2) with the approval of the court.

(b) In approving a resignation, the court may issue orders and impose conditions reasonably necessary for the protection of the trust property.

(c) Any liability of a resigning trustee or of any sureties on the trustee's bond for acts or omissions of the trustee is not discharged or affected by the trustee's resignation.

Notes

A Trustee may be a private individual, a group of individuals, or, as is often the case, a private corporate body such as the United States Trust Company. In all cases, the Trustee is the one who holds legal title to the trust property once it has been transferred by the Settlor. The beneficiaries hold equitable title, allowing for them to enforce their interests upon the Trustee. In order to qualify as a Trustee, the state may require posting a bond or a formal appointment by the court. The corporation may also have requirements under its corporate charter before commencing duties as a corporate Trustee, and in all cases, there may be prohibitions for some. For example, the federal Employee Retirement Income Security Act of 1974 (ERISA) prohibits any person from serving as a fiduciary if the person has been convicted of crimes involving moral turpitude. *See* 29 U.S.C. § 1111 (2004).

Unless the Settlor specifies otherwise, no trust will fail for want of a Trustee; the court is able to appoint another should no Trustee qualify. But once nominated, accepted, and appointed as Trustee, the Trustee may resign only under the terms of the trust instrument or with the approval of the court. More than likely, the reasons given for the Trustee's resignation must include a good faith explanation involving a poor relationship with the beneficiaries or personal family necessities. In some cases, the Trustee may also be the Settlor of the trust, and this invites an added consideration—merger. Each trust must have a separation of legal and equitable interests. Thus, if the Settlor, the Trustee, and the beneficiary are all the same person, then the trust has been terminated and the Trustee's duties are at an end. If however, there are multiple persons, all of whom are Settlors, Trustees, and beneficiaries, then the trust is still viable as there is more than one person, and one may enforce duties against the other. *See, e.g.,* First Alabama Bank v. Webb, 373 So. 2d 631 (Ala. 1979).

C. Beneficiaries

Trusts may have as beneficiaries three categories—private, charitable, and honorary. These categories most often define the scope of the trust and any particular responsibilities. (1) Private beneficiaries are the most common beneficiaries, including family members and friends. (2) Charitable beneficiaries are defined as such through state and federal statutes, as well as common law usage, based mostly on purposes associated with the Statute of Charitable Uses, 43 Eliz. I, c.4 (1601). (3) Honorary beneficiaries may include those beneficiaries similar to both private and charitable enterprise, such as pets and human cemeteries. If the beneficiaries of a trust qualify as charitable, there will be immunity from any Rule Against Perpetuities restraint, and additional tax benefits will likely result. Trusts involving pets invoke deep emotions, but often run afoul of the Rule Against Perpetuities and surviving relatives. The Uniform Trust Code seeks to make some delineation among the three categories.

1. Private Trusts

Uniform Trust Code (2003)

Section 103. Definitions.

(2) "Beneficiary" means a person that:

(A) has a present or future beneficial interest in a trust, vested or contingent; or

(B) in a capacity other than a trustee, holds a power of appointment over trust property.

Clark v. Campbell

Supreme Court of New Hampshire, 1926
82 N.H. 281, 133 A.166

SNOW, J.

The ninth clause of the will of deceased reads:

> My estate will comprise so many and such a variety of articles of personal property such as books, photographic albums, pictures, statuary, bronzes, bric-a-brac, hunting and fishing equipment, antiques, rugs, scrap books, canes and masonic jewels, that probably I shall not distribute all, and perhaps no great part thereof during my life by gift among my friends. Each of my trustees is competent by reason of familiarity with the property, my wishes and friendships, to wisely distribute some portion at least of said property. I therefore give and bequeath to my trustees all my property embraced within the classification aforesaid in trust to make disposal by the way of a memento from myself, of such articles to such of my friends as they, my trustees, shall select. All of said property, not so disposed of by them, my trustees are directed to sell and the proceeds of such sale or sales to become and be disposed of as a part of the residue of my estate.

The question here reserved is whether or not the enumeration of chattels in this clause was intended to be restrictive or merely indicative of the variety of the personal property bequeathed. The question is immaterial, if the bequest for the benefit of the testator's "friends" must fail for the want of certainty of the beneficiaries.

By the common law there cannot be a valid bequest to an indefinite person. There must be a beneficiary or a class of beneficiaries indicated in the will capable of coming into court and claiming the benefit of the bequest. Adye v. Smith, 44 Conn. 60, 26 Am. Rep. 424, 425. This principle applies to private but not to public trusts and charities. Harrington v. Pier, 105 Wis. 485, 82 N. W. 345 ... [citations omitted].

The basis assigned for this distinction is the difference in the enforceability of the two classes of trusts. In the former, there being no definite cestui que trust to assert his right, there is no one who can compel performance, with the consequent unjust enrichment of the trustee; while, in the case of the latter, performance is considered to be sufficiently secured by the authority of the Attorney General to invoke the power of the courts. The soundness of this distinction and the grounds upon which it rests, as applied to cases where the trustee is willing to act, has been questioned by distinguished authorities (5 Harvard Law Review, 390, 394, 395; 65 University of Pennsylvania Law Review, 538, 540; 37 Harvard Law Review, 687, 688) and has been supported by other authorities of equal note (15 Harvard Law Review, 510, 513–515, 530). It is, however, conceded by the former that, since the doctrine was first stated in Morice v. Bishop of Durham, supra, more than a century ago, it has remained unchallenged, and has been followed by the courts in a practically unbroken line of decisions. 5 Harvard Law Review, 392, 397; 65 University of Pennsylvania Law Review, 539; 37 Harvard Law Review, 688; 26 R. C. L. 1189. Although it be conceded that the doctrine is not a legal necessity (15 Harvard Law Review, 515), the fact that it has never been impeached affords strong evidence that in its practical application it has been generally found just and reasonable. This is a sufficient ground for continued adherence to the rule.

* * *

It is difficult to conceive of language more clearly disclosing an intention to create a trust. However, if the trust idea introduced by the words "trustees" and in "trust" were not controlling, all the evidence within the will confirms such ideas. In the first clause of the will the testator nominates three trustees, and an alternate in case of vacancy. Throughout the will these nominees are repeatedly and invariably referred to as "my trustees," whenever the testator is dealing with their trust duties. Whenever rights are conferred upon them individually, as happens in the fifth, sixth, and eighth clauses, they are as invariably severally referred to solely by their individual names. The clause under consideration (ninth) expressly provides for the disposal of only a portion of the classi-fied articles, and imposes upon the trustees the duty of selling the balance thereof and adding the proceeds to the residue which they are to continue to hold, and administer in their capacity as trustees. The proceeds thus accruing under this clause are expressly re-ferred to in the eleventh clause in the enumeration of the ultimate funds to be distrib-uted by them as trustees "in and among such charitable * * * institutions" as they shall select and designate. The conclusion is inescapable that there was no intention to bestow any part of the property enumerated in the ninth clause upon the trustees for their own benefit. This necessarily follows, since the direction to make disposal is clearly as broad as the gift.

It is further sought to sustain the bequest as a power. The distinction apparently re-lied upon is that a power, unlike a trust (Goodale v. Mooney, 60 N. H. 528, 534, 49 Am. Rep. 334), is not imperative and leaves the act to be done at the will of the donee of the power (21 R. C. L. 773; 26 R. C. L. 1169). But the ninth clause by its terms imposes upon the trustees the imperative duty to dispose of the selected articles among the testa-tor's friends. If, therefore, the authority bestowed by the testator by the use of a loose terminology may be called a power, it is not an optional power, but a power coupled with a trust, to which the principles incident to a trust so far as here involved, clearly apply. People v. Kaiser, 137 N. E. 827, 828, 306 Ill. 313; 1 Tiffany on Real Property, § 317; Greenough v. Wells, 10 Cush. (Mass.) 571, 576; Sweeney v. Warren, 28 N. E. 413, 414, 127 N. Y. 426, 24 Am. St. Rep. 468; Read v. Williams, 26 N. E. 730, 731, 125 N. Y. 560, 21 Am. St. Rep. 748; 26 R. C. L. 1169.

We must therefore conclude that this clause presents the case of an attempt to create a private trust, and clearly falls within the principle of well-considered authorities. Nichols v. Allen, 130 Mass. 211, 212, 39 Am. Rep. 445; Blunt v. Taylor, 119 N. E. 954, 230 Mass. 303, 305. In so far as the cases cited by the petitioners upon this phase of the case are not readily distinguishable from the case at bar, they are in conflict with the great weight of authority. The question presented, therefore, is whether or not the ninth clause provides for definite and ascertainable beneficiaries, so that the bequest therein can be sustained as a private trust.

In this state the identity of a beneficiary is a question of fact to be found from the language of the will, construed in the light of all the competent evidence rather than by the application of arbitrary rules of law. It is believed that in no other jurisdiction is there greater liberality shown in seeking the intention of the testator in this, as in other particulars. Trustees of South Newmarket Methodist Seminary v. Peaslee, 15 N. H. 317; Goodhue v. Clark, 37 N. H. 525, 532; Goodale v. Mooney, supra; Harriman v. Harri-man, 59 N. H. 135; Galloway v. Babb, 77 N. H. 259, 260, 90 A. 968; Remick v. Merrill, 80 N. H. 225, 227, 116 A. 344; Adams v. Hospital, 132 A. 525, 81 N. H. ___. We find, however, no case in which our courts have sustained a gift where the testator has attempted to delegate to a trustee the arbitrary selection of the beneficiaries of his bounty through means of a private trust.

Like the direct legatees in a will, the beneficiaries under a trust may be designated by class. But in such case the class must be capable of delimitation, as "brothers and sisters," "children," "issue," "nephews and nieces." A bequest giving the executor authority to distribute his property "among his relatives and for benevolent objects in such sums as in their judgment shall be for the best" was sustained upon evidence within the will that by "relatives" the testator intended such of his relatives within the statute of distributions as were needy, and thus brought the bequest within the line of charitable gifts, and excluded all others as individuals. Goodale v. Mooney, 60 N. H. 528, 536, 49 Am. Rep. 334. See Portsmouth v. Shackford, 46 N. H. 423, 425; Gafney v. Kenison, 64 N. H. 354, 356, 10 A. 706. Where a testator bequeathed his stocks to be apportioned to his "relations" according to the discretion of the trustee, to be enjoyed by them after his decease, it was held to be a power to appoint amongst his relations who were next of kin under the statute of distribution. Varrell v. Wendell, 20 N. H. 431, 436. Likewise where a devise over after a particular estate was to the testator's "next of kin" simpliciter. Pinkham v. Blair, 57 N. H. 226, 243. See Snow v. Durgin, 70 N. H. 121, 122, 47 A. 89. Unless the will discloses a plain purpose to the contrary, the words "relatives" or "relations," to prevent gifts from being void for uncertainty, are commonly construed to mean those who would take under statutes of distribution or descent. 2 Schouler on Wills, § 1008; Thompson on Wills, 181; Thompson v. Thornton, 197 Mass. 273, 83 N. E. 880; Drew v. Wakefield, 54 Me. 291, 298.

In the case now under consideration the cestuis que trust are designated as the "friends" of the testator. The word "friends," unlike "relations," has no accepted statutory or other controlling limitations, and in fact has no precise sense at all. Friendship is a word of broad and varied application. It is commonly used to describe the undefinable relationships which exist, not only between those connected by ties of kinship or marriage, but as well between strangers in blood, and which vary in degree from the greatest intimacy to an acquaintance more or less casual. "Friend" is sometimes used in contradistinction to "enemy." "A friendless man is an outlaw." Cowell, Bouvier. Although the word was formerly sometimes used as synonymous with relatives (5 Com. Dig. 336; Sugden on Powers [1823] 519), there is no evidence that it was so used here. The inference is to the contrary. The testator in the will refers to eight different persons, some of them already deceased, by the title of "friends." He never uses the appellation concurrently with "nephew" or "niece," which words occur several times in describing legatees. Nor is there anything to indicate that the word "friends" in the ninth clause was intended to apply only to those who had been thus referred to in the will. See Hall v. Wiggin, 67 N. H. 89, 90, 29 A. 671. There is no express evidence that the word is used in any restricted sense. The only implied limitation of the class is that fixed by the boundaries of the familiarity of the testator's trustees with his friendships. If such familiarity could be held to constitute such a line of demarcation as to define an ascertainable group, it is to be noted that the gift is not to such group as a class, the members of which are to take in some definite proportion (1 Jarman on Wills, 534; 2 Schouler, § 1011), or according to their needs, but the disposition is to "such of my friends as they, my trustees may select." No sufficient criterion is furnished to govern the selection of the individuals from the class. The assertion of the testator's confidence in the competency of his trustees "to wisely distribute some portion" of the enumerated articles "by reason of familiarity with the property, my wishes and friendships" does not furnish such a criterion. Where, after expressing confidence in the discretion of his executors and trustees, the testator gave the remainder of his estate to them "for certain purposes which I have made known to them," and authorized them to "make such distribution and division of my estate as I have indicated to them, and as they shall deem proper for the fulfillment of my wishes so well known to them," it was held that the trust created was not sufficiently definite for execution. Blunt v. Taylor, 230 Mass, 303, 305, 119 N. E. 954. A bequest to executors "particularly for the purpose of giving to any relatives of mine who without apparent reason I may have overlooked, such sum as may seem to them or him, under all the circumstances, fitting, suitable and proper," was held void for indefiniteness, notwithstanding the aid of the statute of distributions. Minot v. Parker, 189 Mass. 176, 75 N. E. 149. A limitation over, after the death of the testatrix's son without heirs, "to whoever has been his best friend," was held to be "too indefinite for any one to determine who was intended as the object of the testatrix's bounty." Early v. Arnold, 119 Va. 500, 89 S. E. 900. Where an executor was given direction to distribute in a manner calculated to carry out "wishes which I have expressed to him or may express to him," and such wishes had been orally communicated to the executor by the testator, the devise could not be given effect as against the next of kin. Olliffe v. Wells, 130 Mass. 221, 224, 225. Much less can effect be given to the uncommunicated wishes of the testator here.

* * *

Where a gift is impressed with a trust, ineffectively declared, and incapable of taking effect because of the indefiniteness of the cestui que trust, the donee will hold the property in trust for the next taker under the will, or for the next of kin by way of a resulting trust. Varrell v. Wendell, 20 N. H. 431, 438; Lyford v. Laconia, 75 N. H. 220, 223, 72 A. 1085, 22 L. R. A. (N. S.) 1062, 139 Am. St. Rep. 680; Sheedy v. Roach, 124 Mass. 472, 476, 26 Am. Rep. 680; Nichols v. Allen, 130 Mass. 211, 212, 39 Am. Rep. 445; Blunt v. Taylor, supra; Drew v. Wakefield, 54 Me. 291, 295. The trustees therefore hold title to the property enumerated in the paragraph under consideration to be disposed of as a part of the residue, and the trustees are so advised. This conclusion makes it unnecessary to answer the question reserved * * * .

* * *

Case discharged.

All concurred.

2. Charitable Trusts

Uniform Trust Code (2003)

Section 110. Others Treated as Qualified Beneficiaries.

(b) A charitable organization expressly mandated to receive distribution under the terms of a charitable trust or a person appointed to enforce a trust created for the care of an animal or another noncharitable purpose as provided in Section 408 or 409 has the rights of a qualified beneficiary under this [Code].

(c) The [attorney general of this State] has the rights of a qualified beneficiary with respect to a charitable trust having its principal place of administration in this State.

Section 405. Charitable Purposes; Enforcement.

(a) A charitable trust may be created for the relief of poverty, the advancement of education or religion, the promotion of health, governmental or municipal purposes, or other purposes the achievement of which is beneficial to the community.

(b) If the terms of a charitable trust do not indicate a particular charitable purpose or beneficiary, the court may select one or more charitable purposes or beneficiaries. The selection must be consistent with a settlor's intention to the extent it can be ascertained.

(c) The settlor of a charitable trust, among others, may maintain a proceeding to enforce the trust.

Section 413. Cy Pres.

(a) Except as otherwise provided ... if a particular charitable purpose becomes unlawful, impossible to achieve, or wasteful:

(1) the trust does not fail, in whole or in part;

(2) the trust property does not revert to the settlor or the settlor's successors in interest; and

(3) the court may apply cy pres to modify or terminate the trust by directing that the trust property be applied or distributed, in whole of in part, in a manner consistent with the settlor's charitable purposes.

Register of Wills for Baltimore City v. Cook

Court of Appeals of Maryland, 1966
241 Md. 264, 216 A.2d 542

OPPENHEIMER, Judge.

* * *

Jessie Marjorie Cook died December 29, 1960, a resident of Baltimore City, and her will was probated in the Orphans' Court of Baltimore City. The provisions involved read as follows:

> 'TWENTY-SECOND: I give and bequeath unto Helen Elizabeth Brown and Rose S. Zetzer, attorneys at law, the sum of $10,000.00 to be held in Trust for the following purposes: to pay unto the Maryland Branch of the National Woman's Party, One Hundred ($100.) Dollars per year for a period of ten years, if said organization remains in existence and is active for that length of time; the rest and residue of said bequest in trust shall be used to help further the passage of and enactment into law of the EQUAL RIGHTS AMENDMENT to the Constitution of the United States; the said Trustees or their successors, if any, shall have absolute control of said sum of money and use the same as in their joint judgment may seem best to carry out the purposes for which this bequest is intended.
>
> 'TWENTY-THIRD: I give and bequeath unto Helen Elizabeth Brown and Rose S. Zetzer, attorneys at law, in Trust and to their successors, in trust, the sum of $25,000.00 for the purpose of aiding and assisting any woman who may be in distress or suffer any injury to herself or her property as a result of any

inequalities in the laws of the State of Maryland or of any of the United States; said Trustees or their successors in trust shall have absolute control of said trust fund and shall use the same as in their best judgment jointly may be deemed advisable to carry out the purposes for which said bequest is intended and their decision shall be final.

'In the event, however, that said Trustees shall be unable to agree, each Trustee shall select one competent person who shall consider the matter and file their opinion. If these two arbitrators fail to agree, then these two shall mutually select a competent third person and the decision of any two of the three persons thus selected shall be conclusive and be accepted as final.

'TWENTY-EIGHTH: All the rest and residue of my estate, whether real, personal or mixed and wheresoever situate, which I now own, possess or to which I may be entitled to at the time of my death, or at any time thereafter, I give, devise and bequeath in Trust to my Trustees above named; viz: Helen Elizabeth Brown and Rose S. Zetzer, to be used to further the cause of equality for women in civil and economic rights and to carry on the work for women in accordance with the objectives as outlined in paragraphs Nos. 'Twenty-second' and 'Twenty-third' herein.'

Vernon Cook, Jr., the testatrix's brother and executor, filed a bill in equity to test the validity of the bequests and to determine whether his sister's will executed the power of appointment in the will of Vernon Cook, Sr., his father and the father of the testatrix. The litigation resulted in a settlement under which Mr. Cook received one-half of the residue of the trust held by Mercantile-Safe Deposit & Trust Company under the will of Vernon Cook, Sr., and the trustees under Miss Cook's will received the amounts of the specific bequests and the residue of Miss Cook's estate plus the remaining half of the residue of the Mercantile-Safe Deposit fund. The trustees under the testatrix's will received approximately $190,000 from each source, in the total amount of about $380,000, and placed the administration of the fund under the general jurisdiction of the Circuit Court.

* * *

In the hearing before the Maryland Tax Court, the two trustees named in the will, Helen Elizabeth Brown and Rose S. Zetzer, both testified. In addition, various documents were offered in evidence. One exhibit was a statement of the purposes and functions of the Maryland Branch of the National Woman's Party, of which Miss Brown is a past president. The statement reads in part as follows:

'The Maryland Branch of the National Woman's Party has for its fundamental objective to secure for women complete equality under the law with respect to their property, personal, social economic and civil rights and privileges, and to that end to inform, detail and specify what rights and privileges women possess presently, and to what extent these rights and privileges are curtailed or limited. These rights and limitations of rights are brought to focus by way of public discussion and education. Furthermore, to accomplish these purposes, the National Woman's Party, Maryland Branch, whose membership consists of businesswomen, homemakers, lawyers, and civic minded women, arrange, through public meetings and discussion groups, to further the cause of equality of opportunity under the law for women in business, professions and public offices and encourage the enlightened representatives and leaders in our community to remove every vestige of discrimination which is rampant in many of our antiquated customs * * *.'

The testimony shows that the Maryland organization works for the passage of the Equal Rights Amendment, and to remove discriminations in the laws against women throughout the United States. It is a branch of the National Woman's Party, which is incorporated. At the time Miss Cook's will was probated, the Maryland Branch may not have been incorporated.

Another exhibit put into evidence was the report of the President's Commission on the Status of Women made in 1963. This report includes the following statements: 'Eight out of ten women are in paid employment outside of the home at some time during their lives * * *' 'In the face of these amendments, however [the Fifth and Fourteenth Amendments to the Federal Constitution] there remain, especially in certain State laws and official practices, distinctions based on sex which discriminate against women.' 'Lower pay rates for women doing the same work as men are not uncommon.' While in 1963 the Federal Fair Labor Standards Act of 1938 was amended to require equal pay for equal work, 'State laws should establish the principle of equal pay for comparable work.' 'In many specific areas of State law, the disabilities of married women are considerable.'

The testatrix was deeply interested in women's rights. Her trustees conceive their duties as 'educational primarily and charitable.' Miss Zetzer testified that a major legal 'discrimination' in Maryland is the wife's obligation to accept a suitable domicile selected by her husband. The trustees believe, however, that there is greater and more serious legal discrimination in other states. There was also testimony that, in Maryland, discriminations have been found in certain employment practices and that women still do not have equal pay for equal work.

There was testimony about guidelines for the administration of the trust which the trustees formulated under the title 'The Marjorie Cook Foundation.' The testimony is unclear as to whether this formulation was made prior to distribution. There was also testimony as to the scope and nature of the trusts after distribution. However, counsel agree that the legal questions involved in this appeal are to be adjudicated on the basis of the provisions made in the will, irrespective of what may or may not have been done by the trustees after distribution.

The appellant contends that the bequests are not to a trust 'organized and operated exclusively for religious, charitable, scientific, literary or educational purposes.' Counsel have submitted thorough, fair and helpful briefs.

The case, in our view, involves two questions. First, is the general nature of the bequest charitable under the Maryland law?; and, second, if the first question is answered in the affirmative, are the trusts exclusively for charitable purposes, in view of the right of the trustees to employ the funds to support candidates for political office who favor women's rights, to contribute to the Maryland Branch of the National Woman's Party, and to work for the passage of the Equal Rights Amendment? Counsel agree that, if the trusts are not charitable, the bequests are taxable.

* * *

The history of the statutory provision as to the exemption of charitable trusts is set forth in Second Nat'l. Bank of Washington, D. C. v. Second Nat'l. Bank, 171 Md. 547, 555–557, 190 A. 215, 111 A.L.R. 711 (1937). Many gifts for charitable uses had been declared to be invalid because of the indefiniteness of the donees. In 1931, an Act (now Code (1957) Art. 16, sec. 195) was passed declaring that henceforward the statute of 43 Elizabeth Ch. 4 applies to gifts and trusts for charitable purposes. Judge Sloan, for the Court, said:

> 'This statute did not mark the beginning of charitable uses, as courts of equity had, before it was enacted, assumed jurisdiction of charitable trusts. It made legal and enforceable trusts and gifts which had been declared invalid because indefinite and general. Vidal v. [Mayor, Aldermen, etc., of] Philadelphia, 2 How. 127, 196, 11 L.Ed. 205, 233. The courts, in states where the statute had been adopted, did not confine themselves to the charities expressly named, and many objects have been upheld as charities, which the statute neither mentions nor distinctly refers to. Thus a gift 'to the poor' generally, or to the poor of a particular town, parish, age, sex, race, or condition, or to poor emigrants, though not falling within any of the descriptions of poor in the statute, is a good charitable gift.'

* * *

The bequest to the trustees in the Twenty-Second paragraph of the will is for two purposes: Payments to the Maryland Branch of the National Woman's Party and to help further the passage of the Equal Rights Amendment to the Constitution of the United States, which is designed to prohibit discrimination against women by reason of their sex. The bequest to the trustees in the Twenty-Third paragraph is for the purpose of aiding and assisting any woman who may be in distress or suffer any injury to herself or her property as a result of any inequalities in the laws of Maryland or of the United States. The residuary bequest to the trustees in the Twenty-Eighth paragraph is to further the cause of equality of women in civil and economic rights and to carry on the work for women in accordance with the objectives outlined in the Twenty-Second and Twenty-Third paragraphs.

The primary purposes of all the trusts, in our view, are the elimination of discriminations against women and to give relief to women injured by such discriminations. The passage of the Equal Rights Amendment is one of the methods set forth by the testatrix to endeavor to accomplish these objectives, both directly and by contributions to the Maryland Branch of the National Woman's Party.

Trusts to eliminate discriminations and to provide relief for the persons discriminated against have been generally upheld as charitable. Collier v. Lindley, 203 Cal. 641, 266 P. 526 (1928), and Edgeter v. Kemper, Ohio Prob., 136 N.E.2d 630 (1955) (trust to eliminate discriminations against Indians and to provide for their relief); Lewis's Estate, 152 Pa. 477, 25 A. 878 (1893) (trust to eliminate discrimination against Negroes); In re Murphey's Estate, 7 Cal.2d 712, 62 P.2d 374 (1936) (trust to eliminate discriminations against Jews).

> 'If the general purposes for which a trust is created are such as may be reasonably thought to promote the social interest of the community, the mere fact that a majority of the people and the members of the court believe that the particular purpose of the settlor is unwise or not adapted to the accomplishment of the general purposes, does not prevent the trust from being charitable * * *

> 'The Courts do not take sides or attempt to decide which of two conflicting views of promoting the social interest of the community is the better adapted to the purpose, even though the views are opposed to each other * * *' Restatement, Trusts 2d (1959) § 374 comment 1.

By the great weight of authority, if a trust is essentially charitable in nature, it is still charitable even though one of its purposes is to endeavor to effectuate a change of existing law. George v. Braddock, 45 N.J.Eq. 757, 18 A. 881, 6 L.R.A. 511 (1889); Garrison v. Little, 75 Ill.App. 402 (1897); Taylor v. Hoag, 273 Pa. 194, 116 A. 826, 21 A.L.R. 946 (1922); Collier v. Lindley, supra. See also Haines v. Allen, 78 Ind. 100 (1881).

Restatement, Trusts 2d (1959) §374 comment j reads as follows:

> 'Change in existing law. A trust may be charitable although the accomplishment of the purpose for which the trust is created involves a change in the existing law. If the purpose of the trust is to bring about changes in the law by illegal means, such as by revolution, bribery, illegal lobbying or bringing improper pressure to bear upon members of the legislature, the purpose is illegal. See §377. The mere fact, however, that the purpose is to bring about a change in the law, whether indirectly through the education of the electors so as to bring about a public sentiment in favor of the change, or through proper influences brought to bear upon the legislators, does not prevent the purpose from being legal and charitable.'

Bogert and Scott take the same view.

> 'Many American decisions and, it is submitted, the better reasoned cases, declare that trusts which seek to bring about better government by changing laws or constitutional provisions are charitable, so long as the settlor directed that the reforms should be accomplished peaceably, by the established constitutional means, and not by war, riot, or revolution.' Bogert, Trusts & Trustees (2d ed.1964); §378, 'Changes in the Law.'

> 'In the United States the notion that a trust for a purpose otherwise charitable is not charitable if the accomplishment of its purposes involves a change in existing laws has been pretty thoroughly rejected. Many reforms can be accomplished only by a change in the law, and there seems to be no good reason why the mere fact that they can be accomplished only through legislation should prevent them from being valid charitable purposes.' 4 Scott, Trusts (2d ed.1956) §374.4 at 2677.

Two Massachusetts decisions are contrary to what is admitted to be the majority view. In Jackson v. Phillips, 96 Mass. (14 Allen) 539, 555 (1867), the court held that a bequest to secure the passage of laws granting women the right to vote and all other civil rights enjoyed by men could not be sustained as a charity. Justice Gray said, for the court:

> 'But it is the duty of the judicial department to expound and administer the laws as they exist. And trusts whose expressed purpose is to bring about changes in the laws or the political institutions of the country are not charitable in such a sense as to be entitled to peculiar favor, protection and perpetuation from the ministers of those laws which they are designed to modify or subvert.'

The same will involved a trust designed to secure the abolition of slavery and this trust the court held charitable, even though its accomplishment would necessitate a fundamental change in the law. Jackson was followed in Bowditch v. Attorney General, 241 Mass. 168, 134 N.E. 796, 28 A.L.R. 713 (1922), which held a bequest to promote the causes of women's rights not charitable because impliedly it looked to the accomplishment of the testator's intention by legislation.

The above decisions from other states show that the Massachusetts doctrine had not been followed. In *Hoag*, supra, the Pennsylvania Supreme Court, in refusing to follow the Massachusetts cases, said, 273 Pa. at 199–200, 116 A. at 827–828:

> 'We are led to conclude that a trust for a public charity is not invalid merely because it contemplates the procuring of such changes in existing laws as the donor deems beneficial to the people in general, or to a class for whose benefit the trust is created. To hold that an endeavor to procure, by proper means, a change in a law is, in effect, to attempt to violate that law would discourage improvement in legislation and tend to compel us to continue indefinitely to live under laws designed for an entirely different state of society. Such view is opposed to every principle of our government, based on the theory that it is a government 'of the people, by the people, and for the people,' and fails to recognize the right of those who make the laws to change them at their pleasure, when circumstances may seem to require. With the wisdom of the proposed change the courts are not concerned. We perform our duty in determining whether or not the method adopted to make the change violates established law. In the present case we find no apparent intent to violate any law. On the contrary, the trust specifically requires its objects to be accomplished by 'lawful means.' There is nothing inherently unlawful either in the object to be attained or the means to be adopted.'

In Garrison v. Little, supra, the Illinois court said, 75 Ill.App. at 412:

> 'Whether the attainment of the elective franchise by women, to the extent enjoyed by men, would be as beneficial in its results to society as its friends hope or believe, is not a question for us to consider. Upon this subject there are widely divergent opinions; but if the cause was dear to the heart of the testatrix, we see no reason why she should not be permitted to devote a portion of her estate to its advancement. She believed it to be for the benefit of women, and for that purpose and because of her interest in their welfare and not from any selfish motive, she made the bequest in question.'

The appellant cites, in another connection to be hereafter considered, Slee v. Commissioner of Internal Revenue, 42 F.2d 184, 185, 72 A.L.R. 400 (2d Cir.1930). That case involved the deductibility from income of gifts made by the petitioner to the American Birth Control League, which advocates changes in the law. The first question was whether the League was organized for charitable or educational purposes. Judge Learned Hand, in his opinion, said: 'That the League is organized for charitable purposes seems to us clear * * *.'

Great as is our respect for the Massachusetts court, we believe that the majority view should be followed in this case. The provisions of the testatrix's will make it evident to us that her primary objective was to provide funds for the elimination of discriminations against women and that support of the passage of the Equal Rights Amendment and other national or state legislation to this end was merely an incidental means to the accomplishment of the general purpose. All the provisions of the will look only to legal means to effectuate the objective. The bequests to not provide in any way for contributions to a political party as such. Whatever may be the views of individuals, laymen or judges, as to the need or desirability of the passage of the Equal Rights Amendment or similar legislation, our system of government is not opposed to attempts to secure legislative changes by legal means. Indeed, the channelling [sic] of efforts to effect social or political changes to the public discussions involved in proposed constitutional amendments or legislation, rather than by possible violence or subversion, is fundamental to our democracy.

Realistically, a charitable purpose such as that of the testatrix, can often only be effectuated by legislative change. Recognition of that fact by the testatrix does not alter what we have found to be the essentially charitable nature of the bequests here involved.

* * *

Even though the bequests are charitable in nature, the exemption clause of the statute provides in effect that they are taxable unless they are exclusively for religious, charitable or similar purposes. The National Woman's Party and its Maryland Branch are non-profit organizations. In the sense that the bequests here involved do not provide for or permit personal benefit of any private shareholder or individual, except members of the designated class of beneficiaries of the fund, they are exclusively for a charitable purpose. The question remains, however, as to whether the provisions which permit the use of the funds in an endeavor to charge existing laws make the charitable purpose non-exclusive.

The Maryland law contains no provision similar to that in the federal income and estate tax statutes, which specifically provide that the deduction is to be allowed only if no substantial part of the activities of the donee or legatee is carrying on propaganda or otherwise attempting to influence legislation.

If, as we have found the purposes of the trust here involved are charitable, they are no less charitable because of the means authorized to effectuate them, when, as here, those means are legal and not against public policy. Contributions to political parties are not involved. Although efforts to bring about changes in the law are envisioned and authorized, these are only ways to effectuate the purposes; they do not make the purposes themselves less charitable in nature or dilute their nature. Had the General Assembly wished to exclude bequests otherwise charitable from the exemption if a substantial part of a bequest is used in attempts to influence legislation, it could easily have done so by incorporating in the Maryland statute a clause similar to the provisions which the Congress has had in effect for several decades.

The appellant relies on federal cases construing the federal statutes in respect of charitable deductions. It is true that several earlier federal decisions take the same point of view as did the Massachusetts cases as to the effect of efforts to change the law upon the charitable nature of the organizations involved. In Slee v. Commissioner, supra, while the court found that the American Birth Control League was organized for charitable purposes, it held that the taxpayer could not deduct gifts to the League from his gross income because the League worked for the repeal of laws preventing birth control and was therefore not exclusively charitable under the Internal Revenue Act then in effect. Leubuscher v. Commissioner of Internal Revenue, 54 F.2d 998 (2d Cir. 1932) is to the same effect; in that case, a legacy to a club incorporated to advocate the single tax doctrine of Henry George was held not deductible under the estate tax law as a legacy for a corporation organized exclusively for educational purposes, because the organization had for its purposes the effectuation of a change in the existing system of taxation. Vanderbilt v. Commissioner of Internal Revenue, 93 F.2d 360 (1st Cir. 1937) involved the deductibility from the gross estate of a bequest to the National Woman's Party. The court held that although the corporation was not organized for profit and no part of its earnings enured to the benefit of any shareholder or individual, the efforts to enact and repeal laws were political activities and that, therefore, the bequest was not deductible as being exclusively educational.

These cases were decided before the Internal Revenue Code had been amended by the addition of the phrase 'and no substantial part of the activities of which is carrying on propaganda, or otherwise attempting, to influence legislation.' Girard Trust Co. v. Commissioner of Internal Revenue, 122 F.2d 108, 110, 138 A.L.R. 448 (3rd Cir. 1941) was decided after the amendment. In that case, the testatrix had left a bequest to the Board of Temperance, Prohibition and Public Morals of the Methodist Episcopal Church. The commissioner had disallowed the exemption and the Board of Tax Appeals confirmed his action. Part of the activity of the Board of Temperance was an attempt to influence legislation. The court reversed the Board of Tax Appeals and held that the bequest was deductible. Judge Goodrich, for the majority, said:

> '* * * [W]e had Sunday observance laws long before prohibition of alcohol became an important issue. The advocacy of such regulation before party committees and legislative bodies is a part of the achievement of the desired result in a democracy. The safeguards against its undue extension lie in counter-pressures by groups who think differently and the constitutional protection, applied by courts, to check that which interferes with freedom of religion for any.
>
> 'Nor has the law sought to draw such a bright line between the exercise of private and public influence. Judge Hand has pointed out that the promoters of a charity are not unclassed when the charity seeks a special charter or when a society to prevent cruelty to children seeks positive support of law to accomplish its ends or when a university seeks legislation to provide its appropriations. Surely a church would not lose its exemption as a religious institution if, pending a proposal to repeal Sunday observance laws, the congregation held a meeting on church property and authorized a committee to appear before a legislative body to protest against the repeal. The majority of the charitable trust cases recognize the validity of a gift to prohibit or minimize manufacture and sale of intoxicating liquor. They are not directly controlling, of course. But they furnish a strong analogy.'

International Reform Federation v. District Unemployment Compensation Bd., 76 U.S.App.D.C. 282, 131 F.2d 337, 340 (D.C.Cir. 1942) involved an exemption, not under the Internal Revenue laws, but under the District of Columbia Unemployment Compensation Act. The question was whether the Federation was an employer within the meaning of the Act. The Act exempted any corporation or foundation organized exclusively for religious, charitable, scientific, educational, or other similar purposes from the requirement that every employer must make payments to the fund. The Federation had as some of its purposes the enactment of laws prohibiting the alcoholic liquor traffic and traffic in white slaves and narcotics. The Compensation Board contended that, even if the Federation should be classed as a corporation organized for charitable, religious or educational purposes, it was not organized and operated exclusively for those purposes. The court disagreed and held the Federation was not subject to the Act. Chief Judge Groner, for the majority of the court, said:

> 'It would seem to us to be going very far to say that these legislative activities accomplish a metamorphosis in appellant's character whereby it is changed from a charitable or educational to a political organization. Such activities have never been classified as lobbying in the sense in which that activity has been either prohibited or licensed. Hence we see no actual difference between the education of the individual—admittedly proper—and the education of the legislator, where both are directed to a common end, and that end, not the advancement, by political intrigue or otherwise, of the fortunes of a polit-

ical party, but merely the accomplishment of national social improvement. There is nothing new in this position, and it has found support in many cases.'

Marshall v. Commissioner of Internal Revenue, 147 F.2d 75 (2d Cir. 1945) held that bequests in trust to promote the theory of production for use and not for profit, to promote civil liberties and to preserve wilderness areas, were not deductible from the federal estate tax because political activity was a definite purpose of the trust. The court emphasized that the political purposes were substantial and therefore within the exception of the Internal Revenue Code. In Seasongood v. Commissioner of Internal Revenue, 227 F.2d 907 (6th Cir. 1955) it was held that deductions from individual income tax returns for contributions made to a local Good Government League were deductible, even though a minor portion of the time and effort of the League was devoted to activities found to be political. The court held that the statute must be liberally construed to effect its purpose and that the legislative activities of the League in relation to all its other activities were not substantial. Dulles v. Johnson, 273 F.2d 362, 80 A.L.R.2d 1338 (2d Cir. 1959) involved the deductibility under the federal estate tax law of bequests to city, county and state bar associations. Part of the work of the associations was study and report on proposed and existing legislation. Copies of the reports and resolutions were often sent to the legislative and other branches of federal and state governments. The court held that the activities of the associations in respect of impending legislation were not such a substantial part of their activities as to cause the forfeiture of their charitable status.

Taken as a whole, the trend of the federal decisions indicates to us that efforts to change the law do not necessarily affect the exclusive charitable nature of an organization, despite the restriction contained in the Internal Revenue Code, which, as we have pointed out, is not a part of the Maryland law.

We find that the bequests here involved are exclusively charitable within the meaning of the Maryland statute and therefore are deductible.

Order affirmed; costs to be paid by the appellant.

3. Honorary Trusts

Uniform Trust Code (2003)

Section 408. Trust for Care of Animal.

(a) A trust may be created to provide for the care of an animal alive during the settlor's lifetime. The trust terminates upon the death of the animal or, if the trust was created to provide for the care of more than one animal alive during the settlor's lifetime, upon the death of the last surviving animal.

(b) A trust authorized by this section may be enforced by a person appointed in the terms of the trust or, if no person is so appointed, by a person appointed by the court. A person having an interest in the welfare of the animal may request the court to appoint a person to enforce the trust or to remove a person appointed.

(c) Property of a trust authorized by this section may be applied only to its intended use, except to the extent the court determines that the value of the trust property exceeds the amount required for the intended use. Except as otherwise provided in the terms of the trust, property not required for the intended use must be distributed to the settlor, if then living, otherwise to the settlor's successors in interest.

Uniform Probate Code (2003)

Section 2-907(b). Honorary Trusts; Trusts for Pets.

(b) [Trusts for Pets.] Subject to this subsection and subsection (c), a trust for the care of a designated domestic or pet animal is valid. The trust terminates when no living animal is covered by the trust. A governing instrument must be liberally construed to bring the transfer within this subsection, to presume against the merely precatory or honorary nature of the disposition, and to carry out the general intent of the transferor. Extrinsic evidence is admissible in determining the transferor's intent.

In re Searight's Estate

Ohio Court of Appeals, Ninth District, 1950
87 Ohio App. 417, 95 N.E.2d 779

HUNSICKER, Judge.

George P. Searight, a resident of Wayne county, Ohio, died testate on November 27, 1948. Item 'third' of his will provided:

> 'I give and bequeath my dog, Trixie, to Florence Hand of Wooster, Ohio, and I direct my executor to deposit in the Peoples Federal Savings and Loan Association, Wooster, Ohio, the sum of $1000.00 to be used by him to pay Florence Hand at the rate of 75 cents per day for the keep and care of my dog as long as it shall live. If my dog shall die before the said $1000.00 and the interest accruing therefrom shall have been used up, I give and bequeath whatever remains of said $1000.00 to be divided equally among those of the following persons who are living at that time, to wit: Bessie Immler, Florence Hand, Reed Searight, Fern Olson and Willis Horn.'

At the time of his death, all of the persons, and his dog, Trixie, named in such item third, were living.

Florence Hand accepted the bequest of Trixie, and the executor paid to her from the $1000 fund, 75 cents a day for the keep and care of the dog. The value of Trixie was agreed to be $5.

The Probate Court made a determination of inheritance tax due from the estate of George P. Searight, deceased, the pertinent part of this judgment reading as follows:

> 'The court further finds that the value of the dog Trixie is taxable as a succession to Florence Hand; that the said dog inherits the sum of $1000.00 with power to consume both the interest and principal at a limited rate; that the state of Ohio, Sec. 5332, levying a tax on successions to property does not levy a tax upon the succession to any property passing to an animal; that the $1000.00 bequest to said dog is therefore not taxable; that the remainder of the $1000.00, if any, remaining after the death of said dog is taxable in the hands of the remaindermen; that there is no certain life expectancy of said dog, and that a tax should therefore be assessed upon the entire bequest to the contingent beneficiaries, subject to the right of refund as provided in Sec. 5343, Ohio General Code, upon final determination of the exact succession to each of the five remaindermen, or the survivor of them, reserving all rights of

refund to a prior deceased remainderman to the estate of such remainderman, and reserving likewise the rights of the state of Ohio to assess any excess to all remaindermen.

'Wherefore, it is ordered by the court that Florence Hand, as successor to the title of the said dog Trixie, be taxed at the rate prescribed by law on the value of said dog, to wit, $5.00; that Bessie Immler, Florence Hand, Reed Searight, Fern Olson and Willis Horn, as contingent beneficiaries and remaindermen of the said $1000.00, each be taxed on $200.00 at the rate prescribed by law, subject to refund or assessment of any excess as indicated in the findings herein * * *.'

The Department of Taxation of Ohio appeals to this court from such judgment, claiming the Probate Court erred: In holding that the bequest in item third to the extent it was paid to Florence Hand for the care of Trixie, is not a succession to property passing in trust or otherwise, to or for the use of a person; in not holding that the bequest of $1000 to the extent it was to be paid to Florence Hand for the care of Trixie was a bequest or succession to the said Florence Hand, subject to Ohio inheritance taxes; in holding that the bequest of $1000.00 was a bequest to a dog to the extent it is paid to Florence Hand for the care of Trixie; in holding that a bequest of $1000 to the extent it is paid to Florence Hand for the care of Trixie is not subject to Ohio inheritance taxes; in holding that a bequest for the care of Trixie is a valid bequest; in not holding that the sum of $1000 was a succession of property passing to the remaindermen named in item third; in not making a final order holding that the entire bequest of $1000 was subject to Ohio inheritance taxes on the amount of $200 due to each remainderman.

The questions presented by this appeal on questions of law are:

1. Is the testamentary bequest for the care of Trixie (a dog) valid in Ohio–

(a) as a proper subject of a so-called 'honorary trust'?

(b) as not being in violation of the rule against perpetuities?

2. Is the bequest set forth in item third of testator's will subject to the inheritance tax laws of Ohio?

1 (a). The creation of a trust for the benefit of specific animals has not been the subject of much litigation in the courts, and our research, and that of able counsel in this case, have failed to disclose any reported case on the subject in Ohio. The few reported cases in this country, in England and in Ireland have been the subject of considerable comment by the writers of text books and by the law reviews of leading law schools.

* * * [citations omitted].

We do not have, in the instant case, the question of a trust established for the care of dogs in general or of an indefinite number of dogs, but we are here considering the validity of a testamentary bequest for the benefit of a specific dog. This is not a charitable trust, nor is it a gift of money to the Ohio Humane Society or a county humane society, which societies are vested with broad statutory authority, Section 10062, General Code, for the care of animals.

Text writers on the subject of trusts and many law professors designate a bequest for the care of a specific animal as an 'honorary trust'; that is, one binding the conscience of the trustee, since there is no beneficiary capable of enforcing the trust.

The rule in Ohio, that the absence of a beneficiary having a legal standing in court and capable of demanding an accounting of the trustee is fatal and the trust fails, was first announced in Mannix, Assignee, v. Purcell, 46 Ohio St. 102, 19 N.E. 572, 2 L.R.A. 753.

The text writer for Ohio Jurisprudence on the subject of trusts (40 Ohio Jurisprudence, page 85 et seq.), Professor Harry W. Vanneman of Ohio State University Law School, says, in Section 68:

> 'Where property is conveyed or devised to a trustee for certain purposes, such as maintenance of graves, saying of masses, erection of monuments, care of certain animals, and the like, although the object of the bounty cannot enforce the trust, and, the trust not being a charity, the attorney general has no duty with respect to it, nevertheless, contrary to the doctrine of the preceding section, the trust does not fail if the trustee is willing to carry it out and erect the monument, care for the animals, etc., provided the trust will not continue for a period longer than the rule against perpetuities. The trustee cannot hold beneficially, and, if he is unwilling to carry out the power entrusted to him, he will hold as resulting trustee for the proper person. Such a trust has been designated as an 'honorary trust' because there is no beneficiary capable of enforcing it. * * *'

In 1 Scott on the Law of Trusts, Section 124, the author says:

> 'There are certain classes of cases similar to those discussed in the preceding section in that there is no one who as beneficiary can enforce the purpose of the testator, but different in one respect, namely, that the purpose is definite. Such, for example, are bequests for the erection or maintenance of tombstones or monuments or for the care of graves, and bequests for the support of specific animals. It has been held in a number of cases that such bequests as these do not necessarily fail. It is true that the legatee cannot be compelled to carry out the intended purpose, since there is no one to whom he owes a duty to carry out the purpose.

> 'Even though the legatee cannot be compelled to apply the property to the designated purpose, the courts have very generally held that he can properly do so, and that no resulting trust arises so long as he is ready and willing to carry it out. The legatee will not, however, be permitted to retain the property for his own benefit; and if he refuses or neglects to carry out the purpose, a resulting trust will arise in favor of the testator's residuary legatee or next of kin.'

Professor Scott then discusses the position that another eminent scholar, Professor Bogert, takes in his work on the Law of Trusts and Trustees, Sections 165–166.

The object and purpose sought to be accomplished by the testator in the instant case is not capricious or illegal. He sought to effect a worthy purpose—the care of his pet dog.

Whether we designate the gift in this case as an 'honorary trust' or a gift with a power which is valid when exercised is not important, for we do know that the one to whom the dog was given accepted the gift and indicated her willingness to care for such dog, and the executor proceeded to carry out the wishes of the testator.

'Where the owner of property transfers it upon an intended trust for a specific noncharitable purpose and there is no definite or definitely ascertainable beneficiary designated, no trust is created; but the transferee has power to apply the property to the designated purpose, unless he is authorized by the terms of the intended trust so to apply the property beyond the period of the rule against perpetuities, or the purpose is capricious.' I Restatement of the Law of Trusts, Section 124.

To call this bequest for the care of the dog, Trixie, a trust in the accepted sense in which that term is defined is, we know, an unjustified conclusion. The modern authorities, as shown by the cases cited earlier in this discussion, however, uphold the validity of a gift for the purpose designated in the instant case, where the person to whom the power is given is willing to carry out the testator's wishes. Whether called an 'honorary trust' or whatever terminology is used, we conclude that the bequest for the care of the dog, Trixie, is not in and of itself unlawful.

In Ohio, by statute, Section 10512-8, General Code, the rule against perpetuities is specifically defined, and such statute further says:

'It is the intention by the adoption of this section to make effective in Ohio what is generally known as the common law rule against perpetuities.'

It is to be noted, in every situation where the so-called 'honorary trust' is established for specific animals, that, unless the instrument creating such trust limits the duration of the trust—that is, the time during which the power is to be exercised—to human lives, we will have 'honorary trusts' established for animals of great longevity, such as crocodiles, elephants and sea turtles.

* * *

The lives, in being, which are the measure of the period set out in the rule against perpetuities, must be determined from the creating instrument.

If we then examine item third of testator's will, we discover that, although the bequest for his dog is for 'as long as it shall live,' the money given for this purpose is $1000 payable at the rate of 75¢ a day. By simple mathematical computation, this sum of money, expended at the rate determined by the testator, will be fully exhausted in three years and 238-1/3 days. If we assume that this $1000 is deposited in a bank so that interest at the high rate of 6% per annum were earned thereon, the time needed to consume both principal and interest thereon (based on semi-annual computation of such interest on the average unused balance during such six month period) would be four years, 57 1/2 days.

It is thus very apparent that the testator provided a time limit for the exercise of the power given his executor, and that such time limit is much less than the maximum period allowed under the rule against perpetuities.

We must indulge the presumption that the testator was cognizant of the rule against perpetuities and the construction placed upon it by the courts, and that he prepared his will possessed of such knowledge. Everhard et al., Trustees v. Brown, 75 Ohio App. 451, at page 459, 62 N.E.2d 901.

We therefore conclude that the bequest in the instant case for the care of the dog, Trixie, does not, by the terms of the creating instrument, violate the rule against perpetuities.

2. We next consider the problem of the inheritance tax, if any, to be levied on the bequest contained in item third of testator's will.

Section 5332, General Code, says, in part:

'A tax is hereby levied upon the succession to any property passing, in trust or otherwise, to or for the use of a person, institution or corporation, in the following cases:

'1. When the succession is by will or by the intestate laws of this state from a person who was a resident of this state at the time of his death.'* * *

'4. Whenever any person or corporation shall exercise a power of appointment derived from any disposition of property heretofore or hereafter made, such appointment when made shall be deemed a succession taxable under the provisions of this subdivision of this chapter in the same manner as if the property to which such appointment relates belonged absolutely to the donee of such power, and had been bequeathed or devised by said donee by will * * *.'

This statute determines that a tax shall be levied upon succession to all property passing to a person, institution or corporation. Certainly, a dog is neither an institution nor a corporation. Can it be successfully contended that a dog is a person? A 'person' is defined as '3. A human being.' Webster's New International Dictionary, Second Edition.

We have hereinabove indicated that the bequest for the dog, Trixie, comes within the designation of an 'honorary trust,' and, as such, is proper in the instant case. A tax based on the amount expended for the care of the dog cannot lawfully be levied against the monies so expended, since it is not property passing for the use of a 'person, institution or corporation.'

The executor herein had a power granted to him to use the funds for the support of the dog, which he proceeded to fulfill. Is it possible that such a power could be considered as a power of appointment within the terms of subsection 4 of Section 5332, General Code, and, hence, subject to taxation thereunder?

On this point, we need look for no other authority than that contained in 3 Restatement of the Law of Property (Future Interests), Section 318(2), which states the rule as follows:

'(2) The term power of appointment does not include a power of sale, a power of attorney, a power or revocation, a power to cause a gift of income to be augmented out of principal, a power to designate charities, a charitable trust, a discretionary trust, or an honorary trust.'

Thus, an intended trust (honorary trust) for the support of a specific animal does not create a power of appointment, as such term is used in the inheritance tax statute. Section 5332, General Code.

We therefore conclude that no succession tax may be levied against such funds as are expended by the executor in carrying out the power granted to him by item third of testator's will.

The judgment of the Probate Court is affirmed.

Judgment affirmed.

STEVENS, P. J., and DOYLE, J., concur.

Notes

In jurisdictions that do not recognize gifts in favor of animals–usually because (1) there is no beneficiary capable of assuming the equitable interest in the trust and enforcing the obligations of the Trustee, or (2) they violate the Rule Against Perpetuities because the measuring life is not human—a trust with provisions to maintain pet animals or inanimate objects, such as automobiles, for example, are considered void. As a result, either the bequest passes to a designated remainderman or the entire bequest fails and passes by intestacy in the Settlor's estate. *See, e.g.,* Willett v. Willett, 247 S.W. 739, 741 (Ky. 1923) (distribution of property remaining in trust after dog's death was not provided for, so remaining property passed through intestate succession).

The most reliable method to overcome these hurdles is for the Settlor to bequeath the animal and create an enforceable inter vivos or testamentary trust in favor of a human beneficiary, to whom the Trustee is required to make distributions to cover the animal's expenses, provided the beneficiary provides proper care to the animal. This conditional gift in trust provides more flexibility and better assures that the owner's intent is carried out. Of course, a court may reduce the amount of the gift in trust if the gift is unreasonably large. *See, e.g.,* In re Rogers, 412 P.2d 710 (Ariz. 1966) (court adjusted or disallowed specific items for care of dogs that were determined to be unreasonable; attorney/executor suspended from practice of law for sixty days for purchasing automobile to transport dogs and washing machine to launder dog's bedding, among other unreasonable expenditures); Templeton Estate, 4 Fiduciary 2d 172, 175 (Pa. Orphans' Ct. 1984) (gift reduced to an amount sufficient to accomplish owner's intent); *In re* Lyon's Estate, 67 Pa. D. & C.2d 474, 482–83 (Pa. Com. Pl. 1974) (reducing amount left for care of animal because owner miscalculated needs). *See also* Unif. Prob. Code § 2-907(c)(6) (2004) (court may reduce an amount that "substantially exceeds the amount required....").

Although many states validate gifts in favor of animals via the honorary trust, and, consequently, heirs and beneficiaries of the owner may not contest such use of the property, honorary trusts are not enforceable if the Trustee opts *not* to use the property according to the owner's intent. Thus, the conditional gift in trust is the more reliable method for assuring that the owner's intent is fulfilled. In addition, attorneys drafting such trusts must be mindful of the tax consequences. With honorary trusts for pets, the Internal Revenue Code provides that no deduction is allowed for the trust because there is no individual, standing as a beneficiary, who will pay taxes on the trust. However, because such trusts typically do not accumulate income, the trust is not taxed at the normal trust rate; instead, it is taxed at the rate of a married person filing separately. *See* Rev. Rul. 76-486, 1976-2 C.B. 192 (1976). *See also* Rev. Rul. 78-105, 1978-1 CB 295 (1978) (Charitable Remainder Annuity Trust; Care for Pet Animal).

Within the United States, many jurisdictions now recognize enforceable gifts for pets by adopting legislation based on Uniform Probate Code § 2-907 or Uniform Trust Code § 4-408—both of which allow for third party enforcement of the trusts—and by effectively abolishing the Rule Against Perpetuities by including a "perpetuities savings clause." *See* Alaska Stat. § 13.12.907 (2003)("trust may be performed by the trustee for 21 years but not longer, whether or not the terms of the trust contemplate a longer duration"); Ariz. Rev. Stat. § 14-2907 (2004) ("trust may be performed by the trustee for not longer than twenty-one years"); Cal. Prob. Code Ann. § 15212 (West 2004) (trust is valid for the life of the animal); Colo Rev. Stat. § 15-11-901 (2004) (validating trusts for pets "for twenty-one years but no longer, whether or not the terms of the trust contemplate a longer duration"); D.C. Code § 19-1304.08 (2004) ("trust terminates upon the death of the animal or, if the trust was created to provide for the care of more than one animal alive during the settlor's lifetime, upon the death of the last surviving animal"); Fla. Stat. §737.116 (2004) ("trust terminates upon the death of the animal or, if the trust was created to provide for the care of more than one animal alive during the settlor's lifetime, upon the death of the last surviving animal"); 760 Ill. Comp. Stat. §5/15.2 (2004) (trust may be performed until no living animal is covered by the trust); Iowa Code Ann. §633.2105 (2004) (trust may be performed by the Trustee for only twenty-one years); Kan. Stat. Ann. §58A-408 (2003) (terminates upon death of animal or, if to provide for more than one animal, upon death of last surviving animal); 18-B Me. Rev. Stat. Ann. §408 (effective July 1, 2005) (terminates upon death of animal or last surviving animal); Mich. Comp. Laws §700.2722 (2004) (trust may be performed for 21 years); Mo. Rev. Stat. §456.4-408 (2004) (trust terminates at death of animal or last surviving animal); Mont. Code Ann. §72-2-1017 (2003) (trust may be performed for twenty-one years, but no longer); Neb. Rev. Stat. §30-3834 (terminates upon death of animal or last surviving animal) (operative date Jan. 1, 2005); Nev. Rev. Stat. §163.0075 (2003) (terminates upon death of all animals covered by the trust); N.H. Rev. Stat. Ann. §564-B: 4-408 (2004) (trust terminates at death of animal or last surviving animal); N.J. Stat. Ann. §3B:11-38 (2004) ("trust shall terminate when no living animal is covered by the trust, or at the end of 21 years, whichever occurs earlier"); N.M. Stat. Ann. §45-2-907 (2004) (trust limited to twenty-one years); N.M. Stat. Ann. §46A-4-408 (2004) (terminates upon death of animal or last surviving animal; §45-2-907, modeled on the Uniform Probate Code, was not repealed with the enactment of this statute, which is modeled on the Uniform Trust Code); N.Y. Est., Powers & Trusts L. §§7-6.1, 7-8.1 (2004) ("trust shall terminate when no living animal is covered by the trust, or at the end of twenty-one years, whichever occurs earlier"); N.C. Gen. Stat. §36A-147 (2004) ("trust terminates at the death of the animal or last surviving animal"); Or. Rev. Stat. Ann. §128.308 (2003) ("pet trust terminates as provided by the terms of the trust instrument. If the trust instrument makes no provision for termination of the trust, the trust terminates when no living animal is covered by the trust or when all trust assets are exhausted, whichever occurs first"); Tenn. Code Ann. §35-15-408 (2004) (trust may not be enforced for more than twenty-one years); Utah Code Ann. §§75-2-1001, 75-7-408 (2004) (limited to twenty-one years); Wash. Rev. Code §11.118.005 et seq. (2004) ("trust will terminate when no animal that is designated as a beneficiary of the trust remains living"); Wis. Stat. §701.11 (2003) ("no enforceable trust is created; but the transferee has power to apply the property to the designated purpose, unless the purpose is capricious. If the transferee refuses or neglects to apply the property to the designated purpose within a reasonable time and the transferor has not manifested an intention to make a beneficial gift to the transferee, a resulting trust arises in favor of the transferor's estate and the court is authorized to order the transferee to retransfer the property"); Wyo. Stat. Ann. §4-10-409 (2004) (terminates upon death of animal or, where created to provide for care of more than one animal, upon death of last surviving animal). In Virginia, S.B. 506, which mirrors Unif. Trust Code sec. 408, has been continued until 2005. In West Virginia, H.B. 4078—proposed W. Va. Code §44C-4-408—would enact a version of Uniform Trust Code §408; it has been introduced and referred to the Committee of the Judiciary); For federal legislation regarding pet trusts, see the "Morgan Bill," H.R. 1796, 107th Cong. (2001); H.R. 1796, 108th Cong. (2002) (providing for pets and beneficiaries to be cared for for their entire lives, even if beyond twenty-one years).

Other states, like Pennsylvania, for example, accommodate trusts for pets through case law. *See, e.g., In re* Lyon's Estate, 67 Pa. D. & C.2d 474 (Pa. Com. Pl. 1974) (declining to follow rule in Restatement (Second), Trusts, which allows for honorary trust for pets, but holding that trust provisions with regard to animals "should be carried out if it can be done"). *See also In re* Stewart's Estate, 13 Pa. D. & C.3d 488 (Pa. Com. Pl. 1979) (where testatrix bequeathed residue of estate in trust for the care of cats, honorary trust created that cannot be given effect, but reserve of reasonable sum for care of cats may be paid to executrix if she agrees to care for cats). In a leading case in England, *In re* Dean, 41 Ch. D. 552 (1889), the court declined to invalidate a trust for lack of a legal beneficiary, where a testator bequeathed his horses and dogs to a trustee and charged the trustee to care for the animals—including payment for their stables and kennels— with a stated annual sum, for fifty years. The court relied on cases allowing for the up-keep and repair of cemetery monuments, provided the duration of the trust was limited under the Rule Against Perpetuities. Other courts have found that similar gifts of ani-mals, with a sum of money to be used for the care of the animals, are simply absolute gifts. *See, e.g., In re* Myer's Will, 236 N.Y.S.2d 12, 38 Misc. 2d 438 (1962); *In re* John-ston's Estate, 277 A.D. 239, 99 N.Y.S.2d 895 (1950). *See also In re* Andrew's Will, 228 N.Y.S.2d 591, 34 Misc.2d 432 (1962); *In re* Bradley's Estate, 187 Wash. 221, 59 P.2d 1129 (1936) (gift on condition that the legatee care for a named dog is an absolute gift when dog dies before death of testator and performance of condition becomes impossible). In Renner's Estate, 358 Pa. 409, 57 A.2d 836 (1948), the testator gifted two pets "to [the ex-ecutrix's] kind care and judgment," with the residue of the estate held in trust to be used to care for the pets. The court held that no trust was created and that the residue vested in the donee absolutely. Where an attempt was made to care for a particular animal by gifting a plot of land, subject to the care of the animal, with a provision that, if the ani-mal is not cared for, the land shall be gifted to charity, the gift was held to be an invalid executory devise due to its remoteness, and the care of the animal could not be enforced against the donee. *See* Betts v. Snyder, 341 Pa. 465, 19 A.2d 82 (1941).

For web sites addressing the issue of estate planning for pets and pet trusts, see The Estate Planning for Pets Foundation, *Estate Planning for Your Pet*, http://www.es-tateplanningforpets.org (accessed October 21, 2005); Gerry W. Beyer, *Estate Planning for Non-Human Family Members*, http://www.professorbeyer.com/Articles/Animals.htm (last updated July 14, 2005; accessed Oct. 21, 2005); Amy Shever, PetGuardian, LLC, *Pet Trust Plans*, http://www.petguardian.com (accessed Oct. 21, 2005). *See also* Rebecca J. Huss, *Separation, Custody, and Estate Planning Issues Relating to Companion Animals*, 74 U. Colo. L. Rev. 181 (2003); Christine Cave, *Monkeying Around With Our Pets' Fu-tures: Why Oklahoma Should Adopt A Pet-Trust Statute*, 55 Okla. L. Rev. 627 (2002); Gerry W. Beyer, *Pet Animals—What Happens When Their Humans Die?*, 40 Santa Clara L. Rev. 617 (2000).

D. Property: Ascertainable and Contractual

Uniform Trust Code (2003)

Section 103. Definitions.

(11) "Property" means anything that may be the subject of ownership, whether real or personal, real or equitable, or any interest therein.

Brainard v. Commissioner of Internal Revenue

United States Circuit Court of Appeals, Seventh Circuit, 1937
91 F.2d 880

SPARKS, Circuit Judge.

This petition for review involves income taxes for the year 1928. The question presented is whether under the circumstances set forth in the findings of the Board of Tax Appeals, the taxpayer created a valid trust, the income of which was taxable to the beneficiaries under section 162 of the Revenue Act of 1928. * * *

The facts as found by the Board of Tax Appeals are substantially as follows: In December, 1927, the taxpayer, having decided that conditions were favorable, contemplated trading in the stock market during 1928. He consulted a lawyer and was advised that it was possible for him to trade in trust for his children and other members of his family. Taxpayer thereupon discussed the matter with his wife and mother, and stated to them that he declared a trust of his stock trading during 1928 for the benefit of his family upon certain terms and conditions. Taxpayer agreed to assume personally any losses resulting from the venture, and to distribute the profits, if any, in equal shares to his wife, mother, and two minor children after deducting a reasonable compensation for his services. During 1928 taxpayer carried on the trading operations contemplated and at the end of the year determined his compensation at slightly less than $10,000, which he reported in his income tax return for that year. The profits remaining were then divided in approximately equal shares among the members of his family, and the amounts were reported in their respective tax returns for 1928. The amounts allocated to the beneficiaries were credited to them on taxpayer's books, but they did not receive the cash, except taxpayer's mother, to a small extent.

In addition to these findings the record discloses that taxpayer's two children were one and three years of age. Upon these facts the Board held that the income in controversy was taxable to the petitioner as a part of his gross income for 1928, and decided that there was a deficiency. It is here sought to review that decision.

In the determination of the questions here raised it is necessary to consider the nature of the trust, if any, that is said to have been created by the circumstances hereinbefore recited. It is clear that the taxpayer, at the time of his declaration, had no property interest in 'profits in stock trading in 1928, if any,' because there were none in existence at that time. Indeed it is not disclosed that the declarer at that time owned any stock. It is obvious, therefore, that the taxpayer based his declaration of trust upon an interest which at that time had not come into existence and in which no one had a present interest. In the Restatement of the Law of Trusts, vol. 1, Sec. 75, it is said that an interest which has not come into existence or which has ceased to exist can not be held in trust. It is there further said: "A person can, it is true, make a contract binding himself to create a trust of an interest if he should thereafter acquire it; but such an agreement is not binding as a contract unless the requirements of the law of Contracts are complied with * * *

"Thus, if a person gratuitously declares himself trustee of such shares as he may thereafter acquire in a corporation not yet organized, no trust is created. The result is the same where instead of declaring himself trustee, he purports to transfer to another as trustee such shares as he may thereafter acquire in a corporation not yet organized. In such a case there is at most a gratuitous undertaking to create a trust in the future, and such an undertaking is not binding as a contract for lack of consideration * * *

* * * If a person purports to declare himself trustee of an interest not in existence, or if he purports to transfer such an interest to another in trust, he is liable as upon a contract to create a trust if, but only if, the requirements of the law of Contracts are complied with. See, also, Restatement, Sec. 30b; Bogert, Trusts and Trustees, vol. 1, Sec. 112. In 42 Harvard Law Review 561, it is said: 'With logical consistency, the courts have uniformly held that an expectancy cannot be the subject matter of a trust and that an attempted creation, being merely a promise to transfer property in the future, is invalid unless supported by consideration.' Citing Lehigh Valley R. R. Co. v. Woodring, 116 Pa. 513, 9 A. 58. Hence, it is obvious under the facts here presented that taxpayer's declaration amounted to nothing more than a promise to create a trust in the future, and its binding force must be determined by the requirements of the law of contracts.

It is elementary that an executory contract, in order to be enforceable, must be based upon a valuable consideration. Here there was none. The declaration was gratuitous. If we assume that it was based on love and affection that would add nothing to its enforceability, for love and affection, though a sufficient consideration for an executed conveyance, is not a sufficient consideration for a promise. Sullivan v. Sullivan, 122 Ky. 707, 92 S.W. 966, 7 L.R.A. (N.S.) 156, 13 Ann.Cas. 163 * * * [citations omitted].

What has been said, however, does not mean that the taxpayer had no right to carry out his declaration after the subject matter had come into existence, even though there were no consideration. This he did and the trust thereby became effective, after which it was enforceable by the beneficiaries.

The questions with which we are concerned are at what times did the respective earnings which constitute the trust fund come into existence, and at what times did the trust attach to them. It is obvious that the respective profits came into existence when and if such stocks were sold at a profit in 1928. Did they come into existence impressed with the trust, or was there any period of time intervening between the time they came into existence and the time the trust attached? If there were such intervening time, then during that time the taxpayer must be considered as the sole owner of the profits and they were properly taxed to him as a part of his income.

It is said in the Restatement of the Law of Trusts, Sec. 75c: 'If a person purports to declare himself trustee of an interest not in existence or if he purports to transfer such an interest to another in trust, no trust arises even when the interest comes into existence in the absence of a manifestation of intention at that time.' This we think is especially applicable where, as here, there was no consideration for the declaration. It is further stated, however, in the Restatement, Sec. 26k: "If a person manifests an intention to become trustee at a subsequent time, his conduct at that subsequent time considered in connection with his original manifestation *may be* a sufficient manifestation of intention at that subsequent time to create a trust. * * * the act of acquiring the property coupled with the earlier declaration of trust may be a sufficient manifestation of an intention to create a trust at the time of the acquisition of the property. (Our italics, here and hereafter.) In subsection 1 it is said ' * * * Mere silence, however, ordinarily will not be such a manifestation. Whether silence is or is not such a manifestation is a question of interpretation.' In such interpretation, subsection m is quite pertinent and controlling: A promise to create a trust in the future is *enforceable*, if * * * the requirements for an enforceable contract are complied with. Whether a promise to transfer property in trust or to become trustee creates in the promisee a right to recover damages for breach of the promise, and whether such a promise is specifically enforceable, are determined by the law governing contracts. Thus, if the owner of property transfers the property in trust and agrees to pay a sum of money to the trustee to be held upon the same trust, he is not liable for failing to pay the money if the promise was made gratuitously * * * but if the promise was made for consideration * * * the promisor is liable thereon. So also, a promise to create a trust of property if thereafter acquired by the promisor imposes no liability upon the promisor if the promise was gratuitous. * * *"

These matters are discussed by Mr. Bogert in his work on Trusts and Trustees, vol. 1, Sec. 112, and we think there is no contrariety of opinion between his conclusions and those of the Restatement. In speaking of the attitudes of courts of law and equity, he says: "Courts of *law* treat transactions which purport to be present transfers, * * * or trusts of interests in future things as not amounting to *contracts* and as void, with some rare exceptions (referring to potential possession) * * * *Equity* has taken a different attitude toward present efforts to create property interests in future things. It has reasoned that such a transaction could not have been intended to operate as a present transfer because of the inherent impossibility of such an effect. The parties must therefore have expected the only other possible operative result, namely, that there should arise a *contract* to create property interests in the future, by way of absolute transfer, mortgage, trust, or what not * * * Viewed as a *contract* to create property interests in the future, when the things involved are acquired, equity found that in the older common law there was no remedy at all. The law did not recognize the existence of such a *contract*. There was more than inadequacy of remedy; there was total absence of remedy at law. Equity therefore took the position that it would give specific performance or its equivalent. When the things came into existence and into the hands of the intended transferor, they would at once be deemed transferred by way of absolute deed, mortgage, or trust. In other words * * * equity would treat the trust as immediately taking effect and an equitable interest as then passing to the cestui." For instance, he says: "The employee under an existing contract has no present interest in wages to be earned. Such right to receive wages when later earned is a future chose in action. An attempted present conveyance or trust of it can only operate as a *contract* to transfer it when and if acquired, which equity will turn into a perfected transfer when the wages are due." It is obvious that the author's conclusions presuppose, and are based upon, the existence of a valid and enforceable contract between the declarer and the beneficiary. Otherwise the law of contracts would be violated, and equity would be in the attitude of establishing a trust upon an invalid and unenforceable contract, or rather upon no contract at all. The authorities cited by the author in support of his last quoted statement involve valid and enforceable contracts which were based on valuable considerations. In re Bresnan (D.C.) 45 F.(2d) 193; Siter v. Hall, 220 Ky. 43, 294 S.W. 767; Allen v. Chicago Pneumatic Tool Co., 205 Mass. 569, 91 N.E. 887. The same is true as to the additional authority cited by appellant, Bryant v. Shaw, 190 App.Div. 578, 180 N.Y.S. 301.

From what has been said we are convinced that appellant's profits in question were not impressed with a trust when they first came into existence. The Board was obviously of the impression that the trust first attached when appellant credited them to the beneficiaries on his books of account. This act, it seems to us, constituted his first subsequent expression of intention to become a trustee of the fund referred to in his original and gratuitous declaration. Prior to that time we think it is clear that the declaration could not have been enforced against him, and that his mere silence with respect thereto should not be considered as an expression of his intention to establish the trust at a time earlier than the credits. * * *

In the Blair Case, supra, the Supreme Court as a matter of duty followed the construction of the trust by the Appellate Court of Illinois. That case, as we have seen, did not decide the question now before us, nor has it been decided by the Supreme or Appellate Court of Illinois, so far as we have been able to discover, hence it becomes our duty to exercise our own judgment.

Appellant, however, has presented to us a duly authenticated decree of the circuit court of Cook county, Illinois, in a case wherein this appellant filed his complaint in chancery, against his wife and mother, for the construction of this trust with respect to the question now before us. That court differs with us as to the construction and effect of appellant's declaration of trust, and his subsequent acts with respect thereto. With due deference to that court, however, we can not accept the ruling as an expression of the judgment of the state of Illinois as to the property rights of her citizens in the interpretation of the local laws. That court's jurisdiction is limited to Cook county, and there are close to a hundred other circuit courts in Illinois of equal jurisdiction which are not bound by the rulings of the Cook county circuit court. For the interpretation of the laws of Illinois, we must look to the decisions of the Supreme and Appellate Courts of that state, for their rulings are binding upon all the inferior courts of Illinois.

It is no doubt true that the proffered decree is binding upon the parties to that suit, and it will not be appealed from, because all parties thereto are satisfied with it; but we think it can not be binding on the government, which was not a party, and which of course has no right of appeal.

The order of the Board is affirmed.

Unthank v. Rippstein

Supreme Court of Texas, 1964
386 S.W.2d 134

STEAKLEY, Justice.

Three days before his death C. P. Craft penned a lengthy personal letter to Mrs. Iva Rippstein. The letter was not written in terms of his anticipated early death; in fact, Craft spoke in the letter of his plans to go to the Mayo Clinic at a later date. The portion of the letter at issue reads as follows:

> Used most of yesterday and day before to 'round up' my financial affairs, and to be sure I knew just where I stood before I made the statement that I would send you $200.00 cash the first week of each month for the next 5 years, also to send you $200.00 cash for Sept. 1960 and thereafter send that amount in cash the first week of the following months of 1960, October, November and December.'; opposite which in the margin there was written:

> I have stricken out the words 'provided I live that long' and hereby and herewith bind my estate to make the $200.00 monthly payments provided for on this Page One of this letter of 9-17-60.

Mrs. Rippstein, Respondent here, first sought, unsuccessfully, to probate the writing as a codicil to the will of Craft. The Court of Civil Appeals * * * held that the writing was not a testamentary instrument which was subject to probate. We refused the application of Mrs. Rippstein for writ of error with the notation 'no reversible error.' See Rule 483, Texas Rules of Civil Procedure.

The present suit was filed by Mrs. Rippstein against the executors of the estate of Craft, Petitioners here, for judgment in the amount of the monthly installments which had matured, and for declaratory judgment adjudicating the liability of the executors to pay future installments as they mature. The trial court granted the motion of the executors for summary judgment. The Court of Civil Appeals reversed and rendered judgment for Mrs. Rippstein * * * , holding that the writing in question established a voluntary trust under which Craft bound his property to the extent of the promised payments; and that upon his death his legal heirs held the legal title for the benefit of Mrs. Rippstein to that portion of the estate required to make the promised monthly payments.

In her reply to the application for writ of error Mrs. Rippstein states that the sole question before us is whether the marginal notation constitutes 'a declaration of trust whereby (Craft) agrees to thenceforth hold his estate in trust for the explicit purpose of making the payments.' She argues that Craft imposed the obligation for the payment of the monies upon all of his property as if he had said 'I henceforth hold my estate in trust for (such) purpose.' She recognizes that under her position Craft became subject to the Texas Trust Act in the management of his property. Collaterally, however, Mrs. Rippstein takes the position that it being determinable by mathematical computation that less than ten per cent of the property owned by Craft at the time he wrote the letter would be required to discharge the monthly payments, the 'remaining ninety per cent remained in Mr. Craft to do with as he would.' Her theory is that that portion of Craft's property not exhausted in meeting his declared purpose would revert to him by way of a resulting trust eo instante with the legal and equitable title to such surplus merging in him.

These arguments in behalf of Mrs. Rippstein are indeed ingenious and resourceful, but in our opinion there is not sufficient certainty in the language of the marginal notation upon the basis of which a court of equity can declare a trust to exist which is subject to enforcement in such manner. The uncertainties with respect to the intention of Craft and with respect to the subject of the trust are apparent. The language of the notation cannot be expanded to show an intention on the part of Craft to place his property in trust with the result that his exercise of further dominion thereover would be wrongful except in a fiduciary capacity as trustee, and under which Craft would be subject to suit for conversion at the hands of Mrs. Rippstein if he spent or disposed of his property in a manner which would defeat his statement in the notation that a monthly payment of $200.00 in cash would be sent her the first week of each month. It is manifest that Craft did not expressly declare that all of his property, or any specific portion of the assets which he owned at such time, would constitute the corpus or res of a trust for the benefit of Mrs. Rippstein; and inferences may not be drawn from the language used sufficient for a holding to such effect to rest in implication. The conclusion is compelled that the most that Craft did was to express an intention to make monthly gifts to Mrs. Rippstein accompanied by an ineffectual attempt to bind his estate in futuro; the writing was no more than a promise to make similar gifts in the future and as such is unenforceable. The promise to give cannot be tortured into a trust declaration under which Craft while living, and as trustee, and his estate after his death, were under a legally enforceable obligation to pay Mrs. Rippstein the sum of $200.00 monthly for the five-year period.

The controlling tests were stated by this Court in McMurray v. Stanley, 69 Tex. 227, 6 S.W. 412 (1887):

> It has been often said that, in cases of this kind, three things must be shown before a court of equity will declare a trust to exist, and enforce it: First, that the words of the testator ought to be construed as imperative, and hence imposing on the trustee an obligation; secondly, that the subject to which the obligation relates must be certain; thirdly, that the person intended to be the beneficiary under the trust be also certain.

In Fleck v. Baldwin, 141 Tex. 340, 172 S.W.2d 975 (1943), it was said:

> While the transactions under review are in the form of voluntary trusts, they are governed in general by the rules applicable to gifts. The principal difference between such a trust and a gift lies in the fact that in the case of a gift the thing given passess to the donee, while in the case of a voluntary trust only the equitable or beneficial title passes to the cestui qui trust. In each case the equitable title must pass immediately and unconditionally and the transfer thereof must be so complete that the donee might maintain an action for the conversion of the property. Absent a completed gift of the equitable title, no trust is created, for an imperfect gift will not be enforced as a trust merely because of its imperfection. A gift cannot be made to take effect in the future, for the reason that a promise to give is without consideration. Neither can the donor retain the right to use and enjoy the property during his lifetime and direct its disposition after his death in any manner other than by the making of a will. Unless Mrs. Baldwin, therefore, intended at the very time she opened these several accounts and purchased these various stock certificates to pass the equitable title thereto so that the exercise by her of any further dominion over same, except in the fiduciary capacity of trustee, would be wrongful, then no gifts were made or trusts created by such transactions. * * * [citations omitted].

Mrs. Rippstein relies principally on three decisions in support of her theory that the ten per cent of Craft's property required to discharge the monthly payments can be carved out and made to constitute the subject of the trust: McMurray v. Stanley, supra; Estes v. Estes, 267 S.W. 709 (Tex.Com.App.1924); and Monday v. Vance, 92 Tex. 428, 49 S.W. 516 (1899). In Monday v. Vance the husband and wife deeded property in trust for the permanent support of the wife and the children, and for the education of the children. The deed did not prescribe how the property should devolve after the trust was executed, but there was no uncertainty, regarding the establishment of the trust itself. It was held that the effect of the deed was merely to carve out of the estate in the property the usufructuary interest for the support of the wife and the maintenance and education of the children, and to leave what remained unaffected by the conveyance. Estes v. Estes considered a will which created a life estate in B. T. Estes with a vested remainder in fee simple in Bennie Estes; and which also impressed the income from the property in the hands of B. T. Estes with an active trust in favor of Bennie. As relevant here, the court cited what it termed the 'universal rule that, in the absence of express terms defining the estate conferred upon the trustee, the trustee takes exactly that quantity of interest which the purposes of the trust requires, and no more.' But there was no uncertainty regarding the intention of the testatrix. In McMurray v. Stanley this court considered a will under which the testatrix gave all of her property to her husband with full power of disposition, but directed that 'at his death, should he have any of said property still remaining in his possession not disposed of or used by him, that the same shall be given by him' to her nieces. It was held that the intention to create a trust was manifested by the whole instrument, and that the property remaining in the possession of the husband at the time of his death could be shown with as much certainty as any other fact. Here, again, the court was enforcing clear intention, and in so doing it was held that the subject to which the trust attached was sufficiently certain.

We also note that Mrs. Rippstein presented the alternative point in the Court of Civil Appeals (which that court did not reach) that the marginal notation was an instrument in writing which imports consideration; and that she was entitled to summary judgment against the estate of Craft for the monthly payments since the executors of the estate wholly failed to meet their burden of proving a want of consideration. This alternative position was also asserted by counsel for Mrs. Rippstein in oral argument before this Court.

The common law rule was stated by this Court in Jones v. Holliday, 11 Tex. 412 (1854):

> A consideration is essential to the validity of a simple contract, whether it be verbal or in writing. This rule applies to all contracts not under seal, with the exception of bills of exchange and negotiable notes, after they had been negotiated and passed into the hands of an innocent indorsee. * * * In contracts under seal a consideration is implied, in the solemnity of the instrument.

In 1858 the Legislature enacted what became Article 7093 of the 1911 codification providing as follows: '*Every contract in writing* * * * [all italics are added] hereafter made shall be held to import a consideration in the same manner and as fully as sealed instruments have heretofore done.' It was said by this Court in Harris v. Cato, 26 Tex. 338 (1862), that 'The object of this law was to dispense with a mere formality in the execution of a certain class of contracts. And as by the common law *these instruments* when under seal imported a consideration, it was provided, by the clause of the sentence under consideration, that the same effect should be given *to them* when subsequently executed without a scroll or seal.'

Article 7093 of the 1911 codification was omitted in the 1925 codification. Article 27 of the 1925 codification, however read, and still reads, in part, as follows: 'No private seal or scroll shall be required in this State on any written instrument except such as are made by corporations.' In an opinion adopted by this Court in Wright v. Robert & St. John Motor Co., 127 Tex. 278, 58 S.W.2d 67 (1933), it was stated that Article 27 of the 1925 codification included the substance of Articles 7092 and 7093 of the 1911 codification. It was further held that:

> If the seal was required under the common law on simple contracts such as this to import a consideration, and the statute now provides that no seal shall be required, it follows that the only effect the statute can possibly have on such a contract is to dispense with the common-law rule requiring the seal in order to import a consideration.

It is apparent that Article 27 cannot be held to provide that all written instruments import a consideration, regardless of the kind or type of writing the instrument may purport to be. The marginal notation under consideration here does not purport to be a contract, or to embody a bilateral agreement between Craft and Mrs. Rippstein, or to be the result of a meeting of their minds, or to possess the element of mutuality of obligation. A contractual obligation to pay the monthly payments cannot be imposed against the estate of Craft on the theory that the executors thereof were under the burden in this proceeding, which they did not discharge, of alleging and proving a want of consideration.

The judgment of the Court of Civil Appeals is reversed and that of the trial court is affirmed.

Speelman v. Pascal

Court of Appeals of New York, 1961
10 N.Y.2d 313, 178 N.E.2d 723

DESMOND, Chief Judge.

Gabriel Pascal, defendant's intestate who died in 1954, had been for many years a theatrical producer. In 1952 an English corporation named Gabriel Pascal Enterprises, Ltd., of whose 100 shares Gabriel Pascal owned 98, made an agreement with the English Public Trustee who represented the estate of George Bernard Shaw. This agreement granted to Gabriel Pascal Enterprises, Ltd., the exclusive world rights to prepare and produce a musical play to be based on Shaw's play 'Pygmalion' and a motion picture version of the musical play. The agreement recited, as was the fact, that the licensee owned a film scenario written by Pascal and based on 'Pygmalion'. In fact Pascal had, some time previously, produced a nonmusical movie version of 'Pygmalion' under rights obtained by Pascal from George Bernard Shaw during the latter's lifetime. The 1952 agreement required the licensee corporation to pay the Shaw estate an initial advance and thereafter to pay the Shaw estate 3% of the gross receipts of the musical play and musical movie with a provision that the license was to terminate if within certain fixed periods the licensee did not arrange with Lerner and Loewe or other similarly well-known composers to write the musical play and arrange to produce it. Before Pascal's death in July, 1954, he had made a number of unsuccessful efforts to get the musical written and produced and it was not until after his death that arrangements were made, through a New York bank as temporary administrator of his estate, for the writing and production of the highly successful 'My Fair Lady'. Meanwhile, on February 22, 1954, at a time when the license from the Shaw estate still had two years to run, Gabriel Pascal, who died four and a half months later, wrote, signed and delivered to plaintiff a document as follows:

> Dear Miss Kingman
>
> 'This is to confirm to you our understanding that I give you from my shares of profits of the Pygmalion Musical stage version five per cent (5%) in England, and two per cent (2%) of my shares of profits in the United States. From the film version, five per cent (5%) from my profit shares all over the world.
>
> As soon as the contracts are signed, I will send a copy of this letter to my lawyer, Edwin Davies, in London, and he will confirm to you this arrangement in a legal form.
>
> This participation in my shares of profits is a present to you, in recognition for your loyal work for me as my Executive Secretary.
>
> Very sincerely yours,
>
> Gabriel Pascal.

The question in this lawsuit is: Did the delivery of this paper constitute a valid, complete, present gift to plaintiff by way of assignment of a share in future royalties when and if collected from the exhibition of the musical stage version and film version of 'Pygmalion'? A consideration was, of course, unnecessary (Personal Property Law, Consol.Laws, c. 41, § 33, subd. 4).

In pertinent parts the judgment appealed from declares that plaintiff is entitled to receive the percentages set out in the 1954 agreement, requires defendant to render plaintiff accountings from time to time of all moneys received from the musical play and the firm version, and orders defendant to make the payments required by the agreement.

The basic grant from the Shaw estate was to Gabriel Pascal Enterprises, Ltd., a corporation, whereas the document on which plaintiff sues is signed by Gabriel Pascal individually and defendant makes much of this, arguing that Gabriel Pascal, as distinguished from his corporation, owned no rights when he delivered the 1954 document to plaintiff. However, no such point was made in the courts below and no mention of it is made in the motion papers, affidavits, etc., on which plaintiff was granted summary judgment. It is apparent that all concerned in these transactions disregarded any distinction between Pascal's corporation in which he owned practically all the stock, and Pascal individually, as is demonstrated by the agreement between Lerner-Loewe-Levin, writers and producers of 'My Fair Lady', and Gabriel Pascal's estate. Actually, all this makes little difference since what Pascal assigned to plaintiff was a percentage from Pascal's 'shares of profits' and this would cover direct collections or collections through his corporation.

Defendant emphasizes also the use of the word 'profits' in the February, 1954 letter from Pascal to plaintiff, and suggests that this means that plaintiff was not to get a percentage of Pascal's gross royalties but a percentage of some 'profits' remaining after deduction of expenses. Again, the answer is that no such point was made in the proceedings below or in this record and everyone apparently assumed, at least until the case reached this court, that what the defendant Pascal estate will get from the musical play and movie is royalties collectible in full under the agreements pursuant to which 'My Fair Lady' has been and will be produced. In this same connection defendant talks of possible creditors of the Pascal corporation and inquires as to what provision would be made for them if plaintiff were to get her percentages of the full royalties. This, too, is an afterthought and no such matter was litigated below.

The only real question is as to whether the 1954 letter above quoted operated to transfer to plaintiff an enforceable right to the described percentages of the royalties to accrue to Pascal on the production of a stage or film version of a musical play based on 'Pygmalion'. We see no reason why this letter does not have that effect. It is true that at the time of the delivery of the letter there was no musical stage or film play in existence but Pascal, who owned and was conducting negotiations to realize on the stage and film rights, could grant to another a share of the moneys to accrue from the use of those rights by others. There are many instances of courts enforcing assignments of rights to sums which were expected thereafter to become due to the assignor. A typical case is Field v. Mayor of City of New York, 6 N.Y. 179. One Bell, who had done much printing and similar work for the City of New York but had no present contract to do any more such work, gave an assignment in the amount of $1,500 of any moneys that might thereafter become due to Bell for such work. Bell did obtain such contracts or orders from the city and money became due to him therefor. This court held that while there was not at the time of the assignment any presently enforceable or even existing chose in action but merely a possibility that there would be such a chose in action, nevertheless there was a possibility of such which the parties expected to ripen into reality and which did afterwards ripen into reality and that, therefore, the assignment created an equitable title which the courts would enforce. A case similar to the present one in general outline is Central Trust Co. of New York v. West India Improvement Co., 169 N.Y. 314, 62 N.E. 387, where the assignor had a right or concession from the Colony of Jamaica to build a railroad on that island and the courts upheld a mortgage given by the concession owner on any property that would be acquired by the concession owner in consideration of building the railroad if and when the railroad should be built. The Court of Appeals pointed out in Central Trust

Co., at page 323, 62 N.E. at page 389 that the property as to which the mortgage was given had not yet come into existence at the time of the giving of the mortgage but that there was an expectation that such property, consisting of securities, would come into existence and accrue to the concession holder when and if the latter performed the underlying contract. This court held that the assignment would be recognized and enforced in equity. The cases cited by appellant (Young v. Young, 80 N.Y. 422; Vincent v. Rix, 248 N.Y. 76, 161 N.E. 425; Farmers' Loan & Trust Co. v. Winthrop, 207 App.Div. 356, 202 N.Y.S. 456, mod. 238 N.Y. 477, 144 N.E. 686) are not to the contrary. In each of those instances the attempted gifts failed because there had not been such a completed and irrevocable delivery of the subject matter of the gift as to put the gift beyond cancellation by the donor. In every such case the question must be as to whether there was a completed delivery of a kind appropriate to the subject property. Ordinarily, if the property consists of existing stock certificates or corporate bonds, as in the Young and Vincent cases (supra), there must be a completed physical transfer of the stock certificates or bonds. In Farmers' Loan & Trust Co. v. Winthrop (supra) the dispute was as to the effect of a power of attorney but the maker of the power had used language which could not be construed as effectuating a present gift of the property which the donor expected to receive in the future from another estate. The Farmers' Loan & Trust Co. case does not hold that property to be the subject of a valid gift must be in present physical existence and in the possession of the donor but it does hold that the language used in the particular document was not sufficient to show an irrevocable present intention to turn over to the donee securities which would come to the donor on the settlement of another estate. At page 485 of 238 N.Y., at page 687 of 144 N.E. this court held that all that need be established is 'an intention that the title of the donor shall be presently divested and presently transferred' but that in the particular document under scrutiny in the Farmers' Loan & Trust Co. case there was lacking any language to show an irrevocable intent of a gift to become operative at once. In our present case there was nothing left for Pascal to do in order to make an irrevocable transfer to plaintiff of part of Pascal's right to receive royalties from the productions.

* * *

The judgment should be affirmed, with costs.

DYE, FULD, FROESSEL, VAN VOORHIS, BURKE and FOSTER, JJ., concur.

Judgment affirmed.

E. Intent: Precatory and Purpose

The words of a Settlor are often ambiguous, thereby creating various possibilities when the Settlor transfers property to another: Was the transfer intended to be a gift, a loan, a life estate, or a trust? What is the test by which we differentiate one from the other? The result will be important in the eventual distribution of the property. If the property was a gift, there is no further need of court intervention; if the property was a loan, the loan should be repaid upon the death of the "Settlor;" if the property was a life estate, the property reverts to the "Settlor" or successors in interest at the death of the life tenant. If a "trust accountability" will be required of the trustee, and the beneficiary is required to accomplish the purpose of the trust, what then is the test by which a trust, rather than a gift or loan, is established? See the following for assistance.

Uniform Trust Code (2003)

Section 103. Definitions.

(17) "Terms of a trust" means the manifestation of the settlor's intent regarding a trust's provisions as expressed in the trust instrument or as may be established by other evidence that would be admissible in a judicial proceeding.

Jimenez v. Lee

Supreme Court of Oregon, 1976

274 Or. 457, 547 P.2d 126

O'CONNELL, Chief Justice.

This is a suit brought by plaintiff against her father to compel him to account for assets which she alleges were held by defendant as trustee for her. Plaintiff appeals from a decree dismissing her complaint.

Plaintiff's claim against her father is based upon the theory that a trust arose in her favor when two separate gifts were made for her benefit. The first of these gifts was made in 1945, shortly after plaintiff's birth, when her paternal grandmother purchased a $1,000 face value U.S. Savings Bond which was registered in the names of defendant 'and/or' plaintiff 'and/or' Dorothy Lee, plaintiff's mother. It is uncontradicted that the bond was purchased to provide funds to be used for plaintiff's educational needs. A second gift in the amount of $500 was made in 1956 by Mrs. Adolph Diercks, one of defendant's clients. At the same time Mrs. Diercks made identical gifts for the benefit of defendant's two other children. The $1,500 was deposited by the donor in a savings account in the names of defendant and his three children.

In 1960 defendant cashed the savings bond and invested the proceeds in common stock of the Commercial Bank of Salem, Oregon. Ownership of the shares was registered as 'Jason Lee, Custodian under the Laws of Oregon for Betsy Lee (plaintiff).' At the same time, the joint savings account containing the client's gifts to defendant's children was closed and $1,000 of the proceeds invested in Commercial Bank stock.[1] Defendant also took title to this stock as 'custodian' for his children.

The trial court found that defendant did not hold either the savings bond or the savings account in trust for the benefit of plaintiff and that defendant held the shares of the Commercial Bank stock as custodian for plaintiff under the Uniform Gift to Minors Act (ORS 126.805–126.880). Plaintiff contends that the gifts for her educational needs created trusts in each instance and that the trusts survived defendant's investment of the trust assets in the Commercial Bank stock.

It is undisputed that the gifts were made for the educational needs of plaintiff. The respective donors did not expressly direct defendant to hold the subject matter of the gift 'in trust' but this is not essential to create a trust relationship. * * * It is enough if

---

1. The specific disposition of the balance of this account is not revealed in the record. Defendant testified that the portion of the gift not invested in the stock 'was used for other unusual needs of the children.' Defendant could not recall exactly how the money was used but thought some of it was spent for family vacations to Victoria, British Columbia and to satisfy his children's expensive taste in clothing.

the transfer of the property is made with the intent to vest the beneficial ownership in a third person. That was clearly shown in the present case. Even defendant's own testimony establishes such intent. When he was asked whether there was a stated purpose for the gift, he replied:

> * * * Mother said that she felt that the children should all be treated equally and that she was going to supply a bond to help with Elizabeth's educational needs and that she was naming me and Dorothy, the ex-wife and mother of Elizabeth, to use the funds as may be most conducive to the educational needs of Elizabeth.

Defendant also admitted that the gift from Mrs. Diercks was 'for the educational needs of the children.' There was nothing about either of the gifts which would suggest that the beneficial ownership of the subject matter of the gift was to vest in defendant to use as he pleased with an obligation only to pay out of his own funds a similar amount for plaintiff's educational needs. * * *

Defendant himself demonstrated that he knew that the savings bond was held by him in trust. In a letter to his mother, the donor, he wrote: 'Dave and Bitsie (plaintiff) & Dorothy are aware of the fact that I hold $1,000 each for Dave & Bitsie in trust for them on account of your E-Bond gifts.' It is fair to indulge in the presumption that defendant, as a lawyer, used the word 'trust' in the ordinary legal sense of that term.

Defendant further contends that even if the respective donors intended to create trusts, the doctrine of merger defeated that intent because plaintiff acquired both legal and equitable title when the savings bond was registered in her name along with her parents names and when Mrs. Diercks' gift was deposited in the savings account in the name of plaintiff and her father, brother and sister. The answer to this contention is found in II Scott on Trusts §99.4, p. 811 (3d ed 1967):

> A trust may be created in which the trustees are A and B and the sole beneficiary is A. In such a case it might be argued that there is automatically a partial extinguishment of the trust, and that A holds an undivided half interest as joint tenant free of trust, although B holds a similar interest in trust for A. The better view is, however, that there is no such partial merger, and that A and B will hold the property as joint tenants in trust for A. * * *

Having decided that a trust was created for the benefit of plaintiff, it follows that defendant's purchase of the Commercial Bank stock as 'custodian' for plaintiff under the Uniform Gift to Minors Act was ineffectual to expand defendant's powers over the trust property from that of trustee to that of custodian.[4]

---

4. If defendant were 'custodian' of the gifts, he would have the power under the Uniform Gift to Minors Act (ORS 126.820) to use the property 'as he may deem advisable for the support, maintenance, education and general use and benefit of the minor, in such manner, at such time or times, and to such extent as the custodian in his absolute discretion may deem advisable and proper, without court order or without regard to the duty of any person to support the minor, and without regard to any other funds which may be applicable or available for the purpose.' As custodian defendant would not be required to account for his stewardship of the funds unless a petition for accounting were filed in circuit court no later than two years after the end of plaintiff's minority. ORS 126.875. As the trustee of an educational trust, however, defendant has the power to use the trust funds for educational purposes only and has the duty to render clear and accurate accounts showing the funds have been used for trust purposes. See ORS 128.010; Restatement (Second) of Trusts §172 (1959).

Defendant's attempt to broaden his powers over the trust estate by investing the trust funds as custodian violated his duty to the beneficiary 'to administer the trust solely in the interest of the beneficiary.' Restatement (Second) of Trusts § 170, p. 364 (1959).

The money from the savings bond and savings account are clearly traceable into the bank stock. Therefore, plaintiff was entitled to impose a constructive trust or an equitable lien upon the stock so acquired. * * * Plaintiff is also entitled to be credited for any dividends or increment in the value of that part of the stock representing plaintiff's proportional interest. Whether or not the assets of plaintiff's trust are traceable into a product, defendant is personally liable for that amount which would have accrued to plaintiff had there been no breach of trust. * * * Defendant is, of course, entitled to deduct the amount which he expended out of the trust estate for plaintiff's educational needs. However, before he is entitled to be credited for such expenditures, he has the duty as trustee to identify them specifically and prove that they were made for trust purposes. A trustee's duty to maintain and render accurate accounts is a strict one. This strict standard is described in Bogert on Trusts and Trustees § 962, pp. 10–13 (2d ed 1962):

> It is the duty of the trustees to keep full, accurate and orderly records of the status of the trust administration and of all acts thereunder. * * * 'The general rule of law applicable to a trustee burdens him with the duty of showing that the account which he renders and the expenditures which he claims to have been made were correct, just and necessary. * * * He is bound to keep clear and accurate accounts, and if he does not the presumptions are all against him, obscurities and doubts being resolved adversely to him.' (Quoting from White v. Rankin, 46 NYS 228, 18 AppDiv 293, 294, affirmed without opinion 162 NY 622, 57 NE 1128 (1897).) * * * He has the burden of showing on the accounting how much principal and income he has received and from whom, how much disbursed and to whom, and what is on hand at the time. * * *

Defendant did not keep separate records of trust income and trust expenditures. He introduced into evidence a summary of various expenditures which he claimed were made for the benefit of plaintiff. It appears that the summary was prepared for the most part from cancelled checks gathered together for the purpose of defending the present suit. This obviously did not meet the requirement that a trustee 'maintain records of his transactions so complete and accurate that he can show by them his faithfulness to his trust.' * * *

In an even more general way defendant purported to account for the trust assets in a letter dated February 9, 1966, written to plaintiff shortly after her 21st birthday when she was in Europe where she had been receiving instruction and training in ballet. In that letter defendant revealed to plaintiff, apparently for the first time, that her grandmother had made a gift to her of a savings bond and that the proceeds of the bond had been invested in stock. Without revealing the name of the stock, defendant represented that it had doubled in value of the bond from $750 to $1,500. The letter went on to suggest that plaintiff allocate $1,000 to defray the cost of additional ballet classes and that the remaining $500 be held in reserve to defray expenses in returning to the United States and in getting settled in a college or in a ballet company.

Defendant's letter was in no sense a trust accounting. In the first place, it was incomplete; it made no mention of Mrs. Diercks' gift. Moreover, it was inaccurate since it failed to reveal the true value attributable to the Commercial Bank stock. There was evidence which would put the value of plaintiff's interest in the stock at considerably more than $1,500.[9]

Defendant contends that even if a trust is found to exist and that the value of the trust assets is the amount claimed by plaintiff there is sufficient evidence to prove that the trust estate was exhausted by expenditures for legitimate trust purposes. Considering the character of the evidence presented by defendant, it is difficult to understand how such a result could be reached. As we noted above, the trust was for the educational needs of plaintiff. Some of the expenditures made by defendant would seem to fall clearly within the purposes of the trust. These would include the cost of ballet lessons, the cost of subscribing to a ballet magazine, and other items of expenditure related to plaintiff's education.[10] But many of the items defendant lists as trust expenditures are either questionable or clearly outside the purpose of an educational trust. For instance, defendant seeks credit against the trust for tickets to ballet performances on three different occasions while plaintiff was in high school. The cost of plaintiff's ticket to a ballet performance might be regarded as a part of plaintiff's educational program in learning the art of ballet, but defendant claims credit for expenditures made to purchase ballet tickets for himself and other members of the family, disbursements clearly beyond the purposes of the trust.

Other expenditures claimed by defendant in his 'accounting' are clearly not in furtherance of the purposes of the trust. Included in the cancelled checks introduced into evidence in support of defendant's claimed offset against the trust assets were: (1) checks made by defendant in payment of numerous medical bills dating from the time plaintiff was 15 years old (these were obligations which a parent owes to his minor children); (2) checks containing the notation 'Happy Birthday' which plaintiff received from her parents on her 17th, 18th and 22nd birthdays; (3) a 1963 check with a notation 'Honor Roll, Congratulations, Mom and Dad'; (4) defendant's check to a clothier which contains the notation 'Betsy's Slacks and Sweater, Pat's Sweater, Dot's Sweater' (defendant attempted to charge the entire amount against the trust); (5) defendant's check to a Canadian Rotary Club for a meeting attended when he joined plaintiff in Banff after a summer ballet program; (6) $60 sent to plaintiff to enable her to travel from France, where she was studying ballet, to Austria to help care for her sister's newborn babies. There were also other items improperly claimed as expenditures for plaintiff's educational benefit, either because the purpose of the outlay could not be identified or because defendant claimed a double credit.[11]

---

9. It appears that with the accumulation of cash and stock dividends the total value of plaintiff's interest at the time she received defendant's letter would amount to as much as $2,135. This figure is an approximation derived from the incomplete stock price information before us. It is important only to demonstrate that defendant did not render an adequate accounting. Our calculation does not include the value of plaintiff's interest in stock purchased with the proceeds of Mrs. Diercks' gift.

10. Defendant's failure to keep proper records makes it difficult, if not impossible, to determine whether some of these expenditures were made from the trust estate or from defendant' own funds. Moreover, it is unclear in some instances whether the expenditure was for educational purposes or simply for recreation. Thus defendant charges plaintiff with expenses incurred in connection with a European tour taken by plaintiff. It is not disclosed as to whether this was to provide an educational experience for plaintiff or for some other purpose.

11. The double counting occurs where defendant claims credit for cashier's checks sent to plaintiff while she was staying in Europe and at the same time also claims credit for his personal checks used to purchase the cashier's checks.

It is apparent from the foregoing description of defendant's evidence that the trial court erred in finding that 'Plaintiff in these proceedings has received the accounting which she sought and * * * is entitled to no further accounting.' The trial court also erred in finding that 'Defendant did not hold in trust for the benefit of Plaintiff' the product traceable to the two gifts.

The case must, therefore, be remanded for an accounting to be predicated upon a trustee's duty to account, and the trustee's burden to prove that the expenditures were made for trust purposes. There is a moral obligation and in proper cases a legal obligation for a parent to furnish his child with higher education. * * * Where a parent is a trustee of an educational trust, as in the present case, and he makes expenditures out of his own funds, his intent on one hand may be to discharge his moral or legal obligation to educate his child or on the other hand to follow the directions of the trust. * * * It is a question of fact in each case as to which of these two purposes the parent-trustee had in mind at the time of making the expenditures. * * * In determining whether defendant has met this strict burden of proof, the trial court must adhere to the rule that all doubts are resolved against a trustee who maintains an inadequate accounting system.

The decree of the trial court is reversed and the cause is remanded for further proceedings consistent with this opinion.

The Hebrew University Association v. Nye
Supreme Court of Connecticut, 1961
148 Conn. 223, 169 A.2d 641

KING, Associate Justice.

The plaintiff obtained a judgment declaring that it is the rightful owner of the library of Abraham S. Yahuda, a distinguished Hebrew scholar who died in 1951. The library included rare books and manuscripts, mostly relating to the Bible, which Professor Yahuda, with the assistance of his wife, Ethel S. Yahuda, had collected during his lifetime. Some of the library was inventoried in Professor Yahuda's estate and was purchased from the estate by his wife. There is no dispute that all of the library had become the property of Ethel before 1953 and was her property when she died on March 6, 1955, unless by her dealings with the plaintiff between January, 1953, and the time of her death she transferred ownership to the plaintiff. While the defendants in this action are the executors under the will of Ethel, the controversy as to ownership of the library is, in effect, a contest between two Hebrew charitable institutions, the plaintiff and a charitable trust or foundation to which, as hereinafter appears, Ethel bequeathed the bulk of her estate.

The pertinent facts recited in the finding may be summarized as follows: Before his death, Professor Yahuda forwarded certain of the books in his library to a warehouse in New Haven with instructions that they be packed for overseas shipment. The books remained in his name, no consignee was ever specified, and no shipment was made. Although it is not entirely clear, these books were apparently the ones which Ethel purchased from her husband's estate. Professor Yahuda and his wife had indicated to their friends their interest in creating a scholarship research center in Israel which would serve as a memorial to them. In January, 1953, Ethel went to Israel and had several talks with officers of the plaintiff, a university in Jerusalem. One of the departments of the plaintiff is an Institute of Oriental Studies, of outstanding reputation. The library would be very useful to the plaintiff, especially in connection with the work of this institute. On January 28, 1953, a large luncheon was given by the plaintiff in Ethel's honor and was attended by many notables, including officials of the plaintiff and the president of Israel. At this luncheon, Ethel described the library and announced its gift to the plaintiff. The next day, the plaintiff submitted to Ethel a proposed newspaper release which indicated that she had made a gift of the library to the plaintiff. Ethel signed the release as approved by her. From time to time thereafter she stated orally, and in letters to the plaintiff and friends, that she 'had given' the library to the plaintiff. She refused offers of purchase and explained to others that she could not sell the library because it did not belong to her but to the plaintiff. On one occasion, when it was suggested that she give a certain item in the library to a friend, she stated that she could not, since it did not belong to her but to the plaintiff.

Early in 1954, Ethel began the task of arranging and cataloguing the material in the library for crating and shipment to Israel. These activities continued until about the time of her death. She sent some items, which she had finished cataloguing, to a warehouse for crating for overseas shipment. No consignee was named, and they remained in her name until her death. In October, 1954, when she was at the office of the American Friends of the Hebrew University, a fund raising arm of the plaintiff in New York, she stated that she had crated most of the miscellaneous items, was continuously working on cataloguing the balance, and hoped to have the entire library in Israel before the end of the year. Until almost the time of her death, she corresponded with the plaintiff about making delivery to it of the library. In September, 1954, she wrote the president of the plaintiff that she had decided to ship the library and collection, but that it was not to be unpacked unless she was present, so that her husband's ex libris could be affixed to the books, and that she hoped 'to adjust' the matter of her Beth Yahuda and her relations to the plaintiff. A 'beth' is a building or portion of a building dedicated to a particular purpose.

The complaint alleged that the plaintiff was the rightful owner of the library and was entitled to possession. It contained no clue, however, to the theory on which ownership was claimed. The prayers for relief sought a declaratory judgment determining which one of the parties owned the library and an injunction restraining the defendants from disposing of it. The answer amounted to a general denial. The only real issues raised in the pleadings were the ownership and the right to possession of the library. As to these issues, the plaintiff had the burden of proof. Kriedel v. Krampitz, 137 Conn. 532, 534, 79 A.2d 181; Holt v. Wissinger, 145 Conn. 106, 109, 139 A.2d 353. The judgment found the 'issues' for the plaintiff, and further recited that 'a trust [in relation to the library] was created by a declaration of trust made by Ethel S. Yahuda, indicating her intention to create such a trust, made public by her.' We construe this language, in the light of the finding, as a determination, that, at the luncheon in Jerusalem, Ethel orally constituted herself a trustee of the library for future delivery to the plaintiff. The difficulty with the trust theory adopted in the judgment is that the finding contains no facts even intimating that Ethel ever regarded herself as trustee of any trust whatsoever, or as having assumed any enforceable duties with respect to the property. The facts in the finding, in so far as they tend to support the judgment for the plaintiff at all, indicate that Ethel intended to make, and perhaps attempted to make, not a mere promise to give, but an executed, present, legal gift inter vivos of the library to the plaintiff without any delivery whatsoever.

Obviously, if an intended or attempted legal gift inter vivos of personal property fails as such because there was neither actual nor constructive delivery, and the intent to give can nevertheless be carried into effect in equity under the fiction that the donor is presumed to have intended to constitute himself a trustee to make the necessary delivery, then as a practical matter the requirement of delivery is abrogated in any and all cases of intended inter-vivos gifts. Of course this is not the law. A gift which is imperfect for lack of a delivery will not be turned into a declaration of trust for no better reason than that it is imperfect for lack of a delivery. Courts do not supply conveyances where there are none. Cullen v. Chappell, 2 Cir., 116 F.2d 1017, 1018. This is true, even though the intended donee is a charity. Organized Charities Ass'n v. Mansfield, 82 Conn. 504, 510, 74 A. 781. The cases on this point are collected in an annotation in 96 A.L.R. 383, which is supplemented by a later annotation in 123 A.L.R. 1335. The rule is approved in 1 Scott, Trusts § 31.

It is true that one can orally constitute himself a trustee of personal property for the benefit of another and thereby create a trust enforceable in equity, even though without consideration and without delivery. 1 Scott, op. cit. § 28; § 32.2, p. 251. But he must in effect constitute himself a trustee. There must be an express trust, even though oral. It is not sufficient that he declare himself a donor. 1 Scott, op. cit. § 31, p. 239; 4 id. § 462.1. While he need not use the term 'trustee,' nor even manifest an understanding of its technical meaning or the technical meaning of the term 'trust,' he must manifest an intention to impose upon himself enforceable duties of a trust nature. Cullen v. Chappell, supra; Restatement (Second), 1 Trusts §§ 23, 25; 1 Scott, op. cit., pp. 180, 181. There are no subordinate facts in the finding to indicate that Ethel ever intended to, or did, impose upon herself any enforceable duties of a trust nature with respect to this library. The most that could be said is that the subordinate facts in the finding might perhaps have supported a conclusion that at the luncheon she had the requisite donative intent so that, had she subsequently made a delivery of the property while that intent persisted, there would have been a valid, legal gift inter vivos. See cases such as Bachmann v. Reardon, 138 Conn. 665, 667, 88 A.2d 391; Hammond v. Lummis, 106 Conn. 276, 280, 137 A. 767, and Burbank v. Stevens, 104 Conn. 17, 23, 131 A. 742. The judgment, however, is not based on the theory of a legal gift inter vivos but on that of a declaration of trust. Since the subordinate facts give no support for a judgment on that basis, it cannot stand.

While this is dispositive of the appeal adversely to the plaintiff, it may assist in the retrial if certain other matters are briefly mentioned.

By her will, which was executed on November 19, 1953, Ethel provided for the establishment of a foundation in Israel to perpetuate her name and that of her husband, if, as proved to be the case, she failed to establish the foundation during her lifetime. The will also named special trustees, in Israel, to carry out the project in case none were appointed by her before she died. By the second clause of her will, she gave 'all * * * [her] real and the remainder of * * * [her] personal estate' to two named trustees, residing in New Haven, in trust to liquidate and, from the proceeds, to pay debts, funeral and testamentary expenses, death taxes, and legacies. By the third clause, she directed the New Haven trustees to transfer the balance of the proceeds to the trustees of the foundation in Israel. The only other dispositive provision in the will was one in the eighth clause bequeathing to her sister most of the furniture, silver and jewelry. In its memorandum of decision, the trial court seized upon the distinction drawn in the second clause between real estate and personal estate, and the use of the word 'remainder' in connection with the personal estate, as constituting a recognition by Ethel that she had already disposed of the library. Also, in the finding it is stated that the word 'remainder' as used in the second clause meant the personal property other than the library. There is no justification for that finding or for the statement in the memorandum of decision. The word 'remainder' must have been used, not in the technical sense of an estate limited to take effect in possession at the expiration of a prior estate created by the same instrument, but in the loose sense of 'rest' or 'balance.' As such, it would naturally refer to the rest or balance of the personal property owned by the testatrix and not otherwise given by the will, that is, the balance over and above that disposed of in the eighth clause. It could hardly refer to the balance exclusive of the library, because if Ethel did not own the library it would not be affected by her will and there would be no need of excluding it from the operation of the will. A trust res is no part of the trustee's personal estate.

The finding, besides reciting the conclusion of the court that Ethel constituted herself the trustee of an express oral trust for the benefit of the plaintiff, contained the conclusion that she intended 'to give' the library to the plaintiff and 'took all the steps for delivery of possession * * * to the plaintiff which the circumstances afforded'. If the court meant by the quoted language to indicate that a legal inter-vivos gift was effected, there would be a material inconsistency within the finding and between the judgment and the finding. This would be so because there is a well-recognized distinction between a gift inter vivos and a declaration of trust; a single transaction cannot be both. 38 C.J.S. Gifts § 8, p. 785. A similar inconsistency within the finding is indicated, if not established, by the conclusion that the plaintiff acted to its detriment in reliance upon 'the declaration of gift and trust.' Furthermore, while the doctrine of reliance might constitute a reason for the imposition of a constructive trust; 1 Scott, Trusts §§ 31.3, 31.4; note, 12 A.L.R.2d 961, 963; 1 Corbin, Contracts §§ 200–206, 209; Restatement, 1 Contracts § 90; it could play no part in a decision predicated, as the judgment showed the present one was, on an express oral trust, since such a trust needs no consideration for its validity.

To support a factual conclusion of an executed inter-vivos gift, there would have to be a donative intention and at least a constructive delivery. See cases such as Candee v. Connecticut Savings Bank, 81 Conn. 372, 374, 71 A. 551, 22 L.R.A.,N.S., 568; McMahon v. Newtown Savings Bank, 67 Conn. 78, 80, 34 A. 709. It is true that the donative intention need not be expressed, nor the delivery made, in any particular form or mode. Fasano v. Meliso, 146 Conn. 496, 502, 152 A.2d 512, and cases cited. Here, there was no actual delivery of the library; nor was there any constructive delivery. Candee v. Connecticut Savings Bank, supra; Prendergast v. Drew, 103 Conn. 88, 91, 130 A. 75; 24 Am.Jur. 745, § 28; 1 Scott, op. cit., p. 230. No manual delivery of the library could have been made at the time of the expression of the donative intention in Jerusalem, since the library was then in the United States. But there is nothing in the finding to show that constructive delivery was attempted in Jerusalem or that any delivery of any kind was attempted after Ethel's return to the United States. Ethel did not, for instance, make any delivery either of the library or of a document of title purporting to represent the ownership of the library. See McMahon v. Newtown Savings Bank, supra; notes, 63 A.L.R. 537, 550, 48 A.L.R.2d 1405, 1413. For a constructive delivery, the donor must do that which, under the circumstances, will in reason be equivalent to an actual delivery. It must be as nearly perfect and complete as the nature of the property and the circumstances will permit. 24 Am.Jur. 744, § 27. Just what, if any, form of constructive delivery would have been adequate, under the circumstances of this case, when Ethel was in Jerusalem, or what form of actual or constructive delivery would have been adequate after her return to the United States, we have no occasion to determine, since the finding discloses no delivery whatsoever.

The judgment declaring that the plaintiff is the owner of the library is without support in the finding and cannot stand. We cannot, however, as the defendants urge, remand the case for the entry of judgment in their favor, since, as previously pointed out, the finding within itself contains inconsistencies, is at variance with the recitals in the judgment, and is based upon an erroneous view of the controlling law. What finding would have been made had these errors not crept in we have no means of knowing. The case must therefore be remanded for a new trial. See cases such as Thomas F. Rogers, Inc. v. Hochberg, 143 Conn. 22, 25, 118 A.2d 910.

There is error, the judgment is set aside and a new trial is ordered.

In this opinion the other judges concurred.

Notes

The *Hebrew University* case was eventually resolved with a subsequent decision, which held that the delivery of the memorandum, coupled with the decedent's acts and declarations, constituted a *gift* and, thus, Hebrew University was able to obtain the books from the decedent's estate. *See* The Hebrew University Association v. Nye, 26 Conn. Supp. 342, 223 A.2d 397 (1966). Recall that transfer is necessary to make a gift, see *Restatement (Third) of Trusts* § 16(2) (2003). How was that accomplished in the instant decision? If the "Settlor" transfers a legal life estate to a named donee, there is a distinction to be made: The legal life tenant has sole ownership and control over the property, but when there is a trust involved, a trustee has control over the property and is responsible to the court for such things as prudence and management. Finally, note that the intent of the Settlor may not be unlawful: "A trust may be created only to the extent its purposes are lawful, not contrary to public policy, and possible to achieve." Unif. Trust Code § 404 (2004).

II. Classification of Trusts

Even though there are three main categories of trusts—private, charitable and honorary—there are a number of classifications that have arisen, almost all within modern estate planning parameters. These following few classifications are identified to give the student a better understanding of the usage and variety of trust features available today.

Tax Considerations: While a bequest to an heir would not be included within the heir's gross income for income tax purposes, the heir is responsible for payment of inheritance taxes, and the decedent's estate for payment of the appropriate estate or gift taxes. But when an heir receives income as the beneficiary of a trust, the income is subject to income tax (*see* I.R.C. § 102(b)). Generally, the character of the income is the same for the beneficiary as it is for the trust. *See* §§ 1.652(a)-1; 1.662(a)(2). More complications arise when the fiduciary elects to treat any income distribution under a 65-day election rule (*see* I.R.C. § 663(b)), when the income required to be distributed exceeds distributable net income (*see* Reg. § 1.662(a)-2), or when the trust has a net operating loss (*see* Rev. Rul. 61-20, 1961-1 C.B. 248). The items reported on a beneficiary's tax return must be reported in a manner that is consistent with the treatment of such items on the trust's tax return (*see* I.R.C. § 6034A(c)).

Separate from the beneficiary, the trust itself is a taxable entity for federal income tax purposes. The fiduciary (trustee) must file a tax return on Form 1041 for the trust if: (1) the non-exempt trust has income of $600.00 or more; (2) any beneficiary of the trust is a nonresident alien; or (3) an individual's bankruptcy estate has gross income equal to or in excess of the sum of the personal exemption amount plus the basic standard deduction for married individuals filing separately. *See* I.R.C. §§ 6012(a)(3); 6012(a)(4). The taxable year of any trust is the calendar year. *See* I.R.C. § 644. The return must be filed on or before the fifteenth day of the fourth month following the close of the tax year (Reg. § 1.6072-1(a)). If a fiduciary (trustee), judged under a reasonably prudent person standard, has personal knowledge of a tax due the United States and pays expenses other than those associated with funeral expenses and probate costs, to someone other than the United States, the fiduciary becomes personally liable for the tax of the estate to the extent of such payments. *See* 31 U.S.C. § 3713; I.R.C. § 2603.

A. Mandatory Trusts

As the word mandatory implies, the Settlor of a mandatory trust mandates specific acts to be performed by the Trustee. For example: "One million dollars in trust for Sadie, her tuition to be paid each year in any course of legal studies at an accredited law school leading to a juris doctor degree." Even though the tuition will fluctuate, the duties of the Trustee are express and mandatory. Compare this to the following type of trust.

B. Discretionary Trusts

Marsman v. Nasca
Massachusetts Appeals Court, 1991
30 Mass. App. 789, 573 N.E.2d 1025

DREBEN, Justice.

This appeal raises the following questions: Does a trustee, holding a discretionary power to pay principal for the "comfortable support and maintenance" of a beneficiary, have a duty to inquire into the financial resources of that beneficiary so as to recognize his needs? If so, what is the remedy for such failure? A Probate Court judge held that the will involved in this case imposed a duty of inquiry upon the trustee. We agree with this conclusion but disagree with the remedy imposed and accordingly vacate the judgment and remand for further proceedings.

* * *

Sara Wirt Marsman died in September, 1971, survived by her second husband, T. Frederik Marsman (Cappy), and her daughter by her first marriage, Sally Marsman Marlette. Mr. James F. Farr, her lawyer for many years, drew her will and was the trustee thereunder. * * *

Article IIA of Sara's will provided in relevant part:

> It is my desire that my husband, T. Fred Marsman, be provided with *reasonable maintenance, comfort and support* after my death. Accordingly, if my said husband is living at the time of my death, I give to my trustees, who shall set the same aside as a separate trust fund, one-third (1/3) of the rest, residue

and remainder of my estate ... ; they shall pay the net income therefrom to my said husband at least quarterly during his life; and *after having considered the various available sources of support for him,* my trustees shall, if they deem it necessary or desirable from time to time, in their sole and uncontrolled discretion, pay over to him, or use, apply and/or expend for his direct or indirect benefit such amount or amounts of the principal thereof as they shall deem advisable for his *comfortable support and maintenance.* (Emphasis supplied).

Article IIB provided:

> Whatever remains of said separate trust fund, including any accumulated income thereon on the death of my husband, shall be added to the trust fund established under Article IIC....

Article IIC established a trust for the benefit of Sally and her family. Sally was given the right to withdraw principal and, on her death, the trust was to continue for the benefit of her issue and surviving husband.

The will also contained the following exculpatory clause:

> No trustee hereunder shall ever be liable except for his own willful neglect or default.

During their marriage, Sara and Cappy lived well and entertained frequently. Cappy's main interest in life centered around horses. An expert horseman, he was riding director and instructor at the Dana Hall School in Wellesley until he was retired due to age in 1972. Sally, who was also a skilled rider, viewed Cappy as her mentor, and each had great affection for the other. Sara, wealthy from her prior marriage, managed the couple's financial affairs. She treated Cappy as "Lord of the Manor" and gave him money for his personal expenses, including an extensive wardrobe from one of the finest men's stores in Wellesley.

In 1956, Sara and Cappy purchased, as tenants by the entirety, the property in Wellesley which is the subject of this litigation. Although title to the property passed to Cappy by operation of law on Sara's death, Sara's will also indicated an intent to convey her interest in the property to Cappy. In the will, Cappy was also given a life estate in the household furnishings with remainder to Sally.

After Sara's death in 1971, Farr met with Cappy and Sally and held what he termed his "usual family conference" going over the provisions of the will. At the time of Sara's death, the Wellesley property was appraised at $29,000, and the principal of Cappy's trust was about $65,600.

Cappy continued to live in the Wellesley house but was forced by Sara's death and his loss of employment in 1972 to reduce his standard of living substantially. He married Margaret in March, 1972, and, shortly before their marriage, asked her to read Sara's will, but they never discussed it. In 1972, Cappy took out a mortgage for $4,000, the proceeds of which were used to pay bills. Farr was aware of the transaction, as he replied to an inquiry of the mortgagee bank concerning the appraised value of the Wellesley property and the income Cappy expected to receive from Sara's trust.

In 1973, Cappy retained Farr in connection with a new will. The latter drew what he described as a simple will which left most of Cappy's property, including the house, to Margaret. The will was executed on November 7, 1973.

In February, 1974, Cappy informed the trustee that business was at a standstill and that he really needed some funds, if possible. Farr replied in a letter in which he set forth the relevant portion of the will and wrote that he thought the language was "broad enough to permit a distribution of principal." Farr enclosed a check of $300. He asked Cappy to explain in writing the need for some support and why the need had arisen.[5] The judge found that Farr, by his actions, discouraged Cappy from making any requests for principal.

Indeed, Cappy did not reduce his request to writing and never again requested principal. Farr made no investigation whatsoever of Cappy's needs or his "available sources of support" from the date of Sara's death until Cappy's admission to a nursing home in 1983 and, other than the $300 payment, made no additional distributions of principal until Cappy entered the nursing home.

By the fall of 1974, Cappy's difficulty in meeting expenses intensified.[6] Several of his checks were returned for insufficient funds, and in October, 1974, in order that he might remain in the house, Sally and he agreed that she would take over the mortgage payments, the real estate taxes, insurance, and major repairs. In return, she would get the house upon Cappy's death.

Cappy and Sally went to Farr to draw up a deed. Farr was the only lawyer involved, and he billed Sally for the work. He wrote to Sally, stating his understanding of the proposed transaction, and asking, among other things, whether Margaret would have a right to live in the house if Cappy should predecease her. The answer was no. No copy of the letter to Sally was sent to Cappy. A deed was executed by Cappy on November 7, 1974, transferring the property to Sally and her husband Richard T. Marlette (Marlette) as tenants by the entirety, reserving a life estate to Cappy. No writing set forth Sally's obligations to Cappy.

The judge found that there was no indication that Cappy did not understand the transaction, although, in response to a request for certain papers by Farr, Cappy sent a collection of irrelevant documents. The judge also found that Cappy clearly understood that he was preserving no rights for Margaret, and that neither Sally nor Richard nor Farr ever made any representation to Margaret that she would be able to stay in the house after Cappy's death.

Although Farr had read Sara's will to Cappy and had written to him that the will was "broad enough to permit a distribution of principal," the judge found that Farr failed to advise Cappy that the principal of his trust could be used for the expenses of the Wellesley home. The parsimonious distribution of $300 and Farr's knowledge that the purpose of the conveyance to Sally was to enable Cappy to remain in the house, provide support for this finding. After executing the deed, Cappy expressed to Farr that he was

---

5. He also suggested, despite the will's direction that Cappy's trust be set aside as a separate trust, that when principal was paid to Cappy, a proportionate distribution (i.e., twice the sum given to Cappy) be made to Sally. Farr indicated that he was sending a copy of the letter to Sally and hoped "to hear from her." The judge read the letter to imply that Sally should be consulted when and if Cappy requested principal. We need not consider whether this reading is warranted.

6. After Sara's death, Cappy's income was limited, particularly considering the station he had enjoyed while married to Sara. In 1973, including the income from Sara's trust of $2,116, his income was $3,441; in 1974 it was $3,549, including trust income of $2,254; in 1975, $6,624, including trust income of $2,490 and social security income of $2,576. Margaret's income was also minimal; $499 in 1974, $4,084 in 1975, including social security income of $1,686. Cappy's income in 1976 was $8,464; in 1977, $8,955; in 1978, $9,681; in 1979, $10,851; in 1980, $11,261; in 1981, $12,651; in 1982, $13,870; in 1983, $12,711; in 1984, $12,500; in 1985, $12,567; in 1986, $12,558. The largest portion from 1975 on came from social security benefits.

pleased and most appreciative. Margaret testified that Cappy thought Farr was "great" and that he considered him his lawyer.[7]

Sally and Marlette complied with their obligations under the agreement. Sally died in 1983, and Marlette became the sole owner of the property subject to Cappy's life estate. Although Margaret knew before Cappy's death that she did not have any interest in the Wellesley property, she believed that Sally would have allowed her to live in the house because of their friendship. After Cappy's death in 1987, Marlette inquired as to Margaret's plans, and, subsequently, through Farr, sent Margaret a notice to vacate the premises. Margaret brought this action in the Probate Court.

After a two-day trial, the judge held that the trustee was in breach of his duty to Cappy when he neglected to inquire as to the latter's finances. She concluded that, had Farr fulfilled his fiduciary duties, Cappy would not have conveyed the residence owned by him to Sally and Marlette. The judge ordered Marlette to convey the house to Margaret and also ordered Farr to reimburse Marlette from the remaining portion of Cappy's trust for the expenses paid by him and Sally for the upkeep of the property. If Cappy's trust proved insufficient to make such payments, Farr was to be personally liable for such expenses. Both Farr and Marlette appealed from the judgment, from the denial of their motions to amend the findings, and from their motions for a new trial. Margaret appealed from the denial of her motion for attorney's fees. As indicated earlier, we agree with the judge that Sara's will imposed a duty of inquiry on the trustee, but we disagree with the remedy and, therefore, remand for further proceedings.

2. *Breach of trust by the trustee.* Contrary to Farr's contention that it was not incumbent upon him to become familiar with Cappy's finances, Article IIA of Sara's will clearly placed such a duty upon him. In his brief, Farr claims that the will gave Cappy the right to request principal "in extraordinary circumstances" and that the trustee, "was charged by Sara to be wary should Cappy request money beyond that which he quarterly received." Nothing in the will or the record supports this narrow construction. To the contrary, the direction to the trustees was to pay Cappy such amounts "as they shall deem advisable for his comfortable support and maintenance." This language has been interpreted to set an ascertainable standard, namely to maintain the life beneficiary "in accordance with the standard of living which was normal for him before he became a beneficiary of the trust." Woodberry v. Bunker, 359 Mass 239, 243, 268 N.E.2d 841 (1971). Dana v. Gring, 374 Mass. 109, 117, 371 N.E.2d 755 (1977). See Blodget v. Delaney, 201 F.2d 589, 593 (1st Cir.1953).

Even where the only direction to the trustee is that he shall "in his discretion" pay such portion of the principal as he shall "deem advisable," the discretion is not absolute. "Prudence and reasonableness, not caprice or careless good nature, much less a desire on the part of the trustee to be relieved from trouble ... furnish the standard of conduct." Boyden v. Stevens, 285 Mass. 176, 179, 188 N.E. 741 (1934), quoting from Corkery v. Dorsey, 223 Mass. 97, 101, 111 N.E. 795 (1916). Holyoke Natl. Bank v. Wilson, 350 Mass. 223, 227, 214 N.E.2d 42 (1966).

That there is a duty of inquiry into the needs of the beneficiary follows from the requirement that the trustee's power "must be exercised with that soundness of judgment

---

7. The judge noted that Farr, in response to an interrogatory filed by the plaintiff, stated that he rendered legal services to Sara from approximately 1948–1971; to Cappy from approximately 1951–1987; to Sally from 1974 until prior to her death; and to Marlette since 1983.

which follows from a due appreciation of trust responsibility." Boyden v. Stevens, 285 Mass. at 179, 188 N.E. 741. Woodberry v. Bunker, 359 Mass. at 241, 268 N.E.2d 841. In Old Colony Trust Co. v. Rodd, 356 Mass. 584, 586, 254 N.E.2d 886 (1970), the trustee sent a questionnaire to each potential beneficiary to determine which of them required assistance but failed to make further inquiry in cases where the answers were incomplete. The court agreed with the trial judge that the method employed by the trustee in determining the amount of assistance required in each case to attain "comfortable support and maintenance" was inadequate. There, as here, the trustee attempted to argue that it was appropriate to save for the beneficiaries' future medical needs. The court held that the "prospect of illness in old age does not warrant a persistent policy of niggardliness toward individuals for whose comfortable support in life the trust has been established. The payments made to the respondent and several other beneficiaries, viewed in light of their assets and needs, when measured against the assets of the trust show that little consideration has been given to the 'comfortable support' of the beneficiaries." Id. at 589–590, 254 N.E.2d 886. See 3 Scott, Trusts § 187.3 (Fratcher 4th ed. 1988) (action of trustee is "arbitrary" where he "is authorized to make payments to a beneficiary if in his judgment he deems it wise and he refuses to inquire into the circumstances of the beneficiary"). See also Kolodney v. Kolodney, 6 Conn.App. 118, 123, 503 A.2d 625 (1986).

Farr, in our view, did not meet his responsibilities either of inquiry or of distribution under the trust. The conclusion of the trial judge that, had he exercised "sound judgment," he would have made such payments to Cappy "as to allow him to continue to live in the home he had occupied for many years with the settlor" was warranted.

3. *Remedy against Marlette.* The judge, concluding that, had Farr not been in breach of trust, "[C]appy would have died owning the house and thus able to devise it to his widow, the plaintiff," ordered Marlette to convey the house to Margaret. This was an inappropriate remedy in view of the judge's findings. She found that, although the relationship between Cappy and Sally was "close and loving," there was "no fiduciary relation between them" and that Sally and Marlette "were not unjustly enriched by the conveyance." She also found that "Sally and Richard Marlette expended significant monies over a long period of time in maintaining their agreement with [C]appy."

Because the conveyance was supported by sufficient consideration (the agreement to pay the house expenses) and because Sally and Marlette had no notice of a breach of trust and were not themselves guilty of a breach of fiduciary duty, they cannot be charged as constructive trustees of the property. Jones v. Jones, 297 Mass. 198, 207, 7 N.E.2d 1015 (1937). That portion of the judgment which orders Marlette to convey the property is vacated.

4. *Remainder of Cappy's trust.* The amounts that should have been expended for Cappy's benefit are, however, in a different category. More than $80,000 remained in the trust for Cappy at the time of his death. As we have indicated, the trial judge properly concluded that payments of principal should have been made to Cappy from that fund in sufficient amount to enable him to keep the Wellesley property. There is no reason for the beneficiaries of the trust under Article IIC to obtain funds which they would not have received had Farr followed the testatrix's direction. The remedy in such circumstances is to impress a constructive trust on the amounts which should have been distributed to Cappy but were not because of the error of the trustee. Even in cases where beneficiaries have already been paid funds by mistake, the amounts may be collected from them unless the recipients were bona fide purchasers or unless they, without

notice of the improper payments, had so changed their position that it would be inequitable to make them repay. 5 Scott, Trusts § 465, at 341 (Fratcher 4th ed.1989). Allen v. Stewart, 214 Mass. 109, 113, 100 N.E. 1092 (1913). Welch v. Flory, 294 Mass. 138, 144, 200 N.E. 900 (1936). See National Academy of Sciences v. Cambridge Trust Co., 370 Mass. 303, 307, 346 N.E.2d 879 (1976). Here, the remainder of Cappy's trust has not yet been distributed, and there is no reason to depart from the usual rule of impressing a constructive trust in favor of Cappy's estate on the amounts wrongfully withheld. There is also no problem as to the statute of limitations. The period of limitations with respect to those we hold to be constructive trustees (the beneficiaries of the trust under Article IIC) has not run as, at the earliest, their entitlement to funds occurred at Cappy's death in 1987.

That Cappy assented to the accounts is also no bar to recovery by his estate. The judge found that he was in the dark as to his rights to receive principal for the upkeep of the home. An assent may be withdrawn by a judge "if it is deemed improvident or not conducive to justice." Swift v. Hiscock, 344 Mass. 691, 693, 183 N.E.2d 875 (1962). See Akin v. Warner, 318 Mass. 669, 675, 63 N.E.2d 566 (1945). The accounts were not allowed, and we need not consider the effect of G.L. c. 206, § 24, * * * which permits the impeachment of an account after a final decree has been entered only for "fraud or manifest error." See Holyoke Natl. Bank v. Wilson, 350 Mass. at 228, 214 N.E.2d 42; National Academy of Sciences v. Cambridge Trust Co., 370 Mass. at 309, 346 N.E.2d 879.

The amounts to be paid to Cappy's estate have not been determined. * * * On remand, the Probate Court judge is to hold such hearings as are necessary to determine the amounts which should have been paid to Cappy to enable him to retain possession of the house.

5. *Personal liability of the trustee.* Farr raises a number of defenses against the imposition of personal liability, including the statute of limitations, the exculpatory clause in the will, and the fact that Cappy assented to the accounts of the trustee. The judge found that Farr's breach of his fiduciary duty to inquire as to Cappy's needs and his other actions in response to Cappy's request for principal, including the involvement of Sally in distributions of principal despite Sara's provision that Cappy's trust be administered separately, led Cappy to be unaware of his right to receive principal for house expenses. The breach may also be viewed as a continuing one. In these circumstances we do not consider Cappy's assent, see Swift v. Hiscock, 344 Mass. at 693, 183 N.E.2d 875, or the statute of limitations to be a bar. See Greenfield Sav. Bank v. Abercrombie, 211 Mass. 252, 259, 97 N.E. 897 (1912); Allen v. Stewart, 214 Mass. at 113, 100 N.E. 1092; Akin v. Warner, 318 Mass. at 675–676, 63 N.E.2d 566. The judge also found that Margaret learned of Cappy's right to principal for house expenses only when she sought other counsel after his death.

The more difficult question is the effect of the exculpatory clause. As indicated in part 3 of this opinion, we consider the order to Marlette to reconvey the property an inappropriate remedy. In view of the judge's finding that, but for the trustee's breach, Cappy would have retained ownership of the house, the liability of the trustee could be considerable.

Although exculpatory clauses are not looked upon with favor and are strictly construed, such "provisions inserted in the trust instrument without any overreaching or abuse by the trustee of any fiduciary or confidential relationship to the settlor are generally held effective except as to breaches of trust 'committed in bad faith or intentionally or with reckless indifference to the interest of the beneficiary.'" New England Trust Co. v. Paine, 317 Mass. 542, 550, 59 N.E.2d 263 (1945), S.C., 320 Mass. 482, 485, 70 N.E.2d 6 (1946). See Dill v. Boston Safe Deposit & Trust Co., 343 Mass. 97, 100–102, 175 N.E.2d 911 (1961); Boston Safe Deposit & Trust Co. v. Boone, 21 Mass.App.Ct. 637, 644, 489 N.E.2d 209 (1986). The actions of Farr were not of this ilk and also do not fall within the meaning of the term used in the will, "willful neglect or default."

Farr testified that he discussed the exculpatory clause with Sara and that she wanted it included. Nevertheless, the judge, without finding that there was an overreaching or abuse of Farr's fiduciary relation with Sara, held the clause ineffective. Relying on the fact that Farr was Sara's attorney, she stated: "One cannot know at this point in time whether or not Farr specifically called this provision to Sara's attention. Given the total failure of Farr to use his judgment as to [C]appy's needs, it would be unjust and unreasonable to hold him harmless by reason of the exculpatory provisions he himself drafted and inserted in this instrument."

Assuming that the judge disbelieved Farr's testimony that he and Sara discussed the clause, although such disbelief on her part is by no means clear, the conclusion that it "would be unjust and unreasonable to hold [Farr] harmless" is not sufficient to find the overreaching or abuse of a fiduciary relation which is required to hold the provision ineffective. See Restatement (Second) of Trusts §222, comment d (1959).[10] We note that the judge found that Sara managed all the finances of the couple, and from all that appears, was competent in financial matters.

There was no evidence about the preparation and execution of Sara's will except for the questions concerning the exculpatory clause addressed to Farr by his own counsel. No claim was made that the clause was the result of an abuse of confidence. See Boston Safe Deposit & Trust Co. v. Boone, 21 Mass.App.Ct. at 644, 489 N.E.2d 209.

The fact that the trustee drew the instrument and suggested the insertion of the exculpatory clause does not necessarily make the provision ineffective. Restatement (Second) of Trusts §222, comment d. No rule of law requires that an exculpatory clause drawn by a prospective trustee be held ineffective unless the client is advised independently. Cf. Barnum v. Fay, 320 Mass. 177, 181, 69 N.E.2d 470 (1946).

The judge used an incorrect legal standard in invalidating the clause. While recognizing the sensitivity of such clauses, we hold that, since there was no evidence that the insertion of the clause was an abuse of Farr's fiduciary relationship with Sara at the time of the drawing of her will, the clause is effective.

---

10. The Restatement lists six factors which may be considered in determining whether a provision relieving the trustee from liability is ineffective on the ground that it was inserted in the trust instrument as a result of an abuse of a fiduciary relationship at the time of the trust's creation. The six factors are:

> (1) whether the trustee prior to the creation of the trust had been in a fiduciary relationship to the settlor, as where the trustee had been guardian of the settlor; (2) whether the trust instrument was drawn by the trustee or by a person acting wholly or partially on his behalf; (3) whether the settlor has taken independent advice as to the provisions of the trust instrument; (4) whether the settlor is a person of experience and judgment or is a person who is unfamiliar with business affairs or is not a person of much judgment or understanding; (5) whether the insertion of the provision was due to undue influence or other improper conduct on the part of the trustee; (6) the extent and reasonableness of the provision.

Except as provided herein, the motions of the defendants for a new trial and amended findings are denied. The plaintiff's claim of error as to legal fees fails to recognize that fees under G.L. c. 215, §45, are a matter within the discretion of the trial judge. We find no abuse of discretion in the denial of fees.

The judgment is vacated, and the matter is remanded to the Probate Court for further proceedings to determine the amounts which, if paid, would have enabled Cappy to retain ownership of the residence. Such amounts shall be paid to Cappy's estate from the trust for his benefit prior to distributing the balance thereof to the trust under Article IIC of Sara's will. * * *

So ordered.

Uniform Trust Code (2003)

Section 814. Discretionary Powers; Tax Savings.

(a) Notwithstanding the breadth of discretion granted to a trustee in the terms of the trust, including the use of such terms as "absolute", "sole", or "uncontrolled", the trustee shall exercise a discretionary power in good faith and in accordance with the terms and purposes of the trust and the interests of the beneficiaries.

Section 1008. Exculpation of Trustee.

(a) A term of a trust relieving a trustee of liability for breach of trust is unenforceable to the extent that it:

(1) relieves the trustee of liability for breach of trust committed in bad faith or with reckless indifference to the purposes of the trust or the interests of the beneficiaries; or

(2) was inserted as the result of an abuse by the trustee of a fiduciary or confidential relationship to the settlor.

(b) An exculpatory term drafted or caused to be drafted by the trustee is invalid as an abuse of a fiduciary or confidential relationship unless the trustee proves that the exculpatory term is fair under the circumstances and that its existence and contents were adequately communicated to the settlor.

Section 1009. Beneficiary's Consent, Release, or Ratification.

A trustee is not liable to a beneficiary for breach of trust if the beneficiary consented to the conduct constituting the breach, released the trustee from liability for the breach, or ratified the transaction constituting the breach, unless:

(1) the consent, release, or ratification of the beneficiary was induced by improper conduct of the trustee; or

(2) at the time of the consent, release, or ratification, the beneficiary did not know of the beneficiary's rights or of the material facts relating to the breach.

C. Grantor Trusts

Often a Settlor will create a trust of assets to favor a certain class of beneficiaries and to achieve certain tax benefits. For example, in the *Brainard* decision, discussed *supra*, the Settlor declared himself Trustee of undetermined assets for the benefit of his mother, spouse, and children. One incentive for doing so may have been to place whatever income was generated into their income brackets rather than his own. The Settlor was probably responsible for their support and he was providing it with his after-tax dollars from his tax bracket. Why not assist his dependents in meeting their own needs with dollars earned in their lesser tax brackets? The Settlor was attempting to create a Grantor Trust, often called a Clifford trust.

Congress and the Internal Revenue Service have made grantor trusts extremely difficult to create, lessening the incentive to save taxes by shifting income. As a general rule, if the Settlor or the Settlor's spouse retains control over the property, then the Settlor remains the owner of the property and is entitled to the income and the deductions associated with it. Thus, Family Estate Trusts will not avoid income taxes for the Settlor, *see* I.R.C. § 212 (2004), with minor exceptions, income from the trust will be taxed to the Settlor if the trust corpus will revert to the Settlor or the Settlor's spouse, *see id.* at § 673, and the Settlor is taxed on the income if the Settlor or the Settlor's spouse retains administrative powers allowing for financial benefits that would not be available in an arms-length transaction, *see id.* at § 675. The point is that a Grantor trust is a complicated endeavor and should be employed only with expert legal assistance.

Tax Considerations: The taxation of Grantor Trusts needs to be addressed in more detail for those persons seeking a better understanding of their popularity and utilization. The issue arises in the context of a parent seeking to generate income in lower tax bracket dependents rather than themselves. Obviously the point is to pay less income taxes on the money earned, yet meet the needs of family members. When Congress passed legislation taxing a portion of the unearned income of children under the age of 14 at the parents' marginal tax rate if the parents' marginal tax rate is higher than the child's, the ability to shift income was drastically curtailed. *See* I.R.C. § 1(g)(2); Melanie McCoskey, Joanie Sompayrac, and Paul Streer, *Kiddie Tax Raises Costs, Complexity, and Need for Tax Planning*, PRACTICAL TAX STRATEGIES, May 2002, at 279. Indeed, the curtailment of income-shifting—the Kiddie Tax—was an element identified in the Tax Reconciliation Act of 1986 and the Revenue Reconciliation Act of 1990. Parents—Grantors—are left with few options if they wish to reduce income or estate taxes, take advantage of the annual gift tax exclusion, provide for a separate estate for minors, or create a tax-deferred fund to pay for college education. The rules are complicated and require expert assistance. *See, e.g.*, Brenda J. Rediess-Hoosein, *Methods of Transferring Assets to Minors Affected by Recent Tax Changes*, 18 ESTATE PLANNING, March/April 1991, at 86.

Internal Revenue Code Sections 671 through 677 provide labyrinthine income tax rules that determine whether a Grantor will be treated as the owner of an inter vivos trust. Many of these rules focus on a retained power exercisable by a Grantor or a non-adverse party or both. Internal Revenue Code Section 676 provides that the Grantor will be treated as the owner of a trust (including income and capital gains earned by the trust) where at the time the Grantor (or a non-adverse party or both) retains the right to revoke the trust. Internal Revenue Code Section 677(a) provides that a Grantor is treated as the owner of any portion of a trust the income from which is, or may be, distributed to the Grantor or the Grantor's spouse or held or accumulated for future distribution to the Grantor or the Grantor's spouse. These are only some of the rules.

Less complicated than Grantor trusts but often used in conjunction with issue (children) are Internal Revenue Code Section 2503(c) trusts. These devices address the issue raised in I.R.C. § 2503 (b), which requires that the donee of a gift have a present interest in the property transferred to qualify for the annual exclusion amount for each donee child. There is an exception to this rule in I.R.C. § 2503(c), which allows estate planners to create a trust the transfers to which qualify for the annual exclusion under § 2503(b) and at the same time permits the parents to maintain control over the assets given to the trust for the child's benefit. The trust must meet the requirements of I.R.C. § 2503(c), which allows the trustee to have discretionary authority to distribute or accumulate the trust's income or principal to the child before he or she reaches 21. The trustee's discretionary payments may include items such as support, health and education. However, when the child turns 21 the principal and interest must be paid to the child, or if the child dies prior to attaining the age, the principal and income must be paid to the child's estate or such persons as the child appoints pursuant to a general testamentary power of appointment. *See* I.RC. § 2041. The trust may provide specific takers in default if the power is not exercised by the child. Through the trustee, the parent has control over the funds throughout the child's minority, and then at death, if the child does not exercise the power of appointment, the parent has established a control mechanism through takers in default. Powers of appointment will be discussed in greater detail, *infra,* but they play a role in these 2503(c) trusts and in one other similar arrangement, Crummey Trusts.

A Crummey Trust allows a parent to give to the child, for example, assets, in trust, covered by a general power of appointment and in so doing to appoint the asset to himself or herself for a limited period of time. This is the crucial feature. At the end of a limited time period, the power lapses if it is not exercised by the donee (the child) of the power and the property remains in the trust. Because the donee had the power to appoint to himself or herself for a period of time, the donee had a present interest in the assets and thus qualifies for the annual gift tax exclusion in I.R.C. 2503(b) even though the reality is that the parent is still in control of the asset through the trustee. The term "Crummy Trust" derives its name from Crummy v. Commissioner, 397 F.2d 82 (9th Cir. 1968).

Finally, of particular interest to students, tuition paid by someone other than the student on behalf of the student, if paid directly to an educational institution, is not a gift subject to taxation. Also, payments made for medical care are not considered gifts. *See* I.R.C. § 2503(e)(2).

D. Oral Trusts

Uniform Trust Code (2003)

Section 407. Evidence of Oral Trust.

Except as required by a statute other than this [Code], a trust need not be evidenced by a trust instrument, but the creation of an oral trust and its terms may be established only by clear and convincing evidence.

New York Estates, Powers & Trusts Law (2004)

Section 7-1.17 Execution, amendment and revocation of lifetime trusts

(a) Every lifetime trust shall be in writing and shall be executed and acknowledged by the initial creator and, unless such creator is the sole trustee, by at least one trustee thereof, in the manner required by the laws of this state for the recording of a conveyance of real property or, in lieu thereof, executed in the presence of two witnesses who shall affix their signatures to the trust instrument.

(b) Any amendment or revocation authorized by the trust shall be in writing and executed by the person authorized to amend or revoke the trust, and except as otherwise provided in the governing instrument, shall be acknowledged or witnessed in the manner required by paragraph (a) of this section, and shall take effect as of the date of such execution. Written notice of such amendment or revocation shall be delivered to at least one other trustee within a reasonable time if the person executing such amendment or revocation is not the sole trustee, but failure to give such notice shall not affect the validity of the amendment or revocation or the date upon which same shall take effect. No trustee shall be liable for any act reasonably taken in reliance on an existing trust instrument prior to actual receipt of notice of amendment or revocation thereof.

Goodman v. Goodman

Supreme Court of Washington, 1995
128 Wash.2d 366, 907 P.2d 290

JOHNSON, Justice.

This case involves a family dispute between Clive Goodman's mother, Gladys Goodman, and his children over property he transferred to Gladys before his death in 1983. A jury found Gladys held Clive's property in trust for his children and wrongfully withheld the property. The trial judge granted judgment notwithstanding the verdict (JNOV),[1] having found the children commenced the action after the limitations period had run. At issue is whether the trial court erred by granting JNOV because Gladys did not propose jury instructions on the statute of limitations defense, and whether there were disputed facts regarding the limitations period such that it could not be decided as a matter of law. Because in this case the issue of when the statute of limitations began to run was susceptible to more than one reasonable interpretation, it presented a question of fact that could not be decided on a motion for a JNOV. We reverse.

Clive Goodman died in November 1983 after a three-year struggle with a liver disease. His illness required frequent hospitalizations and complicated medical procedures. About five years before his death, Clive gave Gladys general power of attorney. About one year before his death, he transferred his major asset, Ozzie's East Tavern, to Gladys. Gladys sold the tavern on an installment contract in 1982 for $70,000; she deposited the proceeds of the sale in her bank account.

Clive was survived by four children: Scott, Craig, Michelle, and his stepdaughter Tamara. When Clive died in 1983, Scott was seventeen, Craig was sixteen, Michelle was thirteen, and Tamara was twenty-one. He was also survived by Shirley Golden, his first wife and mother of all the children. Shirley and Clive had divorced in 1972, but remained close friends until his death.

Some eight years after Clive's death, when Scott was 25 years old, he asked Gladys for the first time for money from the sale of Ozzie's East and Clive's other assets. When Scott asked Gladys for the money, she reportedly told him she had taken care of Clive and felt she deserved it.

---

1. Under CR 50, as amended, a JNOV is now a judgment as a matter of law.

Scott then hired an attorney and was appointed personal representative of Clive's estate. He sued Gladys in that capacity in 1991, alleging that Clive intended Gladys to hold Clive's property for the benefit of his children until they were the age of majority or were able to receive and manage the property on their own. Gladys pleaded laches as an affirmative defense and counterclaimed for offset of money she had loaned to Clive or had paid on his behalf.

At trial, Shirley testified Clive had a will, had transferred all of his property to Gladys, and intended his children to have his property when they were old enough to responsibly manage it. She testified that shortly after the funeral, Gladys told her there was no will but she would give the children Clive's money when they were old enough to be responsible. Shirley relayed this information to the children. The children did not have a problem with Gladys holding Clive's property in trust. Shirley thought about hiring an attorney at this time but could not afford one. She stated:

> I wasn't concerned at all about the moneys. I felt very confident that there wouldn't be a problem with it. She [Gladys] told me the same things Dee [Clive] had told me.

Report of Proceedings, vol. I at 68. Shirley first became concerned when Scott asked Gladys about the property in 1991.

Clive's stepdaughter Tamara testified she had seen Clive's will in 1977 and briefly discussed it with him. Based on that conversation, she believed Clive's property would be divided among the children. About one year after Clive's death, Tamara heard from relatives that all of Clive's property was in Gladys' name, and the children were not entitled to anything. She believed she discussed this with her siblings and Shirley around Christmas 1983. Shirley does not recall discussing this with Tamara.

Gladys testified she never had a conversation with Shirley regarding Clive's property or a will. She also testified Clive gave her the money to repay numerous loans and out of love and appreciation.

At the close of Scott's case, Gladys moved for a directed verdict on the grounds the limitations period had run. The trial court reserved ruling on this motion.

At the close of testimony, the trial court instructed the jury to decide whether Clive transferred his property to Gladys as a gift or to hold in trust for the benefit of the children. It defined a trust as:

> A trust can be defined as a right of property, real or personal, held by one party for the benefit of another. It is a confidence placed in one person, who is termed a trustee, for the benefit of another, respecting property which is held by the trustee for the benefit of another. A trust need not be in writing. A trust can arise or be implied from circumstances as a result of the presumed intention of the parties as gathered from the nature of the transaction between them.

Clerk's Papers at 28. Gladys did not offer a jury instruction on the statute of limitations defense, nor did she except to the trial court's failure to give one.

The jury found Gladys held the property in trust for the benefit of Clive's children, and the children incurred damages of $60,000 as a result of Gladys' wrongful retention of the trust property. They also found Gladys was entitled to an offset of $11,000.

Following the verdict, the trial court granted Gladys' motion for a JNOV, finding that the children should have discovered the cause of action more than three years before Scott commenced the action. The Court of Appeals agreed. It found the statute of limitations issue presented a factual question, but affirmed the trial court because the facts were susceptible of only one reasonable interpretation: the children were put on notice of facts, which with the exercise of due diligence would have led to discovery of the wrongdoing as each of them turned eighteen and received nothing. Because the youngest child turned eighteen more than three years before the commencement of the action, the suit was time barred. Goodman v. Goodman, No. 13005-3-III, slip op. at 7 (Mar. 28, 1995).

In reviewing a JNOV, this court applies the same standard as the trial court. Peterson v. Littlejohn, 56 Wash.App. 1, 8, 781 P.2d 1329 (1989). A JNOV is proper only when the court can find, "as a matter of law, that there is neither evidence nor reasonable inference therefrom sufficient to sustain the verdict." Brashear v. Puget Sound Power & Light Co., 100 Wash.2d 204, 208–09, 667 P.2d 78 (1983) (quoting Hojem v. Kelly, 93 Wash.2d 143, 145, 606 P.2d 275 (1980)). A motion for a JNOV admits the truth of the opponent's evidence and all inferences that can be reasonably drawn therefrom, and requires the evidence be interpreted most strongly against the moving party and in the light most favorable to the opponent. No element of discretion is involved. Davis v. Early Constr. Co., 63 Wash.2d 252, 254–55, 386 P.2d 958 (1963). Viewing the evidence in the light most favorable to the nonmoving party, we hold the statute of limitations defense presented a question of fact that could not be decided as a matter of law.

The parties and the courts below have referred to the trust as a constructive trust. A constructive trust is an equitable remedy imposed by courts when someone should not in fairness be allowed to retain property. Farrell v. Mentzer, 102 Wash. 629, 174 P. 482 (1918); see generally George T. Bogert, Trusts § 77 (6th ed. 1987). An express trust, on the other hand, arises because of expressed intent and involves a fiduciary relationship in which the trustee holds property for the benefit of a third party. In re Lutz, 74 Wash.App. 356, 365, 873 P.2d 566 (1994).

Scott's theory in this case, consistent with the jury instructions, was that Clive intended Gladys to hold his personal property in trust until the children reached majority or were mature enough to handle it. In support of this theory, Shirley testified:

A. The only thing[ ] that was said, was the day of the funeral.... [Gladys] said that she was not giving them [the children] any money until they got older. Because she didn't want them blowing it.

Q. Did you relay that to the children?

A. Yes.

Q. Did she indicate how much older they would have to get?

A. Until they were responsible. See, we have had a few problems with Scott. And—just took him a little longer than it does other people to grow up.

Report of Proceedings, vol. I at 19–20.

Q. Well, did you ever explain to them what you perceived to be Mrs. Goodman's role in holding onto the property?

A. Well, they just knew that their grandmother was going to—give them the money after they reached a certain age. I didn't know what the certain age was. One child could be—responsible at this age. Another one won't. So I didn't know what she was waiting for. Or—I never questioned it because Dee had told me that they were going to be taken care of, they weren't going to get their money until they were—older.

Report of Proceedings, vol. I at 24.

Consistent with this and other testimony, the jury found Clive intended Gladys to hold his property in trust for the children. This being the case, the trust at issue is properly characterized as an express trust.

An action based on an express (or constructive trust) is subject to the three-year statute of limitations contained in RCW 4.16.080. Viewcrest Coop. Ass'n v. Deer, 70 Wash.2d 290, 294–95, 422 P.2d 832 (1967); Arneman v. Arneman, 43 Wash.2d 787, 800, 264 P.2d 256, 45 A.L.R.2d 370 (1953). The statute of limitations on an express trust action begins to run when the beneficiary of the trust discovers or should have discovered the trust has been terminated or repudiated by the trustee.[2] Rogich v. Dressel, 45 Wash.2d 829, 841, 278 P.2d 367 (1954). A repudiation occurs when the trustee by words or other conduct denies there is a trust and claim the trust property as his or her own. The repudiation must be plain, strong, and unequivocal. O'Steen v. Estate of Wineberg, 30 Wash.App. 923, 932, 640 P.2d 28, review denied, 97 Wash.2d 1016 (1982). Whether the statute of limitations bars a suit is a legal question, but the jury must decide the underlying factual questions unless the facts are susceptible of but one reasonable interpretation. Washburn v. Beatt Equip. Co., 120 Wash.2d 246, 263, 840 P.2d 860 (1992); Richardson v. Denend, 59 Wash.App. 92, 95, 795 P.2d 1192 (1990), review denied, 116 Wash.2d 1005, 803 P.2d 1309 (1991).

Thus, the trial court could only grant a JNOV on this issue as a matter of law if no triable issue of fact existed as to when Gladys repudiated or terminated the trust. See Haslund v. City of Seattle, 86 Wash.2d 607, 621, 547 P.2d 1221 (1976). The jury found Gladys held Clive's property in trust for the children. Although no findings were made concerning the terms of the trust, the trial testimony supports Scott's view that Clive intended Gladys to hold the property until the children reached majority or were mature enough to handle it. Had the evidence only been that Clive intended Gladys to hold his property until the children reached majority, the repudiation would have occurred when each child turned eighteen and received nothing as the trial court found. But given the jury's verdict and the evidence that Clive intended the children to have his property when they were mature enough to handle it, it can hardly be said as a matter of law that the repudiation occurred when each child turned eighteen. A reasonable interpretation of the evidence is the repudiation occurred in 1991 when Gladys told Scott for the first time she deserved Clive's money and would not give him anything. Under these circumstances, when Gladys repudiated the trust is susceptible to more than one reasonable interpretation, and the trial court erred.

Having decided the trial erred by granting JNOV, it is unnecessary to resolve the second issue—whether a trial court may grant a JNOV on the grounds the action is barred by the statute of limitations when the jury is not instructed on the statute of limitations, but the moving party earlier asks for a directed verdict on this issue. We note, however, that the "take out" rule in Browne v. Cassidy, 46 Wash.App. 267, 728 P.2d 1388 (1986) is not implicated because Gladys moved for a directed verdict on the limitations issue.

---

2. The statute of limitations begins to run on a constructive trust when the beneficiary discovers or should have discovered the wrongful act which gave rise to the constructive trust. *Arneman*, 43 Wash.2d at 800, 264 P.2d 256.

Both parties requested attorney's fees in their briefs to the Court of Appeals under RAP 18.1 and RCW 11.96.140. We will not review the Court of Appeals decision denying attorney's fees because Scott's petition for review does not identify attorney's fees as an issue for review. RAP 13.4; RAP 13.7(b).

DURHAM, C.J., DOLLIVER, SMITH, MADSEN, ALEXANDER and TALMADGE, JJ., and PEKELIS, Judge Pro Tem., concur.

SANDERS, J., did not participate.

Notes

Although they should not be, oral trusts are quite common: "I am giving you this now and this is what I want you to do with it." Or perhaps, "In my Last Will and Testament, I am leaving you the farm, and I expect you to take care of Sadie with its proceeds." In each instance, the deed or Will omitted any reference to the oral arrangement. Oral trusts are dangerous devices because of the havoc they play upon written instruments, valid deeds, and Wills. The Statute of Frauds (1677) was an excellent bar to the enforcement of oral trusts but often allowed fraud to be perpetrated. The only recourse was to petition the court to enforce the oral trust on the basis of a constructive trust—an equitable remedy that seeks to right a wrong (unjust enrichment). But before arguing a constructive trust, if there is some writing that can be incorporated into a Will, or allows for the proof of an oral inter vivos arrangement, then the level of proof is often met to sustain the oral arrangement. Please note the UNIFORM TRUST CODE § 407 and N.Y. ESTATES, POWERS & TRUSTS L. § 7-1.17, provided *supra*, and ask how these statutes treat oral trusts.

E. Resulting and Constructive Trusts

A resulting trust arises through operation of law whenever the Settlor has created a trust and it fails for any reason whatsoever. Perhaps the purpose has been accomplished and trust property remains; perhaps the beneficiary dies with property remaining; or the Settlor may have specified a named Trustee and that Trustee dies or is no longer able to perform. Under these circumstances and more, the trust property will revert, through operation of law, back to the Settlor or to the Settlor's estate. Likewise, a constructive trust seeks to remedy bad acts, and it, too, arises by operation of law. Its purpose is to prevent unjust enrichment. It may arise whenever a person should not profit from his or her wrongdoing, such as murder, unfulfilled promises by someone in a confidential relationship, and domestic abuse.

Hieble v. Hieble

Supreme Court of Connecticut, 1972
164 Conn. 56, 316 A.2d 777

SHAPIRO, Associate Justice.

In this action the plaintiff sought a reconveyance of real property in the town of Killingworth which she had transferred to the defendant, claiming that he had agreed to reconvey the same to her, upon request, if she recovered from an illness. The trial court rendered judgment for the plaintiff and the defendant has appealed.

The trial court's finding of facts, which is not attacked, discloses that on May 9, 1959, the plaintiff, without consideration, transferred the title of her real estate by survivorship deed to her son, the defendant, and to her daughter. The plaintiff, who had that year undergone surgery for malignant cancer, feared a recurrence but believed that she would be out of danger if the cancer did not reappear within five years. She and the grantees orally agreed that the transfer would be a temporary arrangement; that she would remain in control of the property and pay all expenses and taxes; that once the danger of recrudescence had passed, the defendant and his sister would reconvey the property to the plaintiff on request. After the transfer, the plaintiff continued to reside on the property with her aged mother, whom she supported, her daughter and the defendant. In 1960, after the plaintiff expressed displeasure over the daughter's marriage, the daughter agreed to relinquish her interest in the property. A deed was prepared and the daughter and son, through a strawman, transferred title to the land to the plaintiff and her son in survivorship. In 1964, five years after the original conveyance, the plaintiff requested that the defendant reconvey his legal title to her, since she considered herself out of risk of a recurrence of cancer.

The plaintiff at that time needed money to make improvements on the land, particularly, to install running water and indoor plumbing facilities as a convenience for her aged mother. The defendant procrastinated, feigning concern about the boundaries of an adjacent forty-acre parcel which the plaintiff had given him in 1956. Although the defendant refused to convey his interest in the jointly-owned premises, some friends of the plaintiff ultimately prevailed on him to sign a mortgage for an improvement loan in 1965. Thereafter, the defendant assured the plaintiff that he would never marry but would continue to live with her. These were his reasons for refusing reconveyance until his marriage plans were disclosed. Although the plaintiff proposed that her son could keep the property if he remained single, he did marry in 1967 and moved out of the house. After her attempts to obtain his voluntary reconveyance failed, the plaintiff brought suit in 1969. Throughout the entire period of time material to this litigation, the plaintiff has borne all expenses and costs of improvement to the property.

From these facts the trial court concluded that a constructive trust * * * should be decreed on the basis of the oral agreement, the confidential relationship of the parties and their conduct with respect to the property. The defendant's appeal raises primarily the claim that the elements necessary to establish a confidential relationship, as the basis for a constructive trust, are lacking.

It hardly needs reciting that under our Statute of Frauds, General Statutes § 52-550, oral agreements concerning interests in land are unenforceable. See Hanney v. Clark, 124 Conn. 140, 144–145, 198 A. 577. In this jurisdiction, however, the law is established that the Statute of Frauds does not apply to trusts arising by operation of law. Reynolds v. Reynolds, 121 Conn. 153, 158, 183 A. 394; Ward v. Ward, 59 Conn. 188, 196, 22 A. 149.

The case before us presents one of the most vexatious problems facing a court of equity in the area of constructive trusts, namely, whether equity should impose a constructive trust where a donee who by deed has received realty under an oral promise to hold and reconvey to the grantor has refused to perform his promise. See 3 Bogert, Trusts and Trustees (2d Ed.) § 495; Costigan, 'Trusts Based on Oral Promises,' 12 Mich.L.Rev. 423, 515. Our task here, however, is considerably alleviated, since the defendant has not attacked the court's finding that the alleged agreement was in fact made, nor does he contest the receipt of parol evidence as having violated the Statute of Frauds. See, for example, Brown v. Brown, 66 Conn. 493, 34 A. 490; Todd v. Munson,

53 Conn. 579, 589, 4 A. 99; Dean v. Dean, 6 Conn. 284, 287–289. Although the deed recited that consideration was given for the 1959 transfer, the defendant does not attack the finding that there was no consideration for the conveyance. Indeed, in his brief the defendant abandons the claim that a recital of consideration suffices to rebut an allegation of a trust. See Andrews v. New Britain National Bank, 113 Conn. 467, 470, 155 A. 838. In addition, the complications typically involved in constructive trusts—for example, the claims of third parties or the testimony of deceased persons—are not present here. See the discussion in Hanney v. Clark, supra, 124 Conn. 144–146, 198 A. 577. In this case the plaintiff was both settlor and beneficiary of the trust.

Since the finding of facts is not challenged, the conclusion of the court that the parties stood in a confidential relationship must stand unless it is unreasonably drawn or unless it involves an erroneous application of law. Johnson v. Zoning Board of Appeals, 156 Conn. 622, 624, 238 A.2d 413; Davis v. Margolis, 107 Conn. 417, 422, 140 A. 823. The defendant's attack on this conclusion is without merit. He argues that because the plaintiff initiated the transfer and was a woman of mature years, and because he was an inexperienced young man, a court of equity should not recognize a relationship of confidentiality between them. We grant that the bond between parent and child is not per se a fiduciary one; it does generate, however, a natural inclination to repose great confidence and trust. See Suchy v. Hajicek, 364 Ill. 502, 509, 510, 4 N.E.2d 836; Wood v. Rabe, 96 N.Y. 414, 426. Coupled with the plaintiff's condition of weakness, her recent surgery, her anticipation of terminal illness, and the defendant's implicit reassurances of his faithfulness, this relationship becomes a classic example of the confidentiality to which equity will fasten consequences. See Restatement (Second), 1 Trusts § 44, pp. 115–16; 3 Bogert, supra, § 482. * * *

The defendant's next contention questions the sufficiency of the evidence to justify the imposition of a constructive trust. Since he does not attack the finding that there was an underlying oral agreement, he cannot question the sufficiency of evidence to support that finding. Brockett v. Jensen, 154 Conn. 328, 331, 225 A.2d 190; Davis v. Margolis, 107 Conn. 417, 422, 140 A. 823. Presumably, the defendant objects to the sufficiency of this 1959 oral agreement, standing by itself, to create a constructive trust. Here, three points are in order. First, the trial court reached its conclusion not only on the basis of that agreement but also on the conduct of the parties and the circumstances surrounding the conveyance, seen as a whole. As we have already noted, the defendant has failed to sustain his attack on the court's conclusion that a confidential relationship existed. Second, where a confidential relationship has been established, there is substantial authority that the burden of proof rests on the party denying the existence of a trust—and then, by clear and convincing evidence to negate such a trust. See Suchy v. Hajicek, supra, 364 Ill. 510, 4 N.E.2d 836; 89 C.J.S. Trusts § 155.[2] Our decision in Wilson v. Warner, 84 Conn. 560, 80 A. 718, is not contrary. There, in regard to an alleged resulting trust in decedent's estate, the court said (pp. 564, 565, 80 A. p. 719): 'But in all cases where the claimed trust title to land is disputed, the facts from which such trust may be implied should be clearly and satisfactorily established.' Third, as this court held in Dowd v. Tucker, 41 Conn. 197, 205, cited in Fisk's Appeal, supra, 81 Conn. 440, 71 A. 559, it is unnecessary to find fraudulent intent for the imposition of a constructive trust. Whether there be fraud at the inception or a repudiation afterward, the whole sig-

---

2. The same allocation of the burden of proof and a similar standard of proof have been imposed where a claimed gift of realty is contested between persons in confidential relationship. See McCutcheon v. Brownfield, 2 Wash.App. 348, 356, 467 P.2d 868; 38 Am.Jur.2d, Gifts, § 106.

nificance of such cases lies in the unjust enrichment of the grantee through his unconscionable retention of the trust res. See Dodson v. Culp, 217 Ga. 299, 122 S.E.2d 109; Kent v. Klein, 352 Mich. 652, 91 N.W.2d 11; Costigan, 'Trusts Based on Oral Promises,' 12 Mich.L.Rev. 536.

The defendant's argument that the reconveyances in 1960 extinguished his obligation has no support in the finding. Rather, the court's finding of facts concerning his conduct subsequent to the 1960 transfers undermines his position. The court found that the defendant countered the plaintiff's request with delay, pretending concern about the boundaries of his adjacent forty-acre parcel; that he gave, as a reason for refusing to reconvey, assurances that he would never marry and that he would continue to reside with his mother. Of more weight to a court of equity, however, is the fact that the 1960 transfers effected no essential legal or equitable change in the defendant's initial undertaking. The finding reveals that his interest remained that of a joint tenant with right of survivorship upon the sister's surrender of her title to the plaintiff. Not only has the defendant failed to substantiate his contention, but his claim that the plaintiff's case must fail for lack of a concomitant renewal of the oral agreement in 1960 misconceives the nature of a constructive trust. See the discussion in Moses v. Moses, 140 N.J.Eq. 575, 580–581, 53 A.2d 805. Indeed, the defendant's assertion could amount to no more than a unilateral attempt to extinguish the original oral agreement. In short, the absence of an express renewal of the defendant's promise does not impair the soundness of the court's conclusion. * * *

Finally, the defendant makes the claim that the plaintiff has unclean hands. There is nothing in the record to suggest that the 1959 transfer was an attempt to defraud creditors or to secrete assets from government agencies. Granted that the plaintiff offered to let her son keep the property in order to dissuade him from taking a wife, it cannot be said, as a matter of law, that her hands are tainted with an attempt to tamper with marriage, especially in view of the defendant's earlier assurances that he would never get married.

In light of the unattacked finding of the court that the defendant in fact had agreed to reconvey the property to the plaintiff upon request and the conclusion of the court, amply supported by the finding of fact, that a confidential relationship existed between the plaintiff and the defendant, the case comes squarely within the provisions of § 44 of the Restatement (Second) of Trusts: 'Where the owner of an interest in land transfers it inter vivos to another in trust for the transferor, but no memorandum properly evidencing the intention to create a trust is signed, as required by the Statute of Frauds, and the transferee refuses to perform the trust, the transferee holds the interest upon a constructive trust for the transferor, if ... (b) the transferee at the time of the transfer was in a confidential relation to the transferor.'

There is no error.

In this opinion the other judges concurred.

F. Spendthrift Trusts

Uniform Trust Code (2003)

Section 502. Spendthrift Provision.

(a) A spendthrift provision is valid only if it restrains both voluntary and involuntary transfer of a beneficiary's interest.

(b) A term of a trust providing that the interest of a beneficiary is held subject to a "spendthrift trust," or words of similar import, is sufficient to restrain both voluntary and involuntary transfer of the beneficiary's interest.

(c) A beneficiary may not transfer an interest in a trust in violation of a valid spendthrift provision and, except as otherwise provided in this [article], a creditor or assignee of the beneficiary may not reach the interest or a distribution by the trustee before its receipt by the beneficiary.

Section 503. Exceptions to Spendthrift Provision.

(a) In this section, "child" includes any person for whom an order or judgment for child support has been entered in this or another State.

(b) Even if a trust contains a spendthrift provision, a beneficiary's child, spouse, or former spouse who has a judgement or court order against the beneficiary for support or maintenance, or a judgment creditor who has provided services for the protection of a beneficiary's interest in the trust, may obtain from a court an order attaching present or future distributions to or for the benefit of the beneficiary.

(c) A spendthrift provision is unenforceable against a claim of this State or the United States to the extent a statute of this State or federal law so provides.

Section 504. Discretionary Trusts; Effect of Standard.

(b) Except as otherwise provided in subsection (c), whether or not a trust contains a spendthrift provision, a creditor of a beneficiary may not compel a distribution that is subject to the trustee's discretion, even if:

(1) the discretion is expressed in the form of a standard of distribution; or

(2) the trustee has abused the discretion.

(c) To the extent a trustee has not complied with a standard of distribution or has abused a discretion:

(1) a distribution may be ordered by the court to satisfy a judgement or court order against the beneficiary for support or maintenance of the beneficiary's child, spouse, or former spouse; and

(2) the court shall direct the trustee to pay to the child, spouse, or former spouse such amount as is equitable under the circumstances but not more than the amount the trustee would have been required to distribute to or for the benefit of the beneficiary had the trustee complied with the standard or not abused the discretion.

Bacardi v. White

Supreme Court of Florida, 1985
463 So.2d 218

ALDERMAN, Justice.

Adriana Bacardi seeks review of the decision of the District Court of Appeal, Third District, in White v. Bacardi, 446 So.2d 150 (Fla. 3d DCA 1984), which expressly and directly conflicts with Gilbert v. Gilbert, 447 So.2d 299 (Fla. 2d DCA 1984).[1]

---

1. The facts in Gilbert, as stated by the Second District Court, are as follows:
    In the judgment of dissolution, the court ordered the husband to pay permanent peri-

The issue presented is whether disbursements from spendthrift trusts can be garnished to satisfy court ordered alimony and attorney's fee payments before such disbursements reach the debtor-beneficiary. The Third District in Bacardi held that a former wife of a spendthrift trust beneficiary may not reach the income of that trust for alimony before it reaches the beneficiary unless she can show by competent and substantial evidence that it was the settlor's intent that she participate as a beneficiary. We quash the decision of the district court and hold that disbursements from spendthrift trusts, in certain limited circumstances, may be garnished to enforce court orders or judgments for alimony before such disbursements reach the debtor-beneficiary.[2] We also hold that an order or judgment for attorney's fees awarded incident to the divorce or the enforcement proceedings may be collected in the same manner.

The facts relevant to this holding are as follows. Luis and Adriana Bacardi were married for approximately two years and had no children. When the marriage ended in divorce, they entered into an agreement whereby Mr. Bacardi agreed to pay Mrs. Bacardi alimony of $2,000 per month until the death of either of them or until she remarried. The final judgment dissolving their marriage incorporated this agreement.

Shortly thereafter Mr. Bacardi ceased paying alimony. Mrs. Bacardi subsequently obtained two judgments for the unpaid alimony, with execution authorized, in the total amount of $14,000. She also obtained a third judgment for attorney's fees in the amount of $1,000 awarded incident to the divorce. In aid of execution on the three judgments, she served a writ of garnishment on Robert White as a trustee of a spendthrift trust created by Mr. Bacardi's father for the benefit of his son Luis. Additionally,

---

odic alimony of $2,500 per month and lump sum alimony in the amount of $35,000 payable in six-month installments of $3,500. The court also required that he be responsible for reasonable and necessary medical expenses of the wife attributable to her multiple sclerosis and that he pay her attorney's fees of $24,750. The husband never paid the attorney's fees and later stopped paying alimony and the wife's medical expenses. The court entered a writ of ne exeat and held him in contempt, but these actions proved futile because he fled the jurisdiction. He is now thought to be living in England. The husband also removed his assets from the state, thereby thwarting the wife's efforts to collect the arrearages.

In her efforts to enforce the dissolution judgment, the wife sought to garnish the husband's interest in a trust established by Emily H. Gilbert for the benefit of various beneficiaries and administered by Southeast Bank as trustee. The trust contained the following paragraph:

5.2—Spendthrift Provision; the interest of each beneficiary in the income or principal of each trust hereunder shall be free from the control or interference of any creditor of a beneficiary or of any spouse of a married beneficiary and shall not be subject to attachment or susceptible of anticipation or alienation.

Notwithstanding this provision, the court entered judgment in garnishment against the bank as trustee for $50,500 arrearages in alimony and medical expenses and $18,000 in attorney's fees. The court also entered a continuing writ of garnishment directing the bank to pay to the wife out of the trust the periodic and lump sum alimony as it becomes due. Id. at 300–01.

The Gilbert court held:

In light of our strong public policy toward requiring persons to support their dependents, we hold that spendthrift trusts can be garnished for the collection of arrearages in alimony. We also believe that a claim for attorney's fees awarded incident to the divorce is collectible in the same manner. Id. at 302.

2. Although this case involves a garnishment to enforce court orders or judgments for alimony, the rationale of our holding would also apply to child support cases.

she obtained a continuing writ of garnishment against the trust income for future alimony payments as they became due.

The trust instrument contained a spendthrift provision which stated:

> No part of the interest of any beneficiary of this trust shall be subject in any event to sale, alienation, hypothecation, pledge, transfer or subject to any debt of said beneficiary or any judgment against said beneficiary or process in aid of execution of said judgment.

Both Luis Bacardi and Mr. White appealed the trial court's garnishment order. They asserted that under this spendthrift provision, the trust could not be garnished for the collection of alimony and incident attorney's fees. The district court agreed, reversed the trial court's order, and remanded the case for further proceedings.

The district court noted that this state has long recognized the validity of spendthrift trust provisions, Waterbury v. Munn, 159 Fla. 754, 32 So.2d 603 (1947), and further that Florida has no statutory law limiting or qualifying spendthrift provisions where alimony payments are involved. In deciding this case, the district court aligned itself with what it believed to be both the modern trend and the best reasoned view. It stated that its holding squares with the public policy of this state as expressed in Waterbury v. Munn. It concluded that the legislature, rather than the courts, should resolve the question whether that public policy should yield to the competing public policy of enforcing support.

Respondents urge that we approve the district court's decision and hold that the settlor's intent prevails over any public policy arguments which would allow the alienation of disbursements from the trust. They contend that an ex-wife's debt is no different than any ordinary debt even though it represents unpaid alimony and related attorney's fees and that, therefore, her claim should be treated the same as the claim of any other creditor. They assert that it is clear from reading the spendthrift provision that the settlor did not intend Adriana Bacardi to participate as a beneficiary and that this intent precludes garnishment.

This case involves competing public policies. On the one hand, there is the long held policy of this state that recognizes the validity of spendthrift trusts. On the other hand, there is the even longer held policy of this state that requires a former spouse or a parent to pay alimony or child support in accordance with court orders. When these competing policies collide, in the absence of an expression of legislative intent, this Court must decide which policy will be accorded the greater weight.

We recognize that spendthrift trusts serve many useful purposes such as protecting beneficiaries from their own improvidence, protecting parties from their financial inabilities, and providing a fund for support, all of which continue to have merit. We acknowledge that one of the basic tenets for the construction of trusts is to ascertain the intent of the settlor and to give effect to this intent. See West Coast Hospital Association v. Florida National Bank, 100 So.2d 807 (Fla.1958). We are also aware that some courts of other jurisdictions have refused to invade spendthrift income for alimony and support solely on the basis that the settlor's intent controls. For example, in Erickson v. Erickson, 197 Minn. 71, 266 N.W. 161 (1936), the Minnesota Supreme Court held that the ex-wife of a spendthrift trust beneficiary could not reach his interest for alimony and support and stated:

> *When unrestrained by statute it is the intent of the donor, not the character of the donee's obligation, which controls the availability and disposition of his gift.* The

> donee's obligation to pay alimony or support money, paramount though it may be, should not, in our opinion, transcend the right of the donor to do as he pleases with his own property and to choose the object of his bounty. Our conclusion does not arise out of any anxiety for the protection of the beneficiary. In the absence of statute and within the limits as to perpetuities, a donor may dispose of his property as he fees fit, and this includes corpus or principal as well as income.

Id. at 78, 266 N.W. at 164 (emphasis supplied). Accord Bucknam v. Bucknam, 294 Mass. 214, 200 N.E. 918 (1936); Dinwiddie v. Baumberger, 18 Ill.App.3d 933, 310 N.E.2d 841 (1974).

Other jurisdictions have permitted an ex-spouse to reach the income of a spendthrift trust for alimony and child support on public policy grounds finding that the legal obligation of support is more compelling than enforcing the settlor's intent. See Safe Deposit & Trust Co. v. Robertson, 192 Md. 653, 65 A.2d 292 (1949) (spendthrift trust provisions should not be extended to alimony claims because the ex-spouse is a favored suitor and the claim is based upon the strongest public policy grounds); Lucas v. Lucas, 365 S.W.2d 372 (Tex.Civ.App.1962) (public policy will not allow a spendthrift trust beneficiary to be well taken care of when those who he has a legal duty to support must do without such support); Dillon v. Dillon, 244 Wis. 122, 11 N.W.2d 628 (1943) (public policy will not prohibit spendthrift trust funds from being reached by a beneficiary's wife). See also Restatement (Second) of Trusts § 157 (1959).

This state has always had a strong public policy favoring the enforcement of both alimony and child support orders. For example, in Brackin v. Brackin, 182 So.2d 1 (Fla.1966), we held that the basis of an order awarding alimony or support money is the obligation imposed by law that a spouse do what in equity and good conscience he or she ought to do under the circumstances. We said: "Unlike judgments and decrees for money or property growing out of other actions, alimony and support money may have no foundation other than the *public policy* which requires the husband to pay what he ought to pay...." Id. at 6 (emphasis supplied). In City of Jacksonville v. Jones, 213 So.2d 259 (Fla. 1st DCA 1968), the district court stated "*[t]he public policy* of this state requires that judicial orders providing for payment of child support be enforceable." Id. at 259.

We have weighed the competing public policies and, although we reaffirm the validity of spendthrift trusts, we conclude that in these types of cases the restraint of spendthrift trusts should not be an absolute bar to the enforcement of alimony orders or judgments. Florida's interest in the enforcement of these awards under certain limited circumstances is paramount to the declared intention of the settlor and the restraint of a spendthrift trust.

In not every case where someone is attempting to enforce alimony orders or judgment, however, will garnishment of a spendthrift trust be appropriate. This enforcement alternative should be allowed only as a last resort. If the debtor himself or his property is within the jurisdiction of this state's courts, the traditional methods of enforcing alimony arrearages may be sufficient. In this event, there would be no overriding reason to defeat the intent of the settlor. Florida courts have a variety of methods available to enforce alimony and child support. When these traditional remedies are not effective, it would be unjust and inequitable to allow the debtor to enjoy the benefits of wealth without being subject to the responsibility to support those whom he has a legal obligation to support.

We further limit this right of garnishment to disbursements that are due to be made or which are actually made from the trust. If, under the terms of the trust, a disbursement of corpus or income is due to the debtor-beneficiary, such disbursement may be subject to garnishment. If disbursements are wholly within the trustee's discretion, the court may not order the trustee to make such disbursements. However, if the trustee exercises its discretion and makes a disbursement, that disbursement may be subject to the writ of garnishment.

This case raises another issue. The trial court ordered a continuing garnishment against the Bacardi trust for future payments of alimony as the sums became due. This order was challenged on appeal by the trustee and the debtor-beneficiary. In light of its holding that the trust was not subject to garnishment, the district court did not consider this issue. Since we quash the district court's holding, it is appropriate that we consider and resolve this issue.

The same point was presented and decided by the Second District in Gilbert v. Gilbert. In that case, the husband objected to a continuing writ of garnishment for future alimony against his spendthrift trust. He argued that section 61.12(2), Florida Statutes (1981), which authorized continuing writs of garnishment to enforce orders for alimony and child support, is applicable only to the garnishment of an employer. The Second District, in responding to this argument, held that the same result could be obtained under the provisions of section 61.11, Florida Statutes (1981), which reads as follows:

> 61.11 *Effect of judgment of alimony.*—A judgment of alimony granted under s. 61.08 or s. 61.09 releases the party receiving the alimony from the control of the other party, and the party receiving the alimony may use his alimony and acquire, use, and dispose of other property uncontrolled by the other party. When either party is about to remove himself or his property out of the state, or fraudulently convey or conceal it, the court may award a ne exeat or injunction against him or his property and make such orders as will secure alimony to the party who should receive it.

The Gilbert court said:

> The remedy is drastic but appropriate to cope with the husband's misconduct. We, therefore, sustain the continuing aspect of the order in lieu of ne exeat as necessary to secure payment of alimony. The bank may continue to administer the trust according to its provisions, but to protect itself it will need to withhold all payments due to the husband in excess of alimony then due and owing in order to secure the future alimony payments. The bank is entitled to seek the court's instructions, and the order is always subject to modification upon a proper showing by any interested party. Id. at 302–03.

We agree that the continuing aspect of such orders may be sustained in lieu of ne exeat as necessary to secure payment of alimony. It should be remembered, however, that a continuing garnishment against a spendthrift trust in lieu of ne exeat is also a "last resort" remedy that is available only when the traditional methods of enforcing alimony arrearages are not effective. We also note that where a continuing garnishment is appropriate, the trustee, if it wishes to make payments to the debtor-beneficiary in excess of alimony then due, should seek court approval before it makes such payments. The court may then authorize such payments if sufficient assets remain in the trust or if other provisions are made to secure the payment of alimony to the person who should receive it.

We also hold that an order awarding attorney's fees or a judgment for such fees which result from the divorce or enforcement proceedings are collectible in the same manner. Such awards represent an integral part of the dissolution process and are subject to the same equitable considerations. If the ex-spouse must pay attorney's fees out of the support awards, it only reduces the amount of support available to the needy party. This is especially true where post-decretal services are required by an attorney to enforce such awards.

Accordingly, we quash the decision of the district court and remand this case for further proceedings consistent with our opinion.

It is so ordered.

ADKINS, OVERTON, McDONALD, EHRLICH and SHAW, JJ., concur.

BOYD, C.J., dissents.

G. Charitable Trusts

Estate of Wilson

New York Court of Appeals, 1983
59 N.Y.2d 461, 452 N.E.2d 1228, 465 N.Y.S.2d 900

Chief Judge Cooke.

These appeals present the question whether the equal protection clause of the Fourteenth Amendment is violated when a court permits the administration of private charitable trusts according to the testators' intent to finance the education of male students and not female students. When a court applies trust law that neither encourages, nor affirmatively promotes, nor compels private discrimination but allows parties to engage in private selection in the devise or bequest of their property, that choice will not be attributable to the State and subjected to the Fourteenth Amendment's strictures.

* * *

The factual patterns in each of these matters are different, but the underlying legal issues are the same. In each there is imposed a decedent's intention to create a testamentary trust under which the class of beneficiaries are members of one sex.

In Matter of Wilson, article ELEVENTH of Clark W. Wilson's will provided that the residuary of his estate be held in trust (Wilson Trust) and that the income "be applied to defraying the education and other expenses of the first year at college of five (5) young men who shall have graduated from the Canastota High School, three (3) of whom shall have attained the highest grades in the study of science and two (2) of whom shall have attained the highest grades in the study of chemistry, as may be certified to by the then Superintendent of Schools for the Canastota Central School District." Wilson died in June, 1969 and for the next 11 years the Wilson Trust was administered according to its terms.

In early 1981, the Civil Rights Office of the United States Department of Education received a complaint alleging that the superintendent's acts in connection with the Wilson Trust violated title IX of the Education Amendments of 1972 (US Code, tit 20, § 1681 et. seq.), which prohibits gender discrimination in Federally financed education programs. The Department of Education informed the Canastota Central School District that the complaint would be investigated. Before the investigation was completed, the school district agreed to refrain from again providing names of students to the trustee. The trustee, Key Bank of Central New York, initiated this proceeding for a determination of the effect and validity of the trust provision of the will.

The Surrogate's Court held that the school superintendent's co-operation with the trustee violated no Federal statute or regulation prohibiting sexual discrimination, nor did it implicate the equal protection clause of the Fourteenth Amendment. The court ordered the trustee to continue administering the trust.

A unanimous Appellate Division, Third Department, modified the Surrogate's decree. The court affirmed the Surrogate's finding that the testator intended the trust to benefit male students only and, noting that the school was under no legal obligation to provide the names of qualified male candidates, found "administration of the trust according to its literal terms is impossible." (87 AD2d, p 101.) The court then exercised its cy pres power to reform the trust by striking the clause in the will providing for the school superintendent's certification of the names of qualified candidates for the scholarships. The candidates were permitted to apply directly to the trustee.

Matter of Johnson also involves a call for judicial construction of a testamentary trust created for the exclusive benefit of male students. By a will dated December 13, 1975, Edwin Irving Johnson left his residuary estate in trust (Johnson Trust). Article SIXTH of the will provided that the income of the trust was to "be used and applied, each year to the extent available, for scholarships or grants for bright and deserving young men who have graduated from the High School of [the Croton-Harmon Union Free] School District, and whose parents are financially unable to send them to college, and who shall be selected by the Board of Education of such School District with the assistance of the Principal of such High School."

Johnson died in 1978. In accordance with the terms of the trust, the board of education, acting as trustee, announced that applications from male students would be accepted on or before May 1, 1979. Before any scholarships were awarded, however, the National Organization for Women, filed a complaint with the Civil Rights Office of the United States Department of Education. This complaint alleged that the school district's involvement in the Johnson Trust constituted illegal gender-based discrimination.

During the pendency of the Department of Education's investigation, a stipulation was entered into between the executrix of the will, the president of the board of education, and the Attorney-General. The parties sought "to avoid administering the educational bequest set forth in Article Sixth in a manner which is in conflict with the law and public policy prohibiting discrimination based on sex". The stipulation provided that "all interested parties agree to the deletion of the word 'men' in Article Sixth of the Will and the insertion of the word 'persons' in its place." The Attorney-General then brought this proceeding by petition to the Surrogate's Court to construe article SIXTH of the will.

The Surrogate found that the trustee's unwillingness to administer the trust according to its terms rendered administration of the trust impossible. The court, however, declined to reform the trust by giving effect to the stipulation. Rather, it reasoned that the testator's primary intent to benefit "deserving young men" would be most closely effected by replacing the school district with a private trustee.

A divided Appellate Division, Second Department, reversed, holding that under the equal protection clause of the Fourteenth Amendment, a court cannot reform a trust that, by its own terms, would deny equal protection of law. The court reasoned that inasmuch as an agent of the State had been appointed trustee, the trust, if administered, would violate the equal protection clause. Judicial reformation of the trust by substituting trustees would, in that court's view, itself constitute State action in violation of the Fourteenth Amendment. The court determined that administration of the trust was impossible and, in an exercise of its cy pres power, reformed the trust by eliminating the gender restriction.

* * *

The court, of course, cannot invoke its cy pres power without first determining that the testator's specific charitable purpose is no longer capable of being performed by the trust (see, e.g., Matter of Scott, supra; Matter of Swan, 237 App Div 454, affd sub nom. Matter of St. Johns Church of Mt. Morris, 263 NY 638; Matter of Fairchild, 15 Misc 2d 272). In establishing these trusts, the testators expressly and unequivocally intended that they provide for the educational expenses of male students. It cannot be said that the accomplishment of the testators' specific expression of charitable intent is "impossible or impracticable." So long as the subject high schools graduate boys with the requisite qualifications, the testators' specific charitable intent can be fulfilled.

Nor are the trusts' particular limitation of beneficiaries by gender invalid and incapable of being accomplished as violative of public policy. It is true that the eradication in this State of gender-based discrimination is an important public policy. Indeed, the Legislature has barred gender–based discrimination in education (see Education Law, § 3201-a), employment (see Labor Law, §§ 194. 197. 220-e; General Business Law, § 187), housing, credit, and many other areas (see Executive Law, § 296). As a result, women, once viewed as able to assume only restricted roles in our society (see Bradwell v State, 16 Wall [83 US] 130, 141), now project significant numbers "in business, in the professions, in government and, indeed, in all walks of life where education is a desirable, if not always a necessary, antecedent" (Stanton v Stanton, 421 US 7, 15). The restrictions in these trusts run contrary to this policy favoring equal opportunity and treatment of men and women. A provision in a charitable trust, however, that is central to the testator's or settlor's charitable purpose, and is not illegal, should not be invalidated on public policy grounds unless that provision, if given effect, would substantially mitigate the general charitable effect of the gift (see 4 Scott, Trusts [3d ed], § 399.4).

Proscribing the enforcement of gender restrictions in private charitable trusts would operate with equal force towards trusts whose benefits are bestowed exclusively on women. "Reduction of the disparity in economic condition between men and women caused by the long history of discrimination against women has been recognized as * * * an important governmental objective" (Califano v Webster, 430 US 313, 317). There can be little doubt that important efforts in effecting this type of social change can be and are performed through private philanthropy (see, generally, Commission on Private Philanthropy and Public Needs, Giving in America: Toward a Stronger Voluntary Section [1975]). And, the private funding of programs for the advancement of women is substantial and growing (see Bernstein, Funding for Women's Higher Education: Looking Backward and Ahead, Grant Magazine, vol 4, No. 4, pp. 225–229; Ford Foundation, Financial Support of Women's Programs in the 1970's [1979]; Yarrow, Feminist Philanthropy Comes Into Its Own, NY Times, May 21, 1983, p 7, col 2). Indeed, one compilation of financial assistance offered primarily or exclusively to women lists 854 sources of funding (see Schlacter, Directory of Financial Aids for Women [2d ed, 1981]; see, also, Note, Sex Restricted Scholarships and the Charitable Trust, 59 Iowa L Rev 1000, 1000–1001, & nn 10, 11). Current thinking in private philanthropic institutions advocates that funding offered by such institutions and the opportunities within the institutions themselves be directly responsive to the needs of particular groups (see Ford Foundation, op cit , at pp 41–44; Fleming, Foundations and Affirmative Action, 4 Foundation News No. 4, at pp 14–17; Griffen, Funding for Women's Programs, 6 Grantsmanship Center News, No. 2, at pp 34–45). It is evident, therefore, that the focusing of private philanthropy on certain classes within society may be consistent with public policy. Consequently, that the restrictions in the trusts before this court may run contrary to public efforts promoting equality of opportunity for women does not justify imposing a per se rule that gender restrictions in private charitable trusts violate public policy.

Finally, this is not an instance in which the restriction of the trusts serves to frustrate a paramount charitable purpose. In Howard Sav. Inst. v Peep (34 NJ 494), for example, the testator made a charitable bequest to Amherst College to be placed in trust and to provide scholarships for "deserving American born, Protestant, Gentile boys of good moral repute, not given to gambling, smoking, drinking or similar acts." Due to the religious restrictions, the college declined to accept the bequest as contrary to its charter. The court found that the college was the principal beneficiary of the trust, so that removing the religious restriction and thereby allowing the college to accept the gift would permit administration of the trust in a manner most closely effectuating the testator's intent (see, also, Matter of Hawley, 32 Misc 2d 624; Coffee v Rice Univ., 408 SW2d 269 [Tex]).

In contrast, the trusts subject to these appeals were not intended to directly benefit the school districts. Although the testators sought the school districts' participation, this was incidental to their primary intent of financing part of the college education of boys who attended the schools. Consequently, severance of the school districts' role in the trusts' administration will not frustrate any part of the testators' charitable purposes. Inasmuch as the specific charitable intent of the testators is not inherently "impossible or impracticable" of being achieved by the trusts, there is no occasion to exercise cy pres power.

Although not inherently so, these trusts are currently incapable of being administered as originally intended because of the school districts' unwillingness to co-operate. These impediments, however, may be remedied by an exercise of a court's general equitable power over all trusts to permit a deviation from the administrative terms of a trust and to appoint a successor trustee.

A testamentary trust will not fail for want of a trustee (see EPTL 8-1.1; see, also, Matter of Thomas, 254 NY 292) and, in the event a trustee is unwilling or unable to act, a court may replace the trustee with another (see EPTL 7-2.6; SCPA 1502; see, also, Matter of Andrews, 233 App Div 547; 2 Scott, Trusts [3d ed], § 108.1). Accordingly, the proper means of continuing the Johnson Trust would be to replace the school district with someone able and willing to administer the trust according to its terms.

* * *

It is argued before this court that the judicial facilitation of the continued administration of gender-restrictive charitable trusts violates the equal protection clause of the Fourteenth Amendment (see US Const, 14th Amdt, § 1). The strictures of the equal protection clause are invoked when the State engages in invidious discrimination (see Moose Lodge No. 107 v Irvis, 407 US 163, 173, 176–177; Burton v Wilmington Parking Auth., 365 US 715, 721; Civil Rights Cases, 109 US 3). Indeed, the State itself cannot, consistent with the Fourteenth Amendment, award scholarships that are gender restrictive (see Mississippi Univ. for Women v Hogan, 458 US 718; Kirchberg v Feenstra, 450 US 455; Stanton v Stanton, 421 US 7, supra).

The Fourteenth Amendment, however, "erects no shield against merely private conduct, however discriminatory or wrongful." * * * [citations omitted]. Private discrimination may violate equal protection of the law when accompanied by State participation in, facilitation of, and, in some cases, acquiescence in the discrimination * * * [citations omitted]. Although there is no conclusive test to determine when State involvement in private discrimination will violate the Fourteenth Amendment (see Reitman v Mulkey, supra, at p 378), the general standard that has evolved is whether "the conduct allegedly causing the deprivation of a federal right [is] fairly attributable to the state" (Lugar v Edmondson Oil Co., 457 US 922, 937). Therefore, it is a question of "state responsibility" and "[o]nly by sifting facts and weighing circumstances can the * * * involvement of the State in private conduct be attributed its true significance" (Burton v Wilmington Parking Auth., 365 US 715, 722, supra).

The Supreme Court has identified various situations in which the State may be deemed responsible for discriminatory conduct with private origins. For example, one such instance appears when the State delegates one of its inherent functions to private parties and those parties engage in discrimination (see Lloyd Corp. v Tanner, 407 US 551; Food Employees v Logan Plaza, 391 US 308; Evans v Newton, 382 US 296; Terry v Adams, 345 US 461; Marsh v Alabama, 326 US 501). Another arises when the State does not directly enforce or abet the private discrimination, but substantially facilitates and profits from it (Burton v Wilmington Parking Auth., 365 US 715, supra).

"The Court has never held, of course, that discrimination by an otherwise private entity would be violative of the Equal Protection Clause if the private entity receives any sort of benefit of service at all from the State, or if it is subject to State regulation in any degree whatever" (Moose Lodge No. 107 v Irvis, 407 US 163, 173, supra). Rather, "the State must have ' significantly involved itself with invidious discriminations' * * * in order for the discriminatory action to fall within the ambit of the constitutional prohibition" (id.; see, also, Rendell-Baker v Kohn, 457 US 830; Gilmore v City of Montgomery, 417 US 556).

The State generally may not be held responsible for private discrimination solely on the basis that it permits the discrimination to occur (see Flagg Bros. v Brooks, 436 US 149, 164; Jackson v Metropolitan Edison Co., 419 US 345, 357, supra; Moose Lodge No. 107 v Irvis, 407 US 163, 176, supra; Evans v Abney, 396 US 435, supra). Nor is the State under an affirmative obligation to prevent purely private discrimination (see Reitman v Mulkey, 387 US 369, 376, 377, supra). Therefore, when the State regulates private dealings it may be responsible for private discrimination occurring in the regulated field only when enforcement of its regulation has the effect of compelling the private discrimination (see Flagg Bros. v Brooks, supra; Moose Lodge No. 107 v Irvis, supra; Shelley v Kraemer, 334 US 1, supra; cf. Adickes v Kress & Co., 398 US 144, 170).

In Shelley v Kraemer (supra), for example, the Supreme Court held that the equal protection clause was violated by judicial enforcement of a private covenant that prohibited the sale of affected properties to "people of Negro or Mongolian Race." When one of the properties was sold to a black family, the other property owners sought to enforce the covenant in State court and the family was ordered to move from the property. The Supreme Court noted "that the restrictive agreements standing alone cannot be regarded as violative of any rights guaranteed to petitioners by the Fourteenth Amendment. So long as the purposes of those agreements are effectuated by voluntary adherence to their terms, it would appear clear that there has been no action by the State and the provisions of the Amendment have not been violated" (334 US, at p 13). The court held, however, that it did have before it cases "in which the States have merely abstained from action leaving private individuals free to impose such discriminations as they see fit. Rather, these are cases in which the States have made available to such individuals the full coercive power of the government to deny petitioners, on the grounds of race or color, the enjoyment of property rights" (id., at p 19). It was not the neutral regulation of contracts permitting parties to enter discriminatory agreements that caused the discrimination to be attributable to the State. Instead, it was that the State court's exercise of its judicial power directly effected a discriminatory act.

In Barrows v Jackson, (346 US 249, supra), the court applied the same reasoning when it held that a court's awarding damages against a party who has breached a racially restrictive covenant also violates the equal protection clause. The court reiterated that "voluntary adherence [to the covenant] would constitute individual action only" (id., at p 253). But, "[t]o compel respondent to respond in damages would be for the State to punish her for failure to perform her covenant to continue to discriminate against non-Caucasians in the use of her property * * * Thus, it becomes not respondent's voluntary choice but the State's choice that she observe her covenant or suffer damages" (id., at p 254).

More recently, the Supreme Court considered whether a State's regulation of private clubs licensed to serve liquor caused a club's restrictive membership policy to be attributable to the State (see Moose Lodge No. 107 v Irvis, 407 US 163, supra). The court held that although the State extensively regulated these private clubs, it was not responsible for the private discrimination simply because the regulation permitted the discrimination to occur. The court stated that "[h]owever detailed this type of regulation may be in some particulars, it cannot be said to in any way foster or encourage * * * discrimination" (407 US, at pp 176–177). The court distinguished the regulatory scheme's general neutral effect on the discrimination from a situation in which that scheme could be used to compel discrimination. One of the regulations provided that "'[e]very club licensee shall adhere to all of the provisions of its Constitution and By-Laws'" (id., at pp 177). The court acknowledged that if this regulation were used (at p 178) "to place state sanctions behind [the licensee's] discriminatory membership rules," the Fourteenth Amendment would be implicated. Accordingly, the court enjoined enforcement of the regulation.

A court's application of its equitable power to permit the continued administration of the trusts involved in these appeals falls outside the ambit of the Fourteenth Amendment. Although the field of trusts is regulated by the State, the Legislature's failure to forbid private discriminatory trusts does not cause such trusts, when they arise, to be attributable to the State (see Flagg Bros. v Brooks, 436 US 149, 165, supra; see, also, Evans v Abney, 396 US 435, 458 [Brennan, J., dissenting], supra). It naturally follows that, when a court applies this trust law and determines that it permits the continued existence of private discriminatory trusts, the Fourteenth Amendment is not implicated.

In the present appeals, the coercive power of the State has never been enlisted to enforce private discrimination. Upon finding that requisite formalities of creating a trust had been met, the courts below determined the testator's intent, and applied the relevant law permitting those intentions to be privately carried out. The court's power compelled no discrimination. That discrimination had been sealed in the private execution of the wills. Recourse to the courts was had here only for the purpose of facilitating the administration of the trusts, not for enforcement of their discriminatory dispositive provisions.

This is not to say that a court's exercise of its power over trusts can never invoke the scrutiny of the Fourteenth Amendment. This court holds only that a trust's discriminatory terms are not fairly attributable to the State when a court applies trust principles that permit private discrimination but do not encourage, affirmatively promote, or compel it.

The testators' intention to involve the State in the administration of these trusts does not alter this result, notwithstanding that the effect of the courts' action respecting the trusts was to eliminate this involvement. The courts' power to replace a trustee who is unwilling to act as in Johnson or to permit a deviation from an incidental administrative term in the trust as in Wilson is a part of the law permitting this private conduct and extends to all trusts regardless of their purposes. It compels no discrimination. Moreover, the minimal State participation in the trusts' administration prior to the time that they reached the courts for the constructions under review did not cause the trusts to take on an indelible public character (see Evans v Newton, 382 US 296, 301; Commonwealth of Pennsylvania v Brown, 392 F2d 120).

In sum, the Fourteenth Amendment does not require the State to exercise the full extent of its power to eradicate private discrimination. It is only when the State itself discriminates, compels another to discriminate, or allows another to assume one of its functions and discriminate that such discrimination will implicate the amendment.

Accordingly, in Matter of Wilson, the order of the Appellate Division should be affirmed, with costs payable out of the estate to all parties appearing separately and filing separate briefs.

In Matter of Johnson, the order of the Appellate Division should be reversed, with costs payable out of the estate to all parties appearing separately and filing separate briefs and the decree of the Surrogate's Court, Westchester County, reinstated.

Meyer, J. (concurring in Matter of Wilson and dissenting in Matter of Johnson).

I would affirm in both cases. Although the Constitution does not proscribe private bias, it does proscribe affirmative State action in furtherance of bias.

In Matter of Wilson the trust is private and the only involvement of a public official (the superintendent of schools) is his certification of a student's class standing, information which is, in any event, available to any student applying to the trustee for a scholarship. There is, therefore, no State action.

In Matter of Johnson, however, the trustee is the board of education, a public body. The establishment of a public trust for a discriminatory purpose is constitutionally improper, as Presiding Justice Mollen has fully spelled out in his opinion. For the State to legitimize that impropriety by replacement of the trustee is unconstitutional State action. The only permissible corrective court action is, as the Appellate Division held, excision of the discriminatory limitation.

In *Matter of Wilson*:

JASEN, JONES, WACHTLER, MEYER and SIMONS, JJ., concur with COOKE, C.J..

MEYER, J., concurs in a memorandum.

Order affirmed, etc.

In *Matter of Johnson*:

JASEN, JONES, WACHTLER and SIMONS, JJ., concur with COOKE, C.J.

MEYER, J., dissents and votes to affirm in a memorandum.

Order reversed, etc.

Notes

Definitions of Charity: The Uniform Trust Code defines charitable trusts along well-established categories, *see* UNIF. TRUST CODE §405(a) (2003), and allows for a similar purpose to be chosen by a court if the original charitable purpose envisioned by the Settlor is no longer a possibility, *Id.* at §405(b). But case law and statutes have made clear that a charitable purpose does not include invidious discrimination, violation of strong public policy, or the promotion of private—as compared to public—aspirations. For example, gifts to aid political parties have been held to be charitable, *see* Liapis' Estate, 88 Pa. D. & C. 303 (1954); George Bernard Shaw's bequest to develop a new English alphabet did not provide a sufficient public benefit to be charitable, *see* In re Public Trustee v. Day (In re Shaw), 1 W.L.R. 729 (1957); and it is questionable if racial or gender restrictions would survive present day scrutiny of valid trust purposes, *see, e.g.,* In re Wilson, 59 N.Y.2d 461, 452 N.E.2d 1228, 465 N.Y.S.2d 900 (1983)(gender restriction) and Podberesky v. Kirwan, 38 F.3d 147 (4th Cir. 1994), *cert. denied*, 514 U.S. 1120 (1995)(race restriction). *See generally* Mary Kay Lundwall, *Inconsistency and Uncertainty in the Charitable Purposes Doctrine*, 41 WAYNE L. REV. 1341 (1995). If gender or racial classifications make the trust invalid, courts have been willing to reform the trust under the doctrine of cy pres and prevent the corpus from reverting to the Settlor, *see, e.g.,* In re Certain Scholarship Funds, 133 N.H. 227, 575 A.2d 1325 (1990). *See generally* Kirk A. Kennedy, *Race-Exclusive Scholarships: Constitutional Vel Non*, 30 WAKE FOREST L. REV. 759 (1995). The Estate of Wilson, *supra*, is a good case with which to discuss the application of cy pres to charitable trusts. *See also* Alex M. Johnson, Jr., *Limiting Dead Hand Control of Charitable Trusts: Expanding Use of the Cy Pres Doctrine*, 21 HAWAII L. REV. 353 (1999); RICHARD POSNER, ECONOMIC ANALYSIS OF LAW (5th ed. 1998); Frances Howell Rudko, *The Cy Pres Doctrine in the United States: From Extreme Reluctance to Affirmative Action*, 46 CLEV. ST. L. REV. 471 (1998).

Enforcement of Charity: The Uniform Trust Code allows for a Settlor, among others, to enforce a charitable trust, thereby providing for a mechanism for enforcement at present and into the future, *see* UNIF. TRUST CODE §405(c) (2003). The state attorney general, who is the other person responsible for enforcement of the charitable purposes, often requires reporting by the trustee, *see, e.g.,* N.Y. EST., POWERS & TRUSTS L. §8-1.4 (2004), thereby furthering the requirements of the Uniform Trust Act, *see* UNIF. TRUST ACT §813 (2003) (Duty to Inform and Report). Matters for supervision by the attorney general would include prudent investing by the trustee. *See, e.g., Restatement of Trusts 2d* §389 (1959); Unif. Prudent Investor Act (1994). Yet, while the attorney general is responsible for enforcement, the courts remain the final arbiters in matters such as cy pres. *See, e.g.,* Town of Brookline v. Barnes, 327 Mass. 201, 97 N.E.2d 651 (1951). Some would argue that the attorney general is a poor choice for enforcement of charitable trusts. *See, e.g.,* Kenneth L. Karst, *The Efficiency of the Charitable Dollar: An Unfulfilled State Responsibility*, 73 HARV. L. REV. 433 (1960). There are few federal or state penalties. The federal Internal Revenue Code imposes tax penalties on private charitable foundations that do not distribute annually at least five percent of the value of the endowment. *See* I.R.C. § 4942 (2004). Failure to do so will result in a 15 % excise tax of any undistributed income. Repeated failure to distribute funds will entail stiffer penalties. *See id.* at § 6684.

Tax Considerations: A contribution made to what may be termed a charity is only deductible as such if made to, or for the use of, the following organizations: (1) The United States, a state, local government, the District of Columbia, or a United States Possession. And the gift must be exclusively for public, rather than private, purposes. (2) A corporation, trust, community chest, fund, or foundation, created in the United States and organized exclusively for religious, charitable, scientific, literary or educational purposes, or for national or international sports competitions, or for the prevention of cruelty to children or to animals. No part of the charity's earnings may go to benefit any private person, and the charity must not be disqualified for tax exemption under I.R.C. § 501(c)(3) by attempting to influence legislation. (3) A cemetery not operated for profit or for the benefit of any private shareholder or individual. (4) A post or organization of war veterans, or its auxiliary society or unit, organized in the United States or its possessions, if no part of the net earnings inures to the benefit of any private shareholder or individual. (5) For individual donors only, a domestic fraternal society, or association, operating under the lodge system, if the contributions are used exclusively for religious, charitable, scientific, literary, or educational purposes, or for the prevention of cruelty to children or animals. I.R.C. § 170(c).

Estates and trusts are allowed unlimited income tax charitable deduction for amounts that are paid to recognized charities out of gross income earned during the tax year (*see* I.R.C. § 642(c)). And if an individual makes a charitable gift during lifetime, he or she is entitled to a gift tax charitable deduction. *See* I.R.C. § 2522. If a decedent makes a charitable gift at death through a valid Last Will and Testament, his or her estate is entitled to the estate tax charitable deduction for the property transferred to charity. *See* I.R.C. § 2055.

Sometimes an individual may make a gift or trust that benefits both the individual and a charity. This type of arrangement is generally referred to as a "split-interest" trust because both an individual and a charity have an interest in the trust. If the transfer is in the form of a trust whereby a charity receives the remainder interest after a life interest is paid to an individual, no charitable deduction is permitted. However, if the trust qualifies as a charitable remainder annuity trust (CRAT) or a charitable remainder unitrust trust (CRUT), the individual will receive a charitable deduction for the value of the remainder interest that will pass to charity under the terms of the trust.

The annuity trust allows for a specified amount not less than five percent, nor more than fifty percent of the initial net fair market value of all of the property placed in the trust to be paid to the individual. And the annuity amount must be paid at least annually to the income beneficiary and the value of the remainder interest must be at least ten percent of the initial net fair market value of all the property in the trust. Furthermore, the trust must prohibit additional future contributions and the term of the trust may be the individual's life or a term of years that does not exceed 20 years. After the death of the individual or the end of the term, the corpus of the trust passes to charity. *See* I.R.C. § 664(d)(1). The advantage of the annuity trust is that the amount the noncharitable beneficiary—the individual—receives is fixed.

A unitrust (CRUT) must pay the income beneficiary, annually, an amount based on a fixed percentage of the net fair market value of the trust's assets that must be valued annually. The fixed percentage cannot be less than five percent, nor more than fifty percent, of the net fair market value of the trust assets. At the death of the beneficiary or after a term of years not to exceed 20, the assets pass to the charity. *See* I.R.C. §§664(d)(2). Unlike the CRAT, additional contributions may be made to the CRUT. There are alternatives to the CRUT described above. First, the unitrust may provide that the non-charitable beneficiary receives the fixed percentage amount of the net fair market value of the assets or the amount of the trust income, whichever is lower (a NICRUT). *See* I.R.C. §664(d)(3)(A). If the trust earns no income, the trust does not pay the income beneficiary. Second, the trust may provide that the non-charitable beneficiary receive the lower of the fixed percentage amount of the net fair market value of the assets or the trust income, whichever is lower and, in years in which the income is lower that the required fixed percentage amount, the trust can distribute amounts of income to the extent previous years income exceeded the amount required to be distributed (a NIMCRUT). *See* I.R.C. §664(d)(3)(B). Third, a trust can start out as a NIMCRUT and upon a certain event, convert to a standard CRUT (a FlipCRUT). *See* I.R.C. §664(f). Drafting charitable annuity trusts or unitrusts is difficult and requires precision. The following decisions is illustrative.

Putnam v. Putnam

Supreme Judicial Court of Massachusetts, 1997
425 Mass. 770, 682 N.E.2d 1351

WILKINS, Chief Justice.

Here on direct appellate review is a reservation and report of an action seeking the reformation of the Stanton W. Putnam charitable remainder unitrust (unitrust). The plaintiff settlor of the unitrust (Putnam) contends that the trust instrument, drafted by a lawyer now deceased, provides for annual distributions to Putnam or to a named successor (King) that (a) are inconsistent with his intent to benefit the charities that have remainder interests in the unitrust and (b) greatly reduce the tax benefits that he intended to flow from the unitrust's creation.

All named defendants have assented to the reformation of the unitrust. The judge reported the case on the facts stated in the complaint and did so on the assumption that the Internal Revenue Service, which is not a party, would be bound only by a decision of this court, a point on which we express no view. The record has been supplemented on appeal by additional facts.

Putnam created the unitrust on December 29, 1989. The trust owns real estate in Truro which has an estimated value of less than $400,000. The property, which is for sale, has produced no income to the trust. Putnam expected to receive no distribution from the trust and did not review the terms of the trust when he executed it. In fact, the trust instrument directs the trustee annually to distribute "first from the net income, and to the extent that such net income is insufficient, from the principal of the trust, an amount (the 'unitrust amount') equal to ten percent of the net fair market value of the trust assets." The distributions are to be made quarterly to Putnam during his life and then to King, if he survives Putnam, for life but for no more than twenty years from Putnam's death. Then the trust assets are to be distributed in equal shares to the named charities.[2]

---

2. The trust instrument grants the trustee the power to amend the terms of the trust for the purpose of complying with the requirements of a qualified charitable remainder unitrust under the Internal Revenue Code.

A charitable remainder trust provides for a specified distribution, at least annually, to one or more beneficiaries, at least one of which is not a charity, for life or for a term of years, with an irrevocable remainder interest in one or more charities. I.R.C. §664 (1994); Treas. Reg. §1.664-1(a) (1997). The plaintiff's unitrust qualifies as a "charitable remainder unitrust" under §664(d)(2) of the I.R.C. Each year, subject to an exception we shall discuss later, a charitable remainder unitrust must distribute a fixed percentage (which may not be less than five per cent) of the net fair market value of the assets valued each year, to one or more noncharitable beneficiaries (also called "income beneficiaries") for a certain term. I.R.C. §664(d)(2)(A). At the end of the term, the trust assets pass to, or for the use of, one or more qualified charities. I.R.C. §664(d)(2)(C). The unitrust conforms to these requirements, but its mandate that ten per cent of the value of the trust assets be distributed annually reduces substantially the prospective value of the charitable remainders.

An exception to the fixed percentage distribution requirements just discussed permits distribution of only net income to a noncharitable beneficiary. I.R.C. §664(d)(3). This method obviously protects the trust principal from intrusion. Putnam relies on this provision in seeking to reform the unitrust instrument to conform to what he intended when he created the unitrust.

We have allowed the reformation of an ambiguous trust instrument based on extrinsic evidence of the settlor's intent and provisions in the instrument that showed that the lawyer who drafted it failed to carry out the settlor's intent. Berman v. Sandler, 379 Mass. 506, 510–511, 399 N.E.2d 17 (1980). We have also allowed reformation of trust instruments that were not ambiguous but which produced results that were proved to be clearly inconsistent with the settlor's estate tax objectives. See Pond v. Pond, 424 Mass. 894, 898–899, 678 N.E.2d 1321 (1997); Simches v. Simches, 423 Mass. 683, 687–688, 671 N.E.2d 1226 (1996); Loeser v. Talbot, 412 Mass. 361, 365, 589 N.E.2d 301 (1992). See Restatement of Property (Donative Transfers) §12.2 (Tent. Draft No. 1 1995). In deciding trust reformation issues, we have made no distinction based on whether the settlor was living when the case was presented for decision. See Berman v. Sandler, supra at 510, 399 N.E.2d 17. Indeed, the crucial evidence of intent and mistake may well be available from the lawyer who drafted (or misdrafted) the instrument rather than from the settlor. Nor have we made any distinction based on whether a trust instrument was or was not ambiguous.[3]

The existence of a mistake in the drafting of a trust instrument must be established by "full, clear, and decisive proof." Berman v. Sandler, supra at 509, 399 N.E.2d 17, quoting Coolidge v. Loring, 235 Mass. 220, 224, 126 N.E. 276 (1920), quoting Richardson v. Adams, 171 Mass. 447, 449, 50 N.E. 941 (1898). That standard is sim-

---

3. We have disallowed extrinsic evidence to "explain" the terms of an unambiguous will. See Putnam v. Putnam, 366 Mass. 261, 266, 316 N.E.2d 729 (1974), and cases cited. The circumstances known to the testator at the time of the will's execution have been admissible, however, in aid of interpreting a will to ascertain the testator's intent. Id. at 266–267, 316 N.E.2d 729.

For reasons that may no longer be meaningful, we have been less willing to recognize the possibility of proof of mistake in the drafting of a will (as opposed to an inter vivos trust) that is unambiguous on its face. The case may be hard to make, however, for denying reformation of a will where, in substantively similar circumstances, we would allow reformation of a trust instrument. See Restatement of Property (Donative Transfers) §12.1 comment c (Tent. Draft No. 1 1995). Evidence of intention, perhaps inadmissible for the purpose of interpretation of a trust instrument, may be relevant and admissible on the issue of mistake, that is, to support the reformation of the instrument.

ilar to proof by "clear and convincing evidence." See Restatement of Property Donative Transfers) § 12.1 (Tent. Draft No. 1 1995). The point is not, however, so much that the burden of proof is heightened as it is that the judge who considers the reformation claim must make thorough and reasoned findings that deal with all relevant facts and must demonstrate a conviction that the proof of mistake was clear and well-founded.

The unitrust with which we are concerned in this case is not ambiguous. One might create such a trust, although in practical terms the trust might generate limited benefits for the charity or charities and thus limited tax benefits for the settlor. In this case, however, it seems clear that the settlor was not interested in receiving significant distributions of principal from the trust. The trust assets, real estate in Truro, had not been sold and had produced no income. The charitable gifts, with the related tax benefits, appear to have been the settlor's goal in creating the unitrust. The provision for distribution of ten per cent of the fair market value of the trust assets each year, made up first from income and then from principal to the extent needed, would considerably deplete the amounts likely to be available for the charities. A reformation of the trust to limit distributions to noncharitable beneficiaries to the income of the trust, as I.R.C. § 664(d)(3) permits, is appropriate in the circumstances.

The request for an award of attorney's fees and costs payable from the assets of the unitrust is denied. The lawyer who made the drafting error was a member of the firm that appears for the plaintiff to correct the error. A judgment shall be entered in the Probate and Family Court allowing the amendment of the unitrust in the form set forth in the first request for relief of the complaint.[4]

So ordered.

H. Pour Over Trusts

Modern estate planning integrates retirement programs (payable-on-death accounts), insurance policies (including long term care insurance), and inter vivos trusts, all of which may coalesce in a valid Last Will and Testament. Needless to say, federal and state taxation policies play a role, and, increasingly, international wealth must be factored. For example, an estate planning attorney may recommend to a client that he or she name as beneficiary on any Keogh or IRA or life insurance policy the testamentary trust established in a valid Last Will and Testament. Conversely, the Last Will and Testament may name as legatee of "all of my property, both real and personal," an inter vivos trust executed during the lifetime of the Settlor. This interaction between inter vivos and testamentary transactions is often referred to as pour over. If a Will bequeaths

---

4. The record in this case is unnecessarily scant. We have not been furnished with calculations showing the difference in the value of the charitable gifts under the trust (a) as drafted and (b) as reformed. We have not even been given the ages of the noncharitable income beneficiaries, facts that are crucial in calculating the date on which the charities will likely be paid. We do not know whether Putnam ever received income from the real estate now in the trust. Nor do we have an affidavit from Putnam (and perhaps others) stating his intention in creating the trust. Although on the facts of this case the charitable giving and tax objectives are sufficiently apparent to permit reformation of the trust instrument, the requirement of clear and decisive proof in such cases counsels that a full factual record supporting reformation be made.

property to a trust, it is a pour over Will; if an inter vivos trust names as beneficiary the Last Will and Testament, it is a pour over trust. Traditionally the inter vivos trust was considered a fact of independent significance, and a valid Will was permitted to name it as a legatee even though it was unfunded.

Pour over practice is evidenced in Uniform Probate Code § 2-512, which follows *infra*. But there was often concern as to whether the pour over was legal if no trust property existed prior to the death of the Testator, when the Will actually pours property into the trust. How could you pour over into something that had no independent significance? To remedy this dilemma, states enacted Uniform Probate Code § 2-511. If the state accepts the provisions of § 2-511, there is no necessity to fund the inter vivos trust during the lifetime of the Settlor. Compare the two following provisions to identify the distinction, remembering that pour over trusts are most often revocable inter vivos trusts, which is the next type of trust to be considered and a valuable estate planning tool.

Uniform Probate Code (2003)

Section 2-512. Events of Independent Significance.

A will may dispose of property by reference to acts and events that have significance apart from their effect upon the dispositions made by the will, whether they occur before or after the execution of the will or before or after the testator's death. The execution or revocation of another individual's will is such an event.

Section 2-511. Testamentary Additions to Trusts.

(a) A will may validly devise property to the trustee of a trust established or to be established (i) during the testator's lifetime by the testator, by the testator and some other person, or by some other person, including a funded or unfunded life insurance trust, although the settlor has reserved any or all rights of ownership of the insurance contracts, or (ii) at the testator's death by the testator's devise to the trustee, if the trust is identified in the testator's will and its terms are set forth in a written instrument, other than a will, executed before, concurrently with, or after the execution of the testator's will or in another individual's will if that other individual has predeceased the testator, regardless of the existence, size, or character of the corpus of the trust. The devise is not invalid because the trust is amendable or revocable, or because the trust was amended after the execution of the will or the testator's death.

(b) Unless the testator's will provides otherwise, property devised to a trust described in subsection (a) is not held under a testamentary trust of the testator, but it becomes a part of the trust to which it is devised, and must be administered and disposed of in accordance with the provisions of the governing instrument setting forth the terms of the trust, including any amendments thereto made before or after the testator's death.

(c) Unless the testator's will provides otherwise, a revocation or termination of the trust before the testator's death causes the devise to lapse.

I. Revocable Inter Vivos Trusts

Clymer v. Mayo

Supreme Court of Massachusetts, 1985
393 Mass. 754, 473 N.E.2d 1084

HENNESSEY, Chief Justice.

This consolidated appeal arises out of the administration of the estate of Clara A. Mayo (decedent). We summarize the findings of the judge of the Probate and Family Court incorporating the parties' agreed statement of uncontested facts.

At the time of her death in November, 1981, the decedent, then fifty years of age, was employed by Boston University as a professor of psychology. She was married to James P. Mayo, Jr. (Mayo), from 1953 to 1978. The couple had no children. The decedent was an only child and her sole heirs at law are her parents, Joseph A. and Maria Weiss.

In 1963, the decedent executed a will designating Mayo as principal beneficiary. In 1964, she named Mayo as the beneficiary of her group annuity contract with John Hancock Mutual Life Insurance Company; and in 1965, made him the beneficiary of her Boston University retirement annuity contracts with Teachers Insurance and Annuity Association (TIAA) and College Retirement Equities Fund (CREF). As a consequence of a $300,000 gift to the couple from the Weisses in 1971, the decedent and Mayo executed new wills and indentures of trust on February 2, 1973, wherein each spouse was made the other's principal beneficiary. Under the terms of the decedent's will, Mayo was to receive her personal property. The residue of her estate was to "pour over" into the inter vivos trust she created that same day.

The decedent's trust instrument named herself and John P. Hill as trustees. As the donor, the decedent retained the right to amend or revoke the trust at any time by written instrument delivered to the trustees. In the event that Mayo survived the decedent, the trust estate was to be divided into two parts. Trust A, the marital deduction trust, was to be funded with an amount "equal to fifty (50%) per cent of the value of the Donor's 'adjusted gross estate,'... for the purpose of the United States Tax Law, less an amount equal to the value of all interest in property, if any, allowable as 'marital deductions' for the purposes of such law...." Mayo was the income beneficiary of Trust A and was entitled to reach the principal at his request or in the trustee's discretion. The trust instrument also gave Mayo a general power of appointment over the assets in Trust A.

The balance of the decedent's estate, excluding personal property passing to Mayo by will, or the entire estate if Mayo did not survive her, composed Trust B. Trust B provided for the payment of five initial specific bequests totalling [sic] $45,000. After those gifts were satisfied, the remaining trust assets were to be held for the benefit of Mayo for life. Upon Mayo's death, the assets in Trust B were to be held for "the benefit of the nephews and nieces of the Donor" living at the time of her death. The trustee was given discretion to spend so much of the income and principal as necessary for their comfort, support, and education. When all of these nephews and nieces reached the age of thirty, the trust was to terminate and its remaining assets were to be divided equally between Clark University and Boston University to assist in graduate education of women.

On the same day she established her trust, the decedent changed the beneficiary of her Boston University group life insurance policy from Mayo to the trustees. One month later, in March, 1973, she also executed a change in her retirement annuity contracts to designate the trustees as beneficiaries. At the time of its creation in 1973, the trust was not funded. Its future assets were to consist solely of the proceeds of these policies and the property which would pour over under the will's residuary clause. The judge found that the remaining trustee has never received any property or held any funds subsequent to the execution of the trust nor has he paid any trust taxes or filed any trust tax returns.

Mayo moved out of the marital home in 1975. In June, 1977, the decedent changed the designation of beneficiary on her Boston University life insurance policy for a second time, substituting Marianne LaFrance for the trustees.[2] LaFrance had lived with the Mayos since 1972, and shared a close friendship with the decedent up until her death. Mayo filed for divorce on September 9, 1977, in New Hampshire. The divorce was decreed on January 3, 1978, and the court incorporated into the decree a permanent stipulation of the parties' property settlement. Under the terms of that settlement, Mayo waived any "right, title or interest" in the decedent's "securities, savings accounts, savings certificates, and retirement fund," as well as her "furniture, furnishings and art." Mayo remarried on August 28, 1978, and later executed a new will in favor of his new wife. The decedent died on November 21, 1981. Her will was allowed on November 18, 1982, and the court appointed John H. Clymer as administrator with the will annexed.

What is primarily at issue in these actions is the effect of the Mayos' divorce upon dispositions provided in the decedent's will and indenture of trust. In the first action, the court-appointed administrator of the decedent's estate petitioned for instructions with respect to the impact of the divorce on the estate's administration. Named as defendants were Mayo, the decedent's parents (the Weisses), and the trustee under the indenture of trust (John P. Hill).

The second case involved a complaint for declaratory and equitable relief filed by the Weisses. Named as defendants were Hill, Mayo, Clymer, the beneficiaries named in Trust B (Hill, Michael Z. Fleming, Renee N. Watkins, LaFrance, Mary Ann Mayo, Boston University, and Clark University), James Mayo's nephews and niece (John Chamberlain, Allan Chamberlain, and Mira Hinman), and the administrators of the Boston University Retirement Plan (TIAA/CREF). The Weisses sought a declaration that the divorce revoked all gifts to Mayo set forth in the will and indenture of trust, including the power of appointment conferred upon Mayo under the trust. The Weisses also alleged that the trust was unfunded, not lawfully created, or alternatively was revoked, and therefore any purported gift to the trust had lapsed. The Weisses asked the court to set aside the trust on the grounds that Mayo and his father allegedly had engaged in fraud, deceit, undue influence, and abuse of a fiduciary relationship in its creation. Additionally, the court was asked to construe the phrase "nephews and nieces" in connection with the trust, and to order that the terms of the Mayos' divorce stipulation precluded Mayo from receiving funds from the decedent's retirement plan. Finally, the plaintiffs sought to have Hill removed as trustee.

In the third action, the Weisses petitioned the court for removal of Clymer as administrator on the ground that he had failed to exercise impartiality in his fiduciary duties.

* * *

---

2. Upon the decedent's death the benefits under said policy were paid to LaFrance.

For the reasons to follow we affirm the judge's conclusions that: (1) the decedent established a valid trust under G.L. c. 203, §3B; (2) Mayo's interest in Trust A was terminated as a result of the divorce; (3) the Chamberlains and Hinman are entitled to take as intended beneficiaries under Trust B, with the remainder interest to be divided equally between Clark University and Boston University; and (4) the Weisses lack standing to petition for removal of the estate's administrator. However, we reverse the judge's ruling that Mayo is to take under Trust B, and we remand the question of attorneys' fees for reconsideration.

* * *

The Weisses claim that the judge erred in ruling that the decedent's trust was validly created despite the fact that it was not funded until her death. They rely on the common law rule that a trust can be created only when a trust res exists. New England Trust Co. v. Sanger, 337 Mass. 342, 348, 149 N.E.2d 598 (1958). Arguing that the trust never came into existence, the Weisses claim they are entitled to the decedent's entire estate as her sole heirs at law.

In upholding the validity of the decedent's pour-over trust, the judge cited the relevant provisions of G.L. c. 203, §3B, inserted by St.1963, c. 418, §1, the Commonwealth's version of the Uniform Testamentary Additions to Trusts Act. "A devise or bequest, the validity of which is determinable by the laws of the commonwealth, may be made to the trustee or trustees of a trust established or to be established by the testator ... including a funded or unfunded life insurance trust, although the trustor has reserved any or all rights of ownership of the insurance contracts, if the trust is identified in the will and the terms of the trust are set forth in a written instrument executed before or concurrently with the execution of the testator's will ... *regardless of the existence, size or character of the corpus of the trust*" (emphasis added). The decedent's trust instrument, which was executed in Massachusetts and states that it is to be governed by the laws of the Commonwealth, satisfies these statutory conditions. The trust is identified in the residuary clause of her will and the terms of the trust are set out in a written instrument executed contemporaneously with the will. However, the Weisses claim that G.L. c. 203, §3B, was not intended to change the common law with respect to the necessity for a trust corpus despite the clear language validating pour-over trusts, "regardless of the existence, size or character of the corpus." The Weisses make no showing of legislative intent that would contradict the plain meaning of these words. It is well established that "the statutory language is the principal source of insight into legislative purpose." Bronstein v. Prudential Ins. Co. of America, 390 Mass. 701, 704, 459 N.E.2d 772 (1984). Moreover, the development of the common law of this Commonwealth with regard to pour-over trusts demonstrates that G.L. c. 203, §3B, takes on practical meaning only if the Legislature meant exactly what the statute says concerning the need for a trust corpus.

This court was one of the first courts to validate pour-over devises to a living trust. In Second Bank-State St. Trust Co. v. Pinion, 341 Mass. 366, 371, 170 N.E.2d 350 (1960), decided prior to the adoption of G.L. c. 203, §3B, we upheld a testamentary gift to a revocable and amendable inter vivos trust established by the testator before the execution of his will and which he amended after the will's execution. Recognizing the importance of the pour-over devise in modern estate planning, we explained that such transfers do not violate the statute of wills despite the testator's ability to amend the trust and thereby change the disposition of property at his death without complying with the statute's formalities. "We agree with modern legal thought that a subsequent amendment is effective because of the applicability of the established equitable doctrine that subsequent acts of independent significance do not require attestation under the statute of wills." Id. at 369, 170 N.E.2d 350.

At that time we noted that "[t]he long established recognition in Massachusetts of the doctrine of independent significance makes unnecessary statutory affirmance of its application to pour-over trusts." Id. at 371, 170 N.E.2d 350. It is evident from Pinion that there was no need for the Legislature to enact G.L. c. 203, § 3B, simply to validate pour-over devises from wills to funded revocable trusts.

However, in Pinion, we were not presented with an unfunded pour-over trust. Nor, prior to G.L. c. 203, § 3B, did other authority exist in this Commonwealth for recognizing testamentary transfers to unfunded trusts. The doctrine of independent significance, upon which we relied in Pinion, assumes that "property was included in the purported inter vivos trust, prior to the testator's death." Restatement (Second) of Trusts § 54, comment f (1959). That is why commentators have recognized that G.L. c. 203, § 3B, "[m]akes some ... modification of the Pinion doctrine. The act does not require that the trust res be more than nominal or even existent." E. Slizewski, Legislation: Uniform Testamentary Additions to Trusts Act, 10 Ann.Surv. of Mass.Law § 2.7, 39 (1963). See Osgood, Pour Over Will: Appraisal of Uniform Testamentary Additions to Trusts Act, 104 Trusts 768, 769 (1965) ("The Act ... eliminates the necessity that there be a trust corpus").

By denying that the statute effected such a change in the existing law, the Weisses render its enactment meaningless. "An intention to enact a barren and ineffective provision is not lightly to be imputed to the Legislature." Insurance Rating Bd. v. Commissioner of Ins., 356 Mass. 184, 189, 248 N.E.2d 500 (1969). By analogy, in Trosch v. Maryland Nat'l Bank, 32 Md.App. 249, 252, 359 N.E.2d 564 (1976), the court construed Maryland's Testamentary Additions to Trusts Act as "conditionally abrogating the common law rule ... that a trust must have a corpus to be in existence." Despite minor differences in the relevant language of Maryland's Estates and Trusts Act, § 4-411,[3] and our G.L. c. 203, § 3B, we agree with the court's conclusion that "the statute is not conditioned upon the existence of a trust but upon the existence of a trust instrument " (emphasis in original). Id. at 253, 359 N.E.2d 564. The Weisses urge us to follow Hageman v. Cleveland Trust Co., 41 Ohio App.2d 160, 324 N.E.2d 594 (1974), rev'd on other grounds, 45 Ohio St.2d 178, 182, 343 N.E.2d 121 (1976), where the court held that an inter vivos trust had to be funded during the settlor's life to receive pour-over assets from a will. However, in reaching this conclusion the court relied on a statute differing from G.L. c. 203, § 3B, in its omission of the critical phrase: "regardless of the existence, size or character of the corpus of the trust." See Ohio Rev.Code Ann. § 2107.63 (Baldwin 1978).

For the foregoing reasons we conclude, in accordance with G.L. c. 203, § 3B, that the decedent established a valid inter vivos trust in 1973 and that its trustee may properly receive the residue of her estate. We affirm the judge's ruling on this issue.

* * *

---

3. Maryland Estates and Trusts Code Ann. § 4-411 (1974), reads:
   A legacy may be made in form or in substance to the trustee in accordance with the terms of a written inter vivos trust, including an unfunded life insurance trust although the settlor has reserved all rights of ownership in the insurance contracts, if the trust instrument has been executed and is in existence prior to or contemporaneously with the execution of the will and is identified in the will, without regard to the size or character of the corpus of the trust or whether the settlor is the testator or a third person.

Because a valid trust existed to receive the decedent's residuary estate, the Weisses' claim to these assets as her sole heirs at law fails. For this reason, the judge properly dismissed their petition to remove Clymer as the estate's administrator on the ground that they had no standing to prevail in such an action. General Laws c. 195, §11, which provides for the removal of administrators for failure to perform their duties, is silent on the question of a petitioner's standing. However, in Massachusetts, as elsewhere, "[c]ourts are not established to enable parties to litigate matters in which they have no interest affecting their liberty, rights or property." Hogarth-Swann v. Weed, 274 Mass. 125, 132, 174 N.E. 314 (1931). As a result, only those with a legal interest in the decedent's estate, such as legatees and creditors, have standing to seek removal. Gay v. Richmond, 9 Mass.App. 334, 337, 400 N.E.2d 1325 (1980). See Estate of Richardson, 74 Cal.App.2d 350, 351–352, 168 P.2d 774 (1946); Hogg v. Hogg, 210 Ga. 809, 810, 82 S.E.2d 818 (1954).

The Weisses' reliance on Quincy Trust Co. v. Taylor, 317 Mass. 195, 57 N.E.2d 573 (1944), is misplaced. In Quincy Trust Co., we were asked to reverse the removal of an executrix for "utter neglect of her duty," because the petitioner allegedly lacked standing as a creditor of the estate. Id. at 197, 57 N.E.2d 573. We concluded that we did not need to reach the issue of standing in light of evidence establishing the obvious unsuitability of the executrix. We stated that in such compelling circumstances the court has both a right and a duty to act sua sponte. Id. at 198, 57 N.E.2d 573. In this case, however, the Weisses have produced no evidence to support their charges of misconduct, nor have their briefs and arguments alleged such facts as would require the court to act on its own. Therefore, we affirm the dismissal of their petition to remove Clymer as administrator.

* * *

The judge terminated Trust A upon finding that its purpose—to qualify the trust for an estate tax marital deduction—became impossible to achieve after the Mayos' divorce. Mayo appeals this ruling. It is well established that the Probate Courts are empowered to terminate or reform a trust in whole or in part where its purposes have become impossible to achieve and the settlor did not contemplate continuation of the trust under the new circumstances. Gordon v. Gordon, 332 Mass. 193, 197, 124 N.E.2d 226 (1955). Ames v. Hall, 313 Mass. 33, 37, 46 N.E.2d 403 (1943).

The language the decedent employed in her indenture of trust makes it clear that by setting off Trusts A and B she intended to reduce estate tax liability in compliance with then existing provisions of the Internal Revenue Code. Therefore we have no disagreement with the judge's reasoning. See Putnam v. Putnam, 366 Mass. 261, 267, 316 N.E.2d 729 (1974). However, we add that our reasoning below—that by operation of G.L. c. 191, §9, Mayo has no beneficial interest in the trust—clearly disposes of Mayo's claim to Trust A.

* * *

The judge's decision to uphold Mayo's beneficial interest in Trust B was appealed by the Weisses, as well as by Boston University and Clark University. The judge reasoned that the decedent intended to create a life interest in Mayo when she established Trust B and failed either to revoke or to amend the trust after the couple's divorce. The appellants argue that we should extend the reach of G.L. c. 191, §9, to revoke all Mayo's interests under the trust.[4] General Laws c. 191, §9, as amended through St.1977, c. 76, §2, provides in relevant part:

---

4. None of the parties contests the judge's ruling that G.L. c. 191, §9, revokes those provisions in the decedent's will which benefitted Mayo.

> If, after executing a will, the testator shall be divorced or his marriage shall be annulled, the divorce or annulment shall revoke any disposition or appointment of property made by the will to the former spouse, any provision conferring a general or special power of appointment on the former spouse, and any nomination of the former spouse, as executor, trustee, conservator or guardian, unless the will shall expressly provide otherwise. Property prevented from passing to a former spouse because of revocation by divorce shall pass as if a former spouse had failed to survive the decedent, and other provisions conferring a power of office on the former spouse shall be interpreted as if the spouse had failed to survive the decedent.

The judge ruled that Mayo's interest in Trust B is unaffected by G.L. c. 191, §9, because his interest in that trust is not derived from a "disposition ... made by the will" but rather from the execution of an inter vivos trust with independent legal significance. We disagree, but in fairness we add that the judge here confronted a question of first impression in this Commonwealth.

General Laws c. 191, §9, was amended by the Legislature in 1976 to provide in the event of divorce for the revocation of testamentary dispositions which benefit the testator's former spouse. St.1976, c. 515, §6. The statute automatically causes such revocations unless the testator expresses a contrary intent. In this case we must determine what effect, if any, G.L. c. 191, §9, has on the former spouse's interest in the testator's pour-over trust.

While, by virtue of G.L. c. 203, §3B, the decedent's trust bore independent significance at the time of its creation in 1973, the trust had no practical significance until her death in 1981. The decedent executed both her will and indenture of trust on February 2, 1973. She transferred no property or funds to the trust at that time. The trust was to receive its funding at the decedent's death, in part through her life insurance policy and retirement benefits, and in part through a pour-over from the will's residuary clause. Mayo, the proposed executor and sole legatee under the will, was also made the primary beneficiary of the trust with power, as to Trust A only, to reach both income and principal.

During her lifetime, the decedent retained power to amend or revoke the trust. Since the trust was unfunded, her co-trustee was subject to no duties or obligations until her death. Similarly, it was only as a result of the decedent's death that Mayo could claim any right to the trust assets. It is evident from the time and manner in which the trust was created and funded, that the decedent's will and trust were integrally related components of a single testamentary scheme. For all practical purposes the trust, like the will, "spoke" only at the decedent's death. For this reason Mayo's interest in the trust was revoked by operation of G.L. c. 191, §9, at the same time his interest under the decedent's will was revoked.

It has reasonably been contended that in enacting G.L. c. 191, §9, the Legislature "intended to bring the law into line with the expectations of most people.... Divorce usually represents a stormy parting, where the last thing one of the parties wishes is to have an earlier will carried out giving everything to the former spouse." Young, Probate Reform, 18 Boston B.J. 7, 11 (1974). To carry out the testator's implied intent, the law revokes "any disposition or appointment of property made by the will to the former spouse." It is indisputable that if the decedent's trust was either testamentary or incorporated by reference into her will, Mayo's beneficial interest in the trust would be revoked by operation of the statute. However, the judge stopped short of mandating the same result in this case because here the trust had "independent significance" by virtue of c. 203, § 3B. While correct, this characterization of the trust does not end our analysis. For example, in Sullivan v. Burkin, 390 Mass. 864, 867, 460 N.E.2d 572 (1984), we ruled prospectively that the assets of a revocable trust will be considered part of the "estate of the decedent" in determining the surviving spouse's statutory share.

Treating the components of the decedent's estate plan separately, and not as parts of an interrelated whole, brings about inconsistent results. Applying c. 191, § 9, the judge correctly revoked the will provisions benefiting Mayo. As a result, the decedent's personal property—originally left to Mayo—fell into the will's residuary clause and passed to the trust. The judge then appropriately terminated Trust A for impossibility of purpose thereby denying Mayo his beneficial interest under Trust A. Yet, by upholding Mayo's interest under Trust B, the judge returned to Mayo a life interest in the same assets that composed the corpus of Trust A—both property passing by way of the decedent's will and the proceeds of her TIAA/CREF annuity contracts.

We are aware of only one case concerning the impact of a statute similar to G.L. c. 191, § 9, on trust provisions benefiting a former spouse. In Miller v. First Nat'l Bank & Trust Co., 637 P.2d 75 (Okla.1981), the testator also simultaneously executed an indenture of trust and will naming his spouse as primary beneficiary. As in this case, the trust was to be funded at the testator's death by insurance proceeds and a will pour-over. Subsequently, the testator divorced his wife but failed to change the terms of his will and trust. The District court revoked the will provisions favoring the testator's former wife by applying a statute similar to G.L. c. 191, § 9.[5] Recognizing that "[t]he will without the trust has no meaning or value to the decedent's estate plan," the Oklahoma Supreme Court revoked the trust benefits as well. Id. at 77. However, we do not agree with the court's reasoning. Because the Oklahoma statute, like G.L. c. 191, § 9, revokes dispositions of property made by will, the court stretched the doctrine of incorporation by reference to render the decedent's trust testamentary. We do not agree that reference to an existing trust in a will's pour-over clause is sufficient to incorporate that trust by reference without evidence that the testator intended such a result. See Second Bank-State St. Trust Co. v. Pinion, 341 Mass. 366, 367, 170 N.E.2d 350 (1960). However, it is not necessary for us to indulge in such reasoning, because we have concluded that the legislative intent under G.L. c. 191, § 9, is that a divorced spouse should not take under a trust executed in these circumstances. In the absence of an expressed contrary intent, that statute implies an intent on the part of a testator to revoke will provisions favoring a former spouse. It is incongruous then to ignore that same intent with regard to a trust funded in part through her will's pour-over at the decedent's death.[6] See State St. Bank & Trust v. United States, 634 F.2d 5, 10 (1st Cir.1980) (trust should be interpreted in light of settlor's contemporaneous execution of interrelated will). As one law review commentator has noted, "[t]ransferors use will substitutes to avoid probate, not to

---

5. Oklahoma Stat. tit. 84, § 114 (1982), states in part: "If, after making a will, the testator is divorced, all provisions in such will in favor of the testator's spouse so divorced are thereby revoked."

6. Although we need not and do not rely on it, we note that extraneous evidence received by the judge regarding the deteriorating relationship between the decedent and Mayo during the years following the execution of her trust and before her death is consistent with the result we have reached. This evidence included the terms of the Mayos' divorce settlement, the decedent's stated desire to draw up a new will after her divorce, her comments to friends expressing relief that her marriage had ended, and frictions developing between the Mayos as a result of his remarriage.

avoid the subsidiary law of wills. The subsidiary rules are the product of centuries of legal experience in attempting to discern transferors' wishes and suppress litigation. These rules should be treated as presumptively correct for will substitutes as well as for wills." Langbien, The Nonprobate Revolution and the Future of the Law of Succession, 97 Harv.L.Rev. 1108, 1136–1137 (1984).

Restricting our holding to the particular facts of this case—specifically the existence of a revocable pour-over trust funded entirely at the time of the decedent's death—we conclude that G.L. c. 191, § 9, revokes Mayo's interest under Trust B.[7]

* * *

According to the terms of G.L. c. 191, § 9, "[p]roperty prevented from passing to a former spouse because of revocation by divorce shall pass as if a former spouse had failed to survive the decedent. ..." In this case, the decedent's indenture of trust provides that if Mayo failed to survive her, "the balance of 'Trust B' shall be held ... for the benefit of the nephews and nieces of the Donor living at the time of the death of the Donor." The trustee is directed to expend as much of the net income and principal as he deems "advisable for [their] reasonable comfort, support and education" until all living nephews and nieces have attained the age of thirty. At that time, the trust is to terminate and Boston University and Clark University are each to receive fifty per cent of the trust property to assist women students in their graduate programs.

The decedent had no siblings and therefore no nephews and nieces who were blood relations. * * * However, when she executed her trust in 1973, her husband, James P. Mayo, Jr., had two nephews and one niece—John and Allan Chamberlain and Mira Hinman. Before her divorce, the decedent maintained friendly relations with these young people and, along with her former husband, contributed toward their educational expenses. The three have survived the decedent.

The Weisses, Boston University, and Clark University appeal the decision of the judge upholding the decedent's gift to these three individuals. They argue that at the time the decedent created her trust she had no "nephews and nieces" by blood and that, at her death, her marital ties to Mayo's nephews and niece had been severed by divorce. Therefore, they contend that the class gift to the donor's "nephews and nieces" lapses for lack of identifiable beneficiaries.

The judge concluded that the trust language created an ambiguity, and thus he considered extrinsic evidence of the decedent's meaning and intent. Based upon that evidence, he decided that the decedent intended to provide for her nieces and nephews by marriage when she created the trust. Because the decedent never revoked this gift, he found that the Chamberlains and Hinman are entitled to their beneficial interests under the trust. We agree.

The appellants claim that no ambiguity is presented by the decedent's gift to her "nephews and nieces" and therefore the judge erred in considering extrinsic evidence of the meaning of this phrase. It is axiomatic that "[t]he intent of the testator governs the

---

7. As an alternative ground the appellants argue that the terms of the Mayos' divorce settlement, in which Mayo waived "any right, title or interest" in the assets that later funded the decedent's trust, amount to a disclaimer of his trust interest. We decline to base our holding on such reasoning because a disclaimer of rights "must be clear and unequivocal." Second Bank-State St. Trust Co. v. Yale Univ. Alumni Fund, 338 Mass. 520, 524, 156 N.E.2d 57 (1959), and we find no such disclaimer in the Mayos' divorce agreement.

interpretation of his will." Sullivan v. Roman Catholic Archbishop of Boston, 368 Mass. 253, 257, 331 N.E.2d 57 (1975). See G.L. c. 191, § 1A. It is equally well established that we "ascertain the intention of the testator from the whole instrument, attributing due weight to all its language, considered in the light of the circumstances known to him at the time of its execution and to give effect to that intent unless some positive rule of law forbids." Fitts v. Powell, 307 Mass. 449, 454, 30 N.E.2d 377 (1940). Gustafson v. Svenson, 373 Mass. 273, 275, 366 N.E.2d 761 (1977). Where "a reading of the whole will produces a conviction that the testator must necessarily have intended an interest to be given which is not bequeathed or devised by express or formal words, the court must supply the defect by implication and so mould the language of the testator as to carry into effect as far as possible the intention which it is of opinion that he has sufficiently declared." Fitts, supra.

The judge was thus well within his discretion in considering the facts and circumstances known to the decedent at the time she executed her indenture of trust. The purpose of his inquiry was not to alter but to explain the language of the trust. Extrinsic evidence is admissible for this purpose even where no ambiguity is presented. Smith, The Admissibility of Extrinsic Evidence in Will Interpretation Cases, 64 Mass.L.Rev. 123 (1979). In fact, however, the decedent's bequest created a latent ambiguity. The gift to the "nephews and nieces of the Donor" posed problems in the identification of the intended donees. See Putnam v. Putnam, 366 Mass. 261, 266, 316 N.E.2d 729 (1974); Hardy v. Smith, 136 Mass. 328 (1884); Dane v. Walker, 109 Mass. 179 (1872). The relevant evidence included the decedent's lack of siblings, her relationship to Mayo's nephews and niece, and her contributions to their education. Combining these facts with the language used by the decedent, it is clear that the Chamberlains and Hinman were her intended beneficiaries.

* * *

The appellants reject these authorities on the ground that the Mayos' divorce left the decedent without any nephews and nieces—by blood or marriage—at the time of her death. They argue that even if the decedent had intended to provide for the Chamberlains and Hinman when she executed her indenture of trust, we should rule that the Mayos' divorce somehow "revoked" this gift. According to Boston University, since the beneficiaries are identified by their relationship to the decedent through her marriage and not by name, we should presume that the decedent no longer intended to benefit her former relatives once her marriage ended. General Laws c. 191, § 9, does not provide the authority for revoking gifts to the blood relatives of a former spouse. The law implies an intent to revoke testamentary gifts between the divorcing parties because of the profound emotional and financial changes divorce normally engenders. There is no indication in the statutory language that the Legislature presumed to know how these changes affect a testator's relations with more distant family members. We therefore conclude that the Chamberlains and Hinman are entitled to take as the decedent's "nephews and nieces" under Trust B.

* * *

Pursuant to G.L. c. 215, § 39B,[9] the judge ordered payment out of the decedent's estate of counsel fees totalling $43,500. Although his order was not accompanied by find-

---

9. General Laws c. 215, § 39B, as appearing in St.1975, c. 400, § 70, states in relevant part: When a judgment or decree is entered in a contested proceeding seeking equitable relief or on an account or to determine the construction of a will or of any trust instrument..., the probate court may, in its discretion as justice and equity may require, provide that such sums as said court may deem reasonable be paid out of the estate ... to any party to

ings or rulings, we conclude, in light of the representations of the parties and the established law, that the judge did not take into consideration all relevant criteria in determining his fee award.

An important factor in assessing the reasonableness of fees awarded in probate cases is the size of the estate. See McMahon v. Krapf, 323 Mass. 118, 123, 80 N.E.2d 314 (1948); Cummings v. National Shawmut Bank, 284 Mass. 563, 569, 188 N.E. 489 (1933). It is a long-standing principle that the judge is to "take into consideration … the amount in controversy, and … prevent the fund from being either entirely or in great part absorbed by counsel fees." Frost v. Belmont, 6 Allen 152, 165 (1863). Accordingly, we have stated that where fees are paid to counsel "who may not have been employed by those whose estates are thus diminished" they are to be awarded on "strictly conservative principles." Holyoke Nat'l Bank v. Wilson, 350 Mass. 223, 230, 214 N.E.2d 42 (1966), quoting Hayden v. Hayden, 326 Mass. 587, 596, 96 N.E.2d 136 (1950). An excessive fee award may itself defeat the decedent's intent by depleting her estate.

According to the testimony of the court-appointed administrator, John Clymer, the value of the decedent's "adjusted gross estate," i.e., undiminished by any estate or inheritance taxes or other governmental charges, stood at approximately $249,000 at the time of the fee award. He stated that he arrived at this estimate after deducting various administrative expenses, as well as counsel fees for the fiduciaries.[10] Assuming that Mayo did not take under the trust, Clymer estimated that the balance of Trust B, after taxes and additional payments, would amount to approximately $100,000. * * * Out of that $100,000, all other attorneys' fees would have to be paid.

* * *

In sum, we conclude that the decedent established a valid trust under G.L. c. 203, § 3B; Mayo's beneficial interest in Trust A and Trust B is revoked by operation of G.L. c. 191, § 9; the Chamberlains and Hinman are entitled to take the interest given to the decedent's "nephews and nieces" under Trust B, leaving the remainder to Clark University and Boston University; the Weisses lack standing to remove the estate administrator; and the judge's award of attorneys' fees is vacated and remanded for reconsideration.

So ordered.

Notes

The case is fascinating because it invites consideration of a modern estate plan, the validity of pour over devices and the challenges they have faced, and the comparison of revocability of inter vivos and testamentary devices. Indeed, the case also considers remedies for mistake and a few of the consequences of divorce, see UNIF. PROB. CODE § 2-804 (2003) (revocation of probate and non-probate transfers by divorce). As a result of legislation, the traditional doctrines of incorporation by reference or facts of independent significance are no longer needed to validate pour over from a Last Will and Testament into an unfunded inter vivos revocable trust.

---

the proceeding on account of counsel fees and other expenses incurred by him in connection therewith.

10. The judge awarded counsel fees of $3,200 to Mira Hinman's guardian ad litem, $4,650 to John Clymer, and $3,000 to the attorney for trustee John Hill.

Today the revocable inter vivos trust is a familiar tool to estate planning attorneys because: (1) it provides the ability to avoid probate, thereby guaranteeing a significant savings in costs, since any assets already placed in the inter vivos trust do not pass according to a Last Will and Testament; (2) property passes quickly, since there is no administration; (3) there is no necessity for publication and disclosure of who got what and how, since the inter vivos trust does not have to pass through the probate procedure; (4) the law of another jurisdiction may be applied—community property rather than common law, for example—and there is no possibility of a change in applicable law, even if the jurisdiction should change; (5) there are far fewer contests because no Last Will and Testament is being probated; (6) ancillary probate is avoided; and (7) more than one party—perhaps two spouses—can create the revocable trust to accommodate their own lifestyles and to provide in a specific way for surviving beneficiaries. The revocable inter vivos trust has few advantages when it comes to the right of the surviving spouse and elective share, *see* UNIF. PROB. CODE § 2-205 (2003), creditors, *see* State Street Bank & Trust Co. v. Reiser, *infra*, or under estate tax laws, *see* I.R.C. §§ 2036 & 2038 (2004).

Because of its advantages, revocable inter vivos trusts have become prolific, *see Restatement (Third) of Trusts* § 25 (2003), far surpassing the nascent origin prophesied by Norman F. Dacey's How TO AVOID PROBATE, which was first published in 1965. *See also* John H. Langbein, *The Nonprobate Revolution and the Future of the Law of Succession,* 97 HARV. L. REV. 1125 (1984). But with the popularity of revocable inter vivos trusts have come professional responsibility issues and concern over the unauthorized practice of law by non-attorneys. These concerns have prompted legislation. *See, e.g.,* 815 Ill. COMP. STAT. ANN. § 505/2BB (2004) (Assembly, drafting, execution and funding of living trust documents by corporations or nonlawyers). Consider the following decisions.

Committee on Professional Ethics v. Baker

Supreme Court of Iowa, 1992
492 N.W.2d 695

LAVORATO, Justice.

Before us is a report of the Grievance Commission recommending that attorney William D. Baker be reprimanded.

The commission found that Baker acted unethically in the following ways: aiding the unauthorized practice of law; permitting others to influence his professional judgment in providing legal services to clients referred to him, resulting in conflicts of interest; and accepting improper referrals.

Baker is a sole practitioner and has practiced law in Des Moines since 1967. He focuses primarily on real estate, probate, estate planning, and trusts.

Rex Voegtlin is a certified financial planner and sole shareholder of Diversified Resource Management, Inc., located in West Des Moines. During 1989 and 1990 Voegtlin was presenting seminars in which he touted living trusts as an estate planning device. (Living or loving trusts have been promoted as a way of avoiding probate.) One of Voegtlin's advertisements concerning these seminars is in evidence. The ad urges people to attend and learn "how to avoid probate and minimize estate taxes with an estate plan that includes a living trust." In a newsletter—also in evidence—Voegtlin condemns probate as too expensive and time consuming.

In 1989 James Miller, a lawyer, was a trust officer for Hawkeye Bank and Trust of Des Moines, a former client of Baker's. In the summer of that year Miller attended one of Voegtlin's seminars and met him for the first time. Sometime after that meeting the two agreed to work jointly in putting on Voegtlin's seminars. Miller's reason for doing so was to attract new business for his bank. The two conducted about eight to ten of these joint seminars from October 1989 to May or June 1990, when Miller quit. About 90 to 100 people attended the first three or four of these seminars. From that point on attendance fell to about 50 or 60.

Shortly before Miller agreed to these joint seminars, he and Voegtlin met with Baker in August 1989. Miller knew Baker because Baker had previously done work for the bank. Miller and Voegtlin asked Baker if he would accept referrals from them. Baker said he was interested but wanted to have several questions answered. Partly for that reason, Miller and Baker attended a seminar in Colorado to see how a living trust seminar might work.

Thereafter, Miller, on behalf of the bank, and Voegtlin agreed to cosponsor seminars on living trusts. Baker told the two he would accept referrals from them for the preparation of living trusts and related documents, and he began doing so in the fall of 1989.

After Baker agreed to accept referrals from Voegtlin and Miller, he attended one seminar the two put on in October 1989. The seminar dealt generally with estate planning and more specifically with the use of a living trust as a way to avoid probate.

Over time the seminars and referrals developed this way. Voegtlin would advertise a free seminar in which the benefits of a living trust would be explained. Voegtlin and Miller would divide up the time during which each would speak. Voegtlin would close the seminar by offering free individual consultations. Usually about half of those attending would seek individual consultations. They did so by filling out a form giving their names, addresses, phone numbers, and their desire for the consultation. The forms were left with Voegtlin who would then follow up and arrange the consultations.

Before the consultations, these "clients"—as Voegtlin described them—would complete a general information planning form in which they would list their names, addresses, family members, and assets. At the consultations, which were held in Voegtlin's office, the clients would present the form at which point Voegtlin and Miller would review it as well as the clients' goals. The primary goal was, of course, to avoid probate.

Voegtlin and Miller would then talk about the various estate planning options the clients had. They would discuss the living trust in a general way—what it can do and what it cannot do. Voegtlin would diagram on a blackboard how a living trust works. The use of marital trusts, family trusts, and generation-skipping trusts was explained— how they worked and how they fit into an estate plan. The diagram would be individualized to include the clients' beneficiaries by name and the names of the trustees.

Voegtlin would also diagram how a will works so the clients could understand the difference between a living trust and a will. Voegtlin would then take a Polaroid picture of the diagrams and give it to the clients. Miller would talk about the duties of a bank trustee and what a bank does on a day-to-day basis when acting as a trustee.

Eventually during the consultations, Voegtlin, Miller, and the clients would reach a consensus as to which estate plan was best for the clients. By this time Voegtlin and Miller had made a determination as to which documents would be necessary to carry out the estate plan.

At this point Voegtlin and Miller would tell the clients that the clients needed to employ a licensed attorney to prepare the documents. If the clients had an attorney, the two would suggest that the clients' attorney be employed. If the clients had no attorney, the two would give the clients a list of attorneys to consider. Baker was among those attorneys listed. The two told the clients that most clients chose Baker because he was a competent attorney, his fees were reasonable, and he was prompt. The evidence shows that from October 1989 through October 1991, Baker accepted about 100 of these referrals. Fewer than ten were received by other attorneys.

Frequently Voegtlin would telephone Baker during the consultations. Voegtlin would tell him that the clients who were there wanted to proceed with the living trust and wanted him to do the legal work. Voegtlin would use a speaker phone so that the clients could also talk to Baker. Voegtlin would remain and listen to the conversation.

Sometimes Voegtlin would not follow this procedure. Instead Voegtlin or Miller would bring the materials discussed at the consultations to Baker and ask if he would accept the referral. A few times clients themselves would go to Baker's office with the materials. The materials would include (1) a copy of the financial form, (2) a general outline of the terms to be included in the clients' living trust, and (3) a description of other necessary documents.

Baker would then call the clients to go over their materials and discuss any questions that either he or they might have. Baker would ask if they were still interested. Some were; others were not. If the clients expressed an interest in proceeding, Baker would tell them that he would prepare a draft of what they wanted and send the draft to them for their review. If the clients did not proceed, Baker would not charge them for any work he might have done for them.

If the clients wanted to proceed, Baker would tell them to bring the trust documents to a meeting at Voegtlin's office. At the meeting Baker would go through the documents and explain them to the clients. Voegtlin was often, but not always, at these meetings. The clients executed the documents at these meetings unless corrections were necessary. If corrections were necessary, the corrections were made and the documents were either executed then or later.

There were times when the clients met Baker at his office. Those times occurred when the clients did not want to involve Voegtlin or the bank.

Not surprisingly, the documents frequently named Voegtlin or Diversified as the person to fund the trust. Voegtlin's wife—also a certified financial planner—usually performed this task. Funding the trust simply means having the clients sign whatever forms or documents that are necessary to transfer personal property from the clients' names to the living trust. Voegtlin's fee for funding the trust and financial advice related to this task was $1000. The advice, for example, might include recommending exchanging a low-interest producing asset for a higher-interest producing one.

In May 1990 Voegtlin asked Baker to furnish him with a sample living trust and accompanying documents that Baker was using for the clients Voegtlin and Miller were referring to him. Voegtlin told Baker he wanted sample documents to show clients who were interested in seeing what Baker's trust looked like. Voegtlin apparently used these documents in his seminars.

The sample living trust and the accompanying documents are in evidence. The accompanying documents included a "Declaration of Trust Ownership," a "Power of Attorney," a "Special Power of Attorney," an "Anatomical Gift," a "Declaration Relating to [the] Use of Life-Sustaining Procedures," a "Petition for Appointment of Guardian (Standby)," a "Declaration of Gift Memorandum," and a "Supplemental Financial Planning Letter." Miller's bank is named in the power of attorney form. The special power of attorney form designates Voegtlin as the attorney-in-fact. The supplemental financial planning letter contains, among other provisions, the following:

> *Financial Planner: This document and related instruments were recommended by Mr. Rex Voegtlin, Certified Financial Planner and Registered Investment Adviser.* He was instrumental in developing a financial and investment framework for my living will as well as death estate. Since Mr. Voegtlin is familiar with my financial planning goals, it is my wish that you notify him upon my demise to help coordinate a smooth financial transition of my invested estate. His address is 1415 28th Street, Suite 110, West Des Moines, Iowa 50265.

(Emphasis added.)

On December 8, 1989, two members of the Commission on the Unauthorized Practice of Law (UPC), a commission established by this court, met with Miller, several bank officials, and Baker. The purpose of the meeting was to determine who actually prepared the living trust documents and to discuss certain misleading statements about Iowa probate fees made in the brochure distributed at the seminars. Miller assured the two UPC members that Baker prepared the living trust documents. Baker concurred. Miller also assured them that the attendees at the seminar who were interested in living trusts were urged to use their attorneys. If they had none they were encouraged to use Baker. Finally, Miller assured the two UPC members that he would continue to urge all attendees to use attorneys to review or prepare all legal instruments. Miller agreed to quit distributing the misleading brochures at the seminars.

Several weeks later one of the two UPC members wrote Miller a letter summarizing what Miller had said. The letter also informed Miller that "[i]n light of our discussion the [UPC] anticipates no further formal action at this time."

In July 1990 the Committee on Professional Ethics and Conduct of the Iowa State Bar Association published interpreting opinions 90-1 and 90-2. Formal opinion 90-32 was published in November 1990. The subject of each opinion was the marketing of living trusts. Opinion 90-32 stated that it was improper for Iowa lawyers to participate in living trust programs like those conducted by Diversified. After publication of opinions 90-1 and 90-2, Baker was the only attorney who continued accepting referrals from Voegtlin.

In February 1991 two members of the UPC met with Baker concerning its investigation of Voegtlin and Diversified. At Baker's disciplinary hearing, one of the two investigating UPC members testified this way:

> Q. According to Mr. Baker, would he attend the first meeting between the client and Mr. Voegtlin? A. The way I understood the process is Mr. Voegtlin would get the client initially interested at the seminars. Mr. Voegtlin would then meet with the individual without Mr. Baker, another attorney present, and discuss what the client needed, what legal documents would be prepared, whether they need a will, a living trust, guardianship, standby guardianship, a trust. And then Mr. Baker would be called in to draw up the documents, but he was not usually in attendance at that first meeting.

Q. So it was your understanding from Mr. Baker that Mr. Voegtlin would discuss at the initial meeting with the client what types of instruments would be needed? A. Yes, and advise the client what the standard package was and what were the varieties of changes they might need for their particular situation.

* * *

Q. Would it be fair to say, based on the information that Mr. Baker gave you, that Mr. Voegtlin would tell Mr. Baker specific documents that would be needed in a given situation? A. That was my understanding, that they had sort of a standard package of documents that Mr. Baker indicated were developed early on that he got from Hawkeye Bank when Hawkeye Bank was involved in doing these trusts, that he had modified them in some respects but the basic package of documents Mr. Baker had and then at Mr. Voegtlin's direction would decide we need will A or will B or trust A or trust B or whatever type was needed.

* * *

Q. ... When does it say Voegtlin's doing this? A. My understanding was that Mr. Voegtlin, when he called Mr. Baker, would tell him that "We need pour-over will A," or, "We need pour-over will B," or, "We need just A or B," and described the client's specific situation and that Voegtlin was giving the legal advice and directing him as to what documents to prepare.

* * *

Q. When you talked with Mr. Baker about what he might recommend to clients, did he tell you that he merely explained the pros and cons of living trusts to the clients and let them make up their own mind, or did he say that he recommended living trusts to his clients? ... A. My understanding is by the time that the people got to Mr. Baker that it was a done deal, in that the decisions had already been discussed with Mr. Voegtlin about what they needed, that they needed the living trust, and that he basically then prepared the documents for their signature.

* * *

Q. Was there any discussion with Mr. Baker as to whether when he got a referral from Mr. Voegtlin he ever recommended anything to them other than the living trust? A. That was one thing I was curious about, is whether as an attorney he was exercising some independent judgment on these clients, and I asked him about that, and he had indicated that he had about 50 to 60 referrals from Mr. Voegtlin over what I understood to be some time period from about 1989, and he indicated he had never suggested to the client that the living trust was not appropriate for their situation.

Baker also told the two UPC investigating members he was worried that he might be aiding in the unauthorized practice of law and might be accepting improper referrals. The two urged Baker to seek an opinion about his concerns from the Committee on Professional Ethics and Conduct.

In March 1991 Baker did write to this committee raising his concerns about opinion 90-32. Baker requested guidance on variations of the scenarios discussed and published in that opinion. Of course, these variations concerned his business referral relationship with Voegtlin.

In May 1991 Baker heard back from the committee. The committee wrote Baker a letter in which it refused to provide him an advisory opinion about his inquiry. This refusal was premised on the rules of the committee, which permit advisory opinions only in "proposed actions of members of the bar." The letter informed Baker that his request was confined to past and/or continuing actions, effectively foreclosing an advisory opinion from that body. The committee, however, did advise Baker that what he described might "involve impropriety and should be reviewed." The committee closed by asking for more information. Baker responded shortly thereafter, providing greater details about Voegtlin's referrals to him.

In April 1991 two members of the UPC met with Voegtlin and his attorney about procedures Voegtlin used in recommending living trusts and referring legal matters. The UPC did not make a determination that Voegtlin was involved in the unauthorized practice of law. Apparently, the UPC is delaying its determination because of this disciplinary proceeding against Baker. The UPC has, however, referred the matter to the attorney general's office for investigation of consumer fraud.

The Committee on Professional Ethics and Conduct filed a complaint against Baker in October 1991. The complaint alleges that Baker's involvement with Voegtlin in the living trust marketing scheme violated several disciplinary rules and ethical considerations of the Iowa Code of Professional Responsibility for Lawyers and formal opinion 90-32.

The record made in the hearing before the commission included the complaint, the committee's requests for admission, witness testimony, and exhibits. Baker responded affirmatively to the majority of both requests for admission and testified in his own behalf.

After finding that the allegations of the complaint were true, the commission recommended that Baker be publicly reprimanded for (1) aiding in the unauthorized practice of law; (2) permitting others to influence his professional judgment in providing legal services to clients referred to him, resulting in a conflict of interest; and (3) accepting improper referrals.

The committee must prove the allegations of the complaint by a convincing preponderance of the evidence. *Committee on Professional Ethics & Conduct v. Lawler*, 342 N.W.2d 486, 487 (Iowa 1984). Although Baker did not appeal, we still review de novo the record made before the commission. Iowa Sup.Ct.R. 118.10. We independently decide the matter and take appropriate action on it. *Id.* In our review we consider the findings of fact made by the commission but are not bound by them. *Committee on Professional Ethics & Conduct v. Conzett*, 476 N.W.2d 43, 44 (Iowa 1991).

* * *

We first turn our attention to the commission's finding that Baker aided Voegtlin in the unauthorized practice of law. Whether we agree with this finding requires a two step analysis. First, did Voegtlin's actions constitute the unauthorized practice of law? If so, did Baker aid those actions?

A. *Voegtlin's actions.* This court has refrained from attempting an all-inclusive definition of the practice of law. Rather it decides each case in this area largely on its own particular facts. *Bump v. Barnett*, 235 Iowa 308, 315, 16 N.W.2d 579, 583 (1944). EC 3-5 of the Iowa Code of Professional Responsibility for Lawyers takes the same tack: "It is neither necessary nor desirable to attempt the formulation of a single, specific definition of what constitutes the practice of law." EC 3-5.

However, EC 3-5 goes on to tell us what the practice of law includes:

However, the practice of law includes, but is not limited to, representing another before the courts; giving of legal advice and counsel to others relating to their rights and obligations under the law; and preparation or *approval of the use of legal instruments by which legal rights of others are either obtained, secured or transferred* even if such matters never become the subject of a court proceeding. Functionally, the practice of law relates to the rendition of services for others that call for the professional judgment of a lawyer. The essence of the professional judgment of the lawyer is his educated ability to relate the general body and philosophy of law to a specific legal problem of a client; and thus, the public interest will be better served if only lawyers are permitted to act in matters involving professional judgment. Where this professional judgment is not involved, nonlawyers, such as court clerks, police officers, abstracters, and many governmental employees, may engage in occupations that require a special knowledge of law in certain areas. But the services of a lawyer are essential in the public interest whenever the exercise of professional legal judgment is required.

(Emphasis added.)

In short, the practice of law includes the obvious: representing another before the court. But the practice of law includes out-of-court services as well. For example, one who gives legal advice about a person's rights and obligations under the law is practicing law. Or one who prepares legal instruments affecting the rights of others is practicing law. Or one who approves the use of legal instruments affecting the rights of others is practicing law.

Practically speaking, professional judgment lies at the core of the practice of law. When lawyers use their educated ability to apply an area of the law to solve a specific problem of a client, they are exercising professional judgment. The phrase "educated ability" in EC 3-5 refers to the system of analysis lawyers learn in law school. They learn to recognize issues first and then how to solve those issues in an ethical manner, using their knowledge of the law. See EC 3-2 ("Competent professional judgment is the product of a trained familiarity with law and legal processes, a disciplined, analytical approach to legal problems, and a firm ethical commitment."). The practice of law is no different: lawyers determine what the issues are and use their knowledge of the law to solve them in an ethical way. This is the art of exercising professional judgment.

In contrast, nonlawyers who use their knowledge of the law for informational purposes alone are not exercising a lawyer's professional judgment. For example, an abstracter must have knowledge of what constitutes a lien on real estate. An abstracter uses this knowledge, which is legal in nature, when the abstracter shows the lien in the abstract of title. In doing so, the abstracter is simply furnishing the title examiner—a lawyer—information that the lawyer needs in advising the client on the marketability of title. In this scenario, the abstracter is simply furnishing information; the title examiner is exercising professional judgment on a legal question. The abstracter is not practicing law; the title examiner is.

From the evidence in this case, it is clear that Voegtlin's actions met one of the practicing law tests articulated in EC 3-5: "approval of the use of legal instruments by which legal rights of others are either obtained, secured or transferred." Voegtlin met with the clients. He advised them about what they needed in the way of estate planning. He advised them in particular about what documents they would need and how those documents would need to be tailored to meet their particular situation. In the words of one UPC investigator, by the time the clients got to Baker "it was a done deal." Baker was merely a scrivener. Voegtlin had already made the major decisions; he, rather than

Baker, was exercising professional judgment. The "smoking gun" on this point is found in the supplemental financial planning letter. This document acknowledges that the financial planning letter and related instruments were recommended by Voegtlin.

Voegtlin's actions fit neatly into what one court considered to be the unauthorized practice of law:

> Giving legal advice, directly or indirectly to individuals or groups concerning the application, preparation, advisability or quality of any legal instrument or document or forms thereof in connection with the disposition of property inter vivos or upon death, including inter vivos trusts and wills.

In re the Florida Bar, 215 So.2d 613, 613–14 (Fla.1968) (per curiam) (petition by state bar and securities broker to determine whether certain activities of securities broker constituted the unauthorized practice of law). We adopt this test as a supplement to EC 3-5 and as an expanded definition of the practice of law.

For all of these reasons, we agree with the commission that Voegtlin was engaged in the unauthorized practice of law.

B. *Baker's actions.* DR 3-101(A) prohibits a lawyer from aiding a nonlawyer in the unauthorized practice of law. EC 3-1 exhorts the legal profession to actively discourage the unauthorized practice of law. EC 3-3 reminds lawyers that the disciplinary rules prohibit a lawyer from submitting to the control of others in the exercise of the lawyer's judgment. EC 3-4 also reminds lawyers that "[p]roper protection of members of the public demands that no person be permitted to act in the confidential and demanding capacity of a lawyer unless he is subject to the regulations of the legal profession."

We agree with the commission that in one way or another Baker violated DR 3-101(A), EC 3-1, EC 3-3, and EC 3-4. From our review of the record, we see Voegtlin's seminars, his newsletters, and his referrals to Baker as nothing more than a scheme on Voegtlin's part to reap substantial fees. Indeed, he targeted clients having estates in excess of $600,000. The scheme worked because Voegtlin preached through his seminars and newsletters that clients should use a living trust because our probate system "takes too long and is too expensive." Voegtlin controlled the whole process from the initial interview to the final meeting when the clients executed the documents in his office. He did so by recommending the living trust, the necessary tailored documents to effectuate it, and a lawyer who he believed would not counsel against his advice. In fact, when Voegtlin sold clients on a living trust, Baker never once counseled against using it.

Instead of discouraging Voegtlin from these actions, Baker actually encouraged them in a number of ways. First, Baker allowed Voegtlin to exercise the professional judgment Baker should have exercised. Second, Baker allowed Voegtlin to act in a confidential capacity with the clients who were referred to Baker. Third, Baker furnished Voegtlin with forms to be used at his seminar. Fourth, Baker accepted approximately 100 referrals from Voegtlin. Last, Baker gave Voegtlin advice on his newsletters.

Our experience with "living trusts" teaches us that they may be a very poor substitute for probate. Unlike probate fees, the fees charged by nonlawyers like Voegtlin who tout living trusts are not subject to court scrutiny. Lack of court scrutiny can easily lead to unnecessary and excessive fees.[1] The point is whether a living trust is appropriate in a given case calls for the exercise of independent professional judgment by a lawyer.

---

1. Recent action taken by the Illinois attorney general has focused on these potentials for abuse. He has sued a group selling living trusts kits to elderly people in Illinois. He alleges that the group

* * *

The commission found that Baker permitted Voegtlin to influence his professional judgment in providing legal services to clients referred to Baker, resulting in a conflict of interest.

This finding is predicated on alleged violations of DR 5-107(B) and EC 5-1.

DR 5-107(B) provides:

> *A lawyer shall not permit a person who recommends, employs, or pays him to render legal services for another to direct or regulate his professional judgment in rendering such legal services.*

(Emphasis added.)

EC 5-1 provides:

> The professional judgment of a lawyer should be exercised, within the bounds of the law, solely for the benefit of his client and free of compromising influences and loyalties. Neither his personal interests, the interests of other clients, *nor the desires of third persons should be permitted to dilute his loyalty to his client.*

(Emphasis added.)

The commission found sufficient evidence to establish a violation of DR 5-107(B) and EC 5-1. We agree.

We have already found that Voegtlin, not Baker, exercised professional judgment as to the appropriateness of a living trust and the particular documents necessary to effectuate it. We have also referred to the reasons why Voegtlin promoted living trusts. All of this is another way of saying that Baker permitted Voegtlin to "direct or regulate his professional judgment" in rendering legal services to the referred clients. DR 5-107(B).

All of this is also another way of saying that Baker permitted Voegtlin's desires to "dilute [Baker's] loyalty to his client[s]." EC 5-1. Like the commission, we find that the prospect of receiving additional referrals constituted the "compromising influences" mentioned in EC 5-1. The number of referrals was many—approximately 100 in all. And the fees generated by them were substantial—approximately $40,000 in total. It is significant to us that Baker came to eventually realize that he was the only lawyer receiving these referrals, and that fact bothered him.

* * *

The commission found that Baker accepted improper referrals in violation of formal opinion 90-32. As we said earlier in division I(B) of this opinion, the referrals were one way Baker aided Voegtlin in the unauthorized practice of law. We offer no opinion on the validity of formal opinion 90-32. We think it would be inappropriate to peg an ethical violation on this opinion for several reasons. First, the opinion is based in part on a disciplinary rule that we hesitate to say has any application to this case. Second, al-

---

has engaged in the unauthorized practice of law and has violated the state's consumer fraud law. Among other things, he alleges that the group is charging as much as $2999 for services which could be obtained at a much lower cost. He has characterized the group's actions as "using a 'one-size-fits-all' approach, [selling] living trusts to individuals for whom the documents [are] neither appropriate nor necessary." David N. Anderson, AG Joins ISBA's 'Living Trust' Battle, Ill.St.B.Ass'n B.News, October 15, 1992, at 1.

though we express no opinion one way or the other, we hesitate to approve the practice of charging an attorney with the violation of a formal opinion. Last, the referrals were inextricably intertwined with the unauthorized practice of law issue. Any discipline resulting from accepting improper referrals should therefore be limited to the allegations of aiding in the unauthorized practice of law.

* * *

Until this court speaks, generally it is not clear what constitutes the practice of law in a particular set of circumstances. We agree with one writer's assessment of this problem:

> Because of the marked lack of precision in the definition of unauthorized practice, it would be intolerable to hold a lawyer to a prophet's standard of clairvoyance about unclear areas of practice in a jurisdiction.

C.W. Wolfram, Modern Legal Ethics 846 (1986). What is implicated here is a potential issue of fair notice. Our rules on the unauthorized practice of law resolve this problem of fair notice by authorizing the UPC to seek an injunction if it believes a person is engaged in the unauthorized practice of law. See Unauthorized Practice of Law Commission Rule 118A.1. Such a person will then be on notice of what specific conduct is prohibited before that person is punished. These reasons, in part, convince us that any discipline here in excess of a reprimand would not be appropriate.

Four additional facts enter our decision on discipline here. First, Baker has for many years enjoyed an excellent reputation as an active practicing lawyer. Second, Baker fully cooperated with all investigations related to the complaint. Third, no client referred by Voegtlin (1) complained about any living trust or other documents Baker prepared or (2) suffered any financial loss based upon these documents. Last, Baker sought clarification from the committee before the complaint was filed and received no satisfaction. Instead, the committee filed the complaint.

We do not condone Baker's behavior in this matter. He was ill-advised to continue accepting referrals from Voegtlin when it became apparent that such conduct might be improper. What he should have done is to follow the old ethics adage, "if you have doubt, don't do it." Baker did the opposite. We view his past professional judgment as misguided, and we expect him to guard against even the appearance of impropriety in his future professional relationships.

We reprimand Baker for aiding Voegtlin in the unauthorized practice of law and for allowing Voegtlin to direct or regulate Baker's professional judgment in rendering legal services to Baker's clients.

Costs are assessed to Baker under Iowa Supreme Court Rule 118.22.

ATTORNEY REPRIMANDED.

State Street Bank & Trust Co. v. Reiser

Massachusetts Appeals Court, 1979
7 Mass. App. Ct. 633, 389 N.E.2d 768

KASS, Justice.

State Street Bank and Trust Company (the bank) seeks to reach the assets of an inter vivos trust in order to pay a debt to the bank owed by the estate of the settlor of the trust. We conclude that the bank can do so.

* * *

Wilfred A. Dunnebier created an inter vivos trust on September 30, 1971, with power to amend or revoke the trust and the right during his lifetime to direct the disposition of principal and income. He conveyed to the trust the capital stock of five closely held corporations. Immediately following execution of this trust, Dunnebier executed a will under which he left his residuary estate to the trust he had established.

About thirteen months later Dunnebier applied to the bank for a $75,000 working capital loan. A bank officer met with Dunnebier, examined a financial statement furnished by him and visited several single family home subdivisions which Dunnebier, or corporations he controlled, had built or were in the process of building. During their conversations, Dunnebier told the bank officer that he had controlling interests in the corporations which owned the most significant assets appearing on the financial statement. On the basis of what he saw of Dunnebier's work, recommendations from another bank, Dunnebier's borrowing history with the bank, and the general cut of Dunnebier's jib, the bank officer decided to make an unsecured loan to Dunnebier for the $75,000 he had asked for. To evidence this loan, Dunnebier, on November 1, 1972, signed a personal demand note to the order of the bank. The probate judge found that Dunnebier did not intend to defraud the bank or misrepresent his financial position by failing to call attention to the fact that he had placed the stock of his corporations in the trust.

Approximately four months after he borrowed this money Dunnebier died in an accident. His estate has insufficient assets to pay the entire indebtedness due the bank.

Under Article Fourteen of his inter vivos trust, Dunnebier's trustees " ... may in their sole discretion pay from the principal and income of this Trust Estate any and all debts and expenses of administration of the Settlor's estate." The bank urges that, since the inter vivos trust was part of an estate plan in which the simultaneously executed will was an integrated document, the instruction in Dunnebier's will that his executor pay his debts * * * should be read into the trust instrument. This must have been Dunnebier's intent, goes the argument.

Leaving to one side whether the precatory language in the will could be read as mandatory, and whether the language of that separate, albeit related, instrument, constitutes a surrounding circumstance (see Hull v. Adams, 286 Mass. 329, 333, 190 N.E. 510 (1934); Dumaine v. Dumaine, 301 Mass. 214, 218, 16 N.E.2d 625 (1938)) which could guide us in interpreting the trust, * * * we find the trust agreement manifests no such intent by Dunnebier. Article Fourteen speaks of the sole discretion of the trustees. Subparagraphs A and B of Article Five, by contrast, direct the trustees unconditionally to pay two $15,000 legacies provided for in Dunnebier's will if his estate has insufficient funds to do so. It is apparent that when Dunnebier wanted his trustees unqualifiedly to discharge his estate's obligations, he knew how to direct them. As to those matters which Dunnebier, as settlor, left to the sole discretion of his trustees, we are not free to substitute our judgment for theirs as to what is wise or most to our taste. The court will substitute its discretion only on those relatively rare occasions when it is necessary to prevent an abuse of discretion. Sylvester v. Newton, 321 Mass. 416, 421–422, 73 N.E.2d 585 (1947); Nexon v. Boston Safe Deposit and Trust Co., 5 Mass.App. —, — — — * * *, 364 N.E.2d 1077 (1977). Restatement (Second) of Trusts § 187 (1959) (see particularly comment (j), which says that where such adjectives as "absolute" or "unlimited" or "uncontrolled" modify the word "discretion" the trustees may act unreasonably, so long as not dishonestly or from a motive other than the accomplishment of the purposes of the trust). Here, the trustees could have considered preservation of the trust corpus for the benefit of the beneficiaries as most consistent with the trust purpose.

During the lifetime of the settlor, to be sure, the bank would have had access to the assets of the trust. When a person creates for his own benefit a trust for support or a discretionary trust, his creditors can reach the maximum amount which the trustee, under the terms of the trust, could pay to him or apply for his benefit. Ware v. Gulda, 331 Mass. 68, 70, 117 N.E.2d 137 (1954). Restatement (Second) of Trusts § 156(2) (1959). This is so even if the trust contains spendthrift provisions. Pacific Natl. Bank v. Windram, 133 Mass. 175, 176–177 (1882). Merchants Natl. Bank v. Morrissey, 329 Mass. 601, 605, 109 N.E.2d 821 (1953). Restatement (Second) of Trusts § 156(1) (1959). Under the terms of Dunnebier's trust, all the income and principal were at his disposal while he lived.

We then face the question whether Dunnebier's death broke the vital chain. His powers to amend or revoke the trust, or to direct payments from it, obviously died with him, and the remainder interests of the beneficiaries of the trust became vested. The contingencies which might defeat those remainder interests could no longer occur. Greenwich Trust Co. v. Tyson, 129 Conn. 211, 225, 27 A.2d 166 (1942). In one jurisdiction, at least, it has been held that when the settlor of a revocable living trust dies, the property is no longer subject to his debts. Schofield v. Cleveland Trust Co., 135 Ohio St. 328, 334, 21 N.E.2d 119 (1939). See generally McGovern, The Payable on Death Account and Other Will Substitutes, 67 N.W.L.Rev. 7, 26–29 (1972). Cf. Griswold, Spendthrift Trusts § 475 (2d ed. 1947).

Traditionally the courts of this Commonwealth have always given full effect to inter vivos trusts, notwithstanding retention of powers to amend and revoke during life, even though this resulted in disinheritance of a spouse or children and nullified the policy which allows a spouse to waive the will and claim a statutory share, G.L. c. 191, § 15. See National Shawmut Bank of Boston v. Joy, 315 Mass. 457, 474–475, 53 N.E.2d 113 (1944); Kerwin v. Donaghy, 317 Mass. 559, 567, 59 N.E.2d 299 (1945); Ascher v. Cohen, 333 Mass. 397, 400, 131 N.E.2d 198 (1956). It might then be argued that a creditor ought to stand in no better position where, as here, the trust device was not employed in fraud of creditors.

There has developed, however, another thread of decisions which takes cognizance of, and gives effect to, the power which a person exercises in life over property. When a person has a general power of appointment, exercisable by will or by deed, and exercises that power, any property so appointed is, in equity, considered part of his assets and becomes available to his creditors in preference to the claims of his voluntary appointees or legatees. Clapp v. Ingraham, 126 Mass. 200, 202 (1879); Shattuck v. Burrage, 229 Mass. 448, 452, 118 N.E. 889 (1918); State Street Trust Co. v. Kissel, 302 Mass. 328, 333, 19 N.E.2d 25 (1939). Compare Prescott v. Wordell, 319 Mass. 118, 120, 65 N.E.2d 19 (1946). These decisions rest on the theory that as to property which a person could appoint to himself or his executors, the property could have been devoted to the payment of debts and, therefore, creditors have an equitable right to reach that property. It taxes the imagination to invent reasons why the same analysis and policy should not apply to trust property over which the settlor retains dominion at least as great as a power of appointment. The Restatement of Property has, in fact, translated the doctrine applicable to powers of appointment to trusts: "When a person transfers property in trust for himself for life and reserves a general power to appoint the remainder and creates no other beneficial interests which he cannot destroy by exercising the power, the property, though the power is unexercised, can be subjected to the payment of the claims of creditors of such person and claims against his estate to whatever extent other available property is insufficient for that purpose." Restatement of Property, § 328 (1940). See also, for the assimilation of a power to revoke to a general power of appointment, concurring opinion of Goodman, J., in Massachusetts Co. v. Berger, 1 Mass.App. 624, 628 n.3, 305 N.E.2d 123 (1973).

As an estate planning vehicle, the inter vivos trust has become common currency. See Second Bank State St. Trust Co. v. Pinion, 341 Mass. 366, 371, 170 N.E.2d 350 (1960). Frequently, as Dunnebier did in the instant case, the settlor retains all the substantial incidents of ownership because access to the trust property is necessary or desirable as a matter of sound financial planning. Psychologically, the settlor thinks of the trust property as "his", as Dunnebier did when he took the bank's officer to visit the real estate owned by the corporation whose stock he had put in trust. See Fiduciary Trust Co. v. First Natl. Bank, 344 Mass. 1, 9, 181 N.E.2d 6 (1962). In other circumstances, persons place property in trust in order to obtain expert management of their assets, while retaining the power to invade principal and to amend and revoke the trust. It is excessive obeisance to the form in which property is held to prevent creditors from reaching property placed in trust under such terms. See Restatement of Property, § 328, Comment a (1940).

This view was adopted in United States v. Ritter, 558 F.2d 1165, 1167 (4th Cir. 1977). In a concurring opinion in that case Judge Widener observed that it violates public policy for an individual to have an estate to live on, but not an estate to pay his debts with. Id. at 1168. The Internal Revenue Code institutionalizes the concept that a settlor of a trust who retains administrative powers, power to revoke or power to control beneficial enjoyment "owns" that trust property and provides that it shall be included in the settlor's personal estate. I.R.C. §§ 2038 and 2041.

We hold, therefore, that where a person places property in trust and reserves the right to amend and revoke, or to direct disposition of principal and income, the settlor's creditors may, following the death of the settlor, reach in satisfaction of the settlor's debts to them, to the extent not satisfied by the settlor's estate, those assets owned by the trust over which the settlor had such control at the time of his death as would have enabled the settlor to use the trust assets for his own benefit. Assets which pour over into such a trust as a consequence of the settlor's death or after the settlor's death, over which the settlor did not have control during his life, are not subject to the reach of creditors since, as to those assets, the equitable principles do not apply which place assets subject to creditors' disposal.

The judgment is reversed, and a new judgment is to enter declaring that the assets owned by the trust (Wilfred A. Dunnebier Trust, I) up to the time of Dunnebier's death can be reached and applied in satisfaction of a judgment entered in favor of the plaintiff against the estate of Dunnebier, to the extent assets of the estate are insufficient to satisfy such a judgment.

So ordered.

J. Dynasty Trusts

Technically, a dynasty trust refers to a trust meant to take advantage of the tax exemption given to successive generations of descendants. *See* I.R.C. § 2601 (2004); Joel C. Dobris, *Changes in the Role and the Form of the Trust at the New Millennium, or, We*

Don't Have to Think of England Anymore, 62 ALBANY L. REV. 543 (1998). However, since the generation skipping tax is scheduled to be repealed along with the estate tax in 2010, *see* I.R.C. §2663 (2004), the reference to dynasty trusts as a tax device is waning. Nonetheless, if the tax is repealed, there will remain a desire on the part of some Settlors to provide assets for successive generations of descendants. Such a desire is made possible in perpetuity—or, with the erosion of the Rule Against Perpetuities, at least until the descendants expire—when applied to all private trusts. Indeed, with the adoption of the Uniform Statutory Rule Against Perpetuities (1990) now incorporated into Part 9 of the Uniform Probate Code, it is possible to create a trust for descendants to last for at least ninety years. *See generally* Jesse Dukeminier, *Dynasty Trusts: Sheltering Descendants From Transfer Taxes,* 23 EST. PLAN. 417 (1996). The parameters of such a trust are quite simple but could be augmented with powers of appointment and a remainder for whenever the trust beneficiaries do cease. For example: Settlor provides one-million dollars in trust, income to provide payment of all law school tuition until the death of the last living descendant of the Settlor.

K. Non-Probate Contracts

While a revocable inter vivos trust is a popular means of avoiding probate and speedily passing property to another, there are other devices commonly used that involve concerns similar to trusts. For example, recipients of all nonprobate transfers can be required to contribute to creditors of the decedent, including statutory allowances, if the probate estate is insufficient. The Uniform Probate Code provides statutory means of assigning liability for decedents' debts. The list following that provision, although not exhaustive, provides other commonly used methods of avoiding probate while retaining liability.

Uniform Probate Code (2003)

Section 6-102. Liability of Nonprobate Transferees for Creditor Claims and Statutory Allowances.

(a) In this section, "nonprobate transfer" means a valid transfer effective at death, other than a transfer of a survivorship interest in a joint tenancy of real estate, by a transferor whose last domicile was in this State to the extent that the transferor immediately before death had power, acting alone, to prevent the transfer by revocation or withdrawal and instead to use the property for the benefit of the transferor or apply it to discharge claims against the transferor's probate estate.

(b) Except as otherwise provided by statute, a transferee of a nonprobate transfer is subject to liability to any probate estate of the decedent for allowed claims against decedent's probate estate and statutory allowances to the decedent's spouse and children to the extent the estate is insufficient to satisfy those claims and allowances. The liability of a nonprobate transferee may not exceed the value of nonprobate transfers received or controlled by that transferee.

(c) Nonprobate transferees are liable for the insufficiency described in subsection (b) in the following order of priority:

> (1) a transferee designated in the decedent's will or any other governing instrument, as provided in the instrument;

(2) the trustee of a trust serving as the principal nonprobate instrument in the decedent's estate plan as shown by its designation as devisee of the decedent's residuary estate or by other facts or circumstances, to the extent of the value of the nonprobate transfer received or controlled;

(3) other nonprobate transferees, in proportion to the values received.

(d) Unless otherwise provided by the trust instrument, interests of beneficiaries in all trusts incurring liabilities under this section abate as necessary to satisfy the liability, as if all of the trust instruments were a single will and the interests were devises under it.

(e) A provision made in one instrument may direct the apportionment of the liability among the nonprobate transferees taking under that or any other governing instrument. If a provision in one instrument conflicts with a provision in another, the later one prevails.

(f) Upon due notice to a nonprobate transferee, the liability imposed by this section is enforceable in proceedings in this State, whether or not the transferee is located in this State.

(g) A proceeding under this section may not be commenced unless the personal representative of the decedent's estate has received a written demand for the proceeding from the surviving spouse or a child, to the extent that statutory allowances are affected, or a creditor. If the personal representative declines or fails to commence a proceeding after demand, a person making demand may commence the proceeding in the name of the decedent's estate, at the expense of the person making the demand and not of the estate. A personal representative who declines in good faith to commence a requested proceeding incurs no personal liability for declining.

(h) A proceeding under this section must be commenced within one year after the decedent's death, but a proceeding on behalf of a creditor whose claim was allowed after proceedings challenging disallowance of the claim may be commenced within 60 days after final allowance of the claim.

(i) Unless a written notice asserting that a decedent's probate estate is nonexistent or insufficient to pay allowed claims and statutory allowances has been received from the decedent's personal representative, the following rules apply:

(1) Payment or delivery of assets by a financial institution, registrar, or other obligor, to a nonprobate transferee in accordance with the terms of the governing instrument controlling the transfer releases the obligor from all claims for amounts paid or assets delivered.

(2) A trustee receiving or controlling a nonprobate transfer is released from liability under this section with respect to any assets distributed to the trust's beneficiaries. Each beneficiary to the extent of the distribution received becomes liable for the amount of the trustee's liability attributable to assets received by the beneficiary.

1. *Payable-on-Death Contracts*

Estate of Hillowitz

Court of Appeals of New York, 1968
22 N.Y.2d 107, 238 N.E.2d 723, 291 N.Y.S.2d 325

Chief Judge Fuld.

This appeal stems from a discovery proceeding brought in the Surrogate's Court by the executors of the estate of Abraham Hillowitz against his widow, the appellant herein. The husband had been a partner in an "investment club" and, after his death, the club, pursuant to a provision of the partnership agreement, paid the widow the sum of $2,800, representing his interest in the partnership. "In the event of the death of any partner," the agreement recited, "his share will be transferred to his wife, with no termination of the partnership." The executors contend in their petition that the above provision was an invalid attempt to make a testamentary disposition of property and that the proceeds should pass under the decedent's will as an asset of his estate. The widow maintains that it was a valid and enforcable contract. Although the Surrogate agreed with her, the Appellate Division held that the agreement was invalid as "an attempted testamentary disposition" (24 A D 2d 891). * * *

A partnership agreement which provides that, upon the death of one partner, his interest shall pass to the surviving partner or partners, resting as it does in contract, is unquestionably valid and may not be defeated by labeling it a testamentary disposition. * * * [citations omitted]. We are unable to perceive a difference in principle between an agreement of this character and one, such as that before us, providing for a deceased partner's widow, rather than a surviving partner, to succeed to the decedent's interest in the partnership. * * * [citations omitted].

These partnership undertakings are, in effect, nothing more or less than third-party beneficiary contracts, performable at death. Like many similar instruments, contractual in nature, which provide for the disposition of property after death, they need not conform to the requirements of the statute of wills. (See, e.g., Matter of Fairbairn, 265 App. Div. 431, 433, mot. for lv. to app. den. 291 N. Y. 828.) Examples of such instruments include (1) a contract to make a will (see, e.g., Ga Nun v. Palmer, 216 N. Y. 603, 610; Phalen v. United States Trust Co., 186 N. Y. 178, 184; Gilman v. McArdle, 99 N. Y. 451, 461); (2) an inter vivos trust in which the settlor reserves a life estate (see, e.g., Matter of Ford, 304 N. Y. 598; City Bank Farmers Trust Co. v. Cannon, 291 N. Y. 125; City Bank Farmers Trust Co. v. Charity Organization Soc., 264 N. Y. 441; and (3) an insurance policy. (See, e.g., Hutchings v. Miner, 46 N. Y. 456, 460–461; Johnston v. Scott, 76 Misc. 641, 648; Ambrose v. United States, 15 F. 2d 52; see, also, Ward v. New York Life Ins. Co., 225 N. Y. 314; Note, 53 A L R 2d 1112.)

In short, members of a partnership may provide, without fear of running afoul of our statute of wills, that, upon the death of a partner, his widow shall be entitled to his interest in the firm. This type of third-party beneficiary contract is not invalid as an attempted testamentary disposition.

The executors may derive little satisfaction from McCarthy v. Pieret (281 N. Y. 407), upon which they heavily rely. In the first place, it is our considered judgment that the decision should be limited to its facts. And, in the second place, the case is clearly distinguishable from the one now before us in that the court expressly noted that the "facts ... indicate a mere intention on the part of the mortgagee to make a testamentary disposition of the property and not an intention to convey an immediate interest" and, in addition, that the named beneficiaries "knew nothing of the provisions of the extension agreement" (p. 413).

The order of the Appellate Division should be reversed, with costs in this court and in the Appellate Division, and the order of the Surrogate's Court reinstated.

Judges Burke, Scileppi, Bergan, Breitel and Jasen concur with Chief Judge Fuld; * * *

Order reversed, etc.

Notes

In order to avoid courts treating arrangements like the one in Estate of Hillowitz as testamentary, the Uniform Probate Code § 6-101 (2003), specifically provides that this and similar transfers at death are nontestamentary. A question then arises as to the revocability of these transfers through such events as divorce, whether statutory anti-lapse should apply if the beneficiary of the payable-on-death arrangement predeceases the decedent survived by issue, and finally, whether there should be a requirement of survivorship by 120 hours. The answer is yes to all three questions. *See* UNIF. PROB. CODE §§ 2-702(c) (survivorship), 2-706 (anti-lapse), and 2-804(b) (revocation) (2003). As to whether the beneficiary of a payable-on-death contract may be changed with a provision in a valid Last Will and Testament, the following decision is illustrative. Please compare the decision with Uniform Probate Code § 6-213(b), which provides that a right of survivorship arising from a contract of deposit between a depositor and a financial institution (checking account, savings account, certificate of deposit) or a payable-on-death designation may not be altered by a Last Will and Testament.

Cook v. Equitable Life Assurance Society

Indiana Court of Appeals, First District, 1981
428 N.E.2d 110

RATLIFF, Judge.

Margaret A. Cook, Administratrix C.T.A. of the Estate of Douglas D. Cook (Douglas); Margaret A. Cook; and Daniel J. Cook (Margaret and Daniel) appeal from an entry of summary judgment granted by the trial court in favor of Doris J. Cook Combs (Doris) in an interpleader action brought by The Equitable Life Assurance Society of the United States (Equitable). We affirm.

* * *

Douglas purchased a whole life insurance policy on March 13, 1953, from Equitable, naming his wife at that time, Doris, as the beneficiary. On March 5, 1965, Douglas and Doris were divorced. The divorce decree made no provision regarding the insurance policy, but did state the following: "It is further understood and agreed between the parties hereto that the provisions of this agreement shall be in full satisfaction of all claims by either of said parties against the other, including alimony, support and maintenance money." Record at 85–86.

After the divorce Douglas ceased paying the premiums on his life insurance policy, and Equitable notified him on July 2, 1965, that because the premium due on March 9, 1965, had not been paid, his whole life policy was automatically converted to a paid-up term policy with an expiration date of June 12, 1986. The policy contained the following provision with respect to beneficiaries:

> BENEFICIARY. The Owner may change the beneficiary from time to time prior to the death of the Insured, by written notice to the Society, but any such change shall be effective only if it is endorsed on this policy by the Society, and, if there is a written assignment of this policy in force and on file with the Society (other than an assignment to the Society as security for an advance), such a change may be made only with the written consent of the assignee. The interest of a beneficiary shall be subject to the rights of any assignee of record with the Society.

Upon endorsement of a change of beneficiary upon this policy by the Society, such change shall take effect as of the date the written notice thereof was signed, whether or not the Insured is living at the time of endorsement, but without further liability on the part of the Society with respect to any proceeds paid by the Society or applied under any option in this policy prior to such endorsement.

If the executors or administrators of the Insured be not expressly designated as beneficiary, any part of the proceeds of this policy with respect to which there is no designated beneficiary living at the death of the Insured and no assignee entitled thereto, will be payable in a single sum to the children of the Insured who survive the Insured, in equal shares, or should none survive, then to the Insured's executors or administrators.

Record at 2 and 59.

On December 24, 1965, Douglas married Margaret, and a son, Daniel, was born to them. On June 7, 1976, Douglas made a holographic will in which he bequeathed his insurance policy with Equitable Life to his wife and son, Margaret and Daniel:

Last Will & Testimint

I Douglas D. Cook

Being of sound mind do Hereby leave all my Worldly posessions to my Wife and son, Margaret A. Cook & Daniel Joseph Cook. being my Bank Accounts at Irwin Union Bank & trust to their Welfair my Insurance policys with Common Welth of Ky. and Equitable Life. all my machinecal tools to be left to my son if He is Interested in Working with them If not to be sold and money used for their welfair all my Gun Collection Kept as long as they, my Wife & Son and then sold and money used for their welfair

I sighn this

June 7-1976
at Barth Conty
Hospital Room
1114 Bed 2

/s/ Douglas D. Cook

/s/ 6-7-76 Margaret A. Cook wife

/s/ Chas. W. Winkler

/s/ Mary A. Winkler"

This will was admitted to probate in Bartholomew Superior Court after Douglas's death on June 9, 1979. On August 24, 1979, Margaret filed a claim with Equitable for the proceeds of Douglas's policy, but Equitable deposited the proceeds, along with its complaint in interpleader, with the Bartholomew Circuit Court on March 14, 1980. Discovery was made; interrogatories and affidavits were filed; and all parties moved for summary judgment. The trial court found that there was no genuine issue as to any material fact respecting Doris's claim to the proceeds of the policy and entered judgment in her favor as to the amount of the proceeds plus interest, a total of $3,154.09. Margaret and Daniel appeal from this award.

* * *

Doris agrees that less than strict compliance with policy change requirements may be adequate to change a beneficiary where circumstances show the insured has done everything within his power to effect the change. Nevertheless, Doris asserts that Indiana adheres to the majority rule finding an attempt to change the beneficiary of a life insurance policy by will, without more, to be ineffectual. We agree with Doris.

Margaret and Daniel are correct in asserting that there are no Indiana cases involving precisely the same set of facts as occur in this case. Nevertheless, there is ample case law in this jurisdiction to support the trial court's determination. Almost one hundred years ago our supreme court in Holland v. Taylor, (1887) 111 Ind. 121, 12 N.E. 116, enunciated the general rule still followed in Indiana: an attempt to change the beneficiary of a life insurance contract * * * by will and in disregard of the methods prescribed under the contract will be unsuccessful. See also, 44 Am.Jur.2d, Insurance § 1785 (1969); 46 C.J.S. Insurance § 1176 (1946); 25 A.L.R.2d 999 (1952) and Later Case Service (1981); 2A J. A. Appleman, Insurance Law & Practice § 1078 (1966). In Holland, the assured and testator, Charles D. Taylor, had been issued a benefit certificate by Royal Arcanum, a mutual benefit society, in which certificate Taylor's daughter, Anna Laura, was the named beneficiary. The certificate provided that Taylor could change the named beneficiary by following certain procedures. On the same day that Taylor applied for the certificate he made his will in which he acknowledged the certificate for his daughter's benefit, but also provided that the certificate benefits, under certain circumstances, were to inure to the benefit of his wife or estate rather than as provided in the certificate for the exclusive benefit of his daughter. After Taylor's death, Holland was appointed guardian of Anna Laura and brought an action requesting that the executors of Taylor's estate pay over to him the fund which they had collected from the Royal Arcanum. The trial court overruled a demurrer to the answer and held that the executors were entitled to dispose of the fund according to the will. On appeal, our supreme court reversed with instructions to the trial court to sustain appellant's demurrer to the answer. In doing so the court stated at 111 Ind. 130–31, 12 N.E. 116:

> Taylor, the assured, neither changed, nor attempted to change, the beneficiary in the mode and manner provided in the by-laws. He could not accomplish that end, nor affect the ultimate rights of the beneficiary by a will. Upon his death, therefore, Anna Laura became entitled to the amount to be paid upon the certificate, as her absolute property; appellees' executors, having collected from the Royal Arcanum, hold the amount so collected in trust for her, but they have no right to control, manage, and dispose of the fund as directed by the will, because, as to that fund, the will is of no effect.

Indiana courts have recognized exceptions to the general rule that strict compliance with policy requirements is necessary to effect a change of beneficiary. Three exceptions were noted by this court in Modern Brotherhood v. Matkovitch, (1914) 56 Ind.App. 8, 14, 104 N.E. 795, and reiterated in Heinzman v. Whiteman, (1923) 81 Ind.App. 29, 36, 139 N.E. 329, trans. denied:

> '1. If the society has waived a strict compliance with its own rules, and in pursuance of a request of the insured to change the beneficiary, has issued a new certificate to him, the original beneficiary will not be heard to complain that the course indicated by the regulations was not pursued. 2. If it be beyond the power of the insured to comply literally with the regulations, a court of equity

will treat the change as having been legally made. 3. If the insured has pursued the course pointed out by the laws of the association, and has done all in his power to change the beneficiary; but before the new certificate is actually issued, he dies, a court of equity will decree that to be done which ought to be done, and act as though the certificate had been issued.'

In Modern Brotherhood the insured had attempted to change the beneficiary of a mutual benefit insurance certificate in accordance with the terms of the certificate, but was thwarted in her attempts to do so by wrongful acts of the original beneficiary. It was impossible, therefore, for the insured to comply literally with the bylaws and regulations of the society for changing beneficiaries even though she notified the society of her desires to change the beneficiary on her certificate and also indicated those desires in her will. The court on appeal held that the trial court had erred in sustaining a demurrer to paragraph three of the complaint which stated facts sufficient to constitute an action upon equitable principles, but had properly sustained a demurrer to paragraph four of the complaint which merely stated that the insured had changed the beneficiaries of her certificate by will. The court repeated the rule of Holland at 56 Ind.App. 16, 104 N.E. 795: "Our courts have indicated that the rule in this State is, that without some other fact or facts, in aid of the change the insured cannot change the beneficiary by the execution of a will."

The public policy considerations undergirding this rule and its limited exceptions involve protection of the rights of all the parties concerned and should not be viewed, as appellants advocate, for the exclusive protection of the insurer. Indiana, in fact, has specifically rejected this position. In Stover v. Stover, (1965) 137 Ind.App. 578, 204 N.E.2d 374, 380, on rehearing 205 N.E.2d 178, trans. denied, the court recognized an insured's right to rely on the provisions of the policy in regard to change of beneficiary:

> We must reject appellant's contention that the provisions set forth in the certificate, as mentioned above, are for the exclusive benefit of the insurance company and may be waived at will. The deceased insured himself is entitled to rely upon such provisions that he may at all times know to whom the proceeds of the insurance shall be payable.

In Holland the court also recognized that the beneficiary had a right in the executed contract which was subject to defeat only by a change of beneficiary which had been executed in accord with the terms of the insurance contract: "In that contract Anna Laura, the beneficiary, had such an interest as that she had, and has, the right to insist that in order to cut her out, the change of beneficiary should be made in the manner provided in the contract." 111 Ind. 127, 12 N.E. 116. And in Borgman v. Borgman, (1981) Ind.App., 420 N.E.2d 1261, trans. denied, this court held that an interpleader action by a life insurance company does not affect the parties' rights.

Clearly it is in the interest of insurance companies to require and to follow certain specified procedures in the change of beneficiaries of its policies so that they may pay over benefits to persons properly entitled to them without subjection to claims by others of whose rights they had no notice or knowledge. Certainly it is also in the interest of beneficiaries themselves to be entitled to prompt payment of benefits by insurance companies which do not withhold payment until the will has been probated in the fear of later litigation which might result from having paid the wrong party. The legislature reflects this concern with certainty in the area of insurance beneficiaries in Ind.Code 27-1-12-14 by permitting changes of beneficiaries in insurance policies upon written notice to the insurance company when accompanied by the policy. Finally, society's interest in the conservation of judicial energy and expense will be served where the rule and its limited exceptions are clearly stated and rigorously applied.

* * *

We may be sympathetic to the cause of the decedent's widow and son, and it might seem that a departure from the general rule in an attempt to do equity under these facts would be noble. Nevertheless, such a course is fraught with the dangers of eroding a solidly paved pathway of the law and leaving in its stead only a gaping hole of uncertainty. Public policy requires that the insurer, insured, and beneficiary alike should be able to rely on the certainty that policy provisions pertaining to the naming and changing of beneficiaries will control except in extreme situations. We, therefore, invoke a maxim equally as venerable as the one upon which appellants rely in the determination of this cause: Equity aids the vigilant, not those who slumber on their rights.

Judgment affirmed.

NEAL, P. J., and ROBERTSON, J., concur.

2. Multiple Party Bank Accounts

Franklin v. Anna National Bank of Anna

Illinois Appellate Court, Fifth District, 1986
140 Ill. App. 3d 533, 488 N.E.2d 1117

WELCH, Justice:

Plaintiff Enola Stevens Franklin, as executor of the Estate of Frank A. Whitehead, deceased, commenced this action in the circuit court of Union County against defendant Anna National Bank, alleging that the funds in a joint savings account were the property of the estate. The bank interpleaded Cora Goddard, who asserted her right to the money as the surviving joint owner. After a bench trial, the circuit court entered judgment for Mrs. Goddard. Mrs. Franklin appeals. We reverse.

* * *

Decedent died December 22, 1980. His wife Muriel Whitehead died in 1974. Mrs. Goddard was Muriel's sister. Decedent had eye surgery in May of 1978, and according to Mrs. Goddard was losing his eyesight in 1978. In April of 1978 Mrs. Goddard moved to Union County to help decedent and live with him. On April 17, 1978, Mrs. Goddard and decedent went to the bank, according to Mrs. Goddard to have his money put in both their names so she could get money when they needed it, "and he wanted me to have this money if I outlived him."

A bank employee prepared a signature card for savings account number 3816 and Mrs. Goddard signed it. A copy of this card was in evidence at trial. The signatures of decedent and Mrs. Goddard appear on both sides of the card. It appears that Muriel Whitehead's signature was "whited out" and Mrs. Goddard's signature added. The front of the card states that one signature is required for withdrawals. The back of the card states that all funds deposited are owned by the signatories as joint tenants with right of survivorship.

Mrs. Goddard testified that she did not deposit any of the money in savings account 3816. She made no withdrawals, though she once took decedent to the bank so he could make a withdrawal. According to Mrs. Goddard, on the day she signed the signature card decedent "asked me if I needed my money because they had bought cemetery lots from me, and I told him, not at this time, that I didn't need it. He wanted to know if I needed any more money at that time and I said, no, and I said, just leave it in here and I will get it out whenever I need it." According to Mrs. Goddard, decedent promised to pay her a thousand dollars for the lots; she was never paid. Asked whether she ever had the passbook for savings account 3816 in her possession, Mrs. Goddard answered, "Only while I was at Frank's. It was there."

Later in 1978, Mrs. Franklin began to care for decedent. In January, 1979, decedent telephoned the bank, then sent Mrs. Franklin to the bank to deliver a letter to Mrs. Kedron Boyer, a bank employee. The handwritten letter, dated January 13, 1979, and signed by decedent, stated: "I Frank Whitehead wish by Bank accounts be changed to Enola Stevens joint intendency [sic]. Nobody go in my lock box but me." According to Mrs. Franklin, Mrs. Boyer told her to tell decedent he would have to specify what type of account he was referring to. Decedent gave Mrs. Franklin a second letter which Mrs. Franklin delivered to Mrs. Carol Williams at the bank (Mrs. Boyer was absent). This handwritten letter, dated January 13, 1979, stated: "I Frank Whitehead want Enola Stevens and me only go in my lock box. Account type Saving and Checking. In case I can't see she is to take care of my bill or sick." According to Mrs. Franklin, Mrs. Williams said she would take care of it and give the letter to Mrs. Boyer. Mrs. Franklin testified that she signed the savings passbook in the presence of decedent and Mrs. Boyer. Mrs. Franklin took her present last name on May 8, 1979.

Mrs. Boyer, Mrs. Williams, and bank president Delano Mowery all testified at trial. These witnesses explained the usual procedures for account changes. None remembered much of the circumstances surrounding the bank's receipt of the January 13, 1979, letters. According to Mr. Mowery, the bank would not remove a signature from a signature card based on a letter; the most recent signature card the bank had for savings account 3816 was signed by decedent and Mrs. Goddard.

Mrs. Goddard's attorney's assertion at trial that there were no monthly statements on savings account 3816 was uncontradicted.

The trial court found that Mrs. Goddard was the sole owner of the funds in savings account 3816 by right of survivorship as surviving joint tenant, and that no part of the funds became part of decedent's estate.

Mrs. Franklin argues that decedent did not intend to make a gift of savings account 3816 to Mrs. Goddard.

The instrument creating a joint tenancy account presumably speaks the whole truth. In order to go behind the terms of the agreement, the one claiming adversely thereto has the burden of establishing by clear and convincing evidence that a gift was not intended. (Murgic v. Granite City Trust & Savings Bank (1964), 31 Ill.2d 587, 590, 202 N.E.2d 470, 472.) Each case involving a joint tenancy account must be evaluated on its own facts and circumstances. (In re Estate of Hayes (1971), 131 Ill.App.2d 563, 568, 268 N.E.2d 501, 505.) The form of the agreement is not conclusive regarding the intention of the depositors between themselves. (In re Estate of Schneider (1955), 6 Ill.2d 180, 186, 127 N.E.2d 445, 449.) Evidence of lack of donative intent must relate back to the time of creation of the joint tenancy. (In re Estate of Stang (1966), 71 Ill.App.2d 314, 317, 218 N.E.2d 854, 856.) The decision of the donor, made subsequent to the creation of the joint tenancy, that he did not want the proceeds to pass to the survivor, would not, in itself, be sufficient to sever the tenancy. (Estate of Zengerle (1971), 2 Ill.App.3d 98, 101, 276 N.E.2d 128, 130.) However, it is proper to consider events occurring after creation of the joint account in determining whether the donor actually intended to transfer his interest in the account at his death to the surviving joint tenant. Matter of Estate of Guzak (1979), 69 Ill.App.3d 552, 555, 26 Ill.Dec. 716, 718, 388 N.E.2d 431, 433.

We examine the instant facts in light of the above principles: There appears no serious doubt that in January of 1979, just nine months after adding Mrs. Goddard's name to savings account 3816, decedent attempted to remove Mrs. Goddard's name and substitute Mrs. Franklin's. The second of decedent's handwritten letters to the bank in January of 1979 indicates decedent's concern that he might lose his sight and be unable to transact his own banking business. These facts show that decedent made Mrs. Goddard (and later Mrs. Franklin) a signatory for his own convenience, in case he could not get his money, and not with intent to effect a present gift. (See Dixon Nat'l Bank v. Morris (1965), 33 Ill.2d 156, 159, 210 N.E.2d 505, 506; Estate of Guzak.) It does not appear that Mrs. Goddard ever exercised any authority or control over the joint account. (See Estate of Guzak.) While decedent's statement that he wanted Mrs. Goddard to have the money in the account if she outlived him suggests decedent's donative intent, taken literally decedent's statement is inconsistent with intent to donate any interest during decedent's lifetime. (See Lipe v. Farmers State Bank of Alto Pass (1970), 131 Ill.App.2d 1024, 1026, 265 N.E.2d 204, 205.) Mrs. Goddard does not argue that there was a valid testamentary disposition in her favor, nor could we so find on the instant facts.

Of the many cases cited by the parties for comparison with the case at bar, the most persuasive is In re Estate of Schneider (1955), 6 Ill.2d 180, 127 N.E.2d 445. In Estate of Schneider the decedent's executor filed a petition alleging the funds in joint bank accounts belonged to the estate and not to Ralston, the surviving joint tenant. Ralston testified that all of the money in the account was deposited by the decedent, that the decedent at no time told Ralston he wanted Ralston to have any of the money, and that when Ralston's name was added to the accounts the decedent said, "I want your name on these bank accounts so that in case I am sick you can go and get the money for me." The trial court concluded that the decedent intended to retain actual ownership of the money. Our supreme court agreed. We reach the same conclusion here. In the case at bar, decedent's attempts to change the account show his consistent view of the account as his own. The surrounding circumstances show decedent's concern for his health and his relatively brief use of Mrs. Goddard (and later Mrs. Franklin) to assure his access to his funds. The money in account 3816 should have been found to be the property of the estate.

For the foregoing reasons, the judgment of the circuit court of Union County is reversed, and this cause is remanded for entry of judgment in favor of plaintiff.

REVERSED.

KARNS and HARRISON, JJ., concur.

Notes

The Uniform Probate Code includes an extensive part on multiple-person accounts at §§6-201 through 6-227, including a sample form for single or multiple party accounts. Compare the following two sections with the holding of the previous decision.

Uniform Probate Code (2003)

Section 6-211. Ownership During Lifetime.

(a) In this section, "net contribution" of a party means the sum of all deposits to an account made by or for the party, less all payments from the account made to or for the party which have not been paid to or applied to the use of another party and a proportionate share of any charges deducted from the account, plus a proportionate share of any interest or dividends earned, whether or not included in the current balance. The term includes deposit life insurance proceeds added to the account by reason of death of the party whose net contribution is in question.

(b) During the lifetime of all parties, an account belongs to the parties in proportion to the net contribution of each to the sums on deposit, unless there is clear and convincing evidence of a different intent. As between parties married to each other, in the absence of proof otherwise, the net contribution of each is presumed to be an equal amount.

(c) A beneficiary in an account having a POD designation has no right to sums on deposit during the lifetime of any party.

(d) An agent in an account with an agency designation has no beneficial right to sums on deposit.

Section 6-212. Rights at Death.

(a) Except as otherwise provided in this part, on death of a party sums on deposit in a multiple-party account belong to the surviving party or parties. If two or more parties survive and one is the surviving spouse of the decedent, the amount to which the decedent, immediately before death, was beneficially entitled under Section 6-211 belongs to the surviving spouse. If two or more parties survive and none is the surviving spouse of the decedent, the amount to which the decedent, immediately before death, was beneficially entitled under Section 6-211 belongs to the surviving parties in equal shares, and augments the proportion to which each survivor, immediately before the decedent's death, was beneficially entitled under Section 6-211, and the right of survivorship continues between the surviving parties.

(b) In an account with a POD designation:

> (1) On death of one of two or more parties, the rights in sums on deposit are governed by subsection (a).

> (2) On death of the sole party or the last survivor of two or more parties, sums on deposit belong to the surviving beneficiary or beneficiaries. If two or more beneficiaries survive, sums on deposit belong to them in equal and undivided shares, and there is no right of survivorship in the event of death of a beneficiary thereafter. If no beneficiary survives, sums on deposit belong to the estate of the last surviving party.

(c) Sums on deposit in a single-party account without a POD designation, or in a multiple-party account that, by the terms of the account, is without right of survivorship, are not affected by death of a party, but the amount to which the decedent, immediately before death, was beneficially entitled under Section 6-211 is transferred as part of the decedent's estate. A POD designation in a multiple-party account without right of survivorship is ineffective. For purposes of this section, designation of an account as a tenancy in common establishes that the account is without right of survivorship.

(d) The ownership right of a surviving party or beneficiary, or of the decedent's estate, in sums on deposit is subject to requests for payment made by a party before the party's death, whether paid by the financial institution before or after death, or unpaid. The surviving party or beneficiary, or the decedent's estate, is liable to the payee of an unpaid request for payment. The liability is limited to a proportionate share of the amount transferred under this section, to the extent necessary to discharge the request for payment.

3. Totten Trusts

Green v. Green

Supreme Court of Rhode Island, 1989
559 A.2d 1047

FAY, Chief Justice.

This case comes before the Supreme Court on the plaintiff's appeal from a Superior Court judgment denying her petition to recover assets distributed to the defendants upon the death of her husband. The trial justice held that the defendants were entitled to the funds of numerous trusts created by the decedent during his lifetime. We affirm that decision.

Initially we shall discuss our standard of review following the decision of a trial justice sitting without a jury. We have consistently held that the findings of a trial justice sitting without a jury are accorded great deference and will not be disturbed unless it is demonstrated that the trial justice misconceived or overlooked material evidence or was otherwise clearly wrong. Oster v. Tellier, 544 A.2d 128, 131 (R.I.1988); Miller v. Dixon Industries Corp., 513 A.2d 597, 601 (R.I.1986); Dickinson v. Killheffer, 497 A.2d 307, 312 (R.I.1985). Furthermore, if findings of fact are supported by substantial evidence, we shall not substitute our decision for that of the trial justice. Millerick v. Fascio, 120 R.I. 9, 15, 384 A.2d 601, 604 (1978). Mindful of our standard of review, we set out the facts pertinent to this appeal as follows.

George L. Green (Green) died intestate on March 7, 1985, and was survived by his wife, Hilda A. Green, plaintiff, and three children from a prior marriage, George L. Green, Jr., Elizabeth A. Swope, and James D. Green, defendants. The plaintiff also has one daughter from a prior marriage.

Green and plaintiff were married in 1949. During the marriage both husband and wife worked to contribute financially to the marriage and also to the upkeep of various properties. The Greens owned some property jointly, and other property was recorded in Green's name alone. Green owned eight cottages on Cape Cod, which he rented to tourists. The plaintiff assisted Green by cleaning and preparing the cottages for the arrival of new guests. Green also owned a condominium in Florida, which was used by Green and plaintiff as a residential unit.

Green assumed responsibility for a majority of the couple's finances, including the purchase and sale of their real estate holdings. Whereas Green paid for the rent, heat, and food, plaintiff was responsible for the telephone bill, laundry bill, and various other miscellaneous bills. The plaintiff kept her own checking account, which she funded with money earned from employment outside the home. The funds in this account were used to buy goods for her daughter and herself.

Throughout the Greens' marriage Green maintained a strong relationship with his three children. Green's daughter, Elizabeth Swope (Swope), was exceptionally close to her father. Green enlisted Swope's aid in filing his tax returns, divulged the contents of his financial record book to Swope, which listed his holdings of stock and trust accounts, and told her of his specific intention to avoid a will and probate. Green also informed Swope that the funds in each of his eight bank accounts were left in trust to be distributed upon his death to the named beneficiaries.

Upon Green's death, his Rhode Island estate-tax return revealed a gross estate of $258,125: $218,574 in eight separate bank accounts, $38,651 in securities, and $900 in personal property. Green had contributed all the money in each of the eight bank accounts, and each account was held in trust for one of his heirs. Green was named as trustee on all eight accounts, and he retained physical possession of the bankbooks throughout his life. Most of his stocks were also held jointly with one of the heirs. Because these assets were held either jointly or in trust, it was unnecessary for them to pass through probate as the remainder of the estate did.

The plaintiff's share of her late husband's estate comprised personal property (stocks) totaling $2,432 and, as the named beneficiary, the contents of two bank accounts totaling $25,000. The funds in the remaining bank accounts were distributed to the other named beneficiaries following Green's death, and the accounts were subsequently closed by each bank.

Thereafter, plaintiff filed a petition with the Pawtucket Probate Court. She requested a widow's allowance and also the recovery of all funds distributed to Green's three children pursuant to the trust accounts. The petition was denied, and plaintiff filed two appeals in the Superior Court, pursuant to G.L.1956 (1984 Reenactment) § 33-23-1. The plaintiff sought the overturn of the denial of a widow's allowance and a determination that the bank accounts were not valid trust accounts, thereby causing the estate to recover all funds formerly distributed.

The two appeals were consolidated and subsequently tried without a jury. The trial justice found that plaintiff was entitled to a widow's allowance totaling $10,000, provided the estate had ample funds. This portion of the decision was not appealed.

Focusing on the trust accounts, the trial justice further noted that throughout the years activity on the trust accounts had been minimal. Although Green had made one withdrawal of approximately $2,000 and also reported all interest earned from said accounts on his tax returns, the trial justice determined that Green fully intended that upon his death the accounts were to be distributed to the named beneficiaries, including plaintiff. Furthermore, the trial justice noted that Green had told his daughter of his specific intent to avoid probate. The trial justice held that the trust accounts were valid totten trusts and as such the funds were properly distributed to each of the named beneficiaries. The plaintiff now appeals this portion of the trial justice's decision.

An initial examination of the law regarding totten trusts will be helpful to our analysis. A totten trust is defined as a deposit in trust by the settlor of his own money for the benefit of another. Black's Law Dictionary 1356 (West 5th ed.1979). The creation of a valid totten trust requires retention of the subject matter of the trust by the settlor or the trustee for the benefit of the named beneficiary. Petition of Atkinson, 16 R.I. 413,

415–16, 16 A. 712, 713 (1889). The settlor may be the named trustee, but this is not necessary to the validity of the trust.[1] Black's Law Dictionary 1356. During the settlor's lifetime the trust is revocable, and the settlor may use the funds for his own benefit. Id. Upon the settlor's death, however, the trust becomes irrevocable and is the exclusive property of the beneficiary. Peoples Savings Bank v. Webb, 21 R.I. 218, 42 A. 874 (1899).

For over one hundred years we have recognized that a totten trust is a valid tool for transferring assets upon the settlor's death. See Slepkow v. McSoley, 54 R.I. 210, 172 A. 328 (1934); Petition of Atkinson, 16 R.I. 413, 16 A. 712 (1889); Ray v. Simmons, 11 R.I. 266 (1875). In our line of cases interpreting totten trusts, we have distinguished a totten trust from a gift. See Slepkow, 54 R.I. at 213, 172 A. at 329; Peoples Savings Bank, 21 R.I. at 220, 42 A. at 874; Atkinson, 16 R.I. at 415, 16 A. at 713. The validity of a totten trust, unlike a gift, does not require delivery of the subject matter to the beneficiary. Slepkow, 54 R.I. at 213, 172 A. at 329; Peoples Savings Bank, 21 R.I. at 220, 42 A. at 874; Atkinson, 16 R.I. at 415, 16 A. at 713.

Because of the distinction between a trust and a gift, the settlor's intention is critical to the validity of a totten trust. The intention to create a trust must be shown by the settlor through a clear act and/or declaration and must be made during his lifetime. Malley v. Malley, 69 R.I. 407, 412, 34 A.2d 761, 763 (1943). The settlor is not required to use any particular form of words to create a trust but must convey the property to another in trust or unequivocally declare that he holds it in praesenti in trust or as trustee for another. Ray, 11 R.I. at 268.

In Atkinson we held that a valid trust was created when the settlor, after making a deposit in trust, communicated that fact to the beneficiary. However, actual notice to the beneficiary is not essential to the creation, existence, or validity of a trust. Ray, 11 R.I. at 268. Nor is an acceptance of or assent to a trust by the beneficiary necessary. Tompkins v. Wheeler, 41 U.S. (16 Pet.) 106, 10 L.Ed. 903 (1842). Finally, we have held that the creation of a valid totten trust is a question of intention and, therefore, a question of fact. Peoples Savings Bank, 21 R.I. at 222, 42 A. at 875.

The factfinder may look to the settlor's statements and conduct regarding the account in discerning the settlor's intent. Malley, 69 R.I. at 413, 34 A.2d at 763. The form of the account creates a rebuttable presumption that a valid trust exists for the named beneficiary. Id. at 412, 34 A.2d at 763. Merely making a deposit in trust for another, however, is not conclusive evidence of the intent to create a trust. Slepkow, 54 R.I. at 213, 172 A. at 329. See also Peoples Savings Bank, 21 R.I. at 222, 42 A. at 875. Nevertheless, if the depositor dies before the beneficiary, leaving an unexplained bank account in the form of a trust and not revoking or disaffirming the trust during his lifetime, then a prima facie case supporting the creation of a valid trust exists. Slepkow, 54 R.I. at 213, 172 A. at 329.

Once the prima facie case is established, the burden of going forward shifts to the party opposing the trust. If that party presents satisfactory evidence to rebut the prima facie case, then the presumption of a valid trust becomes inoperative. The case will then proceed as if no presumption had been invoked. See generally Rules 302 and 303 of the Rhode Island Rules of Evidence (providing for presumptions regarding burden of pro-

---

1. Although the settlor is not required to serve as trustee, in this case the decedent, Green, acted as both the settlor and the trustee.

ducing evidence and stating when such presumptions will be applicable). However, if the prima facie case is not overcome by any reliable testimony and/or substantive evidence, then the trust will be upheld as valid. See Slepkow, 54 R.I. at 213, 172 A. at 329 (beneficiary entitled to bank account in trust because testimony presented failed to rebut presumption created by form of account).

Turning to the instant case, the principal issue is whether defendants are beneficially entitled to the sums of money in each account, which were placed on deposit by their father, Green. It is uncontradicted that all eight accounts were in the name of Green as trustee for each named beneficiary. We believe that Green specifically intended to dispose of his property through totten trusts. Therefore, the beneficiaries are entitled to the full amount of these trusts.

The trial justice ruled that the funds in the trust accounts are properly the funds of the beneficiaries named on each of the accounts. The trial justice stated that Green's intent—as shown by the form of the accounts as trusts, by the testimony that Green wanted to avoid probate, by the statements to Swope, and by the knowledge of all the beneficiaries that they were to inherit from said accounts—was to form totten trusts. Relying upon this evidence, the trial justice determined that at the time of the creation of said accounts Green had established perfectly valid in praesenti trusts and the full effect of the trusts was to take place at the time of his death.

It is clear from Swope's testimony and Green's acts during his lifetime that he fully intended to dispose of his property through bank accounts naming his heirs as beneficiaries. After carefully reviewing the testimony and evidence entered below, we are of the opinion that the trial justice's findings regarding Green's intention and the validity of the totten trusts were not clearly wrong.

The form of the accounts at Green's death created a prima facie case that the accounts were totten trusts. The plaintiff argued that the presumption in favor of a valid trust disappears when any evidence is presented contrary to the prima facie case. The plaintiff presented as contradictory evidence testimony that all the beneficiaries did not know of the existence of the accounts during Green's lifetime, that at all times Green maintained control of the passbooks, and that he withdrew funds from one of the accounts. Although Green retained control of the passbooks, paid taxes on all interest accumulated, and withdrew approximately $2,000 from one of the accounts, his retention of control created valid revocable trusts during his lifetime. We are of the opinion that Green's control, disposition, and appropriation of the funds in the accounts does not invalidate the trusts or render them testamentary. Therefore, we find that plaintiff's evidence is insufficient to rebut the prima facie existence and validity of the accounts as totten trusts.

We also believe that the trial justice's findings of fact are supported by substantial evidence. In making these findings, the trial justice did not misconceive or overlook material evidence. Consequently we find that the trial justice did not err in determining that Green fully intended to create valid totten trust bank accounts during his lifetime. Furthermore, on the basis of this review, we hold that the funds in each account were properly distributed to the named beneficiary and should not revert back to the estate for distribution pursuant to our intestacy laws.

For the reasons stated, the plaintiff's appeal is hereby denied and dismissed. The judgment appealed from is affirmed, and the papers in this case are remanded to the Superior Court with our decision endorsed thereon.

Notes

In order to keep some control over property, Settlors often deposit money with a financial institution simply "in trust" for another, without specifying specific duties, retaining the right to revoke, or changing the name of the beneficiary. The case of In re Totten, 179 N.Y. 112, 71 N.E. 748 (1904), was the first to sustain these trusts against claims that they were invalid testamentary transfers. The absence of specified duties make these Totten Trusts more like payable-on-death accounts, therefore, the Uniform Probate Code abolishes the concept of a Totten Trust and simply calls them P.O.D. accounts. *See* UNIF. PROB. CODE §6-201(8) (2003). States and commentators often refer to these trusts as "tentative trusts" or "saving account trusts," but the nature of the arrangement is the same. *See Restatement (Third) of Trusts* §26 (2003).

4. Joint Tenancy

In common law states, many, if not most, married couples own the homes in which they are living under tenancy by the entirety. This form of ownership is reserved to marriage and exists only in common law jurisdictions. Thus, upon death, the decedent's interest in the property ceases to exist and the surviving spouse owns the real property absolutely, without the necessity of probate. Hence, this is a non-probate device and is very advantageous because of speed. Likewise, if two or more unmarried persons in a common law state or a community property state wish to achieve the same non-probate result, the two parties may hold title as joint tenants. *See* GRACE GANZ BLUMBERG, COMMUNITY PROPERTY IN CALIFORNIA 174–75 (4th ed. 2003). The essential difference between tenancy by the entirety and joint tenancy, and tenants in common is that, in the former two, survivorship is implied in the title; a Last Will and Testament has no effect upon the joint tenancy. Whereas, with tenants in common, one party may devise his or her interest to another; there is a lack of non-probate survivorship.

5. Security Accounts

While bank deposits first come to mind when thinking of multiple party accounts, *see, e.g.,* Franklin v. Anna National Bank of Anna, *supra*, much of today's wealth is held in mutual funds and investor brokerage accounts. To address the concerns generated by these accounts, the Uniform Probate Code §§6-301 through 6-311 provides a procedure similar to payable-on-death provisions (here called transfer-on-death or "TOD"). Specifically, Uniform Probate Code §6-306 provides that: "The designation of a TOD beneficiary on a registration in beneficiary form has no effect on ownership until the owner's death. A registration of a security in beneficiary form may be canceled or changed at any time by the sole owner or all then surviving owners with the consent of the beneficiary."

III. Modification and Termination

Once a trust has been created by a competent Settlor, the traditional argument is that the Settlor's Trustee now has the legal ownership of the property but is responsible to the Settlor for the terms and conditions of the trust purpose. "The founder of [the] trust was the absolute owner of [the] property … [with] the entire right to dispose of it, either by an absolute gift … or by a gift with such restrictions or limitations, not repugnant to law, as [the Settlor] saw fit to impose." Broadway National Bank v. Adams, 133 Mass. 170 (1882). But should the Settlor be able to have a change of heart and terminate (revoke) the trust or modify its purposes? And should the beneficiaries be able to do the same? Finally, under what terms and conditions may the Trustee modify or terminate the trust? Consider the following circumstances.

A. Settlor

Connecticut General Life Insurance Co. v. First National Bank of Minneapolis
Supreme Court of Minnesota, 1977
262 N.W.2d 403

YETKA, Justice.

Appeal from judgment and order denying appellant's motion for amended findings of fact, conclusions of law, and order for judgment. The plaintiff, Connecticut General Life Insurance Co., filed a complaint in interpleader on September 9, 1974. After answers and counterclaims were filed, plaintiff deposited disputed life insurance proceeds with the court and was dismissed from the proceedings. After a trial without a jury, the District Court in Hennepin County determined that the disputed insurance proceeds were to be paid to the First National Bank of Minneapolis, as trustee of the John W. Aughenbaugh Trust. * * * Mrs. Marilyn Aughenbaugh appeals from that determination. We affirm.

On February 2, 1965, Connecticut General Life Insurance Co. (Connecticut General) issued John W. Aughenbaugh a life insurance policy. At that time there was in existence a Last Will and Testament of John W. Aughenbaugh, executed on or about March 16, 1964, which left his estate to Elizabeth Ann Aughenbaugh. On May 4, 1967, John W. Aughenbaugh executed a new will. On the same date he executed an instrument creating the John W. Aughenbaugh Revocable Insurance Trust (the trust). First National Bank of Minneapolis (respondent) was named as trustee. Part of the funding for the trust was to be provided by the Connecticut General policy. The trust was not funded in any respect except by the insurance policies listed. The respondent, First National Bank of Minneapolis, was made beneficiary of the Connecticut General Insurance policy; the trust beneficiaries were Elizabeth Ann Aughenbaugh and three Aughenbaugh children. There were other trusts created in the instrument but they are not in issue in the present case.

In February 1972 the last premium was paid. At that time John W. Aughenbaugh and Elizabeth Ann Aughenbaugh were married and living in Minneapolis. On November 10, 1972, they were divorced, and on February 14, 1973, John W. Aughenbaugh and Marilyn L. Melaas (appellant) were married in Nevada.

In April 1973 Aughenbaugh and his second spouse moved to Arizona. On or about October 16, 1973, John W. Aughenbaugh executed a document entitled "Will." The will purported to "supercede and cancel any previous wills or trusts established by me." It was entrusted by John Aughenbaugh to his wife Marilyn after it was executed. He died on October 21, 1973. The will was probated in Arizona. After several exchanges of documents between Connecticut General and appellant, the present action was instituted raising the issue as to whether the will executed by John W. Aughenbaugh on October

16, 1973, operated to revoke the John W. Aughenbaugh Revocable Insurance Trust, created May 4, 1967. The trial court held in the negative.

Appellant appears to raise five points in her brief, but three of those issues depend primarily upon whether the trust is inter vivos or testamentary in nature. The remaining two issues involve interpretation of the trust agreement itself.

* * *

Unless the trust can be characterized as testamentary, appellant's contentions that it can be revoked without notice and that it was impliedly revoked by the settlor's subsequent divorce and remarriage must fail. Appellant cites no authority for the proposition that a revocable life insurance trust is testamentary, even when the trust instrument is executed contemporaneously with a will. Thus, if the trust was inter vivos, much of the force of appellant's argument is lost.

In Minnesota, as in the overwhelming majority of jurisdictions, * * * a revocable life insurance trust is not testamentary, even though the settlor reserves the right to revoke or otherwise change it. In re Estate of Soper, 196 Minn. 60, 65, 264 N.W. 427, 430 (1935).

The only argument which appellant raises is that the trust would have no funds and would thus not operate or take effect until the death of the testator and is thus similar to other testamentary dispositions. She does not address the authorities or case law and advances no reasons for this court to change well settled trust law. Further, the appellant notes that Minn.St. 525.223, the Uniform Testamentary Additions to Trusts Act, appears to treat such trusts as non-testamentary. This statute allows the creation of "pour over" trusts and allows certain estate assets to be put into trusts which might otherwise fail because of lack of testamentary formalities. Thus, the trust was in force and there was a trustee appointed and acting at the time the new will of Mr. Aughenbaugh was executed in October, 1973.

* * *

It is the general rule that where a settlor reserves the power to revoke a trust by a transaction inter vivos, as for example by notice to the trustee, he cannot revoke the trust by his will. Restatement, Trusts (2d) § 330, comment j; Bogert, Trusts and Trustees, § 1001 (2 ed.); IV Scott on Trusts, § 330.8 (3 ed.). * * * The trust involved in the present case includes the following clause:

> 3.1) *Reservations Affecting the Trust.* Donor reserves the right to amend this agreement from time to time in any and all respects; to revoke the trust hereby created, in whole or in part; and to change the identity or number (or both) of the trustee or trustees hereunder, *by written instrument executed by Donor and delivered to any trustee* (or to Donor's wife if no trustee is acting at a particular time) *during Donor's lifetime*; provided, however, that the duties and responsibilities of the Trustee shall not be substantially increased by any such amendment without its written consent. (Italics supplied.)

The trial court interpreted this clause to mean that the trust could only be revoked by written instrument as set forth above. We agree.

Although the clause is not a model of good drafting, appellant concedes that the obvious intent of the section and the requirement of written notice is to protect the trustee. But once this purpose is conceded, any claimed ambiguity in this section of the trust disappears. Maximum protection for the trustee is provided by requiring all major changes to be made by notice to the trustee. * * *

This position, taken by the trial court, appears reasonable because the trustee would wish to know of any major change in its duties; revocation or amendment of the trust would constitute as major a change as an increase or decrease in the number of trustees. The sense of the clause, taken as a whole, is that changes which do not substantially increase the duties and responsibilities of the trustee may be made unilaterally by giving written notice, but that the trustee must concur in substantial increases in its duties.

Affirmed.

TODD, J., took no part in the consideration or decision of this case.

Notes

Most states provide that all trusts are irrevocable unless the Settlor expressly reserves the right to revoke. *See, e.g.,* N.Y. Est., Powers & Trusts L. §7-1.16 (2004). However, some states and the Uniform Trust Code §602 provide the reverse, stating that "unless the terms of a trust expressly provide that the trust is irrevocable, the settlor may revoke or amend the trust." If the trust is irrevocable, the trust may be modified or terminated only with the consent of the Settlor and all of the beneficiaries. *See* Unif. Trust Code §411(a) (2003). Most problems result from the inability of some of the beneficiaries to consent to termination because they are indeterminate. A provision from the Uniform Trust Code §411(e) is meant to allow a court to fashion an appropriate remedy to protect the non-consenting beneficiaries:

> If not all of the beneficiaries consent to a proposed modification or termination of the trust ... the modification or termination may be approved by the court if the court is satisfied that: (1) if all of the beneficiaries had consented, the trust could have been modified or terminated; and (2) the interests of a beneficiary who does not consent will be adequately protected.

Unif. Trust Code §411(a) (2003).

B. Beneficiaries

Adams v. Link

Supreme Court of Errors of Connecticut, 1958
145 Conn. 634, 145 A.2d 753

KING, Associate Justice.

The defendants Link and the United States Trust Company of New York are the executors and trustees under the will and codicil of Mildred A. Kingsmill, late of Darien. Mrs. Kingsmill left, as her sole heirs at law, two brothers, Orson Adams, Jr., and Alvin P. Adams, and a sister, Ethel A. Martin. This action grows out of, although it is distinct from, an appeal by Orson Adams, Jr., and Alvin P. Adams, two of the three heirs at law, from the admission of the will and codicil to probate.

In the view which we take of the case, only the right to terminate the trust created in paragraph sixth of the will need be considered. This paragraph disposed of the residue by a trust. It provided for the payment of the net income for life, in monthly or quarterly instalments at their written election, to Joan K. Pringle and Mayes M. Foeppel, neither of whom was an heir at law. At the death of the survivor, the trust was to terminate and distribution of the corpus was to be made to the New York Association for the Blind. In fact, Joan K. Pringle, predeceased the testatrix, leaving Mayes M. Foeppel as the sole income beneficiary and entitled, under the terms of the trust, to the entire net income for life.

During the pendency of the appeal from probate, a so-called compromise agreement was entered into between Mayes M. Foeppel, party of the first part, the New York Association for the Blind, party of the second part, and the three heirs at law of the testatrix, parties of the third part. The agreement in effect provided that (1) the appeal from the admission of the will and codicil to probate would be withdrawn; (2) 15 per cent of the residuary estate, i.e. the trust corpus, would be paid outright to the three heirs at law in equal shares; (3) 37 per cent would be paid outright to the New York Association for the Blind; and (4) 48 per cent would be paid outright to Mayes M. Foeppel less a deduction of $15,000 which would be used to establish a new trust, the precise terms of which are not material. Basically, it was for the education of a son of Alvin P. Adams, and upon completion of his education the trust would terminate and any unused corpus and interest would be returned to Mayes M. Foeppel. The compromise agreement was by its express terms made subject to the approval of the Superior Court. The defendant executors and trustees refused to participate in the agreement or to carry it out. The present action, the plaintiffs in which include all parties to the agreement except the New York Association for the Blind, which was made a party defendant, seeks in effect (a) the approval of the agreement by the Superior Court, and (b) a decree compelling the defendant executors and trustees to carry it out. Since the provision for the New York Association for the Blind was a charitable gift, the attorney general was made a defendant to represent the public interest, under the provisions of § 212 of the General Statutes. The court refused to approve the agreement, and from this action the plaintiffs took this appeal.

While the parties have extensively argued and briefed a number of questions, one basic proposition is dispositive of, and fatal to, the position taken by the plaintiffs. No corrections of the finding which could benefit them in this view of the case can be made.

The fundamental effect of the compromise agreement, if approved by the court, would be to abolish the trust. Our rule as to the right of the beneficiaries of a testamentary trust to have it terminated has been set forth in a number of cases, including Ackerman v. Union & New Haven Trust Co., 90 Conn. 63, 71, 96 A. 149; De Ladson v. Crawford, 93 Conn. 402, 411, 106 A. 326, and Hills v. Travelers Bank & Trust Co., 125 Conn. 640, 648, 7 A.2d 652, 173 A.L.R. 1419. The rule has also in effect been applied to the right of the beneficiaries to terminate an inter-vivos trust. Gaess v. Gaess, 132 Conn. 96, 101, 42 A.2d 796, 160 A.L.R. 432. Here a testatrix, in her will, established a trust in admittedly clear and unambiguous language; she has now died; and the trust beneficiaries and the heirs at law have joined in a plan to set aside the trust and substitute a distribution of the testatrix' estate more to their liking. Such a testamentary trust may be terminated only by a decree of a court of equity, regardless of any stipulation by all parties in interest. Peiter v. Degenring, 136 Conn. 331, 336, 71 A.2d 87. Our rule as set forth in Hills v. Travelers Bank & Trust Co., supra, is: Conditions precedent which should concur in order to warrant termination of a testamentary trust by judicial decree are (1) that all the parties in interest unite in seeking the termination, (2) that every reasonable ultimate purpose of the trust's creation and existence has been accomplished, and (3) that no fair and lawful restriction imposed by the testator will be nullified or disturbed by such a result. 'The function of the court [of equity] with reference to trusts is not to remake the trust instrument, reduce or increase the size of the gifts made therein or accord the beneficiary more advantage than the donor directed that he should enjoy, but rather to ascertain what the donor directed that the donee should receive and to secure to him the enjoyment of that interest only.' Hills v. Travelers Bank & Trust Co., supra [125 Conn. 640, 7 A.2d 655]; Peiter v. Degenring, supra. The underlying rationale of our rule is the protection, if reasonably possible, of any reasonable, properly expressed, testamentary desire of a decedent. 3 Scott, Trusts (2d Ed.) § 337.

It appears that all the interested beneficiaries have joined in the agreement under consideration. For the purposes of this case only, we will assume, without in any way deciding, that the plaintiffs are correct in their claim that the defendant executors and trustees have no standing to attack the compromise. This assumption is permissible because the compromise was in terms made contingent upon court approval, and this approval could not be compelled by any agreement of the trust beneficiaries among themselves. Peiter v. Degenring, supra. This we may assume, without deciding, that he first condition precedent under our rule is satisfied. But see Loring, A Trustee's Handbook (5th Ed.) § 122 p. 316, § 123 p. 318. The second and third conditions precedent have not, however, been satisfied. The obvious objectives of the testatrix were to provide (a) an assured income for life for Mayes M. Foeppel, and (b) at her death an intact corpus for the New York Association for the Blind. In carrying out these objectives, the testatrix took two important steps. In the first place, the management of the trust corpus was committed to trustees selected by her and in whose financial judgment she is presumed to have had confidence. Secondly, expenditure of any principal by the life beneficiary was precluded. Taken together, these two steps would tend to achieve, and in all reasonable probability would achieve, the testatrix' two basic objectives. To abolish the trust and turn over a fraction of the corpus outright to the life beneficiary would be to enable her in a moment to lose the protection of the practically assured life income provided by the testatrix. The two basic objectives of the trust's creation and existence were reasonable and commendable and cannot be fully accomplished prior to the death of the life beneficiary. Peiter v. Degenring, supra, 136 Conn. 337, 71 A.2d 90; 3 Scott, op. cit., § 337.1, p. 2454. Obviously, had the testatrix intended to entrust the life beneficiary with the handling of any part of the corpus, she would have so provided by a simple, outright gift.

The plaintiffs attempt to avoid the impact of our rule by two main claims. The first is that since the protection accorded the life beneficiary could be lost by her voluntary alienation of the income or by its involuntary alienation through attachment or seizure under an order in equity, the testatrix could not have intended to protect the beneficiary. This amounts in effect to a claim that only a spendthrift trust is protected from termination by agreement of all interested beneficiaries. The case against termination under our rule is of course even stronger where a spendthrift trust is involved, as in Mason v. Rhode Island Hospital Trust Co., 78 Conn. 81, 84, 61 A. 57. 3 Scott, op. cit., § 337.2. But the operation of our rule is not restricted to such trusts. The mere fact that the testatrix failed to provide the maximum possible protection for the life beneficiary by creating a spendthrift trust under the terms of what is now § 3195d of the 1955 Cumulative Supplement[1] does not warrant a conclusion that she intended no protection at all, so that we can consider that the trust no longer has any purpose. Id., p. 2454.

---

1. Sec. 3195d provides a procedure for the attachment of such an unrestricted life estate as was here created, but further provides:

> When any such trust shall have been expressly provided to be for the support of the beneficiary or his family, a court of equity having jurisdiction may make such order regarding

There is no merit in the plaintiffs' claim that in Peiter v. Degenring, supra, there was a change in, or a relaxation of, our rule. The facts in that case were peculiar. The testator's brother was seventy-eight years old and under a conservator. The testator created a trust for the payment to the brother or his conservator of 'so much of the income and principal of my estate as may be necessary for his support and comfort, using the income first.' In other words, the beneficiary was given neither principal nor income except as necessary for his support and comfort. The parties stipulated that the brother owned personal estate the annual income of which was greatly in excess of his needs for comfort and support, that he had not been entitled to receive and had not received any money from the trust, and that there was no possibility that he would be entitled to received any money from it at any time. The proposal of all interested parties was that the trust be terminated upon the payment to the brother of $10,000, which of course would be under the management of the conservator. We held that a decree terminating the trust could not be granted on any stipulation of the parties but only, if at all, upon the basis of facts found by testimony offered before the court, and that the trust should not be terminated 'unless those facts clearly establish that no purpose it was designed to serve would be defeated or jeopardized.' Id., 136 Conn. 340, 71 A.2d 91. There is nothing in the decision inconsistent with our rule as set forth in the other cases cited by us. The Peiter case does hold that evidence may be offered of facts, not apparent from the provisions of the trust instrument itself, which, if proved, would warrant a conclusion that the trust does not serve a legal and useful purpose and should be terminated. Ibid. We also held in the Peiter case that if satisfactory proof was made of the peculiar facts therein, it might warrant a conclusion by the court that in all reasonable probability the trust would remain inactive during the beneficiary's life and, if so, a termination might be ordered, as in the case of any useless trust. The Peiter case in nowise helps the plaintiffs here.

The case of Johnson's Appeal, 71 Conn. 590, 594, 42 A. 662, is also one wherein it was proven that facts extrinsic to the will made it impossible, as a practical matter, to carry out its terms. These facts were, in substance, that the estate had been distributed in good faith as intestate before any will was discovered; that several of the distributees were under conservators; that the funds distributed had in large part been spent by, or on behalf of, the distributees, so that as a practical matter it would be impossible to recover the funds distributed; and that some of the distributees were going to contest the admission of the will to probate. The actual holding of the case concerned only the scope of what is now, in amplified form, § 7016 of the General Statutes, empowering probate courts to authorize the settlement of disputed claims. The statute was held broad enough to authorize the Court of Probate to approve a compromise settlement of all disputes between all parties in interest, including the threatened appeal from the admission of the will to probate. Johnson's Appeal, supra, 71 Conn. 595, 42 A. 666. The question of the effect of such a settlement on an outstanding life estate was neither considered nor discussed. The further questions decided were that the statute was broad enough to authorize approval of the compromise even though the parties to the settlement included (a) the administrator c. t. a. of the will and (b) the respective conservators of certain distributees. Under the present, amplified wording of the statute, it is unlikely that the questions determined by the court would have arisen. It is implicit in

---

the surplus, if any, not required for the support of the beneficiary or his family, as justice and equity may require.

the opinion that the facts might warrant a conclusion by the Probate Court that it would be impossible, practically speaking, to carry out the terms of the will, even though it was admitted to probate. See 3 Scott, op. cit., § 335. The threatened appeal from probate was an incidental consideration, unnecessary to the decision of the case.

The plaintiffs also claim that whatever the rule may be in cases involving no will contest, a more liberal rule applies where, as here, the termination of the trust is a part of the settlement of such a contest. Some support for this position may be found in cases cited in 3 Scott, Trusts (2d Ed.) § 337.6. The rationale of our rule as to the power to set aside or terminate a trust is not, however, such that its applicability would be affected by the mere fact that the motivation of a trust termination agreement is the compromise of a will contest. It is true that such contests are not infrequently compromised by agreements involving the transfer of legacies or devises, in whole or in part, by beneficiaries under the will. Where such gifts are alienable this is permissible, since no violence is done to the provisions of the will. But that is not this case. Here the provisions of the will itself are being drastically changed so as to abolish a trust contrary to our rule. This cannot be done. It follows that the court below was not in error in denying approval of the agreement. Indeed, it was the only decision which could properly have been made. This conclusion makes unnecessary the consideration of the other grounds of appeal.

There is no error.

In this opinion the other judges concurred.

Notes

The court in Claflin v. Claflin, 149 Mass. 19, 20 N.E. 545 (1889), held that a trust could not be terminated if there still remained a material purpose of the Settlor. Hence, life income or even the presence of a spendthrift clause provided sufficient materiality to prevent termination. The Uniform Trust Code § 411(b) provides that an irrevocable trust may be terminated upon the consent of all of the beneficiaries if the court concludes that continuance of the trust is not necessary to achieve any material purpose of the trust. Furthermore, modification of an irrevocable trust may be achieved with consent of all of the beneficiaries if the court concludes that modification is not inconsistent with a material purpose of the trust. But a less restrictive alternative may be found in Uniform Trust Code § 412, which allows the court to modify or terminate a trust if, because of circumstances not anticipated by the Settlor, modification or termination would further the terms of the trust; administrative terms of the trust may be modified if existing terms would make the trust wasteful or impracticable. This is complemented by Uniform Trust Code § 415, which provides that a court may reform the terms of a trust, even if unambiguous, to conform to the Settlor's intent if there is clear and convincing evidence that both the Settlor's intent and the terms of the trust were affected by a mistake of fact or law.

Typical reasons for seeking modification or termination are changes in the tax law, seeking to take advantage of a marital deduction, disqualification from public assistance, and the need for additional income. See generally RICHARD A. POSNER, ECONOMIC ANALYSIS OF LAW 556 (5th ed. 1998). Often the problem is that unborn beneficiaries are unavailable to give consent to termination of the trust. California provides that "the guardian ad litem may rely on general family benefit accruing to living members of the beneficiary's family as a basis for approving a modification or termination of the trust." CAL. PROB. CODE § 15405 (2004).

C. Trustee

Uniform Trust Code (2003)

Section 414. Modification or Termination of Uneconomic Trust.

(a) After notice to the qualified beneficiaries, the trustee of a trust consisting of trust property having a total value less that [$50,000] may terminate the trust if the trustee concludes that the value of the trust property is insufficient to justify the cost of administration.

(b) The court may modify or terminate a trust or remove the trustee and appoint a different trustee if it determines that the value of the trust property is insufficient to justify the cost of administration.

(c) Upon termination of a trust under this section, the trustee shall distribute the trust property in a manner consistent with the purposes of the trust.

Section 706. Removal of Trustee.

(b) The court may remove a trustee if:

(4) there has been a substantial change of circumstances or removal is requested by all of the qualified beneficiaries, the court finds that removal of the trustee best serves the interests of all of the beneficiaries and is not inconsistent with a material purpose of the trust, and a suitable cotrustee or successor trustee is available.

IV. Administration of Trusts

A. Loyalty and Impartiality Among Beneficiaries

Uniform Trust Code (2003)

Section 802. Duty of Loyalty.

(a) A trustee shall administer the trust solely in the interests of the beneficiaries.

Section 811. Enforcement and Defense of Claims.

A trustee shall take reasonable steps to enforce claims of the trust and to defend claims against the trust.

Section 803. Impartiality.

If a trust has two or more beneficiaries, the trustee shall act impartially in investing, managing, and distributing the trust property, giving due regard to the beneficiaries' respective interests.

Section 813. Duty to Inform and Report.

(a) A trustee shall keep the qualified beneficiaries of the trust reasonably informed about the administration of the trust and of the material facts necessary for them to protect their interests. Unless unreasonable under the circumstances, a trustee shall promptly respond to a beneficiary's request for information related to the administration of the trust.

Section 1002. Damages for Breach of Trust.

(a) A trustee who commits a breach of trust is liable to the beneficiaries affected for the greater of:

(1) the amount required to restore the value of the trust property and trust distributions to what they would have been had the breach not occurred; or

(2) the profit the trustee made by reason of the breach.

Section 814. Discretionary Powers; Tax Savings.

(a) Notwithstanding the breadth of discretion granted to a trustee in the terms of the trust, including the use of such terms as "absolute", "sole", or "uncontrolled", the trustee shall exercise a discretionary power in food faith and in accordance with the terms and purposes of the trust and the interests of the beneficiaries.

In re Rothko

Court of Appeals of New York, 1977
43 N.Y.2d 305, 372 N.E.2d 291, 140 N.Y.S.2d 449

Cooke, J.

Mark Rothko, an abstract expressionist painter whose works through the years gained for him an international reputation of greatness, died testate on February 25, 1970. The principal asset of his estate consisted of 798 paintings of tremendous value, and the dispute underlying this appeal involves the conduct of his three executors in their disposition of these works of art. In sum, that conduct as portrayed in the record and sketched in the opinions was manifestly wrongful and indeed shocking.

Rothkos' will was admitted to probate on April 27, 1970 and letters testamentary were issued to Bernard J. Reis, Theodoros Stamos and Morton Levine. Hastily and within a period of only about three weeks and by virtue of two contracts each dated May 21, 1970, the executors dealt with all 798 paintings.

By a contract of sale, the estate executors agreed to sell to Marlborough AG., a Liechtenstein corporation (hereinafter MAG), 100 Rothko paintings as listed for $1,800,000, $200,000 to be paid on execution of the agreement and the balance of $1,600,000 in 12 equal interest-free installments over a 12-year period. Under the second agreement, the executors consigned to Marlborough Gallery, Inc., a domestic corporation (hereinafter MNY), "approximately 700 paintings listed on a Schedule to be prepared", the consignee to be responsible for costs covering items such as insurance, storage restoration and promotion. By its provisos, MNY could sell up to 35 paintings a year from each of two groups, pre-1947 and post-1947, for 12 years at the best price obtainable but not less than the appraised estate value, and it would receive a 50% commission on each painting sold, except for a commission of 40% on those sold to or through other dealers.

Petitioner Kate Rothko, decedent's daughter and a person entitled to share in his estate by virtue of an election under EPTL 5-3.3, instituted this proceeding to remove the executors, to enjoin MNY and MAG from disposing of the paintings, to rescind the aforesaid agreements between the executors and said corporations, for a return of the paintings still in possession of those corporations, and for damages. She was joined by the guardian of her brother Christopher Rothko, likewise interested in the estate, who answered by adopting the allegations of his sister's petition and by demanding the same relief. The Attorney-General of the State, as the representative of the ultimate beneficiaries of the Mark Rothko Foundation, Inc., a charitable corporation and the residuary legatee under decedent's will, joined in requesting relief substantially similar to that prayed for by petitioner. On June 26, 1972 the Surrogate issued a temporary restraining order and on September 26, 1972 a preliminary injunction enjoining MAG, MNY, and the three executors from selling or otherwise disposing of the paintings referred to in the agreements dated May 21, 1970, except for sales or dispositions made with court permission. The Appellate Division modified the preliminary injunction order by increasing the amount of the bond and otherwise affirmed. By a 1974 petition, the Attorney-General, on behalf of the ultimate charitable beneficiaries of the Mark Rothko Foundation, sought the punishment of MNY, MAG, Lloyd and Reis for contempt and other relief.

Following a nonjury trial covering 89 days and in a thorough opinion, the Surrogate found: that Reis was a director, secretary and treasurer of MNY, the consignee art gallery, in addition to being a coexecutor of the estate; that the testator had a 1969 inter vivos contract with MNY to sell Rothko's work at a commission of only 10% and whether that agreement survived testator's death was problem that a fiduciary in a dual position could not have impartially faced; that Reis was in a position of serious conflict of interest with respect to the contracts of May 21, 1970 and that his dual role and planned purpose benefited the Marlborough interests to the detriment of the estate; that it was to the advantage of coexecutor Stamos as a "not-too-successful artist, financially", to curry favor with Marlborough and that the contract made by him with MNY within months after signing the estate contracts placed him in a position where his personal interests conflicted with those of the estate, especially leading to lax contract enforcement efforts by Stamos; that Stamos acted negligently and improvidently in view of his own knowledge of the conflict of interest of Reis; that the third coexecutor, Levine, while not acting in self-interest or with bad faith, nonetheless failed to exercise ordinary prudence in the performance of his assumed fiduciary obligations since he was aware of Reis' divided loyalty, believed that Stamos was also seeking personal advantage, possessed personal opinions as to the value of the paintings and yet followed the leadership of his coexecutors without investigation of essential facts or consultation with competent and disinterested appraisers, and that the business transactions of the two Marlborough corporations were admittedly controlled and directed by Francis K. Lloyd. It was concluded that the acts and failures of the three executors were clearly improper to such a substantial extent as to mandate their removal under SCPA 711 as estate fiduciaries. The Surrogate also found that MNY, MAG and Lloyd were guilty of contempt in shipping, disposing of and selling 57 paintings in violation of the temporary restraining order dated June 26, 1972 and of the injunction dated September 26, 1972; that the contracts for sale and consignment of paintings between the executors and MNY and MAG provided inadequate value to the estate, amounting to a lack of mutuality and fairness resulting from conflicts on the part of Reis and Stamos and improvidence on the part of all executors; that said contracts were voidable and were set aside by reason of violation of the duty of loyalty and improvidence of the executors, knowingly participated in and induced by MNY and MAG; that the fact that these agreements were voidable did not revive the 1696 inter vivos agreements since the parties by their conduct evinced an intent to abandon and abrogate these compacts. The Surrogate held that the present value at the time of trial of the paintings sold is the proper measure of damages as to MNY, MAG, Lloyd, Reis and Stamos. He imposed a civil fine of $3,332,000 upon MNY, MAG and Lloyd, same being the appreciated value at the time of trial of the 57 paintings sold in violation of the temporary restraining order and injunction.[1] It was held that Levine was liable for $6,464,880 in damages, as he was not in a dual position acting for his own interest and was thus liable only for the actual value of paintings sold MNY and MAG as of the dates of sale, and that Reis, Stamos, MNY and MAG, apart from being jointly and severally liable for the same damages as Levine for negligence, were liable for the greater sum of $9,252,000 "as appreciation damages less amounts previously paid to the estate with regard to sales of paintings." The cross petition of the Attorney-General to reopen the record for submission of newly discovered documentary evidence was denied. The liabilities were held to be congruent so that payment of the highest sum would satisfy all lesser liabilities including the civil fines and the liabilities for damages were to be reduced by payment of the fine levied or by return of any of the 57 paintings disposed of, the new fiduciary to have the option in the first instance to specify which paintings the fiduciary would accept.

The Appellate Division, in an opinion by Justice Lane, modified to the extent of deleting the option given the new fiduciary to specify which paintings he would accept. Except for this modification, the majority affirmed on the opinion of Surrogate Midonick, with additional comments. Among others, it was stated that the entire court agreed that executors Reis and Stamos had a conflict of interest and divided loyalty in view of their nexus to MNY and that a majority were in agreement with the Surrogate's assessment of liability as to executor Levine and his findings of liability against MNY, MAG and Lloyd. The majority agreed with the Surrogate's analysis awarding "appreciation damages" and found further support for his rationale in Menzel v List (24 NY2d 91). Justice Kupferman, in an opinion styled "concurring in part and dissenting in part", stated that, although he had "expressed reservations with respect to various factors to be considered in the calculation of damages", he concurred "in the basic conclusion and, therefore, in order to resolve the matter for the purpose of appeal" voted to modify as per the Lane opinion (56 AD2d 499, 505–506). Justices Capozzoli and Nunez, in separate dissenting in part opinions, viewed Menzel v List as inapplicable and voted to modify and remit to determine the reasonable value of the paintings as of May, 1970, when estate contracts with MNY and MAG had their inception in writing.

* * *

In seeking a reversal, it is urged that an improper legal standard was applied in voiding the estate contracts of May, 1970, that the "no further inquiry" rule applies only to self-dealing and that in case of a conflict of interest, absent self-dealing, a challenged transaction must be shown to be unfair. The subject of fairness of the contracts is intertwined with the issue of whether Reis and Stamos were guilty of conflicts of interest.[2]

---

1. The decree of the Surrogate's Court, New York County, dated January 15, 1976, was amended in this respect pursuant to an order filed April 28, 1976 by substituting "63" for "57" as the number of paintings sold and disposed of and "$3,872,000" as the amount of the fine instead of "$3,332,000".

2. In New York, an executor, as such, takes a qualified legal title to all personalty specifically bequeathed and an unqualified legal title to that not so bequeathed; he holds not in his own right but as a trustee for the benefit of creditors, those entitled to receive under the will and, if all is not bequeathed, those entitled to distribution under the EPTL (Blood v Kane, 130 NY 514, 517; see

Scott is quoted to the effect that "[a] trustee does not necessarily incur liability merely because he has an individual interest in the transaction *** In Bullivant v. First Nat. Bank [246 Mass 324] it was held that *** the fact that the bank was also a creditor of the corporation did not make its assent invalid, if it acted in good faith and the plan was fair" (2 Scott, Trusts, § 170.24, p 1384 [emphasis added]), and our attention has been called to the statement in Phelan v Middle States Oil Corp. (220 F2d 593, 603, cert den sub nom. Cohen v Glass, 349 US 929) that Judge Learned Hand found "no decisions that have applied [the no further inquiry rule] inflexibly to every occasion in which the fiduciary has been shown to have had a personal interest that might in fact have conflicted with his loyalty".

These contentions should be rejected. First, a review of the opinions of the Surrogate and the Appellate Division manifests that they did not rely solely on a "no further inquiry rule", and secondly, there is more than an adequate basis to conclude that the agreements between the Marlborough corporations and the estate were neither fair nor in the best interests of the estate. This is demonstrated, for example, by the comments of the Surrogate concerning the commissions on the consignment of the 698 paintings (see 84 Misc 2d 830, 852–853) and those of the Appellate Division concerning the sale of the 100 paintings (see 56 AD2d, at pp 501–502). The opinions under review demonstrate that neither the Surrogate nor the Appellate Division set aside the contracts by merely applying the no further inquiry rule without regard to fairness. Rather they determined, quite properly indeed, that these agreements were neither fair nor in the best interests of the estate.

To be sure, the assertions that there were no conflicts of interest on the part of Reis or Stamos indulge in sheer fantasy. Besides being a director and officer of MNY, for which there was financial remuneration, however slight, Reis, as noted by the Surrogate, had different inducements to favor the Marlborough interests, including his own aggrandizement of status and financial advantage through sales of almost one million dollars for items from his own and his family's extensive private art collection by the Marlborough interests (see 84 Misc 2d, at pp 843–844). Similarly, Stamos benefited as an artist under contract with Marlborough and, interestingly, Marlborough purchased a Stamos painting from a third party for $4,000 during the week in May, 1970 when the estate contract negotiations were pending (see 84 Misc 2d, at p 845). The conflicts are manifest. Further, as noted in Bogert, Trusts and Trustees (2d ed), "The duty of loyalty imposed on the fiduciary prevents him from accepting employment from a third party who is entering into a business transaction with the trust" (§ 543, subd [S], p 573). "While he [a trustee] is administering the trust he must refrain from placing himself in a position where his personal interest or that of a third person does or may conflict with the interest of the beneficiaries" (Bogert, Trusts [Hornbook Series—5th ed], p 343). Here, Reis was employed and Stamos benefited in a manner contemplated by Bogert (see, also, Meinhard v Salmon, 249 NY 458, 464, 466–467; Schmidt v Chambers, 265 Md 9, 33–38). In short, one must strain the law rather than follow it to reach the result suggested on behalf of Reis and Stamos.

Levine contends that, having acted prudently and upon the advice of counsel, a complete defense was established. Suffice it to say, an executor who knows that his coexecutor is committing breaches of trust and not only fails to exert efforts directed towards prevention but accedes to them is legally accountable even though he was acting on the advice of counsel (Matter of Westerfield, 32 App Div 324, 344; 3 Scott, Trusts [3d ed],

---

Bischoff v Yorkville Bank, 218 NY 106, 110–111; Bankers Sur. Co. v Meyer, 205 NY 219, 223–224; but see Restatement, Trusts 2d, § 6; Bogert, Trusts [Hornbook Series—5th ed], p 31).

§ 201, p 1657). When confronted with the question of whether to enter into the Marlborough contracts, Levine was acting in a business capacity, not a legal one, in which he was required as an executor primarily to employ such diligence and prudence to the care and management of the estate assets and affairs as would prudent persons of discretion and intelligence (King v Talbot, 40 NY 76, 85–86), accented by "[n]ot honesty alone, but the punctilio of an honor the most sensitive" (Meinhard v Salmon, 249 NY 458, 464, supra;). Alleged good faith on the part of a fiduciary forgetful of his duty is not enough (Wendt v Fischer, 243 NY 439, 443). He could not close his eyes, remain passive or move with unconcern in the face of the obvious loss to be visited upon the estate by participation in those business arrangements and then shelter himself behind the claimed counsel of an attorney (see Matter of Niles, 113 NY 547, 558; Matter of Huntley, 13 Misc 375, 380; 3 Warren's Heaton, Surrogates' Courts [6th ed], § 217, subd 3, par [b]).

Further, there is no merit to the argument that MNY and MAG lacked notice of the breach of trust. The record amply supports the determination that they are chargeable with notice of the executors' breach of duty.

The measure of damages was the issue that divided the Appellate Division (see 56 AD2d, at p 500). The contention of Reis, Stamos, MNY and MAG, that the award of appreciation damages was legally erroneous and impermissible, is based on a principle that an executor authorized to sell is not liable for an increase in value if the breach consists only in selling for a figure less than that for which the executor should have sold. For example, Scott states:

"The beneficiaries are not entitled to the value of the property at the time of the decree if it was not the duty of the trustee to retain the property in the trust and the breach of trust consisted *merely* in selling the property for too low a price" (3 Scott, Trusts [3d ed], § 208.3, p 1687 [emphasis added]).

"If the trustee is guilty of a breach of trust in selling trust property for an inadequate price, he is liable for the difference between the amount he should have received and the amount which he did receive. He is not liable, however, for any subsequent rise in value of the property sold". (Id., § 208.6, pp 1689–1690.) A recitation of similar import appears in Comment d under Restatement, Trusts 2d (§ 205): "d. Sale for less than value. If the trustee is authorized to sell trust property, but in breach of trust he sells it for less than he should receive, he is liable for the value of the property at the time of the sale less the amount which he received. If the breach of trust consists only in selling it for too little, he is not chargeable with the amount of any subsequent increase in value of the property under the rule stated in Clause (c), as he would be if he were not authorized to sell the property. See § 208." (Emphasis added.) However, employment of "merely" and "only" as limiting words suggests that where the breach consists of some misfeasance, other than solely for selling "for too low a price" or "for too little", appreciation damages may be appropriate. Under Scott (§ 208.3, pp 1686–1687) and the Restatement (§ 208), the trustee may be held liable for appreciation damages if it was his or her duty to retain the property, the theory being that the beneficiaries are entitled to be placed in the same position they would have been in had the breach not consisted of a sale of property that should have been retained. The same rule should apply where the breach of trust consists of a serious conflict of interest—which is more than merely selling for too little.

The reason for allowing appreciation damages, where there is a duty to retain, and only date of sale damages, where there is authorization to sell, is policy oriented. If a trustee authorized to sell were subjected to a greater measure of damages he might be reluctant to sell (in which event he might run a risk if depreciation ensued). On the other hand, if there is a duty to retain and the trustee sells there is no policy reason to protect the trustee; he has not simply acted imprudently, he has violated an integral condition of the trust.

"If a trustee in breach of trust transfers trust property to a person who takes with notice of the breach of trust, and the transferee has disposed of the property *** [i]t seems proper to charge him with the value at the time of the decree, since if it had not been for the breach of trust the property would still have been a part of the trust estate" (4 Scott, Trusts [3d ed], § 291.2; see, also, United States v Dunn, 268 US 121, 132). This rule of law which applies to the transferees MNY and MAG also supports the imposition of appreciation damages against Reis and Stamos, since if the Marlborough corporations are liable for such damages either as purchaser or consignees with notice, from one in breach of trust, it is only logical to hold that said executors, as sellers and consignors, are liable also pro tanto.

Contrary to assertions of appellants and the dissenters at the Appellate Division, Menzel v List (24 NY2d 91, supra;) is authority for the allowance of appreciation damages. There, the damages involved a breach of warranty of title to a painting which at one time had been stolen from plaintiff and her husband and ultimately sold to defendant. Here, the executors, though authorized to sell, did not merely err in the amount they accepted but sold to one with whom Reis and Stamos had a self-interest. To make the injured party whole, in both instances the quantum of damages should be the same. In other words, since the paintings cannot be returned, the estate is therefore entitled to their value at the time of the decree, i.e., appreciation damages. These are not punitive damages in a true sense, rather they are damages intended to make the estate whole. Of course, as to Reis, Stamos, MNY and MAG, these damages might be considered by some to be exemplary in a sense, in that they serve as a warning to others (see Reynolds v Pegler, 123 F Supp 36, 38, affd 223 F2d 429, cert den 350 US 846), but their true character is ascertained when viewed in the light of overriding policy considerations and in the realization that the sale and consignment were not merely sales below value but inherently wrongful transfers which should allow the owner to be made whole (see Menzel v List, 24 NY2d 91, 97, supra; see, also, Simon v Electrospace Corp., 28 NY2d 136, 144, supra).

The decree of the Surrogate imposed appreciation damages against Reis, Stamos, MNY and MAG in the amount of $7,339,464.72—computed as $9,252,000 (86 works on canvas at $90,000 each and 54 works on paper at $28,000 each) less the aggregate amounts paid the estate under the two rescinded agreements and interest. Appellants chose not to offer evidence of "present value" and the only proof furnished on the subject was that of the expert Heller whose appraisal as of January, 1974 (the month previous to that when trial commenced) on a painting-by-painting basis totaled $15,1000,000. There was also testimony as to bona fide sales of other Rothkos between 1971 and 1974. Under the circumstances, it was impossible to appraise the value of the unreturned works of art with an absolute certainty and, so long as the figure arrived at had a reasonable basis of computation and was not merely speculative, possible or imaginary, the Surrogate had the right to resort to reasonable conjectures and probable estimates and to make the best approximation possible through the exercise of good judgment and common sense in arriving at that amount * * * [citations omitted]. This is particularly so where the conduct of wrongdoers has rendered it difficult to ascertain the damages suffered with the precision otherwise possible (Story Parchment Co. v Paterson Co., supra, at p 563; Eastman Co. v Southern Photo Co., supra, at p 379). Significantly, the Surrogate's factual finding as to the present value of these unreturned paintings was affirmed by the Appellate Division and, since that finding had support in the record and was not legally erroneous, it should not now be subjected to our disturbance.

On February 21, 1969, decedent made a contract with MAG which provided that "Mark Rothko agrees not to sell any works of art for a period of eight years, except to Marlborough A.G. if a supplementary contract is made." A supplementary contract made that same day recited that "Mark Rothko has the option to sell to Marlborough A.G. an additional four paintings each year at prices not below Marlborough A.G.'s then current selling prices, the price to be paid being [90%] of the current selling prices." The Surrogate reasoned that the fact that the 1970 agreements for the sale and consignment of paintings were voidable because of self-dealing did not revive the 1969 inter vivos agreements and found that the parties by their conduct intended to abandon and abrogate these 1969 agreements. In turn and in effect, the Appellate Division agreed with this finding of abandonment (56 AD2d, at p 501). "A voidable contract is one where one or more parties thereto have the power, by a manifestation of election to do so, to avoid the legal relations created by the contract; or by ratification of the contract to extinguish the power of avoidance" (Restatement, Contracts, § 13). Where a contract is voidable on both sides, as where there has been a violation of the duty of loyalty and improvidence by executors knowingly participated in and induced by the other contracting parties (see 84 Misc 2d, at p 858), the transaction is not wholly void, since in order to prevent the contract from having its normal operation the claim or defense must in some manner be asserted and also since the contract is capable of ratification, such a contract affects from the outset the legal relations of the parties (1 Williston, Contracts [3d ed], § 15, pp 28–29). The question of whether there has been an abandonment or abrogation of a contract is usually one of fact (see Green v Doniger, 300 NY 238, 245) and the circumstances disclosed by the record, including a showing of the new agreements in 1970, contained a sufficient basis for the finding of the abandonment or abrogation of those which came into being in 1969 (see Schwartzreich v Bauman-Basch, 231 NY 196, 203).

The Marlborough corporations and Lloyd contend that there was no violation of either the temporary restraining order or the preliminary injunction by the delivery of paintings sold prior to the court's restraints and that, therefore, the finding of contempt was erroneous. The Attorney-General in response contends that the "group" sales did not pass equitable ownership and that even if the invoices had been typed prior to said order and injunction no sale took place until after the injunction. In support of the latter position, the Uniform Commercial Code (§ 2-106, subd [1]; §§ 2-307, 2-401, subds [2], [3]) is cited for the proposition that as a matter of law the questioned sales took place on delivery to the purchasers which in all instances occurred after the injunction, the latter of the two court restraints. MNY, MAG and Lloyd counter with the argument that, under art market custom, invoices of paintings are sales and that the restraining order and preliminary injunction failed to clearly state what acts were prohibited. In any event, the plain and simple import of both the order and the injunction—not to sell or otherwise dispose of the paintings (cf. Matter of Black, 138 App Div 562, 565)—was violated by dispositions of them. Consequently, it is immaterial how the applicable Uniform Commercial Code provisions might be interpreted. If MNY, MAG and Lloyd had invoiced paintings and were acting in good faith, they would have advised the court of their prior commitments.

We have considered the other alleged errors urged by the parties, and find those arguments to be without merit. In short, we find no basis for disturbing the result reached below.

Accordingly, the order of the Appellate Division should be affirmed, with costs to the prevailing parties against appellants, and the question certified answered in the affirmative.

Chief Judge Breitel and Judges Jasen, Gabrielli, Jones, Wachtler and Fuchsberg concur.

Order affirmed, etc.

Notes

Conflict of interest is often in the eye of the beholder. The Uniform Trust Code §802(b) provides that a sale involving the investment or management of trust property, entered into by the trustee for the trustee's own personal account or which is otherwise affected by a conflict between the Trustee's fiduciary and personal interests, is voidable by a beneficiary affected by the transaction unless certain conditions occur. Also, in Uniform Trust Code §802(c), there is a presumption of a conflict between personal and fiduciary interests of the Trustee, if there is a sale of trust property by the Trustee to: (1) the Trustee's spouse; (2) the Trustee's descendants, siblings, or parents, or their spouses; (3) an agent or attorney of the Trustee; or (4) a corporation or other enterprise in which the Trustee has an interest that might affect the Trustee's best judgement. These Code provisions imply a voidable breach of loyalty, but the conflict of interest is rebutted

> if the trustee establishes that the transaction was not affected by a conflict between personal and fiduciary interests. Among the factors tending to rebut the presumption are whether the consideration was fair and whether the other terms of the transaction are similar to those that would be transacted with an independent party.

UNIF. TRUST CODE §802 (2003) (Comment).

Dennis v. Rhode Island Hospital Trust Co.
United States Court of Appeals, First Circuit, 1984
744 F.2d 893

BREYER, Circuit Judge.

The plaintiffs are the great-grandchildren of Alice M. Sullivan and beneficiaries of a trust created under her will. They claimed in the district court that the Bank trustee had breached various fiduciary obligations owed them as beneficiaries of that trust. The trust came into existence in 1920. It will cease to exist in 1991 (twenty-one years after the 1970 death of Alice Sullivan's last surviving child). The trust distributes all its income for the benefit of Alice Sullivan's living issue; the principal is to go to her issue surviving in 1991. Evidently, since the death of their mother, the two plaintiffs are the sole surviving issue, entitled to the trust's income until 1991, and then, as remaindermen, entitled to the principal.

The controversy arises out of the trustee's handling of the most important trust assets, undivided interests in three multi-story commercial buildings in downtown Providence. The buildings (the Jones, Wheaton-Anthony, and Alice Buildings) were all constructed before the beginning of the century, in an area where the value of the property has declined markedly over the last thirty years. During the period that the trust held these interests the buildings were leased to a number of different tenants, including corporations which subsequently subleased the premises. Income distribution from the trust to the life tenants has averaged over $34,000 annually.

At the time of the creation of the trust in 1920, its interests in the three buildings were worth more than $300,000. The trustee was authorized by the will to sell real estate. When the trustee finally sold the buildings in 1945, 1970, and 1979, respectively, it did so at or near the lowest point of their value; the trust received a total of only $185,000 for its interests in them. These losses, in plaintiffs' view, reflect a serious mishandling of assets over the years.

The district court, 571 F.Supp. 623, while rejecting many of plaintiffs' arguments, nonetheless found that the trustee had failed to act impartially, as between the trust's income beneficiaries and the remaindermen; it had favored the former over the latter, and, in doing so, it had reduced the value of the trust assets. To avoid improper favoritism, the trustee should have sold the real estate interests, at least by 1950, and reinvested the proceeds elsewhere. By 1950 the trustee must have, or should have, known that the buildings' value to the remaindermen would be small; the character of downtown commercial Providence was beginning to change; retention of the buildings would work to the disadvantage of the remaindermen. The court ordered a surcharge of $365,000, apparently designed to restore the real value of the trust's principal to its 1950 level.

On appeal, plaintiffs and defendants attack different aspects of the district court's judgment. We have reviewed the record in light of their arguments. We will not overturn a district court's factual determination unless it is "clearly erroneous," Fed.R.Civ.P. 52(a). And, in a diversity case such as this one, involving a technical subject matter primarily of state concern, we are "reluctant to interfere with a reasonable construction of state law made by a district judge, sitting in the state, who is familiar with that state's law and practices." * * * [citations omitted]. Application of these principles leads us, with one minor exception, to affirm the district court's judgment.

* * *

The trustee first argues that the district court's conclusions rest on "hindsight." It points out that Rhode Island law requires a trustee to be "prudent and vigilant and exercise sound judgment," Rhode Island Hospital Trust Co. v. Copeland, 39 R.I. 193, 98 A. 273, 279 (1916), but "[n]either prophecy nor prescience is expected." Stark v. United States Trust Co. of New York, 445 F.Supp. 670, 678 (S.D.N.Y.1978). It adds that a trustee can indulge a preference for keeping the trust's "inception assets," those placed in trust by the settlor and commended to the trustee for retention. See Peckham v. Newton, 15 R.I. 321, 4 A. 758, 760 (1886); Rhode Island Hospital Trust Co. v. Copeland, supra. How then, the trustee asks, can the court have found that it should have sold these property interests in 1950?

The trustee's claim might be persuasive had the district court found that it had acted imprudently in 1950, in retaining the buildings. If that were the case, one might note that every 1950 sale involved both a pessimistic seller and an optimistic buyer; and one might ask how the court could expect the trustee to have known then (in 1950) whose prediction would turn out to be correct. The trustee's argument is less plausible, however, where, as here, the district court basically found that in 1950 the trustee had acted not imprudently, but unfairly, between income beneficiaries and remaindermen.

Suppose, for example, that a trustee of farmland over a number of years overplants the land, thereby increasing short run income, but ruining the soil and making the farm worthless in the long run. The trustee's duty to take corrective action would arise from the fact that he knows (or plainly ought to know) that his present course of action will injure the remaindermen; settled law requires him to act impartially, "with due regard" for the "respective interests" of both the life tenant and the remainderman. Restatement (Second) of Trusts § 232 (1959). See also A. Scott, The Law of Trusts § 183 (1967); G.G. Bogert & G.T. Bogert, The Law of Trusts and Trustees § 612 (1980). The district court here found that a sale in 1950 would have represented one way (perhaps the only practical way) to correct this type of favoritism. It held that instead of correcting the problem, the trustee continued to favor the life tenant to the "very real disadvantage" of the remainder interests, in violation of Rhode Island law. See Industrial Trust Co. v. Parks, 57 R.I. 363, 190 A. 32, 38 (1937); Rhode Island Hospital Trust Co. v. Tucker, 52 R.I. 277, 160 A. 465, 466 (1932).

To be more specific, in the court's view the problem arose out of the trustee's failure to keep up the buildings, to renovate them, to modernize them, or to take other reasonably obvious steps that might have given the remaindermen property roughly capable of continuing to produce a reasonable income. This failure allowed the trustee to make larger income payments during the life of the trust; but the size of those payments reflected the trustee's acquiescence in the gradual deterioration of the property. In a sense, the payments ate away the trust's capital.

The trustee correctly points out that it did take certain steps to keep up the buildings; and events beyond its control made it difficult to do more. In the 1920's, the trustee, with court approval, entered into very longterm leases on the Alice and Wheaton-Anthony buildings. The lessees and the subtenants were supposed to keep the buildings in good repair; some improvements were made. Moreover, the depression made it difficult during the 1930's to find tenants who would pay a high rent and keep up the buildings. After World War II the neighborhood enjoyed a brief renaissance; but, then, with the 1950's flight to the suburbs, it simply deteriorated.

Even if we accept these trustee claims, however, the record provides adequate support for the district court's conclusions. There is considerable evidence indicating that, at least by 1950, the trustee should have been aware of the way in which the buildings' high rents, the upkeep problem, the changing neighborhood, the buildings' age, the failure to modernize, all together were consuming the buildings' value. There is evidence that the trustee did not come to grips with the problem. Indeed, the trustee did not appraise the properties periodically, and it did not keep proper records. It made no formal or informal accounting in 55 years. There is no indication in the record that the trust's officers focused upon the problem or consulted real estate experts about it or made any further rehabilitation efforts. Rather, there is evidence that the trustee did little more than routinely agree to the requests of the trust's income beneficiaries that it manage the trust corpus to produce the largest possible income. The New Jersey courts have pointed out that an impartial trustee must

> view the overall picture as it is presented from all the facts, and not close its eyes to any relevant facts which might result in excessive burden to the one class in preference to the other.

Pennsylvania Co. v. Gillmore, 137 N.J.Eq. 51, 43 A.2d 667, 672 (1945). The record supports a conclusion of failure to satisfy that duty.

The district court also found that the trustee had at least one practical solution available. It might have sold the property in 1950 and reinvested the proceeds in other assets of roughly equivalent total value that did not create a "partiality" problem. The Restatement of Trusts foresees such a solution, for it says that

> the trustee is under a duty to the beneficiary who is ultimately entitled to the principal not to ... retain property which is certain or likely to depreciate in value, although the property yields a large income, unless he makes adequate provision for amortizing the depreciation.

Restatement (Second) of Trusts § 232, comment b. Rhode Island case law also allows the court considerable discretion, in cases of fiduciary breach, to fashion a remedy, including a remedy based on a hypothetical, earlier sale. In, for example, Industrial Trust Co. v. Parks, 190 A. at 42, the court apportioned payments between income and principal "in the same way as they would have been apportioned if [certain] rights had been sold by the trustees immediately after the death of the testator" for a specified hypothetical value, to which the court added hypothetical interest. In the absence of a showing that such a sale and reinvestment would have been impractical or that some equivalent or better curative steps might have been taken, the district court's use of a 1950 sale as a remedial measure of what the trustee ought to have done is within the scope of its lawful powers.

In reaching this conclusion, we have taken account of the trustee's argument that the buildings' values were especially high in 1950 (though not as high as in the late 1920's). As the trustee argues, this fact would make 1950 an unreasonable remedial choice, other things being equal. But the record indicates that other things were not equal. For one thing, the district court chose 1950, not because of then-existing property values, but because that date marks a reasonable outer bound of the time the trustee could plead ignorance of the serious fairness problem. And, this conclusion, as we have noted, has adequate record support. For another thing, the district court could properly understand plaintiffs' expert witness as stating that the suburban flight that led to mid-1950's downtown decline began before 1950; its causes (increased household income; more cars; more mobility) were apparent before 1950. Thus, the court might reasonably have felt that a brief (1948–52) downtown "renaissance" should not have appeared (to the expert eye) to have been permanent or long lasting; it did not relieve the trustee of its obligation to do something about the fairness problem, nor did it make simple "building retention" a plausible cure. Finally, another expert testified that the trustee should have asked for power to sell the property "sometime between 1947 and 1952" when institutional investors generally began to diversify portfolios. For these reasons, reading the record, as we must, simply to see if it contains adequate support for the district court's conclusion as to remedy (as to which its powers are broad), we find that its choice of 1950 as a remedial base year is lawful.

Contrary to the trustee's contention, the case law it cites does not give it an absolute right under Rhode Island law to keep the trust's "inception assets" in disregard of the likely effect of retention on classes of trust beneficiaries. Cf. Peckham v. Newton, supra (original holdings should be retained but only so long as there is no doubt as to their safety); Rhode Island Hospital Trust Co. v. Copeland, supra (court not sufficiently informed on safety of holding to order sale or retention). The district court's conclusion that the trustee should have sold the assets if necessary to prevent the trust corpus from being consumed by the income beneficiaries is reasonable and therefore lawful. Cf. Industrial Trust Co. v. Parks, supra (wasting assets); Rhode Island Hospital Trust v. Tucker, supra (similar).

* * * [Court's discussion of res judicata is omitted].

The trustee challenges the district court's calculation of the surcharge. The court assumed, for purposes of making the trust principal whole, that the trustee had hypothetically sold the trust's interests in the Wheaton-Anthony and the Alice buildings in 1950, at their 1950 values (about $70,000 and $220,000, respectively). It subtracted, from that sum of about $290,000, the $130,000 the trust actually received when the buildings were in fact sold (about $40,000 for the Wheaton-Anthony interest in 1970 and about $90,000 for the Alice interest in 1979). The court considered the difference of $160,000 to be a loss in the value of the principal, suffered as a result of the trustee's failure to prevent the principal from eroding. The court then assumed that, had the trustee sold the buildings in 1950 and reinvested the proceeds, the trustee would have been able to preserve the real value of the principal. It therefore multiplied the $160,000 by 3.6 percent, the average annual increase in the consumer price index from 1950 to 1982, and multiplied again by 32, the number of full years since 1950. Finally, the court multiplied again by an annual 0.4 percent, designed to reflect an "allowance for appreciation." It added the result ($160,000 x 4 percent x 32), about $205,000, to the $160,000 loss and surcharged the trustee $365,000. We are aware of a number of mathematical problems with this calculation. (Why, for example, was no account taken of inflation when subtracting sale receipts from 1950 values?) But, in the context of this specific litigation, fairness as between the parties requires us to restrict our examination to the two particular challenges that the trustee raises.

First, the trustee claims that the court improperly ascertained the 1950 values of the trust's interests because it simply took a proportionate share of the buildings' values. That is to say, it divided the total value of the Alice Building by four to reflect the fact that the trust owned a 1/4 undivided interest. The trustee argues that the building's values should have been discounted further to reflect the facts that the trust owned a fractional interest in the buildings and that fractional interests (with their consequent problems of divided control) typically sell at a discount.

This particular matter in this case, however, was the subject of conflicting evidence. On the one hand, the trustee showed that the marketplace ordinarily discounted the value of fractional interests. On the other hand, the plaintiffs introduced an expert study giving the 1950 values of the trust's interests at precisely the figure shown by the district court. When the trustee finally sold the trust's interests (in 1970 and 1979), their value was not significantly discounted. And, since the trustee also controlled (as a trustee) other fractional interests in the same building, the trustee arguably could have arranged to sell the entire building in 1950 as it did in 1970 and 1979. Evaluating this evidence and the merits of these arguments is a matter for the district court. We see no abuse of the district court's powers to make reasonable judgments as to hypothetical values in its efforts to devise an appropriate remedy for the trustee's breach of duty.

Second, the trustee argues that the district court should not have applied to the 1950 hypothetical sales value a 4 percent interest factor—a factor designed to compensate for 3.6 percent average annual inflation and for 0.4 percent "appreciation." We do not agree with the trustee in respect to the 3.6 percent.

Rhode Island law simply requires that the court's approach be reasonable and its calculations grounded in the record's facts. See generally Industrial Trust Co. v. Parks, supra. The trustee does not claim that it requires the court to follow any one particular calculation method, such as that, for example, contained in Restatement (Second) of

Trusts § 241. And, we believe the inflation adjustment meets Rhode Island's broader requirements.

For one thing, it seems reasonable for the court—in devising a remedy for the trustee's violation of its duty of impartiality—to assume that a fair trustee would have maintained the property's real value from 1950 through 1982. Cf. In re Trusteeship under Agreement with Mayo, 105 N.W.2d 900 (Minn.1960) (ordering modification in trust terms where inflation was reducing real value of trust). Such an assumption is consistent with basic trust law policies of providing income to income beneficiaries while preserving principal for the remaindermen, and, consequently, of avoiding investment in wasting assets, see Industrial Trust Co. v. Parks, supra; Rhode Island Hospital Trust Co. v. Tucker, supra. Moreover, it is consistent with readily ascertainable general economic facts that wages and many asset values as well as prices have on average kept pace with inflation. See generally K. Hirsch, Inflation and the Law of Trusts, 18 Real Prop., Prob. & Tr. J. 601 (Win.1983); Comment, Investment and Management of Trust Funds in an Inflationary Economy, 126 U. of Pa.L.R. 1171, 1197 (1978). While the value of long term bonds has fallen, the value of common stocks and much property has risen. See generally R. Ibbotson & R. Sinquefield, Stocks, Bonds, Bills and Inflation: The Past and the Future (1982); J. Wiedemer, Real Estate Investment (1979). Where a court is trying to create, not a measure of the trustee's duty, but simply a plausible reconstruction of what would have occurred to a hypothetical 1950 reinvestment, we see nothing unreasonable in assuming that the value of the corpus would have kept pace with inflation.

We reach a different conclusion, however, in respect to the additional 0.4 percent, designed to reflect "appreciation." Neither the court nor the parties have provided us with any reason to believe that the trustee would have outperformed inflation. There is no evidence in the record suggesting that a hypothetical reinvestment of hypothetical proceeds from a hypothetical 1950 property sale would have yielded real appreciation over and above inflation's nominal increase. We have found no information about the performance of an average, or typical, trust. And the general publicly available sources offer insufficient support for a claim of likely real increase. See R. Ibbotson & R. Sinquefield, supra. Moreover, one can imagine reasonable disagreement about whether any such hypothetical real appreciation would belong to the life tenant or to the remainderman. These factors lead us to conclude that, in adding 0.4 percent interest for real appreciation, the district court exceeded its broad remedial powers. Our recalculation, omitting the 0.4 percent, reduces the surcharge from $365,781.67 to $345,246.56.

* * * The trustee objects to the court's having removed it as trustee. The removal of a trustee, however, is primarily a matter for the district court. A trustee can be removed even if "the charges of his misconduct" are "not made out." Petition of Slatter, 108 R.I. 326, 275 A.2d 272, 276 (1971). The issue here is whether "ill feeling" might interfere with the administration of the trust. The district court concluded that the course of the litigation in this case itself demonstrated such ill feeling. Nothing in the record shows that the court abused its powers in reaching that conclusion.

* * *

The plaintiffs argue, on their cross appeal, that the district court should have awarded them prejudgment interest on the surcharge, under R.I.Gen.Laws § 9-21-10 (1969), which states that

> [i]n any civil action in which a verdict is rendered or a decision made for pecuniary damages, there shall be added ... to the amount of damages, interest at

the rate of twelve per cent (12%) per annum thereon from the date that the cause of action accrued....

As the plaintiffs note, however, the purpose of this statute is "to compensate plaintiffs for waiting for the recompense to which they were legally entitled." Lombardi v. Merchants Mutual Insurance Co., 429 A.2d 1290, 1293 (R.I.1981), citing Factory Mutual Liability Ins. Co. of America v. Cooper, 106 R.I. 632, 262 A.2d 370, 373 (1970). That purpose would not be served by applying the statute here, for the district court calculated the surcharge in a way that made plaintiffs whole. The value of the corpus is maintained at its real 1950 level; that is the amount that the plaintiffs would (hypothetically) have received had the trustees fulfilled their obligations. Plaintiffs have lost nothing "for waiting for the recompense," as they can in no event receive the trust's corpus prior to 1991. Moreover, the Rhode Island courts have made clear that, despite the statute's language, it does not apply literally to "*any* civil action." R.I.Gen.Laws 9-21-10 (emphasis added). In fact, Rhode Island's Chief Justice has written that its Supreme Court "construe[s] the statute to apply only to those actions sounding in tort or contract. See Gott v. Norberg, R.I., 417 A.2d 1352 (1980)". Andrade v. State, 448 A.2d 1293, 1297 n. 5 (R.I.1982) (Bevilacqua, C.J., dissenting on other grounds). The action in this case is traditionally viewed as one in equity, not in tort or contract. Only by construing the statutory word "damages" broadly can a "surcharge" be brought within its scope. Since neither the purpose nor the language of the Rhode Island statute requires its application here, the district court was correct in not applying it.

* * * Plaintiffs also argue that the district court should have awarded them attorneys' fees to be paid by the trustee from its own pocket. The plaintiffs concede that in an action of this sort, the award of attorneys' fees at the expense of the trustees (not the trust) is an "exercise of [the court's] discretion." Horowitz v. Le Lacheure, 81 R.I. 235, 101 A.2d 483, 488 (1953). Plaintiffs also state that the court, when deciding whether to award fees, should take account of the litigation's outcome, the need to bring suit to correct the trustee's errors, and the trustee's conduct. The district court here found that plaintiffs succeeded in winning only a small part of the money that they claimed the trustee owed them. In its view, had the plaintiffs' claims been less extravagant, eight years of litigation might not have been necessary to obtain the surcharge that they won. The court also characterized the trustee's failing as a simple breach of fiduciary duty not reflecting willfully wrong or egregious conduct. It stated that there was "absolutely no evidence of malice or bad faith on the part of the Trustee." In addition, the court found evidence that plaintiffs' attorneys sought "inflated or unnecessary unsubstantiated charges." Under these circumstances, we believe the court did not abuse its powers in refusing to depart from the ordinary American rule requiring each party to pay its own attorneys' fees. See Alyeska Pipeline Service Co. v. Wilderness Society, 421 U.S. 240, 95 S.Ct. 1612, 44 L.Ed.2d 141 (1975).

The judgment of the district court is modified and as modified affirmed.

B. Prudence and Property

Uniform Trust Code (2003)

Section 809. Control and Protection of Trust Property.

A trustee shall take reasonable steps to take control of and protect the trust property.

Section 810. Recordkeeping and Identification of Trust Property.

(a) A trustee shall keep adequate records of the administration of the trust.

(b) A trustee shall keep trust property separate from the trustee's own property.

(c) Except as otherwise provided in subsection (d), a trustee shall cause the trust property to be designated so that the interest of the trust, to the extent feasible, appears in records maintained by a party other than a trustee or beneficiary.

(d) If a trustee maintains records clearly indicating the respective interests, a trustee may invest as a whole the property of two or more separate trusts.

Section 804. Prudent Administration.

A trustee shall administer the trust as a prudent person would, by considering the purposes, terms, distributional requirements, and other circumstances of the trust. In satisfying this standard, the trustee shall exercise reasonable care, skill, and caution.

Section 805. Costs of Administration.

In administering a trust, the trustee may incur only costs that are reasonable in relation to the trust property, the purposes of the trust, and the skills of the trustee.

Estate of Collins

California Court of Appeal, Second District, 1977
72 Cal. App.3d 663, 139 Cal. Rptr. 644

KAUS, P. J.

Objectors (plaintiffs) are beneficiaries under a testamentary trust established in the will of Ralph Collins, deceased. Carl Lamb and Charles E. Millikan, Jr., (defendants) were, respectively, Collins' business partner and lawyer. They were named in Collins' will as trustees. In 1973 defendants filed a petition for an order approving and settling the first and final account and discharging the trustees. Plaintiffs objected on grounds that defendants had improperly invested $50,000 and requested that defendants be surcharged. After a hearing, the trial court ruled in favor of defendants, and approved the account, terminated the trust, and discharged the trustees. Plaintiff beneficiaries have appealed.

* * *

The primary beneficiaries under the testamentary trust were Collins' wife and children; his mother and father were also named as beneficiaries. General support provisions were included; the will also specifically provided that the trustees pay his daughter $4,000 a year for five years for her undergraduate and graduate education.

Paragraph (d) of the declaration of trust recited the powers of the trustees in the usual, inclusive fashion. Subparagraph (3) authorized the trustees to purchase "every kind of property, real, personal or mixed, and every kind of investment, specifically including, but not by way of limitation, corporate obligations of every kind, and stocks, preferred or common, irrespective of whether said investments are in accordance with the laws then enforced in the State of California pertaining to the investment of trust funds by corporate trustees."

Subparagraph (3) provided: "Unless specifically limited, all discretions conferred upon the Trustee shall be absolute, and their exercise conclusive on all persons interest[ed] in this trust. The enumeration of certain powers of the Trustee shall not limit its general powers, the Trustee, subject always to the discharge of its fiduciary obligations, being vested with and having all the rights, powers and privileges which an absolute owner of the same property would have."

Collins died in 1963 and his will was admitted to probate. In June 1965, the court ordered the estate to be distributed. After various other payments and distributions, defendant trustees received about $80,000 as the trust principal. After other distributions, such as the annual $4,000 payment for the education of Collins' daughter, the trustees had about $50,000 available for investment.

Defendant Millikan's clients included two real property developers, Downing and Ward. In March 1965, Millikan filed an action on behalf of Downing and Ward against a lender who refused to honor a commitment to carry certain construction loans. In June 1965, defendants learned that Downing and Ward wanted to borrow $50,000. Millikan knew that the builders wanted the loan because of their difficulties with the lender who had withdrawn its loan commitment.

The loan would be secured by a second trust deed to 9.38 acres of unimproved real property in San Bernardino County near Upland. This property was subject to a $90,000 first trust deed; the note which secured the first trust deed was payable in quarterly installments of interest only, and due in full in three years, that is, in July 1968. The $50,000 loan to be made by defendants would be payable in monthly installments of interest only, at 10 percent interest with the full amount due in 30 months, that is, in January 1968.

Defendants knew that the property had been sold two years earlier in 1963 for $107,000. Defendants checked with two real estate brokers in the area, one of whom said that property in that area was selling for $18,000 to $20,000 an acre. They did not have the property appraised, they did not check with the county clerk or recorder in either Los Angeles or San Bernardino County to determine whether there were foreclosures or lawsuits pending against the construction company. In fact, when defendants made the loan in July 1965, there were six notices of default and three lawsuits pending against Downing and Ward.

Defendants obtained and reviewed an unaudited company financial statement. This statement indicated that the Downing and Ward Company had a net worth in excess of $2 million.

Downing and Ward told defendants that they were not in default on any of their loans, that they were not defendants in any pending litigation, and that there had never been any liens filed on any of their projects. Defendants phoned the bank with whom Downing and Ward had a line of credit and learned that the bank had a satisfactory relationship with the builders.

Based on this information, on July 23, 1965, defendants lent Downing and Ward $50,000 on the terms described above. In addition to the second trust deed, Downing and Ward pledged 20 percent of the stock in their company as security. However, defendants neither obtained possession of the stock, placed it in escrow, nor placed a legend on the stock certificates. Defendants also obtained the personal guarantees of Downing and Ward and their wives. However, defendants did not obtain financial statements from the guarantors.

When the loan was made in July 1965, construction in the Upland area was, as the trial court said, "enjoying boom times, although the bubble was to burst just a few months later." From July 1965 through September 1966, the builders made the monthly interest payments required by the note. In October 1966, Downing & Ward Construction Corporation was placed in involuntary bankruptcy and thereafter Mr. and Mrs. Ward and Mr. and Mrs. Downing declared personal bankruptcies. Defendants foreclosed their second trust deed in June 1967, and became the owners of the unimproved real property. They spent $10,000 in an unsuccessful effort to salvage the investment by forestalling foreclosure by the holder of the first trust deed. In September 1968, the holder of the first trust deed did foreclose. This extinguished the trustees' interest in the property and the entire investment. In short, about $60,000 of the trust fund was lost. * * *

The trial court made findings of fact and drew conclusions of law. As relevant, the court found that defendant trustees "exercised the judgment and care, under the circumstances then prevailing, which men of prudence, discretion and intelligence exercised in the management of their own affairs, not in regard to speculation, but in regard to the disposition of their funds, considering the probable income, as well as the probable safety of their capital." In making the loan, "the cotrustees used reasonable care, diligence and skill. The cotrustees did not act arbitrarily or in bad faith."

* * *

The trial court's finding that defendants exercised the judgment and care "which men of prudence, discretion and intelligence exercised in the management of their own affairs," reflects the standard imposed upon trustees by Civil Code section 2261. (See also, Rest.2d Trusts, § 227 [Restatement].)

Plaintiffs contend, and we agree, that contrary to the trial court's findings and conclusions, defendants failed to follow the "prudent investor" standard, first, by investing two-thirds of the trust principal in a single investment, second, by investing in real property secured only by a second deed of trust, and third, by making that investment without adequate investigation of either the borrowers or the collateral.

Although California does not limit the trustee's authority to a list of authorized investments, relying instead on the prudent investor rule (see 7 Witkin, Summary of Cal. Law (8th ed.) Trusts, § 63, p. 5424), nevertheless, the prudent investor rule encompasses certain guidelines applicable to this case.

First, "the trustee is under a duty to the beneficiary to distribute the risk of loss by a reasonable diversification of investments, unless under the circumstances it is prudent not to do so." (Rest.2d Trusts, § 228; see also, Estate of Beach (1975) 15 Cal.3d 623, 634, fn. 9 [125 Cal.Rptr. 570, 542 P.2d 994]; Witkin, supra, at p. 5425, see generally, Uniform Management of Institutional Funds Act, Civ. Code, §§ 2290.1–2290.12, 2290.6.)

Second, ordinarily, "second or other junior mortgages are not proper trust investments," unless taking a second mortgage is a reasonable method of settling a claim or making possible the sale of property. (Rest.2d Trusts, § 227, p. 533.) Stated more emphatically: "While loans secured by second mortgages on land are sometimes allowed, they are almost always disapproved by courts of equity. The trustee should not place the trust funds in a position where they may be endangered by the foreclosure of a prior lien.... In rare cases equity will sanction an investment secured by a second mortgage, but only when the security is adequate and unusual circumstances justify the trustee in taking this form of investment." (Bogert, Trusts and Trustees (2d ed.) § 675, p. 274.)

Third, in "buying a mortgage for trust investment, the trustee should give careful attention to the valuation of the property, in order to make certain that his margin of security is adequate. He must use every reasonable endeavor to provide protection which will cover the risks of depreciation in the property and changes in price levels. And he must investigate the status of the property and of the mortgage, as well as the financial situation of the mortgagor." (Bogert, supra, §674, at p. 267.)[2] Similarly, the Restatement rule is that "the trustee cannot properly lend on a mortgage upon real property more than a reasonable proportion of the value of the mortgaged property." (§229.)

We think it apparent that defendants violated every applicable rule. First, they failed totally to diversify the investments in this relatively small trust fund. Second, defendants invested in a junior mortgage on unimproved real property, and left an inadequate margin of security. As noted, the land had most recently sold for $107,000, and was subject to a first trust deed of $90,000. Thus, unless the land was worth more than $140,000, there was no margin of security at all. Defendants did not have the land appraised; the only information they had was the opinion of a real estate broker that property in the area—not that particular parcel—was going for $18,000 to $20,000 an acre. Thus, any assumption that the property was worth about $185,000—and therefore the $140,000 in loans were well-secured—would have been little more than a guess.

Third, the backup security obtained by defendants was no security at all. The builders pledged 20 percent of their stock, but defendants never obtained possession of the stock, placed it in escrow or even had it legended. They accepted the personal guarantees of the builders and their wives without investigating the financial status of these persons. They accepted at face value the claimed $2 million value of the company shown in an unaudited statement. Defendant Millikan apparently ignored the fact that one lender had, for whatever reasons, reneged on a loan commitment to the builders.

Defendants contend that the evidence sustains the trial court's findings that they exercised the judgment and care under the circumstances then prevailing expected of men of prudence. They rely on the rule that the determination whether an investment was proper must be made in light of the circumstances existing at the time of the investment. (E.g., Witkin, supra, §63, p. 5425.) That rule does not help defendants. Nothing that happened after the loan was made can change the fact that defendants invested two-thirds of the principal of the trust in a single second deed of trust on unappraised property, with no knowledge of the borrowers' true financial status, and without any other security.

We recognize, as did the trial court, that the loan was made in 1965, and defendants, some 10 years later, could not be expected to recall the specifics of their investigation. But that is the point of this case turned inside out: Defendants were required to rely on faded memories because their investigation was limited to casual conversations. No documentation existed, not because it was lost, but because it was never obtained. Further, it is defendants' own fault that they filed their "first and final account" more than eight years after assuming their duties.

---

2. Bogert states that where a statutory list still exists, the margin required is usually either 50 or 40 percent "and it is believed that under the prudent man rule a similar standard will be applied, unless there are special circumstances, as where the mortgage is insured." (Bogert, supra, at pp. 268–269.) The Restatement notes that generally a trustee cannot "properly lend on a mortgage upon real property more than from one-half to two-thirds of the value of the mortgaged property." (Rest.2d Trusts, §229, com. a, p. 544.)

Although we do not intimate that either standard is realistic or definitive in California, we do note that when the property involved was sold two years earlier in 1963 for $107,000, the sales agreement called for the owners to carry a $90,000 mortgage, which would amount to about 15 percent cash investment.

Defendants seek to place themselves in the position of the trustee in Day v. First Trust & Sav. Bank (1941) 47 Cal.App.2d 470 [118 P.2d 51], who made investments—most of them in the 1920's—and ran into certain difficulties during the years from 1929 until 1933. Leaving aside the difference between the depression years, covered in Day, and the recession in the construction business in the late 1960's, an examination of some of the investments by the trustee in Day illustrates the difference between a prudent man and what defendants did here: A $300,000 mortgage on property appraised at $700,000 and valued in February 1933 at $555,000; a $225,000 mortgage on property appraised at $725,000; a $30,000 mortgage on property appraised at $112,000; a $35,000 mortgage on property appraised at $83,000; a $15,000 mortgage on property appraised at $37,000. (Id., at pp. 473–475.) Here defendants must be surcharged, not because they lacked prescience of what would happen, but because they both lacked and ignored information about what was happening at the time.

Plainly, defendants' conduct did not meet the prudent-investor standard. They claim, however, that the trust instrument conferred on them an "absolute discretion." Therefore, they argue, their sole obligation was not to act arbitrarily and to use their best judgment. (Coberly v. Superior Court (1965) 231 Cal.App.2d 685, 689 [42 Cal.Rptr. 64].)

We leave aside that even a trustee with "absolute discretion" may not "neglect its trust or abdicate its judgment," (Coberly v. Superior Court, supra, 231 Cal.App.2d at p. 689) or show a "reckless indifference" to the interests of the beneficiary. (Rest.2d Trusts, § 222.) The record before us contains no evidence that defendants satisfied even the lesser standard of care for which they contend.

More fundamentally we do not agree with defendants' premise. While the declaration of trust may possibly enlarge the prudent-investor standard as far as the type of investment is concerned, it cannot be construed as permitting deviations from that standard in investigating the soundness of a specific investment. This distinction is well established. Comment v, to section 227 of the Restatement reads, in part, as follows:

> v. An authorization by the terms of the trust to invest in a particular type of security does not mean that any investment in securities of that type is proper. The trustee must use care and skill and caution in making the selection. Thus, if the trustee is authorized by the terms of the trust to invest in railroad bonds, he is guilty of a breach of trust if he invests in bonds of a railroad company *in which a prudent man would not invest because of the financial condition of the company.* * * *

The provisions on which defendants rely are subparagraphs (3) and (11) to paragraph (d), quoted earlier. Neither supports their position. Subparagraph (3) merely tracks section 2261 of the Civil Code and adds that the investments listed therein are permissible "irrespective of whether said investments are in accordance with the laws then in force in the State of California pertaining to the investment of trust funds by corporate trustees." This adds nothing. (5) Neither Civil Code section 2261 nor any other authority which we can locate authorizes different types of investments for "corporate trustees" as distinguished from amateurs. The difference is, rather, that the corporate trustee is held to a greater standard of care based on its presumed expertise. (Estate of Beach, supra, 15 Cal.3d 623, 635; Coberly v. Superior Court, supra, 231 Cal.App.2d 685, 689; Bogert, supra, § 541, p. 453.)

In any event, even if the trust instrument permitted a type of investment generally frowned on under the prudent-investor rule, it did not authorize the trustees to make it blindly. Defendants might have a point, had they purchased a well-secured second trust deed after careful investigation. Clearly, however, the nature of their investment is the least of their problems.

Alternatively, defendants rely on the language in subparagraph (11) that "all discretions conferred upon the Trustee shall be absolute, ..." This reliance, too, is misplaced.

First, viewed as an exculpatory clause, subparagraph (11) is subject to the rule of strict construction. (Rest.2d Trusts, §222, com. a, p. 517; 3 Scott on Trusts, supra, §222.2 and cases cited.)

Second, the "absolute discretion" is "specifically limited" by the requirement that the trustee is "subject always to the discharge of its fiduciary obligations, ..."

Third, in context subparagraph (11) refers only to "discretions conferred on the Trustee" in paragraph (d) of the trust which, as noted, deals exclusively with powers, as distinguished from the degree of care with which they are to be exercised. Nor does any other part of the declaration of trust mention any relevant discretion which subparagraph (11) would make "absolute." Nowhere did the trustor say anything about a discretion not to diversify, a discretion to invest in a junior encumbrance without ability to protect against the foreclosure of a senior lien, a discretion not to make a businesslike investigation of the credit and net worth of the borrower, or a discretion not to insist on an appraisal of the security given by the borrower.

The orders are reversed with directions to determine the damages to which plaintiffs are entitled.

STEPHENS and ASHBY, JJ., concur.

[A petition for a rehearing was denied December 9, 1977, and respondents' petition for a hearing by the Supreme Court was denied October 6, 1977.]

In re Estate of Cooper

Court of Appeals of Washington, 1996
81 Wash. App. 79, 913 P.2d 393

SWEENEY, Chief Judge.

Washington's prudent investor rule requires a trustee to "exercise the judgment and care under the circumstances then prevailing, which persons of prudence, discretion and intelligence exercise in the management of their own affairs...." RCW 11.100.020(1). This exercise of judgment requires, among other things, "consideration to the role that the proposed investment or investment course of action plays within the overall portfolio of assets." RCW 11.100.020(1). In this case of first impression, we are asked to decide whether the prudent investor rule limits the court's consideration to the overall performance of the trust, or whether, instead, the court may consider the performance of specific assets in the trust. We hold the prudent investor rule focuses on the performance of the trustee, not the results of the trust. The trial court here then appropriately considered individual assets, and groups of assets, in finding that the trustee had improperly weighed trust assets in favor of himself, the income beneficiary. We affirm that portion of the court's judgment which required the trustee to reimburse the trust corpus for the loss caused by that investment strategy. We reverse other court rulings regarding personal representative, trustee and attorney fees.

* * *

De Anne Cooper died on March 6, 1978. In her will, she provided that her one-half of the community property would be held in trust during her husband Fermore B. Cooper's lifetime, and that Mr. Cooper and The Old National Bank of Washington (ONB) would serve as co-trustees of the testamentary trust. The trust required payment of income to Mr. Cooper and distribution of the corpus to her children after Mr. Cooper's death. The nonintervention will named Mr. Cooper personal representative. At the time of her death, Mrs. Cooper had two children, Joyce Johnston and Richard Cooper. Her one-half of the community property was worth about $800,000.

Mr. Cooper filed his wife's will and started a probate. But he took no further steps to conclude the probate until Joyce filed this action. He did not keep a separate estate account and continued to manage all of the former community property as his own.

In 1986, Mr. Cooper asked Joyce to approve the substitution of Richard for ONB as co-trustee of the trust. Joyce refused and asked about Mr. Cooper's management of the estate. At that point, Mr. Cooper funded the trust by depositing in ONB assets valued at approximately $2,000,000. Joyce then petitioned the court to remove Mr. Cooper as personal representative of the estate and trustee of the trust, and for an accounting and a declaration that Mr. Cooper's second wife had no interest in the trust property. Her petition included a request for attorney fees and costs.

* * *

In March 1989, Mr. Cooper filed an inventory of estate assets. The asset mix set out in that inventory generates the primary dispute in this case. The inventory included (1) an unsecured note from Gifford-Hill, Inc., with a balance of $1,200,000 owing on the date of Mrs. Cooper's death; (2) partnership interests in Eight-O-One Investment Company and Hillside Investment Company, which owned interests in the Deaconess Medical Building; and (3) substantial holdings in income-producing assets including tax-exempt bonds. The inventory did not include shares in Comtrex, Inc. Mr. Cooper's son, Richard, was the chief executive officer of Comtrex. After Mrs. Cooper's death, Mr. Cooper bought shares in the company and also loaned it approximately $824,000, which Comtrex never repaid.

Before Mr. Cooper compiled the inventory, he had sold the community's share of stock in a closely held corporation, Western Frontiers. The corporation owned the North Shore, a hotel and restaurant in Coeur d'Alene. Its shares were valued for estate tax purposes in 1978 at 75¢ a share, for a total value of $21,750. Mr. Cooper sold both his and the estate's shares in 1983 to Duane Hagadone at a profit of about $1 million. The stock had appreciated largely because of a bidding war between Mr. Hagadone and Robert Templin. Both wanted control of the company. The purchase gave Mr. Hagadone a majority interest. Mr. Cooper reinvested the proceeds in stocks and bonds.

An accounting filed along with the inventory calculated the current value of Mrs. Cooper's estate at $1,279,433. Mr. Cooper's accountant compiled the accounting from estate tax returns and transaction sheets supplied by Mr. Cooper's stockbroker. The accounting summarized (1) purchases and sales of assets listed in the 1978 estate tax return, (2) capital gains, and (3) income.

On December 26, 1989, the superior court appointed John Cummins "as special master/referee to assist [it] in resolving various disputes that [had] arisen in connection with [the Cooper] estate." At the time, Mr. Cummins was a vice-president of Seattle-

First National Bank and manager of its trust department. The court asked Mr. Cummins to contact the trust department of U.S. Bank (ONB's successor) to "review what has transpired in connection with the assets" deposited by Mr. Cooper in 1987 to fund the trust. The court also asked Mr. Cooper to forward to Mr. Cummins a copy of the estate accounting. After consulting with Mr. Cummins, the court found that "the accounting as accomplished to date in connection with the trust estate is not in accordance with generally recognized format and principles." It then instructed Mr. Cooper's accountant, James McDirmid, "to confer with Mr. Cummins as to what is contemplated to comply with those standards."

Mr. Cooper filed a revised inventory accounting in May 1990 based on Mr. McDirmid's calculations (McDirmid accounting). It set the 1987 fair market value of the inventoried assets at $1,835,821.50. The value of the assets Mr. Cooper had transferred to fund the trust in 1987 had a value of $1,959,113. Thus, the trust was overfunded by $123,291.50. The accounting also valued the partnership interests in Eight-O-One and Hillside, half of which the estate owned, at $192,000 and $86,000, respectively. These values reflected a 60 percent discount because Mr. Cooper's interest was a minority interest and therefore not easily marketable.

Mr. Cummins concluded the amended accounting revealed "no improprieties." The court refused Joyce's request to discover the basis for Mr. Cummins' opinions. It stated Mr. Cummins was appointed "solely for the purpose of deciding whether or not F. BERT COOPER should be removed as Personal Representative."

* * *

On December 12, 1990, the court directed the parties to proceed to a hearing on the final report and petition for distribution. At the hearing, the principal issues were the accuracy of the McDirmid accounting and the propriety of Mr. Cooper's investment strategy. Mr. Cooper and Joyce presented expert opinion testimony in support of their respective positions.

* * *

On December 15, 1992, following the hearing, the court found Mr. Cooper had commingled income from estate assets and proceeds from the sale of estate assets with his own funds. It found the accounting prepared by Mr. Cooper's accountant adequately traced the estate's assets. The court further found, based on the McDirmid accounting, that Mr. Cooper "had more than sufficient funds in his own right as his separate property to make gifts and other distributions to and for the benefit of his children."

The court agreed with Mr. Cooper's valuation of the Eight-O-One and Hillside partnerships. And it held he had acted prudently in negotiating the sale of the Western Frontiers shares. It found that Mr. Cooper had, however, "maintained a policy of investment ... which maximized the income of the estate ... to the detriment of the growth of the corpus of the estate." It valued the loss to the remainder interest at $342,493 as of July 1987. It ordered Mr. Cooper to contribute that additional amount, along with $115,840 of expected appreciation from July 1987 to entry of the judgment.

The court also found that Mr. Cooper had overfunded the trust by $123,292. It credited that sum against the $458,333 surcharge it had levied against Mr. Cooper to compensate the trust for losses it suffered as a result of his investment strategy ($342,493 + $115,840). It held estate taxes, attorney and accounting fees, and expenses of administration were properly charged by Mr. Cooper to the estate. The court set 1984 as the outside date by which Mr. Cooper should have closed the estate. It then awarded him a fee for serving as personal representative from 1978 through 1984. It also awarded him a fee as co-trustee from July 1987 to the date of the judgment. It ordered the trust divided between Richard and Joyce and discharged Mr. Cooper as the trustee over Joyce's half because of the "mutual distrust, conflict, and dissension" between Joyce and Mr. Cooper.

The court further found that "[a]ll parties to this cause have succeeded to some degree herein and have worked for the benefit of the estate and of their respective clients." It therefore awarded all parties a portion of their attorney and accountant fees. Joyce received $45,600 in attorney fees and $12,421.67 for her accountant's fees. The court awarded Mr. Cooper $46,400 of the $115,000 in attorney fees he had requested, and $48,802.50 for his accountant's fees. It awarded Richard $18,400 in attorney fees and $220.47 in costs. The court approved Joyce's additional attorney and professional fees of $156,975, but ordered them charged to her share of the trust.

* * *

The question presented is whether the trial court improperly applied the prudent investor rule. Mr. Cooper and Richard argue the court should have evaluated Mr. Cooper's performance based on the performance of the trust as a whole rather than focusing on specific assets, or groups of assets. They point out that the return on total trust assets exceeded that of the ONB trust department.

The trust's favorable performance, as compared to that of the ONB trust department, was largely due to the gains from Mr. Cooper's sale of the estate's Western Frontiers stock. The balance of the trust assets were weighted heavily toward current income rather than capital appreciation. Common stocks represented 13 percent of the trust's marketable securities; bonds and bond equivalents represented 87 percent. The estate's gain attributable to increases in the value of the securities was only $226,313. This figure represented a 22.23 percent return on those investments, or a 2.15 percent increase per year between 1978 and 1987. Inflation averaged 6 percent a year during that same period. The purchasing power of these assets decreased then just under 4 percent a year.

Overall trust performance is a factor in evaluating the performance of the trustee. But it is not by itself controlling. "The court's focus in applying the Prudent Investor standard is conduct, not the end result." J. Alan Nelson, The Prudent Person Rule: A Shield for the Professional Trustee, 45 Baylor L.Rev. 933, 939 (1993). The American version of the prudent investor rule began with the Harvard College case:

> All that can be required of a trustee to invest, is, that he shall conduct himself faithfully and exercise a sound discretion. He is to observe how men of prudence, discretion, and intelligence manage their own affairs, not in regard to speculation, but in regard to the permanent disposition of their funds, considering the probable income, as well as the probable safety of the capital to be invested.

Nelson, 45 Baylor L.Rev. at 939 (quoting Harvard College v. Amory, 26 Mass. (9 Pick.) 446, 460–61 (1830)). In Harvard College, the court recognized that trust assets could never be fully protected from the uncertainties of the market place; thus, the prudent investor standard was necessarily flexible. Nelson, 45 Baylor L.Rev. at 938.

In the recent New York case of In re Lincoln First Bank, N.A., 165 Misc.2d 743, 630 N.Y.S.2d 472 (Sur.Ct.1995), the court interpreted its own version of the prudent investor rule and made two observations which are helpful here. First, "whether an investment is prudent or not is a question of fact." Lincoln First Bank, 630 N.Y.S.2d at 474 (citing In re Clarke's Estate, 12 N.Y.2d 183, 188 N.E.2d 128, 237 N.Y.S.2d 694 (1962); In re Yarm, 119 A.D.2d 754, 501 N.Y.S.2d 163 (1986)). Second, the prudent investor standard requires "that the fiduciary maintain a balance between the rights of income beneficiaries with those of the remainderman." Lincoln First Bank, 630 N.Y.S.2d at 474. This state's version of the rule also requires that the trustee consider income as well as the safety of the capital and the requirements of the beneficiaries. RCW 11.100.020(1), (2).[1] Clearly, the focus is on the trustee's performance, not simply on the net gain or loss to the trust corpus. Nelson, 45 Baylor L.Rev. at 939.

The trial court here properly applied the prudent investor standard, as set forth above, and its findings of fact on that issue are supported by substantial evidence. Cowiche Canyon Conservancy v. Bosley, 118 Wash.2d 801, 819, 828 P.2d 549 (1992).

Both parties rely on Baker Boyer Nat'l Bank v. Garver, 43 Wash.App. 673, 719 P.2d 583, review denied, 106 Wash.2d 1017 (1986). There, the trust beneficiaries sued for damages resulting from imprudent investments made by Baker Boyer, the trustee bank. They argued the bank had breached a duty to diversify when it invested primarily in fixed-income securities. The bank responded it had no duty to diversify under the prudent investor rule, as codified in former RCW 30.24.020 (now RCW 11.100.020). Even if such a duty existed, the bank contended diversification between fixed-income securities and equity investment in real property satisfied the duty under a "total asset" management approach.

---

1. In 1984, the Legislature amended RCW 34.24.020 and recodified it as RCW 11.100.020. That statute provides in part:

(1) A fiduciary is authorized to acquire and retain every kind of property. In acquiring, investing, reinvesting, exchanging, selling and managing property for the benefit of another, a fiduciary, in determining the prudence of a particular investment, shall give due consideration to the role that the proposed investment or investment course of action plays within the overall portfolio of assets. In applying such total asset management approach, a fiduciary shall exercise the judgment and care under the circumstances then prevailing, which persons of prudence, discretion and intelligence exercise in the management of their own affairs, not in regard to speculation but in regard to the permanent disposition of their funds, and if the fiduciary has special skills or is named trustee on the basis of representations of special skills or expertise, the fiduciary is under a duty to use those skills.

(2) Except as may be provided to the contrary in the instrument, the following are among the factors that should be considered by a fiduciary in applying this total asset management approach:

(a) The probable income as well as the probable safety of their capital;
(b) Marketability of investments;
(c) General economic conditions;
(d) Length of the term of the investments;
(e) Duration of the trust;
(f) Liquidity needs;
(g) Requirements of the beneficiary or beneficiaries;
(h) Other assets of the beneficiary or beneficiaries, including earning capacity; and
(i) Effect of investments in increasing or diminishing liability for taxes.

(Emphasis added.) The Legislature amended the statute in 1995, but the change is not material to the issue presented here.

Before 1984, RCW 30.24.020 provided in part: "[A] fiduciary shall exercise the judgment and care ... which men of prudence, discretion and intelligence exercise in the management of their own affairs ... considering the probable income as well as the probable safety of their capital.

The court agreed with the beneficiaries that the prudent investor standard includes the duty to diversify trust assets. But it found it unnecessary to decide whether former RCW 30.24.020 incorporated the "total asset" approach. The evidence supported the trial court's finding "the Bank had *not* weighed the investment in securities against the investment in the farmland for purposes of diversification." Baker Boyer, 43 Wash.App. at 681, 719 P.2d 583 (emphasis added).

Likewise, Mr. Cooper did not weigh his investment in income-producing securities against his investment in Western Frontiers. The overall trust performance was boosted dramatically by the sale of the Western Frontiers stock in 1983. But Mr. Cooper's investment strategy could not have anticipated the gain from the sale of the stock before it occurred. By 1983, when the stock was sold, he had been administering the estate for five years. Furthermore, after the sale, he invested the estate assets almost exclusively in marketable securities, 87 percent in bonds, favoring again the income beneficiary—him. There was no other asset or group of assets which Mr. Cooper could have balanced against this investment.

Mr. Cooper also claims the amount the trial court awarded to compensate the trust for his investment strategy was error because the court did not deduct state inheritance tax, interest on deferred liability, and interest on tax deficiency from the estate's assets. If the court had done so, the baseline for calculating the estate's loss would have been less, and the overall rate of return would have been greater. He further alleges the court used incorrect tax rates in calculating the amount available to invest. Those arguments were not made in the trial court, which calculated the dollar amount of its judgment based upon the evidence presented. We, accordingly, do not address this assignment of error.

* * * Mr. Cooper and Richard contend the court erred in awarding Joyce attorney fees from the trust. In addition, Richard contends the court erred in awarding him less than half the fees awarded to Mr. Cooper and Joyce. Joyce argues the court should have required that Mr. Cooper, rather than the trust, pay her fees because his mismanagement of the trust assets precipitated the suit. She also challenges the court's award of any attorney fees to Mr. Cooper. She argues those fees were incurred in defending the alleged breach of his fiduciary duties. * * *

Both RCW 11.76 (settlement of estates) and RCW 11.96 (judicial proceedings in probate and trust matters) provide for attorney fees. Under RCW 11.76.070, the court may award fees to a party who brings suit to compel an accounting from the personal representative or to resist an inaccurate accounting. RCW 11.96.140 permits a court to "order costs, including attorneys' fees, to be paid by any party to the proceedings or out of the assets of the estate or trust or nonprobate asset, as justice may require." * * *

In In re Estate of Burmeister, 70 Wash.App. 532, 539, 854 P.2d 653 (1993), rev'd on other grounds, 124 Wash.2d 282, 877 P.2d 195 (1994), the trial court refused to award fees against a party personally. Division One of this court affirmed. The court held that the Legislature in enacting RCW 11.96.140 intended to leave that decision to the discretion of the trial judge, to whom it gave the authority to award fees "'as justice may require.'" Burmeister, 70 Wash.App. at 539, 854 P.2d 653. In approving the award of fees from the estate, the court in Burmeister relied on two factors. First, all of the beneficiaries affected by the litigation were involved in the dispute. Second, arguments by both sides were reasonable and in good faith. Burmeister, 70 Wash.App. at 539–40, 854 P.2d 653. But, Burmeister is distinguishable from the facts here. In Burmeister, the personal representative had not breached his fiduciary duties. If there is a breach of fiduciary duties, the plaintiff has a right to recover fees against the trustee personally. Allard v. Pacific Nat'l Bank, 99 Wash.2d 394, 407, 663 P.2d 104 (1983).

With one exception, the awards here were an appropriate exercise of the court's discretion. Arguments by the parties related to the accuracy of Mr. Cooper's accounting. The court found them to be reasonable and made in good faith. The fact the court awarded Mr. Cooper less than his full request is supported by the fact a portion of those fees were incurred in the defense of Joyce's allegation that he violated the prudent investor rule. Richard complains his award of fees, when compared to the others, is small. The record demonstrates he played a lesser role in the proceedings. That fact supports the lower award. The court, however, should have awarded a portion of Joyce's fees against Mr. Cooper personally, because it found he breached his fiduciary duties. We therefore remand to the trial court to determine what part of Joyce's fees were attributable to her challenge to Mr. Cooper's investment strategy.

Finally, Joyce argues the court erred in awarding Mr. Cooper his accountant fees. In her view, Mr. Cooper incurred those fees for his own benefit, not that of the estate. Her view, however, ignores the fact the trial court found in Mr. Cooper's favor on the question of whether the McDirmid accounting adequately traced the estate's assets.

Joyce specifically challenges Mr. McDirmid's fee of $2,345 to review his own files in preparation for a deposition. She contends Mr. McDirmid was an "actor in the transaction" and therefore was limited to collecting the statutory witness fee.

We first note the trial court ordered the above fee "held in abeyance ... pending further order of the Court." The court ultimately awarded $48,802.50 in fees for Mr. McDirmid's services. The award does not specify whether it includes the fee for $2,345. If it did not, the trial court has not made a final determination and the issue is not ripe for review.

Assuming the judgment included the $2,345 fee, the award was appropriate pursuant to CR 26(b)(5) and 37(a)(4). * * * Joyce relies on Baird v. Larson, 59 Wash.App. 715, 720, 801 P.2d 247 (1990). Her reliance is misplaced. In that case, Dr. Frank Baird sued Dr. David Larson for breach of contract following the sale of Baird's practice to Larson. The appraiser who had valued the practice prior to the sale was called as a witness. The trial court awarded the appraiser an expert witness fee. We reversed, holding that "only opinions acquired and developed in anticipation of litigation are expert opinions." Baird, 59 Wash.App. at 719, 801 P.2d 247. The appraiser's opinion was not acquired in anticipation of litigation. He was, therefore, an occurrence witness, not an expert witness.

The situation here is very different. Although Mr. Cooper had a fiduciary duty to account for trust assets, the actual accounting by Mr. McDirmid was prepared in response to Joyce's petition. His expenses were therefore properly charged to the estate. CR 26(b)(5); CR 37(a)(4).

All parties request attorney fees on appeal. "[T]he court on appeal, may ... order costs, including attorneys' fees, to be paid by any party ... or out of the assets of the estate...." RCW 11.96.140. Since all parties have prevailed on some issues raised in the appeal and the cross-appeal, we award fees to Mr. Cooper, Richard and Joyce in amounts to be determined by this court's commissioner. RAP 18.1(f). The trust shall pay the fees awarded, except Mr. Cooper must pay that portion of Joyce's fees incurred defending the trial court's holding that his investment strategy violated the prudent investor rule.

In summary, we affirm all fees awarded payable out of the estate, save for the fees Joyce incurred in establishing Mr. Cooper's breach of fiduciary duty. We assess those fees against Mr. Cooper personally in an amount to be determined by the superior court.

* * * Mr. Cooper next contends the court's removal of him as trustee over Joyce's half of the trust corpus violates the provisions of Mrs. Cooper's will. The will provided that neither income nor principal of the trust were alienable. He does not explain, however, how his removal as trustee results in an alienation of the trust's income and principal. Nothing in the court's order transfers either the right to the trust's income to someone other than Mr. Cooper, or the right to the trust's principal to someone other than Mrs. Cooper's children, following Mr. Cooper's death.

RCW 11.96.009 allows the court, in the exercise of its jurisdiction over probate and trust matters, to "administer and settle all trusts and trust matters...." A court has a "wide latitude of discretion" to remove the trustee, "when there is sufficient reason to do so to protect the best interests of the trust and its beneficiaries." Schildberg v. Schildberg, 461 N.W.2d 186, 191 (Iowa 1990). Given the relationship between these parties, retaining Mr. Cooper as trustee only insures more litigation. The court did not abuse its discretion in removing Mr. Cooper as trustee.

* * * Both Mr. Cooper and Richard testified that shortly after Mrs. Cooper's death, Mr. Cooper advised his children their mother had left her property in trust with a remainder interest in them. According to them, Joyce responded: "Daddy, I want you to take care of everything just as you always have." They contend this amounted to a waiver of her right to challenge Mr. Cooper's management of the estate. We disagree.

A waiver is an intentional relinquishment of a known right. Wagner v. Wagner, 95 Wash.2d 94, 102, 621 P.2d 1279 (1980). The statement attributed to Joyce does not unambiguously renounce her right to prudent trust management. Her statement was not a waiver.

* * *

As stated in the facts, the court appointed John Cummins to review Mr. Cooper's accounting. Joyce contends the court used Mr. Cummins' report as evidence, and, therefore, it should have given her the opportunity to either cross-examine him or otherwise challenge his report. She argues the court should have followed the procedure for (1) special master provided in Fed.R.Civ.P. 53, (2) referees acting under RCW 4.48.010, or (3) deposing expert witnesses under CR 26(b)(5)(A).

Mr. Cummins' first letter to the court reported he had reviewed the accounting and concluded it was not in accordance with generally accepted accounting principles. On April 3, 1990, the court ordered Mr. Cooper to revise the accounting "in accordance with directions from ... John D. Cummins...." In his second letter, dated April 25, 1990, Mr. Cummins approved the McDirmid accounting as amended.

On January 22, 1991, Joyce moved "[t]hat ... counsel be permitted to depose John D. Cummins, or that, in the alternative, all communications by him ... be stricken, removed from the files..., and completely disregarded by [the] court...." The court denied the motion, stating it considered Mr. Cummins' work product only for the limited purpose of deciding whether to remove Mr. Cooper as personal representative. Joyce contends the court used Mr. Cummins' reports for much more. She relies on the court's Finding of Fact XI: "The accountings were reviewed by the court's special master, John Cummins, and the court has indicated that the accountings submitted on behalf of the Personal Representative were prepared in accordance with generally accepted accounting principles for estates and trusts...."

The court's use of Mr. Cummins' reports and denial of discovery was error. ER 706 provides a court may appoint an expert witness with the consent of the parties. The parties also have the right to depose the expert and call him or her at trial. See Graves v. P.J. Taggares Co., 25 Wash.App. 118, 120, 605 P.2d 348, aff'd, 94 Wash.2d 298, 616 P.2d 1223 (1980); R.E. Barber, Annotation, Trial Court's Appointment, in Civil Case, of Expert Witness, 95 A.L.R.2d 390 (1964). The court did neither. Nor did the court comply with RCW 4.48.010, which provides that the parties may, by written consent, permit the court to refer issues in a civil trial to a referee. The court also did not comply with the procedures outlined in Fed.R.Civ.P. 53. That rule has not been adopted in Washington. It requires, among other things, that the court accept the master's findings unless clearly erroneous, and permit parties to submit written objections. Fed.R.Civ.P. 53(e)(2). Joyce also relies on the Supreme Court's decision in Weyerhaeuser v. Pierce County, 124 Wash.2d 26, 32–33, 873 P.2d 498 (1994). There, the court held that county staff members, who prepared documents for consideration by a hearing examiner, were witnesses and had to be made available for cross-examination. Mr. Cummins was a witness and the trial court should have permitted discovery of his opinions and the reasons for them. CR 26(b)(5)(A).

We cannot, however, find any prejudice to Joyce. Mr. Cummins' opinions were fully disclosed. The only opinion given by Mr. Cummins and relied on by the court was that McDirmid's second accounting was prepared using acceptable accounting methods. Before trial, McDirmid's accounting was subject to extensive discovery. And during trial it was the topic of extensive cross-examination. Further, the court ultimately rejected Mr. Cummins' opinion that the prudence of Mr. Cooper's investment strategy should be judged by the total appreciation of the corpus, not the gain or loss of the marketable securities. The error was therefore harmless. See Rice v. Janovich, 109 Wash.2d 48, 62–63, 742 P.2d 1230 (1987) (ex parte contact by trial judge, absent showing of prejudice, is not ground for reversal).

* * *

In Mr. Cooper's appeal, we affirm the trial court's findings (1) his management of the estate's marketable securities breached his duty to act as a prudent investor, (2) removing him as trustee over half of the trust assets, and (3) rejecting his argument Joyce had waived any right to challenge his management. We also affirm the court's decision to award attorney fees to all parties, but remand for a determination of what portion of Joyce's fees were attributable to her challenging Mr. Cooper's management of the marketable securities. That amount shall be paid by Mr. Cooper personally. We grant Mr. Cooper's, Richard's and Joyce's requests for attorney fees on appeal. In Joyce's cross-appeal, we hold the trial court's use of Mr. Cummins to review the McDirmid accountings was not reversible error.

Affirmed in part; reversed in part.

The remainder of this opinion has no precedential value. Therefore, it will not be published but has been filed for public record. See RCW 2.06.040; CAR 14.

MUNSON, J., and RICHARD W. MILLER, J. Pro Tem., concur.

Uniform Prudent Investor Act (1994)

Section 2. Standard of Care; Portfolio Strategy; Risk and Return Objectives.

(a) A trustee shall invest and manage trust assets as a prudent investor would, by considering the purposes, terms, distribution requirements, and other circumstances of the trust. In satisfying this standard, the trustees shall exercise reasonable care, skill and caution.

(b) A trustee's investment and management decisions respecting individual assets must be evaluated not in isolation but in the context of the trust portfolio as a whole and as a part of an overall investment strategy having risk and return objectives reasonably suited to the trust.

(c) Among circumstances that a trustee shall consider in investing and managing trust assets are such of the following as are relevant to the trust or its beneficiaries:

(1) general economic conditions;

(2) the possible effect of inflation or deflation;

(3) the expected tax consequences of investment decisions or strategies;

(4) the role that each investment or course of action plays within the overall trust portfolio, which may include financial assets, interests in closely held enterprises, tangible and intangible personal property, and real property;

(5) the expected total return from income and the appreciation of capital;

(6) other resources of the beneficiary;

(7) needs for liquidity, regularity of income, and preservation or appreciation of capital; and

(8) an asset's special relationship or special value, if any, to the purposes of the trust or to one or more of the beneficiaries.

Section 3. Diversification.

A trustee shall diversify the investments of the trust unless the trustee reasonably determines that, because of special circumstances, the purposes of the trust are better served without diversifying.

Section 8. Reviewing Compliance.

Compliance with the prudent investor rule is determined in light of the facts and circumstances existing at the time of a trustee's decision or action and not by hindsight.

Shriners Hospital for Crippled Children v. Gardiner

Supreme Court of Arizona, 1987
152 Ariz. 527, 733 P.2d 1110

HAYS, Justice (Retired).

Laurabel Gardiner established a trust to provide income to her daughter, Mary Jane Gardiner; her two grandchildren, Charles Gardiner and Robert Gardiner; and a now-deceased daughter-in-law, Jean Gardiner. The remainder of the estate passes to Shriners Hospitals for Crippled Children (Shriners) upon the death of the life income beneficiaries. In re Estate of Gardiner, 5 Ariz.App. 239, 240, 425 P.2d 427, 428 (1967). Laurabel appointed Mary Jane as trustee, Charles as first alternate trustee, and Robert as second alternate trustee. Mary Jane was not an experienced investor, and she placed the trust assets with Dean Witter Reynolds, a brokerage house. Charles, an investment counselor and stockbroker, made all investment decisions concerning the trust assets. At some point in time, Charles embezzled $317,234.36 from the trust. Shriners brought a petition to surcharge Mary Jane for the full $317,234.36. The trial court denied the petition, but a divided court of appeals reversed. *Shriners Hospitals for Crippled Children v. Gardiner*, 152 Ariz. 519, 733 P.2d 1102, (Ct.App.1986).

We granted review on three issues:

1) Whether Mary Jane's delegation of investment power to Charles was a breach of Mary Jane's fiduciary duty.

2) Whether Mary Jane's delegation to Charles of investment power was the proximate cause of the loss of $317,234.36.

3) Whether Robert can properly continue to act as successor trustee and as guardian and conservator for the predecessor trustee Mary Jane.

* * *

In Arizona, a trustee has the duty to "observe the standard in dealing with the trust assets that would be observed by a prudent man dealing with the property of another." A.R.S. § 14-7302. If the trustee breaches that responsibility, he is personally liable for any resulting loss to the trust assets. Restatement (Second) of Trusts §§ 201, 205(a). A trustee breaches the prudent man standard when he delegates responsibilities that he reasonably can be expected personally to perform. Restatement (Second) of Trusts § 171.

We believe that Mary Jane breached the prudent man standard when she transferred investment power to Charles. Mary Jane argues, and we agree, that a trustee lacking investment experience must seek out expert advice. Although a trustee must seek out expert advice, "he is not ordinarily justified in relying on such advice, but must exercise his own judgment." Restatement (Second) of Trusts § 227. *In re Will of Newhoff*, 107 Misc.2d 589, 595, 435 N.Y.S.2d 632, 637 (1980) (a trustee must not only obtain information concerning investment possibilities but also is "under a duty to use a reasonable degree of skill in selecting an investment"). Mary Jane, though, did not evaluate Charles' advice and then make her own decisions. Charles managed the trust fund, not Mary Jane. A prudent investor would certainly participate, to some degree, in investment decisions.

The dissent in the court of appeals stated that "there is nothing to indicate the trustee 'gave up her trusteeship' or 'delegated' the 'complete management' of trust assets to Charles." *Shriners Hospitals for Crippled Children*, 152 Ariz. at 525, 733 P.2d at 1108, (Froeb, C.J., dissenting). While we agree that the record on appeal is meager, Mary Jane unquestionably transferred trustee discretion to Charles.

Mary Jane's second accounting of the Gardiner trust states:

> From time to time the Trustee made investments ("investments") in the money market and also in the purchase and sale of shares of stock listed on the New York Stock Exchange, the American Stock Exchange and the Over-the-Counter Markets.... *All of said investments were made on behalf of the Trust Estate by a person qualified in that business, [Charles] who was selected by and in whom the Trustee justifiably had the utmost trust and confidence.*

(emphasis added)

Most damning, however, are the admissions of Mary Jane's own attorney.

> Now, we can show, if the Court pleases, by way of evidence if counsel will not accept my avowal, we can show that Charles Gardiner for the past many

years, including several years prior to and since these assets were placed in his hands for investment, was in the business of a consultant and in the business of investing and selecting investments in the stock market, and this he did. And it was only natural that Mary Jane would turn to him to make that selection, to invest those funds and to account in an appropriate proceeding if, as and when required. So the prudent man rule has been adhered to here. She got a man who is capable and fortunately he was a man who was designated as an alternate trustee *and for all practical purposes really served as trustee.*

(emphasis added)

Together, the accounting and admissions establish that Charles was functioning as a surrogate trustee. Mary Jane was not exercising any control over the selection of investments. She clearly breached her duties to act prudently and to personally perform her duties as a trustee. In re Kohler's Estate, 348 Pa. 55, 33 A.2d 920 (1943) (fiduciary may not delegate to another the performance of a duty involving discretion and judgment).

Even on appeal, Mary Jane does not argue that she, in fact, exercised any discretionary investment power. Instead, she argues that her lack of investment experience made it prudent for her to delegate her investment power. She relies on the Restatement (Second) of Torts § 171.

* * *

The trustee is under a duty to the beneficiary not to delegate to others the doing of acts which the trustee can reasonably be required personally to perform.

Mary Jane asserts that her lack of investment experience prevented her from personally exercising investment power and consequently permitted delegation of that power. The standard of care required, however, is measured objectively. In re Mild's Estate, 25 N.J. 467, 480–81, 136 A.2d 875, 882 (1957) (the standard of care required of a trustee does not take into account the "differing degrees of education or intellect possessed by a fiduciary"). The trustee must be reasonable in her delegation. A delegation of investment authority is unreasonable and therefore Mary Jane's delegation is a breach of trust. See Estate of Baldwin, 442 A.2d 529 (Me.1982) (bank trustee liable for losses incurred when it failed to monitor management of grocery store despite bank's lack of expertise in grocery store management).

It is of no import that Charles was named as alternate trustee. A trustee is not permitted to delegate his responsibilities to a co-trustee. Restatement (Second) of Trusts § 224(2)(b); see also id., comment a (improper for co-trustee A to direct co-trustee B to invest trust funds without consulting A). Certainly, then, a trustee is subject to liability when she improperly delegates her investment responsibility to an alternate trustee. Bumbaugh v. Burns, 635 S.W.2d 518, 521 (Tenn.App.1982) (impermissible for trustee to delegate discretion as to investment of funds to co-trustee).

Mary Jane also argues that broad language in the trust document permitted her to delegate her investment authority to Charles. A trust document may allow a trustee to delegate powers ordinarily nondelegable. The Gardiner Trust permits the trustee "to employ and compensate attorneys, accountants, agents and brokers." This language does not bear on Mary Jane's delegation of investment authority. Mary Jane did not simply employ Charles; she allowed him to serve as surrogate trustee. We view this language as merely an express recognition of the trustee's obligation to obtain expert advice, not as a license to remove herself from her role as a trustee.

* * *

Mary Jane next argues that there is no causal connection between her breach and the loss suffered by the trust. The court of appeals rejected this argument in a summary fashion, stating that "the trustee offers no evidence to meet this burden of showing that the loss would have occurred anyway." Shriners Hospitals for Crippled Children, 152 Ariz. at 523, 733 P.2d at 1106. We disagree.

The very nature of the loss indicates that the breach was not causally connected to the loss. The accounting indicates that Charles embezzled the funds.

> Without the knowledge or consent of the Trustee, said person received from said investments, and diverted to his own use, a total believed by the Trustee to aggregate $317,234.36 ($116,695.55 on January 16, 1981 and $200,537.81 on March 4, 1981). The trustee did not learn of said diversions until long after they occurred. No part of the amount so diverted had been returned or paid to the Trustee or the Trust Estate....

If the trust had suffered because poor investments were made, the delegation of investment authority would unquestionably be the cause of the loss. Otherwise, a causal connection between Charles' diversion of funds and Mary Jane's breach is absent unless the delegation of investment authority gave Charles control and dominion over the trust fund that permitted the defalcation.

A causal connection does not exist simply because "but for" Mary Jane's opening of the account at Dean Witter Reynolds, no loss would have occurred. A trustee is not personally liable for losses not resulting from a breach of trust. Restatement (Second) of Trusts § 204; Citizens & Southern Nat'l Bank v. Haskins, 254 Ga. 131, 134, 327 S.E.2d 192, 197 (1985). Mary Jane did not breach her duty by establishing an account at Dean Witter Reynolds, a major brokerage house. Charles was not only the type of person Mary Jane was obliged to seek out for investment advice, but he was a person whom Laurabel Gardiner indicated was trustworthy by naming him as second alternate trustee. Furthermore, the Dean Witter Reynolds account was apparently in Mary Jane's name. If Dean Witter Reynolds wrongfully allowed Charles access to the fund, Mary Jane is not personally liable. Restatement (Second) of Trusts § 225 (trustee not generally liable for wrongful acts of agents employed in administration of estate).

Unfortunately, the record does not reveal the nature of the diversion. The relative culpability of Charles, Mary Jane and Dean Witter Reynolds is unclear. The trial court found that Mary Jane was without fault and, therefore, did not consider the causal connection between Mary Jane's breach and Charles's defalcation. The inadequacy of the record demands a remand for a determination of the relationship between Mary Jane's delegation of investment authority and Charles' diversion of funds.

* * *

If, after remand, the trial court determines that Mary Jane is personally liable for the diversion of funds, Robert must be removed as trustee.[1] A trustee is liable to a beneficiary if he fails to "redress a breach of trust committed by the predecessor [trustee]." Restatement (Second) of Trusts § 223(2). Robert would, therefore, have a duty to enforce the surcharge against his aunt and ward, Mary Jane. The conflict between personal re-

---

1. Robert Gardiner is currently serving as trustee because Mary Jane is an invalid and Charles is untrustworthy. Robert is also Mary Jane's guardian-conservator.

sponsibilities and trust obligations is obvious and great. Estate of Rothko, 43 N.Y.2d 305, 319, 401 N.Y.S.2d 449, 454, 372 N.E.2d 291, 296 (1977) (while a trustee is administering the trust he must refrain from placing himself in position where his personal interest does or may conflict with interest of beneficiaries). Another trustee, without such conflicts, would have to be appointed.

The decision of the court of appeals is vacated, and the case is remanded for further proceedings consistent with this opinion.

GORDON, C.J., and FELDMAN, V.C.J., and HOLOHAN, J., concur.

Note: JAMES DUKE CAMERON, Justice, recused himself from participation in the determination of the foregoing case.

Notes

The Uniform Prudent Investor Act allows a trustee to delegate investment and management functions but cautions as to selecting an agent, keeping the delegation within the terms of the trust, and the need to review performance. *See* UNIF. PRUDENT INV. ACT §9 (2003). The FEDERAL EMPLOYEE RETIREMENT INCOME SECURITY ACT OF 1974 (ERISA) and the Restatement of Trusts (Third): Prudent Investment Rule allow for delegation. *See* 29 U.S.C. §1103(a)(2) (2004)(as amended by PL 108-357, Oct. 22, 2004). This signals a distinct trend towards allowing delegation of investment and management functions. *See generally* Mark R. Gillett, *Investing Trust Assets: Prudence Redefined*, 29 OKLA. CITY U. L. REV. 505 (2004); John H. Langbein, *The Uniform Prudent Investor Act and the Future of Trust Investing*, 81 IOWA L. REV. 641 (1996).

C. Powers of the Trustee

Uniform Trust Code (2003)

Section 816. Specific Powers of Trustee

Without limiting the authority conferred by Section 815, a trustee may:

(1) collect trust property and accept or reject additions to the trust property from a settlor or any other person;

(2) acquire or sell property, for cash or on credit, at public or private sale;

(3) exchange, partition, or otherwise change the character of trust property;

(4) deposit trust money in an account in a regulated financial-service institution;

(5) borrow money, with or without security, and mortgage or pledge trust property for a period within or extending beyond the duration of the trust;

(6) with respect to an interest in a proprietorship, partnership, limited liability company, business trust, corporation, or other form of business or enterprise, continue the business or other enterprise and take any action that may be taken by shareholders, members, or property owners, including merging, dissolving, or otherwise changing the form of business organization or contributing additional capital;

(7) with respect to stocks or other securities, exercise the rights of an absolute owner, including the right to:

(A) vote, or give proxies to vote, with or without power of substitution, or enter into or continue a voting trust agreement;

(B) hold a security in the name of a nominee or in other form without disclosure of the trust so that title may pass by delivery;

(C) pay calls, assessments, and other sums chargeable or accruing against the securities, and sell or exercise stock subscription or conversion rights; and

(D) deposit the securities with a depositary or other regulated financial-service institution;

(8) with respect to an interest in real property, construct, or make ordinary or extraordinary repairs to, alterations to, or improvements in, buildings or other structures, demolish improvements, raze existing or erect new party walls or buildings, subdivide or develop land, dedicate land to public use or grant public or private easements, and make or vacate plats and adjust boundaries;

(9) enter into a lease for any purpose as lessor or lessee, including a lease or other arrangement for exploration and removal of natural resources, with or without the option to purchase or renew, for a period within or extending beyond the duration of the trust;

(10) grant an option involving a sale, lease, or other disposition of trust property or acquire an option for the acquisition of property, including an option exercisable beyond the duration of the trust, and exercise an option so acquired;

(11) insure the property of the trust against damage or loss and insure the trustee, the trustee's agents, and beneficiaries against liability arising from the administration of the trust;

(12) abandon or decline to administer property of no value or of insufficient value to justify its collection or continued administration;

(13) with respect to possible liability for violation of environmental law:

(A) inspect or investigate property the trustee holds or has been asked to hold, or property owned or operated by an organization in which the trustee holds or has been asked to hold an interest, for the purpose of determining the application of environmental law with respect to the property;

(B) take action to prevent, abate, or otherwise remedy any actual or potential violation of any environmental law affecting property held directly or indirectly by the trustee, whether taken before or after the assertion of a claim or the initiation of governmental enforcement;

(C) decline to accept property into trust or disclaim any power with respect to property that is or may be burdened with liability for violation of environmental law;

(D) compromise claims against the trust which may be asserted for an alleged violation of environmental law; and

(E) pay the expense of any inspection, review, abatement, or remedial action to comply with environmental law;

(14) pay or contest any claim, settle a claim by or against the trust, and release, in whole or in part, a claim belonging to the trust;

(15) pay taxes, assessments, compensation of the trustee and of employees and agents of the trust, and other expenses incurred in the administration of the trust;

(16) exercise elections with respect to federal, state, and local taxes;

(17) select a mode of payment under any employee benefit or retirement plan, annuity, or life insurance payable to the trustee, exercise rights thereunder, including exercise of the right to indemnification for expenses and against liabilities, and take appropriate action to collect the proceeds;

(18) make loans out of trust property, including loans to a beneficiary on terms and conditions the trustee considers to be fair and reasonable under the circumstances, and the trustee has a lien on future distributions for repayment of those loans;

(19) pledge trust property to guarantee loans made by others to the beneficiary;

(20) appoint a trustee to act in another jurisdiction with respect to trust property located in the other jurisdiction, confer upon the appointed trustee all of the powers and duties of the appointing trustee, require that the appointed trustee furnish security, and remove any trustee so appointed;

(21) pay an amount distributable to a beneficiary who is under a legal disability or who the trustee reasonably believes is incapacitated, by paying it directly to the beneficiary or applying it for the beneficiary's benefit, or by:

(A) paying it to the beneficiary's [conservator] or, if the beneficiary does not have a [conservator], the beneficiary's [guardian];

(B) paying it to the beneficiary's custodian under [the Uniform Transfers to Minors Act] or custodial trustee under [the Uniform Custodial Trust Act], and, for that purpose, creating a custodianship or custodial trust;

(C) if the trustee does not know of a [conservator], [guardian], custodian, or custodial trustee, paying it to an adult relative or other person having legal or physical care or custody of the beneficiary, to be expended on the beneficiary's behalf; or

(D) managing it as a separate fund on the beneficiary's behalf, subject to the beneficiary's continuing right to withdraw the distribution;

(22) on distribution of trust property or the division or termination of a trust, make distributions in divided or undivided interests, allocate particular assets in proportionate or disproportionate shares, value the trust property for those purposes, and adjust for resulting differences in valuation;

(23) resolve a dispute concerning the interpretation of the trust or its administration by mediation, arbitration, or other procedure for alternative dispute resolution;

(24) prosecute or defend an action, claim, or judicial proceeding in any jurisdiction to protect trust property and the trustee in the performance of the trustee's duties;

(25) sign and deliver contracts and other instruments that are useful to achieve or facilitate the exercise of the trustee's powers; and

(26) on termination of the trust, exercise the powers appropriate to wind up the administration of the trust and distribute the trust property to the persons entitled to it.

Allard v. Pacific National Bank

Supreme Court of Washington, 1983
99 Wash.2d 394, 663 P.2d 104

DOLLIVER, Justice.

* * *

J.T. and Georgiana Stone, both deceased, established trusts in their wills conveying their property upon their deaths to Pacific Bank to be held for their children and the issue of their children. The Stones' children, Evelyn Orkney and Freeman Allard, are life income beneficiaries of the Stone trusts. Upon the death of either life income beneficiary, the trustee is to pay the income from the trust to the issue of the deceased beneficiary. When all the children of the deceased beneficiary reach the age of 21 years, the trusts direct the trustee to distribute the trust corpus equally among the issue of that beneficiary.

In 1978 the sole asset of the Stone trusts was a fee interest in a quarter block located on the northwest corner of Third Avenue and Columbia Street in downtown Seattle. The trust provisions of the wills gave Pacific Bank "full power to ... manage, improve, sell, lease, mortgage, pledge, encumber, and exchange the whole or any part of the assets of [the] trust estate" and required Pacific Bank to

> exercise the judgment and care under the circumstances then prevailing, which prudent men exercise in the management of their own affairs, not in regard to speculation but in regard to the permanent disposition of their funds, considering the probable income as well as the probable safety of their capital.

The Third and Columbia property was subject to a 99-year lease, entered into by the Stones in 1952 with Seattle-First National Bank (Seafirst Bank). The lease contained no rental escalation provision and the rental rate was to remain the same for the entire 99-year term of the lease. The right of first refusal to purchase the lessor's interest in the property was given to the lessee. The lease also contained several restrictive provisions. One paragraph required any repair, reconstruction, or replacement of buildings on the property by the lessee to be completed within 8 months from the date the original building was damaged or destroyed "from any cause whatsoever". Another paragraph provided that, upon termination of lease, the lessee had the option either to surrender possession of all improvements or to remove the improvements. The lease prohibited, without the lessor's consent, any encumbrance which would have priority over the lessor in case of the lessee's insolvency.

In June 1977 Seafirst Bank assigned its leasehold interest in the Third and Columbia property to the City Credit Union of Seattle (Credit Union). Eight months later, on February 14, 1978, Credit Union offered to purchase the property from Pacific Bank for $139,900. On April 25, 1978, Pacific Bank informed Credit Union it was interested in selling the property, but demanded at least $200,000. In early June 1978, Credit Union offered $200,000 for the Third and Columbia property. Pacific Bank accepted Credit Union's offer, and deeded the property to Credit Union on August 17, 1978. On September 26, 1978, Pacific Bank informed Freeman Allard and Evelyn Orkney of the sale to Credit Union.

On May 1, 1979, plaintiffs commenced the present action against Pacific Bank for breach of its fiduciary duties regarding management of the Stone trusts, against Credit Union and Seafirst Bank for participation in the alleged breach, and against Credit

Union for conversion. Plaintiffs' complaint requested money damages from Pacific Bank, Credit Union, and Seafirst Bank. The complaint also requested the imposition of a constructive trust on the Third and Columbia property and the removal of Pacific Bank as trustee. On March 18, 1980, plaintiffs filed their demand for a trial by jury under Const. art. 1, § 21.

Based on its determination plaintiffs' cause of action was primarily equitable in nature, the trial court struck their demand for trial by jury. The trial court also granted motions by Credit Union and Seafirst Bank for a partial summary judgment dismissing them from the case. Plaintiffs did not appeal the summary judgments dismissing Credit Union and Seafirst Bank.

At trial, the primary dispute was over the degree of care owed by Pacific Bank to the Stone trusts and to the Stone trust beneficiaries. Plaintiffs attempted to call expert witnesses to testify Pacific Bank failed to comply with the ordinary standards of trust administration when it sold the Third and Columbia property. Plaintiffs' first expert witness, Edmond R. Davis, was former manager of the trust department legal division of Security First National Bank, now Security Pacific National Bank, in California. Plaintiffs presented an offer of proof Edmond Davis would testify Pacific Bank failed to comply with ordinary standards of trust practice in making its decision to sell the Third and Columbia property and in the steps it took to sell the property. Plaintiffs' other excluded expert witness, McLain Davis, was former manager of the trust department probate division of the National Bank of Commerce, now Rainier Bank. Plaintiffs' offers of proof regarding the testimony of McLain Davis indicated the witness would testify a bank trustee, acting in accordance with ordinary standards of trust practice, would not be excused from obtaining an appraisal by lack of funds in the trust account. Furthermore, according to plaintiffs, McLain Davis would have testified a trustee would not be acting in accordance with ordinary trust practices if the trustee dispensed with obtaining an outside appraisal or other prospective purchasers where its own internal appraisal indicated the sale was for an amount in excess of the property's fair market value.

At trial it was unquestioned that both witnesses were qualified as experts in trust administration. Rather, the trial court sustained defendant's objections to the testimony of plaintiffs' expert witnesses on the grounds the witnesses would testify as to legal opinions, inadmissible under ER 702, 704. The exclusion of plaintiffs' proffered expert witnesses left plaintiffs with no direct testimony regarding ordinary standards of trust administration.

At the culmination of the trial, the court entered judgment dismissing plaintiffs' action against Pacific Bank. It determined Pacific Bank acted in good faith and in conformance with its duties under the Stone trust instruments. The court concluded Pacific Bank neither had a duty to inform the trust beneficiaries prior to sale of the Third and Columbia property nor a duty to obtain an independent appraisal of the property or to place the property on the open market. Finally, the trial court awarded Pacific Bank $51,507.07 attorney fees and costs from the income and principal of the Stone trusts. From this judgment plaintiffs bring appeal.

* * *

[Court's opinion rejecting plaintiffs' right to jury trial is omitted].

We now consider the crux of the case before us. Defendant contends it had full authority under the trust instrument to exercise its own judgment and impartial discretion in deciding how to invest the trust assets and a duty to use reasonable care and skill to make the trust property productive. See findings of fact 12–14. It further contends the sale of the property was conducted in good faith and with honest judgment. Finding of fact 19. Plaintiffs assert this discretion was limited by its fiduciary duties and that defendant in its management of the trusts breached its fiduciary duty.

Plaintiffs' argument regarding Pacific Bank's alleged breach of its fiduciary duties is twofold. First, Pacific Bank had a duty to inform them of the sale of the Third and Columbia property. Second, Pacific Bank breached its fiduciary duties by failing either to obtain an independent appraisal of the Third and Columbia property or to place the property on the open market prior to selling it to Seattle Credit Union. We agree with plaintiffs' position in both instances and hold defendant breached its fiduciary duty in its management of the trusts.

* * *

Initially, plaintiffs and amicus curiae the Attorney General of the State of Washington contend Pacific Bank should be held to a higher standard of care than the ordinary, prudent investor standard provided in RCW 30.24.020. Plaintiffs and amicus curiae argue the ordinary, prudent investor standard is inappropriate where the trustee represents that it has greater skill than that of a nonprofessional trustee. They fail to mention, however, the terms of the Stone trust agreements which specifically adopt the prudent investor standard of care provided in RCW 30.24.020.

RCW 30.24.020 provides:

> In acquiring, investing, reinvesting, exchanging, selling and managing property for the benefit of another, a fiduciary shall exercise the judgment and care *under the circumstances* then prevailing, which *men of prudence, discretion and intelligence exercise in the management of their own affairs*, not in regard to speculation but in regard to the permanent disposition of their funds, considering the probable income as well as the probable safety of their capital.

(Italics ours.) Under the trust agreements, Pacific Bank is required as trustee to

> exercise the judgment and care under the circumstances then prevailing, which prudent men exercise in the management of their own affairs, not in regard to speculation but in regard to the permanent disposition of their funds, considering the probable income as well as the probable safety of their capital.

Significantly, the statute recognizes the standard of care required of a trustee is "subject to any express provisions or limitations contained in any particular trust instrument". RCW 30.24.020. Furthermore, the terms of the trust instrument control as to the investments made by a trustee. RCW 30.24.070. Except where impossible, illegal, or where a change of circumstances occurs which would impair the purposes of the trust, the nature and extent of the duties and powers of a trustee are determined by the trust agreement. See Baldus v. Bank of Cal., 12 Wash.App. at 628, 530 P.2d 1350; Steiner v. Hawaiian Trust Co., 47 Hawaii 548, 562–63, 393 P.2d 96 (1964). Although in some future case we may be called upon to determine if a corporate professional trustee should be held to a higher standard because of the language in the trust instruments, this issue need not be decided here. Cf. Restatement (Second) of Trusts §227, comment d (1959).

* * *

The Stone trusts gave Pacific Bank "full power to ... manage, improve, sell, lease, mortgage, pledge, encumber, and exchange the whole or any part of the assets of [the] trust estate". Under such an agreement, the trustee is not required to secure the consent of trust beneficiaries before selling trust assets. 3 A. Scott, Trusts § 190.5 (3d ed. 1967). Accord, Bulla v. Valley Nat'l Bank, 82 Ariz. 84, 308 P.2d 932 (1957); In re Wellman Estate, 119 Vt. 426, 127 A.2d 279 (1956). The trustee owes to the beneficiaries, however, the highest degree of good faith, care, loyalty, and integrity. Esmieu v. Schrag, 88 Wash.2d 490, 498, 563 P.2d 203 (1977); Monroe v. Winn, 16 Wash.2d 497, 508, 133 P.2d 952 (1943).

Pacific Bank claims it was obligated to sell the property to Credit Union since Credit Union, as assignee of the lease agreement with Seafirst Bank, had a right of first refusal to purchase the property. Since it did not need to obtain the consent of the beneficiaries before selling trust assets, Pacific Bank argues it also was not required to inform the beneficiaries of the sale. We disagree. The beneficiaries could have offered to purchase the property at a higher price than the offer by Credit Union, thereby forcing Credit Union to pay a higher price to exercise its right of first refusal as assignee of the lease agreement. Furthermore, letters from the beneficiaries to Pacific Bank indicated their desire to retain the Third and Columbia property. While the beneficiaries could not have prevented Pacific Bank from selling the property, they presumably could have outbid Credit Union for the property. This opportunity should have been afforded to them.

On a previous occasion, we ruled the trustee's fiduciary duty includes the responsibility to inform the beneficiaries fully of all facts which would aid them in protecting their interests. Esmieu v. Schrag, supra. See United States v. Bennett, 57 F.Supp. 670 (E.D.Wash.1944). We adhere to the view expressed in Esmieu. That the settlor has created a trust and thus required the beneficiaries to enjoy their property interests indirectly does not imply the beneficiaries are to be kept in ignorance of the trust, the nature of the trust property, and the details of its administration. G. Bogert, Trusts and Trustees § 961 (2d ed. 1962). If the beneficiaries are able to hold the trustee to proper standards of care and honesty and procure the benefits to which they are entitled, they must know of what the trust property consists and how it is being managed. G. Bogert, Trusts and Trustees, supra.

The duty to provide information is often performed by corporate trustees by rendering periodic statements to the beneficiaries, usually in the form of copies of the ledger sheets concerning the trust. G. Bogert, Trusts § 141 (5th ed. 1973). For example, such condensed explanations of recent transactions may be mailed to the beneficiaries annually, semiannually, or quarterly. G. Bogert, Trusts, supra. Ordinarily, periodic statements are sufficient to satisfy a trustee's duty to beneficiaries of transactions affecting the trust property. The trust provisions here, for example, provide the trustee

> shall furnish on or before February 15 of each year to each person described in Section 1 of Article IV who is then a beneficiary ... a statement showing how the respective trust assets are invested and all transactions relating thereto for the preceding calendar year.

The trustee must inform beneficiaries, however, of all material facts in connection with a nonroutine transaction which significantly affects the trust estate and the interests of the beneficiaries prior to the transaction taking place. The duty to inform is particularly required in this case where the only asset of the trusts was the property on the corner of Third and Columbia. Under the circumstances found in this case failure to inform was an egregious breach of fiduciary duty and defies the course of conduct any reasonable person would take, much less a prudent investor.

* * *

We also conclude Pacific Bank breached its fiduciary duties regarding management of the Stone trusts by failing to obtain the best possible price for the Third and Columbia property. Pacific Bank made no attempt to obtain a more favorable price for the property from Credit Union by, for example, negotiating to cancel the restrictive provisions in the lease originally negotiated with Seafirst Bank. Cf. Hatcher v. United States Nat'l Bank, 56 Or.App. 643, 643 P.2d 359 (1982) (trustee had not fulfilled its fiduciary duties by merely examining offer to purchase and altering the terms slightly). The bank neither offered the property for sale on the open market, see Rippey v. Denver United States Nat'l Bank, 273 F.Supp. 718 (D.Colo.1967), nor did it obtain an independent, outside appraisal of the Third and Columbia property to determine its fair market value. See Belcher v. Birmingham Trust Nat'l Bank, 348 F.Supp. 61 (N.D.Ala.1968); Webb & Knapp, Inc. v. Hanover Bank, 214 Md. 230, 133 A.2d 450 (1957).

Washington courts have not yet considered the nature of a trustee's duty of care regarding the sale of trust assets. Other courts, however, generally require that a trustee when selling trust assets try to obtain the maximum price for the asset. E.g., Berner v. Equitable Office Bldg. Corp., 175 F.2d 218, 221 (2d Cir.1949); Terry v. Midwest Ref. Co., 64 F.2d 428 (10th Cir.), cert. denied, 290 U.S. 660, 54 S.Ct. 74, 78 L.Ed. 571 (1933); Lockwood v. OFB Corp., 305 A.2d 636, 638 (Del.Ch.1973); Ross v. Wilson, 308 N.Y. 605, 127 N.E.2d 697 (1955). The Oregon Court of Appeals required a trustee to determine the fair market value of trust property prior to selling the property by obtaining an appraisal or by "testing the market" to determine what a willing buyer would pay. Hatcher v. United States Nat'l Bank, 56 Or.App. at 652, 643 P.2d 359. Some courts specifically require trustees to obtain an independent appraisal of the property. See, e.g., Belcher v. Birmingham Trust Nat'l Bank, 348 F.Supp. 61 (N.D.Ala.1968); Webb & Knapp, Inc. v. Hanover Bank, 214 Md. 230, 133 A.2d 450 (1957). Other courts merely require that a trustee determine fair market value by placing the property on the open market. See, e.g., Lockwood v. OFB Corp., supra; State v. Hartman, 54 Wis.2d 47, 194 N.W.2d 653 (1972).

We agree with the Oregon Court of Appeals in Hatcher that a trustee may determine the best possible price for trust property either by obtaining an independent appraisal of the property or by "testing the market" to determine what a willing buyer would pay. The record discloses none of these actions were taken by the defendant. By its failure to obtain the best possible price for the Third and Columbia property, defendant breached its fiduciary duty as the prudent manager of the trusts.

On the issue of the exclusion by the trial court of the testimony regarding ordinary standards of trust administration, we need not express an opinion. The admission of such evidence is at the discretion of the trial court. See Maehren v. Seattle, 92 Wash.2d 480, 488, 599 P.2d 1255 (1979). Although arguably it was an abuse of discretion and the evidence might properly have been admitted, because of our disposition of the case it is unnecessary to reach that issue and we decline to do so.

* * *

Finally, we consider whether the trial court improperly awarded attorney fees to Pacific Bank. A trial court may allow and properly charge attorney fees to a trust estate for litigation that is necessary to the administration of the trust. Peoples Nat'l Bank v.

Jarvis, 58 Wash.2d 627, 632–33, 364 P.2d 436 (1961); Puget Sound Nat'l Bank v. Easterday, 56 Wash.2d 937, 951, 350 P.2d 444, 354 P.2d 24 (1960). The award of attorney fees against the trust estate is vested in the discretion of the trial court. Jarvis, 58 Wash.2d at 632, 364 P.2d 436; Tucker v. Brown, 20 Wash.2d 740, 839, 150 P.2d 604 (1944). A trial court's discretion to award attorney fees, however, is not absolute. The court must determine the litigation is indispensable to the proper administration of the trust; the issues presented are neither immaterial nor trifling; the conduct of the parties or counsel is not vexatious or litigious; and that there has been no unnecessary delay or expense. Jarvis, 58 Wash.2d at 632, 364 P.2d 436. Furthermore, the trial court must consider the result of the litigation. G. Bogert, Trusts and Trustees §871 (2d rev. ed. 1982).

The court's underlying consideration must be whether the litigation and the participation of the party seeking attorney fees caused a benefit to the trust. Estate of Baird, 135 Cal.App.2d 343, 287 P.2d 372 (1955); Kronzer v. First Nat'l Bank, 305 Minn. 415, 235 N.W.2d 187 (1975). A trustee who unsuccessfully defends against charges of breach of fiduciary duties obviously has not caused a benefit to the trust. Therefore, a trial court abuses its discretion when it awards attorney fees to a trustee for litigation caused by the trustee's misconduct. Accord, Estate of Baird, supra; Ellis v. King, 336 Ill.App. 298, 83 N.E.2d 367 (1949).

Here the trial court awarded attorney fees to Pacific Bank based on its decision Pacific Bank properly exercised its discretion in the management of the Stone trusts. Since we rule here that regardless of the discretion of the trustee it breached its fiduciary duties, the award of attorney fees was based on untenable grounds. We hold this was an abuse of discretion. State ex rel. Carroll v. Junker, 79 Wash.2d 12, 26, 482 P.2d 775 (1971). A trustee may be awarded attorney fees and costs for litigation alleging breach of the trust agreement only if the trustee successfully defends against the action. See Annot., 9 A.L.R.2d 1132, 1241–53 (1950).

We also hold that since defendant breached its fiduciary duty plaintiffs should be granted their request to recover all attorney fees expended at both the trial and on appeal on behalf of the plaintiffs and all minor beneficiaries and unknown beneficiaries. See PUD 1 v. Kottsick, 86 Wash.2d 388, 545 P.2d 1 (1976). See Annot., 9 A.L.R.2d 1132, 1241–53 (1950). Ordinarily, the trust estate must bear the general costs of administration of the trust, including the expenses of necessary litigation. Monroe v. Winn, 19 Wash.2d 462, 466, 142 P.2d 1022 (1943). Where litigation is necessitated by the inexcusable conduct of the trustee, however, the trustee individually must pay those expenses. Wolff v. Calla, 288 F.Supp. 891, 894 (E.D. Pa. 1968); Wilmington Trust Co. v. Coulter, 42 Del. Ch. 253, 208 A.2d 677 (1965). Accord, Hsu Ying Li v. Tang, 87 Wash.2d 796, 557 P.2d 342 (1976). As we said in Grein v. Cavano, 61 Wash.2d 498, 506, 379 P.2d 209 (1963) (quoting Weber v. Marine Cooks' & Stewards' Ass'n, 93 Cal.App.2d 327, 340–41, 208 P.2d 1009 (1949)), quoted with approval in DeMonbrun v. Sheet Metal Workers Int'l Ass'n, 140 Cal.App.2d 546, 565, 295 P.2d 881 (1956):

> [T]he successful maintenance by a few for the benefit of many of an equitable action resulting in the protection of [their] contractual rights as originally established is ground for allowing attorney's fees to those who battle to redress the wrong and maintain the previous personal rights although no actual court order to return the erroneously spent funds has been made.

Accord, Peoples Nat'l Bank v. Jarvis, 58 Wash.2d 627, 632–33, 364 P.2d 436 (1961).

We affirm the trial court's refusal to grant plaintiffs a jury trial. We hold defendant breached its fiduciary duty and reverse the trial court on this issue. The award of attorney fees to Pacific Bank is reversed. The case is remanded for a determination of the damages caused to plaintiffs by defendant's breach of its fiduciary duties as trustee of the Stone trusts and a determination of the amount of attorney fees to be awarded plaintiffs from the trustee individually.

WILLIAM H. WILLIAMS, C.J., STAFFORD, DORE, DIMMICK and PEARSON, JJ., and WIELAND and ALEXANDER, JJ. Pro Tem.

Notes

The Uniform Trust Code permits an exculpatory clause in the trust instrument to relieve a Trustee of liability for breach of trust, as long as the breach was not committed in bad faith, by reckless indifference, or as a result of an abuse of the confidential relationship between the Settlor and the Trustee. *See* UNIF. TRUST CODE §1008 (2003). The consent of the beneficiary will also permit the Trustee to escape liability as long as the consent was obtained properly and all the material facts were know to the beneficiary. *See id.* at §1009. A beneficiary may not commence an action against a Trustee more than one year after the date on which the beneficiary was made aware of a potential claim for a breach. *See id.* at §1005. Finally, a Trustee is not personally liable on contracts properly entered into in the course of administration, as long as the Trustee reveals his or her representative capacity and identifies the trust estate in the contract. *See* UNIF. PROB. CODE §7-306 (2003); UNIF. TRUST CODE §1010 (2003).

V. Class Gifts

A class gift is created by a Testator or a Settlor, with the intention of creating a gift in favor of persons belonging to a group that is capable of increasing or decreasing on its own. For example, if, in a Last Will and Testament, the Testator writes: "All of my property, both real and personal, I hereby give, devise, and bequeath to my children." At the time the Testator executes the Will, the Testator has one child, but when the Testator dies some years later and the Will speaks, the Testator has three children. How many children take? Obviously, the Testator intended that all of the children should take because all are members of a "class," and none has been excluded through specific language. Likewise, if, in a valid inter vivos trust, a Settlor, writes: "income to myself for life and then the remainder to my children, to be paid when the youngest turns twenty-one," the Settlor has one child when the trust is created and three when the Settlor dies and the youngest child turns twenty-one, how many children should take? Once again, since a class designation was used, all of the children meeting the description should take when the corpus of the trust becomes available. Class gifts are intended to be fluid and flexible, and these two examples provide illustrations of class members increasing until distribution occurs.

But there also can be decreasing members of a class, and this raises different issues. For example, if, as in the previous example, the Testator writes: "All of my property, both real and personal, I hereby give, devise, and bequeath to my children," what happens if one of these children dies before the Testator, and the child has descendants who survive the Testator? If the state's anti-lapse statute applies to class gifts, then the descendants of the pre-deceasing child will take the portion that his or her deceased parent would have taken as a member of a class, if the parent had survived. Because the child was a relative of the Testator, anti-lapse is free to apply (you may review the material concerning anti-lapse at Chapter Four, Section VII, *supra*). But there may be a decrease in the members of a class in an inter vivos trust—something to which anti-lapse will not apply. Return to the previous example of a Settlor who creates an inter vivos trust and writes: "To myself for life, and then the remainder to my children, to be paid when the youngest turns twenty-one." If the Settlor has a child who dies after the Settlor creates the trust but before the death of the Settlor *and* when the youngest child turns twenty-one, and that predeceasing child leaves descendants and an estate, should a portion of the trust go to the descendants or to the estate? The answer is, "yes," but the portion that would have gone to the child had the child survived as a member of the class now goes to the estate of the deceased child when the Settlor dies and the youngest child turns twenty-one. The descendants do not take as they would have done under the anti-lapse statute. The reason the estate takes is due to vesting.

To explain vesting, we know that when the Settlor established the trust during the Settlor's lifetime, the Settlor provided that the corpus would be distributed to the children whenever the Settlor died and the youngest child then, or in the future, turned twenty-one. But note that the Settlor did not create a condition that the child survive until the later of these two events. Instead, the Settlor provided that the corpus would be paid at that point. *See* Clobberie's Case, 2 Vent. 342, 86 Eng. Rep. 476 (1677). Vesting occurred first; possession or payment occurred in the future. Thus, a child has a vested interest in the remainder simply by being alive or born during the trust period. And at the point of distribution—the death of the Settlor and the youngest child turning twenty-one—the child or the estate takes possession or payment.

There are other issues concerning class gifts, but the issues surrounding increase and decrease abound. Careful drafting and a knowledge of construction issues will prevent a multitude of litigation.

A. Increase of Class

In re Evans' Estate

Supreme Court of Wisconsin, 1957
274 Wis. 459, 80 N.W.2d 408

FAIRCHILD, Chief Justice.

Before taking up the question of whether or not the judgment entered April 17, 1942 is *res judicata* as to grandchildren born after the date of death of the testator, it seems well to pass upon the nature and inclusiveness of the bequest. If the gift grant in Article Third is to a class, and that class is so fixed by the terms of the bequest that there may be an interval of time during which the class may increase, then the gift is one which vests in the existing number of the class and such other persons as thereafter become members of the class. That interval continues to the point of time or event which is specified and certain. The gift we are considering is to 'my grandchildren,' and because of the absence of an alternative gift over or reversion in favor of the testator's heirs, it bespeaks an intention of a vested gift. The grandchildren living at the death of the testator are members of the class, but the class is subject to a change by addition of after-born grandchildren who came into being before the coming of the event which closes forever the membership in the class.

The time fixed for closing the class is set in the bequest: 'After each grandchild reaches the age of thirty years, he is to be paid his full share of the principal sum of this bequest together with the interest which has accumulated thereon.' This controls the increase in membership in the class. The time of the distribution of the *corpus* settles the question of maximum membership. In the absence of words in the will indicating a contrary intent, a testator would naturally desire to include all grandchildren born at the time of the distribution of the *corpus*. In Simes, The Law of Future Interests, we find the following recognition of rules of construction:

> 'The maximum membership in the class is determined when the time for distribution has arrived. The class may increase until that time, and persons born thereafter are excluded.' Sec. 634, p. 69.

> 'The time for distribution arrived when the first member of the class attained the designated age.' Sec. 644, p. 89.

In 5 American Law of Property, the following rules are recognized:

> When a class gift is postponed until the occurrence of some * * * event, such as the attainment of age twenty-one * * *. the class does not normally close until the first member of the class attains the designated age. Sec. 22.44, p. 372.

> 'It must be kept in mind that the probable desire of the average transferor, when he describes his transferees by a group designation, is to benefit as many persons who comply with the description as he can, without at the same time causing too much inconvenience.' Sec. 22.43, p. 364.

The gift may be so made that the class may either increase or decrease after the death of the testator until the arrival of the fixed point of time or the happening of the specified event. It may be so worded that there may be an interval of time during which the class may increase but during which it cannot decrease. The most common example of this kind of gift is one which vests in the existing members of a class and in such other persons as thereafter become members of the class up to the point of time or event which is specified. Page on Wills, sec. 1052. It is considered that the three grandchildren born after the death of the testator and before the distribution of the *corpus* are members of the class and inherit as such.

The question of *res adjudicata* we conclude to be without merit. In his will the deceased made a gift to a class, to wit, his grandchildren. As previously construed herein, such class might increase in membership after his death until the arrival of a fixed point of time to be determined as of the date when the first grandchild reaches the age of thirty. The bequest vested in the existing members of the class and in such other persons as thereafter became members, up until such a point of time when the first distribution of the *corpus* was directed to be made. At the time the will was admitted to probate, there were then in existence six grandchildren who were members of the class, with the possibility of an increase in the membership before the point of distribution would be reached.

The appellant contends that the final decree entered in the estate construed the bequest as not permitting the opening up of the class after the death of the testator to admit after-born grandchildren, and that such determination is *res adjudicata* as to the rights of all after-born grandchildren. The petition propounding the will for probate was made January 27, 1940. In those proceedings it was ordered that notice of hearing be published in the Weekly Home News, a newspaper published in Spring Green, Wisconsin. The publication was made. Prior to the admission of the will to probate, the court appointed a guardian *ad litem*, reciting that the six grandchildren were minors interested in said estate, and included therein the words 'guardian *ad litem* for said minors and all unknown minors and incompetents, for the sole purpose of appearing for them and taking care of their interests in the proceedings in said matter.' On February 7, the will was admitted to probate. On March 17, the letters testamentary were issued, and the inventory properly filed. The final account and petition for settlement were dated August 2, 1941; and on August 6 of that year the court directed that the hearing be held on the final account, and that notice thereof be given by publication in the Weekly Home News. In the order determining the inheritance tax, one-sixth of the $50,000 trust estate was taxed to each of the grandchildren who survived the decedent. On April 17, 1942, final judgment was entered, and in that judgment the court found that the deceased was survived by the widow and his children and by the six grandchildren. The First National Bank of Madison was appointed trustee. The trust estate created by the bequest, and referred to in the final judgment, was assigned in such final decree as follows:

'To Maxine A. Perry, Barbara A. Perry, Evan F. Evans, Thomas E. Evans, Keith A. Pope and Wayne E. Pope, grandchildren, the sum of Fifty Thousand ($50,000.00) less such amounts as have heretofore been paid by said executor for inheritance tax upon the distributive shares of each such grandchild * * * the same to be held in trust by the First National Bank of Madison, Wisconsin, subject to the terms and conditions as set forth in the will of said deceased as follows:

'That the income shall be allowed to accumulate until said grandchildren shall respectively become of legal age.

'That when each such grandchild becomes of legal age he shall receive his proportionate share of such accumulated income, and thereafter all income on his proportionate share shall be paid to him annually until he reaches the age of thirty years.

'That when each such grandchild becomes thirty years of age he shall be paid his full share of the principal of said trust, together with all interest accumulated thereon.'

Thereafter, commencing as of the date that the first grandchild became of age, the trustee has paid interest to the grandchild as provided in the judgment; and on March 26, 1955, when Maxine A. Perry (Tesia), the oldest of such grandchildren, attained the age of thirty years, the trustee paid to her one-sixth of the corpus of the trust and was discharged as trustee to her.

Three children have been born to Alice Pope Draper, one of the children of the deceased, since the death of the deceased: to wit: Walter Draper, born on November 1, 1945; Margaret Anne Draper, born on February 13, 1951; and Susan K. Draper, born on June 30, 1953.

On August 9, 1955, the trustee having been advised of the birth of such subsequent-born grandchildren, and being concerned as to whether they might possibly have an interest in such trust, petitioned the court to construe the judgment and the will of the deceased to so determine. The appellant trustee urges that the judgment entered in

1942 is *res adjudicata* as to all persons, including those born after the death of the decedent. The guardian ad litem, appearing for the after-born grandchildren, urges that they have never had their day in court, that from the time for petition of the probate of the will of John C. Evans, on January 27, 1940, and through the entire proceedings in the county court there has never been any one or some one representing these after-born children, who are plainly members of the class to which the $50,000 was bequeathed. Their interests had never been given consideration until the appointment of a guardian for them on August 15, 1955, which occurred in the instant proceedings.

* * *

Inasmuch as and because the trial court erroneously held that membership in the class opened up each time a new grandchild is born, until such time as the entire trust *corpus* was distributed the order must be modified to correct this error.

We do not continue a discussion of other questions not necessary for a determination of the material issues.

Order modified so as to provide that membership in the class permanently closed when the oldest grandchild arrived at the age of thirty years, and as so modified it is affirmed. Cause remanded for further proceedings according to law.

Notes

Administrative Convenience Closing. The intention of the Testator controls as to when the class closes. Under the Rule of Administrative Convenience, this means that the class will close whenever a member may demand his or her share of the corpus. Remember that this is a rule of convenience and it will result in great inconvenience for the class member born after the first point of distribution. The careful drafter will plan ahead for all contingencies. *See generally* John L. Garvey, *Drafting Wills and Trusts: Anticipating the Birth and Death of Possible Beneficiaries*, 71 Or. L. Rev. 47 (1992). As with many things in life, there are exceptions to the Rule of Administrative Convenience. The first exception is found in the common law and provides that, if, when the interest was to become possessory (a class member could demand a share) and there was no member of the class then in existence to demand a share, then the rule of administrative convenience will not apply; the common law provides that we wait until the class membership has been exhausted. *See Restatement (Second) of Property, Donative Transfers* § 26.1(2) (1988). For example, in the case of a Settlor who creates a trust for himself for life and then the remainder to his grandchildren, at the Settlor's death, no grandchild has yet been born, but there are child-bearing children of the Settlor in existence, so there is no one to demand a share, nor is there an estate to which we may give a share. Thus, the common law holds that, rather than waiting until the first grandchild is born and could demand a share, we wait until there is no longer any possibility of any grandchild being born. Only at the death of all of the children of the Settlor—when there is no longer the possibility of any additional child being born—do we distribute the trust corpus to any of the grandchildren in existence and the estates of any who have predeceased the event. The common law rule leaves the class open for a significant period of time and benefits more class members, but it certainly lessens the share of the first grandchild to be born, who would have taken all under the rule of administrative convenience.

The second exception states that if a specific sum is given to each member of a class, the class closes at the death of the Settlor, regardless of whether any members of the class are then alive. This is really an extension of the rule of administrative convenience, since it would be very inconvenient to guess how many class members might be able to take each of the specific shares. Rather than guess, the class is closed immediately, and if no member of the class is in existence to take, then the trust fails and results back to the estate from which it was generated.

Membership. Who is included in the class is an issue as well. The Uniform Probate Code provides that adopted individuals, non-marital individuals, and the descendants of both are included as class members. Likewise, within the terms "brothers and sisters" and "nephews and nieces" are included relationships of the half blood. *See* Unif. Prob. Code § 2-705(a) (2003). "Terms of relationship that do not differentiate relationships by blood from those of affinity, such as 'uncles,' 'aunts,' 'nieces,' or 'nephews', are construed to exclude relatives by affinity." *Id.*

Distribution. If the class gift refers to issue or descendants—rather than the more exclusive class term of children—how should the class gift be distributed if some members of the "issue" or "descendants" have predeceased and some have survived? The most obvious answer is to look to the intestate statute, *see* Chapter Two, Section IV, C, *supra*, and determine if the state statute used: (1) the old Uniform Probate Code system of complete per stirpes; (2) the new Uniform Probate Code system of complete per capita; (3) a next of kin approach; or (4) the outmoded strict method. The *Restatement (Second) of Property, Donative Transfers* § 28.2, does not utilize the state intestate statute to determine class meaning of issue and descendants but, instead, adopts the old Uniform Probate Code system of per stirpes at each generation.

The latest Uniform Probate Code makes a distinction for whenever the words "issue per stirpes" are used. Strangely, whenever "issue per stirpes" is used, the new Uniform Probate Code utilizes the old Uniform Probate Code system of per stirpes at each generation. Whenever that term is not used, per capita at each generation, in accordance with the New Uniform Probate Code, is used. *See* Unif. Prob. Code §§ 2-708, 2-709 (c) (2003). Sometimes the operative instrument may direct that, upon the occurrence of an event, the property be distributed to "my heirs." Like issue and descendants, this is a class designation, and the question becomes one of determining when the class of heirs should close. Observe the following decision and the Uniform Probate Code section that follows.

Harris Trust and Savings Bank v. Beach

Supreme Court of Illinois, 1987
118 Ill. 2d 1, 513 N.E.2d 833

Justice SIMON delivered the opinion of the court:

In construing either a trust or a will the challenge is to find the settlor's or testator's intent and, provided that the intention is not against public policy, to give it effect. (See Hull v. Adams (1948), 399 Ill. 347, 352, 77 N.E.2d 706.) Courts search for intent by analyzing both the words used in the instrument and the circumstances under which they were drafted, including: "the state of the testator's property, his family, and the like." (Armstrong v. Barber (1909), 239 Ill. 389, 404, 88 N.E.2d 246.) When, however, the instrument fails to make the settlor's or testator's intention clear, courts often resort to rules of construction to determine the meaning of the terms used in the document. (Hull v. Adams (1948), 399 Ill. 347, 352, 77 N.E.2d 706.) Rules of construction, which are applied in the same manner to both wills and trusts, are court created presumptions of what the ordinary settlor or testator would have intended the ambiguous terms to mean; they are merely the court's own assessments of what the person probably meant when the provision was drafted. (Harris Trust & Savings Bank v. Jackson (1952), 412 Ill. 261, 266–67, 106 N.E.2d 188.) Such rules should not be allowed to defeat what the ordinary settlor would have intended. When a rule of construction tends to subvert intentions, the rule is no longer legitimate and must be discarded. H. Carey and D. Schuyler, Illinois Law of Future Interests 190–93 (Cum. Pocket Part 1954).

In this case Harris Trust and Savings Bank, Robert Hixon Glore and William Gray III, trustees of two trusts, sought instructions from the circuit court of Cook County regarding to whom and in what manner the trusts should be distributed. The central controversy is over the proper construction of the remainder over to the heirs following the death of a life tenant: specifically, the question is whether the settlor intended that his heirs be ascertained at his death, or whether he desired that they be determined after the death of his wife, who was the life tenant.

The pertinent facts in this case are as follows: Frank P. Hixon and Alice Green entered into an antenuptial agreement dated March 30, 1921, and following that, they were married. The agreement created a trust consisting of 200 shares of preferred stock of Pioneer Investment Company, a Hixon family holding company. The trust provided that Alice was to receive the net income of the trust for life and that she could "dispose of Fifty Thousand ($50,000) Dollars of said fund in such a manner as she" deemed fit and proper. In exchange for the provisions made for her in the trust, Alice surrendered any interest, including dower, which she might have had in Hixon's estate. If Hixon survived Alice, the trust property was to be reconveyed to him. If Alice survived Hixon, the trust provided that on her death "the balance of said trust fund shall be divided among the heirs of the party of the first part [Hixon], share and share alike."

On May 31, 1926, Hixon created a second trust to provide for Alice. The principal of this trust consisted of 300 shares of stock of Pioneer Investment Company. This trust provided that Alice was to receive the income from the principal for life and upon her death "this trust shall terminate, and the trust fund shall be distributed equally among my [Hixon's] heirs."

In 1930, Hixon executed his will, which was interpreted by our appellate court and is not at issue in this case (Harris Trust & Savings Bank v. Beach (1985), 145 Ill.App.3d 682, 99 Ill.Dec. 438, 495 N.E.2d 1173), leaving gifts to specific individuals and charities. He divided the residue of his estate equally among his daughters, Ellen Glore and Dorothy Clark and in trust for Alice. Hixon died in 1931, when he was 69 years old. He was survived by Alice, who was then 49, by Dorothy and Ellen, who were then 38 and 36, respectively, and by his grandchildren, Frances Glore Beach, Charles F. Glore, Jr., and Robert Hixon Glore, who were then minors.

Alice lived for 51 more years. Both the 1921 and the 1926 trusts continued for her benefit until she died in February 1982. At that time, Hixon's then living descendants were his grandchildren, Frances Glore Beach and Robert Hixon Glore (the grandchildren), and the children of his deceased grandchild, Charles F. Glore, Jr.—Charles F. Glore III, Sallie Glore Farlow, and Edward R. Glore (the great-grandchildren). The parties agree that both the 1921 and the 1926 trust should be distributed in the same manner.

If Hixon's heirs are those surviving at his death, the trust estates will pass under the wills of his two daughters, Ellen H. Glore and Dorothy H. Clark, who both died in

1973. Ellen had three children. One child, as noted above—Charles F. Glore, Jr.—is deceased and survived by three children, Hixon's great-grandchildren. Ellen's other two children—the grandchildren Robert and Frances—are living and are parties to this suit. Dorothy had no children. The devisees under her will are defendants California Institute of Technology, Santa Barbara Foundation, Santa Barbara Cottage Hospital and the Kansas Endowment Association (collectively the charities), and her husband Alfred. Alfred is deceased and his portion of the assets would be distributed to his devisees, Frederick Acker, as special trustee under the will of Charles F. Glore, Jr., and Robert Hixon Glore. On the other hand, if the heirs are determined at the time of Alice's death, the trust estates will be divided among Hixon's now-living descendants—the two grandchildren and three great-grandchildren.

The four charities assert that the heirs should be those heirs alive at Hixon's death; this determination would include them since they were devisees under Dorothy's will. The grandchildren and the great-grandchildren argue that the heirs should be those who were surviving at Alice's death, but they disagree over whether the trust should be divided *per stirpes* (by each share) or *per capita* (by each head).

All parties seeking distribution in their favor filed motions for summary judgment, and the circuit court granted the motion in favor of the charities. That court held that the class of heirs should be ascertained at Hixon's death. The court concluded that the heirs would be only Hixon's two daughters, since Alice was excluded under the terms of the antenuptial agreement. * * *

The word "heirs" refers to "those persons appointed by the law to inherit an estate in case of intestacy." (Le Sourd v. Leinweber (1952), 412 Ill. 100, 105, 105 N.E.2d 722.) When used in its technical sense, the testator's or settlor's heirs are, of course, determined at the time of his or her death. (Hull v. Adams (1948), 399 Ill. 347, 352, 77 N.E.2d 706.) This court, however, has never adopted the technical meaning of the word "heirs" as a rule of law. We have observed that "'heirs' when used in a will does not necessarily have a fixed meaning. It may mean children or, where there are no children, it may mean some other class of heirs * * * if the context of the entire will *plainly shows* such to have been the intention of the testator." (Emphasis added.) (Stites v. Gray (1955), 4 Ill.2d 510, 513, 123 N.E.2d 483.) A determination of the class of heirs, therefore, is governed by the settlor's or testator's intention rather than by a fixed rule of law. The rule in Illinois, however, has been that, unless the settlor's intention to the contrary is "plainly shown" in the trust document, courts will rely upon the technical meaning of the term "heirs" by applying it as a rule of construction. (Harris Trust & Savings Bank v. Jackson (1952), 412 Ill. 261, 266, 106 N.E.2d 188.) The charities are, therefore, correct in their observation that presently our rule of construction requires us to determine heirs at the settlor's death unless the trust or will provides clear evidence to the contrary. (See, e.g., Stites v. Gray (1955), 4 Ill.2d 510, 513, 123 N.E.2d 483; Le Sourd v. Leinweber (1952), 412 Ill. 100, 105, 105 N.E.2d 722; Hull v. Adams (1948), 399 Ill. 347, 352, 77 N.E.2d 706.) The initial question we must address is whether we should continue to adhere to this standard of proof.

The charities contend that this high degree of proof is necessary to rebut the rule of construction because of the policy favoring early vesting of remainders. They refer to one leading commentator's views on implied survivorship and its detrimental effects on early vesting (see Halbach, Future Interests: Express and Implied Conditions of Survival, 49 Cal.L.Rev. 297, 304–07 (1961)), as well as to Evans v. Giles (1980), 83 Ill.2d 448, 47 Ill.Dec. 349, 415 N.E.2d 354, and to Dyslin v. Wolf (1950), 407 Ill. 532, 96

N.E.2d 485, which are factually distinguishable from this case, to bolster their position. However, they overlook that two eminent scholars in the field of Illinois future interest law revised their views regarding the policy in favor of early vesting. In the supplement to their treatise entitled the Illinois Law of Future Interests, Carey and Schuyler observe that "it was the rule regarding the destructibility of contingent remainders that caused courts to favor the early vesting of estates. * * * But now, in this state and in many others, there is no rule of destructibility. If the original reason for favoring early vesting is gone, why continue to favor it?" H. Carey and D. Schuyler, Illinois Law of Future Interests 190 (Cum. Pocket Part 1954); Ill.Rev.Stat.1985, ch. 30, par. 40.

Briefly stated, the destruction of contingent remainders was an archaic device which frequently frustrated grantors' intentions by prematurely defeating an interest subject to a condition. By vesting remainders as quickly as possible the drastic effects of destructibility "could be contained by a rule of construction which resulted in declaring that future interests were vested and hence indestructible." (H. Carey and D. Schuyler, Illinois Law of Future Interests 190 (Cum. Pocket Part 1954)). Our legislature abolished destructibility when it passed "An Act concerning future interests" in 1921 (Ill.Rev.Stat.1985, ch. 30, par. 40). However, despite the passage of this statute, vesting remainders as quickly as possible was such an imbedded rule of construction that in many cases courts continued to adhere to it without question and regardless of the consequences.

Early vesting frequently frustrates intentions by casting property to strangers. (H. Carey and D. Schuyler, Illinois Law of Future Interests 193 (Cum. Pocket Part 1954); see also DeKowin v. First National Bank of Chicago (N.D.Ill.1949), 84 F.Supp. 918, rev'd on other grounds (C.A.Ill.1949), 179 F.2d 347 (property goes to second wife of son-in-law); Peadro v. Peadro (1948), 81 N.E.2d 192, 400 Ill. 482 (property falls into the hands of the second wife of the testator's niece's widower).) Carey and Schuyler observe that if interests following life estates "are said to be contingent on survivorship, * * * children of the life tenant will take all the property, which seems to accord more with what the testator wanted." H. Carey and D. Schuyler, Illinois Law of Future Interests 192 (Cum. Pocket Part 1954).

In their 1954 supplement to their treatise on future interests, Professors Carey and Schuyler re-examined their earlier view that early vesting is axiomatic. (See H. Carey and D. Schuyler, Illinois Law of Future Interests 399 (1941); H. Carey and D. Schuyler, Illinois Law of Future Interests 190–93 (Cum. Pocket Part 1954). They state:

> One does not readily differ from men so learned as Professor Gray and Professor Kales, both of whom seemed satisfied with the axiom that 'the law favors the early vesting of estates.' Accordingly, at the time the principal text was written, and even in 1947, when the first supplement to this was published, the authors were much inclined unquestioningly to accent this ancient dogma. But subsequent further reflection causes one to wonder if the maxim has lost much, if not most of its utility. (H. Carey and D. Schuyler, Illinois Law of Future Interests 190 (Cum. Pocket Part 1954).)

They conclude that "the desirability of retaining the rule of early vesting as a rule of construction * * * warrant[s] a microscopic scrutiny of it by those charged with the administration of justice." (H. Carey and D. Schuyler, Illinois Law of Future Interest 193 (Cum. Pocket Part (1954).) In the instant case, we have an interest following a life estate. If we follow both the circuit and appellate court's decision and vest the heirs' interest as quickly as possible, a large portion of the estate will fall into the hands of strangers. If we reduce the burden of proving that a grantor intended to use "heirs" in a nontechnical sense and if that vests the gift at the termination of the life estate, obviously only those heirs surviving the life tenant will share in the remainder.

Whether survivorship ought to be implied is not a case of first impression before this court. A rule of construction regarding implied survivorship was set forth in Drury v. Drury (1915), 271 Ill. 336, 111 N.E. 140, where this court held that when a gift to a class was "postponed pending the termination of the life estate * * * *only those* took who were in existence at the termination of the life estate." (Emphasis added.) (271 Ill. 336, 341, 111 N.E. 140.) The effect of Drury was to delay the vesting of the gift by adding or implying survivorship for the class of remaindermen to share in the estate.

Hofing v. Willis (1964), 31 Ill.2d 365, 373, 201 N.E.2d 852, clarified Drury by stating that implied survivorship was not a mandatory rule of construction. Rather, according to the court in Hofing, the grantor's intent regarding this issue should remain paramount. While a later case, Evans v. Giles (1980), 83 Ill.2d 448, 456, 47 Ill.Dec. 349, 415 N.E.2d 354, also criticized the Drury rule, the rationale in that case was that implied survivorship defeated the policy against early vesting. In neither Hofing nor Evans did this court hold that it was inappropriate to imply survivorship when there was evidence that the grantor intended to do so. Further, Hofing, Evans and Dyslin are distinguishable in an important respect: the gift was not to a class of heirs—a term which is vague and imports futurity—but rather in Hofing to a group of sisters, in Giles to a specific individual, and in Dyslin to the grandchildren.

We agree with Professors Carey and Schuyler that early vesting of remainders should no longer be followed in this State without question. Early vesting is an axiom which must not get in the way when a contrary intent is demonstrated by a preponderance of the evidence. Requiring *clear and convincing* evidence or a *plain showing* to rebut the presumption in favor of the technical meaning of the term "heirs" (see Stites v. Gray (1955), 4 Ill.2d 510, 513, 123 N.E.2d 483; Le Sourd v. Leinweber (1952), 412 Ill. 100, 105, 105 N.E.2d 722; Hull v. Adams (1948), 399 Ill. 347, 352, 77 N.E.2d 706), has its roots in the maxim favoring early vesting of remainders. Frequently this policy, as is the case here, frustrates what the ordinary settlor would have intended. We hold that because the primary reason for early vesting is no longer as important as it formerly was, proof by the preponderance of the evidence that the settlor, testator, or donor intended to use the term "heirs" in its nontechnical sense is sufficient to delay the vesting of a gift to a time other than at the grantor's death.

The result of delaying a gift to the heirs is not dramatic. The fear that a contingent remainder could be prematurely destroyed no longer exists. Further, should a predeceased member of the class be excluded from the gift, the result is not drastic. If the predeceased "heir" leaves issue, as is the case here, the settlor's own blood still enjoys the gift. If, on the other hand, a predeceased member fails to leave issue, as also occurred here, the gift is prevented from falling into the hands of strangers. In sum, by altering the degree of proof necessary to delay the vesting of a gift to the heirs, we do no harm. Instead, we further the ordinary grantor's intent, which is exactly what a proper rule of construction ought to do. Consequently, in this case we must determine which parties have offered the preponderant proof as to Hixon's intent—the charities or the grandchildren and great-grandchildren.

Hixon's trusts, as the charities stress, do not explicitly state the point at which his heirs should be determined. The 1921 trust provides that the "balance of said trust fund shall be divided among the heirs," and the 1926 trust states that "the trust shall be distributed equally among my [Hixon's] heirs." When the trusts are considered as a whole, however, it becomes apparent that the documents revolve totally around Alice's life and death; Hixon's life and death play only secondary roles. As the grandchildren and great-grandchildren note, the trusts were created for Alice's benefit in exchange for her rights to dower or any other portion of Hixon's estate. The trusts were intended to last throughout her life, and depending upon when she died, the trust principal would either revert to Hixon or be distributed to his heirs. Alice's central role in the trust is indicative of Hixon's intent to make her and not himself the point of reference for determining the heirs. Under similar circumstances, our appellate court found the testator's frequent reference to the life tenant's death to be evidence of his intent to look towards the future and to ascertain the heirs at the life tenant's death rather than at his own. (See Handy v. Shearer (1967), 81 Ill.App.2d 461, 464, 225 N.E.2d 414.) In that case the court stated that the frequent references to the life tenant's death suggested "that it was an event and a point of time that weighed heavily in the testator's plan and in his thinking. * * * By using the date of the widow's remarriage or death as a date for the determination of 'my legal heirs,' testator's plan is complete." 81 Ill.App.2d 461, 464, 225 N.E.2d 414.

The circumstances under which Hixon created the trust provide additional evidence of his intent to vest the gift at Alice's death. Hixon was 20 years older than Alice and he would consequently have expected her trusts to last for a considerable time after his own death. During this time, changes in the family through births and deaths would certainly occur. Rather than leave the remainder of the principal to his daughters, as he left the residue of his estate in his will, his use of an indefinite term such as "heirs" covered the inevitable changes in family circumstances that might occur.

Alice's power of appointment over $50,000 of the trust principal is also evidence of Hixon's intent to ascertain the heirs at her death. The grandchildren and great-grandchildren observe that this power might prevent the heirs from ever enjoying the trust principal; the trust could be worth $50,000 or less when Alice exercised her power of appointment and thus there would be no trust principal left to distribute. The grandchildren's and great-grandchildren's claim that it would be senseless to vest the gift upon Hixon's death when one could not be certain until Alice exercised her power of appointment whether or not there were any assets left for the heirs to possess and enjoy, certainly has merit.

The charities assert that under the common law gifts subject to powers of appointment are always considered to vest at the testator's or settlor's death even though they may be subject to complete or partial divestment. In other words, the charities argue that the remaindermen, in this case Hixon's heirs, would still have a vested right in the trust principal whether or not at the time of distribution it contained any assets. The charities are correct in their interpretation of the common law. (See Moynihan, Introduction to Real Property 120 (1962).) However, they refer to no decision in our State that adopts this position.

Our court has consistently held that the time at which a gift vests ultimately turns upon a "consideration of the whole instrument[, its] creation and by the intent apparently in the mind of their creator as gathered from such instrument." (Jones v. Miller (1918), 283 Ill. 348, 356, 119 N.E. 324; see also Fuller v. Black (1921), 298 Ill. 351, 353, 131 N.E. 641.) As we have already noted, Hixon must have anticipated that the trusts for Alice's benefit would last for some time. The value of the trust principal—stock—was likely to fluctuate during this period. The logical conclusion is that Hixon desired to wait before "dividing and distributing" his assets to see if they had any value; it is unlikely that Hixon would have intended to vest a gift which might be worth nothing.

While the possibility that there might be nothing left for the remaindermen to take, standing by itself, would not be determinative; it is a factor to be considered along with the other circumstances presented in searching for Hixon's intent.

The grandchildren and great-grandchildren also claim that the language in the trusts instructing the trustees to "divide or distribute" the principal "equally among the heirs" invokes the "divide and pay over rule," which would operate to vest the gift at Alice's death. This rule is one of construction to aid courts in determining whether a gift to a class is a vested or contingent remainder. (Hull v. Adams (1948), 399 Ill. 347, 357, 77 N.E.2d 706.) If a gift to a class is vested, it is considered a true legal estate once the trust is executed. On the other hand, if the gift is a contingent, it "is not an estate, but merely the possibility of acquiring one." 399 Ill. 347, 357, 77 N.E.2d 706.

Under the "divide and pay over rule," when a trustee is directed to divide or distribute a gift to a class at a time after the settlor's death, the gift is contingent and possession and enjoyment of that gift are delayed until the time of distribution. The gift is contingent under the rule not only because it is dependent upon the happening of an event—the trustee dividing and distributing the assets—but also because the members of the class who would be alive and able to enjoy the gift would not be ascertained until the trustees performed their duty of distributing the assets. See Hull v. Adams (1948), 399 Ill. 347, 357, 77 N.E.2d 706.

In the present case, Hixon left the trust gift to a class—the heirs—and he employed the key phrase to "divide and/or distribute the trust principal"; it therefore appears that this rule is applicable. However, the charities contend that our court has created this exception to the divide and pay rule: "if such payment or distribution is not deferred for reasons personal to the legatee, but merely because the testator desired to appropriate the subject matter of the legacy to the use and benefit of another * * * the vesting of the gift will not be postponed but will vest at once, the right of enjoyment only being deferred." Knight v. Pottgieser (1898), 176 Ill. 368, 374, 52 N.E. 934.

Pottgieser is the only decision in this State that the charities refer to which set forth this particular exception, and a case decided a half century later never mentions Pottgieser. In Hull v. Adams (1948), 399 Ill. 347, 77 N.E.2d 706, this court concluded that the rule is applicable whenever it is unclear whether the gift to a class is a contingent or vested remainder. This court stated in Hull:

> It is a general rule that where the donees of a testamentary gift constitute a class, and the only words importing the gift are found in the direction to divide, distribute or pay or to sell the property and distribute or pay over the proceeds in the future, the gift will not vest until the time arrives to pay, divide or distribute, and the members of the class who are to take are to be ascertained at that time and not at the death of the testator. It [the rule] is invoked by the courts to aid in determining the vested or contingent character of future interests. (399 Ill. 347, 357, 77 N.E.2d 706.)

In the present case, the gift to the heirs in the 1921 trust was contingent when it was executed because it was conditioned upon Alice surviving Hixon; if she failed to do so the trust would revert and the heirs' interest would be defeated. Whether the gift to the heirs continues to be contingent on the heirs surviving Alice or whether their gift vests at Hixon's death is precisely the issue we are confronted with in this case. Consequently, the divide and pay over rule appears to operate and, in view of the ambiguity confronting us, gives us an additional clue as to Hixon's intent.

The provision in the 1921 trust creating a reversion in Hixon should Alice predecease him also advances the grandchildren's and great-grandchildren's argument that Hixon's intention was that the heirs be determined at Alice's death. The reversionary clause conditioned the duration of the trust on Alice's survival. If Alice failed to survive Hixon, the trust would terminate and Hixon's reversion would operate. On the other hand, if Alice survived Hixon, the reversion would not take effect and the principal would be distributed to the heirs. The grandchildren and great-grandchildren persuasively stress that considering the heirs at Hixon's death would lead to nearly the same result as if the reversion had occurred. In both instances the bulk of the principal would pass through the estates of Hixon's two daughters. Hixon's intention that the result was to be different should Alice survive and the reversion fail is an indication that Hixon must have intended that his heirs be determined at Alice's death. Viewing all of these indications with respect to Hixon's intent together, we conclude that the preponderant proof favors the position of the grandchildren and great-grandchildren and Hixon's heirs should therefore be determined at Alice's death.

* * *

Because we have concluded that it was Hixon's intention that the heirs were to be ascertained at Alice's death, the doctrine of worthier title is not applicable. The doctrine, which was developed in medieval England but abolished there in 1833, voids a gift to the grantor's heirs. It was premised on the notion that it was worthier to take by descent than by devise. (Moynihan, Introduction to the Law of Real Property 152 (1962).) The doctrine was incorporated into American common law, but in Illinois our legislature abolished it in 1955. See Ill.Rev.Stat.1985, ch. 30, par. 188.

In Illinois, the doctrine applies only where the devisees would take *exactly the same* estate by devise as they would by descent. (McNeilly v. Wylie (1945), 389 Ill. 391, 393, 59 N.E.2d 811.) It "is not applicable where there is a difference in kind or quality of the estate or property to be passed under the devise from that which would descend under the statute [the laws of descent and distribution]." (389 Ill. 391, 393, 59 N.E.2d 811, accord Darst v. Swearingen (1906), 224 Ill. 229, 79 N.E. 635; Boldenweck v. City National Bank & Trust Co. (1951), 343 Ill.App. 569, 99 N.E.2d 692.) Therefore, under Illinois law the doctrine is not likely to operate when the heirs are determined after the termination of a life estate; when vesting is postponed the devisees rarely receive either the same amount or the same estate as they would had their gift taken effect at the testator's death. See McCormick v. Sanford (1925), 318 Ill. 544, 546, 149 N.E. 476.

Having already concluded that Hixon's heirs are to be determined at Alice's and not at Hixon's death, those who would take Hixon's estate under the laws of descent and distribution had Hixon died intestate—Alice and the two daughters—are not the same as those who will take after Alice's death—the grandchildren and great-grandchildren. As a result, the doctrine is not relevant and therefore we need not reach the other issues briefed before this court: whether the doctrine is a rule of construction or rule of law and whether the doctrine is an anachronism which should be abandoned in the case of trusts established in Illinois prior to our 1955 statutory abolition of the doctrine.

* * *

The final question is whether the gift to the grandchildren and great-grandchildren should be distributed *per stirpes* or *per capita*. The great-grandchildren contend that because Hixon used the words "share and share alike" and instructed the trustees to distribute the gift "equally," the gift must be divided on a *per capita* basis. The great-grandchildren accurately observe that, "When the words 'equally,' 'equal among,' 'share and share alike,' or other similar words, are used to indicate an equal division among a class, the persons among whom the division is to be made are usually held to take *per capita* unless a contrary intention is discoverable from the will." (Dollander v. Dhaemers (1921), 297 Ill. 274, 278, 130 N.E. 705.) However, "'it is worthy of remark that the leading cases which sustain a distribution *per capita* intimate that a very small indication of intent to the contrary would change the rule.'" (297 Ill. 274, 280, 130 N.E. 705, quoting Eyer v. Beck (1888), 70 Mich. 179, 181, 38 N.W. 20.) When a testator leaves his estate to his or her heirs, courts generally conclude that the testator intended the gift to be distributed in accordance with laws of descent and distribution which provide for a *per stirpes* distribution. (Carlin v. Helm (1928), 331 Ill. 213, 221–22, 162 N.E. 873; see also Ill.Rev.Stat.1985, ch. 110 1/2 , par. 2-1.) Under these circumstances we have stated that "a gift to issue 'equally' and 'share and share alike' does not require that each of such issue shall have an equal share with the other; that the mandate is satisfied if the issue of equal degree taking per stirpes share equally." Condee v. Trout (1942), 379 Ill. 89, 93, 39 N.E.2d 350.

In the present case, Hixon left the remainder in the trust principal to his heirs. That he provided for his heirs to share equally in that gift fails to rebut the presumption in favor of a *per stirpes* distribution; the gift to the class of heirs is a sufficient indication that Hixon intended the remainder to be divided in accordance with the laws of descent and distribution. This conclusion is bolstered by the wording of the statute, in effect both at Hixon's death and when he executed the trusts, which used the terms "equally among" and in "equal parts" in describing the *per stirpes* distribution of estates. That Hixon employed the words "equally" and "share and share alike" in his instructions to the trustees regarding the division of his estate is therefore not inconsistent with an intention that the heirs share equally under a *per stirpes* distribution. See Ill.Rev. Stat.1937, ch. 39, sec. 1.

The cases cited by the great-grandchildren in which the court provided for a *per capita* distribution are distinguishable. In Carlin v. Helm (1928), 331 Ill. 213, 222, 162 N.E. 873, not only was the gift made to *named individuals* and not to a class, but also the court stated that had the gift been devised to the class of heirs, it would have divided the remainder differently. In Northern Trust Co. v. Wheeler (1931), 345 Ill. 182, 177 N.E. 884, another case cited by the great-grandchildren, the language explicitly stated that the remainder be divided *per capita*.

We conclude that the remainder in the heirs should be distributed *per stirpes* with the three great-grandchildren each taking one-ninth of the estate and the two grandchildren each taking one-third. The judgments of both the circuit and appellate courts are reversed and the case is remanded for a distribution of the trust principal in a manner consistent with this opinion.

Judgments reversed; cause remanded.

GOLDENHERSH, J., took no part in the consideration or decision of this case.

Uniform Probate Code (2003)

Section 2-711. Future Interests in "Heirs" and the Like.

If an applicable statute or governing instrument calls for a present or future distribution to or creates a present or future interest in a designated individual's "heirs," "heirs at law," "next of kin," "relatives," or "family," or language of similar import, the property passes to those persons, including the state, and in such shares as would succeed to the designated individual's intestate estate under the intestate succession law of the designated individual's domicile if the designated individual died when the disposition is to take effect in possession or enjoyment. If the designated individual's surviving spouse is living but is remarried at the time the disposition is to take effect in possession or enjoyment, the surviving spouse is not an heir of the designated individual.

B. Decrease of Class

Any decrease in class membership involves the response of the anti-lapse statute, vesting of interests, or both. For example, a Testator provides in a valid Last Will and Testament that, at death, one-million dollars is to be held in trust for any children, income for them for life, and then, at the death of the last child, to be divided among the grandchildren. At the death of the last child of the Testator—the moment when the remainder interest is to be divided among the class of grandchildren—there are three grandchildren then living. Nonetheless, one grandchild dies prior to the Testator, survived by issue, and another grandchild dies after the Testator but before the death of the last child. Into how many shares should the trust corpus be divided? The answer is "five." The three surviving class members take each of their respective shares, the issue of the grandchild who died prior to the Testator take under the state's anti-lapse statute, and the grandchild who survived the Testator but did not survive the last child has a vested interest, and a share will go to his or her estate. If the Testator had directed that the grandchildren must survive the children, then matters could be different. Compare the following decision with the often-criticized Uniform Probate Code provision that follows.

Usry v. Farr
Supreme Court of Georgia, 2001
553 S.E.2d 789

FLETCHER, Chief Justice.

At issue in this appeal is when title to the remainder interest under the will of Watson Usry vested. On summary judgment, the trial court held that the remainder vested at the time of Usry's death and not at the death of the life tenant. Because Usry's will expressed the intention of providing for those who survive him and all five grandchildren survived him, we affirm.

Watson Usry died in 1967. The relevant clause of Usry's will provided successive life estates in his lands, first to his wife Lucille and then to their children, with the remainder to his grandchildren. Usry had three children, the last of whom died in 2000. There are five appellants: the four children of Usry's son Jack, and Jack's widow, Evelyn. Usry's fifth grandson, Hoyt, died in 1970 leaving three young children, all of whom were alive at the time of Usry's death. * * * Hoyt's three children are the appellees. Appellants claim that the remainder vested upon the death of the last life tenant and not upon the death of Usry. Therefore, because they are the only grandchildren who survived the life tenants, they take all lands under the will. Appellees contend that the remainder vested upon Usry's death, and that Hoyt, who survived Usry, had a vested interest under the will, and therefore his children stand in his shoes and take under the will along with appellants.

* * * The construction of a will is a question of law for the court. * * * The cardinal rule for construing wills is to ascertain and give effect to the testator's intent. * * * Item Three of the will provided,

> I will, bequeath and devise all of the land, with improvements thereon, which I may own at my death to my Wife, LUCILLE, to be hers for and during her lifetime, and at her death same is to go to my children who may survive my wife, and to my grandchildren with restrictions as follows: Any of my children taking land under this Item shall have a life interest therein, share and share alike, with any grandchildren who take hereunder taking the part which their father or mother would have taken. Upon the death of my last surviving child title in fee simple to said lands shall vest in my grand-children, per stirpes and not per capita.

The first sentence of Item Three establishes a life estate first in Usry's wife Lucille and then in the children who survive Lucille. This sentence imposes a requirement that the children survive Lucille before taking under Item three. In contrast, no requirement that the grandchildren survive the life tenants is imposed. Therefore, at Usry's death, fee simple title vested in his five grandchildren, who were all alive at that time. The possessory interest vested when Usry's son Ned, the last life tenant, died in April 2000. At that time, the grandchildren were entitled to take possession, with the appellees taking the share that had vested in Hoyt.

The testator's intention that the only survivorship requirement apply to his life appears expressly in Item Eight of the will. In that provision, Usry declared that "my entire plan of disposition is the result of a conscientious effort to provide for the welfare of my loved ones who survive me, and to fairly divide and distribute the worldly goods for which I have worked so hard." Because we must construe the will as a whole, we must consider this clause in construing the remainder of the will. * * * Usry's stated intention of providing for those who survive him is fatal to the claim of appellants who would defer vesting well beyond the death of Usry until the conclusion of the life estates.

The dissent's concern that this construction provides an anomalous result is not well-founded. The testator himself decided to leave successive life estates to his widow and children. Obviously, if his children were to enjoy a life estate that followed their mother's life estate, the children had to survive their mother. Because the testator decided that his children were to enjoy only a life estate, there is nothing unusual about his further providing for title to vest in his loved ones who survive him.

* * * Usry's express intention with regard to a survivorship requirement is consistent with the statutory rule in Georgia favoring vesting of title as of the time of the testator's death. * * * Appellants contend that the last sentence of Item Three demonstrates an intention that the remainder vest, not at the testator's death, but at the conclusion of the life estates. However, this Court has repeatedly held that virtually identical language is not sufficient to divest the remainder share from one who survives the testator but predeceases the life tenant. * * * In view of the strong preference in Georgia for early vesting, the language required to render a remainder contingent upon surviving the life tenant must be clear and unambiguous. * * * The last sentence of Item Three fails to meet this standard when considered along with Item Eight. To the extent that this sentence would permit a construction favoring a contingent remainder, it must give way to the construction favoring a vested remainder, where both constructions are possible. * * *

We construe the final sentence of Item Three, and similar language in Item Five,[9] to refer to the time the grandchildren take possession in the land and become entitled to enjoy the title to the remainder, which had vested at Usry's death. This construction is consistent with our case law that recognizes that a vested remainder will have both a vesting of title and a vesting of possession. * * *

* * * Appellants also rely on a deed of assent executed by Usry's widow as executrix in 1968. That deed refers to property devised in Usry's will as being left to "the living grandchildren of Watson Usry." The deed of assent, prepared after the testator's death, is irrelevant to determining the testator's intent.

Judgment affirmed.

All the Justices concur, except THOMPSON, J., who concurs in the judgment only, and BENHAM, CARLEY and HINES, JJ., who dissent.

* * *

CARLEY, Justice, dissenting.

The law of Georgia favors the early vesting of remainders "in all cases of doubt," but not where "a manifest intention to the contrary shall appear." OCGA § 44-6-66. "[T]his preference for vested interests is only a presumption and will give way to a clear intent to make the interest subject to a contingency." Verner F. Chaffin, Studies in the Georgia Law of Decedents' Estates and Future Interests, p. 332 (1978). Because the controlling terms of Watson Usry's will leave no doubt of his clear intent that his grandchildren must survive their parents to inherit, their remainders are contingent and the preference for early vesting does not apply in this case. Therefore, I dissent to the majority's affirmance of the trial court's erroneous ruling.

Item Three of Mr. Usry's will creates a life estate in his widow and then in those of their children who survived her. Thus, he clearly intended that his children's interests not vest at his death, but at the death of his wife. With regard to the grandchildren, Item 3 provides: "Upon the death of my last surviving child *title in fee simple to said lands shall vest* in my grand-children, per stirpes and not per capita." (Emphasis supplied.) A "fee simple" estate "'is the entire and absolute property in the land; no person can have a greater estate or interest.' [Cit.]" Houston v. Coram, 215 Ga. 101, 102(1), 109 S.E.2d 41 (1959). Thus, Item 3 clearly expresses the testator's intent that his grandchildren would have *no* interest in the property until such time as the entire and absolute estate passed to them at the death of the last life tenant.

Despite this clear expression of Mr. Usry's intent, the majority concludes that what he really meant was for title to pass to his grandchildren at his death and that only possession be postponed until the death of his last surviving child. This is patently erroneous, as *title* cannot vest both at the time of the testator's death and then again at the death of the last life tenant. As the majority correctly notes, "there are two vestings of a *vested remainder*," a vesting of title and a vesting of possession. (Emphasis supplied.) Crawley v. Kendrick, 122 Ga. 183, 184(1), 50 S.E. 41 (1905). However, the issue here is whether the grandchildren's remainders are vested or contingent. OCGA § 44-6-61. The will does not specify that their interests vest at the testator's death with possession delayed until the last life tenant dies. The instrument unambiguously provides that the

---

9. "If my daughter-in-law, EVELYN, has not married again by the time the title to my land vests in my grand-children, as per Item Three of this Will, then I desire that she take a child's part...."

grandchildren take no "title" until that time. One can hold title without possession or possession without title. However, fee simple title in the grandchildren vests either at the time of Mr. Usry's death or when his last child dies. The will expressly indicates that his children must survive his widow to take a life estate and, by postponing the vesting of *title* in his grandchildren, implicitly requires that they survive the life tenants. See Ruth v. First Nat. Bank of Atlanta, 230 Ga. 490, 493, 197 S.E.2d 699 (1973).

> The importance of *Ruth* is that the court did look to the will as a whole rather than focusing on the particular words used in the bequest, and determined that the testator's intention, even though he used the word "absolutely," was that the bequest was not to vest until the death of the testator or the life tenant, whichever last occurred.

Chaffin, supra at p. 355 (1978). See also Fourth Nat. Bank of Columbus v. Brannon, 227 Ga. 191, 192(1), 179 S.E.2d 232 (1971).

The error in the majority's analysis is that it equates the absence of an *express* requirement for survivorship as conclusive evidence of the testator's intent to create vested, rather than contingent, remainders. However, the law favors the early vesting of remainders only in cases of doubt, and no doubt arises simply because the testator did not specifically provide that the remaindermen must survive to take. A postponement of the vesting of title can be the functional equivalent of a survivorship requirement. See Wells v. Ellis, 184 Ga. 645, 646(1), 192 S.E. 380 (1937). The applicable rule of construction is to ascertain the testator's intent based upon a consideration of the entire will and the circumstances surrounding its execution. Timberlake v. Munford, 267 Ga. 631, 632, 481 S.E.2d 217 (1997). Contrary to the majority opinion, the testator's will did not provide "for title to vest in his loved ones who survive him." In Item 8 of Mr. Usry's will, he expressed only the general intent "to provide for the welfare of my loved ones who survive me...." However, the relevant inquiry is the construction of the specific provisions of the instrument so as to determine how he intended to provide for them. There is a distinction between the expression of a general testamentary intent to provide for survivors, as in Item 8, and a specific provision for the vesting of title in those who survive, as in Item 3. In Item 3, Mr. Usry created life estates for his widow and children, and provided that his grandchildren would not take title until the death of the last surviving child. Thus, he obviously did not intend to provide for the welfare of all of his survivors, since only those children who outlived his widow were to take life estates. Under the majority's anomalous construction, the remainder to a grandchild who survived Mr. Usry and died before his or her own parent would be vested, but the parent of that grandchild would have no interest unless he or she outlived Mrs. Usry. Based upon the will as a whole, the more reasonable interpretation is that the testator intended all remainders to be contingent upon survival until the time of vesting. Mr. Usry accomplished that intent by expressly providing that his children survive his widow and by specifically providing that title would not pass to his grandchildren until the death of the last life tenant.

The authority cited by the majority does not support its holding. In Witcher v. Witcher, 231 Ga. 49, 200 S.E.2d 110 (1973), the will did not expressly provide that title would not vest in the testator's four sons until the death of the widow, but it did specify that, in the event a son predeceased the testator or his widow, the child or children of that deceased son would take the dead parent's share. Only three sons outlived their mother, and they urged that the effect of the survivorship language was to create contingent remainders so that the widow of their deceased brother took nothing. This Court rejected that construction. Because the testator did not specify when his sons' interests vested, the will "created a vested remainder interest in a class composed of the testator's sons" and the survivorship language was intended to "prevent a lapse of the devise to any son who died prior to the testator's death, leaving a child or children." Witcher, supra at 51, 200 S.E.2d 110. Thus, that case is entirely consistent with the principle that "words of survivorship shall refer to those survivors living at the time of the death of the testator in order to vest remainders unless a manifest intention to the contrary shall appear." OCGA § 44-6-66.

> Since no language in the will plainly manifested an intention to divest the share of a son who survived the testator but died before the life tenant leaving no children to take the substitutionary gift, the deceased son's remainder was not divested and therefore descended to his heirs.

Chaffin, supra at p. 351 (1978). Witcher does not hold that, in the absence of any express survivorship language, remainders must be construed as vested. The last sentence of Item 3 of Mr. Usry's will contains no survivorship language, but it does expressly provide that his grandchildren take no interest until the death of the last of his children. Thus, this case is controlled by the principle that

> the language of each particular instrument construed as a whole, showing the intent and purpose of the grantor or testator, must be given effect; and if the instrument creating the remainder should by specific language, consistent with a clear intent of the maker as gathered from the entire instrument, make the *remainder itself* subject to a contingency, the intent of the maker, if lawful, will control. (Emphasis in original.)

Britt v. Fincher, 202 Ga. 661, 664(4), 44 S.E.2d 372 (1947). Compare Miller v. Brown, 215 Ga. 148, 109 S.E.2d 741 (1959) (will which did not specify time of vesting in remaindermen construed to create vested remainders at time of testator's death).

The trial court erred in misapplying the preference for early vesting so as to violate the testator's manifest intent to create contingent remainders for his children and grandchildren. Because the majority endorses, rather than corrects that error, I dissent.

I am authorized to state that Justice BENHAM and Justice HINES join in this dissent.

Uniform Probate Code (2003)

Section 2-707. Survivorship With Respect to Future Interests Under Terms of Trust; Substitute Takers.
(b) [Survivorship Required; Substitute Gift]

(3) For the purposes of Section 2-701, words of survivorship attached to a future interest are not, in the absence of additional evidence, a sufficient indication of an intent contrary to the application of this section. Words of survivorship include words of survivorship that relate to the distribution date or to an earlier or unspecified time, whether these words or survivorship are expressed in condition-precedent, condition-subsequent, or any other form.

Notes

The Uniform Probate Code provision is quite revolutionary, both in the section quoted here and in other references to future interests. *See* Chapter Seven, *supra.* For extensive criticism of the Code's policy, *see* Jesse Dukeminier, *The Uniform Probate Code Upends the Law of Remainders*, 94 MICH. L. REV. 148 (1995).

VI. Powers of Appointment

If, in a valid Last Will and Testament or in an inter vivos trust, a Settlor were to give to Sadie one-million dollars, income for life, then the remainder to Sadie's issue, Sadie would have a life income trust, and her issue would have a vested remainder. But if the Settlor were to give to Sadie one-million dollars, income for life, then as she shall appoint in her Last Will and Testament, Sadie would be the beneficiary of a life income trust, but Sadie would also be what is called a Donee of a general testamentary power of appointment. Please note the difference between the two trusts. In both of the trusts, a Trustee is involved, and there is a distribution of life income to Sadie, but in the latter of the two, the Trustee is to distribute the remainder at Sadie's death to those persons named to take in her Last Will and Testament. Thus, Sadie has a power of appointment. If Sadie dies without a Last Will and Testament and, thus, does not appoint, the trust corpus will result back to the Settlor. The scope of the power of appointment, the effectiveness of Sadie's exercise, and the mechanisms by which a court seeks to determine the Settlor's intent, are all part of the realm of powers of appointment. Substantive doctrines regarding mistake, the Rule Against Perpetuities, and even fraud all play a role in powers of appointment. As in most areas of the law, there is a distinctive language that is applicable that must be learned in order to understand the focus and operation of the concept. Consider the following.

A. Elements of a Valid Power

1. The **Definition** of a power of appointment is found in the *Restatement (Third) of Property: Donative Transfers*, § 19.1 (Prelim. Draft No. 4, 1995): "A power of appointment is a power that authorizes the donee to designate recipients of the appointive property." This power is what separates a power of appointment from a life estate; a power provides flexibility by giving the Settlor/Donor the eyes of the Donee of the power, long into the future. It is an indispensable tool of estate planning.

2. The **Donor** of a power of appointment is the person who creates the power. This person is likely a Settlor of the trust, through which the power of appointment operates, or a Testator, if the power is created in a Last Will and Testament. The intention of the Donor is significant: the more restrictive the power of appointment, the more the intention of the Donor will matter.

3. The **Donee** of a power of appointment is the one who exercises the power of appointment. Although rare, the Donee could also be the Donor. The Donee could also possess a life estate in the corpus, thereby being a beneficiary also. And there could be more than one Donee. The validity of the Donee's exercise and the manner in which that exercise will prompt analysis under the Rule Against Perpetuities will be significant.

4. Appointees of a power of appointment are those persons to whom the Donee may appoint. Sometimes they are referred to as the object of the power. Obviously, an appointee may be an institution, and there may be one or more appointees. Issues of class gift, anti-lapse, and vesting will be significant issues when discussing appointees.

5. **Takers in Default** are those persons named by the Donor to take if the Donee does not exercise the power of appointment conferred, or, in the case of special powers, those who are eligible to take the appointment if the Donee exercises ineffectively.

6. **Testamentary/Inter Vivos Power** of appointment regards the time when the Donee may exercise the power of appointment, not when the Donor creates the power. Thus, if the Donor gives to the Donee a life estate, and then the Donee may appoint, the power is testamentary, since the Donee may only exercise at the end of a life estate. Obviously, a valid Last Will and Testament will be necessary for the Donee to have a valid exercise.

7. **General Power** of appointment refers to the scope of the permissible appointees from whom the Donee may choose. The *Restatement (Third) of Property*, § 19.4 (Prelim. Draft No. 4, 1995) states that: "A power of appointment is general if it is exercisable in favor of the donee, the donee's creditors, the donee's estate, or the creditors of the donee's estate." This language results from the Internal Revenue Code § 2041(b), signaling that any general power will be includable in the gross taxable estate of any donee possessing one, and it is subject to the elective share of any surviving spouse, or bona fide creditor. Please note that, in order for a power to be general, the power given to the Donee does not require the Donee to be able to exercise in favor of all three of these groups, but any one of them would be sufficient to make the power general. For example: "One-million dollars to Sadie, income for life, and then as she shall appoint to her estate or among her siblings." The ability to appoint among her siblings would not make this a general power, but the ability to appoint to her estate *would* make this a general power.

8. **Special Power** of appointment occurs whenever a donee is prohibited from appointing to one of the three groups mentioned in the Restatement as creating a general power. Hence, if the Settlor provides: "One-million dollars to Sadie, income for life, and then as she shall appoint among her siblings," the power is a special one. Because a special power limits the choices of the Donee, the Donor retains greater control, thereby prompting the question as to whether the Donor wanted the Donee to "exclude" some members that could be included within the special power, or was the Donee so restricted as to be prohibited from excluding, hence possessing a non-exclusive power? *See Restatement (Third) of Property: Donative Transfers*, § 29.1 (Preliminary Draft No. 4, 1995). If the power is interpreted as being non-exclusive, it creates very little, if any, discretion in the Donee, thus defeating the purposes of powers of appointment. Thus, the Restatement takes the position that, absent a contrary intent, special powers of appointment are presumptively exclusive. *See Restatement (Second) of Property, Donative Transfers*, § 21.1 (1986). The Donor must be very explicit in defining the power as non-exclusive—"to give to all equally"—before the court is likely to define the power as non-exclusive. Please note that the classification of a power as exclusive or non-exclusive may only be accomplished within the scope of a special power. Since a Donee may appoint to anyone in a general power, the ability to exclude is automatic.

No particular form of words is necessary to create a power of appointment; the court will simply look to a modicum of discretion given to the putative Donee. Thus, it is important to be able to identify a power of appointment and to classify its attributes. Being able to do so will lessen the possibility of error when considering what is to follow: release of the power, effective exercise, mistaken exercise, applicability of anti-lapse, fraud upon the power, and the application of the Rule Against Perpetuities and the Relation Back Doctrine. So, before going any further, make certain that you can identify the features of the following trust.

Case: During her lifetime, the Settlor created a valid inter vivos trust of one million dollars, to pay the income to her daughter, Sadie, for life, then at Sadie's death, United States Trust Company was to pay the corpus to those of her issue that Sadie designated in her Last Will and Testament. In the event that Sadie were to die without a Last Will and Testament, duly probated, or she were to die without issue, then United States Trust Company was to pay the remainder to the National Geographic Society.

Even though the words "power of appointment" were never used, Sadie had discretion to pick and choose among her issue at the time of her death, thereby a power was created in Sadie, the Donee. Sadie, of course, had a life estate, but at her death, she could appoint what was a special exclusive testamentary power of appointment, with the National Geographic Society being a taker in default. The power was special because Sadie could not appoint to herself, her creditors, or her estate—her issue do not constitute her estate. Since there was no restriction on the ability of Sadie to "exclude" issue, the power is exclusive. And because the power may be exercised only at her death, the power is testamentary. The fact that the Donor created the power during her lifetime does not make the power an inter vivos one. If you have mastered this, then ask the following questions: (1) What if Sadie wanted to release the power?— how would she do this? (2) What does Sadie have to say in her Last Will and Testament to exercise the power? Does she have to mention it specifically? (3) What should the court do if Sadie exercises the power in favor of her spouse, and not a named appointee? (4) What if Sadie appoints to a particular issue in her Last Will and Testament, but that issue predeceases her, survived by issue? Should we apply anti-lapse? (5) If Sadie exercises the power of appointment by creating yet another trust in favor of one child, and then, at the death of that child, to that child's issue, how should the Rule Against Perpetuities be utilized? We shall discuss these questions in the material that follows.

Tax Considerations: Classifications of powers of appointment as general or special, inter vivos or testamentary, and whether they have been exercised or released are all very important to the treatment powers receive under the Internal Revenue Code. For example, if the donee has the ability to appoint to the donee himself or herself, or to the donee's estate or creditors, the donee has a general power of appointment. If the donee exercises the power or releases the power during the donee's lifetime, the donee has made a transfer and is responsible for the gift tax. *See* I.R.C. § 2514. Gift tax is also imposed if there is a lapse of the power at any time during the life of the donee, so long as the appointment is greater than $5,000 or 5% of the aggregate value, at the time of the lapse, of the assets out of which the exercise of the lapsed powers could have been satisfied. *See* I.R.C. § 2041(b)(2).

If the decedent possesses a general power of appointment over property at death, the value of the property to which the power applies is included in his or her estate even if the power is not exercised. *See* I.R.C. § 2041. If the donee had only a special power of appointment, the value of the property subject to the appointment is not subject to the estate tax. *See* Treasury Reg. § 20.2041-1(c)(1).

There are two exceptions to the rule including property over which the donee had a general power or appointment into either gift tax or estate tax. One is that if the donee is given a power by the donor that could be included within the donee's taxable estate or gift tax, but the donee is "limited by an ascertainable standard relating to health, education, support, or maintenance" of the donee (*see* I.R.C.

§ 2041(b)(1)), the power is not considered as general and hence not includable in the gift and estate tax calculations for the donee. And second, if the donee is given no more than five thousand dollars or five percent of the aggregate value and the donee had the power to consume or invade that amount, then the maximum amount includable within the donee's estate is $5,000 or 5% of the corpus. *See* I.R.C. § 2041(b)(2). The rules regarding the taxation of powers of appointment are not as complicated as others areas, but obviously a careful drafting is required. *See, e.g.,* John G. Steinkamp, *Estate and Gift Taxation of Powers of Appointment Limited by Ascertainable Standards,* 79 MARQ. L. REV. 195 (1995). In Kinney v. Shinholser, 663 So. 2d 643 (Fla. App. 1995), an attorney was liable to the estate of a life tenant who was given a general testamentary power of appoint and the attorney did not explain to the client the consequences of not disclaiming the power upon receipt. Because of the attorney's negligence the life tenant's estate was obligated to pay estate taxes of $320,000. However, even with proper drafting and counsel, issues will arise. The following decision is an example.

Estate of Vissering v. Commissioner
United States Court of Appeals, Tenth Circuit, 1993
990 F.2d 578

LOGAN, Circuit Judge.

The estate of decedent Norman H. Vissering appeals from a judgment of the Tax Court determining that he held at his death a general power of appointment as defined by I.R.C. § 2041, and requiring that the assets of a trust of which he was cotrustee be included in his gross estate for federal estate tax purposes. The appeal turns on whether decedent held powers permitting him to invade the principal of the trust for his own benefit unrestrained by an ascertainable standard relating to health, education, support, or maintenance. The trust was created by decedent's mother in Florida and specifies that Florida law controls in the interpretation and administration of its provisions.

The estate argues that decedent was not a trustee at the time of his death because a New Mexico court's adjudication that he was incapacitated two months before his death divested him of those powers. Decedent was not formally removed as trustee; if he ceased to serve it was by operation of Florida law. However, we assume for purposes of this opinion that decedent continued as trustee until his death and that his powers are to be adjudged as if he were fully competent to exercise them at the time of his death. * * *

The trust at issue was created by decedent's mother, and became irrevocable on her death in 1965. Decedent and a bank served as cotrustees. Under the dispositive provisions decedent received all the income from the trust after his mother's death. On decedent's death (his wife, a contingent beneficiary, predeceased him), remaining trust assets were to be divided into equal parts and passed to decedent's two children or were held for their benefit. Decedent developed Alzheimer's disease and entered into a nursing home in 1984, but he tendered no resignation as trustee, nor did his guardian or conservator do so on his behalf after he was found to be incapacitated.

The Tax Court's decision, based entirely upon stipulated facts, resolved only questions of law, and consequently our review is de novo. First Nat'l Bank v. Commissioner, 921 F.2d 1081, 1086 (10th Cir.1990).

Under I.R.C. § 2041 a decedent has a general power of appointment includable in his estate if he possesses at the time of his death a power over assets that permits him to benefit himself, his estate, his creditors, or creditors of his estate. A power vested in a trustee, even with a cotrustee who has no interest adverse to the exercise of the power, to invade principal of the trust for his own benefit is sufficient to find the decedent trustee to have a general power of appointment, unless the power to invade is limited by an ascertainable standard relating to health, education, support, or maintenance. Treas.Reg. § 20.2041-1(c), -3(c)(2). See, e.g., Estate of Sowell v. Commissioner, 708 F.2d 1564, 1568 (10th Cir.1983) (invasion of trust corpus in case of emergency or illness is an ascertainable standard under § 2041(b)(1)(A)); Gaskill v. United States, 561 F.Supp. 73, 78 (D.Kan.1983) (life estate with power of disposition but not to consume the proceeds did not create general power of appointment under § 2041(b)(1)(A)), aff'd mem., 787 F.2d 1446 (10th Cir.1986); see also Merchants Nat'l Bank v. Commissioner, 320 U.S. 256, 261, 64 S.Ct. 108, 111, 88 L.Ed. 35 (1943) (invasion of trust corpus for "the comfort, support, maintenance and/or happiness of my wife" is not a fixed standard for purposes of charitable deductions); Ithaca Trust Co. v. United States, 279 U.S. 151, 154, 49 S.Ct. 291, 291, 73 L.Ed. 647 (1929) (invasion of trust corpus for any amount "that may be necessary to suitably maintain [decedent's wife] in as much comfort as she now enjoys" is a fixed standard for purposes of charitable deduction).

The relevant provisions of the instant trust agreement are as follows:

> During the term of [this trust], the Trustees shall further be authorized to pay over or to use or expend for the direct or indirect benefit of any of the aforesaid beneficiaries, whatever amount or amounts of the principal of this Trust as may, in the discretion of the Trustees, be required for the continued comfort, support, maintenance, or education of said beneficiary.

Tax Ct. ex. 3-C at 5–6. The Internal Revenue Service (IRS) and the Tax Court focused on portions of the invasion provision providing that the trust principal could be expended for the "comfort" of decedent, declaring that this statement rendered the power of invasion incapable of limitation by the courts.

We look to state law (here Florida's) to determine the legal interests and rights created by a trust instrument, but federal law determines the tax consequences of those interests and rights. Morgan v. Commissioner, 309 U.S. 78, 80, 60 S.Ct. 424, 425–26, 84 L.Ed. 585 (1940); Maytag v. United States, 493 F.2d 995, 998 (10th Cir.1974). The absence of clear and controlling state precedent regarding the use of the term "comfort" in trust documents for purposes of determining a general power of appointment under federal estate tax law has prompted the estate and amici to request that we certify this question to the Supreme Court of Florida. Because recent changes in Florida trust law significantly curtail the number of trusts that might be affected by such a certification, * * * and because the language of each trust document in any event requires individualized attention, we deny the motion to certify to the Florida Supreme Court.

Despite the decision in Barritt v. Tomlinson, 129 F.Supp. 642 (S.D.Fla.1955), which involved a power of invasion broader than the one before us, we believe the Florida Supreme Court would hold that a trust document permitting invasion of principal for "comfort," without further qualifying language, creates a general power of appointment. Treas.Reg. § 20.2041-1(c). See First Virginia Bank v. United States, 490 F.2d 532, 533

(4th Cir.1974) (under Virginia law, right of invasion for beneficiary's "comfort and care as she may see fit" not limited by an ascertainable standard); Lehman v. United States, 448 F.2d 1318, 1320 (5th Cir.1971) (under Texas law, power to invade corpus for "support, maintenance, comfort, and welfare" not limited by ascertainable standard); Miller v. United States, 387 F.2d 866, 869 (3d Cir.1968) (under Pennsylvania law, power to make disbursements from principal in amounts "necessary or expedient for [beneficiary's] proper maintenance, support, medical care, hospitalization, or other expenses incidental to her comfort and well-being" not limited by ascertainable standard); Estate of Schlotterer v. United States, 421 F.Supp. 85, 91 (W.D.Pa.1976) (power of consumption "to the extent deemed by [beneficiary] to be desirable not only for her support and maintenance but also for her comfort and pleasure" not limited by ascertainable standard); Doyle v. United States, 358 F.Supp. 300, 309–10 (E.D.Pa.1973) (under Pennsylvania law, trustees' "uncontrolled discretion" to pay beneficiary "such part or parts of the principal of said trust fund as may be necessary for her comfort, maintenance and support" not limited by ascertainable standard); Stafford v. United States, 236 F.Supp. 132, 134 (E.D.Wisc.1964) (under Wisconsin law, trust permitting husband "for his use, benefit and enjoyment during his lifetime," unlimited power of disposition thereof "without permission of any court, and with the right to use and enjoy the principal, as well as the income, if he shall have need thereof for his care, comfort or enjoyment" not limited by ascertainable standard).

However, there is modifying language in the trust before us that we believe would lead the Florida courts to hold that "comfort," in context, does not permit an unlimited power of invasion. The instant language states that invasion of principal is permitted to the extent "*required* for the *continued* comfort" of the decedent, and is part of a clause referencing the support, maintenance and education of the beneficiary. Invasion of the corpus is not permitted to the extent "determined" or "desired" for the beneficiary's comfort but only to the extent that it is "required." Furthermore, the invasion must be for the beneficiary's "continued" comfort, implying, we believe, more than the minimum necessary for survival, but nevertheless reasonably necessary to maintain the beneficiary in his accustomed manner of living. These words in context state a standard essentially no different from the examples in the Treasury Regulation, in which phrases such as "support in reasonable comfort," "maintenance in health and reasonable comfort," and "support in his accustomed manner of living" are deemed to be limited by an ascertainable standard. Treas.Reg. § 20.2041-1(c)(2). See, e.g., United States v. Powell, 307 F.2d 821, 828 (10th Cir.1962) (under Kansas law, invasion of the corpus if "it is necessary or advisable … for the maintenance, welfare, comfort or happiness" of beneficiaries, and only if the need justifies the reduction in principal, is subject to ascertainable standard); Hunter v. United States, 597 F.Supp. 1293, 1295 (W.D.Pa.1984) (power to invade for "comfortable support and maintenance" of beneficiaries is subject to ascertainable standard).

We believe that had decedent, during his life, sought to use the assets of the trust to increase significantly his standard of living beyond that which he had previously enjoyed, his cotrustee would have been obligated to refuse to consent, and the remainder beneficiaries of the trust could have successfully petitioned the court to disallow such expenditures as inconsistent with the intent of the trust instrument. The Tax Court erred in ruling that this power was a general power of appointment includable in decedent's estate.

REVERSED and REMANDED.

B. Exercise of a Power

Beals v. State Street Bank & Trust Co.
Supreme Judicial Court of Massachusetts, 1975
367 Mass. 318, 326 N.E.2d 896

WILKINS, Justice.

The trustees under the will of Arthur Hunnewell filed this petition for instructions, seeking a determination of the proper distribution to be made of a portion of the trust created under the residuary clause of his will. A judge of the Probate Court reserved decision and reported the case to the Appeals Court on the pleadings and a stipulation of facts. We transferred the case here.

Arthur Hunnewell died, a resident of Wellesley, in 1904, leaving his wife and four daughters. His will placed the residue of his property in a trust, the income of which was to be paid to his wife during her life. At the death of his wife the trust was to be divided in portions, one for each then surviving daughter and one for the then surviving issue of any deceased daughter. Mrs. Hunnewell died in 1930. One of the four daughters predeceased her mother, leaving no issue. The trust was divided, therefore, in three portions at the death of Mrs. Hunnewell. The will directed that the income of each portion held for a surviving daughter should be paid to her during her life and on her death the principal of such portion should 'be paid and disposed of as she may direct and appoint by her last Will and Testament duly probated.' In default of appointment, the will directed that a daughter's share should be distributed to 'the persons who would be entitled to such estate under the laws then governing the distribution of intestate estates.'

This petition concerns the distribution of the trust portion held for the testator's daughter Isabella H. Hunnewell, later Isabella H. Dexter (Isabella). Following the death of her mother, Isabella requested the trustees to exercise their discretionary power to make principal payments by transferring substantially all of her trust share 'to the Dexter family office in Boston, there to be managed in the first instance by her husband, Mr. Gordon Dexter.' This request was granted, and cash and securities were transferred to her account at the Dexter office. The Hunnewell trustees, however, retained in Isabella's share a relatively small cash balance, an undivided one-third interest in a mortgage and undivided one-third interest in various parcels of real estate in the Commonwealth, which Isabella did not want in kind and which the trustees could not sell at a reasonable price at the time. Thereafter, the trustees received payments on the mortgage and proceeds from occasional sales of portions of the real estate. From her one-third share of these receipts, the trustees made further distributions to her of $1,900 in 1937, $22,000 in 1952, and $5,000 in 1953.

In February, 1944, Isabella, who was then a resident of New York, executed and caused to be filed in the Registry of Probate for Norfolk County an instrument which partially released her general power of appointment under the will of her father. See G.L. c. 204, §§ 27–36, inserted by St.1943, c. 152. Isabella released her power of appointment 'to the extent that such power empowers me to appoint to any one other than one or more of the ... descendants me surviving of Arthur Hunnewell.'

On December 14, 1968, Isabella, who survived her husband, died without issue, still a resident of New York, leaving a will dated May 21, 1965. Her share in the trust under her father's will then consisted of an interest in a contract to sell real estate, cash, notes and a certificate of deposit, and was valued at approximately $88,000. Isabella did not expressly exercise her power of appointment under her father's will. The residuary clause of her will provided in effect for the distribution of all 'the rest, residue and remainder of my property' to the issue per stirpes of her sister Margaret Blake, who had predeceased Isabella.[1] The Blake issue would take one-half of Isabella's trust share, as takers in default of appointment, in all events. If, however, Isabella's will should be treated as effectively exercising her power of appointment under her father's will, the Blake issue would take the entire trust share, and the executors of the will of Isabella's sister Jane (who survived Isabella and has since died) would not receive that one-half of the trust share which would go to Jane in default of appointment.[2]

In support of their argument that Isabella's will did not exercise the power of appointment under her father's will, the executors of Jane's estate contend that (1) Massachusetts substantive law governs all questions relating to the power of appointment, including the interpretation of Isabella's will; (2) the power should be treated as a special power of appointment because of its partial release by Isabella; and (3) because Isabella's will neither expresses nor implies any intention to exercise the power, the applicable rule of construction in this Commonwealth is that a general residuary clause does not exercise a special power of appointment. The Blake issue, in support of their argument that the power was exercised, contend that (1) Isabella's will manifests an intention to exercise the power and that no rule of construction need be applied; (2) the law of New York should govern the question whether Isabella's will exercised the power and, if it does, by statute New York has adopted a rule that a special power of appointment is exercised by a testamentary disposition of all of the donee's property; and (3) if Massachusetts law does apply, and the will is silent on the subject of the exercise of the power, the principles underlying our rule of construction that a residuary clause exercises a general power of appointment are applicable in these circumstances.

* * * We turn first to a consideration of the question whether Isabella's will should be construed according to the law of this Commonwealth or the law of New York.[3] There

---

1. The significant portion of the residuary clause reads as follows: 'All the rest, residue and remainder of my property of whatever kind and wherever situated (including any property not effectively disposed of by the preceding provisions of this my will and all property over which I have or may have the power of appointment under or by virtue of the last will and testament dated November 27, 1933 and codicils thereto dated January 7, 1935 and January 8, 1935 of my husband, the late Gordon Dexter) ... I give, devise, bequeath and appoint in equal shares to such of my said nephew GEORGE BATY BLAKE and my said nieces MARGARET CABOT and JULIA O. BEALS as shall survive me and the issue who shall survive me of any of my said nephew or nieces who may predecease me, such issue to take per stirpes.'

2. The parties agree that in these circumstances the intestate recipients, and the proportion due to each, are the same under the laws governing the distribution of intestate estates in Massachusetts and New York.

3. The applicable rules of construction where a donee's intention is not clear from his will differ between the two States. In the absence of a requirement by the donor that the donee refer to the power in order to exercise it, New York provides by statute that a residuary clause in a will exercises not only a general power of appointment but also a special power of appointment, unless the will expressly or by necessary implication shows the contrary. 17B McKinney's Consol.Laws of N.Y.Anno., EPTL, c. 17-b, §10-6.1 (1967). See Matter of Hopkins, 46 Misc.2d 273, 276, 259 N.Y.S.2d 565 (1964). "Necessary implication" exists only where the will permits no other construction. Matter of Deane, 4 N.Y.2d 326, 330, 175 N.Y.S.2d 21, 151 N.E.2d 184 (1958). In Massachusetts, unless the donor has provided that the donee of the power can exercise it only by explicit reference to the power, a general residuary clause in a will exercises a general power of appointment unless there is a clear indication of a contrary intent. Boston Safe Deposit & Trust Co. v. Painter,

are strong, logical reasons for turning to the law of the donee's domicil at the time of death to determine whether a donee's will has exercised a testamentary power of appointment over movables. See Restatement 2d: Conflict of Laws, § 275, comment c (1971); Scott, Trusts, § 642, p. 4065 (3d ed. 1967); Scoles, Goodrich's Conflict of Laws, §§ 175–177, p. 346 (4th ed. 1964). Most courts in this country which have considered the question, however, interpret the donee's will under the law governing the administration of the trust, which is usually the law of the donor's domicil. * * * [Citations omitted]. This has long been the rule in Massachusetts. * * * [Citations omitted]. Indeed, the rule is so well established that parties have conceded the point from time to time. * * * [Citations omitted].[4]

If the question were before us now for the first time, we might well adopt a choice of law rule which would turn to the substantive law of the donee's domicil, for the purpose of determining whether the donee's will exercised a power of appointment. However, in a field where much depends on certainty and consistency as to the applicable rules of law, we think that we should adhere to our well established rule. Thus, in interpreting the will of a donee to determine whether a power of appointment was exercised, we apply the substantive law of the jurisdiction whose law governs the administration of the trust.

* * * Considering the arguments of the parties, we conclude that there is no indication in Isabella's will of an intention to exercise or not to exercise the power of appointment given to her under her father's will. A detailed analysis of the various competing contentions would not add to our jurisprudence.[5] In the absence of an intention disclosed by her will construed in light of circumstances known to her when she executed it, we must adopt some Massachusetts rule of construction to resolve the issue before us. The question is what rule of construction. We are unaware of any decided case which, in this context, has dealt with a testamentary general power, reduced to a special power by action of the donee.[6]

* * * We conclude that the residuary clause of Isabella's will should be presumed to have exercised the power of appointment. We reach this result by a consideration of the reasons underlying the canons of construction applicable to general and special testa-

---

322 Mass. 362, 366–367, 77 N.E.2d 409 (1948); Second Bank-State St. Trust Co. v. Yale Univ. Alumni Fund, 338 Mass. 520, 524, 156 N.E.2d 57 (1959). However, in Fiduciary Trust Co. v. First Natl. Bank, 344 Mass. 1, 6–10, 181 N.E.2d 6 (1962), we held that a general residuary clause did not exercise a special testamentary power of appointment in the circumstances of that case.

4. Of course, the law of the donee's domicil would be applied if the donor expressed such an intention. See Walker v. Treasurer & Recr. Gen., 221 Mass. 600, 603, 109 N.E. 647 (1915); Greenough v. Osgood, 235 Mass. 235, 237–238, 126 N.E. 461 (1920); Amerige v. Attorney Gen., 324 Mass. 648, 657–658, 88 N.E.2d 126 (1949).

5. Isabella's residuary clause disposed of her 'property.' Because the trustees had agreed to distribute her trust portion to her and had largely done so and because, in a sense, she had exercised dominion over the trust assets by executing the partial release, a reasonable argument might be made that she regarded the assets in her portion of the trust as her 'property.' However, a conclusion that she intended by implication to include assets over which she had a special power of appointment within the word 'property' is not justifiable because her residuary clause refers expressly to other property over which she had a special power of appointment under the will of her husband.

6. Clearly Isabella had only a special power of appointment after she partially released the general power given to her under her father's will. See Jeffers Estate, 394 Pa. 393, 398–399, 147 A.2d 402 (1959); Mearkle Estate, 23 Pa.D. & C.2d 661, 665 (1960). And, of course, if she had totally released the power of appointment, her will could have had no effect on the devolution of 'her' portion of the trust under her father's will.

mentary powers of appointment. Considered in this way, we believe that a presumption of exercise is more appropriate in the circumstances of this case than a presumption of nonexercise.

When this court first decided not to extend to a special power of appointment the rule of construction that a general residuary clause executes a general testamentary power (unless a contrary intent is shown by the will), we noted significant distinctions between a general power and a special power. Fiduciary Trust Co. v. First Natl. Bank, supra, 344 Mass. at 6–10, 181 N.E.2d 6. A general power was said to be a close approximation to a property interest, a 'virtually unlimited power of disposition' * * *, while a special power of appointment lacked this quality * * *. We observed that a layman having a general testamentary power over property might not be expected to distinguish between the appointive property and that which he owns outright, and thus 'he can reasonably be presumed to regard this appointive property as his own' * * *. On the other hand, the donee of a special power would not reasonably regard such appointive property as his own: '[h]e would more likely consider himself to be, as the donor of the power intended, merely the person chosen by the donor to decide who of the possible appointees should share in the property (if the power is exclusive), and the respective shares of the appointees' * * *.

Considering the power of appointment given to Isabella and her treatment of that power during her life, the rationale for the canon of construction applicable to general powers of appointment should be applied in this case. This power was a general testamentary power at its inception. During her life, as a result of her request, Isabella had the use and enjoyment of the major portion of the property initially placed in her trust share. Prior use and enjoyment of the appointive property is a factor properly considered as weighing in favor of the exercise of a power of appointment by a will. Fiduciary Trust Co. v. First Natl. Bank, supra, at 10, 181 N.E.2d 6. Isabella voluntarily limited the power by selecting the possible appointees. In thus relinquishing the right to add the trust assets to her estate, she was treating the property as her own. Moreover, the gift under her residuary clause was consistent with the terms of the reduced power which she retained. In these circumstances, the partial release of a general power does not obviate the application of that rule of construction which presumes that a general residuary clause exercises a general power of appointment.

* * * A decree shall be entered determining that Isabella H. Dexter did exercise the power of appointment, partially released by an instrument dated February 25, 1944, given to her by art. Fourth of the will of Arthur Hunnewell and directing that the trustees under the will of Arthur Hunnewell pay over the portion of the trust held under art. Fourth of his will for the benefit of Isabella H. Dexter, as follows: one-third each to George Baty Blake and Julia O. Beals; and one-sixth each to Margaret B. Elwell and to the estate of George B. Cabot. The parties shall be allowed their costs and counsel fees in the discretion of the probate court.

So ordered.

QUIRICO, Justice (with whom TAURO, Chief Justice, joins), concurring in the result.

I concur in the court's conclusion that the general residuary clause in the will of Isabella H. Dexter exercised the power of appointment given to her by art. Fourth of the will of Arthur Hunnewell. However, I would reach that result without regard to whether the power of appointment was, either when it was created or when it was exercised, a general power of appointment or a special power of appointment, and without perpetuating the distinction made between the two types of powers in our decision in Fiduciary Trust ,.co. v. First Natl. Bank, 344 Mass. 1, 6–10, 181 N.E.2d 6–8 (1962). I would hold that the 'settled canon of construction that a general residuary clause will operate as an execution of a general testamentary power unless a contrary intent is shown by the will' (Fiduciary Trust Co. case, 5, 181 N.E.2d), quoting from Second Bank-State St. Trust Co. v. Yale Univ. Alumni Fund, 338 Mass. 520, 524, 156 N.E.2d 57 (1959), which has been a part of the case law of this Commonwealth at least since our decision in Amory v. Meredith, 7 Allen 397 (1863), applies equally to the execution of a special power of appointment, provided, of course, that (a) the residuary clause includes any beneficiary within the scope of the special power of appointment, (b) the instrument creating the special power does not prohibit its exercise by a general residuary clause, and (c) the residuary clause includes no disclaimer of intent to exercise the special power.

It is with reluctance that I advocate a departure from the holding in the Fiduciary Trust Co. case which was decided in 1962 by a quorum of distinguished Justices of this court, but I am persuaded to do so by the policy considerations discussed below. The Fiduciary Trust Co. case itself represented a departure from views expressed, by way of dicta, in several cases which preceded it. In Stone v. Forbes, 189 Mass. 163, 169, 75 N.E. 141, 143 (1905), we said: 'If it were necessary to determine the question we should hesitate to follow the ... [distinction drawn in the English cases between the exercise of general and special powers by a residuary clause]. There is certainly less reason for doing so since Amory v. Meredith than before. There would seem to be no good reason why the question whether a special power of appointment had been exercised should not be determined by the same rules that are applied in other cases to the construction or interpretation of wills.' In several other cases the opportunity to rule that a general residuary clause does not ordinarily exercise a special power of appointment was also declined. Worcester Bank & Trust Co. v. Sibley, 287 Mass. 594, 598, 192 N.E. 31 (1934); Pitman v. Pitman, 314 Mass. 465, 475, 50 N.E.2d 69 (1943). Frye v. Loring, 330 Mass. 389, 394–395, 113 N.E.2d 595 (1953). In the last cited case we referred to Am.Law of Property, § 23.40(a) (1952). That source provides: 'The reasoning supporting the Massachusetts presumption that a residuary clause was intended to exercise powers of appointment applies with equal force whether the power in question is general or special.'

The basic judicial objective in this and similar cases is to ascertain the testamentary intent of the donee of the power. I am unable to accept the proposition that a testator who subscribes to a will which includes a residuary clause in substantially the common form, broadly covering 'all the rest, residue and remainder of my property' does not thereby express quite clearly an intention to dispose of all of the property and estate which can be the subject of testamentary disposition by him. Neither am I able to accept the proposition that such language, reasonably construed, permits any inference that the testator intended, by the use of such broad language, to exercise a general power of appointment but not a special one.

In its decision in the Amory case, supra, from which there evolved the 'settled canon of construction that a general residuary clause will operate as an execution of a general testamentary power unless a contrary intent is shown by the will,' this court first reviewed the development of the law of England on this subject. It cited several English cases which had held that a will would not operate to execute a power of appointment unless it referred expressly to the power or to the subject of the power, and that 'a mere residuary clause gave no sufficient indication of intention to execute a power' (399).

This court then noted criticism of the English rule, particularly because of its emphasis on the distinction between 'power' and 'property,' stating that 'the refinements and subtleties to which this distinction leads are great and perplexing' (398). It then noted that the rule was changed by a statute (St. 7 Will. IV and 1 Vict. c. 26, §27), declaring 'that a general devise of real or personal estate, in wills thereafter made, should operate as an execution of a power of the testator over the same, unless a contrary intention should appear on the will'; and then quoted the comment of Judge Story (1 Story R. 458, note), to the effect that as a result of the statute, '[t]he doctrine, therefore, has at last settled down in that country [England] to what would seem to be the dictate of common sense, unaffected by technical niceties' (400). For further discussions and citations of cases on the development of the law on this subject in England and in this country, see Restatement: Property, §343(1), comment d (1940); Am.Law of Property, §23.40 (1952); 104 Trusts and Estates 814 (1965); 51 Cornell L.Q. 1, 9–10 (1965); 16 A.L.R.3d 911, 920–924 (1967); 62 Am.Jur.2d, Powers, §§51–52 (1972).

It is apparent that in the case of Fiduciary Trust Co. v. First Natl. Bank, 344 Mass. 1, 181 N.E.2d 6 (1962), the court distinguished general powers and special powers in part on the basis of the distinction between powers and property.[1] The latter is the same distinction of which this court said in the Amory case, supra: '[T]he refinements and subtleties to which this distinction leads are great and perplexing' (7 Allen 398). Indeed, the case now before us represents one of the perplexities resulting from a rule based on such a distinction. These unnecessary 'refinements and subtleties' inevitably breed litigation initiated either by competing claimants or by a fiduciary, often a professional fiduciary, seeking to avoid or minimize the risk of liability to himself by obtaining the protection of a judicial declaration, usually at considerable expense to the intended beneficiaries. We should, if possible, develop and apply rules of law which will eliminate the occasion for such litigation. One stop in that direction would be to hold that a general residuary clause in a will is equally competent to execute a special power of appointment as it is to exercise a general power. See Bostwick & Hurstel, — Mass. —, — 304 N.E.2d 186 (1973).

Notes

Whenever a Donee neglects to refer to the Donor's power of appointment in any instrument that may be interpreted as an exercise, for example, a residuary clause of a Last Will and Testament, we may say that the Donee's instrument is "open-ended." An open-ended residuary clause in the Will of a Donee makes no reference to the power of appointment. To address the issue of whether the Donee intended to exercise the power, states have adopted many rules to best accommodate the Donor's intent. The following are illustrative.

First, if the Donor is truly concerned about inadvertent exercise of the power of appointment by an unwitting Donee, the Donor may provide in the instrument creating the power that the Donee must specifically mention the power of appointment

---

1. The court said, 344 Mass. at 9, 181 N.E.2d at 11: 'We think that, unlike a general power, a special power is not 'a close approximation to a property interest ...'. It is our opinion that the traditional common law distinction between 'property' and 'powers'... which with regard to general powers has in effect been overridden in cases cited above, persists with undiminished validity in the case of special powers and would alone serve as a sufficiently sound rationale for the nonapplicability of the canon in question to special powers.'

in order to exercise. *See, e.g.,* Unif. Prob. Code § 2-704 (2003). Any competent drafter should consider addressing this issue when creating a power of appointment in a Donee.

Second, the vast majority of states and code references provide that an open-ended residuary clause (no reference made to power of appointment) *does not* exercise any power of appointment. *See, e.g., Restatement (Third) of Property: Donative Transfers* § 25.3 (Prelim. Draft No. 4, 1995). Often these same states allow for extrinsic evidence to be admitted to demonstrate that the open-ended clause does, in fact, exercise the power, thus creating a presumption against exercise, which may be rebutted through extrinsic proof. *See Restatement (Second) of Property, Donative Transfers* § 17.3 (1986).

Third, a minority of states make a distinction between a general power and a special power, and hold that, barring a necessity of specific reference imposed by a Donor, an open-ended residuary clause *does* exercise a general power of appointment and will exercise a special power if the appointees are proper objects of the special power of appointment. The Uniform Probate Code § 2-608 provides that, in the absence of the Donor's requirement of a specific reference, an open-ended residuary clause in a Last Will and Testament does exercise a general power of appointment, as long as the Donor has not provided for a taker in default. And an open-ended residuary clause never executes a special power of appointment.

To determine which law to apply, some states provide that the law of the Donor's domicile controls. *See, e.g.,* N.Y. Est., Powers & Trusts L. § 3-5.1(g) (2004). At least one decision provides that the law of the Donee's domicile controls. *See, e.g.,* White v. United States, 680 F.2d 1156 (7th Cir. 1982).

C. Scope of a Power

In re Carroll's Will

Court of Appeals of New York, 1937
274 N.Y. 288, 8 N.E.2d 864

HUBBS, Judge.

In 1910 William Carroll died leaving a will by the fourth paragraph of which he devised and bequeathed the residue of his estate to his executors in trust to pay the income to his wife during her life. By the fifth paragraph he directed that upon the death of the wife the residuary trust be divided into two equal shares, the proceeds of one to be for the use and benefit of his daughter, Elsa, during her life, and the proceeds of the other share for the use and benefit of his son, Ralph, during his life. In the fifth paragraph he gave his daughter power by her last will and testament to dispose of the property so set aside for her use 'to and among her children or any other kindred who shall survive her and in such shares and manner as she shall think proper.' A similar power of appointment was given to Ralph to dispose of his share 'to and among his kindred or wife.' With respect to the share set aside for the use of the daughter, Elsa, the will provided that, in the absence of any valid disposition of the corpus by her, it should pass 'to her then surviving child or children, descendant or descendants' and, should there be no surviving child or descendant of the daughter, then the share on her decease should pass to the donor's 'surviving heirs or next-of-kin, according to the nature of the estate.'

Elsa died on June 26, 1933, without leaving any child or descendant her surviving. The mother, Grace Carroll, survived her and was living at the time of the trial, as was also the brother, Ralph. Elsa left a will by which she left $5,000 to her brother, and $250,000 to one Paul Curtis, a cousin, such bequest to go to his son if he predeceased her. The remainder of her share of the estate of her father she gave to her executors in trust.

When Elsa's will was drawn, the petitioning executor, Content, as her attorney, prepared the will and attended to its execution and also prepared a letter directed to Elsa by the legatee Paul Curtis, which letter read as follows: 'I am informed that by your last will and testament you have given and bequeathed to me the sum of Two Hundred and Fifty Thousand Dollars ($250,000). In the event that you should predecease me and I should receive the bequest before mentioned, I hereby promise and agree, in consideration of the said bequest, that I will pay to your husband, Foster Milliken, Jr., the sum of One Hundred Thousand Dollars ($100,000) out of the said bequest which you have given to me by your said will.'

It is not contended by any of the parties to this proceeding that Foster Milliken, Jr., husband of Elsa, was of her kindred, and, therefore, a proper object of the power granted to his wife in her father's will. The question here involved is as to the effect of the attempted provision for her husband upon the bequest to Paul Curtis.

Content testified that he had advised Elsa that she could not lawfully make her husband a beneficiary of any part of her father's estate; that she had drawn a previous will in which she had given the residue of the estate of her father to her brother, Ralph, with a request that he pay to her husband the sum of $10,000 per annum; that he advised her that that provision could not be enforced; that on October 6, 1931, she told him that she was not satisfied; that she was growing away from her brother and that she wanted to increase the bequest to her cousin Paul Curtis; that she had given Curtis $50,000 in a prior will; that she wanted to leave him $250,000 and that he prepared the will with the prior will before him and on October 13 she and Mrs. Elliott came to his office where she executed the will; that after the will was executed she told him: 'Paul would like to do something for Foster. He would like to leave him some of this money I am leaving to him, and Paul is perfectly willing to put this in writing to show his good faith.' He then talked with Paul, dictated the letter, and had it signed. He was not sure whether the letter was delivered to Elsa or whether he kept it for her. Curtis testified that several days before the will was executed Elsa told him she was going to make a new will; that she knew if her brother, Ralph, heard about it he would probably start a row with her mother; that she had previously left Curtis $50,000 and his son $50,000, and that she was going to leave him $150,000 and add to it $100,000 which she would like him to give to Mr. Milliken; that he told her if she wanted him to do so, he would sign a paper to that effect; that she said she did not know whether it would be necessary but if she wanted him to she would make a date for him to go down to Mr. Content's office; that she called him upon the day the will was executed and asked him to meet her there; that he was not present when the will was executed but that he went in afterwards and heard the letter dictated and signed it.

The surrogate determined that the promise made by Curtis so vitiated and permeated the bequest to him that the appointment constituted a fraud upon the power and made the bequest to him void.

The Appellate Division, two justices dissenting, decided that the only reasonable interpretation to be placed upon the transaction is that Elsa desired to appoint $150,000 to her cousin and an additional $100,000 to her husband; accordingly, that the lawful appointment of $150,000 to Curtis is separable from the unlawful appointment of $100,000 to him for the benefit of the husband.

It seems to us that the conclusion is inescapable that the testimony of Content, the attorney who drew the instruments, and of Curtis, who was the legatee, do not affect the true intent and purpose of the letter. Stress is laid upon the fact as testified to by Content that the testatrix, Elsa, did not tell him of the understanding with Curtis until after the will had been executed. Nevertheless, it appears from the testimony of Curtis that she had an understanding with him prior to the execution of the will and the writing constituted only a record of the actual prior agreement. The surrogate had the benefit of hearing the witnesses testify and of observing their conduct. He found nothing in their testimony to detract from the force of the letter signed by Curtis. Concededly, the attempted bequest for the benefit of the husband was not valid. Curtis alone testified that he was to receive $150,000 and the husband $100,000. Content testified that she told him she wanted to leave Curtis $250,000, and that he did not know until after the will was drawn of the understanding between Curtis and the testatrix. The letter says that the agreement to pay the husband $100,000 is in consideration of a bequest of $250,000. No one can say whether she would have left Curtis $100,000, $150,000, or a lesser or greater sum had it not been for the agreement to take care of her husband. Only by speculation can it be said that she would have left him $150,000 had it not been for that agreement. Had it not been for her continued possession either personally or by her attorney of the promise on the part of Curtis, no one can say but what she might have changed the will. Curtis was a party to the attempted fraud on the power. If the bequest to him be sustained to the extent of $150,000 on his own testimony, he suffers no penalty. It seems to us that on the facts, the conclusion of the surrogate was correct; that the entire bequest is involved in the intent to defeat the power and that it is impossible to separate and sustain the bequest to Curtis to the extent of $150,000.

Upon the general question the law of England is correctly stated in Halsbury's Laws of England (vol. 23, p. 58):

> A person having a limited power must exercise it bona fide for the end designed; otherwise the execution is a fraud on the power and void. Fraud in this connection does not necessarily imply any moral turpitude, but is used to cover all cases where the purpose of the appointor is to effect some bye or sinister object, whether such purpose be selfish or, in the appointor's belief, a more beneficial mode of disposition of the property and more consonant with that which he believes would be the real wish of the creator of the power under the circumstances existing at the date of the appointment. In all cases of fraudulent execution, the fraud consists in the exercise of the power for purposes foreign to those for which it was created and the exercise of the power may be held fraudulent on any of the three following grounds:
>
> (1) If the execution was made for a corrupt purpose.
>
> (2) If it was made in pursuance of an antecedent agreement by the appointee to benefit persons not objects of the power, even although the agreement in itself is unobjectionable. An appointment to a child an object of the power, and a contemporaneous settlement by him of the appointed fund, is, however, valid unless it can be shown that the appointment was made in pursuance of a contract inducing the appointment.

(3) If it was made for purposes foreign to the power, although such purposes are not communicated to the appointee before the appointment and although the appointor gets no personal benefit. * * * Appointments cannot be severed, so as to be good to the extent to which they are bona fide exercises of the power, but bad as to the remainder, unless (1) some consideration has been given which cannot be restored, or (2) the court can sever the intentions of the appointor and distinguish the good from the bad.

In a footnote on page 60 it is said: 'The fact that the appointor knows that the object intends to dispose of the fund in favour of a stranger to the power does not necessarily vitiate the appointment, but it may have that effect if it can be shown that the appointment would not have been made but for the agreement. Pryor v. Pryor, 2 DeGex, J. & S. 205, C.A.; Daniel v. Arkwright, 2 Hem. & M. 95; Re Foote and Purdon's Estate (1910) 1 I.R. 365. The question in each case is the character in which the appointee takes the property; if it is for his absolute benefit the appointment is good, but if this is not the appointor's purpose it is bad. Langston v. Blackmore, Amb. 289; FitzRoy v. Richmond, Duke (No. 2), 27 Beav. 190; Birley v. Birley, 25 Beav. 299; Pryor v. Pryor, supra; Cooper v. Cooper, L.R. 8 Eq. 312; Roach v. Trood, 3 Ch.Div. 429, C.A.; In re Turner's Settled Estates, 28 Ch.Div. 205, C.A.'

Halsbury calls attention that powers of jointure are an exception to the rule that the court may not sever appointments except upon the conditions stated. The cases of Lane v. Page, 27 English Reprint, 155; Aleyn v. Belchier, 1 Eden, 132, 28 English Reprint, 634, and Whelan v. Palmer, 39 Ch.Div. 648, cited by the Appellate Division, are jointure cases and distinguishable. Topham v. Duke of Portland, 1 De Gex, J. & S. 517, C.A., is relied upon in support of the doctrine that the appointment is separable. We find nothing in that case that sustains the respondent's position.

In Pryor v. Pryor, supra, it is stated: 'The donee of a limited power of appointment may well execute it in favour of an object of the power, though he believes and knows that the appointee will at once dispose of the property in favour of persons who are not objects of the power. But if, besides this belief and knowledge, there is a bargain between the appointor and appointee that the appointee shall make a disposition in favour of persons not objects of the power, and the just result of the evidence is, that the appointment would not have been made but for the bargain, then the appointment is bad.'

In that case a husband and wife had a power of appointment of certain real estate limited to the use of one or more of their children 'subject to such powers, provisos, remainders and limitations over (such charges, powers, provisos, remainders and limitations over being for the benefit of the said children or some or one of them).' They appointed the property to two of their sons as joint tenants and contemporaneously the sons conveyed the property in trust to pay the income to themselves and their brothers and sisters for life with remainders in favor of their children. The intent there was clearly to provide a benefit for grandchildren of the donees of the power where the power gave them authority only to appoint for the use of their children. The bargain was considered in its entirety and the appointment held invalid. There the bargain apparently was largely a matter of inference but it was found to exist from the acts of the parties.

* * *

In the case at bar we have written evidence which is corroborative of a prior agreement. It seems to us that the surrogate was quite correct in concluding that it is impossible to separate the valid from the invalid disposition. To say that it clearly appears that the donee would have given $150,000 to Curtis had the bargain not been made is not justified. It clearly appears than an object of the appointment to Curtis was to secure a benefit to the husband of the donee who was excluded by the donor of the power from being an appointee or benefiting from the exercise of the power. The purpose of the donee was to accomplish by an agreement with Curtis an end entirely foreign to the intent of the donor of the power. Her act constituted a fraud on the power in which Curtis actively participated. There was a bargain between the donee and Curtis by which, in consideration of the appointment, he agreed to dispose of a part of the legacy in favor of a person who was not an object of the power. That bargain resulted in vitiating not only the provision for donee's husband but also the bequest to Curtis within the meaning of the authorities heretofore cited.

The wording of the letter which he signed was 'in consideration of the said bequest' he would pay to donee's husband $100,000 'out of the said bequest' of $250,000. It is hard to see how those plain words can be construed otherwise than a bargain to share his bequest of $250,000 with another not an object of the power. Such a bargain under all the authorities makes the entire bequest void. Cf. 46 Yale Law Journal, 344; 49 C.J. 1298.

The appellant Ralph C. Carroll contends that, in permitting the donee to appoint to any of her kindred, the donor used the word 'kindred' in a narrow sense and intended to limit the possible beneficiaries of the power to her next of kin. If correct in that contention, since the donee died without children, the result would be that she could appoint only to her brother, the appellant Ralph Carroll. There is no inconsistency or ambiguity in the will of William Carroll evidenced by the fact that he gave to his daughter a power of appointment to her children or any other of her kindred. Kindred has a well-established meaning, 'blood relatives,' as distinguished from that limited number of blood relatives embraced under the term 'next of kin.' William Carroll in his will used the words next of kin where it is apparent that it was his intention that the property was to pass as in the case of intestacy. The surrogate has determined that kindred was used in the generally accepted meaning of the word. That determination has been affirmed by the Appellate Division and there appears no reason for according to it a limited application.

* * *

The order of the Appellate Division should be modified in accordance with this opinion and, as so modified, affirmed, without costs.

CRANE, C. J., and O'BRIEN, LOUGHRAN, FINCH, and RIPPEY, JJ., concur.

LEHMAN, J., dissents and votes to affirm.

Judgment accordingly.

Notes

The Donee of a power of appointment may only do that which is authorized by the Donor. To allow otherwise would be to commit a fraud on the power. *See Restatement (Second) of Property, Donative Transfers,* §20.2 (1986). Thus, if a Donor has given a Donee a general inter vivos power, the Donee may exercise immediately in favor of anyone, but if the general power is testamentary, the Donee may only exercise at death. There are more stringent restrictions on special powers, but if a Donee has a special exclusive testamentary power, it seems reasonable to allow the Donee to exercise the power in a valid Last Will and Testament by creating a trust in favor of only those appointees allowed by the Donor. *See Restatement (Third) of Property: Donative Transfers*, § 27.3 (Prelim. Draft No. 4, 1995). *But see* Loring v. Karrie-Davies, 371 Mass. 346, 357 N.E.2d 11 (1976) (special powers of appointment granted to donee through inter vivos trust and testamentary trust held invalid; default provision effectuated). But the Donee of a special testamentary power of appointment cannot contract to make an appointment during lifetime unless the Donee and the Donor are the same person, *see Restatement (Third) of Property: Donative Transfers*, § 24.2 (Prelim. Draft No. 4, 1995); Cal. Prob. Code § 660 (2004), because if the power is testamentary, it cannot be "exercised" during life.

D. Ineffective Exercise

If the Donee has sufficiently exercised the power of appointment, thereby avoiding the open-ended residuary clause issue, the next issue that may occur is ineffective exercise by the Donee. For example, the Donor of a *general* testamentary power of appointment exercises by creating another trust that violates the Rule Against Perpetuities, results in a lapsed bequest, or violates a condition of the appointment. Or the Donee of a *special* exclusive testamentary power of appointment exercises in favor of a non-permissible appointee. One solution would be to simply result the appointment back to the Donor's estate, which is what would occur if there were no exercise at all by the Donee of a general power. But when there has been an attempted exercise by the Donee, the law proceeds in a different fashion. Consider the following three situations.

1. Allocation of Assets. If the Donee of a special power of appointment properly exercises the power in a valid Last Will and Testament's residuary clause, it is possible that the Donee could inadvertently blend the Donee's personal assets with the Donor's appointment, and, worse, the Donee could appoint to an impermissible appointee and a permissible appointee. May a court "allocate" the estate of the Donee to provide for both appointees? The *Restatement (Third) of Property: Donative Transfers*, § 30.2 (Prelim. Draft No. 4, 1995) provides that a court can allocate. For an illustration, see *Restatement (Third) of Property, Donative Transfers*, § 30.2, illus. 5 (Prelim. Draft No. 4, 1995).

2. General Powers: Capture. Whenever there has been an attempted exercise of the general power by the Donee, courts will apply the doctrine of capture to keep the appointment in the estate of the Donee, rather than have it revert to the estate of the Donor. Allowing the appointment to be "captured' in the Donee reflects "an intent [by the Donee] to assume control of the appointive property for all purposes and not merely for the limited purpose of giving effect to the expressed appointment." *Restatement (Second) of Property, Donative Transfers*, § 23.2 (1986). The fact that a Donor may have included a Taker-in-Default will not defeat capture; the Taker-in-Default provision is applicable only if the Donee attempts no exercise at all or the Donee has expressed an intent that capture not apply.

3. Special Powers: Implied Gift. Whenever a Donor has created a special power, the Donor has delegated far less discretion to the Donee. Thus, capturing the appointment in the estate of the Donee when there is an ineffective exercise is not an option. Courts are willing to create an implied gift in the permissible appointees if the Donee: (1) ineffectively exercises, or (2) does not exercise at all. *See Restatement (Second) of Property, Donative Transfers*, § 24.2 (1986). Please contrast this with general powers and capture, where there must be an attempted exercise and Takers-in-Default do not matter. California does not refer to implied gifts but, instead, uses "imperative powers," providing that: "A power is 'imperative' where the creating instrument manifests an intent that the permissible appointees be benefitted even if the donee fails to exercise the power." CAL. PROB. CODE §§ 613 & 671 (2004). How, then, would implied gift be utilized? Please consider the following decision.

Loring v. Marshall

Supreme Judicial Court of Massachusetts, 1985
396 Mass. 166, 484 N.E.2d 1315

WILKINS, Justice.

This complaint, here on a reservation and report by a single justice of this court, seeks instructions as to the disposition of the remainder of a trust created under the will of Marian Hovey. * * * In Massachusetts Inst. of Technology v. Loring, 327 Mass. 553, 99 N.E.2d 854 (1951), this court held that the President and Fellows of Harvard College, the Boston Museum of Fine Arts, and Massachusetts Institute of Technology (the charities) would not be entitled to the remainder of the trust on its termination. The court, however, did not decide, as we now must, what ultimate disposition should be made of the trust principal.

Marian Hovey died in 1898, survived by a brother, Henry S. Hovey, a sister, Fanny H. Morse, and two nephews, John Torrey Morse, Third, and Cabot Jackson Morse. By her will, Marian Hovey left the residue of her estate in trust, the income payable in equal shares to her brother and sister during their lives. Upon her brother's death in 1900, his share of the income passed to her sister, and, upon her sister's death in 1922, the income was paid in equal shares to her two nephews. John Torrey Morse, Third, died in 1928, unmarried and without issue. His share of the income then passed to his brother, Cabot Jackson Morse, who remained the sole income beneficiary until his death in 1946.

At that point, the death of the last surviving income beneficiary, Marian Hovey's will provided for the treatment of the trust assets in the following language:

> At the death of the last survivor of my said brother and sister and my two said nephews, or at my death, if none of them be then living, the trustees shall divide the trust fund in their hands into two equal parts, and shall transfer and pay over one of such parts to the use of the wife and issue of each of my said nephews as he may by will have appointed; provided, that if his wife was living at my death he shall appoint to her no larger interest in the property possessed by me than a right to the income during her life, and if she was living at the death of my father, he shall appoint to her no larger interest in the property over which I have a power of disposition under the will of my father than a right to the income during her life; and the same limitations shall apply to the appointment of income as aforesaid. If either of my said nephews shall leave no such appointees then living, the whole of the trust fund shall be paid to the appointees of his said brother as aforesaid. If neither of my said nephews leave such appointees then living the whole trust fund shall be paid over and transferred in in [sic] equal shares to the Boston Museum of Fine Arts, the Massachusetts Institute of Technology, and the President and Fellows of Harvard College for the benefit of the Medical School; provided, that if the said Medical School shall not then admit women to instruction on an equal footing with men, the said President and Fellows shall not receive any part of the trust prop-

erty, but it shall be divided equally between the Boston Museum of Fine Arts and the Massachusetts Institute of Technology.[4]

The will thus gave Cabot Jackson Morse, the surviving nephew, a special power to appoint the trust principal to his "wife and issue" with the limitation that only income could be appointed to a widow who was living at Marian Hovey's death.[5] Cabot Jackson Morse was survived by his wife, Anna Braden Morse, who was living at Marian Hovey's death, and by his only child, Cabot Jackson Morse, Jr., a child of an earlier marriage, who died in 1948, two years after his father. Cabot Jackson Morse left a will which contained the following provisions:

> Second: I give to my son, Cabot Jackson Morse, Jr., the sum of one dollar ($1.00), as he is otherwise amply provided for.

> Third: The power of appointment which I have under the wills of my aunt, Marian Hovey, and my uncle, Henry S. Hovey, both late of Gloucester, Massachusetts, I exercise as follows: I appoint to my wife, Anna Braden Morse, the right to the income during her lifetime of all of the property to which my power of appointment applies under the will of Marian Hovey, and I appoint to my wife the right during her widowhood to the income to which I would be entitled under the will of Henry S. Hovey if I were living.

> Fourth: All the rest, residue and remainder of my estate, wherever situated, real or personal, in trust or otherwise, I leave outright and in fee simple to my wife, Anna Braden Morse.

In Welch v. Morse, 323 Mass. 233, 81 N.E.2d 361 (1948), we held that the appointment of a life interest to Anna Braden Morse was valid, notwithstanding Cabot Jackson Morse's failure fully to exercise the power by appointing the trust principal. Consequently, the trust income following Cabot Jackson Morse's death was paid to Anna Braden Morse until her death in 1983, when the principal became distributable. The trustees thereupon brought this complaint for instructions.

The complaint alleges that the trustees "are uncertain as to who is entitled to the remainder of the Marian Hovey Trust now that the trust is distributable and specifically whether the trust principal should be paid in any one of the following manners: (a) to the estate of Cabot Jackson Morse, Jr. as the only permissible appointee of the remainder of the trust living at the death of Cabot Jackson Morse; (b) in equal shares to the estates of Cabot Jackson Morse, Jr. and Anna Braden Morse as the only permissible appointees living at the death of Cabot Jackson Morse; (c) to the estate of Anna Braden Morse as the only actual appointee living at the death of Cabot Jackson Morse; (d) to the intestate takers of Marian Hovey's estate on the basis that Marian Hovey failed to make a complete disposition of her property by her will; (e) to Massachusetts Institute of Technology, Museum of Fine Arts and the President and Fellows of Harvard College in equal shares as remaindermen of the trust; or (f) some other disposition." Before us each named potential taker claims to be entitled to trust principal.

---

4. The parties have stipulated that at the relevant time the Harvard Medical School admitted women to instruction on an equal footing with men.

5. We are concerned here only with "property possessed" by the testatrix at her death and not property over which she had "a power of disposition under the will of [her] father." That property was given outright to his widow under the residuary clause of the will of Cabot Jackson Morse. See Frye v. Loring, 330 Mass. at 396, 113 N.E.2d 595. See also Loring v. Morse, 332 Mass. at 64, 123 N.E.2d 360.

In our 1951 opinion, *Massachusetts Inst. of Technology v. Loring*, 327 Mass. at 555–556, 99 N.E.2d 854, we explained why in the circumstances the charities had no interest in the trust: "The rights of the petitioning charities as remaindermen depend upon the proposition that Cabot J. Morse, Senior, did not leave an 'appointee' although he appointed his wife Anna Braden Morse to receive the income during her life. The time when, if at all, the 'whole trust fund' was to be paid over and transferred to the petitioning charities is the time of the death of Cabot J. Morse, Senior. At that time the whole trust fund could not be paid over and transferred to the petitioning charities, because Anna Braden Morse still retained the income for her life. We think that the phrase no 'such appointees then living' is not the equivalent of an express gift in default of appointment, a phrase used by the testatrix in the preceding paragraph." In *Frye v. Loring*, 330 Mass. 389, 393, 113 N.E.2d 595 (1953), the court reiterated that the charities had no interest in the trust fund.

It is apparent that Marian Hovey knew how to refer to a disposition in default of appointment from her use of the terms elsewhere in her will. She did not use those words in describing the potential gift to the charities. A fair reading of the will's crucial language may rightly be that the charities were not to take the principal unless no class member who could receive principal was then living (i.e., if no possible appointee of principal was living at the death of the surviving donee). Regardless of how the words "no such appointees then living" are construed, the express circumstances under which the charities were to take did not occur. The question is what disposition should be made of the principal in the absence of any explicit direction in the will.

Although in its 1951 opinion this court disavowed making a determination of the "ultimate destination of the trust fund," the opinion cited the Restatement of Property § 367(2) (1940), and 1 A. Scott, Trusts § 27.1 (1st ed.1939) * * * to the effect that, when a special power of appointment is not exercised and absent specific language indicating an express gift in default of appointment, the property not appointed goes in equal shares to the members of the class to whom the property could have been appointed. For more recent authority, see 5 American Law of Property § 23.63, at 645 (A.J. Casner ed.1952 & Supp.1962) ("The fact that the donee has failed to apportion the property within the class should not defeat the donor's intent to benefit the class"); Restatement (Second) of Property § 24.2 (Tent.Draft No. 7, 1984). * * *

Applying this rule of law, we find no specific language in the will which indicates a gift in default of appointment in the event Cabot Jackson Morse should fail to appoint the principal. The charities argue that the will's reference to them suggests that in default of appointment Marian Hovey intended them to take. On the other hand, in *Welch v. Morse*, 323 Mass. at 238, 81 N.E.2d 361, we commented that Marian Hovey's "will discloses an intent to keep her property in the family." The interests Marian Hovey gave to her sister and brother were life interests, as were the interests given to her nephews. The share of any nephew who died unmarried and without issue, as did one, was added to the share of the other nephew. Each nephew was limited to exercising his power of appointment only in favor of his issue and his widow. * * * We think the apparent intent to keep the assets within the family is sufficiently strong to overcome any claim that Marian Hovey's will "expressly" or "in specific language" provides for a gift to the charities in default of appointment. * * *

If we were to depart from the view taken thirty-four years ago in Massachusetts Inst. of Technology v. Loring, 327 Mass. 553, 99 N.E.2d 854 (1951), and now were to conclude that under the terms of Marian Hovey's will the charities were to receive the trust principal, we would face the problem that, under normal principles of res judicata, our earlier decision against the charities is binding on them. Any suggestion that our 1951 decision did not bind the charities because the Attorney General was not a party to that proceeding is not supported by authority. The charities themselves brought the earlier action and chose not to name the Attorney General as a party. That action preceded the enactment of G.L. c. 12, §8G, inserted by St.1954, c. 529, §1, which made the Attorney General a necessary party to the proceedings concerning the application of funds to public charities. Moreover, our 1951 opinion did not concern a compromise settlement between a charity and its adversaries, a situation in which the Attorney General's involvement would then have been required. See Springfield Safe Deposit & Trust Co. v. Stoop, 326 Mass. 363, 95 N.E.2d 161 (1950). To conclude now that the Attorney General's involvement was indispensable to a valid determination in the 1951 action would cast a shadow over hundreds of pre-1954 decisions concerning charitable interests under wills and trusts. See Eustace v. Dickey, 240 Mass. 55, 86, 132 N.E. 852 (1921). * * *

The same arguments made by the charities and the Attorney General in this case were considered and rejected in 1951. Surely in a case such as this, at least in the absence of a statute to the contrary, the public interest in protecting the charities' rights was fully accommodated by the Justices of this court in its prior decision. The Attorney General does not suggest in his answer that, if the named charities could not take, other charities should take in their stead by application of the doctrine of cy-pres.

What we have said disposes of the claim that the trust principal should pass to Marian Hovey's heirs as intestate property, a result generally disfavored in the interpretation of testamentary dispositions. See Fiduciary Trust Co. v. State St. Bank & Trust Co., 360 Mass. 652, 656, 277 N.E.2d 120 (1971); New England Merchants Nat'l Bank v. Frost, 357 Mass. 158, 163, 257 N.E.2d 439 (1970); Loring v. Clapp, 337 Mass. 53, 59, 147 N.E.2d 836 (1958). The claim of the executors of the estate of Anna Braden Morse that her estate should take as the class, or at least as a member of the class, must fail because Marian Hovey's will specifically limits such a widow's potential stake to a life interest.

A judgment shall be entered instructing the trustees under the will of Marian Hovey to distribute the trust principal to the executors of the estate of Cabot Jackson Morse, Jr. The allowance of counsel fees, costs, and expenses from the principal of the trust is to be in the discretion of the single justice.

So ordered.

* * *

E. Release of a Power

Seidel v. Werner

Supreme Court, New York County, 1975
81 Misc.2d 220, 364 N.Y.S.2d 963
aff'd on opinion below, 50 A.D.2d 743, 376 N.Y.S.2d 139

Samuel J. Silverman, J.

* * *

Plaintiffs, trustees of a trust established in 1919 by Abraham L. Werner, sue for a declaratory judgment to determine who is entitled to one half of the principal of the trust fund—the share in which Steven L. Werner, decedent (hereinafter "Steven"), was the life beneficiary and over which he had a testamentary power of appointment. The dispute concerns the manner in which Steven exercised his power of appointment and is between Steven's second wife, Harriet G. Werner (hereinafter "Harriet"), along with their children, Anna G. and Frank S. Werner (hereinafter "Anna" and "Frank") and Steven's third wife, Edith Fisch Werner (hereinafter "Edith").

Anna and Frank claim Steven's entire share of the trust remainder on the basis of a Mexican consent judgment of divorce, obtained by Steven against Harriet on December 9, 1963, which incorporated by reference and approved a separation agreement, entered into between Steven and Harriet on December 1, 1963. That agreement included the following provision:

> 10. The Husband shall make, and hereby promises not to revoke, a will in which he shall exercise his testamentary power of appointment over his share in a trust known as 'Abraham L. Werner Trust No. 1' by establishing with respect to said share a trust for the benefit of the aforesaid Children, for the same purposes and under the same terms and conditions, as the trust provided for in Paragraph '9' of this Agreement, insofar as said terms and conditions are applicable thereto.
>
> Paragraph 9 in relevant part provides for the wife to receive the income of the trust, upon the death of the husband, for the support and maintenance of the children, until they reach 21 years of age, at which time they are to receive the principal in equal shares.

On March 20, 1964, less than four months after entry of the divorce judgment, Steven executed a will in which, instead of exercising his testamentary power of appointment in favor of Anna and Frank, he left everything to his third wife, Edith:

> First, I give, devise and bequeath all of my property ... including ... all property over which I have a power of testamentary disposition, to my wife, EDITH FISCH WERNER.

Steven died in April, 1971 and his will was admitted to probate by the Surrogate's Court of New York County on July 11, 1973.

* * * Paragraph 10 of the separation agreement is a contract to exercise a testamentary power of appointment not presently exercisable (EPTL 10-3.3) and as such is invalid under EPTL 10-5.3, which provides as follows:

> (a) The donee of a power of appointment which is not presently exercisable, or of a postponed power which has not become exercisable, cannot contract to make an appointment. Such a contract, if made cannot be the basis of an action for specific performance or damages, but the promisee can obtain restitution of the value given by him for the promise unless the donee has exercised the power pursuant to the contract.

This is a testamentary power of appointment. The original trust instrument provided in relevant part that:

> "Upon the death of such child [Steven] the principal of such share shall be disposed of as such child shall by its last will direct, and in default of such testamentary disposition then the same shall go to the issue of such child then surviving per stirpes."

It is not disputed that New York law is determinative of the validity of paragraph 10 of the separation agreement; the separation agreement itself provides that New York law shall govern.

The reasoning underlying the refusal to enforce a contract to exercise a testamentary power was stated by Judge Cardozo in the case of Farmers' Loan and Trust Co. v Mortimer (219 NY 290, 293–294):

> The exercise of the power was to represent the final judgment, the last will, of the donee. Up to the last moment of his life he was to have the power to deal with the share as he thought best ... To permit him to bargain that right away would be to defeat the purpose of the donor. Her command was that her property should go to her son's issue unless at the end of his life it remained his will that it go elsewhere. It has not remained his will that it go elsewhere; and his earlier contract cannot nullify the expression of his final purpose. 'It is not, I apprehend, to be doubted,' says Rolt, L. J., in Cooper v Martin (LR [3 Ch App] 47, 58) 'that equity ... will never uphold an act which will defeat what the person creating the power has declared, by expression or necessary implication, to be a material part of his intention. (See also, Matter of Brown, 33 NY2d 211.)

* * * [Court's discussion of res judicata and comity omitted].

* * * As indicated, the statute makes a promise to exercise a testamentary power in a particular way unenforceable. However, EPTL 10-5.3 (subd [b]) permits a donee of a power to release the power, and that release, if in conformity with EPTL 10-9.2, prevents the donee from then exercising the power thereafter.

Under the terms of the trust instrument, if Steven fails to exercise his power of appointment, Anna and Frank (along with the children of Steven's first marriage) take the remainder, i.e., the property which is the subject of Steven's power of appointment. Therefore, Harriet, Anna and Frank argue that at a minimum Steven's agreement should be construed as a release of his power of appointment, and that Anna and Frank should be permitted to take as on default of appointment.

There is respectable authority—by no means unanimous authority, and none binding on this court—to the effect that a promise to appoint a given sum to persons who would take in default of appointment should, to that extent, be deemed a release of the power of appointment. (See Restatement, Property, § 336 [1940]; Simes and Smith, Law of Future Interests, § 1016 [1956].)

This argument has the appeal that it seems to be consistent with the exception that the release statute EPTL 10-5.3 (subd [b]) carves out of EPTL 10-5.3 (subd [a]); and is also consistent with the intentions and reasonable expectations of the parties at the time they entered into the agreement to appoint, here in the separation agreement; and that therefore perhaps in these circumstances the difference between what the parties agreed to and a release of the power of appointment is merely one of form. Whatever may be the possible validity or applicability of this argument to other circumstances and situations, I think it is inapplicable to this situation because:

(a) It is clear that the parties did not intend a release of the power of appointment. (Cf. Matter of Haskell, 59 Misc 2d 797.) Indeed, the agreement—unlike a release of a power of appointment—expressly contemplates that something will be done by the donee of the power in the future, and that that something will be an exercise of the power of appointment. Thus, the agreement, in the very language said to be a release of the power of appointment, says (par 10, supra):

> "The Husband *shall* make ... a will in which he *shall* exercise his testamentary power of appointment." (Emphasis added.)

(b) Nor is the substantial effect of the promised exercise of the power the same as would follow from release of, or failure to exercise the power.

(i) Under the separation agreement, the power is to be exercised so that the entire appointive property shall be for the benefit of Anna and Frank; under the trust instrument, on default of exercise of the power, the property goes to all of Steven's children (Anna, Frank and the two children of Steven's first marriage). Thus the agreement provides for appointment of a greater principal to Anna and Frank than they would get in default of appointment.

(ii) Under the trust instrument, on default of exercise of the power, the property goes to the four children absolutely and in fee. The separation agreement provides that Steven shall create a trust, with income payable to Harriet as trustee, for the support of Anna and Frank until they both reach the age of 21, at which time the principal shall be paid to them or the survivor; and if both fail to attain the age of 21, then the principal shall revert to Steven's estate. Thus, Anna and Frank's interest in the principal would be a defeasible interest if they did not live to be 21; and indeed at Steven's death they were both still under 21 so that their interest was defeasible.

(iii) Finally, under the separation agreement, as just noted, if Anna and Frank failed to qualify to take the principal, either because they both died before Steven or before reaching the age of 21, then the principal would go to Steven's estate. Under the trust instrument, on the other hand, on default of appointment and an inability of Anna and Frank to take, Steven's share of the principal would not go to Steven's estate, but to his other children, if living, and if not, to the settlor's next of kin.

In these circumstances, I think it is too strained and tortuous to construe the separation agreement provision as the equivalent of a release of the power of appointment. If this is a release then the exception of EPTL 10-5.3 (subd [b]) has swallowed and destroyed the principal rule of EPTL 10-5.3 (subd [a]).

I note that in Wood v American Security and Trust Co. (253 F Supp 592, 594), the principal case relied upon by Harriet, Anna and Frank on this point, the court said:

> "The Court finds that it is significant that the disposition resulting from the agreement is in accordance with the wishes of the testator in the event the power should not be exercised."

Furthermore, the language of the instrument in that case was much more consistent with the nonexercise of the powers of appointment than in the case at bar.

Accordingly, I hold that the separation agreement is not the equivalent of a total or partial release of the power of appointment.

* * * Anna and Frank also seek restitution out of the trust fund of the value given by them in exchange for Steven's unfulfilled promise. EPTL 10-5.3 (subd [a]) provides that although the contract to make an appointment cannot be the basis for an action for specific performance or damages, "the promisee can obtain restitution of the value given by him for the promise unless the donee has exercised the power pursuant to contract."

Anna and Frank's remedy is limited, however, to the claim for restitution that they have (and apparently have asserted) against Steven's estate. They may not seek restitution out of the trust fund, even if their allegation that the estate lacks sufficient assets to meet this claim were factually supported, because the trust fund was not the property of Steven, except to the extent of his life estate, so as to be subject to the equitable remedy of restitution, but was the property of the donor of the power of appointment until it vested in someone else. (Farmers' Loan & Trust Co. v Mortimer, 219 NY 290, 295, supra; see Matter of Rosenthal, 283 App Div 316, 319; see, also, EPTL 10-7.1 and 10-7.4.)

* * *

Accordingly, on the motions for summary judgment I direct judgment declaring that defendant Edith Fisch Werner is entitled to the one-half share of Steven C. Werner in the principal of the Abraham L. Werner trust; to the extent that the counterclaims and cross claims asserted by Harriet, Anna and Frank seek relief other than a declaratory judgment, they are dismissed.

California Probate Code (2004)

Section 661. Release of discretionary power.

(a) Unless the creating instrument otherwise provides, a general or special power of appointment that is a discretionary power, whether testamentary or otherwise, may be released, either with or without consideration, by a written instrument signed by the donee and delivered as provided in subsection (c).

Tax Considerations: I.R.C. § 2514(b): "The exercise or release of a general power of appointment created after October 21, 1942, shall be deemed a transfer of property by the individual possessing such power." It is possible to disclaim any general power of appointment and thus avoid taxability. Nonetheless, the disclaimer must be in writing, received by the transferor of the interest, his or her legal representative, or the holder of the legal title to the property to which the interest relates not later than that date which is 9 months after the later of the day on which the transfer creating the interest is made, or the day on which such person attains the age of 21. I.R.C. § 2518(b).

F. Rights of Creditors

Irwin Union Bank & Trust Co. v. Long

Indiana Court of Appeals, 1974
160 Ind. App. 509, 312 N.E.2d 908

LOWDERMILK, Judge.

On February 3, 1957, Victoria Long, appellee herein, obtained a judgment in the amount of $15,000 against Philip W. Long, which judgment emanated from a divorce decree. This action is the result of the filing by appellee of a petition in proceedings supplemental to execution on the prior judgment. Appellee sought satisfaction of that judgment by pursuing funds allegedly owed to Philip W. Long as a result of a trust set up by Laura Long, his mother.

Appellee alleged that the Irwin Union Bank and Trust Company (Union Bank) was indebted to Philip W. Long as the result of its position as trustee of the trust created by Laura Long. On April 24, 1969, the trial court ordered that any income, property, or profits, which were owed to Philip Long and not exempt from execution should be applied to the divorce judgment. Thereafter, on February 13, 1973, the trial court ordered that four percent (4%) of the trust corpus of the trust created by Laura Long which benefited Philip Long was not exempt from execution and could be levied upon by appellee and ordered a writ of execution. Union Bank, as trustee, filed its motion to set aside the writ of execution. Said motion was overruled by the trial court, whereupon Union Bank filed its motion to correct errors, which was by the court overruled.

The pertinent portion of the trust created by Laura Long is as follows, to-wit:

* * *

Withdrawal of Principal.

When Philip W. Long, Jr. has attained the age of twenty-one (21) years and is not a full-time student at an educational institution as a candidate for a Bachelor of Arts or Bachelor of Sciences degree, Philip W. Long shall have the right to withdraw from principal once in any calendar year upon thirty (30) days written notice to the Trustee up to four percent (4%) of the market value of the entire trust principal on the date of such notice, which right shall not be cumulative; provided, however, that the amount distributable hereunder shall not be in excess of the market value of the assets of the trust on the date of such notice other than interests in real estate.

The primary issue raised on this appeal is whether the trial court erred in allowing execution on the 4% of the trust corpus.

Appellant contends that Philip Long's right to withdraw 4% of the trust corpus is, in fact, a general power of appointment. Union Bank further contends that since Philip Long has never exercised his right of withdrawal, pursuant to the provisions of the trust instrument, no creditors of Philip Long can reach the trust corpus. Appellant points out that if the power of appointment is unexercised, the creditors cannot force the exercise of said power and cannot reach the trust corpus in this case.

Appellee posits that the condition precedent to Philip Long's right of withdrawal has been met and therefore Philip Long has an absolute right to the present enjoyment of 4% of the trust corpus simply by making a written request to the trustee. Appellee contends that this is a vested right and is consistent with the intentions of the donor, Laura Long. Appellee further contends in her brief that the right of withdrawal is not a power of appointment, but is, rather, a power of augmentation and relies upon the Restatement of the Law of Property, § 318, which reads as follows, to-wit:

Definition—Power of Appointment.

(1) Except as stated in Subsection (2), a power of appointment, as the term is used in this Restatement, is a power created or reserved by a person (the donor) having property subject to his disposition enabling the donee of the power to designate, within such limits as the donor may prescribe, the transferees of the property or the shares in which it shall be received.

(2) The term power of appointment does not include a power of sale, a power of attorney, a power of revocation, a power to cause a gift of income to

be augmented out of principal, a power to designate charities, a charitable trust, a discretionary trust, or an honorary trust.'

However, in oral argument, appellee stated that the label that is put on the provision of the trust instrument is immaterial.

It is the position of appellee that if the right of withdrawal is not a power of appointment under §318, supra, then the cases and authorities relied upon by appellant which relate to powers of appointment will not be in point.

Appellee also argues that Philip has absolute control and use of the 4% of the corpus and that the bank does not have control over that portion of the corpus if Philip decides to exercise his right of withdrawal. Appellee argues that the intention of Laura Long was to give Philip not only an income interest in the trust but a fixed amount of corpus which he could use as he saw fit. Thus, Philip Long would have a right to the present enjoyment of 4% of the trust corpus. A summation of appellee's argument, as stated in her brief, is as follows: 'So it is with Philip—he can get it if he desires it, so why cannot Victoria get it even if Philip does not desire it?'

We have had no Indiana authority directly in point cited to us by either of the parties and a thorough research of this issue does not reveal any Indiana authority on point. Thus, this issue so far as we can determine is one of first impression in Indiana.

The distinction which appellee seeks to rely upon based on the Restatement of the Law of Property in regard to a power of augmentation is apparently such a distinction only in that authority. We have found no cases or treatises which follow the distinction made in the Restatement. We have found one treatise which expressly refutes the distinction between a power of appointment and a power of augmentation, as set out in the Restatement. Appleman, Basic Estate Planning, Ch. XVI, p. 696, discusses the Restatement distinction as follows:

> The 'Definitions' section of the Restatement of the Law of Property says: 'The term power of appointment does not include * * * a power of revocation, a power to cause a gift of income to be augmented out of principal, * * * a discretionary trust * * *.' Today, for estate and gift tax purposes and consequently for estate planning purposes, this statement must be virtually disregarded.

Further, appellee has failed to point out exactly how the distinction made in the Restatement would affect the case at bar. Appellee cites no authority which says that an unexercised power of augmentation can be reached by creditors.

Appellant, for the sake of argument, conceded that even if the trust language was a power of augmentation, the same rules would be in effect in this case as they would apply to creditors.

Broadly speaking, a power is said to be general if it can be exercised in favor of anyone whom the donee may select. A power is defined in Thompson on Real Property, 1961 Repl., Future Interests, §2025, as follows:

> §2025. What a 'power' is.—Broadly stated, a 'power' is an authority enabling one person to dispose of an interest which is vested in another. It is an authority reserved by or limited to one to do certain acts in relation to the subject matter of the gift for his own benefit or for the benefit of another. The word 'power,' as defined by the Restatement of the Law of Property, 'is an ability on the part of a person to produce a change in a given legal relation by

doing or not doing a given act.' It is an authority to do some act in relation to lands, or the creation of estates therein, or of charges thereon, which the owner granting or reserving such power, might himself lawfully perform.

* * *

Powers are either general or special. They are general when they are capable of being exercised by the donee in favor of any person, including himself, and are not restricted as to the estate or interest over which he may exercise the power, while the power is special if its exercise is restricted to particular persons, or a particular class of persons, or if it can by exercised only for certain named purposes or under certain conditions. The donee under a general power has an absolute disposing power over the estate; but where he cannot exercise the power for his own benefit during his lifetime, the power is not general....

In the case of In Re Kuttler's Estate (1958), 160 Cal.App.2d 332, 337, 325 P.2d 624, 628, 629, a power of appointment was defined as follows:

A power of appointment, which may be created by deed or by will, is defined, generally, as a power or authority given to a person to dispose of property, or an interest therein, which is vested in a person other than the donee of the power.

The Supreme Court of Texas, in the case of Republic National Bank of Dallas v. Fredericks (1955), 155 Tex. 79, 88, 283 S.W.2d 39, 46, discussed and defined power of appointment and stated:

Subject to certain restrictions, the common law accords to the individual a right to delegate to another person the power of designating or selecting the takers of his property. The authority thus to control the disposition of the estate of the grantor or testator is referred to as a 'power of appointment.'

* * *

'A power of appointment is a power of disposition given to a person over property not his own, by some one who directs the mode in which that power shall be exercised by a particular instrument. It is an authority to do an act which the owner granting the power might himself lawfully perform.' Thompson on Wills, 3rd Ed., p. 596, Sec. 400.

See, also, Commissioner of Internal Revenue v. Walston (4 Cir., 1948), 168 F.2d 211.

An examination of the pertinent parts of the trust created by Laura Long indicates that the power which was given to Philip Long in Item V C falls under the definition of power of appointment, as set out above. Philip Long may exercise the power which was delegated to him by Laura Long, that being to distribute property not his own. It is obvious that Laura Long would have had the same power to dispose of her property as that given to Philip Long, had Laura Long decided to dispose of her property in such a manner.

A reading of Item V C, supra, does not disclose any direct reference to a power of appointment. However, it is not necessary that the actual words 'power of appointment' be used in order to create such a power.

In the case of Estate of Rosecrans (1971), 4 Cal.3d 34, 92 Cal.Rptr. 680, 480 P.2d 296, it was held that no particular form of words is necessary to create a power of appointment. In In Re Kuttler's Estate, supra, the court said: 'No particular form of words is necessary to the creation of such a power.' Thompson on Real Property, supra, § 2025, states:

No particular form or words is necessary for the creation of a power; any expression, however, informal, is sufficient if it clearly indicates an intention to give a power. Where the intention to create the power is plain, it should be given effect. All that is necessary is an indication of a clear intention to accomplish some proper purpose by the donor through the donee. It may be conferred by express words, or may be necessarily implied....

Appellee contends that the right of withdrawal of Philip Long is a vested property right rather than a power of appointment. However, it is our opinion that such is not the case. This problem was discussed in 62 Am.Jur.2d, Powers, § 107, p. 206, as follows:

> * * * Creating a general power of appointment is virtually an offer to the donee of the estate or fund that he may receive or reject at will, and like any other offer to donate property to a person, no title can vest until he accepts the offer, nor can a court of equity compel him to accept the property or fund against his will, even for the benefit of creditors.

The leading case on this issue is Gilman v. Bell (1881), 99 Ill. 144, 150, 151, wherein the Illinois Supreme Court discussed powers of appointment and vesting as follows:

> * * * No title or interest in the thing vests in the donee of the power until he exercises the power. It is virtually an offer to him of the estate or fund, that the may receive or reject at will, and like any other offer to donate property to a person, no title can vest until he accepts the offer, nor can a court of equity compel him to accept the property or fund against his will, even for the benefit of creditors. If it should, it would be to convert the property of the person offering to make the donation to the payment of the debts of another person. Until accepted, the person to whom the offer is made has not, nor can he have, the slightest interest or title to the property. So the donee of the power only receives the naked power to make the property or fund his own. And when he exercises the power, he thereby consents to receive it, and the title thereby vests in him, although it may pass out of him *eo instanti*, to the appointee....

See, also, 59 A.L.R. 1510.

In the case of Shattuck v. Burrage (1918), 229 Mass. 449, 118 N.E. 889, it was held that:

> * * * When a donor gives to another power of appointment over property, the donee of the power does not thereby become the owner of the property. The donee has no title whatever to the property. The power is simply a delegation to the donee of authority to act for the donor in the disposition of the latter's property.... The right to exercise the power is not property and cannot be reached by creditors.... On no theory of hard fact is the property appointed the property of the donee of the power....

Contrary to the contention of appellee, it is our opinion that Philip Long has no control over the trust corpus until he exercises his power of appointment and gives notice to the trustee that he wishes to receive his 4% of the trust corpus. Until such an exercise is made, the trustee has the absolute control and benefit of the trust corpus within the terms of the trust instrument.

While not controlling as precedent, we find that the Federal Estate Tax laws are quite analogous to the case at bar. Under § 2041, Powers of Appointment, of the Internal Revenue Code, it is clear that the interest given to Philip Long under Item V C would be considered a power of appointment for estate tax purposes. A general power of appointment is defined in §2041(b)(1) as follows:

> (1) General power of appointment.—The term 'general power of appointment' means a power which is exercisable in favor of the decedent, his estate, his creditors, or the creditors of his estate; ...

The regulations pertinent to this issue discuss a power of appointment as it is used for estate tax purposes as follows:

> (b) Definition of 'power of appointment' (1) In general. The term 'power of appointment' includes all powers which are in substance and effect powers of appointment regardless of the nomenclature used in creating the power and regardless of local property law connotations. For example, if a trust instrument provides that the beneficiary may appropriate or consume the principal of the trust, the power to consume or appropriate is a power of appointment.... 20.2041–1(b)(1).

For estate tax purposes even the failure to exercise a power of appointment may lead to tax consequences. Under §2041(b)(2) the lapse of a power of appointment will be considered a release of such power during the calendar year to the extent of the value of the power in question. However, the lapsed power will only be considered a release and includable in the gross estate of a decedent if the value of the lapsed power is greater than $5,000 or 5% of the aggregate value of the assets out of which the lapsed power could have been satisfied.

The trust instrument was obviously carefully drawn with the tax consequences bearing an important place in the overall intent of the testator. The trust as a whole is set up to give the grandchildren of Laura Long the substantial portion of the assets involved. We note with interest that the percentage of corpus which Philip Long may receive is carefully limited to a percentage less than that which would be includable in the gross estate of Philip Long should he die within a year in which he had allowed his power of appointment to lapse.

It is elementary that courts will seek to ascertain the intention of the testator by giving a full consideration to the entire will. See 29 I.L.E. Wills, §174. The trust created in the will of Laura Long, in our opinion, has the legal effect of creating a power of appointment in Philip Long under Item V C of the trust.

Philip Long has never exercised his power of appointment under the trust. Such a situation is discussed in II Scott on Trusts, §147.3 as follows:

> * * * Where the power is a special power, a power to appoint only among a group of persons, the power is not beneficial to the donee and cannot, of course, be reached by his creditors. Where the power is a general power, that is, a power to appoint to anyone including the donee himself or his estate, the power is beneficial to the donee. If the donee exercises the power by appointing to a volunteer, the property appointed can be reached by his creditors if his other assets are insufficient for the payment of his debts. But where the donee of a general power created by some person other than himself fails to exercise the power, his creditors cannot acquire the power or compel its exercise, nor can they reach the property covered by the power, unless it is otherwise provided by statute....

Indiana has no statute which would authorize a creditor to reach property covered by a power of appointment which is unexercised.

In Gilman v. Bell, supra, the court analyzed the situation where a general power of appointment was unexercised and discussed the position of creditors of the donee of the power as follows:

> But it is insisted, that, conceding it to be a mere naked power of appointment in favor of himself, in favor of creditors he should be compelled by a court of equity to so appoint, or be treated as the owner, and the property subjected to the payment of his debts. The doctrine has been long established in the English courts, that the courts of equity will not aid creditors in case there is a non-execution of the power....

The creditors' rights against an unexercised power of appointment was also discussed in 62 Am.Jur.2d, Powers, § 107, as follows:

> It is established by the great weight of authority, and may be regarded as settled, that an unexercised general power of appointment does not render the property subject thereto equitable assets of the donee, nor make it liable for his debts or the debts of his estate, although his own property is insufficient to pay them....

See, also, Quinn v. Tuttle (1962), 104 N.H. 1, 177 A.2d 391.

Appellee concedes that if we find that Philip Long had merely an unexercised power of appointment then creditors are in no position to either force the exercise of the power or to reach the trust corpus. Thus, it is clear that the trial court erred when it overruled appellant's motion to set aside the writ of execution.

Having found reversible error on the primary issue, it is unnecessary for this court to discuss other issues raised in this appeal.

Reversed and remanded.

ROBERTSON, P. J., and LYBROOK, J., concur.

Notes

As the original owner of the appointment, the Donor is responsible to any and all creditors of the Donor only. The issue for consideration is the Donee's responsibility to the Donee's creditors, and whether the appointment may be used to satisfy those responsibilities. The liability of the Donee to his or her creditors will depend on the power given by the Donor. Obviously, the more power given to the Donee, the more likely will the creditors of the Donee be able to reach the appointment. Consider the following possibilities.

1. General inter vivos power of appointment. Other than if the Donor gave to the Donee outright, with no power attached at all, this is an extensive delegation of power over the appointment, and the creditors of the Donee should always be able to reach the appointment after the personal property of the Donee has been exhausted. *See, e.g.,* CAL. PROB. CODE § 682 (2004). In addition, any general inter vivos power is included in the bankruptcy estate of the Donee during the Donee's lifetime. *See* 11 U.S.C. § 541(b)(1) (2004).

2. General testamentary power of appointment. New York does not permit the creditors of a Donee of a general testamentary power of appointment to reach assets. *See* N.Y. EST., POWERS & TRUSTS L. §§ 10-7.2 & 10-7.4 (1998) (2004). Nonetheless, if the

Donor and the Donee are the same persons, creditors may reach the appointment. *See Restatement (Third) of Property: Donative Transfers* , § 21.3, (Prelim. Draft No. 4, 1995).

3. Special powers, inter vivos and testamentary. Because very little delegation has been given by the Donor to the Donee, creditors of the Donee may not reach the appointment. *See, e.g.,* Cal. Prob. Code § 681 (2004).

4. Spouses. A spouse's claim for support is treated as if it were a creditor's claim. *See, e.g.,* Cal. Prob. Code § 684 (2004). Nonetheless, if a Donee possesses a general testamentary power of appointment, the power is available for inclusion within the augmented estate of the decedent. *See* Unif. Prob. Code § 2-205(1)(I) (2003).

VII. The Rule Against Perpetuities

A. Public Policy

The late Jesse Dukeminier, a renowned professor of both property law and decedents' estates, introduced his casebook material on the Rule Against Perpetuities with an evolution of historical English statutes, commencing with the Statute de Donis (1285), through the decision of the Duke of Norfolk's Case (1682), and the classic law review article by Professor W. Barton Leach, *Perpetuities in a Nutshell*, 51 Harv. L. Rev. 638 (1938). Professor Dukeminier included in his discussion photographs of the Sixth Duke of Norfolk and the First Earl of Nottingham, and, as was his trademark, a few bons mots to capture the background of a duke's beheading and the lament over deadhand control of property. *See* Jesse Dukeminier, Stanley M. Johanson, James Lindgren and Robert H. Sitkoff, Wills, Trusts, and Estates 673 (7th ed. 2005). Any student of decedents' estates soon realized that what was to follow was not a legal bump in the road, but rather a doctrine with lengthy roots in the law's attempt to limit perpetuities, entails, dead hand control, restrictions on land, and family advantage. Modern students might even have seen in the Rule Against Perpetuities an egalitarian tool to foster marketability of property at each generation and a curative device to refashion trust purposes to accommodate present changed circumstances. *See generally* Jesse Dukeminier, *A Modern Guide to Perpetuities*, 74 Cal. L. Rev.1867 (1986); *Restatement (Second) of Property, Donative Transfers*, Pt. 1, Introductory Note (1983); Jesse Dukeminier & James E. Krier, Property 291 (4th ed. 1998).

At its core, the Rule Against Perpetuities is a rule of public policy limiting the ability of persons to control both real and personal property to accommodate private purposes. For example, a Settlor may not prohibit in perpetuity the family home from being sold; a parent may not prohibit in perpetuity alienation of a private trust income and corpus; a private company may not be controlled dynastically throughout successive generations. The law sought to make certain that, within a reasonable time, some person would own a fee simple interest in property not burdened by any trust and, thus, be able to sell, encumber, or re-trust the property in accordance with current objectives. To accomplish this, the law crafted a device to confine all contingent remainders and executory interests created in transferees to a human life in being, plus twenty-one years. If there is any possibility that a contingency may occur to allow vesting to occur in anyone not a life in being, now or within twenty-one years, the entire trust will fail. Often the Rule resulted in the inadvertent termination of trusts because of poor drafting by attorneys, *see, e.g.*, Lucas v. Hamm, 56 Cal.2d 583, 364 P.2d 685 (1961), judicial wizardry, as courts sought to salvage a Settlor's intent, *see, e.g.*, Second National Bank of New Haven v. Harris Trust & Savings Bank, 29 Conn. Supp. 275, 283 A.2d 226 (Sup. Ct. 1971)(decrying "exaltation of verbalism over substance"), or, more recently, judicial and legislative reform devices, *see, e.g.*, 20 PA. STAT. ANN. § 301.4-5 (1950) (wait and see doctrine). More than half of the states have adopted the Uniform Statutory Rule Against Perpetuities (1990), now adopted as Part 9 of the Uniform Probate Code (1990). And in a remarkable break with the past, some states have abolished the Rule completely, often with the avowed goal of providing a mechanism to create dynasty trusts. *See* Joel C. Dobris, *The Death of the Rule Against Perpetuities, or the RAP Has No Friends*, 35 Real PROP, PROB. & TRUST J. 601 (2000); Jesse Dukeminier, *Dynasty Trusts: Sheltering Descendants From Transfer Taxes*, 23 EST. PLAN. 417 (1996).

The evolution of the Rule places a burden on the practitioner of estate planning and administration who seeks to provide competent representation amidst shifting legal parameters. But even greater stakes are involved. The Rule is a public policy formulation providing a limit on private trusts. In their eagerness to abolish the Rule, states within the twenty-first century also abolish the public policy that spawned it. Permeating the following material is the issue of what will occur if the Rule is abolished.

B. Statement of the Rule

The classic statement of the Rule, culled from the accumulations of centuries, was formulated by John Chipman Gray: "No interest is good unless it must vest, if at all, not later than twenty-one years after some life in being at the creation of the interest." JOHN C. GRAY. THE RULE AGAINST PERPETUITIES 191 (4th ed. 1942). Since the Rule applies to all future interests created within testamentary trusts and inter vivos trusts, it is assumed that the trust and the instrument in which it is written are valid under the proper rules applicable to formalities and intentionalities. If so, we progress to the elements of the Rule itself. First, please note the phrase "life in being," used in Professor Chipman's formulation. A life in being must be a human life, hence the concern over honorary trusts and vesting to occur upon the death of a pet—a non-human life. *See* UNIF. PROB. CODE § 2-907 (2004). The life in being may also be a life in gestation, not yet born but able to postpone vesting through the future interest created because, simply by being conceived, the life is treated as being in existence at the creation of the interest. Second, these lives in being may also be what are called "measuring lives." A measuring life is that person or persons, upon whose death or the occurrence of an event, vesting will occur. For example, Settlor creates a testamentary trust and writes: "One-million dollars to my grandchildren, to be paid only if she or he turns twenty-one." The Settlor has created a contingent interest—the grandchild takes only IF the grandchild turns twenty-one. If no grandchild turns twenty-one, the corpus of the trust reverts to the Settlor's estate. Note that the grandchild is a measuring life because, when the grandchild turns twenty-one, there is an occurrence of an event that brings about vesting. *See generally* David M. Becker, *A Methodology for Solving Perpetuities Problems Under the Common Law Rule: A Step-by-Step Process That Carefully Identifies All Testing Lives in Being*, 67 WASH. U. L. REV. 949 (1989); Jesse Dukeminier, *Perpetuities: The Measuring Lives*, 85 COLUM. L. REV.

1648, 1665–74 (1985). Professor Dukeminier suggested that the statement of the Rule should be re-formulated to require vesting after the death of all persons in being when the interest is created who can affect the vesting of the interest. *Id.* at 1713. It is important to be able to identify both of these terms and then apply them in the following question: Standing at the creation of the instrument, is there any possibility that any interest will not vest within a life in being plus twenty-one years? If the answer is yes, the Rule is violated.

1. *Standing at the Creation of the Instrument*

Creation is when the instrument speaks. There are three possibilities: (1) a valid Last Will and Testament speaks at the death of the Testator, not when the Will is executed; (2) in a valid inter vivos trust that is revocable, nothing begins in perpetuity until the death of the Settlor or whenever the Settlor can no longer revoke the trust instrument. If the inter vivos trust is irrevocable (recall that most jurisdictions make all trusts irrevocable unless the trust expressly says otherwise), creation is when the trust is created by the Settlor, not when the Settlor dies or surrenders any power; (3) according to the rules applicable to powers of appointment, if a Donor of a power of appointment creates any power other than a general inter vivos power in a Donee, under the relation back doctrine, any exercise by the Donee must be read back into the creation of the power by the Donor. We will see examples of this relation back doctrine as we progress through the material. For the present, identify the issue in the following decision.

Cook v. Horn
Supreme Court of Georgia, 1958
214 Ga. 289, 104 S.E.2d 461

WYATT, Presiding Justice.

It is first contended that, under the provisions of the trust instrument, the petitioners take a fee-simple interest in the trust fund rather than a life interest, and that, being sui juris and not spendthrifts (it being conceded by all parties that Code, § 108-111.1 does not apply to this instrument), the trust is executed and the petitioners are entitled to have the corpus of the trust distributed to them. While there is language in certain paragraphs of the trust agreement which by themselves could be construed to enlarge the gift to these petitioners into a fee simple interest, a consideration of all the instrument discloses that this was not the settlor's intent. He provided that the trust should be divided into as many parts as he had children, and that each child was to receive the proceeds from his or her trust for and during his or her natural life. This, without more, would, under the law prior to the enactment of Code, § 108-111.1, amount to a gift of a fee-simple interest, the petitioners being sui juris and not spendthrifts. However, the settlor then provided remainders to the issue of his children upon the death of said children, and he set out in detail how the remainders were to be paid and administered. The language appearing in paragraphs F, G, and H of section V. considered in connection with the section V, considered in connection with the clearly apparent intention of the settlor as determined from the whole instrument. Accordingly, as is held above, the petitioners took a life interest in the corpus of the trust estate with remainders to their issue, and the trusts are executory since the remaindermen will not be determined until the petitioners die.

It is next contended that the instrument in question violates the rule against perpetuities, and that since the limitations beyond the petitioners are void, they are entitled to have the property delivered to them. In order to determine this question, it is necessary first to determine when this instrument took effect, whether at the time it was executed and delivered, or at the death of the settlor. This question is settled by the decision of this court in Wilson v. Fulton National Bank, 188 Ga. 691, 4 S.E.2d 660, where an instrument similar in all material respects to that here under consideration was held to create a valid trust, to convey a present interest, and not to be testamentary in character.

It is contended that, if the trust instrument is effective to convey a present interest at the time it was executed and delivered, as is held above, then the limitations beyond the petitioners are void as violative of the rule against perpetuities, because there was a possibility at that time that the settlor would have additional children born to him thereafter, by whose life the duration of the trust would be limited. This result does not necessarily follow. While there is a scarcity of authority on this question, and none that we have found in Georgia, the prevailing opinion by both the courts of other jurisdictions and recognized text writers is that, when a settlor has the power during his lifetime to revoke or destroy the trust estate for his own exclusive personal benefit, the question whether interests, or any of them, created by an instrument or deed of trust are void because in violation of the rule against perpetuities, is to be determined as of the date of the settlor's death and not as of the date the instrument is executed and delivered. * * * [Citations omitted].

While none of these authorities is binding upon this court, the conclusion reached by them is in accord with the aim of and reason for the rule against perpetuities, which is to prevent the tying up of property for an unreasonable length of time and to prohibit unreasonable restraint upon the alienation of property. So long as the settlor of an inter vivos trust has the absolute right to revoke or terminate the trust for his own exclusive personal benefit, there is no tying up of property and no restraint upon the alienability of the property in the trust fund, and thus no reason to include this time during which the trust is so destructible in determining whether a limitation is violative of the rule against perpetuities. Restatement, Property, sec. 373 states: 'The period of time during which an interest is destructible, pursuant to the uncontrolled volition, and for the exclusive personal benefit of the person having such a power of destruction is not included in determining whether the limitation is invalid under the rule against perpetuities.' We conclude that this rule is a sound one, which does no violence to the rule against perpetuities, but is in complete accord with its aim and purpose.

In the instant case, the settlor, during his lifetime, had an absolute right to revoke or terminate the trust, to change the beneficiaries in the policies, and to receive any and all benefits under the policies. Therefore, under the rulings above made, the time from which it will be determined whether any of the limitations in the trust agreement are void for remoteness is the date of the settlor's death. When so considered, it is apparent that none of the limitations in the instrument violate the rule against perpetuities, since all limitations under the instrument will end and all interests vest within twenty-one years after the death of the settlor's children plus the usual period of gestation, and, of course, no children can be born to the settlor after his death plus the usual period of gestation. It follows, the limitations over to the issue of the children of the settlor are valid, and the petitioners are not entitled to have the trust terminated for any reason alleged. The judgment of the court below dismissing the petition on general demurrer was therefore not error.

Judgment affirmed.

All the Justices concur.

2. Is There Any Possibility?

If there is any possibility that any interest will not vest within a life in being, plus twenty-one years, the Rule is violated. Remember that actuality is not what matters to the Rule; rather, possibility—logical possibility to be precise—is what matters. Thus, we are concerned with what might happen with the measuring lives if they are the persons upon whom the contingency depends. For example, if a Testator were to provide in a valid Last Will and Testament the following: "One-million dollars to my children if any one of them turns twenty-five." The date of creation is the death of the Testator. In addition, let us say that there are three children and that all are over the age of four. Therefore, all are in existence; no one is in gestation. We know that the measuring lives are the children because one of them must turn twenty-five to meet the condition of vesting. And since the event of turning twenty-five must occur within the lives of the lives in being (the children), and the event must occur within twenty-one years, there is no violation of the Rule. But, on the other hand, if the interest were created in an irrevocable trust, and the Settlor were still alive and able to have additional children, then the Rule would be violated. In that case, the date of creation would be the creation of the trust by the Settlor. The *possibility* that the Settlor could then have a child, who would be a measuring life (to turn 25) but is not a life in being, creates the possibility that the child will turn twenty-five more than twenty-one years after any life in being. If the Settlor were unable to have children, then this would not be a possibility, and there would be no violation of the Rule. We can review possibilities in the following examples.

a. Afterborn Measuring Lives

Dickerson v. Union National Bank of Little Rock

Supreme Court of Arkansas, 1980
268 Ark. 292, 595 S.W.2d 677

GEORGE ROSE SMITH, Justice.

The principal question on this appeal is whether a trust created by the holographic will of Nina Martin Dickerson, who died on June 21, 1967, is void under the rule against perpetuities, because it is possible that the interest of the various beneficiaries may not vest within the period allowed by that rule. Cecil H. Dickerson, Jr., one of the testatrix's two sons, attacks the validity of the trust. The chancellor rejected Cecil's attack on two grounds: First, Cecil should have raised the question of the validity of the trust in the probate court in connection with the probate of the will and the administration of the estate. His failure to do so makes the issue res judicata. Second, on the merits, the trust does not violate the rule against perpetuities. We disagree with the chancellor on both grounds.

The facts are not in dispute. The testatrix was survived by her two children. Cecil, 50, was single, and Martin, 45, was married. At that time the two sons had a total of seven children, who of course were the testatrix's grandchildren.

The testatrix named the appellee bank as executor and directed that at the close of the administration proceedings the bank transfer to itself as trustee all the assets of the estate. The terms of the trust are quite long, but we may summarize them as follows:

The trust is to continue until the death of both sons and of Martin's widow, *who is not otherwise identified.* The income is to be divided equally between the two sons during their lives, except that Cecil's share is to be used in part to provide for a four-year college education for his two minor children, who are named, and for the support and education of any bodily heirs by a later marriage. When the two named minor children finish college, their share of the income is to revert to Cecil. Upon Martin's death his share of the income is to be paid monthly to his widow and children living in the home, but the share of each child terminates and passes to the widow when that child marries or becomes self-supporting. The trustee is given discretionary power to make advance payments of principal in certain cases of emergency or illness. If either son and his wife and all his bodily heirs die before the final distribution of the trust assets, that son's share in the estate and in the income passes to the other son and then to his bodily heirs.

As far as the rule against perpetuities is concerned, the important part of the will is paragraph VIII, from which we quote:

> VIII. This Trust shall continue until the death of both my sons and my son Martin's widow and until the youngest child of either son has reached the age of twenty-five years, then at that time, the Trust shall terminate and the Union National Bank Trustee shall distribute and pay over the entire balance of the Trust Fund in their hands to the bodily heirs of my son, Cecil H. Dickerson, and the bodily heirs of my son, William Martin Dickerson, in the same manner and in the same proportions as provided for by the general inheritance laws of Arkansas.

Upon the death of the testatrix in 1967, her will was presented to the Faulkner Probate Court by her son Cecil, who lived in Conway, Arkansas. (The other son, Martin, was living in Indiana.) The probate court entered a routine order reciting that the will had been properly executed, admitting the instrument to probate, and appointing the bank as executor, without bond. On May 31, 1968, the probate court entered another routine order approving the executor's first and final accounting, allowing fees to the executor and its attorneys, discharging the executor, and closing the administration of the estate. That order made no reference to the validity of the trust or to the manner in which the assets of the estate were to be distributed.

In fact, the assets of the estate, except for $18,000 set aside for administration expenses and estate taxes, had already been transferred by the bank to itself as trustee. On August 11, 1967, about a month after the probate of the will, the bank filed in the Faulkner Chancery Court an ex parte "Declaration of Trust," in which the bank expressed its desire to perform the trust and asked the court to find and decree that it held the property in trust for the beneficiaries of the testamentary trust. No notice of that filing appears to have been given to anyone. On September 1, 1967, the bank filed a petition in the same ex parte case, asking for an interpretation of the will with respect to the distribution of income derived from capital gains. The court directed the bank to give notice of that petition to all persons interested in the trust estate. Counsel for the trustee certified that such notice of the hearing on the petition for interpretation had been given. On October 4 the chancery court entered an order reciting the appearance of the bank only, finding that the bank had been appointed as administrator of the estate and as trustee of the trust, authorizing the bank to transfer all the real and personal property (except $18,000) to the trust estate, and instructing the trustee as to the proper treatment of capital gains as trust income.

Nothing further appears to have taken place in the case until 1977, when Cecil Dickerson filed in the same proceeding the present complaint against the bank and its trust officer. The complaint, after reciting the background facts, asserts that the trust is void under the rule against perpetuities. The complaint charges the trust officer with violations of his fiduciary duties in failing to deliver all the assets of the estate to the heirs of the testatrix and in failing to ask the probate court to construe the will with respect to violations of the rule against perpetuities. The complaint charges that the trust officer concealed the trust's defects from the court and from the testatrix's two sons. The prayer is for an order restraining the trustee from making further transfers or distributions of the trust funds, for recovery of Cecil's half interest in the estate, for compensatory and punitive damages, and for other proper relief. The charges of negligence and wrongdoing on the part of the bank were later dismissed without prejudice. The other matters were heard upon stipulated facts, culminating in the decree dismissing Cecil's complaint on the two grounds we have mentioned.

First, there is no merit in the argument that Cecil's failure to challenge the validity of the trust in the probate proceedings precludes him from raising that issue now. Under the Probate Code the probate court does have the power to construe a will, but the construction must be necessary to the determination of some issue properly before the court. Ark.Stat.Ann. §60-416 (Repl.1971). Here the probate court made no pertinent decisions except that Mrs. Dickerson's will had been properly executed and that at the end of the administration proceeding the estate should be closed. There was not even an order of distribution, because the trust assets had already been transferred by the bank to itself with the ex parte approval of the chancery court. Just as we said in an earlier case: "The (probate) court was not called upon to determine the validity of the fourth paragraph in Collie's will, for a decision of that issue was not essential to a distribution of the estate." Collie v. Tucker, 229 Ark. 606, 317 S.W.2d 137 (1958).

The doctrine of res judicata is based on the assumption that a litigant has already had his day in court. For that reason it applies to matters that were necessarily within the issues and might have been litigated in the former suit. Crump v. Loggains, 212 Ark. 394, 205 S.W.2d 846 (1947); Robertson v. Evans, 180 Ark. 420, 21 S.W.2d 610 (1929). Here the validity of the trust was not such a matter. The complications that may be presented by the rule against perpetuities are so numerous and difficult that even experienced lawyers and judges must usually consult the authorities to be certain about its application to a given set of facts. There was not the slightest reason for Cecil or Martin Dickerson to suspect a possible invalidity in their mother's testamentary trust, nor any duty on their part to raise such a question. To deprive them of their property on the basis of res judicata would actually be to deny them their day in court.

Indeed, if there was any duty on anyone to raise the issue, that duty rested on the bank. It was a fiduciary, both as executor and as trustee. It owed a duty of good faith and loyalty to all the beneficiaries of the estate and of the trust and a duty to act impartially as between successive beneficiaries. Restatement of Trusts (2d), §§ 170 and 232 (1959), and Arkansas Annotations (1939) to those sections. We do not imply any wrongdoing on the part of this appellee, but it is certainly not in a position to ignore the possible invalidity of the trust both in the probate court and in the ex parte chancery court case and then take advantage, to its own pecuniary benefit, of the beneficiaries' similar course of conduct. A contrary rule would compel the beneficiaries of an estate or trust to hire a lawyer to watch the executor or trustee, when the law actually permits them to rely upon the fiduciary.

Second, the trust is void because there is a possibility that the estate will not vest within a period measured by a life or lives in being at the testatrix's death, plus 21 years. A bare possibility is enough. "The interest must vest within the time allowed by the rule. If there is any possibility that the contingent event may happen beyond the limits of the rule, the transaction is void." Comstock v. Smith, 255 Ark. 564, 501 S.W.2d 617 (1973).

The terms of this trust present an instance of the "unborn widow," a pitfall that is familiar to every student of the rule against perpetuities. This trust is not to terminate until the deaths of Cecil, Martin, and Martin's widow, but the identity of Martin's widow cannot be known until his death. Martin might marry an 18-year-old woman twenty years after his mother's death, have additional children by her, and then die. Cecil also might die. Martin's young widow, however, might live for another 40 or 50 years, after which the interests would finally vest. But since Cecil and Martin would have been the last measuring lives in being at the death of the testatrix, the trust property would not vest until many years past the maximum time allowed by the rule. The rule was formulated to prevent just such a possibility uncertainty about the title to real or personal property for an unreasonably long time in the future.

The violation of the rule, except for the interposition of a trust, is actually so clear that the appellee does not argue the point. Instead, it insists that the property would vest in Cecil and Martin's bodily heirs at their deaths, with only the right of possession of the property being deferred until the termination of the trust.

This argument overlooks the fact that the words "bodily heirs" were used in the decisive paragraph VIII of the will not as words of limitation, to specify the duration of an estate granted to Cecil and Martin, but as words of purchase, to specify the persons who would take at the termination of the trust. Obviously the identity of those persons cannot be determined until the death of Martin's widow; so the ownership would not vest until that time.

A vested remainder, simply stated, is a present interest that cannot be defeated by any contingency. Such an interest can be transferred by deed, by will, or by inheritance, even though the right of possession may not accrue until some time in the future. The simplest example is a conveyance or devise to A for life, remainder to B. Since A must eventually die, B's remainder is a present vested interest which cannot be defeated by any contingency. As we said in Hurst v. Hilderbrandt, 178 Ark. 337, 10 S.W.2d 491 (1928), in describing a vested remainder: "[T]here is some person in esse known and ascertained, who, by the will or deed creating the estate, is to take and enjoy the estate, and whose right to such remainder no contingency can defeat." To the same effect see Steele v. Robinson, 221 Ark. 58, 251 S.W.2d 1001 (1952); National Bank of Commerce v. Ritter, 181 Ark. 439, 26 S.W.2d 113 (1930); Restatement of Property, § 157, Comment f (1936).

Here the testatrix directed that at the termination of the trust the property be distributed as provided by the general inheritance laws of Arkansas. At the time of the deaths of Cecil and Martin it would be utterly impossible to say who would take, in the case we have supposed, at the death of Martin's young widow 50 years later. Under our law the surviving descendants would then take per capita if they were related to Cecil and Martin in equal degree, but per stirpes if in unequal degree. Ark.Stat.Ann. §§ 61-134 and -135 (Repl.1971). If there were no surviving descendants of one brother, the entire property would go to the surviving descendants of the other. If there were no surviving descendants of either, the property would revert to the testatrix's estate and go to her collateral heirs. Thus it is really too plain for argument that the interest of every descendant (or "bodily heir") of Cecil or Martin would be contingent upon his surviving the death of Martin's widow, at which time and only at which time the title would finally vest.

A subordinate issue, that of estoppel is relied upon by the dissenting opinion. Cecil certainly did not represent that the trust, as distinguished from the will, was valid, nor did the bank nor anyone else rely to its detriment upon the supposed validity of the trust.

Reversed and remanded for further proceedings.

HICKMAN, J., dissent[ing] * * * [is omitted].

Notes

This case is often used to illustrate possibility. First, there is a possibility that Martin may have a widow (a status person not otherwise identified) who would not be a life in being when the Testarix died, but nonetheless would be a measuring life for purposes of the Rule. Second, there is the possibility that either son will have a "youngest child," who will be less than four when all of the lives in being die. If that child then turns twenty-five more than twenty-one years from that date to bring about vesting, the Rule would be violated. The court focuses on the first possibility—the unborn widow of Martin—but both possibilities exist to cause havoc with the Rule. The lesson for any competent drafter is to avoid any reference to a "status person" when writing an instrument. For example, "When the pope becomes a Baptist," or, to use a more common occurrence, "For my surviving heirs whenever my estate is distributed." Since a "slothful personal representative"—potentially not a life in being when the Testator dies—may not distribute the estate for more than twenty-one years, long after all of the lives in being are deceased, the event could occur beyond the Rule and, hence, violate the requirement of a life in being plus twenty-one years. New York Est., Powers & Trusts L. §9-1.3(c) (2004) provides that, whenever a status term is used—spouse, executor, widow—"it shall be presumed that the reference is to a person in being on the effective date of the instrument." Likewise, with any contingency related to the estate or transfer tax, it is "presumed that the creator of such estate intended such contingency to occur, if at all, within twenty-one years from the effective date of the instrument creating such estate." *Id.* at §9-1.3(d).

b. Fertile Octogenarians

English law was premised on biblical injunctions, among them that all things were possible to God. Hence, it is possible for God to do all things, including allowing a woman to conceive late in her life, even in her eighties. This is the premise of fertile octogenarian cases, made most famous in the English decision of Jee v. Audley, 1 Cox 324, 29 Eng. Rep. 1186 (1787). The decision concerned a Testator, who created a life estate in his wife, and then to his niece and the issue of her body. But if there be no issue of her body, then to be equally divided among the daughters of Testator's kinsman, John Lee, and his wife, Elizabeth Lee. The kinsman and his wife were in their seventies, but the court read the bequest as saying that, when choosing the daughters, we should choose only those daughters who were alive when the issue of the niece finally expired. This event could happen after any life in being if we could presume that John and Elizabeth could have a daughter who was not a life in being but, nonetheless, is a measuring life. The court held that it was possible for John and Elizabeth to have additional daughters and, hence, the event may not take place within a life in being plus twenty-one years.

Fertile octogenarians involve women and the ability to produce viable eggs; men are commonly thought of as being capable of producing sperm throughout their lives. In order to prevent the application of the possibility of after-born children adversely affecting trusts, states have enacted statutes presuming that a woman is incapable of bearing children after the age of fifty-five. *See, e.g.,* N.Y. Est., Powers & Trusts L. §§ 9-1.2 & 9-1.3 (2004). Some courts take judicial notice of infertility due to such causes as a complete hysterectomy. *See, e.g.,* In re Latouf's Will, 887 N.J. Super. 137, 208 A.2d 411 (Super. App. Div. 1965). New York is also quick to legislate that it is presumed that a male can not have a child before the male reaches the age of fourteen, and that a female may not have a child before the age of twelve. *See* N.Y. Est., Powers & Trusts L. § 9-1.3(e)(1) (2004). Please note the distinction between men and women and the presumption of fertility in the following decision.

Ward v. Van der Loeff
House of Lords, United Kingdom, 1924
[1924] A.C. 653

[Testator, William John Dalzell Burnyeat, died in 1916. He was survived by his wife, Hildegard, by his mother and father, and by two brothers and two sisters. Testator had no children. At the time of Testator's death, Testator's brothers and sisters each had children who were living.

In 1921, Testator's widow married Mr. Van der Loeff, who was not a natural-born British subject. After Testator's death and after the marriage of Hildegard and Van der Loeff, one of the testator's siblings had a child—Philip Ponsonby Burnyeat.

Testator executed a Will in 1915 and a codicil in 1916. In the Will, Testator left his estate in trust for his wife for life, with the remainder to his children. However, as provided in the Will, because Testator died without children, he gave his wife a power to appoint the trust fund among the children of Testator's brothers and sisters. In default of appointment, he gave the trust fund, in equal shares, to all of the children of his brothers and sisters.]

VISCOUNT HALDANE L.C:

* * *

About the validity of these trusts no question arises. But it is otherwise with the codicil made by the testator. It was in these terms:

> I declare that the life interest given to my said wife by my said will shall be terminable on her remarriage unless such remarriage shall be with a natural born British subject. I revoke the power of appointment among the children of my brothers and sisters given to my said wife by my said will. And I declare that after her death my trustees shall stand possessed of the residuary trust funds in trust for all or any the children or child of my brothers and sisters who shall be living at the death of my wife or born at any time afterwards before any one of such children for the time being in existence attains a vested interest and who being a son or sons attain the age of twenty-one, or being a daughter or daughters attain that age or marry if more than one, in equal shares.

On the construction of the will and codicil, two questions arise. The first is, whether the limitation in favour of children, contained in the concluding words of the codicil, is valid, having regard to the rule against perpetuities. The second is whether, if invalid, this new limitation and the wording of the codicil have been at all events efficacious as expressing a revocation of his bequest to children contained in the will. If the limitation to children in the codicil be invalid, and that in the will has not been revoked, then a further question arises, whether the gift in the will operated in favour of any children of the brothers and sisters who were not born until after the testator's death. Philip Ponsonby Burnyeat, who is one of the parties to these appeals, was a son of the testator's brother, Myles Fleming Burnyeat, but was not born until after the testator's death and the remarriage of his widow. It is argued against his claim that the life interest of the widow was effectively determined by the provision in the codicil and that the class of children to take was finally ascertained at that date as the time of distribution. If this be so, Philip Ponsonby Burnyeat is excluded.

P. O. Lawrence J. was the judge before whom this summons came in the first instance. He decided that the gift in the codicil in favour of the children of the testator's brothers and sisters was so framed as to be void for perpetuity. He held further, that the codicil operated to revoke the residuary gift in the will only so far as the substituted provision in the codicil was valid, and that the gift in the will in favour of these children, therefore, took effect, but merely in favour of such of the children as were born before the remarriage of the testator's widow. Philip Ponsonby Burnyeat was thus excluded. * * *

My Lords, the principle to be applied in construing instruments for the purpose of ascertaining whether the direction they contain infringes the rule against perpetuity is a well settled one. It was repeated with emphasis in this House in Pearks v. Moseley * * *, where it was laid down that in construing the words the effect of the rule must in the first instance be left out of sight, and then, having in this way defined the intention expressed, the Court had to test its validity by applying the rule to the meaning thus ascertained. It is only therefore if, as matter of construction, the words in the codicil, taken in the natural sense in which the testator used them, do not violate the rule that they can be regarded as giving a valid direction. Looking at the language of the testator here, I am wholly unable to read it as not postponing the ascertainment of possible members of the class beyond the period of a life in being and twenty-one years afterwards. No doubt if we were warranted in interpreting the testator as having referred only to the children of those of his brother and sisters who were alive at his death we might read his language in a way which would satisfy the law. But for so restricting the natural meaning of his words there is no justification in the language used in the context. He speaks of his brothers and sisters generally, and there is no expression which excludes the children of other possible brothers and sisters of the whole or half blood who might in contemplation of law be born. He has nowhere indicated an intention that his words are not to be construed in this, their natural meaning. I think, therefore, that the class to be benefited was not one all the members of which were, as a necessary result of the words used, to be ascertained within the period which the law prescribes, and that the gift in the codicil in favour of children of brothers and sisters is wholly void.

The next question is whether the codicil, although inoperative to this extent, was yet operative to revoke the gift to children of brothers and sisters contained in the will. After consideration, I have come to the conclusion that it was not so operative. There is indeed a revocation expressed in the codicil, but it is confined to the power of appointment given to the wife. It does not extend to what follows. That is, in terms, an attempt at a substantive and independent gift, and, as it is wholly void, I think, differing on this point from the Court of Appeal, that the provision in the will stands undisturbed. There is nothing else in the codicil which purports to affect it. It can make no difference that the class of children is a new and different class if the constitution of the new class is wholly inoperative in law. If it fails, then unless an independent and valid intention to revoke has been independently of it expressed, no revocation can take place. There is no such independent expression of intention here.

The only other point is at what period the class of children of brothers and sisters who took under the will is to be ascertained. I think that according to a well-known rule, the period is that of distribution; in other words, taking the valid alteration in the codicil into account, the remarriage of the widow with a foreign subject. Philip Ponsonby Burnyeat is thus excluded.

The result is that the judgment of P.O. Lawrence J. should be restored. * * *

[Opinion of VISCOUNT CAVE omitted].

* * *

LORD DUNEDIN:

My Lords, the main question in this case seems to me to be determined by what was said in this House by Lord Cairns in the two cases of Hill v. Crook * * * and Dorin v. Dorin. * * * In the former of these cases that noble and learned Lord laid down that when you wish to vary the meaning of a word denoting a class of relations from what the prima facie meaning of that word is—he actually said it of the words legitimate children, but the application is obviously wider—there are two classes of cases only where the primary signification can be departed from. The one is where it is impossible in the circumstances that any person indicated by the prima facie meaning can take under the bequest. That is not the case here because probably in law, though scarcely in fact, the idea of other brothers and sisters to the testator coming into existence could not be excluded, but in any case the half-brother or sister was a real possibility. The second class of cases is where you find something in the will itself, that is, in the expressions used in the will, to exclude the prima facie interpretation. That also seems to me absent. He has used the words "brother and sister" without explanation or glossary, and I am afraid he must take the consequences. * * * [other opinions omitted].

Notes

Assisted conception makes it possible for women to bear children late in life. There are a number of cases involving paternity, custody, and visitation that concern an older woman using in vitro fertilization with oocytes from a donor. *See, e.g.,* In re C.K.G., 2004 WL 1402560 (Tenn. App. June 22, 2004) (woman impregnated with donor eggs fertilized by partner's sperm is the legal mother of triplets); K.M. v. E.G., 13 Cal. Rptr. 3d 136 (Cal. App. 1 Dist.) (woman who donated her eggs to her same-sex partner so she could become pregnant through in vitro fertilization is not the mother of resulting twins), *rev. granted and op. superseded by,* M.K. v. E.G., 97 P.3d 72, 18 Cal. Rptr. 3d 667 (Cal. 2004), *judgment rev'd by,* K.M. v. E.G., 37 Cal. 4th 130, 117 P.3d 673, 33 Cal. Rptr. 3d 61 (2005); Gillett-Netting v. Barnhart, 29 Fam. L. Rep. 1075 (D. Ariz. Dec. 17, 2002) (twins conceived by a widow via in vitro fertilization with her deceased husband's frozen sperm ten months after his death are not entitled to inherit his property or to survivorship benefits under the Social Security Act), *rev'd and remanded,* 371 F.3d 593

(2004). Mirroring the Uniform Statutory Rule Against Perpetuities, the Uniform Probate Code eliminates the possibility of a child born to an individual after the individual's death. *See* Unif. Prob. Code §2-901(d) (2003). These issues are discussed in Daniel M. Schuyler, *The New Biology and the Rule Against Perpetuities*, 15 UCLA L. Rev. 420 (1968). *See generally*, Robin Fretwell Wilson, *Uncovering the Rationale for Requiring Infertility in Surrogacy Arrangements*, 29 Am. J. L. & Med. 337 (2003); Jennifer L. Rosato, *The Children of ART (Assisted Reproductive Technology): Should the Law Protect Them From Harm?*, 2004 Utah L. Rev. 57 (2004); Gina Kolata, *A Record and Big Questions as Woman Gives Birth at 63*, N.Y. Times, Apr. 24, 1997, at A1.

c. Charitable Trusts

Brown v. Independent Baptist Church

Supreme Judicial Court of Massachusetts, 1950
325 Mass. 645, 91 N.E.2d 922

QUA, Chief Justice.

The object of this suit in equity, originally brought in this court, is to determine the ownership of a parcel of land in Woburn and the persons entitled to share in the proceeds of its sale by a receiver.

Sarah Converse died seised of the land on July 19, 1849, leaving a will in which she specifically devised it 'to the Independent Baptist Church of Woburn, to be holden and enjoyed by them so long as they shall maintain and promulgate their present religious belief and faith and shall continue a Church; and if the said Church shall be dissolved, or if its religious sentiments shall be changed or abandoned, then my will is that this real estate shall go to my legatees hereinafter named, to be divided in equal portions between them. And my will further is, that if my beloved husband, Jesse Converse, shall survive me, that then this devise to the aforesaid Independent Church of Woburn, shall not take effect till from and after his decease; and that so long as he shall live he may enjoy and use the said real estate, and take the rents and profits thereof to his own use.' Then followed ten money legacies in varying amounts to different named persons, after which there was a residuary clause in these words, 'The rest and residue of my estate I give and bequeath to my legatees above named, saving and except therefrom the Independent Baptist Church; this devise to take effect from and after the decease of my husband; I do hereby direct and will that he shall have the use and this rest and residue during his life.'

The husband of the testatrix died in 1864. The church named by the testatrix ceased to 'continue a church' on October 19, 1939.

The parties apparently are in agreement, and the single justice ruled, that the estate of the church in the land was a determinable fee. We concur. First Universalist Society of North Adams v. Boland, 155 Mass. 171, 174, 29 N.E. 524, 15 L.R.A. 231; Institution for Savings in Roxbury and its Vicinity v. Roxbury Home for Aged Women, 244 Mass. 583, 585–586, 139 N.E. 301; Dyer v. Siano, 298 Mass. 537, 540, 11 N.E.2d 451. The estate was a fee, since it might last forever, but it was not an absolute fee, since it might (and did) 'automatically expire upon the occurrence of a stated event.' Restatement: Property, §44. It is also conceded, and was ruled, that the specific executory devise over to the persons 'hereinafter named' as legatees was void for remoteness. This conclusion seems to be required by Proprietors of Church in Brattle Square v. Grant, 3 Gray 142,

152, 155–156, 63 Am.Dec. 725; First Universalist Society of North Adams v. Boland, 155 Mass. 171, 173, 29 N.E. 524, 15 L.R.A. 231, and Institution for Savings in Roxbury and its Vicinity v. Roxbury Home for Aged Women, 244 Mass. 583, 587, 139 N.E. 301. See Restatement: Property, § 44, illustration 20. The reason is stated to be that the determinable fee might not come to an end until long after any life or lives in being and twenty-one years, and in theory at least might never come to an end, and for an indefinite period no clear title to the entire estate could be given.

Since the limitation over failed, it next becomes our duty to consider what became of the possibility of reverter which under our decisions remained after the failure of the limitation. First Universalist Society of North Adams v. Boland, 155 Mass. 171, 175, 29 N.E. 524, 15 L.R.A. 231; Institution for Savings in Roxbury and its Vicinity v. Roxbury Home for Aged Women, 244 Mass. 583, 587, 139 N.E. 301. Restatement: Property, § 228, illustration 2, and Appendix to Volume II, at pages 35–36, including note 2. A possibility of reverter seems, by the better authority, to be assignable inter vivos (Restatement: Property, § 159; Sims, Future Interests, § 715; see Tiffany, Real Property, 3d Ed., § 314, note 31, and must be at least as readily devisable as the other similar reversionary interest known as a right of entry for condition broken, which is devisable, though not assignable. * * * It follows that the possibility of reverter passed under the residuary clause of the will to the same persons designated in the invalid executory devise. It is of no consequence that the persons designated in the two provisions were the same. The same result must be reached as if they were different.

The single justice ruled that the residuary clause was void for remoteness, apparently for the same reason that rendered the executory devise void. With this we cannot agree, since we consider it settled that the rule against perpetuities does not apply to reversionary interests of this general type, including possibilities of reverter. Proprietors of the Church in Brattle Square v. Grant, 3 Gray, 142, 148, 63 Am.Dec. 725. French v. Old South Society in Boston, 106 Mass. 479, 488–489; Tobey v. Moore, 130 Mass. 448, 450. First Universalist Society of North Adams v. Boland, 155 Mass. 171, 175–176, 29 N.E. 524, 15 L.R.A. 231; Restatement: Property, § 372, Tiffany, Real Property, 3d Ed., § 404. See Gray, Rule Against Perpetuities, 4th Ed., §§ 41, 312, 313. For a full understanding of the situation here presented it is necessary to keep in mind the fundamental difference in character between the attempted executory devise to the legatees later named in the will and the residuary gift to the same persons. The executory devise was in form and substance an attempt to limit or create a new future interest which might not arise or vest in anyone until long after the permissible period. It was obviously not intended to pass such a residuum of the testatrix's existing estate as a possibility of reverter, and indeed if the executory devise had been valid according to its terms the whole estate would have passed from the testatrix and no possibility of reverter could have been left to her or her devisees. The residuary devise, on the other hand, was in terms and purpose exactly adapted to carry any interest which might otherwise remain in the testatrix, whether or not she had it in mind or knew it would exist. Thayer v. Wellington, 9 Allen 283, 295, 85 Am.Dec. 753; Wellman v. Carter, 286 Mass. 237, 249–250, 190 N.E. 493.

We cannot accept the contention made in behalf of Mrs. Converse's heirs that the words of the residuary clause 'saving and except therefrom the Independent Baptist Church' were meant to exclude from the operation of that clause any possible rights in the *land* previously given to the church. We construe these words as intended merely to render the will consistent by excluding the church which also had been 'above named' from the list of '*legatees*' who were to take the residue.

The interlocutory decree entered December 16, 1947, is reversed, and a new decree is to be entered providing that the land in question or the proceeds of any sale thereof by the receiver shall go to the persons named as legatees in the will, other than the Independent Baptist Church of Woburn, or their successors in interest. Further proceedings are to be in accord with the new decree. Costs and expenses are to be at the discretion of the single justice.

So ordered.

Note

Traditionally, courts have been willing to reform charitable trusts under the doctrine of "cy pres" to accommodate a purpose "as near as" the original invalidated trust purpose as possible. Most often the cy pres doctrine is used when a charitable beneficiary is no longer in existence. *See, e.g.,* Estate of Crawshaw, 249 Kan. 388, 819 P.2d 613 (Kan. 1991). But the Uniform Trust Code §413(a) makes the doctrine applicable whenever "a particular charitable purpose becomes unlawful, impracticable, or impossible to achieve...." In addition, if the Settlor has provided for distribution of the trust property to a non-charitable beneficiary, this will apply rather than cy pres only if: "(1) the trust property is to revert to the settlor and the settlor is still living; or (2) fewer than 21 years have elapsed since the date of the trust's creation." *Id.* at §413(b). Although the issue of failure of a charitable trust because of violation of the Rule Against Perpetuities is of concern, there is greater concern over discrimination by the charitable institution and violation of the Fourteenth Amendment. *See, e.g.,* Estate of Wilson, 59 N.Y.2d 461, 452 N.E.2d 1228, 465 N.Y.S.2d 900 (1983) (Fourteenth Amendment only bars state discrimination, not private discrimination). *But see* Bob Jones University v. United States, 461 U.S. 574 (1983) (denial of federal tax exemption extended to qualified charities, even though qualifying as charitable for state law).

C. Application to Class Gifts

Much of what has been provided, *supra,* refers to class gifts. For example, if a Settlor were to provide in a testamentary trust: "For my spouse for life, then to my children, issue of my body or adopted by me, for life, and then to my surviving issue per stirpes," we have multiple class designations. Between the time the Settlor executes the Last Will and Testament and the Settlor's death, there is the possibility of increase and decrease of class membership in children and issue. Yet, in neither of the classes is there a Rule violation. Using the analysis provided previously (standing at the creation of the instrument—the Settlor's death—which is when the Will speaks), it is impossible for the Settlor to have a spouse who is not a life in being. In addition, the measuring lives at Settlor's death are the Settlor's children. Since the Uniform Trust Code prohibits the possibility of afterborn children being conceived by using his frozen sperm, there is no possibility of there being a measuring life that is not a life in being. Thus, the Rule will not prohibit a distribution of the trust assets to those issue surviving the death of Settlor's last child. But not all trusts are similarly situated. Traditionally, the Rule is violated if it is POSSIBLE that ANY member of the class may receive a vested interest at a time beyond the lives in being plus twenty-one years. The following case provides an example and a judicial solution.

American Security & Trust Co. v. Cramer

United States District Court, District of Columbia, 1959
175 F. Supp. 367

YOUNGDAHL, District Judge.

Six of the eleven * * * defendants before the Court have moved for summary judgment. A hearing has been held and memoranda of points and authorities have been submitted. Plaintiff, trustee of a testamentary trust, is a stakeholder in this controversy among competing heirs. Since all the material facts have been stipulated, * * * the Court is free to render summary judgment.

Abraham D. Hazen, a resident of the District of Columbia, died in the District on December 4, 1901. His will, executed on October 16, 1900, was admitted to probate on March 11, 1902.

Testator was survived by Hannah E. Duffey, who is referred to in his will as his 'adopted daughter'. At the time of the testator's death, Hannah had two children: Mary Hazen Duffey (now Cramer), born November 12, 1897, and Hugh Clarence Duffey, born July 11, * * * 1899. After the testator's death, Hannah gave birth to two more children: Depue Hazen Duffey, born October 9, 1903, and Horace Duffey, born July 8, 1908.

The will provided for the payment of debts and certain specific bequests and then provided that the residue of the estate be put in trust for the benefit of testator's wife for life. At her death, one-half of the corpus was to be, and has been, given to testator's sister and brothers;[4] the other half, composed of realty, remained in trust for Hannah for life. At Hannah's death, the income was to go to the children of Hannah 'then living or the issue of such of them as may then be dead leaving issue surviving' Hannah, and then 'upon the death of each the share of the one so dying shall go absolutely to the persons who shall then be her or his heirs at law according to the laws of descent now in force in the said District of Columbia'.[5]

---

4. The testator left no mother or father surviving him, and he had no natural children. See files and records in Equity Action No. 52600 for July 22, 1935 (findings of fact by Luhring, J.).

5. The seventh paragraph of testator's will reads:

Seventh. Upon the death of my said wife, the said Company, hereinafter designated as 'my Executor', shall, after the appraisal mentioned in the next preceding item of this will shall have been made, submit the same to my said adopted daughter, who may select one-half in value of the parts or parcels composing said real and personal estate belonging to my estate and remaining at my wife's death, and thereupon said Company shall hold said one-half of said estate and the parcels of land included in the same for the use and benefit of my said adopted daughter during her life, and shall pay to her, and not to any creditor or assign of hers, the net income from said half in monthly or quarterly instalments as such income is received, it being understood that all proper cost, taxes, cost of insurance and repairs shall be first deducted from the gross income collected, and my said adopted daughter may, if she so elect, occupy free of charge or rent any house composing said half of said estate, and upon her death, the said half shall be held for the use and benefit of the children of said adopted daughter then living or the issue of such of them as may then be dead leaving issue surviving my said adopted daughter, but it is my will and I do direct that Mary Hazen Duffey, the daughter of my adopted daughter and the namesake of my wife and for whom my wife and I have the greatest affection, shall if living at the death of her mother take a share three times as large as the share of each of the other children of my said adopted daughter, which other children shall take in equal shares between and among themselves, and each of the children of said adopted daughter shall take only for and during the terms of their respective lives and upon the death of each the share of the

Testator's widow died on October 31, 1916; Hannah died on May 21, 1915.

On October 5, 1917, the heirs of the testator brought an action in equity to have the provisions of the seventh paragraph of the will stricken as being in violation of the rule against perpetuities. The Supreme Court of the District of Columbia held that the interests of Hannah's children under the will were valid and the Court of Appeals affirmed. Hazen v. American Security & Trust Co., 1920, 49 App.D.C. 297, 265 F. 447.[6] The validity of the remainders over, after the death of each child, was expressly not ruled upon as the life estates were not 'so intimately connected with the gift over as to require us now to determine the validity of such gifts.' * * *

Hugh, one of the four life tenants after the death of the widow and Hannah, died on December 19, 1928 and shortly thereafter the trustee brought a bill for instructions; this time the validity of the remainder over to Hugh's heirs was in issue. On January 2, 1930, Judge Bailey ruled that 'the remainder provided by the will after his (Hugh's) death to the persons who shall then be his heirs at law became vested within the period prescribed by law and is valid.' * * *

On December 13, 1954, Depue died and for the fourth time a suit concerning this trust was started in this court. The trustees desired instructions as to the disposition of Depue's one-sixth share. While this action was pending, on December 18, 1957, Horace died. A supplemental bill was then filed, asking for instructions as to the disposition of this one-sixth share as well. The remainder over after the death of the sole living life tenant, Mary, cannot yet take effect; however, due to the request of all the parties concerned, and in order to save both the time of this court and the needless expense it would otherwise cost the estate, the Court will also pass on the validity of this remainder.

The law that governs the questions here involved is the law in effect at the time of the testator's death: December 4, 1901. * * *

The common-law rule against perpetuities, as stated by Professor Gray, is as follows:

> No interest is good unless it must vest, if at all, not later than twenty-one years after some life in being at the creation of the interest. * * *

The effect of the rule is to invalidate ab initio certain future interests that might otherwise remain in existence for a period of time considered inimicable [sic] to society's interest in having reasonable limits to dead-hand control and in facilitating the marketability of property. The policy of the law is to permit a person to control the devolution of his property but only for a human lifetime plus twenty-one years and actual periods of gestation. With careful planning, this period could be as long as one hundred years—and this is long enough.

A gift to a class is a gift of an aggregate amount of property to persons who are collectively described and whose individual share will depend upon the number of persons ultimately constituting the class. Evans v. Ockershausen, 1938, 69 App.D.C. 285, 292, 100 F.2d 695, 702, 128 A.L.R. 177. The members of the class must be finally determined

---

one so dying shall go absolutely to the persons who shall then be her or his heirs at law according to the laws of descent now in force in the said District of Columbia.
Mary took a three-sixth's share; each of the other three children took a one-sixth share.

6. 'The devise of the children of Hannah E. Duffey was a devise to a class, which, of necessity, was made up within her lifetime, and the share of each became fixed and certain at her death, and in no way (was?) affected by the provision as to the remainder.' 49 App.D.C. at page 300, 265 F. at page 450.

within a life or lives in being plus twenty-one years and actual periods of gestation, or the gift will fail. Put another way, the class must close within the period of the rule against perpetuities, if the class gift is to be valid. Unless a contrary intent is indicated by the testator, the class will close when any member of the class is entitled to immediate possession and enjoyment of his share of the class gift. Applying these basic principles to the trust here involved, it is seen that the life estates to Hannah's children had to vest, if at all, at the termination of the preceding life estates of the widow and Hannah. Since Hannah's children had to be born within Hannah's lifetime, and since Hannah was a life in being, the class (Hannah's children) physiologically had to close within the period of the rule.[11] This has already been so held. Hazen v. American Security & Trust Co., supra, at note 6. Furthermore, the remainder over at Hugh's death has been held valid. The Court now holds that the remainder limited to the heirs of Mary is valid. Both Hugh and Mary were lives in being at the testator's death; the remainders limited to their heirs had to vest, if at all, within the period of the rule. Horace and Depue were born after the testator died; the remainders over at their deaths are invalid.

In applying the rule against perpetuities, it does not help to show that the rule might be complied with or that, the way things turned out, it actually was complied with.[12] After the testator's death, Hannah might have had more children; one of these might have lived more than twenty-one years after the death of all the lives in being at the testator's death. The vesting of the remainder in this after-born's heirs would take place after the expiration of lives in being and twenty-one years, since the heirs could not be ascertained until the after-born's death and an interest cannot be vested until the interest holder is ascertained. Consequently, because of the possibility that this could happen, even though, in fact, it did not,[13] the remainders limited to the heirs of Horace and Depue (both after-borns) are invalid as a violation of the rule against perpetuities.

Counsel have not argued the point of whether the invalidity of the remainders to the heirs of Horace and Depue serves to taint the otherwise valid remainders to the heirs of Mary and Hugh. Of course, the remainder after Hugh's life estate has already been distributed and is not properly in issue. Nevertheless, as shall be demonstrated, it (and the remainder to the heirs of Mary) are not affected by the two invalid remainders, since the four remainders are to subclasses and stand (or fall) separately.

---

11. The fact that the will provided 'the said half shall be held for the use and benefit of the children of said adopted daughter then living or the issue of such of them as may then be dead leaving issue surviving my said adopted daughter * * *' (emphasis supplied) does not cast any doubt on the above. If one of Hannah's children predeceased Hannah and also failed to leave issue, the other children would have increased shares; but still, the class would be determined, i.e., close, within a life in being (Hannah's).

12. A few jurisdictions have adopted a 'wait and see' doctrine which has the effect of neutralizing the possible interest-invalidating events and taking into consideration only the actual events. Perhaps this is a desirable change, but the District of Columbia has not adopted this doctrine and to do so this Court is of the opinion a statute would be necessary. See discussion of the doctrine in Simes and Smith, supra, note 10 at §1230 and for an example of such a statute, see Mass.Acts (1954), c. 641, enacted as chapter 184A of Mass.Gen.Laws.

13. Mary, a life in being at testator's death, is still alive. Therefore, the heirs of Horace and Depue would *actually* be taking within the period of the rule, but in this area of imagination-run-wild, actualities do not count; what could happen is all that matters.

In this case, the above suppositions are not unreasonable since Hannah was in her middle thirties when the testator died. But cf. the cases of 'the fertile octogenarian', 'the unborn widow' and 'the magic gravel pit' in Professor Leach's classic article, 'Perpetuities in a Nutshell', 51 Harv.L.R. 638, 642–645 (1938).

Beginning with Jee v. Audley, 1 Cox Eq.Cas. 324 (1787) and flowering with Leake v. Robinson, 2 Mer. 363, 35 Eng.Rep. 979 (Chancery 1817), there has been the curious anomaly in future interests law that if the interest of any potential member of a class can possibly vest too remotely, the interests of all the members of the class fails. In other words, the rule is that a class gift is inseparable. For example, T creates a trust to pay the income to A for life and then to pay the corpus over to such of A's children as attain the age of twenty-five. When A dies he might have a child who is not yet four years of age and who was not in being at T's death; this child would not take a vested interest until he satisfied the contingency of reaching the age of twenty-five; since a child under four could not become twenty-five within twenty-one years, the child's interest is void by virtue of the rule against perpetuities. While this much may be sound, the rule in Leake v. Robinson goes on to invalidate the entire class gift. That is, even if the child under four has two brothers who are over twenty-five when A dies, these two brothers take nothing because the invalid interest of their little brother (who, remember, may only be imagined) is contagious—so says Leake. Unless the testator intended to have all of the twenty-five-year-old sons take, or none at all (and this is difficult to imagine in the absence of an express provision in the will), the rule is a dubious one. Fortunately, the Court need not apply it in this case because of the limitation put on it by a long line of cases beginning with Catlin v. Brown, 11 Hare 372, 68 Eng.Rep. 1318 (Chancery, 1853).

In Catlin, the devise was of mortgaged property to A for life, then to the children of A in equal shares during their lives, and after the death of any such child, his share to his children and their heirs. Some of A's children were in being at the time that the testator died; some were born after his death. Counsel conceded that the remainders over to the heirs of those children of A born after the testator's death were invalid. The question was whether those concededly invalid remainders tainted the otherwise valid remainders and rendered them invalid. The Court held that they did not; the remainders to the heirs of the children in being at the testator's death were valid. Leake was distinguished on the ground that it concerned remainders to *one* class (A's children that reach twenty-five) while the remainders involved in Catlin were to a group of subclasses (the heirs of each of A's children was a subclass). * * * In other words, the limitation placed on Leake by Catlin is that if the ultimate takers are not described as a single class but rather as a group of subclasses, and if the share to which each separate subclass is entitled will finally be determined within the period of the rule, the gifts to the different subclasses are separable for the purpose of the rule.

In the instant case, the language of the will compels the Court to read it as a devise of remainders to subclasses and within the rule of Catlin. The provision in issue reads, in part:

> * * * and *each* of the children of said adopted daughter shall take only for and during the terms of their *respective* lives and upon the death of *each* the share of the *one* so dying shall go absolutely to the persons who shall then be *her or his* heirs at law * * * (Emphasis supplied).

The Court deems it advisable to mention that it thoroughly explored the possible applicability here of the Rule in Shelley's Case. Prior to January 2, 1902, this ancient principle of law * * * was in force in the District of Columbia. * * * Noyes v. Parker, 1937, 68 App.D.C. 13, 92 F.2d 562. If it could be utilized in the case at hand, the remainders limited to the heirs of each of Hannah's children would be converted into a remainder in the child himself. This, for one thing, would save the two remainders found invalid and prevent their defaulting to the heirs of the testator.

Assuming, without deciding, that the remainders here are equitable (because the trust is active), nevertheless the rule does not apply because the remainders were not limited to 'heirs' but instead went to 'her or his heirs at law according to the laws of descent now in force in the said District of Columbia'. * * *

When a remainder in fee after a life estate fails, there is no enlargement or diminution of the life estate; rather there is then a reversion in the heirs of the testator. Hilton v. Kinsey, 1950, 88 U.S.App.D.C. 14, 17, 185 F.2d 885, 888, 23 A.L.R.2d 830; Simes and Smith, supra, at note 10 §1263, and numerous cases cited. The two one-sixth shares held invalid shall pass to the successors in interest to the heirs of Abraham D. Hazen.

Since it is undisputed that the late George E. Sullivan, an attorney, had a contingent fee contract, dated March 16, 1922, with the heirs of the testator, entitling him to twenty percent of whatever property was finally held to pass to the heirs of the testator by virtue of the failure of the remainders, and since this has now been brought to fruition, the estate of Edith B. Sullivan, the sole heir of George E. Sullivan, is entitled to a twenty percent share of the two one-sixth interests.

Counsel have stipulated that Hannah was referred to in testator's will as his 'adopted daughter'; there is no agreement as to whether she actually was legally adopted. No proof of a legal adoption has been offered. On the other hand, there is considerable reason to say that Hannah never was, in fact, legally adopted. In 1927 a full hearing was held on the matter and at that time Hannah's husband, mother and numerous friends were alive and testified; these persons have since passed away and the Court is of the opinion that nothing could be gained by ordering a further hearing at this time.

It is clear from the transcript of the hearing that Hannah was treated by the testator and his wife just as if she were their natural daughter. She lived with them, was always referred to as 'our daughter', and used their name. Her formal wedding invitation referred to her as the Hazens' daughter; the community believed she was the Hazens' natural daughter. While there is little testimony on the question of whether she was ever legally adopted, what there is, leads to the conclusion that she had not been. * * * Moreover, it would appear that it was impossible for her ever to have been legally adopted since the original adoption statute provided for the adoption of 'minor children' only. 28 Stat. 687, ch. 134 (passed February 26, 1895). * * * Hannah was at least twenty-six years of age in 1895. * * *

One matter remains. The Court has been urged to terminate the trust and order distribution of three-sixths of the original corpus to the life tenant, Mary. This life tenant is presently sixty-two years of age; she is a widow and has three adult children. These three children and their wives have signed an 'assignment' of their interests in the trust to Mary. Although the legal significance of this 'assignment', standing alone, is questionable, in light of the fact that the children are not their mother's heirs but only presumptive heirs until she dies, nevertheless, it is significant to show that the only persons likely to become remaindermen are willing to have the income beneficiary take the corpus. The intent of the testator is clear:

> I do direct that Mary Hazen Duffey, the daughter of my adopted daughter and the namesake of my wife and for whom my wife and I have the greatest affection, shall if living at the death of her mother take a share three times as large as the share of each of the other children of my said adopted daughter * * *.

It seems obvious that the testator had Mary's interest uppermost in his mind. Last year, Mary's share of the income from the trust amounted to $750.51 which was hardly sufficient for her subsistence; her needs would be amply provided for were she to receive the share of the corpus. If General Hazen were now alive, there would seem to be little doubt but that he would wish to join with Mary's children to have the trust terminated and the corpus distributed to the one for whom he had 'the greatest affection' and who was to receive 'a share three times as large as the share of each of the other children'. In light of the realities of the situation, the desire of all concerned to have the trust terminated, and the evident purpose of the will, the Court shall order the trust terminated and the corpus distributed to the life tenant. Cf. Wolcott's Petition, 1948, 95 N.H. 23, 56 A.2d 641, 1 A.L.R.2d 1323. This, however, is conditioned upon the furnishing of a bond to protect any unascertained remaindermen.

Defendant Blakelock's motion for summary judgment is granted. Defendant Mary Duffey Cramer's prayer for additional relief is granted to the extent of having her receive that portion of the corpus presently supplying the income to which she is entitled as a life tenant, conditioned on her furnishing a bond or undertaking with surety approved by the court.

Counsel will submit an appropriate order.

Notes

Additional courts have adopted approaches to save at least part of a Settlor's trust that would otherwise be void under the Rule Against Perpetuities. For example, in Estates of Coates, 438 Pa. Super. 195, 652 A.2d 331 (1994), the court applied the doctrine of vertical separability to sustain income through great-grandchildren, thereby acknowledging that gifts to subclasses may be evaluated separately, as long as the number of shares is definitely fixed within the time required by the Rule. But the competent drafter should recognize the pitfalls of the "all or nothing" approach to classes and the Rule and should draft instruments accordingly. To properly draft an instrument, first review the materials regarding increase and decrease of class gifts, *supra*, and eliminate the possibility of any afterborn class members who may take an interest in the trust after the date or creation. *See generally* W. Barton Leach, *The Rule Against Perpetuities and Gifts to Classes*, 51 HARV. L. REV. 1329 (1938).

D. Application to Powers of Appointment

Recall that a power of appointment exists when a Donor—a Settlor of an inter vivos trust, or a Testator of a valid Last Will and Testament—deposits an appointment—corpus—with a Trustee, with the instruction to do whatever the Donee says to do with the appointment at the appropriate time. Because a trust is involved, so too are future interests, and, thus, the Rule may void the trust. To properly evaluate the validity of any power of appointment under the Rule Against Perpetuities, first review the language used to establish the power and the options available to the Donee, *supra*, then there are three distinct steps in any analysis:

(1) Is the power created by the Donor valid? Thus, if the Donor were to create a power of appointment using an instrument that was invalid because of a defect in intentionalities or formalities, then analysis ceases. Likewise, if any of the required ele-

ments of a trust is missing, analysis ceases. These are conditions explored in previous chapters and sections, but it is always necessary to remember that even the most complicated testamentary trust exists because of the validity of the testamentary instrument—the Last Will and Testament. But if a valid power exists, then:

(2) Has the Donee exercised the power within the permissible period under the Rule? Recall that there are rules as to whether the Donee's open-ended residuary clause exercises a power of appointment. If the Donee has exercised the power correctly, then the question becomes whether the exercise is within the period of the Rule. Stated another way, we can ask if there is any possibility, standing at the creation of the power by the Donor, there is any possibility that the Donee may exercise the power beyond the period of the Rule, which is a life in being plus twenty-one years. For example, if a Donor were to establish an irrevocable inter vivos trust to provide life income to his children and then as his last child should appoint in a valid Last Will and Testament, this would be an invalid power. Invalidity results from the possibility that, standing at the creation of the power—during the life of the Settlor, not at the death of the Settlor—there is a possibility that the Settlor could have an additional child who would not be a life in being at creation but may exercise the power more than twenty-one years after the death of the last life in being. If the Donor/Settlor had created a revocable trust and power of appointment, the power would be valid because the date of creation would be at the death of the Donor/Settlor. Likewise, the power would be valid if the power were created in the Last Will and Testament of the Donor/Settlor. If there is no possibility that the power may be exercised by the Donee beyond the period of the Rule, we can then address the last issue.

(3) When the Donee exercises the power created by the Donor, has the Donee created a subsequent trust that, when analyzed from the time of creation, but in light of the facts at the time of exercise, there is a possibility that all interests will not vest within a life in being plus twenty-one years? This final step in the analysis is premised on the "relation back" doctrine. Even if the power is validly created and validly exercised by the Donee within the period of the Rule, it may still be invalid if, when the Donee exercises, the exercise relates back to the Donor's date of creation and, thereby, violates the Rule. The doctrine is logical because it recognizes that, in any power other than a general inter vivos power (presently exercisable), the Donor has retained some control over the Donee's selection. Hence, any exercise should be computed from creation of the power by the Donor, not simply exercise by the Donee. We will see this analysis demonstrated in the following cases, but also keep in mind that if there is a violation of the Rule Against Perpetuities in conjunction with a power of appointment, the court will apply the rules previously discussed regarding ineffective exercise, capture for general powers, and implied gifts for special powers.

Industrial National Bank of Rhode Island v. Barrett

Supreme Court of Rhode Island, 1966
101 R.I. 89, 220 A.2d 517

PAOLINO, Justice.

This is a bill in equity brought by the Industrial National Bank of Rhode Island, executor and trustee, and Aline C. Lathan, co-executor, under the will of Mary M. Tilley, deceased, for construction of the latter's will and for instructions to the executors and trustee thereunder. The adult respondents have filed an answer to the bill and all minor and contingent interests and those of persons unascertainable or not in being are represented by a guardian ad litem appointed for that purpose by the court. The guardian has filed an answer neither admitting nor denying the bill's allegations and submitting the interests of his respective wards to the court's care and protection.

* * *

It appears that Arthur H. Tilley, husband of the deceased, died January 28, 1959. Under the eighth clause of his will, admitted to probate February 5, 1959, he devised the property, which qualified for the full marital deduction, to the Industrial National Bank, in trust, with directions to pay the net income at least quarterly to his wife for life and such amounts of the corpus annually or at more frequent intervals as she should in writing request, for her comfort and support, and without being accountable to any court or remainderman therefor. He also conferred upon her a general testamentary power of appointment over the corpus remaining at her death.

Mary M. Tilley died October 28, 1963. Under the fourth clause of her will, admitted to probate November 7, 1963, she exercised her general testamentary power of appointment to the Industrial National Bank, in trust 'to pay over the net income thereof to and for the use and benefit of my granddaughters, Aline C. Lathan and Evelyn M. Barrett * * * equally for and during the term of their natural lives, and upon the death of either of them, to pay over said net income to her issue, *per stirpes* and not *per capita*.' The trustee was also given uncontrolled discretion to pay over to either of said grandchildren, or the issue of any deceased grandchild, for specific purposes, portions of the principal. Finally, the testatrix provided the trust would terminate 'twenty one (21) years after the death of the last survivor of the younger grandchild or issue of either grandchild of mine living at my death * * *.'

On the date of Arthur H. Tilley's death, Aline C. Lathan and Evelyn M. Barrett and one great-grandchild were in being. On the date of Mary M. Tilley's death the aforesaid respondents plus six additional great-grandchildren were in being. One great-grandchild was born subsequent to her death.

At various times within the three-year period preceding her death, Mrs. Tilley made gifts of stock to her respondent granddaughters which were included in her estate for federal estate tax purposes at a gross valuation of $92,995.50. The corpus of the marital trust created under clause eighth of Arthur H. Tilley's will was reported at a value of $65,610.51. The total valuation of her probate estate exclusive of the trust which she appointed was $25,666.18 and the total charges against her estate, including debts, administration expenses, state and federal inheritance and estate taxes total $28,188.44.

* * *

The complainants contend that Mrs. Tilley's exercise of the power of appointment created under her husband's will does not violate the rule against perpetuities on two alternative grounds.

First, they say, in clause eighth of his will, Arthur H. Tilley manifested a clear intent to bestow upon his wife an unlimited power to consume the trust principal giving her in effect a general power of appointment exercisable during her lifetime. In support of this contention, complainants point to the broad discretionary power bestowed on Mrs.

Tilley to invade the principal for her comfort and support which, coupled with her general testamentary power of appointment, they argue, created an absolute interest although not actually designated as such. In this connection complainants cite cases which hold, in construing language similar to that in clause eighth, that actual 'need' of a beneficiary is not a measure of 'comfort' and 'support'—see In the Matter of Woollard's Will, 295 N.Y. 390, 68 N.E.2d 181; In re Walsh's Will, 193 Misc. 785, 85 N.Y.S.2d 207, and New Jersey Title Guarantee & Trust Co. v. Dailey, 123 N.J.Eq. 205, 196 A. 703—and distinguish those which require the beneficiary to show 'reasonableness,' 'good faith,' or that the beneficiary's other assets are factors to be considered as being premised solely on the principle that a life tenant owes other beneficiaries of the trust or other remaindermen, neither present here, a duty not to consume the principal unnecessarily. See 33 Am.Jur., Life Estates, Remainders, etc., §§ 242, 243, pp. 728, 729.

Consequently complainants urge the perpetuities period should be computed from the date of Mrs. Tilley's death when she exercised the power.

The cardinal principle in the construction of wills is that the intention of the testator if definitely ascertainable and lawful must govern. Rhode Island Hospital Trust Co. v. Bateman, 93 R.I. 116, 172 A.2d 84; Industrial Trust Co. v. Saunders, 71 R.I. 94, 42 A.2d 492.

Clause eighth directs the Industrial National Bank to hold certain property qualifying for the marital deduction:

> in trust, nevertheless, * * * to pay over the net income thereof, at least quarterly, to my wife, Mary M. Tilley, for and during her life, and I authorize and direct my said Trustee, annually or at more frequent intervals, whenever my said wife shall in writing so direct, to pay over to her, *for her own comfort and support*, such part of the principal as she shall direct, and without being accountable to any court or remainderman therefor. Upon the death of my said wife, I confer upon her the power by her Will to appoint the entire corpus of the trust remaining at her death, free of trust, which power is exercisable in favor of the estate of my said wife, or in favor of such other distributees, and in such amounts and upon such terms, trusts, powers and limitations as she shall appoint in her Will. (Italics ours.)

The problem before us is to ascertain the extent of the gift the testator intended to bestow upon his wife. In cases such as these the extent and nature of a restriction depends upon the intent of the testator and accordingly, since different combinations of language and circumstances are endless, each will must be construed separately, rules of construction being guides only in a general sense.

We note first that instead of giving the property outright to his widow, the decedent chose to impress it with a trust. The provisions of that trust reflect his intent to make available to her something more than a life estate but something less than a fee. As we read clause eighth with reference to the provision for principal payments we find no language to indicate the trustee was invested with discretion to make them in consideration of the widow's actual needs or other assets, but rather that the discretion to determine the dollar amount payable rested solely in Mrs. Tilley.

Nevertheless the power must be read in reference to the matter for which it was given. In this context Mrs. Tilley did not have a general disposing power over the corpus because, in good-faith compliance with the settlor's plan of disposition, she could withdraw only those sums which she needed for her comfort and support.

However, complainants argue, since neither the beneficiary nor the trustee was accountable to any court or remainderman in regard to these payments, there was no review for her withdrawals, which, in reality, left her in complete control of the fund.

We do not agree. The pertinent language directs the trustee 'annually or at more frequent intervals, whenever my said wife shall in writing so direct, to pay over to her, for her own comfort and support, such part of the principal as she shall direct, *and without being accountable to any court or remainderman therefor.*' (Italics ours.) As we read this sentence the phrase 'and without being accountable to any court or remainderman therefor' applies to the trustee only, as it is used as a conjunctive thought to the first half of the sentence of which the trustee is the subject. While the discretion thus conferred on the trustee is broad, it is not so broad as to relieve it of the obligation to exercise the responsibility and in good faith. See Industrial National Bank v. Rhode Island Hospital, R.I., 207 A.2d 286, and cases cited on page 290. Moreover, and notwithstanding the discretion conferred on the trustee, Mrs. Tilley would have been accountable for withdrawals not made pursuant to the power bestowed on her. A power including one to direct payments of principal is special or limited if it may be exercised only for the use or support of a certain person, even though that person is the donee of the power. 5 Page on Wills (Bowe-Parker rev.) § 45.2, p. 498.

The complainants next contend that even if Mrs. Tilley had only a general testamentary power of appointment, the better-reasoned authorities hold the perpetuity period should be counted from the date of the power's exercise rather than its creation, which would make the gift here vest within the prescribed time.

Before reaching complainants' contention there is an initial problem we feel necessitates some discussion here. Clause fourth of Mrs. Tilley's will provides the trust created thereunder will terminate 'twenty one (21) years after the death of the last survivor of the younger grandchild or issue of either grandchild of mine living at my death * * *.' It is clear the testatrix set out the measuring lives alternatively as 'the last survivor of the younger grandchild' or the 'issue of either grandchild * * *.' Since both are modified by the phrase 'living at my death' the rule is satisfied on that point.

The difficulty arises in determining what person the testatrix designated when she used the word 'survivor.' After reading the clause as a whole we believe that this was but an inartistic reference by her draftsman to one of her grandchildren's issue. For a general discussion of this problem, see Perpetuities: A Standard Saving Clause To Avoid Violations Of The Rule, by W. Barton Leach and James K. Logan, 74 Harv.L.Rev. 1141 (1961).

Since this provision was manifestly intended as a savings clause to obviate any violation of the rule, we will give effect to the testatrix' obvious intent that this trust be created and will adopt the above interpretation, thereby removing any initial impediment to complainants' contention on this point. See Gray, The Rule Against Perpetuities (4th ed.) § 633, p. 601, where Gray said 'When the expression which a testator uses is really ambiguous, and is fairly capable of two constructions, one of which would produce a legal result, and the other a result that would be bad for remoteness, it is a fair presumption that the testator meant to create a legal rather than an illegal interest.'

For a recent discussion of the problem involved in construing testamentary intent see Manufacturers National Bank of Troy, New York v. McCoy, R.I., 212 A.2d 53, 55, where the court said:

When obscurity exists and the constructional aids are invoked, they are not applied as rules of positive law, or for the purpose of discovering an undisclosed intention of the testator, but to test an otherwise obscure intention by the application of constructional preferences for the purpose of reaching a judicial determination. Rhode Island Hospital Trust Co. v. Thomas (73 R.I. 277, 281, 54 A.2d 432) * * *. This process, according to some of the text writers, involves, within the context of the testamentary language and the circumstances attendant upon the instrument's formulation, an ascertainment of what would have been the probable intention of the average testator faced with the particular problem. 2 Scott, Trusts (2d ed.) § 164.1, p. 1160; 5 American Law of Property § 22.3, p. 248.

It is fundamental law that when the free alienation of a future interest in property is limited, the interest must vest within lives in being plus twenty-one years from the date of the creating instrument. When the persons who will take or the extent of their interests are to be determined by the exercise of a subsequent power of appointment, the rule against perpetuities requires that the vesting time be computed as if the appointment were a part of the instrument creating the limitation, because until it is exercised the limitation is incomplete.

Nevertheless as the primary concern behind the rule is to prevent restraint on alienation, a distinction is made between general and special powers. In the case of a general power of appointment by deed and will, all courts hold that since the donee has absolute disposing power over the property and may bring it into the market place at any time, he has what is tantamount to a fee. Therefore, since whatever estates may be created by one seized in fee may be also created under a general power, the commencement of the limitation is computed from the time of the power's exercise and not its creation.

In the case of a general power of appointment by will, however, the weight of authority counts the perpetuity period from the date of creation on the ground that since the donee cannot freely alienate the property during his life, he is not the practical owner thereof. A minority view disagrees with this position on the theory that the concept of actual ownership clouds the substance of the matter, which is that if the person having the power without the ownership may appoint to whomsoever he pleases at the time he exercises it, he is in the same position *in respect to the perpetuity* as if he were actually the owner. Thorndike, General Powers and Perpetuities, 27 Harv.L.Rev., pp. 705, 717. Also see Northern Trust Co. v. Porter, 368 Ill. 256, 13 N.E.2d 487, for leading citations on both positions.

Since this is a case of first impression, we have read with interest the authorities supporting the above positions. See Gray, General Testamentary Powers And The Rule Against Perpetuities, 26 Harv.L.Rev., p. 720; Thorndike, General Powers And Perpetuities, supra; Annot., 1 A.L.R. 374; and Northern Trust Co. v. Porter, supra. From this reading it appears that the early English cases in counting the perpetuity period did not distinguish between a general power to appoint by deed and will and a general power to appoint by will only and we think the cases following this position are the more persuasive.

In essence the majority jurisdictions characterize a general power of appointment by will as being in the nature of a special power, and, as such, a part of the creating instrument of the donor. They reach this result solely on the ground that because the donor has tied up ownership of the property until the donee's death, the restraint on alienation is sufficient to count the perpetuity period from the power's creation.

We think that this position misapprehends the fundamental concepts involved here. The law does not prohibit an estate being tied up for the life of any one individual, but prohibits only restraint beyond lives in being plus twenty-one years. See Thorndike, supra. When the donee exercises his power, he is at that time the practical owner thereof, for the purposes of the rule, as he can appoint to anyone of his choice as well as his own estate. Furthermore when he exercises the power he can create, unlike the case of a special power, estates entirely independent from those created or controlled by the donor, and so, as to the donee, the power is a general one. See Perpetuities In Perspective: Ending The Rule's Reign Of Terror, by W. Barton Leach, 65 Harv.L.Rev. 721.

Consequently, we hold the trust created by clause fourth of Mrs. Tilley's will pursuant to her general testamentary power of appointment is valid. We arrive at this conclusion not only because logic favors its adoption but also because we believe it is in line with the trend to obviate the technical harshness of the rule against perpetuities and decide cases on the substance of things. 6 American Law of Property § 24.45 (1952), p. 118; 3 Restatement, Property § 343 (1940), p. 1913; Union & New Haven Trust Co. v. Taylor, 133 Conn. 221, 50 A.2d 168. For a learned discussion of this problem, see Perpetuities In A Nutshell, 51 Harv.L.Rev. 638, and Perpetuities: The Nutshell Revisited, 78 Harv.L.Rev. 973, both being articles by W. Barton Leach.

* * *

CONDON, C. J., and POWERS, J., not participating.

Notes

The case provides an example of the relation back doctrine, its rationale, and both sides of the controversy over point of creation. The most significant issue is whether a general testamentary power should be treated as any special power under the Rule Against Perpetuities. The court's conclusion is that it should not be treated as such. Some states have adopted this approach by statute. *See, e.g.,* WIS. STAT. ANN. § 700.16(1) (c) (2003) (only special powers of appointment are computed from the time of creation by the Donor); DEL. CODE ANN. TIT. 25, § 501 (2004) (exercise by the Donee of ANY power is point of creation for the Rule); S. D. CODIFIED LAWS ANN. § 43-5-5 (2004). But the Uniform Probate Code § 2-902(a) adopts principles of general property law, thus accepting the Second Restatement of Property § 1.2, comment d, which provides for computing testamentary and special powers from creation by the Donor. The argument may be made that, by adopting the approach of *Barrett*— that the period of the Rule should commence with exercise by the Donee of a general testamentary power (and any general inter vivos power)—the court is simply applying a policy that will result in a less stringent Rule Against Perpetuities. *See generally* Melanie B. Leslie, *The Case Against Applying the Relation-Back Doctrine to the Exercise of General Powers of Appointment,* 14 CARDOZO L. REV. 219 (1992); Robert L. Fletcher, *Perpetuities: Basic Clarity, Muddled Reform,* 63 WASH. L. REV. 791 (1988); Lawrence M. Jones, *The Rule Against Perpetuities and Powers of Appointment: An Old Controversy Revived,* 54 IOWA L. REV. 456 (1968). If there is a violation of the Rule, analysis must then shift to what to do. Of consequence will be the nature of the power (general or special), the presence of a taker in default (if the power is special), and the willingness of a court to fashion its own remedy. The following case is illustrative of these issues.

Second National Bank of New Haven v. Harris Trust & Savings Bank

Connecticut Superior Court, New Haven County, 1971
29 Conn. Supp. 275, 283 A.2d 226

SHEA, Judge.

* * *

In New Haven on April 21, 1922, Caroline Haven Trowbridge, a resident of that city, created an inter vivos trust with the plaintiff as trustee. The income of the trust was given to the settlor's daughter, Margaret Trowbridge Marsh, and she was also given a general testamentary power of appointment over one-half of the corpus. The remaining one-half, as well as the half subject to the power in default of its exercise, would be distributed to Margaret's surviving children or issue per stirpes or, if there were none, to another daughter of the settlor, Mary Brewster Murray, or her surviving issue per stirpes. During the life of the settlor, a power was reserved to 'revoke, modify or alter' the terms of the trust 'respecting the payment of income.' The settlor, Caroline, died in New Haven on June 26, 1941, without having exercised this power.

Margaret, the life tenant and donee of the testamentary power, a resident of Winnetka, Illinois, died on April 13, 1969, leaving a will purporting to exercise the power by creating another trust, giving the income to her daughter, Mary Marsh Washburne, for a period of thirty years. At that time the trust estate would be distributed to Mary, if living, or, if not, to her surviving children or their descendants per stirpes, with outright distribution at age twenty-one. On April 4, 1949, before she executed her will, Margaret had partially released her power of appointment, converting it into a special testamentary power by limiting its exercise to the benefit of the class described in subsection (2)(A) of §811(f) of the Internal Revenue Code of 1939, as amended, 56 Stat. 942, which included her descendants.

Mary, the named beneficiary of the power of appointment as exercised, was born on October 25, 1929. As one of the two surviving children of Margaret, she would share equally with her brother, Charles Allen Marsh, the half of the trust created by Caroline subject to the power, in default of its exercise. If Margaret's exercise of the power under her will is fully effective, the defendant Harris Trust and Savings Bank, as executor and trustee would receive this half of the trust to pay the income to Mary for thirty years following her mother's death, and ultimately to distribute the corpus to Mary. If she did not live that long, upon her death the defendant trustee would make distribution to Mary's surviving children or their surviving descendants.

It appears that all of the living persons having any interest in the trust have been made parties. A guardian ad litem has been appointed to represent any unborn or undetermined persons who may have an interest and also to represent the five children of Mary, all of whom are minors.

* * *

The first problem is whether the exercise of the testamentary power of appointment by Margaret's will is invalid because of a claimed violation of the rule against perpetuities.

It is well established that a donee of a power of appointment, in exercising the power, acts as a mere conduit of the donor's bounty. 'Whenever such a power is in fact exercised, the validity of the appointment is determined by precisely the same rule as if the original testator, who created the power, had made in his own will the same provision in favor of the same appointee.' Bartlett v. Sears, 81 Conn. 34, 42, 70 A. 33, 36. 'The appointment is 'read back' into the instrument creating the power, as if the donee were filling in blanks in the donor's instrument.' 6 American Law of Property § 24.34.

So far as perpetuities are concerned, the period of the rule is reckoned from the date of creation of the power, not from the date of its exercise. Gray, Rule against Perpetuities (4th Ed.) § 515, p. 499. Where the power has been created by a will, the period is measured from the time of the death of the testator. Gray, op. cit. § 520; Simes & Smith, Future Interests (2d Ed.) § 1226. Where a deed is the source of the power, the date of delivery would ordinarily start the running of the period. Gray, loc. cit.; Simes & Smith, loc. cit.

In the case of inter vivos instruments, there is an exception for revocable transfers, for the reason that the policy of the rule is not violated where the grantor may at will terminate any future interests by revoking the grant. Where such an unconditional power of revocation is reserved, the period of perpetuities is calculated from the time the power of revocation ceased, usually at the death of the grantor unless the power was released earlier. 6 American Law of Property § 24.59; Gray, op. cit. § 524.1.

In this case, the defendants who seek to uphold the validity of the exercise of the power by Margaret's will claim that Caroline did retain a power to revoke the trust. The provision upon which they rely is paragraph (i) of the trust instrument, which reads as follows: '* * * as a measure of protection against possible contingencies, I hereby expressly reserve to myself power to revoke, modify or alter the terms hereof respecting the payment of income during my own life, by an instrument in writing, signed, dated and acknowledged, and delivered to the trustee.' It seems clear that a power 'to revoke, modify or alter the terms * * * respecting the payment of income' would not include a power to revoke the provisions for disposition of the principal of the trust. Such a partial power of revocation could affect only the life tenant, Margaret, during the life of the settlor, Caroline. Such a power would not qualify for the exception applicable to a full and unconditional power of revocation, because the remoteness of the future interests created could not be affected by any exercise of the power. 6 American Law of Property § 24.59.

Since the demise of our Connecticut Statute on Perpetuities in 1895, the common-law rule has been followed that no future interest is good unless it must vest, if at all, not later than twenty-one years after some life in being at the creation of the interest. Wilbur v. Portland Trust Co., 121 Conn. 535, 537, 186 A. 499; Cleaveland, Hewitt & Clark, Probate Law and Practice, §§ 446. 447. As applied to this case, the rule would bar any future interest which might not vest within twenty-one years after the life of some person in being on April 21, 1922, the date the trust was established. Since Mary was not born until October 25, 1929, she was not in being at the creation of the trust and her life cannot be taken as a measuring life under the rule against perpetuities. The only relevant life mentioned in the trust is that of Margaret, and, therefore, any valid future interest must vest no later than twenty-one years after her death on April 13, 1969.

In exercising the power of appointment, Margaret in her will used the language of an absolute gift to Mary of the income for thirty years and then a distribution to her of the principal of the trust. The next sentence adds the provision that upon Mary's death within the thirty-year period (or prior to the death of the testatrix, Margaret) the principal of the trust would be distributed to Mary's children or descendants of deceased children surviving her. Such unconditional words of gift would ordinarily be construed as creating a vested interest subject to defeasance upon the occurrence of the condition subsequent contained in the later clause. Howard v. Batchelder, 143 Conn. 328, 336, 122 A.2d 307, 310. 'If the conditional element is incorporated into the description of, or into the gift to, the remainder-man, then the remainder is contingent; but if, after words giving a vested interest, a clause is added divesting it, the remainder is vested.' Gary, op. cit. § 108; Howard v. Batchelder, supra, 334, 122 A.2d 307. Such exaltation of verbalism over substance has been criticized, but it is rigidly adhered to in the legalistic sophistry which comprises much of the lore of future interests. As it was once remarked, 'I am quite aware that this is all largely (a) matter of words, but so is much of the law of property; and unless we treat such formal distinctions as real, that law will melt away and leave not a rack behind.' Commissioner of Internal Revenue v. City Bank Farmers' Trust Co., 2 Cir., 74 F.2d 242, 247.

'An interest is 'vested' for purposes of the Rule when the following conditions exist: a. any condition precedent attached to the interest is satisfied, and b. the taker is ascertained, and c. where the interest is included in a gift to a class, the exact amount or fraction to be taken is determined.' 6 American Law of Property § 24.18. The language creating the gift to Mary imposes no condition precedent, but rather a condition subsequent, i.e. her death within thirty years after Margaret's death. Since the gift is to a named person the identity of the taker is established. The third requirement (c) is not applicable to a gift to an individual.

The construction of the gift of the remainder to Mary as vested rather than contingent is reinforced by the intermediate gift of the income to her. 6 American Law of Property § 24.19. A gift in favor of a named individual has historically been treated as vested and not subject to the rule unless it is expressly subject to a condition precedent. Restatement, 4 Property § 370, comment g. The preference of the law for vested rather than contingent interests certainly dictates such a construction in this case, where even the grammatical form of a condition subsequent has been observed by the draftsman. That the use of a condition subsequent rather than precedent is often the touchstone of validity in perpetuities cases is demonstrated by the following textbook illustrations: 'Case 20. T bequeaths a fund in trust to pay the income to A for life and then to pay the principal to such of A's children as shall reach the age of twenty-five. Reaching the age of twenty-five is a condition precedent attached to the gift to the children. Assuming that A survives the testator and can have further children, an after-born child of A can reach twenty-five at a date later than twenty-one years after lives in being at T's death. Therefore the remainder to A's children is void. Case 21. T bequeaths a fund in trust to pay the income to A for life and then to pay the principal to A's children, but if all of A's children die under the age of twenty-five, then to pay the principal to B. Again the condition is too remote. But it is a condition subsequent. The remainder to the children is vested subject to divestment upon a remote condition; the divesting contingency is void; therefore the children have an indefeasibly vested remainder.' 6 American Law of Property § 24.19, p. 60. It is well recognized that the form of language used rather than the substance of the condition is determinative as to whether the condition is precedent or subsequent. 5 American Law of Property § 21.31, p. 177. 'Whether a remainder is vested or contingent depends upon the language employed.' Gray, op. cit. § 108.

In a case similar in many respects to this one, an appointment was made to a named great-grandnephew, a year old at the time of exercise of the power, by the will of the donee of a power created by an inter vivos transfer, of income until age twenty-five, and then of principal when he attained that age; in the event of his death prior thereto, the principal would be distributed to the boy's father, who was named. It was held, despite the use of some contingent language, that the remainder to the great-grandnephew was valid under the rule, because it might be construed as vested subject to defeasance upon death prior to age twenty-five. The gift over to the father was ruled invalid as in violation of the terms of the power. Dean v. First National Bank, 217 Or. 340, 341 P.2d 512.

The gift to Mary's children, following the same verbal formalism, is a contingent remainder, because it is expressly subject to the condition that they survive their mother and that she not live until termination of the thirty-year trust. White v. Smith, 87 Conn. 663, 669–673, 89 A. 272. It is also contingent because, as a gift to a class (surviving children and surviving descendants of deceased children), the fractional interest of each member of the class cannot be ascertained until the contingency (Mary's death) happens. Gray, op. cit. §§ 369–375.

'It is well established that the rule against perpetuities does not affect vested interests, even though enjoyment may be postponed beyond the period of the rule. Connecticut Trust & Safe Deposit Co. v. Hollister, 74 Conn. 228, 232, 50 A. 750; Restatement, 4 Property § 386, comment j. It would not operate therefore, to invalidate either the gift of the income to Mary for life or thirty years or the gift of the remainder after the thirty years. Colonial Trust Co. v. Brown, 105 Conn. 261, 272, 135 A. 555; Bartlett v. Sears, 81 Conn. 34, 44, 70 A. 33. Both of these gifts vested in interest at the death of Margaret within the period of the rule, and the postponement of enjoyment beyond the period of the rule would not invalidate them. Howard v. Batchelder, 143 Conn. 328, 336, 122 A.2d 307.

The permissible duration of a trust in not governed by the rule against perpetuities. Restatement, 4 Property § 378; Gray, op. cit. §§ 232–246. It is no objection, therefore, that Mary's life estate may last beyond the period of the rule. It is also of no significance that her remainder interest may be defeated by her death, which may occur after that time. A vested remainder is exempt from the rule even though it may be subject to complete defeasance. Restatement, 4 Property § 370. The rule does bar the contingent remainder to Mary's children because it may vest more than twenty-one years after the death of Margaret, whose life must be taken as the measuring life. This result, abhorrent to the rule, would occur if Mary should die more than twenty-one but less than thirty years after her mother.

It is argued that the court should apply the cy pres doctrine to save the remainder to Mary's children by reducing the period of the trust to a maximum of twenty-one years. In a similar case, the Supreme Court of Hawaii expressly applied this doctrine to revise the testator's will as suggested. In re Estate of Chun Quan Yee Hop, 469 P.2d 183 (Haw.). This judicial innovation has received favorable comment, but such a change in the established law of this state ought to be reserved for our Supreme Court. The earlier case of Edgerly v. Barker, 66 N.H. 434, 31 A. 900, in which the cy pres doctrine was first applied by any court in a perpetuities situation, is the subject of a lengthy condemnation by Professor Gray. Gray, op. cit. §§ 857–893.

It is also claimed that General Statutes § 45-95 is applicable. This statute embodies the so-called 'second look' doctrine, and reads as follows: 'In applying the rule against perpetuities to an interest in real or personal property limited to take effect at or after the termination of one or more life estates in, or lives of, persons in being when the period of said rule commences to run, the validity of the interest shall be determined on the basis of facts existing at the termination of such one or more life estates or lives.

For the purpose of this section, an interest which must terminate not later than the death of one or more persons is a life estate although it may terminate at an earlier time.' This statute permits the validity of the interests created to be determined on the basis of the facts existing upon the death of Margaret, the measuring life under the rule against perpetuities. In fact, this has been the reference point for the court's consideration of the validity of the interests involved, because, apart from the statute, the actual exercise of the power of appointment, and not the possibility of its exercise in some other manner, is the criterion under the rule. Gray, op. cit. § 510. 'In the case of all powers of appointment * * * facts can be considered which exist at the time of the exercise of the power.' 6 American Law of Property § 24.24, p. 77. The conclusion that the remainder to Mary's children is invalid would not be changed unless the statute were construed to authorize a second look after Mary's life, an interpretation which its language does not support.

Another statute relied upon is General Statutes § 45-96, which reads as follows: 'If an interest in real or personal property would violate the rule against perpetuities as modified by section 45-95 because such interest is contingent upon any person attaining or failing to attain an age in excess of twenty-one, the age contingency shall be reduced to twenty-one as to all persons subject to the same age contingency.' It seems too clear for argument that the remainder to Mary's children is not 'contingent upon any person attaining or failing to attain an age in excess of twenty-one.' Section 45-96 is not applicable.

'If future interests created by any instrument are avoided by the Rule against Perpetuities, the prior interests become what they would have been had the limitation of the future estate been omitted from the instrument.' Gray, op. cit. § 247. Obviously, the consequences which follow upon the invalidity of a subsequent interest depend upon the intention of the donor. Restatement, 2 Property § 228; 5 American Law of Property § 21.48. 'A presumption is generally recognized that the precedent interest becomes indefeasible as a result of the ineffectiveness of the divesting interest * * *.' 5 American Law of Property § 21.48; Restatement, 2 Property § 229. 'But it will take clear language to show an intention to have the determining limitation taken separately from the remote gift. * * * If the prior estate be a fee simple the void conditional limitation cannot, it is submitted, thus operate as a contingent termination of the prior estate.' Gray, op. cit. § 250. 'Where a divesting interest is void, the interest which would otherwise have been divested becomes absolute.' 6 American Law of Property § 24.47, p. 124.

A gift of trust principal payable at an age beyond the period of the rule, subject to a limitation over in the event of nonattainment of that age, is a common occasion for the application of these principles to result in an indefeasibly vested remainder. Id., p. 125 (Case 72); Restatement, 4 Property § 384, comment g. 'When a subsequent condition or limitation over is void, * * * the estate becomes vested in the first taker, discharged of the condition or limitation over, according to the terms in which it was granted or devised; if for life, it then takes effect as a life estate; if in fee, then as a fee simple absolute.' Howe v. Hodge, 152 Ill. 252, 279, 38 N.E. 1083, 1090; Safe Deposit & Trust Co. v. Sheehan, 169 Md. 93, 109, 179 A. 536.

Under these principles, the gift of the remainder to Mary becomes indefeasibly vested because of the invalidation of the contingent remainder to her children.

In summary, the court has concluded that Mary has a valid income interest, in the half of the trust subject to the power of appointment, for thirty years and is then entitled to receive the principal. If she dies before then, the principal would be distributed to her estate, because her remainder has become indefeasibly vested.

Accordingly, it is ordered that the plaintiff trustee turn over to the defendant Harris Trust and Savings Bank one-half of the trust, to be held by that defendant to pay the income (including accumulated income) to the defendant Mary Marsh Washburne until April 13, 1999, when the principal shall be distributed to her. In the event of her earlier death, the principal shall be distributed to her estate. The court's advice is not sought with respect to any question pertaining to the remaining half of the trust fund.

* * *

Judgment may enter accordingly.

Notes

The case distinguishes between irrevocability (corpus) and revocability (income) in reference to creation and the relation back doctrine. According to the Connecticut court, in either case, we must compute from creation by the Donor, in light of the facts at exercise by the Donee. Commentators have suggested that the doctrine of marshaling of assets could have saved the appointment, *see, e.g.*, *Second Restatement (Second) of Property* §§ 22.1 & 22.2 (1986), and, of course, if the thirty years could have been reduced to twenty-one, there would have been a simpler solution, *see, e.g.*, In re Estate of Kreuzer, 243 A.D.2d 207, 674 N.Y.S.2d 505 (1998). Of course, the best remedy is proper drafting by competent attorneys. But if in doubt, attorneys should utilize savings clauses as remedy for all types of Rule violations.

E. Savings Clauses

Many publications offer drafting advice to attorneys preparing estate planning documents, to include trusts and Wills. For example, Robert J. Lynn and Grayson M.P. McCouch provide for seven tips of proper drafting, *see* Nutshell Series, Introduction to Estate Planning 276–82 (5th ed. 2004), and there is an ode to justified simplicity in the classic THOMAS L. SHAFFER, THE PLANNING AND DRAFTING OF WILLS AND TRUSTS 169–90 (2d ed. 1979), or even more simply at THOMAS L. SHAFFER, CAROL ANN MOONEY & AMY JO BOETTCHER, THE PLANNING AND DRAFTING OF WILLS AND TRUSTS 191–01(4th ed. 2001). But the temptation to be simple is easily forsaken, and, hence, the prudent drafter would be wise to include a savings clause in any estate plan containing a future interest. Such a clause becomes "operative only if some part of the disposition violates the [Rule and] directs the disposition of the offending interest in such a manner as to prevent such violation." MARK REUTLINGER, WILLS, TRUSTS, AND ESTATES: ESSENTIAL TERMS AND CONCEPTS 206 (1993). One of the earliest and most often used of savings clauses may be found at W. Barton Leach and James K. Logan, *Perpetuities: A Standard Savings Clause to Avoid Violations of the Rule*, 74 HARV. L. REV. 1141 (1961). For more recent suggestions, see DAVID M. BECKER, PERPETUITIES AND ESTATE PLANNING 133–84 (1993). Professor Jesse Dukeminier offers an example of such a clause:

> Notwithstanding any other provision in this instrument, this trust shall terminate, if it has not previously terminated, 21 years after the death of the sur-

vivor of the beneficiaries of the trust living at the date this instrument becomes effective. In case of such termination the then remaining principal and
undistributed income of the trust shall be distributed to the then income
beneficiaries in the same proportions as they were, at the time of termination,
entitled to receive the income. The term "beneficiaries" includes persons originally named as beneficiaries in this instrument as well as persons, living at
the date this instrument becomes effective, subsequently named as beneficiaries by a donee of a power of appointment over the trust assets exercising
such power.

JESSE DUKEMINIER, STANLEY M. JOHANSON, JAMES LINDGREN & ROBERT H. SITKOFF,
WILLS, TRUSTS, AND ESTATES 695–96 (2005).

F. Reformation Devices

The preceding material contains references to reform of the harsh consequences of
the Rule, but they are piecemeal and often parochial. England, on the other hand, has
been quick to reform the Rule. *See generally* Robert J. Lynn, *Perpetuities Reform: An
Analysis of Developments in England and the United States*, 113 U. PA. L. REV. 508 (1965).
Until very recently, domestic courts and legislatures were convinced that the Rule was a
staple in American public policy, and, thus, every attempt should be made to alleviate
any "mistakes" made by drafters of long-term trusts. Scholars and commentators offered multiple views as to how public policy may be served and, at the same time, how
testamentary intent may be fostered. *See, e.g.*, Paul G. Haskell, *A Proposal for a Simple
and Socially Effective Rule Against Perpetuities*, 66 N.C. L. REV. 545 (1988); Lawrence W.
Waggoner, *Perpetuity Reform*, 81 MICH. L. REV. 1718 (1983); W. Barton Leach, *Perpetuities in Perspective: Ending the Rule's Reign of Terror*, 65 HARV. L. REV. 721 (1952). Yet,
even amidst the reform movement, there was an appeal to drafters of legal documents
to draft in conformity with the requirements of the orthodox Rule. *See, e.g.*, Robert
Lynn, *Perpetuities Literacy for the 21st Century*, 50 OHIO ST. L. J. 219 (1989). What follows is a list of reformation devices to validate interests otherwise violating the Rule.

1. Wait and See

Pennsylvania was the first state to adopt a statute allowing actual rather than possible
events to measure the Rule. *See* ROBERT J. LYNN, THE MODERN RULE AGAINST PERPETU-
ITIES 10 (1966). But additional states utilize actuality, either by statute or common law.
See IOWA CODE ANN. § 558.68 (West 2004); KY. REV. STAT. ANN. § 381.216 (West 2004); 33
ME. REV. STAT. ANN. §§ 101–106 (2004); Murphy Exploration Prod. Co. v. Sun Operating
Ltd. P'Ship, 747 So. 2d 260 (Miss. 1999) (for Mississippi); Great Bay Sch. & Training Ctr.,
559 A.2d 1329 (N.H. 1989) (for New Hampshire); OHIO REV. CODE ANN. § 2131.08 (West
2004); 20 PA. CONS. STAT. ANN. § 6104 (West 2004); VT. STAT. ANN. tit. 27, § 501 (2003).

The point of Wait and See is to allow for actual events to occur, even though, standing at the creation of the interest, there may well be a possibility of remote vesting violating the Rule. If a Settlor were to provide in an inter vivos irrevocable trust one million dollars for his children for life and then to his grandchildren surviving, there could
be a Rule violation. The violation would occur because the Settlor could have additional
children, whom the grandchildren survive, and one of the survivor's children could be

born after the creation of the trust and live longer than twenty-one years after any life in being, bringing about the vesting in the surviving grandchildren. But under Wait and See, the courts allow actual events to be considered. Therefore, the trust commences as valid because we are allowed to wait and see what actually happens. According to one proponent of Wait and See, the court should use all of the lives in being and make them the measuring lives for the duration of the trust. If the trust actually vests within this period, then everyone is satisfied, even though, at the creation of the interest, there was the definite possibility of invalidity. Any continuance of the trust beyond this period is void. *See* Jesse Dukeminier, *Perpetuities: The Measuring Lives,* 85 COLUM. L. REV. 1648, 1656 (1985); 20 PA. CONS. STAT. § 6104(b) (2004).

The Second Look Doctrine is a variation of Wait and See and is applicable to powers of appointment, even though Second Look is not equivalent to Wait and See in scope. The doctrine permits courts to take into account all of the facts known by a Donee at the exercise by the Donee. To demonstrate the Second Look doctrine and, impliedly, Wait and See, see the following decision.

Sears v. Coolidge

Supreme Judicial Court of Massachusetts, 1952
329 Mass. 340, 108 N.E.2d 563

WILKINS, Justice.

These two petitions under G.L.(Ter.Ed.) c. 231A seek binding declarations as to the validity of the provisions relating to income and to gifts of principal by way of remainder in a deed of trust executed by Thomas Jefferson Coolidge, late of Manchester, under date of February 12, 1913. The settlor died on November 17, 1920. In each case a decree was entered declaring that the life interests are valid; but that the gifts over of principal are invalid and void, and upon the termination of the trust the personal representatives of the settlor's estate are to receive the principal and any unpaid accumulated income. The petitioners, the trustees, and numerous other persons interested in the trust or in the settlor's estate appealed.

The net income of the trust was payable one third semi-annually to 'such of the issue of my deceased son as shall be living at the time of each such semi-annual payment,' and two thirds, divided into three parts payable semi-annually, one part each to Marian A. Sargent and to Sarah L. Newbold and after their death to their respective issue, and one to the living issue of Eleonora R. Sears, who were the petitioners Eleonora R. Sears and Frederick R. Sears.

The appeals relating to the life interests have been 'waived and withdrawn.' We are now concerned only with the decrees in so far as they affect the remainder interests. Whenever we refer to the appellants, we shall mean all or some of those who are seeking to establish the validity of the remainder interests. The facts are undisputed and, for the most part, are embodied in a written stipulation in the Probate Court. The evidence is reported.

The fundamental issue is whether the remainder interests violate the rule against perpetuities. Paragraph 5 of the trust instrument provides that the capital of the trust is to be distributed 'in equal shares to and among my issue living' at the time of distribution. Distribution is to take place upon 'whichever shall first happen' of two events: (1) 'the death of the last survivor of those of my children, grandchildren and great grandchildren who shall be living at my death'; or (2) 'the attainment of fifty years by the youngest surviving grandchild of mine who shall be living at my death.'[1] The second event first happened. William A. Coolidge, the youngest grandchild living at the settlor's death, attained the age of fifty years on October 21, 1951.

Where a trust instrument contains two alternative conditions, of which the first might be too remote and the second, which actually occurs, is not too remote, the rule is not violated. Jackson v. Phillips, 14 Allen 539, 572–573; Stone v. Bradlee, 183 Mass. 165, 171–172, 66 N.E. 708; Gray v. Whittemore, 192 Mass. 367, 372, 78 N.E. 422, 10 L.R.A.,N.S., 1143; Springfield Safe Deposit & Trust Co. v. Ireland, 268 Mass. 62, 67–68, 167 N.E. 261, 64 A.L.R. 1071. Accordingly, the appellants contend that the attainment by the youngest grandchild of the age of fifty years was certain to occur within the period required by the rule, and that as matter of construction the reference in paragraph 5 to 'the youngest surviving grandchild of mine who shall be living at my death' must be read as if 'grandchild' were qualified by 'now living' or similar words. In support are adduced various facts in the settlor's family situation obvious to him when he executed the deed of trust. He was then eighty-one years of age and had been a widower for twelve years. At that time he had two living children, Marian A. Sargent, who was aged fifty-nine and had been a widow for twenty years, and Sarah L. Newbold, who was then fifty-five years of age. During the preceding year there had died two of his children, T. Jefferson Coolidge and Eleonora R. Sears. The settlor then had ten living grandchildren. Four were the minor sons of his deceased son. Two were the children of his deceased daughter, one being the petitioner, Eleonora R. Sears, and the other Frederick R. Sears, the administrator of whose estate is the petitioner Fiduciary Trust Company. One was the child of Marian A. Sargent, and three were the children of Sarah L. Newbold. The oldest grandchild was thirty-five and the youngest was seven. No further grandchildren were born in the settlor's lifetime, but the youngest of the ten died before the settlor.

The appellees argue, on the other hand, that it is not permissible thus to qualify the clause in paragraph 5, and for present purposes we accept their position on this point, and assume that the phrase 'the youngest surviving grandchild of mine who shall be living at my death' is not to be interpreted as excluding grandchildren who might be born after the trust instrument was created.

The appellants make the contention that the settlor in the trust deed reserved a power which was at least equivalent to a special power of appointment, and that the validity of the remainders must in any event be determined in the light of the facts existing at his death when it was known that his only grandchildren had been lives in being at the time the trust was created. This has been referred to in the arguments as 'a second look.'

Paragraph 9 reads: 'I reserve to myself power at all times to make any additions to the trust property, to change and alter any or all of the trusts herein set forth and to declare

---

1. The full language of paragraph 5 is: 'Upon the death of the last survivor of those of my children, grandchildren and great grandchildren who shall be living at my death, or upon the attainment of fifty years by the youngest surviving grandchild of mine who shall be living at my death, whichever shall first happen, the capital of the trust fund, as then existing, shall be conveyed, transferred and paid over in equal shares to and among my issue living at that time, such issue taking per stirpes and not per capita, and thereupon the trusts established by this instrument shall cease and determine.' The same deed of trust was the subject of the decision in Dexter v. Treasurer & Receiver General, 243 Mass. 523, 137 N.E. 877.

new uses and trusts of the property in any way or manner except such as will vest in myself the trust property or any beneficial interest therein, to name and appoint any other persons than those above specified or hereafter appointed as beneficiaries, whether by way of addition or substitution, and to appoint other trustees instead of or in addition to any or all of those above named. Every such change, alteration, nomination and appointment shall be made by my deed and shall take effect immediately upon the delivery thereof to any person who shall at the time be acting as a trustee under the provisions of these presents.'

The point, which, so far as appears, has not been pressed upon an appellate court before, is based upon the analogy of Minot v. Paine, 230 Mass. 514, 120 N.E. 167, 1 A.L.R. 365. The theory is that at the settlor's death the expiration of the power to divert the property from the takers in default was the same in effect as an appointment of the remainders by the settlor's will.

The reserved power is, at the very least, akin to a power of appointment. National Shawmut Bank v. Joy, 315 Mass. 457, 474, 53 N.E.2d 113; Restatement: Property, § 318, comment i. See Saltonstall v. Treasurer & Receiver General, 256 Mass. 519, 524, 153 N.E. 4; Boston Safe Deposit & Trust Co. v. Commissioner of Corporations & Taxation, 294 Mass. 551, 554, 3 N.E.2d 33, 109 A.L.R. 854; State Street Trust Co. v. Crocker, 306 Mass. 257, 262, 28 N.E.2d 5, 128 A.L.R. 1166. And, for present purposes, we treat it as having attributes of a special power to appoint by deed.

In Minot v. Paine, the power to appoint was, in fact, exercised, and there was presented a question as to the effect of the language used by the donee of the power, who had become, in law, the agent of the donor for the purpose. At page 522 of 230 Mass., at page 170 of 120 N.E., it was said: 'The donee in exercising the power is in effect writing the will of the donor respecting the appointed property. * * * The words used by the donee in exercising the power are to be construed and interpreted as to their meaning in the light of the facts as they are at the time the power is exercised. The will of the donor is projected forward to the time of the exercise of the power so as to receive the benefit of the facts which have appeared since his decease. * * * As applied to the exercise of a power of appointment the words of the rule are satisfied if it appears that in the light of facts as to relationship and longevity existent when the appointment is exercised, the estates created in truth will vest and take effect within the period limited by the rule, although this may not have been certain at the death of the donor of the power.'

In the present instance, no appointment having been made, there were no words expressed by the holder of the reserved power to be read back into the deed of trust. That fact, however, should not be decisive. In every case where there is a power, whether it be exercised or not, there is the common feature that until the opportunity for its exercise ceases to exist, there will persist uncertainty as to the ultimate disposition of the property. Until then nothing final can be known as to what are the provisions for the vesting of the future interests, and it is with such vesting the policy of the rule is concerned. * * * [Citations omitted].

Since it is permissible to make use of the circumstances known when a power, which is special or testamentary, is exercised to determine validity under the rule, it seems reasonable to afford the same opportunity in cases where such a power is not exercised. In the case of the trust instrument under consideration until it became too late for the settlor to exercise the reserved power no one could tell what might be the ultimate disposition of the trust property. As long as there remained a right to change, alter, and make new appointments, no instructions to the trustees or declaratory decree would ordinarily have been given as to the validity of the settlor's limitations. See National Shawmut Bank v. Morey, 320 Mass. 492, 497–500, 70 N.E.2d 316, 174 A.L.R. 871; Young v. Jackson, 321 Mass. 1, 7, 71 N.E.2d 386; Burn v. McAllister, 321 Mass. 660, 662, 75 N.E.2d 114. Upon his death it could be learned for the first time what definitely were to be the terms of the trust. It then could be seen for the first time that there was to be no failure to vest within the period limited by the rule. No further grandchildren had been born. In these precise circumstances there is no compelling decision which prevents taking advantage of facts known at the moment when the power ceased to be exercisable. American Law of Property, § 24.36. We are unwilling to apply the rule so as to invalidate the trust instrument.

The appellees strongly urge that the doctrine of a 'second look' has no place in reading the original limitations in default of appointment, which were capable of examination when created, and which should retain the same meaning throughout. They argue that its adoption would be a nullification of the rule 'that executory limitations are void unless they take effect ex necessitate and in all possible contingencies' within the prescribed period. Hall v. Hall, 123 Mass. 120, 124. But this rule, while recognized, was assuaged as to the exercise of a power of appointment in Minot v. Paine, 230 Mass. 514, 522, 120 N.E. 167, 1 A.L.R. 365. It was there deemed wise not to apply unmodified a remorseless technical principle to a case which it did not fit. That principle seems equally inappropriate here.

The decrees are reversed and the causes are remanded to the Probate Court for the entry of decrees in accordance with this opinion. Costs and expenses of appeal are to be in the discretion of the Probate Court.

So ordered.

2. Cy Pres

By adopting a cy pres statute, a state allows the courts to give effect to the general intent of the Settlor of a trust whenever that general intent may be discerned. For example, the Missouri statute provides, in part:

> When any limitation or provision violates the rule against perpetuities or a rule or policy corollary thereto and reformation would more closely approximate the primary purpose or scheme of the grantor, settlor or testator than total invalidity of the limitation or provision, upon the timely filing of a petition in a court of competent jurisdiction, by an party in interest, all parties in interest having been served by process, the limitation or provision shall be reformed, if possible. To the extent necessary to avoid violation of the rule or policy and, as so reformed, shall be valid and effective.

Mo. Rev. Stat. Ann. § 442.555(2) (West 2004).

In addition to Missouri, Texas has adopted Cy Pres. See Tex. Prop. Code Ann. § 5.043 (2004). States like New York have adopted specific cy pres contingencies, such as ones that reduce offending age contingencies. See, e.g., In re Estate of Kreuzer, 243 A.D.2d 207, 674 N.Y.S.2d 505 (1998); N.Y. Est., Powers & Trusts L. §§ 9-1.2 & 9-1.3 (2004). Traditionally, states liked to combine Wait and See and Cy Pres to allow for modification at the end of the period of waiting for actual events to occur. See Jesse Dukeminier, Kentucky Perpetuity Law Restated and Reformed, 49 Ky. L.J. 3 (1960). Seeking more certainty, scholars crafted a better version of Wait and See, which is modeled on the English model of perpetuity reform. It is called the Uniform Statutory Rule Against Perpetuities (2003) (USRAP).

3. Uniform Statutory Rule Against Perpetuities (2003) (USRAP)

The Uniform Statutory Rule Against Perpetuities, now adopted as part of the Uniform Probate Code, §9, is similar to Wait and See in that the statute does two things: (1) if all interests vest within a life in being plus twenty-one years (the common law rule), all is well; but (2) the statute allows for a fixed 90-year period in which all of the interests have an opportunity to vest, even though there may be a possibility, standing at the creation of the interest, that not all will vest within the Rule. At the end of the 90-year period, any interest that has not vested is reformed by the court to best comply with the intention of the Settlor.

Drafters will still need to know the intricacies of the Rule for determining whether the interest is valid under the common law rule, or from what point to begin in calculating the 90-year period. *See, e.g.,* In re Trust of Wold, 310 N.J. Super. 382, 708 A.2d 787 (1998) (relation-back applies in calculating the 90-year period when evaluating powers of appointment). But the advantage is that lives in being, measuring lives, vesting, and the like, are now protected under the mantle of a 90-year period. To date, in addition to the Uniform Probate Code, the USRAP has been adopted in Arizona, California, Colorado, District of Columbia, Florida, Georgia, Hawaii, Indiana, Kansas, Massachusetts, Michigan, Minnesota, Montana, Nebraska, Nevada, New Mexico, North Carolina, North Dakota, South Carolina, Tennessee, Utah, Virginia, and West Virginia. Why the 90-year period rather than some other number? Some argue that 90 years is the length of an average trust. *See* Lawrence W. Waggoner, *The Uniform Statutory Rule Against Perpetuities: The Rational of the 90-Year Waiting Period*, 73 Cornell L. Rev. 157 (1988). Many other articles have been written on many aspects of USRAP. *See, e.g.,* J. Rodney Johnson, *Wills, Trusts and Estates*, 34 U. Rich. L. Rev. 1069 (2000); Jesse Dukeminier, *The Uniform Statutory Rule Against Perpetuities and the GST Tax: New Perils for Practitioners and New Opportunities*, 30 Real Prop., Prob. & Tr. J. 186 (1995); Amy M. Hess, *Freeing Property Owners from the RAP Trap: Tennessee Adopts the Uniform Statutory Rule Against Perpetuities*, 62 Tenn. L. Rev. 267 (1995); Mary L. Fellows, *Testing Perpetuity Reforms: A Study of Perpetuity Cases 1984–89*, 25 Real Prop., Prob. & Trust J. 579 (1990); Jesse Dukeminier, *The Uniform Statutory Rule Against Perpetuities: Ninety Years in Limbo*, 34 UCLA L. Rev. 1023 (1987).

Uniform Probate Code (2003)

Section 2-901. Statutory Rule Against Perpetuities.

(a) [**Validity of Nonvested Property Interest.**] A nonvested property interest is invalid unless:

> (1) when the interest is created, it is certain to vest or terminate no later than 21 years after the death of an individual then alive; or

> (2) the interest either vests or terminates within 90 years after its creation.

(b) [**Validity of General Power of Appointment Subject to a Condition Precedent.**] A general power of appointment not presently exercisable because of a condition precedent is invalid unless:

(1) when the power is created, the condition precedent is certain to be satisfied or becomes impossible to satisfy no later than 21 years after the death of an individual then alive; or

(2) the condition precedent either is satisfied or becomes impossible to satisfy within 90 years after its creation.

(c) [Validity of Nongeneral or Testamentary Power of Appointment.] A nongeneral power of appointment or a general testamentary power of appointment is invalid unless:

(1) when the power is created, it is certain to be irrevocably exercised or otherwise to terminate no later than 21 years after the death of an individual then alive; or

(2) the power is irrevocably exercised or otherwise terminates within 90 years after its creation.

(d) [Possibility of Post-death Child Disregarded.] In determining whether a nonvested property interest or a power of appointment is valid under subsection (a)(1), (b)(1), or (c)(1), the possibility that a child will be born to an individual after the individual's death is disregarded.

(e) [Effect of Certain "Later-of" Type Language.] If, in measuring a period from the creation of a trust or other property arrangement, language in a governing instrument (i) seeks to disallow the vesting or termination of any interest or trust beyond, (ii) seeks to postpone the vesting or termination of any interest or trust until, or (iii) seeks to operate in effect in any similar fashion upon, the later of (A) the expiration of a period of time not exceeding 21 years after the death of the survivor of specified lives in being at the creation of the trust or other property arrangement or (B) the expiration of a period of time that exceeds or might exceed 21 years after the death of the survivor of lives in being at the creation of the trust or other property arrangement, that language is inoperative to the extent it produces a period of time that exceeds 21 years after the death of the survivor of the specified lives.

Section 2-902. When Nonvested Property Interest or Power of Appointment Created.

(a) Except as provided in subsections (b) and (c) and in Section 2-905(a), the time of creation of a nonvested property interest or a power of appointment is determined under general principles of property law.

(b) For purposes of Subpart 1 of this Part, if there is a person who alone can exercise a power created by a governing instrument to become the unqualified beneficial owner of (i) a nonvested property interest or (ii) a property interest subject to a power of appointment described in Section 2-901(b) or (c), the nonvested property interest or power of appointment is created when the power to become the unqualified beneficial owner terminates. [For purposes of Subpart 1 of this Part, a joint power with respect to community property or to marital property under the Uniform Marital Property Act held by individuals married to each other is a power exercisable by one person alone.]

(c) For purposes of Subpart 1 of this Part, a nonvested property interest or a power of appointment arising from a transfer of property to a previously funded trust or other existing property arrangement is created when the nonvested property interest or power of appointment in the original contribution was created.

Section 2-903. Reformation.

Upon the petition of an interested person, a court shall reform a disposition in the manner that most closely approximates the transferor's manifested plan of distribution and is within the 90 years allowed by Section 2-901(a)(2), 2-901(b)(2), or 2-901(c)(2) if:

(1) a nonvested property interest or a power of appointment becomes invalid under Section 2-901 (statutory rule against perpetuities);

(2) a class gift is not but might become invalid under Section 2-901 (statutory rule against perpetuities) and the time has arrived when the share of any class member is to take effect in possession or enjoyment; or

(3) a nonvested property interest that is not validated by Section 2-901(a)(1) can vest but not within 90 years after its creation.

Section 2-904. Exclusion from Statutory Rule Against Perpetuities.

Section 2-901 (statutory rule against perpetuities) does not apply to:

(1) a nonvested property interest or a power of appointment arising out of a non-donative transfer, except a nonvested property interest or a power of appointment arising out of (i) a premarital or postmarital agreement, (ii) a separation or divorce settlement, (iii) a spouse's election, (iv) a similar arrangement arising out of a prospective, existing, or previous marital relationship between the parties, (v) a contract to make or not to revoke a will or trust, (vi) a contract to exercise or not to exercise a power of appointment, (vii) a transfer in satisfaction of a duty of support, or (viii) a reciprocal transfer;

(2) a fiduciary's power relating to the administration or management of assets, including the power of a fiduciary to sell, lease, or mortgage property, and the power of a fiduciary to determine principal and income;

(3) a power to appoint a fiduciary;

(4) a discretionary power of a trustee to distribute principal before termination of a trust to a beneficiary having an indefeasibly vested interest in the income and principal;

(5) a nonvested property interest held by a charity, government, or governmental agency or subdivision, if the nonvested property interest is preceded by an interest held by another charity, government, or governmental agency or subdivision;

(6) a nonvested property interest in or a power of appointment with respect to a trust or other property arrangement forming part of a pension, profit-sharing, stock bonus, health, disability, death benefit, income deferral, or other current or deferred benefit plan for one or more employees, independent contractors, or their beneficiaries or spouses, to which contributions are made for the purpose of distributing to or for the benefit of the participants or their beneficiaries or spouses the property, income, or principal in the trust or other property arrangement, except a nonvested property interest or a power of appointment that is created by an election of a participant or a beneficiary or spouse; or

(7) a property interest, power of appointment, or arrangement that was not subject to the common-law rule against perpetuities or is excluded by another statute of this State.

Section 2-905. Prospective Application.

(a) Except as extended by subsection (b), Subpart 1 of this Part applies to a nonvested property interest or a power of appointment that is created on or after the effective date of Subpart 1 of this Part. For purposes of this section, a nonvested property interest or a power of appointment created by the exercise of a power of appointment is created when the power is irrevocably exercised or when a revocable exercise becomes irrevocable.

(b) If a nonvested property interest or a power of appointment was created before the effective date of Subpart 1 of this Part and is determined in a judicial proceeding, commenced on or after the effective date of Subpart 1 of this Part, to violate this State's rule against perpetuities as that rule existed before the effective date of Subpart 1 of this Part, a court upon the petition of an interested person may reform the disposition in the manner that most closely approximates the transferor's manifested plan of distribution and is within the limits of the rule against perpetuities applicable when the nonvested property interest or power of appointment was created.

G. Abolition of the Rule

Delaware Code Annotated (West 2004)

Title 25, Section 503. Rule against perpetuities.

(a) No interest created in real property held in trust shall be void by reason of the common law rule against perpetuities and no interest created in personal property held in trust shall be void by reason of any rule against perpetuities, whether the common law rule or otherwise.

(b) In this State, the rule against perpetuities for real property held in trust is that at the expiration of 110 years from the later of the date on which a parcel of real property or an interest in real property is added to or purchased by a trust or the date the trust became irrevocable, such parcel or interest, if still held in such trust, shall be distributed in accordance with the trust instrument regarding distribution of such property upon termination of the trust as though termination occurred at that time, or if no such provisions exist, to the persons then entitled to receive the income of the trust in proportion to the amount of the income so receivable by such beneficiaries, or in equal shares if specific proportions are not specified in the trust instrument. In the event that the trust instrument does not provide for distribution upon termination and there are no income beneficiaries of the trust, such parcel or interest shall be distributed to such then living persons who are then determined to be the trustor's or testator's distributees by the application of the intestacy laws of this State then in effect governing the distribution of intestate real property as though the trustor or testator had died at that particular time, intestate, a resident of this State, and owning the property so distributable.

This rule shall not apply to the following trusts, all of which may be perpetual:

> (1) A trust for the benefit of 1 or more charitable organizations as described in §§ 170(c), 2055(a) and 2522(a) of the United States Internal Revenue Code of 1986 (Title 26 of the United States Code) [26 U.S.C. §§ 170(c), 2055(a) and 2522(a)], or under any similar statute;

(2) A trust created by an employer as part of a stock bonus plan, pension plan, disability or death benefit plan or profit sharing plan for the exclusive benefit of some or all of its employees, to which contributions are made by such employer or employees, or both, for the purpose of distributing to such employees the earnings or the principal, or both earnings and principal, of the fund held in trust;

(3) A statutory trust formed under Chapter 38 of Title 12 for which a certificate of statutory trust is on file in the office of the Secretary of State; or

(4) A trust of real or personal property created for the perpetual care of cemeteries pursuant to the provisions of subchapter IV of Chapter 35 of Title 12.

(c) For purposes of this rule against perpetuities, trusts created by the exercise of a power of appointment, whether limited or general, and whether by will, deed or other instrument, shall be deemed to have become irrevocable by the trustor or testator on the date on which such exercise became irrevocable. Donors, not donees, of limited powers of appointment and donees exercising, not donors of, general powers of appointment, shall be deemed the trustors or testators for purposes of distributions to the trustor's or testator's distributees pursuant to subsection (b) of this section. Notwithstanding the foregoing, in the case of a power of appointment described in § 504 of this title as a "first power," trusts created by the exercise of the power of appointment, whether by will, deed or other instrument, shall be deemed to have become irrevocable by the trustor or testator on the date on which the first power was created.

(d) The rule contained in this section is subject to §§ 501 and 502 of this title concerning powers of appointment.

(e) For purposes of this section, real property does not include any intangible personal property such as an interest in a corporation, limited liability company, partnership, statutory trust, business trust or other entity, regardless of whether such entity is the owner of real property or any interest therein.

Notes

The earlier Rule reformation devices of Wait and See, and then Cy Pres, offered little challenge to the authority of the Rule Against Perpetuities in American law; they were simply corrective measures. But when the Uniform Statutory Rule Against Perpetuities was drafted and enacted in so many states, the prohibitions inherent in lives in being and measuring lives ceased. Drafters of Wills and inter vivos trusts were able to rely upon the assurance that an interest crafted into a document would last at least ninety years, long after anyone could remember having a claim to the trust corpus. Professor Jesse Dukeminier was among the first to predict that, with USRAP, the abolition of the Rule Against Perpetuities was close at hand. *See* Jesse Dukeminier, *The Uniform Statutory Rule Against Perpetuities: Ninety Years in Limbo*, 34 UCLA L. Rev. 1023, 1025–27 (1987). Other commentators suggest that the Rule's demise results from the desire to avoid estate taxation. *See, e.g.*, Ira Mark Blook, *The GST Tax Tail is Killing the Rule Against Perpetuities*, Tax Notes (Apr. 24, 2000); Joel C. Dobris, *The Death of the Rule Against Perpetuities, or the RAP Has No Friends*, 35 Real Prop., Prob. & Trust J. 601 (2000); Angela M. Vallario, *Death by a Thousand Cuts: The Rule Against Perpetuities*, 25 J. Legis. 141 (1999). For some states, the rationale for abolishment may be to provide a mechanism to foster "dynasty" trusts, which pay income to beneficiaries forever. *See* Joel C. Dobris, *Changes in the Role and the Form of the Trust at the New Millen-*

nium, or, We Don't Have to Think of England Anymore, 62 ALB. L. REV. 543 (1998). All of the beneficiaries and the Settlor could remain in a state retaining the Rule, but if the trust is established within a state that has abolished the Rule, a proper dynasty trust may exist in perpetuity. *See* Stewart E. Sterk, *Asset Protection Trusts: Trust Law's Race to the Bottom?*, 85 CORNELL L. REV. 1035 (2000); Verner F. Chaffin, *Georgia's Proposed Dynasty Trust: Giving the Dead Too Much Control*, 35 GA. L. REV. 1 (2000).

A successive number of states have abolished the Rule Against Perpetuities in real or personal property, or both. The Delaware statute is illustrative. *See* DEL CODE ANN. tit. 25, § 503 (2004). *But see* ALASKA STAT. § 34.27.051 (2003) (trustee must have discretion to distribute income or principal to a life in being at creation); IDAHO CODE § 55-111 (2004); 765 ILL. COMP. STAT. ANN. 305/3 (2004); MD. EST. & TRUSTS CODE ANN. § 11-102(e) (2004) (preserving Rule Against Perpetuities but enumerating exceptions); N.J. STAT. ANN. §§ 46:2F-9 (2004); R.I. GEN. LAWS § 34-11-38 (2003); S.D. CODIFIED LAWS § 43-5-8 (2004); WIS. STAT. ANN. § 700.16 (West 2003).

The Rule arose from a public policy focused on providing each generation with the ability to gift property without the restraint of preceding generations. The Rule fostered marketability, taxation of large wealth accumulations, addressing present circumstances, and in all of these circumstances, limiting dead hand control. In wondering about the future of the Rule in American law, the late Professor Jesse Dukeminier liked to quote from a comment allegedly made by Alexis Tocqueville: "What is the most important for democracy is not that great fortunes should not exist, but that great fortunes should not remain in the same hands. In that way there are rich men, but they do not form a class." Melvin L. Oliver, Thomas M. Shapiro & Julie E. Press, *Them That's Got Shall Get: Inheritance and Achievement in Wealth Accumulation*, in THE POLITICS OF WEALTH AND INEQUALITY 73–74 (Richard E. Ratcliff, Melvin L. Oliver & Thomas M. Shapiro eds., 1995).

Tax Considerations: Generation skipping transfer (GST) taxes were imposed by Congress in the Tax Reform Act of 1986, Pub. L. 99-514, §§ 1431, 100 Stat. 2085, 2717–32. The 1986 Act repealed an earlier version of the GST, enacted in the Tax Reform Act of 1976, Pub. L. 94-455, § 2006, 90 Stat. 1520, 1879–90. The provisions are contained in Chapter 13 of the Internal Revenue Code (§§ 2601–2662). The taxes were designed to close a loophole that allowed individuals to avoid gift and estate taxes. To do so, an individual would place his or her assets in a trust that would run for successive generations, the terms of which provided a beneficiary with an income interest and a limited power to withdraw the trust property. At death, the beneficiary, through a non-general (special) power of appointment, appointed the trust to his or her children. This continued for successive generations until the trust terminated under the Rule Against Perpetuities. At each generation nothing was included in the beneficiary's estate.

To address this, Congress enacted the generation-skipping transfer tax to ensure that transfers similar to those above would be subject to a tax liability at least as great as that which would ordinarily have been imposed had the transfers been taxed at each generation level. The GST provisions require that a tax be paid at each generation, imposing the GST on any taxable termination, taxable distribution and direct skip. *See* I.R.C. § 2611(a). In addition, each individual has a GST exemption (currently $1,500,000) that may be applied to transfers of property that will exempt the transfer from the GST tax. But the exemption will increase over the next few years. *See* I.R.C. § 2631(c). The issues raised by the tax are complicated with legislative underpinnings. *See generally* Staff of Joint Comm. On Taxation, 99th Cong., 2d Sess., General Explanation of the Tax Reform Act of 1986, at

1263 (1987); Peterson Marital Trust v. Commissioner of Internal Revenue, 78 F.3d 795 (2d Cir. 1996). Estate planners have sought to address the issues raised. *See, e.g.,* Jon J. Gallo, *Estate Planning and the Generation Skipping Tax*, 33 REAL PROP..PROB. & TRUST J. 457 (1998); DON W. LLEWELLYN, GAIL L. RICHARDSON & BEVERLY R. BUDIN, TAX PLANNING FOR LIFETIME AND TESTAMENTARY DISPOSITIONS—PROTOTYPE PLANS (1997).

The Uniform Statutory Rule Against Perpetuities (USRAP), now adopted as part of the Uniform Probate Code, has elongated the period of the Rule Against Perpetuities to a possible ninety years from creation of the interest. This significant event and the abolition or modification of the Rule in an increasing number of states increase the possibility of the creation of dynasty trusts. If the generation skipping transfer tax exemption continues to rise and eventually be extinct together with the estate tax, the question then arises as to the effect this will have upon successive generations benefitting from the dynasty trust without the generation-skipping tax. Will the number of dynasty trusts increase? Will states adopt taxes to replace the federal GST?

Chapter Eight

Planning for Incapacity

Tool Bar

The first chapter of this book focused on a family attempting to balance financial commitments associated with raising children and the necessity of providing care for an aging parent. The aging parent lives on a pension, very modest Social Security benefits, and health care, paid for with Medicare and a low cost medigap insurance plan with a health insurance company. None of these is sufficient, or even expected, to pay for assisted living or nursing home care, the costs for which often exceed $5,000 a month of after-tax dollars. Today, the question then arises: How should we plan for long-term care? *See, e.g.*, Julia Belian, *Medicaid, Elective Shares, and the Ghosts of Tenures Past*, 38 CREIGHTON L. REV. 1111 (2005). How should we plan for incapacity when income remains static, but health care costs rapidly escalate? All too often in America, this is the dilemma of modern estate planning, not what we have studied in the intervening chapters—wills, trusts, and future interests. As human longevity has lengthened, the issue now is not so much how to dispense wealth to succeeding generations, but, rather, how to ensure that I do not live longer than my wealth. Consider the following excerpt:

Raymond C. O'Brien & Michael T. Flannery, Long Term Care: Federal, State, and Private Options for the Future
191–92 (1997)

It was Leon Trotsky who said: "[O]ld age is the most unexpected of all the things that happen to [you]."* * * [LEON TROTSKY, DIARY IN EXILE 106 (1935: Elena Zarudnaya, trans., Harvard Univ. Press, 1958]. To date, in the United States, this is true. Perhaps with the baby boomers, entering the age of 50 and above, the perspective of

Americans will change and old age will be neither unexpected nor unplanned. The one lesson to be learned is that no one can afford to live in the age of "perhaps," the age of "denial," the age of "not me." The United States has come to a pivotal point and, regardless of private interest groups, government bureaucracy, traditional interests, and plain old inertia, dollars and cents will force U.S. residents to face the future of long-term care.

While it would be possible to say that health care is the issue, such an assertion would not take into account the unique status of long-term care. Certainly, health care has a dramatic and casual effect upon any long-term care proposal. But long term care, particularly as it affects the elderly with their large voting block, the disproportionate number of women, and the existent government programs already in place to assist those persons is unique and deserving of special attention.

Special attention is warranted because of technology, the beast that thrives on longer and longer life, more and more dollars, jobs, and progress. How can anyone suggest a curtailment of technology? Well, there may not be a suggestion but there is a denial of funds from the managed-care industry growing so rapidly in the United States.... The truth of the matter is that managed care serves a very important function when it serves to hold the power of new technology and its irrefragable potential to prolong life without regard for what is or is not extraordinary. The litigation explosion in America fuels the technological advance, and the inattentiveness of so many working-class men and women sustains it. Surely, the politicians are part of the problem. How many times during the most recent presidential election were cuts in Medicare raised to a level of feverish rhetoric. U.S. politicians know how to speak to those who vote.

Thus, American health care is a victim of posturing. Each of the posturing elements has a vociferous following and each a fortress of past or current entitlements. Change will not be easy, but change will come. When it does, change will likely be incremental, perhaps starting with innovative insurance programs. Then change will encompass payment for home care, innovative respite care programs, and other efforts to reduce inefficient overinstitutionalization. Once alternatives appear, reliance on Medicaid spend-down, consideration of assisted suicide, and financing difficulties of Medicaid and Medicare will lessen and reoccupy their traditional roles.

Finally, it is absolutely necessary to remember that long-term care is not simply about money, government, insurance, managed care, nursing homes, deficits, hospice, elderly attorneys, doctors, estate planning, meals, deductibles, eligibility, block grants, portability, premiums and working. Long-term care is about *persons*, real live human persons. In all of our incremental planning, plan for what is best for the human in ourselves.

I. Planning Options

A. Anatomical Gifts

Uniform Anatomical Gift Act (1987)

Section 2. Making, Amending, Revoking, and Refusing to Make Anatomical Gifts by Individual.

(a) An individual who is at least [18] years of age may (i) make an anatomical gift for any of the purposes stated in Section 6(a), (ii) limit an anatomical gift to one or more of those purposes, or (iii) refuse to make an anatomical gift.

(b) An anatomical gift may be made only by a document of gift signed by the donor. If the donor cannot sign, the document of gift must be signed by another individual and by two witnesses, all of whom have signed at the direction and in the presence of the donor and of each other, and state that it has been so signed.

(c) If a document of gift is attached to or imprinted on a donor's motor vehicle operator's or chauffeur's license, the document of gift must comply with subsection (b). Revocation, suspension, expiration, or cancellation of the license does not invalidate the anatomical gift.

(d) A document of gift may designate a particular physician or surgeon to carry out the appropriate procedures. In the absence of a designation or if the designee is not available, the donee or other person authorized to accept the anatomical gift may employ or authorize any physician, surgeon, technician, or enucleator to carry out the appropriate procedures.

(e) An anatomical gift by will takes effect upon death of the testator, whether or not the will is probated. If, after death, the will is declared invalid for testamentary purposes, the validity of the anatomical gift is unaffected.

(f) A donor may amend or revoke an anatomical gift, not made by will, only by:

(1) a signed statement;

(2) an oral statement made in the presence of two individuals;

(3) any form of communication during a terminal illness or injury addressed to a physician or surgeon; or

(4) the delivery of a signed statement to a specified donee to whom a document of gift had been delivered.

(g) The donor of an anatomical gift made by will may amend or revoke the gift in the manner provided for amendment or revocation of wills, or as provided in subsection (f).

(h) An anatomical gift that is not revoked by the donor before death is irrevocable and does not require the consent or concurrence of any person after the donor's death.

Notes

The Act has been adopted in all of the states and the District of Columbia and allows for a person to donate all or part of his or her human body, to take effect upon or after death, without the formalities associated with a Last Will and Testament. Likewise, the Act allows a person to refuse to make a gift, and this will supercede any other person's decision to date at death. If there has been no refusal recorded, then a gift may be authorized by any of the following persons (in hierarchical order): Spouse, adult child, either parent, adult sibling, grandparent or guardian at the time of death. *Id.* at § 3(a). Restrictions apply as to who may be a proper recipient of an anatomical gift, such as a hospital research institute or persons associated with a transplantation. *Id.* at § 6(a). A "person may not knowingly, for valuable consideration, purchase or sell a part for transplantation or therapy, if removal of the part is intended to occur after the death of the decedent." *Id.* at § 10(a). To be convicted of violating this provision is a felony and subject to a fine not exceeding $50,000. *Id.* at § 10(c). For a discussion of advance directives, see generally Carol J. Wessels, *Treated With Respect: Enforcing Patient Autonomy By Defending Advance Directives*, 6 MARQ. ELDER'S ADVISOR 217 (2005).

B. Power of Attorney

During a persons life, there may come a time when he or she may need another to have statutory authority to conduct any of the following: (1) real property transactions; (2) personal property transactions; (3) commodity and option transactions; (4) banking and other financial institution transactions; (5) business operating transactions; (6) insurance and annuity transactions; (7) estate, trust, and other beneficiary transactions; (8) claims and litigation; (9) personal and family maintenance; (10) government program benefits management; (11) retirement plan transactions; and (12) tax matters. To accomplish this, the National Conference of Commissioners on Uniform State Laws has proposed the Uniform Statutory Power of Attorney Act (1988), to include a form meant to be universally recognized. *See* UNIF. STAT. FORM POWER ATTY. ACT § 1 (2003). The Act is not meant to provide a durable power of attorney *unless* words are used to provide that: "This power of attorney will continue to be effective if I become disabled, incapacitated, or incompetent." *Id.* at § 2. Revocation is allowed in the manner specified in the power of attorney or in writing, *see, e.g.,* CAL. PROB. CODE § 4151 (2004), and the attorney-in-fact designated must exercise the standard of care of a prudent person, *see id.* at §§ 4230–38. In order to be valid, notarization is required, as provided in the following California provision.

California Probate Code (2004)

Section 4121. Legal sufficiency; conditions

A power of attorney is legally sufficient if all of the following requirements are satisfied:

(a) The power of attorney contains the date of its execution.

(b) The power of attorney is signed either (1) by the principal or (2) in the principal's name by another adult in the principal's presence and at the principal's direction.

(c) The power of attorney is either (1) acknowledged before a notary public or (2) signed by at least two witnesses who satisfy the requirements of Section 4122 [adults not acting as attorney-in-fact, but witnessing either the signing of the instrument or the principal's acknowledgment of the signature].

C. Durable Power of Attorney

At common law, a power of attorney ceased with the incapacity of the principal. Yet, very often, a principal may most need a person acting quickly on his or her behalf at that time of incapacity, without the necessity of applying to a court for the appointment of a guardian or a conservator. Therefore, states allowed for a power of attorney to survive incapacity if proper language was utilized, stating that the power would continue after incapacity. *See, e.g.,* CAL. PROB. CODE §§ 4018 & 4404 (2004). As the following form indicates, California allows for a power of attorney to be a durable power of attorney, unless the principal provides otherwise. Because the durable power grants extensive authority to the attorney-in-fact, California, for example, requires that there be a warning statement on any printed form of a durable power of attorney sold or distributed in the state. *See id.* at § 4128. Review the following form and compare it to the requirement of specificity in the *Franzen* decision.

California Probate Code (2004)

Section 4401. Form

The following statutory form power of attorney is legally sufficient when the requirements of Section 4402 are satisfied:

UNIFORM STATUTORY FORM POWER OF ATTORNEY
(California Probate Code Section 4401)

NOTICE: THE POWERS GRANTED BY THIS DOCUMENT ARE BROAD AND SWEEPING. THEY ARE EXPLAINED IN THE UNIFORM STATUTORY FORM POWER OF ATTORNEY ACT (CALIFORNIA PROBATE CODE SECTIONS 4400–4465). IF YOU HAVE ANY QUESTIONS ABOUT THESE POWERS, OBTAIN COMPETENT LEGAL ADVICE. THIS DOCUMENT DOES NOT AUTHORIZE ANYONE TO MAKE MEDICAL AND OTHER HEALTH-CARE DECISIONS FOR YOU. YOU MAY REVOKE THIS POWER OF ATTORNEY IF YOU LATER WISH TO DO SO.

I _____
(your name and address)

appoint _____
  (name and address of the person appointed, or of each person appointed
  if you want to designate more than one)

as my agent (attorney-in-fact) to act for me in any lawful way with respect to the following initialed subjects:

TO GRANT ALL OF THE FOLLOWING POWERS, INITIAL THE LINE IN FRONT OF (N) AND IGNORE THE LINES IN FRONT OF THE OTHER POWERS.

TO GRANT ONE OR MORE, BUT FEWER THAN ALL, OF THE FOLLOWING POWERS, INITIAL THE LINE IN FRONT OF EACH POWER YOU ARE GRANTING.

TO WITHHOLD A POWER, DO NOT INITIAL THE LINE IN FRONT OF IT. YOU MAY, BUT NEED NOT, CROSS OUT EACH POWER WITHHELD.

INITIAL

_____ (A) Real property transactions.

_____ (B) Tangible personal property transactions.

_____ (C) Stock and bond transactions.

_____ (D) Commodity and option transactions.

_____ (E) Banking and other financial institution transactions.

_____ (F) Business operating transactions.

_____ (G) Insurance and annuity transactions.

_____ (H) Estate, trust, and other beneficiary transactions.

_____ (I) Claims and litigation.

_____ (J) Personal and family maintenance.

_____ (K) Benefits from social security, medicare, medicaid, or other governmental programs, or civil or military service.

_____ (L) Retirement plan transactions.

_____ (M) Tax matters.

_____ (N) ALL OF THE POWERS LISTED ABOVE.

YOU NEED NOT INITIAL ANY OTHER LINES IF YOU INITIAL LINE (N).

SPECIAL INSTRUCTIONS:

ON THE FOLLOWING LINES YOU MAY GIVE SPECIAL INSTRUCTIONS LIMITING OR EXTENDING THE POWERS GRANTED TO YOUR AGENT.

_____

_____

_____

_____

_____

_____

_____

_____

_____

UNLESS YOU DIRECT OTHERWISE ABOVE, THIS POWER OF ATTORNEY IS EFFECTIVE IMMEDIATELY AND WILL CONTINUE UNTIL IT IS REVOKED.

This power of attorney will continue to be effective even though I become incapacitated.

STRIKE THE PRECEDING SENTENCE IF YOU DO NOT WANT THIS POWER OF ATTORNEY TO CONTINUE IF YOU BECOME INCAPACITATED.

EXERCISE OF POWER OF ATTORNEY
WHERE MORE THAN ONE AGENT DESIGNATED

If I have designated more than one agent, the agents are to act

_____

IF YOU APPOINTED MORE THAN ONE AGENT AND YOU WANT EACH AGENT TO BE ABLE TO ACT ALONE WITHOUT THE OTHER AGENT JOINING, WRITE THE WORD "SEPARATELY" IN THE BLANK SPACE ABOVE. IF YOU DO NOT INSERT ANY WORD IN THE BLANK SPACE, OR IF YOU INSERT THE

WORD "JOINTLY", THEN ALL OF YOUR AGENTS MUST ACT OR SIGN TO-
GETHER.

I agree that any third party who receives a copy of this document may act under it. Revocation of the power of attorney is not effective as to a third party until the third party
has actual knowledge of the revocation. I agree to indemnify the third party for any
claims that arise against the third party because of reliance on this power of attorney.

Signed this ___ day of _____, 19___

_____
(your signature)

_____
(your social security number)

State of _____ County of _____

BY ACCEPTING OR ACTING UNDER THE APPOINTMENT, THE AGENT AS-
SUMES THE FIDUCIARY AND OTHER LEGAL RESPONSIBILITIES OF AN AGENT.

[Include certificate of acknowledgment of notary public in compliance with Section
1189 of the Civil Code or other applicable law.]

Franzen v. Norwest Bank Colorado

Supreme Court of Colorado, 1998
955 P.2d 1018

Justice SCOTT delivered the Opinion of the Court.

This case arises out of a disagreement over the disposition of assets in a trust created
for the benefit of Frances Franzen by her late husband, James Franzen. In Norwest Colorado v. Franzen, No. 95CA0386 (Colo.App. June 27, 1996) (not selected for publication), the court of appeals held that James O'Brien, Mrs. Franzen's brother, was authorized to dissolve the trust by virtue of a power of attorney executed by Mrs. Franzen.
The court of appeals also held, moreover, that the trustee was not liable for litigation
expenses associated with challenging O'Brien's authority to dissolve the trust. We affirm
the judgment of the court of appeals in its entirety. * * *

* * *

On February 4, 1992, James Franzen, the settlor, executed an instrument creating a
trust designed to provide for himself and his wife, Frances Franzen, in their old age.
The corpus of the trust initially consisted of three bank accounts containing a total of
$74,251.19, but it did not include certain other assets held by Mr. and Mrs. Franzen as
joint tenants, such as the family home. Norwest Bank, then known as United Bank of
Denver, * * * was named as the sole trustee in the trust agreement.

James Franzen was terminally ill when he created the trust, and he died four months
later. Upon Mr. Franzen's death, a trust officer at the bank sent a letter to Frances
Franzen, who was living in a nursing home, notifying her that she had "certain rights
regarding the trust." A copy of the trust agreement was enclosed, and the letter referred
to Article 5.1, which states:

> At … [James'] death, if Frances survives … [him], she may direct … [the]
> trustee in writing to deliver the residuary trust estate to her within three
> months of [James'] death. If she does not so direct, this trust shall continue to

be administered as provided in Article 3. If she so directs, the trust shall terminate on the date the trust estate is distributed to her.

The letter asked Mrs. Franzen for a decision in writing by August 1, 1992, "so that we have time to make arrangements for the transfer of assets if necessary." A handwritten note at the bottom of the letter, signed by Mrs. Franzen and dated July 14, 1992, says, "I wish to leave the trust intact for my lifetime."

The bank, concerned about the disposition of the vacant house and other assets not included in the trust, contacted Mrs. Franzen's nephews, who were named as remaindermen of the trust. The two nephews were reluctant to assume responsibility for Mrs. Franzen's affairs, though, and Mrs. Franzen's brother, James O'Brien, intervened. O'Brien moved Mrs. Franzen to a nursing home in Kentucky, where he lived, and asked the bank to turn over Mrs. Franzen's assets to him.

In the course of dealing with the bank, the nephews expressed concerns about O'Brien's motives. The bank declined to comply with O'Brien's request, and filed a Petition for Instruction and Advice in the Denver Probate Court (probate court). Before the hearing, O'Brien sent the bank a copy of a power of attorney purporting to authorize him to act in Mrs. Franzen's behalf and a letter attempting to revoke the trust and to remove the bank as trustee, citing Article 6.2 and Article 8 of the trust agreement.

Article 6.2 of the trust provides that after the death of James Franzen, Frances Franzen "may remove any trustee," and that "[a]ny removal under this ... [paragraph] may be made without cause and without notice of any reason and shall become effective immediately upon delivery of ... [written notice] to the trustee" unless Frances Franzen and the trustee agree otherwise.

Article 8 of the trust agreement gives James Franzen "the right to amend or revoke this trust in whole or in part ... by a writing delivered to ... [the] trustee.... After my death, Frances may exercise these powers with respect to the entire trust estate."

The hearing was continued, and the bank filed a Petition for Appointment of a Conservator, asking the probate court to appoint someone to manage and protect Mrs. Franzen's assets. When the hearing on both petitions was held, the probate court ruled that the power of attorney had created a valid agency but that the trust had not been revoked and continued in existence. The probate court found that Mrs. Franzen needed protection, but a conservator was not available, so the Court appointed the bank as "special fiduciary" with responsibility for both trust and non-trust assets pursuant to sections 15-14-408 and 15-14-409, 5 C.R.S. (1997). The probate court ordered the bank to use the assets to make payments for Mrs. Franzen's benefit.

Franzen appealed the probate court rulings. On appeal, the court of appeals reversed, holding that the power of attorney authorized O'Brien to remove the bank as trustee and to revoke the trust. The court of appeals also held, however, that the bank was not liable for expenditures made in good faith after receiving the removal and revocation letter, including the legal fees incurred in the course of opposing O'Brien's efforts.

While the removal and revocation were effective immediately upon receipt of O'Brien's letter, the court of appeals held, the bank was entitled to disburse trust funds in good faith pending judicial resolution of O'Brien's claim that the trust had been dissolved. The court of appeals found that the probate court's award of administration and attorney fees to be paid by the trust estate to the bank were reasonable and appropriate compensation for the bank's duties as a fiduciary under the circumstances, and hence, declined to hold the bank liable.

* * *

A power of attorney is an instrument by which a principal confers express authority on an agent to perform certain acts or kinds of acts on the principal's behalf. See Willey v. Mayer, 876 P.2d 1260 (Colo.1994). In Colorado, the use and interpretation of such instruments is governed by statute. See §§ 15-14-601 to -610, 5 C.R.S. (1997). Under the power of attorney statute, the scope of an agent's authority to alter a trust is narrowly construed. "An agent may not revoke or amend a trust that is revocable or amendable by the principal without specific authority and specific reference to the trust in the agency instrument." § 15-14-608(2), 5 C.R.S. (1997).

Norwest notes that the power of attorney executed by Mrs. Franzen did not refer specifically to the Franzen trust. Thus, Norwest argues, O'Brien was not authorized to remove the trustee or revoke the trust. The statutory specificity requirement, however, did not take effect until January 1, 1995, almost two years after the power of attorney was executed by Mrs. Franzen.

General principles of statutory construction lead us to conclude that the power of attorney statute is inapplicable to any agency instrument executed prior to its effective date. See § 2-4-202, 1 C.R.S. (1997) (statutes are presumed prospective); see also People v. Munoz, 857 P.2d 546, 548 (Colo.App.1993) (applying the statute). In addition, the General Assembly expressly stated that the power of attorney statute does not "in any way invalidate any agency or power of attorney executed ... prior to January 1, 1995," conclusively demonstrating that no retroactive effect was intended. See § 15-14-611, 5 C.R.S. (1997).

Norwest responds that the specificity requirement in section 15-14-608(2) merely restated the common law in effect prior to its adoption, so the same result should be reached even though the statute was not intended to be applied retroactively. The bank asserts that the common law would require the power of attorney to refer to the trust by name.

Unfortunately for Norwest, the cases it cites state no such common law rule. Instead, these cases stand for the unremarkable proposition that a power of attorney giving an agent broad authority to act on behalf of the principal should be construed in light of the surrounding circumstances. Where a broadly worded power of attorney arguably authorizes acts that may be inconsistent with the principal's interests or intent, the instrument should not be interpreted as allowing the agent to undertake such acts in the absence of specific authority.

For example, in Estate of Casey v. Commissioner of Internal Revenue, 948 F.2d 895 (4th Cir.1991), the Fourth Circuit applied Virginia law to hold that an agent acting under a power of attorney that conferred wide-ranging authority to act on the principal's behalf was not authorized to give away the principal's property. The court said, "[T]he failure to enumerate a specific power, particularly one with the dangerous implications of the power to make unrestricted gifts of the principal's assets, reflects deliberate intention." Id. at 898.

Similarly, in Bryant v. Bryant, 125 Wash.2d 113, 882 P.2d 169 (1994), the Supreme Court of Washington held that an agent acting under a broadly worded power of attorney was not authorized to make gifts of the principal's assets. The court noted the consensus view that "gift transfers or transfers without substantial consideration inuring to the benefit of the principal violate the scope of authority conferred by a general power of attorney to sell, exchange, transfer, or convey property for the benefit of the principal." Id. 882 P.2d at 172 (citation omitted). The other cases cited by Norwest are to the same general effect. See, e.g., De Bueno v. Castro, 543 So.2d 393, 394–95 (Fla.App. 1989); Realty Growth Investors v. Council of Unit Owners, 453 A.2d 450, 454–55 (Dela.1982); Brown v. Laird, 134 Or. 150, 291 P. 352, 354–55 (1930)

The basic rule recognized in these cases logically might extend by analogy to situations where a power of attorney gives an agent wide authority to make decisions on behalf of the principal but makes no mention of the power to alter the principal's rights under any trust. We are willing to assume, for the sake of argument, that the scope of the agent's authority under the common law in such circumstances would not extend to revocation of a trust established to benefit the principal.

Even so, we are not persuaded that under the common law, an agency instrument must expressly refer to a particular trust by name in order to confer authority on the agent to revoke it. Under the reasoning of the cases previously cited, the terms of the power of attorney need only evince an intention to authorize the agent to make decisions concerning the principal's interests in trusts generally, not necessarily a particular trust.

Section 1(c) of the power of attorney executed by Mrs. Franzen expressly authorizes O'Brien to

> manage ... and in any manner deal with any real or personal property, tangible or intangible, or any interest therein ... in my name and for my benefit, upon such terms as ... [O'Brien] shall deem proper, *including the funding, creation, and/or revocation of trusts* or other investments.

(Emphasis added.)

We have little trouble concluding that the quoted language expressly authorizes O'Brien to revoke the Franzen trust, even though it does not mention the trust specifically by name.

* * *

Mrs. Franzen contends that Norwest should be strictly liable for trustee and attorney fees spent after the removal and revocation letter was received from O'Brien. In essence, she argues that a trustee should be held liable for all expenses incurred after a trust it oversees is revoked, even if it incurs the expenses in reliance on a court ruling—later vacated on appeal— that the trust remains in effect.

Mrs. Franzen cites a host of authority in support of her contention that a trustee is liable for any act in excess of his or her authority, even if it was undertaken in good faith or in reliance on the advice of counsel. See, e.g., Morgan v. Indep. Drivers Ass'n Pension Plan, 975 F.2d 1467, 1470 (10th Cir.1992); Moore v. Adkins, 2 Kan.App.2d 139, 576 P.2d 245, 255 (1978).

She acknowledges that a trustee is entitled to indemnification for the expenses of prosecuting and defending actions on behalf of the trust, but notes that indemnification is available only if the need for litigation was not caused by the fault of the trustee. See In re Estate of McCart, 847 P.2d 184, 187–88 (Colo.App.1992); 3A William F. Fratcher, Scott on Trusts § 244 (4th ed.1988).

Nowhere in the authorities cited by Mrs. Franzen can we find support for the view that a trustee is liable for acts in excess of his or her authority when the acts are undertaken in reliance on a court order, even when the ruling underlying the order is overturned on appeal. Both Morgan and Moore involved actions taken by fiduciaries in reliance on mistaken professional advice, not a court order. In fact, the reason why good faith reliance on the advice of counsel is not a defense to liability for a breach of duty is that a trustee has the option of seeking instruction from a court rather than depending on the potentially erroneous advice of a lawyer. See Restatement (Second) Trusts § 226 cmt. b & § 201 cmt. b (1957).

As for the propriety of Norwest's commencement of litigation to determine its responsibilities as trustee, we see no legal or equitable basis for imposing liability on the bank. At the time O'Brien sent the removal and revocation letter, the bank's representatives had reason to suspect that Frances Franzen might be incompetent and hence lack the capacity to execute a valid power of attorney authorizing O'Brien to act in her behalf. In addition, the remaindermen of the trust and others had expressed concerns about whether O'Brien was acting in Mrs. Franzen's interests.[3]

If the bank had turned over the trust assets as requested and Mrs. Franzen were later demonstrated to have been incompetent to execute the power of attorney, or if O'Brien had absconded with the money, then the bank would have faced liability for breach of its duty of care as a fiduciary. The remaindermen would likely have pointed out that they warned the bank about the possibility of irregularity in O'Brien's request.

Of course, to the extent that the bank was entitled to compensation for administering the trust only as long as the trust remained in existence and it remained the trustee, the bank's interests were served by challenging O'Brien's authority under the power of attorney and the terms of the trust agreement. However, the bank's interest in maintaining the trust with itself as trustee does not, ipso facto, demonstrate that the litigation did not benefit the trust estate.

Under the circumstances, then, the bank's decision to obtain a judicial determination of its responsibilities under the trust agreement was not only reasonable, but it appears to have been fully consistent with the bank's duty to protect the interests of the trust and its beneficiaries. Thus, we conclude that the need for litigation did not arise due to any fault on the part of Norwest, and the bank is entitled to indemnification.

* * *

In conclusion, we hold that under the common law, a power of attorney that appears to give the agent sweeping powers to dispose of the principal's property is to be narrowly construed in light of the circumstances surrounding the execution of the agency instrument. However, the principal may confer authority to amend or revoke trusts on an agent without referring to the trusts by name in the power of attorney.

Moreover, a trustee is not liable for administration or related attorney fees incurred in reliance on an order of the probate court that is later vacated on appeal. Where the

---

3. We express no opinion concerning the motivations or credibility of Mrs. Franzen's friends and family members, some of whom claimed that O'Brien was attempting to gain control of the trust assets for personal benefit and was acting without Mrs. Franzen's knowledge or assent. The point is not whether O'Brien was in fact acting in Mrs. Franzen's best interests, but that the bank acted reasonably in light of the available information when it sought instructions from a neutral and detached judicial official rather than immediately complying with O'Brien's instructions.

trustee acts in good faith to seek direction from a court concerning its responsibilities in relation to a trust it oversees, the trustee is entitled to indemnification for any associated legal expenses.

Accordingly, we affirm the judgment of the court of appeals in its entirety.

D. Health Care Decisions

Every state has enacted legislation allowing a competent adult to authorize health care decisions, thereby allowing a person to decline additional health care, among other things, even if this should result in death. Indeed, Congress has decided that every patient admitted to a hospital receiving federal funds must be advised of his or her right to sign a health care directive. *See* Patient Self-Determination Act, Omnibus Budget Reconciliation Act of 1990, Pub. L. No. 101-508, § 4751, 104 Stat. 1388, 1388-204 (Requirements for Advance Directives) (codified in scattered sections of 42 U.S.C. 1396a(a)(58) & (w) (2004). Please note that declining additional health care is not comparable to "causing or aiding a suicide," as that term was discussed in Washington v. Glucksberg, 521 U.S. 702 (1997). In that decision, the Court held that Washington's prohibition of assisted suicide does not violate the Fourteenth Amendment's liberty interest as it extends to a personal choice by a mentally competent, terminally ill adult to commit physician-assisted suicide. The state's prohibition is rationally related to its interest in preserving life, protecting the integrity and ethics of the medical profession, protecting the most vulnerable in society from coercion, and erosion of the ban on voluntary euthanasia. Oregon allows for assisted suicide under careful guidelines. *See* Or. Rev. Stat. Ann. § 127.805. § 2.01 (2003). The statute has been upheld in spite of challenge in federal court. *See* Oregon v. Ashcroft, 192 F. Supp. 2d 1077 (D. Or. 2002).

The competent person may designate an agent, a family member, or a court to make the decision if the principal is unable to do so at the time. Indeed, California allows for a domestic partner to possess the same authority as a spouse in making health care decisions. *See* Cal. Prob. Code § 4716 (2004); Cal. Fam. Code § 297 (2004) (defining domestic partner). Under the Uniform Health Care Decisions Act, the directive made by a principal to an agent may be oral or written, but the actual power of attorney for health care (the form designating an agent) must be in writing. The writing does not have to be witnessed or acknowledged, and it cannot be revoked by a guardian without express court approval. Demonstrating the different applications throughout the different states, California does require signatures of two qualified witnesses or an acknowledgment by a notary. *See* Cal. Prob. Code § 4701 (2004). Finally, a medical institution has the right to refuse to honor the directive for reason of conscience, or if the directive is contrary to applicable health care standards.

Often a state statute will refer to "living wills." These are written directives of the principal, requesting to be allowed to die a "natural" death without the necessity of providing extraordinary medical procedures to prolong life. The importance of these statutes is that they insulate the physician or a medical establishment against civil or criminal liability. *See, e.g.,* Ohio Rev. Code Ann. § 2133.11 (2004); 755 Ill. Comp. Stat. § 35/7) (2004). Obviously, they lack the complexity and the versatility of a health care directive. *See generally* Bretton J. Horttor, *A Survey of Living Will and Advanced Health Care Directives,* 74 N. Dak. L. Rev. 233 (1998).

Health care directives are a recent phenomenon, and there is great variation in state requirements. The Uniform Health-Care Decisions Act (1993) has been enacted in a few states. Other states have different requirements, thus necessitating careful preparation of instruments. Without the written instrument, reliance will be upon what the court defines as "clear and convincing evidence" or intent. Consider the following.

Uniform Health-Care Decisions Act (1993)

Section 2. Advance Health-Care Directives.

(a) An adult or emancipated minor may give an individual instruction. The Instruction may be oral or written. The instruction may be limited to take effect only if a specified condition arises.

(b) An adult or emancipated minor may execute a power of attorney for health care, which may authorize the agent to make any health-care decision the principal could have made while having capacity. The power must be in writing and signed by the principal. The power remains in effect notwithstanding the principal's later incapacity and may include individual instructions. Unless related to the principal by blood, marriage, or adoption, an agent may not be an owner, operator, or employee of [a residential long-term health-care institution] at which the principal is receiving care.

(c) Unless otherwise specified in a power of attorney for health care, the authority of an agent becomes effective only upon a determination that the principal lacks capacity, and ceases to be effective upon a determination that the principal has recovered capacity.

(d) Unless otherwise specified in a written advance health-care directive, a determination that an individual lacks or has recovered capacity, or that another condition exists that affects an individual instruction or the authority of an agent, must be made by the primary physician.

California Probate Code (2004)

Section 4701. Statutory form

The statutory advance health care directive form is as follows:

ADVANCE HEALTH CARE DIRECTIVE
(California Probate Code Section 4701)

Explanation

You have the right to give instructions about your own health care. You also have the right to name someone else to make health care decisions for you. This form lets you do either or both of these things. It also lets you express your wishes regarding donation of organs and the designation of your primary physician. If you use this form, you may complete or modify all or any part of it. You are free to use a different form.

Part 1 of this form is a power of attorney for health care. Part 1 lets you name another individual as agent to make health care decisions for you if you become incapable of making your own decisions or if you want someone else to make those decisions for you now even though you are still capable. You may also name an alternate agent to act for you if your first choice is not willing, able, or reasonably available to make decisions for you. (Your agent may not be an operator or employee of a community care facility or a residential care facility where you are receiving care, or your supervising health care provider or employee of the health care institution where you are receiving care, unless your agent is related to you or is a coworker.)

Unless the form you sign limits the authority of your agent, your agent may make all health care decisions for you. This form has a place for you to limit the authority of your agent. You need not limit the authority of your agent if you wish to rely on your agent for all health care decisions that may have to be made. If you choose not to limit the authority of your agent, your agent will have the right to:

(a) Consent or refuse consent to any care, treatment, service, or procedure to maintain, diagnose, or otherwise affect a physical or mental condition.

(b) Select or discharge health care providers and institutions.

(c) Approve or disapprove diagnostic tests, surgical procedures, and programs of medication.

(d) Direct the provision, withholding, or withdrawal of artificial nutrition and hydration and all other forms of health care, including cardiopulmonary resuscitation.

(e) Make anatomical gifts, authorize an autopsy, and direct disposition of remains.

Part 2 of this form lets you give specific instructions about any aspect of your health care, whether or not you appoint an agent. Choices are provided for you to express your wishes regarding the provision, withholding, or withdrawal of treatment to keep you alive, as well as the provision of pain relief. Space is also provided for you to add to the choices you have made or for you to write out any additional wishes. If you are satisfied to allow your agent to determine what is best for you in making end-of-life decisions, you need not fill out Part 2 of this form.

Part 3 of this form lets you express an intention to donate your bodily organs and tissues following your death.

Part 4 of this form lets you designate a physician to have primary responsibility for your health care.

After completing this form, sign and date the form at the end. The form must be signed by two qualified witnesses or acknowledged before a notary public. Give a copy of the signed and completed form to your physician, to any other health care providers you may have, to any health care institution at which you are receiving care, and to any health care agents you have named. You should talk to the person you have named as agent to make sure that he or she understands your wishes and is willing to take the responsibility.

You have the right to revoke this advance health care directive or replace this form at any time.

* * *

PART 1
POWER OF ATTORNEY FOR HEALTH CARE

(1.1) DESIGNATION OF AGENT: I designate the following individual as my agent to make health care decisions for me:

_____

(name of individual you choose as agent)

_____

(address)   (city)   (state)   (ZIP Code)

_____

(home phone)   (work phone)

OPTIONAL: If I revoke my agent's authority or if my agent is not willing, able, or reasonably available to make a health care decision for me, I designate as my first alternate agent:

_____

(name of individual you choose as first alternate agent)

_____

(address)   (city)   (state)   (ZIP Code)

_____

(home phone)   (work phone)

OPTIONAL: If I revoke the authority of my agent and first alternate agent or if neither is willing, able, or reasonably available to make a health care decision for me, I designate as my second alternate agent:

_____

(name of individual you choose as second alternate agent)

_____

(address)   (city)   (state)   (ZIP Code)

_____

(home phone)   (work phone)

(1.2) AGENT'S AUTHORITY: My agent is authorized to make all health care decisions for me, including decisions to provide, withhold, or withdraw artificial nutrition and hydration and all other forms of health care to keep me alive, except as I state here:

_____

_____

_____

(Add additional sheets if needed.)

(1.3) WHEN AGENT'S AUTHORITY BECOMES EFFECTIVE: My agent's authority becomes effective when my primary physician determines that I am unable to make my own health care decisions unless I mark the following box. If I mark this box [ ], my agent's authority to make health care decisions for me takes effect immediately.

(1.4) AGENT'S OBLIGATION: My agent shall make health care decisions for me in accordance with this power of attorney for health care, any instructions I give in Part 2 of this form, and my other wishes to the extent known to my agent. To the extent my wishes are unknown, my agent shall make health care decisions for me in accordance with what my agent determines to be in my best interest. In determining my best interest, my agent shall consider my personal values to the extent known to my agent.

(1.5) AGENT'S POSTDEATH AUTHORITY: My agent is authorized to make anatomical gifts, authorize an autopsy, and direct disposition of my remains, except as I state here or in Part 3 of this form:

_____

_____

_____

_____

(Add additional sheets if needed.)

(1.6) NOMINATION OF CONSERVATOR: If a conservator of my person needs to be appointed for me by a court, I nominate the agent designated in this form. If that agent is not willing, able, or reasonably available to act as conservator, I nominate the alternate agents whom I have named, in the order designated.

PART 2
INSTRUCTIONS FOR HEALTH CARE

If you fill out this part of the form, you may strike any wording you do not want.

(2.1) END-OF-LIFE DECISIONS: I direct that my health care providers and others involved in my care provide, withhold, or withdraw treatment in accordance with the choice I have marked below:

[ ] (a) Choice Not To Prolong Life

I do not want my life to be prolonged if (1) I have an incurable and irreversible condition that will result in my death within a relatively short time, (2) I become unconscious and, to a reasonable degree of medical certainty, I will not regain consciousness, or (3) the likely risks and burdens of treatment would outweigh the expected benefits, OR

[ ] (b) Choice To Prolong Life

I want my life to be prolonged as long as possible within the limits of generally accepted health care standards.

(2.2) RELIEF FROM PAIN: Except as I state in the following space, I direct that treatment for alleviation of pain or discomfort be provided at all times, even if it hastens my death:

_____

_____

_____

_____

(Add additional sheets if needed.)

(2.3) OTHER WISHES: (If you do not agree with any of the optional choices above and wish to write your own, or if you wish to add to the instructions you have given above, you may do so here.) I direct that:

(Add additional sheets if needed.)

PART 3
DONATION OF ORGANS AT DEATH
(OPTIONAL)

(3.1) Upon my death (mark applicable box):

[ ] (a) I give any needed organs, tissues, or parts, OR

[ ] (b) I give the following organs, tissues, or parts only. * * *

(c) My gift is for the following purposes (strike any of * * * the following you do not
want):

(1) Transplant

(2) Therapy

(3) Research

(4) Education

PART 4
PRIMARY PHYSICIAN
(OPTIONAL)

(4.1) I designate the following physician as my primary * * * physician:

(name of physician)

(address)   (city)   (state)   (ZIP Code)

(phone)

OPTIONAL: If the physician I have designated above is not willing, able, or reasonably
available to act as my primary physician, I designate * * * the following physician as my
primary physician:

(name of physician)

(address)   (city)   (state)   (ZIP Code)

(phone)

* * *

PART 5

(5.1) EFFECT OF COPY: A copy of this form has the same effect as * * * the original.

(5.2) SIGNATURE: Sign and date the form here * * * :

(date)	(sign your name)

(address)	(print your name)

(city)	(state)

(5.3) STATEMENT OF WITNESSES: I declare under penalty of perjury under the laws of California (1) that the individual who signed or acknowledged this advance health care directive is personally known to me, or that the individual's identity was proven to me by convincing evidence, (2) that the individual signed or acknowledged this advance directive in my presence, (3) that the individual appears to be of sound mind and under no duress, fraud, or undue influence, (4) that I am not a person appointed as agent by this advance directive, and (5) that I am not the individual's health care provider, an employee of the individual's health care provider, the operator of a community care facility, an employee of an operator of a community care facility, the operator of a residential care facility for the elderly, nor an employee of an operator of a residential care facility for the elderly.

First witness   Second witness

(print name)	(print name)

(address)	(address)

(city) (state)	(city) (state)

(signature of witness)	(signature of witness)

(date)	(date)

(5.4) ADDITIONAL STATEMENT OF WITNESSES: At least one of the above witnesses must also sign the following declaration:

I further declare under penalty of perjury under the laws of California that I am not related to the individual executing this advance health care directive by blood, marriage, or adoption, and to the best of my knowledge, I am not entitled to any part of the individual's estate upon his or her death under a will now existing or by operation of law.

(signature of witness)	(signature of witness)

PART 6
SPECIAL WITNESS REQUIREMENT

(6.1) The following statement is required only if you are a patient in a skilled nursing facility—a health care facility that provides the following basic services: skilled nursing care and supportive care to patients whose primary need is for availability of skilled nursing care on an extended basis. The patient advocate or ombudsman must sign the following statement:

STATEMENT OF PATIENT ADVOCATE OR OMBUDSMAN

I declare under penalty of perjury under the laws of California that I am a patient advocate or ombudsman as designated by the State Department of Aging and that I am serving as a witness as required by Section 4675 of the Probate Code.

_____	_____
(date)	(sign your name)
_____	_____
(address)	(print your name)

_____	
(city)	(state)

Wendland v. Wendland

Supreme Court of California, 2001
26 Cal. 4th 519, 28 P.3d 151

WERDEGAR, J.

In this case we consider whether a conservator of the person may withhold artificial nutrition and hydration from a conscious conservatee who is not terminally ill, comatose, or in a persistent vegetative state, and who has not left formal instructions for health care or appointed an agent or surrogate for health care decisions. Interpreting Probate Code section 2355 in light of the relevant provisions of the California Constitution, we conclude a conservator may not withhold artificial nutrition and hydration from such a person absent clear and convincing evidence the conservator's decision is in accordance with either the conservatee's own wishes or best interest.[1]

The trial court in the case before us, applying the clear and convincing evidence standard, found the evidence on both points insufficient and, thus, denied the conservator's request for authority to withhold artificial nutrition and hydration. The Court of Appeal, which believed the trial court was required to defer to the conservator's good faith decision, reversed. We reverse the decision of the Court of Appeal.

* * *

On September 29, 1993, Robert Wendland rolled his truck at high speed in a solo accident while driving under the influence of alcohol. The accident injured Robert's brain, leaving him conscious yet severely disabled, both mentally and physically, and dependent on artificial nutrition and hydration.[2] Two years later Rose Wendland, Robert's wife and conservator, proposed to direct his physician to remove his feeding tube and allow him to die. Florence Wendland and Rebekah Vinson (respectively Robert's mother

---

1. While this case was under submission following oral argument, the parties informed us the conservatee had passed away. Rather than dismissing the case as moot, we chose to retain the case for decision. We have discretion to decide otherwise moot cases presenting important issues that are capable of repetition yet tend to evade review. * * * [Citations omitted]. This is such a case. The case raises important issues about the fundamental rights of incompetent conservatees to privacy and life, and the corresponding limitations on conservators' power to withhold life-sustaining treatment. Moreover, as this case demonstrates, these issues tend to evade review because they typically concern persons whose health is seriously impaired.

2. At the time of these proceedings, Robert was receiving food and fluids through a PEG (percutaneous endoscopically placed gastronomy) tube.

and sister) objected to the conservator's decision. This proceeding arose under the provisions of the Probate Code authorizing courts to settle such disputes. (Prob.Code, §§ 2355, 2359.) * * *

Following the accident, Robert remained in a coma, totally unresponsive, for several months. During this period Rose visited him daily, often with their children, and authorized treatment as necessary to maintain his health.

Robert eventually regained consciousness. His subsequent medical history is described in a comprehensive medical evaluation later submitted to the court. According to the report, Rose "first noticed signs of responsiveness sometime in late 1994 or early 1995 and alerted [Robert's] physicians and nursing staff." Intensive therapy followed. Robert's "cognitive responsiveness was observed to improve over a period of several months such that by late spring of 1995 the family and most of his health care providers agreed that he was inconsistently interacting with his environment. A video recording * * * of [Robert] in July 1995 demonstrated clear, though inconsistent, interaction with his environment in response to simple commands. At his highest level of function between February and July, 1995, Robert was able to do such things as throw and catch a ball, operate an electric wheelchair with assistance, turn pages, draw circles, draw an 'R' and perform two-step commands." For example, "[h]e was able to respond appropriately to the command 'close your eyes and open them when I say the number 3.'... He could choose a requested color block out of four color blocks. He could set the right peg in a pegboard. Augmented communication[5] was met with inconsistent success. He remained unable to vocalize. Eye blinking was successfully used as a communication mode for a while, however no consistent method of communication was developed."

Despite improvements made in therapy, Robert remained severely disabled, both mentally and physically. * * * The same medical report summarized his continuing impairments as follows: "severe cognitive impairment that is not possible to fully appreciate due to the concurrent motor and communication impairments ..."; "maladaptive behavior characterized by agitation, aggressiveness and non-compliance"; "severe paralysis on the right and moderate paralysis on the left"; "severely impaired communication, without compensatory augmentative communication system"; "severe swallowing dysfunction, dependent upon non-oral enteric tube feeding for nutrition and hydration"; "incontinence of bowel and bladder"; "moderate spasticity"; "mild to moderate contractures"; "general dysphoria"; "recurrent medical illnesses, including pneumonia, bladder infections, sinusitis"; and "dental issues."

After Robert regained consciousness and while he was undergoing therapy, Rose authorized surgery three times to replace dislodged feeding tubes. When physicians sought her permission a fourth time, she declined. She discussed the decision with her daughters and with Robert's brother Michael, all of whom believed that Robert would not have approved the procedure even if necessary to sustain his life. Rose also discussed the decision with Robert's treating physician, Dr. Kass, other physicians, and the hospital's ombudsman, all of whom apparently supported her decision. Dr. Kass, however, inserted a nasogastric feeding tube to keep Robert alive pending input from the hospital's ethics committee.

---

5. "Augmented communication" refers to communication facilitated by a so-called yes/no board, a machine that pronounces the words "yes" and "no" when corresponding buttons are touched.

Eventually, the 20-member ethics committee unanimously approved Rose's decision. In the course of their deliberations, however, the committee did not speak with Robert's mother or sister. Florence learned, apparently through an anonymous telephone call, that Dr. Kass planned to remove Robert's feeding tube. Florence and Rebekah applied for a temporary restraining order to bar him from so doing, and the court granted the motion ex parte.

Rose immediately thereafter petitioned for appointment as Robert's conservator. In the petition, she asked the court to determine that Robert lacked the capacity to give informed consent for medical treatment and to confirm her authority "to withdraw and/or withhold medical treatment and/or life-sustaining treatment, including, but not limited to, withholding nutrition and hydration." Florence and Rebekah (hereafter sometimes objectors) opposed the petition. After a hearing, the court appointed Rose as conservator but reserved judgment on her request for authority to remove Robert's feeding tube. The court ordered the conservator to continue the current plan of physical therapy for 60 days and then to report back to the court. The court also visited Robert in the hospital.

After the 60-day period elapsed without significant improvement in Robert's condition, the conservator renewed her request for authority to remove his feeding tube. The objectors asked the trial court to appoint independent counsel for the conservatee. The trial court declined, and the Court of Appeal summarily denied the objectors' petition for writ of mandate. We granted review and transferred the case to the Court of Appeal, which then directed the trial court to appoint counsel. (Wendland v. Superior Court (1996) 49 Cal.App.4th 44, 56 Cal.Rptr.2d 595.) Appointed counsel, exercising his independent judgment (see generally Conservatorship of Drabick (1988) 200 Cal.App.3d 185, 212–214, 245 Cal.Rptr. 840 (Drabick)), decided to support the conservator's decision. (Because the conservator's and appointed counsel's positions in this court are essentially identical, we will henceforth refer solely to the conservator for brevity's sake.)

The ensuing proceeding generated two decisions. In the first, the court set out the law to be applied at trial. The court found no "clear cut guidance" on how to evaluate a conservator's proposal to end the life of a conscious conservatee who was neither terminally ill nor in a persistent vegetative state. Nevertheless, drawing what assistance it could from cases involving persistently vegetative patients (Drabick, supra, 200 Cal.App.3d 185, 245 Cal.Rptr. 840; Barber v. Superior Court (1983) 147 Cal.App.3d 1006, 195 Cal.Rptr. 484 (Barber)), the court held the conservator would be allowed to withhold artificial nutrition and hydration only if that would be in the conservatee's best interest, taking into account any pertinent wishes the conservatee may have expressed before becoming incompetent. The court also determined the conservator would have to prove the facts justifying her decision by clear and convincing evidence. A decision by a conservator to withhold life-sustaining treatment, the court reasoned, "should be premised on no lesser showing" than that required to justify involuntary medical treatment not likely to cause death. On this point, the court drew an analogy to Lillian F. v. Superior Court (1984) 160 Cal.App.3d 314, 206 Cal.Rptr. 603, which requires clear and convincing evidence of a conservatee's inability to make treatment decisions as a prerequisite to involuntary electroconvulsive treatment. Finally, the court held the conservator would bear the burdens both of producing evidence and of persuasion. "[F]inding itself in uncharted territory" on this subject too, the court explained that "[w]hen a situation arises where it is proposed to terminate the life of a conscious but severely cognitively impaired person, it seems more rational ... to ask 'why?' of the party proposing the act rather than 'why not?' of the party challenging it."

The trial generated the evidence set out above. The testifying physicians agreed that Robert would not likely experience further cognitive recovery. Dr. Kass, Robert's treating physician, testified that, to the highest degree of medical certainty, Robert would never be able to make medical treatment decisions, walk, talk, feed himself, eat, drink, or control his bowel and bladder functions. Robert was able, however, according to Dr. Kass, to express "certain desires.... Like if he's getting tired in therapy of if he wants to quit therapy, he's usually very adamant about that. He'll either strike out or he'll refuse to perform the task." Dr. Kobrin, Robert's neurologist, testified that Robert recognized certain caregivers and would allow only specific caregivers to bathe and help him. Both Dr. Kass and Dr. Kobrin had prescribed medication for Robert's behavioral problems. Dr. Sundance, who was retained by appointed counsel to evaluate Robert, described him as being in a "minimally conscious state in that he does have some cognitive function" and the ability to "respond to his environment," but not to "interact" with it "in a more proactive way."

On April 29, 1997, Dr. Kass asked Robert a series of questions using the augmented communications device, or "yes/no board." (See ante, 110 Cal.Rptr.2d at p. 416, fn. 5, 28 P.3d at 155, fn. 5.) After a series of questions about Robert's physical state, such as "Are you sitting up?" and "Are you lying down?" that Robert appeared to answer correctly "most times," Dr. Kass asked the following questions and received the following answers:

"Do you have pain? Yes.

"Do your legs hurt? No.

"Does your buttocks hurt? No.

"Do you want us to leave you alone? Yes.

"Do you want more therapy? No.

"Do you want to get into the chair? Yes.

"Do you want to go back to bed? No.

"Do you want to die? No answer.

"Are you angry? Yes.

"At somebody? No."

So far as Dr. Kass knew, no one had previously asked Robert the same questions. Dr. Kass acknowledged there was no way to verify whether Robert "really understood the questions or not," but "[t]he reason I asked those questions," Dr. Kass continued, "is because [Robert] was able to answer the previous questions mostly correctly. So I thought perhaps he could understand more questions." Dr. Kass believed Robert probably understood some but not all of the questions. Robert's speech pathologist, Lowana Brauer, testified generally that Robert used the augmented communications device primarily as therapy and not with enough consistency to justify leaving the device in his room for communication with other people. She did not, however, testify specifically about the interaction between Robert and Dr. Kass.

Robert's wife, brother and daughter recounted preaccident statements Robert had made about his attitude towards life-sustaining health care. Robert's wife recounted specific statements on two occasions. The first occasion was Rose's decision whether to turn off a respirator sustaining the life of her father, who was near death from gangrene. Rose recalls Robert saying: "I would never want to live like that, and I wouldn't want my children to see me like that and look at the hurt you're going through as an adult seeing your father like that." On cross-examination, Rose acknowledged Robert said on this occasion that Rose's father "wouldn't want to live like a vegetable" and "wouldn't want to live in a comatose state."

After his father-in-law's death, Robert developed a serious drinking problem. After a particular incident, Rose asked Michael, Robert's brother, to talk to him. When Robert arrived home the next day he was angry to see Michael there, interfering in what he considered a private family matter. Rose remembers Michael telling Robert: "I'm going to get a call from Rosie one day, and you're going to be in a terrible accident." Robert replied: "If that ever happened to me, you know what my feelings are. Don't let that happen to me. Just let me go. Leave me alone." Robert's brother Michael testified about the same conversation. Michael told Robert: "you're drinking; you're going to get drunk.... [Y]ou're either going to go out and kill yourself or kill someone else, or you're going to end up in the hospital like a vegetable— laying in bed just like a vegetable." Michael remembers Robert saying in response, "Mike, whatever you do[,] don't let that happen. Don't let them do that to me." Robert's daughter Katie remembers him saying on this occasion that "if he could not be a provider for his family, if he could not do all the things that he enjoyed doing, just enjoying the outdoors, just basic things, feeding himself, talking, communicating, if he could not do those things, he would not want to live."

Based on all the evidence, the court issued a second decision setting out its findings of fact and conclusions of law. Specifically, the court found the conservator "ha[d] not met her duty and burden to show by clear and convincing evidence that conservatee Robert Wendland, who is not in a persistent vegetative state nor suffering from a terminal illness would, under the circumstances, want to die. Conservator has likewise not met her burden of establishing that the withdrawal of artificially delivered nutrition and hydration is commensurate with conservatee's best interests, consistent with California Law as embodied in Barber [, supra, 147 Cal.App.3d 1006, 195 Cal.Rptr. 484] and Drabick, supra [, 200 Cal.App.3d 185, 245 Cal.Rptr. 840]." Based on these findings, the court granted the objectors' motion for judgment (Code Civ. Proc., § 631.8), thus denying the conservator's request for confirmation of her proposal to withdraw treatment. The court also found the conservator had acted in good faith and would be permitted to remain in that office. Nevertheless, the court limited her powers by ordering that she would "have no authority to direct ... [any] health care provider to remove the conservatee's life sustaining medical treatment in the form of withholding nutrition and hydration." (See Prob.Code, § 2351.) * * *

The conservator appealed this decision. The Court of Appeal reversed. In the Court of Appeal's view, "[t]he trial court properly placed the burden of producing evidence on [the conservator] and properly applied a clear and convincing evidence standard. However, the court erred in requiring [the conservator] to prove that [the conservatee], while competent, expressed a desire to die in the circumstances and in substituting its own judgment concerning [the conservatee's] best interests...." Instead, the trial court's role was "merely to satisfy itself that the conservator had considered the conservatee's best interests in good faith...." This limited judicial role, the Court of Appeal concluded, was mandated by section 2355, as interpreted in Drabick, supra, 200 Cal.App.3d 185, 245 Cal.Rptr. 840. While acknowledging the trial court had already found the conservator had acted in good faith, the Court of Appeal nevertheless declined to enter judgment for the conservator. Instead, the court remanded to permit the objectors to present any evidence rebutting the conservator's case-in-chief. Finally, recognizing that an amended version of section 2355, effective on July 1, 2000, might "be a factor upon remand," the court determined the new law did not affect the outcome. We granted review of this decision.

* * *

The ultimate focus of our analysis must be section 2355, the statute under which the conservator has claimed the authority to end the conservatee's life and the only statute under which such authority might plausibly be found. Nevertheless, the statute speaks in the context of an array of constitutional, common law, and statutory principles. The Law Revision Commission, which drafted the statute's current version, was aware of these principles and cited them to explain and justify the proposed legislation. Because these principles provide essential background, we set them out briefly here, followed by the history of the statute.[8]

* * *

One relatively certain principle is that a competent adult has the right to refuse medical treatment, even treatment necessary to sustain life. The Legislature has cited this principle to justify legislation governing medical care decisions (§ 4650), and courts have invoked it as a starting point for analysis, even in cases examining the rights of incompetent persons and the duties of surrogate decision makers (e.g., Drabick, supra, 200 Cal.App.3d 185, 206, 245 Cal.Rptr. 840; Barber, supra, 147 Cal.App.3d 1006, 1015, 195 Cal.Rptr. 484). This case requires us to look beyond the rights of a competent person to the rights of incompetent conservatees and the duties of conservators, but the principle just mentioned is a logical place to begin.

That a competent person has the right to refuse treatment is a statement both of common law and of state constitutional law. In its common law form, the principle is often traced to Union Pacific Railway Co. v. Botsford (1891) 141 U.S. 250, 251, 11 S.Ct. 1000, 35 L.Ed. 734, in which the United States Supreme Court wrote that "[n]o right is held more sacred, or is more carefully guarded, by the common law, than the right of every individual to the possession and control of his own person, free from all restraint or interference of others, unless by clear and unquestionable authority of law." Applying this principle, the high court held that the plaintiff in a personal injury case was not required to submit to a surgical examination intended to reveal the extent of her injuries. (Ibid.) Courts in subsequent cases relied on the same principle to award damages for operations performed without the patient's consent. The landmark case is Schloendorff v. Society of New York Hospital (N.Y.1914) 211 N.Y. 125, 105 N.E. 92, 93, in which Judge Cardozo wrote that "[e]very human being of adult years and sound mind has a right to determine what shall be done with his own body; and a surgeon who performs an operation without his patient's consent commits an assault, for which he is liable in damages." We adopted this principle in Cobbs v. Grant (1972) 8 Cal.3d 229, 242, 104

---

8. The current version of section 2355 governs this case. It took effect on July 1, 2000, and defines the powers of conservators in California from that day forward. A trial court's order limiting a conservator's powers, like an injunction, defines the rights of the parties in the future and is subject to modification based on changes in the law. In such a case, a reviewing court applies the law in effect at the time it renders its opinion. (Hunt v. Superior Court (1999) 21 Cal.4th 984, 1008, 90 Cal.Rptr.2d 236, 987 P.2d 705; Tulare Irr. Dist. v. Lindsay-Strathmore Irr. Dist. (1935) 3 Cal.2d 489, 527–528, 45 P.2d 972.)

Cal.Rptr. 505, 502 P.2d 1, adding that "the patient's consent to treatment, to be effective, must be an informed consent." Most recently, in Thor v. Superior Court (1993) 5 Cal.4th 725, 21 Cal.Rptr.2d 357, 855 P.2d 375, we held that the common law right of a competent adult to refuse life-sustaining treatment extends even to a state prisoner; we thus absolved prison officials and medical personnel of any duty to provide artificial hydration and nutrition against the will of a quadriplegic prisoner who needed such treatment to survive.

The Courts of Appeal have found another source for the same right in the California Constitution's privacy clause. (Cal. Const., art. I, § 1.) The court in Bartling v. Superior Court (1984) 163 Cal.App.3d 186, 209 Cal.Rptr. 220 held that a competent adult with serious, probably incurable illnesses was entitled to have life-support equipment disconnected over his physicians' objection even though that would hasten his death. "The right of a competent adult patient to refuse medical treatment," the court explained, "has its origins in the constitutional right of privacy. This right is specifically guaranteed by the California Constitution (art. I, § 1).... The constitutional right of privacy guarantees to the individual the freedom to choose to reject, or refuse to consent to, intrusions of his bodily integrity." (Id. at p. 195, 209 Cal.Rptr. 220.) To the same effect is the decision in Bouvia v. Superior Court (1986) 179 Cal.App.3d 1127, 225 Cal.Rptr. 297, in which the court directed injunctive relief requiring a public hospital to comply with a competent, terminally ill patient's direction to remove a nasogastric feeding tube. "The right to refuse medical treatment," the court wrote, "is basic and fundamental.... Its exercise requires no one's approval. It is not merely one vote subject to being overridden by medical opinion." (Id. at p. 1137, 225 Cal.Rptr. 297; see also Rains v. Belshé (1995) 32 Cal.App.4th 157, 169, 38 Cal.Rptr.2d 185, Drabick, supra, 200 Cal.App.3d 185, 206, fn. 20, 245 Cal.Rptr. 840, Keyhea v. Rushen (1986) 178 Cal.App.3d 526, 540, 223 Cal.Rptr. 746, Foy v. Greenblott (1983) 141 Cal.App.3d 1, 11, 190 Cal.Rptr. 84 [all describing, albeit perhaps in dictum, the competent person's right to refuse medical treatment as protected by the state constitutional right to privacy].)

In Thor v. Superior Court, supra, 5 Cal.4th 725, 21 Cal.Rptr.2d 357, 855 P.2d 375, as mentioned, we based our conclusion that a prisoner had the right to refuse life-sustaining treatment solely on the common law without also considering whether the state Constitution provided similar protection. But Thor does not reject the state Constitution as a basis for the right. More importantly, we have since Thor determined that the privacy clause does protect the fundamental interest in personal autonomy. "Where the case involves an obvious invasion of an interest fundamental to personal autonomy, e.g., freedom from involuntary sterilization or the freedom to pursue consensual familial relationships, a 'compelling interest' must be present to overcome the vital privacy interest." (Hill v. National Collegiate Athletic Assn. (1994) 7 Cal.4th 1, 34, 26 Cal. Rptr.2d 834, 865 P.2d 633; see also American Academy of Pediatrics v. Lungren (1997) 16 Cal.4th 307, 340, 66 Cal.Rptr.2d 210, 940 P.2d 797 [reaffirming Hill and adding to its list of "'obvious invasion[s] of ... interest[s] fundamental to personal autonomy'" (italics omitted) a law interfering with the decision whether to bear a child].) In comparison with these examples, the competent adult's decision to refuse life-sustaining medical treatment must also be seen as fundamental.

Federal law has little to say about the competent person's right to refuse treatment, but what it does say is not to the contrary. The United States Supreme Court spoke provisionally to the point in Cruzan v. Director, Missouri Dept. of Health (1990) 497 U.S. 261, 110 S.Ct. 2841, 111 L.Ed.2d 224 (Cruzan). At issue was the constitutionality of a

Missouri law permitting a conservator to withhold artificial nutrition and hydration from a conservatee in a persistent vegetative state only upon clear and convincing evidence that the conservatee, while competent, had expressed the desire to refuse such treatment. The court concluded the law was constitutional. While the case thus did not present the issue, the court nevertheless acknowledged that "a competent person['s] ... constitutionally protected liberty interest in refusing unwanted medical treatment may be inferred" (id. at p. 278, 110 S.Ct. 2841) from prior decisions holding that state laws requiring persons to submit to involuntary medical procedures must be justified by countervailing state interests. The "logic" of such cases would, the court thought, implicate a competent person's liberty interest in refusing artificially delivered food and water essential to life. (Id. at p. 279, 110 S.Ct. 2841.) Whether any given state law infringed such a liberty interest, however, would have to be determined by balancing the liberty interest against the relevant state interests, in particular the state's interest in preserving life. (Id. at p. 280, 110 S.Ct. 2841.)

In view of these authorities, the competent adult's right to refuse medical treatment may be safely considered established, at least in California.

The same right survives incapacity, in a practical sense, if exercised while competent pursuant to a law giving that act lasting validity. For some time, California law has given competent adults the power to leave formal directions for health care in the event they later become incompetent; over time, the Legislature has afforded ever greater scope to that power. The former Natural Death Act (Health & Saf.Code, former § 7185 et seq., added by Stats.1976, ch. 1439, § 1, p. 6478, and repealed by Stats.1991, ch. 895, § 1, p. 3973), as first enacted in 1976, authorized competent adults to direct health care providers to withhold or withdraw life-sustaining procedures under very narrow circumstances only: specifically, in the event of an incurable condition that would cause death regardless of such procedures and where such procedures would serve only to postpone the moment of death. In findings accompanying the law, the Legislature expressly found "that adult persons have the fundamental right to control the decisions relating to the rendering of their own medical care" (id., § 7186) and explained the law as giving lasting effect to that right: "In recognition of the dignity and privacy which patients have a right to expect, the Legislature hereby declares that the laws of the State of California shall recognize the right of an adult person to make a written directive instructing his physician to withhold or withdraw life-sustaining procedures in the event of a terminal condition." (Ibid.) In 1991, the Legislature amended the law to permit competent adults to refuse, in advance, life-sustaining procedures in the event of a "permanent unconscious condition," defined as an "irreversible coma or persistent vegetative state." (Health & Saf.Code, former §§ 7185.5, 7186, subd. (e), added by Stats.1991, ch. 895, § 2, pp. 3974–3975, and repealed by Stats.1999, ch. 658, § 7.) Intervening legislation also enabled a competent adult to execute a durable power of attorney authorizing an agent to "withhold[ ] or withdraw [ ] ... health care ... so as to permit the natural process of dying," and to make other health care decisions, in the event of the principal's incompetence. (Civ.Code, former § 2443, added by Stats.1983, ch. 1204, § 10, p. 4622, and repealed by Stats.1994, ch. 307, § 7, p.1982.)

Effective July 1, 2000, the Health Care Decisions Law (Stats.1999, ch. 658) gives competent adults extremely broad power to direct all aspects of their health care in the event they become incompetent. The new law, which repeals the former Natural Death Act and amends the durable power of attorney law, draws heavily from the Uniform Health Care Decisions Act adopted in 1993 by the National Conference of Commissioners on Uniform State Laws. (See 2000 Health Care Decisions Law and Revised Power of Attorney Law (March 2000) 30 Cal. Law Revision Com. Rep. (2000) p. 49 [preprint copy] (hereafter California Law Revision Commission Report).) Briefly, and as relevant here, the new law permits a competent person to execute an advance directive about "any aspect" of health care. (§ 4701.) Among other things, a person may direct that life-sustaining treatment be withheld or withdrawn under conditions specified by the person and not limited to terminal illness, permanent coma, or persistent vegetative state. A competent person may still use a power of attorney for health care to give an agent the power to make health care decisions (§ 4683), but a patient may also orally designate a surrogate to make such decisions by personally informing the patient's supervising health care provider. (§ 4711.) Under the new law, agents and surrogates are required to make health care decisions "in accordance with the principal's individual health care instructions, if any, and other wishes to the extent known to the agent." (§ 4684; see also § 4711.)

All of the laws just mentioned merely give effect to the decision of a competent person, in the form either of instructions for health care or the designation of an agent or surrogate for health care decisions. Such laws may accurately be described, as the Legislature has described them, as a means to respect personal autonomy by giving effect to competent decisions: "In recognition of the dignity and privacy a person has a right to expect, the law recognizes that an adult has the fundamental right to control the decisions relating to his or her own health care, including the decision to have life-sustaining treatment withheld or withdrawn." (§ 4650, subd. (a) [legislative findings].) This court made essentially the same point in Thor v. Superior Court, supra, 5 Cal.4th 725, 740, 21 Cal.Rptr.2d 357, 855 P.2d 375, where we described "the [former] Natural Death Act and other statutory provisions permitting an individual or designated surrogate to exercise conclusive control over the administration of life-sustaining treatment [as] evidenc[ing] legislative recognition that fostering self-determination in such matters enhances rather than deprecates the value of life."

In contrast, decisions made by conservators typically derive their authority from a different basis—the parens patriae power of the state to protect incompetent persons. Unlike an agent or a surrogate for health care, who is voluntarily appointed by a competent person, a conservator is appointed by the court because the conservatee "has been adjudicated to lack the capacity to make health care decisions." (§ 2355, subd. (a).) In 1988, the court in Drabick, supra, 200 Cal.App.3d 185, 245 Cal.Rptr. 840, confused these two distinct concepts—the voluntary act of a competent person and the state's parens patriae power—and on that questionable basis took to a novel conclusion the idea that a person's right to refuse treatment survives incompetence. Drabick figures prominently both in the legislative history of section 2355—the statute governing this case—and the parties' arguments. It therefore deserves close attention.

At issue in Drabick, supra, 200 Cal.App.3d 185, 245 Cal.Rptr. 840, was a conservator's proposal to end the life of a conservatee by removing a nasogastric feeding tube. The formerly competent conservatee had been unconscious for five years in a persistent vegetative state; physicians opined he would never regain consciousness. While the conservatee had expressed informally his desire not to be kept alive by artificial life support systems, he had not left formal directions for his health care. Former section 2355, subdivision (a) (added by Stats.1979, ch. 726, § 3, pp. 2379–2380, and repealed by Stats.1990, ch. 79, § 13, p. 463) gave the conservator "exclusive authority to give consent for such medical treatment ... as the conservator in good faith based on medical advice determines to be necessary." The court construed this language as also giving the conservator, "by necessary implication, ... power to withhold or withdraw consent to medical treatment under appropriate circumstances." (Drabick, supra, at p. 200, 245 Cal.Rptr. 840.) Treatment to sustain the life of a permanently unconscious person was not "'necessary'" within the meaning of former section 2355, the court reasoned, "if it offers no reasonable possibility of returning the conservatee to cognitive life and if it is not otherwise in the conservatee's best interests, as determined by the conservator in good faith." (Drabick, supra, at p. 218, 245 Cal.Rptr. 840.)

Counsel appointed to represent the conservatee in Drabick, supra, 200 Cal.App.3d 185, 245 Cal.Rptr. 840, argued that the state's interest in preserving life justified the court in limiting the conservator's powers. The court disagreed. Rather than presenting a conflict between the conservator's decision to terminate life support and the state's interest in preserving life, the Drabick court thought the case was more appropriately viewed as presenting a conflict between two rights belonging to the conservatee: "Both the fundamental right to life—to continue receiving treatment—and the right to terminate unwanted treatment deserve consideration. Someone acting in [the conservatee's] best interests can and must choose between them." (Id. at p. 210, 245 Cal.Rptr. 840.) Viewing the case in this way, the court was "convinced that [it would] deprive [the conservatee] of a fundamental right" were it to bar the conservator from withholding treatment. (Id. at p. 208, 245 Cal.Rptr. 840.) The court candidly acknowledged that "to claim [a permanently unconscious conservatee's] 'right to choose' survives incompetence is a legal fiction at best." (Ibid.) Indeed, such a person's "noncognitive state prevents him from choosing anything." (Ibid.) Nevertheless, the court concluded, "incompetence does not cause the loss of a fundamental right from which the incompetent person can still benefit" through its vicarious exercise by a conservator. (Ibid.) As precedent for this analysis, the Drabick court relied on Conservatorship of Valerie N. (1985) 40 Cal.3d 143, 219 Cal.Rptr. 387, 707 P.2d 760, in which this court held unconstitutional a statute (§ 2356, subd. (d)) barring use of the conservator's statutory powers to authorize sterilization of wards and conservatees. Just as this court in Valerie N. permitted conservators of developmentally disabled women to exercise vicariously their conservatees' right to choose sterilization, the Drabick court explained, the conservator of a persistently vegetative conservatee may exercise vicariously the conservatee's right to refuse medical treatment. (Drabick, supra, at pp. 207–208, 245 Cal.Rptr. 840.) * * *

Having expressly recognized the "fiction [al]" aspect of its analysis (Drabick, supra, 200 Cal.App.3d 185, 208, 245 Cal.Rptr. 840), and seeking perhaps to place its conclusion on firmer ground, the court in Drabick offered this alternative rationale: "In the years since the [Matter of] Quinlan [(1976) 70 N.J. 10, 355 A.2d 647] decision," the Drabick court wrote, "most courts have adopted the formula that a patient's 'right to choose' or 'right to refuse' medical treatment survives incompetence. It would be more accurate to say that incompetent patients retain the right to have appropriate medical decisions made on their behalf. An appropriate medical decision is one that is made in the patient's best interests, as opposed to the interests of the hospital, the physicians, the legal system, or someone else." (Id. at p. 205, 245 Cal.Rptr. 840.) We do not question the Drabick court's conclusion that incompetent persons have a right, based in the California Constitution, to appropriate medical decisions that reflect their own interests and values. (Drabick, supra, at p. 205, 245 Cal.Rptr. 840.) But the right to an appropriate decision by a court-appointed conservator does not necessarily equate with the conservatee's right to refuse treatment, or obviously take precedence over the conservatee's right to life or the state's interest in preserving life.

No published decision in this state has rejected the Drabick court's conclusions. Seven months after Drabick, the court in Conservatorship of Morrison (1988) 206 Cal.App.3d 304, 308–309, 253 Cal.Rptr. 530, viewed Drabick as having settled the question whether former section 2355 empowered a conservator to end the life of a persistently vegetative conservatee by withholding artificial nutrition and hydration. But neither, until the decision presently on review, has the holding in Drabick been extended to cases involving conservatees other than those in persistent vegetative states. This, almost certainly, is because the Drabick court strictly limited its decision to such persons. The "opinion's reasoning," the court wrote, "is predicated upon its subject being a patient for whom there is no reasonable hope of a return to cognitive life. We have not considered any other case, and this opinion would not support a decision to forego treatment if this factual predicate could not be satisfied." (Drabick, supra, 200 Cal.App.3d 185, 217, fn. 36, 245 Cal.Rptr. 840.) Although the court did not explain how its reasoning was predicated on the conservatee's permanently unconscious state, the decision's self-imposed limitation avoids or mitigates a serious constitutional problem: A person whose permanent unconsciousness prevents him from perceiving that artificial hydration and nutrition are being withdrawn arguably has a more attenuated interest in avoiding that result than a person who may consciously perceive the effects of dehydration and starvation.

* * *

The ultimate focus of our analysis, as mentioned at the outset, must be section 2355, the statute under which the conservator claims the authority to end the conservatee's life. The statute's history indicates that the Law Revision Commission, which drafted the current version, was aware of and intended to incorporate some, but not all, of the Drabick, supra, 200 Cal.App.3d 185, 245 Cal.Rptr. 840 court's construction of the former statute.

* * *

In 1990, the Legislature repealed and reenacted former section 2355 without change while reorganizing the Probate Code. But in 1999, section 2355 changed significantly with the Legislature's adoption of the Health Care Decisions Law (§ 4600 et seq., added by Stats.1999, ch. 658). That law took effect on July 1, 2000, about four months after the Court of Appeal filed the opinion on review. Many of the new law's provisions, as already noted, are the same as, or drawn from, the Uniform Health-Care Decisions Act. (See 30 Cal. Law Revision Com. Rep., supra, p. 49.) Section 2355, as a statute addressing medical treatment decisions, was revised to conform to the new law.

The main purpose of the Health Care Decisions Law is to provide "procedures and standards" governing "health care decisions to be made for adults at a time when they are incapable of making decisions on their own and [to] provide [ ] mechanisms for directing their health care in anticipation of a time when they may become incapacitated." (30 Cal. Law Revision Com. Rep., supra, p. 6.) The core provision of the new law, which comes directly from the Uniform Health-Care Decisions Act, sets out uniform standards for the making of health care decisions by third parties. The language embodying this core provision now appears in statutes governing decisions by conservators (§ 2355), agents (§ 4684), and surrogates (§ 4714). This language is set out below in italics, as it appears in the context of section 2355: "If the conservatee has been adjudicated to lack the capacity to make health care decisions, the conservator has the exclusive authority to make health care decisions for the conservatee that the conservator in good faith based on medical advice determines to be necessary. *The conservator shall make health care decisions for the conservatee in accordance with the conservatee's individual health care instructions, if any, and other wishes to the extent known to the conservator. Otherwise, the conservator shall make the decision in accordance with the conservator's determination of the conservatee's best interest. In determining the conservatee's best interest, the conservator shall consider the conservatee's personal values to the extent known to the conservator.* The conservator may require the conservatee to receive the health care, whether or not the conservatee objects. In this case, the health care decision of the conservator alone is sufficient and no person is liable because the health care is administered to the conservatee without the conservatee's consent. For the purposes of this subdivision, 'health care' and 'health care decision' have the meanings provided in Sections 4615 and 4617, respectively." (§ 2355, subd. (a), as amended by Stats.1999, ch. 658, § 12, italics added.)

The last sentence of section 2355, subdivision (a), set out above, incorporates definitional provisions of the Health Care Decisions Law. Of these, section 4615 defines "'[h]ealth care'" as "any care, treatment, service, or procedure to maintain, diagnose, or otherwise affect a patient's physical or mental condition." Section 4617 defines "'[h]ealth care decision'" as "a decision made by a patient or the patient's agent, conservator, or surrogate, regarding the patient's health care, including the following: [¶] (a) Selection and discharge of health care providers and institutions. [¶] (b) Approval or disapproval of diagnostic tests, surgical procedures, and programs of medication. [¶] (c) Directions to provide, *withhold, or withdraw artificial nutrition and hydration* and all other forms of health care, including cardiopulmonary resuscitation." (Italics added.)

* * *

In other respects, the current version of section 2355 departs from the decision in Drabick, supra, 200 Cal.App.3d 185, 245 Cal.Rptr. 840. The Drabick court viewed the informally expressed wishes of the incompetent conservatee simply as a factor for the conservator to consider in determining the conservatee's best interest. (Id. at pp. 211–212, 245 Cal.Rptr. 840.) In contrast to Drabick, section 2355 assigns dispositive weight to the conservatee's informally expressed wishes, when known. Under the statute, "[t]he conservator shall make health care decisions for the conservatee in accordance with the conservatee's individual health care instructions, if any, and other wishes to the extent known to the conservator." (§ 2355, subd. (a).) The best interest standard applies only when the conservatee's wishes are not known, as a fallback standard embodied in the statute's next sentence: "Otherwise, the conservator shall make the decision in accordance with the conservator's determination of the conservatee's best interest. In determining the conservatee's best interest, the conservator shall consider the conservatee's personal values to the extent known to the conservator." (Ibid.)

* * *

This background illuminates the parties' arguments, which reduce in essence to this: The conservator has claimed the power under section 2355, as she interprets it, to direct the conservatee's health care providers to cease providing artificial nutrition and hydration. In opposition, the objectors have contended the statute violates the conservatee's rights to privacy and life under the facts of this case if the conservator's interpretation of the statute is correct. * * *

The conservator asserts she offered sufficient evidence at trial to satisfy the primary statutory standard, which contemplates a decision "in accordance with the conservatee's ... wishes...." (§ 2355, subd. (a).) The trial court, however, determined the evidence on this point was insufficient. The conservator did "not [meet] her duty and burden," the court expressly found, "to show by clear and convincing evidence that [the] conservatee..., who is not in a persistent vegetative state nor suffering from a terminal illness would, under the circumstances, want to die." To be sure, the court made this finding under former section 2355 rather than the current version— and not because the former statute expressly called for such a finding but under the belief that case law required it. (See ante, 110 Cal.Rptr.2d at p. 418, 28 P.3d at p. 156.) But the finding's relevance under the new statute cannot easily be dismissed: The new statute expressly requires the conservator to follow the conservatee's wishes, if known. (§ 2355, subd. (a).)

The conservator argues the Legislature understood and intended that the low preponderance of the evidence standard would apply. Certainly this was the Law Revision Commission's understanding. On this subject, the commission wrote: "[Section 2355] does not specify any special evidentiary standard for the determination of the conservatee's wishes or best interest. Consequently, the general rule applies: the standard is by preponderance of the evidence. Proof is not required by clear and convincing evidence." (30 Cal. Law Revision Com. Rep., supra, p. 264.) We have said that "[e]xplanatory comments by a law revision commission are persuasive evidence of the intent of the Legislature in subsequently enacting its recommendations into law." (Brian W. v. Superior Court (1978) 20 Cal.3d 618, 623, 143 Cal.Rptr. 717, 574 P.2d 788.) Nevertheless, one may legitimately question whether the Legislature can fairly be assumed to have read and endorsed every statement in the commission's 280-page report on the Health Care Decisions Law. (Cf. Van Arsdale v. Hollinger (1968) 68 Cal.2d 245, 250, 66 Cal.Rptr. 20, 437 P.2d 508 [describing the inference of legislative approval as strongest when the commission's comment is brief].)

The objectors, in opposition, argue that section 2355 would be unconstitutional if construed to permit a conservator to end the life of a conscious conservatee based on a finding by the low preponderance of the evidence standard that the latter would not want to live. We see no basis for holding the statute unconstitutional on its face. We do, however, find merit in the objectors' argument. We therefore construe the statute to minimize the possibility of its unconstitutional application by requiring clear and convincing evidence of a conscious conservatee's wish to refuse life-sustaining treatment when the conservator relies on that asserted wish to justify withholding life-sustaining treatment. This construction does not entail a deviation from the language of the statute and constitutes only a partial rejection of the Law Revision Commission's understanding that the preponderance of the evidence standard would apply; we see no constitutional reason to apply the higher evidentiary standard to the majority of health care decisions made by conservators not contemplating a conscious conservatee's death. Our reasons are as follows:

At the time the Legislature was considering the present version of section 2355, no court had interpreted any prior version of the statute as permitting a conservator deliberately to end the life of a *conscious* conservatee. Even today, only the decision on review so holds. The court in Drabick, supra, 200 Cal.App.3d 185, 245 Cal.Rptr. 840, as we have seen, found sufficient authority in the statute to confirm a conservator's decision that artificial hydration and nutrition was not in the best interest of a *permanently unconscious, persistently vegetative conservatee.* The Drabick court, however, expressly limited its decision to cases involving conservatees in the same medical condition and stated that its reasoning was, in some unexplained way, predicated on such facts. (Id. at p. 217, fn. 36, 245 Cal.Rptr. 840.) While the conservator embraces Drabick in other respects, the authoring court, she writes, "was flat-out wrong to limit the applicability of [section] 2355, of its statutory analysis, and of its constitutional insights to permanently unconscious conservatees as these limitations ignore the plain language of the statute as well as logic." To the contrary, by limiting its decision in this way the Drabick court thereby avoided the constitutional problem we confront here, namely, the propriety of a decision to withhold artificial nutrition and hydration from a conscious conservatee who, while incompetent, may nevertheless subjectively perceive the effects of dehydration and starvation. (See ante, 110 Cal.Rptr.2d at p. 426, 28 P.3d at p. 163)

In amending section 2355 in 1999, neither the Legislature, nor the Law Revision Commission in its official report to the Legislature, alluded to the possibility that the statute might be invoked to justify withholding artificial nutrition and hydration from a conscious patient. The conservator sees evidence of specific legislative authority for such a decision in the findings that accompanied the Health Care Decisions Law, but we do not. These findings, which first entered California law as part of the former Natural Death Act (Health & Saf.Code, former § 7185.5; see ante, 110 Cal.Rptr.2d at p. 423, 28 P.3d at p. 160), were revised and recodified in the new legislation as Probate Code section 4650.[11] The Law Revision Commission in its report accurately explained the proposed change in the findings as follows: "The earlier legislative findings were limited to persons with a terminal condition or permanent unconscious condition. This restriction is not continued here in recognition of the broader scope of this division and the development of case law since enactment of the original Natural Death Act in 1976." (30 Cal. Law Revision Com. Rep., supra, p. 61.) From this history, the conservator deduces that the commission, and by inference the Legislature, intended to give conservators the power she has sought in this case to end a conscious conservatee's life. Considering, however, the subject's importance and potentially controversial nature, it seems extremely unlikely that the Legislature intended to regulate the subject through the deletion of a few limiting words from a legislative finding. In any event, the commission's reference to "the broader scope" (ibid.) of the new law more plausibly refers simply to the fact that the new law, unlike the former Natural Death Act, permits a competent person to provide by advance directive for virtually all aspects of his or her future health care rather than, as previously, simply the withdrawal of life support under narrowly circumscribed facts. (See ante, 110 Cal.Rptr.2d at p. 423, 28 P.3d at p. 160.) Certainly the commission's reference to "the development of

---

11. Section 4650, in full, currently provides as follows:

"The Legislature finds the following:

"(a) In recognition of the dignity and privacy a person has a right to expect, the law recognizes that an adult has the fundamental right to control the decisions relating to his or her own health care, including the decision to have life-sustaining treatment withheld or withdrawn.

"(b) Modern medical technology has made possible the artificial prolongation of human life beyond natural limits. In the interest of protecting individual autonomy, this prolongation of the process of dying for a person for whom continued health care does not improve the prognosis for recovery may violate patient dignity and cause unnecessary pain and suffering, while providing nothing medically necessary or beneficial to the person.

"(c) In the absence of controversy, a court is normally not the proper forum in which to make health care decisions, including decisions regarding life-sustaining treatment."

case law" since 1976 cannot be understood as suggesting that conservators may end the life of conscious patients. At the time the commission wrote, no California case had addressed the subject. Moreover, of the four cases the commission cites, two involved competent patients (Bouvia v. Superior Court, supra, 179 Cal.App.3d 1127, 225 Cal.Rptr. 297; Bartling v. Superior Court, supra, 163 Cal.App.3d 186, 209 Cal.Rptr. 220), and two concerned patients in persistent vegetative states (Drabick, supra, 200 Cal.App.3d 185, 245 Cal.Rptr. 840; Barber, supra, 147 Cal.App.3d 1006, 195 Cal.Rptr. 484); none involved withdrawal of life support from a conscious but incompetent patient. One also finds in the commission's lengthy report, albeit in a different comment, the cryptic statement that the amended version of section 2355 is "consistent with ... Drabick." (30 Cal. Law Revision Com. Rep., supra, com. to § 2355, p. 263.) But Drabick was expressly limited to patients in persistent vegetative states. (Drabick, supra, 200 Cal.App.3d 185, 217, fn. 36, 245 Cal.Rptr. 840.) Consistency with Drabick on this point does not support the conservator's position. For all these reasons, we are not convinced the Legislature gave any consideration to the particular problem before us in this case. The prefatory note and comments to the Uniform Health-Care Decisions Act are also silent on the point.

Notwithstanding the foregoing, one must acknowledge that the primary standard for decisionmaking set out in section 2355 does articulate what will in some cases form a constitutional basis for a conservator's decision to end the life of a conscious patient: deference to the patient's own wishes. This standard also appears in the new provisions governing decisions by agents and surrogates designated by competent adults. (§§ 4684, 4714.) As applied in that context, the requirement that decisions be made "in accordance with the principal's individual health care instructions ... and other wishes" (§ 4684) merely respects the principal-agent relationship and gives effect to the properly expressed wishes of a competent adult. Because a competent adult may refuse life-sustaining treatment (see ante, 110 Cal.Rptr.2d at p. 420, 28 P.3d at p. 158 et seq.), it follows that an agent properly and voluntarily designated by the principal may refuse treatment on the principal's behalf unless, of course, such authority is revoked. (See, e.g., §§ 4682, 4689, 4695 [providing various ways in which the authority of an agent for health care decisions may be revoked or the agent's instructions countermanded].)

The only apparent purpose of requiring conservators to make decisions in accordance with the conservatee's wishes, when those wishes are known, is to enforce the fundamental principle of personal autonomy. The same requirement, as applied to agents and surrogates freely designated by competent persons, enforces the principles of agency. A reasonable person presumably will designate for such purposes only a person in whom the former reposes the highest degree of confidence. A conservator, in contrast, is not an agent of the conservatee, and unlike a freely designated agent cannot be presumed to have special knowledge of the conservatee's health care wishes. A person with "sufficient capacity ... to form an intelligent preference" may nominate his or her own conservator (§ 1810), but the nomination is not binding because the appointment remains "solely in the discretion of the court" (§ 1812, subd. (a)). Furthermore, while statutory law gives preference to spouses and other persons related to the conservatee (id., subd. (b)), who might know something of the conservatee's health care preferences, the law also permits the court in its sole discretion to appoint unrelated persons and even public conservators (ibid.). While it may be constitutionally permissible to assume that an agent freely designated by a formerly competent person to make all health care decisions, including life-ending ones, will resolve such questions "in accordance with the principal's ... wishes" (§ 4684), one cannot apply the same assumption to conservators and conservatees (cf. § 2355, subd. (a)). For this reason, when the legal premise of a conservator's decision to end a conservatee's life by withholding medical care is that the conservatee would refuse such care, to apply a high standard of proof will help to ensure the reliability of the decision.

* * *

In this case, the importance of the ultimate decision and the risk of error are manifest. So too should be the degree of confidence required in the necessary findings of fact. The ultimate decision is whether a conservatee lives or dies, and the risk is that a conservator, claiming statutory authority to end a conscious conservatee's life "in accordance with the conservatee's ... wishes" (§ 2355, subd. (a)) by withdrawing artificial nutrition and hydration, will make a decision with which the conservatee subjectively disagrees and which subjects the conservatee to starvation, dehydration and death. This would represent the gravest possible affront to a conservatee's state constitutional right to privacy, in the sense of freedom from unwanted bodily intrusions, and to life. While the practical ability to make autonomous health care decisions does not survive incompetence,[13] the ability to perceive unwanted intrusions may. Certainly it is possible, as the conservator here urges, that an incompetent and uncommunicative but conscious conservatee might perceive the efforts to keep him alive as unwanted intrusion and the withdrawal of those efforts as welcome release. But the decision to treat is reversible. The decision to withdraw treatment is not. The role of a high evidentiary standard in such a case is to adjust the risk of error to favor the less perilous result. The high court has aptly explained the benefits of a high evidentiary standard in a similar context: "An erroneous decision not to terminate results in a maintenance of the status quo; the possibility of subsequent developments such as advancements in medical science, the discovery of new evidence regarding the patient's intent, changes in the law, or simply the unexpected death of the patient despite the administration of life-sustaining treatment at least create the potential that a wrong decision will eventually be corrected or its impact mitigated. An erroneous decision to withdraw life-sustaining treatment, however, is not susceptible of correction."[14] (Cruzan, supra, 497 U.S. 261, 283, 110 S.Ct. 2841, 111 L.Ed.2d 224; see also In re Martin (1995) 450 Mich. 204, 538 N.W.2d 399, 409–411 [requiring, under Michigan law, clear and convincing evidence of a conscious but incompetent conservatee's desire to refuse artificial nutrition and hydration].)

In conclusion, to interpret section 2355 to permit a conservator to withdraw artificial nutrition and hydration from a conscious conservatee based on a finding, by a mere preponderance of the evidence, that the conservatee would refuse treatment creates a serious risk that the law will be unconstitutionally applied in some cases, with grave injury to fundamental rights. Under these circumstances, we may properly ask whether the statute may be construed in a way that mitigates the risk. "If a statute is susceptible of two constructions, one of which will render it constitutional and the other unconstitu-

---

13. Except, of course, when a person has before incompetence left legally cognizable instructions for health care or designated an agent or surrogate for health care decisions.

14. The court in Cruzan, supra, 497 U.S. 261, 110 S.Ct. 2841, 111 L.Ed.2d 224, upheld Missouri's choice of an evidentiary standard; the court did not purport to impose that standard as a matter of federal constitutional law. No such question was presented. Nevertheless, the court's pertinent observations on standards of proof have persuasive value on a question we must decide under California law.

tional in whole or in part, or raise serious and doubtful constitutional questions, the court will adopt the construction which, without doing violence to the reasonable meaning of the language used, will render it valid in its entirety, or free from doubt as to its constitutionality, even though the other construction is equally reasonable. [Citations.] The basis of this rule is the presumption that the Legislature intended, not to violate the Constitution, but to enact a valid statute within the scope of its constitutional powers." * * * [Citations omitted]. Here, where the risk to conservatees' rights is grave and the proposed construction is consistent with the language of the statute, to construe the statute to avoid the constitutional risk is an appropriate exercise of judicial power.

* * *

The highest courts of three other states have spoken to the matter. Of these decisions, In re Martin, supra, 450 Mich. 204, 538 N.W.2d 399, is most like the case before us. Conservatee Michael Martin, like the conservatee here, suffered a head injury in an automobile accident that left him minimally conscious, unable to walk or talk, and dependent on artificial nutrition and hydration. At his highest level of functioning, Michael could move his leg or arm in response to a therapist's request and move his head in response to questions seeking a yes or no answer. On one occasion he indicated "no" in response to the question whether there were ever times when he felt he did not want to go on living; the witnesses, however, disagreed about the consistency and significance of Michael's responses to questions. (Id. at pp. 402–403.) The Supreme Court of Michigan, applying that state's common law, did not permit the conservator, Michael's wife, to withdraw artificial nutrition and hydration because clear and convincing evidence did not show he had expressed a desire to refuse such treatment under his present circumstances. The court adopted the clear and convincing standard for essentially the same reasons we do so here, namely, to ensure that a decision to refuse treatment drawing its legal justification from the conservatee's right to make autonomous medical decisions actually enjoys the conservatee's approval (id. at pp. 406–409), and to impose the risk of an erroneous decision on those seeking to withdraw treatment in view of the decision's grave consequences (id. at pp. 409–410). "Only when the patient's prior statements," the court held, "clearly illustrate a serious, well thought out, consistent decision to refuse treatment under these exact circumstances, or circumstances highly similar to the current situation, should treatment be refused or withdrawn." (Id. at p. 411.) Michael's wife testified that he had demanded she promise not to let him live "like a vegetable" or "on machines" in reaction to movies depicting persons who were vegetative, had terminal illnesses, or could not care for themselves because of serious disabilities. (Id. at p. 412.) Michael's coworkers also testified that he had expressed disdain for living in a vegetative state, but they did not understand him as having referred to his present, minimally conscious condition. Considering all this evidence, the court did not find clear and convincing evidence of a "decision to refuse life-sustaining medical treatment under the present circumstances." (Id. at p. 413.)

The Supreme Courts of Wisconsin and New Jersey have also refused permission, under their own states' common law, to withhold artificial nutrition and hydration from incompetent but conscious patients. The Wisconsin court required a "clear statement" of the conservatee's desires, proved by a preponderance of the evidence. (Matter of Edna M.F. (1997) 210 Wis.2d 557, 563 N.W.2d 485, 490.) The court described the necessary "clear statement" as an exceptional requirement, not applicable to "other, less permanent, decisions," and justified by "the interest of the state in preserving human life and the irreversible nature of the decision to withdraw nutrition from a person." (Ibid., fn. omitted.) Ruling in the case of a woman with Alzheimer's dementia, the court did not find a sufficiently clear statement of the desire to refuse treatment in her pre-dementia comment that she "'would rather die of cancer than lose [her] mind'"; she had not, the court noted, said anything specifically about withdrawing life-sustaining medical treatment. (Id. at p. 487.) The court also specifically refused to extend to conscious patients its earlier decision giving conservators, as a matter of law, the power to withhold life-sustaining treatment from persistently vegetative patients. (Id. at pp. 488–490; see Matter of Guardianship of L.W. (1992) 167 Wis.2d 53, 482 N.W.2d 60.)

The Supreme Court of New Jersey, articulating that state's common law, adopted a fairly complex three-part test. (Matter of Conroy (1985) 98 N.J. 321, 486 A.2d 1209.) Under a "pure-objective test" (id. at p. 1232), essentially a best interests test, the court would not require any evidence of the patient's wishes when the patient was in such "recurring, unavoidable and severe pain ... that the effect of administering life-sustaining treatment would be inhumane." (Ibid.) Under a "limited-objective test" (id. at p. 1232), the court would permit treatment to be withdrawn for those in "unavoidable pain" of less severity when there is "some trustworthy evidence" the patient would have refused treatment and "it is clear that the burdens of the patient's continued life with the treatment outweigh the benefits of that life for him." (Ibid.) In other circumstances, however, the court would permit treatment to be withdrawn only "when it is clear that the particular patient would have refused the treatment under the circumstances involved." (Id. at p. 1229.) That standard, the court explained, "is a subjective one, consistent with the notion that the right that we are seeking to effectuate is a very personal right to control one's own life. The question is not what a reasonable or average person would have chosen to do under the circumstances but what the particular patient would have done if able to choose for himself." (Ibid.) Under this "subjective test," the court did not find a sufficiently "'clear' showing of intent" to refuse treatment in a bedridden, severely demented and unresponsive woman's history of scorning medicine and refusing hospitalization. (Id. at pp. 1218, 1242–1243.)

About these three decisions one point deserves emphasis: In each case, the court required a clear statement by the patient of the intent to refuse life-sustaining treatment when a conservator or guardian proposed to withdraw treatment from a conscious conservatee or ward in order to effectuate the latter's own right to refuse treatment. (In re Martin, supra, 450 Mich. 204, 538 N.W.2d 399, 406–411; Matter of Edna M.F., supra, 210 Wis.2d 557, 563 N.W.2d 485, 488–491; Matter of Conroy, supra, 98 N.J. 321, 486 A.2d 1209, 1229.) As we have explained, the only apparent purpose of California's statutory language requiring a decision "in accordance with the conservatee's ... wishes" (§ 2355, subd. (a)) is to enforce the fundamental principle of personal autonomy, in the same way that the identical language in other provisions (§§ 4684, 4714) governing agents and surrogates freely designated by competent persons enforces the principles of agency. While we place no great emphasis on the out-of-state cases, they nevertheless support the fundamental principles that underlie our conclusions, including the imposition of a high standard of proof.

* * *

The "clear and convincing evidence" test requires a finding of high probability, based on evidence "'"so clear as to leave no substantial doubt" [and] "sufficiently strong to command the unhesitating assent of every reasonable mind."'" (In re Angelia P., supra, 28 Cal.3d 908, 919, 171 Cal.Rptr. 637, 623 P.2d 198; accord, Sheehan v. Sullivan (1899) 126 Cal. 189, 193, 58 P. 543.) Applying that standard here, we ask whether the evidence the conservatee would have refused treatment under the circumstances of this case has that degree of clarity, bearing in mind that what we are asking, in essence, is whether the conservatee would actually have wished to die.

On this point the trial court wrote: "[T]he testimony adduced focuses upon two pre-accident conversations during which the conservatee allegedly expressed a desire not to live like a 'vegetable.' These two conversations do not establish by clear and convincing evidence that the conservatee would desire to have his life-sustaining medical treatment terminated under the circumstances in which he now finds himself. One of these conversations allegedly occurred when the conservatee was apparently recovering from a night's bout of drinking. The other alleged conversation occurred following the loss of conservatee's father-in-law, with whom he was very close. The court finds that neither of these conversations reflect an exact 'on all-fours' description of conservatee's present medical condition. More explicit direction than just 'I don't want to live like a vegetable' is required in order to justify a surrogate decision-maker terminating the life of ... someone who is not in a PVS [persistent vegetative state]." We agree with the trial court's assessment of the evidence. That assessment is essentially in accord with the only case directly on point, in which the Michigan Supreme Court found no clear and convincing evidence of a desire to refuse treatment under very similar facts. (See In re Martin, supra, 450 Mich. 204, 538 N.W.2d 399, discussed ante, 110 Cal.Rptr.2d at p. 435, 28 P.3d at p. 170 et seq.) We add to the trial court's assessment only that Rose acknowledged Robert did not describe the precise condition in which he later found himself (see ante, 110 Cal.Rptr.2d at p. 419, 28 P.3d at p. 157) and that, while experts dispute the consistency and accuracy of Robert's responses to questions, it is difficult to ignore the fact that he declined to answer the question "Do you want to die?" while giving facially plausible "yes" or "no" answers to a variety of other questions about his wishes. (See ante, 110 Cal.Rptr.2d at p. 419, 28 P.3d at p. 157 et seq.) On this record, we see no reason to hold that the evidence does not support the trial court's finding.

* * *

Having rejected the conservator's argument that withdrawing artificial hydration and nutrition would have been "in accordance with the conservatee's ... wishes" (§ 2355, subd. (a)), we must next consider her contention that the same action would have been proper under the fallback best interest standard. Under that standard, "the conservator shall make the decision in accordance with the conservator's determination of the conservatee's best interest. In determining the conservatee's best interest, the conservator shall consider the conservatee's personal values to the extent known to the conservator." (Ibid.) The trial court, as noted, ruled the conservator had the burden of establishing that the withdrawal of artificially delivered nutrition and hydration was in the conservatee's best interest, and had not met that burden.

Here, as before, the conservator argues that the trial court applied too high a standard of proof. This follows, she contends, from section 2355, which gives her as conservator "the exclusive authority" to give consent for such medical treatment as she "in good faith based on medical advice determines to be necessary" (§ 2355, subd. (a), italics added), and from the decision in Drabick, supra, 200 Cal.App.3d 185, 200, 245 Cal.Rptr. 840, which emphasized that a court should not substitute its judgment for the conservator's. The legislative findings to the Health Care Decisions Law, the conservator notes, declare that "[i]n the absence of controversy, a court is normally not the proper forum in which to make health care decisions, including decisions regarding life-sustaining treatment" (§ 4650, subd. (c)); similarly, the Law Revision Commission has explained that "[c]ourt control or intervention in this process is neither required by statute, nor desired by the courts." (30 Cal. Law Revision Com. Rep., supra, com. to § 2355, p. 264.) Based on these statements, the conservator argues the trial court has no power other than to verify that she has made the decision for which the Probate Code expressly calls: a "good faith" decision "based on medical advice" and " consider[ing] the conservatee's personal values" whether treatment is " necessary" in the conservatee's "best interest." (§ 2355, subd. (a).) The trial court, as noted, rejected the conservator's assessment of the conservatee's best interest but nevertheless found by clear and convincing evidence that she had acted "in good faith, based on medical evidence and after consideration of the conservatee's best interests, including his likely wishes, based on his previous statements." This finding, the conservator concludes, should end the litigation as a matter of law in her favor.

The conservator's understanding of section 2355 is not correct. To be sure, the statute provides that "the conservator shall make the decision in accordance with the conservator's determination of the conservatee's best interest." (§ 2355, subd. (a), italics added.) But the conservator herself concedes the court must be able to review her decision for abuse of discretion. This much, at least, follows from the conservator's status as an officer of the court subject to judicial supervision. While the assessment of a conservatee's best interest belongs in the first instance to the conservator, this does not mean the court must invariably defer to the conservator regardless of the evidence.

In the exceptional case where a conservator proposes to end the life of a conscious but incompetent conservatee, we believe the same factor that principally justifies applying the clear and convincing evidence standard to a determination of the conservatee's wishes also justifies applying that standard to a determination of the conservatee's best interest: The decision threatens the conservatee's fundamental rights to privacy and life. While section 2355 is written with sufficient breadth to cover all health care decisions, the Legislature cannot have intended to authorize every conceivable application without meaningful judicial review. Taken to its literal extremes, the statute would permit a conservator to withdraw health care necessary to life from any conservatee who had been adjudicated incompetent to make health care decisions, regardless of the degree of mental and physical impairment, and on no greater showing than that the conservator in good faith considered treatment not to be in the conservatee's best interest. The result would be to permit a conservator freely to end a conservatee's life based on the conservator's subjective assessment, albeit "in good faith [and] based on medical advice" (§ 2355, subd.(a)), that the conservatee enjoys an unacceptable quality of life. We find no reason to believe the Legislature intended section 2355 to confer power so unlimited and no authority for such a result in any judicial decision. Under these circumstances, we may properly construe the statute to require proof by clear and convincing evidence to avoid grave injury to the fundamental rights of conscious but incompetent conservatees. (See ante, 110 Cal.Rptr.2d at p. 433, 28 P.3d at p. 169 et seq.)

We need not in this case attempt to define the extreme factual predicates that, if proved by clear and convincing evidence, might support a conservator's decision that withdrawing life support would be in the best interest of a conscious conservatee. Here, the conservator offered no basis for such a finding other than her own subjective judgment that the conservatee did not enjoy a satisfactory quality of life and legally insufficient evidence to the effect that he would have wished to die. On this record, the trial court's decision was correct.

* * *

For the reasons set out above, we conclude the superior court correctly required the conservator to prove, by clear and convincing evidence, either that the conservatee wished to refuse life-sustaining treatment or that to withhold such treatment would have been in his best interest; lacking such evidence, the superior court correctly denied the conservator's request for permission to withdraw artificial hydration and nutrition. We emphasize, however, that the clear and convincing evidence standard does not apply to the vast majority of health care decisions made by conservators under section 2355. Only the decision to withdraw life-sustaining treatment, because of its effect on a conscious conservatee's fundamental rights, justifies imposing that high standard of proof. Therefore, our decision today affects only a narrow class of persons: conscious conservatees who have not left formal directions for health care and whose conservators propose to withhold life-sustaining treatment for the purpose of causing their conservatees' deaths. Our conclusion does not affect permanently unconscious patients, including those who are comatose or in a persistent vegetative state (see generally Conservatorship of Morrison, supra, 206 Cal.App.3d 304, 253 Cal.Rptr. 530; Drabick, supra, 200 Cal.App.3d 185, 245 Cal.Rptr. 840; Barber, supra, 147 Cal.App.3d 1006, 195 Cal.Rptr. 484), persons who have left legally cognizable instructions for health care (see §§ 4670, 4673, 4700), persons who have designated agents or other surrogates for health care (see §§ 4671, 4680, 4711), or conservatees for whom conservators have made medical decisions other than those intended to bring about the death of a conscious conservatee.

The decision of the Court of Appeal is reversed.

GEORGE, C.J., KENNARD, J., BAXTER, J., CHIN, J., BROWN, J., concur.

Notes

These are difficult decisions. Often parents challenge the decisions of spouses and domestic partners, as was evidenced in the *Wendland* decision. More frequently, challenges involve nutrition and hydration, and an appropriate standard of proof when there is no written health-care directive. In 2004, the Supreme Court of Florida ruled on a case that involved a husband seeking to withhold nutrition and hydration to his wife of fourteen years. She did not have a health-care directive, but the husband petitioned the guardianship court to authorize termination of life-prolonging procedures. The husband argued that his wife, who suffered cardiac arrest and has been in a persistent vegetative state for eight years, with no hope of improvement, would not choose to continue constant nursing care with hope of a miracle. Rather, he argued, she would want a natural death to occur so her family could go on with their lives. The guardianship court allowed for the cessation of nutrition and hydration, but the wife's parents objected, arguing that new medical evidence indicated potential improvement of their daughter; they asked that life support continue. The guardianship court nonetheless rejected the parents' argument, holding that there was clear and convincing evidence that the woman maintained on total life support would want to discontinue all nutrition and hydration. *See* In re Guardianship of Schiavo, 780 So. 2d 176, 177 (Fla. 2d Dist. App. 2001). The parents appealed, and the Florida court affirmed, denying relief to the parents, stating:

> But in the end, this case is not about the aspirations that loving parents have for their children. It is about Theresa Schiavo's right to make her own decision, independent of her parents and independent of her husband.... It may be unfortunate that when families cannot agree, the best forum we can offer for this private, personal decision is a public courtroom and the best decision-maker

we can provide is a judge with no prior knowledge of the ward, but the law currently provides no better solution that adequately protects the interests of promoting the value of life.

In re Guardianship of Schiavo, 851 S.2d 182, 186–87 (Fla. 2d Dist. App. 2003).

After the court's decision to remove the nutrition and hydration tube, the tube was removed on October 15, 2003. On October 21, 2003, the Florida legislature enacted a statute that allowed the governor of the state broad powers to issue a one-time stay to prevent the withholding of nutrition and hydration if the patient has no written advance directive, the court finds the patient to be in a persistent vegetative state, the patient has had nutrition and hydration withheld, and a member of the patient's family has challenged the withholding of nutrition and hydration. *See* Terri's Law, Fla. Stat. Ann. § 744.3215 (2004). The nutrition and hydration tube was then reinserted. But one year later, the Supreme Court of Florida ruled that the legislature's enactment of the statute encroaches upon the power of the judicial branch, thereby violating separation of powers. *See* Bush v. Schiavo, 885 So. 2d 321 (Fla. 2004). The court held:

> In enacting [the statute], the Legislature failed to provide any standards by which the Governor should determine whether, in any given case, a stay should be issued and how long a stay should remain in effect. Further, the Legislature has failed to provide any criteria for lifting the stay. This absolute, unfettered discretion to decide whether to issue and then when to lift a stay makes the Governor's decision virtually unreviewable.

Id. at 334.

In concluding, the court stated:

> The trial court's decision regarding Theresa Schiavo was made in accordance with the procedures and protections set forth by the judicial branch and in accordance with the statutes passed by the Legislature in effect at that time. That decision is final and the Legislature's attempt to alter that final adjudication is unconstitutional as applied to Theresa Schiavo.

Id. at 337.

Subsequently, the U.S. Supreme Court declined to hear an appeal brought by the government in January 2005. One day before Terri Schiavo's feeding tube was to be removed at the request of her husband, a Florida circuit judge granted a motion for a temporary stay, which was requested by Terri Schiavo's parents, who claimed that the husband was not acting in Terri Schiavo's best interest. However, the stay was subsequently lifted, and the feeding tube was removed on March 18, 2005. In response, the U.S. Senate and House of Representatives deliberated overnight and passed emergency legislation "for the relief of the parents of" Terri Schiavo. The President signed the legislation—the Schiavo Bill—on March 21, 2005. The legislation provided for injunctive relief to safeguard the right to continued medical treatment. Despite this, the federal district court declined to issue relief. The parents appealed to the Florida Supreme Court and the U.S. Supreme Court, but both declined to intervene. Terri Schiavo died on March 31, 2005. *See* Laura Stanton, *The Battle Over Terri Schiavo*, Wash. Post, Apr. 1, 2005, at A13.

E. Conservator

Uniform Probate Code (2003)

Section 5-102. Definitions.

(1) "Conservator" means a person who is appointed by a court to manage the estate of a protected person.

* * *

(4) "Incapacitated Person" means an individual who, for reasons other than being a minor, is unable to receive and evaluate information or make or communicate decisions to such an extent that the individual lacks the ability to meet essential requirements for physical health, safety, or self-care, even with appropriate technological assistance.

* * *

Section 5-403. Original Petition for Appointment or Protective Order

(a) The following may petition for the appointment of a conservator or for any other appropriate protective order:

(1) the person to be protected;

(2) an individual interested in the estate, affairs, or welfare of the person to be protected, including a parent, guardian, or custodian; or

(3) a person who would be adversely affected by lack of effective management of the property and business affairs of the person to be protected.

* * *

Section 5-413. Who May Be Conservator: Priorities

(a) Except as otherwise provided in subsection (d), the court, in appointing a conservator, shall consider persons otherwise qualified in the following order of priority:

(1) a conservator, guardian or the estate, or other like fiduciary appointed or recognized by an appropriate court of any other jurisdiction in which the protected person resides;

(2) a person nominated as conservator by the respondent, including the respondent's most recent nomination made in a durable power of attorney, if the respondent has attained the age or 14 years of age and at the time of the nomination had sufficient capacity to express a preference.

(3) an agent appointed by the respondent to manage the respondent's property under a durable power of attorney;

(4) the spouse of the respondent;

(5) an adult child of the respondent;

(6) a parent of the respondent; and

(7) an adult with whom the respondent has resided for more than six months before the filing of the petition.

* * *

Section 5-418. General Duties of Conservator; Plan

(a) A conservator, in relation to powers conferred by this [part] or implicit in the title acquired by virtue of the proceeding, is a fiduciary and shall observe the standards of care applicable to a trustee.

(b) A conservator may exercise authority only as necessitated by the limitations of the protected person, and to the extent possible, shall encourage the person to participate in decisions, act in the person's own behalf, and develop or regain the ability to manage the person's estate and business affairs.

(c) Within 60 days after appointment, a conservator shall file with the appointing court a plan for protecting, managing, expending, and distributing the assets of the protected person's estate. The plan must be based on the actual needs of the person and take into consideration the best interests of the person. The conservator shall include in the plan steps to develop or restore the person's ability to manage the person's property, and estimate of the duration of the conservatorship, and projections of expenses and resources.

(d) In investing an estate, selecting assets of the estate for distribution, and invoking powers of revocation or withdrawal available for the use and benefit of the protected person and exercisable by the conservator, a conservator shall take into account any estate plan of the person known to the conservator and may examine the will and any other donative, nominative, or other appointive instrument of the person.

Uniform Custodial Trust Act (2003)

Section 2. Custodial Trust; General

(a) A person may create a custodial trust of property by a written transfer of the property to another person, evidenced by registration or by other instrument of transfer, executed in any lawful manner, naming as beneficiary, an individual who may be the transferor, in which the transferee is designated, in substance, as custodial trustee under the [Enacting state] Uniform Custodial Trust Act.

* * *

Notes

While the Uniform Custodial Trust Act (1987) is analogous to the Uniform Transfers to Minors Act, this Act is often used to provide protection to persons who, while most often are not affluent, are represented by attorneys or others appointed by the court. The Act does not require that a person be incapacitated to benefit from its provisions; it provides only that the adult person has a need for management. It may be used to provide for anticipated incapacity and to ensure proper management at that time; eventual incapacity will not terminate the trust.

F. Guardian

Uniform Probate Code (2004)

Section 5-102. Definitions.

(3) "Guardian" means a person who has qualified as a guardian of a minor or incapacitated person pursuant to appointment by a parent or spouse, or by the court. The term includes a limited, emergency, and temporary substitute guardian but not a guardian ad litem.

Section 5-301. Appointment and Status of Guardian.

A person becomes a guardian of an incapacitated person by a parental or spousal appointment or upon appointment by the court. The guardianship continues until terminated, without regard to the location of the guardian or ward.

Section 5-306. Judicial Appointment of Guardian: Professional Evaluation.

At or before a hearing under this [part], the court may order a professional evaluation of the respondent and shall order the evaluation if the respondent so demands. If the court orders the evaluation, the respondent must be examined by a physician, psychologist, or other individual appointed by the court who is qualified to evaluate the respondent's alleged impairment. The examiner shall promptly file a written report with the court. Unless otherwise directed by the court, the report must contain:

(1) a description of the nature, type, and extent of the respondent's specific cognitive and functional limitations;

(2) an evaluation of the respondent's mental and physical condition and, if appropriate, educational potential, adaptive behavior, and social skills;

(3) a prognosis for improvement and a recommendation as to the appropriate treatment or habitation plan; and

(4) the date of any assessment or examination upon which the report is based.

Section 5-311. Findings; Order of Appointment

(a) The court may:

(1) appoint a limited or unlimited guardian for a respondent only if it finds by clear and convincing evidence that:

    (A) the respondent is an incapacitated person; and

    (B) the respondent's identified needs cannot be met by less restrictive means, including the use of appropriate technological assistance; or

(2) with appropriate findings, treat the petition as one for a protective order under Section 5-401, enter any other appropriate order, or dismiss the proceeding.

(b) The court, whenever feasible, shall grant to a guardian only those powers necessitated by the ward's limitations and demonstrated needs and make appointive and other orders that will encourage the development of the ward's maximum self-reliance and independence.

(c) Within 14 days after an appointment, a guardian shall send or deliver to the ward and to all other persons given notice of the hearing on the petition a copy of the order of appointment, together with a notice of the right to request termination or modification.

Section 5-314. Duties of Guardian

(a) Except as otherwise limited by the court, a guardian shall make decisions regarding the ward's support, care, education, health, and welfare. A guardian shall exercise authority only as necessitated by the ward's limitations and, to the extent possible, shall encourage the ward to participate in decisions, act on the ward's own behalf, and develop or regain the capacity to manage the ward's personal affairs. A guardian, in making decisions, shall consider the expressed desires and personal values of the ward to the extent known to the guardian. A guardian at all times shall act in the ward's best interests and exercise reasonable care, diligence, and prudence.

(b) A guardian shall:

(1) become or remain personally acquainted with the ward and maintain sufficient contact with the ward to know of the ward's capacities, limitations, needs, opportunities, and physical and mental health;

(2) take reasonable care of the ward's personal effects and bring protective proceedings if necessary to protect the property of the ward;

(3) expend money of the ward that has been receive by the guardian for the ward's current needs for support, care, education, health, and welfare;

(4) conserve any excess money of the ward for the ward's future needs, but if a conservator has been appointed for the estate of the ward, the guardian shall pay the money to the conservator, at least quarterly, to be conserved for the ward's future needs;

(5) immediately notify the court if the ward's condition has changed so that the ward is capable of exercising rights previously removed; and

(6) inform the court of any changes in the ward's custodial dwelling or address.

In re Maher

New York Supreme Court, Appellate Division, 1994
207 A.D.2d 133, 621 N.Y.S.2d 617

Friedmann, J.

On this appeal—which appears to represent a case of first impression at the appellate level—we are asked to consider the propriety of a determination by the Supreme Court, Kings County (Leone, J.), embodied in a judgment entered October 8, 1993, that the respondent, Francis E. Maher, was not incapacitated as that term is defined in the recently enacted Mental Hygiene Law article 81. Based upon this determination, the court dismissed, with prejudice, the petition for a guardian for the respondent's property which had been brought by Francis E. Maher, Jr., the respondent's son. Since the court properly applied the standards and carried out the legislative intent of Mental Hygiene Law article 81, we now affirm.

* * *

On December 11, 1992, the respondent, attorney Francis E. Maher, suffered a stroke which left him with right-sided hemiplegia and aphasia. He was admitted to St. Luke's-Roosevelt Hospital where, on December 12, he underwent surgery, *inter alia*, to evacuate a hematoma from the frontal portion of his brain. For some time after the operation, the respondent remained partially paralyzed and aphasic, although occasionally he was able to speak a few words and to move a bit on his right side.

By order to show cause dated December 17, 1992, the appellant commenced a proceeding pursuant to Mental Hygiene Law article 77 for the appointment of a conservator. On December 17, 1992, the Honorable Sebastian Leone, Justice of the Supreme Court, appointed Ronald M. LaRocca, Esq., as temporary receiver, and Margaret M. Bomba, Esq., as the guardian ad litem, for the respondent. The guardian ad litem filed a report dated January 4, 1993, wherein she stated that due to the respondent's physical condition "he is presently incapable of managing his own business and financial affairs", and she recommended the appointment of a conservator of his property. The guardian ad litem objected to the appointment of Ronald M. LaRocca as conservator because of a "perceived conflict of interest"—due to the fact that LaRocca also represented a hospital that owed the respondent considerable sums in attorneys' fees for services rendered in past litigation. By order dated January 20, 1993, the Supreme Court permitted LaRocca to withdraw as temporary receiver and appointed the appellant and Elizabeth Maher, the respondent's sister and for many years his office manager, as temporary receivers pending the conservatorship hearing, upon the posting of an undertaking in the sum of $1,000,000 with an authorized surety company. LaRocca subsequently became the attorney for the appellant in the instant proceeding.

On March 31, 1993—the day on which the respondent executed a power of attorney naming the appellant as his "attorney-in-fact"—the temporary receivers advised the court that the respondent's condition had "improved dramatically" and that the appellant wished to discontinue the proceeding. The guardian ad litem joined in the application, and the court granted the request orally, directing the parties to settle an order withdrawing the petition.

However, according to the appellant, on the very night of the withdrawal petition, namely March 31, 1993, the respondent's condition abruptly deteriorated, and he began to behave in an irrational and abusive manner. At about this same time, the respondent also declared his intention to marry Ms. Helen Kelly, an attorney formerly associated with his law firm, whom he had been seeing since shortly after the death of his first wife in March of 1992. It was the guardian ad litem's considered opinion that the respondent's agitation was provoked by his sons' attempts to isolate him from Ms. Kelly and other friends, as well as by their refusal to permit him access to funds of any kind.

On May 7, 1993, the appellant announced his intention to go forward with the conservatorship proceeding, based on his allegation that the respondent had become "confused and irrational". On May 19, 1993, the respondent revoked the previously issued power of attorney in favor of the appellant, and executed a new power of attorney in favor of Irwin F. Simon, an attorney who had done per diem work for the respondent's law firm for many years. The guardian ad litem submitted her interim report dated May 20, 1993, along with a proposed order to withdraw the petition. The appellant promptly opposed the guardian ad litem's motion to dismiss, and requested a hearing to explore the need for the appointment of a conservator. The guardian ad litem submitted a "Supplemental Report" on June 1, 1993, defending herself against the appellant's charges of bias, and again urging the dismissal of the petition.

On June 1, 1993, the respondent disappeared from the home that he had shared with the appellant and another of his sons. On June 17, 1993, the respondent married Ms. Kelly.

At the outset of the hearing, which was held on June 21, 1993 and July 16, 1993, the proceeding was converted, with the consent of all parties, to one for the appointment of a guardian for property management under Mental Hygiene Law article 81. At the hearing, testimony was taken from the respondent's sister, Betty Maher, two of his sons, George and the appellant, his speech pathologist, Susan Sachs, and Dr. Valerie Lanyi, a rehabilitation specialist who had treated the respondent at the Rusk Institute, and who had seen him in consultation as recently as June 10, 1993. Testifying for the respondent were the respondent himself, and his wife, Mrs. Helen Kelly Maher. At the conclusion of the hearing, the court found that the appellant had not carried his burden of proving by the requisite clear and convincing evidence that (1) the respondent was incapacitated, and (2) a guardian was necessary to manage his property and financial affairs.

* * *

The Legislature enacted Mental Hygiene Law article 81 (L 1992, ch 698), effective April 1, 1993, to remedy the perceived deficiencies in Mental Hygiene Law former articles 77 and 78, which had authorized the appointment of a conservator for the property or a committee for the person, respectively, of individuals whose ability to care for their property was substantially impaired or who were adjudged to be incompetent.

Former Mental Hygiene Law former article 78, the committee statute, required a finding of complete incompetence. That statute provided no guidance regarding what constituted incompetence, no standard governing the type of proof required to establish incompetence, and no specification respecting the range of powers assumed by a "committee of the person". However, a finding of incompetence resulted in a complete loss of civil rights and the accompanying stigma of total incapacity. Because of this stigma and loss of civil rights, the judiciary became increasingly reluctant to invoke article 78. This reluctance, together with the statutory preference for a conservator which appeared in both Mental Hygiene Law former articles 77 and 78, resulted in the virtual abandonment of the committee procedure (Koppell and Munnelly, *The New Guardian Statute: Article 81 of the Mental Hygiene Law,* 65 NY St BJ [No. 2] 16 [Feb. 1993] [hereinafter Koppell and Munnelly]).

Mental Hygiene Law article 77, the conservatorship statute, enacted in 1972, allowed for the appointment of a conservator for property only. While certain language in article 77 regarding the "personal well-being" of the conservatee suggested the possibility of using conservators of the property to exercise authority over the person of the individual, the needs of the population to be served by guardianship statutes proved so varied that the relief ostensibly offered by article 77 simply did not in fact afford either the authority or the flexibility necessary to address them all (Koppell and Munnelly, *op. cit.*).

On April 30, 1991, the Court of Appeals decided *Matter of Grinker (Rose)* (77 NY2d 703), holding, *inter alia*, that Mental Hygiene Law article 77 did not authorize a court to grant to a conservator the power to commit the conservatee to a nursing home. Such power to so significantly displace personal liberty, the Court explained, can be granted only pursuant to Mental Hygiene Law article 78, the committee statute, "with its full panoply of procedural due process safeguards" *(Matter of Grinker [Rose], supra,* at 710). That decision, although it clarified the respective reaches of articles 77 and 78, reinstated the courts' earlier dilemma. It further left without recourse the majority of incapacitated individuals who, although somewhat handicapped, were not hopelessly incompetent, and who, notwithstanding their need for varying degrees of assistance with their personal affairs as well as with property management, were not prepared utterly to relinquish in exchange therefor a lifetime's investment in integrity, autonomy, and dignity *(see,* Mental Hygiene Law § 81.01).

* * *

In response to this predicament, in 1992 the New York State Law Revision Commission proposed the creation of a single statute to replace Mental Hygiene Law articles 77 and 78. The projected legislation envisioned "a new type of guardianship proceeding based on the concept of the least restrictive alternative—one that authorizes the appointment of a guardian whose authority is appropriate to satisfy the needs of an incapacitated person, either personal or financial, while at the same time tailored and limited to only those activities for which a person needs assistance. The standard for appointment under this new procedure focuses on the decisional capacity and functional limitations of the person for whom the appointment is sought, rather than on some underlying mental or physical condition of the person. The proposal encouraged the participation of the allegedly incapacitated person in the proceeding to the greatest extent possible" (Koppell and Munnelly, *op. cit.,* at 17).

As a threshold matter, the new legislation emphasizes that "it is desirable for and beneficial to persons with incapacities to make available to them the least restrictive form of intervention which assists them in meeting their needs", while at the same time permitting them "to exercise the independence and self-determination of which they are capable". Such intervention was therefore to be "tailored to the individual needs of that person", taking into account "the personal wishes, preferences and desires of the person", and affording the person "the greatest amount of independence and self-determination and participation in all the decisions affecting [his] life" (Mental Hygiene Law § 81.01).

In exercising its discretion to appoint a guardian for an individual's property (the focus of the instant proceeding), a court must make a two-pronged determination: first, that the appointment is necessary to manage the property or financial affairs of that person, and, second, that the individual either agrees to the appointment or that the individual is "incapacitated" as defined in Mental Hygiene Law § 81.02 (b) (Mental Hygiene Law § 81.02 [a]).

As to the first prong, "the court shall consider the report of the court evaluator [heretofore the guardian ad litem, although with certain significant differences, as laid out in Mental Hygiene Law § 81.09] ... and the sufficiency and reliability of available resources [e.g., powers of attorney, trusts, representatives and protective payees] ... to provide for personal needs or property management without the appointment of a guardian" (Mental Hygiene Law § 81.02 [a] [2]; § 81.03 [e]).

As to the second prong, a determination of incapacity must be based upon clear and convincing evidence that the person is likely to suffer harm because he is unable to provide for property management and cannot adequately understand and appreciate the nature and consequences of such inability. The burden of proof is on the petitioner (*see,* Mental Hygiene Law § 81.02 [b]; § 81.12 [a]). In reaching its determination, the court must give primary consideration to the functional level and functional limitations of the person, including an assessment of the person's ability to manage the activities of daily living related to property management (e.g., mobility, money management, and banking), his understanding and appreciation of the nature and consequences of any inability to manage these activities, his preferences, wishes, and values regarding management of these affairs, and the nature and extent of the person's property and finances, in the context of his ability to manage them (Mental Hygiene Law § 81.02 [c]; § 81.03 [h]).

Even if all of the elements of incapacity are present, a guardian should be appointed only as a last resort, and should not be imposed if available resources or other alternatives will adequately protect the person (see, Law Rev Commn Comments, reprinted in McKinney's Cons Laws of NY, Book 34A, Mental Hygiene Law §81.02, 1994 Pocket Part, at 241–242).

* * *

Upon our review of the record before us, we are satisfied that the Supreme Court properly assessed the evidence in accordance with both the letter and the spirit of the new Mental Hygiene Law article 81.

Contrary to the appellant's contention, the clear and convincing evidence in the hearing record establishes only that the respondent suffers from certain functional limitations in speaking and writing, but not that he is likely to suffer harm because he is unable to provide for the management of his property, or that he is incapable of adequately understanding and appreciating the nature and consequences of his disabilities. Indeed, by granting a power of attorney to Irwin Simon, and by adding his wife as a signatory on certain of his bank accounts, the respondent evidenced that he appreciated his own handicaps to the extent that he effectuated a plan for assistance in managing his financial affairs without the need for a guardian.

Several witnesses testified to the respondent's ability to understand what he was told and to make his wishes known demonstratively. For example, the respondent's sister testified that she believed that her brother understood her when she provided him with information about the office. The appellant himself conceded that he routinely discussed collection and related business matters with the respondent, and that the respondent had regularly indicated his satisfaction with the appellant's management of his law firm's affairs. Dr. Lanyi, the physician in charge of the respondent's rehabilitation, expressed her doubt that at the time of his discharge from the Rusk Institute in mid-March 1993, the respondent could have managed his checkbook as he had formerly done, but opined that he was nonetheless, even at that time, aware of the magnitude of the sums he was spending. Moreover, according to Dr. Lanyi, when she last saw the respondent on June 10, 1993, her patient appeared to understand everything she said to him or asked of him, noting that on that occasion he had consistently responded to her remarks and inquiries in a prompt, calm manner, with appropriate words or gestures. The respondent's speech therapist, too, documented a steady improvement in her patient's ability to comprehend and respond to the tests she administered. Generally, the consensus among all witnesses was that the respondent had made, and was continuing to make, dramatic progress in his ability to comprehend information and to express himself—as well as in his mobility, which seemed essentially restored to normal—since the initial cerebrovascular episode.

Moreover, the court, which was in the best position to observe the respondent throughout the hearing, remarked that he reacted fittingly to the proceedings— even to the point of making it clear to his attorney and the court when he felt that certain questions or answers were objectionable. The court was further persuaded that the respondent knew the correct responses to the questions put to him on the stand, although he was not able verbally to express them.

This case is therefore distinguishable from those relied upon by the appellant, where the respondent had demonstrably ceased to comprehend his practical affairs, as evidenced, *inter alia,* by a documented dissipation or impending loss of substantial assets (*see, e.g., Matter of Ginsberg [Ginsberg]*, NYLJ, Jan. 3, 1992, at 27, col 6; *Matter of Flowers [Dove]*, 197 AD2d 515; *Matter of Rochester Gen. Hosp. [Levin]*, 158 Misc 2d 522). No such loss or imminent threat of loss has been even alleged, let alone proven, in the case at bar. It is further worthy of note that two of these cases, *Ginsberg* and *Flowers,* were decided under now-repealed Mental Hygiene Law article 77, where the legal standard for a determination of incapacity—whether the respondent suffered from a substantial impairment of his ability to care for his property and manage his finances—was expressly found wanting by the Legislature in fashioning Mental Hygiene Law article 81 (*see,* Law Rev Commn Comments, reprinted at McKinney's Cons Laws of NY, Book 34A, Mental Hygiene Law art 81, 1994 Pocket Part, at 242–243).

The instant case more closely resembles those where the allegedly incapacitated person has effectuated a plan for the management of his affairs which obviated the need for a guardian (*see, e.g., Matter of Tait*, NYLJ, May 31, 1994, at 28, col 1; *Matter of Lambriger*, NYLJ, May 31, 1994, at 37, col 1; *Matter of Gelezewski*, NYLJ, Nov. 17, 1993, at 30, col 2; *Matter of Anonymous, R.A.,*NYLJ, Sept. 28, 1993, at 27, col 2; *Matter of Presbyterian Hosp. [Early]*, NYLJ, July 2, 1993, at 22, col 2 [Sup Ct, NY County]).

Although the appellant tries to distinguish the foregoing cases on the ground that the assets at issue were far more modest than the very substantial estate involved here, we do not find the size of the property involved, standing alone, to be dispositive. Rather, in the matter before us, there has been no showing that the respondent has lost the ability to appreciate his financial circumstances, or that others have taken control of his affairs without his comprehension or rational supervision. There has further been no demonstration of any waste, real or imminent, of the respondent's assets. There is an absence of proof that the respondent's chosen attorney and his wife (who is also an attorney) are incapable of managing the property at issue in accordance with the respondent's wishes.[1] Under such circumstances, the appellant has failed to demonstrate the need for a guardian under the standards enunciated in Mental Hygiene Law article 81.

The court did not err in excluding from evidence certain "tests" or "demonstrations" of the respondent's inability to expatiate on the meaning of a complicated legal text, to write checks in differing amounts to different payees, to separate and count diverse kinds of currency, and to explain his execution of two successive powers of attorney. The court was already well aware of the respondent's difficulty—due to his expressive aphasia and apraxia—in verbally communicating his understanding of the questions posed to him, and in writing or counting numbers clearly—although he could make himself understood to those to whom he could demonstrate nonverbally. Therefore, such "tests" would not have served to inform the court about the material issue before it—namely, whether the respondent appreciated the nature and consequences of his alleged inability personally to manage his property, and that he could suffer harm as a result (*see,* Mental Hygiene Law §81.02 [b]). As the evidence sought to be elicited would merely have distracted the court from the main point at issue, the court properly exercised its discretion in denying the admission of that evidence (*see, Harvey v Mazal Am.*

---

1. It is further worthy of note that there has been no serious allegation, let alone demonstration, that either Ms. Kelly or Mr. Simon— two individuals with whom the respondent had long been acquainted (*cf., Matter of Ginsberg [Ginsberg]*, NYLJ, Jan. 3, 1992, at 27, col 6, *supra*)— used fraud, duress, or undue influence on the respondent in order to bring about either his marriage or his execution of a second power of attorney.

Partners, 79 NY2d 218, 223–224; *People v Acevedo,* 40 NY2d 701, 704–705; *Clark v Brooklyn Hgts. R. R. Co.,* 177 NY 359, 361; *Riddle v Memorial Hosp.,* 43 AD2d 750, 751; Richardson, Evidence §§ 134, 136 [Prince 10th ed]).

The court was similarly justified in refusing to allow the appellant's expert, Dr. Gannon, who had never examined the respondent, to testify to the respondent's alleged incapacitation based upon his appearance in the courtroom. As the court correctly ruled, the appellant could not compensate for his failure to request a timely psychiatric examination of the respondent by permitting Dr. Gannon to draw professional conclusions about the respondent in such an improper setting and under such stressful conditions. Dr. Gannon was also correctly precluded from testifying to the respondent's competence based upon his review of the respondent's hospital records, which the appellant's counsel had subpoenaed to his office on May 24, 1993, pursuant to his client's power of attorney, some five days after that power of attorney had been revoked. There is further no merit to the appellant's contention that the respondent had waived his physician-patient privilege by permitting the appellant's witness, Dr. Lanyi, to testify "full[y]" to her assessment of his inpatient condition, because the record reveals that Dr. Lanyi relied only upon her own notes during the hearing, and at no point consulted the respondent's charts from St. Luke's-Roosevelt Hospital or the Rusk Institute.

Finally, the hearing court erred in admitting into evidence the report of the court evaluator because, although present at the hearing, the court evaluator did not take the stand and submit to cross-examination (*see,* Mental Hygiene Law § 81.12 [b]). We conclude that this error was harmless, however, in view of the fact that the court expressly based its decision upon its own observations of the respondent during the proceedings, and upon the testimony of the various witnesses. Moreover, the record amply supports the Supreme Court's conclusion that the appellant failed to establish by the requisite clear and convincing evidence the respondent's need for a guardian of his property under the standards enunciated in Mental Hygiene Law article 81, independently of the improperly admitted court evaluator's report (*see, e.g., Berger v Estate of Berger,* 203 AD2d 502; *Matter of Wieczorek,* 186 AD2d 204; *Matter of LoGuidice,* 186 AD2d 659, 660; *Turner v Danker,* 30 AD2d 564).

Therefore, the judgment is affirmed insofar as appealed from.

O'Brien, J. P., Joy and Krausman, JJ., concur.

Ordered that the judgment is affirmed insofar as appealed from, with costs.

II. Entitlement Programs

A. Social Security

The Federal Insurance Contributions Act requires an employer to withhold social security taxes from wages paid to an employee. Included within the tax is the Medicare premium for hospital insurance. The employer must also match the contribution, but there is a cap on the wages subject to the Social Security tax ($87,900 in 2004). There is no cap on wages subject to the Medicare tax. In 2003, the combined tax was 7.65%. *See* I.R.C. §§ 3101 & 3111 (2004).Enacted by Congress in 1930, the federal objective was to provide a financial cushion for the elderly and their dependents when they need to retire, become disabled, or die. A worker whose wages have been subject to withholding normally is eligible to receive payments whenever he or she reaches the age of 62, or earlier if disabled. The worker may postpone payment and boost monthly earnings when payment is eventually taken. It takes ten years or forty quarters to be fully insured under Social Security. But the benefits may not be bequeathed through a Last Will and Testament or designated in a trust. Congress has provided that only a surviving spouse or a dependent child may receive benefits. If the worker should die without a surviving spouse or child, and funds accumulated in Social Security are forfeited.

The Social Security Administration periodically mails a form to persons enrolled in the program, providing information on the amount of payment upon retirement and a web address and phone number to call (800-772-1213) for further information. Recently, Congress provided tax relief to those persons receiving Social Security income and income from additional investments or employment. The rules calculating the amount of tax due are complicated and require the assistance of an accountant, but up to 85 percent of an individual's benefits may be included in gross income.

The most recent Social Security publications reveal that more than 50 million people receive some form of benefits from Social Security. This accounts for at least half of the income of 64% of elderly persons. *See* Social Security Administration Online, Press Office, Facts and Figures, http://www.ssa.gov/SSA_Home.html; *path* The Press/Facts and Figures (accessed Oct. 21, 2005). In September 2004, there were 52,018,000 beneficiaries of Social Security, Supplemental Security Income, or both, 34,483,000 of whom were age 65 or over. *See* http://www.socialsecurity.gov/policy/docs/quickfacts/stat_snapshot/index.html (accessed Oct. 12, 2005). The total monthly benefits of Social Security benefits only for September 2004 was $47,468,000,000.00. The average monthly benefit was $846.80. For a description of social security plans throughout the world in 2004, see http://www.ssa.gov/policy/docs/progdesc/ssptw/2004-2005/europe/index.html (accessed Oct. 12, 2005). For a description of social security programs of every state, *see* Social Security Administration Online, Geographic Statistics Fact Sheets (2005), http://www.socialsecurity.gov/pressoffice/statefctshts.htm (accessed Oct. 21, 2005).

B. Medicare

California Probate Code (2004)

Section 4461. Social security or other government programs; civil or military benefit; powers granted

In a statutory form power of attorney, the language granting power with respect to benefits from social security, medicare, medicaid, or other governmental programs, or civil or military service, empowers the agent to do all of the following:

* * *

(c) Prepare, file, and prosecute a claim of the principal to a benefit or assistance, financial or otherwise, to which the principal claims to be entitled, under a statute or governmental regulation.

(d) Prosecute, defend, submit to arbitration, settle, and propose or accept a compromise with respect to any benefits the principal may be entitled to receive.

(e) Receive the financial proceeds of a claim of the type described in this section, conserve, invest, disburse, or use anything received fro a lawful purpose.

Like Social Security, Medicare is a federal program to benefit older Americans— those who reach the age of 65, or those less than 65 but are disabled. Within a few months of eligibility, a person applies for a Medicare card, and this will entitle the person to hospital insurance (Part A) and medical insurance (Part B). For a hospital accepting Medicare payment, the hospital insurance will cover a portion of the hospital costs and a short period of nursing home care. If a physician accepts Medicare, the medical insurance portion will pay for at least a portion of the fee and any attendant diagnostic fees. There is a monthly fee associated with Medicare, in addition to the fees paid through Social Security while employed, plus there is an annual deductible. Since Medicare pays only a "portion" of the total costs, there is a co-payment required. For Medicare recipients with additional income, the way in which these additional costs are met is through what is called Medigap insurance. Medigap insurance is offered through private insurance companies and, to lessen exploitation of the elderly, there is a Medicare Hotline at 800-638-6833, offering assistance in choosing a plan to complement Medicare coverage and personal needs. To find a physician willing to accept Medicare patients, persons may look into the Medicare Participating Physician/Supplier Directory. Often, assistance may be obtained through the American Association of Retired Persons (AARP) (800-424-3410) or state and local agencies on aging, *see, e.g.,* United Seniors Health Cooperative (202-393-6222). Because of rising and often exorbitant costs of prescription drugs, Congress recently amended the benefits available under Medicare to provide for drug prescription cards. *See generally* Thomas E. Bush, *Disabled Adult Children*, 6 MARQ. ELDER'S ADVISOR 243 (2005); Judith Stein, *Introduction to Medicare for People With Multiple Sclerosis*, 6 MARQ. ELDER'S ADVISOR 265 (2005); Karen M. Wieghaus, *The Medicare Prescription Drug, Improvement, and Modernization Act of 2003: The Wrong Prescription for Our Nation's Senior Citizens?*, 11 CONN. INS. L.J. 401 (2004–2005); Brook Ames, *Paying Less for Celebrex: A Comparative Study of Medicaid Prescription Drug Cost-Containment Programs and a Recommendation for Medicare's Increasing Drug Costs*, 85 B.U. L. REV. 517 (2005).

The cost of Medicare associated with an increasing number of eligible recipients is of constant concern. Also of concern is the effectiveness of Medicare in an age of medical technological breakthroughs. Consider the following:

Raymond C. O'Brien & Michael T. Flannery, Long-Term Care: Federal, State, and Private Options for the Future
16–17, 35–36 (1997)

The health status of the elderly has been improving constantly with the concomitant increase in the percentage of the population that is becoming elderly.* * * The present increase in the elderly population is small compared to that which is expected in 15 years. The newcomers to the elderly population now are those who were born during the depression, which accounted for the lowest birth rate in the country's history. But by 2010, the elderly population will be flooded with baby boomers reaching retirement age.* * *

[T]he number of elderly is rising,* * * and those who comprise the elderly population are living longer. For example, in 1900, total life expectancy was approximately 37 years.* * * When social security was founded in 1935, life expectancy at age 65 was only 12.6 years.* * * In 1950, it was 13.9 years, and this figure increased to 17.2 years in 1989.* * * This figure will increase to as high as 21.3 years by the middle of the twenty-first century, when it is estimated there will be 392 million people inhabiting the United States.* * * Because of continuing advancements in medical technology and its ability to prolong life,* * * [in] 2000, there [were] 10 million more Americans over age 65 than there were in 1980.* * *

When Medicare was create [more than] 30 years ago, it was designed "to cover acute but not chronic care—the heart attack patient in the hospital, for example, not the [Alzheimer's] patient in a nursing home."* * * As of 1988, Medicare extended its services to include catastrophic illnesses.* * * Nevertheless, protection against the increasing costs of catastrophic and long-term health care under Medicare is minimal.* * * In fact, since 1986, "[o]lder persons [have paid] a larger portion of their income for health care than they did before Medicare was enacted."* * *

Medicare's hospital insurance is available at no cost to everyone who is entitled to Social Security.* * * Still, in 1987, Medicare costs were approximately $67 billion.* * * By the year 2040, this figure could rise as high as $200 billion.* * * Under the catastrophic health insurance plans of this country, however, less than 3 percent of Medicare's 31 million beneficiaries receive help with the care they need.* * * In 1985, Medicare paid only 1.7 percent of all nursing home bills, and private insurance covered less—0.8 percent, while 51.4 percent was paid out-of-pocket by consumers.* * *

C. Medicaid

Unlike Social Security (age 62) and Medicare (age 65), Medicaid eligibility is not activated by reaching a certain age, but rather upon qualifying as poor. While Medicaid is another federal program, eligibility is determined by each state, most specifying that a single person cannot own more than $2,000, with corresponding very little income. Obviously, disability and marital status will affect the qualification, but the qualification rules are so complicated that it is advisable to consult an attorney specializing in elder law in the state. If a person qualifies at an age less than 65, he or she is entitled to physician and hospital services, diagnostic tests, and related services. Of course, the persons and institutions providing the services must agree to accept Medicaid reimbursement. If the recipient is over the age of 65, then Medicaid may work in tandem with Medicare to provide medical services. *See, e.g.*, Linda S. Ershow-Levenberg, *Court Approval of Medicaid Spend-Down Planning By Guardians*, 6 MARQ. ELDER'S ADVISOR 197 (2005).

Medicaid offers a type of assistance not available under either Social Security or Medicare: long-term nursing home payments. That is, if a person qualifies as eligible, and a nursing home will accept Medicaid reimbursement, the cost of a nursing home—often exceeding $4,000 a month—will be paid for with Medicaid funds. This is a very important feature, often prompting persons anticipating extended nursing home residency to "spend-down" assets until reaching the Medicaid eligibility level of being poor. Indeed, estate planning often includes consideration of spend-down procedures so that clients may obtain long-term nursing home care and still have assets available for distribution to surviving family members. *See, e.g.*, Barbara J. Collins, *Medicaid*, 239 PLI/EST 55 (1995). Because individual states are involved, qualification is best left to a seasoned estate planning attorney, who can balance the tax consequences, government rules, and personal situation of each client. But in general, eligibility will depend upon income and resources available to the applicant for the last 36 months. *See* 42 U.S.C. § 1396p(c)(1) (2004). Of concern will be transfers for less than market value, often made to family members, with the intent of avoiding their inclusion in total assets. But also included in assets are self-owned property, jointly held property, and trusts, whereby income or corpus is or may become available to the applicant. When the spouse of an applicant is dependent on jointly held assets, there are exemptions; Congress allows for property to remain in the possession of the non-applicant spouse without the counting the asset as eligible and not requiring the couple to divorce to separate assets. Many people from more affluent backgrounds have qualified for Medicaid eligibility for nursing home care. Public policy questions the appropriateness of persons "making themselves poor" to obtain assistance with the catastrophic costs associated with long term care. Consider the following:

Raymond C. O'Brien & Michael T. Flannery, Long-Term Care: Federal, State and Private Options for the Future
3, 60 (1997)

By 1975, Medicaid provided nursing home care to approximately 1.31 million persons.* * * By 1982, Medicaid assisted 1.39 million persons; in 1989, 1.45 million persons; in 1990, 1.46 million persons.* * * By 1991 the number had expanded more rapidly—1.5 million persons were assisted, or a 40,000 increase in recipients. By 1992, there was a one-year growth of 80,000 to 1.58 million persons.* * * During 1992, state Medicaid programs spent over $21 billion providing nursing home—and long-term care—assistance to nearly 1.6 million persons. This amount was more than one-quarter of all Medicaid expenditures.* * * For an index of Medicaid topics, see Centers for Medicare & Medicaid Services, Medicaid Index, http://www.cms.hhs.gov/medicaid/medicaidindex.asp (accessed Oct. 21, 2005). For a list of state Medicaid plan descriptions, see, State Medicaid Plan Search Application, http://www.cms.hhs.gov/medicaid/stateplans/map.asp (accessed Oct. 21, 2005). For a description of Medicaid eligibility, see Centers for Medicare & Medicaid Services, Medicaid Eligibility, http://www.cms.hhs.gov/medicaid/eligibility/criteria.asp (accessed Oct. 21, 2005).

Index